Human Geography

Culture, Society, and Space

Sixth Edition

Human Geography
Culture, Society, and Space
Sixth Edition

H.J. de Blij
John Deaver Drinko Chair in Geography
Marshall University

Alexander B. Murphy
Rippey Chair in Liberal Arts and Sciences and Professor of Geography
University of Oregon

John Wiley & Sons, Inc.
New York Chichester Weinheim Brisbane Singapore Toronto

Acquisitions Editor: Nanette Kauffman
Associate Director of Development: Johnna Barto
Assistant Editor: Barbara Bredenko
Marketing Manager: Catherine Beckham
Production Manager: Linda Muriello
Production Editor: Jeanine Furino/Edward Winkleman
Cover and Text Designer: Dawn L. Stanley
Back Cover Photo: Patti McConville/The Image Bank
Photo Editor: Kim Khatchatourian/Jennifer Atkins
Illustration Editor: Edward Starr
Front Cover Photo: Gary John Norman/Tony Stone Images
Back Cover Photo: Patti McConville/The Image Bank
Maps: Magellan Geographix/Mapping Specialists

This book was set in 10/12 ITC Garamond Light by UG division of GGS Information Services and printed and bound by Von Hoffman Press. The cover was printed by Phoenix Color Corp.

This book is printed on acid-free paper. ♾

The paper in this book was manufactured by a mill whose forest management programs include sustained yield harvesting of its timberlands. Sustained yield harvesting principles ensure that the numbers of trees cut each year does not exceed the amount of new growth.

Library of Congress Cataloging in Publication Data:

de Blij, Harm J.
Human geography : culture, society, and space / H.J. de Blij, Alexander B. Murphy. — 6th ed.
p. cm.
Includes index.
ISBN 0-471-24208-X (pbk. : alk. paper)
ISBN 0-471-35595-X (cloth: alk. paper)
1. Human geography. I. Murphy, Alexander B., 1954– . II. Title.
GF41.D4 1998
304.2—dc21 98-34843
CIP

10 9 8 7 6 5 4 3 2

Preface

For nearly a quarter of a century, ***Human Geography: Culture, Society, and Space*** has been a standard work for the introductory course on this subject. During this period, the world has changed quite dramatically, and so has the discipline of geography. Natural environments are changing—often spurred by human action. Cultures everywhere are influenced by globalizing forces. Political systems and frameworks are buckling under powerful pressures. Economic developments transform entire regions.

Geographers chronicle, analyze, and often predict such changes. The old image of place-name and product-list geography has finally faded in the face of spatial and territorial transformations brought on by recent economic and political changes, of satellite imagery and computer cartography, of Geographic Information Systems (GIS) and spatial analysis. In today's truly global world, a sense of *scale* is a prominent component of geographic analysis. But geography's overarching, encompassing character has not changed.

The Sixth Edition retains the depth and breadth of content and scholarship that have been its hallmark. However, with a new co-author, it has been thoroughly revised to address contemporary economic and environmental issues such as deindustrialization and the rise of the service sector, and the human alteration of the physical environment. While chapters have been condensed, new pedagogy has been incorporated to help guide students through the complexities of modern human geography.

THE STUDY OF GEOGRAPHY

In the broadest terms, geography consists of two subdisciplines: human geography and physical (natural) geography. Each of these, in turn, consists of several fields. *Physical geography* incorporates such diverse fields as climatology, geomorphology, aspects of biogeography, glaciology, and much more. *Human geography*, too, is wide-ranging and diverse and includes, among other fields, cultural geography, economic geography, urban geography, and political geography. Rarely is any of these fields studied in isolation. When physical geographers analyze the natural processes shaping coastlines, their conclusions also tell us about these areas as places of human habitation and impact. When human geographers study cities, they often do so with reference to the physical landscape on which the urban area lies, and the role this physical stage has played in the city's evolution. This relationship between human endeavor and natural setting forms one of the discipline's unifying themes.

Another such bond lies in the spatial perspective: human *and* physical geographers depend on this to formulate their research questions and to look for solutions. Maps, representing spatial information, are therefore indispensable to geography.

When a book is entitled *Human Geography*, therefore, that title reveals its emphasis, not the whole story of its contents. Nor could it cover all the many fields of human geography: there is much more to this part of the discipline than one book or course could convey. But ***Human Geography*** does comprise the core of one of geography's major components, as reflected by its subtitle ***Culture, Society, and Space***.

THE SIXTH EDITION

For this new edition, H.J. de Blij is joined by co-author Alexander B. Murphy of the University of Oregon, and the result is a thoroughly restructured, extensively revised, and completely updated book. A new organization, new chapters, new pedagogy, and yet a condensed text combine to create an improved and contemporary edition of ***Human Geography***.

Organization

The order of presentation of topics has changed significantly. Part 1 now focuses on cultural geography, followed immediately by population, language, and religion. On the advice of colleagues and student readers, the lengthy discussion of human origins has been deleted. Following Part 5 (the Rural Sector) and 6 (Urbanization), the discussion of Modern Economic Change (Part 7) now centers on core-periphery relationships, as opposed to developed-underdeveloped dichotomies, and on the rise of the service sector. After Part 8 (The Political Imprint), the final two parts deal with social geography, notably problems of inequality, and global change in natural as well as human contexts.

New chapters in this edition include "Deindustrialization and the Rise of the Service Sector" (24) and "Confronting Human-Induced Global Environmental Change" (33). Major segments of other chapters also have been rewritten, including "Concepts of Development" (21) and "Toward a New World Order? The Changing Global Political Landscape" (35). As in previous editions, we still include separate chapters on ethnicity (30) and gender (31).

Structurally, the book now contains 10 parts and 35 brief chapters, retaining the flexibility that has long been one of its strengths. Each Part addresses a major field of human geography such as culture, population, language, religion, agriculture, urbanization, economics, politics, society, and environment and change. The crucial concept of *scale* is introduced in Part I and used as a frame of reference throughout the book. Within the parts, each of 3 or 4 brief chapters focuses on a particular dimension of a major field, such as population growth, language diffusion, religious origins, urban structure, and concepts of economic development.

Pedagogical Structure

Since students are our audience, we have asked for their opinions in shaping this edition. This feedback has resulted in the new, open design for the Sixth Edition. As part of this student-oriented plan, students will be presented with many opportunities to apply geographic perspectives and methods to the problems and issues they face in this fast-changing world.

• ***At Issue*** — Every part opens with a key contemporary issue, such as who should inhibit world population growth or if a global system should be established to regulate industrial pollution, raised at the beginning, discussed in various contexts during the chapter sequence, and reconsidered at the conclusion. This guides readers toward an awareness of the utility of the geographic perspective in addressing some of our world's major challenges.

• ***Key Points*** — The most important concepts to be covered in the chapter are listed on the opening page of each chapter. These can serve the student as a preview organizer and as a review after completing the chapter.

• ***Headings and Subheadings*** — The hierarchy of headings and subheadings has been strengthened to help readers discern and grasp the main geographical concepts and their relationships.

• ***From the Field Notes*** — All photographs in this book were taken by the authors and are accompanied by the notes they wrote in the field. This unique feature has drawn praise from our adopters, because of its ability to convey a geographer's unique vision. Because of their popularity, we have chosen to open each chapter with the "From the Field Notes" feature.

• ***Sense of Scale*** — To illustrate the crucial role that the concept of scale plays in geographic analysis, each part includes a special 'Sense of Scale' feature, such as Euroregions in southwestern Poland, social and economic change and the Los Angeles riots, Nike and economic globalization.

• ***Focus On*** — special boxes highlight topics that provide background (such as theories of migration) or illustrate geographic concepts (such as acculturation and transculturation).

• ***Key Terms & Concepts*** — As a helpful review, the main terms and concepts discussed in the chapter are listed at the end. These terms are also defined in the Glossary at the end of the book.

• ***Applying Geographic Knowledge*** — To encourage students to think as geographers do, every chapter ends with two or more questions that require some spatial analysis.

• ***Selected Bibliographies*** — As with all sciences, geographic knowledge is established by research. The Selected Bibliography, including important work of geographers past and present, has been reorganized and moved forward from the back of the book to follow the appropriate parts and is thoroughly updated in this edition.

• ***Demographic Table*** — A new World Population Data Table (Resource B) reflects the global situation as of 1998.

Maps and Photos

Maps are among the most important tools of geographers and the de Blij text has long been known for accurate and up-to-date maps. All cartography has been restylized and updated to enhance clarity and effectiveness of the maps. New maps have been prepared. ***Human Geography*** also retains its signature photography: all photographs were taken by the authors and are accompanied by the notes they wrote in the field. Looking at the world through a geographer's eyes is part of a geographic education.

SUPPLEMENTS

For the Student

Study Companion, ***Virtual Field Guide*** and ***Web Site*** and ***Take Note***! This three-part student resource is packaged at no extra charge with every textbook.

The ***Virtual Field Guide*** gives students firsthand experience with the geographic principles discussed in the main text by presenting them with a framework to apply their knowledge at the local and global scales. Through a range of hands-on experiences that were created by geography professors Margaret Gripshover and Glenn Miller, the *Guide* promotes interactive learning, demonstrates linkages between global and local issues, and exposes students to contemporary trends in geographic research.

Each of the 10 parts in *Human Geography* has a corresponding activity in the *Virtual Field Guide.* Activities in the *Guide* prompt students to explore their local communities via group discussion, fieldwork, data analysis, and research, and to apply their empirical work to problem solving. Each activity utilizes the Internet by way of a special Web site created for the *Virtual Field Guide.* The ***Virtual Field Guide Web Site*** chiefly will give users front-end guidance and access to such pre-selected Web sites as the Population Reference Bureau, UNICEF, U.S. Bureau of Labor Statistics, and the Urban Land Institute. The *Web Site* is a restricted site that requires a password, which can be set up with the wallet-size identification card found inside the Field Guide cover. A sample of the *Virtual Field Guide Web Site* may be viewed at ⟨www.wiley.com/college/human⟩. Click Student Resources.

A complete ***Study Companion***, written by A. Steele Becker and Jacqueline Becker, gives students a pedagogical framework to use while reading in preparation for class and for studying for examinations. Since Becker and Becker have written the *Test Bank* too, the *Study Companion* is correlated directly to the goals of their examination questions. In addition to the *Virtual Field Guide* and the *Study Companion*, students will receive with each copy of the main text, all the art work from the overhead transparencies in black and white format as well as multiple copies of a base map of the world. This resource is called ***Take Note!***, and was created to enable better note-taking during class discussions that involve the overheads from the text.

• ***Microsoft Encarta Virtual Globe, Web Site, and Pocket Activity Guide*** — Instructors and students will be able to explore the globe thematically and regionally using a variety of resources, including a wide range of maps and map styles, videos, sounds, animations, up-to-date statistics, and links to Web sites that provide an amazing range of resources for every country. The ***Pocket Activity Guide***, included at no extra charge with every ***Encarta Virtual Globe*** CD-ROM, links the content of the CD directly to every chapter of de Blij and Murphy's *Human Geography* text. See the book's Web site for sample material from the *Pocket Activity Guide.* Our offer of *Encarta Virtual Globe* is tied to an exclusive agreement between Microsoft and John Wiley & Sons, which allows us to offer the product at a deeply discounted price when shrink-wrapped with our textbooks. To order de Blij and Murphy's *Human Geography* Sixth Edition packaged with the *Microsoft Encarta Virtual Globe*, please use ISBN 047132732-4.

• ***Kuby, Gober and Harner's Human Geography in Action*** — Used as a supplement or a stand-alone text, this 13-chapter workbook integrates the most fundamental concepts of human geography with interactive, hands-on applications located on a dual-platform CD-ROM in the back of the book. Students can manipulate data, create maps, and explore the implications of these concepts using this first-hand data. Guidance for using *Human Geography in Action* in conjunction *Human Geography* by de Blij and Murphy is offered on the *Human Geography in Action* Web site at ⟨www.wiley.com/college/kuby⟩.

For the Instructor

• ***Transparencies and Slides*** — 100 full-color maps, illustrations, and tables from the text are included in each of these presentation packages. The Sixth Edition cartography and illustration program uses a richer color palette than the Fifth Edition. The effect this has on transparencies and slides, when combined with enhanced labeling of the type, is a set of strong, clear images when projected in the classroom.

• ***H.J. de Blij's Worldview Geography CD-ROM (Dual-Platform)*** — This rich collection of multimedia resources allows professors to design presentations and on-line projects. The resources include: 15 videos, animations that bring geographic themes to life; over 350 unique photographs with detailed field notes and captions; 65 detailed maps with a unique thematic layering feature. Although *Worldview Geography* is organized regionally, it is an effective resource of media for a thematic approach. The book's main Web site hosts a range of resources for the instructor, including electronic files that advance organize *Worldview Geography's* photos, maps, videos and animations according to each chapter in *Human Geography.* Used in conjunction with the CD itself, these files will run *Worldview Geography* from a thematic perspective. Of course, you may also create your own presentations!

• ***Geography On-Location with H.J. de Blij Video Series*** — Each video in this three-video set comprises fifty minutes of original, current footage taken during the author's travels. The tapes cover a range of themes. Although *Worldview Geography* is organized regionally, it too is an effective resource of media for a thematic approach. The book's main Web site, under "Instructor's Resources," catalogs each of the *Series'* many video segments from a systematic perspective.

• ***Web Site*** —The book's main Web site features a secure Instructor's Resources section. Organized by book part, it includes an *Instructor's Manual*, *Test Bank*, and detailed descriptions of the various media and supplements (Overheads, Slides, Encarta Virtual Globe CD, Virtual Field Guide & Web Site, Worldview Geography CD, Geography On-Location Videos) that support the part.

ACKNOWLEDGMENTS

In preparing this Sixth Edition of ***Human Geography*** we have benefited from the advice and assistance of numerous colleagues. Some told us of their experiences using the Fifth Edition; others helped us formulate the revision plan now reflected by our Table of Contents; still others responded, sometimes in remarkably helpful detail, to the survey we distributed to solicit views on the revision plan; and ten colleagues reviewed the messy manuscript of this new edition as it was going into production. The list that follows acknowledges this support, but it cannot begin to measure our gratitude for all they contributed:

Ian Ackroyd-Kelly *East Stroudsburg University*
James Ashley *University of Toledo*
Sarah W. Bednarz *Texas A&M University*
Sari Bennett *University of Maryland, Baltimore County*
J. Best *Frostburg State University*
Brian Blouet *College of William & Mary*
Margaret F. Boorstein *C. W. Post College of Long Island University*
Evan Denney *University of Montana*
Sr. James Dyer *Mount St. Mary's College*
Adrian X. Esparza *University of Arizona*
Stephen Frenkel *University of Washington, Seattle*
Lay James Gibson *University of Arizona*
Abe Goldman *University of Florida*
Alyson Greiner *Oklahoma State University*
Jeffrey A. Gritzner *University of Montana*
Qian Guo *Northern Michigan University*
Peter R. Hoffmann *Loyola Marymount University*
Peter Hugill *Texas A&M University*
Tarek A. Joseph *Central Michigan University*
Artimus Keiffer *Indiana University/Purdue University*
Les King *McMaster University*
Ann Legreid *Central Missouri State University*
Jess A. Le Vine *Brookdale Community College*
David Lyons *University of Minnesota, Duluth*
Ian MacLachlan *University of Lethbridge*
Wayne McKim *Towson University*
Glenn Miller *Bridgewater State College*
Katharyne Mitchell *University of Washington, Seattle*
John M. Morris *University of Texas, San Antonio*
Garth A. Myers *University of Kansas*
Darrell Norris *SUNY Geneseo*
Walter Peace *McMaster University*
Jeffrey Richetto *University of Alabama*
James Saku *Frostburg State University*
Joseph E. Schwartzberg *University of Minnesota*
Gary W. Shannon *University of Kentucky*
Betty Shimshak *Towson University*
Andrew Sluyter *Pennsylvania State University*
Herschel Stern *Mira Costa College*
Neva Duncan Tabb *University of South Florida*
James A. Tyner *University of Southern California*
George W. White *Frostburg State University*
Donald Zeigler *Old Dominion University*
Robert C. Ziegenfus *Kutztown University*

In addition, we are grateful to Roberto Serralles, Sarah Shafer, Nancy Leeper, and Joanna Kepka, graduate students at the University of Oregon, for valuable research and technical assistance during the preparation of this edition. Finally, we would like to thank the staff of John Wiley & Sons, who have contributed to this project: Nanette Kauffman, geography editor; Tammy McGinnis, editorial assistant; Catherine Beckham, marketing manager; Johnna Barto, associate director of development; Carolyn Smith, development editor; Barbara Bredenko, assistant editor; Edward Starr, illustration editor; Dawn Stanley, designer; Kim Khatchatourian, photo editor; Jeanine Furino and Edward Winkleman, senior production editors; Betty Pessagno, copyeditor; and Shelley Flannery, Pamela Landau, and Christine Marra, proofreaders.

H.J. de Blij
Alexander B. Murphy

About the Authors

H.J. de Blij

Harm de Blij received his early schooling in Europe, his college education in Africa, and his higher degrees in geography in the United States (Ph.D. Northwestern, 1959). He has published more than 30 books and over 100 articles, and has received honorary degrees in the humanities as well as the sciences. Several of his books have been translated into French, Italian, Russian, and Chinese.

Dr. de Blij was for 7 years the Geography Editor for ABC's "Good Morning America," and later Geography Analyst for NBC News. He has taught at several universities, including Michigan State University, the Colorado School of Mines, and Georgetown University, where he was George Landegger Distinguished Professor in the School of Foreign Service. He presently holds the John Deaver Drinko Chair of Geography at Marshall University.

Prof. de Blij is a member of the Committee for Research and Exploration of the National Geographic Society. He is an avid wine collector and one of his books on this topic, *Wine: a Geographic Appreciation*, was awarded the 1984 medal by the O.I.V. in Paris, France. He also is an amateur violinist and has performed with orchestras and chamber groups.

Alexander B. Murphy

Alexander B. Murphy grew up in the western United States, but he spent several of his early years in Europe and Japan where his father was teaching and doing research in geography. Dr. Murphy went to college at Yale University, studied law at the Columbia University School of Law, practiced law for a short time in Chicago, and then pursued a doctoral degree in geography (Ph.D. University of Chicago, 1987). After graduating he joined the faculty of the University of Oregon, where is he now Head of the Department of Geography and holder of the James F. and Shirley K. Rippey Chair in Liberal Arts and Sciences. Professor Murphy is a widely published scholar in the fields of political, cultural, and environmental geography, with a regional emphasis on Europe. His work has been supported by the National Science Foundation, the National Endowment for the Humanities, and the Fulbright-Hays foreign fellowship program.

Professor Murphy is Vice-President of the American Geographical Society and a National Councillor of the Association of American Geographers. He is also one of the editors of *Progress in Human Geography*. He currently chairs the national committee that is overseeing the addition of Geography to the College Board's Advanced Placement program. His interests include hiking, skiing, camping, music—and of course exploring the diverse places that make up our planet.

To Esther Bailey Murphy,
for the love and support she has given
two generations of geographers.

Contents

Part Nine
Social Geographies of the Modern World, *385*

Part Ten
Coping with a Rapidly Changing World, *453*

Resources

Human Geography

Culture, Society, and Space

Sixth Edition

Part One

GEOGRAPHY, CULTURE, AND THE ENVIRONMENT

At Issue

The past decade has seen extraordinary, rapid changes in political, social, and environmental arrangements. The Cold War order has come to an end, ethnic conflicts have intensified in many places, and we increasingly read about the myriad ways in which humans are altering the environment. In the midst of these developments, policy makers and scholars are scrambling to find new ways ofmaking sense of the world—and a growing number are involving geographical concepts and tools in the process. They are seeking out new maps that go beyond the map of states, they are using Geographic Information Systems (GIS) to study the relationship among spatial data, and such terms as "place," "region," and even "geography" are cropping up more and more. ***Why is geography so much a part of the effort to come to terms with our rapidly changing world? What does it mean to think geographically? Can geography offer insights into the diversity of changes unfolding around us?***

GIS is crucial in Tokyo's earthquake warning system.

Part Outline

Chapter 1

Introduction: Geography and Human Geography

From the field notes

"On the main street of Dalian, Northeast China, I watched this artist create an image full of symbolism: the computer in the land (and the hand) of the Manchus. This was no mass-produced billboard. He had painted these images on large sheets of paper, had pasted these up, and was now adding the finishing touches. I pointed to the computer and asked if he knew how to use it. He shook his head, grabbed a paint brush, and pointed it to himself. But his work symbolized the modernization of our ever-more interconnected world."

KEY POINTS

◆ Physical and human geography are two great branches of the discipline, but environmental geography is emerging as a link between the two.

◆ During the twentieth century geography has been marked by four durable traditions: earth-science, culture-environment, locational, and area-analysis.

◆ The National Geographic Society in the 1980s proposed a useful five-theme framework for geography; focused on the concepts of location, interaction between humans and the environment, regions, place, and movement.

◆ The spatial perspective is geography's unifying bond and is demonstrated through the use of maps.

◆ Maps are used to portray the distinctive character of places; their relationship to environmental issues; the movements of people, goods, and ideas; and regions of various types.

◆ People's perceptions of places and regions are influenced by their individual mental maps as well as by printed maps.

Geography is destiny. For the vast majority of the Earth's inhabitants, place of birth is the most powerful determinant of a lifetime's experiences. Even in the modern era of migration and travel, global interaction, and mass communication, place of birth remains crucial. The first language you learn, the first foods you eat, the first religion of which you become aware, the first clothing with which you become comfortable—all these, and much else, are associated with your birthplace. And unless your family belongs to a small elite, your chances of surviving through infancy and childhood, and later your opportunities for advancement in a competitive world, are greatly influenced by your place of birth.

We live in an age of increasing globalization. Peoples and economies throughout the world are interconnected as never before. Nevertheless, our world remains a jigsaw of countries, a patchwork of religions, a Babel of thousands of languages, a mosaic of innumerable customs and traditions. Ours still is a world of endlessly diverse places, most of which are *birth*places. Understanding and explaining this diversity is the mission of ***human geography***.

Geography sometimes is referred to as the "study of place," but it is much more than that. Knowing where countries and important places are located is useful, but it is only a beginning, a bit like knowing some introductory vocabulary when you start studying a foreign language. Knowing *why* places and things are where they are; *what* their location means in the past, present, and future, and *how* their location affects other places—knowing these things brings us much closer to knowing what geography is about.

Note that we just referred to places and things. This book is mainly about places and their human inhabitants. It also deals with how the world has become organized, and in many places transformed, by human activity. But make no mistake: there is more to geography than human geography. The other half of geography is termed ***physical geography***. Actually, a better name for this group would be ***natural geography***, because it deals not only with mountains, glaciers, coastlines, and climates but also with soils, plants, and animals. As we will see, it is often difficult to discuss human geography without also referring to the physical stage on which the human drama is being played out. Indeed, so many contemporary issues occur at the intersection of human and physical geography that ***environmental geography*** is emerging as a third basic subdivision of geography. However, in this book our focus will be on human geography. Although it represents only part of the discipline, human geography encompasses several subfields (Fig. 1-1). Each of these has an environmental component that connects it to the domains of physical and environmental geography.

◆ THE COMMON BOND: A SPATIAL PERSPECTIVE

If geography deals with so many aspects of our world, ranging from people and places to coastlines and cli-

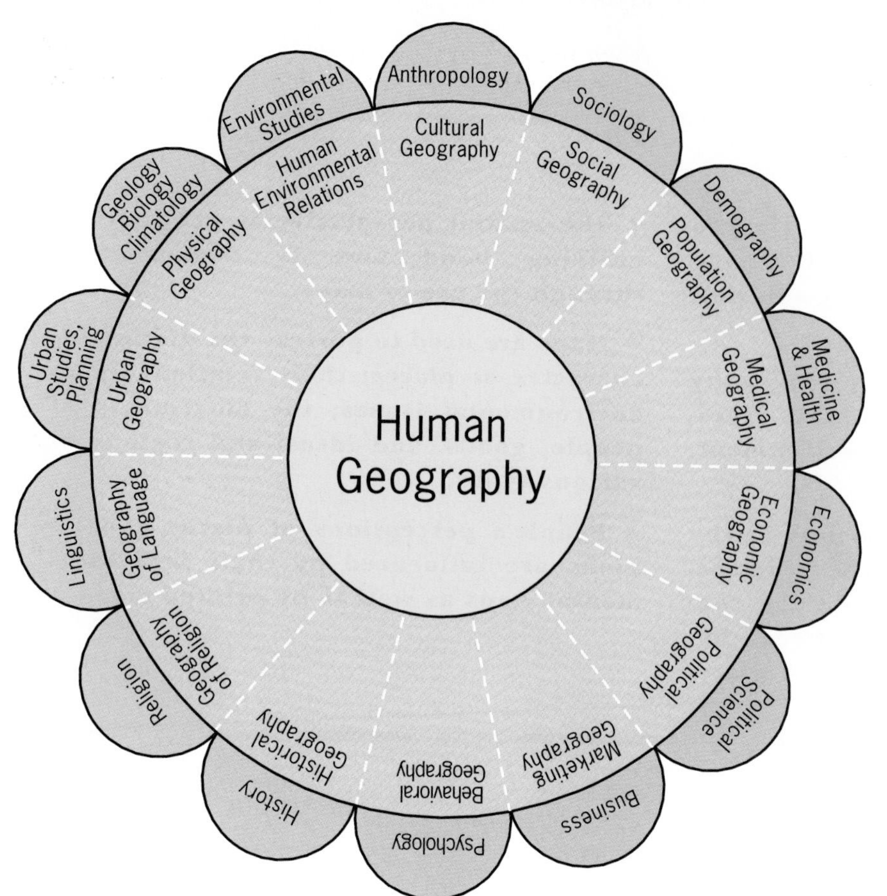

Figure 1-1 Fields of Human Geography. A schematic diagram showing the relationships among the fields of human geography and related fields outside the discipline. *Source: From authors' sketch.*

mates, what do the various facets of this wide-ranging discipline have in common? The answer lies in a term that often is used most effectively as an adjective: *spatial.* Whether they are human geographers or physical geographers, virtually all geographers are interested in the way places and things are laid out, organized, and arranged on the surface of the Earth. Sometimes a particular spatial arrangement of human activities or conditions leads geographers to raise questions as to how this arrangement has come about, what processes create and sustain particular ***patterns***, and what relationships exist between different places and things. In such instances, the spatial pattern already is evident, and the search is on for an explanation. But at other times, the spatial arrangement may not be evident at all and must be discovered before it can lead to answers. As we will see in our discussions of medical geography, the mapping of the ***distribution*** of people afflicted by certain illnesses led researchers directly to the sources of the illnesses and thus to remedies for them.

Medical geography is just one part of human geography in which spatial analysis has practical application. Yet another interest of geographers is the impact of particular spatial patterns on some process or idea. Political geographers, for example, are interested in how the division of the world into discrete countries influences everything from concepts of nationality—"I am a German, Russian, Pole"—to how environmental issues are understood and addressed.

Study of the spatial arrangement of things is not a monopoly of human geography. Physical and human geographers are drawn together because they have a similar way of looking at the world. Early in this century a climatologist, Alfred Wegener, became convinced—from decades of observation—that the jigsaw-like fit of the continental landmasses on opposite sides of the North and South Atlantic oceans could not be a matter of chance. He marshaled a vast array of geographical and geological evidence, most of it spatial in nature, and on the basis of this evidence he proposed a hypothesis of continental drift. His theory was that the continental landmasses were once united as a giant supercontinent that later broke apart. Wegener's geographic hypothesis, based on the spatial layout of the physical world he knew so well, set the direction for the geological research that was to lead (a half century later) to the discovery of plate tectonics and crustal spreading, the mechanism that drives the continents apart.

Human and physical geographers thus share this ***spatial perspective***, this way of looking at the world's—and the Earth's—layout. So the language of geography is not only the language of places and things but also a whole vocabulary of spatial terms, many of which will become familiar (though occasionally from a new viewpoint) as we proceed. We have already used some of these terms: *location* is one, and *pattern* and *distribution* are others. In due course we will become familiar with others, making geographic communication in the pages that follow not only easier but also more efficient and accurate.

The important point here is that we cannot hope to understand the complexity and diversity of our planet if we do not think geographically. No amount of information about the workings of the Russian government can provide insight into the future of the Russian state if we do not understand the distribution of ethnic groups in and around Russia and their differing ideas about territory and place. And no amount of analysis of data on trade among countries in Pacific Asia can provide a sense of the economic challenges facing the region if we do not consider patterns of advantage and disadvantage within individual countries. Geography, in short, is indispensable to an appreciation of who we are, where we came from, and where we are going.

◆ TRADITIONS AND THEMES IN GEOGRAPHY

Before we begin our journey through the world of human geography, we should equip ourselves with some insights into the traditions and themes that have developed in this wide-ranging discipline. With its spatial perspective and its human as well as physical contexts, geography can appear to be an all-encompassing, but poorly defined, field. In fact, some geographers have spent their careers trying to define the nature of geography. Such philosophical musings need not concern us here, but we will have occasion to refer to some of the long-term legacies and customs that have developed in geography.

Traditions

As long ago as 1964, a University of Chicago geographer, W. D. Pattison, published an article in the *Journal of Geography* entitled "The Four Traditions of Geography." In that much-debated publication, Pattison identified four areas in which geographic research, teaching, and other activity were so concentrated that they could be designated as ***traditions*** within the discipline:

1. An earth-science tradition, represented by many decades of work in physical (natural) geography.
2. A culture-environment tradition, in which the dominant questions have to do with the relationships between human societies and their natural environments.
3. A locational tradition (the spatial unifying theme referred to earlier).
4. An area-analysis tradition, which at the time was represented mainly by studies in regional geography.

The Earth-Science Tradition Today, more than three decades later, geography is a much more complex discipline. But the traditions Pattison identified are still evident. As noted earlier, physical geography (the ***earth-science*** tradition) remains one of the cornerstones of the discipline. Physical geographers report on the processes, cycles, and systems that modify the natural world. They interpret the landscape, analyze it, and predict how it will change. Although the focus is on the physical world, what physical geographers learn is often of urgent importance to the Earth's human inhabitants. When they study the silting up of a delta, the movement of a glacier, the carving of a shoreline, or the shifting of a dune, physical geographers help us comprehend the changing nature of our world. As we will see, our study of human geography cannot be carried out without frequent reference to what physical geographers have learned about soil fertility, climatic patterns, river dynamics, and so on.

The Culture-Environment Tradition The ***culture-environment*** tradition has a difficult, even controversial, history. This tradition encompasses a wide range of topics, some of them quite straightforward (for example, the impact of deforestation on traditional societies in the Amazon region or in Congo). But more complicated questions have proven risky for reasons that will be discussed in the next chapter of this book. Many years ago, some geographers were tempted to generalize about the relationships between the natural environment (mainly climate) and the technological development of societies, concluding that the natural environment is a determinant of progress. This led to assumptions about predictable advantages and disadvantages, which were misused by demagogues. For a long time the culture-environment tradition was burdened by criticism that was often unfair. Yet societies and cultures do evolve and develop in a physical-environmental context that has much to do with their properties, patterns, and prospects. The old questions are still there, and modern techniques of analysis have ushered in a new age for this geographic tradition.

The Locational Tradition What Professor Pattison described as the locational tradition lies at the heart of all geography, because this is the spatial focus of the discipline. This dimension of geography has experienced explosive growth, during the past three decades, especially in areas of human geography. The methods used to gather data have expanded dramatically and now include techniques ranging from Earth satellite recording to sophisticated electronic sampling. Methods of analysis also have changed, so that geographers now deal with unprecedented quantities of data.

Location theory has become a modern element of human geography, often using quantitative tech-

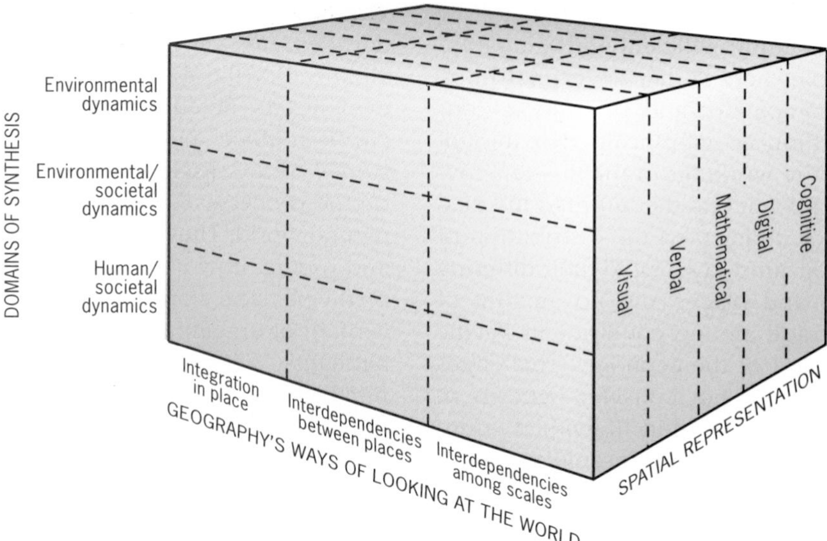

Figure 1-2 Matrix of Geographic Perspectives. Geography's ways of looking at the world—through its focus on place and scale (horizontal axis)—cuts across its three domains of synthesis: human-societal dynamics, environmental dynamics, and environmental-societal dynamics (vertical axis). Spatial representation, the third dimension of the matrix, underpins and sometimes drives research in other branches of geography. *Source: National Research Council, 1997.* Rediscovering Geography: New Relevance for Science and Society. *Washington, D.C.: National Academy Press.*

niques to seek answers to a wide range of questions—some of them theoretical, others highly practical: Why are villages, towns, and cities spaced the way they are? Given a market of a certain size and wealth, where in the surrounding countryside should particular products be grown or raised? What would be the best location for a new shopping center, given existing urban patterns?

The Area-Analysis Tradition The fourth tradition, area analysis, also has undergone a transformation. In the early 1960s, area analysis still focused primarily on the description of areas and regions. Regional geography of a more sophisticated type still forms an important part of the discipline. But the area-analysis tradition also has given rise to ***regional science***, the application of modern spatial analytical techniques to regional problems and issues. In whatever form it exists and whatever it is called, regional study will survive as one of the central traditions of geography. James Michener once wrote that whenever he started writing a new book, he first prepared himself by turning to books written by regional geographers about the area where the action was to occur. Geography's regional dimension is, indeed, one of its permanent traditions.

Themes

During the 1980s, when concern about geographic illiteracy in the United States was growing, several organizations began campaigns to reintroduce geography into school curricula.

Leading these campaigns was the National Geographic Society, and this organization's contribution went beyond the financial; it played a key role in facilitating the work of the Geography Education National Implementation Project (GENIP)—an initiative of the four major U.S. geographical organizations. The National Geographic Society published a document entitled *Maps, the Landscape, and Fundamental Themes in Geography* (1986), which discussed the "Five Themes" of geography developed by GENIP. Several million copies of the publication were disseminated to the schools, and the "Five Themes" became, for many students, an introduction to the discipline of geography.

Three of the ***themes*** correspond to traditions identified earlier: location, interaction between humans and environments, and regions. These durable traditions continue to anchor the study of geography.

In addition to these three traditional themes, the National Geographic Society's publication identified two others. The fourth theme is represented by the simple word ***place***. All places on the surface of the Earth have distinguishing human and physical characteristics, and one of the purposes of geography is to study places and understand how they function. The fifth theme, ***movement***, refers to the mobility of people, goods, and ideas. Interactions of many kinds shape the human geography of the world, and understanding these is an important aspect of geography.

The National Geographic Society's Five Themes of 1986 have much in common with the Four Traditions of 1964, with one important exception: their neglect of physical geography. We should remember this even as we focus on human geography: we are dealing with only part of a discipline that is bound not by a set of facts but by a perspective that applies to the physical as well as to the human world.

The importance of the perspectives that unite geography is highlighted in a recently released report by the National Research Council: *Rediscovering Geography: New Relevance for Science and Society.* This report was developed in response to what the Council's chairman describes as a "renaissance of geography in the United States." The report identifies three key perspectives at the core of the discipline: integration in place, interdependencies between places, and interdependencies among scales (Fig. 1-2). Each of these arises out of geography's fundamental concern with the evolving spatial organization and material character of the Earth's surface. They highlight geography's role as an integrative discipline concerned with how and why things come together to create particular places, regions, and landscapes, and the implications of the resulting patterns and processes.

◆ USING THE SPATIAL PERSPECTIVE

There is no better way to demonstrate the insights gained through spatial analysis than through the use of ***maps***. Maps and geography are practically synonymous, and mapmaking is as old as geography itself. (For details on cartography, see Resource A at the end of this book.) Maps are used to wage war, to make political propaganda, to solve medical problems, to locate shopping centers, to bring relief to refugees, to warn of natural hazards—in short, for countless purposes.

The theme of location is fundamental to geography. Maps tell us where places are located in relation to other places. However, there is more to this than first meets the eye. True, maps provide the locations of places in terms of the Earth's latitude-longitude grid, but it really means very little to know that Chicago lies at 41 degrees, 53 minutes North Latitude and 87 degrees, 38 minutes West Longitude. Those data identify Chicago's ***absolute location***. They become interesting when compared to other absolute locations, but for our purposes they are not useful for much else. By checking a map, we can deter-

SENSE OF SCALE

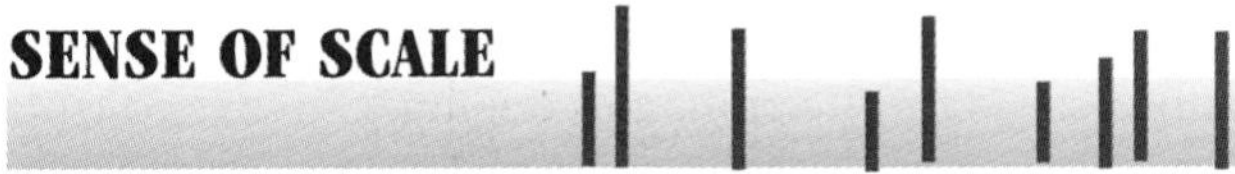

Geography and Scale

Geographers examine places and patterns at a variety of scales, from local to regional to global. Indeed, geography's concern with space puts scale at the center of its agenda. After all, the very process of examining and mapping a phenomenon involves making choices about scale. The things one might say about the distribution of French speakers will change depending on whether one looks at that distribution throughout the world, in Europe, in France, or in a Paris neighborhood. And geographers' sensitivity to scale leads them always to question what is revealed and what is hidden when a generalization is made about a people or a place at a particular scale.

The geographer's concern with scale goes beyond an interest in the scale of individual phenomena to a concern with how processes operating at different scales influence one another. If one is to understand the conflict between the Tutsi and the Hutu people in Rwanda, for example, one cannot look solely at this small African country. That conflict is influenced by developments at a variety of different scales, including patterns of migration and interaction in Central Africa, the economic and political relations between Rwanda and parts of Europe, and the variable impacts of globalization—economic, political, and cultural. The extent to which phenomena at one scale are influenced by those at other scales is so great that some scholars talk about a "local-global continuum."

It is impossible for a single text to cover all the complexities of the local-global continuum. We have therefore chosen to focus on the global and regional scales, both because this book is designed as an introductory survey of the field and because an understanding of developments at larger scales is critical to an appreciation of what is happening at smaller scales. Nevertheless, it is important to understand that influences flow not just from top to bottom, but in the other direction as well, and we talk about some of these in the book. It is also important to recognize that the tools of inquiry that we employ in this book can be employed at smaller scales as well: population can be mapped and analyzed in a neighborhood, cultural landscapes can be studied in a village, and the environmental impacts of agriculture can be studied in a watershed. To help highlight this point, the Sense of Scale boxes scattered through the text highlight local manifestations of larger-scale phenomena and show how developments at one scale influence those at another scale.

mine that Chicago lies approximately at the same latitude as Madrid, Spain, and Beijing, China, and (this may surprise you) at the same longitude as the Galapagos Islands in the Pacific Ocean. So the coordinates of absolute location are useful mainly in determining exact distances and directions.

The ***relative location*** of a place is a very different matter. This is its location relative to other human and physical features on the landscape. Where does Chicago lie in relation to Lake Michigan, its important waterway; to Milwaukee, its not-too-distant neighbor; to the mineral resources and farmlands of the Midwest; or to the road and railroad networks? All of these could be represented on maps. Note that a vast system of roads and railroads converges on Chicago from all parts of the surrounding region (Fig. 1-3). This means that the city's interconnections with the region around it are exceptionally efficient. Whether you wanted to distribute something from Chicago to the four states that lie within 60 miles (100 kilometers) of it, or reach the Chicago market from someplace in the region, surface communications are readily available. What the map does not show is Chicago's role as a hub of airline transportation. As urban geographers (those who study cities) say, Chicago has great ***centrality***. Centrality is a function of location, relative to other urban places, resources, productive farmlands, and efficient transport linkages.

Whereas the absolute location of a place does not change, its relative location is subject to constant modification. From its beginning, Chicago was an important city in the interior of North America, but its relative location changed markedly in 1959 when the St. Lawrence Seaway was opened and the city acquired a direct maritime connection to the North Atlantic Ocean. Although the seaway closes in the winter when ice blocks navigation, Chicago can be reached by oceangoing vessels throughout the rest of the year. As an inland port, its relative location has changed substantially. Ships that could once get no closer than the eastern ports of North America now dock in sight of Chicago's downtown skyline.

An especially dramatic change in relative location has affected an entire country, Japan, during the past century. As late as the mid-nineteenth century, Japan was relatively isolated from the developing global

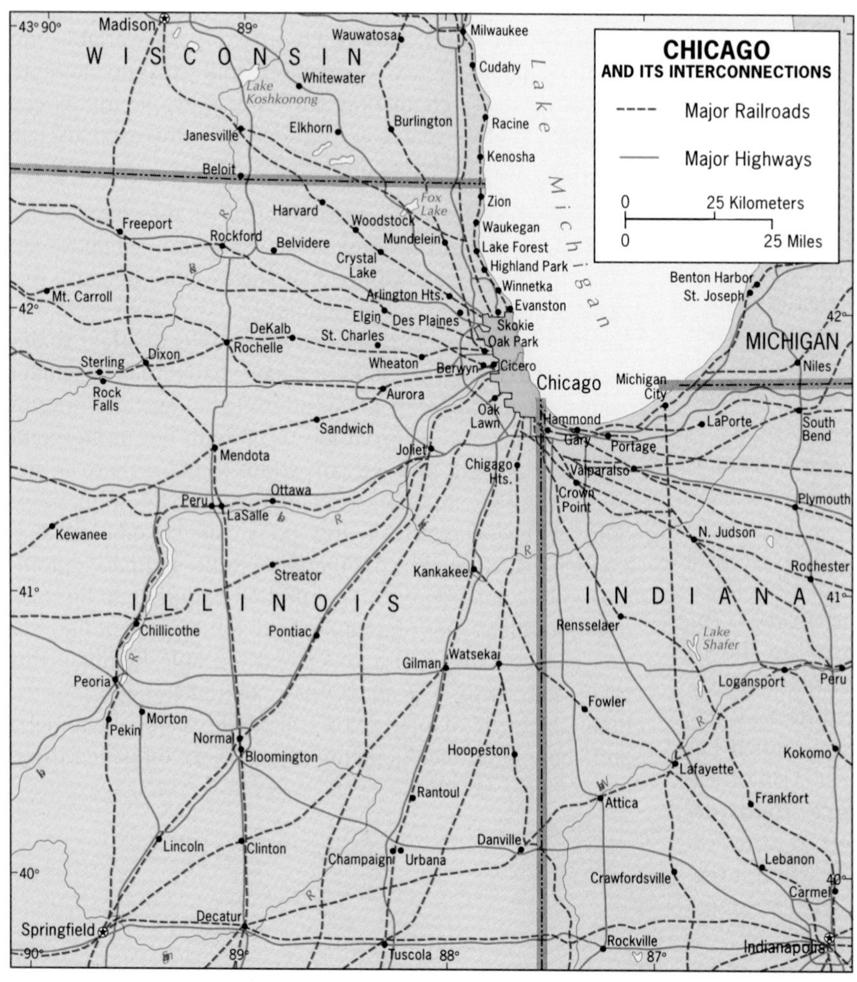

Figure 1-3 Chicago and Its Interconnections. Surface communication lines converge on Chicago.

economy. When the Japanese decided to embark on the road to industrialization, they chose Britain as their model (which is why they still drive on the left side of the road). However, Japan was half a world removed from Europe, the center of the industrial world at the time. Then during the twentieth century, the United States took this position from the Europeans, and now Japan lay directly across the Pacific from the newly powerful American market. Today, Japan's relative location is changing again as China, right across the East China Sea, becomes a growing trading partner and Russia beckons from across the Sea of Japan. Japan thus has gone from remote isolation to global hub—but its absolute location never changed!

◆ THE ROLE OF MAPS IN HUMAN GEOGRAPHY

One of the ways geographers can gain a better understanding of places and issues is by comparing spatial data. Frequently, these comparisons make use of geographic information systems (GISs), a powerful new tool that allows geographers to combine layers of data in a computerized environment, creating maps in which patterns and processes are superimposed. GISs are used not only to *display* spatial data, but also to *analyze* those data, creating new insights in the process. Some of the figures in this book are based on information from GISs.

Maps and Places

Maps demonstrate a vital rule of geography: that places on the Earth have their own distinctive properties that, taken together, give each place its own character. No place is exactly like another, and a map is the best way to prove this. Geographers study both the physical and human properties of places. The Earth's surface, its elevation and relief, slopes and drainage, soils, natural vegetation, and atmospheric conditions (climate and weather) form the physical setting. The uses of this setting, in the form of settlement layout, population patterns, transport networks, land use, and other activity, create the human imprint. Together, these physical and human features constitute the overall geographic character of a particular place.

Geographers therefore have a special interest in the quality of places. Whether it's a fishing village on China's coast or a bustling Arab town, geographers want to know how the people have implanted their traditions on that locale, why they have done so, what sustains them now, and how they interact with the outside world (Fig. 1-4). It is impossible, of course, to study all these aspects at once, so geographers tend to specialize in certain features of places. Some study the street layout and architecture of a town; others concentrate on the transport systems that serve it. Still others focus on the business and industry that sustain the local economy. In the process, a kind of geographic overview of the place emerges. If you were to become a professional geographer and found yourself assigned to study, say, the growth of suburbs around Santiago, the capital of Chile, you would first read what geographers (and others) have already written about that city. With the many specialized maps they have prepared, you would be well informed before you ever set foot in the field.

Maps and Environmental Issues

Throughout this book the theme of human interaction with the environment emerges time and again. Human geography, whether economic, political, urban, or agricultural, cannot be studied without reference to the

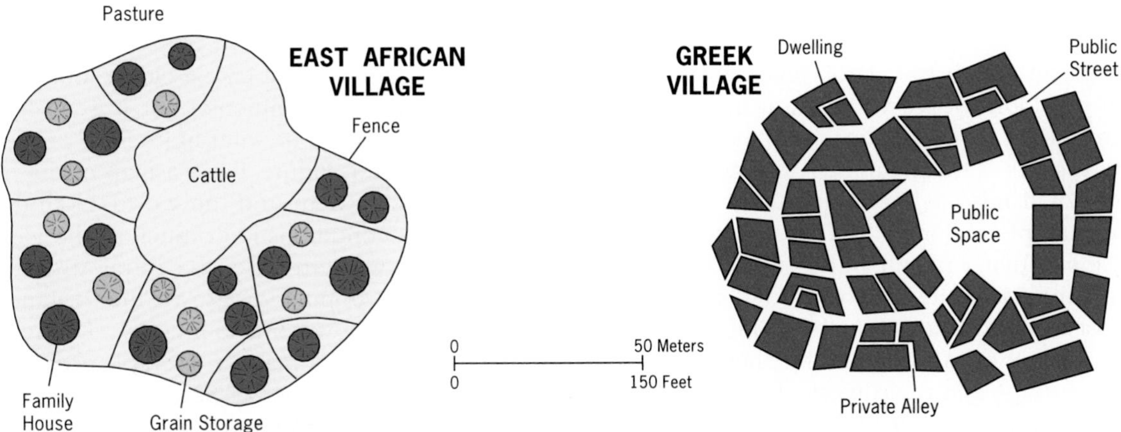

Figure 1-4 Contrasting Village Forms in Africa and Europe. East Africa and Greek villages differ. *Source: From authors' sketch.*

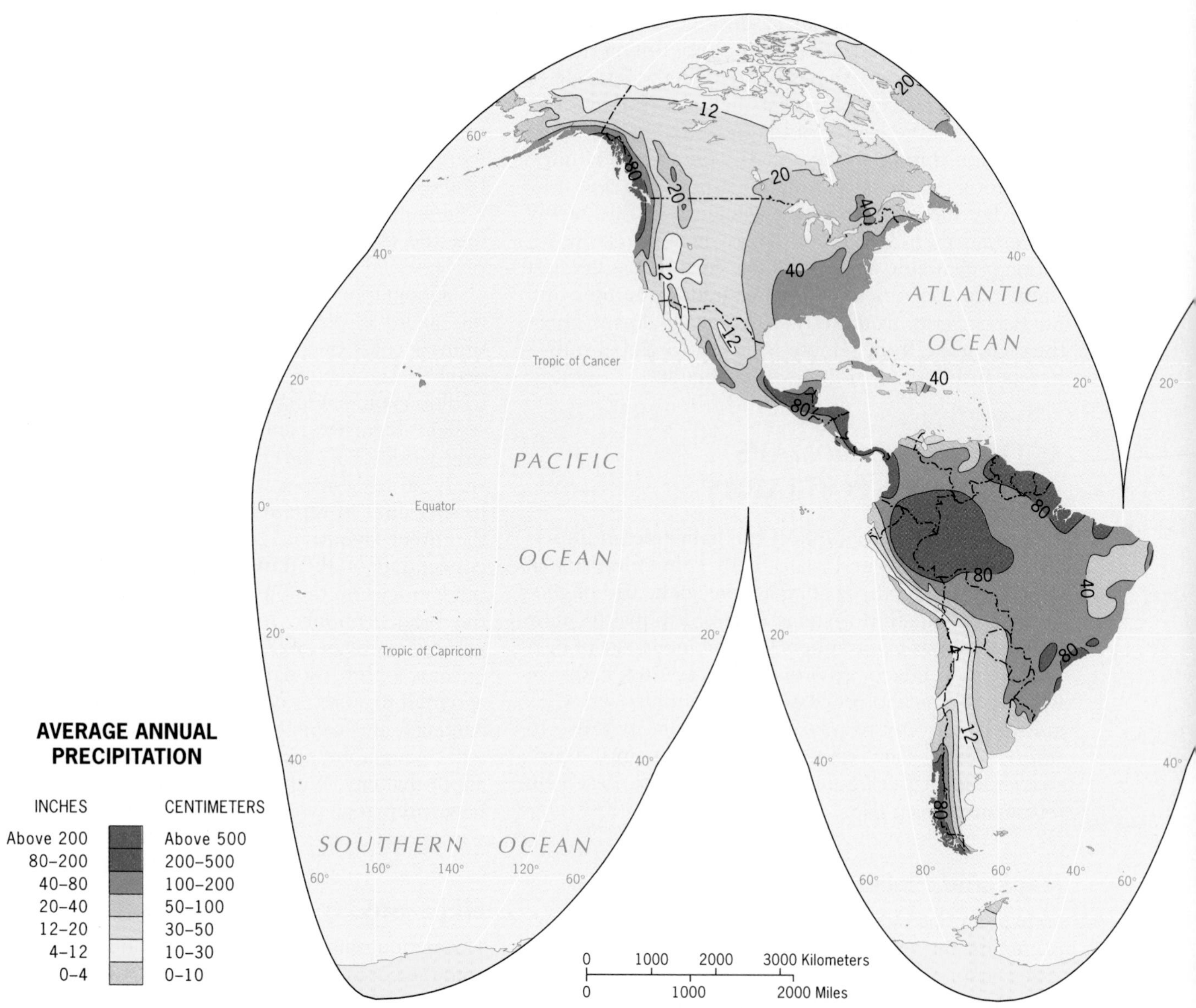

Figure 1-5 Average Annual Precipitation of the World. A generalized map of the mean annual precipitation received around the world. Note that this map projection (see Resource A) is interrupted in the oceans, allowing for maximum clarity of detail on the landmasses.

environment in which the action takes place. In the course of our journey, we will look at maps of "acid rain" distribution, deforestation, river basins, ice ages, and other aspects of the natural environment. Some of these maps will raise as many questions as they answer. For example, if Bangladesh faces certain disaster from cyclones that can kill hundreds of thousands, why do people continue to inhabit low-lying ground in the most dangerous areas? Is the southward spread of the Sahara in West Africa a natural phenomenon, or are human groups and their livestock responsible for this devastating process? If the Amazonian rainforest in Brazil and adjacent countries continues to be destroyed at present rates, what will happen to rainfall patterns there?

In Part One we will take a closer look at past and present global environments, but it is useful now to consider a map of one vital ingredient of our Earthly existence: water. Figure 1-5 is a map of the mean annual precipitation around the world. Note the prevalence of dry conditions over much of the globe, from inner Asia to western Africa to central Australia. As the Earth's human population grows, the demands on this limited supply of water also increase. Drought-caused famines have struck many vulnerable areas, including the northeastern corner of South America, the southern margins of the Sahara in Africa, and south-central Asia. Often such death-dealing droughts cause people to seek relief elsewhere, creating migration streams that cause further dislocation in neighboring zones.

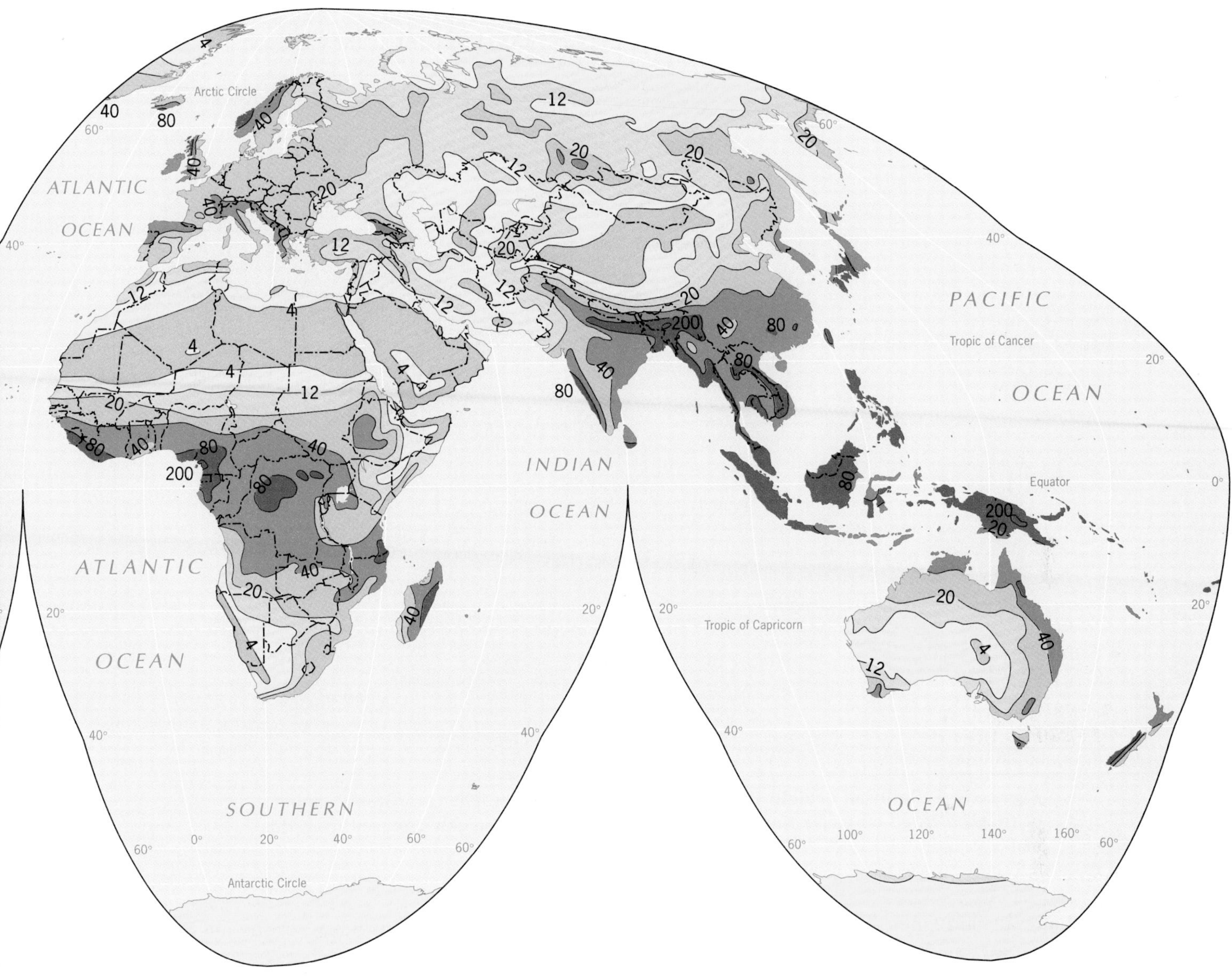

For example, thousands of people and their livestock, fleeing from the last drought in West Africa, migrated southward into the moister savanna lands of coastal countries. There cattle trampled crops and destroyed harvests, and the result was armed conflict between the local farmers and the invading migrants.

Water shortages are not confined to desert-edge grazing lands in remote corners of the world. Water rationing became a fact of life in California in the early 1990s, yet people continue to move not only into California but also into other water-deficient areas of the Southwest. As Figure 1-5 suggests, the prospects for water supply in a burgeoning world are worrisome. Expensive desalinization plants, using ocean water, modeled after those on the Arabian shore of the Persian Gulf, are making their appearance in California. But their capacity is a drop in the proverbial bucket.

The map of world precipitation also emphasizes the importance of the Atlantic Ocean. Note that except for South Asia and Southeast Asia, the moistest areas of the world lie clustered against Atlantic shores, from water-warmed Western Europe to Amazonian South America and from the southeastern United States to West and equatorial Africa. These regions owe most of their annual water supply to the Atlantic Ocean, whose slowly circulating waters bring warmth and moisture to areas from Britain to Brazil. Even the peaks of the Andes Mountains in western South America, and the densely populated highlands of eastern Africa, get most of their snow and rain not from the neighboring Pacific and Indian Oceans, but from the faraway Atlantic. Here again we see that a map can tell far more than mere distribution.

Remote sensing is an important technique used for understanding the scale and rate of many types of environmental change. Remote sensing data collected by

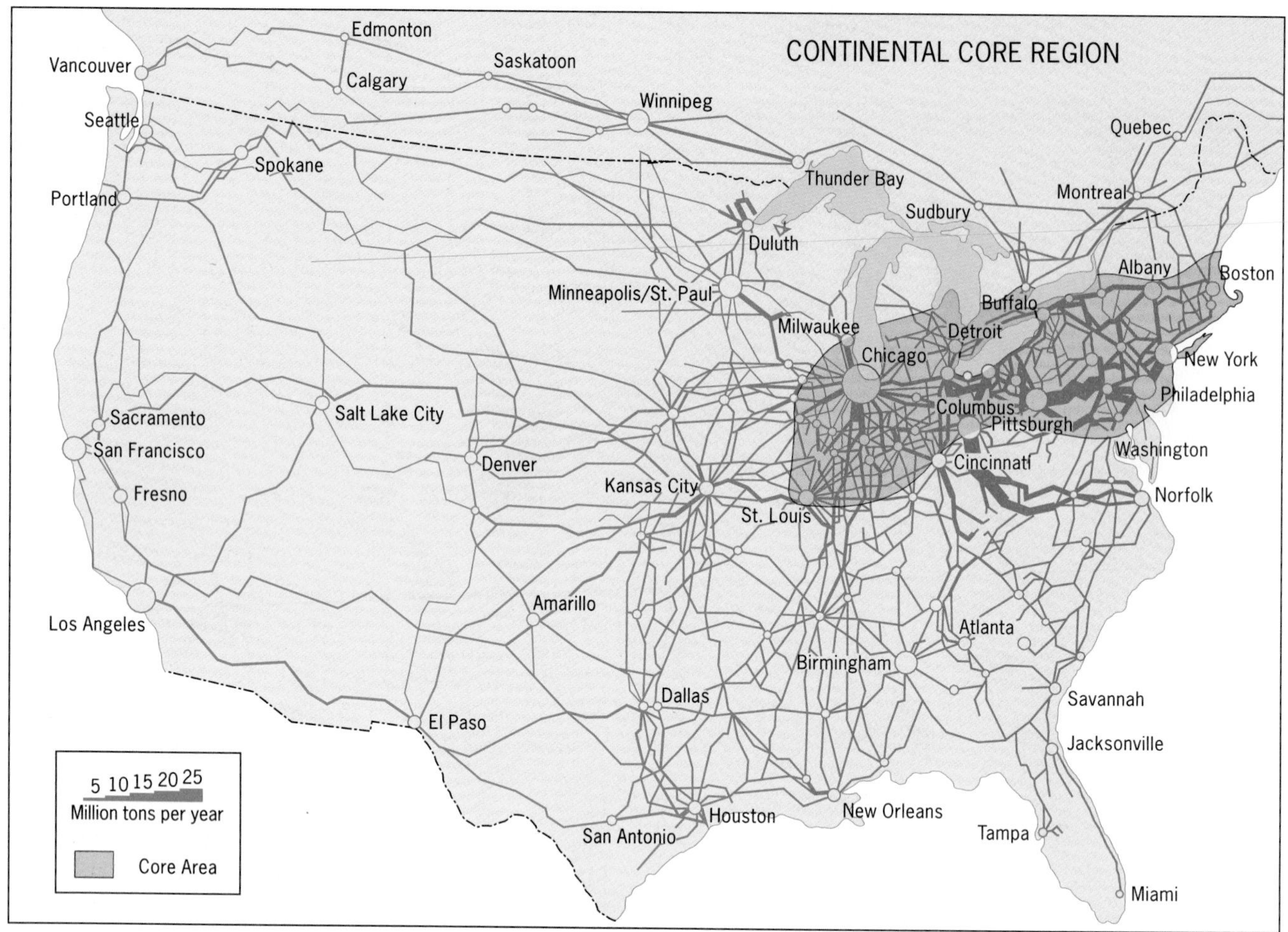

Figure 1-6 Railroad Freight in Continental Core Region. The comparative amount of freight carried on major North American railroads can be quickly assessed from this map.

satellites and aircraft (airplanes, balloons, etc.) reveal both physical changes, such as the extent of flooding in the Mississippi River Valley, and changes that are more directly due to human activity, such as deforestation in the Brazilian Amazon resulting from agricultural activities. More recently, the establishment of a satellite-based global positioning system (GPS) has allowed us to locate things on the surface of the Earth with extraordinary accuracy. Not only does this permit locational data to be collected more quickly and easily in the field, but GPS units also have more mundane uses, such as helping lost campers find their way out of the woods.

Maps and Human Mobility

It is one thing to map static features, such as existing patterns and distributions or the locations of cities and towns, but it is quite another to represent movement on the map. Yet movement is a central theme of geography. Whether it is the movement of goods from factories to markets, the flow of oil from Middle Eastern wells to American consumers, or the migration of people from one region to another, movement must be recorded on maps and interpreted.

To indicate movement, cartographers use many symbols. For example, you can represent the numbers of travelers on key highways or major airline routes using arrows of varying width: the widths of the arrows reveal the comparative quantities of traffic (Fig. 1-6). Such maps show at a glance the intensity of movement along certain routes, and more careful examination reveals the actual numbers or volumes involved.

But there are times when it is not so much the actual volume, but the *direction* of movement that matters most. Where capital flows, for example, can be just as important as how capital is moving out of a particular place. More often it is the movement of ideas, notions, and innovations that matters, but such movement cannot be quantified. The geographic term for this is ***diffusion***, the spread of ideas or knowledge from their origins to areas where they are adopted. Much as we would like to, we cannot always measure such diffusion quantitatively, but we can trace its direction. So some maps representing this process have arrows that reflect direction only, not volume.

Maps showing movement of various kinds are among the most interesting in geography. In the chapter on medical geography, you will find a series of maps with arrows showing the routes of invasion of cholera, a dreaded illness of the nineteenth century. At the time, no one knew what caused cholera; hundreds of thousands of people died of it. But others were somehow spared. As it turned out, a map was the key to discovering the answer, and a medical geographer solved the problem. Today, similar efforts are being made to combat AIDS, another dreaded disease affecting millions. And again medical geographers are using maps to help.

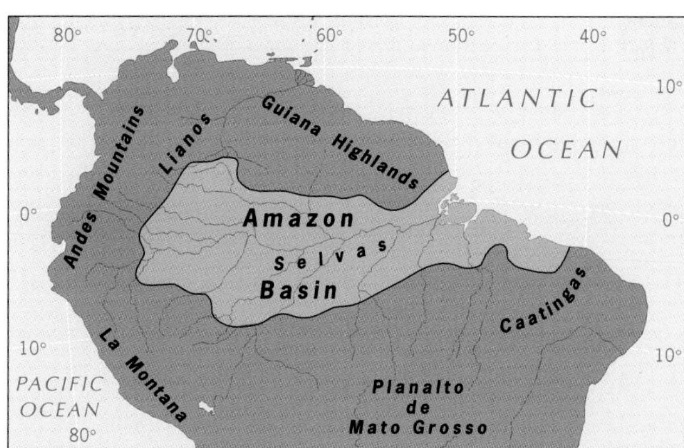

Figure 1-7 Amazon Basin. The Amazon Basin as a region defined by catchment area and topography.

Regions on the Map

Throughout this book we will use *regions*, and the *regional concept*, to clarify what is being discussed. Actually, we use some form of the regional idea all the time, even in everyday conversation. When you plan a vacation in "the Rockies," or a hiking trip in New England, or a cruise in the Caribbean, you are using regional notions to convey what you have in mind. Regions, used this way, serve as informal frames of reference.

In geography, the regional concept is, of course, more specific. To refer to "the Rockies" as a perceived region summarizes what is prominent about this region: steep slopes, high relief, dramatic mountain scenery, snowcapped peaks, and ski slopes. But as a geographer you might be asked to *define* and *delimit* a Rocky Mountains region. Exactly where are the boundaries of "the Rockies"? In some places, the answer is easily found as the mountains rise suddenly from the adjacent Great Plains (another region). But elsewhere the mountainous terrain rises gradually; the plains become hilly and the slopes become steeper. Where, and on what basis, do you draw the regional boundary?

To identify and delimit regions, we must establish *criteria* for them. Imagine that, as an exercise in physical geography, you were asked to delimit the Amazon River Basin as a geographic region. There would be various ways to do this: you might use vegetation distribution, soil properties, slope angles, or drainage patterns. When you presented your results, you would first state the basis on which you had mapped the region and then produce the resulting map. On a small scale, the map might resemble Figure 1-7, which uses drainage lines and defines the Amazon Basin on the basis of the rivers and tributaries that ultimately drain into this great South American river.

Thus we know that all regions have certain characteristics. These include ***area***, that is, they all have some defined spatial extent; ***location***, in that all regions lie somewhere on the Earth's surface; and limits or ***boundaries***, which are sometimes evident on the ground and sometimes not, and are often based on specifically chosen criteria.

Regions are not all of the same type. Some are marked by visible uniformity, for example, a desert basin marked by severe aridity, sandy surface, and steep surrounding mountain slopes. Geographers refer to such a homogeneous region as a ***formal region***. Formal regions also are defined by cultural (as opposed to physical) criteria. A region within which French is spoken by, say, 90 percent or more of the population, is also a formal region. A ***functional region***, on the other hand, is the product of interactions, of movement of various kinds. A city, for example, has a surrounding region within which workers commute, either to the downtown area or to subsidiary centers such as office parks and shopping malls (Fig. 1-8). That entire urban area, defined by people

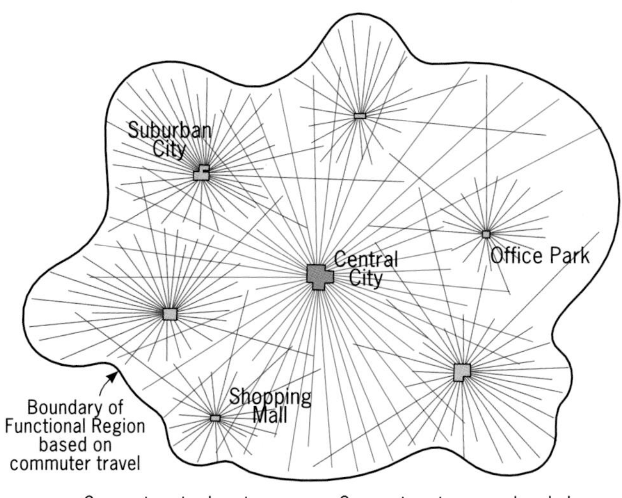

Figure 1-8 Commuter Travel Patterns. Commuter travel patterns in an urban area. *Source: From authors' sketch.*

moving toward and within it, is a functional region. Thus a functional region is a spatial system; its boundaries are defined by the limits of that system. Finally, regions may be primarily in the minds of people. These ***perceptual regions*** are not just curiosities. How people think about regions has influenced everything from daily activity patterns to large-scale international conflict.

Regions can be seen in a vertical order or ***hierarchy***. The French-speaking region to which we referred earlier is a region within a larger region, namely, Western Europe. Western Europe, in turn, is a region of the European geographic realm. Regions form a hierarchy based on size and importance.

Regions, therefore, are ways of organizing humans geographically. They are a form of spatial classification, a means of handling large amounts of information so that it makes sense. The regional concept thus is an indispensable aid in our journey through human geography.

Maps in the Mind

Whether we like it or not, we see and study things from our particular viewpoint, which is shaped by our cultural environment. No matter how hard we try to be objective, our view of the world and its problems (geographic and otherwise) is not the same as the view from Africa or China. Certainly, a map of mountain ranges or known oil reserves might look the same whether it was drawn in China or America, but when we study more subjective things—culture and tradition, politics, or development—we may have quite a different outlook. Take, for example, a standard picture of a major city in another country, such as Mexico (Mexico City) or Kenya (Nairobi). Such a picture is likely to show the modern, high-rise buildings of the "downtown" area, the heart of the city. However, the fact is that the great majority of the people of Mexico City and Nairobi (and dozens of other large cities) live in modest, often inadequate dwellings in vast, sprawling housing tracts that surround the urban core. For many of these people, the skyscrapers of the central city are irrelevant, and city life is a battle for survival in quite a different environment. Shouldn't a "typical" picture of Mexico City or Nairobi show *that* image rather than the downtown area?

It is important to realize that our study of the human world contains some cultural bias, no matter how hard we try to see alternative viewpoints. As you get to know geographers, you will find that they tend to be drawn to the field partly because of their interest in, and respect for, other societies and cultures. That, however, does not make us immune to bias or insensitivity. After all, human geography deals with population growth and control, race and religion, economic development, and political institutions, all of which can be touchy subjects.

Mental Maps Imagine that you are attending a seminar discussion on the political geography of Southern Africa, but there is no wall map to which you can refer. What is your frame of reference? Obviously, it is the countries of the region: South Africa, Namibia, Swaziland, Lesotho, Botswana, Zimbabwe, and their neighbors. As you speak, you will use the map that is in your mind, your ***mental map*** of that part of the world. That mental map has developed over years of looking at wall maps, atlas maps, maps in books, magazines, and newspapers.

Mental maps are a fundamental part of our general knowledge; we use them constantly. If someone were to call you to suggest that you go to the theater, a mental map would come to mind: the hallway, the front door, the walk to your car, the lane to choose in order to be prepared for the left turn you must make, where you would prefer to park, and so forth. If your mental map is vague, you will need a city map to find your way. However, if the issue is more serious than a trip to the theater, and a large number of people are poorly informed, vague mental maps can lead to major policy mistakes.

Environmental Perception Mental maps (also called cognitive maps) are derived from visual observation of the real world (your city or town, college campus, shopping center) and from the scrutiny and study of printed maps. Sights are supplemented by sounds and smells, and the total impression is ***environmental perception***. This is the impression that generates our mental map.

Since geographers are interested in both the physical world and the human organization of it, environmental perception is a popular geographic topic. We have perceptions of places we know by personal experience, but we also carry images of places we have never visited. What shapes these perceptions? To what extent are they accurate or distorted? In a fascinating book titled *Mental Maps* (1982), geographers Peter Gould and Rodney White begin by asking the following question: If you could move to any place of your choice, without any of the usual financial and other obstacles, where would you like to live? (For their respondents' answers, see Fig. 1-9.) Perhaps you would select a location that you perceive as attractive but have never personally experienced. However, the actual environment may turn out to be quite different from your perception of it.

A crucial part of our perception of a place lies in

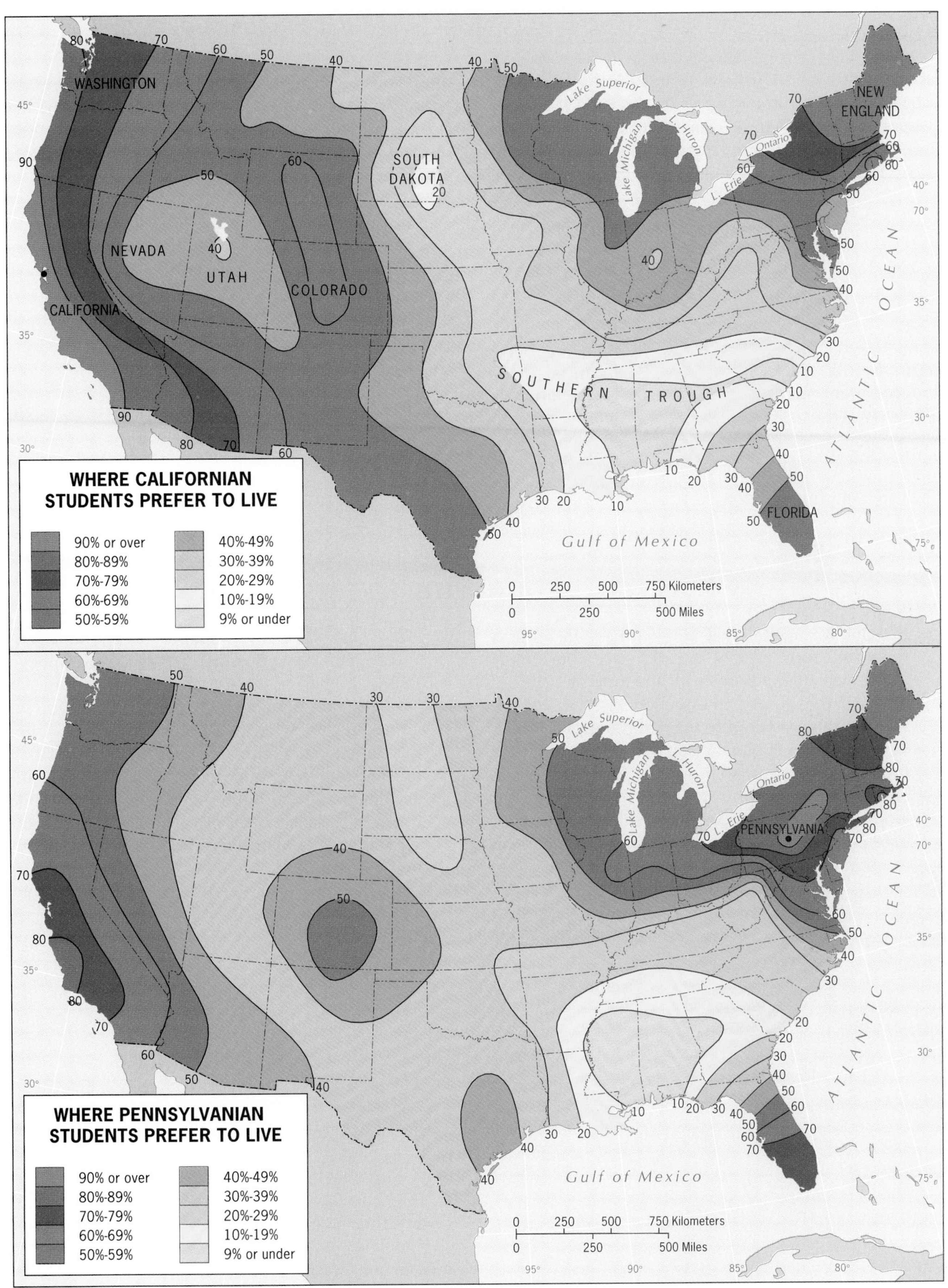

Figure 1-9 Different Living Preferences. Where Californians and Pennsylvanians would prefer to live. *Source: From P. R. Gould and R. White.* Mental Maps. *Harmondsworth: Penguin Books, 1986, pp. 55 and 58. Redrawn by permission of the publisher.*

its layout, that is, its spatial arrangement and organization. To know the location of a country (whether it is Laos or Afghanistan or Bolivia) is only a beginning. From maps we can gain impressions of topography and relief, climate and weather, the quality of roads, the layout of villages and towns, and countless other conditions—without ever having been there. The map is thus our window on the world.

See Resource A, Maps, at the end of the book for guidelines on how to read and use maps.

◆ KEY TERMS ◆

absolute location
area
boundary
centrality
culture-environment
diffusion
distribution
earth-science
environmental geography
environmental perception
functional region
hierarchy
human geography
location (absolute, relative)
location theory
map
mental map
movement
pattern
perceptual region
physical (natural) geography
place
regional science
regions (formal, functional)
relative location
spatial perspective
themes
traditions

◆ APPLYING GEOGRAPHIC KNOWLEDGE ◆

1. Imagine yourself living and working in a small town in a rural area of the Midwest. Your family owns and operates a small department store located at the busiest intersection in town, where the through road crosses the main shopping street. Now the State Highway Department is building a four-lane highway that will bypass your town about six miles away. How will this change your store's relative location? How will it affect your market? What might you and other shopowners do to counter the impact of the new highway?

2. The editor of a city newspaper has appointed you to her staff, and your first job as a geographer is to draw a map of the region within which the paper sells, that is, its market. Describe how you will go about this: what will be the criteria on which this functional region is based? When you have finished your map, the region turns out to be quite asymmetrical; the paper sells as far as 100 miles north of the city, but only 60 miles to the south. What might explain this variable "reach" of the newspaper?

Chapter 2

Culture, Environments, and Regions

From the field notes

"The Atlantic-coast city of Bergen, Norway, displayed the Norse cultural landscape more comprehensively, it seemed, than any other Norwegian city, including Oslo. The high-relief site of Bergen creates great vistas, but also long shadows: windows are large to let in maximum light. Red-tiled roofs are pitched steeply to enhance runoff and inhibit snow accumulation; streets are narrow and houses clustered, conserving warmth."

KEY POINTS

◆ **The concept of culture lies at the heart of human geography.**

◆ **The components of culture include culture regions, culture traits, culture complexes, and culture systems.**

◆ **Key topics in cultural geography are cultural landscape, culture hearths, cultural diffusion, cultural perception, and cultural environment.**

◆ **Culture hearths are the sources of civilizations; ideas, innovation, and ideologies radiate outward from them.**

◆ **Several types of cultural diffusion exist. Expansion diffusion may take the form of contagious diffusion, hierarchical diffusion, or stimulus diffusion. Relocation diffusion involves the actual movement of individuals.**

◆ **Perceptual regions can differ considerably, depending on the individual's mental maps of various communities and cultures.**

◆ **The doctrine of environmental determinism, which holds that human behavior is limited or controlled by the environment, has been a subject of intense debate, and broad generalizations about the impact of environment on humans have been discredited.**

Human geography, as we saw in Chapter 1, encompasses a large part of the discipline. Figure 1-1 reveals human geography's numerous branches as well as its links to other disciplines, ranging from anthropology to zoology. Unifying all these branches of human geography is the spatial perspective. How are humanity's works arranged on the surface of the Earth? What forces and factors influenced their location and distribution? Do different societies organize their space in different ways, and if so, what can be learned from the patterns we observe?

◆ CULTURE AND HUMAN GEOGRAPHY

At the heart of the wide-ranging subdiscipline of human geography lies the concept of ***culture***, for location decisions, patterns, and landscapes are fundamentally influenced by cultural attitudes and practices. Like the regional concept discussed in Chapter 1, the concept of culture appears to be deceptively simple but in fact is complex and challenging. You can prove this just by looking up *culture* in several dictionaries and introductory anthropology texts and noting how widely their definitions of the term vary. Our uses of the word also vary. When we speak of a "cultured" individual, we tend to mean someone with refined tastes in music and the arts, a highly educated, well-read person who knows and appreciates the "best" attributes of society. As a scientific term, however, culture refers not only to the music, literature, and arts of a society but also to all the other features of its way of life: prevailing modes of dress; routine living habits; food preferences; the architecture of houses and public buildings; the layout of fields and farms; and systems of education, government, and law. Thus *culture* is an all-encompassing term that identifies not only the whole tangible lifestyle of a people, but also their prevailing values and beliefs.

The concept of culture is closely identified with the discipline of anthropology, and over the course of more than a century anthropologists have defined it in many different ways. The noted scholar M. J. Herskovits defined culture tersely as "the man-made part of the environment." Another anthropologist, M. Harris, called it "the learned patterns of thought and behavior characteristic of a population or society." Still another anthropologist, E. Adamson Hoebel, defined culture as:

> The integrated system of learned behavior patterns which are characteristic of the members of a society and which are not the result of biological inheritance . . . culture is not geneti-

cally predetermined; it is noninstinctive . . . [culture] is wholly the result of social invention and is transmitted and maintained solely through communication and learning.

This definition touches on a hotly debated issue: the transmission of culture from one generation to the next. Older definitions such as Hoebel's routinely suggest that culture can be transmitted only through learning, but recent advances in sociobiology and related fields suggest that certain behaviors may be genetically determined, so that culture has an "instinctive" component as well as a "learned" one.

Hoebel's emphasis on communication and learning anticipated the current view that culture is a system of meaning, not just a set of acts, customs, or material products. Clifford Geertz advances this view in his classic work, *The Interpretation of Cultures* (1973); much recent work in human geography has been influenced by it. Hence, human geographers are interested not just in the different patterns and landscapes associated with different culture groups, but in the ways in which cultural understandings affect both the creation and significance of those patterns and landscapes.

Components of Culture

Culture is so complex that it is necessary to unravel its interconnected parts. Certain of these parts tie in directly with geography's emphasis on space. A ***culture region*** (the area within which a particular culture system prevails) is marked by all the attributes of a culture, including modes of dress, building styles, farms and fields, and other material manifestations. Cultural geographers identify a single attribute of a culture as a ***culture trait***. For example, the wearing of a turban is a culture trait of Muslim society; for centuries, it was obligatory for men to wear this headgear. Although it is no longer required, the turban continues to be a distinctive trait of Muslim culture. The use of simple tools also constitutes a culture trait, and eating with certain utensils (knife and fork or chopsticks) is a culture trait.

Culture traits are not necessarily confined to a single culture. More than one culture may exhibit a particular culture trait, but each will consist of a discrete *combination* of traits. Such a combination is referred to as a ***culture complex***. In many cultures, the herding of cattle is a trait. However, cattle are regarded and used in different ways by different cultures. The Maasai of East Africa follow their herds along seasonal migration paths, consuming blood and milk as important ingredients of a unique diet. Cattle occupy a central place in Maasai existence; they are the essence of survival, security, and prestige. Although the Maasai culture complex is only one of many cattle-keeping complexes, no other culture complex exhibits exactly the same combination of traits. In Europe, cattle are milked and dairy products, such as butter, yogurt, and cheese, are consumed as part of a diet very different from that of the Maasai.

Thus culture complexes have traits in common, and so it is possible to group certain complexes together as ***culture systems***. Ethnicity, language, religion, and other cultural elements enter into the definition of a culture system; for example, much of China may be so designated. China's culture system consists of a number of quite distinct culture complexes, united by strong cultural bonds. Northern Chinese people may eat wheat and those in the south may eat rice as their staple, and the Chinese language as spoken in the north may not be quite the same as that spoken in the south, but history, philosophy, environmental adaptation and modification, and numerous cultural traditions and attitudes give coherence to the Chinese culture systems.

On the map, an entire culture system is represented by a culture region. West Africa, Polynesia, and Central America may be designated as culture regions of sorts, each consisting of a combination of culture complexes of considerable diversity but still substantial uniformity. Many geographers, however, prefer to describe regions such as Han China, West Africa, and Polynesia as ***geographic regions*** rather than as culture regions, because their definition is based not only on cultural properties but on locational and environmental circumstances as well.

An assemblage of culture (or geographic) regions forms a ***culture realm***, the most highly generalized regionalization of culture and geography on the world map. Together, the culture regions of West, East, equatorial, and Southern Africa constitute the sub-Saharan African culture realm. Once again, there are good reasons for calling these ***geographic realms*** of the human world: the criteria on which they are based, though dominated by cultural characteristics, extend beyond culture.

Cultural Geographies Past and Present

The colonization and Europeanization of the world have obliterated much of the cultural geography of earlier times. Very little is left of the map we might have constructed of indigenous North American cultures (Fig. 2-1); a map of aboriginal Australian cultures would differ radically from the contemporary version. It is important, therefore, to view any map showing culture regions or geographic realms in temporal perspective. Maps of indigenous or "traditional" culture

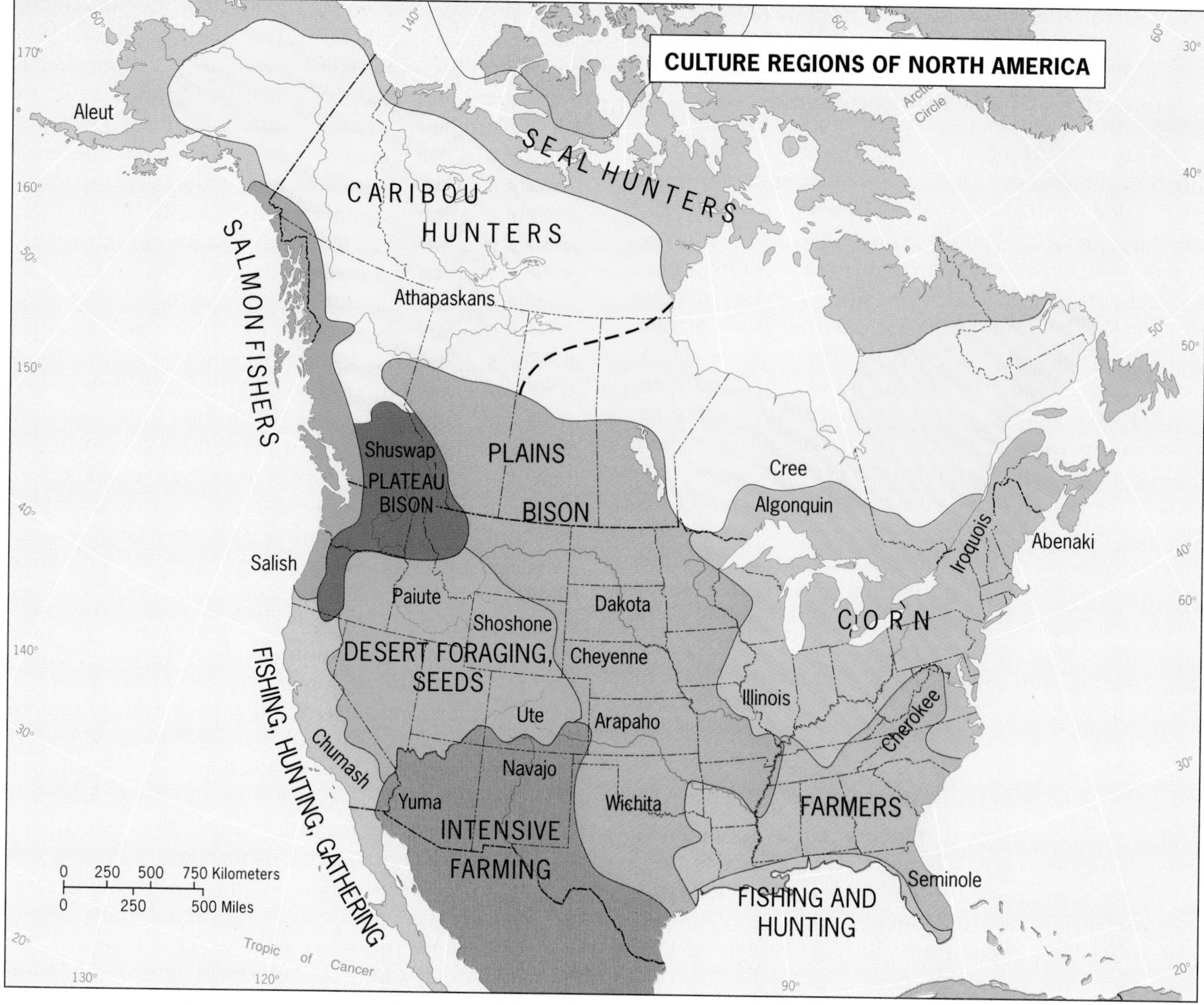

Figure 2-1 Culture Regions of North America. A consensus regionalization of indigenous American cultures. Modern boundary lines are included for spatial references.

complexes do not show the regional patterns resulting from the world's Europeanization and its associated migrations. Consider, for example a map of indigenous African culture regions (Fig. 2-2).

On another map of this sort, New Zealand would be shown as a part of Polynesia because its indigenous Maori population has Polynesian origins. Maps of "modern" culture regions and geographic realms do not reflect historical patterns; instead they represent dominant present-day realities. In a modern context, New Zealand would constitute a segment of a geographic realm shared with Australia and dominated by European cultural norms. The world's cultural mosaic is a jigsaw of traditional and modern regions.

◆ KEY TOPICS IN CULTURAL GEOGRAPHY

The field of cultural geography is wide-ranging and comprehensive. To organize it, we focus on five prominent areas of study and research.

1. ***Cultural Landscape.*** The imprint of cultures on the land creates distinct and characteristic cultural landscapes.
2. ***Culture Hearths.*** Several sources, crucibles, of cultural growth and achievement developed in Eurasia, Africa, and America.
3. ***Cultural Diffusion.*** From their sources, cultural

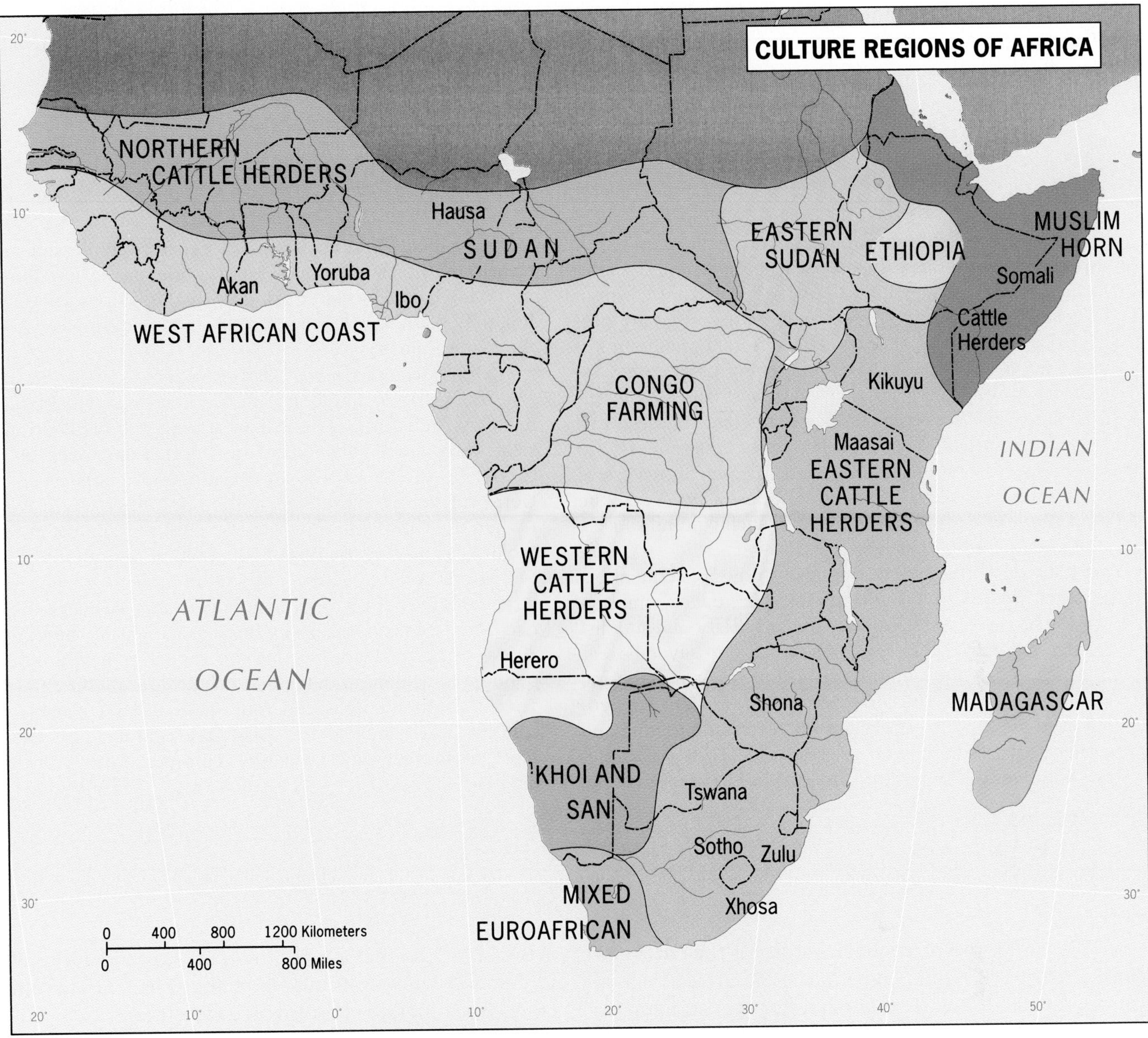

Figure 2-2 Culture Regions of Africa. Generalized regionalization of indigenous cultures in mainland Africa south of the Sahara.

innovations and ideas spread to other areas. The process of cultural diffusion continues to this day.

4. ***Cultural Perception.*** Culture groups have varying ideas and attitudes about space, place, and territory.
5. ***Cultural Environments.*** This area deals with the role of culture in human understanding, use, and alteration of the environment.

In the remainder of this chapter, we focus on these areas in more detail.

The Cultural Landscape

A culture gives character to an area. Often, a single scene, a photograph or picture, can reveal the cultural milieu in which it was made. The architecture, the mode of dress of the people, the means of transportation, and perhaps the goods being carried—all reveal a distinctive cultural environment.

The people of any particular culture transform their living space by building structures on it, creating lines of contact and communication, tilling the land, and channeling the water (see Focus on: Sequent Occupance). There are a few exceptions: nomadic peoples may leave a minimum of permanent evidence on the land, and some peoples living in desert margins (such as the few remaining San clans) and in tropical forest zones (Pygmy groups) do not greatly alter their natural environment. However, most of the time there is change; asphalt roads, irrigation canals, terraced hillslopes.

Focus On

Sequent Occupance

The concept of cultural landscape takes on a practical aspect when an area has been inhabited—and transformed—by a succession of residents, each of whom leaves a lasting imprint. A place and its resources are perceived differently by peoples with different technological and cultural traditions. These contrasting perceptions are reflected in their respective cultural landscapes. The cultural landscape we observe today is a collage of these various contributions, and the challenge for geographers is to reconstruct the contributions made by each successive community. In 1929, Derwent Whittlesey proposed the term ***sequent occupance*** to refer to such cultural succession and its lasting imprints.

Obviously, the most productive studies of sequent occupance are performed at locations where the cultural succession has involved societies with fairly elaborate and distinctive material cultures, as was the case in several areas of Africa. Sequent occupance has left its mark in both rural and urban settings. Thus, for example, the ancient San people used the hillsides and valleys of Swaziland to hunt and gather roots, berries, and other edibles. Then the cattle-herding Bantu found those slopes to be good for grazing, and they planted corn and other food crops in the valleys. Next came the Europeans who laid out sugar plantations in the lowlands, but after using the higher slopes for grazing, they planted extensive forests, and lumbering became the major industry.

The Tanzanian city of Dar es Salaam provides an interesting urban example. Its site was first chosen for settlement by Arabs from Zanzibar who sought a mainland retreat. Next it was selected by the German colonizers as a capital for their East African domain, and it was given a German layout and architectural imprint. After World War I when the Germans were ousted, a British administration took over and the city began still another period of transformation. A large Asian population created a zone of three- and four-story apartment houses that look as if they had been transplanted from Bombay. Then, in the early 1960s, Dar es Salaam became the capital of newly independent Tanzania, under African control for the first time. Thus the city experienced four quite distinct stages of cultural dominance in less than one century, and each stage of the sequence remains imprinted in its cultural landscape.

This composite of artificial features is the ***cultural landscape***, a term that came into general use in geography in the 1920s. The geographer whose name is still most closely identified with this concept is University of California Professor Carl Sauer. In 1927 Sauer wrote an article entitled "Recent Developments in Cultural Geography," in which he produced a deceptively simple definition. The cultural landscape, he said, constitutes "the forms superimposed on the physical landscape by the activities of man." However, when human activities change the physical or natural landscape, does the physical landscape then become a cultural landscape? For example, a dam built in the upper course of a river can affect the whole character of the river downstream, even hundreds of miles away. It can alter the strength of the river's flow and the rate of deposition of sediments in a delta. Does this mean that the river is no longer part of the natural landscape and, therefore, has become a cultural landscape feature? Similar issues are raised by human-induced erosion of untilled soil and by regenerated forests that were formerly cut over. Anyone who is interested can trace this debate in the geographic literature. For our purposes perhaps the best definition is the broadest: that the cultural landscape includes all identifiably human-induced changes in the natural landscape, changes that involve the surface as well as the biosphere.

Thus a cultural landscape consists of buildings and roads and fields and more, but it also has an intangible quality, an "atmosphere," which is often so easy to perceive and yet so difficult to define. The smells and sights and sounds of a traditional African market are unmistakable, but try to record those qualities on maps or in some other way for comparative study! Geographers have long grappled with this problem of recording the less tangible characteristics of the cultural landscape that are often so significant in producing the regional personality.

The more concrete properties of a cultural landscape are a bit easier to observe and record. Take, for example, the urban "townscape" (a prominent element of the overall cultural landscape), and compare a major U.S. city with, say, a leading Japanese city. Visual representations would quickly reveal the differences, of course, but so would maps of the two urban places. The U.S. central city, with its rectangular layout of the central business district (CBD) and its far-

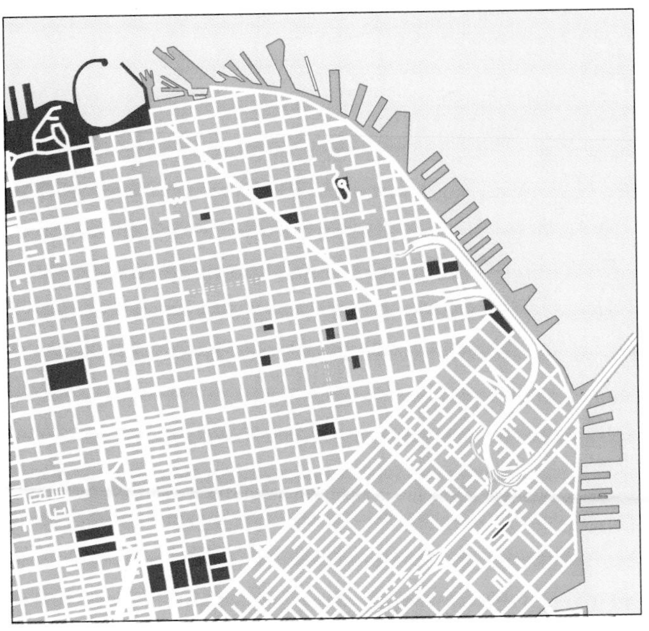

Figure 2-3 San Francisco and Tokyo Maps. Both San Francisco and Tokyo are laid out on a comparatively high-relief urban topography. But their functional structures differ markedly.

flung, sprawling suburbs, contrasts sharply with the clustered, space-conserving Japanese city (Fig. 2-3). Again, the subdivision and ownership of American farmland, represented on a map, looks unmistakably different from that of a traditional African rural area, with its irregular, often tiny patches of land surrounding a village. Still, the whole of a cultural landscape can never be represented on a map. The personality of a region involves not only its prevailing spatial organization, but also its visual appearance, its noises and odors, and even its pace of life.

Culture Hearths

For as long as human communities have existed on Earth, there have been places where people have succeeded, where invention and effort have been rewarded by an increase in numbers, growing strength, comparative stability, and general progress. Conversely, there have been areas where communities have not done well at all. The areas where success and progress prevailed were the places where the first large clusters of human population developed, both because of sustained natural increase and because other people were attracted to those places. The increasing numbers led to the development of new ways to exploit locally available resources and gain power over resources located farther away. Progress was made in farming techniques and, consequently, in crop yields. Settlements could expand. Societies grew more complex, and there were people who could afford to spend time not merely in subsisting, but in such pursuits as politics and the arts. The circulation of goods and ideas intensified. Traditions developed, along with ways of life that set an example for people in other places, far and near. These areas were humanity's early ***culture hearths***, the sources of civilization, outward from which radiated the ideas, innovations, and ideologies that would change the world beyond.

Culture hearths should be viewed in the context of time as well as space. Long before human communities began to depend on cultivated crops or domesticated animals, culture hearths developed in response to the discovery and development of a tool or weapon that made subsistence easier or more efficient. Fishing techniques improved, and waterside communities prospered and grew. Thus the Inuit people, with their early and inventive adaptation to their frigid, watery environment, developed a culture hearth, just as the ancient Mesopotamians did. The nomadic Maasai and their remarkable cattle-based culture still inhabit the region in which they achieved their culture hearth.

Some culture hearths, therefore, remain comparatively isolated and self-contained, but others have an impact far beyond their bounds. When the innovation of agriculture was added to the culture complexes that already existed in the zone of the Fertile Crescent, it soon diffused to areas where it was not yet practiced and affected other culture complexes far and wide. In

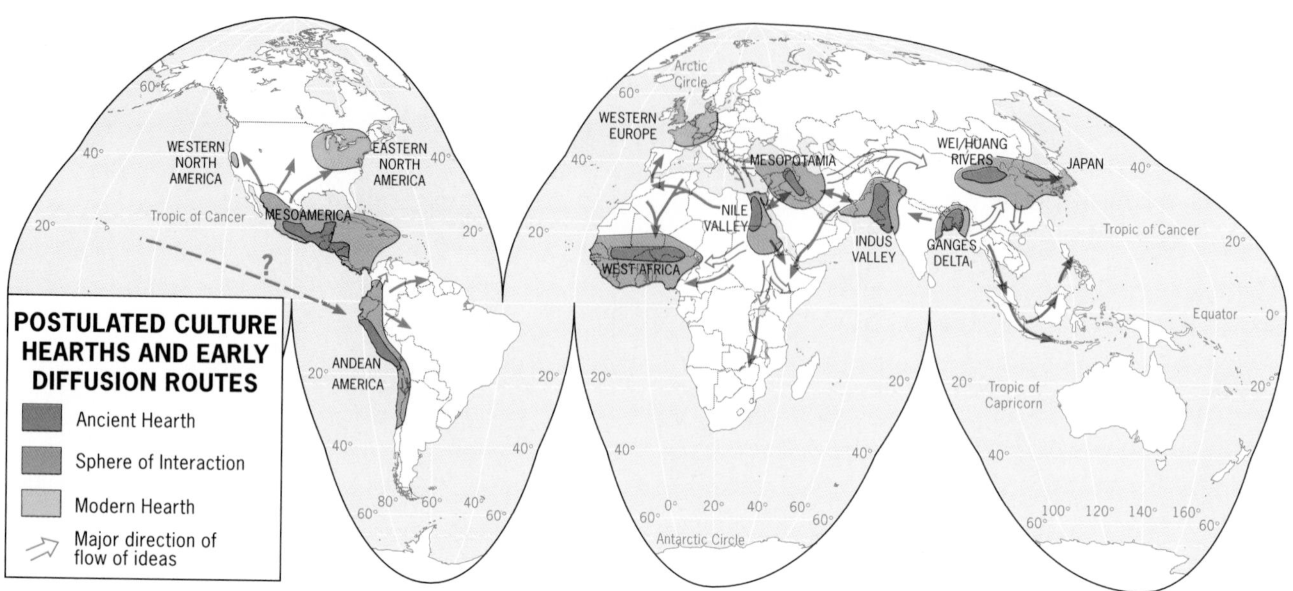

Figure 2-4 Postulated Culture Hearths and Early Diffusion Routes. Ancient and modern culture hearths. The ancient hearths and their diffusion routes are speculative; today's industrial and technological culture hearths are superimposed. *Source: Authors' sketch.*

the culture hearth itself, the practice of cultivation led to the evolution of an infinitely more elaborate civilization, where one innovation followed another.

Thus it is appropriate to distinguish between culture hearths, thousands of which have evolved across the Earth from the Inuit Arctic to Maori New Zealand, and the source areas of ***civilizations***. These latter also began as culture hearths, but their growth and development had a wider, sometimes global impact. Early culture hearths (Fig. 2-4) developed in Southwest Asia and North Africa, South and Southeast Asia, and East Asia in the valleys and basins of the great river systems. The Middle and South American culture hearths evolved thousands of years later, not in river valleys but in highlands. The West African culture hearth emerged later still, strongly influenced by innovations by the peoples of the Nile Valley and Southwest Asia.

It is important to note that all the ancient culture hearths shown in Figure 2-4 achieved breakthroughs in agriculture. Irrigation techniques, crop domestication, planting, seeding and weeding methods, harvesting, storage, and distribution systems all progressed, and individual cultures achieved remarkable adaptations in order to maximize the opportunities offered by their environment.

Shifts in Culture Hearths The locations and nature of the cultural innovations of recent centuries are very different. With the onset of the Industrial Revolution, the world was transformed by the spread of innovations from new hearths, new sources of invention and diffusion. The ancient agricultural and urban revolutions were followed, millennia later, by equally consequential industrial and technological revolutions that created totally new cultural landscapes. These revolutions were (and are) centered in Europe, North America, and East Asia (Fig. 2-4).

Think of the ways in which our daily lives have been changed by the inventions made in these hearths of innovation and how effective modern dissemination systems are. Also note that in the nineteenth century, Western Europe was the dominant industrial hearth—a position that was taken over by the United States during the twentieth century. Now Japan has eroded North America's lead, and despite current difficulties other East Asian industrial-technological giants have emerged as well. Will the next century witness yet another shift?

Cultural Diffusion

The ancient culture hearths were focal points of innovation and invention. They were sources of ideas and stimuli. From these source areas, newly invented techniques, tools, instruments, and ideas about ways of doing things radiated outward, carried by caravans and armies, merchant mariners, teachers, and clergy. Some of the innovations that eventually reached distant peoples were quickly adopted and often modified or refined; others fell on barren ground.

The process of dissemination, the spread of an idea or innovation from its source area to other cultures, is known as ***cultural diffusion***. Today the great majority of the world's cultures are the products of innumerable ideas and innovations that have arrived in an endless, centuries-long stream. Often it is possible to isolate and trace the origin, route, and timing of the adoption of a particular innovation. The phenomenon of ***diffusion*** is therefore an essential part of the study of cultural geography.

The appearance of a particular technique or device in widely separated areas does not necessarily prove that diffusion occurred. Various cultures in parts of Asia, Africa, and the Americas developed methods of irrigation, learned to domesticate animals and plants, and reached other achievements through ***independent invention***. Moreover, a major invention did not guarantee rapid diffusion and adoption everywhere. The wheel, surely a momentous invention, was not adopted in Egypt until 20 centuries after its introduction in nearby Mesopotamia.

Diffusion occurs through the movement of people, goods, or ideas. Carl Sauer focused attention on this process in *Agricultural Origins and Dispersals* (1952), which was published at about the same time that the pioneering diffusion research by the Swedish geographer Torsten Hägerstrand began to appear in print. This fascinating research attracted many geographers to the study of diffusion processes.

Geographers have identified several different processes whereby diffusion takes place. The differences have to do with various conditions: whatever it is that is diffusing through a population, the distribution and character of that population, the distances involved, and much more. Consider two examples: the diffusion of a disease such as Asian "flu" through a population and the diffusion of FAX machines. The first case involves involuntary exposure and the second voluntary adoption. Both, however, are manifestations of diffusion processes.

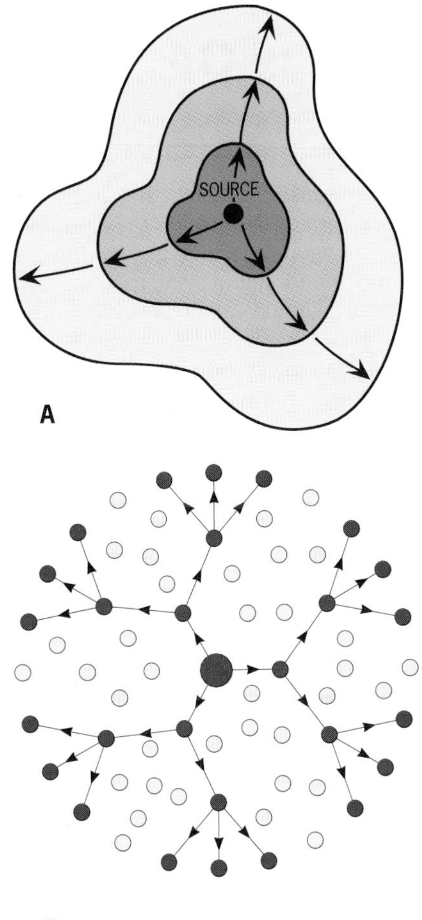

Figure 2-5 Types of Diffusion. Expansion diffusion (A) and hierarchical diffusion (B).

Expansion Diffusion Geographers classify diffusion processes into two broad categories: expansion diffusion and relocation diffusion. In the case of expansion diffusion, an innovation or idea develops in a source area and remains strong there while also spreading outward. Later, for example, we will study the spread of Islam from its hearth on the Arabian Peninsula to Egypt and North Africa, through Southwest Asia, and into West Africa. This is a case of expansion diffusion. If we were to draw a series of maps of the Islamic faithful at 50-year intervals beginning in A.D. 620, the area of adoption of the Muslim religion would be larger in every successive period. Expansion diffusion thus is a very appropriate term (Fig. 2-5).

Expansion diffusion takes several forms. The spread of Islam is an example of ***contagious diffusion***, a form of expansion diffusion in which nearly all adjacent individuals are affected. A disease can spread in this way, infecting almost everyone in a population (although not everyone may show symptoms of the disease).

However, an idea (or a disease, for that matter) may not always spread throughout a fixed population. For example, the spread of AIDS in the United States has not affected everyone in the population. Instead, it has affected particularly vulnerable groups, leapfrogging over wide areas and appearing on maps as clusters in distantly separated cities. This represents another kind of expansion diffusion, ***hierarchical diffusion***, in which the main channel of diffusion is some segment of those who are susceptible to (or adopting) what is being diffused. In the case of the diffusion of AIDS, the hierarchy is the urban structure in the United States; the sizes of cities, towns, and villages are reflected in the clusters of infected people.

Hierarchical diffusion is also illustrated by the spread of the use of fax machines. Here the hierarchy is determined by the equipment's affordability and the potential users' perception of need. Again, the pattern is likely to show an urban-based order. But not all in-

Focus On

Acculturation and Transculturation

When cultures make contact, the dominant culture prevails. The culture of the smaller or weaker society may be somewhat changed, considerably modified, or even completely transformed. But in every case the dominant culture will contribute certain qualities to the smaller or weaker one. This process, in which a culture is substantially changed through interaction with another culture, is called ***acculturation***. It is obviously related to cultural diffusion.

Actually, acculturation is not the one-way street suggested by our definition. Dominant cultures do impose many of their attributes on weaker ones, but they may also adopt aspects of the latter's culture.

After Spanish invaders overthrew the Aztec kingdom, Spanish culture began to prevail: towns were transformed; a new religious order was introduced, new crops were planted. Acculturation proceeded, but Spanish culture also absorbed some Aztec influences. Aztec motifs pervaded Spanish architecture. Aztec crops were transplanted to Iberia. Spaniards began to wear clothing that revealed Aztec influences. In Mexico, there is a saying that citizens who do not have Aztec blood in their veins nonetheless have the Aztec spirit in their minds.

Some small isolated culture groups in remote locales have experienced little acculturation, while others have been strongly affected. Until the recent penetration and destruction of the rainforest reached them, Brazil's Yanomami people remained beyond acculturation's reach. At the other end of the continuum are societies that have been radically changed—notably Japan, which intentionally adopted European technology. Japan's voluntary Westernization stands in strong contrast to the acculturation imposed by European colonial powers on their overseas domains.

Although acculturation is not a one-way process, the flow of innovations, ideas, and practices (voluntary or forced) occurs predominantly in one direction, overshadowing any "reverse" movement. Occasionally, there is contact between culture complexes that are more nearly equal in numbers, strength, and complexity. In such cases a genuine exchange follows, in which both cultures function as sources and adopters. This process is referred to as ***transculturation***.

novations are adopted in cities and towns. The diffusion pattern for an improved piece of farm machinery will be quite different.

A third form of expansion diffusion is ***stimulus diffusion***. Not all ideas can be readily adopted by a receiving population; some are simply too vague, too unattainable, or too practical for immediate adoption. But this does not mean that such ideas have no impact at all. They may result in local experimentation and eventual changes in ways of doing things. At first, for example, the idea of industrialization was not transmitted to pre- or nonindustrial societies through any particular artifact. Nevertheless, industrialization stimulated attempts to mechanize local handicraft manufacturing and thus had an indirect impact.

Relocation Diffusion As noted earlier, expansion diffusion takes place through populations that are stable and fixed. It is the innovation, the idea, or the disease that does the moving. Relocation diffusion, in contrast, involves the actual movement of individuals who have already adopted the idea or innovation, and who carry it to a new, perhaps distant, locale, where they proceed to disseminate it (see Focus on: Acculturation and Transculturation).

Another form of relocation diffusion is ***migrant diffusion***. There are times when an innovation originates somewhere and enjoys strong—but brief—adoption there. By the time it reaches distant places, it has already lost its strength at the place where it started. The diffusion map thus would show a continuous outward shift to new adopters, but there would be no stable core area. Some diseases, such as milder influenza pandemics, display this process as well. By the time these reach North America and Europe, they already have faded away in China, so that the diffusion pattern is one of migrant, rather than contagious, diffusion.

These are some of the leading processes of diffusion and the factors involved. However, there are also forces that work against diffusion and the adoption of new ideas and innovations. One of these is distance; another is time. The farther it is from its source, the less likely an innovation is to be adopted, and the "innovation waves" become weaker. Similarly, the acceptance of an innovation becomes less likely the longer it takes to reach its potential adopters. In combination, time and distance cause *time-distance decay* in the diffusion process.

Another force working against diffusion processes is cultural barriers. Certain innovations, ideas, or practices are not acceptable or adoptable in particular cultures because of prevailing attitudes or even taboos. Prohibitions against alcoholic beverages, as well as certain forms of meat, fish, and other foods, have restricted their consumption. Cultural barriers against other practices, such as the use of contraceptives, also have inhibited diffusion processes. Cultural barriers can pose powerful obstacles to the spread of ideas as well as artifacts.

Cultural Perception

Although architecture—even simple dwellings in remote forests or mountains—dominates the cultural landscape, other aspects of daily life also contribute to the character of places. One of those aspects is the face of life as it is lived in a given area. During the 1960s, when thousands of students from African countries came to study in the United States, a geography professor conducted a survey of their perceptions of this country. Among the top five impressions was a variation of the following: "People and things move so fast here! Everyone seems to be running from one appointment to the next!"

The pace of life is not something that shows up on maps, but it is an important aspect of place. Courtesy is another. A similar survey in Britain produced many references to the British habit of "queueing," or lining up neatly to await one's turn boarding a bus or paying a bill. Again, while tradition does not have the permanence of an architectural style, it is nonetheless part of the cultural character of places.

Such intangible elements help define the personality of a region. They also can contribute to cultural conflict. Violation of such traditions by outsiders can even lead to strife.

Perceptual Regions How is the cultural landscape perceived? In Chapter 1, we noted that people of all cultures have spatial memories, or *mental maps*, that influence their perception. Thus, from the viewpoint of the United States, many countries are underdeveloped and poor. But from the perspective of those countries, U.S. society may seem overdeveloped and wasteful. So it is with culture and the cultural landscape. Our perceptions of our own community and culture may differ quite sharply from those of people in other cultures. ***Perceptual regions*** are intellectual constructs designed to help us understand the nature and distribution of phenomena in human geography. Geographers do not agree entirely on their properties, but they do concur that we all have impressions and images of various regions and cultures. These perceptions are based on our accumulated knowledge about such regions and cultures. The natural environment, too, is part of this inventory. Think of Swiss culture, and the image of a single Alpine environment may come to mind, even though, in fact Swiss culture is divided into several distinct regions by language, religion, and tradition.

Although we can easily explain in general terms how we perceive a culture region, it is much more difficult to put our impressions on a map. For example, consider the *Mid-Atlantic Region.* Weather forecasters refer to the "Mid-Atlantic area" or the "Mid-Atlantic States" as they divide their maps into manageable pieces. But where is this Mid-Atlantic region? If Maryland and Delaware are part of it, then eastern Pennsylvania is, too. But where across Pennsylvania lies the boundary of this partly cultural, partly physical region, and on what basis can it be drawn? There is no single best answer (Fig. 2-6).

Again, we all have a mental map of the *South* as a culture region of the United States. But if you drive southward from, say, Pittsburgh or Detroit, you will not pass a specific place where you enter this perceptual region. You will note features in the cultural landscape that you perceive to be associated with the South, and at some stage of the trip they will begin to dominate the area to such a degree that you will say, "I am really in the South now." This may result from a combination of features of the region's material as well as nonmaterial culture: the form of houses and their porches, items on a roadside restaurant menu (grits, for example), a local radio station's music, the sound of accents that you perceive to be Southern, a succession of Baptist churches in a town along the way. These combined impressions become part of your overall perception of the South as a region.

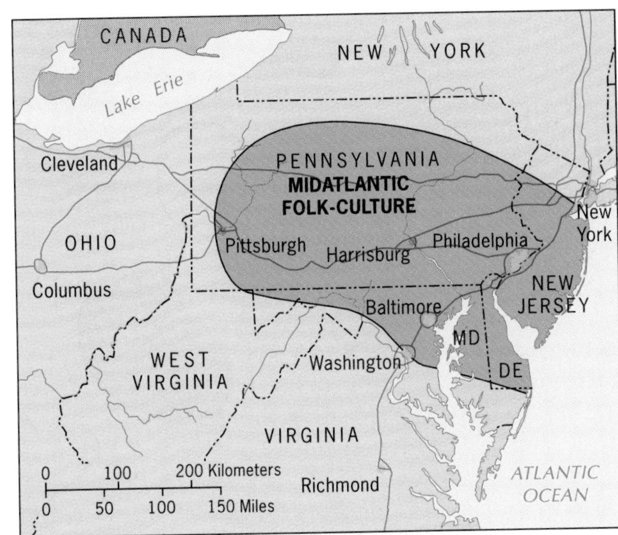

Figure 2-6 Mid-Atlantic Folk-Culture Region. One delimitation of a Mid-Atlantic culture region. *Source: H. Glassie*, Pattern in the Material Folk Culture of the Eastern United States. *Philadelphia: University of Pennsylvania Press, 1968, p. 39.*

Perceptual regions can be studied at a variety of levels. The 12 world geographic realms that form the basis of many courses in world regional geography are perceptual units at the smallest of scales; at the opposite, largest end of the scale would be a tiny region defined by one of the remaining communities of Amish people in the United States. Quite possibly, our perceptions are weakest and least accurate at each end of the scale: at the small scale because so much information must be synthesized that images become distorted, and at the large scale because most diminutive cultures within cultures are not well-defined parts of our general spatial knowledge. An interesting example of regional definition at an intermediate scale occurs in an article by Terry Jordan entitled "Perceptual Regions in Texas" (1978). Like all of us, Texans use regional-cultural names for various parts of their state, and in this article Jordan identifies where names such as *Panhandle, Gulf Coast, Permian Basin,* and *Metroplex* actually apply (Fig. 2-7).

Perceptual Regions in the United States The cultural geographer Wilbur Zelinsky tackled the enormous, complex task of defining and delimiting the perceptual regions of the United States and southern Canada. In an article entitled "North America's Vernacular Regions" (1980), he identified 12 major perceptual regions on a series of maps. Figure 2-5 summarizes these regions. Of necessity, it shows overlaps between certain units. For example, the more general term "the West" obviously incorporates more specific regions, such as the Pacific Region and part of the Northwest.

The problem of defining and delimiting perceptual regions can be approached in several ways. One is to conduct interviews in which people residing within as well as outside a region are asked to respond to questions about their home and cultural environment. Zelinsky used a different technique; he analyzed the telephone directories of 276 metropolitan areas in the United States and Canada, noting the frequencies with which businesses and other enterprises use regional or locational terms (such as "*Southern* Printing Company") in their listings. The resulting maps show a close similarity between these perceptual regions and culture regions identified by geographers.

Regional Identity Culture regions also represent an emotional commitment. Among the perceptual regions shown in Figure 2-8, one, the South, is unlike any of the others. Even today, five generations after the Civil War, the Confederate flag still has a regional connotation; the "Bible belt" still prevails; and the South's unique position among American regions is en-

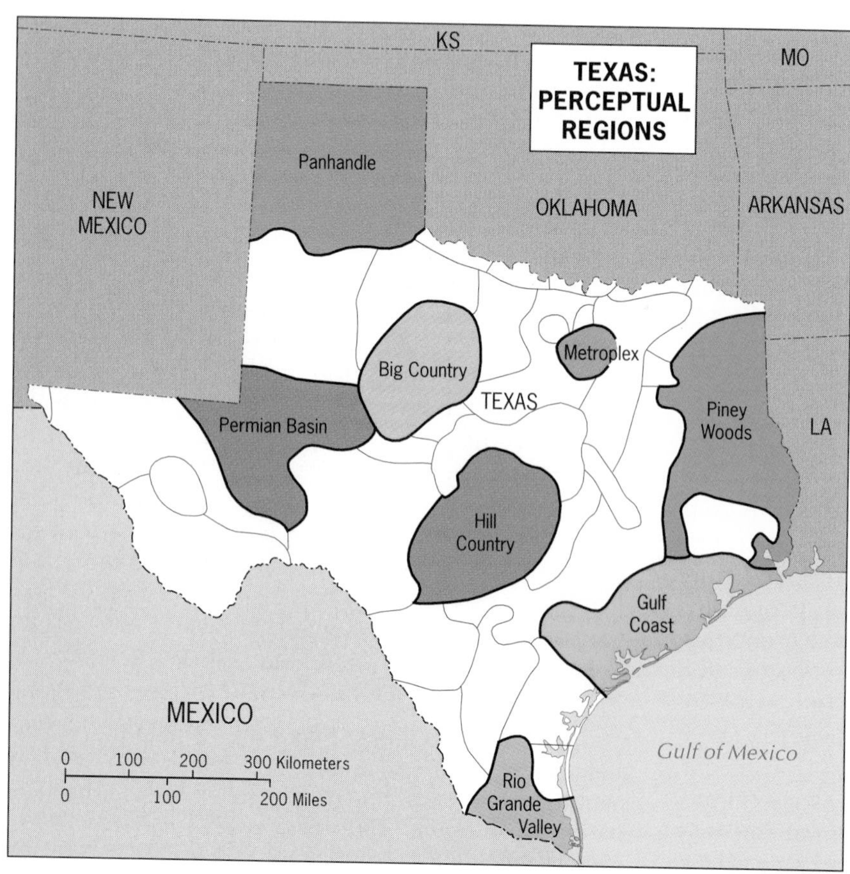

Figure 2-7 Perceptual Regions of Texas. Prominent perceptual regions of Texas. *Source: From T. G. Jordan, "Perceptual Regions in Texas."* Geographical Review *68, 1978, p. 295.*

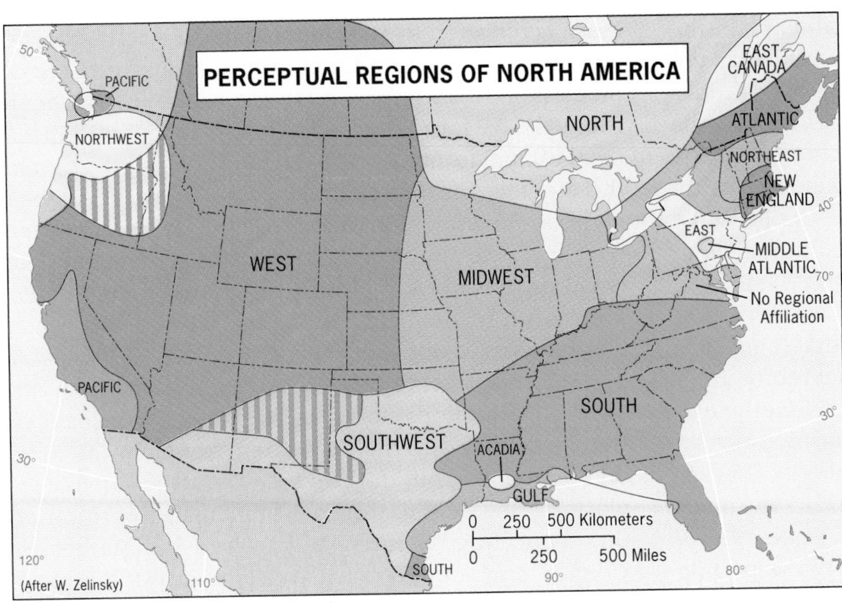

Figure 2-8 Perceptual Regions of North America *Source: From W. Zelinsky, "North America's Vernacular Regions,"* Annals of the AAG, *1980, p. 14.*

trenched in songs and dialects. Certainly a "New South" has emerged over the past several decades, forged by Hispanic immigration, urbanization, Sunbelt movements, and other processes. But the South—especially the rural South—continues to carry imprints of a material culture long past. Its legacy of nonmaterial culture is equally strong, preserved in language, religion, music, food preferences, and other traditions and customs.

Such cultural attributes give a certain social atmosphere to the region, an atmosphere that is appreciated by many of its residents and is sometimes advertised as an attraction for potential visitors. "Experience the South's warmth, courtesy, and pace of life," said one such commercial, which portrayed a sun-drenched seaside landscape, a bowing host, and a couple strolling along a palm-lined path. Such images may or may not represent the perceptions of most inhabitants of the region, but few Southerners would object to publicity of this kind.

The South has its vigorous supporters and defenders, and occasionally a politician uses its embattled history to arouse racial antagonism. But today the South is so multifaceted, so diverse, so vigorous, and so interconnected with the rest of the United States that its regional identity is mainly a matter of academic interest. No group, or combination of groups, in the South today seeks to mobilize the region or to secede from the United States. No one is proposing any form of autonomy for a state or group of states south of the Mason-Dixon line.

Elsewhere, however, discrete and strongly defined culture regions have become political (and even actual) battlegrounds. Emotional attachments to territory and tradition can run so strong that they supersede feelings of national (state) identity, an issue we take up in Chapter 27.

Culture and Environment The relationships between human societies and the natural environment are complex. Environment affects society in countless ways, some of which are reflected by the different types of houses people build, the diverse crops they grow, and the kinds of livestock they can maintain. Societies modify their natural environments in ways that range from slight to severe. In this book we will frequently encounter evidence of human impact on natural environments. Public art and monumental architecture are parts of the cultural landscape, but so are pollution-belching smokestacks, contaminant-oozing landfills, and sludge-clogged streams.

But there is another question involving society and environment. Human cultures exist in a long-term accommodation with their physical environments, seizing opportunities presented by those environments and suffering from the limitations and extremes they sometimes impose. No culture, no matter how sophisticated technologically, can completely escape the forces of nature, as can be seen in the annual list of tornado casualties in the United States. But some cultures have overcome the apparent limitations of their natural environments more effectively than others. How can this be explained?

In the 1940s, the geographer Harlan Barrows argued that this is a central question for geographers, and he proposed the term *cultural ecology* to identify the arena in which the necessary research would take place. Actually, the whole issue of nature and culture had already taken central stage, albeit under a different heading.

Environmental Determinism Efforts to explain the achievements of certain cultures under particular environmental regimes had been going on for decades before Barrows tried to focus the debate. In fact, the fundamental questions were raised much earlier. The ancient Greeks, noting that some of the peoples subjugated by their expanding Empire were docile while others were rebellious, attributed such differences to variations in climate.

In this connection, let us look again at the map of ancient culture hearths (Fig. 2-4). Note that these crucibles of cultural achievement lay in apparently unfavorable climatic zones such as deserts. Nonetheless, 23 centuries ago, Aristotle described the peoples of cold, distant Europe as being "full of spirit . . . but incapable of ruling others" and those of Asia as "intelligent and inventive . . . [but] always in a state of subjection and slavery." How easy it is to view people living in cold climates as "hardy, but not very intelligent," those of the warm tropics as "lazy and passive," and those in the intermediate zones as productive and progressive? Aristotle's views on this topic were nothing if not durable. As recently as the first half of the twentieth century, similar notions still had strong support.

Here is how Ellsworth Huntington (1876–1947), a twentieth-century geographer, stated this idea in *Principles of Human Geography*, published in 1940:

> The well-known contrast between the energetic people of the most progressive parts of the temperate zone and the inert inhabitants of the tropics and even of intermediate regions, such as Persia, is largely due to climate . . . the people of the cyclonic regions rank so far above those of the other parts of the world that they are the natural leaders.

The doctrine expressed by these statements is referred to as environmentalism or, more precisely, ***environmental determinism***. It holds that human behavior, individually and collectively, is strongly affected by, and even controlled or determined by, the environment. It suggests that climate is the critical factor: for progress and productiveness in culture, politics, and technology, the "ideal" climate would be, say, that of Western Europe or northeastern United States. Following such reasoning, the people of hot, tropical areas or cold, near-polar zones might as well abandon hope. This position is effectively summarized in Huntington's map of "level of civilization" (Fig. 2-9).

For a time, some geographers attempted to explain the distribution of centers of culture in terms of the "dictating environment." Quite soon, however, some geographers doubted whether these sweeping generalizations were valid. They recognized exceptions to the environmentalists' postulations (e.g., the Maya civilization in Mesoamerica arose under tropical conditions) and argued that humanity was capable of much more than merely adapting to the natural environment. As for the supposed "efficiency" produced by the climate of Western Europe, this idea ignored the fact that for millennia the most highly developed civilizations were found outside of Western Europe (North Africa, Southeast Asia, East Asia, etc.). Surely it was best not to base "laws" of environmental determinism on inadequate data in the face of apparently contradictory evidence.

Such arguments helped guide the search for answers to questions about the relationships between human society and the natural environment in different directions, but for several decades some geographers still held to the environmentalist position. In this connection it is interesting to read S. F. Markham's *Climate and the Energy of Nations* (1947). Markham thought that he could detect in the migration of the center of power in the Mediterranean (from Egypt to Greece to Rome and onward) the changing climates of that part of Europe during several thousand years of glacial retreat. Markham saw the northward movement of *isotherms*—lines connecting points of equal temperature values—as a key factor in the shifting centers of power in the Ancient World.

Geographers grew increasingly cautious about such speculative notions, however, and they began asking new questions about societal-environmental relationships. If generalizations are to be made, they felt they ought to arise from detailed, carefully designed research. Everyone agrees that human activity is affected by the natural environment, but people are decision makers and the modifiers, not the slaves of environmental forces. And the decisions people make about their environment are influenced by culture.

Reactions to environmentalism produced counterarguments. An approach known as ***possibilism*** emerged—espoused by geographers who argued that the natural environment merely serves to limit the range of choices available to a culture. The choices that a society makes depend on its members' requirements and the technology available to them.

One obvious conclusion is that the influence of the natural environment declines with increasing technological sophistication. Those of us who spend the majority of our time in "artificial" heated and air-conditioned environments are much less dependent on the natural environment than people who live more traditional, generally rural lives. In that sense, humans have the capacity to modify, indeed to transform, their natural environments. Yet this leaves some unanswered questions. Geographers have studied all kinds of human behavior in modern communities and have found that no matter how insulated we are from the natural environment, some influences persist. Change-

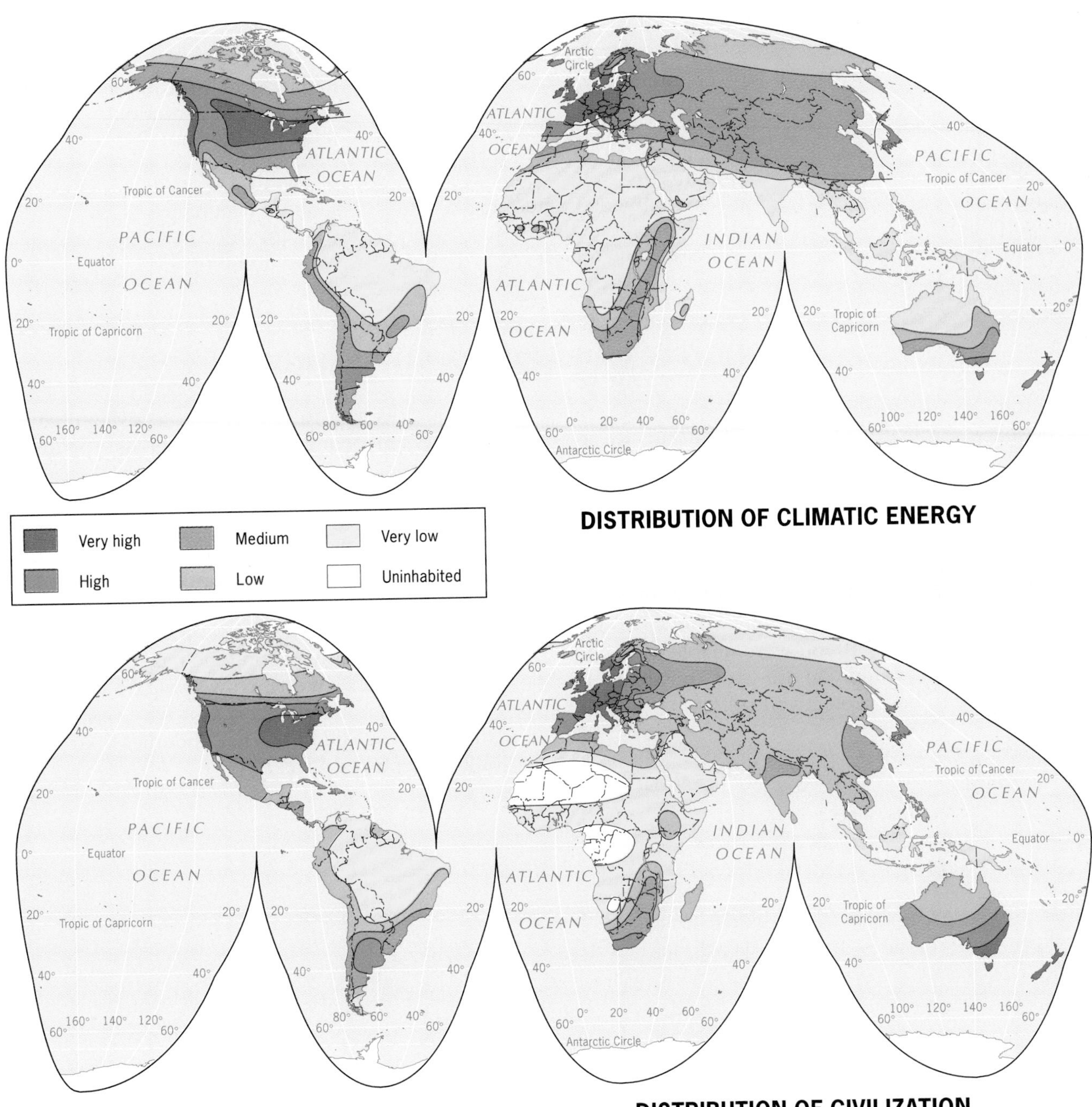

Figure 2-9 Distribution of Climatic Energy and of Civilization. This is how E. Huntington viewed climate and civilization. Below these maps, the author states that they are "based on the opinion of fifty experts in many countries." *Source: E. Huntington,* Principles of Human Geography. *New York: Wiley, 1940, p. 352.*

able weather, heat and cold waves, influence the activities of significant numbers of people, even when they spend most of their time indoors in controlled environments. No wonder cultural ecology has stimulated some intense debates.

What is clear, however, is that broad generalizations about the impact of the environment on humans are rarely sustained. Human societies are sufficiently diverse and the human will is too powerful to be the mere objects of nature's designs. We cannot escape the environmental contexts in which we are situated—nor should we try if the environmental degradation that has followed such efforts is any guide. But any explanation of human–environment relations that does not give credence to the extraordinary power of cultural ideas and practices embarks on a path that has consistently been shown to be simplistic, if not fundamentally wrong.

◆ KEY TERMS ◆

acculturation
civilization
contagious diffusion
cultural diffusion
cultural landscape
culture
culture complex
culture hearth
culture realm
culture region
culture system
culture trait
diffusion
environmental determinism
geographic realm
geographic region
hierarchical diffusion
independent invention
migrant diffusion
perceptual region
possibilism
sequent occupance
stimulus diffusion
transculturation

◆ APPLYING GEOGRAPHIC KNOWLEDGE ◆

1. During a certain week some years ago, several people in a village near a large East Asian city got the flu. Within days, hundreds of people in the city came down with it. In the surrounding countryside, numerous villagers in an ever-widening area became ill. Meanwhile, this Asian flu appeared in such cities as San Francisco, New York, London, and Moscow. What processes spreading this malady were at work in China and worldwide, and how do they differ? If you were unable to be immunized, how would you use your knowledge of geography to best protect yourself?

2. Ask a classmate to join you in a geographic experiment involving perceptual regions. The idea is to confirm, through a simple test, how regional perceptions can vary. First, agree on a U.S. or Canadian region to be defined; this should *not* be the region in which either of you resides. Next, take a blank outline map of North America (or at a larger scale, the United States or Canada), and separately draw a boundary that, in your view, delimits the region in question (such as the U.S. South or the Canadian West). Now compare your maps and, most importantly, *explain* why you defined the region as you did. What underlies your differing perceptions?

Chapter 3

The Earth As Humanity's Home

From the field notes

"Borneo, February 1998. The island's natural environment is being devastated by drought and fires. El Niño has desiccated the forests; people are setting the fires. One of the last refuges of the orangutan is under what may be a final attack. I am driving from Sandakan, where I have visited an orangutan sanctuary, to Kota Kinabalu. A gray, sulfurous smog smothers the countryside, searing the eyes. Mount Kinabalu, the highest point (over 13,000 ft/4000 m), on the Texas-size island, is barely visible. Surrounding valleys are smoke-filled. Nature and culture combine to do irreversible damage here."

KEY POINTS

◆ Environmental change is humanity's constant companion and is a key to understanding the geography of culture.

◆ The Earth currently is in the grip of a long series of glacial advances and retreats; modern human civilization has emerged during a warm spell between glaciations.

◆ Technological progress notwithstanding, terrain and climate continue to influence the distribution and nature of human life and activity.

◆ The innovations of plant and animal domestication may have occurred nearly simultaneously in areas as far removed as the Middle East and Southeast Asia.

◆ The earliest states appear to have emerged about 5500 years ago in the Middle East and southeastern Turkey.

◆ Human population growth and pressure on resources have reached unprecedented levels over the last 200 years, rendering environmental change one of the key issues for the twenty-first century.

The study of human geography is a search for answers to some of the most fascinating questions about humanity, behavior, and environment. Why do ethnic hostilities run so deep when the advantages of accommodation appear so obvious to outsiders? How did food supply catch up with population growth when the threat of mass starvation seemed inescapable? What enables certain great cities to prosper and grow while others wither and decline? Such questions range from the global to the local, from national cultures to village life.

Frequently, the answers to our questions have an environmental dimension. Whether we study ethnic conflict in the former Yugoslavia, rice cultivation in India, or urbanization in Indonesia, we should never lose sight of the environmental context. The better we know the physical geography of our planet, the better we are able to understand its cultural mosaics.

This is our objective in Chapter 3: to define the physical stage on which the human action takes place and to consider some of the most fundamental ways humans have interacted with it. Such knowledge will help us understand the challenges faced by human cultures now and in the past, the advantages and obstacles experienced by migrants, the unifying bonds as well as the divisive forces affecting nations. We will return in Chapter 32 to a matter that must be kept in mind here: natural environments are not static but change over time. Only in recent years have scientists become fully aware of the dimensions of this change. And in the process our understanding of the emergence of humanity and the patterns of civilization has been altered.

◆ THE CHANGING EARTH

From the surface of the moon, our Earth, as seen by America's first lunar astronauts, was a pearl of bright colors in a black sky. Great swirls of white clouds partly veiled blue oceans and brown-gray continents. Emerald-green patches of land drew the eye to the oases of life on Earth. The glistening white snows of the polar regions really did look like ice caps. It was a lesson in geography that no ordinary Earthling had ever had and may not soon have again (see Focus on: Apollo's Promise).

The photographs taken on that lunar mission have become commonplace. Again and again we see the Earth from space—in books and journals, in advertising, and on television and film. But what about the geography lesson? How well do we remember just how small our Earth really is, how thin that layer of clouds, how tiny those specks of life-giving green? Nearly 6 billion people depend on the air, water, and land of this small planet. The term *spaceship earth* came into use to signify the finiteness of these and

Apollo's Promise

In the early evening of July 20, 1969, virtually everyone in the United States (and much of the Western world) paused to witness on television, or to hear on radio, an event of surpassing importance: the first landing on the Moon. We saw, heard, and felt it all, the tense descent of the vehicle, which set down on the very edge of a crater with 17 seconds of maneuvering fuel remaining; the sense of relief at the words "The Eagle Has Landed"; the emergence of space-suited astronauts Armstrong and Aldrin; and the feeling of awe at the first words spoken to Earth from another place in space. It was a historic moment, and many people envisioned Moon bases, Mars voyages, and space exploration in the years ahead.

But now, more than a quarter of a century later, the Apollo Moon program looks like a dead end, and the Saturn 5 rocket engines no longer roar. President Kennedy's exhortation to "put a man on the Moon in this decade and return him safely to Earth" galvanized public opinion and energized Congress, but even before the end of that decade, even before Apollo orbited the Moon, his successors were cutting budgets and canceling missions. The National Aeronautics and Space Administration (NASA), symbol of engineering excellence and global technological supremacy, was reduced to a shuttle program that would make space travel routine, dependable, cheap, and safe. It turned out to be none of these things. Recent projects such as the launch of the Hubble telescope and the discovery of gamma ray fountains at the center of our galaxy have raised NASA's profile somewhat, but the future remains uncertain, with Congress bickering over funds to sustain an orbiting space station that would grow by accretion.

Opponents of space exploration argue that dollars spent on a revived space program would be better spent on social programs on Earth, but those who remember the 1960s recall the social impact of Apollo. A nation at war in Vietnam and at war with itself, divided over ideology, racial issues, crime, and poverty, was temporarily united by Apollo. It was America taking a "giant leap for mankind," that promised a postwar frontier in space, a unifying, inspiring goal for the future.

Later that evening we stood outside, looking anew at the Moon, awestruck, hoping that the return would be safe, talking of the next mission and who would go. No one believed that those pictures of the rising Earth over the lunar landscape would be the last we would see in our lifetimes.

other resources. However, the real meaning of this notion did not seem to strike home. The triumph of technology that sent the astronauts to the moon was not followed by a victory on Earth. Weapons of mass destruction were manufactured in growing quantities, resource exploitation intensified, and air, water, and soil absorbed increasing amounts of pollutants, raising fears for the planet's environmental future.

From the moon, the astronauts saw the Earth at a single instant in its nearly 5-billion-year history. They saw an Earth on which the blue of the oceans was the dominant color because approximately 70 percent of the planet's surface is water. They saw landmasses colored gray and brown because more than 70 percent of the land surface is desert, steppe, rock, or otherwise sparsely vegetated. The swirls of clouds seemed thin because the atmosphere that envelops our planet is so shallow. The Earth was described as an oasis of life, but, as in any oasis, the environment is fragile and subject to damage and destruction.

What the astronauts could not see in that moment of revelation was the changeable nature of the Earth's environments. If they had stood on the Moon's surface just 20,000 years earlier (not long ago, given the age of our planet), they would have seen larger ice caps, huge ice sheets in North America and Eurasia, lower sea levels, and very different continental outlines. If they had been there 20 million years ago, the continents themselves would have been in locations quite different from those of today.

So what the astronauts saw was a still frame in a moving picture: the Earth at a moment in time. They saw an Earth with small ice caps and large oceans, continents with flooded margins, and an Earth warmer than it has been for much of the past 3 million years. During these past 3 million years, and for some time previously, the Earth has been in an ice age, referred to by physical geographers as the Late Cenozoic Ice Age. During this ice age, the most recent of several in the Earth's history, the global temperature fell repeatedly, causing the polar ice caps to expand and ice sheets to form over high latitudes. These ice sheets pushed relentlessly into lower latitudes, scouring the rocky surface and carrying millions of tons of debris as they expanded. In highlands, such as the Rocky Mountains and Europe's Alps, great Alpine glaciers filled the valleys and the whole landscape was practically buried under ice and snow. It was a frigid time, and the Earth's livable space was much reduced. Animals and plants migrated to warmer latitudes, but many, deprived of suitable environments, died out. Others managed to adjust and even thrive, and as a result the biological map changed continuously.

The ice covered much land in the Northern Hemisphere, as Figure 3-1 shows. In the Southern Hemisphere it not only buried Antarctica but also extended far northward on the Southern Ocean. However, it was in the northern lands that its impact was greatest. Virtually all of Canada, the whole Great Lakes region, and the Northeast of the United States were icebound. Note on the map that a corridor in Alaska remained ice-free. (It is believed that this may have been an avenue for human immigration from Asia into North America.) Also note the large glaciers in the high mountains of the West.

The whole world looked different. In fact, the continental outlines are shown on this map for reference only. They did not look like this when glaciation was at its maximum extent. Sea levels were lower, since so much water was taken up in the ice. The Mediterranean Sea was shallower. Possibly the myth of a submerged Atlantis, the lost continent, was born when the ice melted and the Mediterranean rose, flooding human settlements along its shores.

◆ TIME AND SPACE

To get a clearer picture of the complex interrelationships among environmental change, human evolution, and Earth's history, we should be familiar with what we might call the "calendar" of geologic time (Table 3-1). Just as we name the days of the week and the months of the year, and number the years and centuries, Earth time has been divided into stages.

Geologic Eras

On the basis of analyses of rocks and fossils, the last billion years have been divided into three ***geologic eras***: the Paleozoic, the oldest, dating from about 220 million years and older; the middle era, or Mesozoic, from about 220 million to 65 million years ago; and the Cenozoic, which began approximately 65 million years ago and still continues. The boundary between

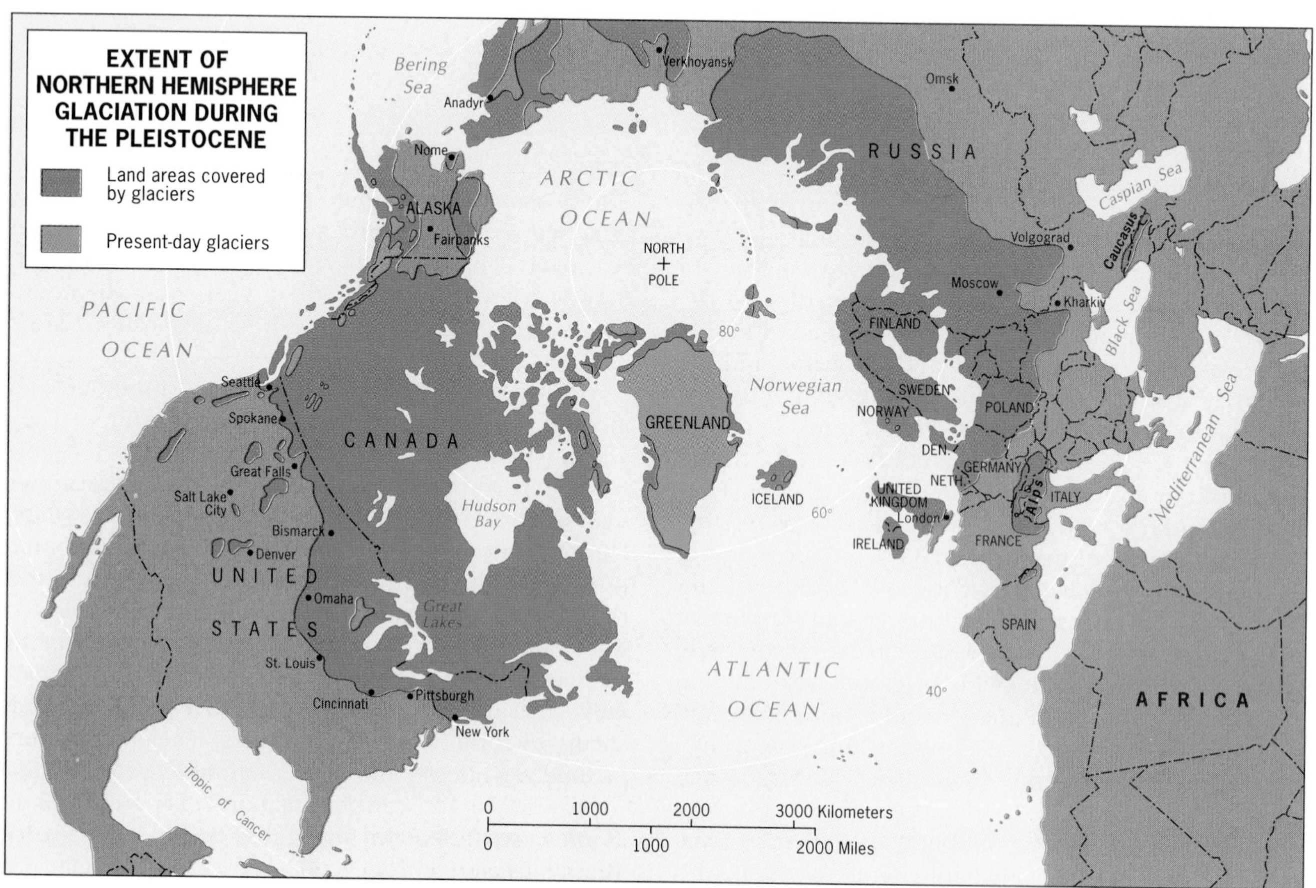

Figure 3-1 Extent of Northern Hemisphere Glaciation During the Pleistocene. The evidence on which this map is based includes glacial deposits and the marks of glaciers' erosion on bedrock.

Table 3-1 Stages in Earth History

Era[a]	Period[b]	MYA	Epoch
Cenozoic	Quaternary		Holocene (Recent)[c]
		3	Pleistocene
	Tertiary	6	Pliocene
		25	Miocene
		40	Oligocene
		60	Eocene
			Paleocene
	K/T Boundary	65	
Mesozoic	Cretaceous	130	
	Jurassic	190	
	Triassic	220	
Paleozoic	Permian	270	
	Pennsylvanian	310	
	Mississippian	350	
	Devonian	400	
	Silurian	440	
	Ordovician	500	
	Cambrian	625	
	Precambrian	↓	

[a]The numbers represent millions of years ago and are very approximate, even for the Tertiary period.

[b]The second half of the Cenozoic era has been marked by the onset of a global ice age that prevailed throughout the Quaternary period.

[c]The Holocene epoch is merely the latest of many interglaciations (warm periods) during this ice age and has lasted only about 10,000 years.

the Mesozoic and the Cenozoic has become quite famous: It is the so-called ***K/T boundary***, a sharp transition marking the extinction of many animals and plants, including the great dinosaurs. (The term *K/T boundary* derives from the German words for Cretaceous and Tertiary.) The cause of this widespread extinction has long been debated by scientists, a growing majority of whom prefer the theory that the Earth was struck by a giant meteor or a swarm of meteors, with calamitous consequences for all life existing at the time.

Periods and Epochs

Geologic eras are in turn divided into *periods*. The last period of the Mesozoic era was the Cretaceous, and the first period of the Cenozoic was the Tertiary. The Tertiary period covers most of the Cenozoic era, ending only about 3 million years ago, to give way to the present period, the Quaternary.

Periods are divided into *epochs*. The Quaternary period is divided into the Pleistocene and Holocene (or Recent) epochs. The Tertiary period is divided into five epochs. We now know that the ***Late Cenozoic Ice Age*** began during the late Tertiary, perhaps even before the Pliocene epoch. But the ice age reached its climax during the Pleistocene epoch, and many scientists continue to call it the Pleistocene (rather than the Late Cenozoic) Ice Age.

How many times the Pleistocene ice has expanded and contracted over the past several million years is a scientific question that lacks a final answer. To recon-

From the field notes

"As we flew over the ice sheet, I imagined that this is what much of the world—at higher latitudes and altitudes—must have looked like during the most recent advance of the Late Cenozoic Ice Age. Whole expanses of continent, plateaus, plains, hills, as well as mountains, lay buried under thousands of feet of ice, only the highest crests protruding. It must have been a cold, forbidding world of climatic extremes in which only the most adaptable of our ancestors survived."

struct the ice age, physical geographers have studied the crushed and powdered rock debris left behind by the successive advances of the ice sheets. Geologists have sampled the oxygen content of the ice caps to identify periods of comparatively cold and warm climate. They have concluded that there may have been as many as 30 glacial periods, some more severe than others. What is certain is that each cold period, or ***glaciation***, was followed by a warmer time during which the ice melted and balmier climates prevailed. These warmer periods, or ***interglaciations***, saw plants and animals move into regions newly vacated by the melting ice, only to be thrown back again by a new glaciation.

Today we live during such an interglaciation. The Earth now is warm, and the space available for terrestrial life is comparatively large. Not much more than 12,000 years ago, a glacial period was still in progress, and winter was "permanent" as far south as the Ohio River. Where Chicago now lies, conditions were similar to those prevailing in northern Siberia today. However, the most recent warming trend came quickly, and the ice and snow melted as far north as Alaska. Today Canada, Norway, Sweden, and Finland have balmy, mild summers compared with those of just a few thousand years ago.

The evolution of humankind, therefore, has taken place during times of great environmental variation. Much of that evolution occurred in eastern Africa, a region that was not affected by the ice sheets—but certainly was affected by the intense cold that swept the globe during glacial times. We should remember that global cooling not only spreads ice sheets from polar areas into lower latitudes; it also affects mountains and highlands, even near the equator. Today Africa's tallest mountain, Kilimanjaro, has permanent ice and snow on its crest, even though it lies in sight of the equator. During glaciations the ice on Kilimanjaro (and the other high mountains on the East African plateau) increased in volume and size, creating ice caps and glaciers that moved far downslope. Warm tropical weather changed to much colder conditions on the adjacent plains. Lake levels dropped, forests died out, and animals migrated away in a quest for survival. Our distant ancestors also saw their survival threatened. From fossil evidence we know that some of the early branches of the human family tree died out. Certain of our ancestors were better equipped to overcome the rigors of changing environments than others.

Holocene Humanity

Table 3-1 refers to the most recent 10,000 plus years of Earth history as the ***Holocene epoch***, thus differentiating it from the ***Pleistocene epoch*** that preceded it. However, there is no evidence that this so-called new epoch is, in fact, a new stage in our planet's environmental history. All the evidence indicates that the Holocene epoch is really the most recent (indeed, the current) interglaciation of the continuing Late Cenozoic Ice Age.

The Holocene epoch merits distinction not because of its geological qualities but because of its cultural-geographical characteristics. Compared to other epochs, which lasted millions of years, the Holocene has lasted only about 10,000 years. But within that short time humanity did what it had not done during previous interglaciations. In the wake of the retreating ice and in the comfort of a warming planet, a tremendous drama began: plants and animals were domesticated, agriculture developed, and surpluses were stored for future use; villages grew larger, towns and cities emerged, and political organization became increasingly complex; inventions multiplied, and tools became more efficient. Certain communities thrived and expanded, sometimes at the expense of others.

Religious ideas appeared. The spiral leading toward states and empires, colonial realms, and global power struggles had begun.

Another spiral also began: that of population growth. No one knows how many people were living on Earth at the beginning of the Holocene epoch. Perhaps there were 4 million, possibly as many as 8 million. Throughout the Pleistocene, these numbers had grown and declined. During the Holocene epoch, however, human population growth began—slowly at first, then ever faster. Modern humanity is indeed the product of the Holocene epoch.

During the Holocene the Earth changed as never before, not because of geologic forces but because of the imprint of humanity. As we will see, that imprint has become stronger over time. Especially during the past two centuries, the Earth has been transformed by the expansion of the human population and the impact of human activities. Not all of this impact has had negative results: hillslopes have been carefully terraced and made productive; wild, flood-prone rivers have been controlled and their floodplains converted into fertile farmlands; land has even been reclaimed from the sea and made livable. However, the Earth, especially during the twentieth century, has begun to feel the strains created by the growing human population. Soil erosion is more severe than ever. Rivers, lakes, and even parts of the oceans are polluted. Gases of many kinds are spewed into the atmosphere. Raw materials such as fuels and ores are used up at an ever faster rate. Our need to dispose of wastes (many of them hazardous or poisonous) has led to the contamination of drinking water and the fouling of the air we breathe. And as humanity and its activities expand, nature recedes. Many species of animals and plants are becoming extinct, and we may never know what role some of them might have played in sciences such as medicine and plant physiology.

◆ ORGANIZING HUMANITY

After more than 30 glaciations and ensuing deglaciations, and after more than 2.5 million years of environmental shifts, the present warm period began in much the same way as preceding periods. Humans of the Paleolithic period (the earliest and longest stage of the Stone Age, marking the period when simple stone tools were made and fire was used) lived in scattered groups and depended on hunting and gathering for their survival. As had happened before, the retreat of the ice expanded the amount of available living space and widened the range of environments open to the moving bands. There was plenty of wildlife to be hunted, fish to be caught, and edible plants and fruits to be gathered. There is evidence that goods (such as cured animal skins for clothing, flint, and obsidian weapons and tools) were traded. Nevertheless, a map of the human population of 12,000 years ago would show mostly small, isolated groups of people numbering perhaps 20 to 60 members, their cultures diverging as a result of contrasting ecological settings.

Although survival was the principal objective of those hunting-and-gathering communities, there was time for other things. From the cave-wall paintings of European Paleolithic groups, we have learned how and what they hunted, what kinds of weapons they used, and other aspects of their culture. In addition to art, there were local developments in language, religion, and customs (such as burial of the dead). Recent research shows that hunting (sometimes accompanied by burning of grassland or forest to drive herds toward the hunters) often went far beyond what the community needed, destroying vast numbers of plains and forest animals. Something akin to the destruction of the present Amazon rainforest occurred as more numerous and efficient hunters exterminated entire species of animals in Northern America, Eurasia, and Africa.

◆ A DIFFERENT EPOCH

The early Holocene was not very different from earlier warm periods of the late Pleistocene; there was little to foreshadow the momentous events soon to come. But the Holocene proved to be unique for many reasons.

Long before the revolutionary changes of modern times began, some hunter-gatherer groups probably were using plants in new ways. The notion that useful or sacred plants could be protected by pulling weeds away from them added a new dimension to food production. But since a patch of food-producing plants could not move with a migrating band, the idea of plant care is likely to have taken hold around stable, long-term settlements assured of a dependable supply of food from other sources.

Domestication of Plants

Simply caring for plants that yield desired products is not the same as ***plant domestication*** and organized, planned farming, but it was an important step in that direction. Human groups lived in widely diverse environments, and they learned to exploit them in diverse ways. The domestication of root crops, plants that grow as tubers in the tropics (such as manioc or cassava, yams, and sweet potatoes) is not the same as the sowing of seed for fields of barley or wheat under more temperate environments. So the domestication of plants took different paths in different places at different times—but this was a process unique to the Holocene; it was to transform patterns of human livelihood.

Where did plant domestication begin? Cultural geographer Carl Sauer, who spent a lifetime studying cultural origins and diffusion, suggested that southeastern Asia may have been the scene, more than 14,000 years ago, of the first domestication of tropical plants. There, he believed, the combination of human settlements, forest margins, and freshwater streams may have given rise to the earliest planned cultivation (Fig. 3-2). A similar but later development may have taken place in northwestern South America.

The planned cultivation of seed plants is a more complex process, involving seed selection, sowing, watering, and well-timed harvesting. Again, the practice seems to have developed in more than one area and at different times. Some scholars believe that the first domestication of seed plants may have occurred in the Nile River Valley in North Africa, but the majority view is that this crucial development took place in a region of southwestern Asia, through which flow the two major rivers of present-day Iraq, the Tigris and the Euphrates. This marked the beginning of what has been called the First Agricultural Revolution, and the area where it occurred is known as the ***Fertile Crescent***. The grain crops, wheat and barley, grew in the warming southwest Asian climate. When rainfall diminished as the interglaciation wore on, the river-inundated plains of Mesopotamia provided alternate, irrigable fields for farming (Fig. 3-3). Food surpluses could now be stored for long-term distribution and use.

Domestication of Animals

The domestication of animals appears to have taken place during the same period, also in different ways and different areas and times. As with the growing of root crops, the notion of ***animal domestication*** must have emerged quite naturally (see also Part 5, Chapter 14). Hungry animals foraged through garbage near human settlements; orphaned young probably were adopted as pets; some wild animals were docile and easily penned up. Goats were domesticated in the Zagros Mountains as long as 10,000 years ago; sheep some 9500 years ago in Anatolia (Turkey); pigs and cattle shortly thereafter. The advantages of animal domestication—their use as beasts of burden, as a source of meat, and as providers of milk—stimulated the rapid diffusion of this idea throughout the inhabited world and gave the sedentary farmers of southwestern Asia and elsewhere a new measure of security. Again, an idea that was probably not totally new to the Holocene took on revolutionary form in the present epoch.

Early Networks

The domestication of plants and animals allowed humans to live in stable, permanent settlements for the first time in human history. About 10,000 years ago, a network of farm villages appeared across the area between the Mediterranean Sea, the Persian Gulf, the Caspian Sea, and the Black Sea. These villages were not large by modern standards, but they contained hundreds of inhabitants, rather than the dozens that were typical of nomadic hunter-gatherer settlements.

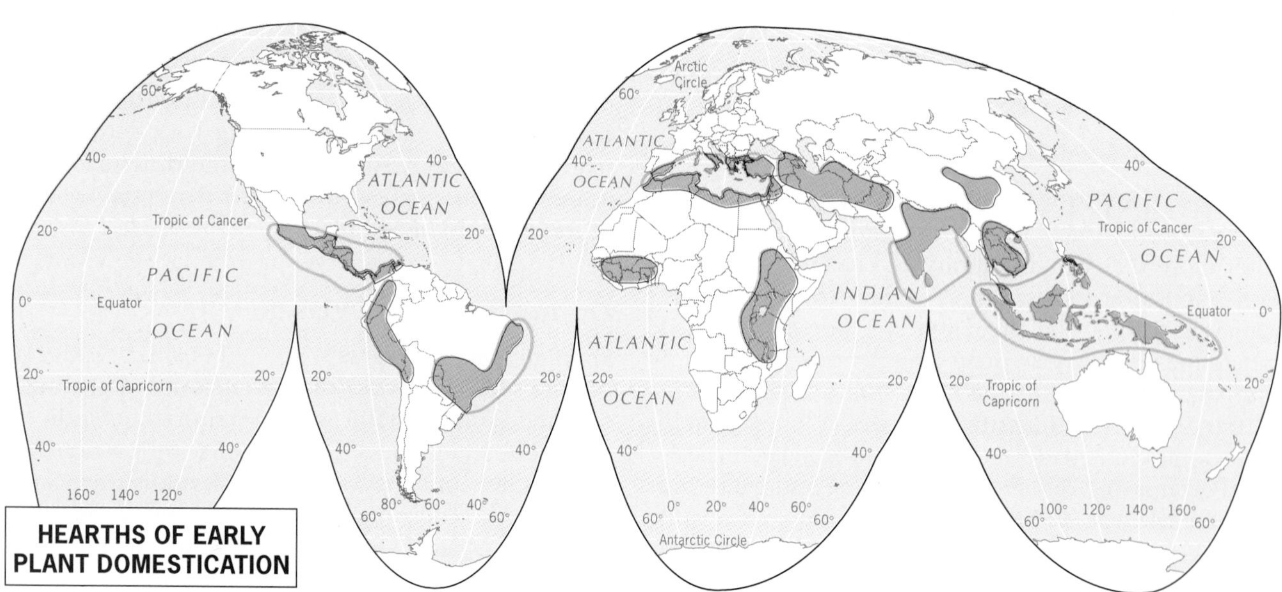

Figure 3-2 Hearths of Early Plant Domestication. Areas of earliest plant domestication, as postulated by C. O. Sauer. *Source: From J. E. Spencer & W. L. Thomas,* Introducing Cultural Geography. *New York: Wiley, 1973, p. 67.*

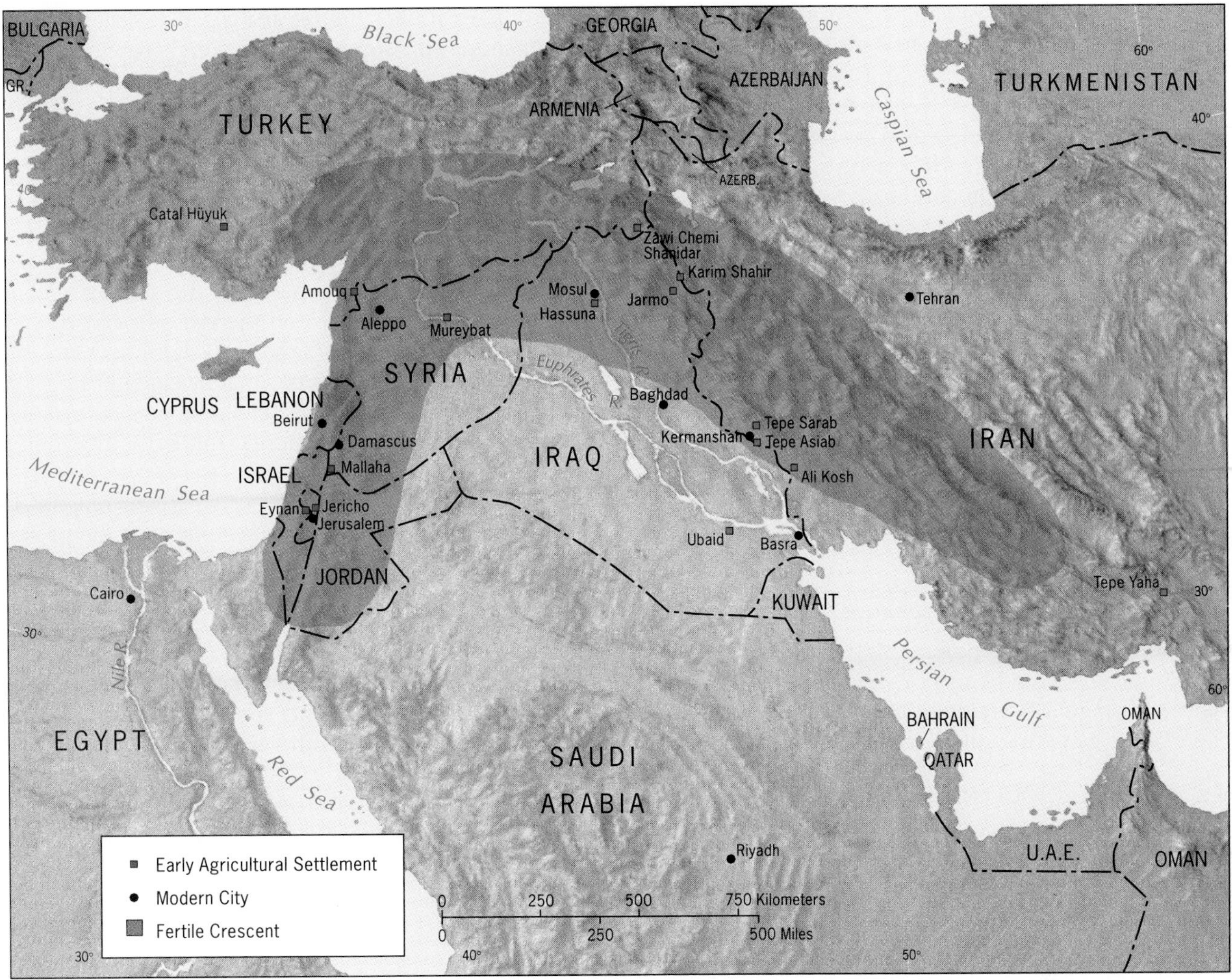

Figure 3-3 The Fertile Crescent. The Fertile Crescent, early agricultural settlement, and modern state boundaries in Southwest Asia.

The implications of this transformation were far-reaching. Some of the people in the farm villages were nonfarmers who performed other work, including not only activities directly related to farming (toolmaking, bagging, transport) but also teaching, administration, and policing. Thus a set of social strata or layers, termed ***social stratification***, developed. People found themselves on different rungs on a social ladder. At the top were those with prestige, influence, and power (the elite). Below them were the lower classes engaged in production and provision.

Conflict and competition also arose. Some villages had more productive lands; others were less fortunate. Stronger villages took control over weaker ones, and some became regional centers. The transition from village to city was under way.

Just what stimulated the rise of cities in Southwest Asia is not yet certain. It may have been a combination of circumstances: prospering regional centers, strong militias, the strength of numbers, and the rise of larger scale, well-organized religious orders. Possibly the role of irrigation was crucial, because towns that controlled irrigation works could deny their competitors access to water. Perhaps some villages grew stronger and larger because technological inventions enhanced their productivity and power. Some geographers believe that the rise of certain cities (and the decline of other places) was related to continuing climatic change. For example, when the region's rainfall declined, the Fertile Crescent's towns located on the slopes, far from controllable river water, were at a disadvantage relative to those in the river basins. Whatever the cause(s), urbanization had begun and would eventually affect all of humanity everywhere on the Earth.

Although there can be no doubt that the development of sedentary and irrigated agriculture and the rise of villages and towns initially occurred in Southwest Asia, we should remember that the dispersal of humans into other regions had already taken place. During the period from about 10,000 to 5000 years ago, important advances were being made in those regions as well as in the Fertile Crescent. In Africa, the Nile River Valley was a ribbon of agriculture. Rice-farming villages arose in Southeast Asia. And in China, momentous developments were occurring in the basins of the Chang (Yangtzi) and the Yellow (Huang) rivers, where rice and millet farmers supplied villages in networks not unlike those of Southwest Asia. On the North China Plain, the Shang Dynasty emerged, with its capital at Anyang and its core area in the confluence of the Huang and Wei rivers (Fig. 3-4). Whether these were independent innovations or the consequence of the diffusion of ideas from Southwest Asia remains an open question.

◆ EARLY STATES

Even after the development of the first villages, it would not yet have been possible to draw a map of the next stage of regional organization: the state. There were networks of farm settlements and established trade routes; fields and pastures marked the countryside; and some villages were growing larger. But political states, with capitals and boundaries and military forces, had not yet developed.

This next stage of human organization was not long in coming. The cities of the Fertile Crescent became centers not only of political power and economic strength, but of religious dominance as well (see Focus on: Ancient Babylon). Although scholars are not in complete agreement on the subject, clearly a relationship exists between the rise of powerful cities and the emergence of large and durable states. We will discuss the character of ancient cities in Part Six, but it is worth noting here that momentous political and geographic developments followed the emergence of large cities.

The Sumerian state arose in the lower reaches of Mesopotamia at about the same time that Egypt was unified politically for the first time (Fig. 3-5). The state of Uruk developed on the southwest slopes of the Zagros Mountains in what is now Iran. These states arose between 6000 and 5000 years ago, soon to be followed by Babylon (north of Sumer) and Assyria (a state in the Tigris Valley). Later the Hittites forged a state in Anatolia, but by then Southwest Asia no longer had a

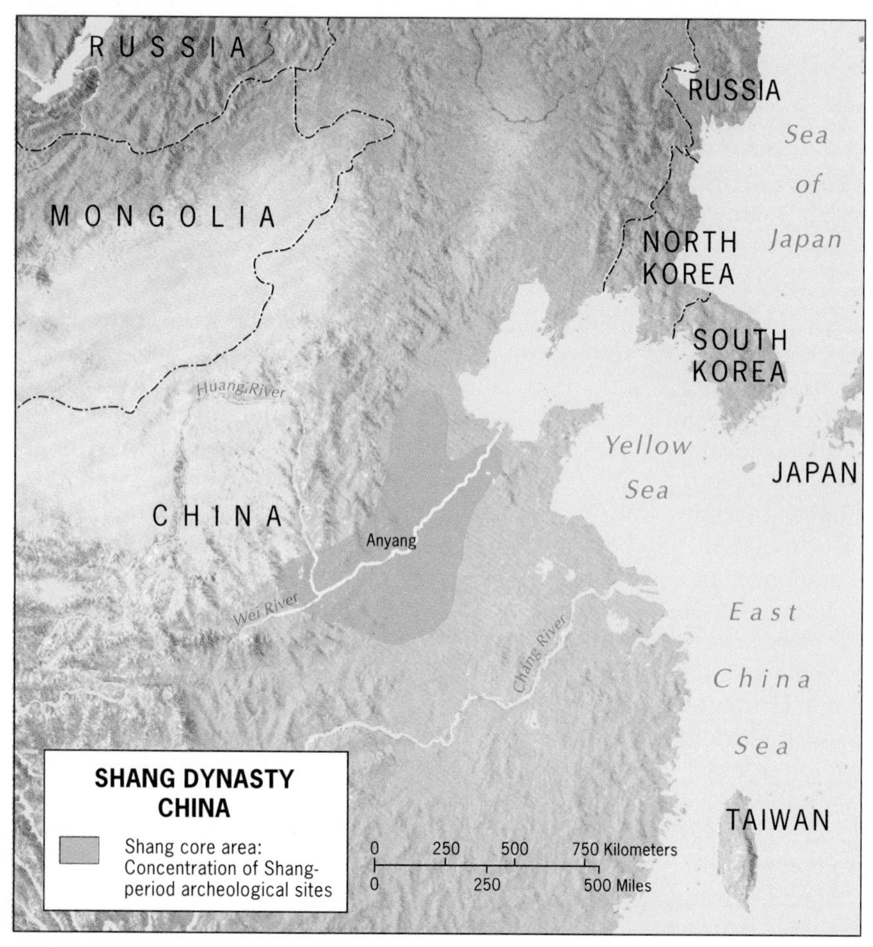

Figure 3-4 Shang Dynasty in China. The geographical origins of what may be the world's oldest continuous civilization.

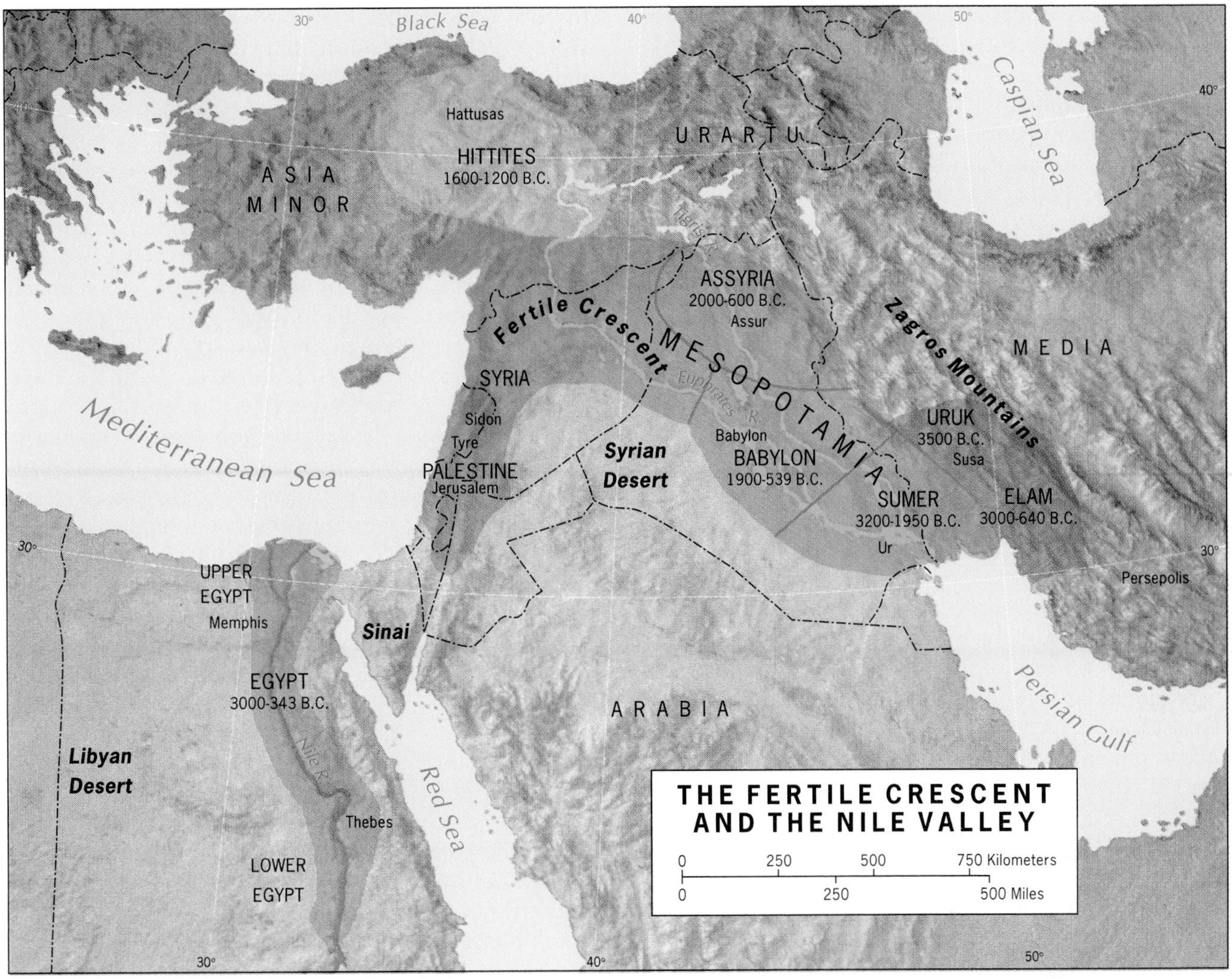

Figure 3-5 The Fertile Crescent and the Nile Valley. Ancient states in Mesopotamia and adjacent areas, and in the Nile Valley.

Ancient Babylon

Babylon was one of the largest and most powerful cities of antiquity, the capital of a powerful Mesopotamian state, and the headquarters of formidable rulers, including Nebuchadnezzar.

Situated on the Euphrates River in present-day Iraq, Babylon endured for nearly 2000 years (from 4100 B.P.) as a walled, fortified center endowed with temples, towers, and palaces. A bridge of stone and wood crossed the river, and docks accommodated the many boats that carried goods to and from what was, at the time, the world's largest city. Rising above the townscape was the tallest structure in Mesopotamian cities of the time: the ***Ziggurat***, or tower of the great temple. When Nebuchadnezzar ruled Babylon, he oversaw the building of the highest *ziggurat* yet constructed, to mark the temple of Marduk. The tower's base was 90 m (300 ft) square, and its height, in seven levels, reached more than 90 m as well. The uppermost level of the Babylon ziggurat consisted of a magnificent temple glazed sky-blue. On the flat floodplain of the Euphrates, this symbol of power could be seen for many miles.

Babylon was laid out in a grid pattern, with wide and magnificently decorated processional roadways. Beyond the city's fortified walls lay a second line of defense, and between these were irrigated fields. Here too, lay an artificial, terraced hill built and planted over an elaborate, vaulted foundation. When the Greeks of Alexander the Great conquered the city in 331 B.C., they called these "Hanging Gardens" one of the Seven Wonders of the World.

monopoly over the development of states. Large states had arisen in the Indus Valley (in present-day Pakistan) and China, and the stage was set for the rise of Greece and Rome.

As we know, not only urban life but also the idea of the state spread throughout the world. Today, as a result, the planet's living space is compartmentalized into over 200 states, dependencies, and other bounded territories. From a comparatively small number of migrating hunter-gatherer groups that represented the most complex spatial-organizational system on Earth just 12,000 years ago, we have reached a point where theirs is now the simplest form, represented now by a few surviving hunter-gatherer groups like the San of Botswana's Kalahari Desert.

◆ IMPRINTS OF HUMAN ORGANIZATION

Time and again over the past million years, deglaciation was followed by sustained interglaciation, and during the warm interglaciations our hominid ancestors spread far and wide. They left their imprint on the landscape: they burned forests, killed wildlife, built encampments, inhabited caves, and in some instances buried their dead. Their bone and stone tools are found at fossil sites, sometimes in large quantities. But until about 12,000 years ago, when the present interglaciation began, our ancestors had left only the slightest imprint on the Earth as a whole.

Why Is the Holocene Different?

Indeed, the Holocene began with little indication that this interglaciation would be different. Perhaps this was so because for the first time humans living in more or less stable communities had to adapt to changing environments in particular settings. People were living, for example, in the tundras and grasslands of northern Europe, following migratory herds and killing animals for meat whenever they needed it. But the warming climate caused the tundras and grasslands to shift to the north, and forests of pine, oak, and birch developed in their place. Some human groups moved northward, but others adapted to this new environment, in which hunting was more difficult. Those who stayed behind learned to make new weapons that were better suited to hunting in the woods. Their fossil teeth indicate that they also changed their diets. They collected wild grains, caught fish, and gathered mollusks. Importantly, they began to fashion better stone axes and were able to cut down trees. Now they could build log houses and hollow out trees to make canoes. Their settlements took on the look of permanence.

But even then, toward the end of the Mesolithic, there was no indication of what lay ahead. Had the Holocene interglaciation come to a close, there would have been little to differentiate it from previous warm phases. Human communities remained small, and most still were migratory.

Human populations also remained very small. Because the data can be interpreted in different ways, there is no consensus on this subject. But around the beginning of the Neolithic, some 10,000 years ago, when animal and plant domestication commenced, the total human population was almost certainly below 6 million. Although they had spread far and wide, humans occupied a tiny fraction of the Earth's surface.

And yet the world has been transformed during the Holocene epoch. Several theories have been proposed to explain why the transformation occurred *this* time. After all, humans had been confronted by environmental change during previous interglaciations as well, and nothing comparable had happened. In truth, there still is no satisfactory answer. Some historical geographers suggest that this enormous change was the result of comparatively rapid population growth in the Middle East, which pushed people into less hospitable regions where their knowledge of agriculture helped them to adapt. Adaptation led to the domestication of animals and plants, and this set in motion the First Agricultural Revolution. It is true that population differences stand out when we try to identify ways in which the early Holocene differed from the previous interglaciation. *Homo sapiens* was not nearly as numerous, nor as widely dispersed, during the previous warm phase.

Yet in other areas population numbers were substantial, and yet no revolutionary changes occurred there. The special combination of conditions that was to propel the world into its modern age seems to have existed in only a few places.

How Did Holocene Humanity Transform the Earth?

Let us consider the human imprint on the Earth during the Holocene. We will look at several major areas, although of course many others could be mentioned.

Farming The First Agricultural Revolution has been followed by two more, one organizational and the other (still in progress) genetic. Entire regions of the Earth have been plowed, terraced, fenced, and covered with crops; huge herds of livestock graze on fields from Tierra del Fuego to Finland. No human activity transforms as much of the Earth's surface as farming does.

Administration The world has been compartmentalized into more than 200 countries and other entities, heirs to the state idea that first arose about 5500 years ago. The imprint of the modern state is complex and includes its capital city, its provincial or other subsidiary capitals, its heartland or core area (see Part Eight), and its boundaries, the last often marked by walls, fences, or posts.

Urbanization In a matter of centuries, urban dwellers, rather than villagers, have become the majority of the world population. The earliest cities, established less than 6000 years ago, had successors (such as Babylon, Damascus, Athens) that anchored growing civilizations, but until the twentieth century they were relatively rare. Today many cities house more people than entire nations. Nothing symbolizes Holocene humanity as much as the great cities of the present day.

Industrialization Even in the context of the Holocene (as opposed to the period of *H. sapiens'* presence or hominid evolution), industrialization as we know it is a late development. Industries existed 6000 years ago, and they spread throughout the world. "Pre-industrial" India and Japan had major complexes of workshops that produced goods ranging from textiles to ceramics. The Industrial Revolution occurred little more than two centuries ago; but it transformed manufacturing and vastly expanded the demand for natural resources. From the great industrial complexes to the slag heaps at the mines, the impact of industrialization is etched in the landscape.

Transportation and Communication Another symbol of humanity's imprint is the global network of transportation and communication routes and lines crisscrossing the Earth's surface. Railroads, highways, ports, pipelines, airfields, power lines, and other signs of the transportation age bear witness to modern civilization; not even a new glaciation could erase all of this evidence.

Population Overshadowing everything else is the almost unimaginable expansion of the human population during the Holocene, especially in recent centuries. Every month, more people are added to the world population than existed on the entire planet at the beginning of the Holocene. From 6 million the population has grown to 6 billion, a thousandfold increase, most of which has taken place in less than two centuries. In Part 2 we begin our geographic look at the modern world by turning our attention to population.

◆ HUMAN GEOGRAPHY AND THE NATURAL ENVIRONMENT

The relationship between human society and the natural environment is central to human geography. The emergence of *Homo sapiens* may have spanned 6 million years or more, but the expansion of humanity to unprecedented numbers has taken only two centuries. This expansion has had an unprecedented impact on the natural environment—local, regional, and global.

The Human Impact

We should be aware of two kinds of change that can affect elements of our natural environment. We have reason to believe that the warm Holocene will not last forever. Some climatologists have suggested that the current period of interglaciation may soon come to an end. This swing between cold glaciation and warm interglaciation is a natural phenomenon. But now the human impact on the natural environment is taking on powerful dimensions. We are pouring so much pollution into the atmosphere that global environments may be modified as a result. The loss of high-altitude ozone, for example, is attributed to the emanation of chlorofluorocarbons (CFCs) from air conditioners and other equipment; as the ozone layer thins, its ability to absorb ultraviolet radiation is diminished. Plants, animals, and people are affected by overexposure; photosynthesis is impaired, skin cancer rates increase, and eye problems multiply.

Beginning in the 1980s, many scientists warned that atmospheric pollution was creating a ***greenhouse warming effect*** in the atmosphere that could lead to global temperature increases, rapid melting of the remaining glaciers, and rising sea levels. But while there was some evidence of a temporary warming trend in many regions of the world, other areas did not record any such a trend. Such variation is not inconsistent with global warming, and a sequence of warm years in the 1990s appeared to confirm predictions based on computer models that a human-induced global-warming trend was at hand. A minority of scientists, though (including some geographers), continued to view this recent warming episode as a primarily natural cycle, only slightly affected by human actions.

Geographers did not, however, ignore the evidence that global environments were experiencing wider fluctuations, greater deviations from the norm. Regional warming was only one of these variations. In the Pacific Ocean, ***El Niño Southern/Oscillation (ENSO)*** events, involving changes in normal patterns of water circulation, occurred with greater frequency and had wider impact; ENSO events were correlated with floods in Texas and droughts in Africa. During a short span of time North America experienced a hundred-year storm (one so severe that it is calculated to occur just once in 100 years), a blizzard of the century, and two floods, one a 500-year event and the other a "flood of the millennium."

Is it possible that our continuing pollution of the atmosphere is contributing to these environmental extremes? Or are these wide variations of climate an early warning that a major environmental reversal lies ahead? At present we cannot answer these questions definitively, but one thing is certain: our befouling of the atmosphere can interfere with natural changes.

Whatever the course of events, it has become clear that we should be prepared for environmental change. Two ways to do so are to become aware of the layout of the habitable world, that is, its geography, and to appreciate the possible directions change might take. We deal with the first challenge in this chapter and with the second at the end of the book, in Chapter 32.

Land and Space

In the remainder of this chapter we present two important maps, each containing information about the habitable space on our planet. It is hardly necessary to remind ourselves that only about 30 percent of the Earth's surface consists of land, but Figure 3-6 emphasizes how little of this 30 percent is capable of sustaining dense human populations. Much of the land surface of the Earth is mountainous and rugged.

Certainly, mountains can sustain people in sizable clusters (the Inca Empire was a mountain-based state in the Andes of South America), but generally mountains do not support populations comparable to those found in river basins and plains, where accessibility,

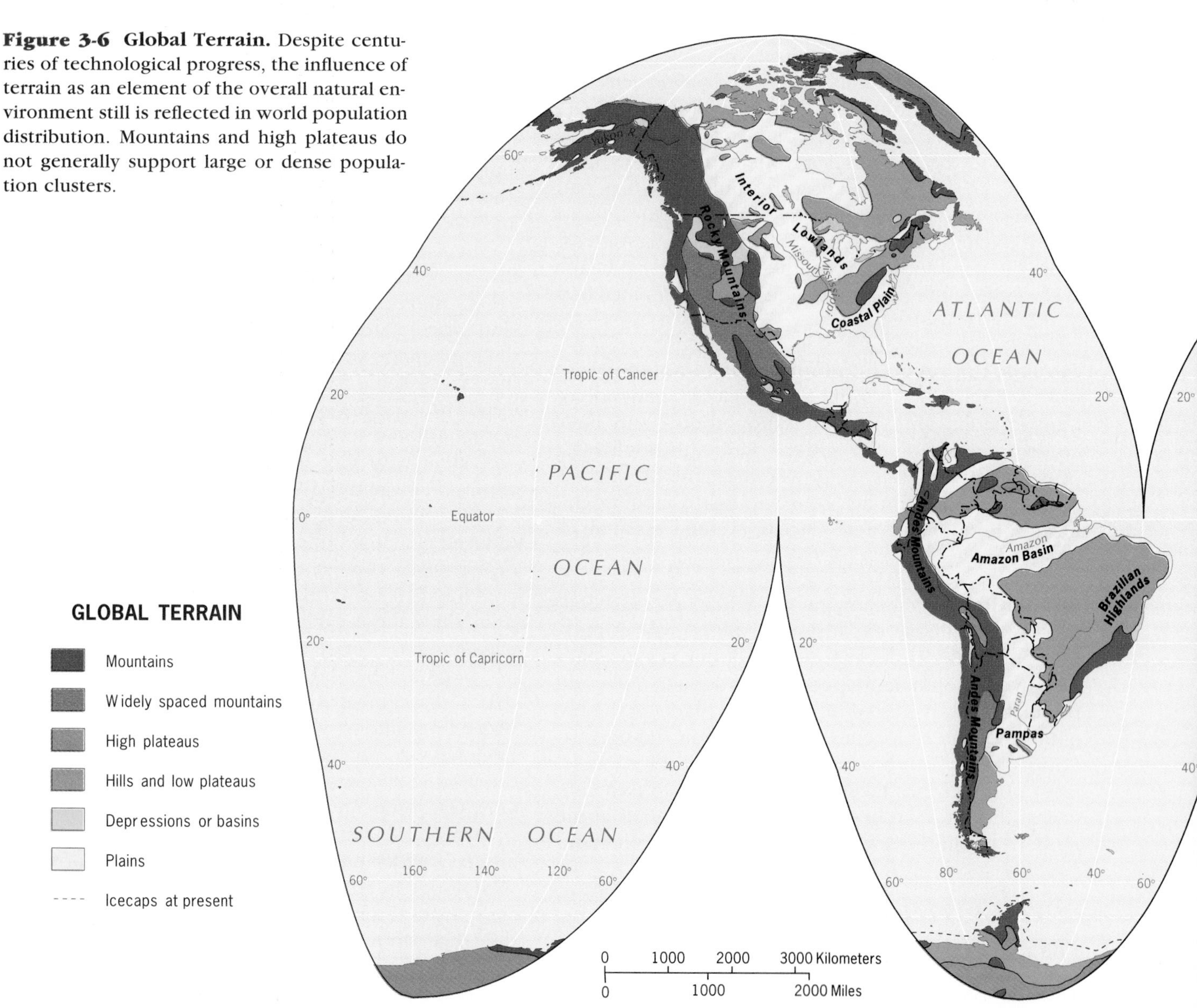

Figure 3-6 Global Terrain. Despite centuries of technological progress, the influence of terrain as an element of the overall natural environment still is reflected in world population distribution. Mountains and high plateaus do not generally support large or dense population clusters.

circulation, and movement of people and goods are easier. In Part Two, where we focus on present population patterns, distribution, and density, Figure 4-1 when compared with Figure 3-6, reveals the sparseness of population in the mountainous regions of the world.

High plateaus also tend to support sparse populations. It is no coincidence that the entire continent of Africa, much of which consists of plateau, sustains fewer people than the single country of India. The elevation of high plateaus like that of Tibet makes living conditions difficult. Severe erosion can create problems similar to those presented by mountainous terrain. Again, the high-plateau regions stand out as low-population areas.

Land and Climate

In combination, all the elements of weather, the sweep of the Sun's energy, the rotation of the Earth, the circulation of the oceans, the movement of weather systems, the rush of air in jet streams—produce a pattern of climates that may appear complicated but is actually remarkably simple. This is one of those maps that's worth a million words, because it allows us to determine at a glance what climate and weather are like anywhere on the Earth.

We owe this remarkable map to the work of Wladimir Köppen (1846–1940), who devised a scheme for classifying the world's climates on the basis of temperature and precipitation. Many efforts have been

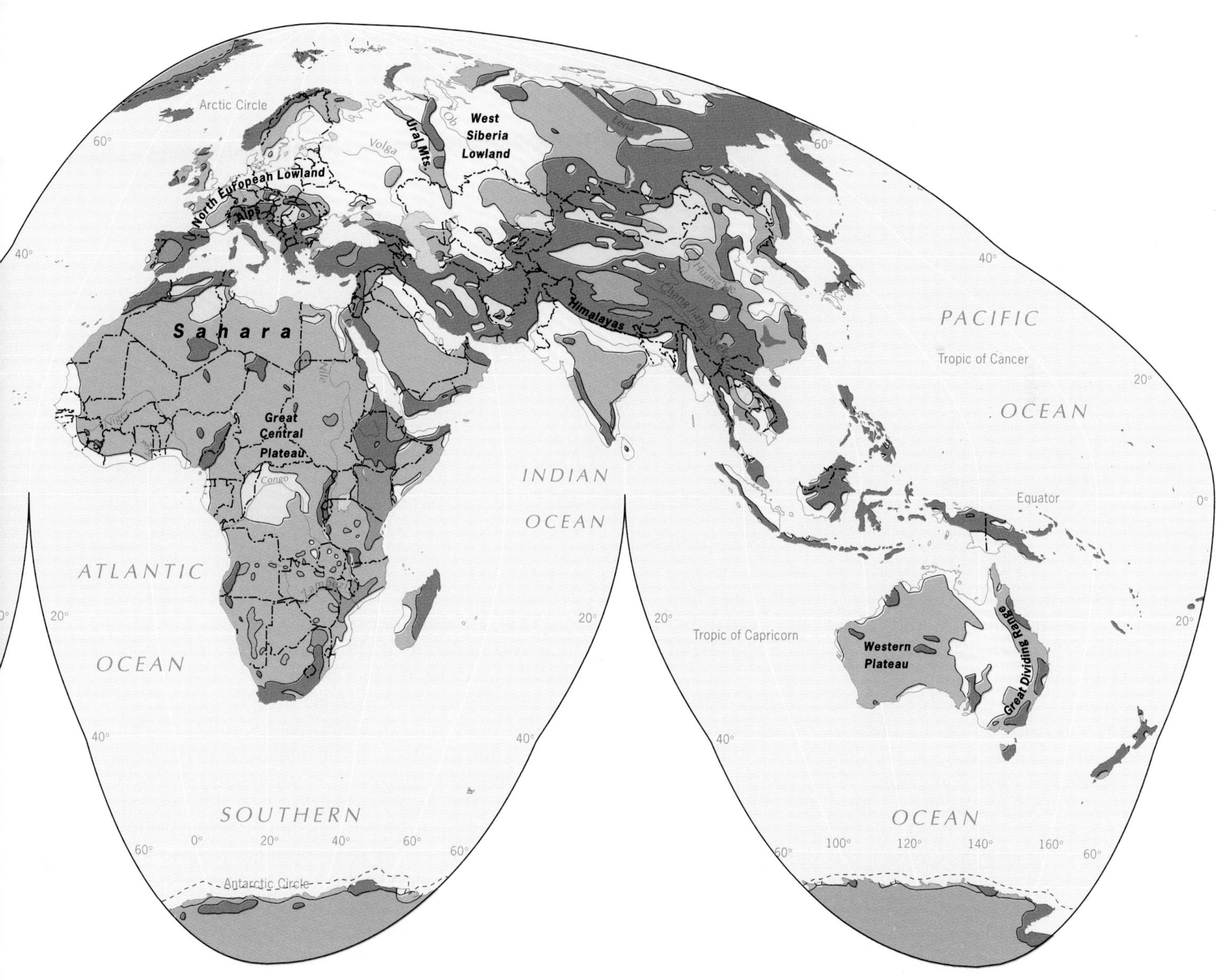

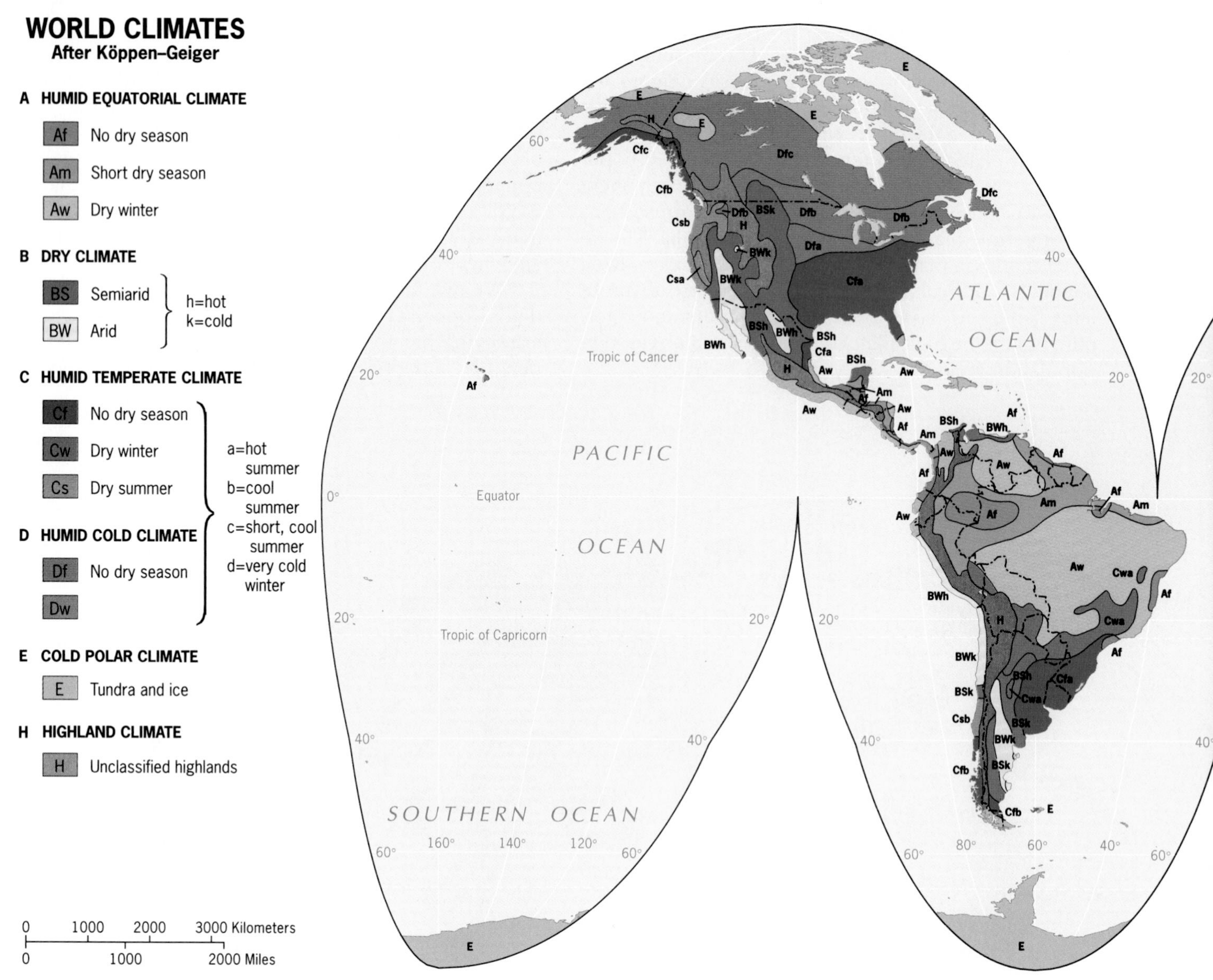

made to improve on Köppen's scheme, but nearly a century after its creation, and despite the availability of more accurate climatic data, it has stood the test of time (Fig. 3-7).

Köppen's map displays the present distribution of ***climatic regions*** across the planet. The legend looks complicated, but it really is not; here is one of those maps worth spending some time on. For our purposes, it is enough to get a sense of the distribution of the major types of climate. The letter categories in the legend give a clear indication of the conditions they represent.

The (A) climates are hot or very warm and generally humid. The "no dry season" (Af) regions are *equatorial rainforest* regions. The "short dry season" (Am) climate is known as the *monsoon* climate. And if you can envisage an African savanna, you know what the (Aw, *savanna*) designation means.

Once you realize that the yellow and light beige colors on the map represent dry climates (BW, *desert* and BS, *steppe*), it becomes clear how much of the world is always in need of water. As we will see later, some very large population clusters have developed in these water-deficient regions, especially at lower (and warmer) latitudes. The world faces a long-term water crisis, and the Köppen map helps explain why.

The (C) climates also have familiar names. The (Cf) climate, represented by dark green, prevails over the southeastern United States. If you know the local weather in Atlanta or Nashville or Jacksonville, you understand why this climate is often called "humid temperate." It's moist, and it doesn't get as cold as it

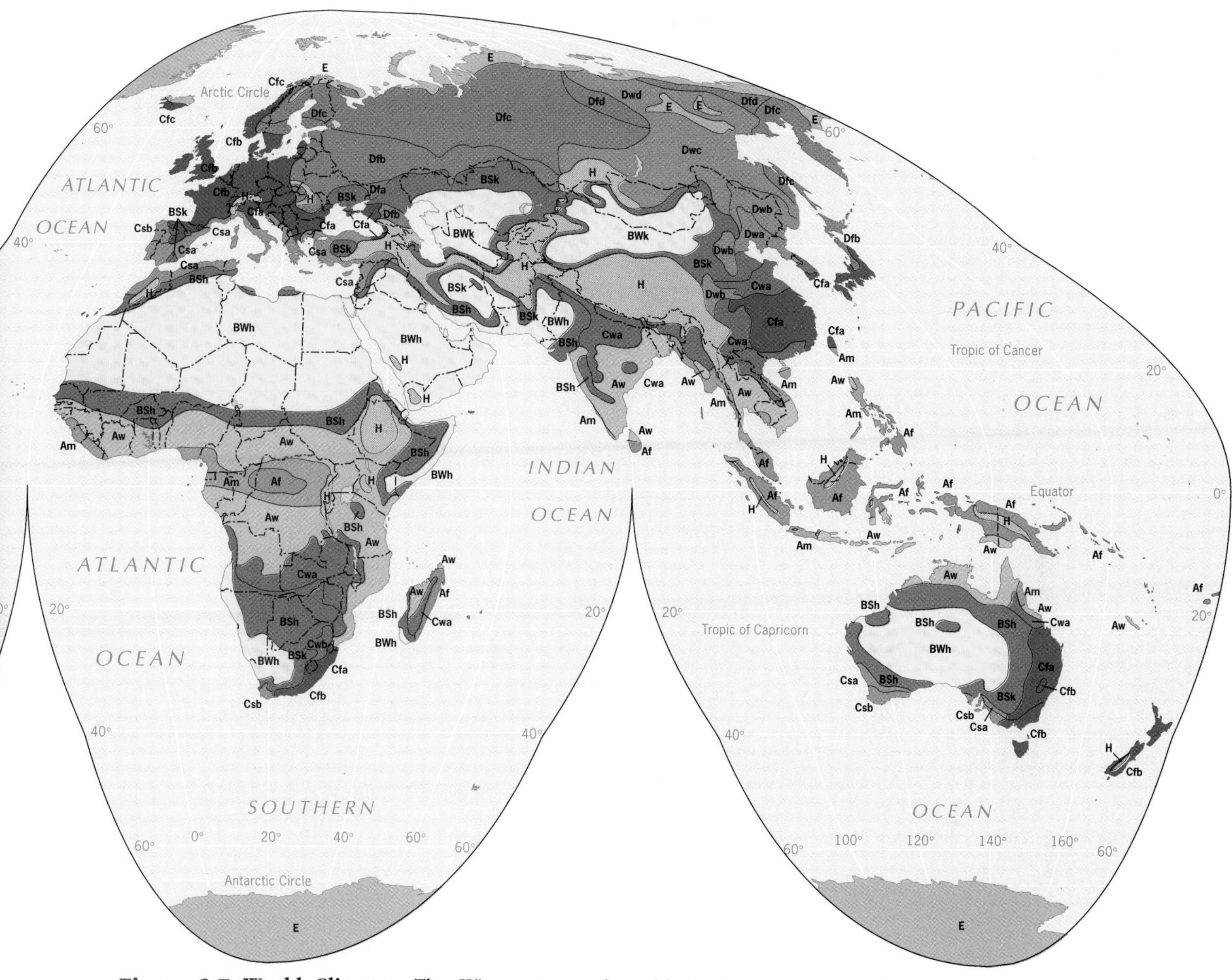

Figure 3-7 World Climates. The Köppen map of world climates as modified by R. Geiger. These, of course, are macroclimatic regions; microclimates are set within these but cannot be shown at this scale.

does in Canada or as warm (continuously, anyway) as in the Amazon Basin. If you have experienced this kind of climate, the map gives you a good idea of what it's like in much of eastern China, southeastern Australia, and a large part of southeastern South America.

The "dry summer" (C) climates are known as *Mediterranean* climates (the small s in Cs means that summers are dry). This mild climate occurs not only around the Mediterranean Sea, and thus in the famous wine countries of France, Italy, and Spain, but also in California, Chile, South Africa's Cape, and southern parts of Australia. So you know what kind of weather to expect in Rome, San Francisco, Santiago, Cape Town, and Adelaide.

Farther toward the poles, the planet gets rather cold. Note that the (D) climates dominate in the upper Midwest and Canada, but it gets even colder in Siberia. The "milder" (Da) climates (here the key is the small (a), which denotes a warm summer) have very limited extent in Eurasia. Winters are very cold in all the (D) climates and downright frigid (and long) in the (Dfb) and (Dfc) regions. The latter merge into the polar climates, where tundra and ice prevail.

The climate map, like the landscape map, reflects the limited habitable areas of the Earth. Vast portions of the planet's landmasses are extremely arid or frigid or excessively hot and humid and therefore cannot sustain large populations that depend directly on the land for their sustenance. And despite technological advances, hundreds of millions of people still live off the land.

Figure 3-7, like Figure 3-1, is a still photo of a changing pattern. When the conditions shown in Figure 3-1 prevailed, the habitable zone of the Earth was much narrower, and polar (E) climates reached as far south as the central Great Plains and the Alpine slopes of southern Europe. Today the Earth is much warmer, but it will not remain warm forever. Before long the Köppen map will look quite different.

The two world maps presented here provide a good portrait of the physical stage on which the events described in the rest of this book take place. For example, we will discuss places like Nigeria (Africa's most populous country) and Quebec (the Canadian province where separatism is a popular sentiment). From these maps we can deduce the terrain, the climate, and the precipitation in those places, and thus obtain some notion of what their environments are like. Such information can be useful in understanding the local human geography.

◆ KEY TERMS ◆

animal domestication
climatic regions
El Niño Southern Oscillation (ENSO)
Fertile Crescent
geologic eras
glaciation
greenhouse (enhanced) warming effect
Holocene epoch
interglaciation
K/T boundary
Late Cenozoic Ice Age
plant domestication
Pleistocene epoch
social stratification
ziggurat

◆ APPLYING GEOGRAPHIC KNOWLEDGE ◆

1. We live today during an interglacial period. The Earth is experiencing a warm phase: sea level is high, coastal plains lie partially submerged, climates are comparatively mild. How would your place of residence be affected by (a) a further warming of the atmosphere and (b) a return to glacial conditions?
2. You have been offered the opportunity to lead a tour group consisting of travelers from North America to New Zealand and Australia. How will you use Figure 3-7 to answer questions about the climate and weather in those countries? If your guests resided in Vancouver, British Columbia, where would they find a familiar environment "downunder?" In Phoenix, Arizona? Jacksonville, Florida? San Francisco, California?

Part One
GEOGRAPHY, CULTURE, AND THE ENVIRONMENT

Why is geography so much a part of the effort to come to terms with our rapidly changing world? What does it mean to think geographically? Can geography offer insights into the diversity of changes unfolding around us? The developments of the past decade have shown that we live in a world of constant change—a world that defies easy generalization. Differences from place to place matter, and no one map can capture the dynamism of our situation. At the same time, the practice of separating the study of physical and human phenomena seems increasingly problematic. Small wonder, then, that geography is being looked to for ideas and approaches. As one geographer put it, place matters—as does the relationship among phenomena in place and space. The concepts and tools of geography are thus an indispensable part of our effort to come to terms with the world around us.

◆ SELECTED REFERENCES ◆

Part One **Geography, Culture, and the Environment**

Abler, R., et al., eds. *Human Geography in a Shrinking World* (North Scituate, Mass.: Duxbury Press, 1975).

Abler, R., et al. *Spatial Organization: The Geographer's View of the World* (Englewood Cliffs, N.J.: Prentice-Hall, 1971).

Allen, J., & Massey, D., eds. *Geographical Worlds* (Oxford, U.K.: Oxford University Press, 1995).

Amedeo, D., & Golledge, R. *An Introduction to Scientific Reasoning in Geography* (New York: John Wiley & Sons, 1975).

Bailey, R., ed. *The True State of the Planet* (New York: The Free Press, 1995).

Bradley, R. S. *Quaternary Paleoclimatology: Methods of Paleoclimatological Reconstruction* (Boston: Allen & Unwin, 1985).

Brown, L. A. *Innovation Diffusion: A New Perspective* (New York: Methuen, 1981).

Campbell, B., ed. *Humankind Emerging* (Glenville, Ill. Scott, Foresman, 5th rev. ed., 1988).

Campbell, J. *Map Use and Analysis* (Dubuque, Iowa: Wm. C. Brown, 1991).

Cox, C. B., & Moore, P. D. *Biogeography: An Ecological and Evolutionary Approach* (Oxford, U.K.: Blackwell Scientific Publications, 5th ed., 1993).

de Blij, H. J. & Muller, P. O. *Geography: Realms, Regions and Concepts*, 8th rev. ed. (New York: John Wiley & Sons, 1998).

Dent, B. *Principles of Thematic Map Design* (Reading, Mass.: Addison-Wesley, 1984).

Ember, C. R., & Ember, M. E. *Anthropology* (Englewood Cliffs, N.J.: Prentice-Hall, 6th rev. ed., 1990).

Espenshade, E. B., Jr., ed. Goode's *World Atlas* (Chicago: Rand McNally, 19th rev. ed., 1995).

Fagan, B. M. *People of the Earth: An Introduction to World Pre-history* (Glenville, Ill.: Scott, Foresman, 1989).

Gaile, G. L., and Willmott, C. J., eds., *Geography in America* (Columbus, Ohio: Merrill, 1989).

Geertz, C. *The Interpretation of Cultures* (New York: Basic Books, 1973).

Gibbons, A. "First Hominid Finds from Ethiopia in a Decade." *Science*, 22 March 1991, p. 1428.

Gold, J. *An Introduction to Behavioral Geography* (New York: Oxford University Press, 1980).

Gould, P. *The Geographer at Work* (London: Routledge & Kegan Paul, 1985).

Gould, P., & White, R. *Mental Maps* (Boston: Allen & Unwin, 2nd rev. ed., 1982).

Graedel, T. E., & Crutzen, P. J. *Atmosphere, Climate and Change* (New York: Scientific American Library, 1995).

Gregory, D. *Ideology, Science and Human Geography* (London: Hutchinson, 1978).

Gregory, D., & Walford, R., eds. *Horizons in Human Geography* (Totowa, N.J.: Barnes & Noble Books, 1989).

Grove, J. M. *The Little Ice Age* (London: Methuen, 1988).

Harris, C. D., ed. *A Geographical Bibliography for American Libraries* (Washington, D.C.: Association of American Geographers and the National Geographic Society, 1985).

Hartshorne, R. *The Nature of Geography* (Washington, D.C.: Association of American Geographers, 1939).

Hartshorne, R. *Perspective on the Nature of Geography* (Chicago: Rand McNally, 1959).

Holz, R., ed. *The Surveillant Science: Remote Sensing of the Environment* (New York: John Wiley & Sons, 2nd rev. ed, 1984).

Huntington, E., and Cushing, S.W., *Principles of Human Geography, 5th ed.* (New York: John Wiley, 1940).

Intergovernmental Panel on Climate Change (IPCC). *Climate Change 1995—The Science of Climate Change* (Cambridge, U.K.: Cambridge University Press, 1996).

Jackson, P. *Maps of Meaning* (London: Unwin Hyman, 1989).

James, P. E., & Jones, C. F., eds. *American Geography: Inventory and Prospect* (Syracuse, N.Y.: Syracuse University Press, 1954).

James, P. E., & Martin, G. *All Possible Worlds: A History of Geographical Ideas* (New York: John Wiley & Sons, 3rd rev. ed., 1981).

Johnston, R. *The Nature of Human Geography* (Oxford, U.K.: Basil Blackwell, 5th ed., 1996).

Johnston, R., et al., eds. *The Dictionary of Human Geography* (Oxford, U.K.: Basil Blackwell, 2nd ed., 1994).

Keates, J. S. *Cartographic Design and Production* (Essex, U.K.: Longmans, 1989).

Levenson, T. *Ice Time: Climate, Science and Life on Earth* (New York: Harper & Row, 1989).

Markham, S. F. *Climate and the Energy of Nations* (London and New York: Oxford University Press, 1947).

Massey, D., & Allen, J., eds. *Geography Matters! A Reader* (New York: Cambridge University Press, 1985).

Maunder, W. J. *The Human Impact of Climate Uncertainty* (New York: Routledge, Chapman & Hall, 1989).

Michener, J. "The Mature Social Studies Teacher," *Social Education*, November 1970, pp. 760–766.

Monmonier, M. S. *Computer-Assisted Cartography: Principles and Prospects* (Englewood Cliffs, N.J.: Prentice-Hall, 1982).

Monmonier, M. S. *How to Lie with Maps* (Chicago: University of Chicago Press, 1990).

Monmonier, M. S. *Mapping It Out: Expository Cartography for the Humanities and Social Sciences* (Chicago: University of Chicago Press, 1993).

Monmonier, M. S. *Maps with the News* (Chicago: University of Chicago Press, 1989).

National Geographic Society, *Maps, the Landscape, and Fundamental Themes in Geography* (Washington, D.C., 1986).

National Geographic Society. *Atlas of the World* (Washington, D.C.: National Geographic Society, 6th rev. ed., 1990).

National Geographic Society. *Historical Atlas of the United States* (Washington, D.C.: National Geographic Society, 1988).

National Research Council. *Rediscovering Geography: New Relevance for Science and Society* (Washington, D.C.: National Academy Press, 1997).

Pattison, W. "The Four Traditions of Geography," *Journal of Geography* 63 (1964), 211–216.

Peet, R., & Thrift, N. J., eds. *New Models in Geography* (2 vols.) (London: Unwin Hyman, 1989).

Pielou, E. C. *After the Ice Age: The Return of Life to Glaciated North America* (Chicago: University of Chicago Press, 1991).

Rand McNally & Co. *The New International Atlas* (Chicago: Rand McNally, 2nd rev. ed., 1996).

Roberts, N. *The Holocene: An Environmental History* (New York: Basil Blackwell, 1989).

Robinson, A. H., et al. *Elements of Cartography* (New York: John Wiley & Sons, 6th rev. ed., 1990).

Sauer, Carl "Recent Developments in Cultural Geography" in *Recent Developments in the Social Sciences*, Elwood, C. A., Wissler, C., and Gault, R. H., eds. (Philadelphia: J.B. Lippincott, 1927), pp. 154–212.

Schneider, S. H. *Global Warming: Are We Entering the Greenhouse Century?* (New York: Vintage Books, 1990).

Schneider, S. H. *Laboratory Earth: The Planetary Gamble We Can't Afford to Lose* (New York: Basic Books, 1997).

Sheffield, C. *Man on Earth: How Civilization and Technology Changed the Face of the World—A Survey from Space* (New York: Macmillan, 1983).

Simons, E. L., "Human Origin," *Science*, 22 September 1989, pp. 133–135.

Soja, E. W. *Postmodern Geographies* (London: Verson, 1989).

Strahler, A. N., & Strahler, A. H. *Modern Physical Geography* (New York: John Wiley & Sons, 4th rev. ed., 1992).

Thomas, W., ed. *Man's Role in Changing the Face of the Earth* (Chicago: University of Chicago Press, 1956).

Tufte, E. R. *Envisioning Information* (Chesire, Conn.: Graphics Press, 1990).

Weaver, K. "The Search for Our Ancestors," *National Geographic*, November 1985, pp. 560–623.

Wegener, A. *The Origin of Continents and Oceans* (New York: Dover, trans. J. Biram, 1966).

Wenke, R. J. *Patterns in Prehistory: Humankind's First Three Million Years* (New York: Oxford University Press, 3rd rev. ed., 1990).

Williams, M. A. J., et al. *Quaternary Environments* (London: Edward Arnold, 1993).

Part Two

POPULATION PATTERNS AND PROCESSES

At Issue

The world's growing human population is poised to pass the 6-billion mark, four times the number just one century ago. The rate of overall growth is declining, but the actual increase continues to exceed 90 million per year. Reducing this annual increment is an objective advocated vigorously by the wealthier, low-growth, Western countries. Improved living standards, they argue, can be achieved only by controlling the population explosion. Some poorer countries, notably China, have adopted policies designed to reduce their population growth rates. But a world population conference held by the United Nations in 1994 revealed some deep disagreements among the participants. Many Islamic countries argued that population control of the kind advocated by Western nations violated Muslim precepts. (They found support in the Vatican, also represented at the conference.) Other countries maintained that the high rate of consumption in the rich Western countries constitutes a larger problem than rapid population growth in poorer regions. In a lifetime, an American will consume 30 times as much as, say, a Bangladeshi of the world's food and other resources. ***So who should inhibit population growth? Should lowering the world's population growth rate be a global objective at all?***

A warning from the authorities in Chengdu, China.

Part Outline

Chapter 4

Fundamentals of Population Geography

From the field notes

"No matter where you are, the Indonesian island of Jawa (Java) leaves no doubt that this is one of the most densely populated places on Earth. The back roads I traveled seemed to be lined with houses for endless miles, the houses clustering into villages and towns every few minutes. Here in Jakarta, the national capital, the crush of people reminds you that this is the world's fourth-most populous country. Traffic is so congested that it crawls along, so that pedestrians simply mix with road vehicles. It is all a sign of a burgeoning economy, but what happens when the economy falters? Will food supply always suffice, as it does today?"

KEY POINTS

◆ **The world's population is currently growing by about 90 million per year; the bulk of this growth is occurring in the world's poorer countries.**

◆ **The world's three largest population concentrations all lie on the Eurasian landmass, and the smallest of the three is the most highly developed and urbanized.**

◆ **Population data often are unreliable because of the high cost and organizational challenges of census taking.**

◆ **Population density can be measured on the basis of several different criteria, revealing contrasting aspects of a country's demography.**

For some 200,000 years after the emergence of *Homo sapiens* in Africa, the Earth's human population grew very slowly, its numbers rising and falling in response to environmental change, disease, and availability of food. But then, as the ice of the last glaciation retreated and the amount of habitable space expanded, the momentous events of the Holocene began. At this point in the text it is appropriate for us to focus on the growth and spread of the planet's population, because virtually everything discussed in later chapters flows from it.

The study of population is termed ***demography*** (from the ancient Greek words *demos*, meaning populace or people, and *graphe*, meaning to describe or write about). The focus of ***population geography*** is on the spatial aspects of demography. The key questions in geography are *where?* and *why there?*, and as you will discover, these lead to some penetrating insights into population issues.

◆ KEY ISSUES IN POPULATION GEOGRAPHY

What are these issues? At present the dominant one is *population growth*. The Earth's environments and natural resources are strained by the needs of the mushrooming human population, which farms and erodes its soils, fishes and depletes its oceans, mines and consumes its minerals and fuels, and cuts and destroys its forests. These problems have become especially acute in the twentieth century as the world's population has increased *fourfold* from its level just a hundred years earlier. A continued high rate of population growth in the twenty-first century could have a calamitous impact, causing irreversible damage to the natural systems on which we depend for our existence and survival.

Another, related issue involves *food supply*. During the 1960s, when population growth was outrunning the rate of increase in grain harvests, widespread malnutrition and hunger seemed likely to occur. Soon, however, technological advances produced higher-yielding strains of rice, wheat, and other crops, and the gap between demand and supply narrowed. But in the 1990s scientists warned that a combination of continued population growth and changing eating habits—especially higher consumption of meat—could lead to a global food crisis.

A further concern is *health*. Rapidly growing numbers of people can produce "reservoirs" of disease—for example, in remote equatorial areas, where immunizations are rare, and in burgeoning slums around cities, where public health and sanitation are lacking. The possibility that virulent diseases might spread rapidly throughout the world has brought health issues to center stage. Other aspects of health, including infant and child mortality and life expectancy, are also matters of concern, particularly in the poorest nations.

Yet another dimension of population geography centers on the *status of women*. Statistics about populations (total numbers, density, percentage living in cities, life expectancy), are usually given by country. These data do not always reflect differences between men and women. When certain governments instituted measures to reduce the rate of population growth, the impact fell disproportionately on women. In those societies millions of infant girls are abandoned; girls are malnourished and deprived of medical care; and women are denied the opportunities available to men.

Still another important issue related to population is *migration*. The movement of millions of people across international borders—in search of jobs and a better life, to escape the ravages of war, to evade environmental disasters—is a significant factor in population change. Immigration into some countries adds more to the total population than natural population increase in those countries. Governments have tried to stem the tide of immigration in various ways, but these measures have had limited success. It should also be noted that major population movements can take place *within* a country because of ethnic conflict and civil war, impoverishment of rural areas, and other causes.

◆ ELEMENTS OF POPULATION GEOGRAPHY

How can a geographic approach to issues such as those just described improve our understanding of them? To begin with, we should consider some of the spatial aspects of the human world. Not only does less than 30 percent of the Earth's surface consist of solid ground, but of that living space, only a fraction (at most, around one-third) is arable—that is, able to produce crops and livestock. Vast stretches of land are desert, frigid, mountainous, or otherwise agriculturally unproductive, or of such low productivity that only very small human populations can subsist there.

Population and Space

From the very beginning, humanity has been unevenly distributed over the land, and the contrasts between crowded countrysides and bustling cities on the one hand, and empty reaches on the other, have only intensified—especially during the twentieth century. Even countries with huge populations, such as China and India, have large areas where people are absent or sparsely distributed. The peoples of China and India still depend quite heavily on the food their farmers can produce, so the clustering of the population in those countries continues to reflect the availability and fertility of farmland. China's interior deserts, cold, windswept plateaus, and snowcapped mountains remain as empty as they have always been, except for small settlements in areas where minerals or fuels are mined.

In countries with more technologically advanced economies, people tend to leave the land and to cluster in cities and towns. Mushrooming urbanization, in which rural, farm-based societies are transformed into urban, trade-based ones, is a dominant theme of twentieth-century human geography. To be sure, cities are also growing in such countries as India and China, but the percentage of those countries' population that is urbanized remains far below that of, say the United States or Western Europe. (For comparisons among these and other countries, consult Resource B, page R-10, where demographic data for all the world's principal countries are provided.)

Population Distribution and Density

To represent contrasts of the kind just discussed on maps, population geographers use measures of population ***distribution*** and ***density***.

The distribution of population describes the locations on the Earth's surface where individuals or groups (depending on the scale) live. It is represented most efficiently by a so-called *dot map*. At the largest scale—for example, part of a rural county in the United States—such a map can actually show the location of every individual, with each dot representing one person. At a medium scale—say an entire country such as France—one dot would represent a cluster of perhaps 5000 people, and the map would reveal where the population is concentrated and where the number of people in an area would not add up to 5000. At the smallest scale, a world map of population density would use a single dot to represent as many as 100,000 people.

Maps of population distribution have many uses. Famine-relief campaigns, for example, use them in their efforts to deliver supplies to remote areas more efficiently. Closer to home, electoral redistricting maps cannot be drawn without data on where voters live. For such purposes, too, distribution maps are needed.

Population density is another matter. Here the measure is of the number of people per unit area, such as a square kilometer or square mile. The data in Resource B (page R-10) provide the area, total population, and density per square mile for every country (but see "Focus on: Reliability of Population Data").

Note, however, that no country has an evenly distributed population, so that the average derived by dividing the national area by the total number of people may not have much practical meaning. The United States, for example, with a territory of 3,787,425 square miles (9,809,430 square kilometers) had a population of 269 million in 1998. Its average population density would be calculated as 71 per square mile or 27 per square kilometer.* This figure is the nation's ***arithmetic population density***, and in a very general way it confirms the contrast between this country and Asian countries such as Bangladesh (2478 per square mile/957 per square kilometer), Japan (870/335), and India (861/332). These averages do not, however, take account of the clustering of people

*In 1991 the U.S. Census Bureau changed its definition of what constitutes the area of each of the 50 states by including the water areas of ponds, streams, and the territorial sea up to the 3-mile limit. This increases the total area of the United States by 168,655 square miles (436,816 square kilometers), thus creating a total of 3,787,425 square miles (9,809,430 square kilometers). See *New York Times*, Sunday, December 15, 1991, p. 26.

Reliability of Population Data

When the United States conducted its 1990 population ***census*** and the results began to be published, there was an uproar from several quarters. Mayors of major cities insisted that the census had undercounted their populations. This would put them at a financial disadvantage during coming years because federal aid is based on ***population data***. Governors complained that undependable population data could affect the number of congressional seats allotted to their states. Independent observers found that the census had been carried out well, but that as many as 2 million people may not have been counted.

If a prosperous country such as the United States has problems conducting an accurate census, imagine the difficulties that must be overcome in less well-off countries. The cost, organization, and reporting of a census go beyond what many countries can afford or handle.

World population data are collected by several agencies. The United Nations records official statistics that have been assembled and reported by national governments. The U.S. Census Bureau also gathers global population data. The World Bank and the Population Reference Bureau are among other organizations that conduct research and report on the population of the world and of individual countries.

The population data published by these and other organizations frequently are inconsistent. If you examine various statistical tables in detail, inconsistencies will inevitably emerge. Growth rates and other vital statistics, data on food availability, health conditions, and incomes are at times informed estimates rather than hard facts. Thus, while the figures used in this book are based on careful assessments, they are still subject to error.

within a country. In the case of the United States, the average fails to reflect the emptiness of Alaska, the sparseness of the population in much of the West, or the concentration of people in the eastern cities.

An even clearer example of the misleading nature of average density figures can be seen in the case of Egypt. As noted earlier, nearly all of Egypt's over 66 million inhabitants live in the Nile Valley. However, Egypt's total area is 386,660 square miles (about 1 million square kilometers), so the average population density is about 172 per square mile or 66 per square kilometer. Obviously, this figure is rather meaningless when all those people are crowded onto the irrigable land and cultivable soils of the Nile Valley and the rest of the country is desert! It has been estimated that 98 percent of Egypt's population occupies just 3 percent of its total area. For a country like Egypt, then, arithmetic population density measures have little practical relevance.

Arithmetic and Physiologic Densities

Can we arrive at a more meaningful index of population density in individual countries? Yes—by relating the total population to the amount of cultivated land in the country, rather than to its whole area (see Table 4-1). In those heavily populated Asian countries, after

Table 4-1 Population Densities for Selected Countries, 1998

Country	1995 Population (millions)	Area (thousand sq mi/km)	Arithmetic Density (sq mi/km)	Physiologic Density (sq mi/km)
Egypt	66.2	386.7/1001.6	172/66	8161/3150
Japan	126.5	145.7/377.4	870/335	6788/2620
Netherlands	15.6	15.9/41.2	981/379	4431/1711
Bangladesh	124.6	55.6/144.0	2478/956	3779/1459
Colombia	38.2	439.7/1138.8	87/34	1709/660
India	988.1	1237.1/3204.1	798/308	1491/576
Nigeria	110.3	356.7/923.9	309/119	901/348
Argentina	36.0	1068.3/2766.9	34/14	689/266
United States	269.3	3787.4/9808.4	71/27	367/142

Sources: Calculated from World Population Data Sheet published by the Population Reference Bureau, Inc., from data on agriculture in the Encyclopaedia Britannica *Book of the Year* 1997, and from the United Nations Food and Agriculture Organization (FAO) *Production Yearbook* 1996. Note that population data in this table may not correspond to statistics drawn from other sources. (See "Focus on: Reliability of Population Data.")

Figure 4-1 World Population Distribution.

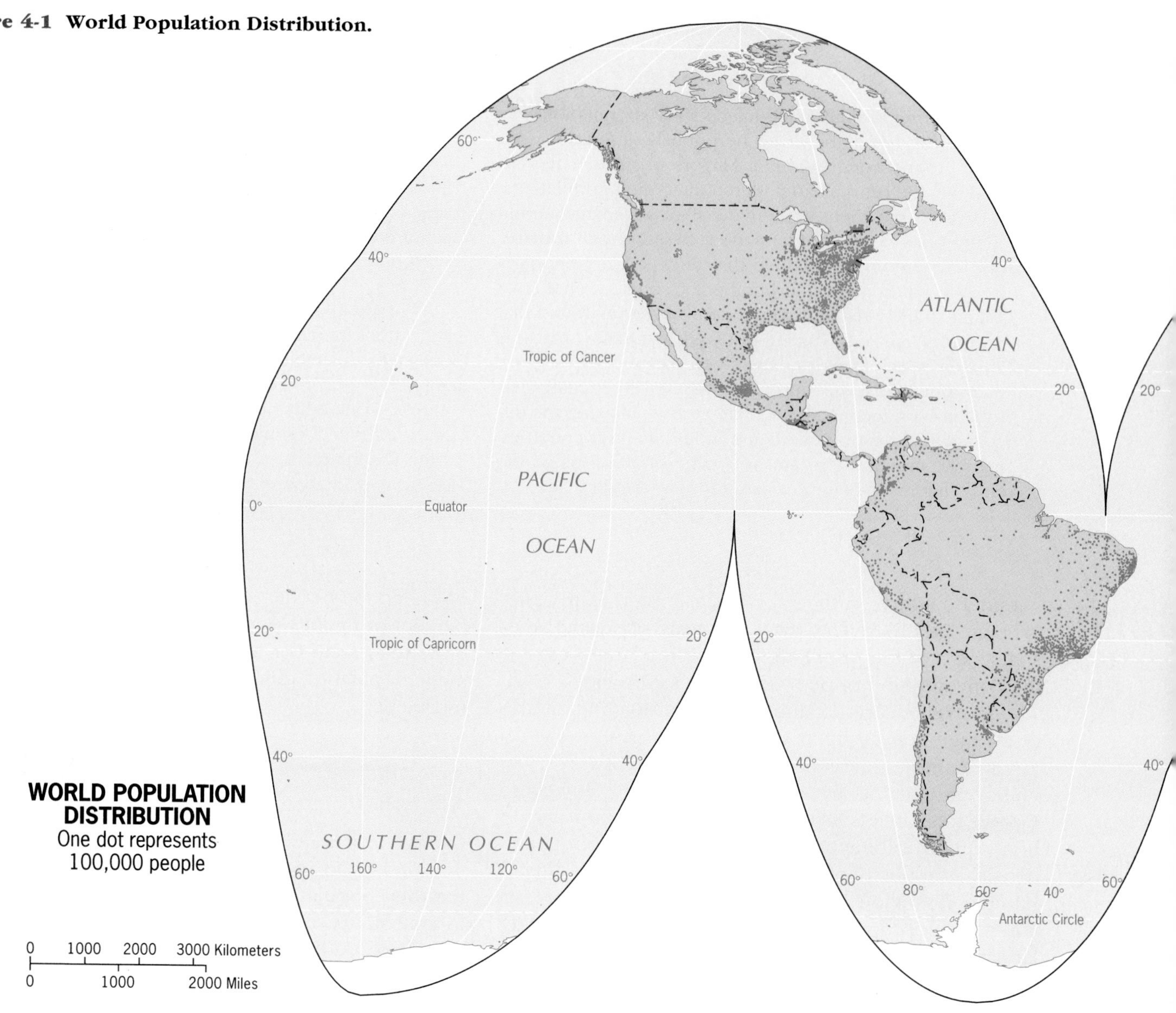

all, it is the arable (farmable) land that matters, not the dry areas or the inhospitable mountains. Instead of the arithmetic density, we calculate the ***physiologic density***, the number of people per unit area of agriculturally productive land. In the case of Egypt, while the arithmetic density is 160 per square mile (61 per square kilometer), the physiologic density is nearly *8000* people per cultivable square mile (3070 per square kilometer). In Japan, the physiologic density also is very high: 6770 per square mile (2613 per square kilometer). In Europe, the country with the highest physiologic density is the Netherlands, reporting 4425 people per square mile (1708 per square kilometer).

Even these calculations are subject to error, however. In every country there are farmlands of different productivity. Some lands produce high crop yields (more than once a year in many Asian countries), while others are marginal or can sustain only livestock. All these variable levels of production are treated equally in our calculation of physiologic density. Still, the measure is much more useful than the arithmetic density index. Table 4-1 provides an indication of the usefulness of the concept of physiologic density. Note, for example, that the United States and Colombia have almost the same arithmetic density, but Colombia has a physiologic density more than four times that of the United States. Egypt's arithmetic density does not look especially high, but its physiologic density tells us what the real situation is in terms of cultivable land and the growing pressure on it. Argentina is the only country on the list with both relatively low arithmetic and physiologic densities. Also note that India's phys-

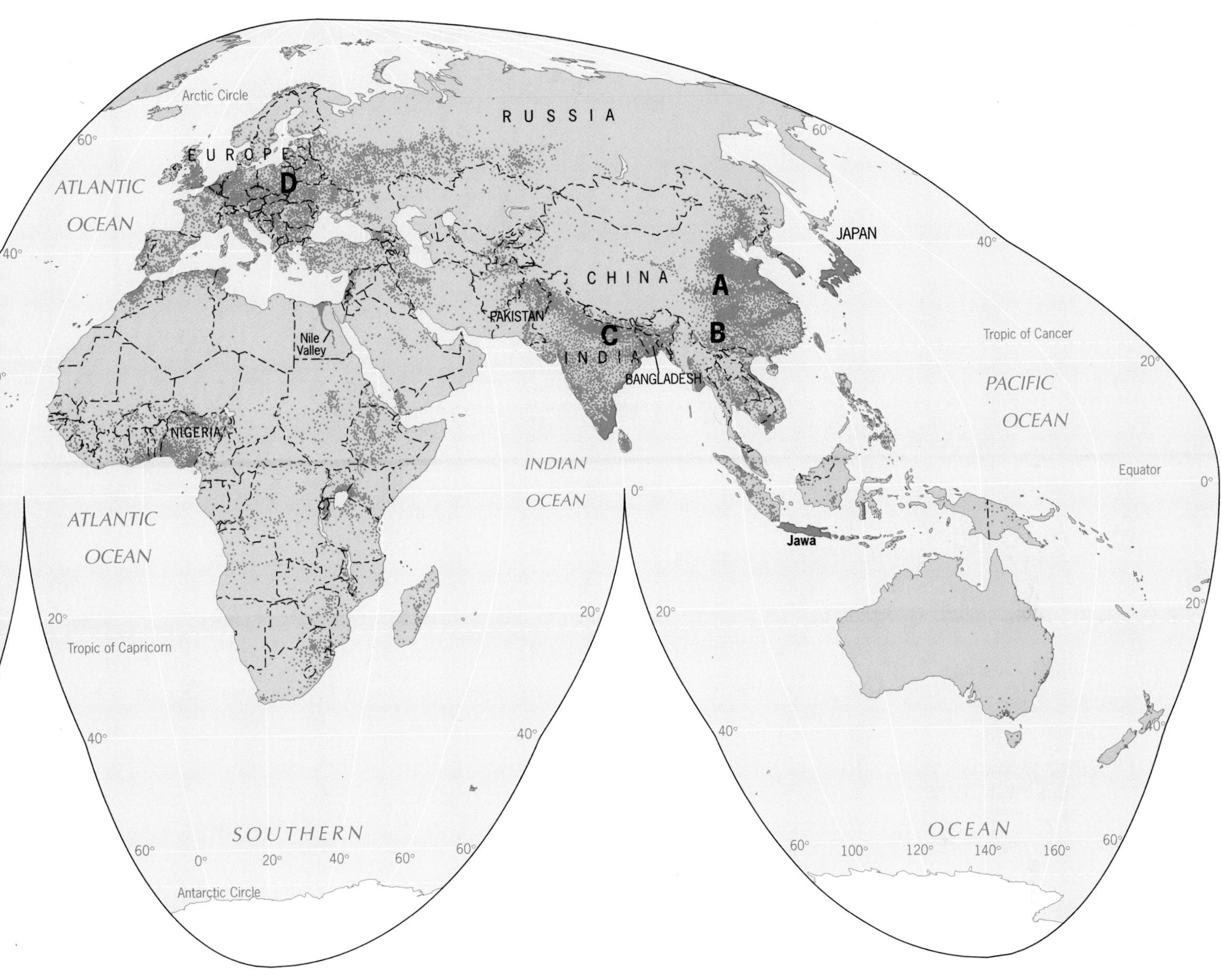

iologic density, while high, is still moderate compared to those of its neighbor Bangladesh, or Japan.

◆ MAJOR POPULATION CONCENTRATIONS

Figures 4-1 and 4-2 show patterns of distribution and density in the world population. Figure 4-1 displays distribution using the dot method, whereas Figure 4-2 illustrates density via the isopleth method. Both maps confirm that the world's three largest ***population concentrations*** are all found on the same landmass: Eurasia. They also remind us that the overwhelming majority of the world's population inhabits the Northern Hemisphere.

The three Eurasian concentrations are in East Asia, South Asia, and Europe. Each is associated with a major civilization: China, India, and Western Europe. The fourth-ranking concentration, North America, is centered in the United States and represents still another important civilization. In this section we explore some of the significant differences among these leading population clusters.

East Asia

While the distribution map (Fig. 4-1) requires no color contrasts, Figure 4-2 depicts population density through shading: the darker the color, the larger the number of people per unit area. The most extensive area of dark shading lies in *East Asia*, primarily in

Figure 4-2 World Population Density.

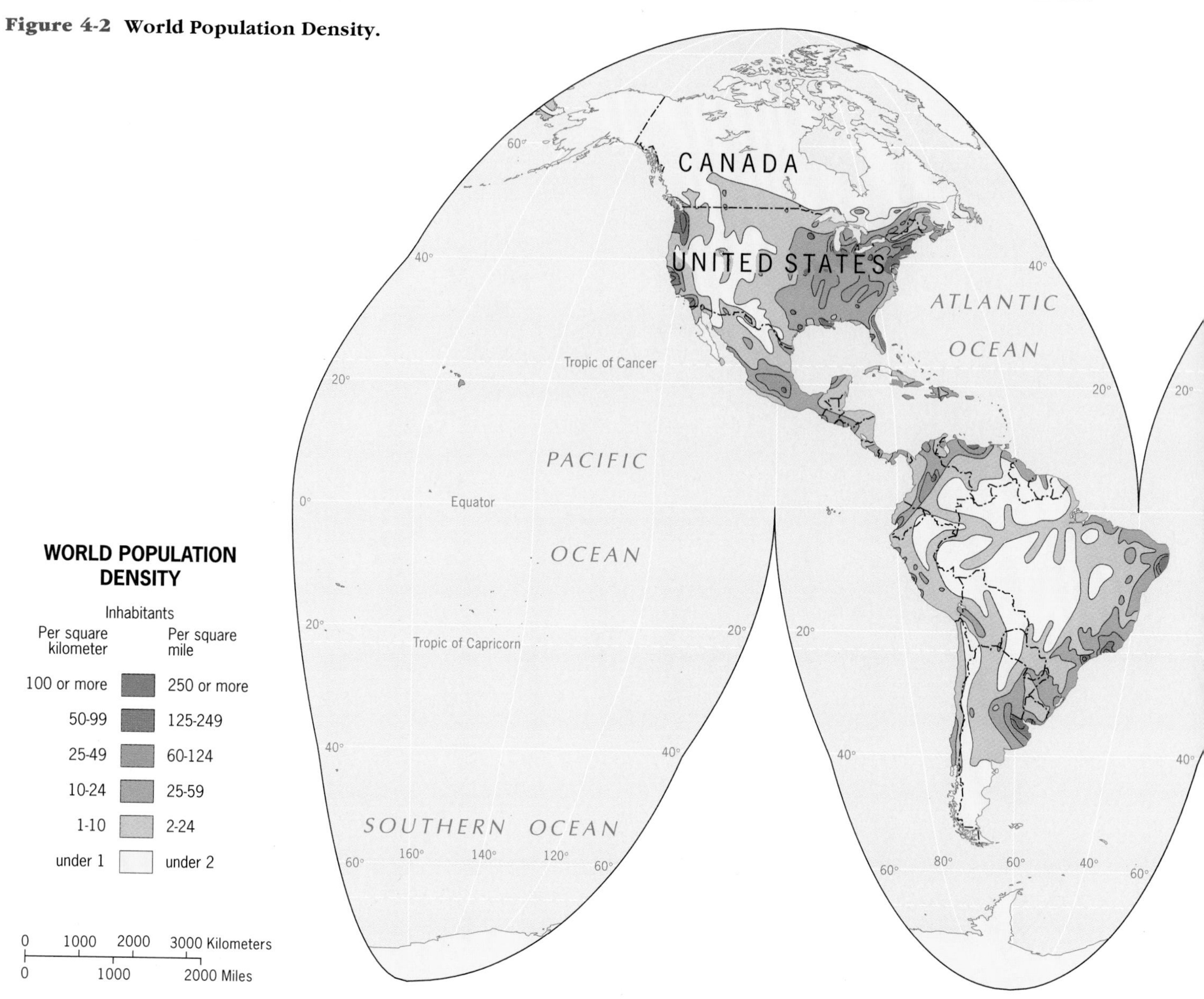

China but also in Korea and Japan. About one-quarter of the world's population is concentrated here—nearly 1.3 billion people in China alone.

The East Asian population cluster adjoins the Pacific Ocean from Korea to Vietnam; the number of people per unit area tends to decline from this coastal zone toward the interior. Also visible are several ribbon-like extensions of dense population (Fig. 4-2 A and B). These extensions represent populations that are clustered in the basins and lowlands of China's major rivers. This serves to remind us that the great majority of people in East Asia are farmers, not city dwellers. True, China has large cities, such as Shanghai and Beijing. However, the total population of these and other cities is far outnumbered by the farmers, who produce crops of wheat and rice to feed not only themselves but also those in the cities and towns.

South Asia

The second major population concentration also lies in Asia and is similar in many ways to that of East Asia. At the heart of this cluster lies India, but the concentration also extends into Pakistan and Bangladesh and onto the island of Sri Lanka. Again, note the riverine and coastal orientation of the most densely inhabited zones and the finger-like extension of dense population on the plain of the Ganges River in northern India (Fig. 4-2 C). This is one of the greatest concentrations of people on the Earth.

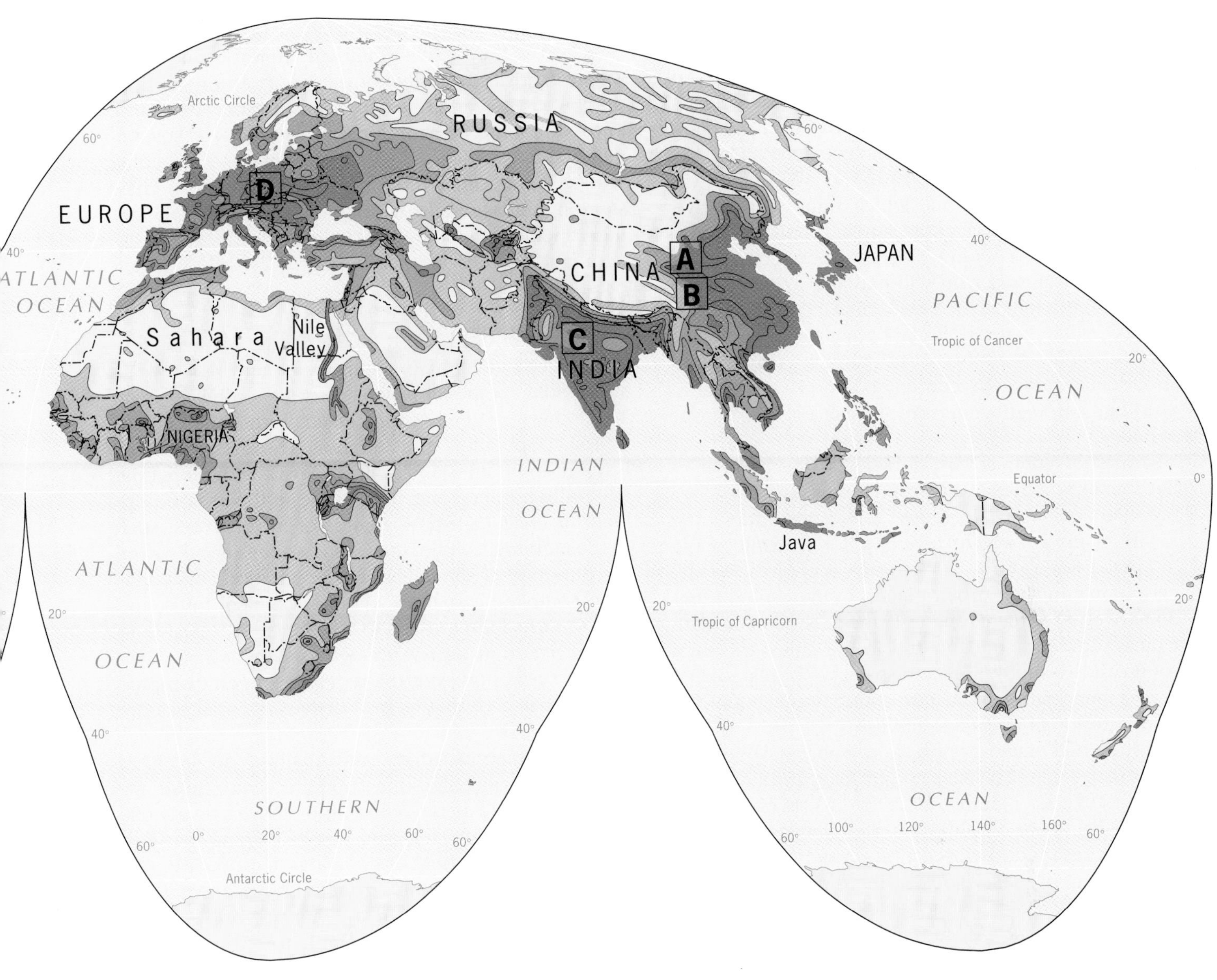

There are about 1.5 billion people in the South Asia population cluster. Our map shows how sharply this region is marked off by physical barriers: the Himalaya Mountains to the north and the desert west of the Indus River Valley in Pakistan. This is a confined region with a rapidly growing population. The capacity of the region to support this population has, by almost any estimate, already been exceeded. As in East Asia, the overwhelming majority of the people here are farmers, but in South Asia the pressure on the land is even greater. In Bangladesh, nearly 125 million people, almost all of them farmers, are crowded into an area about the size of Iowa. Over large parts of Bangladesh the rural population density is between 3000 and 5000 people per square mile. By comparison, in 1998 the population of Iowa was about 3 million people, and less than 40 percent lived on the land rather than in cities and towns. The rural population density was under 30 people per square mile.

Europe

Further inspection of Figures 4-1 and 4-2 reveals that the third-ranking population cluster also lies in Eurasia—at the opposite end from China. An axis of dense population extends from the British Isles into Russia and includes large parts of Germany, Poland, Ukraine, and Belarus. It also includes the Netherlands and Belgium, parts of France, and northern Italy. This European cluster contains about 700 million inhabitants, which puts it in a class with the South Asia concentration—but there the similarity ends. A comparison of the population and physical maps indicates that in Europe terrain and environment are not as closely related to population distribution as they are in East and South Asia. For example, note that lengthy extension marked D in Figure 4-2, which protrudes far into Russia. Unlike the Asian extensions, which reflect fertile river valleys, the European extension reflects the orientation of Europe's coal-fields. If you look more closely at the physical map, you will note that comparatively dense population occurs even in mountainous, rugged country, such as the boundary zone between Poland and its neighbors to the south. A much greater correspondence exists between coastal and river lowlands and high population density in Asia than in Europe generally.

Another contrast can be seen in the number of Europeans who live in cities and towns. The European population cluster includes numerous cities and towns, many of which developed as a result of the Industrial Revolution. In Germany, 85 percent of the people live in such urban places; in the United Kingdom, over 90 percent; and in France, 74 percent. With so many people concentrated in the cities, the rural countryside is more open and sparsely populated than in East and South Asia, where about 30 percent of the people reside in cities and towns.

The three major population concentrations we have discussed—East Asia, South Asia, and Europe—account for over 4 billion of the total world population of approximately 6 billion people. Nowhere else on the globe is there a population cluster even half as great as any of these. Look at the dimensions of the landmasses in Figure 4-1 and note that the populations of South America, Africa, and Australia combined barely exceed that of India alone.

North America

The population cluster comprising the east-central United States and southeastern Canada is only about one-quarter the size of the smallest of the Eurasian concentrations. As Figure 4-2 shows, the North American region does not have large, contiguous high-density zones like those of Europe or East and South Asia.

The North American population cluster outdoes Europe in some respects. As in the European region, much of the population is concentrated in major cities while rural areas are relatively sparsely populated. The major focus of the North America cluster lies in the urban complex along the eastern seaboard from Boston to Washington, which includes New York, Philadelphia, and Baltimore. Urban geographers use the term ***megalopolis*** to refer to such huge urban agglomerations, and predict that it is only a matter of time before they coalesce into an enormous megacity. Other major focal points of the North American population cluster are Chicago, Detroit, and Cleveland, and with some interruptions, San Francisco, Los Angeles, and San Diego. If you study Figure 4-1 carefully, you will note other prominent North American cities standing out as small areas of high-density population; they include Pittsburgh, St. Louis, Minneapolis–St. Paul, and Seattle.

Other Regions

Further examination of Figures 4-1 and 4-2 reveals substantial population clusters in Southeast Asia. These are actually discrete clusters rather than a contiguous population concentration. The largest of them is the Indonesian island of Jawa (Java), with more than 120 million inhabitants. Elsewhere in the region populations cluster in the lowlands of major rivers, such as the Mekong. Neither these river valleys nor the rural surroundings of the cities have population concentrations comparable to those of either China or India, and under normal circumstances Southeast Asia is able to export rice to its hungrier neighbors. Over many decades of strife, however, the region has been disrupted to such a degree that its productive potential has not been attained.

South America, Africa, and Australia do not have population concentrations comparable to those we have considered so far. Subsaharan Africa's nearly 600 million inhabitants cluster in above-average densities in West Africa (where Nigeria has a population of some 100 million) and in a zone in the east extending from Ethiopia to South Africa. Only in North Africa is there an agglomeration comparable to those found on the crowded riverine plains of Asia. This cluster is in the Nile Valley and Delta, which has over 66 million residents. Note that the *pattern* of the Nile agglomeration—not the dimensions—resembles the pattern seen in Asia. As in East and South Asia, the Nile Valley and Delta teem with farmers who cultivate every foot of the rich and fertile soil. However, the lowlands of the Ganges, Chang Jiang (Yangtzi), and Huang He (Yellow) rivers contain far more inhabitants.

The large light-shaded spaces in South America and Australia, and the peripheral distribution of the modest populations of these continents, suggest that there is some space here for the world's huge population. Indeed, South America could probably sustain more than its present 330 million people if reforms were made in patterns of land ownership and use in the region. At present, while the people of South America as a whole are well fed, poverty and malnutrition occur in some areas, such as northeast Brazil.

This raises an issue that is central to any study of population density and the capacity of a country to support its people: level of technology. You will note that Japan, a small island country, has a population of over 126 million. Its population density is at least as great as that of parts of China and India, but its farmlands are quite limited, not only by its small size but also by its mountainous character. What makes such a large population in Japan possible is Japan's technological prowess, industrial capacity, and money-producing exports. Japan imports raw materials from all over the world, converts them into finished products, and exports those products to most parts of the globe. With the income brought in by these exports, Japan can buy the food that it cannot produce at home. Thus it is not enough to say that a country cannot support more than a specific number of people. We should qualify this statement by observing that under present economic, political, and technological conditions it can or cannot support a given population, depending on its status in the world market. So, while Australia could not find a place for tens of millions of Chinese farmers, if tens of millions of Japanese came to Australia with their skills, technologies, factories, and international connections, Australia would be quite capable of accommodating them—and many more.

Having examined the distribution and general density of global and regional populations, we now come to the crucial issue: population growth—its history, dimensions, and spatial expression. The next chapter links the maps of distribution and density with the dynamics of demographic change.

◆ KEY TERMS ◆

arithmetic density
census
demography
density
distribution
megalopolis
physiologic density
population concentration
population data
population density
population geography

◆ APPLYING GEOGRAPHIC KNOWLEDGE ◆

1. If the arithmetic density measure is of so little practical use, why do you suppose it is listed in virtually every database published by population-monitoring agencies? Which State in the United States has the lowest arithmetic density, and how meaningful is that statistic? When it comes to physiologic density, this measure is much more relevant, in practical terms, for some countries than for others. Compare the Netherlands and Bangladesh in this context.
2. Some of the world's largest cities, such as Mumbai (Bombay), Shanghai, and Cairo, lie in countries that rank among the world's least urbanized societies. Explain this apparent contradiction.
3. An international food-relief agency has asked you to prepare a report to help make food distribution in a certain area, threatened by famine, more efficient. Will you use maps of population distribution (dot maps) or population density (isopleth maps) to support your case? What role will scale play in your presentation?

Chapter 5

Processes and Cycles of Population Change

From the field notes

China, 1981. In town after town, we were the first Westerners people had seen, and they followed us in droves, curious, friendly, yet reticent. Here, in a town on the outskirts of Anyang, we had hoped to find archeological items from the Shang dynasty in a long-shuttered museum. The news of our visit had spread and a crowd was waiting. As with all the others, what struck me was the predominance of youngsters. In the rural villages and towns, the population seemed to practically *consist* of children. No wonder the new leadership in Beijing was trying to devise ways to reduce family size throughout the country. (No archaeological treasures remained. Destroyed during the Cultural Revolution, we were told)."

KEY POINTS

◆ **The population explosion of the past 200 years has increased the world's population from under 1 billion to approximately 6 billion.**

◆ **Although hundreds of millions of people remain inadequately nourished, the threat of global hunger has receded—perhaps temporarily.**

◆ **Rapid population growth varies over time and space. Europe's rapid growth occurred during the nineteenth century; over the past 30 years, South America's growth rates have declined whereas Africa's have increased.**

◆ **Keys to the reduction of population growth rates include providing greater access to education for women and securing their rights in society.**

◆ **The demographic transition model suggests that the world's population will stabilize in the twenty-first century, but the model may not be universally applicable.**

If there are reasons to doubt the accuracy of some published population statistics, there is no uncertainty about another dimension of world population: its accelerating growth. Never before in human history have so many people filled the Earth's living space, and never has world population grown as rapidly as it has during the past 100 years. In 1975 the world's population reached 4 billion; it passed 5 billion in 1987 and will have reached 6 billion in 1998. It took from the dawn of history to the year 1820 for the Earth's population to reach 1 billion. It required just 12 years to add the same number in the 1970s, and now it is taking only a decade to add the next billion. Even if the global rate of population growth stabilizes or declines somewhat in years to come, there still may be 10 billion human inhabitants on the planet before the middle of the twenty-first century.

◆ WORLDWIDE POPULATION TRENDS

About 177 million babies are born every year, and approximately 86 million people die. This means that we are adding about 90 million inhabitants to the world's population every year. Most of the increase is occurring in areas that are least able to support the new arrivals, and of those who die, many millions are young children who succumb to disease or starvation.

Can these trends continue forever? Obviously not. There are signs that explosive population growth will be followed by a marked slowdown in the rate of increase and that the world's population will actually stabilize during the twenty-first century (see "Focus on: A Stabilizing Population?"). This has already happened in some parts of the world: in the United Kingdom, France, and several other developed countries, population growth has slowed to a trickle after a period of rapid increase. But the population of France is less than one-twelfth that of India. Real change requires a decrease in the rate of growth in countries with large populations and high rates of increase—not only India but also Indonesia, Bangladesh, Nigeria, Brazil, Mexico, and others.

Sometimes there are signs that a slowdown may be coming. In 1990 the U.S. Census Bureau reported that the overall growth rate of the world's population had declined from approximately 2.1 percent per year during the 1965–1969 period to 1.6 percent during 1985–1989. But when the growth rate was 2.1 percent, the world's population was approaching 4 billion, resulting in 80 million additional inhabitants each year. By the time the rate was down to 1.6 percent per year (possibly a low estimate), the population base was already 5 billion. Calculate it for yourself: a 1.6-percent increase, on a base of 5.0 billion, *still* produces over 80 million additional people.

Even while the global population growth rate has continued to decline, the reduction has been offset by the ever larger total on which it is based. The consensus is that in 1997 the world's population grew at a rate of just under 1.5 percent; this figure is encouraging—until we calculate that growth rate based on a population of nearly 6 billion. The outcome: at the lower growth rate, world population is now growing by 90 million annually—10 million *more* than during the 1970s.

The world map of population growth rates by country (Fig. 5-1) also reveals the wide range of growth rates in different regions. These variations

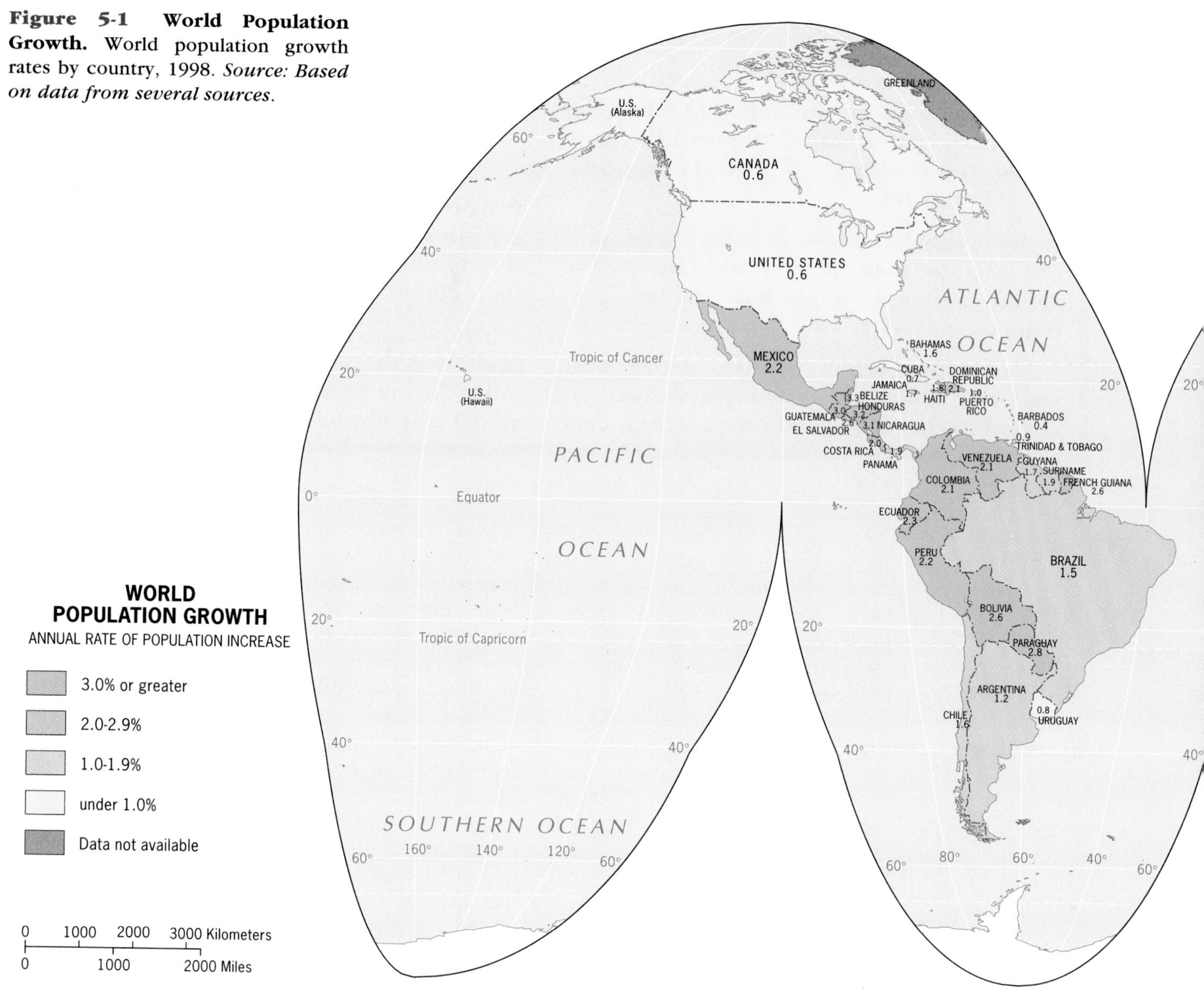

Figure 5-1 World Population Growth. World population growth rates by country, 1998. *Source: Based on data from several sources.*

have existed as long as records have been kept: countries and regions go through stages of expansion (and in some cases even decline) at varying times. Thirty years ago, for example, population geographers worried about India's high growth rate, certain that mass starvation lay ahead. In those days India's population was growing more rapidly than Africa's. But today India's growth rate is down from 2.6 percent to 1.9 percent, whereas Africa's overall growth rate has increased from 2.4 percent to 2.8 percent.

Figure 5-1 reflects not only the rapid population growth of countries south of the Sahara, but also the increased growth rates in Muslim countries of North Africa and Southwest Asia. Today Iran's is one of the world's most rapidly growing populations, followed closely by those of Saudi Arabia, Yemen, and Libya. The growth rates of some Muslim countries are higher today than they were 30 years ago. In Subsaharan Africa, the end of colonialism and the failure of national economies are often cited as reasons for the upward population curve. In Africa as in the Muslim realm, cultural traditions and constricted opportunities for women also contribute to rapid population growth.

Population growth in one of the two largest human agglomerations, South Asia, continues to be rapid. India's population approaches 1 billion as its growth rate slowly declines, but at a rate of 1.9 percent India is still growing faster than the world as a whole. But China, which in the 1980s imposed severely restrictive population policies (see Chapter 34) to bring down its growth rate to 1.2 percent, has seen this rate continue to decline: in 1997, China reported a growth rate of 1.0 percent, and East Asia as a whole is now growing at 0.9 percent—half the rate of just 20 years ago.

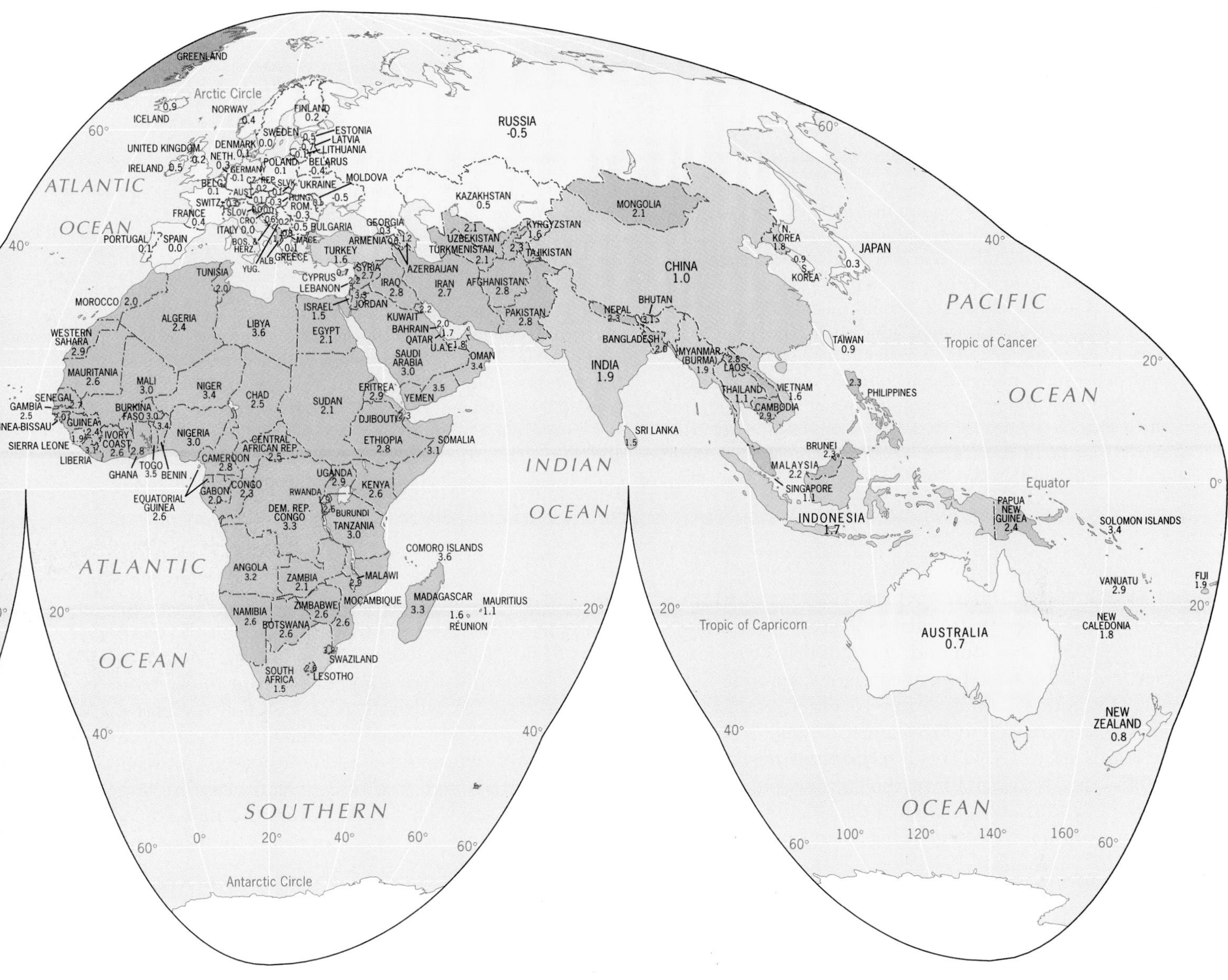

Today marked declines in population growth rates are occurring in South America. Although the populations of most South American countries are still growing faster than the world average, the growth rate for South America as a whole has decreased from over 3.0 to 1.7 percent. Brazil's growth rate, for example, has fallen from 2.9 percent in the mid-1960s to 1.5 percent today. Brazil's neighbors have all recorded significant declines; 30 years ago their populations were growing at rates of 3.2 to 3.4 percent. And the populations of the southern cone (Argentina, Chile, and Uruguay) are growing at rates well below the world rate.

As Figure 5-1 shows, the slowest growing countries (under 1 percent annual increase) lie in the economically wealthier zone extending from the United States and Canada across Western Europe to Japan. In fact, not all of these countries are rich; for example, the nations of the former Soviet Union are not well off at all. In those countries population growth is hindered by adverse political and social conditions. Indeed, by some accounts, Russia is experiencing negative population growth, which means that deaths outnumber births.

◆ DIMENSIONS OF POPULATION GROWTH

As the figures just quoted indicate, the human population has not expanded in a *linear* manner, in which increases occur in uniform amount during a series of equal time periods. If you have $100 and add $10 to it the first year and each successive year, your $100 will become $200 after 10 years, $300 after 20 years,

Focus On

A Stabilizing Population?

Agencies monitoring global population growth occasionally publish new projections for various countries. Such projections sometimes suggest that most (if not all) countries' populations will stop growing at some time during the twenty-first century, reaching a so-called ***stationary population level (SPL)***—as some Western European countries already have. This would mean, of course, that the world's population would stabilize, that the population explosion would be over, and that the major problems to be faced would involve the aged rather than the young.

But such predictions require frequent revision, and the anticipated dates for population stabilization are often moved back. In the late 1980s, for example, the World Bank predicted that the United States would reach SPL in 2035 with 276 million inhabitants. Brazil's population would stabilize at 353 million in 2070, Mexico's at 254 million in 2075, and China's at 1.4 billion in 2090. India, destined to become the world's most populous country, would reach SPL at 1.6 billion in 2150.

In the late 1990s those figures seem unrealistic. China's population passed the 1.2 billion mark in 1994; India's reached 1 billion in 1998. If we were to project an optimistic decline in growth rates for both countries, China's population would "stabilize" at 1.7 billion in 2070 and India's at 2.0 billion in the same year. But population increase is a cyclic phenomenon, and overall declines mask lags and spurts (not to mention regional disparities). It is too early to be confident about predictions of SPL.

and so on. This is ***linear growth*** (Fig. 5-2A). However, if you invested your initial $100 at an interest rate of 10 percent, compounded continuously, each increase would be based on the original amount *plus* previously added interest. After 10 years, your $100 would have increased to $259; after 20 years, it would have increased to $673. This is ***exponential growth***. The difference between linear and exponential growth is obvious, and it is equally clear that the world's human population has been growing at exponential rates (Fig. 5-2B).

Doubling Time

Another way of looking at exponential growth is to compare a population's rate of growth to its ***doubling time***. Every rate of growth has a doubling time; for example, your $100 invested at 10 percent took about 7 years to double to $200, and then another 7 years to become $400, and then another 7 years to become $800. When the growth rate is 10 percent, therefore, the doubling time is around 7 years. During the middle of this century, when the world's population was increasing at an average rate of 2 percent, its doubling time was 35 years (Fig. 5-2C). During the mid-1980s, when the rate declined to 1.8 percent, the doubling time rose to 39 years.

It is interesting to read the data for various countries in Figure 5-1 in the context of Table 5-1. In 1995, the U.S. population was growing at a rate of 0.7 percent, yielding a doubling time of 98 years. The populations of Nigeria and several other African countries,

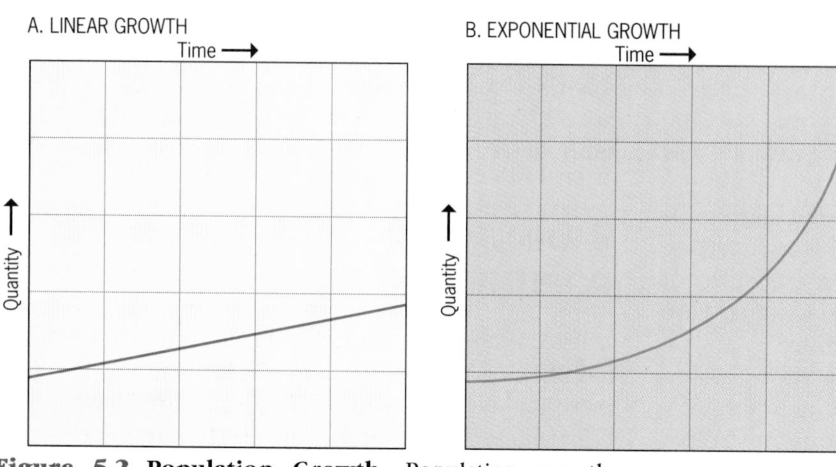

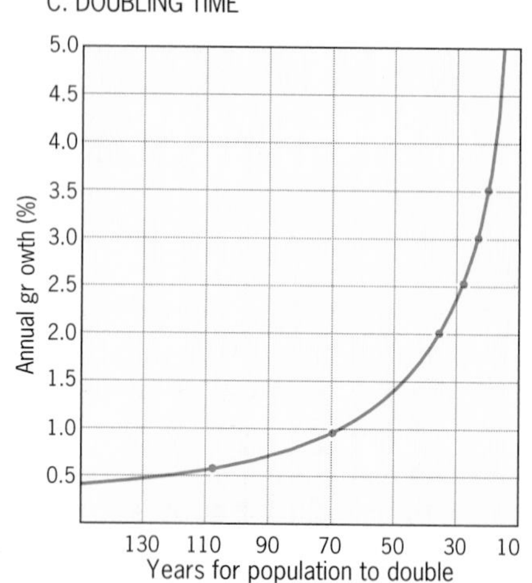

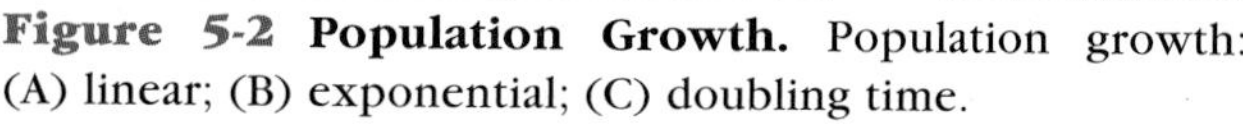

Figure 5-2 Population Growth. Population growth: (A) linear; (B) exponential; (C) doubling time.

Table 5-1 Rates of Population Growth and Doubling Times

Rate of Increase (percent)	Doubling Time (years)	Current (1998) Example
0.50	141	Ireland
0.75	94	Australia
1.00	70	China
1.50	46	Brazil
2.00	35	Costa Rica
2.50	28	Chad
3.00	24	Nigeria
3.50	20	Yemen

with growth rates in the 3.0 percent range, are doubling in as little as 20 years. Always, however, remember the actual numbers involved. Doubling the populations of the three largest East African countries (Kenya, Tanzania, and Uganda) would result in an increase from about 75 million to 150 million in little more than 30 years. Doubling India's population of 988 million (1998) might take longer (36 years) but would add nearly 1 billion people over that period.

The Population Explosion

It is estimated that 2000 years ago the world's population was about 250 million. More than 16 centuries passed before this total had doubled to 500 million, the estimated population in 1650. Just 170 years later, in 1820, the population had doubled again, to 1 billion (Fig. 5-3). And barely more than a century after this, in 1930, it reached 2 billion. Now the doubling time was down to 100 years and dropping fast; the ***population explosion*** was in full gear. Only 45 years elapsed during the next doubling, to 4 billion (1975). In that decade the rate of growth was approximately 2 percent per year, and the doubling time (Fig. 5-2) had declined to 35 years. The history of humanity thus is one of growing numbers *and* ever-higher rates of increase.

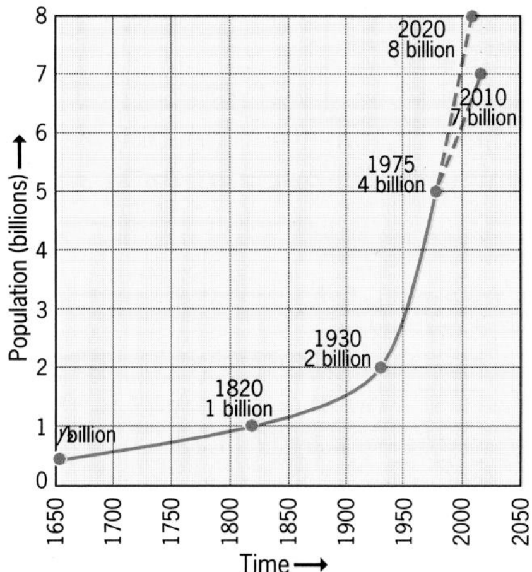

Figure 5-3 Population Growth, 1650 to (estimated) 2020. The dotted lines indicate different scenarios depending on birth rate trends in the coming decades.

◆ EARLY WARNINGS

Concern over population growth arose even before the full impact of the population explosion was felt. As long ago as 1798, a British economist named Thomas Malthus published *An Essay on the Principle of Population as It Affects the Future Improvement of Society.* In this work he sounded the alarm: the world's population was increasing faster than the food supplies needed to sustain it. Recognizing the nature of exponential growth, Malthus pointed out that population increases at what he called a *geometric* rate. The means of subsistence, in contrast, grow at an *arithmetic* (linear) rate. From 1803 to 1826, Malthus issued revised editions of his essay and responded vigorously to a barrage of criticism. He suggested that population growth in Britain might be checked by hunger within 50 years after the first appearance of his warning.

Malthus could not have foreseen the impacts of colonization and migration, and he would not have believed that the United Kingdom could sustain between 50 and 60 million people, as it does today. Nor was he correct about the linear increase of food production. It, too, has grown exponentially as the acreage under cultivation has expanded, improved strains of seed have been developed, and more fertilizers have been used. Those who continue to share Malthus' concerns (even if they do not agree with every detail of his argument) are sometimes called neo-Malthusians, and their number is growing. They point out that human suffering is now occurring on a scale unimagined even by Malthus, and they argue that it is not enough simply to assert that this is an inevitable stage in the history of the world's population. Despite predictions that the population will stabilize in the twenty-first century, they believe that the problem must be addressed now.

Once one moves below the global scale, it becomes increasingly difficult to apply Malthus' ideas. Some commentators speak of a "Malthusian crisis" occurring in particular regions or countries, by which they mean that population growth is outstripping food supplies. But at the time that Malthus was writing, he could treat Britain as a more or less closed system and confine his analysis to the population trends and re-

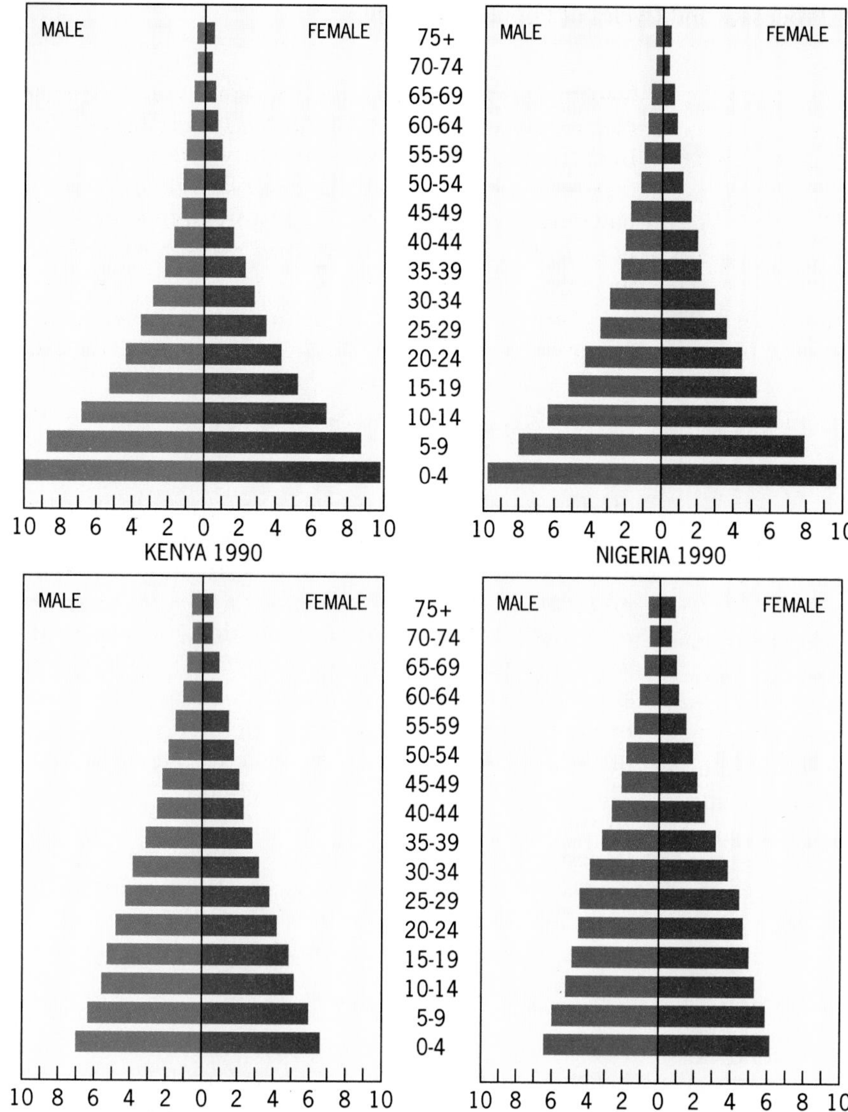

Figure 5-4 Age-Sex Pyramids for Countries with High Growth Rates. *Source: Data from World Bank* Population Projections, 1991–1992.

sources of the British Isles. Few places in the world come close to being closed systems anymore. Switzerland and Japan are countries with large numbers of people living in areas with relatively few natural resources and limited agricultural land. Yet there is little hunger or suffering in those countries because of the strength of their political and economic institutions and their global economic position.

Hence, analysis of population growth at the regional scale requires a level of geographic understanding that is often missing. It requires seeing regions not as discrete places but as places whose nature and character are shaped both by their internal characteristics and by their external geographical relationships.

◆ POPULATION STRUCTURE

Maps showing the regional distribution and density of populations tell us about the numbers of people in countries or regions, but they cannot reveal two other aspects of those populations: the numbers of men and women and their ages. These aspects are important, because a populous country in which half the population is very young has very different problems than a country in which a large proportion of the population is elderly. When geographers study populations, therefore, they are concerned not only with spatial distribution but also with ***population structure***.

Age-Sex Pyramids

The structure of a population is created by the number of people in its various age groups. It is represented visually by an ***age-sex pyramid***. These pyramids display the percentages of the total population in various age groups (normally five-year groups). The sexes are placed on the left (males) and right (females) of the pyramid's center line.

Populations with high fertility as well as mortality rates have pyramids with broad bases because large percentages of the population are in the youngest age groups. Populations with lower fertility and mortality rates have pyramids with narrower bases and a more rectangular shape. Figure 5-4 shows the 1990 population pyramids for four countries with high growth rates: Kenya, Nigeria, India, and Brazil. Note that the percentages of people in the three youngest age groups are much larger in Kenya and Nigeria than in India or Brazil, indicating that the rate of natural increase is declining in the latter two populations. The data bear this out: in 1991 Kenya still had a birth rate of 46 per thousand and a death rate of 7, while India's birth rate had declined to under 31 per thousand with a mortality rate of just over 10. In Nigeria the comparable figures were 44 and 17, but in Brazil they were 27 and 8.

Figure 5-5 shows what happens to the population pyramid when both birth and death rates decline, narrowing the gap and thus reducing the rate of increase. Mexico's pyramid is still broad-based, but less so than India's and much less so than Nigeria's. China's population pyramid vividly reveals the impact of Beijing's restrictive population policies: the percentages in the three lowest age groups are actually smaller than those in the next three groups.

Other factors produced the nearly rectangular age-sex pyramids for France and Japan. Economic development, urbanization, and general modernization resulted in smaller families—not by government edict but through family planning and economic and life-style changes. As the pyramids show, there are nearly as many people in the upper age groups as in the lower ones. But the incomes of those in the middle groups must support those in the younger and older groups. Thus, while a pyramid like Japan's may be more desirable than one like Kenya's, Japan's pyramid

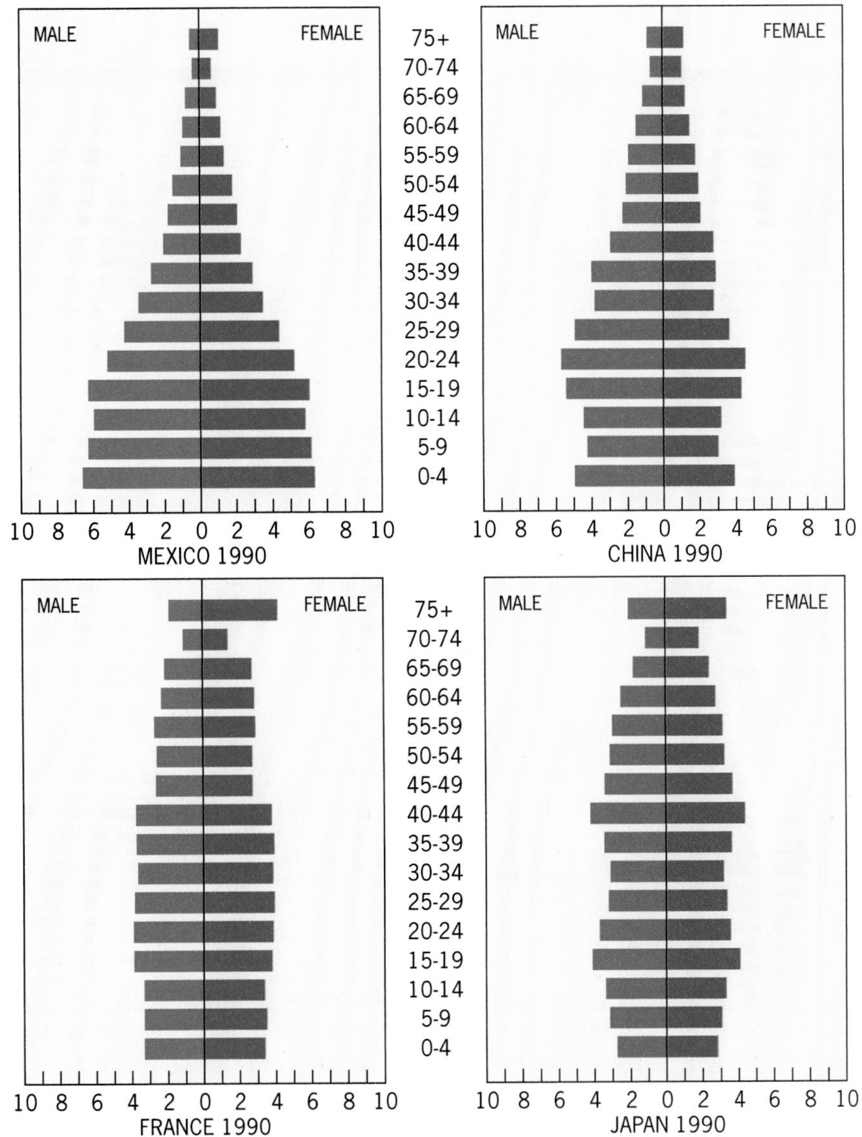

Figure 5-5 Age-Sex Pyramids for Countries with Declining Birth and Death Rates. *Source: Data from World Bank* Population Projections, 1991–1992.

Figure 5-6 World Birth Rate. World birth rates by country. *Source: Based on data from several sources.*

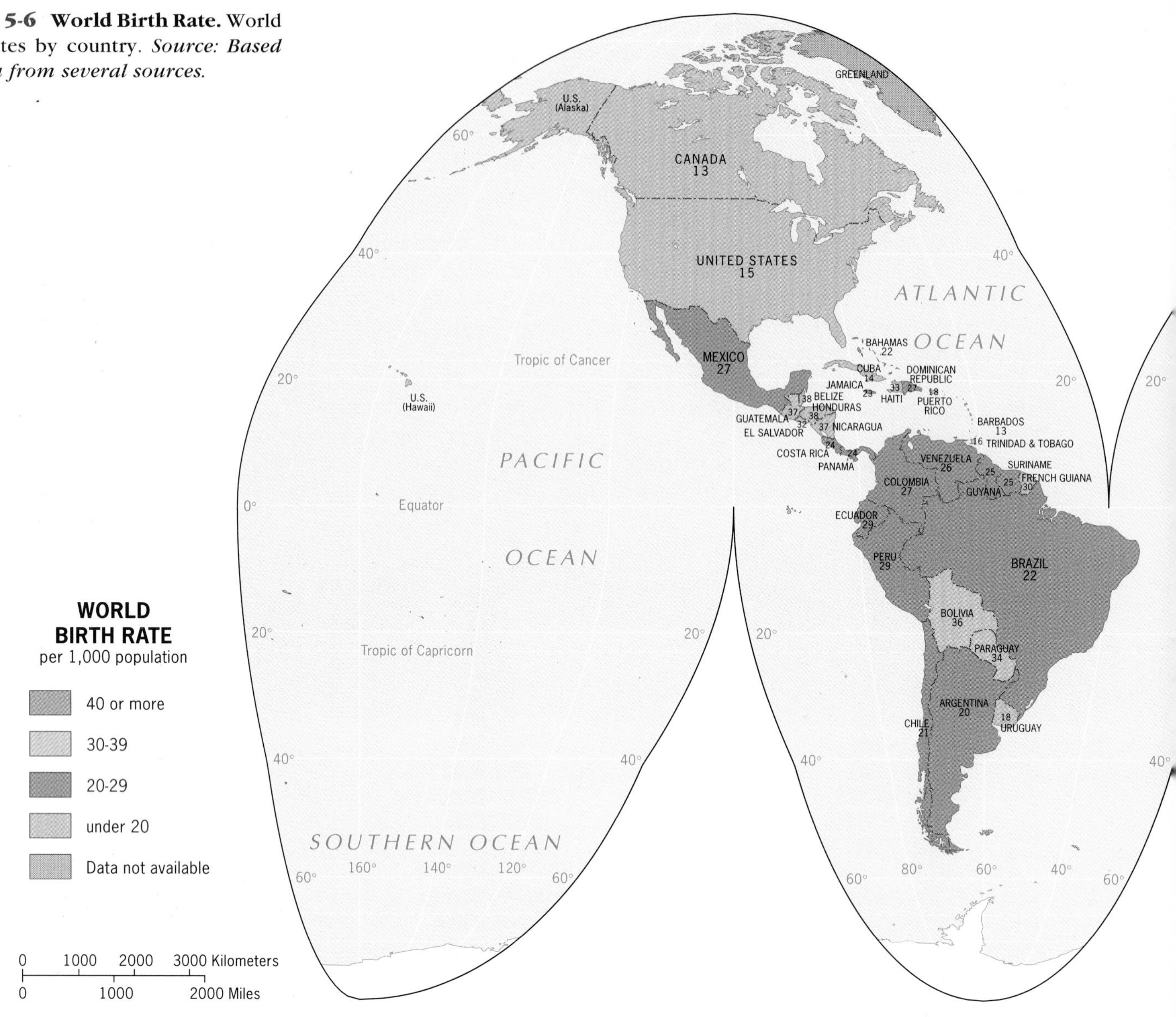

has its own problems, including a shortage of young workers. In France, a similar situation has led to the immigration of foreign laborers from North Africa, with a significant impact on social conditions in that country.

◆ DEMOGRAPHIC CYCLES

The study of population is called *demography*, and its spatial component is *population geography*. We now turn to the demographic factors that underlie the patterns shown in Figure 5-1. So far we have viewed *global* population growth. But while some countries and regions are growing faster than the world average, others are growing much more slowly. And some countries actually have declining populations, that is, "negative" population growth.

A population goes through stages of growth each of which forms part of its *demographic cycle*. Populations in different parts of the world, and sometimes even in different parts of the same country, are at different stages in their demographic cycles—and these differences can have serious economic and political consequences.

Natural Increase

The rate of ***natural increase*** of a population is the difference between the number of births and the number of deaths during a specific period. These two measures, the birth rate and death rate, are commonly ex-

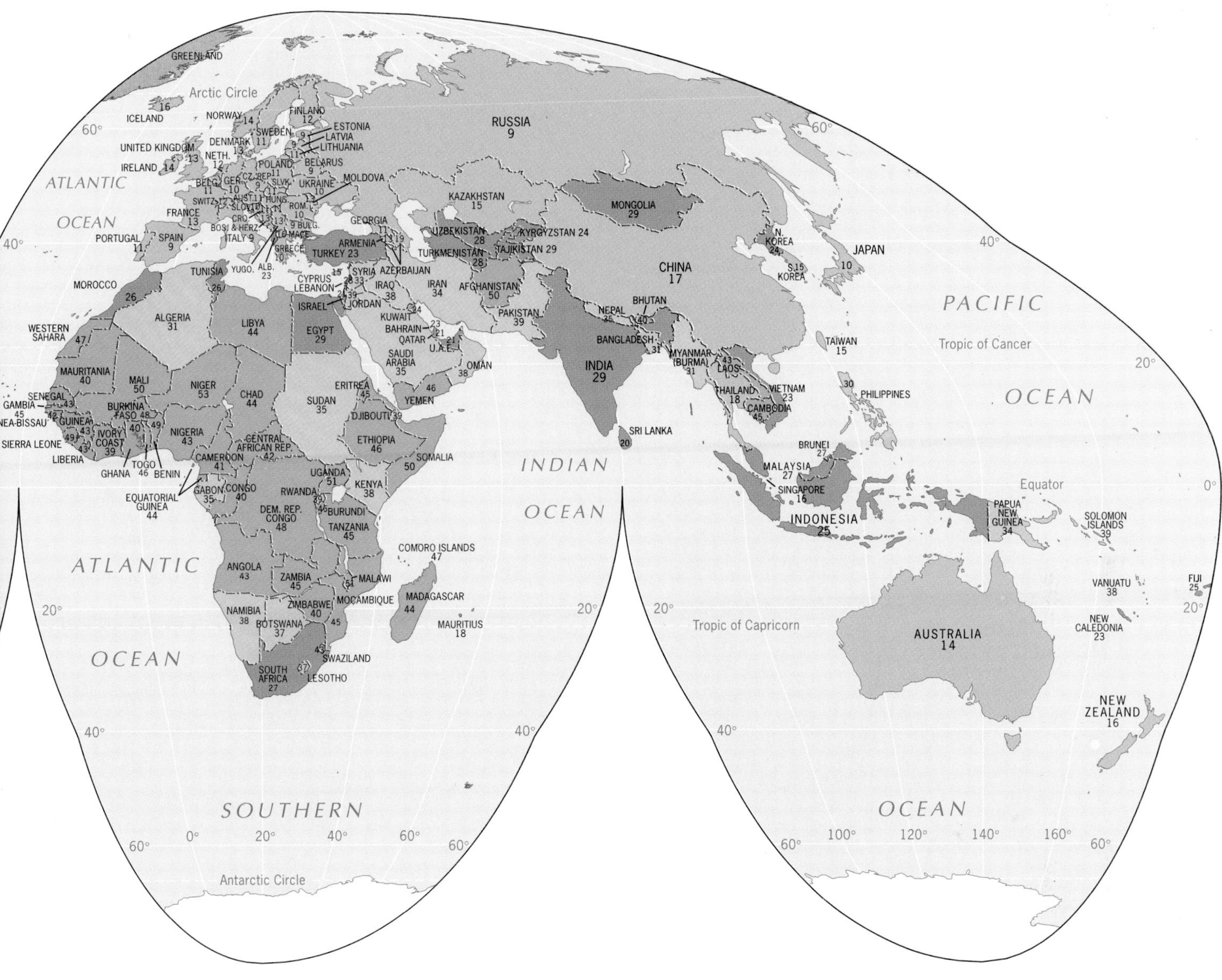

pressed in terms of the number of individuals per thousand. In statistical tables these are reported as the ***crude birth rate (CBR)***, the number of live births per year per thousand people in the population, and the ***crude death rate (CDR)***, the number of deaths per thousand.

The Birth Rate

As Figure 5-6 shows, birth rates vary widely around the world. The highest birth rates today are in Africa and Southwest Asia. For many years countries in East Africa have had the highest birth rates in the world; during the 1980s Kenya, Tanzania, and Uganda all reported 50 or more births per thousand per year. Demographers describe birth rates above 30 as high, which puts many tropical American, African, and Asian countries in that category.

The lowest birth rates are in Europe, where several countries have CBRs below 15. Other areas with low birth rates are North America, Australia, New Zealand, Japan, and China. It is clear that low birth rates are associated with modernization—industrialization and urbanization—except in the case of China. Just one generation ago China still had high birth rates. Although it is not yet an industrialized, urbanized nation, China achieved its present low birth rate by imposing stringent population controls.

Looking more closely at Figure 5-6, we can see that a number of countries that are somewhere between poor and prosperous, such as Argentina, Colombia, and Thailand, also have intermediate (or tran-

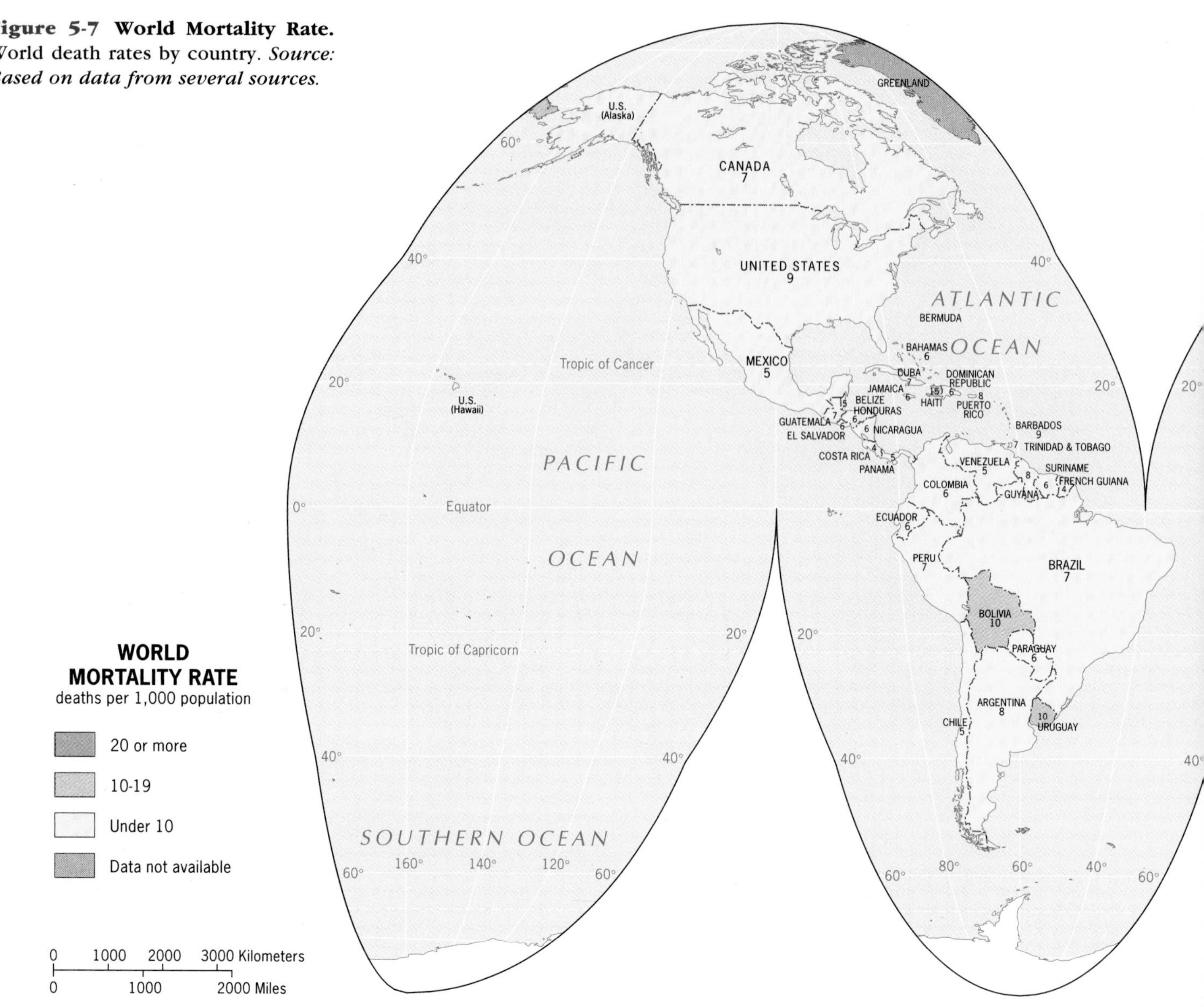

Figure 5-7 World Mortality Rate. World death rates by country. *Source: Based on data from several sources.*

sitional) birth rates. This would suggest that birth rates are related to the country's level of economic development. Again this generalization does not hold in the case of China. Economic development is crucial, but other factors, including cultural traditions, affect the patterns shown on Figure 5-6.

The Total Fertility Rate

Another measure of the reproductive status of a population is the ***total fertility rate (TFR)***. This is a measure of the number of children born to women of childbearing age. The TFR is usually reported as the number of children per woman, and it is a revealing statistic. For example, at the height of Kenya's population explosion in the 1980s, the number of children per woman of childbearing age was 8.1! In 1997, it was still high at 5.4. In China just 30 years ago the TFR was 6.0; today it is 1.8.

TFRs in many countries have declined in recent years, which is a major reason for the optimism of some demographers. Not only China but also India, Egypt, Brazil, and Mexico have lower TFRs today than they did one generation ago. India's TFR has declined from 5.8 to 3.4, Egypt's from 7.2 to 3.6, Brazil's from 6.3 to 2.5, and Mexico's from 6.7 to 3.1. On the other hand, Nigeria's TFR still exceeds 6.0 (as does that for all of Africa combined), and Pakistani women still bear an average of nearly 6 children.

Both birth rates and fertility rates show much spatial variation, but an overall decline has been in progress for several decades. This is why the growth rate of the world's population has declined from over 2.1 percent to 1.5 percent over the past 25 years. As noted

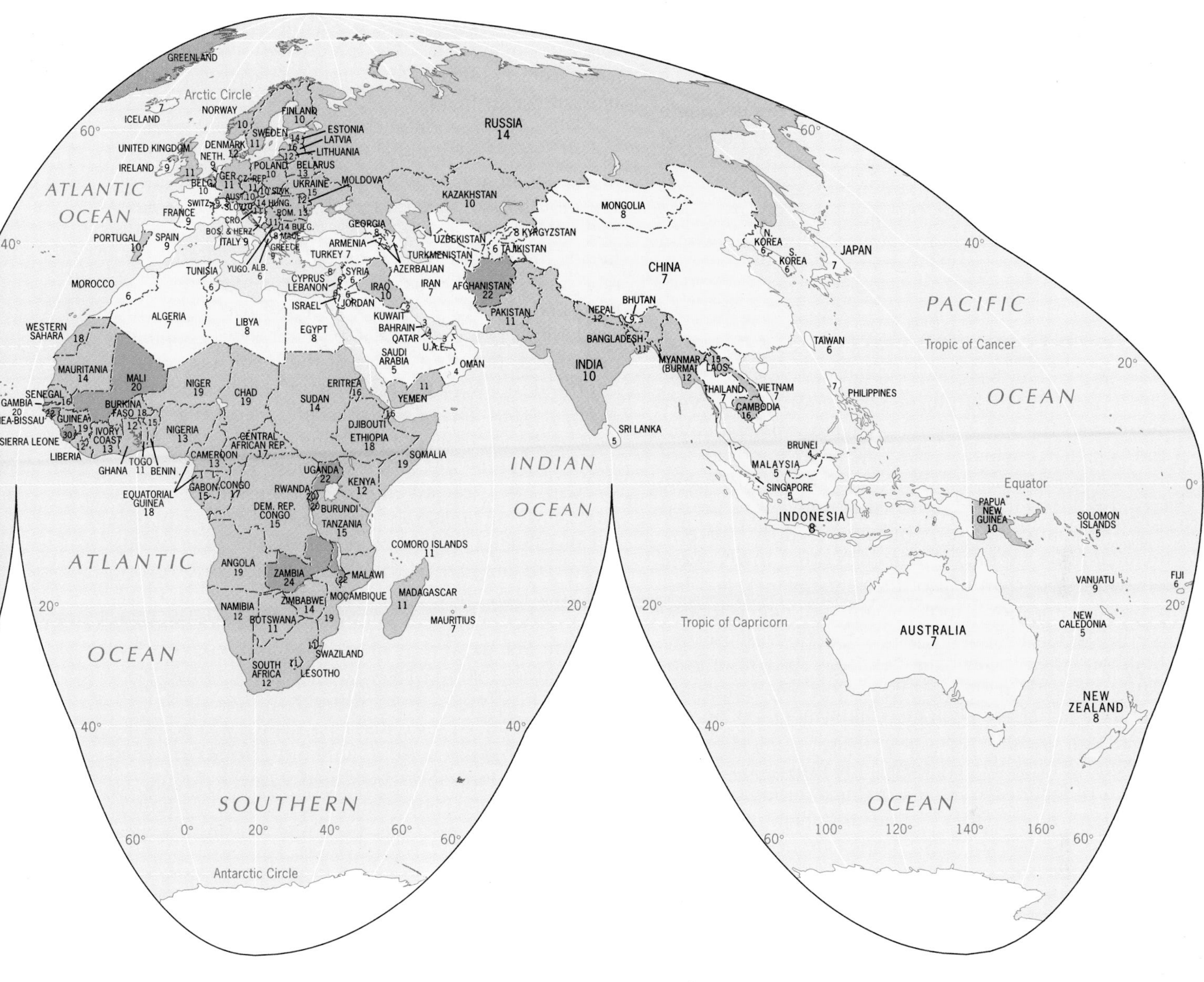

earlier, however, the lower rate of natural increase still results in the addition of more people than before.

The Death Rate

The crude death rate (CDR) is the number of deaths per thousand people in a given year. Also called the *mortality rate*, this figure has declined more dramatically than birth and fertility rates (Fig. 5-7). During the global population explosion, the widening gap between still-high birth rates and falling death rates signaled the rapid growth of the total human population.

As Figure 5-7 shows, death rates are highest in tropical Africa, where they are still above 20 per thousand in several countries. They are lowest in North America and most of South America, parts of Europe, Japan, China, and Australia. Also noteworthy are the low CDRs of several Southeast Asian countries. Here the correlation between economic development and low or declining death rates is less evident than appeared to be the case with birth rates. Otherwise we would not find Sri Lanka, Vietnam, or Paraguay recording lower rates. Figure 5-7 testifies not only to the role of economic development but also to the diffusion of health facilities and medicines, hygienic practices, pesticide use, and improved nutrition to less developed countries.

Crude death rates should be viewed in the context of ***infant mortality***. Many children (more than 1 in 10 in many countries) die before reaching their first birthday, so high CDRs tend to reflect high infant mortality. We will discuss this topic in detail in Part 9, where we study medical geography, health, and nutrition.

◆ POPULATION CHANGES IN THE PAST

Because of the population explosion of the twentieth century, we have become accustomed to thinking of population change in terms of growth. But there have been times when populations have declined, sometimes dramatically, and the number of deaths per thousand far exceeded the number of births in certain regions.

Limits on Population Growth

We noted earlier that the world's population increased slowly until the early nineteenth century. What were the reasons for this? A significant factor was epidemics and plagues, which often claimed hundreds of thousands of lives. Between 1348 and 1350 Europe was ravaged by the bubonic plague, and it is estimated that one-quarter of the population died. In this epidemic and its aftermath, many cities and towns were left with fewer than half of their inhabitants. It is believed that the population of England, which totaled nearly 4 million when the plague began, was just over 2 million when it was over. Clearly, a student of population change in the second half of the fourteenth century would have been more likely to talk of annual population decrease than of growth.

Famines also limited population growth. There are records of famines in India and China during the eighteenth and nineteenth centuries in which millions of people perished. Nor was Europe safe from such disasters. From Britain to Russia, unusual weather conditions periodically caused crops to fail, resulting in famine (the Little Ice Age had a major impact). At other times population gains were largely wiped out by destructive wars. Thus the apparent slow and steady increase of the world's population from 250 million at A.D. 0 to 500 million in 1650 and 1 billion in 1820 does not reflect countless unrevealed ups and downs. Birth rates were high, but death rates were also high, and there were times when there were many more deaths than live births.

The Second Agricultural Revolution and the Industrial Revolution

Eventually things began to change. In Europe there was a marked increase in the growth rate during the eighteenth century, and this time there was no major setback to erase the gains. This was the time of the Second Agricultural Revolution, when farming methods improved, crop yields increased, storage capacities were expanded, and distribution systems were improved. The Continental European Industrial Revolution of the nineteenth century also had a major impact: sanitation facilities made the towns and cities safer from epidemics, and modern medical practices became widespread.

Disease prevention through vaccination introduced a new era in public health. Death rates declined markedly. Before 1750 they probably averaged 35 per 1000 (births averaged under 40), but by 1850 the death rate was about 16 per thousand. Consider what this means in terms of natural growth: if in 1750 the birth rate was 39 per thousand and the death rate 35 per thousand, the rate of natural increase was 4 per thousand, or 0.4 percent. In 1850 birth rates were still high, perhaps 36 per thousand, but the death rate was 16 per thousand. Now the rate of natural increase was 2.0 percent. The change is especially spectacular when viewed in the context of doubling time. In 1750, it was about 150 years; in 1850, it was only 35 years.

One effect of this increase in the rate of natural growth was increased migration. Millions of people left the squalid, crowded industrial cities (and farms as well) to emigrate to other parts of the world—North and South America, Australia, South Africa, and elsewhere. They were not the first to make this journey. Adventurers, explorers, merchants, and colonists had gone before them. Those early immigrants had decimated native populations through conquest, slavery, and the introduction of diseases against which the local people had no natural immunity. However, when European colonization began in earnest during the nineteenth century, the Europeans brought with them their newfound methods of sanitation and medical techniques, and these had the opposite effect. In Africa, India, and South America death rates began to decline as they had in Europe, and populations that had long been caught in cycles of gains and losses began to grow—and to grow at increasing rates.

We can only speculate about the native populations of the Americas, Africa, Asia, and Australia before the arrival of the Europeans. At about the time of the first European contact, there were probably fewer than 25 million people in all of North and South America; in Africa south of the Sahara there may have been 70 million. (Some recent estimates place these totals somewhat higher.) In China in the mid-seventeenth century, the population may have been less than 200 million; India probably had fewer than 100 million inhabitants. However, there is no doubt about the consequences of European colonization: it reduced the impact of periodic natural checks on population growth.

◆ DEMOGRAPHIC CHANGE

The population of a country (or a city or region) changes as a result of four conditions: births and inmigration (immigration), which add to the total; and deaths and outmigration (emigration), which subtract from it. Births (fertility), deaths (mortality), and migration are the three demographic *variables*.

To calculate demographic change in a country or region, we use the simple formula

$$TP = OP + B - D + I - E$$

where TP (total population) equals OP (original population) plus B (births) minus D (deaths) plus I (immigration) minus E (emigration). As noted earlier, only births and deaths are used in calculating a population's natural increase. You can calculate the natural increase for various countries by subtracting figures on the map of world mortality (Fig. 5-7) from those of births (Fig. 5-6).

The demographic change formula explains why calculations based only on births and deaths do not correspond to the figures in Figure 5-1 (World Population Growth). Population change, as recorded in Figure 5-1, takes into account emigration and immigration. Obviously, the world population figures referred to previously represent the natural increase for the world as a whole, because our planet does not (yet) experience immigration or emigration.

The Demographic Transition

Demographers who have studied population growth in various parts of the world believe that the high rates of increase now occurring in many less developed countries are not necessarily permanent. In Europe, for example, the situation is very different today than it was a century ago. In the United Kingdom in 1997, the crude birth rate was 13 and the crude death rate was 11, producing a rate of natural increase of just 0.2 percent. In the preindustrial period there also was a small difference between birth and death rates, but both rates were high; now both are low. It is in the intervening stage, when birth rates remained high but death rates fell rapidly, that Britain's population explosion took place. It is not difficult, then, to discern four stages in the United Kingdom's demographic cycle: (1) high birth rates and high death rates and a low rate of growth; (2) continuing high birth rates, but declining and low death rates and a high rate of growth; (3) declining and low death rates but a still substantial growth rate; and (4) low birth and low death rates and, thus, a low rate of growth.

This sequence of stages has been observed in the population records of several European countries, and on this basis demographers have defined what they call the ***demographic cycle*** or ***demographic transition***. Its four stages (Fig. 5-8) are:

1. ***High stationary stage,*** with high fertility (births) and high mortality (deaths) and variable population, but little long-term growth.
2. ***Early expanding stage,*** with high fertility and declining mortality.
3. ***Late expanding stage,*** with declining fertility but, as a result of already-low mortality, continuing significant growth.
4. ***Low stationary stage,*** with low fertility and low mortality, and a very low rate of growth.

The *demographic transition* is represented by stages 2 and 3, during which high birth and death rates decline. The initial rapid drop in death rates is not matched by lowered birth rates, so a period of high natural increase results. The dimensions of the expansion depend on the size of the base population and the rate of decline in the death rate.

This is what happened in the United Kingdom and in much of Europe. Europe as a whole currently has a population growth rate of close to zero. It appears, therefore, that the population "bomb" may eventually fizzle out and that in due course the European model of low birth and death rates and a nearly stable population will prevail everywhere—or will it?

Demographic Change in Developing Countries

In Europe the birth rate declined largely because of the effects of industrialization, urbanization, and general modernization. In contrast, in much of the developing world, the majority of the people have not been greatly affected by such changes. Moreover, there are quantitative differences between the situation in Europe during the nineteenth century and that prevailing in certain parts of the world today. When Europe's population revolution began, the base was small. Britain had between 6 and 7 million residents; Germany had 7 million; France, Belgium, and the Netherlands combined had 18 million. Asia's major population clusters were already much larger when the population revolution began there. China may have had over 200 million inhabitants and India over 100 million. If you superimpose the growth rates of the second and third stages on these large bases, the resulting population increases take on astronomical proportions.

Therefore, it may be unwise to assume that all countries' demographic cycles will follow the sequence that occurred in industrializing Europe or to believe that the explosive growth now taking place in Bangladesh, Mexico, and numerous other countries will simply subside. Optimistic projections suggest that a leveling off will occur when an "ultimate" population is reached, but there is no firm evidence for this outcome. Occasionally there are hopeful signs. In Sri Lanka, for example, the birth rate is declining, and so is the overall growth rate—*without* the kind of economic development that is usually considered a prerequisite for such a decline. A similar noteworthy reduction in the population growth rate has been recorded in the Indian state of Kerala, where the growth rate now stands at 1.1 percent compared to 1.9 percent for India as a whole. It is interesting that the literacy rate for Kerala is about 90 percent of the population, compared to just over 50 percent for all of India.

These remain isolated instances, however, and as yet there is no proof of a permanent, worldwide reversal in population expansion. Indeed, the demographic transition model is useful primarily in explaining developments in one place—Western Europe. To assume that it can be applied anywhere is to fail to think geographically or historically about the world around us. Places differ in time and space, and the conditions that prevailed in one place at a particular time may not apply in another. Hence, even though there are some grounds for optimism, the population "bomb" remains a very real issue as we enter the twenty-first century.

◆ KEY TERMS ◆

age-sex pyramid
crude birth rate (CBR)
crude death rate (CDR)
demographic transition (cycle)
doubling time
exponential growth
infant mortality
linear growth
natural increase
population explosion
population structure
stationary population level (SPL)
total fertility rate (TFR)

◆ APPLYING GEOGRAPHIC KNOWLEDGE ◆

1. The debate over population growth and food supply, started by Malthus 200 years ago, still continues. Neo-Malthusians argue that what Malthus wrote about Britain two centuries ago can be applied to the world as a whole today—recent gains in global food supplies notwithstanding. Take a pro- or anti-Malthusian position and argue your case, using your geographic knowledge of population distribution, urbanization, resource availability, and demographic processes.

2. Some argue that the demographic transition model (see Fig. 5-8) is not necessarily an appropriate tool for understanding likely future population trends in Subsaharan African countries. What is different about those countries now and the Western European countries at the time they went through the demographic transition? Are those differences likely to render the demographic transition model inapplicable to Subsaharan Africa? If so, why? If not, why not?

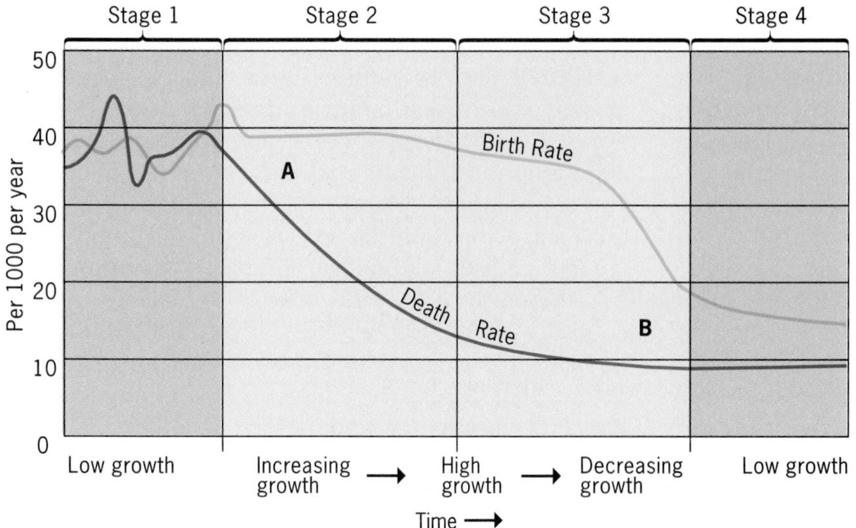

Figure 5-8 The Demographic Cycle. Four stages of the demographic cycle.

Chapter 6

Migration and Its Causes

From the field notes

"A truly ugly sight, this spiked, barbed-wire fence along the waterfront of (still-Portuguese) Macau. To the right, the beach belongs to China; the road to the left lies in Macau. To stop the Chinese from leaving the communist state and entering the colony, barriers like this were constructed (the border between Hong Kong and China was reinforced in a similar way). As the transfer of these last European colonies approaches, these barriers to migration are losing their relevance. But illegal emigration from China continues, and barriers to migration are being built in many other areas of the world—including the U.S.-Mexican border."

KEY POINTS

◆ Many factors stimulate the migration process. They include conflict, economic conditions, political strife, cultural circumstances, environmental change, and technological advances.

◆ Migrants move on the basis of their perceptions of particular destinations; distance tends to affect the accuracy of these perceptions.

◆ Migration usually takes place in stages. Rural-to-urban movement occurs in steps, often from smaller to larger centers. Migrants tend to relocate repeatedly after reaching the land of their destination.

◆ Voluntary migrations, such as the movement toward the Sunbelt in North America, are stimulated by "pull" as well as "push" factors.

◆ Forced migrations result from the imposition of power by stronger peoples over weaker ones. A modern example is the repatriation of illegal migrants by governments that are unwilling to accept them.

What impelled our East African ancestors to leave their familiar abode for the unknown, to cross into Arabia, eventually into India, and ultimately into Australia? What could have persuaded early *Homo sapiens* to venture into the cold regions of Pleistocene Europe? To cross the Bering land bridge from Asia to America? To risk survival in flimsy boats on the open sea?

These questions go to the heart of a basic human behavior. Throughout history humans have sought new frontiers—new islands and continents. Risks have been taken and lives lost, but the search for new frontiers has continued and still continues today. Our efforts to reach the moon stemmed from the same urge that dispersed *H. sapiens* in the first place.

The U.S. population is the most mobile in the world. More than 5 million people move from one state to another every year, and nearly seven times as many—an average of 35 million—move within their state, county, or community. On average, an American citizen moves once in about every six years.

Human mobility is of central interest in human geography because it is an inherently spatial process. Human movement speeds the diffusion of ideas and innovations. It intensifies spatial interaction and transforms regions. And as we will see, it is often closely linked to environmental conditions.

◆ KEY FACTORS IN HUMAN MOVEMENT

Human movement often results from a perception that conditions are better, safer, easier, or in some other way superior (or at least different) in some distant place. We took note of the role of perception in human geography in Chapter 1. Here we will consider it in relation to migration and its causes.

Absolute and Relative Direction

When people move, either permanently to a new abode or temporarily (for example, for a long vacation), they think in terms of the *direction* their travel should take. Direction, like location, can be viewed in two ways: *absolute* and *relative*. Just as absolute location refers to the global grid system, so ***absolute direction*** refers to astronomically determined direction. From any given location, absolute north and south point to the north and south poles, respectively. Absolute east and west are exactly parallel to latitude lines. Intervening directions are stated in terms of measured degree; for example, SE is south 45° east. Absolute direction thus is what we think of as *compass* direction.

Relative direction, on the other hand, is more perceptual. During a cold winter, a Michigan family may contemplate a vacation (or perhaps a relocation) to the Sunbelt. Exactly where is this Sunbelt? It lies to the south, obviously, but people's perceptions of it vary. Almost everyone would agree that Florida is part of the Sunbelt, but other areas (Arkansas and Utah, for example) are viewed differently. So it is with such directional images as the "Middle East," which implies that there is a "Near East" and a "Far East." Those perceptions are derived from older British usage: the "Near East," viewed from London, consisted of Turkey, Egypt, Libya, and the coastal countries of the eastern Mediterranean; the "Middle East" was centered on Iraq and the Persian Gulf; and the "Far East" was the East Asian region.

Absolute and Relative Distance

A second perception that affects human mobility is *distance*. Again, distance can be measured in both absolute and relative terms. Absolute distances can be read on maps, using the scales discussed in Resource A at the end of this book. But distance "as the crow flies" more often than not is irrelevant when it comes to human movement. The U.S. system of interstate highways did not change the ***absolute distance*** between places that it connects, but it did alter the time it takes to travel by automobile between those places. Commuters are always looking for alternate routes between their homes and places of work, not because the absolute distance between these points changes but because the ***relative distance*** is shortened by using a quicker route (Fig. 6-1).

Research has shown that people's perceptions of both distance and direction are often greatly distorted, and this means that many travel decisions are based on inadequate information. Add to this people's tendency to have an incomplete geographic picture of areas to which they relocate, and it is understandable that a sizable percentage of movers return to their original home.

External and Internal Migration

In Chapter 5, we saw that the growth or decline of a country's population involves not only natural increase or decrease but also the movement of people into or out of the country. In the case of the United States, the natural increase of the population is substantially lower than its overall growth because inmigration from other countries exceeds outmigration by several hundred thousand people every year. The low growth rates recorded in several European countries, on the other hand, reflect the permanent departure of many citizens as well as declining fertility rates.

Emigration (outmigration) and immigration (inmigration) are forms of ***migration***, the long-term relocation of an individual, household, or group to a new location outside the community of origin. Many migrants, after having moved, may move again, while others are unable to adjust or establish themselves in their new surroundings and return home.

When migrants move from one country to another, they become part of the vital statistics of the countries they leave and enter (see "Focus on: Migration and Demographic Structure"). But countries also experience *internal* migration—often in well-defined streams that change over time. In the United States during the 1980s and 1990s, internal migration streams were moving people from east to west and from north to south. The older industrial states of the North and East were losing people to the Sunbelt; the U.S. Census Bureau reported that between 1981 and 1988, New York alone lost 330,000 people to Florida and nearly 70,000 to California. But these are recent movements. Early in the twentieth century, a major internal migration stream carried tens of thousands of black families from the South to the industrializing cities of the "rustbelt" that people are leaving today.

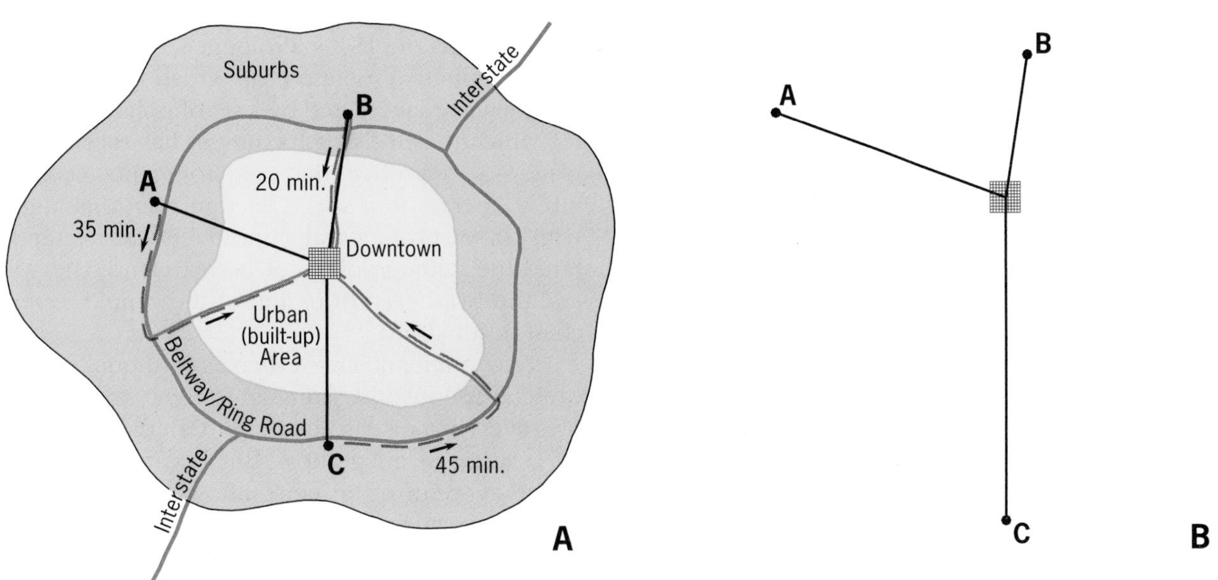

Figure 6-1 Relative Distances. The absolute distance of three homes just outside an urban beltway (A) and their relative distance, once the travel times to the central city are measured (B).

Focus On

Migration and Demographic Structure

The age-sex pyramids of individual countries (see Figs. 5-4 and 5-5) summarize the structure of the population as a whole, but they conceal internal differences. The age compositions of cities often differ markedly from those of rural areas. Families in cities tend to be smaller, and there are fewer children, proportionally, than in the countryside. Contrasts occur even within cities, for the population pyramid of the affluent sector may differ substantially from that of poorer sectors. Obviously, the migration process that brings people to cities from the countryside has an impact on urban and rural population structures, because many of the migrants are young adults seeking jobs. This age-selective migration is revealed in the charts.

Migration, whether forced or voluntary, can also be sex-selective. For example, far more male than female Africans were taken to the New World as slaves. In modern times, the number of male emigrants from European countries to America was much larger than the number of female emigrants. At the beginning of the century, there were about 107 males in the United States for every 100 females, but over time the disparity has decreased, and now women are a slight majority. Greater losses of males in wartime and the longer life expectancy of women have contributed to the reversal. In cities in India and Africa, in contrast, males continue to outnumber females, sometimes overwhelmingly—partly as a result of sex-selective migration. This disparity has caused serious problems of social adjustment.

◆ CATALYSTS OF MIGRATION

What impels people to pull up stakes and leave the familiar for the uncertain? Research has shown that usually it is not just one factor but a combination of factors that leads to the decision to move. In this section we look briefly at several key factors.

Economic Conditions

Poverty has driven countless millions from their homelands and continues to do so. Perceived opportunities in destinations such as Western Europe and North America impel numerous migrants, both legal and illegal, to cross the Mediterranean, the Caribbean, and the Rio Grande in search of a better life.

Political Circumstances

Throughout history oppressive regimes have engendered migration streams. More than 125,000 Cubans left their country in 1980 on the "Mariel Boatlift" to escape communist dictatorship. Desperate "boat people" fled Vietnam by the hundreds of thousands after communist insurgents took control of the country. In 1972 Uganda's dictator, Idi Amin, expelled 50,000 Asians and Ugandans of Asian descent from his country. Migrations driven by politics thus are marked by both escape and expulsion.

Armed Conflict and Civil War

The dreadful conflict that engulfed the former Yugoslavia during the 1990s drove as many as 3 million people from their homes. Many of those people became permanent emigrants, unable to return home. During the mid-1990s a civil war engulfed Rwanda in Equatorial Africa, a conflict that pitted militant Hutu against the minority Tutsi and "moderate" Hutu. The carnage may have claimed as many as 600,000 lives and produced huge outmigrations into neighboring Zaïre (now Congo) and Tanzania. It is estimated that more than 2 million Rwandans left their homeland.

Environmental Conditions

A major example of migration induced by environmental conditions is the movement of hundreds of thousands of Irish citizens from Ireland to the New World during the 1840s. Prolonged excessive rains rotted the country's potato crop, creating a famine. The famine was exacerbated by a set of political conditions for which the British government has recently apologized—a reminder that environmental conditions rarely operate in a social vacuum. But this migration with an environmental component permanently altered the demographics of both Ireland (the source) and the Northeastern region of the United States (the chief destination).

Environmental crises such as earthquakes and volcanic eruptions also stimulate migrations. For example, every major earthquake in California is followed by a surge in emigration. But because many of the emigrants return, the net outflow generated by such momentary crises is comparatively small.

Culture and Traditions

People who fear that their culture and traditions will not survive a major political transition, and who are able to migrate to places they perceive as safer, will often do so. When British India was partitioned into a mainly Hindu India and an almost exclusively Muslim Pakistan, millions of Muslim residents of India migrated across the border to the new Islamic state. Similarly, in the 1990s after decades of Soviet obstruction, more than 2 million Jews left the former USSR for Israel and other destinations. And turbulent political conditions in South Africa during the mid-1990s impelled many whites to emigrate to Australia, Europe, and North America.

Technological Advances

For many migrants emigration is no longer the difficult and hazardous journey it used to be. While many migrants still move by simple and even difficult means, millions more now use modern forms of transportation whose availability can itself encourage migration. Moreover, technological innovations have made certain parts of the planet more attractive to migrants. For example, it has been suggested that the growing availability of air conditioning greatly reduced return migration from the Sunbelt back to the North, resulting in a larger net flow of migrants within the United States.

Flow of Information

Gone is the time when would-be emigrants waited months, even years, for information about distant places. News today travels faster than ever, including news of job opportunities and ways to reach desired destinations. Television, radio, and telephone have stimulated millions of people to migrate by relaying information about relatives, opportunities, and already established communities in destination lands. Thus Turks quickly heard about Germany's need for immigrant labor. Algerians knew where the most favorable destinations were in France. Haitians knew that a "Little Haiti" had sprung up in the Miami area.

◆ "PUSH" AND "PULL" FACTORS

Geographers who study human migration have identified conditions and perceptions that tend to induce people to leave their abodes ***(push factors)***. They have also identified circumstances that effectively attract people to certain locales from other places ***(pull factors)*** (see "Focus on: Theories About Migration").

The decision to migrate usually results from a combination of push and pull factors, along with perceived obstacles (or lack thereof) that are not directly

ocus On

Theories About Migration

What causes people to decide to migrate? This question has intrigued researchers for more than a century. Studies indicate that the intensity of a migration flow varies with such factors as the degree of difference between the source and the destination, the effectiveness of the flow of information from the destination back to the source, and the physical distance between the source and the (ultimate) destination.

As long ago as 1885, the British demographer Ernst Ravenstein studied internal migration in England. On the basis of his data he proposed several "laws" of migration. These "laws" are still relevant today.

1. ***Net migration amounts to a fraction of the gross migration between two places.*** Every migration flow generates a "return" or "counter" migration, so the actual migration is the volume of the original flow minus that of the return flow.
2. ***The majority of migrants move a short distance.*** Average migration distance undoubtedly has increased since Ravenstein's time, but step migration still prevails.
3. ***Migrants who move longer distances tend to choose big-city destinations.*** London was the great magnet in Ravenstein's time, and other British cities were mushrooming as a result of migration.
4. ***Urban residents are less migratory than inhabitants of rural areas.*** In England in Ravenstein's time, urbanization was drawing people toward towns and cities. The same phenomenon can be observed today in the developing countries.
5. ***Families are less likely to make international moves than young adults.*** Throughout the world young adults are the most mobile population group.

Ravenstein also posited an inverse relationship between the volume of migration and the distance between source and destination; that is, the number of migrants declines as the distance they must travel increases. This proposal anticipated the ***gravity model***, a measure of the interaction of places. The gravity model predicts this interaction on the basis of the size of population in the respective places and the distance between them. It states that spatial interaction (such as migration) is directly related to the populations and inversely related to the distance between them. In mathematical terms, the model holds that interaction is proportional to the multiplication of the two populations divided by the distance between them. Variants of this notion are applicable in many areas of human geography, especially economic geography.

related to the place of origin or destination. Because a migrant is likely to be more familiar with his or her place of residence (source) than with the locale to which he or she is moving (destination), push factors are likely to be perceived more accurately than pull factors. Push factors include individual considerations such as work or retirement conditions, cost of living, personal safety and security, and, for many, weather and climate. Pull factors tend to be more vague and may depend on several visits to the destination. Many migrants move on the basis of excessively positive images and expectations regarding their destinations.

Distance Decay

The principle of ***distance decay*** comes into play here (Fig. 6-2). Prospective migrants are likely to have more complete and accurate perceptions of nearer places than of farther ones, which confirms the notion that the intensity of human activity, process, or function declines as distance from its source increases. Since interaction with faraway places decreases as distance increases, prospective migrants are likely to feel much less certain about distant destinations than about nearer ones. This leads many migrants to move less far than they originally contemplated. Indeed, many migration streams that appear on maps as long, unbroken routes in fact consist of a series of stages, a phenomenon known as ***step migration***. A peasant family in Brazil, for example, is likely to move first to a village, then to a nearby town, later to a city, and finally to a metropolis such as São Paulo or Rio de Janeiro. At each stage a new set of pull factors comes into play.

Intervening Opportunity

Not all migrants complete all of these steps. When 1000 people leave a village and migrate to a town in a given year, most if not all of them may dream of making it to—and in—the "big city." But only about 500 may actually move from town to city, and of these, only 200 eventually reach the metropolis that impelled them to move in the first place. Along the way the majority are captured by ***intervening opportunity***. This is what happened when African Americans migrated northward after World War I to seek work in growing cities like Chicago and Cleveland. Many found employment in St. Louis and Cincinnati; that is, they encountered intervening opportunities along their northbound routes.

Like distance decay, intervening opportunity is a geographic principle that is relevant to the study of migration as well as other human activities. A special kind of temporary migrants—tourists—also respond to intervening opportunities. Other things being equal, cost-conscious vacationers will choose a nearer, and hence cheaper, resort over a more distant one (e.g., Vermont instead of Maine for New Yorkers). Intervening opportunity is the constant worry of every resort that depends on attracting visitors from distant places.

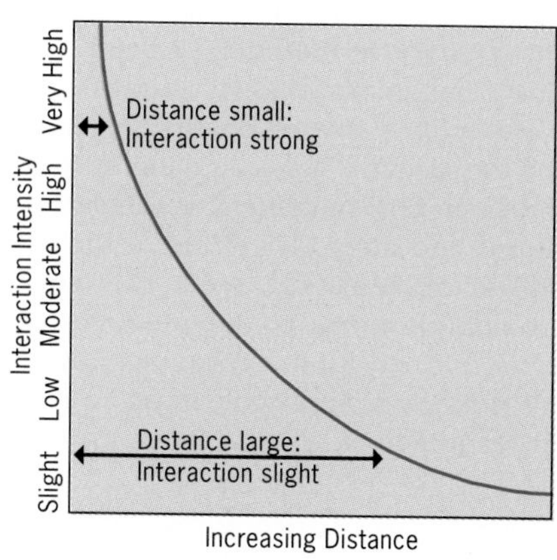

Figure 6-2 Distance Decay.

◆ VOLUNTARY AND FORCED MIGRATIONS

Our final look at the reasons people move focuses on a pair of opposites: the luxury of choice and the fear of compulsion. Two major migration flows—of Europeans to overseas colonies and Africans to the Americas—illustrate the difference between the two, which may be classified as ***voluntary*** and ***forced migrations***. However, there are different cases within each of these categories. Africans were captured and transported as prisoners, then sold into slavery. Other migrants who were forced to move faced quite different circumstances. During the early 1970s, for example, the rulers of Uganda decided to oust nearly all individuals of Asian descent from that country. Many of those people were shopkeepers, traders, or otherwise engaged in commerce. They were given very little time to get out of a country in which many of them had been born. As approximately 50,000 Asians were transported out of Uganda with only the belongings they could carry, this was obviously a forced migration—but still a very different type of forced migration from that of the African slaves transported to America. We should therefore focus more closely on our two classes of migratory movements.

Voluntary Migration

Of the millions of Europeans who came to the Americas, most were seeking opportunity and better living standards. These same motives carried others from Europe to the African and Asian colonies—Portuguese and British to Angola and Kenya, Belgians and Dutch to the Congo and Netherlands East Indies. Some of the emigrants, among them many Irish families, left for the New World because of declining harvests, so there is an element of force in this case. The prevailing force, however, was the "pull" of opportunity. Today, as noted earlier, this is the force that leads people to leave rural areas and head for the cities.

Another kind of voluntary migration involves people's desire to be with others who share their cultural attributes or political beliefs. The world is a mosaic of languages, religions, and ways of life, and there are minorities everywhere. Most of these minorities have become adjusted to their circumstances, but times do change. When Africa's European colonies won independence, some of the white settlers were able to adjust to the new situation. Others could not adjust, so they departed, some to South Africa, others to Europe. Unlike the Asians forced out of Uganda, these Europeans were not ousted. If there was a "push" factor, it often lay more in what they perceived might happen than in what actually did occur. Theirs was a voluntary emigration. Similarly, communities may decide to seek new homes in places where they will enjoy more religious freedom, as many Muslims did when the separate states of India and Pakistan were created.

In the United States, a major migration flow is the movement of people who reach retirement age and leave their long-time homes for Florida, Arizona, and other Sunbelt locales where the weather is milder and costs are lower. Again, this is mainly a voluntary migration that is often planned for many years before the move is actually made. There are elements of cultural migration here as well. Older people often wish to live in places where other retirees also reside so that they may share their interests and activities. The impact of this migration flow on the landscape can be seen in Florida's myriad high-rise condominiums and Arizona's sprawling retirement communities.

Forced Migration

Several of the world's largest migration streams have been forced migrations. By far the most important of these was the transatlantic ***slave trade***, which carried tens of millions of Africans from their homes to the Americas with huge loss of life. How many Africans were sold into slavery will probably never be known (estimates range from 12 million to over 30 million); Figure 6-3 indicates only their destinations and the proportions transported to each of them. The largest numbers of Africans were brought to plantations in the Caribbean and eastern South America. Today the descendants of these people make up an overwhelming majority of the populations of several Caribbean countries. Despite the substantial proportion of blacks in the U.S. population, the number of enslaved Africans who were taken to the United States was quite small compared to the many who were taken to the Caribbean and South America. In 1800 the black population of the United States was just 1 million (Fig. 6-3).

The quest for slaves had a significant effect on Africa as well. For the most part, emigrants from Europe left by choice (some were exiled prisoners or indentured laborers), and to some extent their departure relieved the very pressures that forced them to go. In Africa, on the other hand, there was no such freedom of choice, and far from improving the situation, the forced emigration greatly damaged the societies involved. Whole families left Europe and joined communities in America, thereby cushioning, to some degree, the effects of migration. In Africa, however, families were destroyed, children orphaned, and communities disrupted—and once in America the African slaves faced not only terror but loneliness as well. In Africa the communities that were raided for slaves, if they survived at all, lost most of their younger men; in Amer-

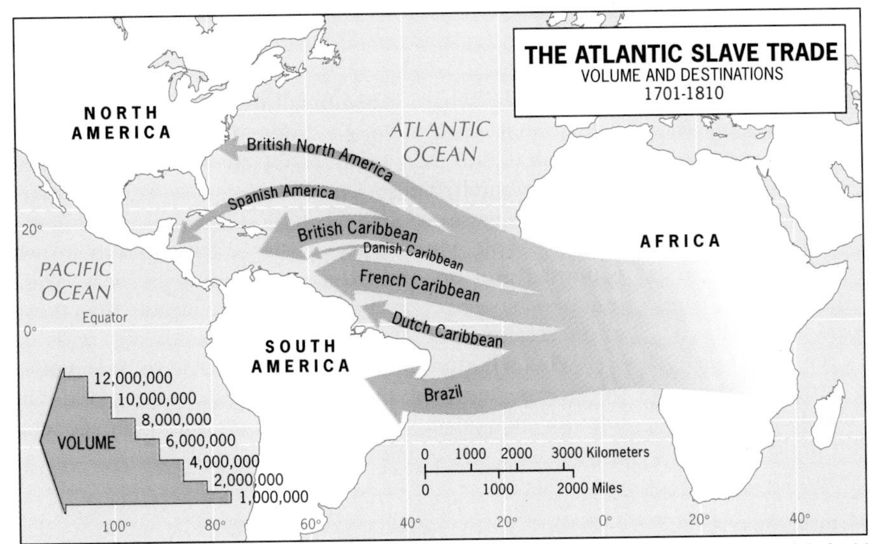

Figure 6-3 The Atlantic Slave Trade. Dimensions of the Atlantic slave trade. *Source: After a map in P. Curtin,* The Atlantic Slave Trade *(Madison: University of Wisconsin Press, 1969), p. 57.*

ica, the number of African-American women lagged behind the number of African-American men for a long time, even after emancipation. Generations passed before the demographic effects of the slave trade were overcome and the long-term balance of population structures in Africa and the Americas was restored.

Nothing in human history compares to the North Atlantic slave trade, but other forced migrations also changed the world's demographic map. For 50 years beginning in 1788, tens of thousands of convicts were shipped from Britain to Australia, where they had a lasting impact on the continent's population geography. In the 1800s, thousands of Native Americans were forced onto reservations—some far from their traditional homelands. In the then-Soviet Union during Stalin's ruthless rule earlier in this century, many millions of non-Russians were forcibly moved from their homes to remote parts of Central Asia and Siberia for political reasons. Nor is forced migration unknown today. It continues to occur in the form of ***counter migration***, in which governments send back migrants caught entering their countries illegally. In the 1990s the United States has repatriated Haitian arrivals from Florida. Vietnamese escapees have been expelled from Hong Kong. By comparison, other migration streams—whatever their causes—are benign.

Whenever we observe migrations, we should realize that the flow of migrants represents only a small fraction of the population at the source; the migrants have made a choice that is not available to those who were moved forcibly. Another contrast lies in the "return" migration. All voluntary migration flows generate a return, or counter, migration. For example, some Soviet-Jewish emigrants have returned to Russia. Some Canadians find that they cannot adjust to life in Florida and return home. In short, any voluntary migration flow represents the numbers going from the source to the destination *minus* those returning from the destination to the source. This cannot be said of forced migrations.

◆ THE GEOGRAPHY OF DISLOCATION

Forced migrations tend to produce social crises. Large numbers of people have been ousted from their homes, exhausted by the rigors of the trek, faced with starvation, and ravaged by disease. In the aftermath of the conflict in Rwanda, for example, huge camps holding hundreds of thousands of Hutu sprang up on the Congo side of the border, and thousands died of hunger or disease.

The Rwanda tragedy may have been the largest-ever crisis of its kind, but in truth it was only the latest in a series of human dislocations that have created a growing global dilemma. In 1970, there were about 2.9 million ***refugees*** in the world. Just a decade later, this number had grown to 8 million. In 1997, the United Nations High Commission for Refugees (UNHCR) reported that some 22 million people qualified as refugees and that another 25 million had been forced to abandon their homes. The world's refugee population is growing much faster than the total population, and the overused words "global crisis" certainly apply here (see "Focus on: Dimensions of the Refugee Problem").

Focus On

Dimensions of the Refugee Problem

When the refugee problem is viewed in a geographic context, a key problem involves numbers. The official UN agency that monitors refugee concerns (UNHCR) is one of several offices that seek information on refugees and their needs, and UNHCR data often are contradicted by data from other sources.

Why is this so? Several reasons exist. First, there are different definitions of what constitutes a refugee. The United Nations defines a refugee as "a person who has a well-founded fear of being persecuted for reasons of race, religion, nationality, membership of a particular social group, or political opinion." Countries interpret this definition in various ways; the phrase "well-founded" leaves much room for judgment. Second, refugees often flee into remote areas where it is difficult to count them, let alone provide help. And third, governments manipulate refugee numbers to suit their political objectives, so reported statistics are unreliable.

The biggest problem has to do with internal refugees, that is, people who have been displaced within their own countries and do not cross international borders. Their numbers have been growing even more rapidly than those of international refugees, although estimates vary widely.

Whatever their numbers, refugees tend to be the most powerless, deprived, threatened people in the world. Often they face death while governments and relief agencies quarrel over rescue plans.

UNHCR and other agencies distinguish between ***international refugees***, who have crossed one or more international borders during their move and have encamped in a country other than their own, and ***intranational refugees***, who have abandoned their homes but not their countries. Resettlement efforts have been more successful with intranational than international refugees simply because those fleeing their countries often resist repatriation.

Because the status of refugee has an official, internationally sanctioned basis, UNHCR and other agencies must make difficult decisions when they distinguish between genuine refugees and migrants who may be just as poor or desperate, but who do not qualify for refugee status. When a refugee meets the official criteria, he or she becomes eligible for assistance, including possible asylum, to which other migrants are not entitled. Such assistance can extend over decades and become the very basis for a way of life, as has happened in the Middle East. In Jordan, Palestinian refugees have become so integrated into the host country's national life that they are regarded as ***permanent refugees***, but in Lebanon other Palestinians wait in refugee camps for resettlement and still qualify as ***temporary refugees***.

While it is not always easy to distinguish between a refugee and a voluntary (if desperate) migrant, refugees can be identified by at least three characteristics, individual or aggregate:

1. ***Most refugees move without any more tangible property than they can carry or transport with them.*** When the Gulf War's aftermath generated a vast refugee flow among Iraq's Kurds, these people walked in a giant column across the Turkish and Iranian borders. A minority were able to load possessions on trucks, cars, or animals.

2. ***Most refugees make their first "step" on foot, by bicycle, wagon, or open boat.*** In other words, the technological factor that facilitates modern migration (see above) is inoperative here. Refugees are suddenly displaced, limiting their options, and the great majority have few resources to invest in their journey.

3. ***Refugees move without the official documents that accompany channeled migration.*** External refugees almost without exception migrate without authorization and often carry few or no identifying papers.

As recent events in Africa underscore, refugee movements often happen suddenly and can involve millions in a matter of weeks, if not days. This means that the refugee map changes frequently. Usually, it is difficult to predict where the next crisis will occur (and impossible where natural calamities are concerned), so that preparing for a refugee exodus yet to come is mainly a fruitless exercise. In a recent study, the International Red Cross identified nearly 2000 locales in Africa where conflict or natural catastrophes might precipitate refugee movements at some future time. Other parts of the world may be less threatened today, but no place on Earth is immune to the forces of dislocation.

Figure 6-4 shows the location (by country) and numbers of refugees as reported by the United Nations High Commission for Refugees in December 1997. The map differentiates between international and intranational refugees; only one country, Sudan, has substantial numbers of both (4 million international refugees and 4 million internally dislocated people). Note that these numbers represent people officially recognized to be refugees, not the additional estimated 25 million dislocated persons not yet accorded this status.

Regions of Dislocation

The refugee situation changes frequently as some refugees return home, conditions permitting, and as other, new streams suddenly form. Yet the overall geography of refugees has a certain continuity. In the late 1990s, Africa south of the Sahara had the largest number of refugees in the world as well as the greatest potential for new refugee flows. The second-ranking geographic realm in terms of refugee numbers was Southwest Asia and North Africa, the realm that includes the Middle East, Iran, and Afghanistan. South Asia, as a result of Pakistan's proximity to Afghanistan, ranked third.

Subsaharan Africa The burgeoning population of Subsaharan Africa is severely affected by dislocation—and not just in terms of the nearly 8 million "official" refugees accounted for by international agencies. Many more are intranational refugees, and their numbers also are in the millions.

Four of the world's largest refugee crises plagued Africa during the 1990s: the collapse of order in Somalia, the civil wars in Liberia and Sierra Leone, the ongoing conflict in Sudan, and the disaster in Rwanda and its neighbors. Among the causes are those endemic to Africa: undemocratic, weak, corrupt governments; historic ethnic rivalries; excess of weapons (mostly supplied by the superpowers during the Cold War); and lack of national cohesion.

The situation in Somalia resulted from cultural-political as well as environmental causes. A famine-producing drought led to a UN relief effort, which in turn entangled the relief operation in Somalia's clan-based politics. Although the relief effort saved thousands of lives, the UN forces delegated to protect

Figure 6-4 Location of Refugees, 1997. This map shows the number and areas of international and intranational refugees. *Source: United Nations High Commission for Refugees, 1997.*

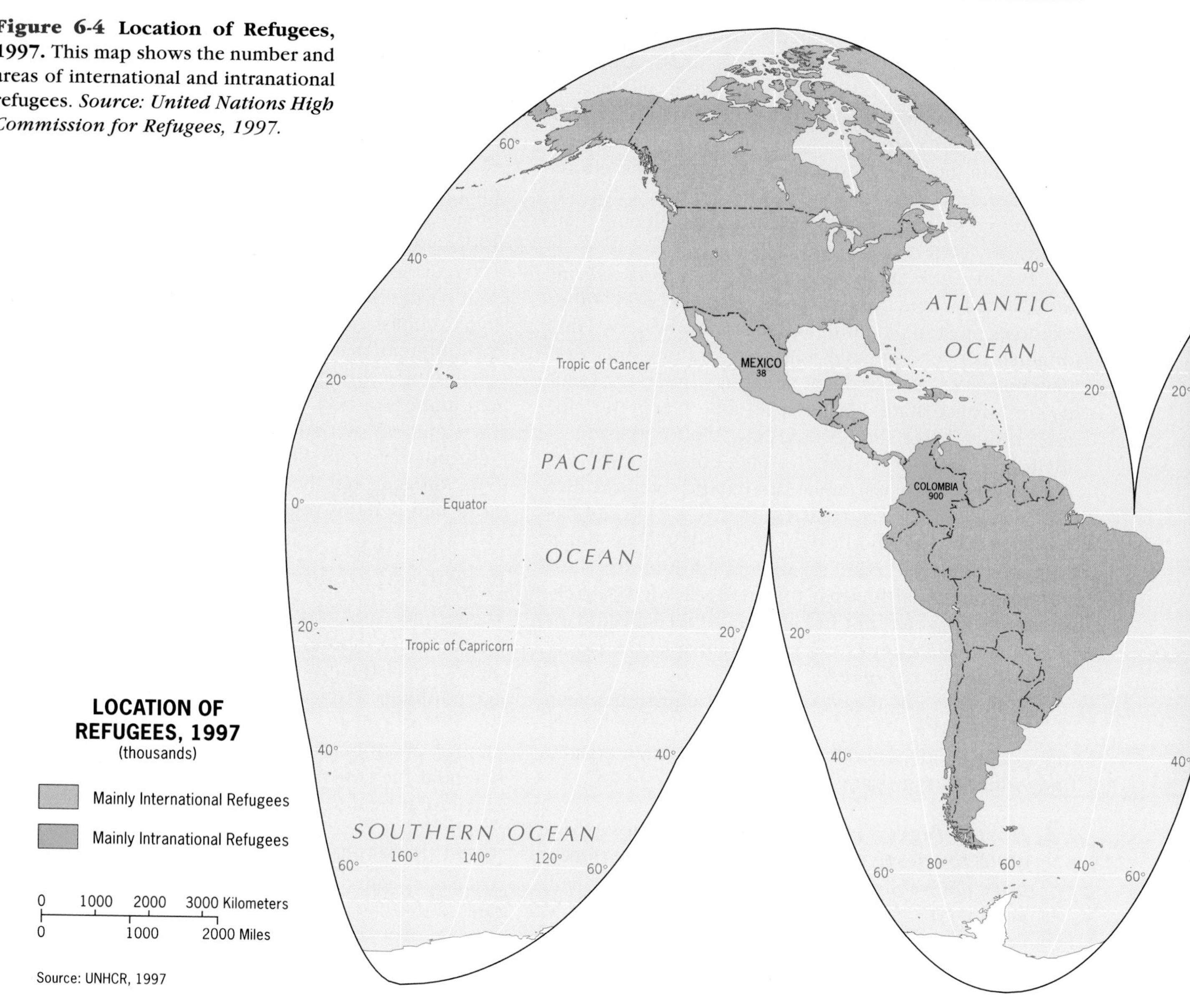

the operation suffered numerous casualties and the initiative ended. In 1997, unprecedented floods struck southern Somalia, creating hundreds of thousands of refugees; this time, the UN relief project involved air drops of food supplies but no other assistance. In West Africa, Liberia and Guinea suffered from civil wars that generated massive flows of refugees.

In Equatorial Africa, a cyclic conflict between Hutu and Tutsi in Rwanda sent millions of refugees into neighboring countries, contributing to a successful revolution in one of those neighbors, Congo (then still called Zaïre). Tutsi support for revolutionary forces in eastern Zaïre enabled those forces to move westward and take the capital, Kinshasa. In their wake lay huge refugee camps and countless casualties. And in Sudan, a 30-year conflict between northern, Arabized Muslims and southern animists and Christians continues to create millions of refugees constantly threatened by hunger and famine.

Political conflicts, environmental deterioration, and ideological changes have dislocated millions of Africans over the past generations. Mushrooming population and latent civil strife will unfortunately ensure that the refugee cycle in Africa will not soon be broken.

Southwest Asia and North Africa The geographic realm of Southwest Asia and North Africa includes major refugee concentrations and exhibits qualities that are likely to generate additional refugee flow in the future. One of the most serious refugee crises in Southwest Asia took place in 1991, when, in the aftermath

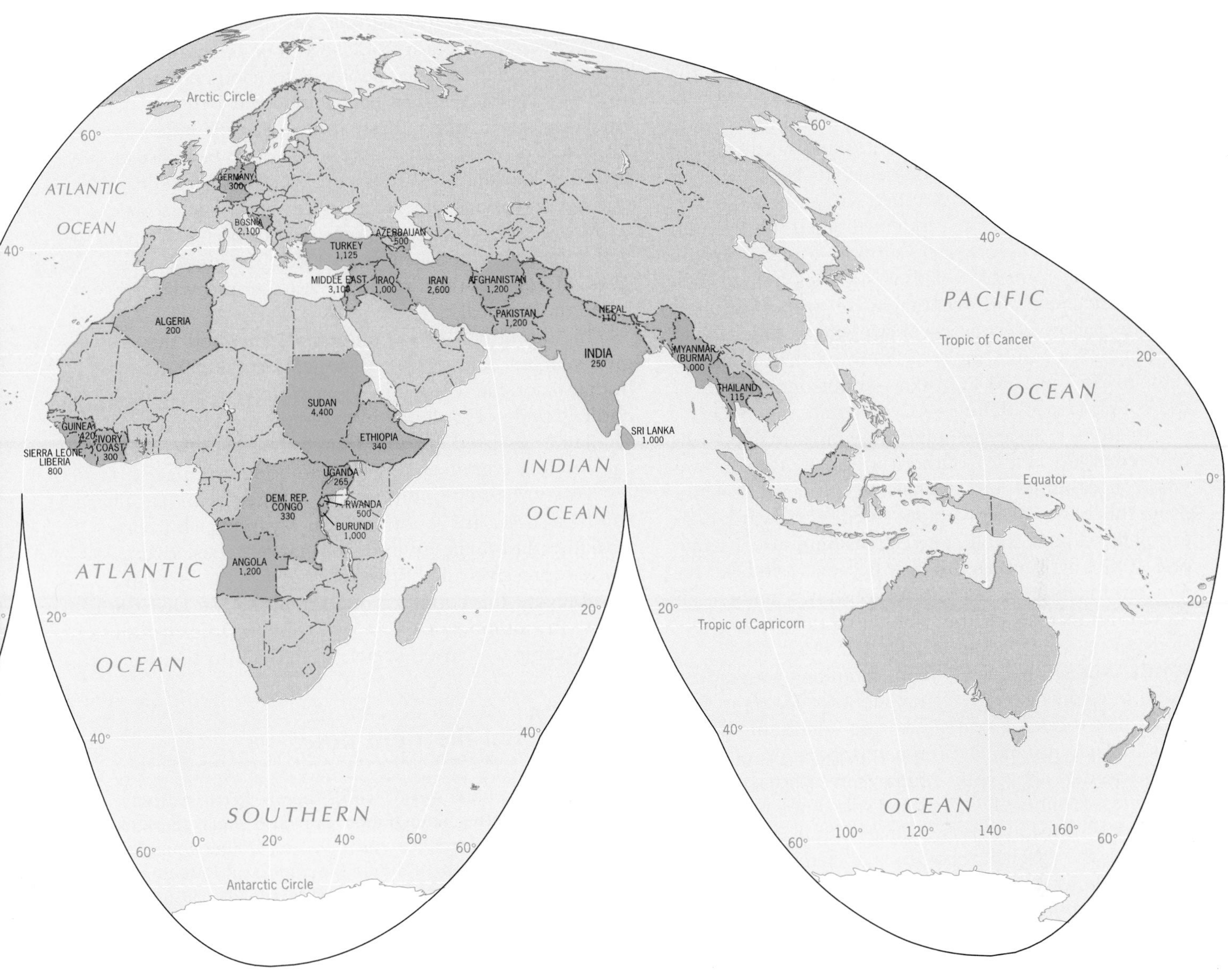

of the Gulf War, the Kurdish population of northern Iraq, threatened by the surviving military apparatus and under Baghdad's control, abandoned their villages and towns and streamed toward and across the Turkish and Iranian borders. The refugee movement of Iraq's Kurds involved as many as 2.5 million people and riveted world attention on the plight of people who are condemned to such status by the actions of others. It led the United States and its allies to create a secure zone for Kurds in extreme northern Iraq to persuade Kurds in Turkey and Iran to return to their country.

But this effort was only partially successful. The Kurdish people of Iraq were severely dislocated by the events surrounding the Gulf War; as Figure 6-4 shows, many remain refugees in Turkey as well as Iran.

The Kurds are among the stateless nations of the world that are especially susceptible to dislocation at the will (and hands) of others. Ever since the creation of the state of Israel in what was formerly the British Mandate of Palestine, hundreds of thousands of Arabs who called Palestine their homeland have lived as refugees in neighboring countries. Over time—now five decades—many of the Palestinians have been assimilated into the societies of Israel's neighbors, but a still larger number live in makeshift refugee camps. The Palestinians also call themselves a nation without a state (much as the Jews were before Israel was founded), and they have kept the issue of a national homeland alive in the political forums of the world.

During the 1980s Afghanistan was caught in the last campaign of Soviet imperialism and paid an enormous price for it. The Soviet invasion, in support of a puppet regime, and Afghan resistance generated a double migration stream that carried millions westward into Iran and eastward into Pakistan. At the height of the exodus, 2.5 million Afghans were estimated to be living in camps in Iran, and some 3.7 million gathered in tent camps in Pakistan's northwestern province and in southern Baluchistan. The Soviet invasion of 1979 seemed destined to succeed quickly, but the Russian generals underestimated the strength of Afghan opposition. U.S. support for the Muslim forces in the form of weapons supplies helped produce a stalemate and eventual Soviet withdrawal, but this was followed by a power struggle among Afghan factions. As a result, most of the more than 6 million refugees in Iran and Pakistan—about one-quarter of the country's population—stayed where they were.

In 1996, a Fundamentalist movement named Taliban emerged in the southern areas of Afghanistan, where it captured and consolidated a large domain. From this base, the movement swept northward, capturing the capital, Kabul, and establishing strict Islamic rule. Taliban's success did not, however, end the region's refugee crisis. As Figure 6-4 shows, millions of Afghan refugees remain in Iran and Pakistan.

South Asia South Asia is the third-ranking geographic realm in terms of refugee numbers (see Fig. 6-4), but about half the total stems from the continuing problems in Afghanistan. The refugee population of Pakistan's border area with Afghanistan (the so-called Northwest Frontier) has declined substantially; during the Soviet intrusion it was estimated to exceed 3 million. Still, the UNHCR recognizes as many as 1.2 million people as refugees in Pakistan. Most will not return until stability, and some relaxation of the Taliban's harsh rule, have been achieved in their home country.

The other major refugee problem in South Asia stems from a civil war in Sri Lanka. This conflict, arising from demands by minority Tamils for an independent state on the Sinhalese-dominated island, has cost tens of thousands of lives and has severely damaged the economy; the United Nations reports that about 1 million people (out of a population of 19 million) are now intranational refugees.

Europe The collapse of Yugoslavia and its associated conflicts created the largest refugee crisis in Europe since the end of World War II. In 1995, the UNHCR reported the staggering total of 6,056,600 refugees, a number that some observers felt was inflated by the Europeans' unusually liberal interpretations of the United Nations' rules for refugee recognition. Nevertheless, even after the cessation of armed conflict and the implementation of a peace agreement known as the Dayton Accords, the UNHCR still reports as many as 2.1 million intranational refugees in the area—people dislocated and unable to return to their homes.

Southeast Asia Southeast Asia was the scene of one of the twentieth century's most desperate refugee crises—the stream of "boat people" who fled communist rule in postwar Vietnam by risking their lives on the open ocean in often flimsy boats. It will never be known how many left Vietnam's shores, but all estimates exceed 1 million. It is estimated that between 40 and 70 percent of the escapees fell victim to storms, exposure, starvation, or pirates. By 1990, the United States had accepted nearly 900,000 Vietnamese refugees, about one-third of them boat people who survived their ordeal.

In the early 1990s, Cambodia generated the region's largest refugee flow; as many as 300,000 Cambodians sought to escape their country's seemingly endless cycle of violence by crossing the border into Thailand. Assisted by the United Nations, the Thai government continues to help Cambodia's refugees.

Today, however, the largest refugee numbers in Southeast Asia are reported from Myanmar (Burma); virtually all of them are intranational refugees, victims of the repressive rule of the generals who are seeking to subjugate the country's minorities. As the UNHCR states, the number itself is an estimate; information from Myanmar's closed society is difficult to secure.

From the field notes

"This public war of words seen in Perth, Australia was a reminder that immigration can raise social tensions and produce ugly reactions. Australia was among countries that agreed to accept a limited number of Indochina's "boat people"; subsequently, several boatloads of Chinese would-be migrants arrived at the port of Darwin and appealed for refugee status. Australia's Asian population still is small but growing, and in the country's more politically conservative areas, extremist organizations such as the Australian Nationalist Movement proclaimed their opposition in various ways. I saw posters such as this not only in Perth but also in several smaller towns in Western Australia and in Queensland."

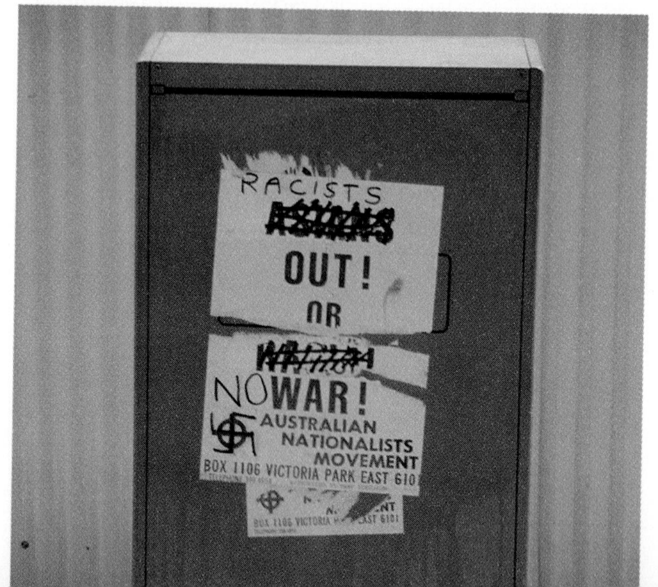

Elsewhere

As Figure 6-4 shows, the number of refugees in other geographic realms is much smaller. In the Western Hemisphere, only Colombia in 1997 had a serious refugee problem, caused by the country's chronic instability associated with its struggle against narcotics. Large areas of Colombia's countryside are vulnerable to armed attack by "narcoterrorists" and paramilitary units; these rural areas are essentially beyond government control, and thousands of villagers have died in the crossfire. Hundreds of thousands more, as the map indicates, have left their homes to seek protection as refugees.

As recently as 1995, the UNHCR reported that North America harbored more than 1 million refugees from Asian and Middle American sources. Today, it states that the number in North America is negligible—primarily because political conflicts in Middle America (El Salvador, Haiti) have been resolved; and Asian refugees have been absorbed into society. The days of the Cuban refugee flow and the Mariel Boatlift are long past; the number of genuine refugees from communist Cuba has slowed to a trickle. All this illustrates how rapidly the international refugee picture can change.

◆ PERSPECTIVE

This chapter has focused on the world's current major refugee problems. The price of a mushrooming global population, political and ethnic strife, and environmental deterioration is human dislocation. While we discussed salient refugee streams, we did not account for many other refugee populations: the de facto partition of Cyprus, which dislocated tens of thousands of Greeks and Turks; the Guatemalans in Mexico; the Vietnamese in Malaysia; the New Guineans under Indonesian rule who have crossed into Papua New Guinea; and hundreds of thousands more. Inevitably, the next decade will experience refugee crises unforeseen today.

Several circumstances point to a further increase in the global numbers of refugees as well. Twenty years ago, when the globe-girdling droughts of the 1970s developed, the Earth's population was nearly 2 billion people less than it is today. An ever larger number of people are at risk. Concurrently, the pace of environmental degradation is increasing as well. And the "New World Order" increasingly seems to be a misnomer for widespread political disorder. Virtually everywhere on the globe, political systems are under stress, incapable of accommodating the pressures of modern times. It is a combination destined to dislocate peoples the world over.

People who abandon their familiar surroundings because conditions there have become unlivable commit an ultimate act of desperation. In the process, the habits of civilization vanish as survival becomes the sole imperative. The Earth's refugee population is a barometer of the world's future.

◆ KEY TERMS ◆

absolute direction
absolute distance
counter migration
distance decay
forced migration
gravity model
international refugees
intervening opportunity
intranational refugees
migration
permanent refugees
pull factors
push factors
refugee
relative direction
relative distance
slave trade
step migration
temporary refugees
voluntary migration

◆ APPLYING GEOGRAPHIC KNOWLEDGE ◆

1. A recent newspaper headline read as follows: POPULATION GROWTH CAUSES MIGRATION. The article beneath this headline described current global population growth trends and suggested that the pressure on people to migrate would not end until population growth had declined. Write a letter to the Editor commenting on this issue from a geographic perspective.

2. The world's refugee population (counting both internal and external refugees) is at an all-time high today. Account for the factors that explain this situation. What conditions and circumstances might cause the number of dislocated people to increase even more? Wherein lies the hope for improvement?

Chapter 7

Routes of Human Mobility

From the field notes

"Human mobility takes many forms, and commuting is one way activity space is defined. But the daily commute in Delhi, India is a bit unlike that in, say London or Chicago. I watched the trains roll in during the early morning rush hour, most without doors or windows, with people literally hanging out of the cars as they passed by. Uncomfortable this may be, especially during the monsoon season, but these commuters share in India's economic growth, and they are willing to accept it. Their activity space is measured in miles; take the train out of Delhi for a half hour, and you reach villages where life is confined to the few hundred yards between room and paddy."

KEY POINTS

◆ **Mobility is among the qualities that define the character of a culture, and American society today is the world's most mobile.**

◆ **A society's mobility is measured as the sum of cyclic, periodic, and migratory movements by its population.**

◆ **The voluntary migration of Europeans to the New World, the forced migration of Africans to the Americas, and the migration of Europeans to their overseas colonial empires are among migration streams that have transformed the world.**

◆ **Internal migrations, involving major population shifts, have occurred in the former Soviet Union, the United States, China, and other large countries.**

◆ **In the United States, the Northeast and the Midwest have been losing population for decades, while the South and West have been gaining.**

◆ **Physical as well as legal barriers are placed in the way of migrants, but few countries have succeeded in controlling immigration effectively.**

Having noted the factors that cause people to move, we now turn to the question of where the major migration routes are located. Every day millions of people are on the move, some across oceans, others from villages to towns. Migration occurs in surges, sometimes overwhelming the authorities who try to control it. At other times the surge may be encouraged. For example, after World War II, when Western Europe experienced an economic boom, Europeans spurned jobs that Turkish and North African immigrants were willing to do. As a result, migrants arrived by the millions. We turn to these major migrations later in the chapter, after considering the many different forms human mobility can take.

The great majority of people have a daily routine that takes them through a regular sequence of short moves. These moves create what geographers call ***activity* (or *action*) *space***. The magnitude of activity space varies in different societies. North Americans' activity space, on average, is very large compared to that of, say, Africans or Southwest Asians. Millions of American commuters travel a greater distance each day than many Chinese village dwellers do in a year. Technology has vastly expanded daily activity spaces, as reflected by the continuous shuttle flights between major cities such as Washington, D.C. and New York City.

◆ TYPES OF MOVEMENT

Migration is not the only form of movement that affects populations and communities. Mobility of all kinds is one of the defining characteristics of a culture.

Consider your own lifestyle. You may go to classes every weekday and perhaps to a job as well. This is a form of ***cyclic movement***, and it defines your activity space. However, you may also have come from another town, perhaps another State, to study at the college or university you now attend. Your arrival for the fall semester and your return trip after the spring is a different form of movement. This ***periodic movement*** involves a lengthy period of residence following your trip. After graduation you may decide to take a job in a foreign country, perhaps as an employee of a business with international connections. That might lead to long-term residence in that country, and your move would be an example of ***migratory movement***.

We have already noted that migration takes many forms. Cyclic and periodic movements also occur in numerous ways. We are creatures of habit, and our habits, from commuting to vacationing, define our activity spaces.

Cyclic Movement

Cyclic movement involves journeys that begin at our home base and bring us back to it. In farming villages around the world, farmers walk or ride to the fields each morning, spend the day working on the land, and return to the village at night. In urbanized societies this *daily* cyclic movement has its equivalent in the daily journey to work, ***commuting***, a trip that sometimes involves hours of travel in automobiles, buses, trains, or subways. People who work in the central business districts of large cities, such as New York and Chicago, are prepared to travel an hour or more each way every working day. Thus, despite the recent suburbanization of economic activity (see Part Seven), these central cities still attract a large portion of the surrounding labor force. For example, thousands of workers travel from New Jersey into and out of New York City every day.

Your trip to classes each day may be shorter, but it is nonetheless a form of cyclic movement. So, too, are shopping trips; if you kept a record of those journeys, you would find yourself returning time and again to the same store or gasoline station. Again, visits to friends and other trips for social purposes are usually made during the same day and with approximately the same frequency during the week or month.

More time-consuming and less frequent are cyclic movements termed ***seasonal movements***. Many of us take our vacations and holidays during the same period each year. We undertake a trip that may cover thousands of miles and extend over several weeks. Every spring, thousands of college students find their way to the beach towns of Florida on the warm Atlantic coast. Every winter, skiers from all over the country try the slopes of Colorado. Many people, of course, cannot afford the luxury of vacation travel. Still the flood of tourists in search of winter warmth or the challenge of ski slopes has the magnitude of a small-scale migration!

Not all seasonal travel is for fun and recreation, however. The herring fleets of Western Europe wait in port until the fish run, and then fan out into the North Sea and adjacent waters to pursue their catches. Again, such fishing trips may take one or more days, but the boats return to the port that is their home base, thus engaging in cyclic movement.

The cyclic movements discussed so far occur on given days (working days) or during given seasons (the Christmas and New Year's holidays, for example). Some cyclic movements, by contrast, are irregular in their timing. A common form of movement in this category is the business trip. People involved in sales and marketing take numerous long-distance trips every year, but not normally according to regular and recurrent schedules. This form of movement is of an intensity that is surely a hallmark of our particular society. Every day tens of thousands of salespersons are in transit by air and automobile, traveling from one prospective buyer to another, before returning to the home base for recordkeeping and restocking.

Quite another form of irregular, yet cyclic, movement is ***nomadism***. Some may envisage nomadic groups of people as wandering aimlessly across steppe or desert, but in fact, most nomadic movement takes place according to travel patterns that are repeated time and again. Often, the climate and its seasonal changes influence the nomads' decisions to break camp and move, and, in that sense, this is to some degree a seasonal form of cyclic movement.

In those arid areas where nomadic peoples trek, year-to-year climatic patterns can vary enormously. Furthermore, nomadic people frequently do have a base to which they return for a period each year. The Maasai of East Africa, for example, establish a village where they remain while the rains permit a sedentary life. They even try to grow some crops nearby. When the rains begin to fail and drought encroaches, everyone packs their belongings on the backs of donkeys, and the cattle and goats are driven in pursuit of the essential ingredient of life: water. Eventually, the group will return to the village and, if the rains permit, will remain at the site for some months. In some years there is hardly any rain, and the stay at the village base is brief.

Periodic Movement

Some forms of movement involve a longer period of residence away from the home base than normal cyclic movements. In the United States alone, over 2 million students are attending colleges and universities, the majority of them away from home. When you leave home to go to college, you are likely to be away for nine months of the year, except perhaps for a few brief vacations. Moreover, whereas you may have gone off to college intending eventually to return to your hometown, that may never happen. The chances are great that you will go on to still another location for graduate school or employment.

Other hundreds of thousands of people are relocated through *military service*. This also is periodic movement—to military bases, training schools, and combat zones. At the height of the Persian Gulf War, the United States had a half-million people in Southwest Asia, a mass movement whose total numbers amounted to more than twice the whole population of Iceland. In a given year in the United States, perhaps as many as 10 million people, including military personnel and their families, are moved to new locations. Many of them become familiar with the area to which they are moved and remain there after their tour of duty has ended.

The movement of *migrant laborers* and their families is also periodic, although it is more cyclic than that of college students or military personnel. The migrant labor force moves from place to place as crops ripen in different areas, creating a temporary demand for labor there. This happens according to recurrent cycles, but the climate in various parts of the country is inconsistent, and sometimes there is less work in certain areas during a particular year. If crops are late in ripening, the migrants may arrive too early and must wait until they are needed. If crops fail or the harvest is poor, there may not be enough demand for labor to put everyone to work. It is a precarious and difficult existence, and as a result poverty is widespread among migrant farm workers. Unlike college graduates and discharged military personnel, migrant laborers do not have the opportunity to choose where they will live. They are trapped in a system of transience.

Another form of periodic movement is ***transhumance***. This term refers to a system of pastoral farming in which livestock and their keepers move in response to the seasonal availability of pastures. In Switzerland, for example, cattle are driven up the mountain slopes to high, fresh pastures during the summer; farm families follow the herds, taking up residence in cottages that are abandoned during the cold winter. In the "Horn" of Northeast Africa, hundreds of thousands of people follow their livestock from highland to lowland and back in search of pastures renewed by seasonal rainfall.

◆ PERMANENT RELOCATION

Migratory movement is the most significant form of movement we will discuss here. It involves permanent relocation, leaving behind the old and making a new beginning. It has numerous causes and many manifestations, so many that, as we have noted, it is often impossible to discern the exact reasons underlying the decision to seek a new home. Obviously, some factors *push* people away from their homes, and other forces *pull* them to new, more promising locations. These forces are difficult to identify and measure. Oppression, discrimination, and the threat of war or natural catastrophe can drive people away; the attraction of better economic opportunities, greater freedom, or increased security can pull them to new homelands. Always, however, some people will move while others stay behind.

Major Modern Migrations

The past five centuries have witnessed human migration on an unprecedented scale, much of it generated by events in Europe. Major modern migration flows are shown in Figure 7-1. They include movements from Europe to North America ①; from Southern Europe to South and Middle America ②; from Britain and Ireland to Africa and Australia ③; from Africa to the Americas during the period of slavery ④; from India to eastern Africa, Southeast Asia, and Caribbean America ⑤; from China to Southeast Asia ⑥; from the eastern United States westward ⑦; and from western Russia eastward ⑧. These last two migrations are internal to the United States and Russia. Our map does not show some other significant internal migrations, for example, the south-to-north movement of black Americans during the twentieth century. We return to these great population shifts later in the chapter.

European Emigration

Among the greatest human migrations in recent centuries was the flow from Europe to the Americas. When we discussed the period of explosive popula-

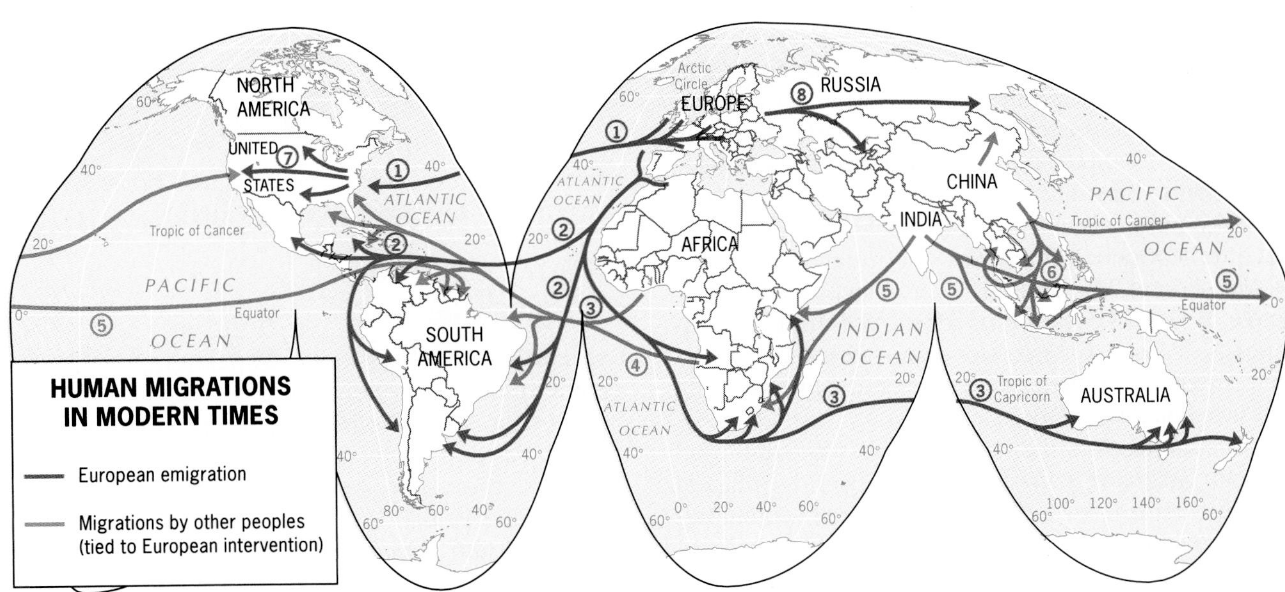

Figure 7-1 Human Migrations in Modern Times. Major routes of migrants.

tion growth in nineteenth-century Europe (Chapter 5), we did not fully account for this process, which kept the total increase far below what it might have been. The great emigration from Europe (① and ② in Fig. 7-1) began slowly. Before the 1830s perhaps 2.75 million Europeans left to settle overseas. After that, however, the rate of emigration increased sharply; between 1835 and 1935 perhaps as many as 75 million departed for the New World and other overseas territories. The British went to North America, Australia, New Zealand, and South Africa. From Spain and Portugal, many hundreds of thousands emigrated to Middle and South America. Early European colonial settlements grew, even in such places as Angola, Kenya, and Java. Although millions of Europeans eventually returned to their homelands, the net outflow from Europe was enormous.

African Forced Migration

This European emigration has had no counterpart in modern world history in terms of size and numbers, but it is not the only major migration flow that has occurred in recent centuries. As we saw in Chapter 6, the Americas were the destination of another mass of immigrants: African slaves. This forced migration began during the sixteenth century, when Africans were first brought to the Caribbean. In the early decades of the seventeenth century, they arrived in small numbers on the plantations that were developing in coastal eastern North America. They were among the very first settlers in this country.

The terror and destruction of slave raiding afflicted large areas of Africa. Most of West Africa was exploited, from Liberia to Nigeria and from the coast to the margins of the Sahara. So many Africans were taken from the area that is now Benin to Bahia in Brazil that significant elements of the local culture remained intact in the transition. Today there are strong ties between Bahia and Benin, and cultural exchanges are growing stronger. The entire Equatorial African coastal region was victimized as well, and Portuguese slave traders raided freely in the Portuguese domains of Angola and Moçambique. Arab slave raiders were active in East Africa and the Horn, penetrating Equatorial Africa and often cooperating with the Europeans. Zanzibar, off the coast of mainland Tanzania, long was a major slave market.

In combination, the forced migrations from these ***African migrant sources*** (④ in Fig. 7-1) inflicted dreadful damage on African societies and communities and changed the cultural and ethnic geography of Brazil, Middle America, and the United States. While it is just one among many migrations, its immense impact on both sides of the Atlantic sets it apart from all the others.

◆ EXTERNAL AND INTERNAL MIGRATIONS

When our ancestors began migrating from Africa to Eurasia, Australia, and the Americas, the only boundaries they crossed were natural ones. Rivers, mountain ranges, and forest margins must have presented barriers, but they did not stop the inexorable march of human migration.

Today's migrants face a very different situation. Political boundaries, not natural barriers, are the most difficult obstacles for people on the move. Agencies that monitor the annual stream of human migration use the world's political framework to keep track of migrants. Collecting information from embassies and consulates (where visas for legal immigrants are issued), border stations, refugee camps, and other formal as well as informal sources, these agencies try to identify migration flows, record the numbers of people involved, and gauge the resulting net population changes. To facilitate this work, they differentiate between migrants who cross international borders (***external migrants***) and those who relocate within their national boundaries (***internal migrants***). In any given year, internal migrants greatly outnumber external migrants. But it is the external migrants who change countries' vital statistics, affect their economies, and often influence their politics.

A complicating factor is the impermanence (and uncertain status) of many external migrants. Turks who are long-term residents of Germany are able to acquire German citizenship; Algerians and other North Africans in France also have been able to gain French citizenship. But the rules of admission *and* naturalization have recently been tightened in response to political pressures in the destination countries. In all countries that have accepted large numbers of foreign worker-immigrants, there are substantial numbers of immigrants with uncertain status. With this in mind, we now examine some major past and present migration streams, internal as well as external.

External Migrations

External migrations took Europeans to America and to other parts of the world; the arrival of the Europeans, in turn, caused other people to move. We have already considered the movement of Africans to the Americas, but other peoples were induced to move as well. The British brought indentured Indian labor to Natal, South Africa, and areas of East Africa. This intercontinental migration (⑤ in Fig. 7-1) greatly changed the ethnic mosaic of eastern Africa. Free Asian entrepreneurs followed the stream of indentured laborers, and eventually much of the local trade

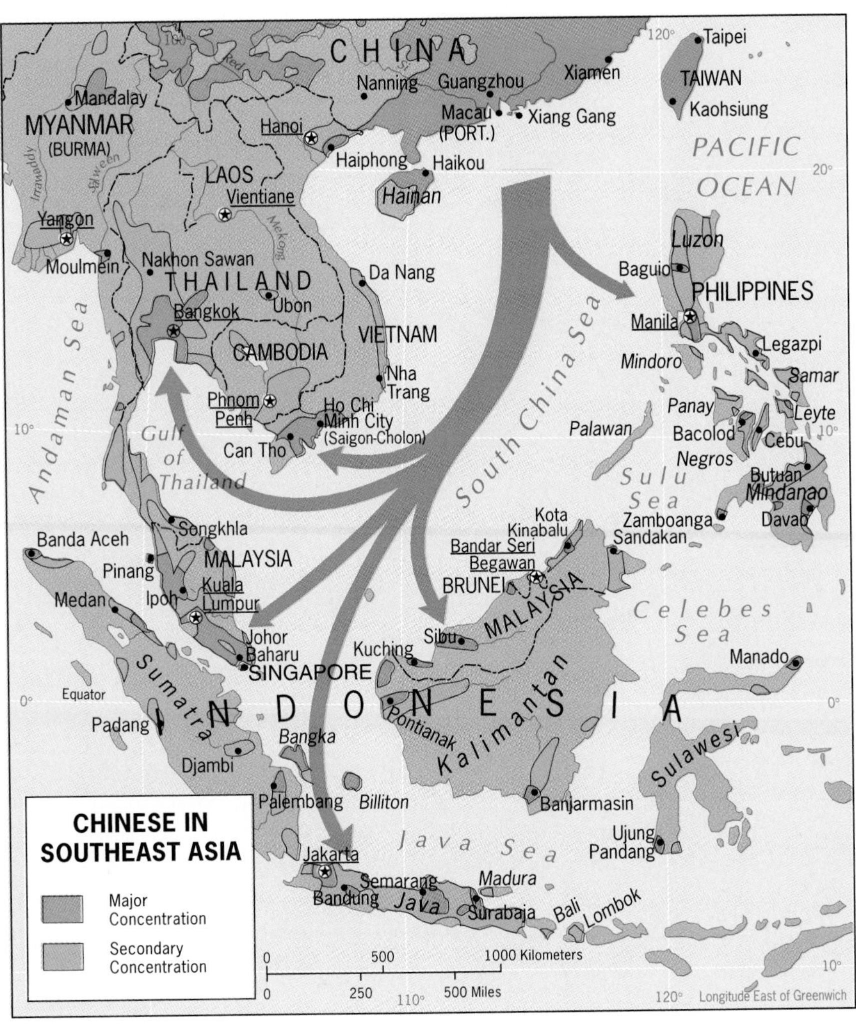

Figure 7-2 Chinese in Southeast Asia. The great majority of Chinese emigrants left from southeast China.

and commerce along the East African coast was in the hands of Asians.

The British were also instrumental in relocating Asians, mainly from India, to such Caribbean countries as Trinidad and Tobago and Guyana (the trans-Pacific stream marked ⑤ in Fig. 7-1). The Dutch brought many Javanese from what is today Indonesia to their former dependency of Suriname along the same route. Meanwhile, the colonial occupation of Southeast Asia presented opportunities for the Chinese to function as middlemen, and many Chinese immigrated to this region (⑥ in Fig. 7-1). Chinese minorities in Southeast Asian countries (Fig. 7-2) account for substantial portions of national populations: 14 percent in Thailand, 32 percent in Malaysia, and no less than 76 percent in Singapore. The Chinese minority in Indonesia accounts for only about 3 percent of the total population, but Indonesia has more than 200 million people, so its Chinese minority is one of Southeast Asia's largest clusters. Several twentieth-century governments in Southeast Asia have discouraged and restricted Chinese immigration. Like the Asians in East Africa, the Chinese minorities in Southeast Asia tend to be urban and to engage in trade, commerce, and finance.

Jewish Migration to Israel A modern external migration, albeit on a smaller scale, is the flow of Jewish immigrants to Israel. This migration has occurred mainly in the twentieth century. At the turn of the century, there were probably fewer than 50,000 Jewish residents in what was then Palestine. From 1919 to 1948 the United Kingdom held a mandate over Palestine, originally under the auspices of the League of Nations, and Britain encouraged the immigration of Jews from Europe. By 1948 there were perhaps 750,000 Jewish residents in Palestine, and the independent state of Israel was established through UN intervention and the partition of the area (Fig. 7-3). This in turn led to another migration stream: the displacement of 600,000 Palestinian Arabs who sought refuge in neighboring Jordan, Egypt, Syria, and elsewhere.

Jewish migrants continued to arrive from Europe,

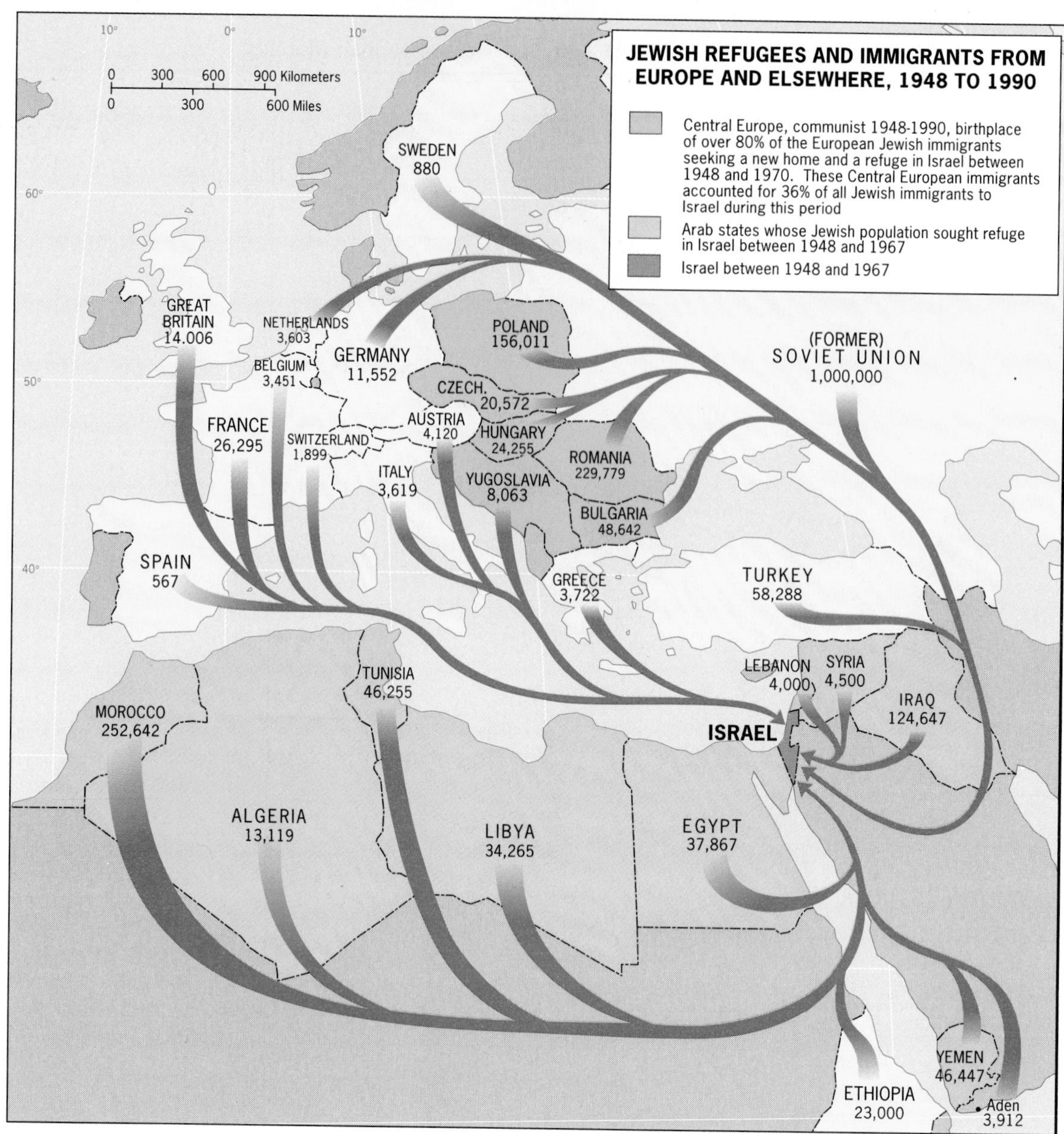

Figure 7-3A Jewish Refugees and Immigrants from Europe and Elsewhere, 1948 to 1990. *Source: From a map in M. Gilbert,* Atlas of the Arab-Israeli Conflict *(New York: Macmillan, 1974), p. 38.*

America, South Africa, and even the former Soviet Union. Since 1989 the number of Russian Jews arriving in Israel has increased sharply as a result of changed emigration policies. Israel's total population is approaching 6 million, and it continues to expand through migration.

Postwar Movements External migrations (authorized movements and organized resettlements, as well as refugee movements) usually occur after wars. One of the major resettlements of the twentieth century occurred after the end of World War II, when as many as 15 million Germans migrated westward from their homes in Eastern Europe, either voluntarily or because they were forced to leave. Before the Berlin Wall went up and the Iron Curtain was lowered, several million Germans fled Soviet-controlled East Germany into what was then West Germany. And millions of migrants left Europe altogether to go to the United States (1.8 million), Canada (1.1 million), Australia (1 million), Israel (750,000), Argentina (750,000), Brazil (500,000), Venezuela (500,000), and other countries. As many as 8 million Europeans emigrated from Europe in this postwar stream.

As often happens, this outmigration stimulated a counter migration. European countries that were rebuilding their economies now found themselves in need of labor. Not only did millions of workers move from one European country to another (notably from Italy, Spain, Greece, and Ireland to the industrial heartland), but also additional millions of foreign workers migrated from North Africa (mainly to France) and Turkey (mostly to Germany).

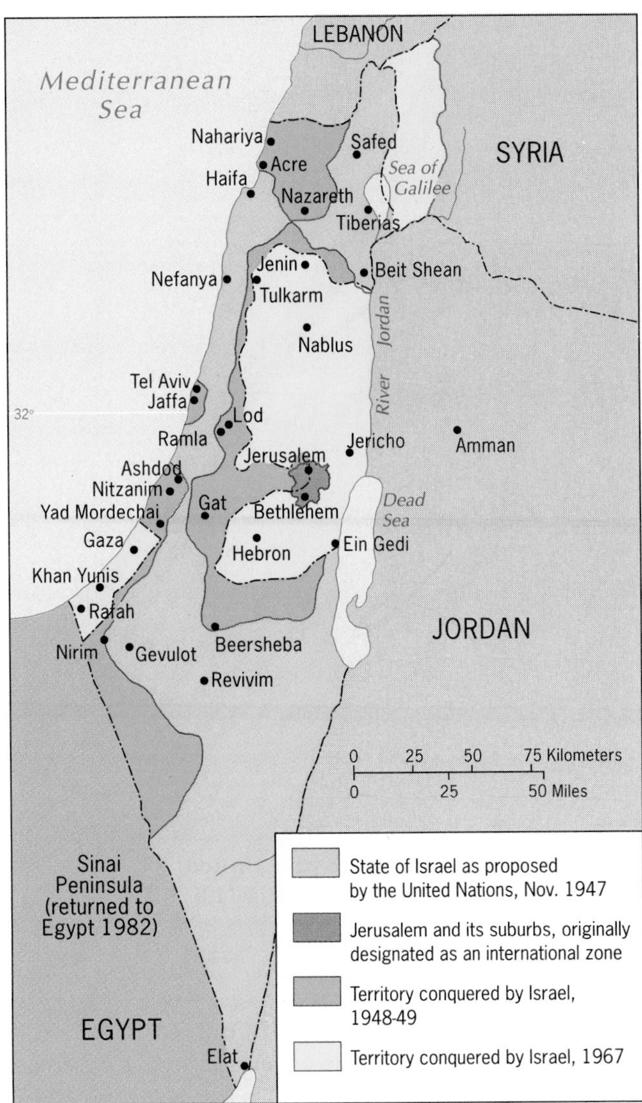

Figure 7-3B Different Israel, Boundaries *Source: From a map in M. Gilbert,* Atlas of the Arab-Israeli Conflict *(New York: Macmillan, 1974), p. 38.*

Effects of European Unification In 1992 European unification created even greater opportunities for intra-European (but still international) migrants in search of work. Among many of the countries of the European Union, circulation is almost as free as it is among States in the United States, and despite recent efforts by European governments to control their movements, foreign workers also have found new doors opened.

Italy provides an example of the impact of migration on the demographic makeup of Europe. Before the formation of the European Union, Italy was the natural stepping stone from North Africa into Europe, but it was not yet easy for North African workers to cross from Italy into France or Germany. As more immigrants arrived, southern Italy, known as the Mezzogiorno region, became North-Africanized. Muslim workers and families arrived, but their further migration was obstructed. As Italy struggled to accommodate the influx, the already-poor Mezzogiorno experienced even higher unemployment, social unrest, and cultural animosity. In the process, Italy's north-south divide, already a major factor in the country's national life, grew even stronger.

In 1992 a significant development occurred in Algeria that may ultimately lead to further emigration from that country to Europe. In elections for the Algerian parliament, a party called the Islamic Salvation Front triumphed on a platform of Islamic Fundamentalism. For three decades Algeria had been a secular state in which religion and state were separate. But as Algeria's economy deteriorated and social conditions worsened, frustration and unrest reigned, and the Islamic Salvation Front seemed to offer an alternative. Its leaders proposed the institution of an "Islamic Republic" similar to those in Iran, Pakistan, and Sudan. But in Algeria the large urbanized and Westernized segment of the population was opposed to such a traditional regime. The situation had the potential to produce further emigration of Algerians to Europe at a time when the immigrant communities already in Europe were facing difficult times both economically and socially.

As the political stalemate wore on, it was punctuated by a murderous campaign of intimidation in which, by early 1998, more than 100,000 Algerians, mostly villagers, had been killed. European Union countries across the Mediterranean from North Africa, facing the potential of a mass emigration from the region, sought to mediate but were rebuffed by the Algerian government. The situation has the potential to generate a major refugee crisis.

Migration to North America Even before Cuba became a socialist state, thousands of Cuban citizens applied for residency in the United States. During the 1960s this migration stream intensified and was formalized as the Cuban Airlift, an authorized movement of persons desiring to escape from a communist government. The great majority of the Cuban immigrants arrived and remained in the greater Miami area. In southern Florida they developed a core of Hispanic culture, and in due course Dade County declared itself bicultural and bilingual (Fig. 7-4).

Throughout the 1960s and 1970s Cubans continued to arrive in the United States as refugees (see Chapter 6) until in 1980 another massive, organized exodus occurred during the Mariel Boatlift, which brought more than 100,000 Cubans to U.S. shores; the migrants qualified for refugee status under U.S. regulations. The Cuban influx persisted throughout the 1980s, so that at the end of the decade, the official number of Cuban arrivals was 488,770.

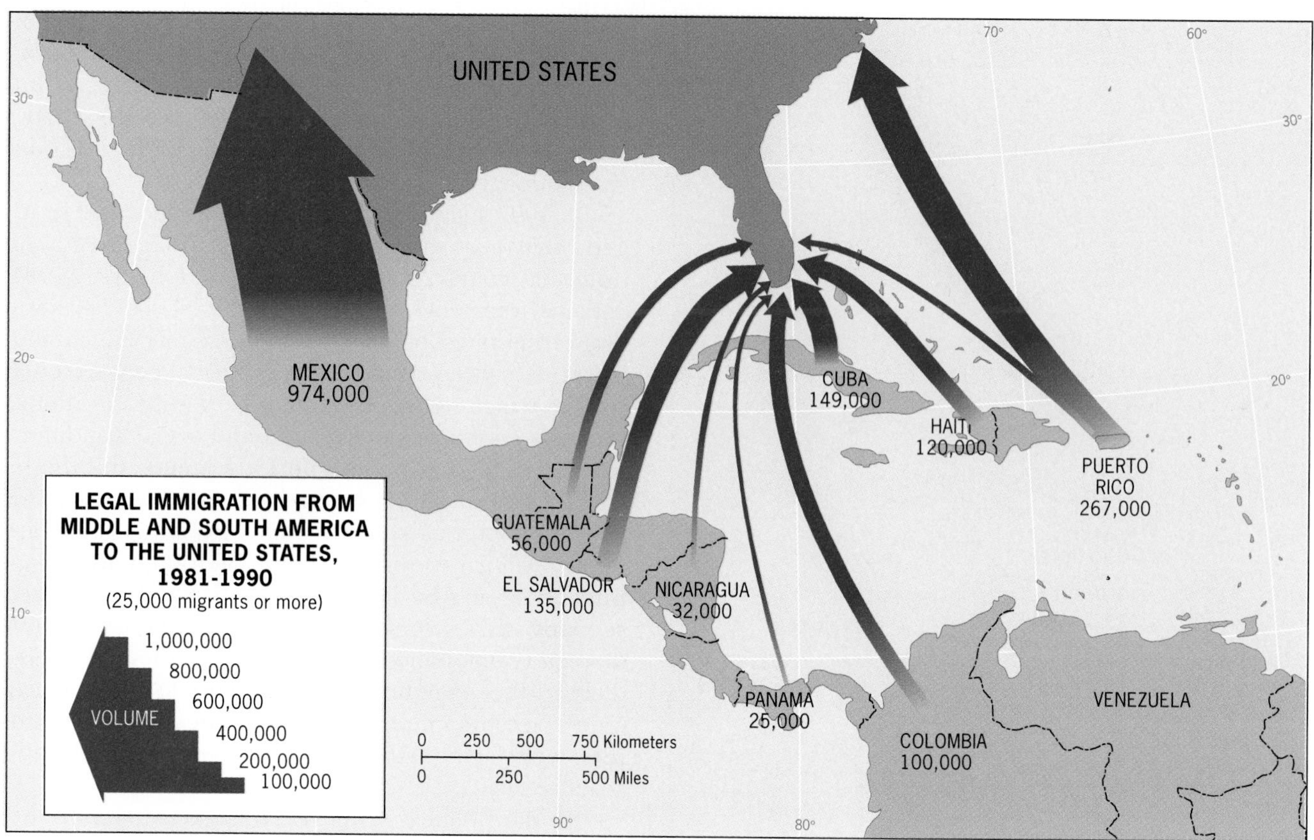

Figure 7-4 Legal Immigration from Middle and South America to the United States, 1981–1990. *Source: Based on data in U.S. Bureau of the Census,* Statistical Abstract of the United States: 1991, *111th ed. (Washington, D.C., 1991), p. 10.*

An even larger immigration stream was reaching the southwestern United States from Mexico (Table 7-1). So much of this movement has been unauthorized that demographers cannot estimate its magnitude even within hundreds of thousands. During the 1990s, legal immigration from Mexico exceeded 1 million; since 1961 it has surpassed 2.5 million. This migration stream has transformed the southwestern borderland of the United States.

As Table 7-1 shows, immigration from Asia during the 1980s exceeded even that from Middle America. Nearly 2.5 million Asians entered the United States legally. The Philippines was the leading source country, followed closely by Vietnam and three East Asian countries. Europe, once the primary U.S. source area, contributed only 9.8 percent of the immigrants (about 0.59 million) in the period from 1960 to 1990.

Internal Migrations

Internal migration involves relocation within a country. Such movements can also produce significant population shifts, even though the migrants do not cross any international borders.

Russia During the last decades of the czarist period in Russia, the Siberian expanses east of the Urals were invaded by growing numbers of peasant farmers seeking new lands and opportunities. Beginning in 1892, this flow was strengthened by the construction of the Trans-Siberian Railroad to Vladivostok. Eventually, World War I and the Russian Revolution stemmed the tide of eastward migration, but after the reorganization of the 1920s, new efforts were made to stimulate the development of Siberia. Natural resources were opened up, industrialization was supported, and various incentives were used to induce people to move eastward to places such as Novosibirsk and Krasnoyarsk.

The German invasion from the west during World War II further strengthened the Soviets' resolve to develop the nation's eastern regions, and more than 2 million people were resettled east of the Ural Mountains. Until the collapse of the Soviet Union, relatively rapid growth in the east continued, spurred by official policy. Also contributing to the population shift was the comparatively fast rate of natural increase in the Muslim republics of Central Asia.

Today long-term trends and developments in the

Table 7-1 Sources of Legal Immigrants into the United States, 1981–1989 (thousands)

Realm		Leading Countries	
Africa	156.4		
Asia	2478.8		
		Philippines	431.5
		Vietnam	352.6
		China and Taiwan	341.8
		South Korea	306.5
Europe	593.2		
		United Kingdom	126.2
		Poland	76.9
Middle America	2065.0		
		Mexico	974.2
		Dominican Republic	209.6
		Jamaica	188.8
		Cuba	148.6
		El Salvador	134.4
		Haiti	119.9
North America	102.4		
		Canada	102.4
South America	370.1		
		Colombia	100.2
		Guyana	84.0
Other realms	35.6		

Source: U.S. Department of Commerce, Bureau of the Census, *Statistical Abstract of the United States, 1991*, 111th ed. (Washington, D.C., 1991), p. 10.

former Soviet Union have been interrupted by the breakdown of order, but the map of the region still bears the mark of one of the great long-term internal migrations anywhere in the world. It is identified as flow ⑧ in Figure 7-1.

China Other major internal migrations have changed the population map of China. When China's communist planners embarked on their industrialization program, China's Northeast (formerly called Manchuria) became a principal focus because of its raw materials and existing infrastructure. (The Japanese had previously held Manchuria as a colony.) Huge state industrial complexes were built, and workers were encouraged to move to the new heartland. Millions did so and the Northeast grew rapidly, a product of officially sanctioned migration.

Today, China is pursuing new economic policies and the Northeast has become something of a rustbelt, its inefficient state enterprises running far below capacity. China's new economic focus lies on its eastern and southern Pacific coast, and large numbers of workers are moving to this part of the country. When the authorities in Shanghai announced the establishment of a new development area, the Pudong District, as many as 3 million job-seekers descended on the city. The migration of workers to the more southerly growth zones has been larger still. In China, with its huge population numbers, economic reorientation leads to massive human movements.

Migration Destinations in the United States We noted earlier that Americans are the world's most mobile people. The effects of two historic internal migrations are etched on the U.S. population map: the westward movement of the population as a whole, and the northward migration of black Americans from the rural South to the urban North.

The West is still a major migration destination, as can be seen from the continual westward shift of the U.S. population's center of gravity (Fig. 7-5). Note that this map also reflects the southward movement of recent decades; after 1960 the center of the U.S. population moved not only westward but also southward.

The northward migration of African Americans from the South was a small stream until World War I, when the inmigrations from Europe were cut off. In-

Figure 7-5 Changing Center of Population. *Source: From U.S. Bureau of the Census,* Statistical Abstract, 1991, *p. 8.*

A SENSE OF SCALE

Factors Influencing Migration

Economic conditions, political circumstances, and environmental factors help explain why people throughout the world move to other parts of the world. Yet it is important to remember that migration occurs on a variety of scales. People not only move from one continent or country to another; they also move between regions within countries, and even between neighborhoods in a city. Many of the factors influencing migration on the global scale help explain local movements of people, but the circumstances of individual places can profoundly influence where and why those movements occur.

Compare, for example, patterns of mobility within the United States with those in Peru. The fact that the United States is a relatively prosperous country with a diverse, flexible economy means that patterns of mobility are quite complex. The past few decades have seen substantial numbers of people move to economically dynamic regions such as the Sunbelt and the Far West, the movement of people from both large cities and rural areas to medium-sized cities, and the colonization of environmentally attractive rural areas by individuals ranging from the wealthy to those seeking alternative lifestyles. Moreover, interregional migration in the United States is influenced by a variety of social and demographic factors, including age, marital status, and cohort size (the size of a group of a similar age level). Thus geographers have found that in recent decades there has been an inverse relationship between cohort size and mobility; when large numbers of "baby boomers" reached their early 20s in the mid-1970s, mobility among young adults decreased. This is presumably because the large young adult cohort faced stiffer competition for jobs—and was aware of that fact.

Internal migration in Peru is also influenced by economic factors, but the resultant pattern is much simpler. For decades a single migration stream has dominated: that between rural, small-town Peru and the burgeoning metropolis of Lima. As a country where external pressures have exposed small-scale enterprises to intense competition and where investment capital is concentrated in the dominant capital city, Lima represents the only major focus of economic opportunity for a rural population with diminishing economic prospects. As such, not only is Lima the recipient of the vast majority of Peru's migrants, but also the migration stream to the Peruvian capital is less sensitive to matters of age, marital status, or cohort size. So when considering influences on migration, it is important to recognize that general economic, political, and social forces must be seen in the context of the spaces and places that define migration patterns.

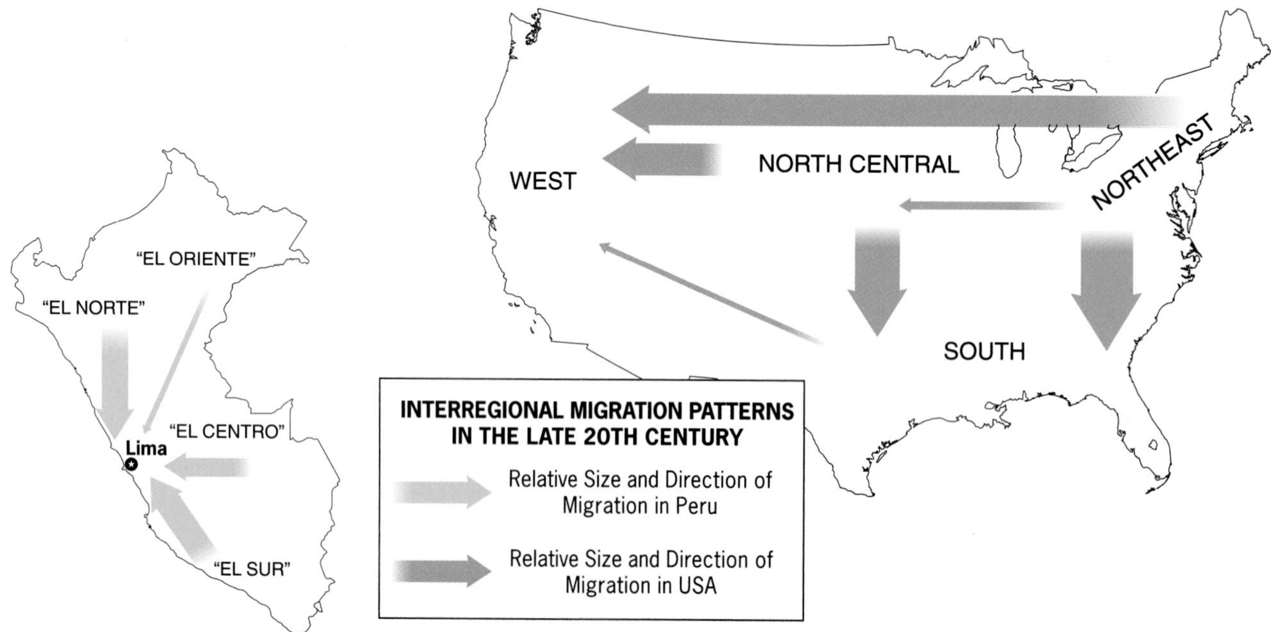

Dominant migration patterns in Peru and the United States. *Source: Schematic Peru map based in part on data from: D. Collier,* Squatters and Oliogarchs *(Baltimore, Md.: Johns Hopkins University Press, 1976 and schematic U.S. map based on data from: W.A.V. Clark,* Human Migration *(Beverly Hills, CA: Sage, 1985).*

dustries continued to expand and the labor market grew rapidly, requiring more employees. Now a campaign began to recruit black workers from the South, and blacks responded by the hundreds of thousands. Most moved to the cities of the Northeast and Midwest. The flow continued after the end of the war and, indeed, accelerated during the 1920s after newly legislated quotas sharply curtailed European immigration. After a decline during the depression years of the 1930s, it resumed its upward climb. At the turn of the century, only 10 percent of the black population lived outside the South; in 1990, the proportion was about 50 percent. This means that the black population of the United States became urbanized even more rapidly than the white population did, for the vast majority of those who went to the industrial North came from rural areas in the South.

Today about 80 percent of African Americans living in rural areas remain in the South; of those in the North, over 90 percent reside in metropolitan areas. This helps explain the apparent Southern concentration of the African-American population shown in Figure 7-6: the southeastern core area is extensive but largely rural. The urban concentrations of the North show less spatial extent but represent much larger numbers of people.

During the 1970s the long-term pattern of African-American migration from the South to northern and western cities changed in a surprising way: more African Americans were leaving the North and returning to the South than were leaving the South for northern destinations. This reversal of a trend that had continued for many decades appeared to have several causes. Undoubtedly, it resulted in part from changed civil rights conditions in the South. Disillusionment with living conditions in the urban North and West was another factor. Perceived economic opportunities in the growing cities of the South played a role as well. One effect of this new situation could be observed in the growth statistics of southern cities. Black residents of northern cities migrate to southern cities, not to rural areas. Thus, the rural black Southerner became urbanized in the North and then relocated to a southern city. On the map, this adds up to a rural-to-urban flow in the South, which is now experiencing one of its most dramatic periods of growth.

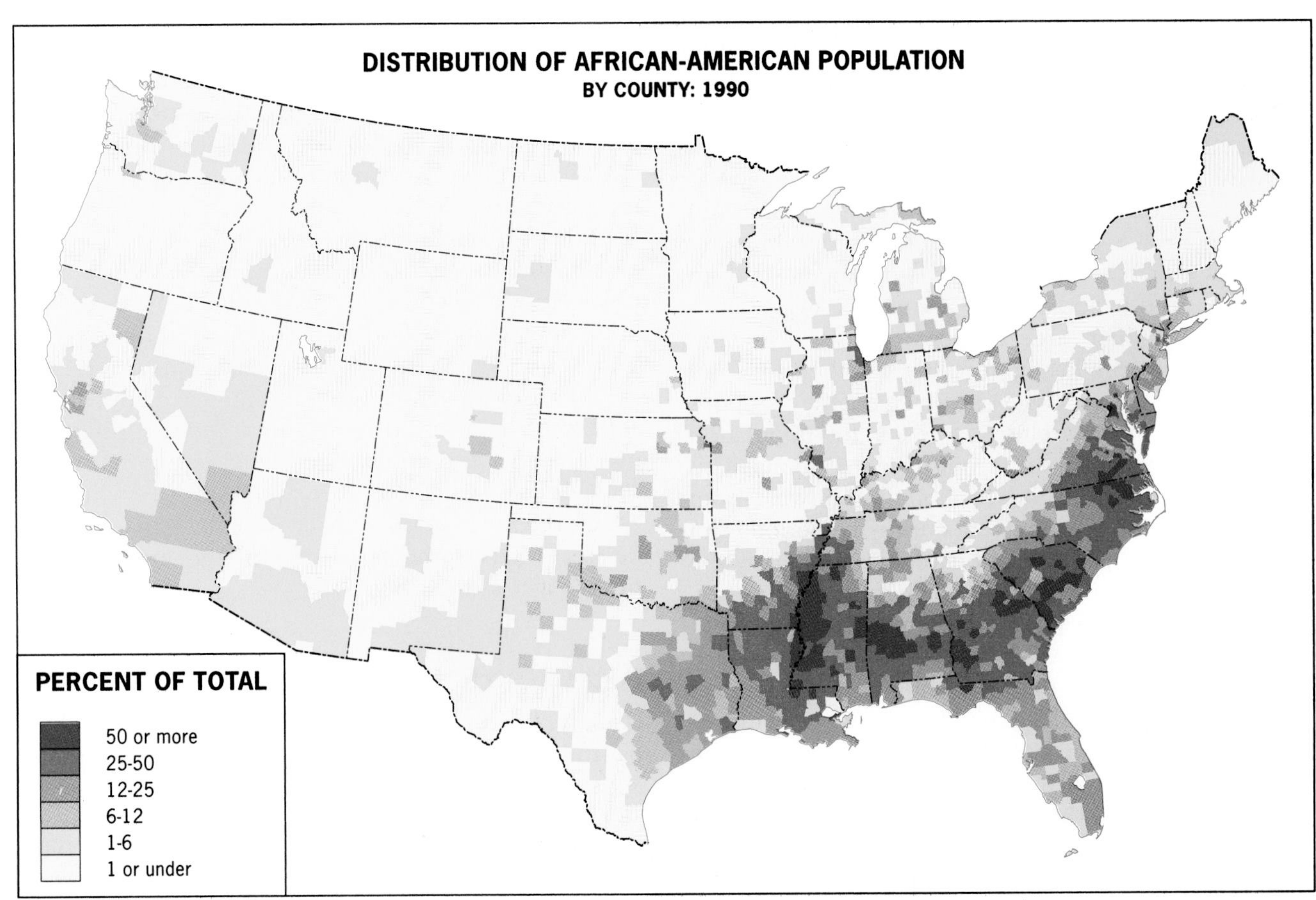

Figure 7-6 Distribution of African-American Population. African-Americans, by count, 1990. *Source: U.S. Department of Commerce, Economics and Statistics Administration, Bureau of the Census.*

Table 7-2 U.S. Population Percentage by Region, 1960–1990

Region	1960	1970	1980	1990
Northeast	24.9	24.1	21.7	20.4
Midwest	28.8	27.8	26.0	24.0
South	30.7	30.9	33.3	34.4
West	15.6	17.1	19.1	21.2

Source: U.S. Department of Commerce, Bureau of the Census, *Statistical Abstract of the United States: 1991*, 111th ed. (Washington, D.C., 1991), p. 19.

Regional Migration in the United States A migration stream is never a one-way flow of migrants. It is the *net* movement of people: the flow from source to destination minus the return flow from destination to source. Even some Jewish migrants who left Russia for Israel in the late 1980s and early 1990s decided to return because they were unable to settle down in the land of their original destination. This return flow reduced the net movement of people from Russia to Israel.

Internal population movements in the United States also involve multiple streams. The U.S. Bureau of the Census divides the United States into four regions: the Northeast (including New York, Pennsylvania, New Jersey, and the New England states); the Midwest (from Ohio westward to the Dakotas, Nebraska, and Kansas); the South (from Maryland and Delaware to Texas, and including West Virginia and Kentucky); and the West (from the mountain states to California, and including Hawaii and Alaska).

For more than three decades the Northeast and Midwest have been losing population to the South and West. Table 7-2 reports the percentage of the U.S. population living in each region. Note that the population of the Northeast declined from nearly 25 percent to just over 20 percent and that of the Midwest from nearly 30 percent to 24 percent during the period from 1960 to 1990. The population of the South, on the other hand, rose from under 31 percent to over 34 percent, and that of the West rose from under 16 percent to over 21 percent.

When we look at the actual numbers of migrants, however, we can see that these are not one-way movements. Take the year 1987 to 1988, for example (the latest year for which detailed data were available at the time of writing). In that year, some 679,000 people left the Northeast, and about 444,000 of them moved to the South. But 448,000 people moved *into* the Northeast, so the outmigration for that year amounted to only 231,000—the *net* difference between emigration and immigration. For the Midwest, this net difference was even less: 829,000 emigrants but 741,000 immigrants, for a loss of just 88,000. Again, the South and West may be gaining population, but not everyone who moves there stays there. In 1987–1988, 1.36 million people entered the South, but 946,000 moved away. And in that year the West actually had a slight loss of population after many years of continuous gains.

Over the long term, the southward and westward shift in the U.S. population has continued, with the southward component becoming stronger. Add to this the arrival of external immigrants, the majority of whom arrive on southern and western shores or cross southern land borders, and we can see that a new population map of the United States is in the making.

◆ CONTROLLING MIGRATION

Migration control and its attendant problems have become hot issues around the world. In Europe, right-wing political parties whip up anti-immigrant sentiment. In California, the state government demands federal help to provide services for hundreds of thousands of illegal immigrants; if the federal government cannot control its borders, the argument goes, the states should not have to foot the bill. In Cuba, the Castro regime has used migration as a threat: in August 1994 Castro threatened to open Cuba's doors to a flood of emigrants that "will make the Mariel Boatlift look like child's play." And in the United States the government faced reproach for preventing tens of thousands of Haitians from entering Florida.

Efforts to restrict migrations are nothing new, however. Media coverage, democratic debate, and political wrangling only make it seem so. China's Great Wall was built in part as a defensive measure but also as a barrier to emigration (by Chinese beyond the sphere of their authorities) and immigration (mainly by Mongol "barbarians" from the northern plains). The Berlin Wall, the Korean DMZ (demilitarized zone), the fences along the Rio Grande—all evince the desire of governments to control the movement of people across their borders.

Legal Restrictions

Usually, however, the obstacles placed in the way of potential immigrants are legal, not physical. Restrictive legislation made its appearance in the United States in 1882, when Congress approved the Oriental Exclusion Acts (1882 to 1907). These ***immigration laws*** were designed to restrict the immigration of Chinese people to California. In 1901 Australia's government approved the Immigration Restriction Act, which terminated all nonwhite immigration into the newly united Commonwealth. This act, too, was aimed primarily at Japanese and Chinese immigrants (but it included South Asians as well). It also had the effect of prohibiting immigration by South Pacific islanders who had entered Australia to work on the large sugar plantations. These workers, the Kanakas, were the target of a provision that facilitated their deportation by the end of 1906. The White Australia Policy was one of the issues on which the Australian colonies were united prior to the establishment of the Commonwealth, and it remained in effect until it was modified in 1972 and again in 1979.

In the United States, restrictive legislation affecting European immigrants was passed in 1921. The balance of European immigrants had been shifting from Western Europe to Southern and Eastern Europe, and many immigrants had no training or resources—at a time when industry's need for skilled labor was declining. The 1921 legislation was a quota law. Each year each European country could permit the emigration to the United States of 3 percent of the number of its nationals living in America in 1910. This had the effect of limiting annual immigration to about 357,000 Europeans, most of them from Western Europe. In 1924 the Immigration Act lowered the quota to 2 percent and made 1890 the base year; this further reduced the annual total to 150,000 immigrants.

The National Origins Law took effect in 1929. It sustained the limit of 150,000 immigrants per year, but it also tied immigration quotas to the national origins of the U.S. population in 1920. This law had the effect of preventing the immigration of Asians. Immigration slowed to a trickle during the 1930s, and in some years emigration actually exceeded immigration.

After 1940 the restrictions on immigration to the United States were modified. In 1943 China was given equal status with European countries, and in 1952 Japan received similar status. A new Immigration and Nationality Act (1952) was designed to incorporate all preceding legislation, establishing quotas for all countries and limiting total immigration to under 160,000. However, far more immigrants entered the country as displaced persons (refugees), thereby filling quotas for years ahead. Estimates vary, but more than 7 million immigrants may have entered the United States as refugees between 1945 (the end of World War II in Europe) and 1970. The 1952 law was acknowledged to be a failure, and in 1965 the quota system was abolished. New limits were set: 170,000 immigrants per year from countries outside the Western Hemisphere and 120,000 from countries in the Americas. Nevertheless, in the 1970s and 1980s the numbers of Cuban, Haitian, and Mexican arrivals far exceeded these limitations.

The United States and Australia are not the only countries that have restricted immigration. Many countries practice selective immigration, in which individuals with certain backgrounds (criminal records, poor health, subversive activities) are barred from entering. Other countries have specific requirements. For example, South Africa long demanded "pure" European descent; New Zealand favored persons of British birth and parentage; Brazil preferred people with a farming background; and Singapore courts financially secure persons of Chinese ancestry. Today South American countries place limits on the number of immigrants who may cross their borders, and quota systems are being instituted. Thailand has restricted Chinese immigration, and Myanmar (Burma) limits immigration from neighboring India. In France, problems associ-

From the field notes

"When I first saw China's Great Wall, I felt that this was more than a wall: it was a giant building, complete with towers and roadways. It had taken us nearly three hours from central Beijing to get here (today a four-lane highway cuts that time to less than one hour), and along the way you can see collapsed sections of the various walls China's early rulers built. During Mao Zedong's regime, parts of the Great Wall were torn down to provide building materials for collectives, but the current government is restoring it. As a result the wall, built to keep Chinese farmers in and Mongol horsemen out, now generates its own population movement; an endless stream of tourists who throng the section nearest the capital. The Great Wall stretches from the Yellow Sea to Xinjiang, up mountain slopes and across plains, perhaps humanity's greatest effort ever to control population movement."

ated with the large and growing Arab population from North Africa have resulted in calls for repatriation of those without residency permits and for restrictions on further immigration from the former French North African dependencies (Algeria, Morocco, and Tunisia).

As the world's population mushrooms, the volume of migrants will likewise expand. In an increasingly open and interconnected world, neither physical barriers nor politically motivated legislation will stem tides that are as old as human history.

◆ KEY TERMS ◆

activity space
African migrant sources
commuting
cyclic movement
external migrant
immigration laws
internal migrant
migration control
migratory movement
nomadism
periodic movement
seasonal movement
transhumance

◆ APPLYING GEOGRAPHIC KNOWLEDGE ◆

1. Migrations tend to leave their marks on the landscape. Take a map of the upper Midwest and see if you can discern, from the place names, the transatlantic links of certain communities. (The most detailed maps for this purpose are those found in the *National Geographic* Atlas.) Next, look at the map of Spain. Do any of the place names you encounter suggest an earlier immigration by a non-Iberian culture?

2. What factors are promoting illegal immigration into the United States? What geographical factors influence where the illegal immigrants end up, and why? In what ways are illegal immigrants altering the landscapes of the places they reside? Give concrete examples.

Part Two
POPULATION PATTERNS AND PROCESSES

Who should inhibit population growth? Should lowering the world's poopulation growth rate be a global objective? Any attempt to address the hard questions about population growth must begin with the fundamental geographical concept of scale. Continued rapid global population growth presents troubling problems for the twenty-first century, but look regionally instead of globally and it is clear that numbers aren't the only issue. As we confront the population issue, different regions face different challenges. No place, however, can afford to exempt itself from those challenges, for in the mix of expanding numbers, consumption, economic development, technology, and women's rights lies the future of the Earth's environments and the people who inhabit them.

◆ SELECTED REFERENCES ◆

Part Two: Population Patterns and Processes

Alonso, W., & Starr, P., eds. *The Politics of Numbers* (New York: Russell Sage, 1987).

Bennett, D. G. *World Population Problems* (Delray Beach, Fla.: Park Press, 1984).

Berardi, G. M., ed. *World Food, Population and Development* (Totowa, N.J.: Rowman & Allanheld, 1985).

Boserup, E. *Population and Technological Change* (Chicago: University of Chicago Press, 1981).

Brown, L., & Wolf, E. *Soil Erosion: Quiet Crisis in the World Economy* (Washington, D.C., Paper No. 60, 1984).

Boswell, T., & Curtis, J. *The Cuban-American Experience: Culture, Images, and Perspective* (Totowa, N.J.: Rowman & Allanheld, 1984).

Brown, L. R., et al. *State of the World* (New York: W. W. Norton, Annual).

Clark, W. A. V. *Human Migration* (Beverly Hills, Calif.: Sage, 1986).

Clark, W. A. V. "Comparing Cross-sectional and Longitudinal Analyses of Residential Mobility and Migration," *Environment and Planning A* (1992), 1291–1302.

Clarke, G. *Interregional Migration: National Policy and Social Justice* (Totowa, N.J.: Rowman & Allanheld, 1983).

Curtin, P. D. *Death by Migration: Europe's Encounter with the Tropical World in the Nineteenth Century* (New York: Cambridge University Press, 1989).

Ehrlich, P., & Ehrlich, A. *The Population Explosion* (New York: Simon & Schuster, 1990).

Ehrlich, P., & Ehrlich, A. *Healing the Planet: Strategies for Resolving the Environmental Crisis* (Reading, Mass.: Addison-Wesley Publishing Co., 1991).

Goldscheider, C., ed. *Population, Ethnicity, and Nation-Building* (Boulder, Colo.: Westview Press, 1995).

Gould, W. T. S., & Findlay, A. M., eds. *Population Migration and the Changing World Order* (New York, N.Y.: John Wiley, 1994).

Grossman, J. R. *Land of Hope: Black Southerners and the Great Migration* (Chicago: University of Chicago Press, 1989).

Gugler, J., ed. *The Urbanization of the Third World* (New York: Oxford University Press, 1988).

Heer, D. M., & Grigsby, J. S. *Society and Population* (Englewood Cliffs, N.J.: Prentice-Hall, 2nd ed., 1992).

Hornby, W., & Jones, M. *An Introduction to Population Geography* (New York: Cambridge University Press, 2nd ed., 1993).

Jones, R., ed. *Patterns of Undocumented Migration in Mexico and the United States* (Totowa, N.J.: Rowman & Allanheld, 1984).

Kane, H. *The Hour of Departure: The Forces That Create Refugees and Migrants* (Washington, D.C.: Worldwatch Institute, 1995).

Kleinman, D. *Human Adaptation and Population Growth: A Non-Malthusian Perspective* (Totowa, N.J.: Rowman & Allanheld, 1980).

Lewis, G. *Human Migration: A Geographical Perspective* (New York: St. Martin's Press, 1982).

Ley, D. *A Social Geography of the City* (New York: Harper & Row, 1983).

Malthus, T. R. *An Essay on the Principles of Population.* Edited by A. Appelman (New York: W.W. Norton, 1976).

McHugh, K. E. "Hispanic Migration and Population Redistribution in the United States," *The Professional Geographer*, 41, 1989, pp. 429–439.

Mortimore, M. *Adapting to Drought: Farmers, Famines, and Desertification in West Africa* (Cambridge, U.K.: Cambridge University Press, 1989).

Newman, J., & Matzke, G. *Population: Patterns, Dynamics, and Prospects* (Englewood Cliffs, N.J.: Prentice-Hall, 1984).

Ogden, P. E. *Migration and Geographical Change* (Cambridge, U.K.: Cambridge University Press, 1984).

Plane, D. A. "Demographic Influences on Migration," *Regional Studies* 27 (1993), 375–383.

Plane, D. A., & Rogerson, P. A. "Tracking the Baby Boom, the Baby Bust, and the Echo Generations: How Age Composition Regulates US Migration,"*Professional Geographer* 43, no. 4 (1991), 416–430.

Population Reference Bureau. *1997 World Population Data Sheet* (Washington, D.C., 1997).

Preston, S. H., ed. *World Population: Approaching the Year 2000.* Special edition of the *Annals of the American Acadamy of Political and Social Science*, July 1990, Vol. 510.

Roberts, G. *Population Policy: Contemporary Issues* (New York: Praeger, 1990).

Rogge, J. *Too Many Too Long: Sudan's Twenty-Year Refugee Dilemma* (Totowa, N.J.: Rowman & Allanheld, 1985).

Roseman, C. "Cities in Flux: Migration, Mobility, and Political Change," in Christian, C., & Harper, R. eds., *Modern Metropolitan Systems* (Columbus, Ohio: Charles E. Merrill, 1982), pp. 277–298.

Simon, R., & Brettell, C., eds. *International Migration. The Female Experience* (Totowa, N.J.: Rowman & Allanheld, 1986).

Swann, M. M. *Migrants in the Mexican North: Mobility, Economy, and Society in a Colonial World* (Boulder, Colo.: Westview Press, 1989).

Teitelbaum, M. S., & Winter, J. M., eds. *Population and Resources in Western Intellectual Traditions* (Cambridge, U.K.: Cambridge University Press, 1989).

White, P., & Woods, R., eds. *The Geographical Impact of Migration* (London: Longman, 1980).

Wood, W. B. "Forced Migration: Local Conflicts and International Dilemmas." *Annals of the Association of American Geographers*, 84, no. 4 (1994), 607–635.

Woods, R. *Theoretical Population Geography* (London and New York: Longman, 1982).

World Bank. *World Development Report 1990: Poverty* (New York: Oxford University Press, 1990).

World Bank. *World Development Report 1994* (New York: Oxford University Press, 1994).

Zegeye, A., & Ishemo, S., eds. *Forced Labor Migration: Movement Within Africa* (London: Hans Zell Publishers, 1989).

Part Three

THE GLOBAL LINGUISTIC MOSAIC

Language is one of the cornerstones of national identity, of cultural unity, of community cohesion. Old languages with historic roots, and languages spoken by threatened minorities, are nurtured and fostered by their speakers. But language also can be a weapon in cultural conflict and in political strife. In the United States, the growth of the Spanish-speaking population has led to demands for the use of Spanish in public affairs; this movement, in turn, spawned national countermovements called "English Only" and "English First." In Quebec, a campaign for political independence from Canada was accompanied by the official demotion of English in favor of Quebec's distinctive version of French. Language is a powerful component of local nationalisms in many areas. It is English, however, that has become the world's most frequently used language of cross-cultural communication, science, and business. The issue now is: *What role should English play in the increasingly internationalized world of the twenty-first century?*

English, global lingua franca? Dubai, Arabian Peninsula.

Part Outline

Chapter 8

A Geography of Language

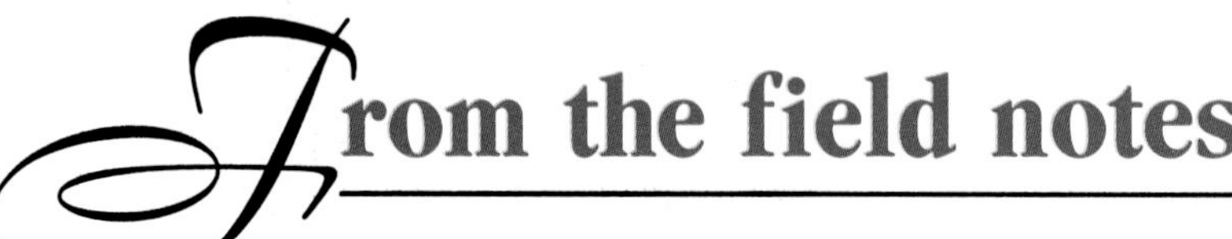

From the field notes

"Efforts to maintain and nurture indigenous and precolonial languages continue to multiply and can often be seen in the cultural landscape. Here in Ireland, official signs give the names of towns and other geographic features in Gaelic as well as English. I started to take notes, and soon I had a list not only of Gaelic equivalents of English place names, but also of geographic features such as, on this sign on the outskirts of Kilkenney, 'city center'."

KEY POINTS

- **Language is the essence of culture, and no culture exists without it. When a people's language is threatened, the response often is passionate and protective.**
- **Mature and complex cultures attempt to maintain a standard language sustained by national institutions and official state examinations. In the modern world, where innovations diffuse rapidly, such standards are difficult to uphold.**
- **More people speak languages belonging to the Indo-European language family than languages in any other family. Indo-European languages are also more widely distributed than any others.**
- **Chinese is spoken by more people than any other language, but English has become the principal language of cross-cultural communication, economics, and science.**
- **The present distribution of languages, as revealed on maps, is useful in understanding cultural development and change.**

People tend to feel passionately about their language, especially when they sense that it is threatened. Language is at the heart of culture, and culture is the glue of society; without language, culture could not be transmitted from one generation to the next.

Such passion is not the exclusive preserve of small groups whose languages are threatened by extinction (of which there are many). It is also exhibited by cultures whose languages are spoken by the tens, even hundreds of millions. Many French citizens, for example, are fiercely, even aggressively protective of their language. A former French president, Georges Pompidou, once stated that "It is through our language that we exist in the world other than as just another country."

About 25 years ago these words were given the force of law: in 1975 the French government banned the use of foreign words in advertisements, television and radio broadcasts, and official documents unless no French equivalent could be found. In 1992, France amended its constitution to make French the official language of the Republic. And in 1994 still another law was passed to stop the use of foreign (mainly English) words in France, with a hefty fine for violators. The French, said the government, would have to get used to saying something other than *le meeting*, *le corner*, *le drugstore*, and *le hamburger*.

Such legislation is unlikely to stop the "pollution" of French. In our modern, interconnected world, where innovations diffuse rapidly, words will be borrowed and languages will change. But French is in no danger of disappearing. Communities that perceive a real threat to their culture's survival will protect it even more forcefully.

Preliterate societies (peoples who speak their language but do not write it) are at a disadvantage. Although they can transmit their culture from one generation to the next, they do not have a written literature that can serve as a foundation for cultural preservation. Like endangered species, there are languages that are on the verge of extinction, and others are threatened. The language mosaic of the world is constantly changing.

Linguists estimate that between 5000 and 6000 languages are in use in the world today, some spoken by many millions of people, others by a few hundred. As we note in Chapter 9, there are many unanswered questions about the origins and diffusion of all these languages; but clearly the same migrations that led to spatial isolation among early human communities also led to linguistic differences. Modern research is reconstructing the paths of ***linguistic diversification*** and throwing new light on ancient migrations.

◆ DEFINING LANGUAGE

The term ***language*** has been defined in numerous ways. Webster's Dictionary defines it as "a systematic means of communicating ideas or feelings by the use of conventionalized signs, gestures, marks, or especially articulate vocal sounds." Communication of sound (***vocalization***) is the crucial part of this definition. Such communication is *symbolic*; that is, in each language the meanings of sounds and combination of sounds must be learned.

The definition is correct in stating that other means of communication also constitute "language." Nonhuman primates such as chimpanzees can also communicate through symbolic calls, such as combinations of gestures and sounds that alert the group to the presence of a predator or the availability of food. Elephants and dolphins, too, use sounds to communicate. But only humans have developed complex vocal communication systems that change over time and space. How these systems first emerged remains an unanswered question. We do know that the vocal systems of nonhuman primates are so basic and static that they are unlikely to have been forerunners of human language.

This means that human languages, even those spoken in preliterate societies, are fundamentally different from those of nonhuman primates. The Khoisan-speaking peoples of southwestern Africa may not have a word for *helicopter*, but they have the symbols that they can use to describe this piece of unfamiliar technology. The potential vocabulary of any language is infinite, whether it is spoken by large-scale industrialized societies or by nonindustrial peoples like the San or the Yanomami of the Amazonian rainforest. The languages of such peoples are *not* primitive or intermediate.

Languages are not static but change continuously. A vital culture requires a flexible language. If you read a few pages from one of Shakespeare's plays, you will realize how much English has changed over several centuries. Today we can see changes in American English; the computer revolution, for example, has greatly expanded the vocabulary of commonly used words.

In this chapter we examine the geographic aspects of the world's language mosaic. This will prepare us for an introduction to the fascinating study of language origins and diffusion, the subject of Chapter 9. In Chapter 10 we will look at some topics of special interest, including the language of place names.

Standard Language

In technologically advanced societies, there is likely to be a ***standard language***, whose quality is a matter of cultural identity and national concern. The standard language may be sustained by official state examinations for teachers, civil servants, and others. The phrase "the King's English" is a popular reference to the fact that the English spoken by well-educated people in London and its environs is regarded as *British Received Pronunciation* (BRP) English—that is, the standard.

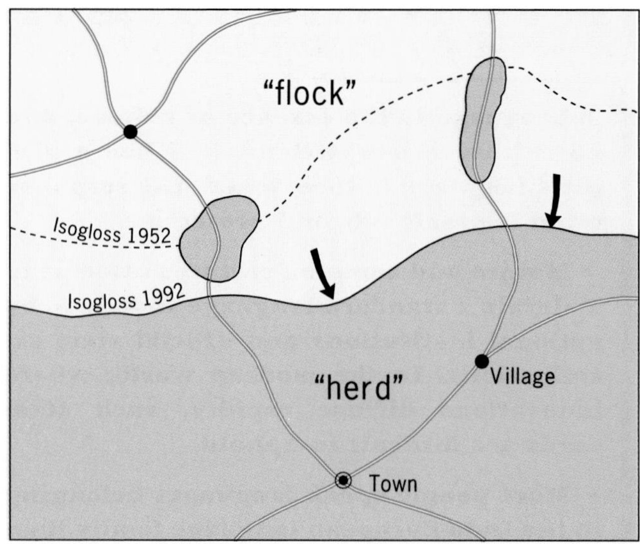

Figure 8-1 Isoglosses. Isoglosses move over time. In this hypothetical case, the use of "herd" has receded in favor of "flock," but some outliers of "herd" remain.

Who decides what the standard language will be? Not surprisingly, the answer has to do with influence and power. In France, the French spoken in and around Paris was made the official, standard language during the sixteenth century. In China, standard Chinese is the Northern Mandarin Chinese heard in and around the capital, Beijing. Although this is China's official standard language, the linguistic term "Chinese" actually incorporates many variants. This distinction between the standard language and other versions of it is not unique to China; it is found in all but the smallest societies. The Italian of Sicily is very different from that spoken north of Venice, and both tongues differ from the standard Italian of Latium, the region around Rome.

Dialects

As we will see, the distinction between a language and a dialect is not always clear, but ***dialects*** can generally be thought of as regional variants of a standard language. Differences in vocabulary, syntax (the way words are put together to form phrases), pronunciation, cadence (the rhythm of speech), and even the pace of speech all mark a speaker's dialect. Even if the written form of a statement adheres to the standard language, an *accent* can reveal the regional home of a person who reads the statement aloud. The words "horse" and "oil" are written the same way in New England and in the South, but to the Southerner, the New Englander may be saying "hahse," while to the New Englander the Southerner seems to be saying "all."

More often, however, dialects are marked by actual differences in vocabulary. A single word or group of words can reveal the source area of the dialect used. Linguistic geographers map the areal extent of particular words, marking their limits as ***isoglosses*** (Fig. 8-1). An isogloss is a geographic boundary within which a particular linguistic feature occurs, but such a boundary is rarely a simple line. Usually there are outlying areas of usage, as in Figure 8-1. This may signify either that use of the dialect has expanded or that it has contracted, leaving the outliers as dwindling remnants. A series of large-scale maps over time will tell the story of that dialect's advance or retreat.

◆ CLASSIFICATION AND DISTRIBUTION OF LANGUAGES

In the context of cultural geography, we are interested in how languages are distributed throughout the world, what processes created this distribution, and how the present pattern is changing.

Before we view maps of language distribution, however, let us briefly consider the problem of language classification. This obviously relates to the definition of language: What is a language and what is a dialect? That issue is a complex one. Some scholars have classified Quebecan French as a language, whereas others insist that it is a dialect of European French. In regions of Africa where Bantu languages are spoken, many of those languages are closely related and share major portions of their vocabulary.

What is clear is that the distinction between a language and a dialect is not based on an objective measure of mutual intelligibility; if it were, Chinese would not be considered one language, whereas Norwegian and Danish might be. Instead, we must recognize that what we consider a language is a function of society's view of what constitutes a cultural community—a matter that in turn is influenced by historical developments in the political arena. The ability of the Chinese political elite to build and sustain a state encompassing speakers of different, albeit closely related, Sino-Tibetan tongues helps explain why we think of Chinese as one language. By contrast, the disintegration of the Danish and Swedish empires is partly responsible for our tendency to recognize several distinct lanuages in Scandinavia. Under the circumstances, the actual number of languages in use remains a matter of debate. The most conservative calculation, which would recognize the maximum number of dialects, puts the number at about 3000. Most linguistic geographers today would recognize between 5000 and 6000 languages, including more than 600 in India and over 1000 in Africa alone.

In classifying languages we use terms that are also employed in biology, and for the same reasons: some languages are related and some are not. Languages that are grouped in ***language families*** are thought to have a shared, but fairly distant, origin; in a ***language subfamily***, their commonality is more definite. Subfamilies are divided into ***language groups***, which consist of sets of individual languages.

Figure 8-2 shows the distribution of 20 major language families. On this map, only the Indo-European language family is broken down into subfamilies (greater detail is shown in Figure 8-3). Spatially, the Indo-European languages are the most widely dispersed language family. As Figure 8-2 indicates, the Indo-European language family dominates not only in Europe but also in much of Asia (including Russia and India), North and South America, Australia, and parts of Southern Africa. ***Indo-European languages*** are spoken by about half the world's peoples, and English is the most widely used Indo-European language.

Geolinguists theorize that a lost language (or set of languages) they call Proto-Indo-European existed somewhere in the vicinity of the Black Sea or east-central Europe (see the discussion in the next chapter) and that the present languages of the Indo-European family evolved from it. As Indo-European speakers dispersed, vocabularies grew and linguistic differentiation took place. Latin arose during this early period and was disseminated over much of Europe during the rise of the Roman Empire. Later, Latin died out and was supplanted by Italian, French, and the other Romance languages.

As Figure 8-2 indicates, the Indo-European language family includes not only the major languages of Europe and the former Soviet Union but also those of northern India and Bangladesh, Pakistan, Afghanistan, and Iran. This reflects the probable route of ancient migration from the west to South Asia. More modern migrations carried Indo-European languages (principally English, Spanish, Portuguese, and French) to the Americas, Australia, and Africa.

◆ THE MAJOR WORLD LANGUAGES

Although more of the world's peoples speak Indo-European languages than languages in any other family, Chinese is the single most important language in terms of number of speakers (Table 8-1), with English ranking second. The numbers in Table 8-1 should be viewed as approximations. English, for example, is not only spoken by 270 million North Americans, 60 million Britons and Irish, nearly 20 million Australians and New Zealanders, and millions more in countries with smaller populations; it is also used as a second

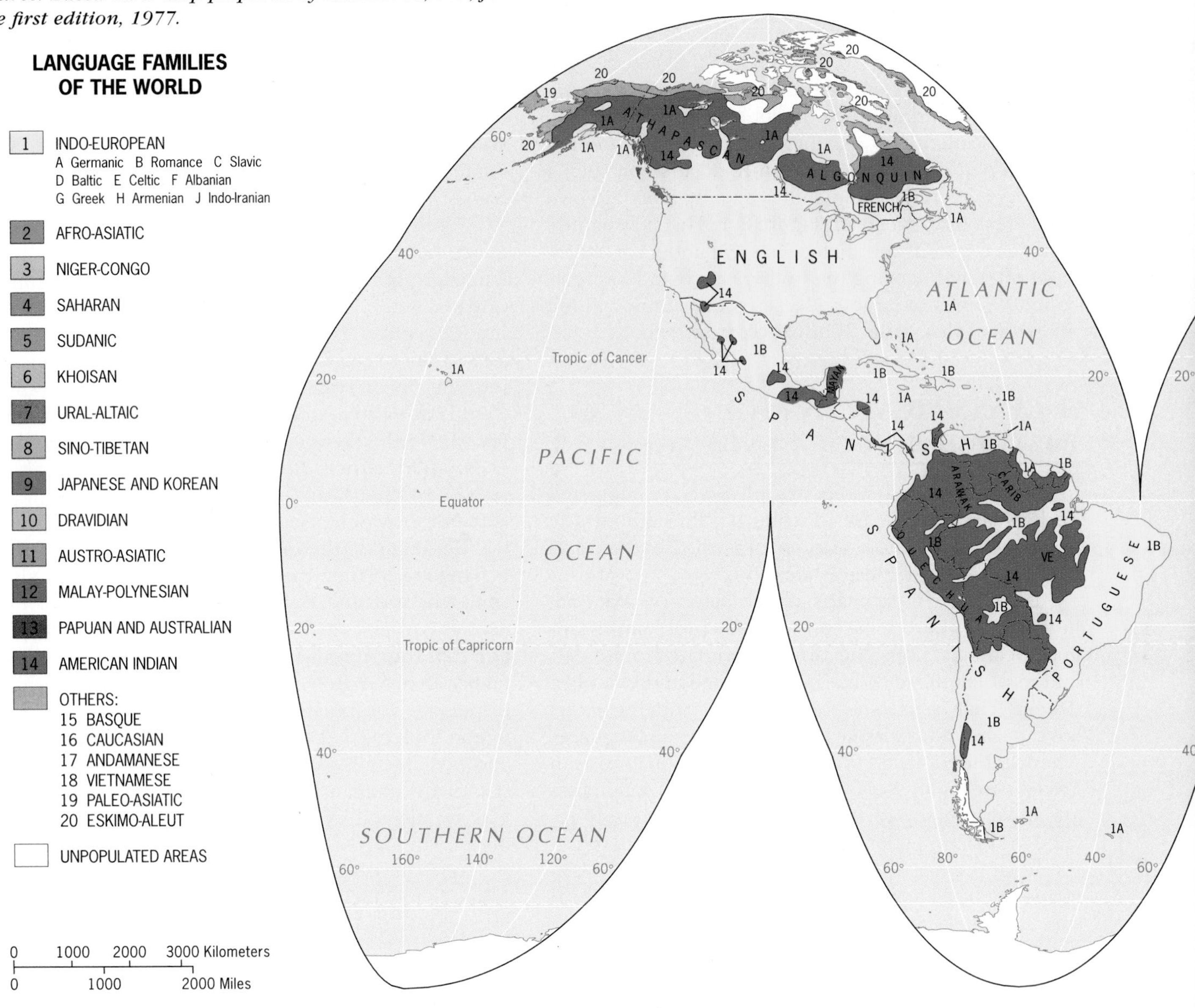

Figure 8-2 Language Families of the World. Generalized map of the world distribution of language families. *Source: Based on a map prepared by Hammond, Inc., for the first edition, 1977.*

language by hundreds of millions of people in India, Africa, and elsewhere. French is the first language of 90 million people (some sources report as many as 100 million) but it is also widely used as a second language. Note also that some of the numbers in Table 8-1 are based on population data that are not reliable. The regional languages of India (Indo-European as well as Dravidian) are among the most used, but exact data on the number of speakers are not available.

Table 8-1 (p. 117) does not list any languages spoken south of the Sahara as major world languages. One reason can be seen in Figure 8-2: the African language map is highly fragmented. Subsaharan Africa still has a relatively small population (about 600 million people in the late-1990s), but more than 1000 languages are spoken there. These languages are grouped into four families (3, 4, 5, and 6 in Figure 8-2). In terms of number of speakers, Hausa is estimated to be the most important Subsaharan African language, with perhaps as many as 50 million speakers. Hundreds of African languages have fewer than 1 million speakers.

Figure 8-2 also shows other language families that are spoken by dwindling, often marginally located or isolated groups. Austro-Asiatic languages (11), spoken in interior locales of eastern India and in Cambodia (Khmer) and Laos, are thought to be survivors of ancient languages spoken before modern invasions and cultural diffusion took place. Some scholars place Vietnamese in this family, but others do not. The Papuan and indigenous Australian languages (13), though numerous and quite diverse, are spoken by fewer than 10 million people. The languages of Native Americans (14) remain strong only in areas of Middle America,

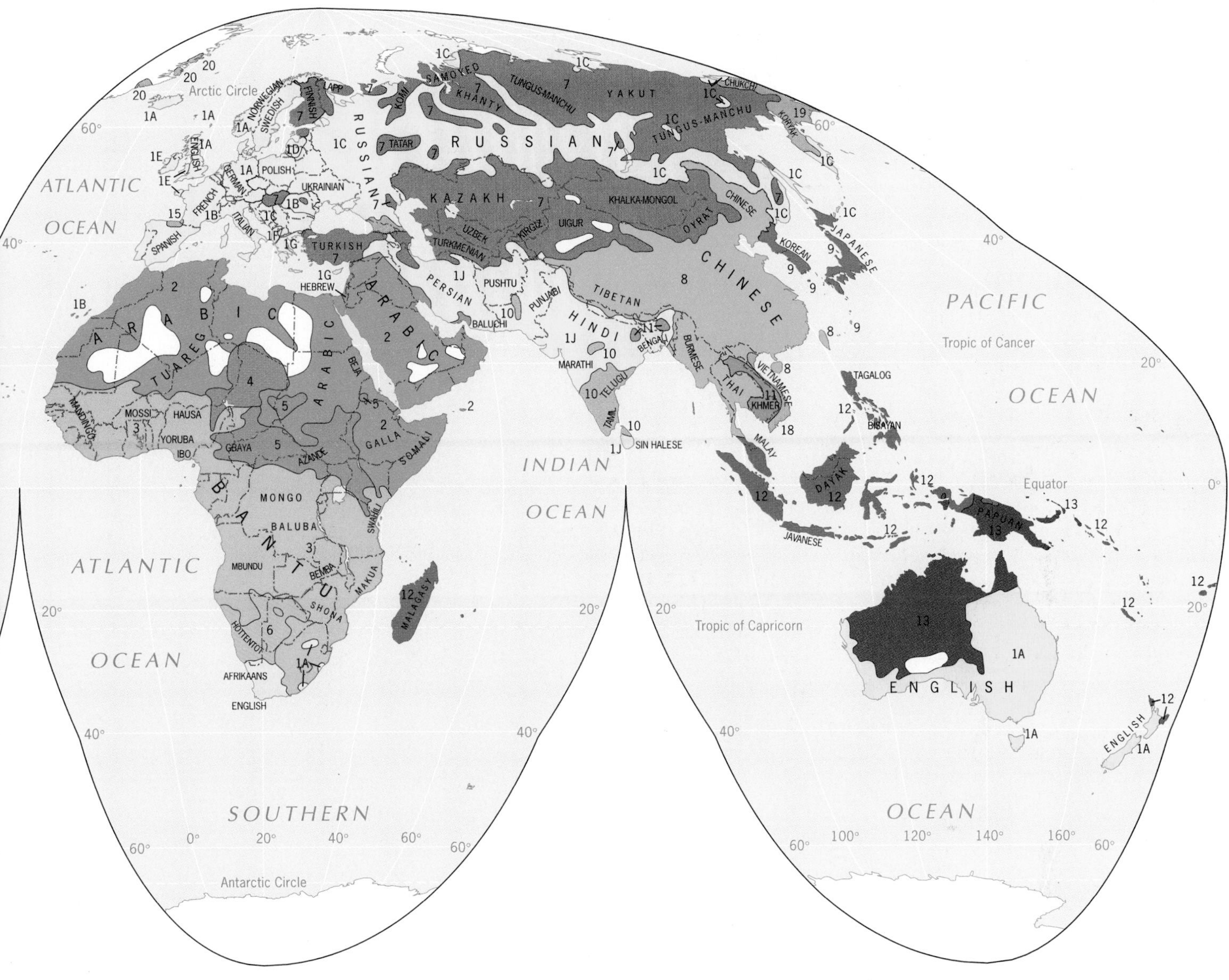

the high Andes, and northern Canada. Languages of the Eskimo-Aleut family (20) survive on the Arctic margins of Greenland, North America, and eastern Asia.

If we look carefully at the map of world languages, some interesting questions arise. Consider, for example, the island of Madagascar off the East African coast. The primary languages spoken on Madagascar belong not to an African language family but to the Malay-Polynesian family, the languages of Indonesia and its neighbors. How did this happen on an island so close to Africa? Actually, the map reveals a piece of ancient history that is not well understood. Long ago, seafarers from the islands of Southeast Asia crossed the Indian Ocean. They may have reached the East African coast first and then sailed on to Madagascar, where they settled. Africans had not yet sailed across the strait, so there was no threat to the Indonesian-Malayan settlements. The settlements grew and prospered, and large states evolved. Later, Africans began to come to Madagascar, but by that time the cultural landscape had been established. If you compare the names of Madagascar's places to those across the water in Africa, you can see evidence of a fascinating piece of geographic history.

The Languages of Europe

The language map of Europe (Fig. 8-3) shows that the Indo-European language family prevails in this region, with pockets of the Ural-Altaic family occurring in Finland and adjacent areas, Hungary (the Ugric subfamily), and Turkey west of the Sea of Marmara. Subfamilies include the Germanic languages (English, German, Danish, Norwegian, and Swedish), the Ro-

Figure 8-3 Languages of Europe. Generalized map of language-use regions in Europe. *Source: Based on a map in Murphy, A. B. 1998 "European Languages," T. Unwin, ed.,* A European Geography. *London: Longman.*

Table 8-1 Numbers of Speakers of Major Languages of the World, 1999 (estimated)[a]

Language Family	Major Language	Number of Speakers (Millions)
Indo-European	English	405
	Spanish	300
	Hindi	300
	Bengali	195
	Russian	205
	Portuguese	165
	German	100
	Punjabi	90
	French	90
	Italian	60
Sino-Tibetan	Chinese	1160
	Thai	50
	Burmese	35
Japanese-Korean	Japanese	125
	Korean	75
Afro-Asiatic	Arabic	170
Dravidian	Telugu	80
	Tamil	75
Malay-Polynesian	Indonesian	150

[a]Estimates extrapolated from several sources.

mance languages (French, Spanish, Italian, Romanian, and Portuguese), the Slavic languages (Russian, Polish, Czech, Slovak, Ukrainian, Slovenian, Serbo-Croatian, and Bulgarian), and the Celtic languages (Breton, Welsh, and Gaelic). Language groups in Europe are represented by clusters, such as the Scandinavian languages, the Iberian languages, and the Slavic languages of Eastern Europe.

A comparison of Europe's linguistic and political maps shows a high correlation between the languages spoken and the political organization of space. The Romance languages, of Romanic-Latin origin, dominate in five countries, including Romania. The eastern boundaries of Germany coincide almost exactly with the transition from Germanic to Slavic tongues. Even at the level of individual languages, boundaries can be seen on the political map: between French and Spanish, between Norwegian and Swedish, and between Bulgarian and Greek.

Although Figure 8-3 shows a significant correlation between political and linguistic boundaries, there are some important exceptions. The French linguistic region extends into Belgium, Switzerland, and Italy, but in France itself it coexists with a Celtic tongue in the Bretagne (Brittany) Peninsula. The Celtic languages survive not only in Brittany (Breton) but also in Wales (Welsh), western Ireland (Irish Gaelic), and Scotland (Scots Gaelic), where they constitute remnants of an early period of European history before modern languages displaced them toward the realm's westernmost fringes. The use of Romanian extends well into Moldavia, signifying a past loss of national territory. Greek and Albanian are also Indo-European languages, and their regional distribution corresponds significantly (though not exactly) with national territories. Figure 8-3 underscores the complex cultural pattern of Eastern Europe: there are German speakers in Hungary; Hungarian speakers in Slovakia, Romania, and Yugoslavia; Romanian speakers in Greece and Moldavia; Turkish speakers in Bulgaria; and Albanian speakers in Serbia.

Although the overwhelming majority of Europeans and Russians speak Indo-European languages, the Ural-Altaic language family is also represented in this realm. Finnish, Estonian, and Hungarian are major languages of this family, which, as Figure 8-2 shows, extends across Eurasia to the Pacific coast and includes Turkish, Kazakh, Uigur, Kyrgyz, and Uzbek, among other languages. Not all students of linguistic geography view the Ural-Altaic languages as a single family; some separate the more northerly *Uralic* from the southern *Altaic* families. However, there are reasons to group these languages together. It is believed that they spread into Europe between 7000 and 10,000 years ago and later were overtaken in most places by the Indo-European languages. Their source area may have been a longitudinal zone along the Ural Mountains from which migrations occurred both westward into Europe and eastward into Asia. Whatever their origins, the Ural-Altaic languages survive as the national languages of Finland and Hungary.

The Languages of India

The mosaic of languages in India (Fig. 8-4) includes four language families, but only two of these—the Indo-European family and the Dravidian family—have significant numbers of speakers among India's nearly 1 billion inhabitants. In the Karakoram Mountains of Jammu and Kashmir (the far northwest) there are small numbers of Tibetan speakers, and along the border with Myanmar (Burma) in the east lies a cluster of Naga (Burmese) speakers. Also in the east are small groups of Austro-Asiatic speakers. Otherwise, the people of India speak about 15 major languages, all but 4 of them Indo-European, and more than 1600 lesser languages, some of which are spoken by only a few thousand persons.

As Figure 8-4 indicates, the four Dravidian languages are all spoken in a compact region in the south of the Indian Peninsula. The map suggests that these

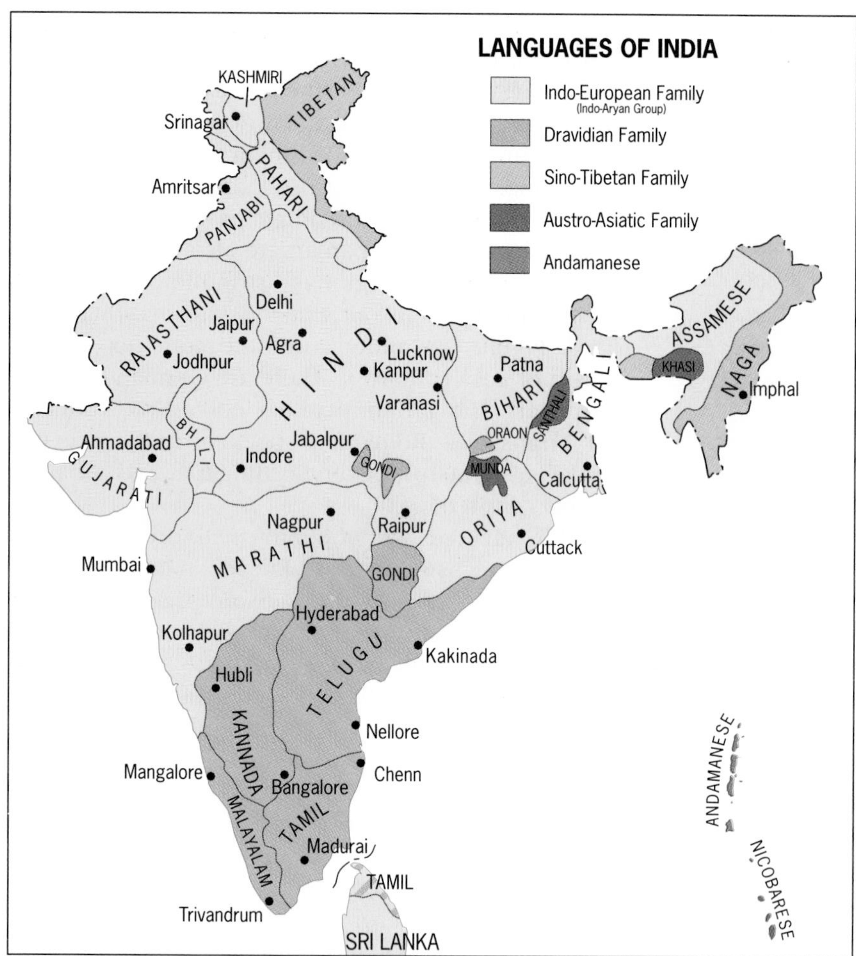

Figure 8-4 Languages of India. Major languages of the Indian subcontinent. *Source: From a map prepared by Hammond, Inc., for the first edition, 1977.*

languages and the cultures they represent were "pushed" southward by the advancing Indo-European speakers. The Dravidian languages are older, although their origins are unclear. Some scholars believe that Dravidian emerged in India. Others suggest that Dravidian speakers arrived thousands of years ago from Central Asia and that Dravidian is related to Ural-Altaic languages. Still others link the Dravidians with the ancient Indus civilization that arose in what is today Pakistan. Indeed, there is a cluster of about 350,000 speakers of a form of Dravidian in north-central Pakistan.

Today the largest Dravidian language, with about 80 million speakers, is Telugu, the language of the Indian state of Andhra Pradesh. Tamil, with its rich literature, is spoken by approximately 75 million persons in Tamil Nadu. Kannada (also called Kanarese), the language of Karnataka, has approximately 35 million speakers, about the same number as Malayalam, which is spoken in the state of Kerala.

This close relationship between regional languages and political divisions in southern India also prevails in the north. Indeed, a comparison of Figure 8-4 with an atlas map of India's federal system underscores the important role of languages in the development of this spatial structure. Hindi, the principal Indo-European language with approximately 300 million speakers, extends across several north-central Indian states. But east as well as west of India's Hindi-speaking core lie states where other languages prevail: Orissa (Oriya), Bihar (Bihari), West Bengal (Bengali), Punjab (Punjabi), Rajasthan (Rajasthani), Gujarat (Gujarati), and Maharashtra (Marathi). In the northeast the linguistic map is especially complex, as is reflected in the existence of seven comparatively small states.

In addition to more than a dozen major languages, India has hundreds of lesser languages, both Indo-European and Dravidian, that cannot be shown on a map on the scale of Figure 8-4. Nevertheless, for such a large population the Indian language mosaic is not as intensely fragmented as Africa's. Instead, like that of Europe, it is dominated by several major regional languages with more speakers than many national tongues.

The Languages of Africa

As noted earlier, more than 1000 languages are spoken in Subsaharan Africa, and linguists have been working to record many of these; most are unwritten. The resulting data offer some significant insights into Africa's cultural past.

The languages of Africa (Fig. 8-5) are grouped into four families, the largest of which is the Niger-Congo family, which extends from West Africa all the way to the south. This family can be subdivided into five subfamilies. One of these is the Bantu subfamily, whose languages are spoken by most of the people near the equator and south of it. The languages spoken in West Africa are of the Atlantic, Voltaic, Guinea, and Hausa subfamilies. The oldest languages of Subsaharan Africa are the *Khoisan* languages, which include a "click" sound. Among these is the language of the San, spoken by only a few thousand people in southwestern Africa. Perhaps the Khoisan languages were once the main languages of much of Africa, but they have been reduced to comparative insignificance by the Bantu invasion, just as the Celtic languages were in Europe.

How can languages help us reconstruct the cultural development of Africa? Consider what has happened in Europe, where the subfamily of Romance languages has differentiated into French, Italian, Spanish, and Portuguese. Even within these individual languages we see evidence of differentiation—for example, between Castilian Spanish and Catalan, and between Northern and Southern French and Walloon. Such differentiation develops over time, and it is reasonable to assume that the more time elapses, the greater the individuality of each language. Therefore, if the peoples of a large region speak languages that are somewhat different but still closely related, it is reasonable to conclude that they have migrated into that region relatively recently. On the other hand, languages that clearly have common roots and yet are very different must have undergone modification over a lengthy period.

Among the languages of the Niger-Congo family, those of the Bantu subfamily are much more closely related than those of other subfamilies. We can therefore deduce that the Bantu peoples and cultures of Central and Southern Africa are of more recent origin

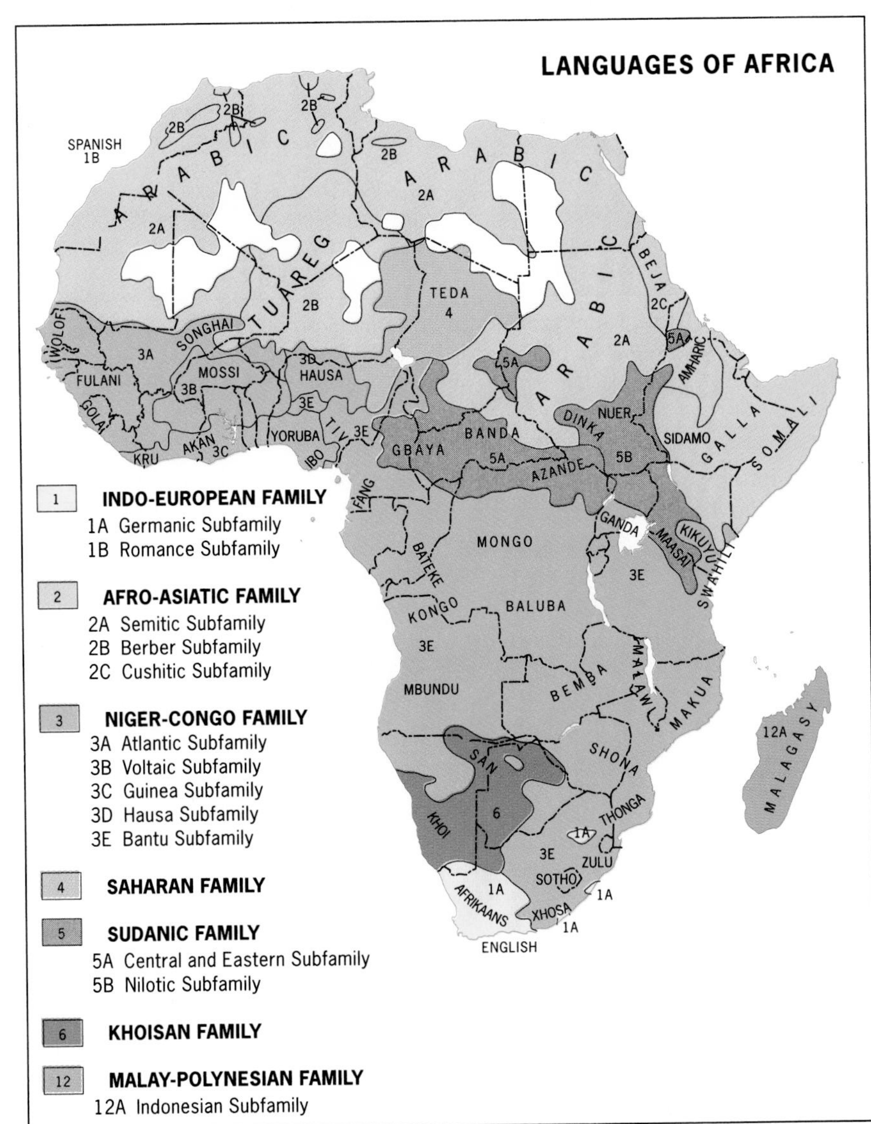

Figure 8-5 Languages of Africa. Regional classification of African languages. *Source: From a map prepared by Hammond, Inc., for the first edition 1977.*

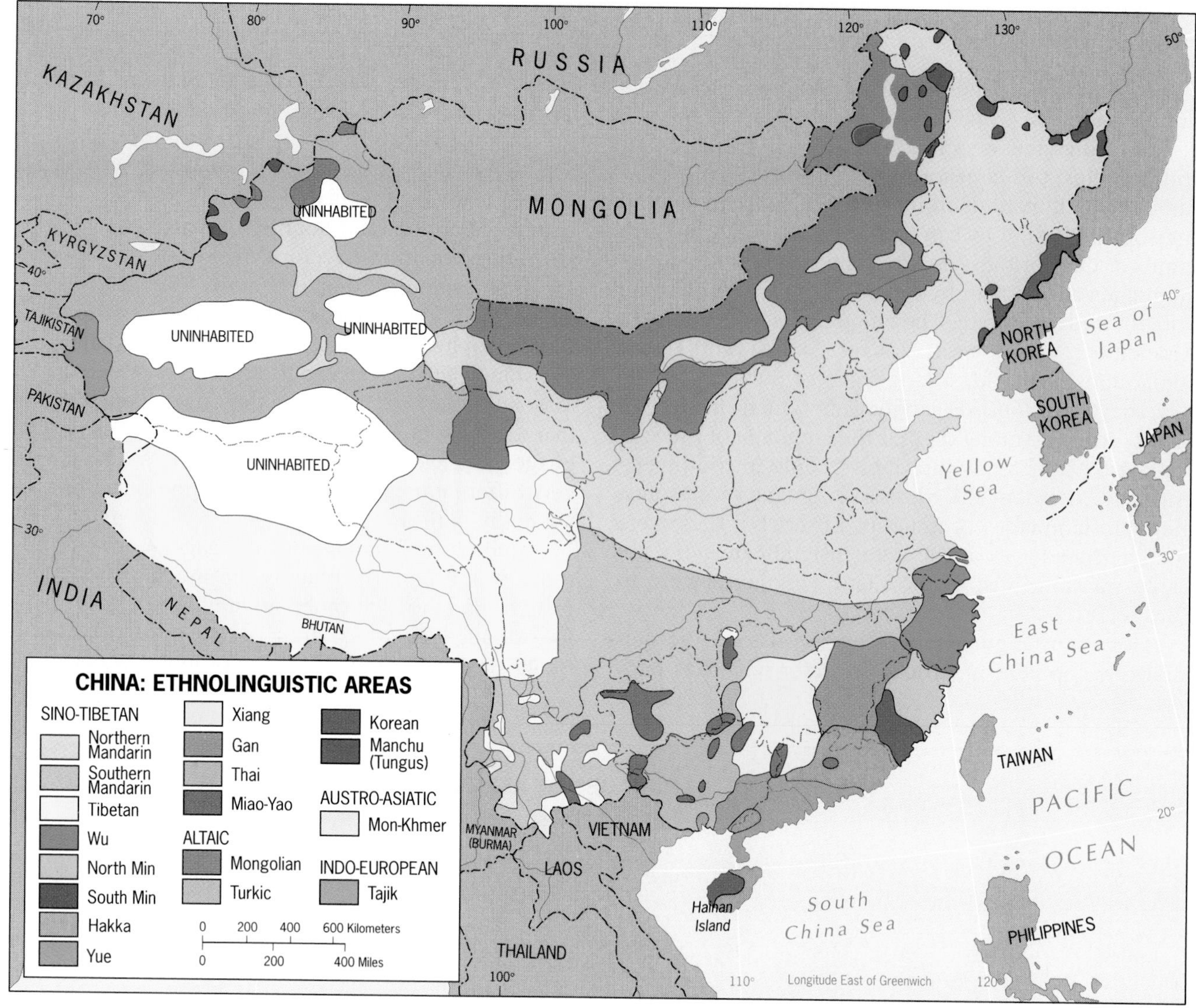

Figure 8-6 Ethnolinguistic Areas of China. Languages in use in China. *Source: From several sources including Academia Sinica, Republic of China Yearbook, and university publications.*

than West Africans. This is reflected in African names. The word "Bantu" should actually be written *BaNtu* (people), with the *Ba* being a prefix. Sometimes the prefix is retained in common usage, sometimes not. The *Watusi*, for example, are now usually called Tutsi. The people of southeastern Uganda are the BaGanda or Ganda. The Zulu of South Africa are actually the *Ama*Zulu. Stories about Zimbabwe often mention the *Ma*Shona or Shona. Remember Basutoland, now called Lesotho? It was originally named after the Sotho, and BaSotholand became Basutoland. *Ba, Ma, Wa,* and *Ama* are not very far removed linguistically, and they reveal close associations between languages and peoples spread across Africa from Uganda to Kwazulu-Natal.

It is not just a matter of prefixes, of course. Bantu languages reflect their close relationships in vocabulary and in numerous other respects. Geolinguists have traced the changes that occur over space in a single word and have found that thousands of miles away a word is often quite close to its original form. Consider the familiar Swahili greeting, *jambo*, used in coastal East Africa. In the eastern Transvaal of South Africa and Swaziland, people will recognize *jabo*.

The situation in West Africa is quite different. There are languages that are closely associated, but the major languages of the West African subfamilies are much more discrete. Of course, there are other kinds of evidence supporting the conclusion that the peoples of Bantu Africa have a shorter history in that area than those of West Africa, but the primary evidence is linguistic.

Chinese: One Language or Many?

The map of China's ethnolinguistic areas (Fig. 8-6) should be compared to the map of world population distribution (Fig. 4-1). That comparison will reveal that the great majority of China's people speak Mandarin, either Northern or Southern. Chinese is one of the world's oldest languages and is spoken by the greatest contiguous population cluster on the Earth.

As the map shows, a number of Chinese dialects prevail in large areas of the country, notably in the south. Most of these dialects are mutually unintelligible, and some scholars therefore argue that Chinese is not one but several languages, among which Mandarin dominates with about 700 million speakers. Wu Chinese ranks next with over 100 million, and Yue (Cantonese) is third with about 70 million.

In mid-1997, when the government of China took over control of Hong Kong from the British, Beijing's leaders all made their speeches in Northern Mandarin, and the Cantonese familiar to the great majority of Hong Kong's population was never heard. Thus China's rulers used language to underscore the nature of the new authority to which the local people would now be subject.

During the twentieth century several efforts were made to create a truly national language in China. The latest of these is the so-called *pinyin* system, a phonetic-spelling system based on the pronunciation of Chinese characters in Northern Mandarin, China's standard language. But China's population contains many minorities, as Figure 8-6 reminds us, and as a result linguistic integration may never be achieved.

One of the most interesting and challenging dimensions of the geography of language is the reconstruction of the routes of diffusion of peoples and their languages. While linguists attempt to establish the family tree of languages, geographers focus on the spatial implications of this effort: the routes of migration and linguistic diffusion. We turn next to this complicated topic, about which new information is constantly emerging.

◆ KEY TERMS ◆

dialect
Indo-European languages
isogloss
language
language family
language group
language subfamily
linguistic diversification
preliterate society
standard language
vocalization

◆ APPLYING GEOGRAPHIC KNOWLEDGE ◆

1. Why is the language spoken by more people in this world than any other *not* the language of international trade and communication? What factors put another language in this position? Can you foresee a twenty-first-century scenario that might alter the balance?
2. In 1997 several dozen "Francophone" countries convened in Hanoi, Vietnam, to discuss ways to promote the use of French and to (in the words of the conference report) "reverse the deterioration" of the language. In the social, economic, and political geography of the world today, why do French-speakers feel a threat to their language?
3. In terms of the geographic pattern (not the origins) of language, what do Subsaharan Africa and New Guinea have in common?

Chapter 9

The Diffusion of Languages

From the field notes

"Latin Spoken here . . . two thousand years ago. Travel the British countryside from Hampshire to Hadrian's Wall, and marvel at the impact the Romans made on their distant western outpost. Even here in the rugged Cumbrian Mountains facing the Irish Sea, where winters are severe and surface travel is difficult to this day, the Romans established a presence whose remnants still survive. But their linguistic legacy does not; what might have become another Romance-language-speaking area fell to the Anglo-Saxons. Today English, a member of the Germanic subfamily of languages, prevails here, and these ruins evince a linguistic diffusion that failed."

KEY POINTS

◆ **The search for the origins of language goes back tens of thousands of years. It has yielded information not only about how language changes but also about the environments where early languages were spoken.**

◆ **Scientists do not yet agree on how long ago language emerged. Some believe that the use of language began with the rise of *Homo sapiens* 200,000 or more years ago; others argue that simple vocal communication began much earlier.**

◆ **Languages change through divergence, convergence, and replacement, making the spatial search for origins problematic.**

◆ **The Pacific and American realms, where languages spread relatively recently, provide useful information for the reconstruction of language-diffusion routes and processes.**

◆ **Writing, technology, and political organization play a key role in the diffusion of individual languages.**

The world today is a Babel of languages, a patchwork of tongues. Nevertheless, it is possible to identify some languages that are related, such as Spanish and Portuguese, which are so similar that their common origin and recent divergence are beyond doubt. In fact, there is a historical record of this process. It reveals how the Latin of Roman times gave rise to the Romance languages of today (the major ones being Italian, Spanish, Portuguese, French, and Romanian). In just a few centuries Latin, which had been spoken in territories extending from Britain to the Bosporus, was replaced by a set of derivative languages.

Given the speed and thoroughness of this process, can we hope to unlock the mysteries of much earlier languages and retrace the evolution of modern languages from what linguists call the Mother Tongue, the first language spoken by *Homo sapiens sapiens* perhaps as long as 200,000 years ago? That remains an elusive goal, but with the help of computers, remarkable progress is being made in the reconstruction of ancient languages and their paths of diffusion. This chapter focuses on the relevance of linguistic theory and research to historical geography.

◆ TRACING LINGUISTIC DIVERSIFICATION

The diversification of languages has long been charted through the analysis of ***sound shifts***. Take the Latin word for milk (*lacte*) and note that it becomes *latta* in Italian, *leche* in Spanish, and *lait* in French. Or the Latin for the number eight (*octo*), which becomes *otto*, *ocho*, and *huit*, respectively. Even if the Latin roots for these words had never been known, linguists would have been able to deduce them.

This technique of backward reconstruction is crucial to linguistic research. If it is possible to deduce a large part of the vocabulary of an extinct language, it may be feasible to go even further and re-create the language that preceded it. This technique, called ***deep reconstruction***, has yielded some important results. It takes humanity's linguistic family tree back thousands of years.

More than two centuries ago William Jones, an Englishman living in South Asia, undertook a study of Sanskrit, the language in which ancient Indian religious and literary texts were written. Jones discovered that the vocabulary and grammatical forms of Sanskrit bore a striking resemblance to the ancient Greek and Latin he had learned while in college. "No philologer [student of literature] could examine all three," Jones wrote, "without believing them to have sprung from some common source, which, perhaps, no longer exists." In the late eighteenth century this was a revolutionary notion indeed.

During the nineteenth century Jacob Grimm, a scholar as well as a writer of fairy tales, suggested that sound shifts might prove the relationships between languages in a scientific manner. He pointed out that related languages have similar, but not identical, consonants. (Consonants are formed by the constriction of the sound channel.) He believed that these consonants would change over time in a predictable way. Hard consonants, such as the **v** and **t** in the German word *vater*, would soften into va**d**er (Dutch) and **f**ather (English). Looking backward, we should expect to find the opposite: a hardening of consonants.

From Jones's notions and Grimm's ideas came the first major linguistic hypothesis, which proposed the existence of an ancestral ***(Proto) Indo-European*** language (or closely related languages), the predecessor of Latin, Greek, and Sanskrit, among other ancient languages. This concept had major implications because the proposed ancestral language(s) would link not only the present and past Romance language but also a number of other languages spoken from Britain to North Africa and South Asia.

Several research tasks followed from this hypothesis. First, the vocabulary of the proposed ancestral language must be reconstructed. Second, the hearth or source where this language originated, and from which it spread, must be located. Third, the routes of diffusion by which this dispersal took place should be traced. And fourth, researchers should attempt to learn about the ways of life of those who spoke this language.

◆ THE LANGUAGE TREE

Proto-Indo-European gave rise to more than Latin, Greek, and Sanskrit. As Figure 8-2 reminds us, the Indo-European language realm includes not only languages derived from Latin but also the Slavonic (Slavic) languages, including Russian, Ukrainian, Polish, Czech, Slovak, Bulgarian, and Slovenian, and the Germanic languages, including German, Swedish, Danish, and Norwegian. These, too, must have had common ancestors, branches of the Proto-Indo-European "tree."

Divergence

The first scholar to compare the world's language families to the branches of a tree was August Schleicher, a German linguist. In the mid-nineteenth century he suggested that the basic process of language formation is ***language divergence***, that is, differentiation over time and space. Languages would branch into dialects; isolation then increased the differences between dialects. Over time, dialects would become discrete languages, as happened with Spanish and Portuguese and is now happening with Quebecois French. Although this idea was later challenged, it stood the test of time, and the language-tree model remains central to language research (Fig. 9-1).

Convergence

A complicating factor, however is human mobility. While languages diverged, people migrated as well. Languages did not merely diffuse through static populations; they were also spread by relocation diffusion (see Chapter 2). Sometimes such diffusion caused long-isolated languages to make contact, creating ***language convergence***. Such instances create special problems for researchers because the rules of reconstruction may not apply or may be unreliable.

Replacement

A further complication should be considered in view of modern cultural events. We know that the languages of traditional, numerically smaller, and technologically less advanced peoples have been replaced, or greatly modified, by the languages of invaders. This process of ***language replacement*** goes on today, and there is every reason to believe that it has happened ever since humans began to use language. (In the next chapter we discuss the process of *creolization*, a form of language replacement now occurring in the Caribbean region and elsewhere.)

Reconstructing even a small branch of the language tree, therefore, is a complicated task. Look again at the language map of Europe (Fig. 8-3). If only *all* the languages were members of the same family, the same branch of the tree! But things are not that simple. Hungarian, completely surrounded by Indo-European languages, is not in the same family as any of its neighbors. Finnish is another non-Indo-European language, apparently distantly related to Hungarian but mapped as a member of a discrete subfamily. Estonian is more closely related to Finnish, as the map suggests. But a tantalizing enigma is presented by Basque, a family that is now isolated in a small region of northern Spain and southwestern France. What ancient proto-language gave rise to Basque? Similar questions arise in hundreds of places throughout the world, where linguistic islands survive despite later waves of language diffusion.

◆ THEORIES OF LANGUAGE DIFFUSION

While linguists reconstructed Proto-Indo-European vocabulary, human geographers and other scholars searched for the source of Proto-Indo-European. Identifying this hearth would enormously increase their understanding of Eurasian historical geography.

The linguists' research produced many valuable clues. Reconstructions by scholars working independently often produced remarkably similar results. The proto-language(s) had words for certain landforms, trees, and other features of the natural landscape, but it lacked others. Such information helps reveal the environment in which a language may have developed. For example, if a reconstructed language has no word for *snow*, this would suggest a tropical or equatorial

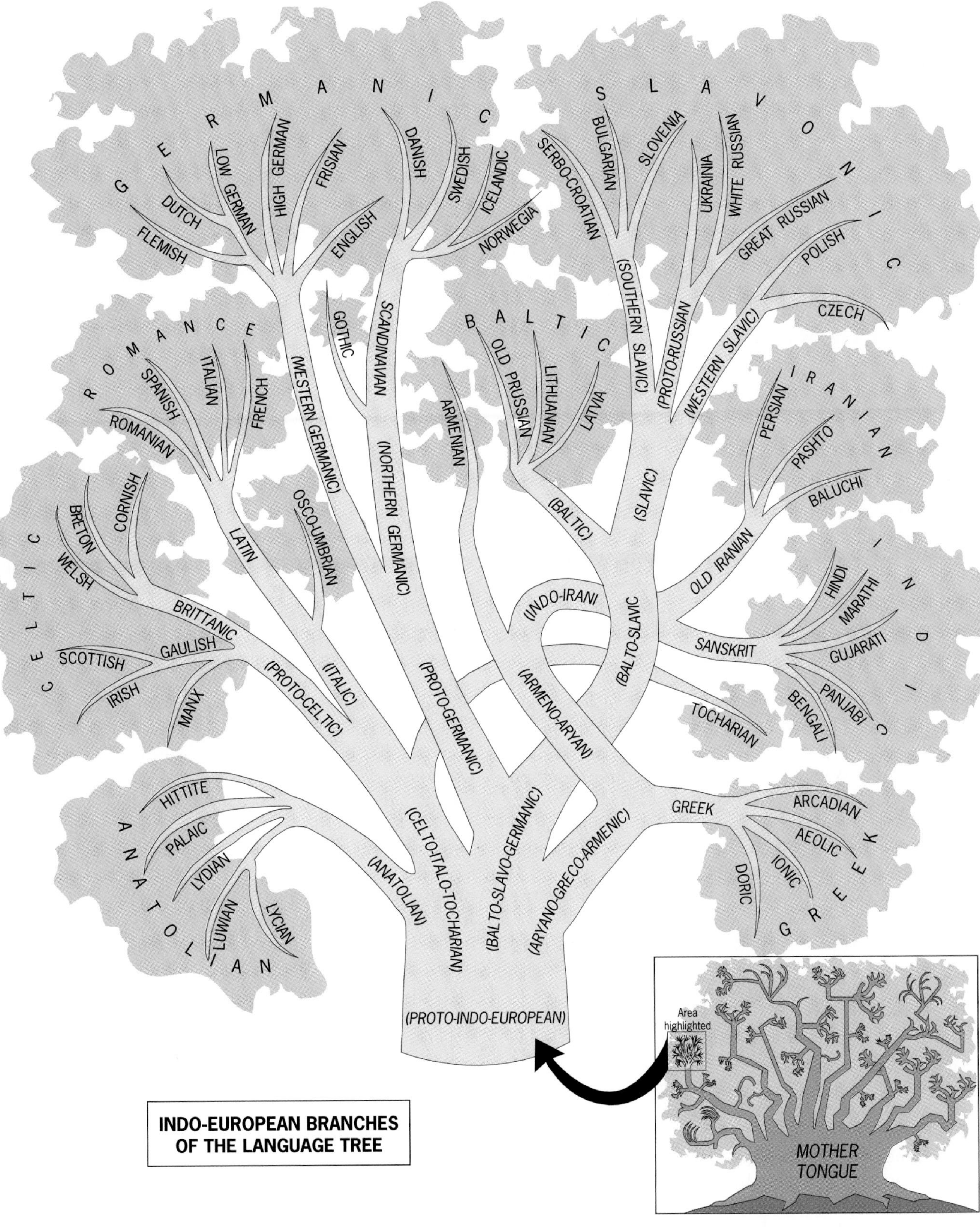

Figure 9-1 Indo-European Branches of the Language Tree. *Source: From T. V. Gamkrelidze and V. V. Ivanov, "The Early History of Indo-European Languages,"* Scientific American, *March 1990, p. 111.*

origin. If there is no word for *palm* tree, the language is likely to have emerged in a cold region. More specifically, if a certain type of vegetation (oak, pine, beech, birch, tall or short grass) is part of the vocabulary, the search for the environment where the language developed can be narrowed down—although researchers must factor in a time dimension, as environments have changed even during the Holocene. Time is less an issue when vocabulary refers to physiographic features of the landscape. If there are many words for mountains and hills but few for flat land, we can conclude that the source area was mountainous.

Conquest Theory

Analyses of this kind produced a tentative answer to the geographic question. The Proto-Indo-European homeland source, it seemed, lay somewhere north of the Black Sea in the vast steppes of present-day Ukraine and Russia. The time, it was suggested, was more than 5000 years ago, and judging from the reconstructed vocabulary, the people used horses, had developed the wheel, and traded widely in many goods. The logical conclusion seemed to be that these early speakers of Proto-Indo-European spread westward on horseback, overpowering earlier inhabitants and beginning the diffusion and differentiation of Latin, Germanic, and Slavonic languages.

This ***conquest theory*** of language dispersal in Europe west of the Russian plains was long supported by a majority of archeologists, linguists, and human geographers. The sound shifts in the derivative languages (*vater* to *vader* to *father*, for example) seemed to represent a long period of westward divergence. The location of older Indo-European languages on western margins (Breton in France, Scottish Gaelic and Welsh in Britain, and Irish Gaelic in Ireland) appeared to be due to the arrival of newer languages from the east.

Agriculture Theory

But not all scholars were convinced. As the archeological record in Europe became better known, other hypotheses were proposed. Luca Cavalli-Sforza and Robert Ammerman suggested that it was the spread of agriculture, not conquest, that diffused the Proto-Indo-European language through Europe. This, of course, meant that the source area of the ancient language would have had to lie in an area of agricultural innovation, not in the Ukrainian-Russian grasslands where pastoralism was the prevailing way of life. But where was this hearth? Was it in the Fertile Crescent of the Middle East? Apparently not, because the vocabulary of Proto-Indo-European has few words for plains but many terms for high and low mountains, valleys, mountain streams, rapids, lakes, and other high-relief landforms.

In 1984 the Soviet scholars Thomas Gamkrelidze and Victor Ivanov, who reconstructed much of the known vocabulary of Proto-Indo-European, published a book in which they reported that these terms were supplemented by words for trees such as mountain oak, pine, fir, willow, and ash. The language also had names for animals such as lions, leopards, and monkeys—none of which lived in the plains north of the Black Sea. Thus arose the ***agriculture theory*** (as opposed to the conquest theory) and its proposed source area: the mountainous, well-watered terrain of Anatolia in modern Turkey. The archeological record indicates that there, between 7000 and 9000 years ago, the horse had been domesticated and the wheel was in use. The realm's leading hearth of agricultural innovation lay in nearby Mesopotamia.

Support for the Theory In 1991 the agriculture theory received support from analyses of the protein (that is, gene) content of individuals from several thousand locations across Europe. This research confirmed the presence of distance decay in the geographic pattern: certain genes became steadily less common from southern Turkey across the Balkans and into Western and northern Europe. This pattern was interpreted as showing that the farming peoples of Anatolia moved steadily westward and northward. As they did so, they mixed with nonfarming peoples, diluting their genetic identity as the distance from their source area increased. Archeologists Robert Sokal, Neal Olden, and Chester Wilson argued that farming led to an unprecedented increase in population and that this in turn stimulated migration. As a result, a slow but steady wave of farmers dispersed into Europe.

The agriculture theory can be used to explain a number of features of the language map of Europe. Ammerman and Cavalli-Sforza proposed that for every generation (25 years) the agricultural frontier moved approximately 18 kilometers (11 miles). This would mean that the European frontier would have been completely penetrated by farmers in about 1500 years, which is close to what the archeological record suggests. But some of the nonfarming societies in their path held out, and their languages did not change. Thus Etruscan did not become extinct until Roman times, and Basque survives to this day as a direct link to Europe's pre-farming era.

Drawbacks of the Theory The agriculture theory has some drawbacks, however. The Anatolian region is not an ideal environment for farming, and there is no strong archeological evidence for an agricultural culture hearth there. In addition, despite the genetic gradient identified in Europe, some language geographers

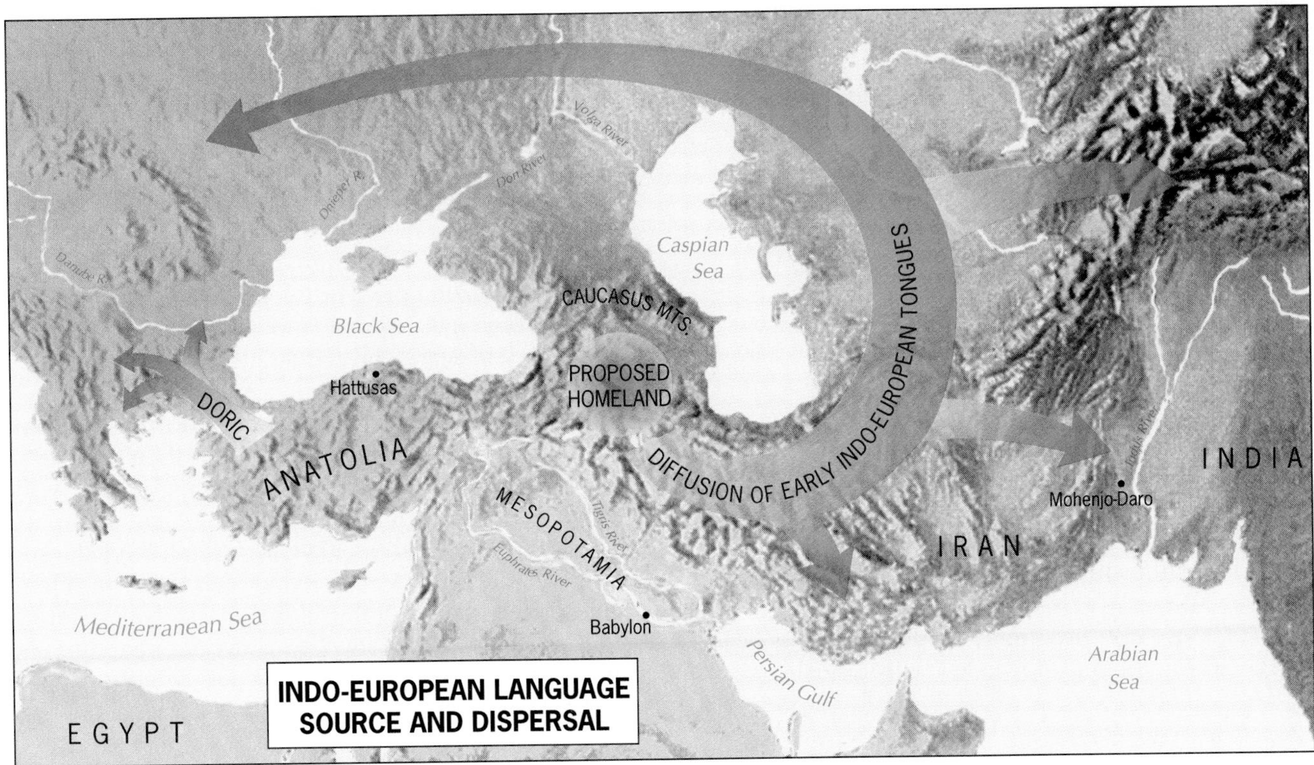

Figure 9-2 Indo-European Language Source and Dispersal. Postulated diffusion of an Indo-European proto-language. *Source: From T. V. Gamkrelidze and V. V. Ivanov,* Scientific American, *March 1990, p. 112.*

continued to prefer the dispersal hypothesis, which holds that the Indo-European languages that arose from the proto-language(s) were first carried eastward into Southwest Asia, then around the Caspian Sea, and then across the Russian-Ukrainian plains and on into the Balkans (Fig. 9-2). As is so often the case, there may be some truth in both hypotheses. If Anatolia was the source, the diffusion of Indo-European languages (that is, dialects of Proto-Indo-European) could have spread both westward across southern Europe *and* in the broad arc shown in Figure 9-3. In any case, an eastward diffusion must have occurred in view of the re-

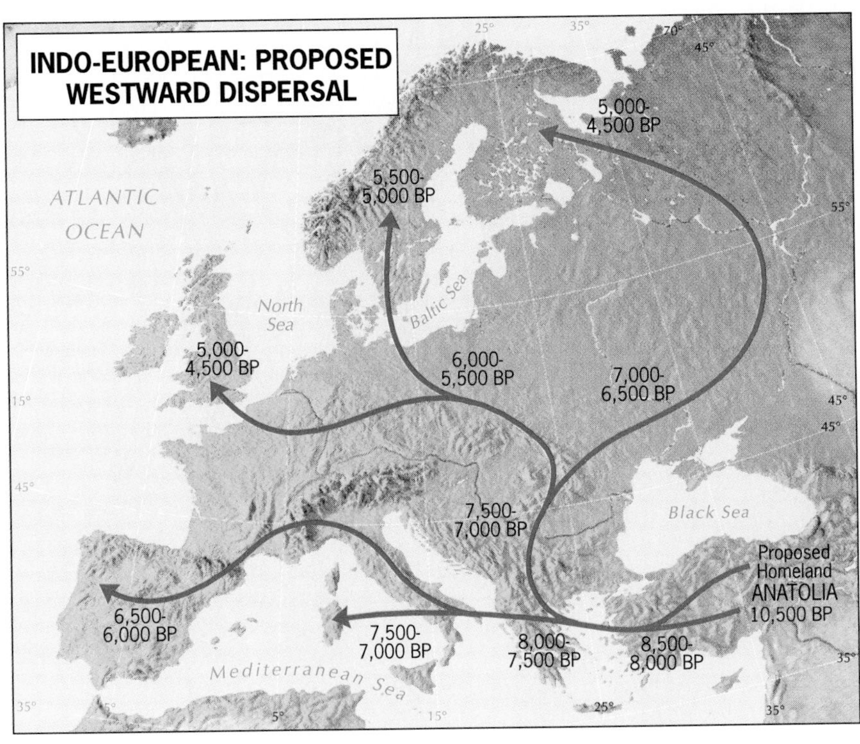

Figure 9-3 Indo-European Proposed Westward Dispersal. The approximate timing of the westward dispersal of the Indo-European languages.

lationships between Sanskrit and ancient Latin and Greek described by William Jones.

The geographic story of Proto-Indo-European is still unfolding, but this has not deterred researchers from going back even further. What was the ancestral language for Proto-Indo-European?

◆ THE SEARCH FOR A SUPERFAMILY

The evolution and diffusion of Proto-Indo-European occurred over a period of, at most, 9000 years. But language development and divergence have been going on for ten times as long or more; we have just dissected a thin branch of an old, gnarled tree (Fig. 9-4).

This does not discourage modern linguists or language geographers, however. The British scholar Colin Renfrew carried the agriculture theory a step further by proposing that not just one but three agricultural hearths gave rise to language families (Fig. 9-5). From the Anatolian source diffused Europe's Indo-European languages; from the western arc of the Fertile Crescent came the languages of North Africa and Arabia; and from the Fertile Crescent's eastern arc ancient languages spread into present-day Iran, Afghanistan, Pakistan, and India, later to be replaced by Indo-European languages.

Russian scholars have long been in the forefront of research on ancient languages, but their work was not well known in the West until recently. The work of two scholars in particular has had great impact. Starting in the 1960s, Vladislav Illich-Svitych and Aharon Dolgopolsky tackled a daunting problem: deep reconstruction of the language that was ancestral to Proto-Indo-European. Using words that are assumed to be the most stable and dependable parts of

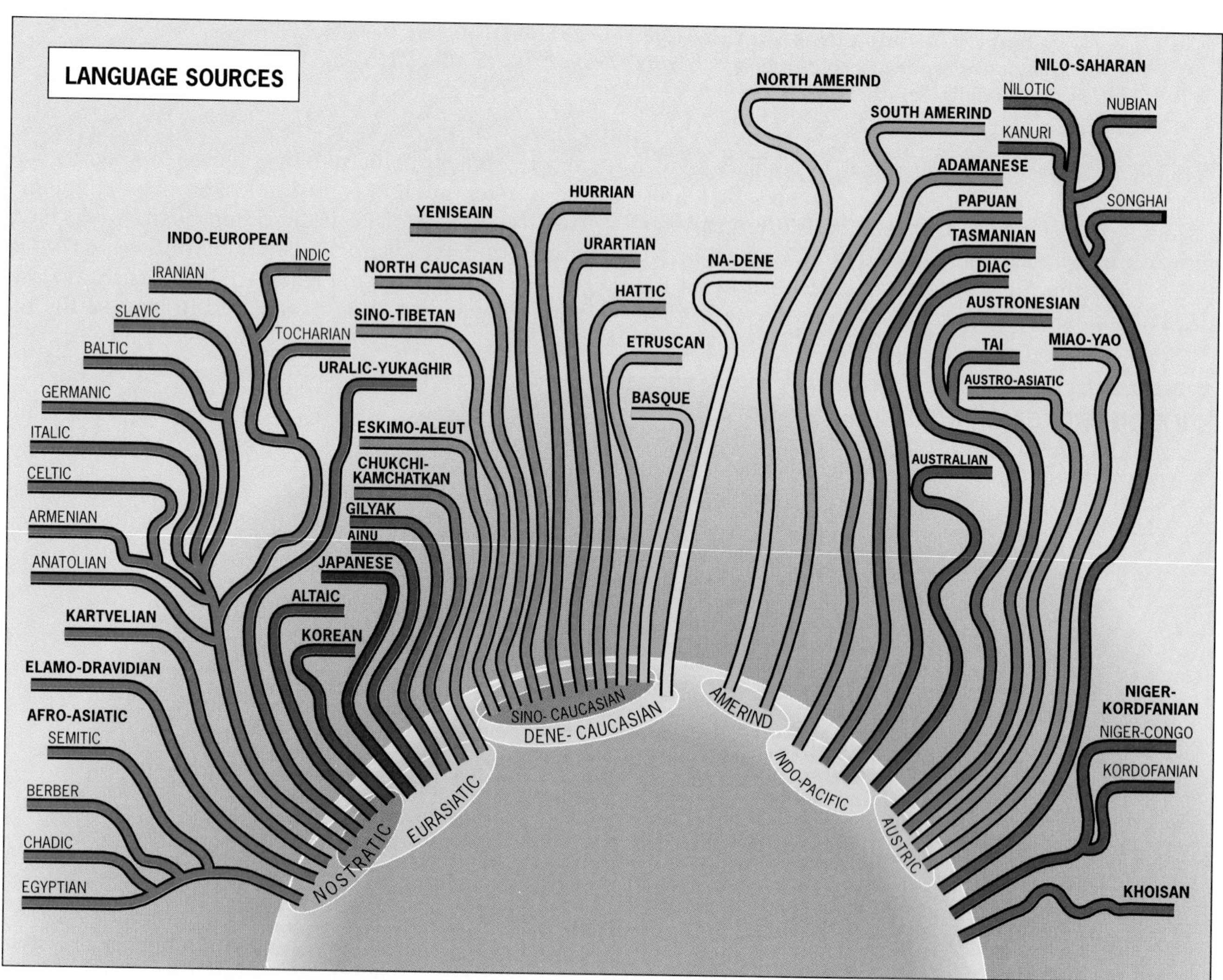

Figure 9-4 Language Sources. *Source: After a diagram in Philip E. Ross, "Hard Words,"* Scientific American, *April 1991, p. 139.*

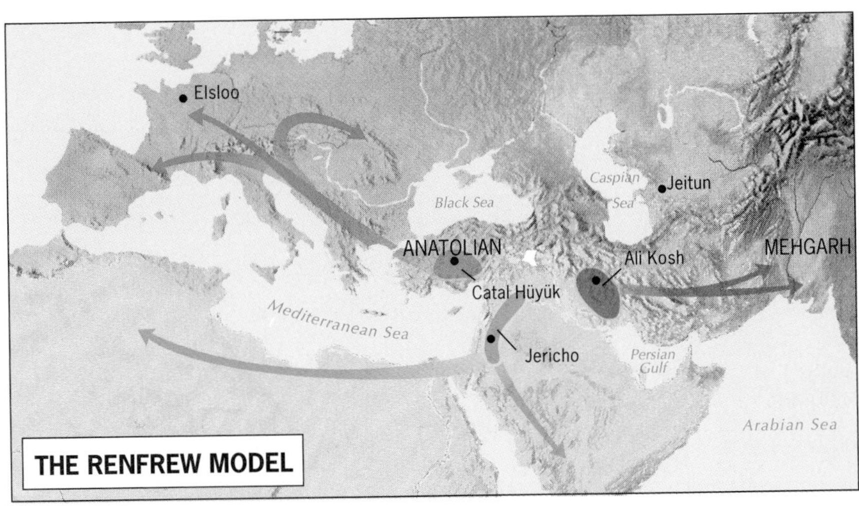

Figure 9-5 The Renfrew Model. The Renfrew Model poses that three source areas of agriculture each gave rise to a great language family. *Source: From "The Origins of Indo-European Languages,"* Scientific American, *1989, p. 114.*

a language's vocabulary (such as those identifying arms, legs, feet, hands, and other body parts, and terms for the sun, moon, and other elements of the natural environment), they reconstructed an inventory of several hundred words. What was most remarkable is that they did this independently, each unaware of the other's work for many years. When finally they met and compared their inventories, they found that they were amazingly similar. They agreed that they had established the core of a pre-Proto-Indo-European language, which they named ***Nostratic***.

As with Proto-Indo-European, the evolving vocabulary of the Nostratic language revealed much about the lives and environments of its speakers. There apparently were no names for domesticated plants or animals, so Nostratic-speakers were hunter-gatherers, not farmers. An especially interesting conclusion had to do with the words for *dog* and *wolf*, which turned out to be the same, suggesting that the domestication of wolves may have been occurring at the time. The oldest known bones of dogs excavated at archeological sites date from about 14,000 years ago, so Nostratic may have been in use at about that time, well before the First Agricultural Revolution.

Nostratic is believed to be the ancestral language not only of Proto-Indo-European, and thus the Indo-European language family as a whole, but also of the Kartvelian languages of the southern Caucasus region (16 in Fig. 8-2), the Uralic-Altaic languages (which include Hungarian and Finnish, Turkish and Mongolian), the Dravidian languages of India (Fig. 8-5), and the Afro-Asiatic language family, in which Arabic is dominant.

How long *before* 14,000 years B.P. (Before the Present) it may have been in use has not yet been established. The same is true of Nostratic's geography. Where Nostratic was born, and what tongues gave rise to it, are unanswered questions. However, Nostratic links languages that are separated even more widely than those of the Indo-European family today. Some scholars have suggested that Nostratic (and its contemporaries, variously named Eurasiatic, Indo-Pacific, Amerind, and Austric) is a direct successor of a proto-world language that goes back to the dawn of human history, but this notion is highly speculative. The inset in Figure 9-1 reminds us how little of the human language tree we know with any certainty.

◆ DIFFUSION TO THE PACIFIC AND THE AMERICAS

The final stages of the dispersal of the older languages—before the global diffusion of English and other Indo-European languages—occurred in the Pacific realm and in the Americas. One would assume that the historical geography of these events would be easier to reconstruct than the complex situation in western Eurasia. After all, the peoples who canoed across the Pacific brought their languages to unpopulated islands. Similarly, there was no linguistic convergence with preexisting languages in the Americas. Therefore, if we needed a testing ground for linguistic divergence without "noise," the Pacific islands and the Americas would seem to be fine natural laboratories. But when we examine the debates over Pacific and American native languages, we find that the problems involved are not simple at all.

Pacific Diffusion

In our discussion of human dispersal, we noted how late people first arrived in the Pacific islands; Polynesians reached New Zealand little more than 1000 years ago. On the other hand, Australia was reached between 50,000 and 60,000 years ago, and New Guinea's first human population must have arrived even earlier because the route to the southern landmass passed

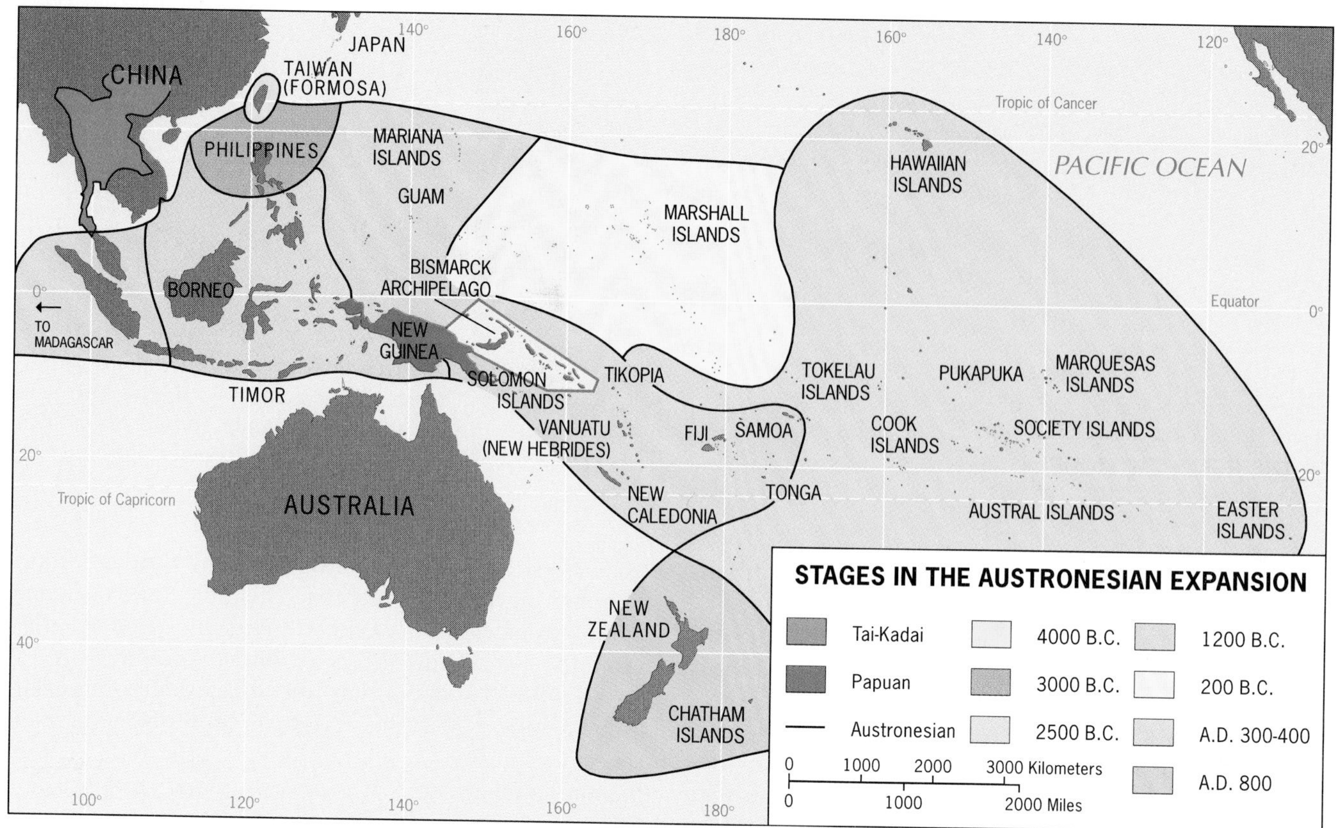

Figure 9-6 Stages in the Austronesian Expansion. Bellwood's Pacific-realm model shows the stages in the expansion of Austronesian languages. *Source: Adapted from P. Bellwood, "The Austronesian Dispersal and the Origin of Languages,"* Scientific American, *1991, p. 88.*

through it. Papuans as well as Native Australians were hunter-gatherers, although there is archeological evidence that root-crop cultivation began in New Guinea as long as 6000 years ago, leading to population growth and the expansion of Papuan populations eastward into the Solomon Islands and westward into present-day Indonesia. This expansion brought farmers into contact with foragers, and as a result the language mosaic of New Guinea and nearby islands is extremely complex.

But the diffusion of peoples and their languages into the Pacific north of Indonesia and New Guinea did not begin from these areas. Instead, it began in coastal China, where farming was well established. The languages of China and Southeast Asia had undergone several transitions; the sequence probably was similar to that from the pre-farmers' Nostratic to the farmers' Proto-Indo-European. An ancestral language gave rise to the Austro-Tai family of languages, and out of this family arose ***Austronesian***. Language geographers believe that speakers of this language (with many words for rice, field, farm, water buffalo, plow, and canoe) reached Taiwan about 6000 years ago. Several centuries later, Austronesian speakers managed to reach the Philippines. This movement resulted in the division of Austronesian into two dialects that later developed into major subfamilies. One of these, ***Malayo-Polynesian***, became the forerunner of a large number of languages, including those spoken by the first settlers of Madagascar, the islands of Melanesia and Micronesia, Fiji (where ***Fijian*** was a discrete Malayo-Polynesian offshoot), and New Zealand, whose Maori people speak ***Polynesian***, another derivative of this branch.

Considering the water-fragmented nature of the Pacific realm, this process of diffusion took place remarkably quickly. We may wonder why it took so long for the Agricultural Revolution in East Asia to stimulate emigration onto the islands off Asia's coast; but then the migrants rapidly spread from Madagascar in the west to Easter Island in the east. The whole eastern region of Polynesia was settled within several centuries (Fig. 9-6).

Although the lineages of Austronesian languages are better understood today, much remains to be learned about the reasons behind the complexity of the Pacific language map. Did successive waves of invasion stimulate divergence among the Malayo-

Polynesian languages? Or was differentiation due to isolation? And there remains the question of Austronesian ancestries. Linguists do not have a model similar to Nostratic for the languages of the Asian mainland. The Pacific language arena thus is anything but simple.

Diffusion in the Americas

As Figure 8-2 indicates, the current language map of the Americas is dominated by Indo-European languages. These have engulfed the languages spoken in America for thousands of years—the languages of Native Americans.

The Native American population never was very large by modern standards. Estimates of its pre-Columbian population have increased over the years as anthropologists have learned more about these peoples, but even the highest estimate puts the number of Native Americans at 40 million just before the European invasion. As noted previously, it was long believed that the Native Americans arrived via the Bering land bridge from Asia and that the earliest immigrations occurred just 12,000 to 13,000 years ago. Given the modest numbers of people involved and their recent arrival, one would assume under this scenario that the linguistic situation should be fairly simple. There were no preexisting peoples to be absorbed and no lifeways to be transformed. At the very least, the pattern should be much simpler than that of Eurasia.

These conclusions may be wrong, however. While some 40 language families have been recognized in the Old World, linguists have identified as many as 200 Native American language families, each different from the others. It thus appears that the first American languages diverged into the most intricately divided branch of the human language tree—within a very brief period if one accepts the Bering land bridge hypothesis.

The Greenberg Hypothesis Or did they? Not all linguists agree. In *Language in the Americas* (1987), Joseph Greenberg proposed that there are three families of indigenous American languages, each corresponding to a major wave of migration from Asia into the New World (Fig. 9-7). The oldest and largest and most widely distributed family is the ***Amerind*** superfamily, which spread from the shores of Hudson Bay to the coast of Tierra del Fuego. The next oldest, next largest, but much less widely diffused family is the ***Na-Dene***, whose languages are spoken by Native Americans of northwest Canada and part of Alaska as well as by the Apache and Navajo (the outlier in the southwestern United States shown in Figure 9-7). Last to arrive in North America were speakers of the

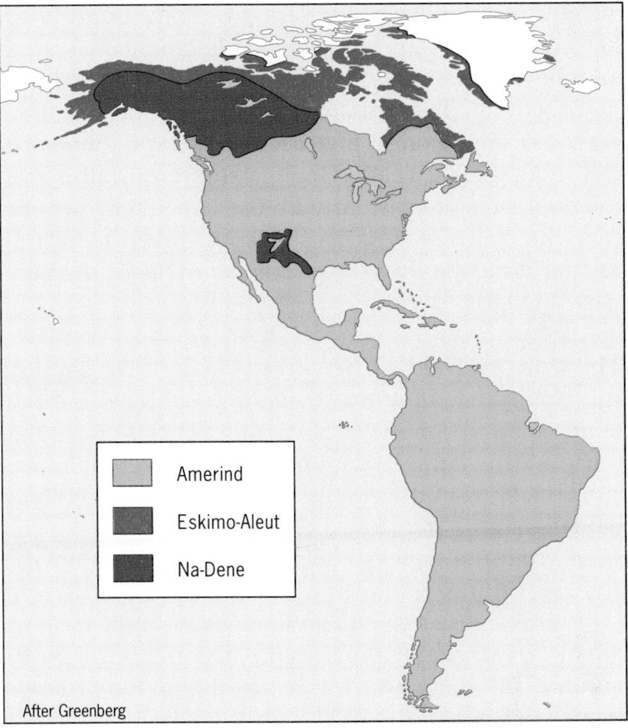

Figure 9-7 Greenberg's Three Indigenous Language Families. Greenberg's indigenous language families include Amerind, Eskimo-Aleut, and Na-Dene. *Source: From R. Lewin, "American Indian Language Dispute,"* Science *242, 1988, p. 1633.*

Eskimo-Aleut family of languages, who are still concentrated along Arctic and near-Arctic shores.

Critics of Greenberg's hypothesis contended that Greenberg did not follow proper procedures of reconstruction. Rather than studying sound shifts and other details, he compared similar-sounding words in contemporary languages. Similar work in Africa produced the map shown in Figure 8-5, which also came under heavy fire when it was first published. Today, however, that map is widely accepted.

The implications of Greenberg's hypothesis are far-reaching. If the Amerind languages are indeed members of the same family, their divergence must have occurred during a period of more than the 12,000 to 13,000 years allowed for by the dating of the first immigration. That would require a revision of the long-held view of the peopling of the Americas.

In the late 1980s and early 1990s new archeological data gave support to such a revision. A rock shelter in Pennsylvania produced artifacts dated at about 16,000 years B.P., and a site in Chile yielded material tentatively dated at 33,000 B.P. If the latter date can be confirmed, the first wave of migrants may have crossed the Pacific more than 40,000 years ago. Crucial evidence may come to light in the next several years, but at the moment the archeological evidence for very early American immigration is still tentative.

Stronger support has come from other directions. For many years Christy Turner studied dental variation among Native Americans. On the basis of dental data he concluded that the Americas were peopled in three waves of immigration that occurred over a longer period than 12,000 years. Genetic studies are also producing results consistent with the Greenberg hypothesis: the Native American speakers appear to belong to one large group whose languages have diverged over a lengthy period.

The Continuing Controversy A majority of linguists still doubt the three-wave hypothesis and the three-family map of American languages. They believe that the ultimate family relationships will eventually become clear from the careful reconstruction of individual languages. They also believe that drawing conclusions from the data Greenberg used is inappropriate and misleading.

Genetic research and archeological studies will ultimately resolve the issue. In the meantime we are reminded of the gaps still remaining in our knowledge—not just of the early development of humanity and its acquisition of language but even of its most recent precolonial migrations. The modern map of languages conceals a complex and fascinating past whose unraveling will help tell us not only where we were but also why we are the way we are.

◆ INFLUENCES ON INDIVIDUAL LANGUAGES

Each of the languages in the world's language families has its own story of origin and dispersal. We cannot hope to tell the story of even a fraction of these languages here, but we can identify some of the critical influences on the diffusion of individual tongues. First, it is clear that speakers of nonwritten languages will not retain the same language very long if they lose contact with one another. This is what led to the proliferation of languages before the advent of writing. By the same logic, the diffusion of a single tongue over a large area occurs only when people remain in contact with one another and continue to rely on a common linguistic frame of reference. Three critical components therefore have influenced the world's linguistic mosaic: writing, technology, and political organization. Writing is critical because texts are the primary means by which language can become stabilized. Technology is important because it influences both the production of written texts and the interaction of distant peoples. Political organization is key because it affects both what people have access to and which areas are in close contact with one another.

Armed with these insights, we can begin to see how the global linguistic pattern has changed. Just a few thousand years ago most habitable parts of the Earth's surface were characterized by a tremendous diversity of languages—much as one finds in interior New Guinea today. There were no literate societies and no means of bringing together peoples who were separated even by short distances. With the rise of larger-scale, more technologically sophisticated literate societies, some languages began to spread over larger areas. By two thousand years ago certain languages (notably Chinese and Latin) had successfully diffused over entire subcontinents. This was possible because these languages were associated with political systems that knit together large swaths of territory—although it should be noted that the dominant languages often coexisted with local languages that shaped the direction of regional linguistic change. Not surprisingly, then, when large-scale political systems disintegrated—as happened in the case of the Roman Empire—linguistic divergence took place.

Given the importance of writing, technology, and politics for the diffusion of languages, two developments in the late Middle Ages were of particular importance in the emergence of the modern language pattern: the invention of the printing press and the rise of nation-states. The printing press was invented in Germany in 1588, and during the next hundred years it spread to other parts of Europe and beyond. The printing press allowed for an unprecedented production of texts. Many of the early printed texts were religious, and these helped determine the standard form of various languages. The Luther Bible played this role for German, as did the King James Bible for English. The rise of nation-states was equally important, however, for these states had a strong interest in creating a more integrated state territory, and in some cases they asserted their interests in faraway places as well. Political elites thus brought peoples together and exposed them to common linguistic influences. Indeed, they played a key role in distributing printed texts. And as the leaders of countries such as England and Spain sought to expand their influence overseas, they established networks of communication and interaction that brought distant areas into closer contact than would have been conceivable just a few centuries earlier. In the process, certain languages came to be spread over vast portions of the Earth's surface.

As interesting as the historical geography of language is, the problems of language in the modern world are many and urgent. Language is a powerful component of ethnicity and lies at the heart of many current conflicts. It can be a barrier to advancement, a source of misunderstanding, and a divisive force. Governments manipulate language to bridge cultural and ethnic chasms; traders modify it to facilitate business. We consider these matters in the next chapter.

◆ KEY TERMS ◆

agriculture theory
Amerind
Austronesian
conquest theory
deep reconstruction
Eskimo-Aleut
Fijian
language convergence
language divergence
language replacement
Malayo-Polynesian
Na-Dene
Nostratic
Polynesian
Proto-Indo-European
sound shifts

◆ APPLYING GEOGRAPHIC KNOWLEDGE ◆

1. Language divergence involves the differentiation of languages over time and space. Where in North America is language divergence in progress today? What geographic factors contribute to this process here and elsewhere in the world?
2. After perhaps as long as 200,000 years of diffusion, the final phase of language dispersal (before the modern colonial period) occurred in the Americas and the Pacific. Explain how the distribution and content of indigenous languages in the Americas are analyzed to help in the reconstruction of the human settlement of this last frontier. Archeological and linguistic evidence are not always in agreement—why?

Chapter 10

Modern Language Mosaics

From the field notes

"The government of the Indian State of Maharashtra wasted no time once it had decided to scrap the name of its largest city! Even before all the legalities had been completed, the old signs showing Bombay were taken down and new ones erected. I saw this one near the harbor entrance, and asked a uniformed guard about it. 'It's the Hindu party, all politics,' he said. 'Bombay was a world name, but Mumbai refers to some Hindu goddess that is supposed to have lived here centuries ago. A lot of people in the city don't like it.' The guard was a Muslim, but he said that the city's large Sikh community also opposed the change. But a group of commuters at the railroad station were pleased. Bombay, they said, was a colonial name derived from the Portuguese, inappropriate in modern times. What was wrong with Mumbai? 'This is a Hindu country!' "

KEY POINTS

◆ **English, an Indo-European language that diffused throughout the world during the era of colonialism, has become the global language of elites, commerce, and business.**

◆ **Virtually no country is truly monolingual today. Multilingual countries sometimes solve the problem of intercultural communication by making a foreign tongue their official language.**

◆ **In several areas of the world, linguistic convergence due to trade has produced languages of mixed origin. Some of these have developed into major regional languages.**

◆ **The study of place names (toponymy) can reveal a great deal about the contents and historical geography of a culture region.**

In the 1990s a language debate has been raging in the United States. Large-scale immigration of Hispanic (primarily Mexican) people is changing the country's cultural composition. In less than three decades the ethnic balance of States from Florida to California has been transformed. In little more than a decade from now, Hispanics will constitute the largest minority in the country. The American melting pot is being stirred again.

With the growing Hispanic presence has come an expanded role for Spanish in many places. This—together with the sheer numbers of Spanish-speaking immigrants—has generated strong reactions, official as well as unofficial. Some state and local governments have sought to reaffirm the primacy of English. Organizations such as *English First* and *English Only* have spread their own message in the media. One of their oft-repeated arguments reminds Americans of their nation's history of admitting immigrant groups with foreign tongues: Germans, Italians, Swedes, and, most recently, hundreds of thousands of Asians from Vietnam and elsewhere. They ask why Spanish should be treated any differently.

To answer that question, Hispanics need only point to the map. Not only are their numbers growing faster than those of any other major ethnic community in the country, but the regional concentrations of Hispanics in several Southern, Southwestern, and Western States is marked. In this mobile, migrating nation, where ethnic Easterners have moved westward, black Southerners have moved northward, and white Midwesterners have moved southward, the Hispanic sector has begun to redefine the southern tier of the United States because it is anchored there. True, large Hispanic communities have grown in cities from New York to Denver. But the "Hispanicization" of America is a regional phenomenon, and from this comes the community's cultural strength in the national mosaic.

More than ethnic pride is at stake. Those who oppose giving special status to Spanish point to the problems faced by bilingual (two-language) countries like Canada and Belgium, where linguistic differences create strong regional divisions. Supporters of greater recognition for Spanish argue that in bilingual countries the cultures of the different ethnic communities have been preserved and weaker ones have not been submerged by stronger ones.

Nevertheless, the issue has also divided Hispanic communities themselves. In 1990 a national Hispanic policy organization published the results of a study that showed that well over half of all Hispanic adults were functionally illiterate in English and that the educational attainment of Hispanics was declining compared to the national average. Some Hispanic educators blamed much of this on the failure of many Spanish speakers to learn English. Others argued that the data reflected the disadvantaged socioeconomic position of Hispanics. Still others pointed out that in the nineteenth and early twentieth centuries many European immigrants did not learn English very well either. They went on to note that the current outcry over Spanish is a matter of cultural insecurity and even racism, and may actually work against the desire of second-generation Spanish speakers to learn English. They cited the many cases around the world where legal efforts to mandate language use have backfired because the learning of another language is seen as a concession to the dominant society.

◆ LANGUAGE AND CULTURE

Debates of this kind are ongoing in many countries. Note that the issue is not the preservation of the English language so much as its primacy in the national culture. Command of English undoubtedly is an advantage throughout the world. English has become the primary medium of international communication, especially in business, and for many the advantages of being able to use English outweigh cultural considerations. That, at least, is the position of several governments.

In Malaysia, for example, for four decades after independence the government promoted the Malay language, Bahasa Melayu. (This was less a reversal of the norms introduced by the former colonizer, Britain, than a boosting of the Malay language as opposed to Chinese, spoken by about one-third of the country's population.) But in 1994, the government of Malaysia announced that university courses in scientific and technical fields would henceforth be taught in English, not Bahasa Melayu. Malaysian nationalists were outraged, but the government held its ground. Proficiency in English, it argued, was essential to the country's economic competitiveness. Lack of such proficiency was creating a bottleneck for foreign investors and for Malaysians involved in international trade.

There was another problem as well. Malays learning English as a second language in the country's state schools were not doing nearly as well as Chinese citizens of Malaysia, many of whom were going to private schools where English was taught rigorously. Greater command of English among educated Malays would improve their competitiveness at home, too.

As we will see, some countries have made English (or another foreign language) their official language, giving indigenous languages secondary status. This provokes charges of neocolonialism or favoring the interest of educated elites. Again we see that emotional attachment to language is not just a matter of protecting threatened tongues. It is also a practical issue.

◆ LANGUAGE AND TRADE

As we saw in the previous chapter, the position of traditional native languages has changed greatly over the past several centuries—not for linguistic but for political reasons. The European subfamily of Indo-European spread rapidly over much of the globe, replacing and modifying local languages virtually everywhere. Then the world developed a boundary system that confined the speakers of many languages within specific territories. Although these borders often separated people speaking the same language, they more often threw together peoples with mutually unintelligible tongues. This created a host of difficulties both between and within states, problems that persist today.

The Esperanto Experiment

Early in the twentieth century a major effort was launched to create a world language, an artificial tongue that would eventually become the first or second language of all peoples everywhere. Called ***Esperanto***, this invented language was based on Latin and a combination of words from modern European languages. European schools introduced Esperanto, and Esperanto societies were formed in many countries during the interwar period. Even the League of Nations endorsed the idea. But Esperanto was not a global tongue. It was another Indo-European language, and therefore its applicability was limited. Moreover, Europeans were becoming increasingly multilingual, and few wanted to learn another language that did not have obvious practical utility. The Esperanto initiative therefore failed.

Lingua Franca

Where language planners failed, traders succeeded. Long before the rise of the global economy, centuries before the global diffusion of English (the Esperanto of today), and before the invention of Esperanto, people speaking different languages were forced to find ways to communicate for trade. This need resulted in the emergence of a ***lingua franca***.

The term comes from the Mediterranean Sea and its numerous trading ports during the period following the Crusades. As seaborne commerce in the Mediterranean expanded, traders from the ports of southern France—the *Franks*—revitalized the ports of the eastern Mediterranean. But the local traders did not speak the seafarers' language. Thus began a process of convergence in which the tongue of the Franks was mixed with Italian, Greek, Spanish, and Arabic. This mixture was known as the *Frankish language*, or *lingua franca*, and it served for centuries as the common tongue of Mediterranean commerce.

Today the term *lingua franca* is still used to denote any common language spoken by peoples with different native tongues. Arabic became a lingua franca during the expansion of Islam, and English did so in many areas during the colonial era. But the term is most appropriate for languages that are products of linguistic convergence. One of the best modern examples is Swahili, the lingua franca of East Africa. Over centuries of contact and interaction, Swahili developed from African Bantu languages, Arabic, and Persian. Although not a tone language like many other African languages, Swahili has a complex vocabulary

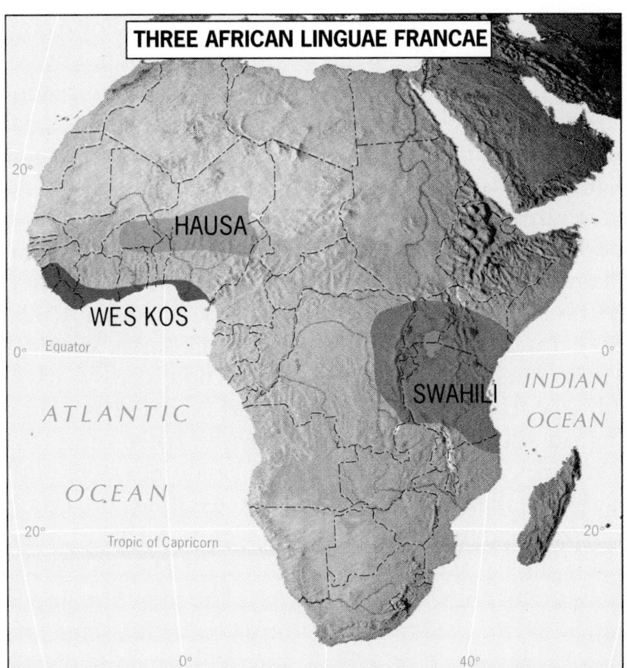

Figure 10-1 Three African Linguae Francae. The three African linguae francae are Swahili, Wes Kos, and Hausa.

and structure. It has become the Esperanto of a region that extends from southern Somalia to northern Moçambique and from coastal Kenya and Tanzania to Uganda and the East African Great Lakes region; it is even used in eastern Congo.

During the period when West Africa's interior kingdom thrived and trade between the arid north and the moist, forested coast was intense, a lingua franca emerged in the cities and bustling markets of the Sudanic zone extending from northern Nigeria westward to Senegal. That language, Hausa, is still a regional tongue used by speakers of other languages to communicate. Hausa is heard today not only in Nigeria but also in western Chad, southern Niger, and even Burkina Faso and eastern Mali (Fig. 10-1).

Creolization

When relocation diffusion sends speakers of a language far from their homeland, their language is likely to change, if not grammatically, then in terms of pronunciation, rhythm, and speed. Australian English is not very different from standard English in vocabulary, but its cadence makes it unmistakable. English as spoken in India and South Africa also sounds quite different from standard English.

In some instances, however, a language changes much more radically. Through contact with other languages, it can be simplified and modified to become what linguists call a ***pidgin***. In the Caribbean region, for example, English speakers met peoples speaking African languages, and before long a form of pidgin English developed. Ordinary people—not the colonialists or the elites—communicated in this pidgin, which diffused throughout the islands. It even reached mainland South America, not only in English-speaking Guyana but also in Dutch-speaking Suriname.

Over time a pidgin language may itself become the mother tongue as the original languages of its speakers are forgotten. African languages heard in the Caribbean in the years following the first involuntary migration faded away and were replaced by an ever more complex pidgin. This important form of language replacement is known as ***creolization***. The original pidgin becomes a lingua franca and is referred to as a ***creole*** language. A process similar to that just described occurred in the western Pacific region, where Melanesian pidgin is evolving into a regional creole language that was originally based on English but is now quite distinct. In coastal West Africa, a pidgin language called *Wes Kos* is also continuing to develop. Swahili, on the other hand, cannot be classified as a pidgin or a successor to a creole language. Because of its complex structure and vocabulary, it is a full-fledged Bantu language, though a distinct one. A former president of Tanzania, Julius Nyerere, proved the depth and capacity of Swahili by translating Shakespeare's plays into that language.

Pidgin and creole languages are important unifying forces in a linguistically divided world. They tend to be simple and accessible, and therefore disseminate rapidly. In Southeast Asia a trade language called *Bazaar Malay* can be heard from Myanmar (Burma) to Indonesia and from the Philippines to Malaysia; it has become a lingua franca in the region. A simplified form of Chinese also serves as a language of commerce even beyond the borders of China.

Sometimes the difference between a dialect and a pidgin or creole language becomes blurred. As mentioned in the preceding chapter, some linguists regard Quebecois French as a dialect, but others consider it a distinct language derived from French. It is not a creole language; neither is Afrikaans, originally a dialect of Dutch spoken in South Africa but now a distinct language with Dutch, French, and even Malay components.

◆ MULTILINGUALISM

At the beginning of the chapter we touched upon the sensitive issue of language and status. Languages, including pidgin and creole forms, can promote understanding and interaction between different peoples, but they can also divide. There are only a few ***monolingual states***, countries in which only one language is spoken. They include Japan in Asia; Uruguay and

Venezuela in South America; Iceland, Portugal, and Poland in Europe; and Lesotho in Africa. However, even in these countries there are small numbers of people who speak other languages; for example, more than a half-million Koreans live in Japan. In fact, there is no truly monolingual country today. English-speaking Australia has more than 180,000 speakers of aboriginal languages. Predominantly Portuguese-speaking Brazil has nearly 1.5 million speakers of Native American languages.

Countries in which more than one language is in use are called ***multilingual states***. In some of these countries linguistic fragmentation reflects strong cultural pluralism as well as divisive forces. This is true in former colonial areas where peoples speaking different languages were thrown together, as happened in Africa and Asia. This also occurred in the Americas: as Figure 10-2 shows, Native American languages are spoken by more than half of the people in large areas of Guatemala and Mexico, although these countries tend to be viewed as Spanish speaking.

Multilingualism, therefore, takes several forms. In effectively bilingual Canada and Belgium, it is reflected in regional divisions; that is, the two major languages each dominate in particular areas of the country. In multilingual Switzerland there are four such regions (Fig. 10-3). In Peru, centuries of acculturation have not erased the regional identities of the Native American tongues spoken in the Andean Mountains and the Amazonian interior, and of Spanish, spoken on the coast. We noted previously the jigsaw of languages in India, where entire states correspond to linguistic majorities.

But multilingualism has another dimension. In some countries (far fewer), there is less regional separation of speakers of different languages. For example, members of the white (European) community of South Africa speak two majority languages (Afrikaans and English) and several other tongues. Although Afrikaans remains the dominant language in part of South Africa's rural interior, the country has no linguistic regionalism comparable to that of Canada or the former Czechoslovakia (where Czech was the language of the west and Slovak of the east). In addition to the European languages spoken in South Africa, there are many African languages, of course, but their spatial interlocking is nonetheless noteworthy. Kwazulu-Natal and especially the city of Durban have large English-speaking minorities; Cape Town and the Western Cape Province have large numbers of Afrikaner speakers. But neither group excludes the other.

This pattern is what Soviet planners had in mind when they organized the communist state after the Russian Revolution: Russian would become the lingua franca of the USSR, and the diffusion of Russians and their language would create a state in which linguistic communities retained their identities while "Russification" progressed around them. But today the region is a patchwork of ethnolinguistic areas, in many of which the local language is being aggressively promoted and supported.

Another country in which a multilingual experiment failed is Cyprus, where Greeks and Turks shared a small but comparatively prosperous island. Although the Greek majority and the Turkish minority were often at odds, there was much mingling between the two groups in the years after the country gained independence in 1960, as Figure 10-4 shows. But a political crisis in 1974 led to armed intervention by Turkey. Cyprus was partitioned, and both Turks and Greeks became refugees in their own country. Virtually all the Turks moved north of the "Green Line" shown in Figure 10-4, while all the Greeks were confined to the south of it.

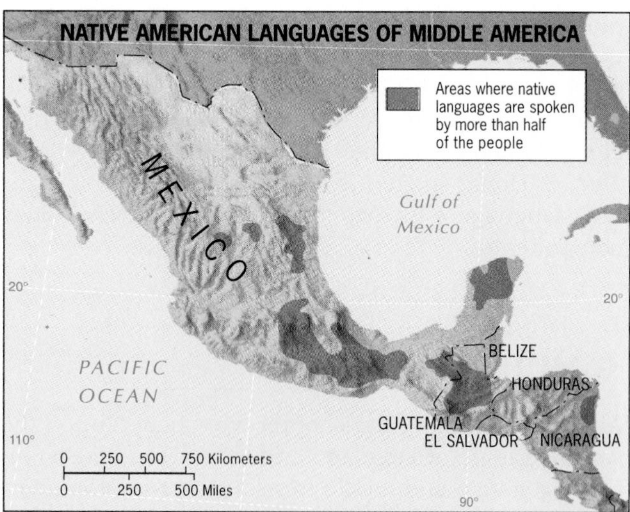

Figure 10-2 Native American Languages in Middle America. This map shows areas where native languages are spoken by more than half of the people.

Canada

The modern state of Canada is the product of a sequence of events that had the effect of combining a large, dominantly French-speaking territory, Quebec, with an even larger, mainly English-speaking area centered on neighboring Ontario. Under the British North America Act of 1867, which created the Canadian federation, Quebec was given important guarantees: the French civil code was sustained, and the French language was protected in parliament and in the courts.

More than five generations later Canada is still a divided society, and language lies at the heart of the division. More than 85 percent of Quebec's population of over 7 million speak French at home, but that still leaves a significant minority of non-French speakers

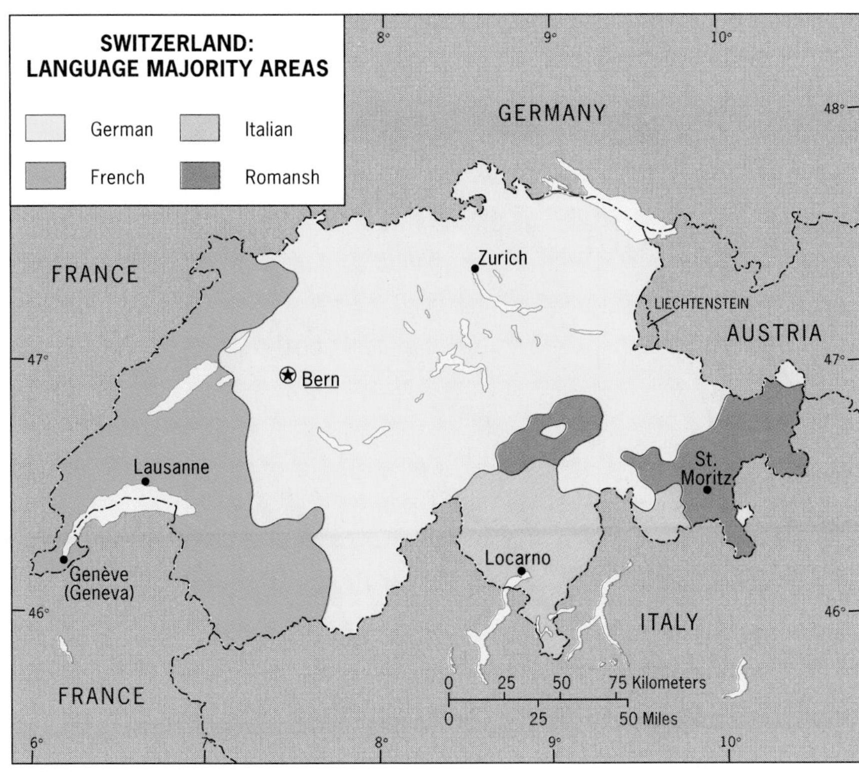

Figure 10-3 Language Majority Areas in Switzerland. German, French, Italian, and Romansh are spoken in different areas of Switzerland. *Source: From a map in W. A. D. Jackson,* The Shaping of Our World. *New York: Wiley, 1985, p. 224.*

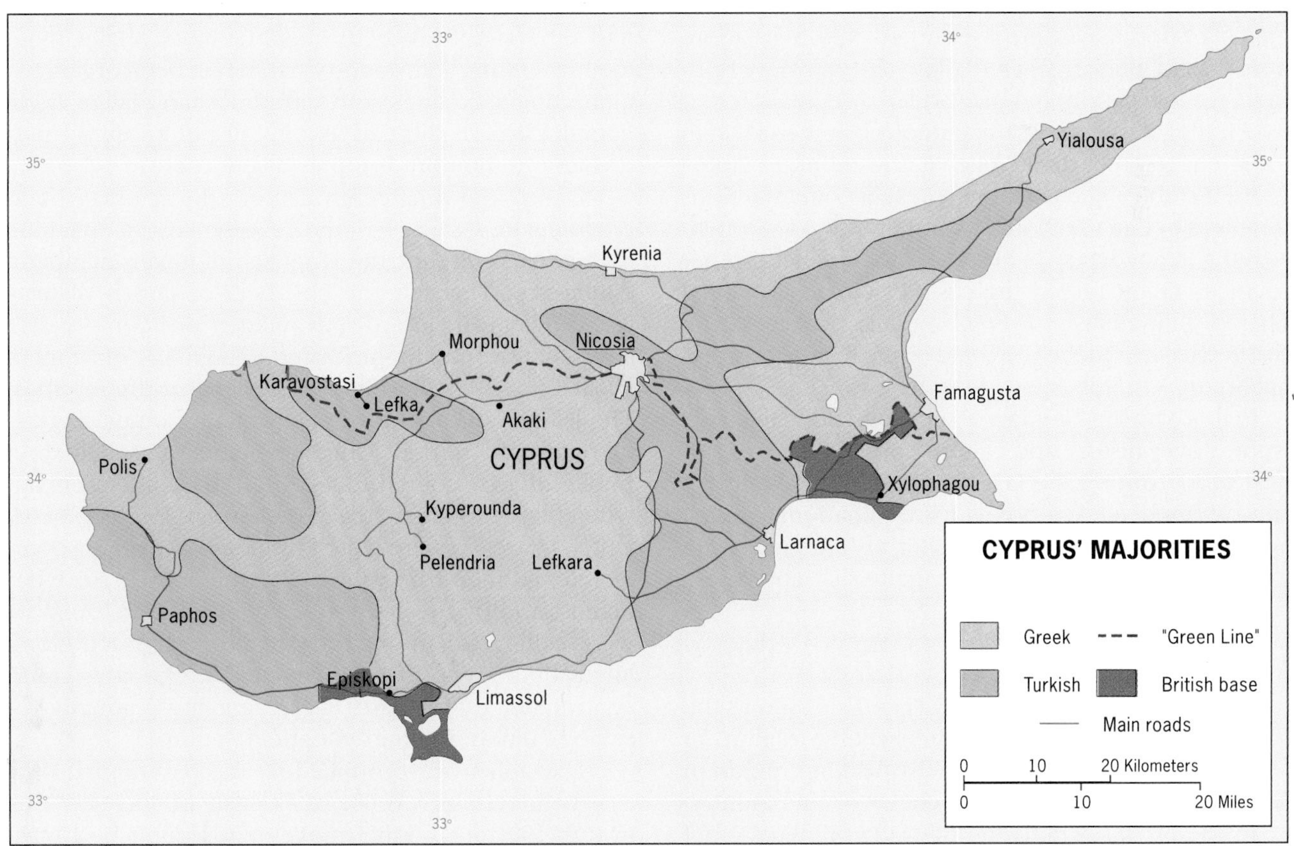

Figure 10-4 Cyprus's Majorities before 1974. This map shows Greek and Turkish areas and British bases. *Source: From a map in D. Downing,* An Atlas of Territorial Border Disputes. *London: New English Library, 1980, p. 30.*

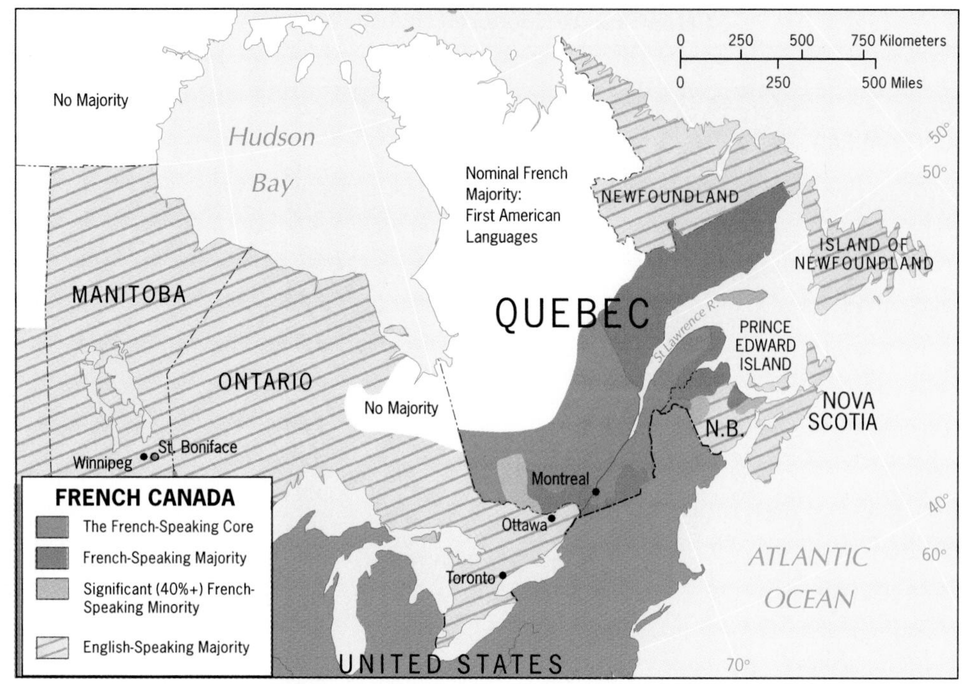

Figure 10-5 French Speakers in Canada. *Sources: Canada Census, Statistics Canada,* The National Atlas of Canada *(1985), and* The Canada Year Book.

(Fig. 10-5). Many Quebecers feel threatened by this situation. In 1977 the Quebec provincial parliament passed a law that compelled all businesses in the province to demonstrate that they functioned in French. Canada's Supreme Court overturned this legislation, but in 1988 Quebec enacted a law that not only reinstated the legislation, but also added a regulation that made it illegal to exhibit any outdoor commercial sign in a language other than French in the entire province.

Predictably, such actions caused counteractions elsewhere in Canada. With fewer than 700,000 French-speaking Canadians living outside Quebec, other provinces reconsidered the costs of Canada's official policy of bilingualism. If English could be treated the way it was in Quebec, should French be accorded equality in, say, Alberta or Saskatchewan?

In this way the language issue, embedded in larger disputes over history and culture, tore at Canada's political fabric during the last decades of the twentieth century. Language is a potent force in national affairs, and the strongly regional character of bilingualism in Canada poses a daunting challenge to that country.

Belgium

A contemporary map of Belgium (Fig. 10-6) shows the country divided into a Dutch-speaking region in the north (Flanders) and a French-speaking region in the south (Wallonia). Near the center of the country, just inside of Flanders, is the officially bilingual—but majority French-speaking—capital of Brussels. These language regions reflect the fact that Belgium straddles the line separating the Romance and Germanic branches of Indo-European. Language has been a divisive issue in Belgium almost since its founding in 1830, but it has not always been associated with regionalism. The formal language regions of Belgium had little significance throughout most of the nineteenth century. The country had never been organized along linguistic lines, and differences in dialect made communication difficult among all but an elite—particularly in the northern part of the country.

During the nineteenth century the effort to build an integrated state led the largely French-speaking elite to make French the language of government and commerce. This left the speakers of Dutch dialects (called Flemish) in a disadvantaged position—a situation that eventually produced a language movement spearheaded by the elites of several northern cities. The leaders of that movement initially sought linguistic rights (the right of Dutch speakers to use Dutch in public affairs, court proceedings, schools, etc.), but when that failed they began demanding protection for Dutch in areas where Dutch or Flemish speakers dominated. Further frustrations led to more radical demands, and by the 1920s a growing cadre of activists were calling for the country to be partitioned along linguistic lines so that Dutch-speaking peoples could control their own affairs. These demands gradually became reality in the mid-twentieth century.

The upheavals produced by the partitioning process helped forge a sense of Flemish identity, and this in turn fueled a countermovement among Belgium's French speakers—the Walloons. With language-group identity on the rise, conflicts between linguistic "communities" became an increasingly central feature of

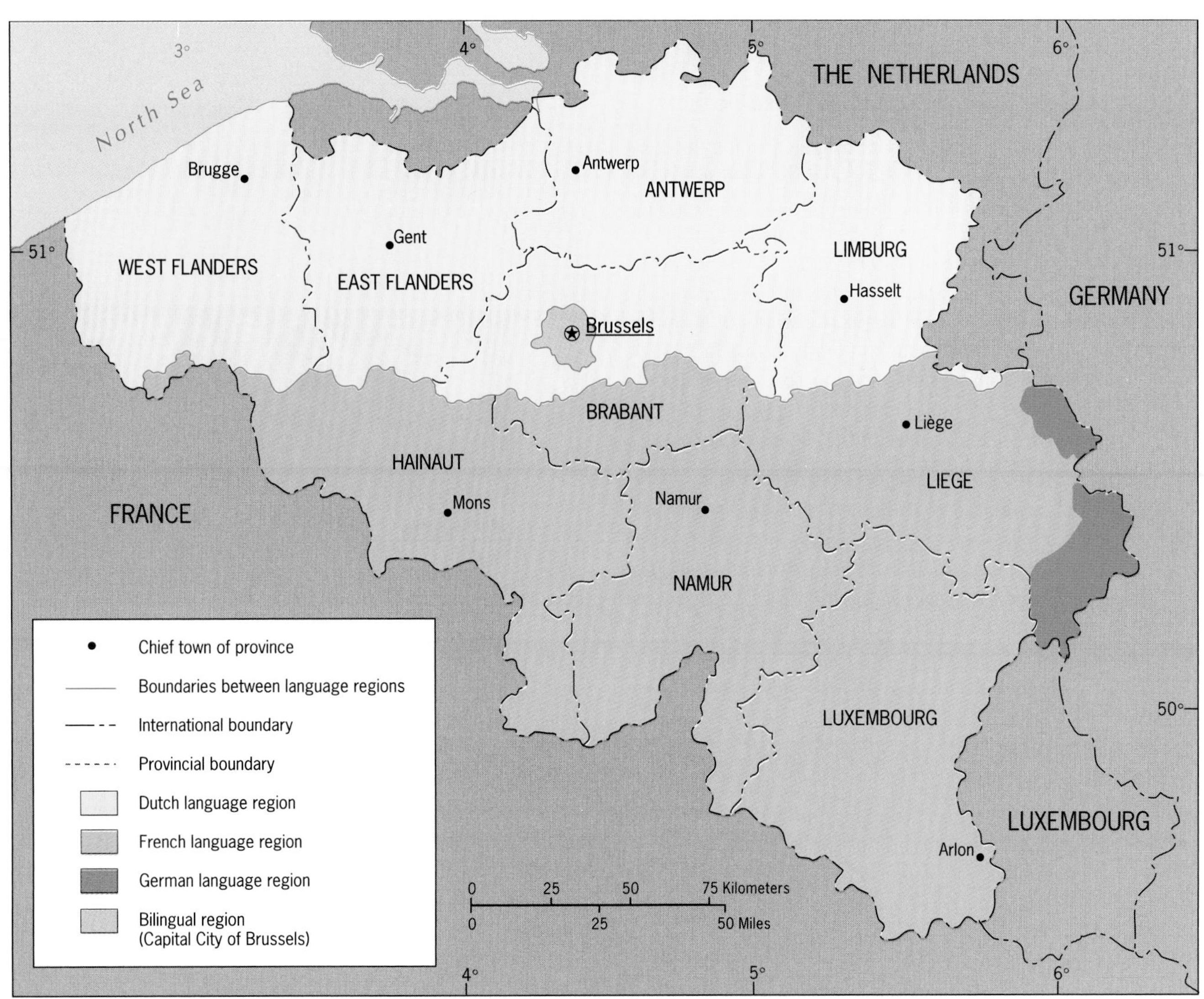

Figure 10-6 Divided Belgium and Its Neighbors. Dutch, French, and German are spoken in different areas of Belgium. *Source: Murphy, A. B. 1995. "Belgium's Regional Divergence along the Road to Federation,"* Federalism: The Multiethnic Challenge, *G. Smith, ed., London: Longman.*

Belgian political life. The conflict has been largely nonviolent, but it has led to the fall of several governments and has dominated the political agenda on numerous occasions. It is also responsible for Belgium's recent changeover from a unitary to a federal state. (The language regions shown in Figure 10-6 are the constituent units of the federation.)

The partitioning of Belgium along language lines does not signal the end of linguistic conflict. With the country divided between two major language regions, many issues are cast in regional linguistic terms—even issues that are not overtly cultural. The language regions of Belgium thus are not just a product of the coalescence of language communities; their existence actually tends to *foster* regionalism. Some even wonder whether Belgium will follow Czechoslovakia's lead and split into two countries. This is not impossible, but the situation of Brussels works against it. Both Flanders and Wallonia have a vested interest in Brussels, so neither would abandon it lightly. And the French-speaking majority in Brussels has little interest in casting its lot with the region in which it is situated—Flanders. Thus, for the time being, Belgium is likely to continue to look for the compromises that have kept the language issue alive for so long, but have also kept it from spilling over into violence.

Nigeria

Nigeria's multilingualism is much more complicated than that of either Canada or Belgium. Nigeria, with a population of over 100 million, is a former colony characterized by almost unimaginable linguistic diversity. It has three major regional languages, more than

A SENSE OF SCALE

Linguistic Transition Zones

Behind many of the neat lines on language maps lie complicated, at times contentious, linguistic transition zones. This is certainly the case in Belgium, where the language regions shown on Figure 10-6 hide complexities that are evident only when language patterns are considered at the local scale. Brussels, the capital of Belgium, lies north of the line separating the two major language regions of Belgium. Most maps show the city as an officially bilingual area—and indeed many of its inhabitants can speak both French and Dutch. But the internal situation is more complicated than that—and it is fraught with political significance.

For centuries Brussels was a Flemish city dominated by a Germanic dialect related to Dutch. In the eighteenth century when French was the language of international politics and culture in Europe, a process of "Frenchification" began. Official promotion of French, together with the use of French in government in this heavily administrative city, led to a growing use of French during the nineteenth century. By the mid-twentieth century, a majority of the city's residents spoke French.

Brussels' linguistic history placed it at the center of Belgium's struggles over language. For the Dutch-speaking peoples of northern Belgium, the Frenchification of the city became a symbol of the creeping dominance of French. Their efforts to combat that process were interpreted by Belgium's French-speaking population as confrontational and undemocratic. An uneasy compromise now accords the city a bilingual status and places strict limits on the use of French in surrounding communes. Behind these legal arrangements lies a complex urban-cultural geography. No one knows precisely where speakers of French and Dutch live—language questions became so sensitive that they were banned from the Belgian census after 1947—but some areas are clearly dominated by one group or the other. As such, social and economic inequalities that reflect these patterns of dominance often take on larger meaning. Similarly, any departure from the principle of bilingualism can generate heated exchanges and, if official in nature, can have wide-ranging political repercussions.

Brussels is but one of many cities around the world where language communities come together. From Montreal to Jerusalem to Johannesburg, the local geography of language use is a matter that is imbued with larger cultural significance. The spatial distribution of language groups and the controversies that rage over language use in public spaces help to define the character of such places, as well as the ways that different groups view themselves and one another.

a dozen major local languages spoken by 1 to 5 million people, and 230 lesser tongues (Fig. 10-7). The three major regional languages, Hausa (the old lingua franca of the north, now spoken by some 35 million northerners), Yoruba (the leading language of the southwest, with 25 million speakers), and Ibo (the major language of the southeast, spoken by more than 20 million people), are strongly associated with regional cultures, and thus are unsuitable as national languages. Upon becoming independent, Nigeria decided to adopt English as its "official" language, as India had done earlier. When Nigeria's 20 million schoolchildren go to school, they first must learn English, which is used for all subsequent instruction.

Certainly, the use of English has helped Nigeria avoid cultural conflicts based on language, but Nigerian educators are having second thoughts about the policy. Upon entering school, children who have grown up speaking a local language are suddenly confronted with a new, unfamiliar language. The time and energy that must be spent learning the lingua franca are taken away from the learning of other important subjects. Moreover, for many students knowledge of English is irrelevant if they emerge from school (as many do after only six years) unable to function in local Nigerian society. Nigeria thus is having serious doubts about its relationship with the lingua franca brought here by the colonists who established their multiethnic country in the first place.

◆ OFFICIAL LANGUAGES

India and Nigeria are not the only countries that have chosen to use an "umbrella" language. Several dozen countries have embraced the concept of an ***official language***. In theory, an official language, already used by the educated and politically powerful elite, will enhance communication and interaction among peoples who speak different traditional languages.

As Table 10-1 shows, many former African colonies have adopted the colonists' language as their official language, even though they may have gained their independence in a violent revolution against those colonists. Thus Portuguese is the official language of Angola, English is the language of Nigeria and Ghana, and French is the language of Côte d'Ivoire.

Such a policy is not without risks. As we noted in the case of Nigeria, the long-term results of the use of a foreign language may not always be positive. In some countries, including India, citizens objected to using a language that they associated with colonial repression. In response, some former colonies chose not just one but two official languages: the European colonial language plus one of the country's own major languages. As Table 10-1 shows, English *and* Hindi are official languages of India. English and Swahili are official languages of Tanzania. In Mauritania, French and Arabic are official languages. But this solution was not always enough. When Hindi was given official status in India, riots and disorder broke out in non-Hindi areas of the country. Kenya, which at first made English and Swahili its official languages, decided to drop English in the face of public opposition to "archaic" rules requiring candidates for public office to pass a test of their ability to use English.

Further inspection of Table 10-1 reveals some noteworthy relationships. French and English are both official languages in the African country of Cameroon because an English-speaking province was welded to the French-dominated colony shortly after independence. In Peru, Spanish and the Native American (Amerindian) language Quechuan have official status and are found in distinct regions. In the Philippines, English and a creolized Spanish, Pilipino, are both official languages. Tiny Singapore, the city-state at the tip of the Malay Peninsula, has four official languages: English, Chinese, Malay, and Tamil, an Indian tongue. South Africa has the largest number of official languages—eleven.

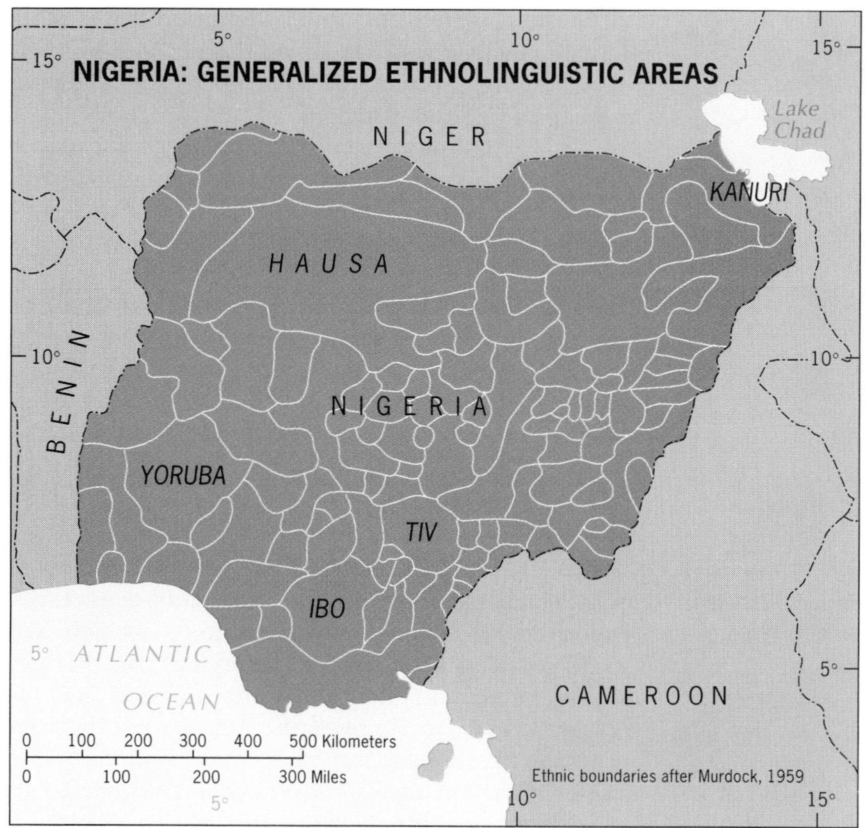

Figure 10-7 Generalized Ethnolinguistic Areas of Nigeria. This map is actually a simplification of the ethnolinguistic mosaic of Nigeria. *Source: Detail from a map in G. P. Murdock,* Africa: Its Peoples and their Culture History. *New York: McGraw-Hill, 1972.*

Table 10-1 Official Languages of Selected Countries, 1998

Country	Language(s)
Angola	Portuguese
Benin	French
Botswana	English
Brunei	English, Malay
Burundi	French
Cameroon	French, English
Canada	English, French
Central African Republic	French
Chad	French
Congo	French
Djibouti	French, Arabic
Dominica	English
Equatorial Guinea	Spanish
Fiji	English, Fijian
Gabon	French
Ghana	English
Guinea	French
India	English, Hindi
Indonesia	Bahasa, Indonesian
Ivory Coast (Côte d'Ivoire)	French
Kenya	Swahili
Lesotho	English, Sesotho
Madagascar	French, Malagasy
Malawi	English, Chichewa
Mali	French
Mauritania	French, Arabic
Moçambique	Portuguese
Niger	French
Nigeria	English
Peru	Spanish, Quechuan
Philippines	English, Pilipino (Tagalog)
Rwanda	French, Kinyarwanda
Senegal	French
Seychelles	French, English
Sierra Leone	English
Singapore	English, Malay, Chinese, Tamil
Somalia	English, Somali
South Africa	English, Xhosa and 9 others
Suriname	Dutch
Swaziland	English, SiSwati
Tanzania	English, Swahili
Togo	French
Uganda	English
Zimbabwe	English

As would be expected, Canada recognizes both English and French not only as official languages but as equals in all governmental settings. The United States, on the other hand, has never proclaimed an official language, although there have been many demands that it do so.

◆ TOPONYMY

The systematic study of place names, or ***toponymy***, leads to many valuable and useful insights. A classic work on this topic is George Stewart's *Names on the Land: A Historical Account of Place-Naming in the United States* (1958). There are also numerous studies dealing with the significance of place names in individual states or regions.

Place names can reveal much about a culture area even when time has erased other evidence. A cluster of Welsh place names in Pennsylvania, French place names in Louisiana, or Dutch place names in Michigan not only reveals national origins but may also provide insight into language and dialect, routes of diffusion, and ways of life. For example, amid the Portuguese place names of Santa Catarina State, Brazil, lies the town named Blumenau. If you check more closely, you will discover that German immigrants played major roles in the development of this southern Brazilian state. The fondness for flowers reflected in so many German place names (Blumberg, Blumenhof, Blumenort, Blumenthal, Blumenstein) is reflected on the map in this part of South America.

Toponyms (place names) make reading a map a fruitful and sometimes revealing exercise. A careful eye will spot Roman names on the map of Britain, German names on the map of France, and Dutch names in Australia. Sometimes the links are harder to find. The Brazilian state of Bahia has a number of place names that seem to have originated in West Africa, especially Benin and Nigeria. And indeed, these two areas were linked by the forced migration of enslaved Africans.

Two-Part Names

Many place names consist of two parts, sometimes connected and sometimes separate: a *specific* (or given) part and a *generic* (or classifying) part. For example, the capital of the Netherlands, Amster/dam, refers to the city's major river (the Amstel) and the dam that made possible the settlement of the site. The name Battle Creek (Michigan) consists of a reference to an event (specific) and a landscape feature (generic). Johns/town, Pitts/burgh, Nash/ville, Chapel Hill, and

Little Rock are among the many additional examples that could be cited.

Such generic names can sometimes be linked to each of the three source areas of U.S. dialects and their westward diffusion. In the North, towns and cities were typically laid out by compass directions. To this day, foreign visitors are impressed by the use of these directions to show the way ("go four blocks east, then three blocks north"). This led to the naming of adjacent settlements by direction as well: *East* Lansing (Michigan), *West* Chester (Pennsylvania), *North* Chicago (Illinois), *South* St. Paul (Minnesota). This pattern is mainly (though not exclusively) a northern phenomenon.

Classification of Place Names

The historian George Stewart classified place names into ten categories, as follows:

descriptive names (Rocky Mountains)
associative names (Mill Valley, California)
incident names (Battle Creek, Michigan)
possessive names (Johnson City, Texas)
commemorative names (San Francisco)
commendatory names (Paradise Valley, Arizona)
folk-etymology names (Plains, Georgia, or Academia, Pennsylvania)
manufactured names (Truth or Consequences, New Mexico)
mistake names, involving historic errors in identification or translation (such as Lasker, North Carolina, named after the state of Alaska!)
so-called **shift** names (relocated names; double names for the same feature—For example, Alpine Mountain)

Each of these categories contains cultural-geographic evidence. For example, the capital of Russia has an associative place name. Moscow is actually spelled *Moskva* in Russian, but *kva* is Finnish for water. A check on other toponyms in the Moscow region confirms the ancient presence of Finnish peoples in what is now the Russian heartland. Another example is the southern tip of South America, Cape Horn, which can be categorized as a mistake name. The Dutch named this area Cape Hoorn, after a Dutch town. The English interpreted this as Cape Horn, which the Spanish, in turn, translated into *Cabo Hornos*—meaning Cape of Ovens!

Changing Place Names

Like language itself, the names of places can elicit strong passions. When African colonies became independent countries, one of the first acts of many of the new governments was to change the names of places that had been named after colonial figures. Not only were the names of cities and towns changed, but also several countries were renamed: Upper Volta to Burkina Faso, Gold Coast to Ghana, Nyasaland to Malawi, Northern and Southern Rhodesia to Zambia and Zimbabwe, and many more. New names such as Sri Lanka (Ceylon), Bangladesh (East Pakistan), and Indonesia (Netherlands East Indies) appeared on the map of Asia. (See "Focus on: What's in a Name?").

Changes in the names of cities and towns, however, seemed to evoke stronger reactions than changes in the names of territories. Some governments carried this campaign further than others, changing not only European names but even indigenous names that were thought to have a colonial tinge. Thus Leopoldville (named after a Belgian king) became Kinshasa, capital of the Congo; Salisbury (Zimbabwe), named after a British leader, was renamed Harare; and Lourenço Marques, commemorating a Portuguese naval hero, became Maputo. On the other hand, Etoile (the Congo), Colleen Bawn (Zimbabwe), and Cabo Delgado (Moçambique) remained on the postcolonial map.

The next round of name-changing occurred during and after the collapse of the Soviet Union. Thousands of places named after Soviet-era personalities or slogans were renamed—sometimes to their earlier Czarist-era names. Leningrad became St. Petersburg, Sverdlovsk went back to Yekaterinburg, its name under the Czars, and Andropov was renamed Rybinsk, which is how it was known before the communist ruler Yuri Andropov died. Reformers, nationalists, and unreformed communists argued bitterly over these changes, and many people continued to address their mail according to the older usage.

Today, the still-new government of South Africa is wrestling with pressures for and against place-name changes. It has restructured the country's administrative framework, creating nine provinces out of four and giving some of the new ones African names (Mpumalanga for the new Eastern Transvaal, Gauteng for a new central province). One of the old provinces, Natal, has become Kwazulu-Natal. Some names of towns and villages have been changed, but South Africa's map still includes many names from the Boer-British and Apartheid periods. Name changes can evoke strong reactions, and the government is trying to move slowly and carefully to avoid arousing emotions in this still-divided country.

Obviously, language provides a wide range of opportunities for research and study. It is a vital element in the reconstruction of past cultures. The transmittal of oral literature and its interpretation opens up whole new possibilities. The professional storyteller in an Af-

Focus On

What's in a Name?

Some years after General Mobutu Sese Seko seized control of the former Belgian Congo in Equatorial Africa, he renamed the country Zaïre. At first other governments and international agencies did not take this move seriously, but Mobutu's decision eventually had to be recognized. Maps and atlases were changed. The Congo's money, the franc, became the newly printed zaïre. Even the fabled Congo River was renamed the Zaïre.

In 1997, when the revolutionary leader Laurent Kabila ousted Mobutu and established his regime in the capital, Kinshasa, one of his first acts was to rename the country. It became the Democratic Republic of the Congo, and Zaïre thus got its colonial name back—at least in its short form.

Renaming countries after revolutionary successes or military coups has become commonplace—and a cartographer's nightmare. In 1989 the generals who had taken over the government of Burma changed their country's thousand-year-old name to Myanmar. This name, too, may not outlast the next revolution.

Some embattled locales have more than one name at the same time. Argentinians refer to the Islas Malvinas, a small archipelago in the southwest Atlantic that is called the Falkland Islands by the British and most other countries. In 1982 Argentina's invasion of the Malvinas was repelled by British forces, and the Falklands remained under the British Crown. The war ended in a matter of weeks, but the underlying dispute lingers, and so do both names.

In the western Pacific, between Japan's Okinawa and Taiwan, lies a group of eight uninhabited islands that are claimed both by China, which calls them the Diaoyu, and by Japan, which calls them the Senkakus. In 1996 a band of Japanese nationalist activists built a lighthouse and memorial on one of the islands, enraging Chinese authorities. This issue is far from settled, and both names will remain on maps for years to come.

Sometimes a name change is viewed as a move toward justice and satisfaction. The Dutch province of Friesland, locals insist, was known as Fryslan, an independent entity, 3000 years ago. Then came the Romans, who conquered Fryslan and renamed it Frisia; then the French, who called it La Frise; and next the Hollanders, who attached it to the Kingdom of the Netherlands as the province of Friesland. After years of agitation the Frysk National Party achieved its goal: Dutch maps will show the province as Fryslan. Will the next demand be to make Frisian an official language?

rican village is not just a picturesque figure; his tales contain the history and psyche of his people. The study of dialects and the spatial character of word changes can tell us much about the movement of people, their external contacts or isolation, their former distribution, and more.

Language can also reveal much about the way people view reality. In their structure and vocabulary and in their ability (or inability) to express certain concepts and ideas, languages reflect the way people think about and perceive their world. There are African languages that have no word or term for the concept of a god. Some Asian languages have no tenses, no system for reporting chronological events. Given our own culture's preoccupation with dating and timing, it would be difficult for us to understand how speakers of those languages perceive the world about them.

Language and religion are two cornerstones of culture. Ethnic consciousness is aroused as deeply by religious fervor as it is by issues of language. Like language, religion has ancient roots that are not well understood. From a cluster of sources, the world's great religions diffused widely—a process that continues today. We turn next to this vital dimension of human culture in a spatial context.

◆ KEY TERMS ◆

creole
creolization
Esperanto
lingua franca
monolingual states
multilingual states
official language
pidgin
toponymy

◆ APPLYING GEOGRAPHIC KNOWLEDGE ◆

1. Over the more than two centuries of its existence, the United States has been a largely English-speaking country. For African Americans, European Americans, and Asian Americans, English became the first (often the only) language. Today, Spanish is challenging this English monopoly. Geographic factors play a major role in this process. Explain how and why.
2. You have been put in charge of a group of Peace Corps volunteers who are going to Kenya to assist in the country's schools. An intensive language-training period will form part of the volunteers' preparation, but the group will study only one of Kenya's numerous languages. How will you decide on the language to be studied? Should it be that of the most powerful political group that dominates the government in Nairobi? Should it be one of the languages spoken in the rural areas? Is there another option?

Part Three

THE GLOBAL LINGUISTIC MOSAIC

At Issue: Revisited

What role should English play in the increasingly international world of the twenty-first century? During the twentieth century, English assumed a position of dominance in the international arena. The growing influence of technology—with its strong English-language base—is likely to spread the influence of English yet further in the decades ahead. As English becomes more widespread, however, reactions to its dominant position mount. Language embodies deeply held cultural values and is a basic feature of cultural identity. As such, few are willing to abandon their native tongues in favor of a single, universal language tied to its own set of values and traditions. Instead, the twenty-first century is likely to see a widely used English coexist—sometimes uneasily—with the great diversity of languages and dialects that give places and people meaning.

◆ SELECTED REFERENCES ◆

Part Three The Global Linguistic Model

Baron, D. *The English Only Question* (New Haven: Yale University Press, 1990).

Bellwood, P. "The Austronesian Dispersal and the Origin of Languages," *Scientific American,* July 1991, pp. 88–93.

Brenton, R.J.L. *Geolinguistics: Language Dynamics and Ethnolinguistic Geography.* Translated by H. F. Schiffman (Ottawa: University of Ottawa Press, 1991).

Cavalli-Sforza, L. L. "Genes, Peoples and Languages," *Scientific American,* November 1991, pp. 104–110.

de Carvalho, C. "The Geography of Languages," in P. Wagner & M. Mikesell, eds. *Readings in Cultural Geography* (Chicago: University of Chicago Press, 1962), pp. 75–93.

Dixon, R.M.W. *Searching for Aboriginal Languages* (Chicago: University of Chicago Press, 1989).

Dugdale, J. *The Linguistic Map of Europe* (London: Hutchinson University Library, 1969).

Frazer, T. C. *Geolinguistics: Language Dynamics and Ethnolinguistic Geography* (Concord: Paul & Company Publishers Consortium, 1992).

Gamkrelidze, T. V., & Ivanov, V. V. "The Early History of Indo-European Languages," *Scientific American,* March 1990, pp. 110–116.

Greenberg, J. *The Languages of Africa* (Bloomington: Indiana University Press, 1963).

Greenberg, J. *Languages in the Americas* (Bloomington: Indiana University Press, 1987).

Kaplan, D. H. "Population and Politics in a Plural Society: The Changing Geography of Canada's Linguistic Groups," *Annals of the Association of American Geographers,* 84 (1), 1994, pp. 46–67.

Kirk, J., et al., eds. *Studies in Linguistic Geography* (Dover, N.J.: Longwood, 1985).

Krantz, G. S. *Geographical Development of European Languages* (New York: Peter Lang, 1988).

Laponce, J. A. *Languages and their Territories* (Toronto: University of Toronto Press, 1987).

Lewin, R. "American Indian Language Dispute," *Science,* 23 December 1988, pp. 1632–1633.

Lewin, R. "Ancestral Voices at War," *New Scientist,* 16 June 1990, pp. 42–44.

McDavid, R., Jr., & O'Cain, R., eds., *Linguistic Atlas of the Middle and South Atlantic States* (Chicago: University of Chicago Press, 1980).

Moseley, C., & Asher, R. E., eds. *Atlas of the World's Languages* (London and New York: Routledge, 1994).

Murphy, A. B. "European Languages," in *A European Geography,* T. Unwin, ed. (London: Longman, 1998).

Murphy, A. B. *The Regional Dynamics of Language Differentiation in Belgium: A Study in Cultural-Political Geography* (Chicago: University of Chicago Geographical Research Paper No. 227, 1988).

Pred, A. R. *Lost Words and Lost Worlds: Modernity and the Language of Everyday Life in Nineteenth-Century Stockholm* (Cambridge: Cambridge University Press, 1990).

Renfrew, C. *Archaeology and Language: The Puzzle of Indo-European Origins* (Cambridge: Cambridge University Press, 1988).

Renfrew, C. "The Origins of Indo-European Languages," *Scientific American,* October 1989, pp. 106–114.

Schwartzberg, J. *An Historical Atlas of South Asia* (Chicago: University of Chicago Press, 1978).

Sopher, D., ed. *An Exploration of India: Geographical Perspectives on Society and Culture* (Ithaca, N.Y.: Cornell University Press, 1980).

Stewart, G. *Names on the Globe* (New York: Oxford University Press, 1975).

Stewart, G. *Names on the Land: A Historical Account of Place-Naming in the United States* (Boston: Houghton Mifflin, 2nd rev. ed., 1958).

Trudgill, P. "Linguistic Geography and Geographical Linguistics," in C. Board et al., eds., *Progress in Geography,* Vol. 7 (New York: St. Martin's Press, 1975), pp. 227–252.

Tuan, Yi-Fu "Language and the Making of Place: A Narrative-Descriptive Approach," *Annals of the Association of American Geographers,* 81 (4), 1991, pp. 684–696.

Williams, C. H., ed. *Language in Geographic Context* (Clevedon, Avon, England and Philadelphia: Multilingual Matters, 1988).

Wixman, R. *Language Aspects of Ethnic Patterns and Processes in the North Caucasus* (Chicago: University of Chicago Geographical Research Paper no. 191, 1980).

Wurm, S., & Hattori, S., eds. *Linguistic Atlas of the Pacific Area* (Canberra, Austr.: Australian Academy of the Humanities, 1982).

Part Four

THE GEOGRAPHY OF RELIGION

At Issue

Religious fundamentalism is resurgent throughout the world. From the pulpits of Alabama to the mosques of Algeria, the drive is toward the foundations of the faith. And from the villages of Northern Ireland to the contested lands of the Middle East, religion lies at the heart of nationalism. Religion stokes the fires of war in Bosnia, Kashmir, and the Transcaucasus. Some express the fear that the cold ideological war of the twentieth century may be followed by a hot religious war along the Islamic front of the twenty-first. Others note the fragmentation within, as well as among, major religions and see a future of multiple, smaller-scale religious conflicts. Here is the key issue: *Can modern-secular and fundamentalist-religious communities and countries coexist?*

Orthodox Christian revival at the core of atheism: St. Petersburg, Russia.

Part Outline

Chapter 11

The Origin and Distribution of Religions

From the field notes

"I took the elevator to the top of the tallest hotel tower in the city, and was rewarded with a sweeping view over Singapore. At once I was reminded of two tenets of cultural geography: that small-scale maps of religious distributions obscure the intermixing of religious in much of the world, and that Christian religious institutions in non-Christian areas of the world often look prosperous and well-maintained (Muslim mosques in non-Muslim areas tend to display similar affluence). Here, Saint Andrew's Cathedral reflects such wealth: its spacious grounds occupy some of Singapore's most costly real estate between the commercial center and the hotel district in a city that is predominantly Chinese with Buddhist, Hindu, and Muslim minorities. Around the world, the competition for adherents never ceases."

KEY POINTS

◆ **Despite the urbanization and secularization of modern societies, religion still dominates the lives and behaviors of billions of people.**

◆ **The several faiths of Christianity, having been diffused through European colonialism and aggressive proselytism, constitute the largest and most widely dispersed religion today.**

◆ **Islam is the world's fastest growing major religion, but like other major religions it has more than one branch.**

◆ **Christianity and Islam together hold the allegiance of nearly half the world's population; no other faith comes close, and the third largest religion, Hinduism, is not a global but a cultural faith.**

Religion and language lie at the foundation of culture; they are vital strands in the fabric of society. Like language but in a different way, religion confers identity. In societies that are not dominated by technology, religion is the great binding force, the guiding rule of daily life. From eating habits to dress codes, religion sets the standards for members of those societies.

Like languages, religions are constantly changing. Although religious leaders and bureaucracies attempt to slow the pace of change, religions nevertheless change with the times. In the process, the great religions of the world have diffused across cultural barriers and language boundaries. Persuasion will not lead people to change the language they speak, but it can induce them to convert to a new faith. Conversion still goes on as missionaries spread their beliefs far and wide. The new climate of freedom in the countries of the former Soviet Union has opened the door to proselytizing in a region where until a few years ago religious practice was carried on furtively and quietly. Just as the map of languages continues to change, so do patterns of religious affiliation.

The cultural landscape is marked by religion—by churches and mosques, cemeteries and shrines, statues and symbols. Religion is proclaimed in modes of dress (veils, turbans) and personal habits (beards, scars). In industrialized societies, such overt religious displays have declined, but they are still common in more traditional societies. In the Islamic Republic of Pakistan, the government proclaimed in 1991 that henceforth possessing a beard would be a condition for the appointment of judges.

In Part 4, we consider the sources, diffusion, and transformation of the world's great religions, their regional distribution, and their cultural landscapes. Again like language, religion can be a strong unifying force, but it can also divide and foster conflict. Such strife is occurring in Northern Ireland, the former Yugoslavia, the Middle East, India, Ethiopia, and elsewhere. The study of religion thus has many geographic dimensions.

◆ THE GEOGRAPHY OF RELIGION

In many parts of the world, especially in non-Western areas, ***religion*** is such a vital part of culture that it practically constitutes culture. Thus it is not surprising that it is difficult to define exactly what a religion is. Religion manifests itself in so many different ways: in the worship of the souls of ancestors living in natural objects such as mountains, animals, or trees; in the belief that a certain living person possesses special abilities granted by a supernatural power; in belief in a deity or deities, as in the great world religions. In some societies, religion—at least in organized form—has become less significant in the lives of many people. However, in many societies in Africa and Asia, religious doctrine exerts tight control over behavior, during the daytime through ritual and practice, and even at night in prescribing the orientation of the sleeping body. And even where religion is less dominant, its expression is still evident in many practices and beliefs.

If we cannot define religion precisely, we can at least observe some of its key characteristics. There are, of course, sets of doctrines and beliefs relating to a god or gods. There are also a number of rituals for expressing these beliefs. Such rituals may mark important events in people's lives: birth and death, attainment of adulthood, marriage. They are also expressed at regular intervals in a routine manner, as is done on Sundays in most of the Western world. A

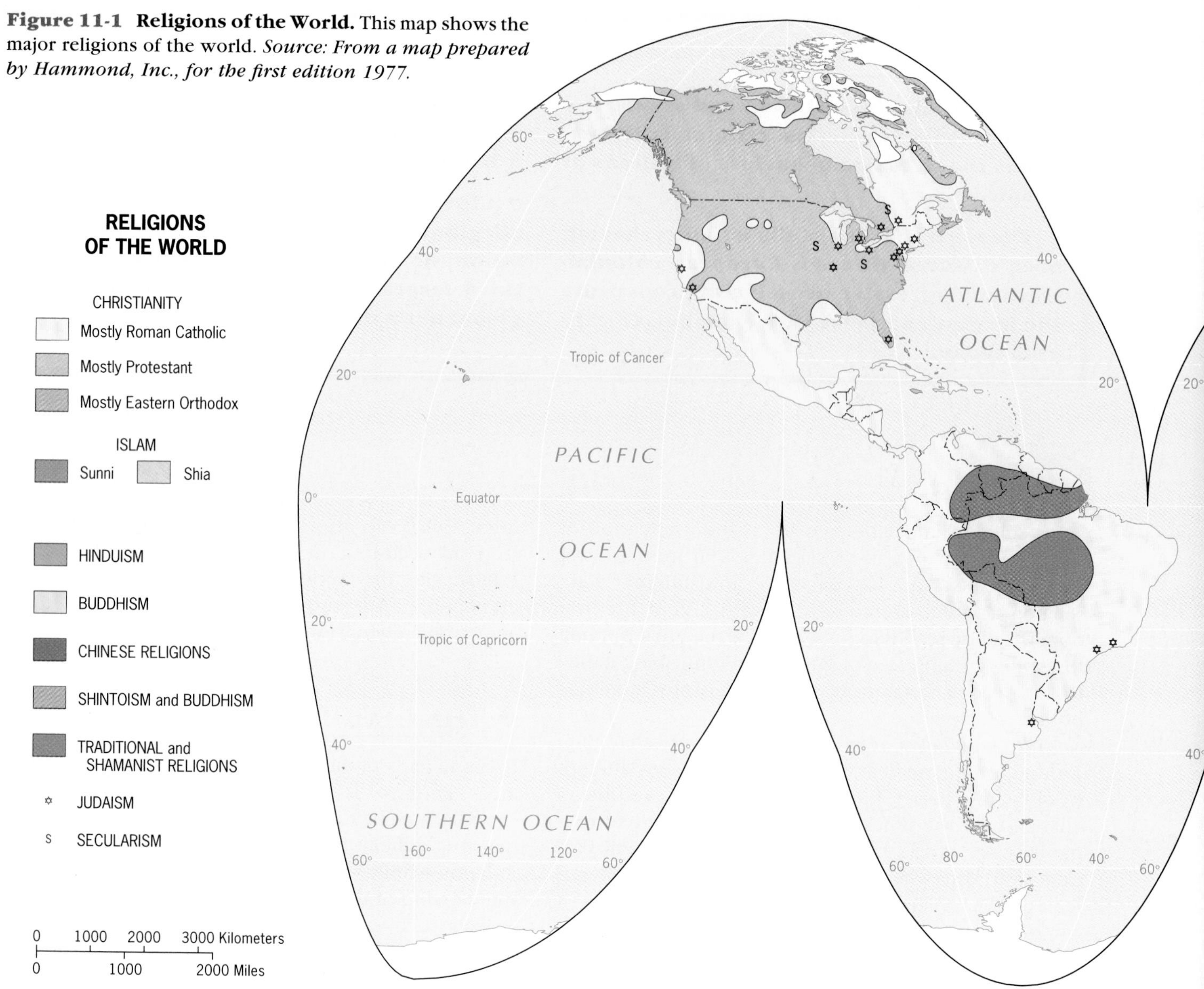

Figure 11-1 Religions of the World. This map shows the major religions of the world. *Source: From a map prepared by Hammond, Inc., for the first edition 1977.*

common ritual is prayer, whether at mealtime, at sunrise and sundown, at night upon retiring, or in the morning when arising. Ritual is likely to involve the religion's literature, if such a literature exists (the Bible and the Koran are familiar examples).

Religions, especially the major faiths like Christianity and Islam, have produced vast and complex organizational structures. These bureaucracies have a hierarchy of officers and command a great deal of wealth and authority over people's lives. Religious officers seek to maintain the approved set of standards and the code of ethics prescribed by the religion.

By now it should be clear how strongly a culture may be dominated by religious precepts. The idea that a "good" life has rewards and "bad" behavior risks punishment has an enormous effect. Modes of dress, the kinds of food people should and should not eat, commerical practices, and even the location and structure of houses may be determined by religious rules. The daily influence of religion can be seen in our calendar, our holidays, architectural landmarks, many place names, even the slogan "In God We Trust" on coins and currency. Even in societies that have sought to divest themselves of religion, such as China, religion has continued to affect living conditions and cultural landscapes.

Organized religion has had powerful effects on human societies. It has been a major force in combating social ills, sustaining the poor, promoting the arts, educating the deprived, and advancing medical knowledge. However, religion has also blocked scientific study, encouraged the oppression of dissidents, supported colonialism and exploitation, and condemned women to an inferior status in many societies.

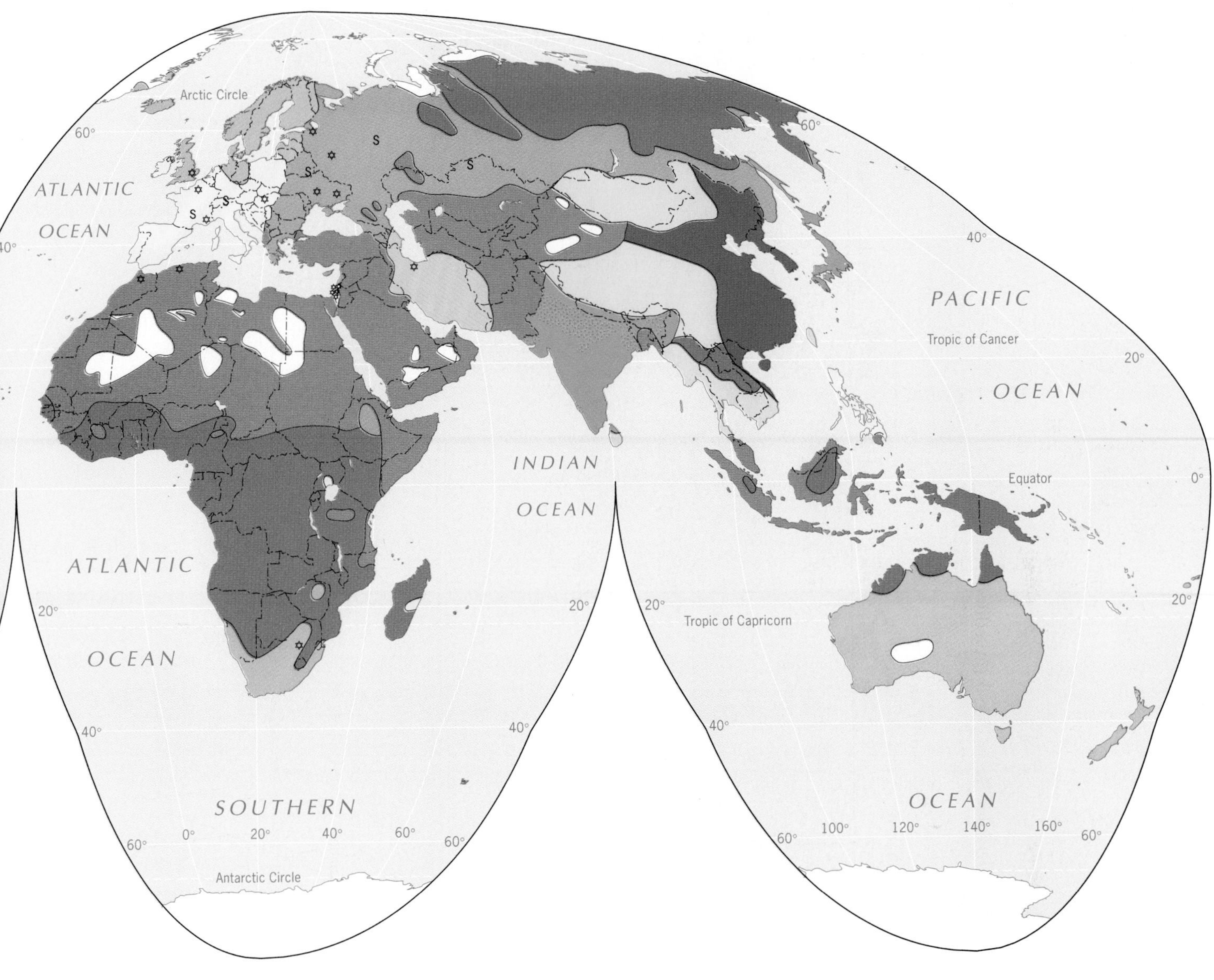

Like other bureaucracies, large-scale organized religion has all too often been unable to adjust to the times.

Sources and Distributions

Human geographers are interested in the locational characteristics of the major religions, their source areas, their distribution, and patterns of religious affiliation. The distribution of the major religions among various world regions is depicted in Figure 11-1. The information on this map should be viewed as a generalization of a much more intricate set of distributions. For example, India (except for the northwest) is shown as a Hindu region, but other religious faiths survive there (Islam remains strong in several parts of the country). Nevertheless, the map does reveal the dominance of the Christian religions, the wide dispersal of Islam, the connection between Hinduism and one of the world's major population concentrations, and the survival of Buddhism.

Figure 11-1 should be viewed in conjunction with Table 11-1, which reports the latest available data on religious affiliation. Tables like this one should be used cautiously, however, because the information on which they are based is not reliable. When you compare similar tabulations from other sources, you will find major discrepancies. This is due not only to undependable census data but also to problems of definition. Some census counts take a much broader view than others do. Consider, for instance, the table in the *Encyclopaedia Britannica Book of the Year 1997*, which reports the "religious population" of the world. It gives the number of Christians in North America (the

Table 11-1 Estimated Adherents to Major World Religions, By Geographic Realm, 1996 (in millions)*

Religion	Americas			Europe	Subsaharan Africa	North Africa and Southwest Asia	Asia			Russia	Pacific	Totals
	North	Middle	South				South	Southeast	East			
Christianity	208.1	140.8	296.2	409.6	253.1	5.0	24.7	90.5	50.0	110.7	15.3	1,604.0
Roman Catholic	94.7	128.6	281.8	255.3	109.1	0.3	5.5	69.7	13.0**	4.9	6.9	969.8
Protestant	107.4	12.1	14.2	107.2	114.6	4.3	19.2	20.8	37.0**	9.1	7.9	453.8
Orthodox	6.0	0.1	0.2	47.1	29.4	0.4	—	—	—	96.7	0.5	180.4
Islam	6.1	0.2	0.3	13.9	171.9	401.3	327.1	182.6	29.3	3.2	0.2	1,136.1
Sunni	6.0	0.2	0.3	11.9	164.5	260.4	319.4	180.1	29.3	3.2	0.2	975.5
Shiite	0.1	—	—	2.0	7.4	140.9	8.7	2.5	—	—	—	160.6
Hinduism	1.0	0.3	0.4	0.7	1.7	2.3	741.3	5.9	0.3	—	0.4	754.3
Buddhism	0.6	0.1	0.4	0.3	—	0.1	22.5	168.7	151.2	0.9	—	343.9
Chinese religions	0.1	—	0.1	0.1	—	—	0.1	9.1	253.0	—	—	262.5
Sikhism	0.3	—	—	0.2	—	—	20.1	—	—	—	—	20.6
Judaism	7.4	0.2	0.7	2.1	0.1	5.1	—	—	—	2.5	0.1	18.2

*Geographic realms in accordance with the de Blij/Muller definition.

**Official count is 7.7 million Christians in state-sanctioned churches, but counting unregistered Christian worshippers, the actual total may be about 50 million. Data from various sources, including *The 1997 Encyclopaedia Britannica Book of the Year*, United Nations statistics, and official church bulletins. Published statistics vary widely, so these figures should be viewed as rough approximations. Data extrapolated to 1996.

United States and Canada) as 255,542,000. But the *1993 Yearbook of American and Canadian Churches* reports only 147,130,000 "members of religious groups" in the United States. The larger estimate, therefore, includes a huge number of people "assumed" to be Christians, many of whom probably are agnostics.

Table 11-1, therefore, should be viewed as a very rough estimate. But certain conclusions are beyond doubt: the Christian religions have the largest number of adherents and are geographically the most widely dispersed. There are more than 1.6 billion Christians, including about 520 million in Europe and the former Soviet Union; approximately 350 million in North and Middle America; approximately 300 million in South America; perhaps 250 million in Africa; and an estimated 165 million in Asia. Christians thus account for nearly 40 percent of the members of the world's major religions. Islam, with more than 1 billion adherents, ranks second, and in fact there are about 165 million more Muslims than Roman Catholics.

Christianity As we note in more detail later, the world's religions are themselves divided. Roman Catholicism is the largest segment of ***Christianity***. Figure 11-1 reveals the strength of Roman Catholicism in Europe, areas of North America, and Middle and South America. The Protestant churches prevail in northern Europe and in much of North America, as well as in Australia, New Zealand and South Africa. The Eastern Orthodox churches have as many as 180 million adherents in Europe, Russia and its neighboring states, Africa (where a major cluster survives in Ethiopia), and North America.

Islam *Islam*, the fastest growing of the world's major religions, dominates in Northern Africa and Southwest Asia, extending into the former Soviet Union and China and including clusters in Indonesia, Bangladesh, and southern Mindanao in the Philippines. Islam is strongly represented along the East African coast, survives in Bosnia and Albania, has an outlier at South Africa's Cape of Good Hope, and has adherents in the United States (see "Focus on: America's Black Muslims"). As noted earlier, Islam has well over 1 billion adherents, of whom more than half are outside the culture realm often called the Islamic World. There are 120 million Muslims in India, and approximately 170 million Muslims reside in Subsaharan Africa, including about 55 million in Nigeria alone (see Table 11-1). Southwest Asia and Northern Africa, however, remain the Islamic heartland, with about 400 million adherents.

The main division within Islam is between Sunni Muslims (the great majority, as can be seen in Fig. 11-1 and Table 11-1) and the Shiah or Shiite cluster, which is concentrated in Iran. A comparison between Figures 11-1 and 7-1 shows that the largest Muslim country is Indonesia, with about 165 million believers.

Hinduism In terms of number of adherents, ***Hinduism*** ranks after Islam as a world religion, but there are some important structural differences between Hinduism, Christianity, and Islam. The Hindu religion lacks the kind of bureaucracy that is familiar to Christians and Muslims. It has holy men, but they represent literally thousands of gods. Thus, unlike Christianity or Islam, Hinduism is polytheistic and is fragmented by numerous cults. There are stories—*Vedas*—but Hinduism does not have a prescriptive book like the Bible or the Koran. Also unlike Christianity or Islam, Hinduism is concentrated in a single geographic realm, its source region (it is regarded as the world's oldest organized religion). The vast majority of the 750 million Hindus live in India, although Hinduism extends into Bangladesh, Myanmar, Sri Lanka, and Nepal.

Buddhism and Shintoism *Buddhism*, another religion that originated in India, is now a minority faith in that country but remains strong in Southeast Asia, China, and Japan. Buddhism's various branches have an estimated 340 million adherents. Again, this is a strongly regional religion, as Figure 11-1 shows. ***Shintoism***, a Japanese ethnic religion that is closely related to Buddhism, has numerous followers, but just how many is uncertain. The reported figures depend on varying definitions of who is a Shinto adherent; the number of registered worshippers is given as under 3.4 million, but Japanese publications refer to as many as 45 million "followers." It is generally agreed, however, that modernization is reducing the importance of Shintoism in Japanese culture.

The Chinese Religions The ***Chinese religions*** also have elements of Buddhism mixed with local belief systems. The traditional Chinese religions never involved concepts of supernatural omnipotence. ***Confucianism*** was mainly a philosophy of life, and ***Taoism*** held that human happiness lies in maintaining the proper relationship with nature. Chinese Buddhism was a pragmatic version of what the Buddha originally preached. These faiths survive in China today, but there are no reliable data on the numbers of people adhering to them. The data given in Table 11-1 are rough estimates.

Judaism Our map shows that ***Judaism*** is distributed throughout parts of the Middle East and North Africa, Russia, Ukraine, and Europe, and parts of North and South America. Judaism is one of the world's great religions, but outside of Israel it is scattered across much of the world. Today it has about 18 million adherents.

Focus On

America's Black Muslims

The faith of Islam has a foothold in the United States on the strength of an African-American religious movement commonly called the Black Muslims (officially the ***Nation of Islam***). The movement was born in the 1930s, although it traces its roots to Ali's Moorish Science Temple of America, founded in 1913. In 1930 a split developed in the Temple movement, and one of the fragments became the Nation of Islam under the leadership of W. D. Fard.

The Nation of Islam was founded on the desire of American blacks to be freed from white oppression. Believing themselves to be members of a lost Islamic tribe, the Black Muslims await the arrival of a messiah; they often compare themselves to the tribes of Israel in bondage to Egypt. Fard preached this message in the Nation's first temple in Detroit. In 1933 the Chicago Temple of Elijah Muhammad was founded, and upon Fard's sudden disappearance Muhammad became the Nation's leader. Fard became a Mahdi or a savior, but it was Elijah Muhammad who brought new strength to the Nation of Islam. In 1935 membership in the Nation was just a few hundred; by 1960 it was probably over 10,000, and when Elijah died in 1975 there were perhaps a half-million members and active sympathizers. The largest temples (now called mosques) are No. 7 in New York and No. 27 in Los Angeles.

The ideology of the Nation of Islam had been a mixture of nationalism (including a separate homeland as a primary objective) and a modified form of Islam. Tight discipline, large contributions from members, business enterprises, educational programs, a newspaper (*Muhammad Speaks*), and an annual convention all contributed to the Nation's cohesion and appeal.

In the late 1950s and early 1960s a young member named Malcolm X rose to prominence in the movement, bringing it unprecedented national visibility. A clash with orthodox leadership followed. The assassination of Malcolm X in February 1965 was a low point for the Nation.

Elijah Muhammad's death in 1975 marked the end of an era. His son, Wallace Muhammad, ended the Black Muslim's aloofness from politics (Elijah had condemned participation as sinful), strengthened the movement's ties with African and Caribbean countries by creating mosques there, permitted the first white person to join the movement, and brought the Nation's rituals and practices more in line with those of orthodox Islam.

In the early 1980s Wallace changed the name of the organization to the American Muslim Mission. In 1985 the mission announced that it was disbanding, but encouraged its local member groups to move into the mainstream of the Islamic faith. The Nation of Islam survived this transition as well. During the late 1980s, it regained national attention through its role as a force against drug use in black neighborhoods and through its espousal of international Islamic causes. In addition, Muslim leader Louis Farrakhan's anti-Semitic rhetoric thrust the Nation of Islam into the national spotlight.

By the early 1990s, the Nation of Islam was benefiting from its increased credibility in the black community and from the growth of Islam in America generally. In 1998, there were nearly 7 million practicing Muslims in the United States, most of them immigrants from Asia, North Africa, and Southwest Asia. There are now more than 1,200 mosques, many of which have been joined by African-American adherents. Present estimates suggest that more than 1 million black Americans are Muslims. Islam is now the nation's fastest-growing faith.

The Nation of Islam is still associated with aloofness and separatism. Only a small minority of black American Muslims are members. The recent hardening of anti-Semitic rhetoric on the part of some of the organization's leaders threatens a return to the divisiveness of earlier years, but cutting the other way is the Nation's role in such broad-based initiatives as the 1995 Million Man March on Washington—an effort to encourage empowerment through self-sufficiency among African Americans. If the Nation of Islam continues its move toward the mainstream of American Islam, we can expect it to increase in importance.

The three main branches of Judaism are Orthodox, Conservative, and Reform. Significant differences in ideas and practices are associated with these three branches, but Judaism is united by a strong sense of ethnic distinctiveness. As such, it does not actively seek converts.

Shamanism and Traditional Religions Finally, Figure 11-1 identifies large areas in Africa and several other parts of the world as "Traditional and Shamanist." ***Shamanism*** is a community faith in which people follow their *shaman*, a religious leader, teacher, healer, and visionary. Such a shaman appeared at various times to various peoples in Africa, Native America, Southeast Asia, and East Asia. These appearances had similar effects on the cultures of widely scattered peoples. Perhaps if these shamanist religions had developed elaborate bureaucracies and sent representatives to international congresses, they would have become more similar and might have evolved into another world religion. Unlike Christianity or Islam the shamanist faiths are small and comparatively isolated.

Shamanism is a ***traditional religion***, an intimate part of a local culture and society. But not all traditional religions are shamanist. Traditional African religions involve beliefs in a god as creator and provider, in divinities both superhuman and human, in spirits, and in a life hereafter. Christianity and Islam have made inroads into traditional religions, but as the map indicates, they have failed to convert most African peoples, except in limited areas. Where Figure 11-1 shows that traditional religions continue to exist, their adherents remain in the majority.

Source Areas

All the major religions originated in a remarkably small area of the world. Judaism and Christianity developed in what is today Israel and Jordan. Islam arose through the teachings of Muhammad, a resident of Mecca in western Arabia. The Hindu religion originated in the Indus region of what is today Pakistan, long before Christianity or Islam. Buddhism emerged from the teachings of Prince Siddhartha, who renounced his claim to his kingdom, located in northern India, to seek salvation and enlightenment in religious meditation.

These source areas coincide quite strongly with the culture hearths shown in Figure 2-4, and there can be no doubt that while other developments were occurring in these regions—urbanization, irrigated agriculture, political growth, increasingly complex social orders, and legal systems—religious systems became more sophisticated. Like technological innovations, the resulting faiths diffused far and wide.

◆ THE RISE OF SECULARISM

Figure 11-1 might mislead us into assuming that populations in areas portrayed as Christian or Buddhist do in fact adhere to these faiths. This is not the case, as Table 11-1 emphasizes. Even the most careful analysis of worldwide church and religious membership produces a total of about 4 billion adherents—in a population of about 6 billion. Hundreds of millions of peoples are not counted in Table 11-1 because they practice traditional religions. But even when they are taken into account, it is clear that additional hundreds of millions do not practice a religion at all. Moreover, even church membership figures do *not* accurately reflect the number of active members of the church. These discrepancies underscore the rise of ***secularism***—indifference to or rejection of religious ideas—in the modern world.

This should not surprise us in North America, where the church plays only a modest role in culture and society. However, in other countries antireligious ideologies have contributed to the decline of organized religion. Church membership in the former Soviet Union dropped drastically during the twentieth century under communist rule, rebounding, but to much lower numbers, after the collapse of the USSR. Maoist China's drive against Confucianism was, in part, an antireligious effort as well, and reports of religious persecution continued to emanate from China in the late 1990s. Elsewhere, communist regimes such as that in pre-1989 Poland found it necessary to accommodate powerful religious structures.

Secularism has become more widespread during the twentieth century, but it is not a new phenomenon. After the collapse of the Roman Empire, Europe was controlled by the Catholic Church: politics, sci-

From the field notes

"One of the noteworthy aspects of cityscapes in China is the virtual absence of houses of worship. Old pagodas still stand, protected now as monuments and serving as overlooks for the public. But when you scan an urban landscape such as this in Zhengzhou, you are struck by this lack. Even in Russia under communism, many of the old churches survived, and you could see them in the townscapes, neglected, sometimes crumbling, but still there as witnesses to the precommunist, Christian period. Not here in China—although a religious revival may be in the offing, and things may change."

ence, farming, and all other spheres of life were dominated, if not directly managed, by the church. After the rise of Protestantism, the priests became less powerful and the fortunes of the monasteries crumbled. The state took over functions that the church once held, and separation of church and state became a political cornerstone. Even in modern-day Rome, the bastion of Roman Catholicism, church and state exist side by side, each with its own bureaucracy and hierarchy.

With this separation came the freedom to choose—not only whom to worship with but whether to worship at all. People abandoned organized religion in growing numbers. Even if they continued to be members of a church, their participation in church activities declined. Traditions also weakened. For example, there was a time when almost all shops and businesses were closed on Sundays and the "seventh day" was a day of sermons, rest, and introspection. But today shopping centers are mostly open as usual, and Sunday is increasingly devoted to business and personal affairs, not church.

There are some exceptions to these developments. Traditions are stronger in some culture regions than in others, and Sunday observance does continue, for example, in the Mormon culture area of the United States. Moreover, Evangelical and other alternative churches are growing rapidly in some parts of the United States and Western Europe. However, in the Christian realms, from Canada to Australia and from the United States to Western Europe, the decline of organized religion as a cultural force is evident. This is so even in the strongly Roman Catholic regions of Southern Europe and Latin America. In Europe, many people are dissatisfied with religious rules regarding birth control. In Latin America, the church finds itself in a difficult position in the face of rapid social change.

Although the rise of secularism and the decline of church affiliation are evident in the Christian realms, other important trends are occurring elsewhere. In the Muslim world, a newfound power based on oil revenues and a resurgence of revolutionary fervor have strenghtened Islam's position. Moreover, although there may be an overall decline in adherence to the major faiths, several smaller religions are growing in importance. They include Baha'i, Cao Dai, Jainism, and the Spiritual Church of Brazil. The rise of secularism may be primarily a condition of industrialization and urbanization, reflecting the church's failure to adjust to modernizing society. (The fate of Shintoism in Japan seems to confirm this notion.) In contrast, in more conservative, rural societies, the faiths remain strong.

◆ GLOBAL AND REGIONAL RELIGIONS

The world's many religions can be classified according to several different sets of criteria, each with its particular advantages. Here we will examine two commonly used classification systems.

Reach

One such typology is based on the "reach" of religions. The true ***global religions*** are Christianity, Islam, and the various forms of Buddhism. These faiths have adherents around the world. These global religions are sometimes called *universal* or *universalizing religions* because their adherents actively seek converts and aim to become universal. ***Cultural religions*** are faiths that dominate a single national culture, as Hinduism does in India, Confucianism and Taoism in China, and Shintoism in Japan (see "Focus on: Shintoism"). These

Shintoism

Emperor worship, reverence for nature, and a strong feeling for land and nation are central elements of the *Shinto* religion of Japan. Early Shintoism arose from shamanism and other traditional religious faiths and developed into a national religion that unified religion and government. Then Buddhism made substantial inroads, and Shinto was much modified. However, Japanese determination to reject external influences brought Shinto back as a religious and political force. After the Meiji Restoration in 1868, Buddhists were persecuted, Buddhism was attacked, and Buddhist shrines were removed. Later these campaigns became less intense, but Shinto remained the state religion.

After Japan's defeat in World War II, Shinto's role as the official state religion was terminated, and the doctrine relating to the emperor's divine descent was also rejected. This has led to a further decline of Shintoism, while Buddhism has experienced some revival. Shintoism is a prime example of a cultural religion: its rise and decline are closely related to the vigor of the regional culture.

religions are sometimes referred to as *regional* or *ethnic* religions. (Judaism is a special case because of its global dispersal.) The traditional religions of Africa form the focus of a third group of religions. They are also found in Native South America, interior areas of Southeast Asia, and New Guinea and northern Australia. The traditional religions are also referred to as *local* religions in recognition of their limited extent.

Focus

Religions can also be classified on the basis of their central focus. ***Monotheistic religions*** worship a single deity, a God or Allah. ***Polytheistic religions*** worship more than one deity, even thousands, as in the case of Hinduism. ***Animistic religions*** are centered on the belief that inanimate objects, such as mountains, boulders, rivers, and trees, possess spirits and should therefore be revered.

The map of the distribution of the world's religions reveals that Christianity is not only the largest but also the most widespread religion, dispersed throughout the world by conquest and colonialism. Islam has also diffused widely, but mainly in Africa and Asia. At the scale of Figure 11-1, Islam's foothold in the United States, South Africa, and other outposts cannot be shown, but Islam is a universal faith nonetheless. Buddhism, though concentrated mainly in Southeast and East Asia, also transcends global cultural and political boundaries.

Compared to these "universal" faiths, Hinduism, Confucianism, Taoism, and Shintoism are regional rather than global religions. Once again the map shows a general picture, not the details. In many areas of India beliefs other than Hinduism prevail, but Hinduism's domination of India, and its virtual (but not total) confinement to South Asia, are accurately shown. Confucianism and Taoism are found almost exclusively in China, while Shintoism is virtually confined to Japan.

The traditional religions still prevail in parts of the world where the impact of external forces is weakest. For centuries these local faiths have been repressed by missionaries and conquerors, yet they still survive. Again, the map cannot show a detailed pattern for several reasons. Even where Christianity and Islam have penetrated, as in much of Africa, the new faith is often adopted not in place of, but rather alongside, the old ones. Many "Christian" Africans continue to believe in traditional powers.

Having viewed the spatial distribution of the world's major religions and assessed their strengths in terms of number of adherents, we turn next to three geographic characteristics of religions: their locational origins, their routes of diffusion, and their imprints on the cultural landscape.

◆ KEY TERMS ◆

animistic religion
Buddhism
Chinese religions
Christianity
Confucianism
cultural religion
global religion
Hinduism
Islam
Judaism
monotheistic religion
Nation of Islam
polytheistic religion
religion
secularism
Shamanism
Shintoism
Taoism
traditional religion

◆ APPLYING GEOGRAPHIC KNOWLEDGE ◆

1. You have been asked to guide a group of students from a Muslim country around the United States. You will point out that this is a society in which the separation of church and state is enshrined in the Constitution. Your guests, however, note that religion remains quite evident in the cultural landscape, in annual and weekly cycles of life, in daily transactions, in government and education—more prominently, though, in some parts of the United States than in others. Explain both the phenomenon and its geographic variability to a group of newcomers.
2. The map of world religions (Fig. 11-1) reveals that one geographic realm remains dominated by traditional and shamanist religions, while global and cultural religions dominate all others. What geographic factors contributed to this development? Considering precedents in other areas of the world, how might the African religious map change during the next century?

Chapter 12

Religion: Location, Diffusion, and Cultural Landscape

From the field notes

"After a rather difficult (and, my colleague said, unsafe) trip from Phnom Penh we reached the temple complex at Angkor Wat in Cambodia. This extensive, walled structure, now suffering from neglect and destruction, marks the earliest period of Hinduism's diffusion into Southeast Asia and forms a reminder of six centuries of Khmer empire in this realm. Hinduism inspired magnificent architecture and art, and left its imprint not only on Cambodia but also on Java and Bali (Indonesia). But Buddhism supplanted Hinduism in Cambodia, and Islam did the same in Java."

KEY POINTS

◆ **Hinduism is the oldest of the world's major religions; it is a cultural religion, strongly influencing Indian cultural landscapes.**

◆ **Buddhism, with fewer than half as many adherents as Hinduism, arose as a reaction to Hinduism and became a global religion. It continues to expand today.**

◆ **The more liberal atmosphere in communist China is reviving both the Chinese religions of old *and* the Christian and Islamic faiths; Confucianism and Taoism continue to shape Chinese society.**

◆ **Judaism is the oldest religion to arise west of the Indus River. With only about 18 million adherents, it has a global importance far greater than its numbers would suggest.**

◆ **Christianity's three major branches (Roman Catholicism, Protestantism, and Orthodoxy) have diffused throughout the world. The Orthodox churches are experiencing a revival in Russia.**

◆ **Islam, the youngest of the world religions, has two major sects, the majority Sunni and the minority Shiah. This division occurred almost immediately after the prophet Muhammad's death and took on regional overtones when Shiism became the state religion of Persia (now Iran).**

The major religions arose and diffused much later than the great language families. Even the oldest, Hinduism, emerged long after the First Agricultural Revolution had transformed the cultural landscape of Southwest Asia. Christianity appeared while the Roman Empire was at its height, and Islam was founded several centuries later. As a result, the historical geography of the global religions is better known than that of the earliest languages.

In this chapter we trace the spread of the belief systems that have contributed so strongly to the formation of modern culture regions. It is remarkable that, after tens of thousands of years of human development and migration, the great faiths all arose within a few thousand years and within a few thousand kilometers of each other in South and Southwest Asia (Fig. 12-1).

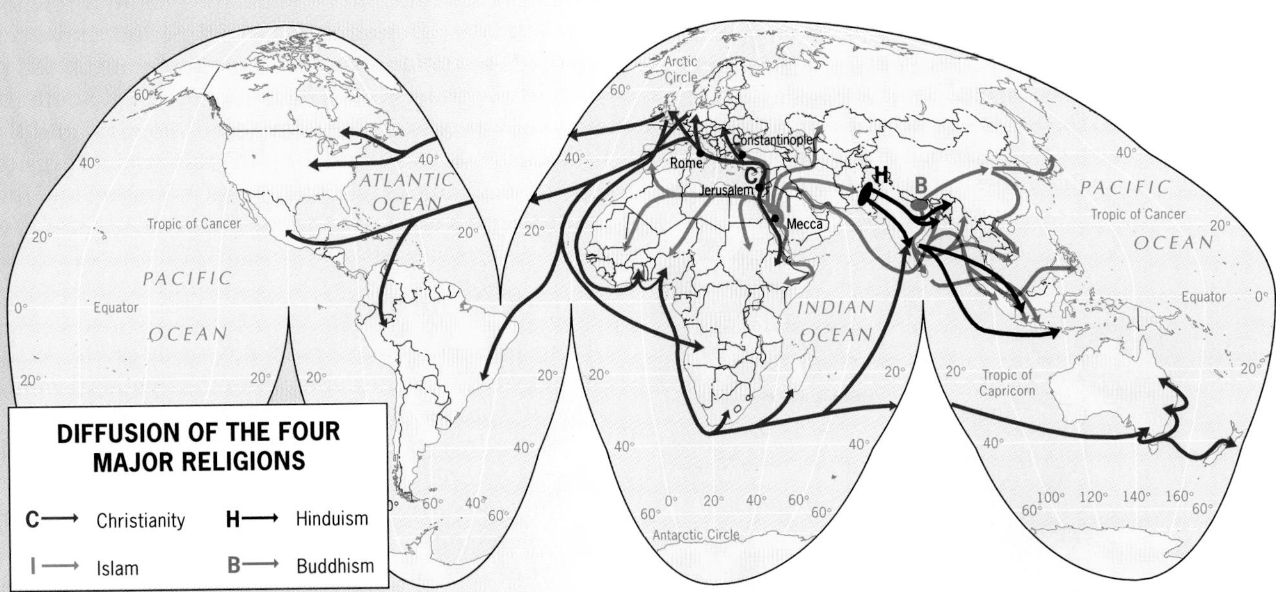

Figure 12-1 Diffusion of the Four Major Religions. Major routes of religious dispersal are shown on this map. It does not show smaller diffusion streams; Islam, for example, is gaining strength in North America, although its numbers are still comparatively small.

◆ HINDUISM

The Hindu religion is the oldest of the major religions and one of the oldest extant religions in the world. It emerged without a prophet or a book of scriptures and without evolving a bureaucratic structure comparable to that of the Christian religions. Hinduism appears to have originated in the region of the Indus Valley, perhaps as much as 4000 years ago. Its fundamental doctrine is ***karma***, which has to do with the transferability of the soul. According to Hindu doctrine, all beings have souls and are arranged in a hierarchy. The ideal is to move upward in the hierarchy and then to escape from the eternal cycle through union with the ***Brahman***. A soul moves upward or downward according to the individual's behavior in the present life. Good deeds and adherence to the faith lead to a higher level in the next life, whereas bad behavior leads to demotion to a lower level. All souls, those of animals as well as humans, participate in this process.

The principle of ***reincarnation*** is a cornerstone of Hinduism. If you mistreat an animal in this life, chances are you will *be* that animal in a future life.

Hinduism's doctrines are closely bound to the Indian society's ***caste system***, for castes themselves are steps on the universal ladder. However, the caste system locks people into particular social classes and imposes many restrictions, especially in the lowest of the castes, the ***untouchables***. Until a generation ago, the untouchables could not enter temples, were excluded from certain schools, and were restricted to performing the most unpleasant tasks. The coming of other religions to India, the effects of modernization during the colonial period, and especially the work of Mahatma Gandhi loosened the social barriers of the caste system and somewhat improved the lot of the 80 million untouchables.

Hinduism was born in the western part of the Indian subcontinent and spread eastward. Before the advent of Christianity it had spread into Southeast Asia. It would first attach itself to traditional faiths and then slowly supplant them. Later, when Islam and Christianity appeared and were actively spread in Hindu areas, Hindu thinkers attempted to assimilate certain of the new teachings into their own religion. For example, elements of the Sermon on the Mount now form part of Hindu preaching, and Christian beliefs contributed to the weakness of caste barriers. In other instances, the confrontation between Hinduism and other faiths led to the emergence of a compromise religion. Thus the monotheism of Islam stimulated the rise of ***Sikhism***, whose followers disapproved of the worship of idols and disliked the caste system, but retained the concepts of reincarnation and karma.

As Figure 12-1 shows, Hinduism evolved in what is today Pakistan, reached its fullest development in India, and spread into Southeast Asia. It has not been widely disseminated. However, in Southeast Asia, it was overtaken by Islam and Buddhism. In overwhelmingly Muslim Indonesia, the island of Bali remains a Hindu outpost (see "Focus on: Hindu Bali"), but Java retains only architectural remnants of its Hindu age.

From the field notes

"The various religions approach in different ways the disposition of the deceased. We in the dominantly Christian, Western world are familiar with large, sometimes elaborate cemeteries. The Hindu faith requires cremation of the body. Wherever large Hindu communities exist outside India itself you will see this equivalent of the funeral parlor, pictured here in Mombasa, Kenya."

Diffusion

Hinduism has remained essentially a cultural religion of South Asia. During the colonial period, however, hundreds of thousands of Indians were transported to other areas of the world, including East and South Africa, the Caribbean, northern South America, and the Pacific islands (notably Fiji). This relocation diffusion did not result in new Hindu regions, however, and few non-Indians were converted to the faith.

Cultural Landscape

Hinduism is more than a faith; it is a way of life. Meals are religious rites; prohibitions and commands multiply as the ladder of caste is ascended. Pilgrimages follow prescribed routes, and rituals are attended by millions of people. Festivals and feasts are frequent, colorful, and noisy. Hindu doctrines include the belief that the erection of a temple, whether modest or elaborate, bestows merit on the builder and will be rewarded. As a result, the Hindu cultural landscape—urban as well as rural—is dotted with countless shrines, ranging from small village temples to struc-

Focus On

Hindu Bali

The Indonesian island of Bali became a refuge for Hindu holy men, nobles, and intellectuals during the sixteenth century, when Islam engulfed neighboring Java. Since then, the Balinese have developed a unique faith, still based on Hindu principles but mixed with elements of Buddhism, animism, and ancestor worship. The caste system prevails, but the lower castes outnumber the higher castes by nearly ten to one, so that the system divides the society less than is the case in India. Holy men, military personnel, and merchants rank at the top of the hierarchy.

Religion is at the focus of life in Bali, and temples and shrines dominate the cultural landscape, which is also characterized by some of the world's most meticulously terraced hillslopes. Religious festivals, feasts, and other ceremonies occur frequently, and streets and roads are colorfully decorated to mark each event. Participation is almost universal, and although Bali only has about 3 million inhabitants, it has numerous orchestras, actors and actresses, dancers, and artists. The island's unique religion is at the heart of a culture that has been described as a celebration of life.

tures so large and elaborate that they are virtually holy cities. The location of shrines is important because there should be minimal disruption of the natural landscape. Whenever possible the temple should be in a "comfortable" position (for example, under a large, shady tree) and near water, because many gods will not venture far from water and because water has a holy function in Hinduism. A village temple should face the village from a prominent position, and offerings must be made frequently. Small offerings of fruit and flowers lie before the sanctuary of the deity honored by the shrine.

Thus the cultural landscape of Hinduism is the cultural landscape of India, the cultural region. Temples and shrines, holy animals by the tens of millions, distinctively garbed holy men, and the sights and sounds of endless processions and rituals all contribute to a unique atmosphere. The faith is a visual as well as an emotional experience.

◆ BUDDHISM

Buddhism appeared in India during the sixth century B.C. as a reaction to the less desirable features of Hinduism such as its strict social hierarchy that protected the privileged and kept millions mired in poverty. It was by no means the only protest of its kind (***Jainism*** was another), but it was the strongest and most effective. Buddhism was founded by Prince Siddhartha, known to his followers as Gautama, the heir to a wealthy kingdom in what is now Nepal. Siddhartha was profoundly shaken by the misery he saw about him, which contrasted so sharply with the splendor and wealth in which he had been raised. The Buddha (enlightened one) was perhaps the first prominent In-

From the field notes

"To reach the capital of Myanmar (Burma) we had to transfer to a ferry and sail up the Rangoon River for several hours. One of Southeast Asia's most spectacular Buddhist shrines is the golden Shwedogon Pagoda in the heart of Yangon. The golden dome (or *chedi*) is one of the finest in the entire realm, and its religious importance also is superior: here are preserved eight hairs of the Buddha. Vast amounts of gold have gone into the creation and preservation of the Shwedogon Pagoda; local rulers often gave the monks their weight in gold—or more. Today, the pagoda is a cornerstone of Buddhism, drawing millions of faithful to the site. It also is slowly becoming a tourist attraction as Myanmar's door to the outside world is slightly ajar and foreign visitors are arriving again."

dian religious leader to speak out against Hinduism's caste system. Salvation, he preached, could be attained by anyone, no matter what his or her caste. Enlightenment would come through knowledge, especially self-knowledge; elimination of greed, craving, and desire; complete honesty; and never hurting another person or animal.

Diffusion

After the Buddha's death in 489 B.C. at the age of 80, the faith grew rather slowly until the middle of the third century B.C., when the Emperor Asoka became a convert. Asoka was the leader of a large and powerful Indian state that extended from the Punjab to Bengal and from the Himalayan foothills to Mysore. He not only set out to rule his country in accordance with the teachings of the Buddha, but he also sent missionaries to carry the Buddha's teachings to distant peoples. Buddhism spread as far south as Sri Lanka and later spread west toward the Mediterranean, north into Tibet, and east into China, Korea, Japan, Vietnam, and Indonesia, over a span of about 10 centuries (Fig. 12-1). While Buddhism spread to distant lands, it began to decline in its region of origin. During Asoka's rule there may have been more Buddhists than Hindu adherents in India, but after that period the strength of Hinduism began to reassert itself. Today Buddhism is practically extinct in India, although it still thrives in Sri Lanka, Southeast Asia, Nepal, Tibet, and Korea. Along with other faiths, it also survives in Japan.

Buddhism is fragmented into numerous branches, the leading ones being Mahayana Buddhism and Theravada Buddhism. Theravada Buddhism is a monastic faith that survives in Sri Lanka, Myanmar (Burma), Thailand, Laos, and Cambodia. It holds that salvation is a personal matter, achieved through good behavior and religious activities, including periods of service as a monk or nun. Mahayana Buddhism, which is practiced mainly in Vietnam, Korea, Japan, and China, holds that salvation can be aided by appeals to superhuman, holy sources of merit. The Buddha is regarded as a divine savior. Mahayana Buddhists do not serve as monks, but they spend much time in personal meditation and worship. Other branches of Buddhism include the Lamaism of Xizang (Tibet), which combines monastic Buddhism with the worship of local demons and deities, and Zen Buddhism, the contemplative form that is prevalent in Japan.

Buddhism is experiencing a revival that started two centuries ago and has recently intensified. It has become a global religion and has diffused to many areas of the world. However, the faith has suffered in its modern hearth in Southeast Asia. Militant communist regimes have attacked the faith in Cambodia, Laos, and Vietnam. In Thailand also, Buddhism has been under pressure owing to rising political tensions. Nevertheless, the appeal of Buddhism's principles has ensured its continued diffusion, notably in the Western world.

Cultural Landscape

When the Buddha received enlightenment he sat under a large tree, the Bodhi (enlightenment) tree at Bodh Gaya in India. (The Bodhi tree now growing on the site is believed to be a descendant of the original tree.) The Bodhi tree has a thick, banyan-like trunk and a wide canopy of leafy branches. Because of its association with the Buddha, the tree is revered and protected, and is the object of pilgrimages to Bodh Gaya and other places where the Buddha may have taught beneath its branches. The tree has also been diffused as far as China and Japan and marks the cultural landscape of numerous villages and towns.

Buddhism's architecture includes some magnificent achievements, including the famed structures at Borobudur in central Java (Indonesia). The shrines of Buddhism include bell-shaped structures that protect burial mounds, temples that enshrine an image of the Buddha in his familiar cross-legged pose, and large monasteries that tower over the local landscape. The pagoda is perhaps Buddhism's most familiar structure. Its shape is derived from the relic (often funeral) mounds of old. Every fragment of its construction is a meaningful representation of Buddhist philosophy.

◆ THE CHINESE RELIGIONS

While the Buddha's teachings were gaining converts in India, a religious revolution of another kind was taking place in China. Confucius (551–479 B.C.) and his followers constructed a blueprint for Chinese civilization in almost every field—philosophy, government, education, and others. In religion, Confucius addressed the traditional Chinese cults that included belief in heaven and the existence of the soul, ancestor worship, sacrificial rites, and shamanism. He held that the real meaning of life lay in the present, not in some future abstract existence, and that service to one's fellow humans should supersede service to spirits.

Taoism

At the same time Chinese philosophy was being influenced by another school. The beginnings of ***Taoism*** are unclear, but many scholars believe that an older contemporary of Confucius, Lao-Tsu, published a volume titled *Tao-te-ching*, or "Book of the Way." In his teachings, Lao-Tsu focused on the proper form of political rule and on the oneness of humanity and nature:

Focus On

Feng Shui

Chinese cultural traditions include a deep appreciation for nature. The need to exist in harmony with nature is a precept of both Taoism and Confucianism, and this principle, known as ***Feng Shui***, is to be adhered to in life as well as in death.

In life, Feng Shui revealed itself through opposition to modernization. Together with the ancient belief that the powerful spirits of ancestors, dragons, tigers, and other beings all occupy natural phenomena (mountains, hills, rivers, and trees), it was also held that disturbing nature would incur their wrath. Nothing should be done to nature without consulting the geomancers, men who knew the desires of the spirits. When, in 1876, engineers tried to lay the first railroad inland from the port of Shanghai without consulting the geomancers, local opposition was so strong that the project had to be abandoned. The geomancers had not approved it.

In the 1950s the communist regime also confronted Feng Shui. China's geomancers had long identified suitable gravesites for the deceased so as to leave the dead in perfect harmony with their natural surroundings. Burial mounds were an important part of rural Chinese communities, taking up much land that could have been farmed. The pragmatic communists had little regard for such practices, and they leveled burial mounds during their communization program. This generated strong opposition by tradition-bound villagers, producing a reserve of deep resentment that was to explode much later and contribute to the revolutionary changes of the 1970s. Geomancy is still a powerful force in China today—even in areas undergoing rapid urbanization.

people, he said, should learn to live in harmony with nature (see "Focus on: Feng Shui"). The Taoist virtues were simplicity and spontaneity, tenderness, and tranquility. Competition, possession, and even the pursuit of knowledge were to be avoided. War, punishment, taxation, and ceremonial ostentation were viewed as evils. The best government, according to Lao-Tsu, was the least government.

Taoism became a cult of the masses. Lao-Tsu himself was worshipped as a god, something of which he would have disapproved. People, animals, even dragons became objects of worship as well, and a sort of Taoist witchcraft emerged.

Confucianism

Both Taoism and ***Confucianism*** had great and lasting impacts on Chinese life. Confucius was appalled at the suffering of ordinary people at the hands of feudal lords, and he urged the poor to assert themselves. He was not a prophet who dealt in promises of heaven and threats of hell. He denied the divine ancestry of China's aristocratic rulers, educated the landless and the weak, disliked supernatural mysticism, and argued that human virtues and abilities, not heritage, should determine a person's position and responsibilities in society.

Despite these views, Confucius came to be revered as a spiritual leader after his death in 479 B.C. His teachings diffused widely throughout East and Southeast Asia. Temples were built in his honor all over China. From his writings and sayings emerged the *Confucian Classics*, a set of 13 texts that became the

From the field notes

"Here is evidence that Feng Shui remains a powerful force in Chinese life. Every bookstore that carries English-language books has a section under the heading *geomancy*, with a large number of books describing the rules and rewards of Feng Shui. When I asked a colleague in Hong Kong about this, he told me that in Chinese-language bookstores, the geomancy sections are even larger. "No one, not a banker, lawyer, or doctor, would build an office without consulting a geomancer," he said. Another local resident told me that all the problems encountered by the last British governor were caused by the orientation of his mansion. The British had built it without asking the geomancers, and it was destined to be a troubled place."

focus of education in China for 2000 years. In government, law, literature, religion, morality, and many other ways, the *Confucian Classics* were the guide for Chinese civilization.

Elements of Buddhism, introduced into China during the Han Dynasty, also formed part of the society's belief system. Buddhism's reverence for the aged, ancestors, and nature made it easily adaptable to Chinese philosophies. Thus elements of several existing religions were combined to create, if not a distinct faith, certainly a religious way of life. Over the centuries, Confucianism (with its Taoist and Buddhist ingredients) became China's state ethic, although Confucius' ideals were modified over time. (For example, worship of and obedience to the emperor became a part of Confucianism.)

During the twentieth century political upheavals in China led to reactions against Confucian philosophies, first during the Republican period after 1912 and later under the communist regimes after 1949. However, Confucianism has been China's beacon for a very long time. It will be difficult to eradicate two millennia of cultural conditioning in a few decades.

◆ JUDAISM

Judaism grew out of the belief system of the Jews, one of several, nomadic Semitic tribes living in Southwest Asia about 2000 B.C. The history of the Jews is filled with upheavals. Moses led them from Egypt, where they had been enslaved, to Canaan, where an internal conflict developed and the nation split into two branches, Israel and Judah. Israel was subsequently wiped out by enemies, but Judah survived longer, only to be conquered by the Babylonians. The Jews regrouped to rebuild their headquarters, Jerusalem, but then fell victim to a series of foreign powers. The Romans destroyed their holy city in A.D. 70, at which time the Jews were driven away and scattered far and wide. Those who went north into Central Europe came to be known as ***Ashkenazim***; those who scattered across North Africa and into the Iberian Peninsula were called ***Sephardim***. Both the Ashkenazim and the Sephardim were persecuted, denied citizenship, driven into ghettos, and massacred.

In the face of such constant threats to their existence, the Jews have been sustained by their faith. The roots of Jewish religious tradition lie in the teachings of Abraham, who united his people. Among the religions of the ancient Semitic tribes, that of the Jews was unique in that it involved the worship of only one god, who, the Jews believed, had selected them to bear witness to his existence and his works. However, the Jewish faith also incorporated elements of other religions. From ***Zoroastrianism***, which arose in Persia during the sixth century B.C., Judaism acquired its concept of paradise and hell, angels and devils, judgment day, and resurrection.

Modern times have seen a division of Judaism into many branches. During the nineteenth century a reform movement developed with the objective of adjusting the faith and its practices to current times. However, many feared that this would cause a loss of identity and cohesion, and the orthodox movement sought to retain the old precepts. Between those two extremes is a sector that is less strictly orthodox but not as liberal as the reformers; it is known as the conservative movement.

The idea of a homeland for the Jewish people, which became popular during the nineteenth century, developed into the ideology of ***Zionism***. Zionist ideals were rooted in the belief that Jews should not be absorbed into other societies. The goal of a Jewish state became a reality in 1948, when Israel was created under UN auspices on the shores of the eastern Mediterranean.

As Table 11-1 shows, the Jewish faith has about 18 million adherents, but the distribution of Jews proves that Judaism is indeed a world religion. Seven million Jews reside in North America and about 5 million in Europe and the former Soviet Union. The total for Asia, over 5 million, includes the Jewish population of Israel itself.

◆ CHRISTIANITY

The Christian religions had their beginnings in the Jews' desire to be free from Roman oppression and in the appearance of Jesus. Many saw in Jesus a manifestation of God, but probably even a greater number hoped that he would be more than a spiritual leader and would lead them to freedom as well as salvation. Among the Apostles was Paul, a Jew who had received a Greek education and who, after the crucifixion, began offering the teachings of Jesus to non-Jews. Paul played a central role in organizing the Christian church and disseminating Jesus' teachings. But Paul's Christian church, with its center in Rome, was not the only Christian center. Alexandria, Constantinople, and Jerusalem were also important centers.

After Paul's death, his church continued to grow but met the resistance of Roman authority. Christians were persecuted, and many lost their lives. A crucial event in the rise of Christianity was the conversion of the Emperor Constantine in 312. From that time on, Christianity was the Roman state religion. The Roman Empire soon declined and broke up, and the western half, centered on Rome, fell on hard times. The eastern half, with Constantinople (now Istanbul in Turkey) at its heart, became the new focus of the empire. Christianity thrived there and radiated into other areas, including the Balkan Peninsula. Today the Eastern or Orthodox Church is still one of the three major branches of the faith (Fig. 12-1), despite the blows it suffered when Constantinople fell to the Turks and Islam invaded Eastern Europe (in the fifteenth century), and again when the church was threatened by the rise of communism in Russia (in the twentieth century).

In Rome, the papacy was established and the second branch of the faith, Roman Catholicism, arose. In the Middle Ages the power of the church was at its peak, with all the excesses this involved. The inevitable reaction came during the fifteenth and sixteenth centuries with the teachings of Luther, Calvin, and others. There followed widespread friction and open warfare among Christians holding different views. However, the Protestant movement—the third major branch—grew steadily stronger.

Diffusion

The dissemination of Christianity occurred as a result of expansion combined with relocation diffusion. The worldwide dispersal of Christianity was accomplished during the era of European colonialism in the sixteenth century. Spain invaded Middle and South America, bringing the Catholic faith to those areas. Protestant refugees, tired of conflict and oppression, came to North America in large numbers. Through the efforts of missionaries, Catholicism made inroads in Congo, Angola, and Moçambique. A very small percentage of the people in formerly British India were converted to Christianity, but Catholicism scored heavily in the Philippines during the period of Spanish control.

Today Christianity is the largest and most widespread of the world religions, and although the numbers of its adherents may be declining in some places, it is still gaining adherents in many areas. The faith has always been characterized by aggressive and persistent proselytism, and Christian missionaries created an almost worldwide network of conversion during the colonial period (Fig. 12-1).

Cultural Landscape

The cultural landscapes of Christianity's branches reflect the changes the faith has undergone over the centuries. In Medieval Europe the cathedral, church, or monastery was the focus of life. Other buildings clustered around the tower, steeple, and spire of the church that could be seen (and whose bells could be heard) for miles in the surrounding countryside. In the square or plaza in front of the church, crowds would gather for ceremonies and festivals in which the church played a role whether or not the event was primarily religious. Good harvests, military victories, public announcements, and much else was done in the shadow of the symbol of religious authority.

The Reformation, the rise of secularism, and the decline of organized religion are reflected in the cultural landscape as well. The cathedral towns of Europe are reminders of the region's Roman Catholic-dominated history. For Protestants, in contrast, a house of worship need not be large, imposing, or ornate. In Protestant regions, therefore, churches often blend into the local architecture and may be identified only by a sign.

In some large cities, cathedral and church now stand in the shadow of another kind of structure, the skyscraper—a symbol of the power of commerce and money. Churches are likely to be built outside the central business district, where land costs less. Except for some large-scale projects (such as the Washington Cathedral), most modern religious structures are not as impressive and elaborate as those of earlier times. Other kinds of symbols are needed to sustain the church in an age of television and automobiles.

From the field notes

"In the light of dawn I looked toward the city of Bordeaux and saw a sight that must be representative of a Christian Europe that once was: the tower and steeple of a cathedral rising tall over the townscape. Today, the commercial skyscraper, not the symbol of the faith, tends to dominate urban landscapes."

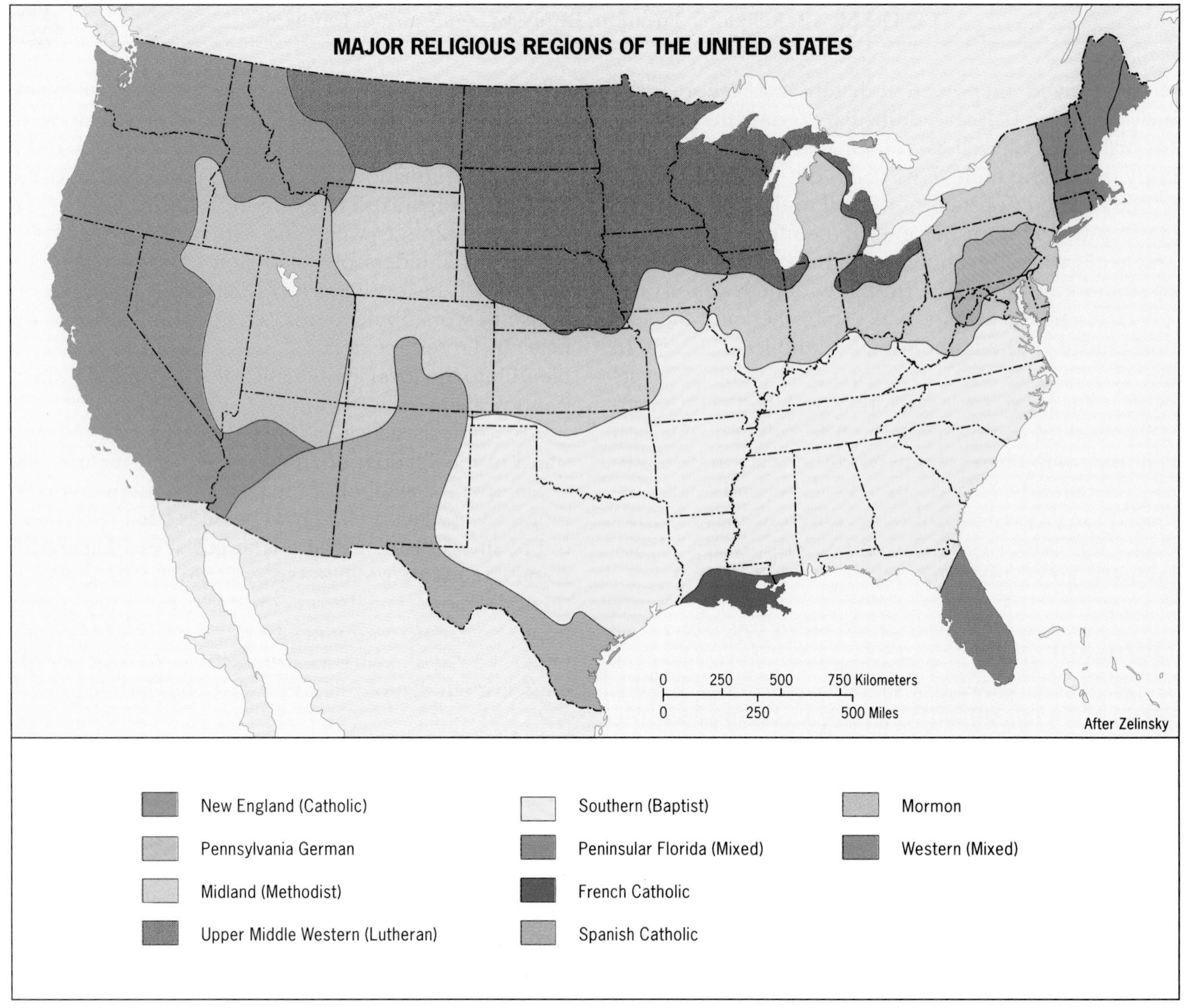

Figure 12-2 Major Religious Regions of the United States. A generalized map of religious regions in the United States shows concentrations of the major religions. *Source: Modified from W. Zelinksy, "An Approach to the Religious Geography of the United States,"* Annals of the AAG *51, 1961, p. 139.*

We should note that certain denominations have more durable cultural landscapes in which the authority and influence of the church remain visible. In the United States, the best example is the Mormon culture region. The Northeast is another, with its history of places dominated by Catholicism or particular combinations of Protestant denominations.

The cultural landscape also carries the imprint of death. It is appropriate to relate this topic to the cultural landscape of Christianity, because no other faith uses so much land for burial. Hindus, Buddhists, and Shintoists cremate the dead, and it is noteworthy that this practice prevails in regions where living space and farmland are at a premium. However, Christian faiths bury their dead, often with elaborate rituals and in parklike cemeteries. Class differences are reflected here: some graves are marked by a simple tombstone, whereas others are elaborate structures. A more impressive aspect of this culture trait, however, is the amount of space that is devoted to graveyards and cemeteries, even in crowded urban areas where land prices have risen enormously. This is a reflection not only of the power of the church but also of the fact that cemeteries and funeral establishments constitute a significant economic enterprise in Western cultures.

Religion and Culture Regions in the United States

The Mormon culture region is only one of several regions in the United States of which religion is a crucial cultural component. In "An Approach to the Religious Geography of the United States" (1961), Wilbur Zelinksy constructed a map of religious regions that identifies seven such regions (Fig. 12-2). These regions will be familiar to anyone who has even the most general impression of the United States. The New England region, for example, is strongly Catholic; the South's leading denomination is Baptist; the Upper Middle West has large numbers of Lutherans; and the Southwest is predominantly Spanish Catholic. A broad region extending from the Middle Atlantic to the Mormon region has a mixture of denominations in which no single church dominates; this is also true of the West. As Zelinsky's map shows, several of the major regions can be subdivided on the basis of local clustering, such as the French Catholic area centered in New Orleans and the mixed denominations of Peninsular Florida, where a large Spanish Catholic cluster has emerged in metropolitan Miami.

The culture regions of Christian denominations in the United States are better known and understood than similar regions in other geographic realms. Data on religious affiliation are more accurate and available for the United States, Canada, and Europe, but similar information for the former communist countries is not provided, and the same is true for Africa and the Subsaharan Islamic world. It is obvious that a great deal of research remains to be done in this interesting field.

◆ ISLAM

Islam, the youngest of the major religions, arose out of the teachings of Muhammad, who was born in A.D. 571. According to Muslim belief, Muhammad received the truth directly from Allah in a series of revelations that began when the prophet was about 42 years old. During these revelations Muhammad spoke the verses of the Koran (Qur-an), the Muslims' holy book. Muhammad admired the monotheism of Christianity and Judaism; he believed that Allah had already revealed himself through other prophets (including Jesus). However, he also believed that he, Muhammad, was the real and ultimate prophet.

After his visions, Muhammad at first had doubts that he could have been chosen to be a prophet, but he was convinced by further revelations. He thereupon devoted his life to the fulfillment of the divine commands. In those days the Arab world was in religious and social disarray, with Christianity and Judaism coexisting with polytheistic religions. The political order was, at best, feudal. Muhammad's opponents, sensing his strength and purpose, began to combat his efforts. The prophet was forced to flee Mecca (Makkah), where he had been raised, for Medina (al Madinah), and he continued his work from this new base.

In many ways, the precepts of Islam constituted a revision of Judaic and Christian beliefs and traditions. The central precept is that there is but one god, who occasionally reveals himself through prophets. Jesus was such a prophet. Another key precept is that Earthly matters are profane; only Allah is pure. Allah's will is absolute; he is omnipotent and omniscient. All humans live in a world that was created for their use but only until the final judgment day.

Playing off the elitism of the Middle Eastern Christian Church and appealing to the common person, Islam spread rapidly and brought to the Arab world not only a unifying faith but also a new set of values and a new way of life. Adherents were required to observe the "five pillars" of Islam (repeated expressions of the basic creed, frequent prayer, a month of daytime fasting, almsgiving, and at least one pilgrimage to Mecca). The faith dictated behavior in other spheres of life as well. Alcohol, smoking, and gambling were forbidden. Polygamy was tolerated, although monogamy was preferred. Mosques were built in Arab settlements, not only for the Friday prayer but also to serve as social gathering places. Mecca became the spiritual center of a divided, far-flung people.

The spiritual and political stimulus provided by Muhammad was so great that the Arab world was transformed overnight. The prophet died in A.D. 632, but his fame continued to spread. Arab armies were formed. They invaded and conquered, and Islam was diffused throughout North Africa. By the early ninth century A.D., the Muslim world included emirates extending from Egypt to Morocco, a caliphate occupying most of Spain and Portugal, and a unified realm encompassing Arabia, the Middle East, Iran, and most of what is today Pakistan (Fig. 12-3). Muslim influences had penetrated France, Italy, and Turkestan in Central Asia as far as the Aral Sea. Ultimately, the Arab empire extended from Morocco to India and from Turkey to Ethiopia. The original capital was at Medina, but in response to these strategic successes it was moved, first to Damascus and then to Baghdad. In the fields of architecture, mathematics, and science, the Arabs far overshadowed their European contemporaries, and they established institutions of higher learning in many cities, including Baghdad, Cairo, and Toledo (Spain). The Muslim faith had spawned a culture, and it remains at the heart of that culture today.

Regions and Sects

Islam is a divided faith (see Fig. 11-1). The main division occurred almost immediately after the prophet's death, and it was caused by a conflict over his succession. To some, the rightful heir to the prophet's *caliphate* (Muslim community) was Muhammad's son-in-law, Ali. Others preferred different candidates. The ensuing conflict was marked by murder, warfare, and

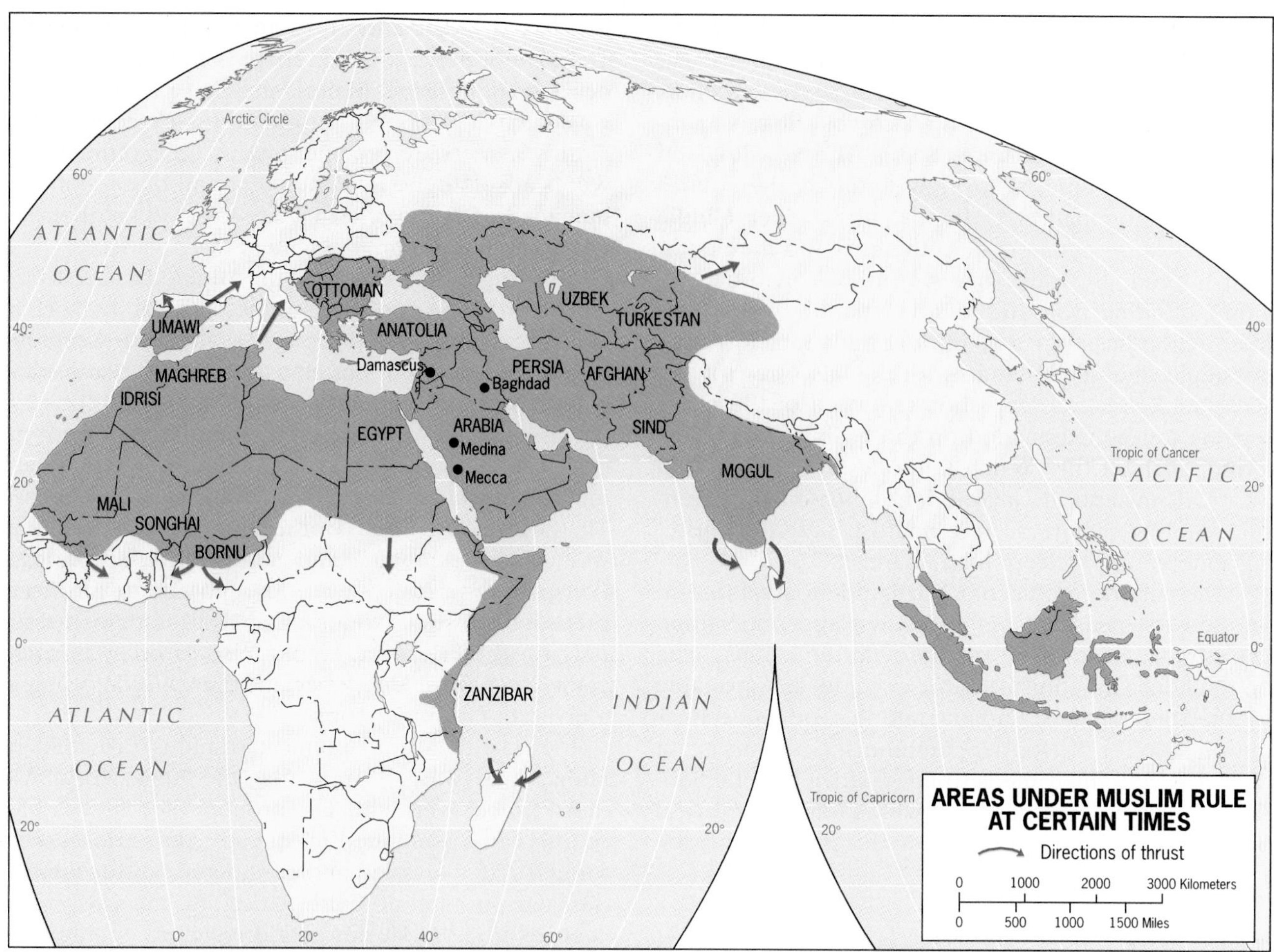

Figure 12-3 Areas under Muslim Rule at Certain Times. Some Muslims believe that areas that were at any time in history under Islamic sway remain Islamic forever—even if Islam is temporarily ousted.

lasting doctrinal disagreements. The orthodox ***Sunni*** Muslims eventually prevailed, but the ***Shiite*** Muslims, the followers of Ali, survived as small minorities. Then, early in the sixteenth century, an Iranian (Persian) ruling dynasty made Shiism (or ***Shiah***) the only legitimate faith of that empire—which extended into what is now southern Azerbaijan, eastern Iraq, and western Afghanistan and Pakistan. This gave the Shiite sect unprecedented strength and created the foundations of its modern-day culture region centered on the state of Iran (Fig. 12-3). Approximately 13 percent of all Muslims (about 160 million persons) are Shiites.

The differences between the Sunnis and the Shiites may be viewed as a matter of practicality and Earthly knowledge as opposed to idealism and the supernatural. Sunni Muslims believe in the effectiveness of family and community in solving life's problems; Shiites believe that the *imam* is the sole source of true knowledge. ***Imams*** are Shiite Muslim leaders whose appointments are regarded as sanctioned by Allah. They are thought to be without sin and infallible, and are therefore a potent social as well as political force. Shiite Muslim ceremonies are especially passionate and emotional in Western Christian eyes. Religious anniversaries are observed with intense processions during which marchers beat themselves with chains and cut themselves with sharp metal instruments.

Shiah Islam has influenced Sunni Islam in several ways. The passionate quality of the faith has diffused eastward into Pakistan, Afghanistan, and India, where Sunnis now engage in similar rituals. The veneration of Ali has diffused throughout Sunni Islam and is reflected in the respect shown to his family's descendants, the *sayyids* of East Africa and the *sharifs* of North Africa, by all Muslims. The revolutionary fervor of Iran during the late 1970s and 1980s stirred all of

Islam, although it also produced violent conflict along the political-cultural boundary between Iran and its Sunni-dominated neighbor, Iraq.

Diffusion

The spread of Islam from its Arabian source area is a classic example of expansion diffusion. Its subsequent dispersal to Malaysia, Indonesia, South Africa, and the New World resulted from relocation diffusion (Fig. 12-4). Unlike Hinduism, which also diffused through relocation, Islam attracted converts wherever it took hold, and new core areas became source areas for further dispersal. As Figure 12-3 shows, Islam's regions include not only North Africa and Southwest Asia but also Bangladesh, Malaysia (to be a Malay *is* to be a Muslim), and Indonesia. Although Islam's adherents are concentrated mostly in Asia (nearly 540 million), Africa south of the Sahara (about 170 million), and Southwest Asia/North Africa (400 million), there are also about 41 million Muslims in the nations of the former Soviet Union north of Iran and Afghanistan, and perhaps 14 million in Europe and 6 million in the Americas (see Table 12-1). Islam is experiencing a resurgence, and its expansion is likely to continue.

Cultural Landscape

Islamic cities, towns, and villages are dominated by the elaborate, ornate, sometimes magnificently designed mosques whose balconied minarets rise above the townscape. Often the mosque is the town's most imposing and most carefully maintained building. From the towering minarets the faithful are called to prayer, filling the streets as they converge on the holy place, there to bend to the ground in disciplined worship.

At the height of Islam's expansion into eastern North Africa and Southern Europe, Muslim architects incorporated earlier Roman models into their designs. The results included some of the world's greatest architectural masterpieces, such as the Alhambra Palace in Granada and the Great Mosque of Cordoba in Spain. During the eleventh century Muslim builders began

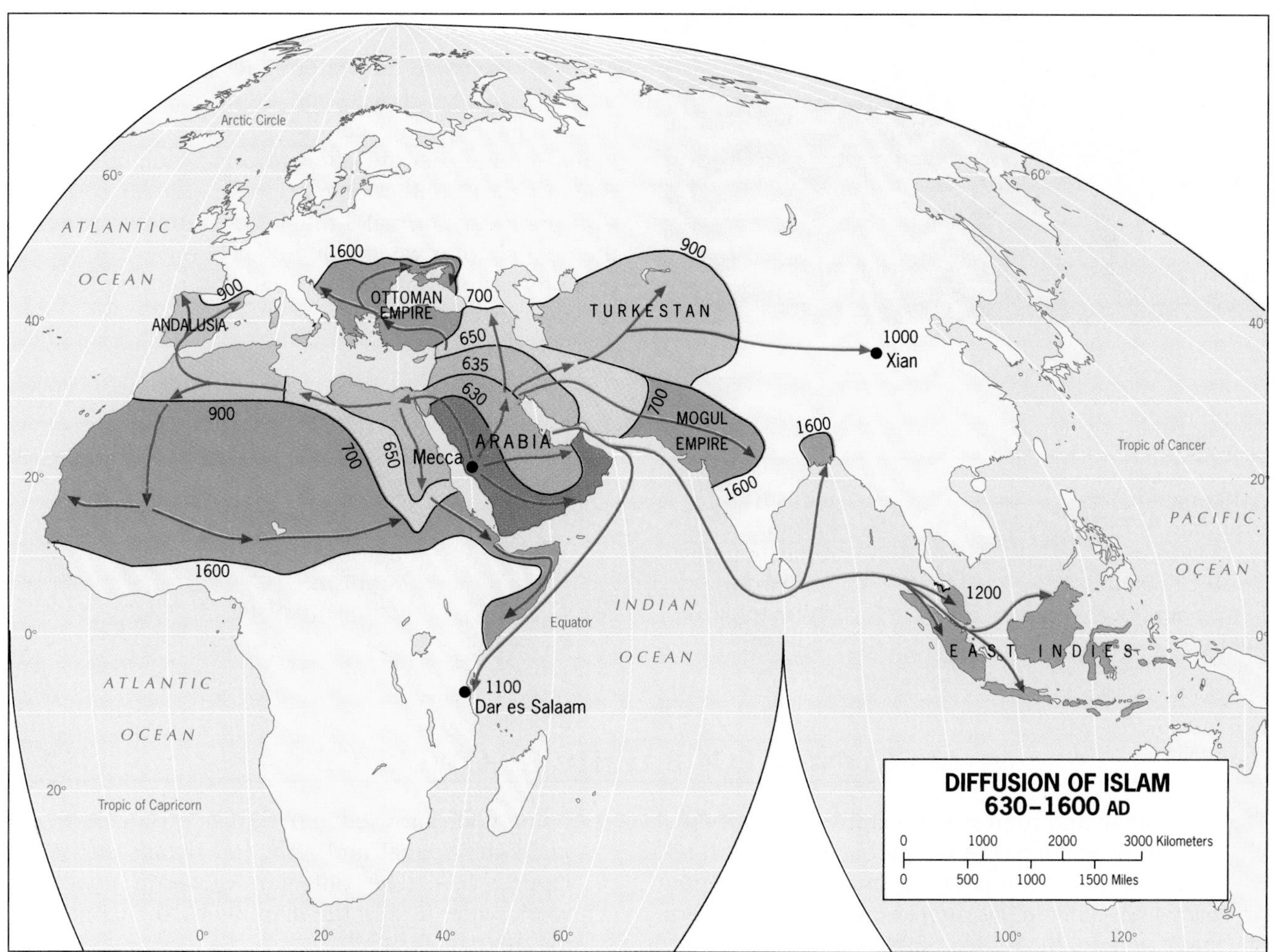

Figure 12-4 Diffusion of Islam. This map shows the diffusion of Islam from 630–1600 A.D.

From the field notes

"Golden domes and soaring minarets mark Islam's mosques from Morocco to Malaysia, and beautify townscapes from Casablanca to Kota Kinabalu. You can see this, Malaysian Sabah's most impressive mosque, from afar."

glazing the tiles of domes and roofs. To the beautiful arcades and arched courtyards were added the exquisite beauty of glass-like, perfectly symmetrical cupolas. Muslim architecture represents the unifying concept of Islamic monotheism: the perfection and vastness of the spirit of Allah.

Islam achieved its greatest artistic expression, its most distinctive visible element, in architecture. Even in the smallest town, the community helps build and maintain its mosque. The mosque symbolizes the power of the faith and its role in the community. Its primacy in the cultural landscape confirms that in the Muslim world religion and culture are one.

This chapter has focused on the world's major religions, but to hundreds of millions of people, local variants of the global or regional faiths are more important. In the United States alone, for example, there are more than 60 Christian denominations, including such churches as the Christadelphians, the Evangelicals, the Moravians, the Schwenkfelders, and the Wesleyans. Some of these denominations, such as the Pentecostal Churches, encompass a dozen or more groups with memberships ranging from under 5000 people to over a half-million.

It is often said that "all politics is local"; the same may be said of church and faith. So when outside forces challenge the comfort and familiarity of religious routine, people often respond violently. Memories of past conflict or repression, or fear of future uncertainties, can make religion a source of strife. In the next chapter we conclude our overview of the geography of religion with a discussion of the problems of religious coexistence.

◆ KEY TERMS ◆

Ashkenazim
Brahman
caste system
Confucianism
Feng Shui
imam
Jainism
karma
reincarnation
Sephardim
Shiite (Shiah)
Sikhism
Sunni
Taoism
untouchables
Zionism
Zoroastrianism

◆ APPLYING GEOGRAPHIC KNOWLEDGE ◆

1. Both urban and rural cultural landscapes carry the imprint of religion. But the global and cultural religions differ in terms of the intensity of this impact, especially in the rural areas. Can you discern some geographic reasons for the differences?

2. Using your knowledge of diffusion processes, explain the spatial and temporal details shown in Figure 12-4. The diffusion of Islam continues worldwide; how is the map likely to change over the next 100 years?

Chapter 13

Religion, Culture, and Conflict

From the field notes

"First trip to the Soviet Union, 1964. We are driven from Leningrad to Moscow. In every town we pass, and in many villages along the way, churches lie in ruins, their roofs collapsed, their steeples toppled. The bells are gone, stained-glass windows now are gaping holes. My host does not want me to photograph these churches. "Why let them collapse?" I ask. "Why not remove them altogether?" He points his finger. "Religion causes conflict. We had many religions in the Soviet Union, and they set Soviet against Soviet. And the Orthodox Church opposed our communist victory. That's what these useless relics are for. They remind the people of our victory and their freedom." I wondered what might be happening to the monumental mosques in Soviet Asia, and other great religious architecture now under Soviet sway."

KEY POINTS

- ◆ **Boundaries between major religions that cross countries can be powerful sources of conflict.**
- ◆ **Boundaries between branches of a major religion, though generally less divisive than boundaries between religions, still are capable of producing cultural conflict.**
- ◆ **Religious fundamentalism is a worldwide phenomenon that affects virtually all religions, including Islam, Christianity, and Hinduism.**
- ◆ **The cultural cores of Christianity and Islam lie in close proximity in Europe and Southwest Asia/North Africa; the prospect of disharmony and conflict between them is growing.**

Language and religion are two of the most powerful forces shaping the geography of culture. In Part 3 we noted the role of language as a unifying and culture-conserving force; a threat to the language is perceived as a threat to the culture as a whole. But language can also create a gulf between peoples otherwise united by cultural traits and traditions, and even by a political border. In many countries language disputes fuel the fires of division.

So it is with religion. Religious beliefs and histories can bitterly divide peoples who speak the same language, have the same ethnic background, and make their living in similar ways. Such divisions arise not only between people adhering to different major religions (as with Muslims and Christians in the former Yugoslavia) but also among adherents of the same religion. Some of the most destructive conflict has pitted Christian against Christian and Muslim against Muslim.

Religious conflicts usually involve more than differences in spiritual practices and beliefs. Religion functions as a symbol of a wider set of cultural and political differences. As we will see, the "religious" conflict in Northern Ireland is not just about different views of Christianity, and the conflict between Hindus and Sikhs in India has a strong political as well as religious dimension. Nevertheless, in these and other cases religion serves as the principal symbolic category around which conflict is organized. In this chapter we examine the role of religion in cultural strife and use our geographic perspective to anticipate future problems.

◆ INTERFAITH BOUNDARIES

A comparison between Figure 11-1 and a political map reveals that some countries lie entirely within the realms of individual world religions, while other countries straddle ***interfaith boundaries***, the boundaries between the world's major faiths. Many countries that lie astride interfaith boundaries are subject to divisive cultural forces, with serious implications for political cohesion and stability. As Figure 13-1 shows, several countries in Africa are in this situation, including Nigeria, Africa's most populous state.

Nigeria

With about 110 million inhabitants, Nigeria is a multilingual country. Superimposed on its linguistic diversity is religious regionalism: the north is a Muslim zone, whereas Christianity prevails in the south along with local traditional religions.

This north-south division puts the main ethnic group of the north, the Hausa-Fulani, in the Muslim camp. The two main culture cores of the south, the Yoruba of the southwest and the Ibo of the southeast, are in the Christian-animist sphere. These groups have

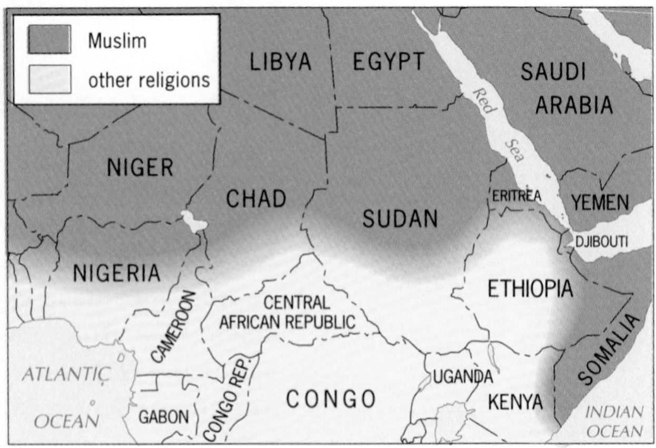

Figure 13-1 The African Transition Zone. Religious areas are shown across political boundaries in the African Transition Zone.

considerable disdain for each other. Muslim Hausa sometimes say that Yoruba are godless and uncultured. Ibo at times characterize the Hausa as backward and uneducated. Northerners may see the Ibo as money-mad merchants who will do anything for a price.

When Nigeria conducted a census in 1991, the people were not asked to state their religious preference. The numbers, however, are estimated as follows: Muslims, 55 million; Christians, 37 million; others (chiefly animists), 12 million. A substantial number of Yoruba, perhaps 2 million, are Muslims. Islam has a moderate tone in Yorubaland, however, and some geographers describe the Yoruba as "middlemen" between Christian easterners and more dogmatic Muslim northerners, defusing the tensions that might long ago have led to religious conflict. In 1993 a Muslim Yoruba was elected president of Nigeria, but the military regime then in power would not allow him to take office.

Islam predominates in the north, but Christian communities do exist—and coexistence has been the rule despite sporadic skirmishes. But during the 1990s Nigeria's fundamental religious division began to threaten the future of the state. In the north, Muslim preachers are calling for an "Islamic Republic," emboldened by the president's decision to allow Nigeria to join the Islamic Conference Organization (ICO), the global association of Islamic countries. In the south, Christian leaders are outraged by these developments. Calls for secession are being heard in the south, notably in the southeast (where the Ibo tried to secede once before, with disastrous results).

Will Nigeria's location astride an interfaith boundary ultimately destroy the country? The domination of national affairs by Muslims is becoming an issue in the south, and the aggressive expansion of Islam among smaller population groups adds to the problem. The potential for a fracture along religious lines is growing.

Any such development would have enormous social and political consequences. Nigeria is a crucible of West African culture, rich in literature and the arts. In the late 1990s Nigeria was OPEC's (Organization of Petroleum Exporting Countries) fourth largest oil producer. Nigeria's survival as a multicultural society is an achievement on a par with India's, and its Christian-Islamic coexistence has served as a model for other countries with two or more major religious groups within their borders. The breakup of Nigeria thus would have far-reaching implications.

Sudan

As Figure 11-1 shows, several other countries, including Chad, Sudan, and Ethiopia, straddle the Islamic–non-Islamic interfaith boundary in Africa. In Sudan the Muslim north and the Christian-traditional south have waged war since soon after the country gained independence. But the conflict is more complicated than that. Sudan's northern provinces contain about 60 percent of the total population, but while this region is overwhelmingly Muslim, only about two-thirds of the northerners speak Arabic as their native language. These Muslim but non-Arab northerners have been targets of anti-Islamic propaganda from the south.

Intensifying the struggle between the north and the south was the decision by the Muslim-dominated regime in Khartum to impose Islam's ***sharia religious laws*** on the entire country. Sharia laws, especially the criminal code, are harsh (prescribing, for example, the amputation of hands or limbs for theft). In the south, where people are ethnically and culturally African and where Christianity has made inroads among traditional religions, that action canceled any prospect of a compromise.

The war in Sudan has caused immense damage. Millions of people have been dislocated, and hundreds of thousands have starved; both sides have interfered with the efforts of international agencies to help the refugees. In 1992 Nigeria sought to broker a peace, and in the Nigerian capital of Abuja the northerners promised to rescind the sharia regulations and allow freedom of belief and religious observance. But by 1994 the north seemed to have victory in its grasp and declined to honor these commitments. In the late 1990s, the war raged on.

The lesson of Sudan is not lost on Nigeria: the cost of religious conflict there would be immeasurable. But both Nigeria and Sudan underscore the risks of a location that crosses interfaith boundaries.

The African Horn

Developments in the so-called Horn of Africa in the mid-1990s have changed the map. As Figure 11-1 shows, Ethiopia's religious map is even more complicated than that of Nigeria or Sudan. At the heart of the former mountain kingdom lies the cultural core area of Amharic (Coptic) Christians. From their nearly impregnable natural fortress, the Amharics controlled the lowlands in all directions. Islam won some adherents at the base of the mountains, but the Christian rulers maintained control (Fig. 13-1). When the last of Ethiopia's emperors fell in 1974, the Amharic rulers still controlled the Muslim Eritreans in the north, the Muslim Somalis in the east, and a huge arc-shaped region to the west and south. But a revolution was brewing, and in 1991 the military dictatorship that had overthrown the imperial dynasty was overthrown in its turn.

In the late 1990s, the future of Ethiopia remains uncertain. The revolution that destroyed the old order created a new state: Eritrea. Predominantly Muslim, Eritrea is culturally distinct from the empire of which it was a part. But Eritrea's secession did not end Ethiopia's religious multiculturalism. Ethiopia still contains a large Muslim population of Somalis in its eastern zone; the south and west are non-Muslim; and Coptic Christians still cluster in their highland domain. The separation of Eritrea is likely to be only one step in a series of changes that underscore the perils of straddling an interfaith border.

South Asia

Britain's South Asian colonial empire extended from Pakistan in the west to Bangladesh in the east and from Kashmir to Sri Lanka. This giant domain lay astride a deep and divisive interfaith boundary. In 1947 that boundary became the political border between Islamic Pakistan and multicultural India. The establishment of that political boundary produced one of the largest human migrations of modern times as millions of Muslims crossed into Pakistan and Hindus moved eastward into India.

While Pakistan became an almost exclusively Islamic state, India proclaimed itself a secular federation in which all faiths would be tolerated and freedom of religion would prevail. However, India continued to experience problems created by location. Within its borders large religious communities faced each other across deep cultural divides.

For more than 30 years following independence, religious conflict in India was sporadic and relatively minor. But during the 1980s several events occurred that led to more intense conflict. The first was a campaign by Sikhs for greater independence. The Sikhs found themselves at a disadvantage in a nation that was dominated by Hindus and in which the Muslims were the most powerful religious minority. The Sikhs demanded a separate state in the Punjab. When this demand was not met, they reacted with militancy and terrorism. In 1984 the Indian Army raided the Sikhs' holiest shrine, the Golden Temple in Amritsar, causing more than 1000 deaths. Four months later India's prime minister, Indira Gandhi, was assassinated by Sikh members of her bodyguard.

The Sikhs' demand for a separate State (to be named Khalistan, if it ever comes about) is based in part on the concentration of Sikhs in the Panjab (Punjab) region of northwestern India (Fig. 13-2). As we saw in Chapter 11, Sikhism arose as a reaction to Hinduism and Islam. By world standards, it is not a large religion; it has about 20 million adherents, more than 90 percent of whom are in northwest India. But as the map shows, although Sikhs are in the majority in most of the districts of Punjab, the state also includes significant Hindu minorities. The situation is somewhat similar to that in Northern Ireland and is no closer to a solution.

The second development that threatened India's stability occurred during the late 1980s, when the site of a holy shrine claimed by both Muslims and Hindus became a battleground. This struggle focused on a shrine at Ayodhya in the State of Uttar Pradesh. A building housing both a temple and a mosque sat atop a hill that was holy to both Hindus and Muslims, but in 1986 a local judge ruled it to be a Hindu site. Hindu pilgrims came to the site by the thousands, and a militant Hindu group announced plans to tear down the mosque portion of the building and expand the temple section. Muslims protested, but Hindus argued that the site was in fact the birthplace of the Hindu god Rama

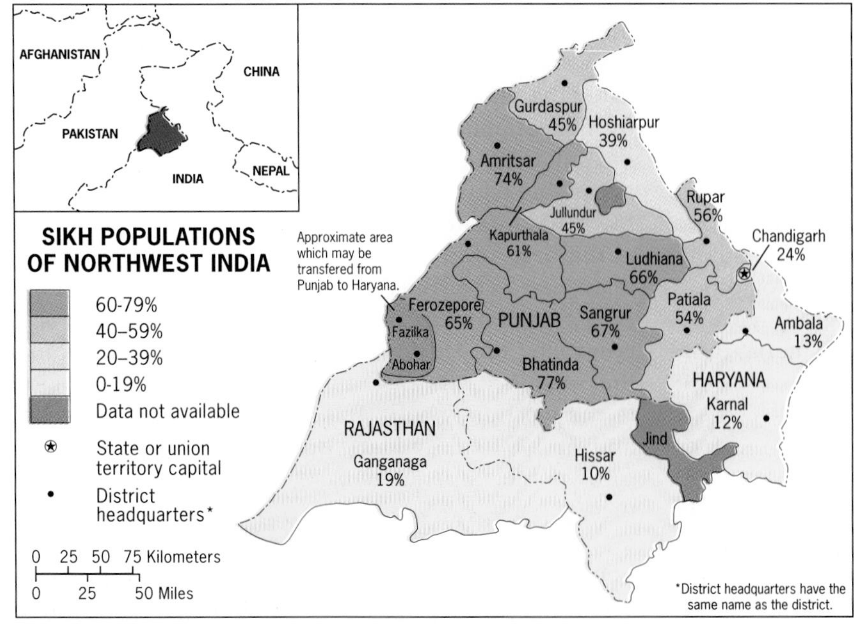

Figure 13-2 Sikh Populations of Northwest India. *Source: From a map in M. I. Glassner and H. J. de Blij,* Systematic Political Geography, 4th ed. *New York: Wiley, 1989, p. 402.*

and that its original temple had been torn down by the Muslims during the Moghul period. In 1989 the issue aroused religious passions throughout India, and the resulting clashes killed nearly 400 people.

The third threat to India's continuity arose in part from the kinds of skirmishes just described. For the first time in memory, Hinduism began to exhibit the sort of fundamentalism and militancy that had long been associated with other faiths. The beginnings of this trend can be traced to 1983, when reactions to Sikh and Muslim militancy led to "Save Hinduism" marches across the country. Ten years later Hindu fundamentalism had become a major force in Indian politics. It is strongest in the north-central region of the country, but it is spreading. To many observers, Hindu militancy and fundamentalism seem contradictory; Hinduism has never been an aggressive faith. But Hindu leaders see the results of militancy and appeals to fundamentalism elsewhere, and they understand the potential rewards.

The surge of Hindu fundamentalism is reflected on the map. In 1990 political leaders in the state of Maharashtra proclaimed that the city of Bombay would henceforth be named Mumbai (its precolonial name, after a Hindu goddess). The change was fiercely opposed by Muslims, Sikhs, and other communities in the giant city. Soon after, the change was approved by the Indian government, Hindu leaders in Madras announced that their city would henceforth be known as Chennai. These developments show that fundamentalism is often tied to the rejection of outside influence—whether historical or contemporary.

The rise of fundamentalism is affecting virtually all religions today, and we will devote further attention to this serious development later in the chapter. The appearance of fundamentalism in India is evidence that returning to the "basics" of faith has worldwide appeal.

The Former Soviet Union

When the Soviet Union was forged from the czar's empire three generations ago, the socialist planners faced the task of satisfying the territorial demands of dozens of diverse peoples. Most of these peoples had participated in the revolution, and many were rewarded with territory, producing a multitiered political mosaic. The top tier consisted of the 15 Soviet Republics; other territories were of lower rank. Russia, the largest and dominant Soviet Republic, itself was divided into more than 70 territories, each of which had some degree of autonomy.

The Republics not only inherited more than 100 "nationalities" or ethnic groups with their languages, beliefs, and lifeways; they were also heir to parts of two great religious realms. Under the czars' rule, the Russian branch of the Eastern Orthodox Church had thrived, marking the Russian cultural landscape from Kiev to St. Petersburg (Leningrad). The czars also had subjugated the vast steppes and deserts of Central Asia, where Islam was the prevailing faith. East of the Caspian Sea, the Soviet empire included the physical and cultural landscapes of Southwest Asia.

Between the Caspian and Black seas, the Soviets acquired two neighboring territories that were strongly infused with religion. The Armenians, mainly on the Black Sea side, were Christians.

The Azerbaijani, on the Caspian Sea side, were Shiite Muslims. The Soviet communists were determined to create an atheistic state, and so they discouraged religious practice on both sides of the interfaith boundary that extended from the Black Sea to the Chinese border. In Russia, they seized church bells and other religious paraphernalia and demolished many churches, converting others to secular uses. In the Soviet Muslim realm, they tolerated Islamic practice among the old but not among the young. Time, they believed, would erase the imprints of both Christianity and Islam.

In laying out an administrative framework, however, the Soviet planners proved to be poor geographers. In Armenia and Azerbaijan they tried to establish boundaries that would facilitate local control and discourage separatism. The result (Fig. 13-3) was a layout that could function as long as Soviet authorities controlled both "republics," but was a blueprint for religious conflict when that control diminished. A large ***exclave*** of Christian Armenia, called Nagorno-Karabakh, was created as an ***enclave*** within Muslim Azerbaijan. Azerbaijan was also divided through the creation of an exclave called Nakhichevan, which was established on the Iranian border.

When the USSR collapsed, the Soviet Republics became independent states, and ethnic strife broke out almost immediately. Azerbaijani Muslims, long cut off from their Iranian Shiite counterparts, broke through the southern border, acquiring weapons in the process. Soon Muslims and Christians were locked in combat, and Armenian refugees were streaming from Nagorno-Karabakh westward and even fleeing by boat across the Caspian Sea. More than 70 years of Soviet domination had done little to soften Armenian-Christian memories of Islamic oppression or to lessen the intensity of Azerbaijani-Muslim disdain for Christian unbelievers.

Another interfaith boundary extended across the vast region of Central Asia called Turkestan (see Fig. 11-1). There the Soviets subjugated a Muslim population numbering between 40 and 50 million. (Soviet census figures for this region were always suspect.)

The Soviet communist policy of promoting atheism applied to Central Asian Muslims as well as Rus-

Figure 13-3 Two Exclaves in Transcaucasia. This map shows two Transcaucasian exclaves: Muslim-Azerbaijan Nakhichevan, cut off by Christian Armenia, and Christian-Armenian Nagorno-Karabakh, surrounded by Muslim Azerbaijan.

sian Christians. But centuries of Muslim history and ideology could not quickly be stamped out, and when the Soviet Union collapsed, Islam quickly revived in the Central Asian republics. Most of Turkestan's Muslims adhere to Sunni Islam, although there are pockets of Shiism in the region. Simultaneously, the Russian Orthodox (Christian) Church is experiencing a resurrection in Russia and among Russians living in other countries; these events create the potential for friction.

The most serious problem could develop in Kazakhstan, the largest state in Central Asia. The Islamic-Christian interfaith boundary runs right across Kazakhstan, whose north is strongly Russified and whose south remains Islamic (Fig. 11-1). An estimated 47 percent of the population of between 17 and 19 million adheres to Islam, while about 17 percent now belong to the Russian Orthodox Church. Virtually all the Christians live in the north, and almost all the Muslims live in the south. There is a high degree of spatial separation between the Islamic and Christian communities, but Christians and Muslims do not have their own countries—unless the interfaith boundary becomes a political border at some future time. In the case of Kazakhstan, therefore, the religious map suggests, the future holds a major challenge.

Europe

No discussion of the impact of interfaith boundaries would be complete without some mention of Yugoslavia. Ever since the Ottoman Turks brought soldiers to their northwestern military frontier and converted some Slavic communities, the region has had Muslim pockets—and, hence, interfaith boundaries. In the former Yugoslavia these clusters were quite large in terms of both territory and population. They centered on Bosnia and its capital, Sarajevo.

The scale of Figure 11-1 cannot illustrate the complexity of Yugoslavia's cultural map, but it can be imagined when one considers the fact that the Muslim-Christian interfaith boundary there lay in an area where an intrafaith boundary also prevailed: a boundary between the Serbian Orthodox Church and the Catholic Church. The Muslims were caught in the middle, and when Yugoslavia's political system collapsed, they were attacked by both Christian camps. The term ***ethnic cleansing*** came into use to describe the ouster of Muslims and others from their homes and lands. Serbs and Croats ousted Muslims, but they also "cleansed" each other's territories. Where they could, Muslims drove their Christian adversaries away, but it was the Muslim minority that suffered most.

The case of Yugoslavia illustrates the risk an interfaith boundary poses to any state, no matter how long peoples of different religions have lived within its boundaries. Yugoslavia was a relatively young state, having been formed from the chaotic aftermath of World War I before 1920. But its 7 major and 17 smaller cultural groups had managed to live together for nearly three generations before disaster struck. During World War II, Nazi-supporting Croats fought anti-Nazi Serbs, but after 1945 Yugoslavia resumed its quest for nationhood under communist rule imposed by its strongman president, Tito. After Tito's death, and following an uneasy period of rule by committee, Yugoslavia was swept up in the winds of change produced by the disintegration of the Soviet Union, and religious differences became grounds for combat.

The result has been disastrous not just for Yugoslavia. After World War II Europeans proclaimed that what had happened during the war would never happen again. In Yugoslavia Europe had a chance to prove that its collective power and influence would indeed prevent outrages like those that happened during World War II. But it failed to do so, and the case of Yugoslavia can truly be seen as Europe's tragedy.

Other Interfaith Boundaries

The problems of religious militancy plague several other countries with various degrees of intensity. In populous Bangladesh, where the southern lowland regions are mainly Muslim and the interior is Hindu, the level of interfaith conflict has been lower than in India. Hindu fundamentalism has not yet made inroads here, and the level of Muslim militancy has until recently been relatively low. (In 1994, however, evidence of growing Muslim fundamentalism in Bangladesh came in the form of the arrest and forced exile of the author of a book that was deemed blasphemous by Islamic religious authorities.)

The future of the interfaith boundary in Bangladesh will depend on the religious situation in neighboring India. If India manages to accommodate its huge Muslim minority and if conflict with Islamic Pakistan can be avoided, Bangladesh is likely to remain calm. Should serious interfaith strife occur in India, Bangladesh will feel the effects.

Sri Lanka Another neighbor of India, the island country of Sri Lanka, has experienced conflict with religious overtones. About 70 percent of Sri Lanka's 19 million inhabitants are Buddhists, but in the north and northeast a Tamil-speaking minority, ethnically Dravidian and religiously Hindu, has developed. Since 1984 this group has fought a war of secession in which religion has become an ever stronger force. Buddhist shrines were targeted, and Hindu holy sites were attacked in retaliation. The Indian government tried to assist the Sri Lanka government to settle the issue, even through armed intervention. In India, Hindu fundamentalists protested this support for Buddhists against Hindus, and this may have led to the assassination of Prime Minister Rajiv Gandhi in 1991.

In the mid-1990s, a change of government promised negotiations and perhaps a settlement. But a series of attacks in the capital, Colombo, in 1997 proved that Tamil extremists would settle for nothing less than a sovereign Hindu state. As the decade drew to a close, the interfaith conflict continued.

From the field notes

"A field trip in the area of Vienna, Austria included a reminder of the changing religious mosaic of Europe, and the evolving pattern of interfaith boundaries there. This thriving mosque stands near the banks of the Danube Canal. Turkish workers, refugee Bosnian Muslims, and other adherents of Islam came here to worship, to play (there were many children on the grounds), and to patronize the sizeable bazaar. Islam's presence in Europe is growing and changing."

Southeast and Southwest Asia In Southeast Asia, an interfaith boundary between Islam and Christianity touches the southern Philippines. The southernmost islands of the Philippines have Muslim populations that are small minorities in a Catholic-dominated country (see Fig. 11-1). Although Muslims account for only about 5 percent of the population of the Philippines, they have campaigned vigorously, and sometimes violently, for improved status.

One of the most significant interfaith boundaries prevails in Southwest Asia, in Israel and between Israel and its neighbors. The Jewish presence in Gaza always was small, but Jewish settlement in the West Bank blurred the interfaith boundary between Israel and Jordan. Israel's control over Gaza, the West Bank, and the Golan Heights put many miles of interfaith boundaries within that nation's jurisdiction.

Events in the early- and mid-1990s began to change this religious-political mosaic as self-government was awarded to Gaza and to small areas inside the West Bank. Palestinian Arabs were empowered to run their own affairs within these zones. Stability and satisfactory coexistence could lead to further adjustments and, as seen from the Arab side, a legitimate Palestinian state. But Israel lies astride what may well be the world's most sensitive interfaith boundaries. Recent challenges to the framework for peace hammered out in Oslo in 1995—including suicide bombings and retaliatory curfews and arrests—show that a successful transition is by no means assured.

◆ INTRAFAITH BOUNDARIES

Interfaith boundaries can threaten the stability of entire countries. Countries that contain ***intrafaith boundaries*** would seem to be less troubled.

A SENSE OF SCALE

The Geography of Religious Diversity

The spatial scale of maps showing the distribution of religions throughout the world influences our understanding of the relative importance of a religion in a particular place or region. Figure 11-1, for example, shows the distribution of religions on a global scale. By looking at this small-scale map we may think that most of the United States is Protestant or that most of Western Europe is Catholic. Yet this understanding of the distribution of religions is adequate only when we are trying to identify patterns at a *macro* or global scale. As soon as we turn our attention to a more intermediate or *meso* scale, such as that depicted in Figure 12-2, a different picture emerges. The United States appears as a more culturally complex region. If taken a step further, a map showing the *micro*-scale distribution of religions in a city such as New York City would show some neighborhoods as predominantly Catholic, Protestant, or Jewish, and others as quite mixed.

A diversity of religions are found in cities like New York, but no specific sites within the city are critically important to members of more than one religious group. In fact, in the whole of the United States virtually no sites are considered holy or otherwise essential to the identity of more than one religion. For example, the holy sites of Mormonism in Utah are critically important only to Mormons. Other sites of supreme importance to only one group are the Vatican City in Italy for Catholics and Mecca in Saudi Arabia for Muslims. However, throughout the world many sites are in some way claimed as holy or important to adherents of more than one religious faith. In India, for example, several locations are considered holy by Hindus, Buddhists, and Jains. Specifically, Volture Peak in Rajgir, India, is holy to Buddhists because it is the site where the Buddha first proclaimed the Heart Sutra, a very important canon of Buddhism. Hindus and Jains also consider the site holy because they consider Buddha to be a god or prophet. There has been no serious discord among religious groups over this site, however. Pilgrims of all faiths peacefully congregate there year after year.

Unfortunately, the same cannot be said of religious sites in the ancient city of Jerusalem. There sacred space has been bitterly contested among Jews, Christians, and Muslims since the seventh century, when Muslim armies took control over the city from the Byzantine empire. Rivalry over the control of Jerusalem is based on the fact that three religions attach historic and religious significance to overlapping spaces in the city. The most contested site within Jerusalem (and arguably one of the most contested sites in the world) is the walled rise in the southeast corner of the Old City known to Jews as the Temple Mount and to Muslims as *al-Haram al-Sharif* (the Noble Sanctuary). This 144,000 square

meter area is the place where Jews and Christians believe that God commanded Abraham to sacrifice his son, and where Muslims believe that Muhammad arrived from his extraordinary one-night journey from Mecca to Jerusalem. Attempts by members of different religious groups to control this small site have created tensions that echo far beyond Jerusalem to a world of great religious diversity.

In general, that is indeed the case. A number of Western European countries have Catholic as well as Protestant communities, and often these are reflected in the regional distribution of the population, as in the case of Switzerland (Fig. 13-4). In the late 1990s the great majority of these countries were not experiencing religious or ethnic conflict. Factors other than (or in addition to) religious ones lay at the root of the strife in Eastern Europe.

Northern Ireland

The single most intractable problem in Western Europe is Northern Ireland, where a Protestant majority and a Catholic minority are in conflict over their coexistence and their future. The issue stems from the period when all of Ireland was a British dependency. A substantial Protestant British population immigrated into Ireland during this time, many from Scotland. Most settled in the northeastern corner of the island.

When the Catholic Irish rebelled against British colonialism, Ireland was partitioned so as to protect the Protestant minority in the northeast. But Northern

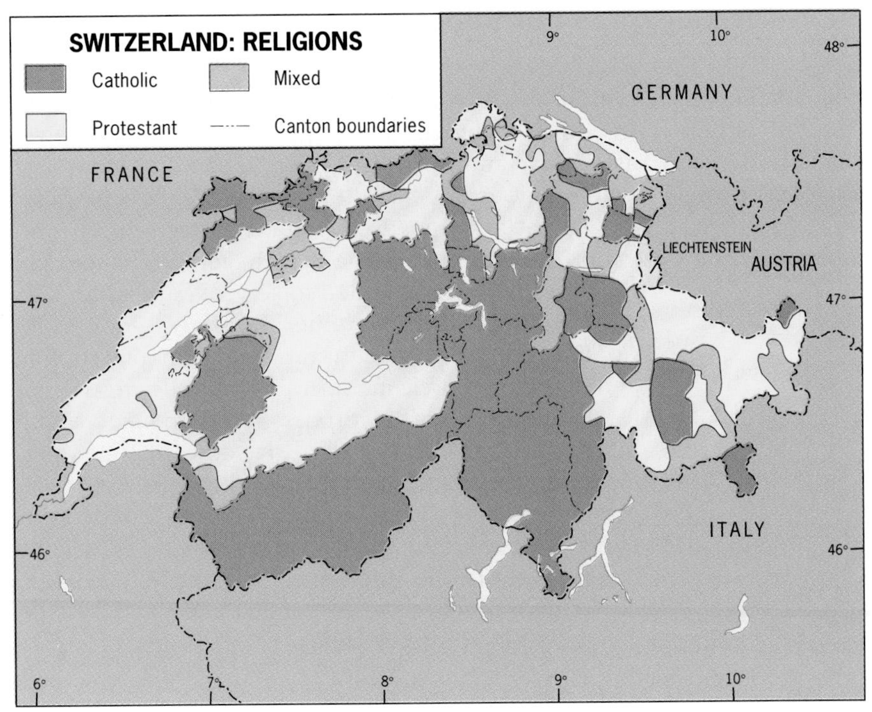

Figure 13-4 Religions of Switzerland. Switzerland includes Catholic, Protestant, and mixed religion areas. *Source: From M. I. Glassner and H. J. de Blij,* Systematic Political Geography, 4th ed., *1989, p. 535.*

Ireland also contained a substantial Catholic minority, which was left unprotected. In the 1920s, when the new map of Ireland was being drawn, it was assumed that time and economic development would soften the religious animosities in "the North" (Fig. 13-5).

This was not to be. The Protestant majority in Northern Ireland, constituting about two-thirds of the total population (about 1.6 million) held all the economic and political advantages. Charges of discrimination and repression of Catholics were underscored by terrorist acts, bringing British troops into the area. As time went on, the situation was worsened by economic stagnation. Although the Republic of Ireland was sensitive to the plight of Catholics in the North, no official help was extended to those who were engaging in violence.

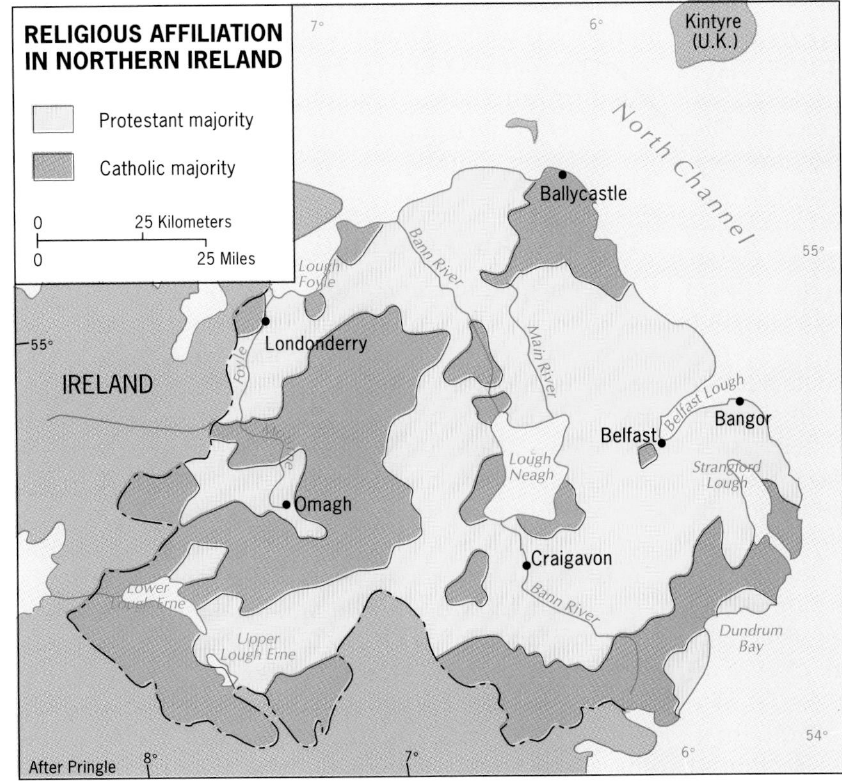

Figure 13-5 Religious Affiliation in Northern Ireland. Areas of Catholic and Protestant majorities are scattered throughout Northern Ireland. *Source: From D. G. Pringle,* One Island, Two Nations? *Letchworth: Research Studies Press/Wiley, 1985, p. 21.*

As many observers have noted, the conflict in Northern Ireland is not strictly religious; it is a conflict over access to opportunities, over civil rights, and over political influence. But religion and religious history are the banners beneath which the opposing sides march, and church and cathedral have become symbols of strife rather than peace.

The Islamic Realm

In the Islamic realm, conflicts between the majority Sunni and minority Shiite branches have pitted followers of Islam against each other. Undoubtedly the most destructive war of its kind in modern times, the Iran-Iraq conflict of the 1980s, was a battle between Sunni-dominated Iraq and Shiite-ruled Iran. The war began over a territorial issue, but religious enmity helped to sustain it. Although the Shiites constitute only about 12 percent of all Muslims, they proclaim themselves the true followers of Muhammad and often resent the less dogmatic, more worldly Sunni.

The depth of this division was revealed in the aftermath of the Persian Gulf War, when the Sunni-controlled army of defeated Iraq immediately moved against the Shiite communities of the south to preclude any opposition or cooperation with neighboring Iran (see Figure 11-1). Shiite and Sunni factions have also been in conflict in Lebanon, and factional conflict has occurred during the annual pilgrimage to Mecca, claiming thousands of lives.

◆ RELIGIOUS FUNDAMENTALISM

Today, throughout the world, religious leaders and millions of their followers are seeking to return to the basics of their faith. This drive toward ***religious fundamentalism*** is often born of frustration at the perceived breakdown of society's mores and values, loss of religious authority, failure to achieve economic goals, corruption of political systems, and loss of a sense of local control in the face of the globalization of culture and economy.

People in one society often fear fundamentalism in other societies without recognizing it in their own. In the United States, fundamentalism is often associated with Islam. Such incidents as the Iranian religious regime's pronouncement of a death sentence for the author of an allegedly blasphemous book seem alien to adherents of Christianity. But other cultures view religious zealots' killings of physicians who are willing to perform legal abortions in this country as equally alien. Fundamentalism and extremism are closely related, and their appeal is global.

Today religions are affected by modernization. Education, radio, television, and travel have diffused notions of individual liberties, sexual equality, and freedom of choice; questions about religious as well as secular authority; and other ideas that may clash with religious dogma. They have also greatly amplifed the extent and speed of cultural diffusion and innovation. Some churches have managed to change with the times, allowing women to serve as priests and liberalizing their doctrines. But others have gone in the opposite direction, reaffirming fundamental dogma and trying to block modernization and external cultural influence. In the process, some believe, battle lines are being drawn. The drive toward fundamentalism in Christianity and Islam alike is creating a climate of mistrust that could lead to strife. On the other hand, fragmentation within the Christian and Islamic realms is more the rule than the exception, creating doubt that any large-scale conflict can or will be organized along interfaith lines.

Christian Fundamentalism

Among Christian religions, the Roman Catholic Church has resisted innovations deemed to be incompatible with the fundamentals of the faith. Among the issues giving rise to disputes are birth control, family planning, and the role of women in the religious bureaucracy. The major religions tend to be male-dominated, and few women have managed to enter the hierarchy. More important from a global viewpoint is the Roman Catholic Church's position on family planning. In a world of exploding populations, the church continues to militate against the use of artificial means of birth control as well as abortion. During the September 1994 United Nations Conference on Population and Development, the Roman Catholic Church even sought to ally itelf with Islamic countries against advocates of population control.

Islamic Fundamentalism

Other major faiths must also confront the pressures of change. Not all Muslim communities, for example, adhere with equal strictness to the rules of the Koran such as the prohibition of alcohol. The laws of Islam, which are very strict and call for severe punishment of offenders, are not applied with equal force throughout the Muslim religious realm.

Such inconsistency produces a reaction, not only in the religious bureaucracies but also among the masses of believers. In general, the clergy tend to be conservative, with some more liberal members reflecting the forces of modernization. Church and mosque memberships are divided in response. The geographic dimension is not difficult to find: in the Catholic Church, the modernizers are located far from the heartland, in the Netherlands and in the United States.

In the Muslim realm, conservatism is strongest in a tier of countries extending from Sudan to Pakistan, becoming weaker in Turkey to the northwest and Malaysia and Indonesia to the east, where the so-called laissez-faire Islam prevails.

Even in those "moderate" wings of Islam, however, fundamentalism is gaining ground. In Malaysia, the Chinese and other minorities reacted fearfully when the government considered demands for the general application of Sharia law. In Indonesia, a fundamentalist drive by Islamic preachers has found fertile soil, especially among rural people who remain remote from the changes affecting Indonesian society elsewhere.

Countering religious fundamentalism entails political risks, as is evident in the care U.S. politicians take to avoid offending the "religious right." When the former Shah of Iran tried to limit the power of the imams as he sought to modernize the state, he provoked a religious movement that eventually led to his overthrow. During the revolution in Iran, the imams imposed the most basic of Shiite religious rules and practices upon their followers. After the Shah was replaced by an ***ayatollah***, a supreme religious leader, those rules and practices became law. Women, whose situation had improved under the Shah's regime, suffered setbacks. Those who had adopted Western modes of dress were arrested and forced to wear Muslim headgear, veils, and long robes. Many lost positions in commerce and administration.

What happened in Iran during the 1970s and 1980s was perhaps the most significant manifestation of the trend toward fundamentalism in organized religion in contemporary times. The process took a violent course in Iran, but it was, and is, happening in other regions and countries as well. When religion becomes a political force, when the power of religion is threatened by secularization, when the revered shrines of a faith are imperiled or damaged, when modernization is opposed by those who prefer traditional ways, or when ethnic conflict arises over other issues, people often turn to the most basic precepts of their fath. Thus religion becomes a binding force, a bulwark against adversity, and a proclamation of strength and unity.

Like religion generally, therefore, fundamentalism can constitute both a unifying and a divisive force. In the United States, fundamentalist "preachers" and their massive following have divided the Protestant churches, especially when the personal and financial excesses of certain evangelists became public knowledge. The debate within the Catholic Church has created a split between orthodox and liberal members. In Muslim societies, fundamentalism has stimulated the formation of political movements whose aim is to reverse the move toward secularization and, if possible, to seize political power.

In Algeria such a movement has come close to overthrowing the government. In 1991 a conservative Muslim political party was poised to win in the national elections, having appealed to voters who were eager to replace a corrupt secular administration with an Islamic regime. Rather than allowing the final round of voting to take place, the Algerian government canceled the election. The Muslim movement then began a campaign of violent opposition. Some saw a parallel with Iran, and Muslim leaders called for an ***Islamic republic*** in Algeria. Dozens of foreigners were killed; but thousands of Algerians lost their lives in a continuing exchange of reprisals. France, fearful of a mass exodus of Algerians to French shores, tried to mediate. But both the Algerian government and the Muslim fundamentalists rejected both French and European Union efforts to involve themselves in Algeria's internal struggle. Meanwhile, attacks on remote villages by unidentified bands of assailants cost tens of thousands of

From the field notes

"The Lautoka Muslim School reminded me that communities try hard to maintain their traditions, no matter how far from their source areas they may be. Lautoka is a town on the northwest coast of Viti Levu, the most populous island of Fiji in the Pacific Ocean. This is a cosmopolitan place, on the boundary between Melanesia and Polynesia, with a large population of (South Asian) Indians brought here during (British) colonial times. Among these South Asians the Hindus are in the majority, but the smaller Muslim community is determined to protect its identity and ways of life. The Lautoka Muslim School is coeducational, though girls must wear elaborate dress that covers them from head to ankles while boys wear shorts and short-sleeved shirts—which, I am sure, is why the boys played ball on the field while the girls stood in the shade of the tent to the right. I asked a teacher about the relations between Muslim and Hindu communities in Lautoka, "They are good," he said. "We keep to ourselves." Then he told me where to find the town's largest mosque, and urged me to pay a visit."

lives; the identity of the killers, and their goals, remained a mystery. The war between Islamists and secularists dealt Algeria a damaging setback.

The struggle in Algeria emboldened Muslim fundamentalists to challenge government authority elsewhere. In Tunisia, Muslim clerics called for the end of secular government; in Egypt, Muslim radicals attacked foreign tourists, thus destroying one of the country's major sources of income. It was believed that disorder would generate dissatisfaction, and dissatisfaction would lead to the creation of an Islamic state.

It is often said that we live in an age of religious tolerance. Compared to the Middle Ages, that certainly is true. But religious feelings can quickly be translated into hostility and conflict. When the rise of fundamentalism is added to the divisions created by interfaith and intrafaith boundaries, religion can plunge entire societies into conflict.

◆ KEY TERMS ◆

ayatollah
enclave
ethnic cleansing
exclave
interfaith boundary
intrafaith boundary
Islamic republic
religious fundamentalism
sharia religious law

◆ APPLYING GEOGRAPHIC KNOWLEDGE ◆

1. In this chapter we focus on interfaith, as compared to intrafaith, boundaries in the cultural landscape. Select two of the world's countries, one astride an interfaith boundary and the other marked by an intrafaith boundary, and compare the level of conflict. Is such conflict inevitable when religious boundaries cross national territories?

2. One of the important consequences of the collapse of the Soviet Union has been the revival of religion, not only in Russia, but also in the former Soviet republics, notably in Turkestan. What cultural-geographic factors are contributing to this revival? Can you disern new or reemerging interfaith or intrafaith boundaries in what used to be the Soviet realm?

Part Four
THE GEOGRAPHY OF RELIGION

At Issue: Revisited

Can modern-secular and fundamentalist-religious communities and countries coexist? The growth of secularism in most industrialized societies does not spell the end of religion as a major social force. Instead, religion continues to shape the lives of billions and to define critical social boundaries around the world. In many places the disorienting and depersonalizing effects of modernism have strengthened religious fundamentalism and have placed religion at the center of volatile conflicts. Such conflicts are not just between believers in different world religions, however. They are just as often between Protestant and Catholic, Shiite and Sunni, ecclesiastical conservative and liberal. Thus, religious fragmentation presents a challenge not just at the meeting points of world religions, but for all societies confronting rapid social, economic, and environmental change.

◆ SELECTED REFERENCES ◆

Part Four The Geography of Religion

al Faruqi, I., & Sopher, D., eds. *Historical Atlas of the Religions of the World* (New York: Macmillan, 1974).

Barakat, H. *The Arab World: Society, Culture, and State* (Berkeley: University of California Press, 1993).

Bhardwaj, S. *Hindu Places of Pilgrimage in India: A Study in Cultural Geography* (Berkeley and Los Angeles: University of California Press, 1973).

de Blij, H. J. "Islam in South Africa," in J. Kritzeck, & W. H. Lewis, eds., *Islam in Africa* (New York: Van Nostrand, 1970).

Eliade, M. *The Sacred and the Profane: The Nature of Religion* (New York: Harcourt, Brace & World, 1959).

Finegan, J. *An Archaeological History of Religions of Indian Asia* (New York: Paragon House, 1989).

Gaustad, E. *Historical Atlas of Religion in America* (New York: Harper & Row, 1962).

Griffith, J. S. *Beliefs and Holy Places: A Spiritual Geography of the Pimeria Alta* (Tucson: University of Arizona Press, 1992).

Halvorson, P., & Newman, W. *Atlas of Religious Change in America, 1952–1990* (Washington, D.C.: Glenmary Research Center, 1994).

Halvorson, P., & Newman, W. *Patterns in Pluralism: A Portrait of American Religion* (Washington, D.C.: Glenmary Research Center, 1980).

Isaac, E. "The Pilgrimage of Mecca," *Geographical Review* 63 (1973), 405–409.

Khalidi, R. *Palestinian Identity: The Construction of Modern National Consciousness* (New York: Columbia University Press, 1997).

Korp, M. *The Sacred Geography of the American Mound Builders* (Lewiston, N.Y.: E. Mellen Press, 1990).

Levine, G. J. "On the Geography of Religion," *Transactions of the Institute of British Geographers,* 11, 1987, pp. 248–440.

Lewis, B., ed. *The World of Islam: Faith, People, Culture* (London, U.K.: Thames & Hudson, 1976).

Marty, M. E. *Pilgrims in Their Own Land: 500 Years of Religion in America* (Boston: Little, Brown, 1984).

Mitchell, G. *The Hindu Temple: An Introduction to Its Meaning and Forms* (New York: Harper & Row, 1977).

Noble, A. G., & Efrat, E. "Geography of the Intifada," *The Geographical Review,* July 1990, pp. 288–307.

Park, C. *Sacred Worlds: An Introduction to Geography and Religion* (London: Routledge, 1994).

Rahman, M., ed. *Muslim World: Geography and Development* (Lanham, Md: University Press of America, 1987).

Romann, M. & Weingrod, A. *Living Together Separately: Arabs and Jews in Contemporary Jerusalem* (Princeton, N.J.: Princeton University Press, 1991).

Rowland, B. *The Art and Architecture of India: Buddhist, Hindu, Jain* (New York: Penguin, 1977).

Schwartzberg, J. *An Historical Atlas of South Asia* (Chicago: University of Chicago Press, rev. ed., 1978).

Scott, J. & Simpson-Housley, P., eds. *Sacred Places and Profane Spaces: Essays in the Geographics of Judaism, Christianity, and Islam* (New York: Greenwood Press, 1991).

Shortridge, J. R. "Patterns of Religion in the United States," *Geographical Review,* 66, 1976, pp. 420–434.

Sopher, D. E. *Geography of Religions* (Englewood Cliffs, N.J.: Prentice-Hall, 1967).

Sopher, D., ed. *An Exploration of India: Geographical Perspectives on Society and Culture* (Ithaca, N.Y.: Cornell University Press, 1980).

Swartz, M. J. *The Way the World Is* (Berkeley: University of California Press, 1991).

Thernstrom, S., ed. *Harvard Encyclopedia of American Ethnic Groups* (Cambridge, Mass.: Belknap-Harvard University Press, 1980).

Wurm, S., & Hattori, S., eds. *Linguistic Atlas of the Pacific Area* (Canberra: Australian Academy of the Humanities, 1982).

Zelinsky, W. "An Approach to the Religious Geography of the United States,"*Annals of the Association of American Geographers* 51 (1961), 139–167.

Part Five

LAND AND LAND USE IN THE RURAL SECTOR

At Issue

The farmers on the land produce what the consumers in the cities need, but it is the consumers, not the producers, who dictate what the farmers will be paid. This core-periphery relationship prevails at global as well as regional levels: North Americans and Europeans determine the prices of bananas grown in the Caribbean and Central America; food prices are kept artificially low by governments in African capitals for political reasons and the farmers suffer. Now the World Trade Organization is sweeping away the last vestiges of price support for poor-country farmers, and economies from St. Lucia to Mauritius face adversity. At issue: *Should poor-country commercial farmers be protected against the avarice of the rich markets?*

Cattle on a Kenya pasture: but who will set the price of meat?

Part Outline

Chapter 14

Livelihoods of Rural Peoples

From the field notes

"Were it not for the telephone wires, this photo, taken in Greece, could represent a scene five thousand years ago. Short-stemmed wheat, the staple of the Fertile Crescent, stands at right; grapevines are in the foreground. If the grapevines do not conform to our image of neat rows, it is because they are grown here in the eastern Mediterranean in a time-honored way. High winds (a property of this climatic regime) would blow over any trellised rows of vines, so the plant is allowed to form a tangled knot of gnarled wood close to the surface, from which the grape-bearing shoots sprout each growing season."

KEY POINTS

◆ **Rural life has long been dominated by primary economic activities, particularly farming and fishing.**

◆ **Agriculture, the deliberate tending of crops and livestock in order to produce food and fiber, may be less than 12,000 years old and emerged sequentially in several regions of the world.**

◆ **The First Agricultural Revolution achieved plant domestication; the Second Agricultural Revolution involved improved methods of cultivation, production, and storage; and the Third Agricultural Revolution (now in progress) is based on research and technology in plant genetics.**

◆ **Subsistence agriculture, which produces little or no surplus and involves hundreds of millions of people in a struggle for survival, still prevails in large regions of tropical Africa, Asia, and the Americas.**

◆ **One of the earliest models of the spatial economy was developed by J. H. von Thünen and accounted for agricultural patterns around urban market centers.**

When we examined the problems involved in attempts to define culture, it was obvious that this term encompasses all human thought and activity, from belief systems to technological implements. Human geographers are especially interested in the imprints made by human culture on the landscape. These include not only the marks of religion and language, but also the impress of economic and political activities.

It is not difficult to visualize the cultural landscapes of farming. Agriculture transforms whole countrysides. The range of agricultural landscapes is enormous, from the vast, rolling wheatlands of the Great Plains in America to the terraced hillslopes of Asia; from the vineyards of France to the pastures of New Zealand. In Part 5, we begin a discussion of economic geography that will carry us from farmlands to factories to urban complexes. Economic geography is concerned with the various ways in which people earn a living and with how the goods and services they produce are spatially expressed and organized. It is also concerned with the impacts of the spatial organization of economic activity on society, politics, and the environment.

◆ CLASSIFYING ECONOMIC ACTIVITIES

Economic activities range from the simple to the complex and from the ancient to the modern. One way to classify those activities is to distinguish among different types of activities. For a long time three basic types of economic activities were recognized: primary, secondary, and tertiary.

Primary Activities

Hunting and gathering (ancient means of survival), farming of all kinds, livestock herding, fishing and aquaculture, forestry and lumbering, mining and quarrying are all primary activities. They are carried on in the *extractive sector*, in which workers and the natural environment come into direct contact; in the process, the environment sometimes suffers.

Secondary Activities

Manufacturing industries convert raw materials into intermediate or finished products, an activity that dates from the time stones and bones were first shaped into tools. Major stages in human history are based on various forms of conversion of raw materials (the Bronze Age and the Iron Age are examples). Today secondary activities include the *production* of an almost infinite range of commodities. Toys, warships, pottery, steel, chemicals, buildings—all are products of secondary activities.

Tertiary Activities

Today hundreds of millions of workers are employed in the so-called *service industries*. The people in the offices, banks, hospitals, and shops in the downtown of an American city represent the tertiary sector. They connect producers to consumers, thus facilitating commerce and trade; as lawyers, doctors, dentists, teachers, and librarians, they provide essential services in a complex society. As we will see in Part Seven, the tertiary sector has become so complicated that specialized service activities are now grouped into quaternary and quinary categories. Grouping economic activities into categories helps us discuss and analyze them, but it is evident that such categories are actually points on a continuum. Take the case of farming. Most farm products are marketed in the form in which they are harvested (rice, oranges, potatoes), but some are cooked, dried, salted, or otherwise converted before distribution. These latter products may be classified as secondary manufactures, since raw materials have been converted into different commodities. Nevertheless, all farming industries, from subsistence rice growing on small plots to commercial wheat cultivation on huge estates, are regarded as primary activities. These activities are the focus of this chapter.

◆ THE PERSISTENCE OF AGRICULTURE

In this part of the book we focus on ***agriculture***, the deliberate tending of crops and livestock in order to produce food and fiber. Yet in the United States this activity has become less and less important. In 1994 the U.S. Bureau of the Census announced that the number of farmers in the United States had fallen below 2 million. Not since the mid-nineteenth century, when the American population was barely over 20 million, had the Census counted so few farming families.

Does this mean that farming is no longer a major component of the U.S. economy? Hardly. Total agricultural production is at an all-time high. But the nature of farming has changed: mechanization and farm consolidation have driven millions of small farmers off the land. The transformation of the U.S. economy from an agricultural to an industrial and technological one has altered the pattern of employment. Still, American farm output is enormous and remains among the world's largest.

In the chapters that follow, we will move our focus from farming to industry and technology, but it is well to remember that in the majority of countries agriculture remains the leading employment sector. Indeed, in some societies people continue to live and work as they did thousands of years ago. The revolutionary changes that are so commonplace to us have barely touched the existence of many millions of people in Asia and Africa. *We* may be witnessing the beginnings of a postindustrial age, but they are not. The first half of this chapter, therefore, focuses on the way these people make their living.

◆ ANCIENT LIVELIHOODS IN A MODERN WORLD

The processes whereby food is produced, distributed, and consumed form a fundamental part of every culture. The way in which land is allocated to individuals or families (or bought or sold), the manner in which it is used for food production, the functions of livestock, and the consumption of food from crops and animals are all aspects of culture. In earlier chapters we noted that food consumption is often related to religious influence and dogma. Adherents of Islam and Judaism avoid pork; Hindus do not consume beef (Fig. 14-1). Various other forms of partial or total abstinence occur among human cultures, including periodic fasts. Such rules, like the religions that generate them, tend to be old and persistent, and change only slowly. In other cases food avoidance is due to intolerance for particular substances, such as dairy products, eggs, or fish.

From the field notes

"It was harvest time on the North China Plain, and everywhere you looked, farm workers by the thousands were cutting the wheat, carting it in, threshing it, piling up the chaff. Not a sign of any equipment: it was all done by hand. What will all these workers do when China mechanizes and modernizes?" (This note written at a collective near Anyang in 1981; today the question is: How many of these workers are employed by Beijing's building boom or in the factories of the Pacific Rim?").

Before Farming

Most of the food eaten by humans comes, directly or indirectly, from the soil. ***Farming*** therefore has long been the basis of existence all over the world. However, there was a time before the invention of agriculture when human existence was based on methods other than farming. Viewed in the context of human history as a whole, farming is a very recent innovation (its beginnings date back a mere 12,000 years). Even

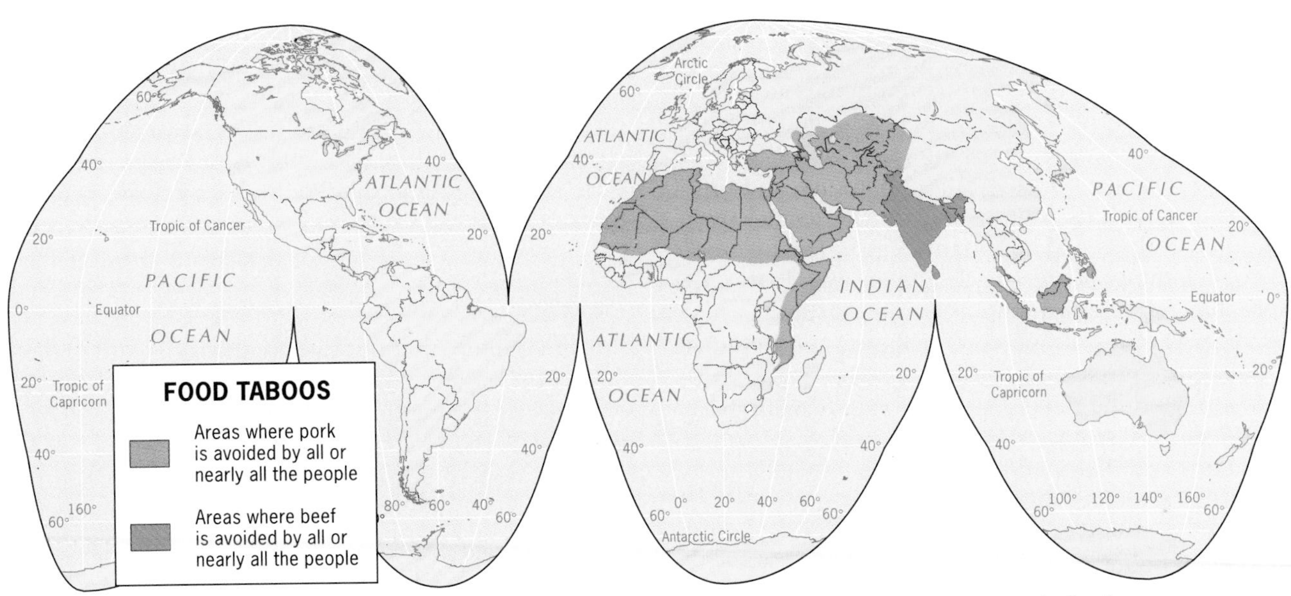

Figure 14-1 World Areas of Food Taboos. Prohibitions and bans against certain foods affect diets in many areas of the world. Here only the major taboos are mapped.

today, a few small societies survive much as they did before agriculture was developed: by ***hunting and gathering*** whatever food nature has to offer, and sometimes by fishing.

Peoples who still subsist in this way have been pushed into difficult environments by more powerful competitors (as the San of Southern Africa were by the Bantu and the white invaders), and their survival seems to involve one crisis after another. Cyclical drought is the worst enemy. It withers vegetation, kills or drives off wildlife, and cuts off natural water supplies such as springs. Still, the San of Southern Africa, the aboriginal peoples of Australia, the Native Americans of Brazil, and several other groups in the Americas, Africa, and Asia manage to survive in the face of great odds. They do so by knowing and fully exploiting their environment. Every seed, root, fruit, berry, and beetle is sought out and consumed. Hunting is done with poisoned spears, bows and arrows, clubs, and sticks.

When the people do not depend on a particular water hole for their own water supply, they may poison it and follow the animals that have drunk there until they succumb. Thus the community is on the move much of the time. The group cannot become too large, nor can settlements be permanent. However, without agriculture and the storage of food for the future, life is difficult. It was easier where the land was more productive, but most of the surviving hunting-and-gathering peoples have been driven into dry, cold, and otherwise less hospitable environments.

We should not assume that the hunting-and-gathering groups that survive today are entirely representative of early hunter-gatherer communities. When Europe's plains opened up after the most recent glacial retreat, our distant ancestors hunted mammoth and other plentiful wildlife. They set elaborate traps and cooperated in driving wildlife to areas where it would be vulnerable. Communities were much larger than present-day San clans. Very early on, there were peoples who subsisted on hunting and gathering and fishing who had learned to specialize to some extent in some area of production. The oak forests of parts of North America provided an abundant harvest of nuts, sometimes enough to last more than a full year, so Native American communities collected and stored this food source. Others living near the Pacific Ocean became adept at salmon fishing. The buffalo herds of interior North America provided sustenance for centuries before being virtually wiped out. In more northerly regions, people followed the migrations of the caribou herds. The Aleut and the Ainu (now confined to northern Japan) developed specialized fishing techniques.

We can deduce to some extent the means by which our preagricultural ancestors survived. Undoubtedly, some hunting-and-gathering communities found themselves in more favorable locations than others. For example, people living on the forest margins could gather food in the forest when hunting yielded poor results and return to hunting when the opportunities improved again. Possibly those communities could stay in one place for some time, creating a more or less permanent settlement. That is one of the key contributions of agriculture: it permitted people to settle permanently in one location with the assurance that food would be available in seasons to come.

Terrain and Tools

The capacity of early human communities to sustain themselves was enhanced by their knowledge of the terrain and its exploitable resources, as well as by their ability to improve on their tools, weapons, and other equipment. Such technological advances came slowly, but some of them had important effects. The first tools used in hunting were simple clubs, tree limbs that were thin at one end and thick and heavy at the other. These were not only used to strike trapped animals but also thrown at hunted wildlife. The use of bone and stone and the development of spears made hunting far more effective. The fashioning of stone into hand axes and, later, handle axes was a crucial innovation that enabled hunters to skin their prey and cut the meat. It now was possible to cut down trees and build even better shelters and tools.

The controlled use of fire was another important early achievement of human communities. The first opportunities to control fire were offered by natural conditions (lightning, spontaneous combustion of surface-heated coal). Excavations of ancient settlement sites suggest that attempts were made to keep a fire burning continuously once it was captured. Later it was learned that fire could be generated by rapid hand rotation of a wooden stick in a small hole surrounded by dry tinder. Fire became the focal point of the settlement, and the campfire became a symbol of the community. It was a means of making foods digestible and was used to drive animals into traps or over cliffs. This greatly enhanced the capacity of ancient communities to modify the natural landscape.

In the meantime, tools and equipment were developed as well. Perhaps the first transportation tool ever devised was a strong stick carried by two men; over the stick hung the limp body of a freshly killed gazelle. Simple baskets were fashioned to hold berries, nuts, and roots. Various kinds of racks, packing frames, and sleds were developed to transport logs, stones, firewood, and other heavy goods. Fishing became a more important means of survival for communities situated along rivers or on shorelines, and primitive rafts and canoes soon made their appearance. (Controlled use of fire made the dugout canoe possible.)

Even before the domestication of animals and plants, rudimentary forms of metal-working had emerged, although true ***metallurgy***, the technique of separating metals from their ores, came later. There is evidence that fragments of copper, nuggets of gold, and pieces of iron from meteorites were hammered into arrowheads and other shapes. Equipment made of stone also went far beyond simple knives and axes. Stone pots and pounders, grinders, and simple mills were developed to prepare seeds, grains, and other edible foods. Meat was roasted and other foods were cooked; dietary patterns and preferences began to develop. Thus, long before animal and plant domestication, preagricultural human communities were characterized by considerable complexity not only in forms of shelter, but also in tools, utensils and weapons, food preferences and taboos, and related cultural traits.

Fishing

It is quite likely that our distant ancestors added dried fish to their diets during the warming period that accompanied the melting of the latest of the Pleistocene glaciers. Perhaps 12,000 to 15,000 years ago, as the glaciers melted, sea levels began to rise. Coastal flatlands were inundated as the seawater encroached on the continental shelves. Until this time, coastal waters over much of the Earth had been cold and rough, and shorelines were often steep cliffs. Therefore, most coastal areas were not hospitable to the humans, and marine life was not nearly as plentiful as it was to become later.

When glacial melting began and water levels rose, the continental shelves became shallow seas, full of coastal lagoons and patches of standing water. The sun warmed these thin layers of water very quickly, and soon marine fauna flourished. Coastal regions became warmer and more habitable, and communities moved to the water's edge. There people were able to harvest all kinds of shellfish, and they learned to trap fish by cutting small patches of standing water off from the open sea. And they invented tools for catching fish: harpoons for spearing larger fish, and baskets suspended in streams where fish were known to run.

In several regions human communities achieved a degree of permanence by combining hunting and fishing with some gathering and by making use of the migration cycles of fish and animal life. Native American peoples along the Pacific coast and on Arctic shores, the Ainu of Japan and coastal East Asia, and communities in coastal Western Europe caught salmon as they swam up rivers and negotiated rapids and falls. (Huge accumulations of fish bones have been found at prehistoric sites near such locations.)

When the salmon runs ended, people stalked deer during their annual spring and fall movements, trapping them where they crossed rivers or in narrow valleys. The summer salmon runs and the wildlife migrations of fall and spring provided food for all the year except winter. People had learned, however, that dried meat could remain edible for months, and the winter cold provided natural refrigeration.

The early fishers and hunters had their bad years as well as good ones. Sometimes winter brought hunger and death. The riverside dwellers were forced to abandon their settlements and pursue distant herds.

Along with the development of fishing as a means of subsistence came the invention of a wide range of tools. Among the earliest means of catching fish and other aquatic life was a simple stone trap used in tidal channels. Stones would be removed during the incoming tide, permitting fish to enter an inlet; the stones would be replaced at high tide. When the next low tide drained the closed-off pool, water could seep out between the stones, but the fish would be trapped. Crescent-shaped stone traps on a tidal flat had the same effect, but eventually traps were refined by the creation of basketlike wicker devices that could be used in stream channels and nets of rough twine that could be stretched across an inlet or placed off a shoreline.

The fishing spear was to fishing what the arrow was to hunting, and various kinds of spears were invented, ranging from simple pointed sticks to more refined harpoonlike spears. The use of hooks and bait led to the invention of hooks made from wood, bone, horn, and seashells. Most important, however, was the invention of boats. From the first simple rafts were developed more elaborate canoes and sailing boats. The role of these innovations in the worldwide diffusion of humans is obvious.

◆ AGRICULTURAL ORIGINS

Plant Domestication

We noted in Part 1 that the domestication of plants and animals may have begun nearly simultaneously in several parts of the world. The first conscious cultivation of plants may have involved root crops and may have occurred in South and Southeast Asia. Not long afterward—possibly as long as 12,000 years ago—the ***First Agricultural Revolution*** was in progress. Wherever it took hold, this First Agricultural Revolution was accompanied by a modest population explosion, the outmigration by farmers with their new techniques, and the absorption of foraging peoples.

Events in the Americas, where agricultural techniques developed much later than in South and Southwest Asia, prove that the First Agricultural Revolution extended over thousands of years. Here, too, it appears that cultivation of roots and cuttings occurred first, followed by more sophisticated seeding methods.

When the source regions of ***plant domestication*** are mapped, the results show a surprisingly global distribution (Fig. 14-2). In *Cultural Geography* (1969), where this map first appeared, cultural geographers Joseph Spencer and William Thomas emphasized that local groupings of plants formed the basis for each regional agricultural zone. For example, in the Mesoamerican region (Region 6 in Figure 14-2), the basic plants were maize (corn), squashes, and several kinds of beans. In Southeast Asia (Region 1), on the other hand, taro, yams, and bananas were the leading food plants. In Southwest Asia (Region 4), plant domestication centered on wheat, barley, and other grains.

Agricultural origins in China (Region 7) have recently attracted greater attention because they may have occurred earlier than was long believed—so early, in fact, that Chinese farmers may have been among the world's first. The resulting food surpluses and population increases produced the wave of emigration that peopled Taiwan, the Philippines, and the Pacific islands.

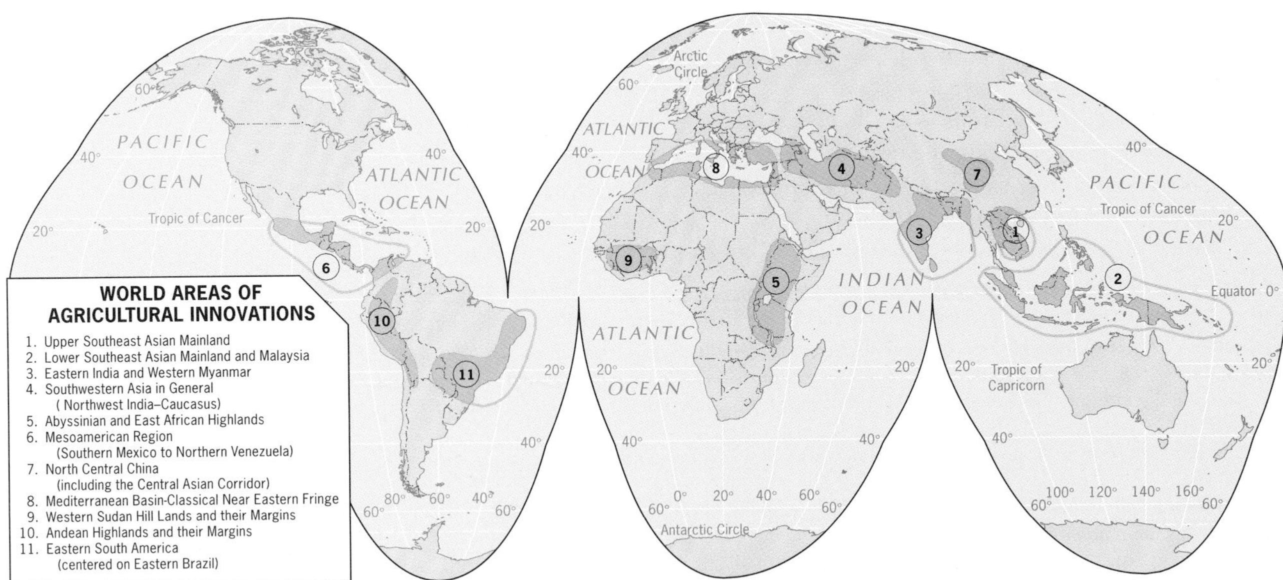

Figure 14-2 World Areas of Agricultural Innovations. Cultural geographer Carl Sauer identified 11 areas where agricultural innovations occurred. *Source: From C. O. Sauer,* Agricultural Origins and Dispersals. *New York: American Geographical Society, 1952, p. 24.*

Table 14-1 Chief Source Regions of Important Crop Plant Domestications (after J. E. Spencer and W. L. Thomas)

A. Primary Regions of Domestications

1. The Upper Southeast Asian Mainland

Citrus fruits*	Bamboos*	Yams*	Rices*	Eugenias*	Lichi	Teas	Ramie
Bananas*	Taros*	Cabbages*	Beans*	Job's tears	Longan	Tung oils	Water chestnut

2. Lower Southeast Asian Mainland and Malaysia (including New Guinea)

Citrus fruits*	Taros*	Pandanuses	Breadfruits	Lanzones	Vine peppers*	Nutmeg	Areca
Bananas*	Yams*	Cucumbers*	Jackfruits	Durian	Gingers*	Clove	Abaca
Bamboos*	Almonds*	Sugarcanes	Coconuts	Rambutan	Brinjals*	Cardamom	

3. Eastern India and Western Burma

Bananas*	Beans*	Millets*	Grams	Vine peppers*	Mangoes	Safflower	Lotus
Yams*	Rices*	Sorghums*	Eggplants	Gingers*	Kapok*	Jute	Turmeric
Taros*	Amaranths*	Peas*	Brinjals*	Palms*	Indigo	Sunn Hemp	

4. Southwestern Asia (Northwest India-Caucasus)

Soft wheats*	Peas*	Rye*	Beets*	Hemp	Soft Pears*	Pomegranates	Walnuts
Barleys*	Oil seeds*	Onions	Spinach	Apples	Cherries*	Grapes*	Melons
Lentils*	Poppies	Carrots*	Sesames	Almonds*	Plums*	Jujubes*	Tamarind
Beans*	Oats*	Turnips	Flax	Peaches*	Figs	Pistachio	Alfalfa

5. Ethiopian and East African Highlands

Hard wheats*	Sorghums*	Barleys	Beans*	Oil seeds*	Melons*	Coffees	Okras
Millets*	Rices*	Peas*	Vetches	Cucumbers*	Gourds*	Castor beans	Cottons*

6. Meso-American Region (Southern Mexico to Northern Venezuela)

Maizes	Taros*	Tomatoes*	Avocados	Muskmelons	Cottons*
Amaranths*	Sweet potatoes	Chilli peppers	Sapotes	Palms*	Agaves
Beans*	Squashes	Custard apples	Plums*	Manioc	Kapok

B. Secondary Regions of Domestications

7. North-Central China (including the Central Asian corridor)

Millets*	Soybeans	Naked oat*	Mulberries	Bush cherries*	Peaches*
Barleys*	Cabbages*	Mustards	Persimmons	Hard pears*	Jujubes*
Buckwheats	Radishes*	Rhubarb	Plums*	Apricots	

8. Mediterranean Basin—Classical Near Eastern Fringe

Barleys*	Lentils*	Grapes*	Dates	Parsnips	Lettuces	Carrots*	Sugar beet
Oats*	Peas*	Olives	Carobs	Asparagus	Celeries	Garlic	Leek

9. Western Sudan Hill Lands and Their Margins

Sorghums*	Rices*	Yams*	Peas*	Melons*	Oil palms	Kola nut
Millets*	Fonio	Beans*	Oil seeds*	Gourds*	Tamarind*	

10. Andean Highlands and Their Margins

White potatoes	Tomatoes*	Beans*	Quinoa	Cubio	Ulluco
Pumpkins	Strawberries	Papayas	Oca	Arrocacha	

11. Eastern South America (centered on Eastern Brazil)

Taros*	Peanuts	Cashew nut	Cacao	Cottons*
Beans*	Pineapples	Brazil nut	Passion fruits	Tobaccos

Source: J. E. Spencer and W. L. Thomas, *Introducing Cultural Geography*, 1978. Reproduced by permission from John Wiley & Sons.

*The asterisk indicates domestication of related species or hybridized development of new species during domestication in some other region or regions. Some of these secondary domestications were later than in the original region, but evidence of chronologic priority seldom is clear-cut.

The plural rendering of the crop name indicates that several different varieties/species either were involved in initial domestication or followed thereafter.

The term *oil seeds* indicates several varieties/species of small-seeded crop plants grown for the production of edible oils, without further breakdown.

In regions 2 and 3 the brinjals refer to the spicy members of the eggplant group used in curries, whereas in region 3 the eggplants refer to the sweet vegetable members.

None of the regional lists attempts a complete listing of all crop plants/species domesticated within the region.

The table has been compiled from a wide variety of sources.

Another agricultural source region lies in West Africa (Region 9). This region was recognized quite late, and it is not certain that agriculture developed independently there. As Table 14-1 indicates, however, secondary domestication clearly did take place in West Africa.

Table 14-1 is worth careful attention, if only because it reveals the enormous range of crops that were cultivated around the world. At various times and in different locales, particular groups of crops became the mainstays of life. Soon the knowledge needed to farm such crops diffused outward from these agricultural hearths. It is thought that millet, a small-seed grain, was introduced to India from West Africa, and sorghum, another grain crop, from West Africa to China. The watermelon spread from West Africa, first to nearby regions but eventually all over the world. Corn (maize) spread from Middle America into North America. After the Portuguese brought it across the Atlantic, it became a staple in much of Africa. The banana came from Southeast Asia, as did a variety of yams. Dispersal occurred slowly for many thousands of years, but it was greatly accelerated by the worldwide trade and communications networks established with the colonial expansion of Europe.

Animal Domestication

While our distant ancestors were learning to plant crops, they were also beginning to keep animals as livestock. As we saw in Chapter 9, the Nostratic proto-language word for *wolf* also meant *dog*, suggesting that domestication was in progress as long as 14,000 years ago.

Perhaps ***animal domestication*** became possible when communities became more sedentary. Animals were kept as pets or for other reasons (e.g., for ceremonial purposes). Quite possibly, animals attached themselves to human settlements as scavengers and even for protection against predators, thus reinforcing the idea that they might be tamed and kept. Any visitor to an African wildlife reserve can observe that when night falls, a permanent camp is approached by animals such as gazelle, zebra, and monkeys, which spend the night near and sometimes even within the camp. At daybreak the animals wander off, returning at nightfall. Similar behavior probably brought animals to the settlements of the ancient forest farmers. Hunters might bring back the young offspring of an animal that had been killed in the field and raise it. The concept of animal domestication probably developed out of such events.

Just when this happened is still a subject of debate. Some scholars believe that animal domestication began earlier than plant cultivation, but others argue that animal domestication began as recently as 8000 years ago—well after crop agriculture. In any case, goats, pigs, and sheep became part of a rapidly growing array of domestic animals, and in captivity they changed considerably from their wild state. Archeological research indicates that when animals such as wild cattle are penned in a corral, they undergo physical changes as time goes by. Protection from predators led to the survival of animals that would have been eliminated in the wild, and modifications that nature would have wiped out were preserved through inbreeding. Our domestic versions of the pig, the cow, and the horse differ considerably from those first kept by our ancestors.

How did the ancient communities select their livestock, and for what purposes were livestock kept? It is thought that wild cattle may originally have been domesticated for religious purposes, perhaps because the shape of their horns looked like a crescent moon. Apparently, cattle were strongly associated with religious ritual from the earliest times, and they remain holy animals in some societies today. However, those religious functions may also have led to the use of cows as draft animals and suppliers of milk. If cattle could pull sled-like platforms used in religious ceremonies, they could also pull plows. If cattle whose calves were taken away continued to produce milk, and in fact needed to be milked, cattle could be kept for that purpose as well.

As with plant domestication, it is possible to identify certain regions where the domestication of particular animals occurred. In Southeast Asia, the presence of several kinds of pigs led to their domestication, along with the water buffalo, chickens, and some other bird species (ducks, geese). In South Asia, cattle were domesticated and came to occupy an important place in the regional culture. Later, the Indian elephant was domesticated, to be used as a ceremonial animal, a beast of burden, and a weapon of war. However, elephants were never successfully bred in captivity, and some scholars argue that the elephant never really became a domesticated animal. In Southwest Asia and adjacent areas of Northeast Africa, domesticated animals included the goat, sheep, and camel. In inner Asia, the yak, horse, some species of goats and sheep, and reindeer were domesticated. In the Mesoamerican region (including the Andes from Peru northward and Middle America up to central Mexico), the llama and alpaca were domesticated, along with a species of pig and the turkey.

Although we can identify regions of domestication like those just described, they should be regarded with caution. When animal domestication began, there were numerous species of a large variety of fauna, and these were domesticated simultaneously. The water buffalo, for example, was probably domesticated in both Southeast and South Asia during the same period.

Camels may have been domesticated in inner Asia as well as in Southwest Asia. The pig was domesticated in numerous areas. Different species of cattle were domesticated in regions other than South Asia. Dogs and cats attached themselves to human settlements very early (they may have been the first animals to be domesticated) and in widely separated regions. Specific sources can be identified for only a few animals, including the llama and the alpaca, the yak, the turkey, and the reindeer.

◆ DIFFUSION

As in the case of crops, the dispersal of domesticated animals—first regionally and later throughout the world—blurred the original spatial patterns of domestication. Successful domestication depended on the presence of wild animals suitable for domestication. The great majority of these inhabited Eurasia; far fewer species were available in the Americas, Australia, or Africa. Among Africa's numerous wild animals, only the guinea fowl was domesticated early. All other species resisted domestication. This greatly affected Subsaharan Africa's cultural and economic development, leaving Africans without the kinds of dependable livestock that benefited societies in Eurasia.

Africans became cattle herders only after cattle were introduced via Southwest Asia. Other livestock spread worldwide. Chickens can now be found in virtually every rural village, from Indonesia to Ecuador. Donkeys (probably first domesticated in Southwest Asia) serve as beasts of burden around the world. Goats and sheep, cattle and horses, and dogs and cats are globally distributed. Even the Asian elephant made its appearance not only in China but also in ancient Europe as part of Hannibal's forces.

Efforts to domesticate animals continue today. Now it may be possible to domesticate some African species as livestock. An example is the eland, a potential source of meat in a region where one is greatly needed. Several experiment stations in the savannalands are trying to find ways to breed the region's wildlife. They have had some success with a species of eland but less with various species of gazelles, and they have been unable to domesticate the buffalo. Indeed, throughout the world only about 40 species of higher animals have been domesticated.

Thus the process of animal domestication, set in motion more than 8000 (and perhaps as long as 12,000) years ago, still continues. Communities that were able to combine the cultivation of plants and the domestication of animals greatly reduced their dependence on limited food resources. This was a critical step in the evolution of human civilization.

◆ SUBSISTENCE FARMING

We tend to think of agricultural geography in terms of cash cropping (i.e., farming for sale and profit): plantations, ranches, mechanization, irrigation, the movement of farm products, and so on. When we associate certain crops with particular countries, these are usually cash commodities: Brazilian coffee, Colombian tobacco, Egyptian cotton, Australian wool, Argentinian beef. But large numbers of farmers are not involved in commercial agriculture at all. Hundreds of millions of farmers grow only enough food to survive. They are ***subsistence farmers***. Like nomadic pastoralists, they often move from place to place in search of better land (see "Focus on: Shifting Cultivation"). However, in many areas subsistence farmers cannot migrate but are confined to a small field of more fertile soil that they farm intensively year after year. Very likely, they do not own the soil they till.

Scholars classify agricultural societies as "subsistence," "intermediate," and "developed" or as "primitive," "traditional," and "modern." These divisions are made for purposes of discussion and are not absolute. Nor is the term *subsistence*. It is sometimes used in the strictest sense of the word—that is, to refer to farmers who grow food only to sustain themselves and their families, find building materials and firewood in the natural environment, and do not enter

From the field notes

"Attempts to tame wildlife started in ancient times, and still continue. At Hunter's Lodge on the Nairobi-Mombasa road we met an agricultural officer who reported that an animal domestication experiment station was located not far into the bush, about 10 miles south. On his invitation, we spent the next day observing this work. In some herds, domestic animals (goats) were combined with wild gazelles, all penned together in a large enclosure. This was not working well; the gazelles continued all day to seek escape. By comparison, these eland were docile, manageable, and in good health. Importantly, they also were reproducing in captivity. Here, our host describes the program."

Focus On

Shifting Cultivation

Early farmers learned to plant crops, but they knew little about soil chemistry, fertilizing, or irrigation. It is likely that they had to abandon land in tropical and subtropical zones after the soil became infertile and the crops stopped growing. They would move to another parcel of land, clear the vegetation, turn the soil, and try again. This practice of ***shifting cultivation***, like hunting and gathering, still goes on today. In tropical areas, where the redness of the soil signifies heavy leaching of soil nutrients and yet natural vegetation thrives, a plot of cleared soil will carry a good crop at least once and perhaps two or three times. Then, however, the land is best left alone to regenerate its natural vegetative cover and replenish the soil with nutrients lost during cultivation. Several years later, the plot may yield a good harvest once again.

Shifting cultivation is a way of life for many more people than hunting and gathering. Between 150 million and 200 million people still sustain themselves in this way in Africa, Middle America, tropical South America, and parts of Southeast Asia. At one time this was the chief form of agriculture. It goes by various names: *slash-and-burn* agriculture, *milpa* agriculture, *patch* agriculture, and others. As a system of cultivation, it has changed little over thousands of years.

The controlled use of fire played a major role in shifting agriculture. Trees were cut down and all existing vegetation was burned off. The resulting layer of ash contributed to the soil's fertility. In these cleared patches were planted crops that were native to the region: tubers in the humid, warm tropical areas, grains in the more humid subtropics, and vegetables and fruits in cooler zones. Shifting cultivation gave ancient farmers opportunities to experiment with various plants, to learn the effects of weeding and crop care, to cope with environmental vagaries, and to discern the decreased fertility of soil after sustained farming.

The process of shifting agriculture thus involves a kind of natural rotation system in which areas of forest are used without being destroyed. It does not require a nomadic existence. Usually there is a central village surrounded by parcels of land that are worked successively. When the village grows too large and the distance to usable land becomes too great, part of the village's population may establish a new settlement some distance away. This implies, of course, that population densities in areas of shifting agriculture cannot be very high. However, high population densities were rare in ancient times, and today shifting agriculture continues only in areas where population densities are far lower than in crowded regions like the Nile Delta or the Ganges Valley.

Shifting agriculture appears destructive, wasteful, and disorganized to people who are accustomed to more intensive types of farming. There are no neat rows of plants, carefully turned soil, or precisely laid-out fields. In fact, however, shifting agriculture conserves both forest and soil; its harvests are substantial given the environmental limitations; and it requires better organization than one might assume. It also requires substantially less energy than more modern techniques of farming.

into the cash economy at all. This definition fits farmers in societies where shifting agriculture is practiced, in remote areas of South and Middle America, Africa, and South and Southeast Asia (Fig. 14-3). On the other hand, farm families that are living at the subsistence level but sometimes sell a small quantity of produce (perhaps to pay taxes) are not subsistence farmers in the strict sense. Yet the term *subsistence* is surely applicable to societies where farmers with small plots sometimes sell a few pounds of grain on the market but where poverty, indebtedness, and (sometimes) tenancy are ways of life. For the Native American peoples in the Amazon Basin, the sedentary farmers of Africa's savanna areas, villagers in much of India, and peasants in Indonesia, subsistence is not only a way of life but a state of mind. Experience has taught farmers and their families that times of comparative plenty will be followed by times of scarcity.

Alternatives to Subsistence Farming

How might subsistence farmers escape from this situation, achieving not only higher productivity but also better nutrition and longer life spans? European powers seeking to "modernize" the economies of their dependencies also tried to improve the farmers' conditions of life. Sometimes their methods were harsh: by demanding that farmers pay some taxes, they forced subsistence farmers to begin selling some of their produce to raise the necessary cash. They also compelled many subsistence farmers to devote some land to a cash crop such as cotton, thus bringing them into the commercial economy. The colonial powers also provided genuine assistance by conducting soil surveys, building irrigation systems, and establishing lending agencies that would provide loans to farmers. In addition, the colonial powers sought to make profits, and

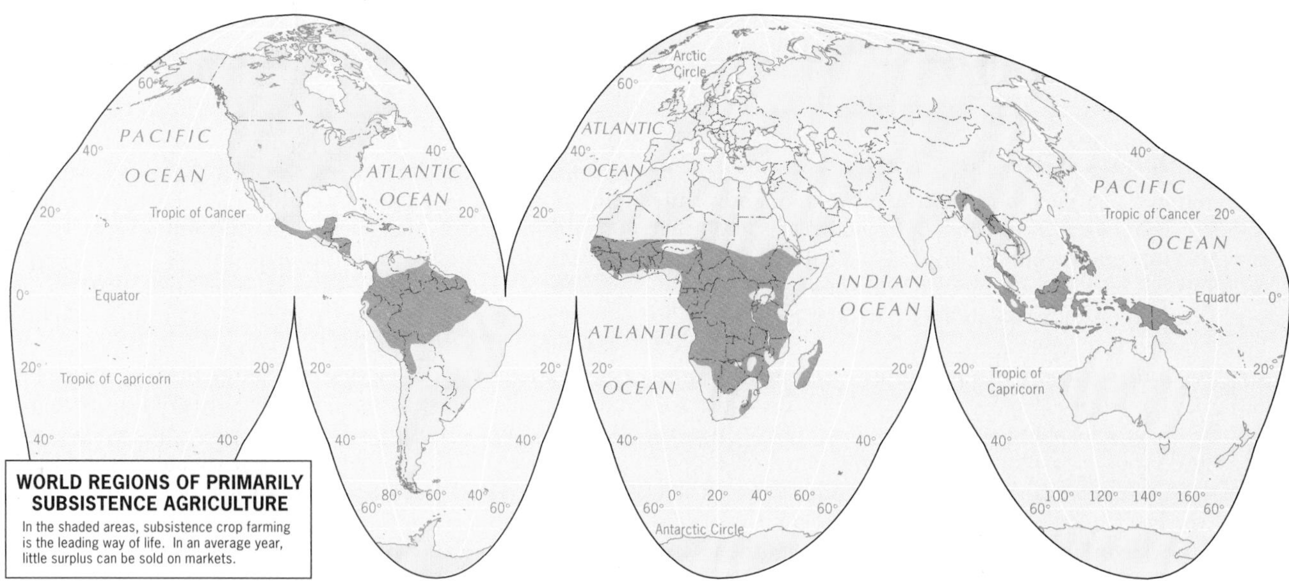

Figure 14-3 World Regions of Primarily Subsistence Agriculture. Definitions of subsistence farming vary. India and China are not shaded because farmers sell some produce on markets; in equatorial Africa and South America, subsistence allows little of this.

it was difficult to squeeze very much from subsistence-farming areas. Forced cropping schemes were designed to solve this problem. If farmers in a subsistence area cultivated a certain acreage of, say, corn, they were required to grow a specified acreage of a cash crop, such as cotton, as well. Whether this crop would be grown on old land that was formerly used for grain, or on newly cleared land, was the farmers' decision. If no new land was available, the farmers would have to give up food crops for the compulsory cash crops. In many areas, severe famines resulted and local economies were disrupted.

Many scholars have considered the question of how "to tempt [subsistence farmers] into wanting cash by the availability of suitable consumer goods," as agricultural specialists A. N. Duckham and G. B. Masefield wrote in *Farming Systems of the World* (1970). In the interests of "progress" and "modernization," subsistence farmers are pushed away from their traditional modes of livelihood. Yet some aspects of subsistence farming may be worth preserving. Changing farmers' attitudes could result in a less cohesive society. Subsistence farmers often hold land in common; surpluses are shared by all the members of the community; accumulation of personal wealth is restricted; and individual advancement at the cost of the group as a whole is limited. As economist A. H. Bunting wrote in *Change in Agriculture* (1970):

> To allocate the land or manage the seasonal migrations, and to survive through hardship and calamity these societies have to be cohesive, communal and relatively little differentiated socially and economically: the chiefs, elders or elected headmen may be little richer than their fellows—to many of whom they are in addition linked by ties of relationship within the extended family. Mutual dependence, imposed by the environment and the state of the agricultural art, is maintained and reinforced by genetic relationships. The community is enclosed socially and may even tend to be isolated culturally. Landlords and feudal rulers are unknown; the cultivators are poor but free.

This description could also be applied to the human communities that first developed agriculture as a way of life and have shown such amazing durability. Changing the economic system could lead to unpredictable changes in the social fabric.

And such changes are occurring. Subsistence land use is giving way to more intensive farming and cash cropping—even to mechanized farming in which equipment does much of the actual work. In the process, societies from South America to Southeast Asia are being profoundly affected. Land that was once held communally is being parceled out to individuals for cash cropping. The system that ensured an equitable distribution of resources is breaking down. And the distribution of wealth has become stratified, with poor people at the bottom and rich landowners at the top.

◆ THE SECOND AGRICULTURAL REVOLUTION

We sometimes regard the Industrial Revolution as the beginning of a new era of development and modernization. In doing so, we lose sight of another revolution, which began even earlier and had an enormous impact on Europe and other parts of the world. This was the ***Second Agricultural Revolution***. While it was less dramatic than the Industrial Revolution, it had far-reaching consequences nonetheless.

The Second Agricultural Revolution began slowly during the latter phase of the so-called Middle Ages. At first it took hold in a few widely scattered places. Its origins and diffusion cannot be readily traced, but it seems clear that, after centuries of comparative stagnation and lack of innovation, farming in seventeenth- and eighteenth-century Europe underwent significant changes. Tools and equipment were modified. Methods of soil preparation, fertilization, crop care, and harvesting improved. The general organization of agriculture, food storage, and distribution was made more efficient. Productivity increased to meet rising demands. Europe's cities were growing, creating problems for existing food supply systems. But by the time the Industrial Revolution gathered momentum, progress in agriculture made possible the clustering of even larger urban populations than before.

Agriculture and the Industrial Revolution

The Industrial Revolution helped sustain the Second Agricultural Revolution. Tractors and other machines took over the work that for so long had been done by animals and humans. In some regions the cultural landscape of commercial agriculture changed as much as the urban landscape of industrializing cities. Fields of wheat and other grains, sown and harvested by machine, cloaked entire countrysides. Even where tradition continued to prevail—in the vineyards of France's Bordeaux and the ricefields of East Asia, for example—the impact of modernization was felt in the form of research leading to improved fertilizers and more productive crop strains.

Farming obviously is not possible everywhere. Vast deserts, steep mountain slopes, frigid polar zones, and other environmental obstacles prevent farming in many parts of the world. Where farming *is* possible, the land and soil are not put to the same uses everywhere. The huge cattle ranches of Texas represent a very different sort of land use than the dairy farms of Wisconsin or the paddies of Taiwan.

Within a few miles of the subsistence farms of Middle America lie rich plantations whose products are shipped to North American markets by sea. We can observe such differences around our own cities: if you travel by car or train from Chicago, Cincinnati, or St. Louis into the countryside, you can see how land use changes. Close to the city, the soil is used most intensively, perhaps for vegetable gardens yielding crops that can be sent quickly to nearby markets. Farther away, the fields are larger and time becomes less important. The cornfields of Iowa are dotted with grain elevators, and some of the grain stored in them may be consumed not in Chicago or St. Louis, but in India or Bangladesh.

Still farther from the Midwestern cities, we enter the pasturelands of the Great Plains, almost the opposite of the vegetable garden. Here land is measured in hundreds of square miles rather than by the acre. Distance from the market is a powerful factor in shaping the country's economic geography.

Understanding the Spatial Layout of Agriculture

What factors have combined to produce the spatial distribution of farming systems (see "Focus on: Von Thünen's Spatial Model of Farming")? This is a very complicated question. It not only involves the effects of different climate and soil conditions, variations in farming methods and technology, market distributions, and transportation costs, but also has to do with the economic dominance of the United States, Canada, and Europe.

Decisions made by colonial powers in Europe led to the establishment of plantations from Middle America to Malaysia. The plantations grew crops not for local markets but for consumers in Europe; similarly, U.S. companies founded huge plantations in the Americas. Over the past few centuries the impact of this plantation system transformed the map of world agriculture. The end of colonial rule did not merely signal the end of the agricultural practices and systems that had been imposed on the former colonial areas. Even food-poor countries must continue to grow commercial crops for export on some of their best soils where their own food should be harvested. Long-entrenched agricultural systems and patterns are not quickly or easily transformed.

◆ THE THIRD AGRICULTURAL REVOLUTION

We noted earlier that the "Green Revolution" occurred at a time when the population explosion seemed to threaten the kind of global famine Malthus had pre-

Focus On

Von Thünen's Spatial Model of Farming

One of the first economic geographers who tried to analyze the location of agricultural activities was Johann Heinrich von Thünen (1783–1850). Von Thünen experienced the Second Agricultural Revolution firsthand: he farmed an estate not far from the town of Rostock in northeast Germany. Studying the spatial patterns of farming around towns such as Rostock, von Thünen noted that one commodity or crop gave way to another in Rostock's hinterland—without any visible change in the soil or climate or terrain. When he mapped this pattern, he found that each town or market center was surrounded by a set of concentric rings within which particular commodities or crops dominated.

Nearest the town, farmers produced commodities that were perishable and commanded high prices, such as dairy products and strawberries and similar specialized crops. In von Thünen's time the town was still surrounded by a belt of forest that provided wood for fuel and building; but immediately beyond the forest the ring-like pattern of agriculture continued. In the next ring the crops were less perishable and bulkier, including wheat and other grains. Still farther out, livestock raising began to replace field crops.

Von Thünen used these observations to build a model of the spatial distribution of agricultural activities. As with all models, he had to make certain assumptions. For example, he assumed that the terrain was flat, that soils and other environmental conditions were the same everywhere, and that there were no barriers to transportation to market. Under such circumstances, he reasoned, transport costs would govern the use of land. The greater the distance to market, the higher the transport costs that had to be added to the cost of producing of a crop or commodity. At a given distance to market, it would become unprofitable to produce high-cost, perishable commodities—and market gardens would give way to field crops such as grains and potatoes. Still farther away, livestock raising would replace field agriculture.

Von Thünen's model (including the ring of forest) is often described as the first effort to analyze the spatial character of economic activity (Fig. 14-4). He published it as part of a monumental series of works called *Der Isolierte Staat* (The Isolated State), which, in many ways, constitutes the foundation of the geographic field known as *location theory*. Today ***Thünian patterns*** are discerned in many parts of the world. But often such patterns are not solely the result of the forces modeled by von Thünen. Consider the hinterland of Chicago. If you take the train to Denver, you cannot miss a certain concentric zonation that puts dairying and market gardening nearest the city, cash grains such as corn (plus soybeans) in the next "ring," more extensive grain farming and livestock raising beyond, and cattle ranching in the outermost zone. This clearly has something to do with von Thünen's ideas, but it also reflects soil quality and climate changes. Hence, the logic of von Thünen's model is only partially reflected in what we actually observe.

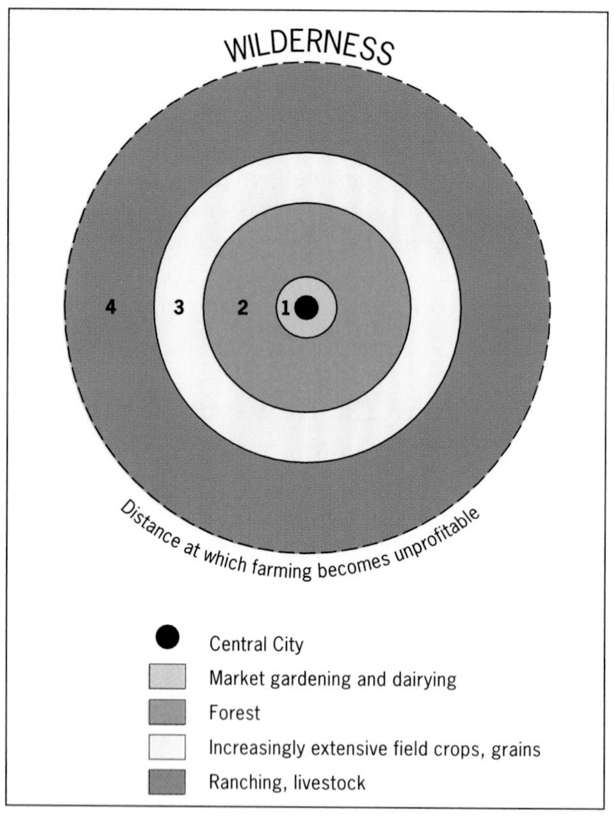

Figure 14-4 Von Thünen's Model.

dicted two centuries earlier. This ***Third Agricultural Revolution*** is still in progress. It is based on new, higher-yielding strains of grains and other crops developed in laboratories using modern techniques of genetic engineering. Some scholars suggest that this revolutionary development will erase the threat of famine because ever-better strains will be invented. Others argue that the capacities of the new strains will be limited and that population expansion will again reach the limits of agricultural production.

In 1994 Lester Brown of the Worldwatch Institute predicted that the benefits of the Third Agricultural Revolution would be used up by the third decade of the twenty-first century. Weeks after the appearance of Brown's study, researchers announced the development of a new strain of rice that would counter the threat Brown had described. The race between population growth and food production is not over—and if significant climate changes were to occur, even the Third Agricultural Revolution might not be enough to overcome the challenge.

Farming practices, from the plowing of fields to the terracing of slopes, have changed entire countrysides into cultural landscapes, a prime example of the transformation of the Earth by human action. And farmers, responding to needs, opportunities, and limitations imposed by nature, have created a host of dwellings, hamlets, and villages. We turn next to a discussion of rural settlements and lifestyles.

◆ KEY TERMS ◆

agricultural origins
agriculture
animal domestication
farming
First Agricultural Revolution
hunting and gathering
metallurgy
plant domestication
Second Agricultural Revolution
shifting cultivation
subsistence farmers
Third Agricultural Revolution
Thünian patterns

◆ APPLYING GEOGRAPHIC KNOWLEDGE ◆

1. It may be said that in all countries where subsistence agriculture still forms the way of life of a substantial number of people, governments seek ways to improve these farm families' lives. What impels governments to do so? What methods have they used to convert subsistence farming into cash agriculture? What are the rewards—and the risks—to the subsistence farmers?

2. The Earth has witnessed three Agricultural Revolutions; each had enormous impact on human civilization. Geographically, each occurred in a distinct area (or group of areas) of the world. Each had a technological dimension. Explain the spatial settings of the three Agricultural Revolutions in cultural, environmental, and technological contexts.

Chapter 15

Rural Settlement Forms

From the field notes

"Having climbed the Dragon's Gate near Kunming, I could see a large area of farmland with numerous villages. The scene provided a reminder that farm villages, not just here in East Asia but in many areas of the world, are space-conserving. The farmland is too important to allow individual houses to invade it: villages like the one seen here have no outskirts. The paddies begin on the very doorsteps of the houses. The homes in the village are tightly clustered, keeping the space it occupies as small as possible."

KEY POINTS

- ◆ **About half the world's population still resides in rural areas.**
- ◆ **The forms, functions, materials, and spacing of rural dwellings reveal much about a region and its culture, including social and economic opportunities and needs, natural environments, and traditions.**
- ◆ **Wattle, wood, brick, and stone are among the building materials used in domestic architecture.**
- ◆ **Village forms reflect historical circumstances, the nature of the land, and economic conditions. They range from linear and clustered to circular and grid-patterned.**

Shelter ranks high on the list of human needs. Throughout the world, in the coldest regions as well as in the warmest, in the rainiest areas as well as in deserts, people build dwellings that are the focal points of their daily lives. These dwellings have several functions, and protection against cold, wind, and precipitation is only one of them. In residential quarters people find privacy, a certain degree of comfort, a place to store belongings, and even an opportunity to display their values and achievements.

Geographers have many reasons to be interested in the nature of human settlements. A house reveals much about a region and its culture: the building materials that are available, the social and economic needs as well as the cultural traditions of the occupants, and the natural environment that the house must withstand. In the *form* of houses, we can sometimes see one culture give way to another. If you were to take a trip southward on a Nile riverboat, you would see the square, flat-roofed Arab houses of Egypt and northern Sudan yield to the round, steep-roofed African houses of southern Sudan and Uganda. House types thus can be valuable indicators of cultural traditions and transitions.

In the layout and *function* of houses, we get an impression of social values and economic needs: in parts of rural Eastern Europe, for example, people and some of their livestock live under the same roof, so that the building is part house and part barn. Consider the contrast with a suburban American home, in which different rooms serve different purposes such as cooking, bathing, eating, and sleeping.

The *materials* used in the construction of dwellings in many areas still reflect local availability and purpose. In the cold, forested areas of Northern Europe, the log cabin, with its thick walls and pitched roof, developed to withstand extreme cold and heavy snowfalls. In low-lying tropical areas, cold weather is not a problem, and you will find leaves, branches, and matting used in the construction of traditional dwellings. Today it is easier to transport building materials from one place to another, so local availability is not as important as it was in the past. Nevertheless, there are still places where location dictates the types of materials used.

We are also interested in the *spacing* of houses. There is a relationship between the density of houses and the intensity of crop cultivation, but that relationship can vary. In the U.S. Midwest, for example, individual farmhouses lie quite far apart in what we call a ***dispersed settlement*** pattern: the land is intensively cultivated but by machine rather than by hand. In the populous Indonesian island of Java, villages are located every half-mile or so along a rural road, and settlement there is defined as *nucleated.* Land use is just as intense, but the work is done by people and animals. So when we consider the density of human settlement as it relates to the intensity of land use, we should keep in mind the way the land is cultivated.

Nucleated settlement is by far the most prevalent rural residential pattern in agricultural areas. When houses are grouped together in tiny clusters or *hamlets*, or in slightly larger clusters we call *villages*, their spatial arrangement also has significance. Sometimes it is possible to identify the prevailing culture just by looking at the ground plan of a village. In parts of Africa where cattle herding is the primary means of existence, the houses in a village are arranged in a circle (that of the chief or headman will be larger and somewhat separated from the others) surrounding a central corral where the livestock are kept at night. In the low-lying areas of Western Europe, the houses of a village are often situated on a strip of higher ground (such as a dike or a levee). When you look at the map of such a village, it is simply a row of evenly spaced units, perhaps on two sides of a road but often on only one side.

In such different regions as Eastern Europe, western Nigeria, and northern Spain, the houses of older villages are not regularly arranged but are closely clustered together, a defensive measure that included the construction of a surrounding outer wall. The need for such defenses has disappeared, but the traditional village is still part of the landscape and people continue to build new villages similar to those of bygone centuries. The arrangement of houses in villages therefore takes many different forms. Tradition, political organization, physical characteristics of the land, and many other factors underlie the development of the villages we see today.

◆ HOUSING AND LANDSCAPE

We may assume that our distant ancestors lived in bands containing from a dozen to 50 or 60 individuals, which moved from place to place, setting up a temporary campsite in each place. We can only speculate on the appearance of these campsites, because nothing very permanent was built. Perhaps holes were dug and covered with branches and leaves to serve as shelters. Later, these burrows may have been improved and enlarged, with posts to support rafters. In any case, it is unlikely that the earliest dwelling was the cave, despite the many myths and stories about "cave men." Our ancestors lived in many parts of the world, including those where no convenient natural housing was available. Efforts were made to construct shelters wherever the earliest human communities clustered.

Functional Differentiation

Such communal living gave way to family structures as human society developed, and dwellings came to accommodate single families rather than larger groups. As the capacity to domesticate animals, grow crops, and store food increased, so did the size and complexity of human groupings. Communities became larger and more highly organized, and they developed rules governing marriage, inheritance, food allocation, domestic duties, and so on. It also became necessary to construct buildings other than those used for living. The chief or headman's residence must appear more imposing than others, and facilities were needed for the storage of food and implements, for guest quarters, and for the sheltering of livestock. Thus we begin to see some ***functional differentiation*** in buildings.

An example of functional differentiation can be seen in a comparison of lifestyles and dwellings in Africa. In the Kalahari Desert, some San bands probably resemble those of the distant past: their shelters are often mere windbreaks made of a few branches across which an animal skin is stretched. Campsites are occupied only temporarily, for the people must hunt wandering animals in their constant struggle for survival. In contrast, the villages of cattle-raising peoples in the eastern highlands are permanent, and larger communities construct centralized buildings that reflect the increasing complexity of society.

Environmental Influences

There is ample evidence that human communities existed in widely separated areas as early as 100,000 years ago, occupying warm as well as cold regions, moist as well as dry zones, coastal as well as interior locations, and river valleys as well as uplands. Early migrations propelled human groups into unfamiliar environments, and conflict and war drove others into new and sometimes difficult situations. From the beginning humans were confronted by variable environmental conditions—floods, storms, severe cold, and heavy winter snows—and began to build shelters for protection against the elements. The physical structures built by ancient human groups differed in form and function, starting traditions that in some cases have survived for thousands of years. People in flood-prone areas learned to construct stilt houses. Where heavy snow prevailed, the steep-sided roof offered protection against the enormous weight of a winter's accumulation. Nomadic peoples needing lightweight, transportable shelters developed various kinds of tents. Among the truly amazing adaptations was the invention of the igloo by Inuit peoples in the frozen northlands, using as building material the very snow and ice against which they sought to protect themselves.

Thus the diversity of dwellings around the world has ancient origins. The distribution pattern was further complicated by migration, which diffused building practices along numerous routes. Sometimes the introduction of new construction techniques led to the abandonment or modification of existing practices. During the period of European colonial expansion this occurred in many parts of the Americas, Africa, and Asia. In other cases, societies retained their building methods even when they were displaced. Some builders of stilt houses, for instance, continued to construct elevated dwellings even after they had been relocated to areas where floods were not a threat. Building on stilts had become an integral part of their culture.

Cultural geographers have tried to reconstruct the diffusion of building forms, a task that has at times proved to be extremely difficult. Barns and other outbuildings, and even fences, have been the subjects of such studies, and influences have been traced halfway around the world. (For example, historical linkages from Western Europe to New England to California, and ultimately to Hawaii, have been identified.) The dynamic geography of ***domestic architecture*** is a complex and fascinating field.

◆ CHANGING RESIDENTIAL TRADITIONS

Although cultural traditions promote continuity in building types and styles, time does bring change. In certain parts of the world, dwellings appear much as they did centuries ago. In portions of Africa, for example, dwellings in rural areas and even in some cities are still built according to centuries-old patterns. You can walk some of the streets of Kano, Nigeria, and readily imagine that you are in another age. On the other hand, the effects of modernization can be seen even in the African bush, where many houses have corrugated metal instead of thatch roofs. Today, the floor plan of a house may remain the same, but the building materials are no longer limited to those available in the region. Thus we can classify dwellings into four groups: (1) unchanged-traditional, (2) modified-traditional, (3) modernized-traditional (where change affects both building materials and floor plan), and (4) modern.

From the field notes

"Between the Tana River and the Somali border, the bush becomes thinner and building materials are less easy to come by. Still, some houses here are very substantial, requiring a large amount of wood for their frames. This house not far from Ijara is ready for roofing (thatch will be used) and wall construction. The walls are made of a mixture of pebbles and soil mixed with termite-mound clay, dried and hardened by the sun."

From the field notes

"A large number of buildings in the town of Torshavn (Faroe Islands) display a characteristic Scandinavian feature: a sod-covered roof. It conserves warmth during the cold winter, but it does present rot problems (judging by the repairs under way all over town) in the supporting wood."

Unchanged-Traditional Dwellings

Unchanged-traditional houses (both permanent and temporary) are those in which layout, construction, and appearance have not been significantly altered by external influences. Such houses may be modified over time—but as a result of changes within the culture, not borrowing from other cultures. Such is the domestic architecture seen in Arab towns, African villages, rural settlements in China, and other places that are remote from or resistant to foreign influences. Villages all over the world contain a mixture of traditional and modified housing, but unchanged-traditional dwellings survive as well. These range from wood-framed, mat-walled, thatch-roofed Micronesian houses to rough-stone structures in Native American areas of Andean South America; also included are mud-walled houses in China, log cabins in northern Europe, and cloth tents in North Africa.

Traditional houses of European and other Western cultures also belong in this category of domestic architecture. Log houses with sod roofs in Scandinavia, single-story stone houses with thatched roofs in Ireland, and barrel-tiled, whitewashed houses in Spain all represent local or regional traditions. In Canada, domestic architecture is represented by two types of houses, the French-Canadian house of Quebec and the British-Canadian house of Ontario. The French-Canadian house tends to be more elaborate, with

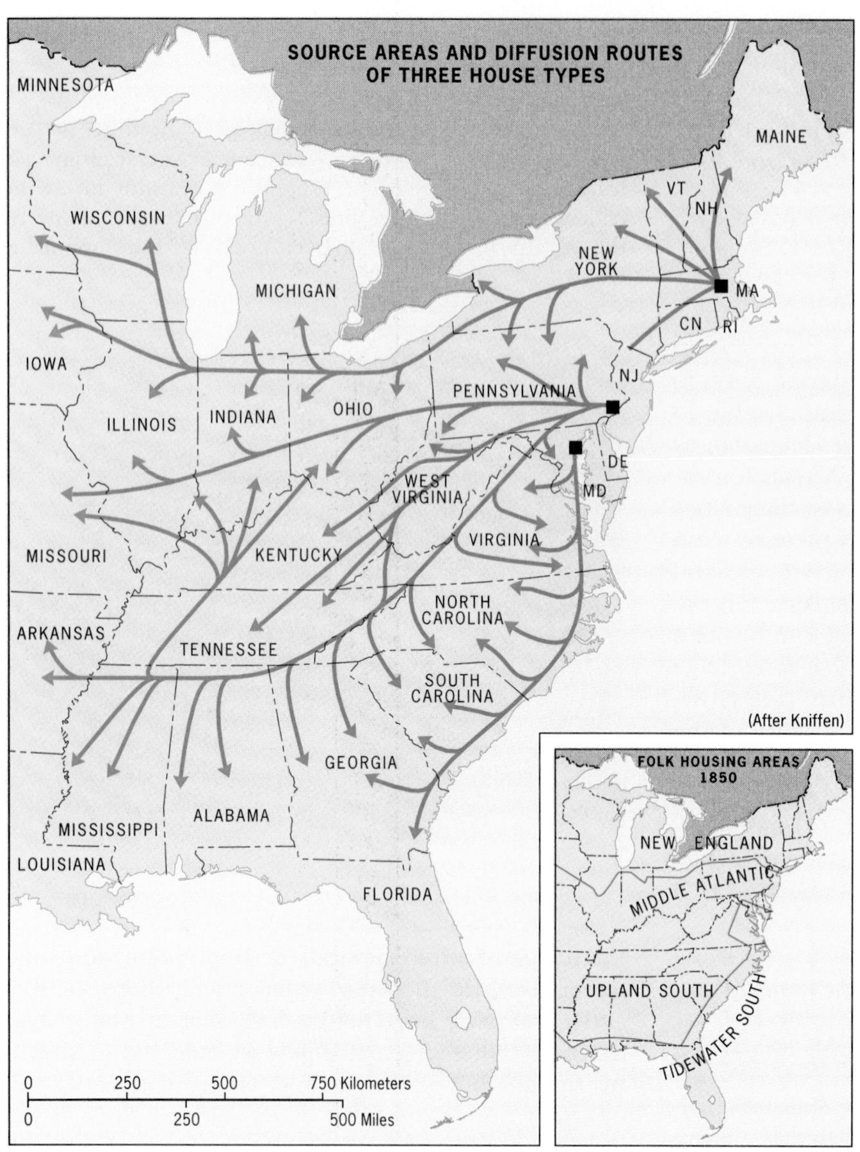

Figure 15-1 Source Areas and Diffusion Routes of Three House Types. This map shows New England, Middle Atlantic, and Southern house styles and their diffusion. *Source: From F. B. Kniffen, "Folk Housing: Key to Diffusion,"* Annals of the AAG *55, 1965, p. 560.*

curved roof lines, attic or dormer windows, and a raised balcony across the front; attached to one side is a summer kitchen that is closed off during the winter. The British-Canadian house is most common in Ontario, and it is more compact and austere. Stone and brick are used in the construction of these two traditional house types.

In the United States, three types of traditional houses can be identified: the New England, Middle Atlantic, and Southern styles. The New England house, unlike its Canadian counterparts, is of wood-frame construction. This style dates from colonial times and diffused from its source area across the northern United States to Michigan, Wisconsin, and beyond (see Fig. 15-1). The Middle Atlantic style originated as a one-room log cabin with a stone chimney and fireplace at one end. Later, additional rooms, a porch, and a second floor were added. In the South, the size and construction of houses reflected the modest means of most of their builders and the comparative warmth of the climate. Smaller than New England houses, Southern dwellings had only one story (sometimes with a small attic room) and a characteristic porch. Often the house was built on a raised platform to reduce interior heat. In low-lying areas, houses were built on raised stone foundations to guard against flood damage.

Modified-Traditional Dwellings

As noted earlier, traditional houses the world over have been modified in many ways. In modified-traditional dwellings, new building materials have been used or elements added that do not fundamentally alter their original structure or layout. The use of corrugated iron as a roofing material, for example, has diffused to many areas of the world and has affected housing everywhere. From Polynesia to West Africa, traditional thatch-roofed dwellings stand next to houses with corrugated-iron roofs. This does not improve the aesthetics of the cultural landscape, since the iron sheeting is subject to ugly rusting. However, the iron roof provides better protection against rain and moisture, cannot be infested by disease-carrying vermin or insects, and often serves as a catchment for fresh water.

Other modifications of traditional houses include the addition of windows and wooden doors. The wall openings are especially important in village houses in Africa, where fires burn inside closed dwellings and smoke-related diseases (especially glaucoma, an affliction of the eyes) are prevalent. Improved air circulation helps reduce the negative effects of the smoke, particularly for newborns and young children. Another modification of traditional dwellings is the raised floor. Without changing the basic structure, the practice of raising the floor has the effect of reducing the amount of moisture inside the dwelling, thus reducing discomfort and disease. Colonial governments therefore encouraged builders of traditional dwellings to raise their floors. Still other improvements are less obvious, yet also important. Thatched roofs were improved through the use of wire mesh and metal ties. Walls made of sun-dried brick were coated with mortar rather than smeared with mud. While these did not materially change the appearance of the traditional dwelling, they did result in better protection and greater durability.

Modernized-Traditional Dwellings

In the case of modern-traditional house types, the modifications are more far-reaching, involving not only building materials but also the floor plan and general layout. Elements of the traditional house persist, but modernization has overtaken tradition. When the New England house type emerged (from European traditions), it had a single bathroom quite unlike those of today, no two-car garage, and almost none of the interior specialization found in modern versions. Remnants of traditional styles still exist—for example, in the Cape-Dutch facades of South Africa, upturned roof lines of Japan, and "Mediterranean" forms in Central and South America—but these are mere vestiges of the originals. European styles have also changed traditional housing in former colonies, where the idea of multiple rooms and specialized facilities has produced imitations of Western houses displaying a mixture of modern and traditional forms and building materials.

Modern Dwellings

The modern house type is most common in the United States. This category has itself become an American tradition, a reflection of advanced technology, upward mobility, practicality, comfort, and hygiene—and large-scale suburbanization. There was a time when the two-story house reflected a family's socioeconomic status and well-being, but the practical advantages of the ranch-style house (once called the "California bungalow") overtook such considerations. Originating in the designs of Elbert Hubbard in Buffalo and Frank Lloyd Wright and his associates in Oak Park, outside Chicago, the ranch-style house took root in Southern California and diffused in various forms to suburbs, where it was much less practical, with its low-angle roof, screened porches and patios, pool and deck, barbecue pit, and other space-demanding, energy-consuming features. Modern domestic architecture in the United States may be less aesthetically pleasing than other dwelling forms, but there are compensations. With its plumbing and electrical systems, temperature- and humidity-control mechanisms, kitchen and bathroom facilities, and automated equipment ranging from garage-door openers to pool-maintenance devices, many would say that the modern American house makes up in technology for what it lacks in style.

Modern domestic architecture tends to sacrifice tradition for practicality and efficiency. Modern house types in Tokyo, Sydney, Nairobi, São Paulo, and Vancouver are far more similar to each other than to the traditional houses in and around these cities. Clearly, tradition remains strongest in the domestic architecture of rural areas.

◆ STRUCTURE AND MATERIALS

Dwellings may also be studied from the viewpoint of their physical structure, their complexity, and the materials from which they are constructed. Cultural geographers classify dwelling types according to these criteria. At one end of the scale are the cave dwelling (people still live in caves in some areas of the world), the windbreak of wandering food-gathering peoples, the pit dwelling, and the simplest huts (little more than stacked-up sticks, branches, grass, and leaves). At the other end are imposing mansions in the wealthy suburbs of Western cities, as well as millions of simpler single-family homes. Between these two ends of the scale are dozens of intermediate dwelling types, ranging from the beehive-shaped Zulu house to the complex houses of several cultures of South, Southeast, and East Asia.

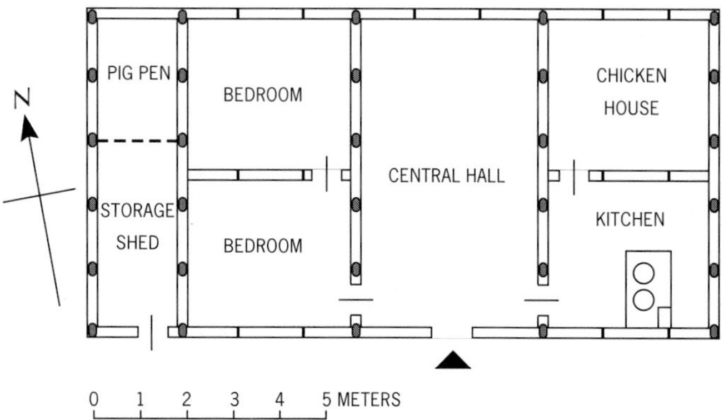

Figure 15-2 Traditional House from Jiangsu Province, China. *Source: From R. G. Knapp,* China's Traditional Architecture. *Honolulu: University of Hawaii Press, 1986, p. 80.*

Maps of the distribution of dwelling-structure types show regions where particular characteristics prevail (Fig. 15-2). In China, for example, farmhouses as well as village houses are now most often built of baked-mud walls and thatch roofs, but older villages contain houses with walls of brick and tile roofs. Most such villages are in the hinterland of Shanghai in the Chang Jiang's middle basin. The many less durable dwellings reflect the scarcity of building materials and the explosive population growth of recent times, which created widespread housing shortages.

In Africa, the transition from the Arab dwelling of the north to the traditional African house of the mid-continent region has already been noted. The existence of Arab and African structures side by side in the transition zone shows how the two culture regions penetrate each other in that zone.

In South America, a map of house structures would reveal not only the diffusion of modern and modernized-traditional forms but also the persistence of older styles such as the rough-stone houses of the Andean Indians, the mud-walled dwellings of the west and south, and the Amazonian Indians' structures of branches and leaves. Maps of this kind have been drawn for local regions, but not for entire geographic realms. However, as in the case of languages, it is often difficult to distinguish what is truly traditional from what has been introduced—the original from the modified.

Building Materials

Another way of studying dwellings is to examine the materials from which they are constructed. In this section we will examine several of the most common types of building materials, bearing in mind that a wide variety of other types are used as well.

Wood Houses made principally of wood still reveal some links to the distribution of forests, although, of course, wood is shipped to all parts of the world today. The log house, which probably originated in the cold forest zones of northern Europe, was brought by early European settlers to northern North America, where forests were plentiful and the cold was at least as severe. Comparatively few log houses are constructed today. These days, log cabins are built in remote areas as recreational homes rather than as year-round residential structures. You could build a log house or cabin with an ax, but modern sawmills produce cut lumber that makes building with wood even easier. Thus the frame house became common in and near forested areas. In this type of structure, walls and ceilings are attached to a frame of cut lumber. The walls may be constructed of wooden planks or boards, and the ceilings of paper; both products are derived from

From the field notes

"I drove northward from Bergen, Norway, and then inland. Roads narrowed from four lanes to two, then to one, and turned from asphalt to dirt. Houses became simpler. Here, near Stalheim, is a house that well represents the area, where the building materials are in ample supply. Wood forms the walls; large slabs of slate create the roof."

trees. The roof is normally made of wood as well, with a protective layer of tarpaper, shingles, or tiles.

Houses made primarily of wood are found in a zone that extends across Eurasia from central Scandinavia and Eastern Europe through Russia to the Pacific coast, including Korea and Japan as well. Wood-frame houses prevail throughout North America from New England to California and from Florida to Alaska. In South America, wood is the primary material for houses in southern Chile and southeastern Brazil, where local forests yield wood for building. Wood is also important in the domestic architecture of Australia and New Zealand.

Brick Where wood is not so readily available, houses are likely to be built of ***brick***. We tend to define a brick as a hard, cement, and oven-baked block that comes in various standard sizes. Elsewhere in the world, however, bricks are made from different raw materials. In the Middle East (as well as in the southwestern United States and Mexico), wet mud is poured into wooden frames, allowed to dry briefly, and then placed in the sun to harden. These bricks are then used in wall construction. Moister mud is used as mortar, and after the newly built structure dries out, the walls are smeared with mud. To construct the roof, a frame of sticks, branches, and straw is covered with mud. In arid regions such dwellings provide adequate protection against both heat and cold; however, the infrequent heavy rains create havoc because the sun-baked mud bricks never become as hard as the oven-baked bricks and tiles used in the Western world. Variations of the method just described are found in many parts of the world.

Sun-dried brick is widely used as a building material. It is the main component of traditional dwellings, not only in the Middle East and the Arab culture realm generally, but also in much of Middle and South America (especially west of the Andes and south of Brazil), the savannalands of Africa, and northern India. The mud-brick house is also common in timber-poor, fairly dry northern China, and some scholars believe that the homebuilding method used there may have diffused from the Middle East.

The fired or baked brick, a more modern innovation, has become a major element of modern construction all over the world. Traditional houses in a Mexican village are made of sun-dried brick, but homes in the towns and cities are built with oven-baked bricks. So it is in the cities of the Arab realm, Africa, and South America (although traditional dwellings cluster on the outskirts of the modern towns). In a few parts of the world, notably Southern Africa and central China, the use of fired brick developed as a traditional building method before modern building technologies were introduced.

From the field notes

"The countryside in Armenia between Yerevan and Lake Sevan is dry and rocky, and the rocks are piled up to mark lot and field lines. They are also used in the construction of houses. As we approached the lake near the town of Akhta you could see the same house form in all directions. The stones are only roughly cut square, and then used to build thick walls with much cement. Windows are small, roofs not very steep (not much rain here). Many residents were changing their roofs from stripped-down tarpaper over wood to corrugated iron sheeting."

Stone Houses also are built of natural stone. In the high Andes of Peru, house-builders pile rough stones on top of each other without mortar, caulk the remaining openings with mud, and add a thatched roof.

Traditional European homes, such as English cottages, also are made of natural stone with cement mortar and have thatched roofs. Southern and interior Egypt, where natural building stone is plentiful, is another area where stone houses are common. Building with available stone developed as ***traditional architecture*** in central and southern India, Xizang (Tibet) and neighboring areas of western China, Yucatan and adjacent parts of Mexico, and south-central Africa (where the great ruins of Zimbabwe provide evidence of the higher level of technology achieved in stone building). Overall, however, wood and mud brick are far more common building materials. In the United States and other Western countries, natural stone is also sometimes used as a decorative material on homes constructed mainly of wood and brick.

Wattle We use the term ***wattle*** to refer to houses built from poles and sticks, which are woven into a tight network and plastered with mud. In fact, these dwellings are built of a combination of wood (the poles and sticks) and the same material from which mud bricks are made. Many African houses are constructed this way, with a thick thatched roof to protect against the occasionally heavy rains.

Regions where poles, sticks, bamboo, bark, leaves, and similar materials are used for building purposes obviously correspond to zones where these materials are readily available. In terms of population, Southeast Asia is the leading region in this category; the traditional houses of Indonesia, the Philippines, and the mainland countries south of China and east of India are made of wattle. In Africa, these materials prevail along the west coast and throughout the lowland basin. And in South America, the sparsely populated Amazon Basin provides ample building material for traditional Native American settlements.

Grass and Brush Between the wattle dwellings of the equatorial rainforest areas and the earthen construction of the drier subtropical zones lie the low-latitude regions where grass and brush are the most common building materials. The African savannalands, including interior West Africa south of the Sahel, East Africa's highlands, and upland South Africa, form the major region of this type, but many traditional dwellings on the Africa savanna also contain sun-dried mud. Grass-and-brush construction also prevails in the Brazilian and Venezuelan highlands to the south of the forested Amazon Basin. Northern Australia's indigenous peoples also build their simple dwellings from vegetation growing on the savanna.

Our enumeration of building materials is by no means complete. The Zulu's beehive-shaped dwellings are made almost exclusively of African tall grass. The tents of nomadic peoples are made of cloth or skins. Even blocks of ice are used as building materials, as noted earlier. Bamboo is used as a building material in parts of Southeast Asia. In northernmost Europe, sod may be piled on the roof to enhance insulation, and in summer you can see goats grazing on the new grass that grows up there. People live permanently on boats and in trailers. The variations are almost infinite.

◆ DIFFUSION OF HOUSE TYPES

Around the world, houses display great variety in form and layout. When people migrate, they carry with them notions of how a home should be planned and constructed, but in new environments those ideas may need to be modified. Differences in available materials and new environmental conditions cause changes that contribute to the development of new styles.

A good example of this process comes from the eastern seaboard of the United States. Fred Kniffen, who conducted extensive research on house types and their diffusion in North America, concluded that three principal types appeared more or less simultaneously in New England, the Middle Atlantic region, and the "Tidewater South" of lower Chesapeake Bay (Fig. 15-1). From these sources, the diverse building styles diffused westward and southward in several parallel streams. By the middle of the nineteenth century these streams had created three distinct ***folk-housing regions*** (see the inset in Figure 15-1).

We have only to look around us to see how things have changed since about 1850. In the Midwest and the South and elsewhere, we still find many single-family houses that are structural variations of the Atlantic-coast types described by Kniffen. However, we also find L-shaped ranch houses, T-shaped homes with the bedrooms separated in the two wings of the T, and U-shaped houses with a patio and perhaps a pool in the enclosed courtyard.

The present cultural landscape thus is a composite of older and newer forms. Figure 15-1 shows the ***diffusion routes*** of the three original types into the U.S. interior. Note that the New England house type was confined to a northern corridor, whereas the Middle Atlantic and Lower Chesapeake types spread more widely. What the map does not show is the eastward diffusion of ranch-style houses from the West. This house style evolved during the 1920s in California and became a cultural symbol of a lifestyle. Expansion diffusion had carried Eastern styles westward, but now Western styles diffused in the opposite direction, first along the Sunbelt corridor and then more widely. But the ranch house is designed for a balmy climate and outdoor living; its single-story, open construction is not really suitable for climates with greater extremes of temperature. Nevertheless, ranch houses are now found virtually everywhere in the United States, even in areas where they are not appropriate. This results from a period of ***maladaptive diffusion*** in which image took precedence over practicality. There are many other examples of such diffusion. To cite just one, the New England style diffused as far as Hawaii, where clusters of these houses still stand—strangely out of place in a tropical environment.

◆ VILLAGES

We now turn our attention from individual dwellings to *settlements*: purposely grouped, organized clusters of houses and nonresidential buildings. The smallest such clusters are known as ***hamlets*** and may contain only about a dozen such buildings. The largest clustered settlements, of course, are cities, the subject of Part Six of this book. Here we are interested in the smallest settlements—hamlets and villages.

Before proceeding, we should note that the definition of a ***village*** varies. We have a mental picture of a village as a small settlement without high-rise buildings or large commercial enterprises, but it is difficult to be precise. What is the upper limit of a village's population? When does a village become a town? In Canada, the official definition of a village limits it to 1000 people; in the United States, the limit is 2500. In India, a place can have up to 5000 residents and still be officially classified as a village. And in Japan a settlement cannot be called an "urban" place until it has 30,000 inhabitants or more. International statistics reporting "rural" (village) and "urban" (city) populations, therefore, are meaningless unless standardized definitions are used.

Village Forms

Rural settlements tend to be small. People who live in them either farm the surrounding land or provide services to those who do the farming. Thus they are closely connected to the land, and most of their livelihoods depend, directly or indirectly, on the cultivation of nearby farmland. As such, they tend to reflect historical and environmental conditions. Houses in Japanese farming villages, for example, are so tightly packed together that only the narrowest passageways remain between them. This reflects the need to allocate every possible square foot of land to farming; villages must not use land where crops could grow.

In the hilly regions of Europe, villages frequently are clustered on hillslopes, leaving the level land for farming. Often an old castle sits atop the hill, so in earlier times the site offered protection as well as land conservation. In many low-lying areas of Western Europe, villages are located on dikes and levees, so that they often take on *linear* characteristics (Fig. 15-3A). Where there is space, a house and outbuildings may be surrounded by a small garden; the farms and pasturelands lie just beyond. In other cases a village may take on the characteristics of a *cluster* (Fig. 15-3B). It may have begun as a small hamlet at the intersection of two roads and then developed by accretion. The European version of the East African circular village, with its central cattle corral, is the *round* village or *rundling* (Fig. 15-3C). This layout was first used by Slavic farmer-herdsmen in Eastern Europe and was later modified by Germanic settlers.

In many parts of the world, farm villages were fortified to protect their inhabitants against marauders. Ten thousand years ago, the first farmers in the Fertile Crescent faced attacks from the horsemen of Asia's steppes and clustered together to ward off this danger.

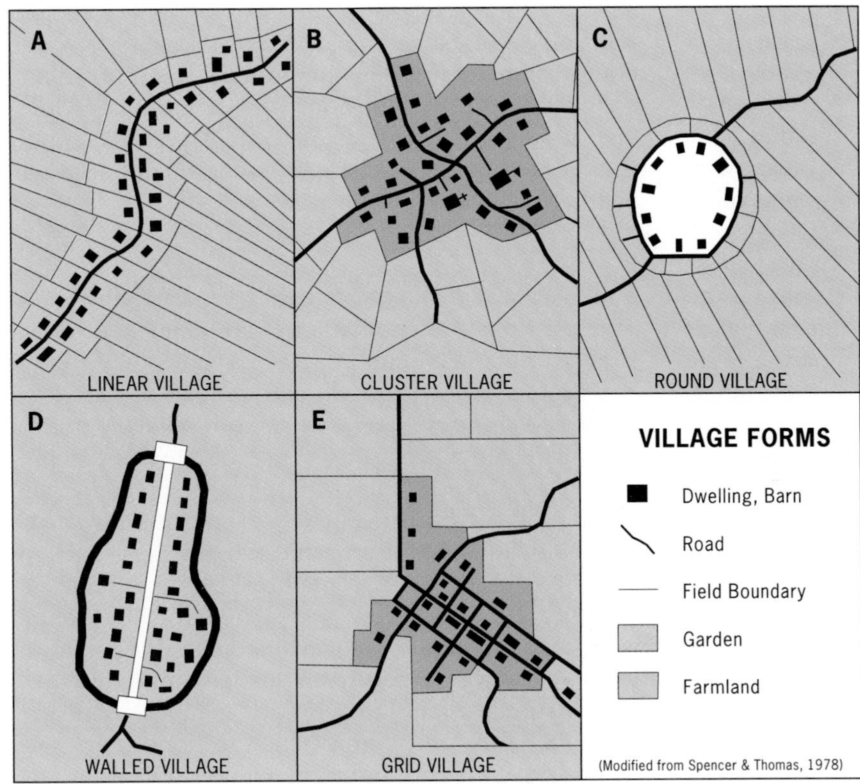

Figure 15-3 Village Forms. Five different representative village layouts are shown here. *Source: From J. E. Spencer and W. H. Thomas,* Introducing Cultural Geography. *New York: Wiley, 1978, p. 154.*

In Nigeria's Yorubaland, the farmers would go out into the surrounding fields by day but retreat to the protection of walled villages at night. Villages, as well as larger towns and cities in Europe, were frequently walled and surrounded by moats. When the population became so large that people had to build houses outside the original wall, a new wall would be built to protect them as well. Walled villages (Fig. 15-3D) still exist in rural areas of many countries, reminders of a turbulent past.

More modern villages, notably planned rural settlements, may be arranged on a *grid* pattern (Fig. 15-3E). This is not, however, a twentieth-century novelty. Centuries ago the Spanish invaders of Middle America laid out grid villages and towns, as did other colonial powers elsewhere in the world. In urban Africa, as we will see in Part 6, such imprints of colonization are pervasive.

Although the twentieth century has witnessed unprecedented urban growth throughout the world, a majority of the world's people still reside in villages and rural areas. In China alone, more than 800 million people (in a country of over 1.2 billion) inhabit villages and hamlets. In India, with a population approaching 1 billion, three out of four people live in villages. Small rural settlements are home to most of the inhabitants of Indonesia, Bangladesh, Pakistan, and other developing countries, including those in Africa. Thus the agrarian village remains the most common form of settlement on Earth despite the industrial and technological revolutions.

Regional Contrasts

Village life varies from one region to another. The modern comforts of a farm village in Wisconsin, with its paved streets, electricity, water supply, and other urban amenities, are a far cry from the dusty, isolated, poverty-ridden village of eastern India. In the industrialized West, modernization has reached all but the remotest rural areas, and on most of the farmlands mechanization prevails. In some other parts of the world, farm villages lie far removed from the sources of change, and there are few material comforts. In South Asia there may be as many as 1 million farm villages, most with fewer than 1000 inhabitants. From a distance, many appear picturesque, rising from emerald-green ricefields or clinging to rocky slopes. However, a closer look often reveals poorly fed, underdressed children, open sores, insects, the absence of sanitation, and inadequate housing.

Clearly, it is not easy to generalize about village life. Villages in areas where subsistence modes of life prevail share certain qualities, whether they lie in South Asia, Subsaharan Africa, or Middle America. Karl Marx once remarked that such places confine the human mind within the narrowest possible bounds, but he failed to understand the inner strength of the inhabitants—their relationship with God or Allah, their confidence in ultimate salvation. Villages in regions where commercial agriculture prevails share a more materialistic orientation, whether they exist in Western Europe, Japan, or the U.S. Midwest. Villages may be viewed as lying along a continuum from the most communal (the multiple-family "long-house" communities of some Pacific, Native American, and Asian cultures) to the most individualistic (the affluent villages of rural North America). Between these extremes are the collective farms of communist societies (such as the *kolkhoz* of the former Soviet Union), other forms of communal agrarian living (Israel's *kibbutzim*), closely knit farm villages in Asian, African, or Native American societies, and looser clusters in rural Europe.

Despite these differences, villages everywhere display certain common qualities, including evidence of social stratification and differentiation of buildings. Social stratification is reflected by the range in size and quality of houses, which represents their owners' wealth and standing in the community. Material well-being is the chief determinant of stratification in Western commercial agricultural regions, where it translates into more elaborate homes. In Africa, a higher social position in the community is associated with a more impressive house. The house of the chief or headman may not only be superior to others but may also stand in a more prominent location. In India, caste still determines the overall quality of daily life, including village housing; the manors of landlords, often comprising large walled compounds, stand in striking contrast to the modest houses of domestic servants, farm workers, carpenters, and craftspeople. The poorest people of the lowest castes live in small one-room, wattle-and-thatch dwellings.

Functional Differentiation in Villages

The functional differentiation of buildings in farm villages is more elaborate in some societies than in others. Protection of livestock and storage of harvested crops are primary functions of farm villages, and in many villages where subsistence farming is the prevailing way of life, the storage place for grains and other food is constructed with as much care as the best-built house. Moisture and vermin must be kept away from stored food; containers of grain often stand on stilts under a carefully thatched roof or behind walls made of carefully maintained sun-dried mud. In India's villages, the paddy-bin made of mud (in which rice is stored) often stands inside the house. Similarly, livestock pens are often attached to houses or, as in Africa, dwellings are built in a circle surrounding the corral or *kraal*.

The functional differentiation of buildings is greatest in Western cultures, where a single farmstead may contain as many buildings as an entire hamlet elsewhere in the world. A prosperous North American farm is likely to include a two-story farmhouse, a stable, a barn, and various outbuildings, including a garage for motorized equipment, a workshop, a shed for tools, and a silo for grain storage. The space these structures occupy often exceeds that used by entire villages in Japan, China, and other agrarian regions where space must be conserved. In the United States, such farmsteads are often separated from each other in a characteristic dispersed pattern; this spatial pattern results from the ***township-and-range system***, a rectangular land-division scheme that was designed to disperse settlers evenly across farmlands of the U.S interior. Even when farms are arranged in a more nucleated pattern in the United States or Europe, they are much more elaborate than farms in many other areas.

Thus villages display an enormous variety of sizes and spatial forms. Their unifying quality is their traditional agricultural orientation: until recently, the great majority of their residents made their living by farming. These settlements typically contain barns, storage sheds, and other buildings related to farming. Villages are also likely to include a place of worship, perhaps a medical clinic, a school, and a public gathering place; in larger villages one may find professional people such as teachers, doctors, and ministers, as well as shopkeepers and mechanics. However, all of these people serve a population whose major tie is to the surrounding land—except in parts of the industrialized West, where rural life is changing rapidly.

Throughout this book we take note of various core-periphery contrasts our world presents. Such contrasts are prominent in rural as well as urban areas. Our examples of farm-village life have been drawn from such countries and regions as India, Subsaharan Africa, China, and Southeast Asia. In the world's core areas, agriculture has taken on a very different form, and true farm villages, in which farming or providing services for farmers are the dominant activities, are disappearing. In India, farming, much of it subsistence farming, still occupies nearly 70 percent of the population. In the United States, where farming once was the leading economic activity, only some 2 percent of the labor force remains engaged in agriculture. The small farmer, it is often said, is a disappearing species.

In the next chapter we examine the spatial features and cultural landscapes of the kind of farming that has come to dominate in the world's economic core areas and in isolated places in the periphery as well: commercial farming. This is the farming of huge corporate grain producers and cattle ranches, mechanized equipment and factory-type labor forces, plantations and profit. As we will see, it is a world apart from the traditional farms of Asia and Africa.

◆ KEY TERMS ◆

brick
building resources
diffusion routes
dispersed settlement
domestic architecture
folk-housing region
functional differentiation
hamlet
maladaptive diffusion
nucleated settlement
township-and-range system
traditional architecture
village
wattle

◆ APPLYING GEOGRAPHIC KNOWLEDGE ◆

1. Do some research on a rural dwelling in the hinterland of the city or town in which you live. Is there evidence that traditional use of local resources (such as wood shingles for the roof, cut stone for the foundation) continues? If not, what has replaced these materials? In the area where you perform this study, do older houses display consistently different characteristics from newer ones? If so, approximately when, and why, did the transition occur?

2. Farm villages are disappearing in the industrialized world, where less than 5 percent of the population still resides in such settlements; but they remain prevalent in Africa and South Asia, where as many as 70 percent of the people inhabit them. What do farm villages in these contrasting core-pheriphery regions have in common? In what ways do they differ? Use your knowledge of cultural landscape and religious geography in your response.

Chapter 16

Commercial Agriculture

From the field notes

"Wherever I went in the wine country of Oregon, orchards were retreating and vineyards are advancing. A high-risk but also high-return agricultural industry, winegrowing is diffusing worldwide, aided by global warming, consumer prosperity, and biotechnology. Parts of Oregon, notably in the Willamette Valley, proved especially suited to the cultivation of the Pinot Noir, the great red grape that made Burgundy famous. Rapid expansion of vineyards planted to this varietal, shown in progress here at Knudsen-Erath, made Oregon one of the world's leading producers of Pinot Noir wines. This is commercial agriculture at its most specialized."

KEY POINTS

◆ Modern commercial agriculture developed out of a global system of commodity exchange established by European colonial powers.

◆ Suitable natural environments and plentiful labor led colonial powers to establish plantation- and luxury-crop agriculture that persists today largely because poorer countries need the cash generated by these crops.

◆ In general, the world's two key grain crops represent different societies: wheat tends to be grown on large landholdings by mechanized means in the richer countries, whereas rice is grown labor-intensively on small plots in poorer countries.

◆ Mediterranean agriculture, a specialized form of farming in a dry-summer climate, yields typical crops in five regions where these conditions prevail.

The roots of modern commercial agriculture can be traced to the vast colonial empires established by European powers in the eighteenth and nineteenth centuries. Europe became a market for agricultural products from around the world but with an added dimension: European countries manufactured and sold in their colonies the finished products made from imported raw materials. Thus cotton grown in Egypt, Sudan, India, and other countries colonized by Europe was bought cheaply, imported to European factories, and made into clothes, many of which were then exported and sold, often in the very colonies where the cotton had been grown in the first place.

Obviously, much has happened to alter the patterns established during the colonial era. The evolution of a worldwide transport network with ever-greater capacity and efficiency changed the competitive position of various agricultural activities. The beef industry of Argentina, for example, secured a world market when the invention of refrigerated ships made it possible to transport a highly perishable commodity over long distances. Yet global agricultural patterns are still influenced by the fact that European colonial powers required farmers in their colonies to cultivate specific crops. Ghanaians still grow cacas. Moçambiquans still raise cotton. Sri Lankans still produce tea.

We have already noted that the Industrial Revolution had a major impact on agriculture. When we attempt to describe the relationships between the urbanized core areas and agricultural patterns, we should view those urban centers as urban-industrial cores, not merely as markets. To these urban-industrial cores, in Europe, North America, Japan, and Russia, flow agricultural (and industrial) raw materials and resources from virtually all parts of the inhabited world. This creates a world spatial system that is represented by Figure 16-1. To make sense of this figure, we need to examine its components in some detail.

◆ EMERGING WORLD PATTERNS

Nonsubsistence farming in many poorer countries is a leftover from colonial times. Such "cash" farming continues to provide badly needed money, even if the conditions of sale to the urban-industrial world are unfavorable. In the Caribbean region, for example, whole national economies depend on sugar exports (sugar having been introduced by the European colonists centuries ago). These island countries naturally wish to sell the sugar at the highest possible price, but they are not in a position to dictate prices. Sugar is produced by many countries in various parts of the world, as well as by farmers in the technologically advanced countries (Fig. 16-1). Thus it is the importing countries that set tariffs and quotas, not the exporters, although regional and global agreements limit what can be done in this respect.

The extent of the importers' power can be seen in the case of Cuba. During its ideological quarrel with Cuba, the United States cut off all imports of Cuban sugar. Although Canada and the Soviet bloc continued to buy sugar from Cuba, this was a staggering blow. The wealthy importing countries can threaten the very survival of the economies of the producers—much like the farmers in von Thünen's Isolated State, who were at the mercy of decisions made by the buyers in the central-city marketplace.

There are occasional signs that the producing countries are seeking to form a cartel in order to pres-

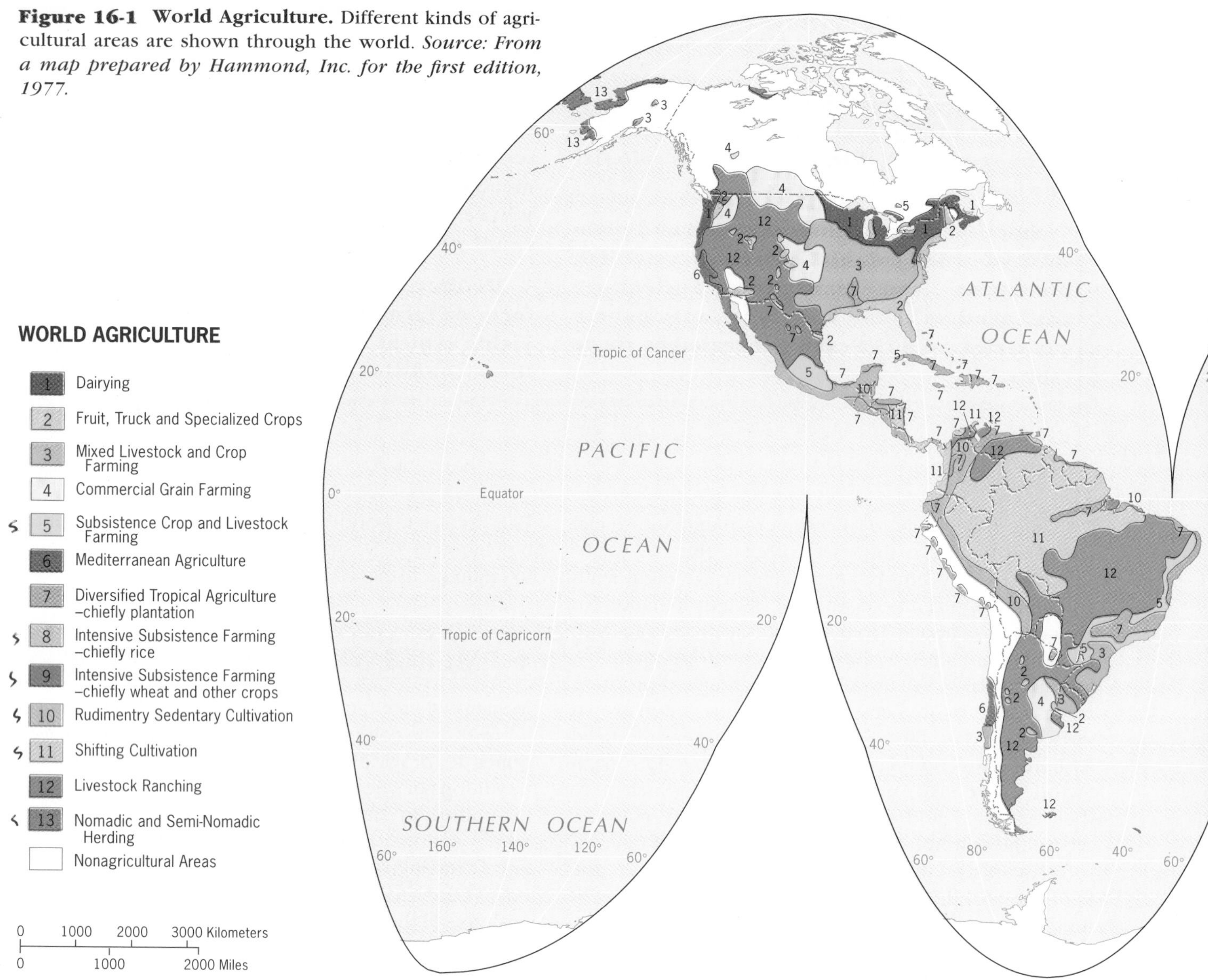

Figure 16-1 World Agriculture. Different kinds of agricultural areas are shown through the world. *Source: From a map prepared by Hammond, Inc. for the first edition, 1977.*

ent a united front to the importing countries, as the oil producing states did during the 1970s. (The OPEC cartel was eventually defeated.) Such collective action is difficult, for several reasons. First, the wealthy importing countries can make deals with countries that are not members of the cartel. Second, the withholding of produce in the exporting countries may stimulate domestic production among the importers. For example, although cane sugar accounts for more than 70 percent of the commercial world sugar crop each year, farmers in the United States, Europe, and Russia produce sugar from sugar beets. In Europe and Russia these beets already produce 25 percent of the annual world sugar harvest. Collective action by countries producing sugarcane could easily cause that percentage to increase.

Cotton and Rubber

As noted earlier, in many former colonies the colonial powers stimulated the production of specific crops. Cotton and rubber are good examples. Today cotton is grown in the United States, northeast China, and several Central Asian Republics. Another large producer, India, began producing cotton under the influence of British colonists. However, cotton cultivation was promoted on a smaller scale in numerous other countries: in Egypt's Nile Delta, in the Punjab region shared by Pakistan and India, and in Sudan, Uganda, Mexico, and Brazil.

Cotton cultivation expanded greatly during the nineteenth century, when the Industrial Revolution produced machines for cotton ginning, spinning, and weaving that increased productive capacity, brought

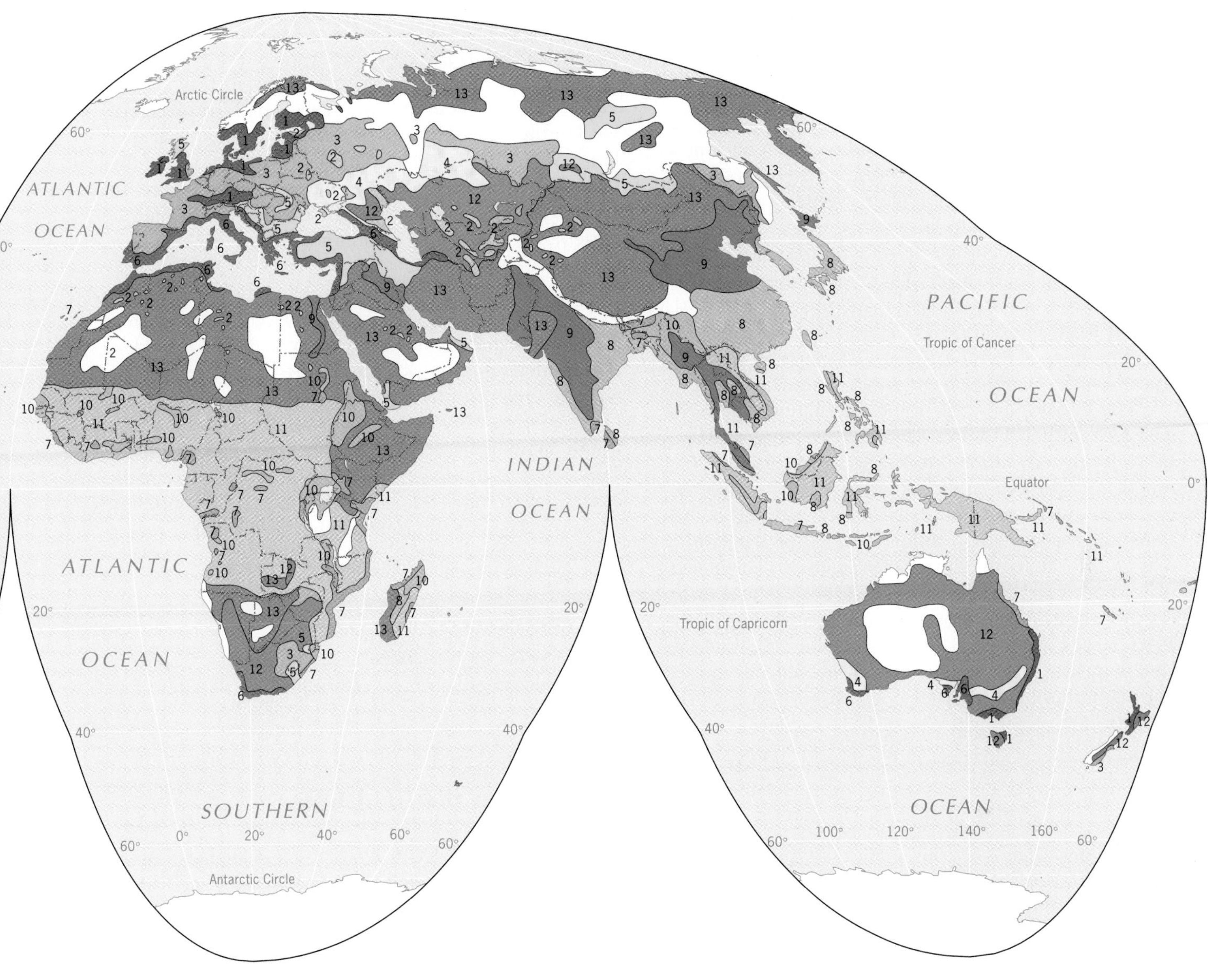

prices down, and put cotton goods within the reach of mass markets. As with sugar, the colonial powers laid out large-scale cotton plantations, sometimes under irrigation (e.g., the famed Jezira Scheme, in the triangle between the White Nile and Blue Nile Rivers in Sudan). The colonial producers received low prices for their cotton, and the European industries prospered as cheap raw materials were converted into large quantities of items for sale at home and abroad.

Today many of the former colonial countries have established their own factories to produce goods for the domestic market, and synthetics, such as nylon and rayon, compete with cotton. Still, the developed countries have not stopped buying cotton, and cotton sales remain important for some developing countries. Japan, the United Kingdom, and Western European countries continue to import cotton fiber, but much of it comes from the United States rather than from the developing countries.

The case of rubber is more complicated. Initially, rubber was collected from rubber-producing trees in equatorial rainforests, mainly in the Amazon Basin in northern South America. In those days, around 1900, the town of Manaus on the Amazon River experienced a rubber boom. Rubber companies in the Congo Basin in Africa experienced a similar period of prosperity.

The boom in wild rubber was short-lived, however. Rubber-tree plantations were created to make rubber collection easier and more efficient. Seedlings of Brazilian rubber trees were planted elsewhere, and they did especially well in Southeast Asia. Within two decades nearly 90 percent of the world's rubber came from new plantations in colonial territories in Malaya, the Netherlands East Indies (now Indonesia), and neighboring colonies.

As time went on, more and more uses for rubber were found, and consumer demand grew continuously. The advent of the automobile was an enormous boost for the industry, and most of the rubber now produced is used to manufacture vehicle tires. World War II created a need for alternative sources of rubber, since Japan had occupied much of Southeast Asia. This stimulated the production of synthetic rubber. In 1997, world rubber production totaled approximately 16 million tons, more than 11 million of it synthetic; of the remaining 4.8 million tons, 75 percent was produced on the plantations of Southeast Asia.

The development of rubber plantations in Southeast Asia, rather than in sections of the Amazon Basin or the Congo Basin, is due less to environmental factors than to the availability of labor. The colonial powers were aware that Southeast Asia combined conditions of tropical environment and labor availability that neither Amazon South America nor equatorial Africa could match. Eventually, a large-scale rubber industry developed in Liberia (West Africa), but in the 1990s it was destroyed during the country's disastrous civil war. Lately, efforts have been made to introduce the plantation system along the Amazon River in the heart of northern Brazil.

Luxury Crops

Similar conditions—a combination of suitable environment and available labor—led the European colonial powers to establish huge plantations for the cultivation of ***luxury crops*** such as tea, cacao, coffee, and tobacco. Coffee was first domesticated in the region of present-day Ethiopia, but today it thrives in Middle and South America, where approximatley 70 percent of the world's annual production is harvested. The United States buys more than half of all the coffee sold on world markets annually, and Western Europe imports most of the rest.

Compared to coffee, tea is consumed in greater amounts in areas where it is grown: India, China, Sri Lanka, and Japan. Whereas coffee is cultivated and consumed mainly in the Americas, tea is the dominant beverage in Eurasia. It goes from the Asian producing areas to the United Kingdom and the rest of Europe. Tea is a rather recent addition to Western diets. It was grown in China perhaps 2000 years ago, but it became popular in Europe only during the nineteenth century. The colonial powers (mainly the British) established enormous tea plantations in Asia and thus began the full-scale flow of tea into European markets.

◆ GLOBAL DISTRIBUTION OF COMMERCIAL AGRICULTURE

The total area occupied by such crops as rubber, coffee, and tea constitutes a tiny fraction of all cultivated land. So small are these patches of luxury crops that they appear as mere dots on maps such as Figure 16-1. The larger regions depicted on the world map of agriculture represent sustenance crops: rice, wheat, and other grains.

Figure 16-1 reveals that virtually all countries have more than one kind of agricultural economy. Even at the small scale required by a global view, it is clear that numerous countries are divided into subsistence-farming areas and commercial-crop production zones. Later, when we investigate secondary and tertiary economic activities, we will see similar regionalisms. In China, for example, the eastern provinces along the Pacific coast have strongly commercial economies, while much of the interior remains largely subsistence-based.

Plantations

Commercial agriculture is the hallmark of modern, industrialized economies, although one version of it,

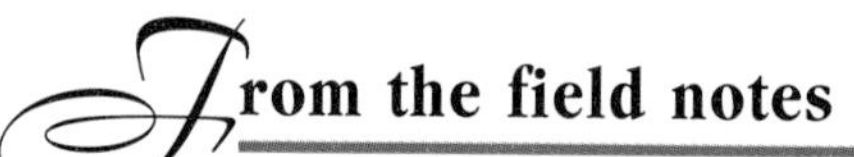

From the field notes

"In Durban, South Africa, I was reminded of an old field lesson: if you cannot do an excursion and want to know what the city's rural environs yield, go to the farmer's market. On Grey Street near the port city's downtown is just such a market. Citrus fruits were the bargain of the day, grown on the sunny slopes of the Province of Natal, now Kwazulu-Natal."

A SENSE OF SCALE

The Impact of Changing Agricultural Practices

Recent shifts from subsistence agriculture to commercial agriculture have had dramatic impacts on rural life. Land-use patterns, land ownership arrangements, and agricultural labor conditions have all changed as rural residents cope with shifting economic, political, and environmental conditions. Interestingly, changes in agricultural practices have affected different parts of the world in different ways. In the more industrialized realms, we have witnessed increased mechanization, consolidation of smaller farms into larger corporate units (***agribusiness***), and increased crop specialization. In the less industrialized world, changes in agricultural practices have had a variety of impacts.

In Latin America, dramatic increases in the production of export crops (or *cash crops* like fruits and coffee) have occurred at the expense of crop production for local consumption. In the process, subsistence farming has been pushed to ever more marginal lands. In Asia, where the "Green Revolution" has had the greatest impact, the production of cereal crops (grains such as rice and wheat) has increased for both foreign and domestic markets. Agricultural production in this region remains relatively small in scale and quite dependent on manual labor. In Subsaharan Africa, total commercialized agriculture has increased but overall agricultural exports have decreased. As in Asia, farm units in Subsaharan Africa have remained relatively small and dependent on intensified manual labor.

What this regional-scale analysis does not tell us is how these changes have affected local rural communities. These changes can be environmental, economic, and social. A recent study in the small country of Gambia (West Africa) by geographer Judith Carney has shown how changing agricultural practices have altered not only the rural environment and economy, but also relations between men and women. Over the last 30 years international developmental assistance of Gambia has led to ambitious projects designed to convert wetlands to irrigated agricultural lands, making possible year-round production of rice. By the late 1980s virtually all of the country's suitable wetlands had been converted to year-round rice production. This transformation created tensions within rural households by converting lands traditionally used by women for family subsistence into commercialized farming plots. In addition, when rice production was turned into a year-round occupation, women found themselves with less time for other activities crucial for household maintenance. This situation underscores the fact that in Africa, as in much of the rest of the less-industrialized world, agricultural work is overwhelmingly carried out by women. In Subsaharan Africa over 85 percent of all women in the labor force work in agriculture, while in China the number is close to 75 percent and in India 70 percent. A geographical perspective that is sensitive to scale helps to shed light on how changes in agricultural practices throughout the world not only alter rural landscapes but also affect family and community relationships.

plantation agriculture, persists in poorer countries along with subsistence farming. Figure 16-1 shows that plantation agriculture (7 in the legend) continues in tropical Middle and South America, Africa, and South Asia. Laid out to produce bananas and sugar, coffee and cocoa in Middle and South America, rubber, cocoa, and tea in West and East Africa, tea in South Asia, and rubber in Southeast Asia, these plantations have outlasted the period of decolonization and continue to provide specialized crops to wealthier markets. Many plantations in former colonies are still owned by European or American individuals or corporations, but even when they were taken over by the governments of newly independent countries, they were kept in operation—because they were an important source of income.

Commercial Agriculture

By far the largest areas of commercial agriculture (1 through 4 in the legend) lie outside the tropics. ***Dairying*** (1) is widespread in the northeastern United States and in northwestern Europe. Fruit, truck, and specialized crops (2), including the market gardens von Thünen observed around Rostock, are found in the eastern and southeastern United States and in widely dispersed small areas where environments are favorable. (Major oases can be seen in the Sahara and in Central Asia.)

Mixed livestock and crop farming (3) extends over much of the eastern United States, Western Europe, western Russia, and smaller areas in Uruguay, Brazil, and South Africa. Commercial grain farming (4) prevails in the southern prairie provinces of Canada, in the Dakotas and Montana in the United States, as well as in Kansas and adjacent areas. Spring wheat (sown in the spring and harvested in the summer) grows in the northern zone, and winter wheat (sown in the autumn and harvested in the spring of the following year) is used in the southern area. An even larger belt of wheat farming extends from Ukraine through Russia into Kazakhstan. The Argentinian and Australian wheat zones are smaller in area, but their exports are an important component of world trade.

Rice Growing

Note that commercial rice growing does not appear as a separate item in the legend, although we know that it exists. The United States is the world's leading exporter of rice, followed by Thailand and Vietnam. The reason has to do with the nature of rice production. Wheat farming is carried out on huge landholdings with large machines that sow and harvest the grain. Rice, in contrast, is grown on small plots and is labor-intensive, so that subsistence and export production (at least in Southeast Asia) occur side by side.

The Third Agricultural Revolution

Twelve thousand years ago, momentous developments were taking place in a few small areas of Southwest Asia. These involved sowing seed and harvesting grain, and they produced the First Agricultural Revolution. Three hundred years ago, a Second Agricultural Revolution occurred as improved equipment, better farming methods, and other innovations greatly increased the productivity of European farming. The Industrial Revolution stimulated the modernization of farming and helped spread it around the world.

Over the past several decades, a ***Third Agricultural Revolution*** has been in progress. Also called the ***Green Revolution***, this revolution occurred in laboratories and plant nurseries. It is the product of the age of ***biotechnology***.

The Third Agricultural Revolution began in the 1960s, when scientists at a research institution in the Philippines crossed a dwarf Chinese variety of rice with an Indonesian variety and produced IR8. This "artificial" rice plant had a number of desirable properties: it developed a bigger "head" of grain and had a stronger stem that did not collapse under the added weight. IR8 produced much better yields than either of its "parents," but the researchers were not satisfied. In 1982 they produced IR36, which was bred from 13 parents to achieve genetic resistance against 15 pests and a growing cycle of 110 days under warm conditions, thus making possible three crops per year. By 1992, IR36 was the most widely grown crop on Earth.

In September 1994 scientists announced yet another breakthrough: the development of a strain of rice that was even more productive than IR36. Still greater achievements may lie ahead. Researchers at the International Rice Research Institute are working to breed a "super rice" that will not have to be transplanted as seedlings but can be seeded directly in the paddy soil. It will have the virtues of its predecessors but will yield nearly twice as much rice per acre than the average for strains in current use. The charting of the genome of rice (the 12 chromosomes that carry all of the plant's characteristics) is under way, so it may also be possible to transform rice genetically so that it will continuously acquire more desirable properties. Not only could yields improve; so could resistance to diseases and pests.

Other crops, from wheat and corn to tomatoes and bananas, have already benefited from research in biotechnology. Advances in this field have produced methods for fattening livestock faster and improving the appearance of fruits. The results of the ongoing revolution in agriculture are already evident. The disastrous famines of the past have abated as a result of increased yields of grains. But the social and environmental consequences of the Green Revolution are not always benign. Growing genetically altered crops often requires higher inputs of chemical fertilizers and pesticides, and these in turn can lead to a reduction of organic matter in the soil and to groundwater pollution. Moreover, many small-scale farmers lack the resources to acquire genetically enhanced seeds and the necessary fertilizers and pesticides. Hence, these farmers are in a poor competitive position, and some are being driven out of business. Nevertheless, the Third Agricultural Revolution is clearly here to stay, and it may transform the world in ways not yet imagined.

Despite the region's significant rice exports, most Southeast Asian farmers are subsistence farmers. Thus Southeast Asia appears on the map as primarily a subsistence grain-growing area. The increases in production associated with recent "Green Revolution" developments are especially evident here (see "Focus on: The Third Agricultural Revolution").

Livestock Ranching

Even a cursory glance at Figure 16-1 reveals the wide distribution of ***livestock ranching*** (12). The raising of cattle for meat and of sheep for meat and wool developed in the wake of European colonization on vast tracts of natural pasture. In addition to the large cattle-ranching areas in the United States, Canada, and Mexico, much of eastern Brazil and Argentina are devoted to ranching, along with large tracts of Australia and New Zealand, as well as South Africa. You may see a Thünian pattern here: livestock ranching on the periphery and consumers in the cities. Refrigeration has overcome the problem of perishability, and high volume has lowered the unit cost of transporting beef, lamb, and other animal products.

From the field notes

"The technology of refrigeration has kept pace with the containerization of seaborne freight traffic. When we sailed into the port of Dunedin, New Zealand, I was unsure of just what those red boxes were. Closer inspection revealed that they are refrigeration units, to which incoming containers are attached. Meats and other perishables can thus be kept frozen until they are transferred to a refrigertor ship."

Much of the land devoted to this form of commercial agriculture is unsuitable for cultivation (see the map of world climate, Figure 3-7) because it is arid or semiarid. But the natural vegetation in these areas cannot always sustain the herds, especially during prolonged droughts. This leads to ecological damage and, in some areas, to desertification. In recent years the popularity of fast-food chains that serve hamburgers has led to the deforestation of wooded areas in order to open up additional pastures for beef cattle, notably in Central and South America.

Mediterranean Agriculture

Only one form of agriculture mentioned in the legend of Figure 16-1 refers to a particular climate: ***Mediterranean agriculture*** (6). As the map shows, this kind of specialized farming occurs in areas where the dry-summer Mediterranean climate prevails: along the shores of the Mediterranean Sea, in parts of California and Oregon, in central Chile, at South Africa's Cape, and in parts of southwestern and southern Australia. Here grows a special combination of crops: grapes, olives, citrus fruits, figs, certain vegetables, dates, and others. From these areas come many wines; these and other commodities are exported to distant markets because Mediterranean products tend to be popular and command high prices.

Numerous factors have shaped the world distribution of subsistence and commercial agricultural systems. History and tradition play important roles, as do environment and technology. Many governments encourage their citizens to limit family size in an attempt to lift the population above the subsistence level. Some governments, notably those of the former Soviet Union and Maoist China, tried to control agricultural output by creating collective farms and agricultural communes, a giant experiment that resulted in untold hardship and mixed results in terms of output. Today farming reprivatization is under way in both countries.

Most of all, the map reveals the capacity of markets to control the activities of farmers. The range and variety of products on the shelves of city supermarkets is uncommon in a world where simple meals and often inadequately balanced diets predominate. A global network of farm production is oriented to the one-fifth of the world's population that is highly urbanized, wealthy, and powerful. Few farmers in distant lands have real control over land-use decisions, for the developed nations continue to decide what will be bought at what price. The colonial era may have come to an end, but, as Figure 16-1 reminds us, its imprint remains strong.

◆ KEY TERMS ◆

agribusiness
biotechnology
commercial agriculture
dairying
Green Revolution
livestock ranching
luxury crops
Mediterranean agriculture
plantation agriculture
Third Agricultural Revolution

◆ APPLYING GEOGRAPHIC KNOWLEDGE ◆

1. For many years, Caribbean islands such as St. Lucia have been exporting bananas to markets in North America and Europe, their industries protected by preferential trade agreements. Now those agreements are ending as trade barriers fall all over the world, and the single-crop economies of the Caribbean are in trouble. What are the options for the farmers of St. Lucia and its neighbors? Can the small-island economies be diversified? Relate your answer to core-periphery contrasts in the modern world.
2. Why is it difficult for producing countries in the periphery to create and sustain cooperative cartels that might protect their joint interests on markets of countries in the core?

Part Five

LAND AND LAND USE IN THE RURAL SECTOR

Should poor-country commercial farmers be protected against the avarice of the rich markets? The liberalization of trade has fostered an extraordinary global movement of agricultural products. The beneficiaries of this trade range from consumers in wealthier parts of the world to the owners of lands on which high-value crops are produced. But the economic fortunes of many commercial farmers in the poor parts of the world are vulnerable to the whims of the international market, and the environmental costs of shifting to large-scale commercial farming are often high. It is difficult to confront such issues without protective measures, yet the major players in the international economy show no signs of abandoning the free trade principle. As pressure grows on the economies and environments of farmers in less well-off areas, steps for improvement will become increasingly necessary. Effective measures will require cooperation among farmers and the political/business elite in poorer parts of the world—a difficult prospect given the vested interests of much of that elite in the status quo.

◆ SELECTED BIBLIOGRAPHY ◆

PART FIVE **Land and Land Use in the Rural Sector**

Blaikie, P. *The Political Economy of Soil Erosion in Developing Countries* (London: Longman, 1985).

Blaikie, P., & Brookfield, H. *Land Degradation and Society* (London: Methuen, 1987).

Boserup. E. *The Conditions of Agricultural Growth: The Economics of Agrarian Change Under Population Pressure* (Chicago: Aldine, 1966).

Bowler, I. R., ed. *The Geography of Agriculture in Developed Market Economies* (New York: Wiley, 1992).

Carney, J. A. "Converting the Wetlands, Engendering the Environment: The Intersection of Gender with Agrarian Change in Gambia." In R. Peet, & M. J. Watts, eds. *Liberation Ecologies* (London: Routledge, 1996).

Dalal-Clayton, D., ed. *Black's Agricultural Dictionary* (Totowa, N.J.: Barnes & Noble, 2nd rev. ed., 1986).

de Blij, H. *Wine: A Geographic Appreciation* (Totowa, N.J.: Rowman & Allanheld, 1983).

de Blij, H. *Wine Regions of the Southern Hemisphere* (Totowa, N.J.: Rowman & Allanheld, 1985).

de Souza, A. *World Space-Economy* (Columbus, Ohio: Charles E. Merrill, 2nd rev. ed., 1989).

Duckham, A. N., & Masefield, G. B. *Farming Systems of the World* (New York: Praeger, 1970).

Goodman, D., & Redclift, M. *Refashioning Nature: Food, Ecology, and Culture* (London: Routledge, 1991).

Gourou, P. *The Tropical World: Its Social and Economic Conditions and Its Future Status* (London and New York: Longman, 5th rev. ed., trans. S. Beaver, 1980).

Grigg, D. *An Introduction to Agricultural Geography* (London, U.K.: Routledge, 2nd ed., 1995).

Grigg, D. *Population Growth and Agrarian Change* (London, U.K.: Cambridge University Press, 1980).

Gritzner, J. A. *The West African Sahel: Human Agency and Environmental Change* (Chicago: University of Chicago Geography Research Paper No. 226, 1988).

Harris, D., ed. *Human Ecology in Savanna Environments* (New York and London; Academic Press, 1980).

Hart, J. F. *The Land that Feeds Us* (New York: W. W. Norton, 1991).

Heiser, C., Jr., *Seed to Civilization: The Story of Food* (Cambridge: Harvard University Press, 1990).

Horvath, R. "Von Thünen's Isolated State and the Area Around Addis Ababa, Ethiopia." *Annals of the Association of American Geographers* 59 (1969) 308–323.

Ilbery, B. W. *Agricultural Geography: A Social and Economic Analysis* (Oxford: Oxford University Press, 1985).

Ilbery, B. W., et al., eds. *Agricultural Restructuring and Sustainability: A Geographical Perspective* (New York: CAB International, 1997).

Keen, E. A. *Ownership and Productivity of Marine Fishery Resources* (Blacksburg, Va.: McDonald & Woodward, 1988).

Klee, G., ed. *World Systems of Traditional Resource Management* (New York: Halsted Press N.H. Winston, 1980).

Knox, P., & Agnew, J. *The Geography of the World Economy* (London: Edward Arnold, 2nd ed. 1994).

Levi, J., & Havinden, M. *Economics of African Agriculture* (Harlow, U.K.: Longman, 1982).

Little, P. D., & Watts, M. J. *Living Under Contract: Contract Farming and Agrarian Transformation in Sub-Saharan Africa* (Madison: University of Wisconsin Press, 1994).

Moris, J. R., & Thom, D. J. *Irrigation Development in Africa: Lessons of Experience* (Boulder, Colo.: Westview Press, 1990).

Sauer, C. O. *Agricultural Origins and Dispersals* (Cambridge, Mass.: MIT Press, 2nd rev. ed., 1969).

Spencer, J., & Horvath, R. "How Does an Agricultural Region Originate?" *Annals of the Association of American Geographers* 53 (1963), 74–82.

Von Thünen, J. H. *Der Isolierte Staat.* Translated by C. M. Wartenberg. In P. Hall, ed., *Von Thünen's Isolated State* (Elmsford, N.Y.: Pergamon, 1966).

Yellen, J. E. "The Transformation of the Kalahari !Kung," *Scientific American*, April 1990, pp. 96–105.

Part Six

THE URBANIZING WORLD

At Issue

During the post-World War II era, a house in the suburbs became the American ideal, and suburbanization pulled an ever-larger number of residents from central cities to the outskirts. A single, spacious home, a two-car garage, a patio, perhaps a pool, separation, and privacy were the attractions of suburban life. In the decaying inner cities, push factors abounded: deteriorating schools, disintegrating neighborhoods, declining services, frightening crime. Suburbanization has robbed the central city of much of its tax base, leaving city governments without the means to reverse the tide. In the United States today, the future of the urban core is in question. ***Should the central city be saved, and should suburbanites, who commute downtown every day to earn their salaries, help pay for this? Or should it be left to be transformed by the forces that are reshaping America's urban areas?***

Should they support the downtown? Miami, Florida.

Part Outline

Chapter 17

Civilization and Urbanization

From the field notes

"The Greek Island of Delos is a window on a time when this was a pivotal place in the Aegean Sea, and indeed in a much larger maritime region. Delos was the Hong Kong of the Mediterranean, a place of magnificent temples, sculptures, theaters, and aqueducts. It had a bustling harbor at least 3,000 years ago, an entrepot that housed and transferred slaves, wild animals, and goods from Africa and Asia. Delos fell to the Greeks and later to the Romans, and for a time was a free port. But the foci of trade in the region changed, and Delos collapsed. All this happened before the birth of Christ; later, this magnificent site was quarried for building stone by, among others, Venetians and Turks. Today Delos is a national monument, uninhabited, to preserve what remains of a creative and turbulent past."

KEY POINTS

◆ Urbanization and the formation of states transformed egalitarian societies into stratified, functionally specialized ones. This process occurred independently in several regions, probably first in the Fertile Crescent.

◆ The ancient Greeks assimilated concepts of urban life from Mesopotamia as well as Minoa. They produced the most highly urbanized society of their time, 2500 years ago.

◆ The ancient Romans combined local traditions with Greek customs in building an urban system that extended from Britain to Mesopotamia. All of the urban centers of the Roman Empire were linked together by a network of land and water routes.

◆ Greek and Roman concepts of urbanization diffused into Western Europe, but Europe's preindustrial cities were poorly organized, unsanitary, overcrowded, and uncomfortable places to live for the majority of their inhabitants.

◆ Cities evolve in stages. The traders' mercantile city gave way to the factory-dominated manufacturing center, and the automobile enabled the evolution of the suburbanized modern city. Today's "post-modern" cities reflect the age of high technology.

Virtually everywhere in the world, people are moving from the countryside to towns and cities. This migration is happening so fast that the various agencies that monitor it, such as the United Nations and the World Bank, cannot agree on the pace. In 1994, one such bureau announced that by its observations, the world's urban population was about to outnumber the rural one. Newspapers and television newscasts marked this as a momentous occasion: from 1994 on, more people would live in towns and cities than in rural areas. Other tabulators disagreed, however, and reported that the 50 percent benchmark would not be reached until early in the twenty-first century. The problem of undependable census data (Chapter 4) and inconsistent definitions (Chapter 15) made agreement all but impossible. Nevertheless, every indicator pointed to the same conclusion: in the twenty-first century, the world will be predominantly urban.

But urbanization is not evenly distributed around the globe. In Western Europe, the United States, Canada, and Japan, four out of five citizens live in cities or towns. But in India and China, the figure is closer to three out of ten. Yet even where urbanization remains low, people are moving to towns and cities. The city of Shenzhen in China was the world's fastest-growing urban area during the second half of the twentieth century; its population increased from about 20,000 to 2.5 million in three decades. When a major development project was announced in Shanghai, nearly 3 million people rushed to the area, hoping to find work. Two of the world's fastest-growing cities, Calcutta and Mumbai in India, also rank among the ten largest.

It is difficult to think of a human world without cities. Cities are the centers of political power and industrial might, higher education and technological innovation, artistic achievement and medical advances. They are the great markets, centers of specialization and interaction, sources of news and information, suppliers of services, and providers of sports and entertainment. Cities are the anchors of culture: the urban system and its spokes form the structural skeleton of society.

And yet, the rise of the city is a very recent phenomenon in human history. If human communities have existed for 200,000 years, they did not cluster into towns until more than 190,000 years had passed. Humans migrated far and wide, glaciations came and went, and climates warmed and cooled. But not until about 8000 years ago did some human settlements begin to grow into larger places.

In Part Six we trace the evolution of urbanization in geographic context, identify the factors that influenced the location and growth (or decline) of cities, investigate the internal structure of cities in various cultural settings, and note the serious problems created by rapid urban growth. We start by looking back at the beginnings of urbanization.

◆ ANCIENT CITIES AND EARLY CIVILIZATIONS

In earlier chapters we noted the beginnings of the diffusion of agriculture between 10,000 and 12,000 years ago. Populations grew and people migrated outward from the early agricultural hearths, carrying their knowledge of farming with them. Settlements became more sedentary; languages diffused and diversified.

But for several thousand years those settlements remained true villages. They were small and did not vary much in size. The households they contained had about the same amount of possessions and status. Apparently, no governmental authority existed beyond the village. There were no public buildings and no workshops. ***Egalitarian societies*** persisted long after agriculture was introduced.

Scholars are fairly certain that this was the situation in the region of the Fertile Crescent and the areas into which agricultural innovations diffused. There is evidence that the same conditions prevailed in other, later hearths of agricultural innovation. In Southwest Asia things began to change in about 6000 B.P. as agricultural societies became more complex with the introduction of irrigation and larger-scale farming. There is evidence that social inequality was developing. The size of houses began to vary. Some people had more property than others and were buried with the best of their Earthly belongings. Specialization developed as some people remained farmers, while others were craftspeople or became involved in government. Government buildings and workshops appeared, and the village became more diversified.

Cities and States

None of this made a city out of a village, but now an important political development occurred. As some villages grew larger and increasing specialization took place in the work that people did, there was a greater need for political systems and structures. Thus it is not surprising that groups of settlements came under the control of a central authority. This was the beginning of the formation of the ***state***, a process that was to lead to the rise of ancient Egypt, Greece, the Roman Empire, and ultimately, the modern state.

The rise of the earliest states is closely linked to the evolution of the first cities. But when did a group of villages controlled by a central government become a state? In a 1975 article anthropologists Henry Wright and Gregory Johnson proposed that the existence of an early state can be deduced from the presence of a centralized political hierarchy with at least three levels of administration. They analyzed an area in present-day southwestern Iran that contained evidence of more than four dozen settlements. The great majority of these settlements were small villages, but four larger "towns" could be identified, and one center was even larger than these towns. So there was a dominant urban center, the probable capital, where the power likely was concentrated, and two levels of settlement below it. This suggests that a state had arisen there more than 5000 years ago.

The period between about 7000 B.P. and 5000 B.P. is called the ***formative era*** for both the development of states and urbanization—the two obviously went hand in hand—in Southwest Asia. Toward the end of that period there was a large state in the lower basin of the Tigris-Euphrates (Mesopotamia) with a number of cities, including Ur. Sumer's cities had impressive temples on high artificial mounds, as well as imposing public buildings, army barracks, numerous workshops, and dwellings of various sizes. The egalitarian society had become a ***stratified society***. Now there were priests, merchants, administrators, soldiers, farmers, craftspeople, and slaves. The city had become the focus of civilization.

Function and Location

The ancient city was also the organizational focus of the state. Agriculture had to be planned so as to guarantee a flow of food into the city—a task that became even more complicated when irrigation systems developed. Some scholars believe that the earliest civilizations emerged from the need for organization that arose when irrigation was invented. The collection of taxes and tribute from an expanding region under the city's control also had to be organized. Soon the city needed to be protected against enemies, and this required collective action—for example, to build fortified walls.

The geographic advantages of certain locations, as well as the organization of the community, influenced the growth of ancient towns and cities. Not only proximity to productive farmlands but also the availability of water and the defensibility of the site contributed to the durability of certain towns. Towns in Mesopotamia enjoyed secure food supplies (see Fig. 3-3). In the Indus Basin, the first cities were served by carefully maintained stone-lined wells (see Harappa and Mohenjo-Daro in Fig. 17-1). Also significant was the position of towns on ancient travel and trade routes. Where such routes converged on an urban place, there were contact, interaction, and growth. Less accessible, more isolated places were at a disadvantage.

Urban growth tested the ingenuity of the town's leaders. Food must not only be acquired and stored but also distributed. This required an ***urban elite***, a group of decision makers and organizers who controlled the resources, and sometimes the lives, of others. An urban elite could afford to devote time to such

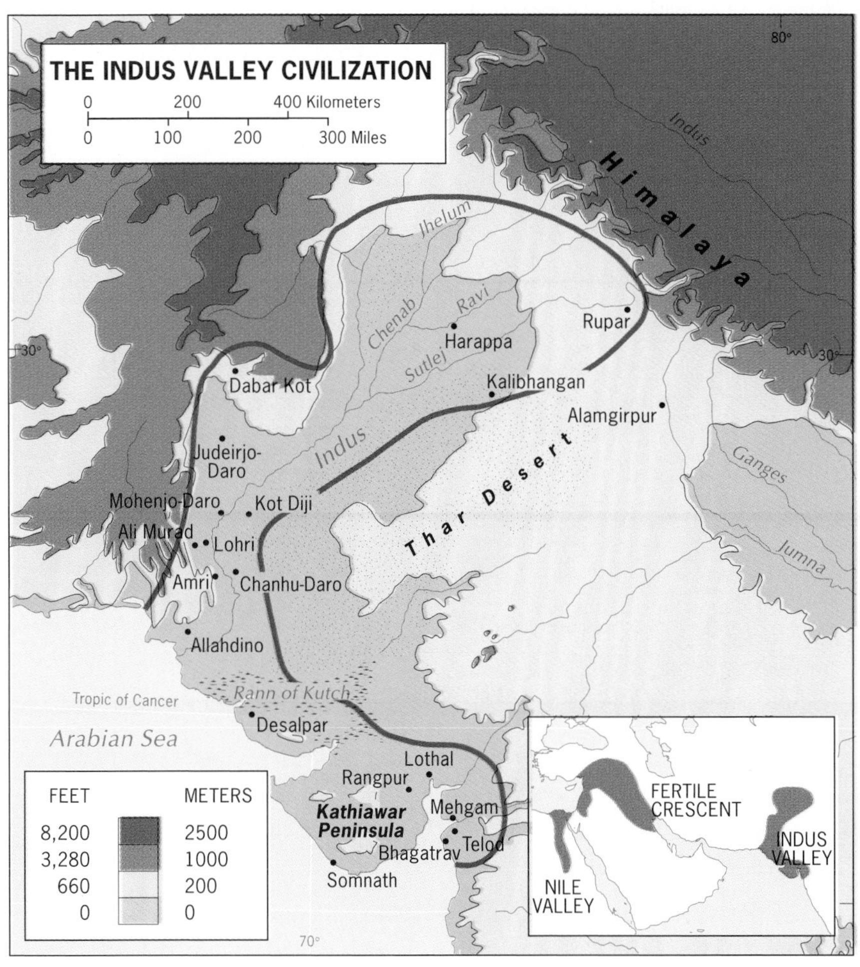

Figure 17-1 The Indus Valley Civilization. The Indus Basin was a crucible, a hearth of culture whose innovations diffused into India.

pursuits as religion and philosophy. Out of such pursuits came the concept of writing and recordkeeping. Writing made possible the codification of laws and the preservation of traditions. It was a crucial element in the development of systematic administration in Mesopotamia and in the evolution of its religious-political ideology. The rulers in the cities were both priests and kings, and the harvest brought by the peasants to be stored in urban granaries was a tribute as well as a tax.

Thus ancient cities had several functions (see "Focus on: The Ancient Mesopotamian City"). As centers of power, they became the headquarters of the first state-like entities the world had seen. As religious centers, their authority was augmented by the presence of priests, temples, and shrines. Many ancient cities were ***theocratic centers*** where rulers were deemed to have divine authority and were, in effect, god-kings. Examples include the great structures of Yucatan, Guatemala, and Honduras built by the Maya Indians (including Tikal, Chichén-Itzá, Uxmal, and Copán) (Fig. 17-2). As economic centers, they were the chief markets, the bases from which wealthy merchants, land and livestock owners, and traders operated. As educational centers, their residents included teachers and philosophers. They also had handicraft industries, which attracted the best craftspeople and inventors. Therefore, ancient cities were the anchors of culture and society, the focal points of power, authority, and change.

As noted earlier, urbanization did not occur simultaneously in all culture hearths. Figure 17-3 shows that it probably occurred first in Mesopotamia and neighboring areas; in the Nile Valley the formative era came less than a millennium later. The formation of cities in China and in the Indus Valley may have occurred at about the same time. European and West African urbanization came later, and in Mesoamerica the formative era probably began during the middle of the third millennium B.P.

As the principal centers, crossroads, markets, places of authority, and religious headquarters, the earliest towns drew talent, trade, and travelers from far around. Where else would metallurgy have developed? Where would a traveler, tradesman, priest, or pilgrim rest before continuing the journey? Towns had to have facilities that would not be found in farm villages: buildings to entertain visitors, package food, process raw materials, provide a place for worship, and house those who defended the town.

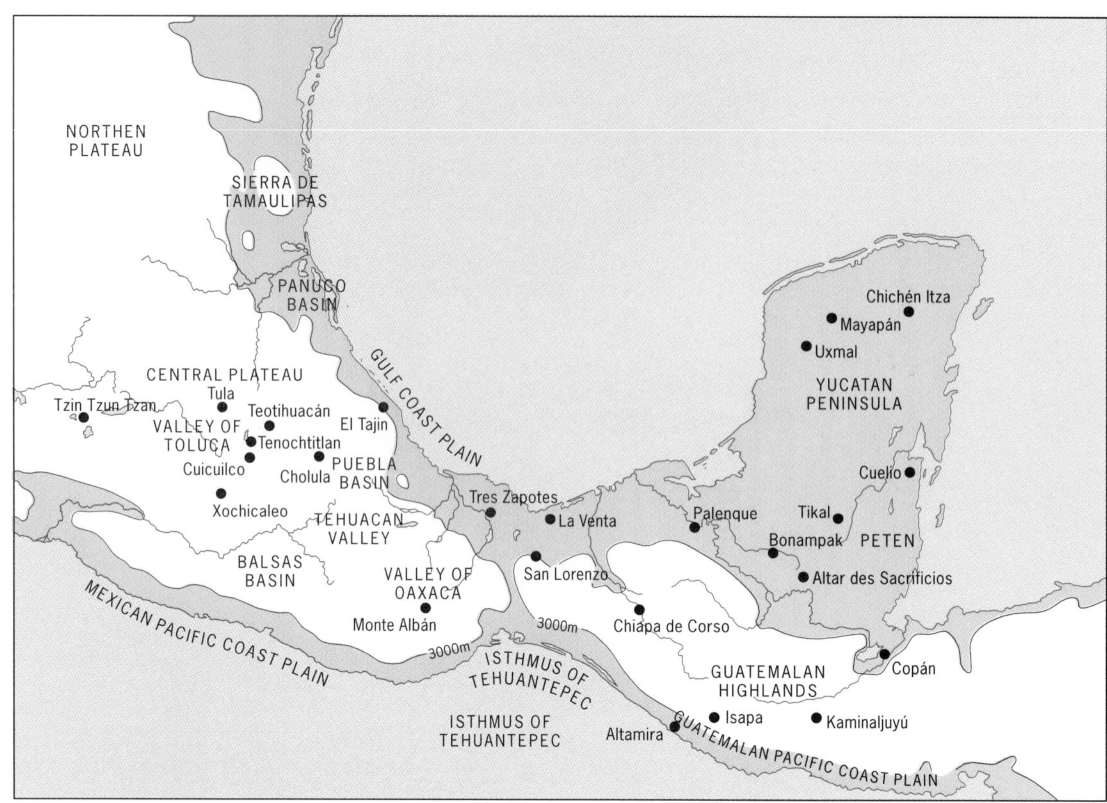

Figure 17-2 Maya and Aztec America. This map indicates early centers of culture in Maya and Aztec America.

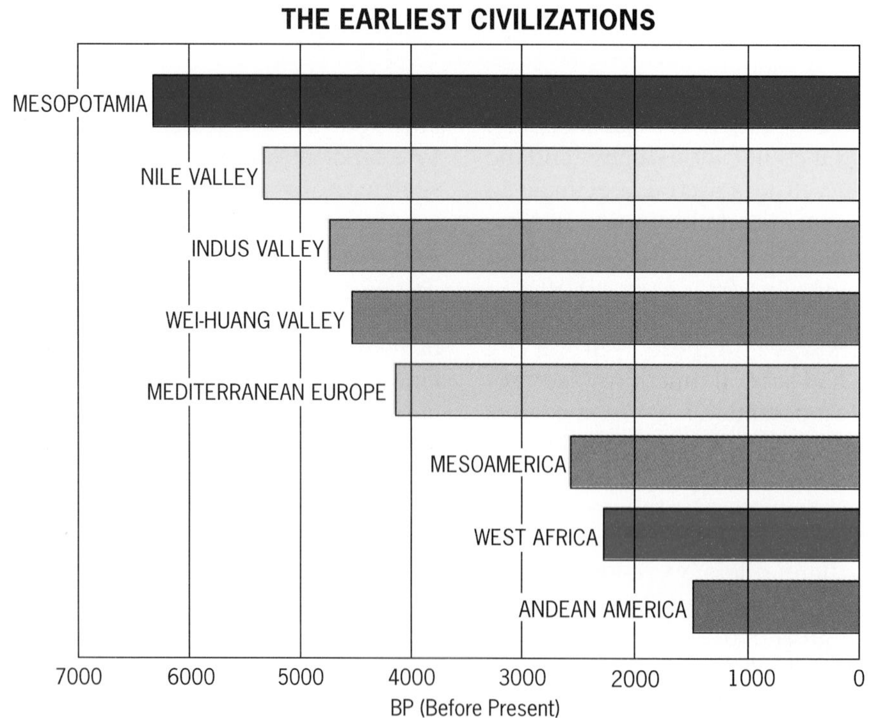

Figure 17-3 The Earliest Civilizations. Approximate dates of birth of the world's early civilizations are shown on this graph.

Focus On

The Ancient Mesopotamian City

The ancient Mesopotamian city was usually protected by an earthen wall that surrounded the entire community, or, sometimes, the cluster of temples and shrines at its center. Temples dominated the urban landscape, not only because they were the largest structures in town but also because they were built on artificial mounds often over 100 feet (30 meters) high.

Priests and other authorities resided in substantial buildings, many of which might be called palaces. Ordinary citizens lived in mud-walled houses packed closely together and separated only by narrow lanes. Facing these lanes were shops and the workplaces of craftspeople. On the outskirts of the city were the homes of the poorest inhabitants. These were little more than tiny huts, often with mud-smeared reed walls. Slaves were held in prison-like accommodations, sometimes outside the city wall.

Lacking waste-disposal or sewage facilities, ancient cities were far from sanitary. Mesopotamians threw their garbage and refuse into the streets and other open spaces, and layers of this waste accumulated to a depth of several yards. In a way this was fortunate, because archeologists have been able to sift through the garbage for clues to life in the ancient city. Not surprisingly, disease was among the reasons why the populations of ancient cities remained small.

How large were the ancient cities? We have only estimates, because it is impossible to judge from excavated ruins the dimensions of a city at its height, or the number of people who might have occupied each residential unit. By modern standards, the ancient cities were not large. The cities of Mesopotamia and the Nile Valley may have had between 10,000 and 15,000 inhabitants after nearly 2000 years of growth and development. That, scholars conclude, is about the maximum size that could have been sustained by existing systems of food gathering and distribution, and by social organization. These urban places were geographical exceptions in an overwhelmingly rural society. Urbanized societies such as those we know today did not emerge until several thousand years later.

◆ DIFFUSION TO GREECE

Urbanization spread from Mesopotamia in several directions. Whether cities emerged in the Nile Valley as a result of expansion diffusion or by independent invention is uncertain. There is no doubt, however, regarding the early development of cities on the Mediterranean island of Crete. There, more than 3500 years ago, Knossos was the cornerstone of a system of towns of the Minoan civilization. Ideas about city life therefore may have reached Greece from several directions. During the third millennium B.P., Greece became one of the most highly urbanized areas on Earth.

The urbanization of ancient Greece ushered in a new stage in the evolution of cities. By the middle of the third millennium B.P. (600 to 500 B.C.), Greece had a network of more than 500 cities and towns, not only on the mainland but also on the many Greek islands. Seafarers connected these urban places with trade routes and carried the notion of urban life throughout the Mediterranean region. Athens and Sparta, often vying with each other for power, were Greece's leading cities. Athens may have been the largest city in the world at the time, with an estimated 250,000 inhabitants.

We should remember that 2500 years ago urbanization was also occurring in several other parts of the world, including China, South Asia, and Mesoamerica. But the developments in ancient Greece had a global, not just regional, impact. Greece inherited Southwest Asian innovations. It transmitted its own urban traditions to the Roman Empire, and Roman urban culture diffused to Western Europe. From there, "Western" concepts of city life were carried around the world on the wings of colonialism and imperialism. From Washington, D.C., to Canberra, Australia, the urban landscape shows the imprints of Greco-Roman urban culture.

In hilly Greece, there was no need to build earthen mounds on which to perch temples; these were provided by nature. Every city had its ***acropolis*** (*acro* = high point; *polis* = city), upon which the most impressive structures—usually religious buildings—were built. The Parthenon of Athens remains the most famous of all, surviving to this day despite nearly 2500 years of war, earth tremors, vandalism, and environmental impact. This magnificent columned structure, designed by the Athenian architect-engineer Phidias, was begun in 447 B.C.; its rows of tapering columns have inspired architects ever since.

Like the older Southwest Asian cities, Greece's cities also had public places. In the Southwest Asian towns these seem to have been rather cramped, crowded, and bustling with activity, but in ancient Greece they were open, spacious squares, often in a low part of town with steps leading down to them. On these steps the Greeks debated, lectured, judged each other, planned military campaigns, and socialized. As time went on, the ***agora*** (meaning market) also became the focus of commercial activity.

Greece's cities also had excellent theaters, another innovation that was transmitted to the Romans. But while the aristocracy attended plays and listened to philosophical discourses, for many people life was miserable. Housing for ordinary people was no better than it had been in the Mesopotamian cities thousands of years earlier. Sanitation and health conditions were poor. And much of the grandeur designed by Greece's urban planners was built by hundreds of thousands of slaves.

From the field notes

"The rocky, hilly peninsulas of Greece provided every ancient Greek city with its *acro* (high point). We waited for the sunrise on the most famous acropolis of all, the acropolis of Athens, still crowned by the great Parthenon, still standing after nearly 25 centuries (*above*). As daylight spread across the modern city, it revealed the commanding position on which the Parthenon was built; in all directions you could see how remnants of the old stand among the urban sprawl of the present (*below*). Athens was the greatest city of ancient Greece; today it is the capital of a modern state, an unbroken urban tradition of nearly three millennia. You can't help thinking about the philosophers, scholars, artists, architects who walked these same hills and streets."

◆ THE ROMAN URBAN SYSTEM

The great majority of Greece's cities and towns were located near the Mediterranean Sea, linking peninsulas and islands. When the Romans succeeded the Greeks as rulers of the region, their empire incorporated not only the Mediterranean shores but also a large part of interior Europe and North Africa (Fig. 17-4). The Roman ***urban system*** was the largest yet. The capital, Rome, was the apex of a hierarchy of settlements ranging from small villages to large cities. A ***transport network*** linked these places by road, river, and sea. Roman regional planners displayed a remarkable capacity for identifying suitable locales for settlements. They also chose surface routes, many of which still serve European motorists today. Efficiency was a Roman hallmark: urban places were positioned a modest distance from each other so that they could be reached in a reasonable amount of time. Roman road builders created a grid of communications to link the empire together.

An urban tradition already existed on the Italian peninsula before Rome emerged. The Etruscans built cities centered on temples. These cities, which still are not well understood by researchers, served as nodes for a thriving agricultural and commercial civilization. Etruscan cities extended from present-day Tuscany into the valley of the Po River; thus, the Etruscan state occupied much of what was to become the heart of the Roman Empire. The Romans, therefore, had domestic as well as foreign traditions on which to build.

Greek imprints on the layout of Roman cities are unmistakable. The Greeks had learned to plan their colonial cities in a rectangular grid pattern (the early cities of mainland Greece were jumbled and congested). This plan was adopted by the Romans wherever surface conditions made it possible. The notion of an open market found expression in the Roman

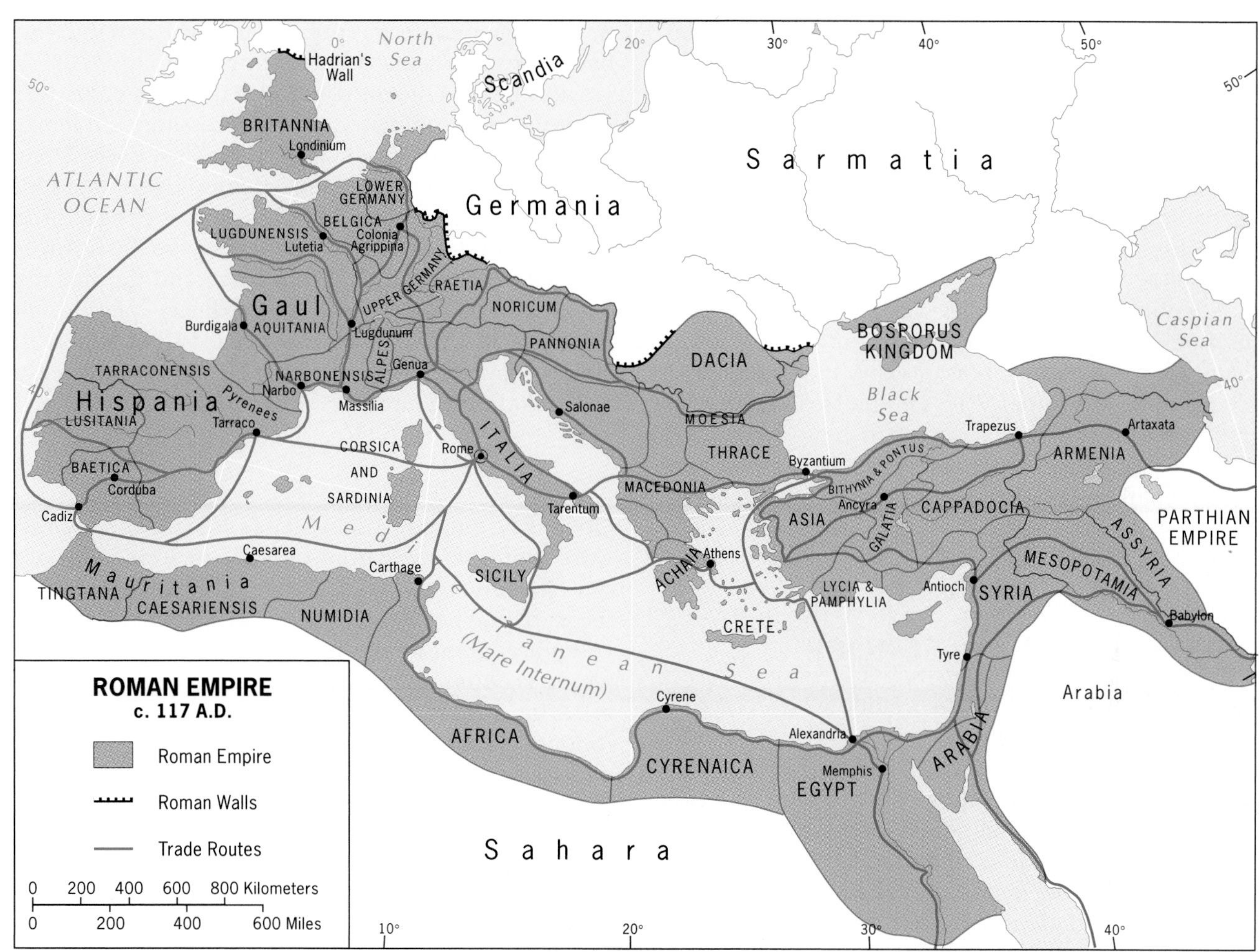

Figure 17-4 The Roman Empire, circa 117 A.D. The Romans established a system of cities linked by a network of land and sea routes. Many of the Roman cities have grown into modern metropolises.

city's *forum*, the focus of public life. The Romans expanded on the Greek theater to build the world's first great *stadium*, the Colosseum in Rome. (All Roman cities of any size had such an arena in which competitions, war games, ceremonies, and other public events took place.) Wild animals imported from Africa were killed before crowds of onlookers in the Colosseum. And after Christianity was diffused to Rome, Christians were forced into the Colosseum to be attacked and eaten by hungry lions as thousands watched.

The Roman city was a place of cultural contrasts: of monumental buildings, impressive villas, spacious avenues, ingenious aqueducts and baths, and sewage systems built of stone and pipe. But the Roman city also was home to the most wretchedly poor, who were crammed into overcrowded tenements. Even worse off were the slaves, many from North Africa. The Roman city, like the city of today, was home to both rich and poor and reflected both the greatest achievements and the worst failings of Roman civilization.

The Post–Roman Decline

The collapse of the Roman Empire was accompanied by the disintegration of its urban system and the decay of many of its cities. The causes underlying the empire's failure include misrule, corruption, and environmental degradation. Trade and transport networks broke down, the social order fell apart, and once-vibrant cities went to ruin. Between about A.D. 500 and 1000, little was left of the urban tradition Rome had bequeathed to its empire. The weakness of the now-fragmented empire was evident in the invasion of Iberia by the armies of the Moorish Empire of North Africa, which brought order, new architectural and scientific ideas, and Islam into what had been one of Rome's principal provinces.

Urban Growth Elsewhere

Elsewhere in the world, however, the growth of cities was proceeding vigorously. China's urban system was developing rapidly, and Xian was known as the Rome of East Asia. In West Africa, trading cities were developing along the southern margin of the Sahara. By 1350, Timbuktu was a major city—a seat of government, a university town, a market, and a religious center. In the upper valley of the Nile River, Meroë was a leading center of metallurgy, specializing in the smelting of iron and the manufacture of weapons. Trade routes from a wide region focused on this populous city.

Significant urban growth was also taking place in the Americas. In the Maya civilization of the Yucatan Peninsula and adjacent areas (Mexico and Guatemala), urbanization was under way. On the Mexican Plateau to the northwest, even larger urban centers emerged. Mexico's largest pre-Columbian city, the Aztec capital of Tenochtitlán, may have had more than 100,000 inhabitants and was growing vigorously while many European cities lay in ruins.

◆ PREINDUSTRIAL EUROPE

The Roman-European urban traditions were weakened, but they were not extinguished. The Muslim invasion helped galvanize Europeans into action; the invaders were halted as they were about to enter southern Italy after penetrating southern France and Sicily, and the Christian counterthrust began. Soon the Crusades carried the battle to the heartland of Islamic power, and old trade routes were reopened.

In the cities the pulse of commerce picked up, there was work to be had, and population growth resumed. Paris, Amsterdam, Antwerp, Lisbon, Venice, Naples, and many other cities and towns revived. It is important to remember that these cities were still small by today's standards. By the middle of the fifteenth century, London had perhaps 80,000 inhabitants and Paris had 120,000. Around the beginning of the nineteenth century, while riches poured into Europe from the colonies, London still had fewer than 1 million residents and Paris only 670,000.

Urban Environments

What were the preindustrial cities like as places to live and work? Well, the adage of the "good old days" hardly applies. If today's cities are no bargain for many of their residents, neither were preindustrial Ghent or Warsaw. With more efficient weapons and the invention of gunpowder, cities faced threats that they had not confronted before. Walls and moats could no longer withstand armies, so cities developed more extensive fortifications at a time when they were also required to accommodate growing numbers of people. Once built, the new fortifications could not simply be moved outward. The only way to house greater numbers of people was to build upward, and four- and five-story tenements began to appear.

By the seventeenth century European cities were slum-ridden, unsanitary, and depressing. Epidemics, fires, crime, and social dislocation prevailed. Picturesque four-story merchants' homes overlooked the sparkling canals of Amsterdam and the lush green parks of London, but their residents were the fortunate few who controlled the labor force and the lucrative overseas commerce. For the ordinary people, the overcrowded cities were no place to be. When the chance came, many decided to leave for America, Australia, and other parts of the world.

Models of Urban Places

Obviously, preindustrial cities in Renaissance Europe were quite different from preindustrial cities in India or China, and the cities of Roman Europe differed from those of medieval times. Scholars have tried to develop a general model of preindustrial urbanism that would account for the different characteristics of cities at various times in history and in different societies. Among the most effective models was that proposed by Gideon Sjoberg in *The Preindustrial City: Past and Present* (1960). Sjoberg argued that cities should be viewed as products of their societies and, as such, could be divided into four categories: (1) ***folk-preliterate***; (2) ***feudal***; (3) ***preindustrial***; and (4) ***urban-industrial***.

Cities can be placed on a continuum reflecting the nature of their societies at each stage of their development. Thus during feudal times a European city was little more than a town, its houses modest and its streets unpaved. The landlords' estates and the monasteries were more imposing. The medieval revival brought the first stage in the rise of the preindustrial European city. The consolidation of political power and the expansion of states were reflected in the growth of the cities, now the focal points of a new order. Architecture and the arts, as well as commerce and trade, moved forward, but the dominant aspect of the preindustrial city, as we saw earlier, was the imposing complex of religious and governmental structures at its heart. Much later, when Europe entered its urban-industrial age, the high-rise buildings of financial and commercial organization took over the dominant position in the urban cores.

Primate Cities

Focusing on the preindustrial city around the world, Sjoberg suggested that prior to the industrial age almost all cities shared certain basic characteristics. Whether in medieval Europe, West Africa, East Asia, the Islamic culture realm, or the Americas, preindus-

The "Law" of the Primate City

Great cities have always reflected regional cultures. In 1939, geographer Mark Jefferson published an article, "The Law of the Primate City," in which he described the dominant city much as Sjoberg did later—as a place that reflects the culture of its region. The "law" states that "a country's leading city is always disproportionately large and exceptionally expressive of national capacity and feeling." It refers, obviously, to cities representing national cultures of modern times, but the notion can be extended to earlier periods. As Sjoberg stated, cities of preindustrial, feudal, and preliterate societies were also products as well as reflections of their cultures.

Although Jefferson's notion is rather imprecise, it is supported by numerous cases, past and present: Kyoto as the primate city reflecting old Japan, and Tokyo of the new; Paris as the reflection of France; and London, where the culture and history of a nation and empire are deeply etched in the urban landscape. In Europe, such cities as Athens, Lisbon, Prague, and Amsterdam may no longer be disproportionately large, but they remain exceptionally expressive of the cultures they represent. Beijing in China, Lahore in Pakistan, Ibadan in Nigeria, and Mexico City are other examples of primate cities—in some cases, no longer the largest in their region, yet still representative of its culture. Jefferson's generalization, like Sjoberg's, might be adapted to conform to stages in a culture's growth. Thus Beijing is the primate city of the old China, Shanghai (now China's largest) of the new; Rio de Janeiro reflects Brazil's historic evolution, whereas São Paulo represents the vigor of modern Brazilian society.

Today, the primate city also exists in three general types of countries: (1) those with dominantly agriculture-based economies, such as Bangladesh, Indonesia, and Ethiopia; (2) those with a recent history of colonial rule, including Kenya, Zimbabwe, and Senegal; and (3) poor countries with a more distant colonial past such as Sri Lanka, Liberia, and Nicaragua. In many of these cases, only part of Jefferson's thesis is fulfilled: the cities are disproportionately large, but they do not necessarily express "national capacity and feeling" because of past foreign influence.

trial cities were similar in form, function, and atmosphere. Sjoberg recognized the emergence of what geographers refer to as the ***primate city*** (see "Focus on: The 'Law' of the Primate City") that expressed the culture and ideology of its society. Primate cities were not large by modern standards, but they were certainly dominant, their influence underscored by the cluster of religious or governmental buildings at their center and by their spaciousness and wealth. Close identification with the center of influence and power was valued, so the wealthy and powerful had homes near the center of the city. The center may also have been viewed as desirable because of its comparative safety. Toward the outskirts, and sometimes even beyond the city's walls, lived the less privileged, the poor and the misfits.

These generalizations about preindustrial cities are open to debate. Not all preindustrial cities were structured as Sjoberg suggested. In Muslim cities, with their impressive central mosques, the surrounding housing is less variable than in Europe's preindustrial cities, and commerce and crafts are concentrated within a bazaar that is without an equivalent in European cities. In the theocratic states of Middle America, the city centers, with their great temples, served as ceremonial sites where thousands of people were present during rituals, but at other times they were vacant. In Africa, no religious or governmental structures dominated the townscape the way they did in preindustrial European or Muslim cities. Nevertheless, Sjoberg's thesis provides a useful basis for comparison.

Another viewpoint holds that the term *preindustrial* is inaccurate because so-called preindustrial cities of various historic periods (Roman, medieval European) and in various realms (Africa, South Asia, China) were so different in form that they cannot be grouped together. For example, "preindustrial" cities did have industries. These were not modern manufacturing industries, but they were industries nonetheless. In the urban places of Japan and India, for example, there was much handicraft industry. Thus the preindustrial city's character *was* shaped by activities of an industrial type. The industries were small, but they often were quite numerous. Some geographers, therefore, avoid the adjective "preindustrial" entirely; others use it only in referring to the Western city before the Industrial Revolution.

◆ THE MODERN WESTERN CITY

To reconstruct the form and features of Europe's preindustrial cities, historical geographers have used old maps, personal diaries, even paintings of the time. In Flanders and northern Italy, medieval urbanism reached its highest form, and the cities in these regions were quite advanced for the period. But in most cases the *medieval city* was a bleak, often grimy place with few wide streets and many narrow alleys. The tallest building was usually the church with its tower; there was no dominant downtown area. Each major neighborhood had its cluster of economic activity in the form of workshops, stores, and a market. Most streets were unpaved; sanitary conditions were poor.

Certain areas of the city fared better than others. In the ***mercantile city***, the colonial era brought a revival and sometimes prosperity. Successful merchants built ornate mansions and patronized the arts. A central square became the focus of the city, flanked by royal, religious, public, and private buildings; streets leading to such squares formed the beginnings of a downtown.

During the sixteenth and seventeenth centuries, mercantile cities such as Amsterdam, Antwerp, Copenhagen, London, Lisbon, and others became the nodes of a global network of regional, national, and international commerce. The power of trading companies and wealthy merchants was so great that they were able to establish settlements in distant lands. The earliest colonial cities in North America were products of this period, as were Dakar, Cape Town, and Lourenço Marques (now Maputo) in Africa, Madras (now Chennai) and Hong Kong in Asia, and many other settlements, most of them coastal.

Therefore, when the impacts of the Industrial Revolution began to be felt during the last quarter of the eighteenth century, many European cities were already undergoing a revival. But none was prepared for what lay ahead: an avalanche of changes that ripped the fabric of urban life. Cities had to adapt to the mushrooming of factories and supply facilities, the expansion of transport systems, and the construction of tenements for the growing labor force. They bulged—and sometimes broke—at the seams. The ***manufacturing city*** now emerged, first in the British Midlands and soon in Western Europe. Some European cities, such as Paris and Amsterdam, managed to retain the character of their historic centers, but many others were totally or partially destroyed. Cities became unregulated jumbles of activity. Private homes were engulfed by factories. Open spaces became refuse dumps. Elegant housing was converted into overcrowded slums. Ugly railroad tracks knifed through long-stable neighborhoods. Sanitation systems failed, and water supplies were inadequate and often polluted.

And yet, people migrated to the manufacturing cities, not only in Europe but wherever factory towns emerged. Living conditions were dreadful for the workers, and working conditions were shocking. Children worked 12-hour shifts in textile mills. Health con-

From the field notes

"From the Eiffel Tower, one can see why Paris is one of the world's best-defined primate cities. The historic old city contains numerous military, political, and religious icons. Several of these can be seen on this photograph, notably the Arc de Triomphe rising above the townscape."

ditions were worse than they had been in medieval times; the air was polluted and the water contaminated. The grimy, soot-covered cities of the English Midlands were appropriately called the "black towns."

In time, conditions in the European manufacturing city improved as a result of government intervention, legislation, the introduction of city planning and zoning, and the recognition of workers' rights. Many manufacturing cities in the New World never suffered as much as their European predecessors, although living and working conditions for factory workers (and "blue-collar" workers generally) were far from satisfactory. During the late nineteenth and early twentieth centuries, the American manufacturing city still shared some of the characteristics of its European forerunners.

The modernization of the American manufacturing city occurred in the late nineteenth century and resulted from innovation in transportation. The introduction of the electric trolley transformed the geographical pattern of cities. In a chapter titled "Geography and Human Mobility: The Perpetual Revolution in Transportation" (1988), James Vance states that the trolley brought "public mass transit to the edge of the built-up city, and, importantly, for the first time the transit system was circumferential as well as radial in its pattern. It became possible to work in factories in the older industrial satellites embedded within the suburban band, to shop in the central business district, and to patronize clusters of shops sited at the junction points where several trolley lines converged." The suburbanization of the ***modern city*** had begun, soon to be augmented by what Vance calls the "revolution of the 1920s," the introduction of the affordable automobile.

The modern city of the twentieth century is the city as we know it in the United States: a sprawling, expanding urban region with many parts and functions, from downtown to suburb, from shopping mall to business park. It is a reflection of an entrepreneurial culture, a showplace of technology. But the modern city has not stabilized. Some urban geographers see what is often referred to as ***postmodernism*** in the cities of technologically advanced societies. We now turn, therefore, to the structuring and spacing of urban centers on the eve of the twenty-first century.

◆ KEY TERMS ◆

acropolis
agora
egalitarian society
feudal city
folk-preliterate city
formative era
manufacturing city
mercantile city
modern city
postmodernism
preindustrial city
primate city
state
stratified society
theocratic center
transport network
urban elite
urban-industrial city
urban system

◆ APPLYING GEOGRAPHIC KNOWLEDGE ◆

1. Since the onset of the Industrial Revolution, cities have grown and urbanized areas have expanded almost continuously, their populations today reaching unprecedented numbers—even in countries whose populations remain mostly agricultural. Is this growth phase a continuation of preindustrial trends, or have cities undergone periods of growth and subsequent decline in the past? How do you view the demographic and economic prospects of today's megacities in the future?

2. A number of governments today are repositioning their capital cities away from the very primate cities that embody the national culture, or have done so during the twentieth century (Brazil, Australia, Nigeria, Malaysia, and others). What cultural-geographic considerations might motivate a government to take this action?

Chapter 18

Urbanization and Location

From the field notes

"I took the elevator to the top of the tallest building in sight to get a sense of the dimensions of what was the fastest-growing city in the world: Shenzhen, China. Just a fishing village one generation earlier, Shenzhen is now a city with about 3 million inhabitants, and still expanding. Geographic location boosted Shenzhen's fortunes. It lies right across the border from Hong Kong, and when the Chinese government established a Special Economic Zone (SEZ) here, business and industry mushroomed. Hundreds of industries moved from Hong Kong to Shenzhen, attracted by lower labor costs; many foreign corporations set up factories and outlets in Shenzhen. Hundreds of thousands of workers moved to the SEZ. Everything you see in this photograph is less than 20 years old; all of it stands where duck ponds and paddies lay less than three decades ago. As my Chinese colleague said as we surveyed this scene, Shenzhen has three great advantages: location, location, and location."

KEY POINTS

◆ **An urban center's location strongly influences its fortunes. Its position in a large and productive hinterland can ensure its well-being.**

◆ **An urban center's site may have played a key role in its origin and early survival, for example, as a defensive locale; but in modern times that same site may limit its growth and expansion.**

◆ **As a percentage of total population, urban dwellers are most numerous in Western Europe, North America, Japan, and Australia. However, urbanization is occurring rapidly elsewhere, especially in Subsaharan Africa.**

◆ **Several of the world's great urban complexes, notably in eastern North America, Western Europe, and Japan, are the products of megalopolitan coalescence. The fastest-growing megacities, however, are in South and East Asia.**

◆ **Despite wretched living conditions for many of their inhabitants, cities continue to attract new residents by the millions.**

When the medieval and mercantile cities of Europe were torn by the forces of the Industrial Revolution, a new map was in the making. For all its famous cities, Europe's population around 1800 was overwhelmingly rural. Less than two centuries later, Western Europe is about 85 percent urban. This astonishing transformation was the beginning of a worldwide process set in motion by colonialism and the diffusion of industrial know-how.

The growth of ***urbanization*** in Western Europe and in the world as a whole is charted in Figure 18-1. The increase in urbanization in Western Europe (Fig. 18-1A) shows that as recently as 1950, only slightly more than 50 percent of Western Europeans lived in cities and towns with 5000 inhabitants or more. Urbanization has raced ahead there during the past half-century.

By some measures, Western Europe is even more highly urbanized than Figure 18-1A suggests. As noted in Chapter 15, various countries use different criteria for defining urban residents. Some regard almost any clustered settlement, even a village of a few hundred people, as urbanized. Others put the limit higher. Still others use employment as the chief criterion. Since the criteria vary, so do the resulting statistics. Figure 18-1A uses the limit of 5000, which gives a regional estimate of urbanization of about 75 percent. But this is arbitrary. By other calculations, urbanization in Western Europe exceeds 85 percent.

The same caveat applies to Figure 18-1B, which shows the growth of urbanization worldwide. As we noted in Chapter 17, the world has just reached the level Western Europe did 50 years ago: one in two world citizens now lives in an urban setting.

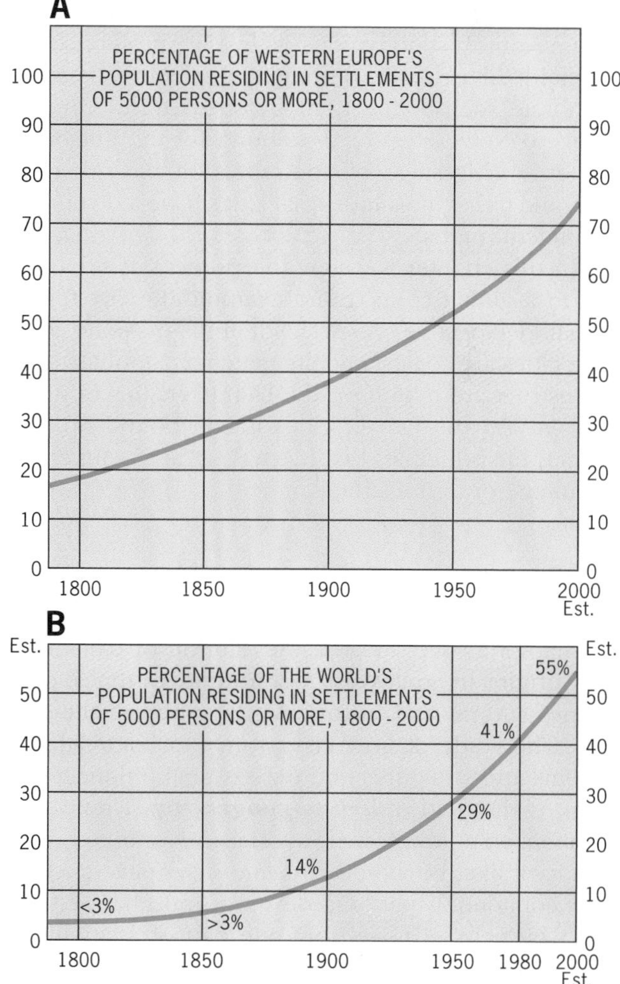

Figure 18-1 Percentage of Population Residing in Settlements of 5000 + Persons. Data on urbanization vary by country; the level of 5000 residents for a settlement to qualify as urban is arbitrary.

In Britain and mainland Europe, industrialization brought far-reaching change to cities, but not all cities were affected in the same way. Relative location played a major role. Some cities were favorably located with respect to resources and other essentials, and had an advantage. Others could not keep pace; some even declined under the withering competition industrialization brought.

In the growing manufacturing cities, raw materials were consumed at enormous rates, and products poured forth from the factories in ever greater quantities. Industrialists found that there was an advantage in sharing the services of raw-material suppliers, transporters, builders, glassmakers, and other businesses, and these businesses found ready markets for their products. Cities grew by ***agglomeration***, the spatial process of clustering by commercial enterprises for mutual advantage and benefit.

The industrial cities also went through a phase of ***specialization***. In some cities, certain industries grew to dominate the manufacturing sector to such a degree that their products and the names of the cities became almost synonymous, as in Manchester textiles, Sheffield silver, and Birmingham steel. (We commemorate such connections by speaking of carrying "coals to Newcastle" or by rooting for the Pittsburgh Steelers.) This stage of specialization passed, however, and today most industrial cities have a diversified manufacturing base.

In this chapter we view the process of urbanization in a global context and examine the city from a spatial perspective. As we will find, in some areas large cities are coalescing into giant metropolitan complexes that are taking on the characteristics of urban regions. Yet the fate of cities is still bound up with geographic principles that place them at a competitive advantage or disadvantage.

◆ URBAN GEOGRAPHY

In Chapter 17 we traced the evolution of cities from their origins in Southwest Asia to modern times, combining cultural and historical geography in the process. The study of how cities function, their internal systems and structures and the external influences on them, is the field of ***urban geography***. Urban geographers want to know how cities are arranged, what they look like, how their circulation systems function, how commuting patterns develop and change, how and why people move from one part of a city to another. What is it that attracts millions of people to cities every year, even while millions of others "escape" from the city to the suburbs?

Cities, too, display spatial variation; that is, they possess internal regional contrasts. Urban regions (such as the "downtown" or the "inner city") can be better understood if they are clearly delineated. Urban geographers therefore conduct detailed studies of economic, cultural, political, and other aspects of cities. Such studies show that the layout of Western cities contrasts quite sharply with that of many East Asian, African, or South American cities. In later chapters we focus on these contrasts.

◆ RANKING URBAN CENTERS

Before proceeding, we should deal with a problem of terminology. Terms such as "city," "town," "village," and even "urban" do not have consistent, universally accepted meanings. Inconsistent use of these terms can lead to confusion and invalid comparisons.

Take, for example, the term *urban*. Earlier we compared the dispersed settlements of rural areas to clustered urban settlements. If clustering is the hallmark of urbanization, even a hamlet is an urban settlement, although it may contain only 100 residents. But at what point does a hamlet become a village, a village a town, and a town a city?

One way to approach this question is to use the notion of ***urban hierarchy*** and consider the *functions* of clustered settlements in addition to their size. Take the case of the hamlet. If a hamlet is a group of farmers' dwellings, it offers no services, such as a gas station, general store, or coffee shop—in short, it has no ***urban function***. But if a hamlet provides some basic services for the people living there and for some of those living nearby, it is an urban place on the bottom step of the urban hierarchy.

A village, the next larger urban settlement, is likely to offer several dozen services. The key here is specialization. Stores sell certain goods; gas stations sell competing brands. As an urban center, the village serves a larger area and more people than a hamlet.

A town is not merely larger than a village; its functions reveal a higher level of specialization. Bank and postal services, medical services, educational institutions (school, library), and stores selling such goods as furniture, appliances, and hardware are among the functions of towns. Rather than relying solely on population size, we define a town as a place where a certain assemblage of goods and services is available, with a ***hinterland*** (surrounding service area) that includes smaller villages and hamlets. The hinterland reveals the *economic reach* of each settlement, the maximum distance from the town or village at which people are still attracted to it for business purposes. A settlement's functions as well as its economic reach produce a measure of its *centrality*, its economic power relative to that of competitors.

The city is next in the urban hierarchy. Not only does a city have more functional specialization than a town, but it has a larger hinterland and greater centrality. To distinguish between town and city, we also should look at the urban layout. A city has a well-defined commercial center, a so-called *central business district* (CBD). A town may have outskirts, but a city has *suburbs*—subsidiary urban areas surrounding and connected to the central city. Many suburbs are exclusively residential, but others have their own commercial centers or shopping malls.

Urban areas that are larger than cities have various names. The term *metropolis* is sometimes used, and in television weather forecasts you may hear the term *metropolitan area*. In many parts of the world, large metropolises are coalescing to create megacities called ***megalopolises***. One such megalopolis stretches along the U.S. East Coast from Boston to beyond Washington, D.C.—this is the so-called Bosnywash megalopolis. Obviously, its economic reach is not just regional but global.

◆ PLACE AND LOCATION

In Guangdong, a province in southern China, there is a city named Shenzhen. Less than three decades ago, Shenzhen was a fishing village with perhaps 20,000 inhabitants and few services. Thatch houses and duck ponds marked the distinctly nonurban scene. Today, Shenzhen has a population of 3.1 million and is the world's fastest-growing urban area (Fig. 18-2). The thatch houses are long gone; skyscrapers tower over the townscape.

Urban Situation

What has propelled Shenzhen to megacity status? The answer is geography. Shenzhen happens to lie next to one of the world's most successful economic centers,

Figure 18-2 Xianggang–Shenzhen. Shenzhen, China's most successful Special Economic Zone, lies adjacent to Xianggang (Hong Kong), one of the economic "tigers" of the Pacific Rim. This proximity has propelled Shenzhen's SEZ ahead of all others. *Source: From a map in H. J. de Blij and P. O. Muller,* Geography: Realms, Regions, and Concepts, *8th ed. New York: Wiley, 1997).*

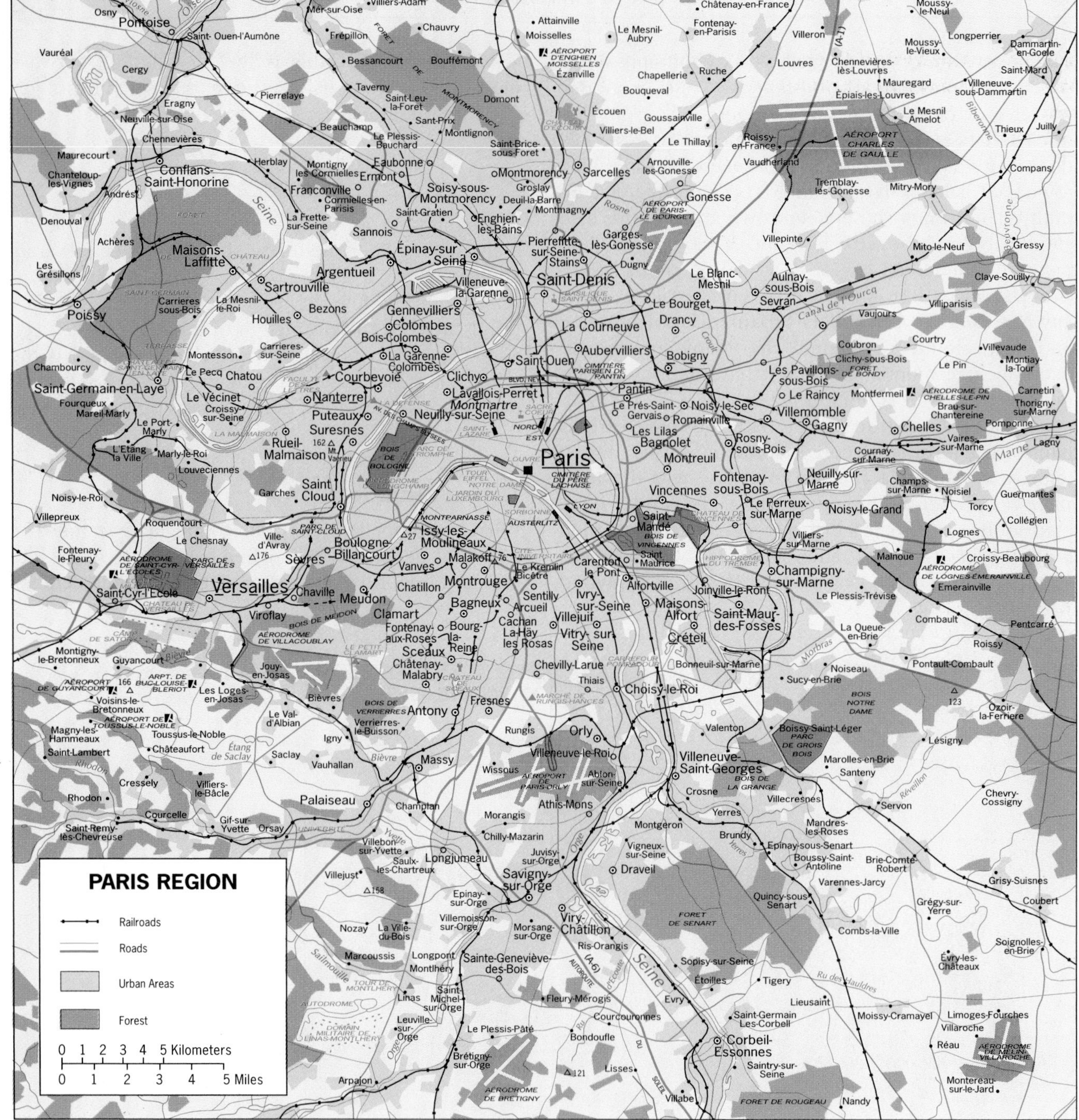

Figure 18-3 Paris Region. *Source: From a map drawn for H. J. de Blij and P. O. Muller*, Geography: Regions and Concepts, *2nd ed. New York: Wiley, 1978.*

Hong Kong. Shenzhen's relative location—its ***situation***, as urban geographers call it—has enabled it to benefit immensely from commerce and trade, and rapid growth has ensued.

When it comes to explaining the growth and success of certain cities, situation often is the key. A city's situation describes its position relative to much-traveled transport routes, productive farmlands, manufacturing complexes, other towns and cities—in short, its near and distant surroundings. Indeed, the size, growth, and character of a city are reflections of its situation.

A city's situation can change. The world's largest and most enduring cities have seen their situation improve with the times. In Paris, for example, settlement may have begun in pre-Roman times, long before the Seine River became a major transport route and before the Seine Basin became one of Europe's most productive areas. Over time the city's situational advantage grew. As its hinterland prospered, so did the city. Paris became increasingly multifunctional—a religious center, a crucible of culture, a political capital, an industrial giant, a focus of high technology. Centrally situated not only in relation to the prosperous Seine Basin but also in relation to the country as a whole, Paris eclipsed every other city in France. Today, with a population of 10 million, it is a ***megacity***, a vast metropolitan area (Fig. 18-3). The next largest city in France, Lyon, is only one-seventh the size of Paris.

Closer to home, we can observe the effect of a long-term favorable situation on the growth of the Chicago urban area. Chicago lies at the landward end of the Great Lakes waterway, where it meets the water routes of the Mississippi system; it lies where the western end of the country's largest manufacturing belt yields to the vast farmlands of one of the world's most productive agricultural zones; it is situated at an ideal location for the convergence of rail, road, and air routes; and it has major natural resources in its vast and populous hinterland. Chicago has long been the dominant city of the North American interior, a place with unparalleled situational advantages.

A city's situation can also deteriorate over time. When parts of the U.S. northeastern manufacturing belt began to decline, the downturn was reflected in many cities and towns. Exhaustion of resources, repeated crop failure, climatic change, and political developments all can change a city's situation. Berlin suffered severely not only from its destruction during World War II but also from the subsequent division of Germany, which deprived the city of much of its hinterland. At a different level of scale, note what happens to the busy commercial center of a small town when a new expressway bypasses it. Gas stations, restaurants, and other services feel the effects as traffic through the town decreases.

Urban Site

A second locational factor affecting the development of cities and towns is their ***site***. This term refers to the actual physical qualities of the place a city occupies: whether it lies in a confining valley, on a coastal plain, on the edge of a plateau, or perhaps on an island. It was site, not situation, that led to the founding of Paris. The first settlement was built on an island in the middle of the Seine River, where security and easy defense were available, where the river could be easily crossed—and the cross traffic controlled. This island, *Île de la Cité*, soon proved to be too small, and Paris spread onto both banks of the Seine (Fig. 18-4).

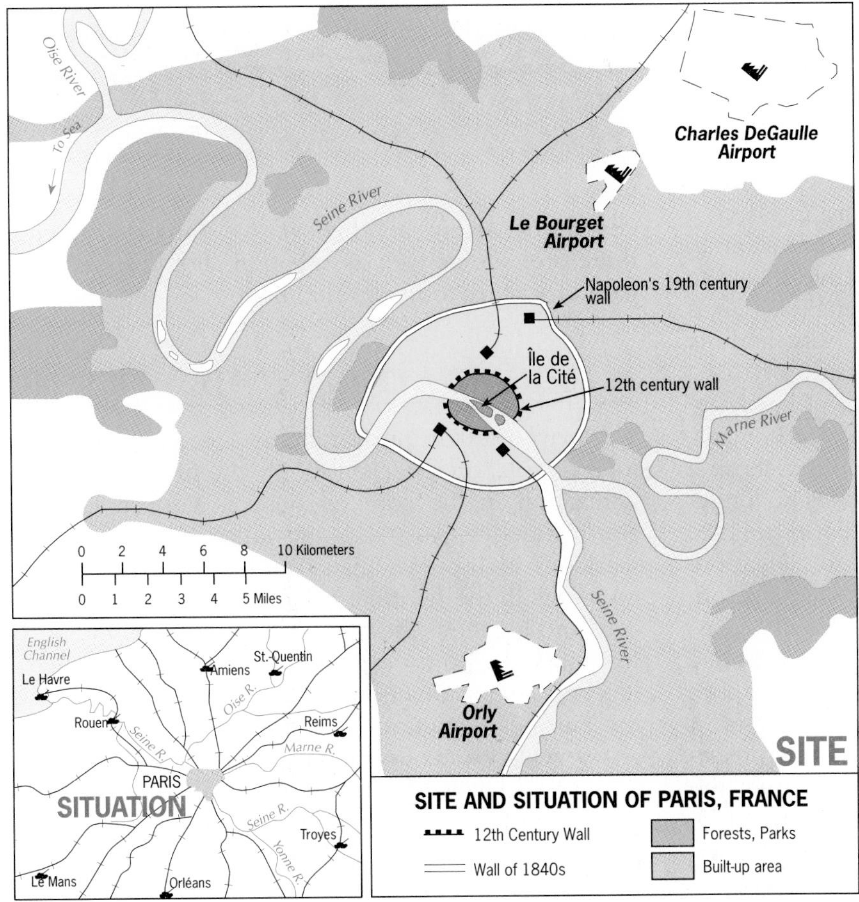

Figure 18-4 Site and Situation of Paris, France. The Île de la Cité was—and remains—at the heart of Paris.

Paris was fortunate: no physical obstacles stood in the way of the city's expansion. Other cities have seen their growth stunted by site problems of various kinds or have experienced environmental deterioration resulting in part from site factors. The world's second largest urban area, Mexico City, lies in a mountain-flanked basin at an elevation of more than 2100 m (7000 ft). Underlain by the now-dry bed of a former lake, the city is vulnerable to earthquakes, is chronically short of water, cannot dispose of its wastes effectively, and has smog-choked air. Once one of the most gracious and attractive cities in the Americas, with magnificent public and private buildings and tree-lined avenues, Mexico City today is a noisy, crowded, traffic-congested central city dominated by high-rises and encircled by about 500 slums, beyond which lies a ring consisting of some of the most squalid squatter camps in the world. It is probably true that no physical site could have accommodated Mexico City's rapid growth (the city receives about 1000 immigrants each day to add to a natural increase of about the same number, creating an annual total growth of about 750,000 inhabitants). But Mexico City's site has greatly complicated an already difficult set of urban problems.

Other fast-growing cities in developing countries confront site problems of various kinds. Bangkok (10 million), the capital of Thailand, lies on the delta of the Chao Phraya, the major river in this part of the country. Fresh water is provided by numerous wells. But the pumping of water from the wells has contributed to a serious site problem: southern Bangkok is sinking into the Gulf of Thailand at a rate of more than 2 cm (nearly 1 in.) per year. Already the city is honeycombed by countless canals that form, in effect, a second network of streets. Millions of people stand to lose their homes if the subsidence continues. Add to this the fact that on an average day Bangkok's air is even more polluted than that of Mexico City, and the enormity of the problem comes into focus.

The role of site in the development of cities obviously has changed over time. The ancient Romans, who founded many of Europe's cities, often chose a site that was easy to defend; that function is no longer relevant. A city's site can still play a role in political struggles, however. Geographers often use Singapore to illustrate the advantages of a favorable situation; Singapore's situational advantages helped it emerge as one of the successful "economic tigers" on the Pacific Rim. But in 1965, when Chinese-dominated Singapore opted to secede from Malay-dominated Malaysia, it was Singapore's site that helped make this step feasible. Singapore lies on an island separated from the Malaysian mainland by the Johore Strait (Fig. 18-5). That clear site definition created geographic identity; without it, Singapore probably would not have seceded from Malaysia. Whenever we study a major city, therefore, site as well as situation should be investigated for clues to its development.

From the field notes

"Although many miles of Bangkok's canals (*khlongs*) have been drained and replaced by roads, a large part of the right bank of the Chao Phraya, the city's major river, still is honeycombed by waterways. And on the left bank, a network remains for use by "river taxis." I asked the driver of my boat to go slowly so that I could map the many waterfront businesses along the *khlongs*; they ranged from laundries to grocery stores, the latter often displaying a wide range of goods, here including one with a familiar logo. But the site of canal-riddled Bangkok is presenting serious problems: it is sinking relative to sea level, and the sea is not far away. Already, many waterfront structures show signs of flooding and deterioration. The future of the "Venice of Southeast Asia" is in doubt."

◆ URBANIZATION IN THE 1990S

The map of urban population as a percentage of the total population reveals not only the high level of urbanization in the core regions of Western Europe, North America, Australia, and Japan but also the remarkably high percentages of urbanization in several countries in the periphery (Fig. 18-6). Taking 70 percent and higher as the highest category, we find Mexico and Cuba on a par with France. In fact, Mexico's level of urbanization is higher than that of several Eastern European countries.

Seventy years of communist rule and industrialization raised levels of urbanization throughout most of the former Soviet Union. Today Russia's population is 73 percent urbanized; in Ukraine the figure is just below 70 percent. In Transcaucasia urbanization exceeds

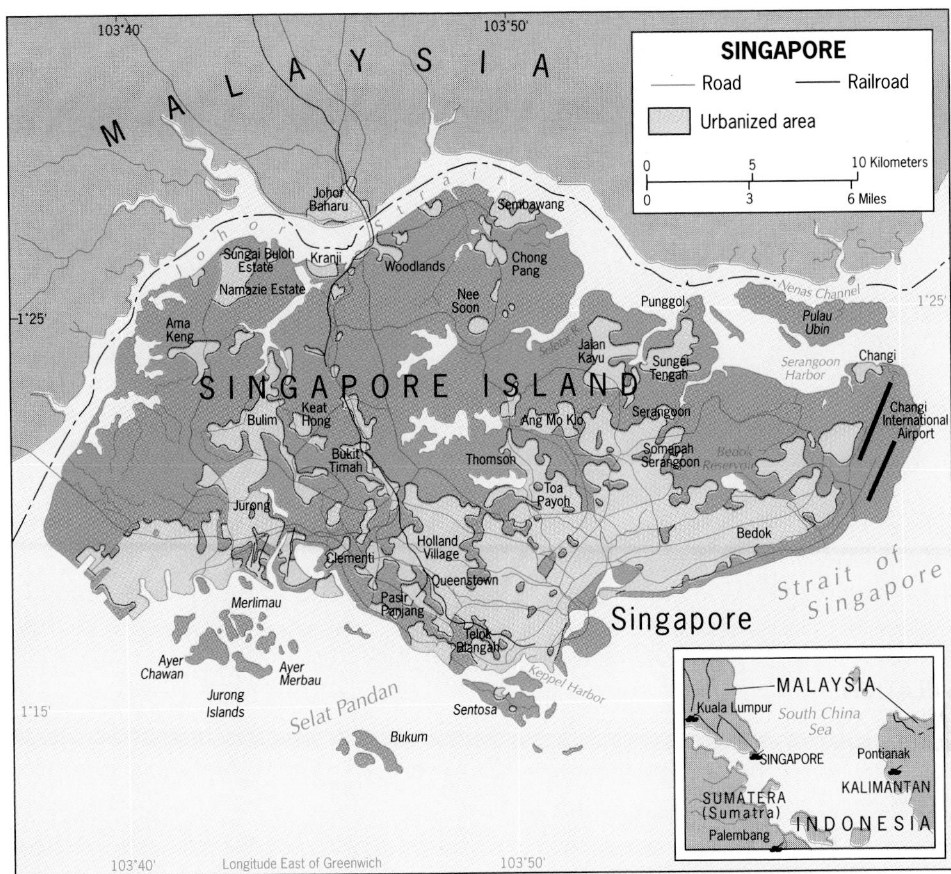

Figure 18-5 Singapore. Singapore's physiographic separation from the Malayan Peninsula facilitated its secession from the Malaysian Federation. The city-state's relative location (inset) helped boost its economy. *Source: From a map in H. J. de Blij and P. O. Muller*, Geography: Realms, Regions, and Concepts, *8th ed. New York: Wiley, 1997.*

55 percent, although Armenia is well ahead of Georgia and Azerbaijan. The former Soviet colonial domain in Central Asia is the least urbanized of the former Soviet realms, ranging from 56 percent in strongly Russified Kazakhstan to a mere 28 percent in remote and poorer Tajikistan.

The progress of urbanization in South America is also obvious from the map. Not only are the three countries of the South American "cone" (Argentina, Chile, and Uruguay) highly urbanized, but Brazil and Venezuela also rank high. In the late 1990s only the landlocked countries (Paraguay and Bolivia) lagged well behind their neighbors, but the lowest levels of urbanization were reported by the three countries on the north coast, Guyana, Suriname, and French Guiana. These "three Guianas" with their Caribbean (and otherwise non-Iberian) cultural characteristics stand apart from the rest of South America in other geographic ways as well.

In the late 1990s the Subsaharan African geographic realm included countries with some of the world's lowest levels of urbanization. Nigeria was just 16 percent urban in 1997. Even lower percentages were reported by Ethiopia, Rwanda, Burundi, and Uganda. In tropical Africa, only a few countries were more than 40 percent urban. South Africa had a level of urbanization of 57 percent, but that figure should be seen in light of that country's strong regional diversity. The mining-industrial heartland is highly urbanized, approaching Western European levels, but beyond this core area the country is predominantly rural and resembles tropical Africa.

The culturally and economically diverse realm of Southwest Asia and North Africa displays remarkable variation in levels of urbanization. This variation is related to differences in national economies and cultures. Much of the realm, the Middle East and the Arabian Peninsula, is quite highly urbanized. ***Nucleation*** resulting from the oil industry has much to do with this situation, although this does not explain the urbanization of Jordan, where the urban tradition is old. At the southern end of the Arabian Peninsula, urbanization has not reached high levels because industrialization and the exploitation of energy resources have not altered traditional livelihoods as much as in Iraq and Saudi Arabia. To the east and west similar

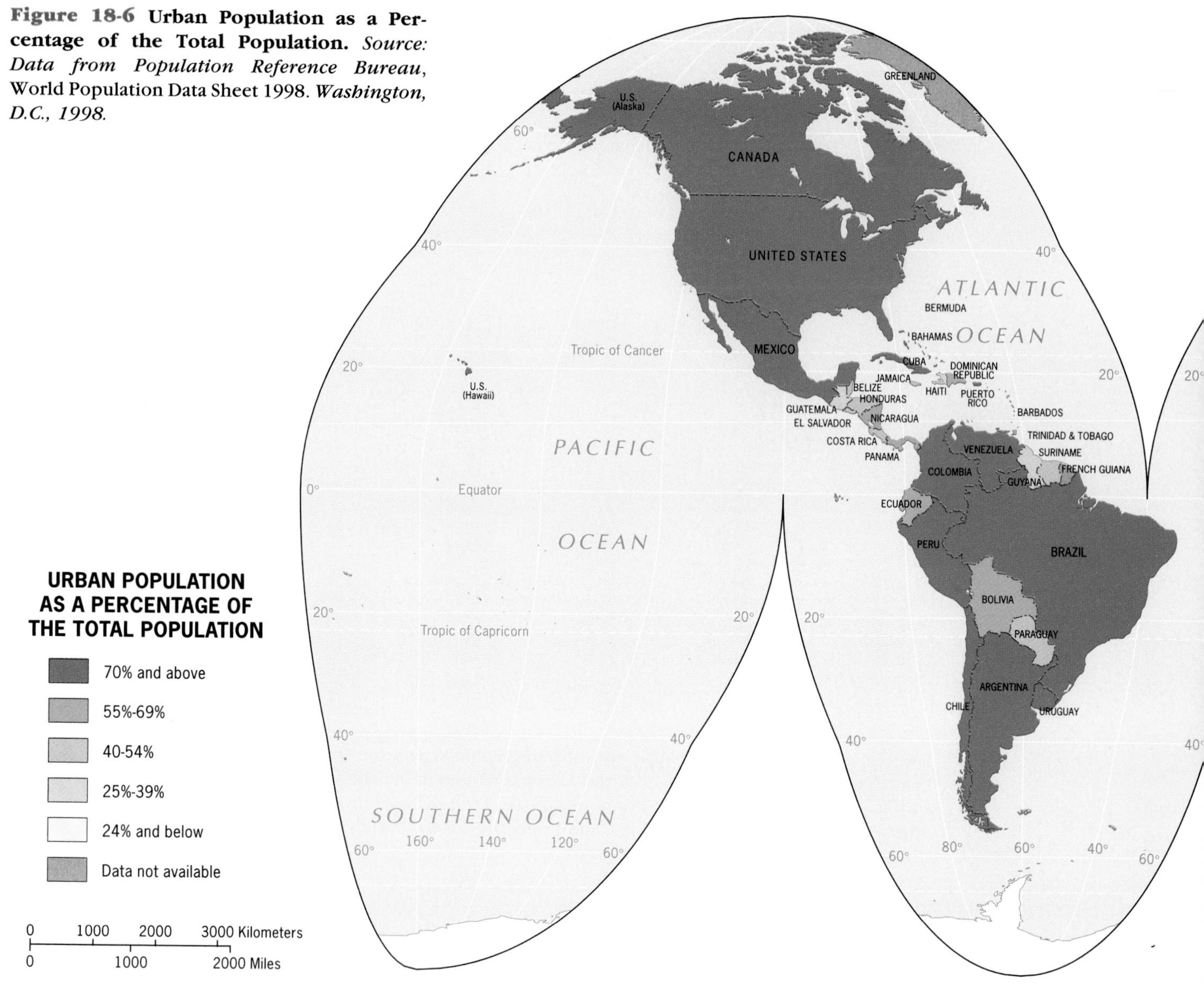

Figure 18-6 Urban Population as a Percentage of the Total Population. *Source: Data from Population Reference Bureau,* World Population Data Sheet 1998. *Washington, D.C., 1998.*

variations are found; note the low level of urbanization in resource-poor Afghanistan and the high level in oil-rich Libya.

Despite great cities such as Mumbai and Calcutta, urbanization in South Asia remains low. For the realm as a whole, urbanization remains well below 30 percent. India today is about 26 percent urbanized, Pakistan 28 percent, and populous Bangladesh only 16 percent. As noted earlier, farming (including subsistence farming) remains the dominant way of life in this realm, and this condition is reflected in the level of urbanization.

Southeast Asia includes the only country in the world that is 100 percent urban: the city-state of Singapore. But overall, this geographic realm is marked by low levels of urbanization. In addition to Singapore, Brunei, the ministate on the Island of Borneo, and Malaysia are more than 50 percent urbanized. Elsewhere the figures were more characteristic of the developing world: Myanmar (25 percent), Vietnam (20), and Thailand (19). Indonesia, the fourth most populous country in the world, remains only 31 percent urbanized.

These days we hear a great deal about the rapid rate of economic growth on the western Pacific Rim and the explosive growth of urban centers there (such as Shenzhen). And yet only Japan, South Korea, and Taiwan are highly urbanized here. As a whole, East Asia is only about 36 percent urbanized, and in China, despite its great cities, barely over one in four citizens lives in urban centers. Shanghai and Beijing between them have about 25 million inhabitants, and there are

many other large cities, but their populations must be compared with China's total population of 1.2 billion. Urbanization in China thus continues to proceed slowly.

The Great Cities

It is useful to compare Figure 18-6 to a map showing the distribution of the more than 300 cities with populations over 1 million (Fig. 18-7). The latter map shows the concentration of large cities in eastern North America, Western Europe, and East Asia, notably Japan. Africa's low level of urbanization is clearly evident.

North America displays the anchors of several megalopolitan regions. These include the Boston–Washington, D.C., Chicago–Detroit–Pittsburgh, San Francisco–Los Angeles–San Diego, and Montreal–Toronto–Windsor conurbations. Yet another, in Florida, is still marked only as a set of discrete, comparatively small cities, but as a result of recent population growth a regional megalopolis is developing quickly. Centered on Miami–Fort Lauderdale–West Palm Beach, it is growing northward along the Atlantic coast toward Jacksonville and westward across central Florida.

In England, a major megalopolitan region is developing around London. That city and its environs lie at the center of an expanding population cluster of nearly 20 million, and the industrial cities of South Wales and the Midlands are now just a short distance away. On the European mainland, a major urban com-

Figure 18-7 World Metropolitan Area Population. Based on data from numerous, often contradictory, sources, data on urban centers often are inconsistent. *Source: From United Nations, U.S. Census Bureau, Encyclopaedia Britannica Yearbooks, World Bank, Statesman's Yearbook, and other sources.*

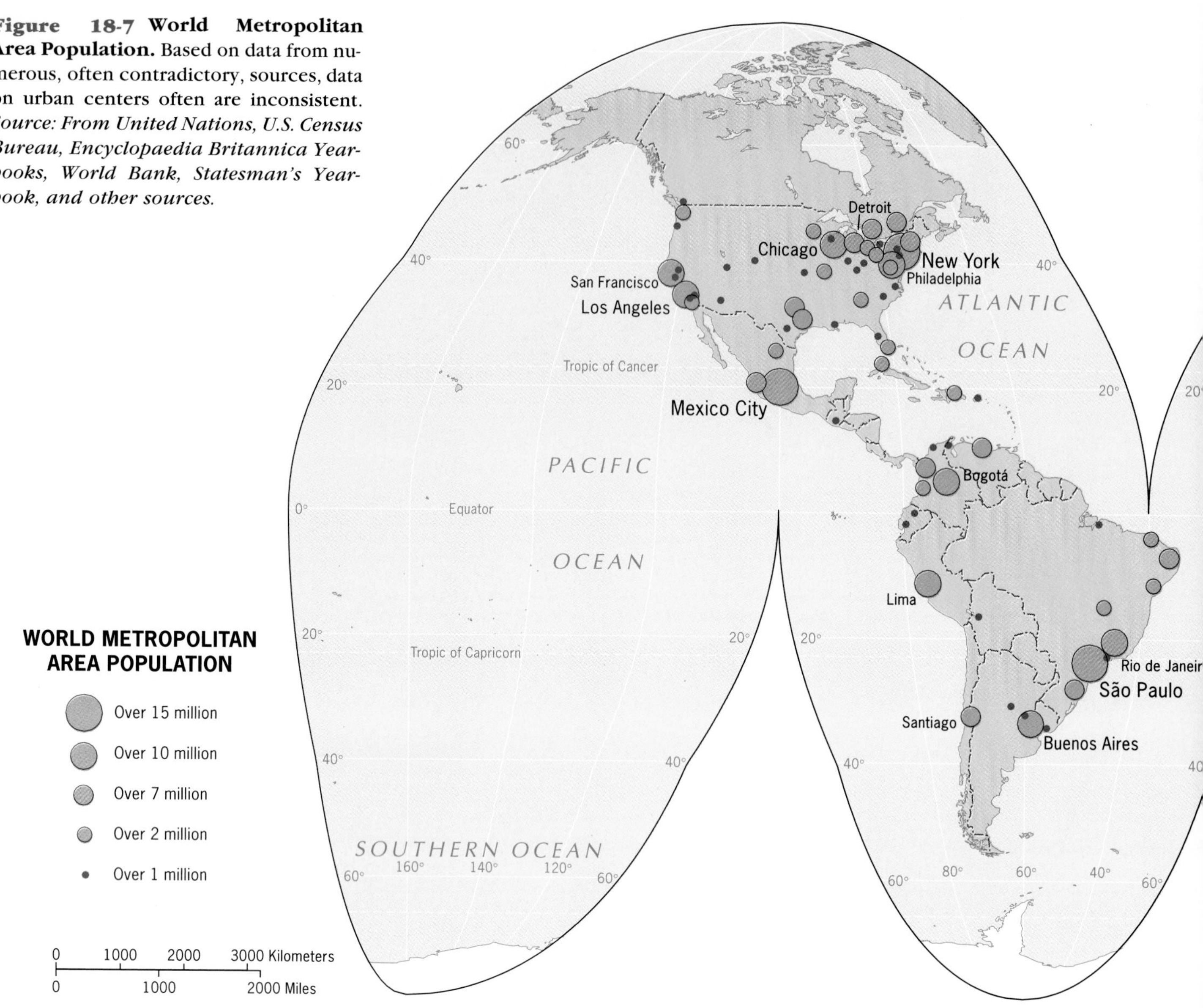

plex is emerging in western Germany in the Ruhr–Rhine zone, which includes such cities as Düsseldorf, Essen, and Cologne. In Belgium, an urban complex is developing centered on Brussels and Antwerp. In the Netherlands, planning for a triangular megalopolis (Amsterdam–Rotterdam–The Hague) is high on the national agenda. An attempt is being made to make this megalopolis, called *Randstad* ("ring-city"), a model megacity, complete with parks, spacious housing, good communications and public transportation, and well-distributed social services.

Other major urban agglomerations in Europe include the region centered on Paris, the rapidly developing Po Plain of northern Italy, and the Central European complex that extends from Saxony in Germany to Silesia in Poland. Elsewhere, there are major cities, such as Moscow, St. Petersburg, and Madrid, that have not yet developed into multicity urban regions. Of course, we should keep the *dimensions* of these developments in perspective. The whole urbanized area of Europe, from Britain's Midlands to Germany's Ruhr–Rhine region, extends over an area not much larger than the North American megalopolis. Yet Europe's historic political fragmentation and cultural diversity lead us to identify discrete urban units on a country-by-country basis.

Major megalopolitan development outside North America and Western Europe is occurring only in Japan. The Tokyo–Yokohama and Osaka–Kobe–Kyoto conurbations are enormous, and they are growing toward each other along Honshu Island's Pacific coast. This is not to suggest that the urbanizing trend that

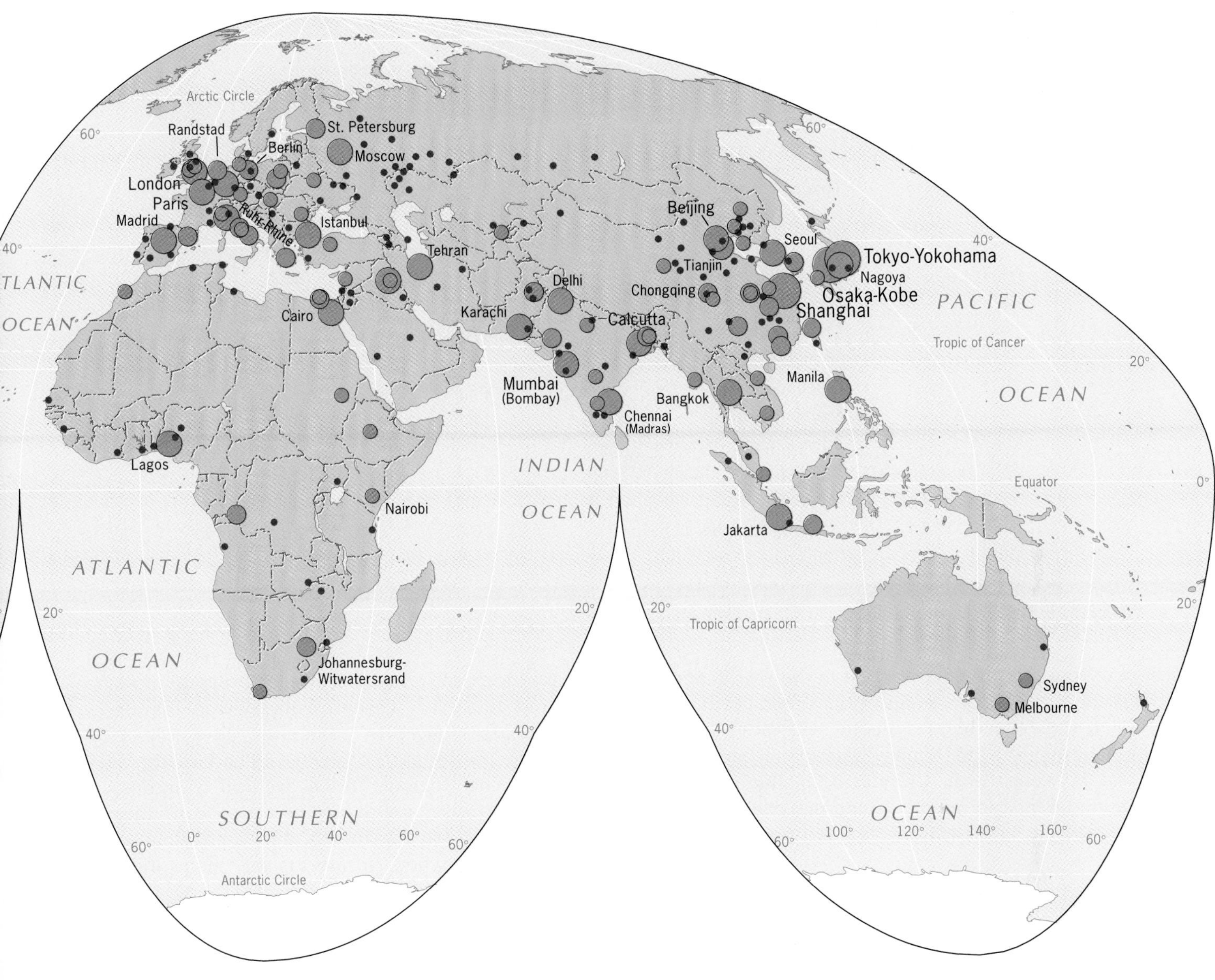

has generated the Bosnywash megalopolis and Randstad–Holland cannot be seen in other parts of the world. Johannesburg in South Africa, for example, lies at the center of a substantial megalopolis that includes several medium-sized cities in the Witwatersrand region. However, in general, conurbanization outside Europe, the United States, and Japan has not yet reached massive proportions. A high level of urbanization does not necessarily produce conurbation, as the widely spaced cities of Australia and Argentina reveal.

Megacities

As Table 18-1 shows, many of the world's most populous cities are found in poorer countries. These great human agglomerations stand alone in their vast rural hinterlands. Mexico City, Shanghai, Calcutta, Mumbai, and Cairo are in this group, and Bangkok, Lima-Callao, and Saigon-Cholon are not far behind. United Nations studies suggest that by 2025 there may be as many as 15 cities with populations over 20 million. Some, such as Mexico City, São Paulo, and Shanghai, may have close to 30 million inhabitants. Thus several of these huge urban areas will have more people than some of the megalopolitan conurbations in Europe and the United States. This prediction suggests that the greatest challenges posed by urbanization still lie ahead.

Table 18-1 also indicates how fast individual cities in poorer countries are growing compared to conurbations in richer countries. By the turn of the century, the New York–New Jersey conurbation will have

Table 18-1 Populations of the World's Largest Conurbations from 1990 to 2000[a] (in millions)

Rank					
1990	2000	Urban Area	1990	1995	2000
1	2	Tokyo–Yokohama–Kawasaki, *Japan*	27.1	27.9	28.7
2	1	Mexico City, *Mexico*	20.9	24.5	29.6
3	3	São Paulo, *Brazil*	18.1	21.7	26.1
4	4	Seoul, *South Korea*	16.7	19.4	22.4
5	8	New York–New Jersey, *U.S.A.*	14.6	14.7	14.7
6	9	Osaka–Kobe–Kyoto, *Japan*	13.8	14.1	14.5
7	7	Shanghai, *China*	13.0	14.0	15.2
8	5	Calcutta, *India*	11.7	13.1	15.9
9	6	Mumbai, *India*	11.7	13.0	15.3
10	12	Buenos Aires, *Argentina*	11.5	12.2	12.9
11	10	Rio de Janeiro, *Brazil*	11.4	12.8	14.3
12	13	Moscow, *Russia*	10.4	10.7	11.1
13	14	Los Angeles Area, *U.S.A.*	10.0	10.4	10.7
14	11	Cairo, *Egypt*	10.0	11.2	13.2

[a]Reports and estimates of urban-area populations vary quite widely. Various sources may cite different figures.

dropped from fifth to eighth largest in the world, and the Osaka–Kobe–Kyoto megalopolis from sixth to ninth. On the other hand, Calcutta will move from eighth place to fifth, and Bombay (Mumbai) from ninth to sixth. Between them, Calcutta and Mumbai will have gained 8 million people during the 1990s, while Tokyo and New York will have gained fewer than 2 million.

As we noted in Part Two, people continue to migrate to cities in response to "pull" factors that are more imaginary than real; their expectations of a better life mostly fail to materialize. Particularly in the less-developed realms, but in the industrial cities of developed regions as well, the new arrivals (and many long-term residents, too) are crowded together in overpopulated apartment buildings, dismal tenements, and teeming slums. New arrivals come from other cities and towns and from the rural countryside, often as large families; they add to the cities' rate of natural growth. Housing cannot keep up with this massive inflow. Almost overnight huge shantytowns, mostly without the barest amenities, develop around these cities. These do not deter additional urban in-migration, and as a result millions of people spend their entire lives in urban housing of wretched quality.

Despite the miserable living conditions of large numbers of urban immigrants, the cities continue to beckon. During the 1990s, Africa had the world's fastest-growing cities, followed by those in South Asia and mainland East Asia and South and Middle America. In contrast, the cities of North America, southern South America, and Australia were growing more slowly, and those of Western Europe were barely growing at all. Figure 18-7 therefore shows much change in the poorer parts of the world and relatively little in the richer regions. In less well-off countries, villages are becoming towns, towns are growing into cities, and cities are expanding into metropolises. There was a time when New York was the world's largest city, its skyline of skyscrapers a symbol of the economic power of the Western world. Then Tokyo's population overtook New York's. Now Mexico City is poised to become the world's most populous city, an agglomeration of slums and squatter settlements encircling a deteriorating central city. By 2025 New York will no longer rank among the world's 10 largest cities.

The fast-growing cities of Asia, Africa, and South America reveal much regional variation. Shanghai and Calcutta, for example, are both located at the mouths of rivers with clear colonial imprints—the British built prominent landmarks along both the Huangpu and the Hooghly Rivers. Although the Chinese have decided to preserve the colonial frontage along the famous Bund of Shanghai, much of the legacy of colonialism there is disappearing under an extensive urban-renewal program. In addition, China's government has designated a triangle of land between the Huangpu and Chang (Yangtzi) Rivers as a zone for special economic development. This zone, called Pudong, has been almost totally rid of older, traditional Chinese urban and rural dwellings. When word of the jobs available in Pudong and in Shanghai's redevelopment program spread into the hinterland, 3 million job-seekers converged on the city. Those who did not find jobs were speedily sent away. Such decisions can be made and implemented more easily in nondemocratic China than in India, where individual rights are stronger. Still, Shanghai is enormously overcrowded, although it does not have squatter settlements like those of Calcutta; nor are there thousands of people living under bridges, in cardboard boxes, even in drainpipes. The deprivation that is a hallmark of Calcutta's urban landscape is not immediately evident in Shanghai.

Cities in poorer parts of the world generally lack enforceable ***zoning*** laws, which are drawn up to ensure the orderly use of space. These laws determine how urban land may be used. Thus a fast-food franchise could not occupy a corner lot in a leafy suburb, because all the lots in that suburban block would be zoned exclusively for single-family residences. In cities in less-developed countries, zoning practices are typically inadequate, ineffective, or unenforced. In Chennai (Madras) and other Indian cities, open space between high-rise buildings is often occupied by squatter settlements. In Bangkok, elementary schools and noisy, polluting factories stand side by side. In Nairobi, hillside villas overlook some of Africa's worst slums. Over time such incongruities may disappear, as is happening in many cities in East Asia. Rising land values and greater demand for enforced zoning regulations are helping transform the central cities there. But in South Asia, Subsaharan Africa, Southwest Asia and North Africa, and Middle and South America, unregulated, helter-skelter growth continues.

Perhaps the most obvious characteristic of megacities in these realms is the stark contrasts they display. If you stand on the roof of the Nile Hilton Hotel in Cairo, Egypt, overlooking the square and avenues leading into it, you see what appears to be a modern, Mediterranean-European metropolis. But if you get on a bus and ride it toward the city's outskirts, that impression fades almost immediately as paved streets give way to dusty alleys, apartment buildings to harsh tenements, sidewalk coffee shops to broken doors and windows. Traffic-choked, garbage-strewn, polluted Cairo is home to an estimated 12.5 million people, about one-fifth of Egypt's population; the city is bursting at the seams. And still people continue to arrive, seeking the better life that pulls countless migrants from the countryside year after year.

From the field notes

"From atop one of the tallest hotels in central Cairo, the city's townscape is reminiscent of a Mediterranean-European scene. But a bus ride to the outskirts gave us quite another view of this metropolis: Asphalt roads gave way to dusty tracks, apartments to tenements and then to shacks. Parched, poor, garbage-strewn outer Cairo is a world away from the elegance and comfort of the center."

◆ CITY AND CULTURE

The world's great cities are crucibles of culture, arenas of transculturation and often difficult accommodation. The millions of people who are drawn to the cities (or forced off their land) represent countless histories and traditions, habits and practices. We acknowledge the geographical imprint of this multiculturalism by identifying urban regions with names such as "Chinatown," "Little Havana," and "the French Quarter."

From the Algerian sectors of Paris and the Turkish neighborhoods of Frankfurt to the Indian suburbs of Durban and the Chinese quarters of Bangkok, cities the world over are culturally regionalized. New arrivals tend to seek—or sometimes are forced to seek—living space among those whose background they share; as a result, various parts of the city become ethnic and cultural entities. In African cities such as Lagos (Nigeria), Mombasa (Kenya), and Johannesburg (South Africa), the residential areas, ranging from suburbs to squatter camps, incorporate a wide range of cultures both from within and from outside the countries in which they are located.

To understand the city better, we must investigate its spatial layout and the influences on it. In the next chapter we begin by studying the kind of city that is most familiar to us, the North American version. Later we expand our horizons to South America, Asia, and Africa.

◆ KEY TERMS ◆

agglomeration
hinterland
megacity
megalopolis
nucleation
site
situation
specialization
urban function
urban geography
urban hierarchy
urbanization
zoning

◆ APPLYING GEOGRAPHIC KNOWLEDGE ◆

1. On July 1, 1997, the People's Republic of China took control of the British dependency of Hong Kong. Initially, Beijing is committed to maintain Hong Kong as a distinct entity under the "one country, two systems" program. But in the long term, Hong Kong will be fully integrated into the Chinese state. How will this affect Hong Kong's geographic situation?

2. As Figure 18-7 shows, Mexico City is one of the Americas'—and the world's—largest cities. As a country, however, Mexico is by no means one of the Americas' (or the world's) most populous. What is the geographic explanation for Mexico City's enormous growth?

Chapter 19

Urban Pattern and Structure

From the field notes

"Urban regions are defined by specific features: high-rise buildings in the city center, open spaces in the suburbs. Often you can tell at a glance, from the skyline, what city is being pictured. Modern buildings such as the World Trade Center (New York), Sears Tower (Chicago), and Transamerica Pyramid (San Francisco) make them unmistakable. Still, city centers have lost much of their older character and atmosphere. This photograph could depict many an American downtown; it is probably not the popular image of San Francisco, where it was taken."

KEY POINTS

◆ **In the United States, the urban system evolved through five stages of development determined by prevailing modes of transport and industry; today's period of high technology, still in the process of transforming the modern city, dates from the 1970s.**

◆ **Every urban center has an economic base, with workers employed in basic (that is, goods-producing) and nonbasic (service) jobs; this employment structure reveals the primary functions a city performs.**

◆ **Central place theory helps explain why, under ideal circumstances, small urban places such as villages lie close together while larger cities lie far apart.**

◆ **Models of urban structure reveal how the forces that shape the internal layout of cities have changed, transforming the single-center city with one dominant downtown into the polycentric metropolis with several commercial nodes.**

The study of urban settlements encompasses a broad range of approaches and interests. We have already noted the application of the cultural landscape concept to urban areas. But geographers have also recognized that the relationships between cities and the surrounding countryside can be measured and mapped. Every city and town has an adjacent region within which its influence is dominant. Farmers in that region sell many of their products on the city's markets, and customers from smaller towns and villages come to the city to shop and to conduct other business. The city's newspapers are read and its television stations watched in the surrounding region. The city's dominance can be seen in many other areas of life as well. The term ***hinterland***, a German word meaning the land "behind" the city, is used in referring to such a region.

When cities lie some distance apart, where does the hinterland of one city end and that of the other begin? That question leads us to investigate the factors that influence the *spacing* of cities. In general, large cities tend to lie farther apart than smaller ones; towns lie still closer together, and villages are separated by even shorter distances. What forces influence the evolution of this pattern? Can von Thünen's method of model building be used to interpret what the map shows?

This chapter takes up these questions. As we will see, they lead quite naturally to the anatomy of the city itself, its internal structure and functions. A city's spatial organization can reveal much about its efficiency and productivity, and hence its capacity to compete not only for dominance over a large hinterland but also for more distant linkages.

◆ INTERURBAN SPATIAL ORGANIZATION

The Industrial Revolution occurred almost a century later in the United States than in Europe. When it finally did cross the Atlantic in the 1870s, it progressed so robustly that only 50 years later America surpassed Europe as the world's mightiest industrial power. Thus the far-reaching economic, demographic, and societal changes experienced in Europe's industrializing countries were greatly accelerated in the United States. Those changes were further fueled by the arrival of more than 25 million European immigrants who were overwhelmingly concentrated in the major manufacturing centers.

The impact of industrial urbanization was felt at two levels. At the national level there quickly emerged a network or system of cities specializing in the collection, processing, and distribution of raw materials and manufactured goods, and linked together by an ever more efficient web of transport routes. Within that urban system, individual cities prospered in their new roles as manufacturing centers, generating a new internal structure that still forms the spatial framework of most industrial cities. Their constantly growing incomes, in turn, permitted the newly industrialized cities to invest in private and public services, as well as housing, and thereby convert each round of industrial expansion into a new stage of urban development. This whole process unfolded so quickly that planning was impossible. Almost literally, near the turn of the twentieth century America awoke to discover that it had built a number of large cities. This rise of the national urban system, unintended though it may have been, was a necessary byproduct of industrialization, without which rapid U.S. economic development could not have taken place. A network of cities and towns now blanketed the continent, providing local populations with the conveniences of modern life.

◆ THE EVOLUTION OF THE AMERICAN URBAN SYSTEM

Even though it became highly visible as the nation industrialized between 1870 and 1910, the U.S. urban system had been in the process of formation for several decades before that time. In a 1967 article titled "American Metropolitan Evolution," John Borchert proposed a four-stage model of the evolution of the American urban system. Borchert's model summarizes two centuries of urban development, based on key changes in transportation technology and industrial energy.

The Sail-Wagon Epoch

The first stage was the preindustrial *Sail-Wagon Epoch* (1790–1830). During this period interaction was limited by slow and primitive overland and waterway transport. The leading cities of the time were those of the Northeast, such as Boston, New York, and Philadelphia, which were oriented as much to European overseas trade as to their still rather inaccessible hinterlands.

The Iron Horse Epoch

Next came the *Iron Horse Epoch* (1830–1870), which was dominated by the diffusion of the steam-powered railroad. The railroad network expanded steadily from east to west until the first transcontinental line was completed at the end of the epoch. A nationwide transport system had been forged. Coal-mining centers boomed (to keep locomotives running), and, aided by the easier and cheaper movement of raw materials, small-scale urban manufacturing began to spread outward from its New England hearth. The national urban system started to take shape. By 1850 New York was the primate city, and at the next level in the hierarchy were booming new industrial centers like Pittsburgh, Detroit, and Chicago.

The Steel-Rail Epoch

This economic-urban development process crystallized during the third stage, the *Steel-Rail Epoch* (1870–1920), which coincided with the Industrial Revolution. Among the massive forces now shaping the growth of the national metropolitan system were the rise of the all-important steel industry along the Chicago–Detroit–Pittsburgh axis (as well as its coal and iron ore supply areas in the northern Appalachians and Lake Superior district, respectively); the increasing scale of manufacturing, which led to greater agglomeration in the most advantageous raw material and market locations; and the physical improvement of the railroads. The latter included much more durable tracks made of steel (which replaced iron), more powerful steam locomotives, and heavier and larger freight cars (including refrigerated cars), which permitted significantly higher speeds, longer hauls, and more effective linking of rail nodes.

The Auto-Air-Amenity Epoch

The *Auto-Air-Amenity Epoch* (1920–1970) comprised the ultimate stage in the evolution of the national urban hierarchy. The key innovation during this epoch was the gasoline-powered internal combustion engine, which made possible ever greater automobile- and truck-based regional and metropolitan dispersal. Moreover, as technological advances in manufacturing

From the field notes

"In many U.S. cities, only vestiges of the steel-rail epoch remain. But in a few places, the tram still services—or rather, serves again—on limited routes linking the downtown to nearby areas. This surface version of the elevated 'people mover' in Portland, Oregon, is a reminder of a bygone era."

resulted in increasing automation of blue-collar jobs, the labor force steadily shifted toward white-collar personal and professional services to manage the industrial economy. These new activities responded less to traditional cost- and distance-based location forces and more strongly to the amenities (pleasant environments) available in suburbs—as well as in the Sunbelt states—in a nation that was now fully interconnected by jet travel and long-distance communication networks.

A High-Technology Epoch?

Although Professor Borchert's model extends only to 1970, its final stage continues to shape the country's urban framework today. Intercity commuting is no longer rare (some residents of Santa Fe, New Mexico, commute weekly to jobs in Los Angeles, for example), and the decline of "rustbelt" cities continues. But there are signs that we are entering a *High-Technology Epoch*, a time when service and information industries, with their growing capacity to operate in locations outside cities, will stimulate an even greater dispersal of city populations. Might the city now begin sending people back into the countryside to repopulate with high-tech specialists the very rural areas it once depopulated by offering factory jobs? Charting this trend will be one of the exciting tasks facing geographers in the years ahead.

◆ URBAN SPATIAL STRUCTURE

When we look at an atlas map of the United States or Canada, or at a road map of a state or province, we see an array of places of different sizes, with varying distances between them. The map looks like a jumble, yet each place is where it is because of some decision, some perception of the site or its situation, or perhaps some incident that led to settlement at that particular place.

The Rank-Size Rule

Even a general map provides an impression of the sizes and locations of settlements in an area. There are many villages with unfamiliar names, a number of towns named in larger print and situated on highways, several cities where transportation routes converge, and perhaps one familiar, dominant city. We can conclude that the larger places become, the fewer there are: there is only one dominant metropolis, but there are several large cities, a greater number of towns, and many villages. We discern not only the hierarchy of urban places but also the so-called ***rank-size rule***. This rule holds that in a model urban hierarchy, the population of a city or town will be inversely proportional to its rank in the hierarchy. For example, if the largest city has 12 million people, the second city will have about 6 million (that is, half the population of the largest city); the third city will have 4 million (one-third); the fourth city 3 million; and so on. Note that the differences between cities become smaller at lower levels of the hierarchy so that the tenth-largest city would have 1.2 million inhabitants.

The rank-size rule does not apply in all countries, especially countries with dominant primate cities, such as France or Mexico. But it does seem to apply in several countries with complex economies, such as the United States. However, the map tells us little about the reasons behind the distribution of places at various levels in the hierarchy. We can use our knowledge of site and situation to speculate on the dominance of Boston compared to, say, Portland, Maine. But what governs the distances from city to city in about the same rank or from village to village?

Urban Functions

Before we try to answer this question, we should note the functions performed by cities and other urban places. Every city and town has an ***economic base***. Geographers classify the activities of workers in cities according to their purpose: a percentage of workers produce goods or services to satisfy demand in the hinterland or in markets even farther away, while others do things that keep the city itself going. For example, workers in a manufacturing plant that produces microwave ovens (the first category) are in the city's ***basic sector***; their work produces goods for export and generates an inflow of money. On the other hand, workers who maintain city streets, clerks who work in offices, and teachers who teach in city schools are responsible for the functioning of the city itself. They constitute the ***nonbasic sector*** (also called the *service sector*). Many people who work in a city, of course, do some of each. An attorney may serve clients from a village in the city's hinterland, where there is no lawyer's office, but also serve city residents.

The ratio of basic to nonbasic workers gives an impression of the city's economic base. The number of nonbasic workers is always greater than the number of basic workers, and this ratio tends to increase as a city grows. Therein lies a danger: when the products or services exported from the basic sector fail to find a market and jobs in the basic sector are lost, many more jobs in the nonbasic sector are affected.

Functional Specialization

From data on the number of people employed in various basic and nonbasic jobs (the ***employment structure***) we can discern the primary functions a city per-

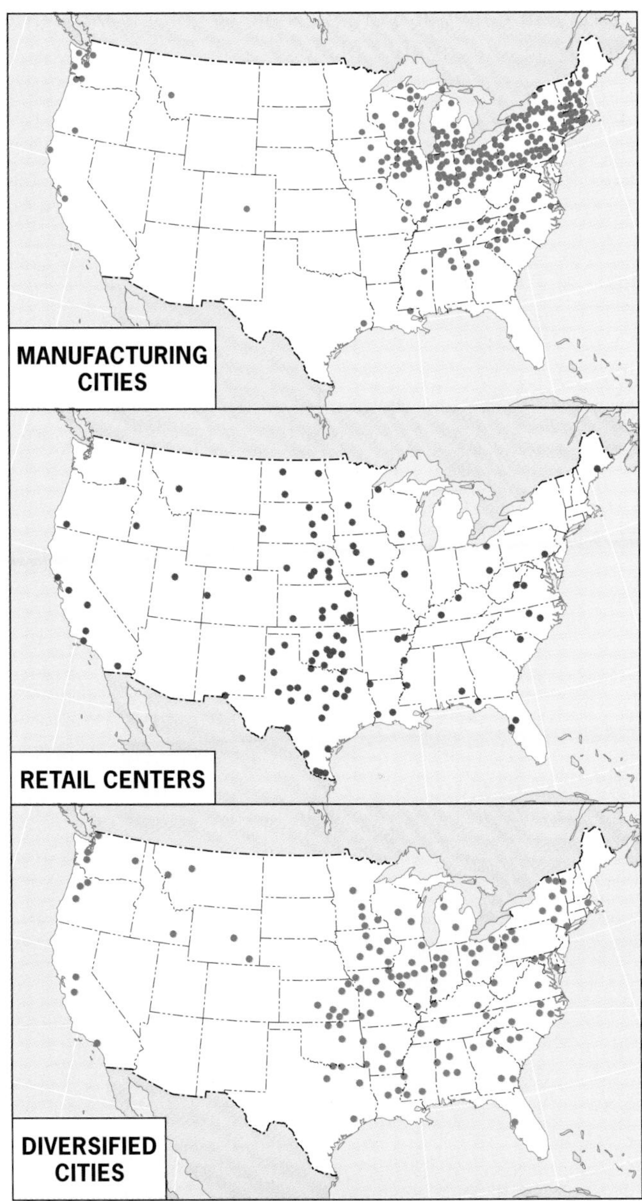

Figure 19-1 Distribution of Cities According to Function. This map shows the distribution of cities according to function: manufacturing, retail-dominated, and diversified cities in the early 1940s. *Source: From C. Harris, "A Functional Classification of Cities in the United States,"* The Geographical Review 33 (1943), p. 88.

forms. Note that all cities have multiple functions, and the larger the city, the larger the number of functions. As we saw at the beginning of the chapter, however, some cities are dominated by one particular activity. This ***functional specialization*** was a characteristic of European cities even before the Industrial Revolution, but the Industrial Revolution gave it new meaning. To most of us the associations between the names of cities and their functional specialties have little relevance today, but there was a time when many cities were closely identified with certain products. But even when automobile production was Detroit's dominant function, other functions also made important contributions to the city's economic base.

In 1943 Chauncy Harris published a detailed study of the distribution of U.S. cities according to their dominant functions. In an article titled "A Functional Classification of Cities in the United States," he described the concentration of manufacturing-dominated cities in the Northeast, the wide dispersal of retail centers, and the western diffusion of cities that were already so diversified that no primary or dominant function could be discerned from the employment data (Fig. 19-1).

The three maps included in Figure 19-1 reveal a situation that no longer exists. Only slightly more than a dozen northeastern cities could still be mapped as manufacturing centers, including such cities as Flint, Michigan; Gary, Indiana; and Wilmington, Delaware; most of the other northeastern cities on Harris's maps have become diversified centers. Retail-dominated cities are fewer still; they include Phoenix, Arizona; San Antonio, Texas; and Orlando, Florida. Thus with growing size has come greater diversification.

This is not to say that specialization no longer exists. As noted at the beginning of the chapter, we can still identify educational centers (college towns), gambling cities (Las Vegas, Atlantic City), resort and retirement towns (Vero Beach, Florida), government headquarters (Augusta, Maine), and mining centers (Leadville, Colorado). But many of these places remain small—or their main industry is unusually dominant. As urban centers grow, they tend to lose their functional specialization.

Another implication of urban growth emerges from the ratio between workers in the basic sector and those in the nonbasic sector. This ratio is about the same (1 to 2) for most large cities. When a business is established with 50 production (basic) workers, it adds 100 nonbasic workers to the work force. Economic expansion of this kind therefore has a ***multiplier effect***, not only on the work force but also on the urban population as a whole, because most workers have dependents who also consume goods and services.

Central Places

Earlier we encountered the notion of a *hierarchy* of urban settlements ranging from hamlets to metropolises. That hierarchy is based not only on population but also on functions and services. These functions and services attract consumers not just from the urban areas themselves but also from areas beyond the urban limits. Thus every urban center has a certain ***economic reach*** that can be used as a measure of its centrality.

Centrality is a characteristic of urban situations that is crucial to the development of urban places and their service areas. For these hinterlands, towns and cities are *central places*; even a village is a central place for its small surrounding area. How do service areas relate to each other? Do they overlap? Do towns of approximately the same size lie about the same distance away from each other? What rules govern the arrangement of urban places on the landscape? These questions are important if we are to understand the structuring of urban hierarchies. Let us therefore take a closer look at the arrangement of urban places.

◆ CENTRAL PLACE THEORY

In a 1933 book titled *The Central Places in Southern Germany*, Walter Christaller laid the groundwork for ***central place theory***. He attempted to develop a model that would show how and where central places in the urban hierarchy (hamlets, villages, towns, and cities) would be functionally and spatially distributed. In his effort to discover the laws that govern this distribution, Christaller began with a set of assumptions. The surface of the ideal region would be flat and have no physical barriers. Soil fertility would be the same everywhere. Christaller also assumed an even distribution of population and purchasing power and a uniform transportation network that permitted direct travel from each settlement to the other. Finally, he assumed that a constant maximum distance or range for the sale of any good or service produced in a town would prevail in all directions from that urban center.

Christaller's idea was to calculate the nature of the central place system that would develop under such conditions, and then to compare that model to real-world situations and try to explain any variations and exceptions. Some places, he realized, would have more centrality than others. The central functions of larger towns would cover regions within which several smaller places with lesser central functions and service areas are nested. What was needed, he reasoned, was a way to calculate the *degree* of centrality of various places. In order to do this, Christaller defined *central goods and services* as those provided only at a central place. These are the goods and services that a central place makes available to its consumers in a surrounding region—as opposed to services that might be available anywhere or are produced for distant markets. Next came the *range of sale* of such central goods and services: the distance people would be willing to travel to acquire them. The limit would lie halfway between one central place and the next place where the same product was sold at the same price, because under the assumptions Christaller used, a person would not be expected to travel 11 miles to one place to buy an item if it were possible to go only 9 miles to purchase it at another place.

Hexagonal Hinterlands

In Christaller's ***urban model***, each central place has a surrounding *complementary region*, an exclusive

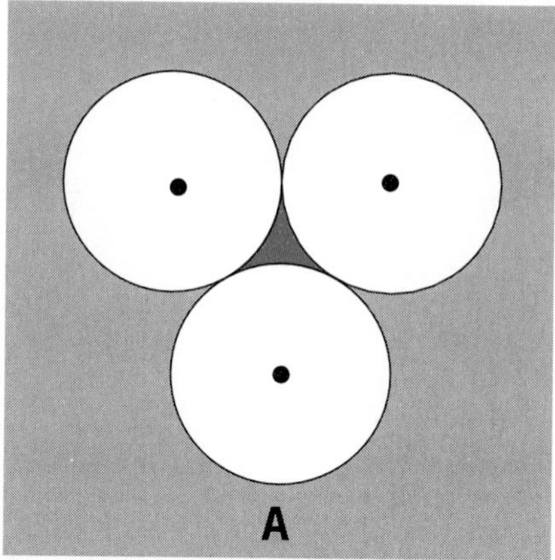

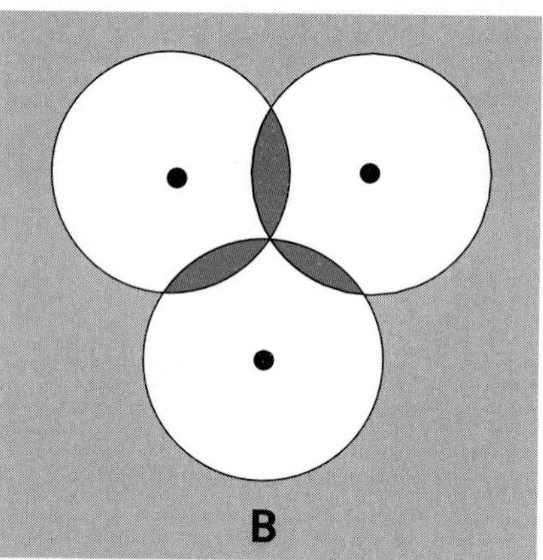

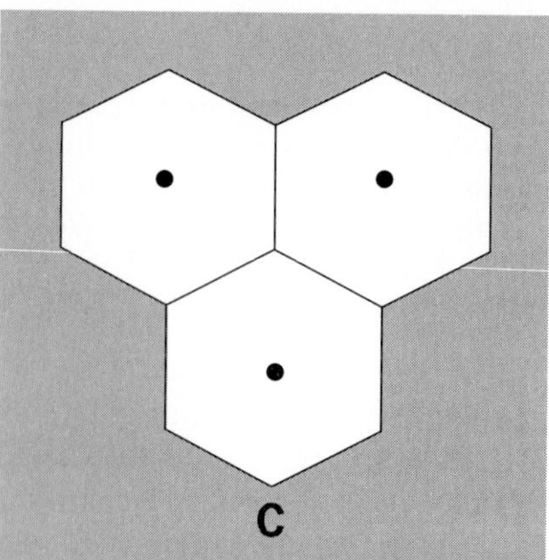

Figure 19-2 Christaller's Hexagonal Trade Areas Surrounding Urban Centers. Constructing Christaller's hexagonal trade areas surrounding urban centers involves: (A) unserved areas shown in purple; (B) purple areas indicate places where the conditions of monopoly would not be fulfilled; and (C) hexagons completely fill an area without overlap.

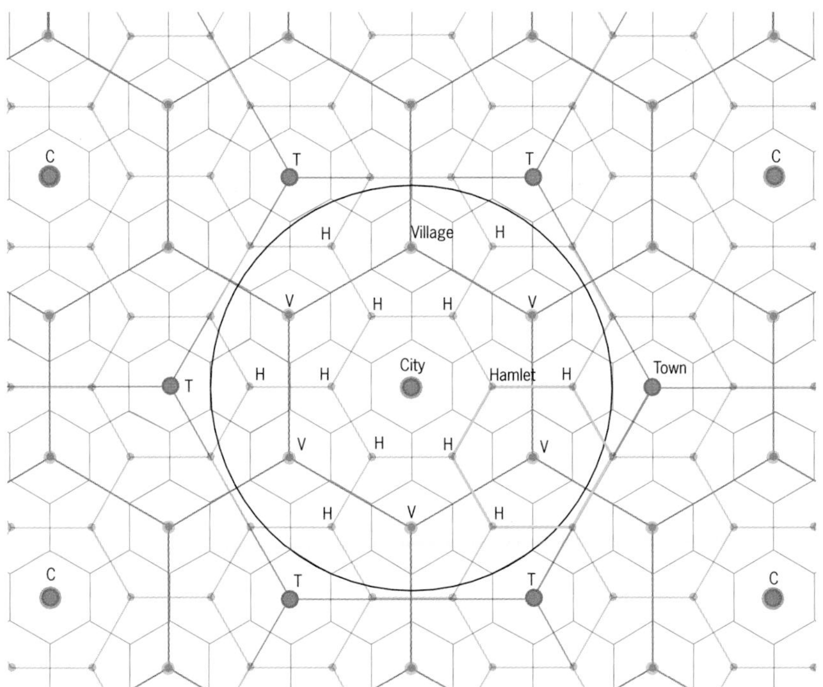

Figure 19-3 Christaller's Hierarchy of Settlements and Their Service Areas. Christaller's interlocking model of a hierarchy of settlements and their service areas include: T = town; C = city; H = hamlet; V = village.

hinterland within which the town has a monopoly on the sale of certain goods because it alone can provide such goods at a given price and within a certain range of travel. From what has just been said, we would expect such complementary regions to be circular. However, when we construct the model on that basis, problems arise: either the circles adjoin and leave unserved areas, or they overlap; in the latter situation the central place no longer has a monopoly. These two problems are resolved by a model consisting of perfectly fitted hexagonal regions, as shown in Figure 19-2.

The logical extension of this conclusion is shown in Figure 19-3. If the hexagonal complementary region shown in Figure 19-2 is centered on a hamlet, where the fewest goods and services are available, that hamlet and its region must form a part of the complementary region of a village. And that village and its complementary region would be part of a town's complementary region. The central place system thus reveals a *nesting* (region-within-region) pattern; each larger complementary region is centered on a higher-order urban place.

Like von Thünen, whose economic-geographic model was also based on a series of assumptions, Christaller knew that conditions would be different in the real world. But his model yielded a number of practical conclusions. First, he showed that the ranks of urban places do in fact form an orderly hierarchy of central places in spatial balance. If one component is removed, the whole system will move toward a new equilibrium. Second, Christaller's model implied that places of the same size with the same number of functions would be spaced the same distance apart. Third, larger cities would be spaced farther from each other than smaller towns or villages. What the model confirmed, therefore, was that the general pattern on the map is not an accident but a product of specific forces that tend to create regular rank-size patterns.

The Real World

If you fly over the rural landscape of southern Germany or any other countryside, you are reminded that Christaller's proposed hexagonal pattern is a model, not reality. Physical barriers, uneven resource distributions, and other factors create modifications of the spatial pattern. Because of such modifications, geographers were divided on the relevance of the model. Some saw hexagonal systems everywhere; others saw none at all. Soon attempts were made to alter the model and relate it to specific parts of the world. Christaller himself joined the debate: in 1950, he published an article, "The Foundations of Spatial Organization in Europe," in which he insisted that he had been correct all along:

> When we connect the metropolitan areas with each other through lines, and draw such a network of systems of the map of Europe, it indeed becomes eminently clear how the metropolitan areas everywhere lie in hexagonal arrangements.

Christaller received support from the research of geographers who applied his ideas to regions in Europe, North America, and elsewhere. In China, both the North China Plain and the Sichuan Basin display the kind of uninterrupted flatness assumed by Christaller's model. When G. William Skinner examined the distribution of villages, towns, and cities there in 1964, he found a spatial pattern closely resembling the one predicted by Christaller's model. Studies in the U.S. Midwest suggested that while the square layout of the township-and-range system imposed a different kind of regularity on the landscape, the spatial forces at work there tended to confirm Christaller's theory.

Christaller's main contribution was the stimulus he gave to urban and economic geography in general and to location theory in particular. Since the 1950s a large number of articles have been published in which geographers have attempted to refine Christaller's model. In the process, our understanding of the functioning of urban places and the forces that influence their distribution has been strengthened.

◆ MODELS OF URBAN STRUCTURE

Cities are not simply random collections of buildings and people. They exhibit ***functional structure***: they are spatially organized to perform their functions as places of commerce, production, education, and much more. Just as Christaller developed a model to explain the spacing of cities and towns, we could prepare a model of the internal layout of a city. How and where are the various residential and nonresidential components of the city positioned with respect to each other? If there are forces that govern the distribution of central places on the landscape, then surely there are forces that affect the way cities are organized. It is not difficult to think of one of these forces: the price of land. This tends to be highest in the downtown area and declines as one moves outward from the center; one would not expect to find a spacious residential area in the central business district.

Before proceeding, let us define some terms that are commonly used in referring to parts of the city—particularly those in North America. The ***central business district (CBD)*** (or "downtown") is the core of the city. High land values, tall buildings, busy traffic, converging highways, and mass transit systems mark the American CBD. An urban *zone* is a sector of a city within which land use is relatively uniform (an industrial or residential zone, for example). The term ***central city*** is often used to denote the part of an urban area that lies within the outer ring of residential suburbs. In effect, it refers to the older city as opposed to the newer suburbs. A ***suburb*** is an outlying, functionally uniform part of an urban area, often (but not always) adjacent to the central city. Most suburbs are residential, but some have other land uses, including schools, shopping malls, and office parks.

Just by using such terms as *residential area* and *central business district*, we acknowledge the existence of a regional structure within cities. When you refer to downtown, or to the airport, or to the municipal zoo, you are in fact referring to urban regions where certain functions prevail (business activity, transportation, and recreation, in the three just mentioned). All of these urban regions or zones, of course, lie near or adjacent to each other and together make up the metropolis. But how are they arranged? Is there any regularity or recurrent pattern in the location of the various zones, perhaps reflecting certain prevailing growth processes? In other words, do the city's regions constitute elements of a metropolitan structure that can be recognized in every metropolis, perhaps with modifications related to a city's particular site, size, shape, and relief?

One way to attack this problem is to study the layout of a large number of cities, compare the resulting maps, and determine which features recur. If we were to do this in North America, we would find that cities generally have *central zones*, consisting mainly of the CBD, and *outer zones* where lower-density suburbs and their new business and shopping centers lie. Between the central and outer zones, one may sometimes discern a *middle zone*, an ill-defined, often rather mixed and disorganized area; this zone is characterized by change, as in the aging of housing and the development of slums.

Throughout the past century urban geographers have attempted to construct models that would account for the geographic layout of cities (see "Focus on: Three Classic Models of Urban Structure"). But as manufacturing cities became modern cities and as modern cities became postmodern, this task grew more complicated. Today urban geographers identify superregions that they call urban realms, and they create models that show cities within cities.

Urban Realms

Even the multiple nuclei model fails to account for all the spatial-structural complexities of the American metropolis. Although this model accurately reflects the decentralization and nucleation of certain urban functions, much has changed since 1945. In the early postwar period, rapid population dispersal to the outer suburbs not only created distant nuclei but also reduced the volume and level of interaction between the central city and these emerging suburban cities. This situation made the new *outer cities* of the suburban

Three Classic Models of Urban Structure

The three models of ***urban structure*** shown in Figure 19-4 display not only three alternative interpretations of the layout of cities, but also the increasing complexity of urban structure over time. The *concentric zone model* (Fig. 19-4*A*) resulted from sociologist Ernest Burgess's study of Chicago in the 1920s. He recognized five concentric functional zones. At the center was the CBD (1), itself subdivided into several subdistricts (financial, retail, theater, etc.). The zone of transition (2) was characterized by residential deterioration and encroachment by business and light manufacturing. Zone 3 was a ring of closely spaced but adequate homes occupied by the blue-collar labor force. Zone 4 consisted of middle-class residences, and zone 5 was the suburban ring. Burgess described his model as dynamic: as the city grew, inner zones encroached on outer ones, so that CBD functions invaded zone 2 and the problems of zone 2 affected the inner margins of zone 3.

In the late 1930s Homer Hoyt published his *sector model* (Fig. 19-4*B*), partly as an answer to the drawbacks of the Burgess model. Hoyt argued that growth alone created a pie-shaped urban structure. From the concentric zone model we would conclude that rent paid for residential use would increase steadily from the tenements of zone 2 to the suburbs of zone 5. But in reality, Hoyt discovered, a low-rent area could extend all the way from the CBD to the city's outer edge, as in sector 3; the same could be true for a high-rent sector (1). Transport (5) and industrial (6) sectors also did not reflect the concentric character proposed by Burgess.

In fact, we can recognize both concentric and sector layouts in the urban structure of many cities. In the 1940s Chauncy Harris and Edward Ullman, arguing that neither of the earlier models adequately reflected city structure, proposed the *multiple nuclei model* (Fig. 19-4*C*). This model was based on the notion that the CBD was losing its dominant position as the nucleus of the urban area. Several of the urban regions shown in the figure therefore have their own subsidiary but competing "nuclei."

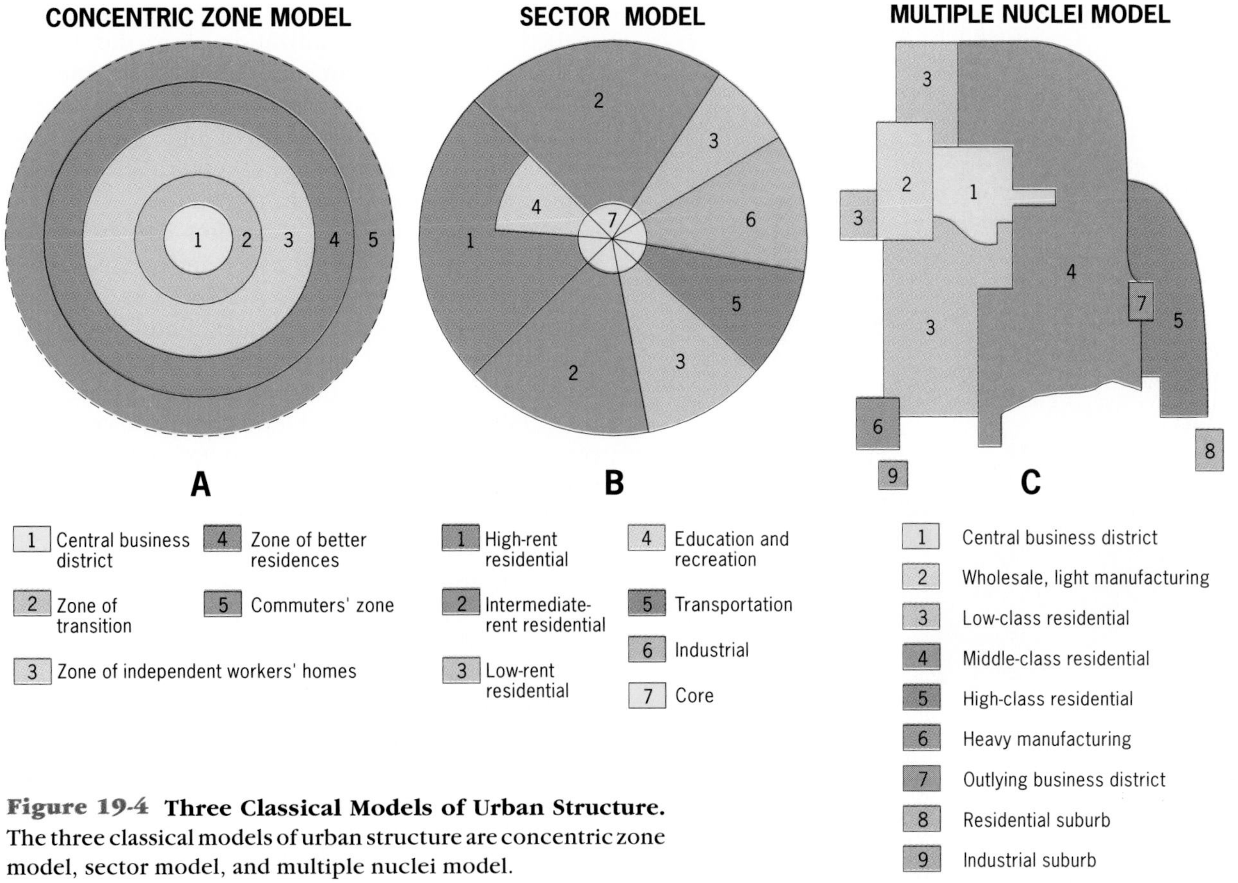

CONCENTRIC ZONE MODEL

A

1 Central business district
2 Zone of transition
3 Zone of independent workers' homes
4 Zone of better residences
5 Commuters' zone

SECTOR MODEL

B

1 High-rent residential
2 Intermediate-rent residential
3 Low-rent residential
4 Education and recreation
5 Transportation
6 Industrial
7 Core

MULTIPLE NUCLEI MODEL

C

1 Central business district
2 Wholesale, light manufacturing
3 Low-class residential
4 Middle-class residential
5 High-class residential
6 Heavy manufacturing
7 Outlying business district
8 Residential suburb
9 Industrial suburb

Figure 19-4 Three Classical Models of Urban Structure. The three classical models of urban structure are concentric zone model, sector model, and multiple nuclei model.

ring more self-sufficient as locational advantages produced an ever-greater range of retailing and employment activity. By the 1970s, outer cities were becoming increasingly independent of the CBD to which these former suburbs had once been closely tied, and they began to duplicate certain functions of the central city. In the 1980s, the increasingly complex American metropolitan area revealed combinations of the classic models described previously, as well as a redistribution of activities and zones in the urban fringe. Regional shopping centers in the suburban zone were becoming the CBDs of the outer nuclei. Business and industrial parks were locating outside the central city as well (Fig. 19-5). The term ***urban realm*** came into use to describe the spatial components of the metropolis of the 1990s, each a separate and distinct economic, social, and political entity within the larger urban framework.

The realm structure is readily apparent in metropolitan Los Angeles. Five discrete urban realms have emerged around the central city (Fig. 19-6), creating a suburban ring that extends as far as 50 miles (80 kilometers) from the CBD. Clockwise from the west, these are:

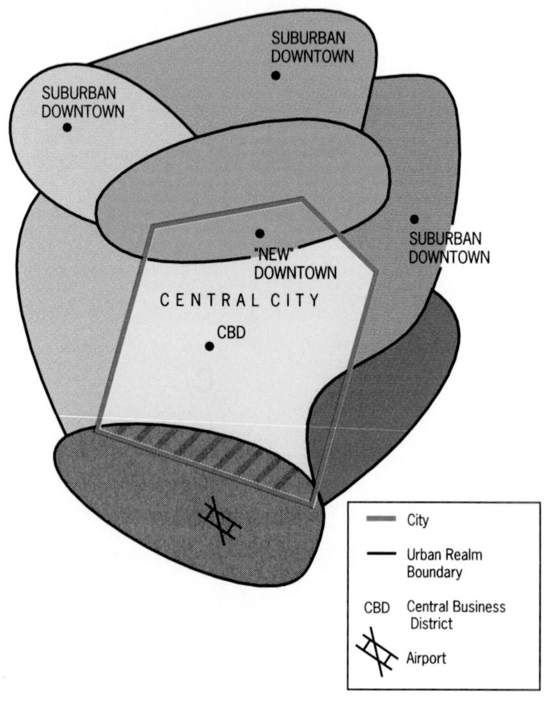

Figure 19-5 Urban Realms Model. The Urban Realms Model includes central business district, central city, new downtown, and suburban downtown. *Source: From T. Hartshorn and P. O. Muller, "Suburban Downtowns and the Transformation of Metropolitan Atlanta's Business Landscape,"* Urban Geography 10 (1989), p. 375. *Reproduced by permission of* Urban Geography.

1. The *West Realm*, typified by Santa Monica, Beverly Hills, and the ribbon extending along the coast toward Santa Barbara.
2. The *Northwest Realm*, the San Fernando Valley between the Santa Monica and the San Gabriel Mountains.
3. The *East Realm*, which follows the San Gabriel Valley eastward to the desert margin.
4. The *Southeast Realm*, Orange County, one of America's fastest growing urban areas, centered on Costa Mesa and Anaheim.
5. The *Southwest Realm*, straddling the San Diego Freeway from near Inglewood in the north to Long Beach in the south, and dominated economically by Los Angeles International Airport (LAX) and aerospace activities.

Approximately in the middle lies the sixth urban realm, *Central Los Angeles*, which is located at the hub of the freeway network but serves more as a crossroads than as a regional core. The CBD itself does contain a cluster of high-rise commercial buildings and a group of cultural and sports facilities, but it is overshadowed economically by Orange County.

The growth of the outer cities has been the hallmark of American urbanization since the 1960s. As early as 1973, American suburbs surpassed the central cities in total employment. By the mid-1980s the suburbanization of a critical mass of jobs (greater than 50 percent of the urban-area total) could be seen even in some major metropolises in the Sunbelt.

After about 1970, as the outer city grew rapidly and became more functionally independent of the central city, new suburban downtowns emerged to serve their new local economies. Often located near key freeway intersections, these multipurpose activity nodes developed mainly around big regional shopping centers and attracted industrial parks, office complexes, hotels, restaurants, entertainment facilities, and even major league sports stadiums to locate nearby. As these new outer city downtowns flourish, they attract tens of thousands of nearby suburbanites—offering workplaces, shopping, leisure activities, and all the other elements of a complete urban environment—thereby loosening remaining ties not only to the central city but to other suburban areas as well.

Thus the urban realms model constitutes the latest step forward in the interpretation of urban structure. It clearly demonstrates that today's outer cities are not satellites of the central city—they have become equal partners in the shaping of the polycentric metropolis.

Urban Form

In addition to the situation and internal spatial organization of cities, geographers have been interested in

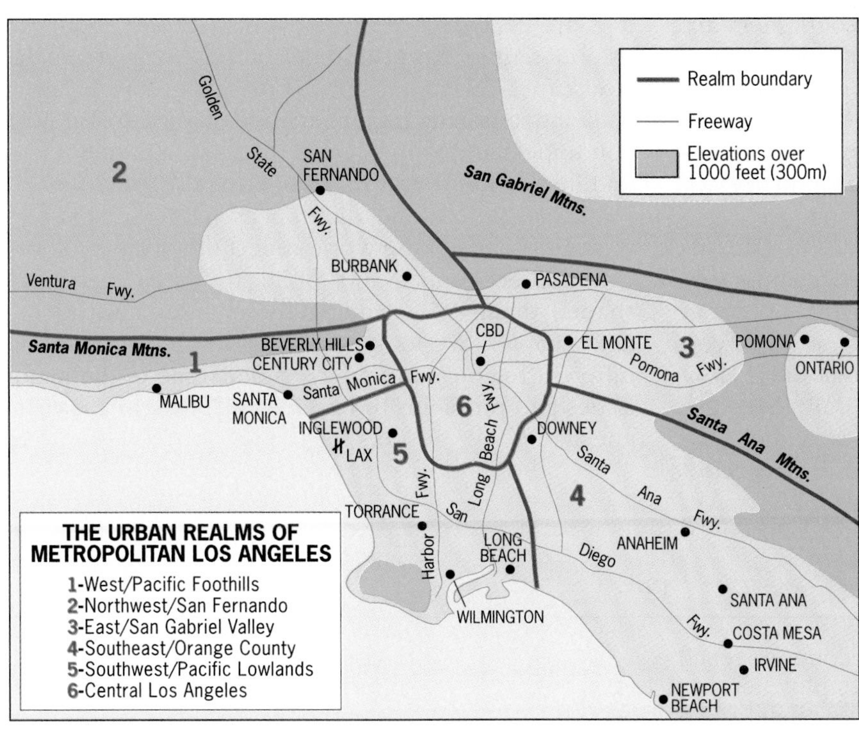

Figure 19-6 The Urban Realms of Metropolitan Los Angeles. *Source: From a map in H. J. de Blij and P. O. Muller,* Geography: Regions and Concepts, *5th ed. New York: Wiley, 1988, p. 220, designed by P. O. Muller.**

their physical attributes. They have sought to understand why ***cityscapes*** look the way they do and how the organization of elements in a city—buildings, streets, parks, public and private spaces—reflect and shape human ideas and practices. Geographers look at cityscapes, as they do to all landscapes, for clues to how societies develop, what they value, and how they

A special field note

"Imagine that you have been on a trip into space, and you are returning to Earth. Below you is a city, but you do not even know what continent you are passing over on your way to the landing site. Is this an American city or not? Does it display any structural features you are able to relate to the urban models discussed in this chapter? Can you guess what city this might be?"

function. If you were to be transported into the center of Paris or Cairo, you would know immediately that you were not in the United States. Why? And what might that tell you about the different social, cultural, and economic histories and geographies of the places you were visiting? Such questions have captured the interest of many geographers.

The term ***urban morphology*** is often used in referring to the geographic study of urban form. *Morphology* is a biological term meaning the form and structure of an organism. It came into geography nearly 100 years ago, when certain European historical geographers began charting the ways in which the physical character of cities changed over time. Earlier in this century Carl Sauer built on this tradition when he proposed that urban places should be viewed as manifestations of the relationship between human societies and natural landscapes. For Sauer, culture was the *factor*, the natural landscapes were the *medium*, and urban plan and structure were the *forms*. This raised questions about the resulting cityscape. How did the actual, physical place where a city grew affect its development? How were cultural ideas grafted onto physical landscapes in ways that produced distinctive urban forms? What clues does the urban landscape provide to the culture(s) that produced it?

The growth of cities and technology have distanced city dwellers from the natural environment, but they still live in physical places whose attributes are shaped both by nature and by humans. The human impact is so great that most recent analyses focus more on the human than the natural. But geographers are still interested in the tangible character of the spaces and structures that make up the city. They focus on the social and cultural bases of urban landscapes as well as on the role of particular urban forms in advancing certain social/cultural ideas and practices or in favoring some groups over others.

The significance of such undertakings can be appreciated by carefully observing the urban landscape. The next time you take a walk, try looking closely at what you pass—and ask questions about what you see. How much space is devoted to automobiles? How is residential space organized? Whose daily lives are inconvenienced by that use? What activities are grouped together on the same block, and what activities are excluded? What does this tell you about the priorities and cultural attitudes of those who create the landscape? Questions such as these can turn a casual walk into a fascinating experience. They can also help you understand why so many geographers seek ideas and inspiration from the study of landscape.

At the global scale, differences in the form of cities in various parts of the world reflect the diversity of the cultural, economic, and political forces that have shaped them. We examine these differences in the next chapter. We look at how cities are organized in different regions, and we consider some of the major issues and problems those cities will face in the years ahead.

◆ KEY TERMS ◆

basic sector
central business district (CBD)
central city
centrality
central place theory
cityscape
economic base
economic reach
employment structure
functional specialization
functional structure
hinterland
multiplier effect
nonbasic sector
rank-size rule
suburb
urban model
urban morphology
urban realm
urban structure

◆ APPLYING GEOGRAPHIC KNOWLEDGE ◆

1. The growth of towns and cities is boosted by the multiplier effect, one of the linkages between basic and nonbasic employment in any urban area. But what are the implications of the multiplier effect when basic employment in a city declines?
2. The popular image of a city still tends to be dominated by the impressive, skyscraper-dominated skyline that symbolizes the supremacy of the "downtown." But behind that image lies a changing reality. How is the downtown-dominant model of the American city changing? Relate the new model to the North American city you know best.
3. You are a geographer on a corporate team that is going to a city in China to position and build a factory. You will need maps to assess the site of this factory as well as its situation in the urban area. At what scales will you request that maps be made available to you?

SPECIAL FIELD NOTE FOLLOW-UP—The city pictured on page 263 is Salt Lake City, Utah.

Chapter 20

Changing Cities in a Changing World

From the field notes

"Our field trip focused on the degeneration of what Burgess would have called St. Louis's middle zone, west of the CBD. Here at Wellston, off Page Boulevard, stood a symbol of decay on the urban fringe: the gutted frame of a once-thriving electrical manufacturing plant. Surrounded by a tall chain-link fence with a locked gate and posted warnings that the site was dangerous because of severe PCB pollution, this wreckage was nevertheless flanked by housing in all directions—some of the poorest housing in the St. Louis area. It was a world (but just a few miles) away from the city center, ballpark, and famous Arch."

KEY POINTS

◆ **The problems of urban America are especially severe in the inner cities and in the older central business districts.**

◆ **Suburbanization has expanded the American city far into the surrounding countryside, contributed to the impoverishment of the central cities, and has had a major impact on community life.**

◆ **European cities have not yet experienced the dispersal of their U.S. counterparts, and remain more compact and clustered. Modern CBDs have emerged near the historic cores of these cities.**

◆ **South American, Southeast Asian, and Subsaharan African cities reflect their colonial beginnings as well as more recent domestic developments.**

The cultural geography of the modern world is affected by urban influences as never before. Two centuries ago, demographers estimate, less than 5 percent of the world's population was urbanized. Today the figure approaches 50 percent. In certain countries, such as Germany, Spain, and Belgium, over 90 percent of the people now live in cities and towns. In some parts of the world, megalopolises are evolving from formerly separate cities. In others, megacities are emerging with populations that exceed those of many countries.

This concluding chapter of Part Six discusses these regional changes and focuses on several of the critical problems rapid urbanization has produced. As we will see, the problems of large cities are cross-cultural; they differ in degree, not in kind. Cities all over the world suffer from pollution, inadequate sanitation, substandard housing, congestion, crime, and other ills. Such conditions stand in sharp contrast to the modernity and energy that are also associated with cities. Softening and reducing those contrasts is the great challenge facing cities and their governments today.

◆ PROBLEMS IN URBAN AMERICA

The American metropolis is a place of contradictions. While urban sprawl continues and cities are coalescing (Fig. 20-1), people have left the inner cities by the millions and moved to the suburbs. No longer the dominant center for urban goods and services, the ***central business district (CBD)*** is being reduced to serving the innermost portion of the metropolis. As manufacturing employment in the core area has declined during the last two decades, many large cities have adapted by promoting a shift toward service industries. Beyond the CBDs of many large cities, however, the vast ***inner cities*** remain problem-ridden domains of low- and moderate-income people, most of whom live there because they have nowhere else to go. Financially ailing big-city governments are unable to fund adequate schools, crime-prevention programs, public housing, and social services, so the downward spiral, including abandonment in the old industrial cities, has continued in the 1990s.

In the older industrial cities, the inner city has become a landscape of inadequate housing, substandard living, and widespread decay. New York City typifies the situation: there nearly 3 million people (plus a substantial number of aliens who are not officially tabulated in the census), many of them minorities, are crowded into apartment buildings averaging five stories high that were built as walkups 75 to 100 years ago. Most of these buildings are now worn out and unsanitary; many are infested by rats and cockroaches. These apartments are overfilled with people who cannot escape the vicious cycle that forces them to live there.

Yet there is something of value that remains in many of the aging neighborhoods of New York and other "manufacturing belt" cities. In the squalid poverty of ghetto and slum life, there persists a sense of neighborhood, social structure, and continuity. Urban renewal in the form of anonymous high-rises and relocation of people to new neighborhoods may so disrupt this sense of community that the costs outweigh the benefits. Drug abuse, crime, vandalism, and other social problems afflict newer areas of the inner city as well as older ones. Relationships between communities and law enforcement officers usually are tense; a single incident can set off massive disturbances.

Smaller cities have been spared some of the worst problems of the largest cities, but the transformation of their central cores has been dramatic. The rise of suburban shopping malls has devastated the commer-

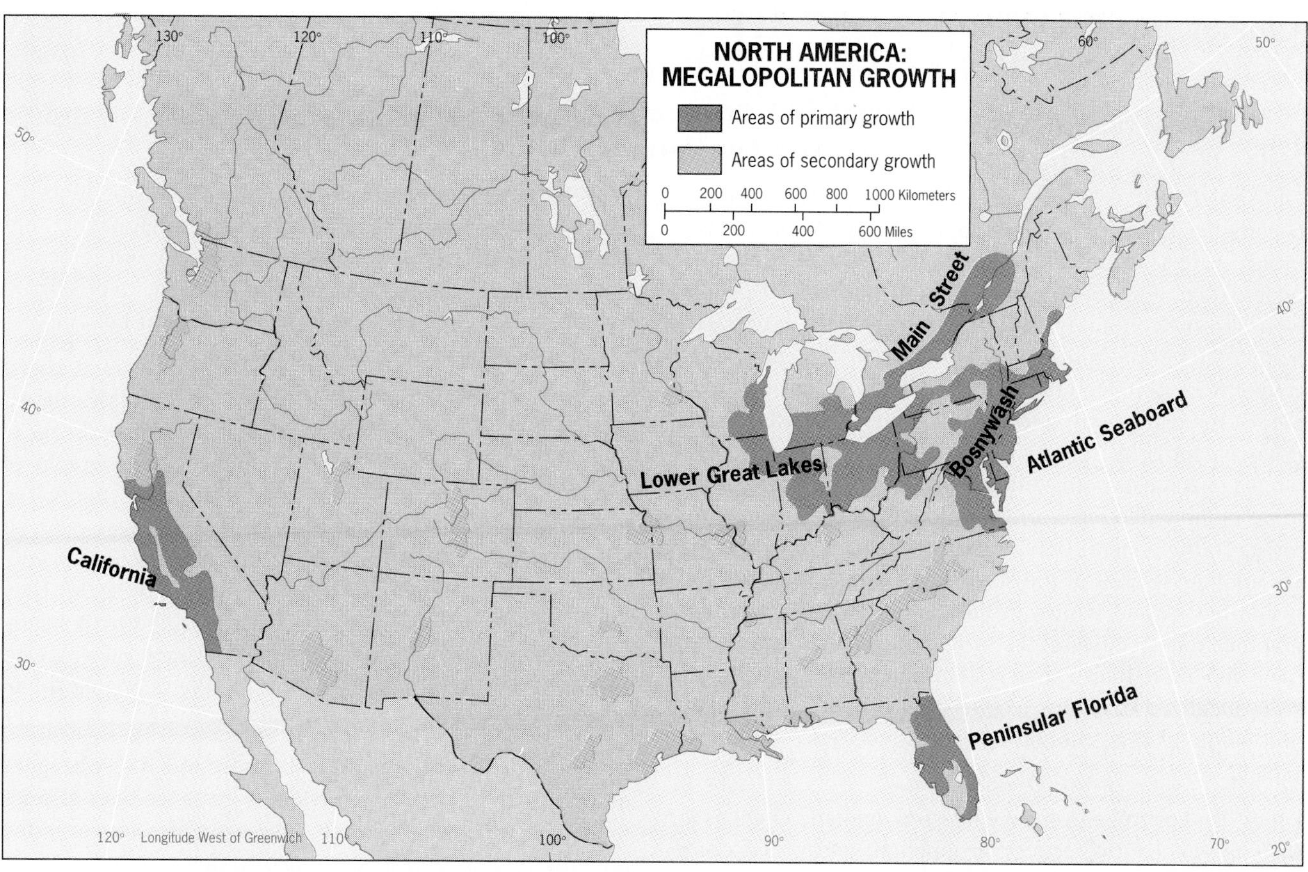

Figure 20-1 North American Megalopolitan Growth. This map shows evolving megalopolises in North America. *Source: From a map in H. J. de Blij and P. O. Muller,* Geography: Realms, Regions, and Concepts, *7th ed. New York: Wiley, 1994.*

cial core of many a modest-sized city, and without the sheer numbers of people and services of their larger counterparts, these cities' downtowns have become hollow reflections of what they once were. And as people and money leave, it becomes very difficult to reverse the downward spiral.

During the 1990s the deterioration of central cities became a major issue of public debate. Many CBDs are surrounded by blighted inner cities. Is the central city worth saving? Let us remember that the downtown area of larger cities still contains many of a city's crucial assets. Although many establishments and businesses have moved to the suburbs, others have not, at least not yet. Great museums, research libraries, world-renowned orchestras, leading universities, attractive recreational facilities, and other amenities still exist in the centers of many American cities. Crowds still fill the sidewalks of the cities each business day, and traffic jams evince their continuing vitality.

But this is a different sort of vigor than the kind that first made the downtown the heart of the city. It is a residual vitality that is engendered by activities and facilities still based in or near the CBD. Central banks, old educational institutions, major museums, governmental agencies, and large hotels are among the kinds of organizations that remain, often because their physical facilities cannot be moved or replaced. But the former advantages of agglomeration are fading fast. Publishing companies, for example, formerly shared the pool of specialized services available in Manhattan, but now many of those services can be performed anywhere in the country and transmitted electronically. The high cost of a downtown location now outweighs the advantages of agglomeration, and publishing companies have moved from New York to as far away as Florida and Texas. Geographers call this process ***deglomeration***, and it is affecting older downtowns everywhere in America.

Revitalizing the Center

In recent years city governments have taken a number of steps to counter the deterioration of the urban core. One of these involves new residential construction in the hope of luring middle- and upper-class residents (and their taxes and spending) back to the heart of the city. But the number of people who have actually moved back downtown is relatively small. Most of the

A SENSE OF SCALE

Social and Economic Change Incite the Los Angeles Riots

On April 29–30, 1992, the city of Los Angeles, California, became engulfed in the worst incident of widespread civil unrest in U.S. history. During the two days of rioting 43 people died, 2383 people were injured, and 16,291 people were arrested. Property damage was estimated at approximately $1 billion, and over 22,700 law enforcement personnel were deployed to quell the unrest. According to the media, the main catalyst for the mass upheaval was the announcement of a "not-guilty" verdict in the trial of four white Los Angeles police officers accused of using excessive force in the videotaped arrest of Rodney King, a black motorist. To the general public, the Los Angeles riots became yet another symbol of the sorry state of race relations between blacks and whites in the United States. Yet a geographical perspective on the Los Angeles riots suggests that they were more than a snap response to a single event; they were localized reactions to sweeping economic, political, and ethnic changes unfolding at regional and even global scales.

Cities like Los Angeles have witnessed dramatic changes in their physical form, economic function, and social composition over the last century. Many of these changes are responses to shifting economic conditions and dramatic technological advances, including the invention of the automobile and the advent of telecommunications. They affect not only the economic health of cities and their hinterlands, but also the social composition and stability of neighborhoods within those cities. This is certainly the case in post–1970 south-central Los Angeles, which experienced a substantial decrease in the availability of high-paying, unionized manufacturing jobs as plants closed and relocated to the city's periphery and beyond. Indeed, over 70,000 manufacturing jobs were lost in south-central Los Angeles between 1978 and 1982 alone.

An interest in understanding the significance of this development led geographer James Johnson and his colleagues to explore its impact on the ethnic and social geography of south-central Los Angeles. Johnson et al. found that while the population of south-central Los Angeles was over 90 percent African American in 1970, it had become evenly split between Latinos and African Americans by 1990. They also found that this change was accompanied by a steady influx of Korean residents and small-business owners who were trying to find a niche in the rapidly changing urban area.

Armed with this information, Johnson and his colleagues argued that the Los Angeles riots were more than a spontaneous reaction to a verdict. They were also rooted in the growing despair and frustration of different ethnic groups competing for a decreasing number of jobs in an environment of declining housing conditions and scarce public resources. Their work shows the importance of looking beyond the immediate catalysts of particular events to the local, national, and international geographical contexts in which they unfold.

---

reinvestment was done by people who were already living in the central city, and a hoped-for "return to the city" movement by suburban dwellers never fully materialized.

Residential construction within and near the downtown has created some attractive high-rise buildings with modern amenities and advantageous locations, but it has not reversed the net outward flow of the urban population. However, the ***gentrification*** of rundown areas of the inner city has had a greater impact. Gentrification is the rehabilitation of deteriorated, often abandoned inner-city housing with favorable locations relative to the CBD and central city places of employment. The growing interest in such inner-city housing results in part from the changing character of American society: the proportion of childless couples and single people in the population is growing, and for these urbanites, the suburbs do not look so attractive. Living within walking distance of the workplace, and very near the cultural and recreational amenities the central city still offers, attracts more residents every year. For them, the gentrified neighborhood is a good choice. For those displaced by gentrification, however, the consequences can be serious. Rising housing costs associated with gentrification have played a key role in the growing problem of homelessness.

Another program for inner-city revival is the ***commercialization*** of part of the downtown. Several cities, including Miami, New York, and Baltimore, have created waterfront "theme" areas to attract visitors. Such ventures have been successful in attracting tourists and generating business, but they have not substantially revived the downtowns because they cannot

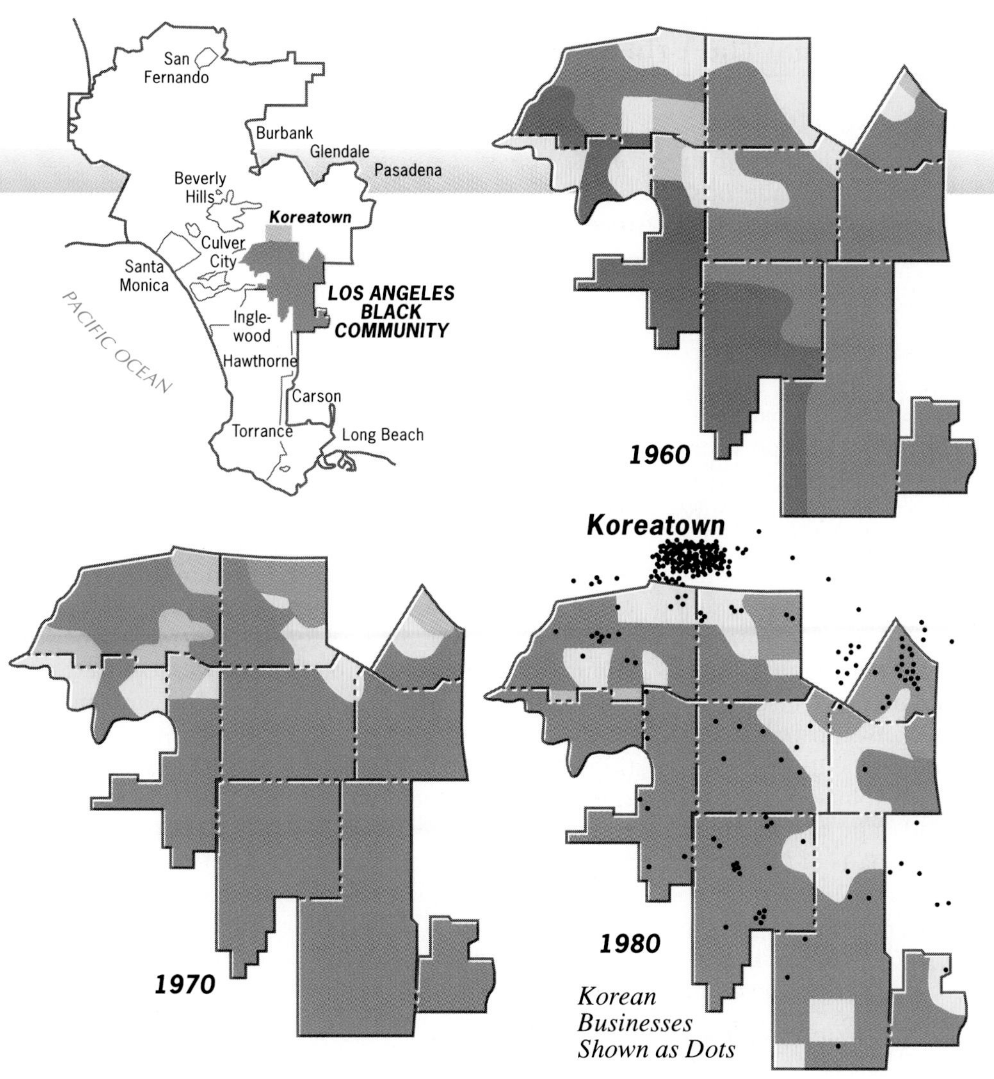

The Changing Ethnic Composition of South-central Los Angeles, 1960–1980. *Source: J. H. Johnson, Jr., C. K. Jones, W. C. Farrell, Jr., & M. L. Oliver. "The Los Angeles Rebellion: A Retrospective in View,* "Economic Development Quarterly *6 (4) (1992), p. 356-372.*

attract what the core of the city needs most: permanent residents with a stake in its future.

Does it matter over the long term? Sweeping changes have affected cities for 200 years, so if the time of downtown prosperity has come and gone, why try to stem the tide? Apparently, the answer is that it does not matter enough to change people's habits or governments' investment priorities. The office towers of Denver, Houston, and other cities contain thousands of suburban commuters whose only contact with the city is the short drive between the freeway exit and their building's parking garage. Again, the shining skyscrapers that were built to attract businesses (or keep them) downtown have not had a major effect on the social fabric of the CBD, and they have actually contributed to the abandonment of older commercial buildings, thus adding to the region's blight. Even more significant, the federal government has not provided nearly enough financial support to help the major cities reverse their decline. Services are being reduced, staff and workers in the nonbasic sector are being laid off, and the city's essential functions (sanitation, maintenance, security, transportation, and education) are suffering, affecting the downtown severely. As a result, the livability of the core of the city continues to decline and its relevance in America's urban culture is diminished.

The Suburban City

For many decades the attraction of country life with city amenities, reinforced by the discomforts of living in the heart of many central cities, has propelled people to move to the suburbs and more distant urban fringes. In postwar times, the automobile made possible mass commuting from suburban residences to downtown workplaces. As a result, the kind of suburbanization that is familiar to North Americans and other Westerners became a characteristic of urbanization in mobile, highly developed societies.

Suburbanization holds special interest for human geographers because it involves the transformation of large areas of land from rural to urban uses, affects large numbers of people who can afford to move to more expensive suburban homes, and rapidly creates distinct urban regions complete with industrial, commercial, and educational, as well as residential, components. In a sense, the suburbs reveal their occupants' idealized living patterns more accurately than any other urban zone because their layout can be planned in response to choice and demand. Elsewhere in the metropolis, there are too many constraints imposed by preexisting land-use arrangements. In a 1974 book titled *Suburban Growth*, J. H. Johnson suggests that in the suburbs "life and landscape are in much closer adjustment" than in the older parts of the urban area, providing geographers with a direct expression of the behavior of contemporary urban society. Suburban life also provides important clues about the nature of the urban future.

Among the earliest and most comprehensive geographic analyses of the rapid and dramatic changes affecting U.S. cities was a book by P. O. Muller, *Contemporary Suburban America* (1981). In it the author points out that suburbia has "now evolved into a self-sufficient urban entity, containing its own major economic and cultural activities, that is no longer an appendage to the central city" (p. 7). As such, suburban cities were ready not just to be self-sufficient but to compete with the central city for leading urban economic activities such as telecommunications, high-technology industries, and corporate headquarters.

In the current era of ***globalization***, America's suburban cities are proving their power to attract such activities, thereby sustaining the suburbanizing process. In a recent article, "The Suburban Transformation of the Globalizing American City" (1997), Muller shows that the ***world city*** model, which views today's suburbanized cities as polycentric metropolises consisting of "realms" of activity such as international company headquarters, telecommunications hubs, and communities of foreigners, describes the typical large American city today. "A new urban future is being shaped as fully developed suburbs become the engine driving metropolitan and world city growth," Muller writes.

The overall importance of suburban life in the United States is underscored by the results of the 1990 census, which indicated that no less than 46 percent of the entire American population resided in the suburbs (up from 37 percent in 1970); the remaining 54 percent were divided between the central cities (31 percent) and nonmetropolitan or rural areas (23 percent). Of the population living in metropolitan areas, 60 percent resided in the suburbs, which in 1990 had 115 million inhabitants, whereas the central cities had 78 million residents. Another indication of the importance of suburbia comes from regional growth-rate figures: during the 1980s the nation's suburban population grew by 15.2 percent, whereas the population of the central cities grew by only 6.6 percent (+4.8 million on a base of 73 million). During the 1990s, suburban growth has continued, as the 2000 Census will confirm. Thus the suburbs have become the essence of the late-twentieth-century American city (see "Focus on: Atlanta: Capital of the New South").

From the field notes

"The Renaissance Center on Detroit's waterfront represented an attempt to reverse the decline of the city's downtown through commercialization. The Center contains hotel facilities, business offices, restaurants, and shops. It continues to dominate the city's skyline, but it was not the success its investors had hoped. Urban blight began right across the street; the contrast between this gleaming skyscraper and the decaying city it overlooked was sharp and jarring. For a time the Center was both a financial and a social failure, and it never did become the symbol of a reviving Detroit."

◆ THE CANADIAN CITY

If you fly into Toronto, Canada's largest city, you may get the impression that Canadian and American cities

Atlanta: Capital of the New South

Atlanta is in the vanguard of American cities. A half-century ago, it was a nearly perfect example of the Burgess and Hoyt models, showing well-developed concentricity around its dominant CBD with some sector development. Today it is a polycentric metropolis, a real-life manifestation of the urban realms model. Emerging downtowns lie scattered across the urban area in what geographers Truman Hartshorn and Peter Muller have called a "pepperoni-pizza pattern."

In Atlanta, as in other U.S. cities, inner-city neighborhoods suffer from deterioration, crime, and dislocation. But Atlanta also is the destination, rather than the source, of relocating companies. Its economic vitality has helped mitigate its social problems.

Atlanta is the largest metropolitan area in a huge triangle extending from the southern end of Bosnywash to South Florida to Texas. With more than 3 million inhabitants, the city is growing faster than any other large metropolitan area in the country. It now extends over an area that incorporates 20 counties, and it has the largest toll-free telephone dialing area in the world.

Numerous multinational firms have established their corporate headquarters in "edge cities" on Atlanta's urban perimeter. Today the original downtown is no longer either the primary retail center or the major corporate headquarters location; it is now mainly a government, hotel, entertainment, sports, and ceremonial center.

Atlanta began as a railroad junction; today it is one of the world's busiest airport hubs, with over 300 international flights to 23 countries each day. It has become a truly international city, with more than 40 foreign consulates. At the same time, it is becoming truly multicultural. The Asian population has grown by more than 300 percent since 1980; the Hispanic population approaches 70,000. In 1995 a Buddhist monastery was under construction in the city.

Atlanta's international image is strengthened by its telecommunications role. The world's first global television network, CNN, is based there. And the city has taken the lead in creating a fiberoptic cable system: in 1995 more than 100,000 miles of fiberoptics were in place. High-tech companies have been attracted to Atlanta as a result.

Unlike the coalescing cities of the megalopolis, Atlanta is a single center that has grown outward and spun off its own satellites, some of which overshadow the old city center. Positioned at the center of the South, it reflects the region's new vitality.

are pretty much the same. A cluster of skyscrapers creates an impressive CBD. Highways carry busy traffic. Tree-lined streets mark suburban neighborhoods. Groups of high-rises near major intersections mark suburban downtowns.

That impression, however, would be mistaken. Canada's major cities suffer far less from the problems that plague their American counterparts. Large as the Toronto urban area may seem, for example, it is much less dispersed than an American city with the same population. Urban population densities are higher; multiple-family dwellings are more common; and most important, suburbanization has not gone nearly as far as it has in the United States. This means that far more high- and middle-income workers have remained in the central city, resulting in a stronger tax base and, generally, better services, ranging from public transit to police protection.

Downtown Toronto still is the functional heart of the Toronto urban area (and the same is true for several other Canadian cities). Although not immune to the forces of globalization and the development of world cities, Canadian central cities have retained a larger share of overall economic activity than their U.S. counterparts have. The kinds of urban amenities that make a central city attractive have not moved to the outer ring of suburbs. In general, the suburbs of Canadian cities are neither as wealthy nor as far from downtown as their American counterparts. The severe decline of inner-city low-income housing that marks so many American cities is not seen in urban Canada. Indeed, Canadian cities do not display the sharp contrasts in wealth that are so evident in American cities.

All this should not suggest that Toronto and other Canadian cities do not share some of the problems affecting American urban areas. The integration of foreign-born residents has not always gone smoothly in Canada's cities. Violent crime, though much less serious than it is in the United States, also afflicts Canada's cities. Circulation in several cities, while eased by the general use of mass transit, is hampered by inadequate road building. But overall Canada's cities have not (at least not yet) developed into competing urban realms. Stability and cohesion have produced an urban model that is beyond the reach of the politically and socially fragmented cities of the United States.

From the field notes

"An unusual itinerary: directly from St. John's Newfoundland, to St. John, New Brunswick. Canadian cities and towns, including those of the Atlantic Provinces, also have experienced central-city problems. Here in the east, factory closings and the decline of the fishing industry have hurt cities and towns. In St. John, New Brunswick, old warehouses have been converted into shopping malls, and the wharf now is a tourist attraction; the city even invites visits from cruise ships. The economic base is changing."

◆ THE EUROPEAN CITY

European cities are older than North American cities, but they, too, were transformed by the Industrial Revolution. Indeed, industrialization struck many of Europe's dormant medieval towns and vibrant mercantile cities like a landslide. But there are some differences between the European experience and that of North America.

In terms of population numbers, the great European cities are in the same class as major North American cities. London (6.4 million) and Paris (10.2 million), like Rome, Berlin, Madrid, and Athens, are megacities by world standards. These, however, are among Europe's many historic urban centers, which have been affected but not engulfed by the industrial tide. The cities of the British Midlands and the megalopolis of Germany's Ruhr are more representative of the manufacturing era. Individually, these cities are smaller, but in a regional context they are major urban complexes.

The industrial cities have lost much of their historic heritage, but in Europe's largest cities the legacy of the past is better preserved. Large, dominant cities such as Paris, Athens, and Lisbon (many of which are primate cities) proved to be the most durable in the face of the impact of the Industrial Age. Wars have taken their toll, of course. In the London CBD, for example, historic and modern buildings vie for space. Many of the modern structures stand on sites where historic buildings were destroyed during World War II. In Paris, Madrid, Rome, and Lisbon, on the other hand, the historic cores are well preserved and protected.

Greenbelts

The central city of London contains residential sectors of varying quality that radiate outward from the CBD. It also contains the city's main industrial zones. But unlike American cities, London's central city is not flanked by a zone of expanding suburbs. Indeed, the central city today is about the same areal size as it was in the early 1960s. The reason for this is the so-called Metropolitan Greenbelt, a zone of open country averaging more than 30 km (20 mi) wide that contains scattered small towns but is otherwise open country. This had the effect of containing London's built-up area within its 1960 limits throughout the period of rapid suburbanization in the United States. Although there are some settlements within the greenbelt, suburbanization has had to proceed beyond it—a long train ride away from the CBD (Fig. 20-2).

The greenbelt phenomenon is not unique to London; many European cities have a version of it. This preservation of near-urban open space is a legacy of governments' reaction to the impact of the Industrial Revolution during the nineteenth century. It has limited not only urban sprawl but also suburbanization. Beyond the greenbelt, suburbs are too far away from the CBD for commuting. And since the cost of gasoline is as much as three times higher in Europe than in the United States, people have an incentive to use rapid transit. This makes it more practical to cluster homes close together, and as a result the suburbs of European cities tend to be high-density villages or towns set in open countryside.

As in the United States, the outlying smaller towns in the urban hinterlands of cities such as London, Paris, and Frankfurt have attracted high-tech industries, corporate headquarters of multinational firms, and other activities typical of the modern world city. But in general, the suburban towns around Europe's major cities do not yet compete with the urban center as American suburban cities do. European governments make every effort to sustain their central cities' dominance; a prime example is the massive La Défense business district in the heart of Paris, west of the historic CBD. The largest project of its kind in Europe, La Défense is a symbol of the world city. Glass-fronted

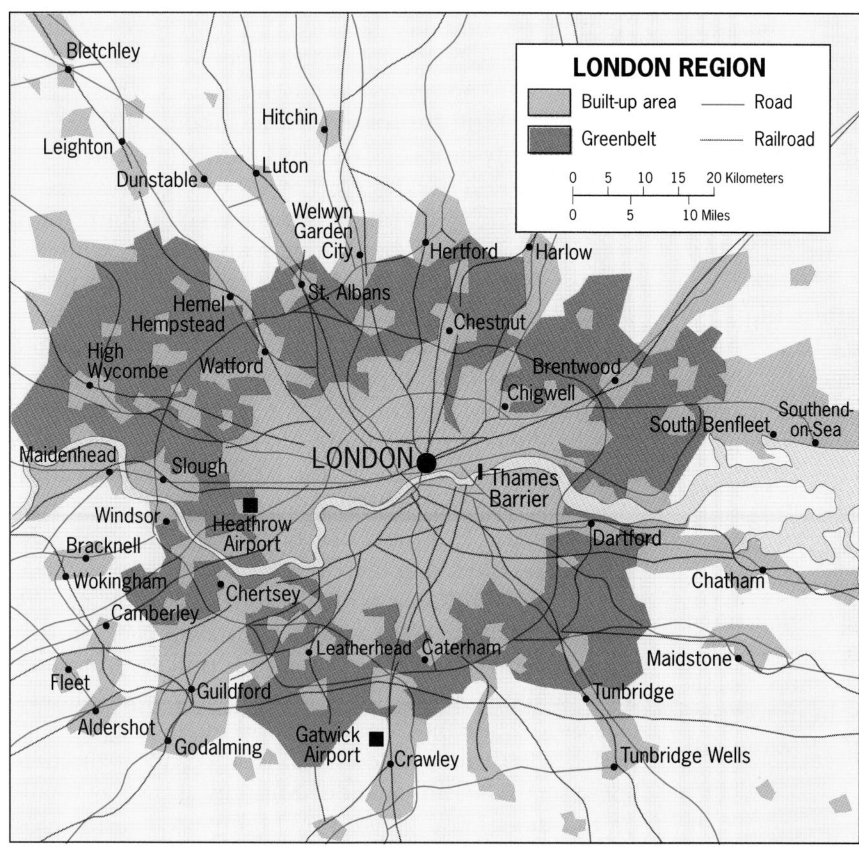

Figure 20-2 London Region. London's greenbelt and the built-up area adjacent are indicated on this map.

high-rises tower over wide avenues, huge parking garages, and every modern amenity—all within sight of the Arc de Triomphe. La Défense has become the hub of greater Paris, far outpacing all of its suburban competitors combined.

For reasons such as this, cities in Western Europe tend to be even more compact than Canadian cities. Highway and beltway development still lag, with mixed results: the central cities are clogged with cars, but mass transit, bicycles, and walking are the primary means of getting to work. Zoning rules are restrictive and strictly enforced. As a result, the European city remains clustered and crowded—which is good for the financial health of its CBD.

Microdistricts

Note that we are referring to *Western* Europe here. Just as there are significant differences between American and Canadian cities, so the cities of Europe show regional contrasts. The cities of Eastern Europe, many of which are old primate cities, were affected by communist planning that tended to neglect their cultural and historic heritage and attempted to reorganize urban life into so-called ***microdistricts***. This plan entailed the creation of a huge, dominant square at the center of the city and wide, radiating avenues fronted by ugly apartment blocks. Assemblages of these apartment blocks, generally 7 to 11 stories high, were designed to form microdistricts with workplaces, schools, recreational facilities, stores, and other amenities either within them or nearby. Thus there was no need for a large CBD, as the districts were supposed to be largely self-sufficient. Neither would there be suburbanization, mass commuting, class contrasts in neighborhoods, or traffic congestion. The emptiness of those vast, multilane avenues became a hallmark of the "socialist city."

In Eastern Europe the impact of communist city planning varied. Prague and Budapest were less severely affected than Bucharest (Romania), where the communist regime destroyed much of the city's historic townscape and replaced it with the faceless apartment blocks that make socialist cities so monotonous and dull. Today the cities of Eastern Europe are undergoing still another transformation as glass towers rise above the city.

The communist urban model was imposed most extensively in the cities of the former Soviet Union. Russia's original primate city, St. Petersburg, was heavily damaged during World War II, and its resultant open spaces were laid out in accordance with communist planning. Fortunately, the city's historic buildings were repaired and renovated, with the result that the urban landscape became a study in stark contrasts. Moscow fared better in the war, but its population grew faster afterward and is now about 11 million. Apart from some dominant Soviet-era buildings (such as the main tower of Moscow University), Moscow did not develop anything resembling an American skyline. The city's growing population lived in hundreds of microdistricts along avenues radiating outward from Red Square.

How will the postcommunist era affect the East European and Soviet city? It is too early to tell. These cities already boast high-rise hotels and modern apartment buildings, symbols of the new age. But a half-century of communist planning will not be erased overnight.

◆ THE IBERO-AMERICAN CITY

South and Middle America are among the world's most rapidly urbanizing realms today, and the largest cities are growing in regions where Iberian cultures dominate. There the urban population grew from 41 percent to 74 percent between 1950 and 1997. Although the urban experience has been a varied one—a function of diverse historical, cultural, and economic influences—there are many common threads. These commonalities form the basis of the model of the Latin American city proposed by Ernst Griffin and Larry Ford in 1980 and revised by Ford in 1996 (Fig. 20-3).

From the field notes

"It was not easy to gain permission to go to the roof of the building overlooking Lima's Plaza de San Martin, one of the Peruvian capital's most impressive public squares. The political situation was tense; the orange tent on the grass was a police post. Only in the company of an armed guard was I able to survey the square, which is flanked by some of the city's architectural treasures, several of them recently restored. The great plazas of Middle and South America's major cities often are named (as this one is) after revolutionary heroes and are flanked by cathedrals and churches as well as public buildings."

The basic spatial framework, which blends traditional elements of Latin American culture with the forces of modernization that are reshaping the urban scene, combines radial sectors and concentric zones. Anchoring the model is the thriving CBD, which, like its European counterpart, remains the city's primary business, employment, and entertainment focus. The CBD is divided into a traditional market sector and a more modern high-rise sector. Adequate public transit systems and nearby affluent residential areas assure the dominance of the CBD. Emanating outward from the urban core along the city's most prestigious axis is the *commercial spine*, which is surrounded by the *elite residential sector*. This widening corridor is essentially an extension of the CBD. It features offices, shopping, high-quality housing for the upper- and upper-middle classes, restaurants, theaters, and such amenities as parks, zoos, and golf courses. At the end of the elite spine sector lies an incipient edge city shown as "mall" on the model and flanked by high-priced residences. This reflects the emergence of suburban nodes on the North American model in South America's cities.

The remaining concentric zones are home to less well-off residents (the great majority of the urban population). Socioeconomic levels and housing quality decrease markedly with greater distance from the city center. The zone of *maturity* in the inner city contains the best housing outside the spine sector, attracting the middle classes, who invest sufficiently to keep their solidly built but aging dwellings from deteriorating. The adjacent zone of *in situ accretion* is one of much more modest housing. Interspersed with it are unkempt areas, which represent a transition from inner-ring affluence to outer-ring poverty. The residential density of this zone is usually quite high, reflecting the uneven assimilation of its occupants into the social and economic fabric of the city. The outermost *zone of peripheral squatter settlements* is home to the impoverished and unskilled. Although this ring consists mainly of teeming, high-density shantytowns, residents here are surprisingly optimistic about finding work and improving their living conditions.

A structural element of many Latin American cities is the ***disamenity sector***, which contains relatively unchanging slums known as *barrios* or *favelas*. The worst of these poverty-stricken areas often include large numbers of people who are so poor that they are forced to live in the streets. Such conditions also prevail beyond the ring highway or *periférico*, now a feature of most South American cities.

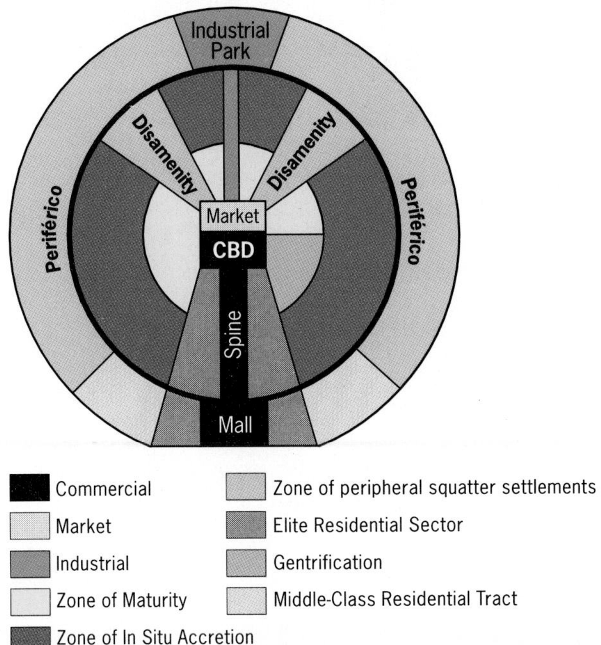

Figure 20-3 A Generalized Model of Latin American City Structure. This model includes commercial/industrial zones, elite residential sector, zone of maturity, zone of *in situ* accretion, and zone of peripheral squatter settlements. *Source: From E. Griffin and L. Ford, "A Model of Latin American City Structure,"* The Geographical Review *70 (1980), p. 406.*

Finally, the Ford model displays two smaller sectors: an industrial park, reflecting the ongoing concentration of industrial activity in the city, and a gentrification zone, where historic buildings are preserved. Gentrification remains much less common in South American cities than in North America, but it is an emerging phenomenon.

To what extent is the Griffin-Ford model a realistic portrayal of the Ibero-American city? In truth, the cities of South and Middle America display so much diversity that no simple model can represent all of their aspects. Elements of sector development can be seen in many large South American cities, for example, and the concentricity suggested by the model seems to be breaking down. Nevertheless, this model remains a useful abstraction of the "Latin" American city.

◆ THE SOUTHEAST ASIAN CITY

When we think of urbanization in Southeast Asia, we tend to focus on Singapore as the prime example. But other cities in this geographic realm also are growing and modernizing, and some of them are surpassing Singapore in certain respects. Anyone who has not seen Kuala Lumpur, the capital of Malaysia, in recent years is in for a surprise: the city is a complex of high-rise development (including the 1483-foot-tall Petronas Towers, now the world's tallest buildings). The Malaysian government is building an entirely new, $30 billion capital at Putrajaya, 40 km (25 mi) to the south.

Urban centers in Southeast Asia are growing rapidly. Between 1950 and the mid-1990s, the realm's urban population doubled in relative size (from 15 to more than 29 percent) and increased fivefold in absolute numbers (from 26 million to 132 million). Foreign influences and investments continue to play a major role in urban development. Urban growth has been most dramatic in the realm's large coastal cities (or cities connected by water to the open ocean). For example, Ho Chi Minh City (Saigon), the largest city in Vietnam, now contains more than 10 percent of the country's population of 75 million.

Urban geographers studying the growth of Southeast Asia's cities report that these cities exhibit similar land-use patterns. These patterns were identified and summarized by T. G. McGee as long ago as 1967 in *The Southeast Asian City* (Fig. 20-4). The old colonial port zone is the city's focus, together with the largely commercial district that surrounds it. Although there is no formal central business district, its elements are present as separate clusters within the belt beyond the port: the government zone, the Western commercial zone (practically a CBD by itself), the alien commercial zone, usually dominated by Chinese merchants whose residences are attached to their places of business, and the mixed land-use zone that contains miscellaneous economic activities, including light industry. The other nonresidential areas are the market-gardening zone at the urban periphery and, still farther from the city, a recently built industrial park or "estate." The residential zones in McGee's model are similar to those in the Griffin-Ford model of the Latin American city (Fig. 20-3). Among the similarities between the two are the hybrid structure of sectors and zones, an elite residential sector that includes new suburbs, an inner-city zone of middle-income housing (with new suburban offshoots in the McGee model), and peripheral low-income squatter settlements. The differences are relatively minor and are partly accounted for by local cultural and historical variations.

◆ THE AFRICAN CITY

Africa south of the Sahara is both the least urbanized *and* the most rapidly urbanizing realm in the world. As yet no city in Subsaharan Africa has reached the dimensions of Shanghai or Calcutta, or even of Cairo.

From the field notes

"Cities in the developing world often seem to be a jumble of inadequate housing and poorly maintained (or absent) facilities. But despite their appearance, clusters of housing such as those shown in this photo are far superior to the rudimentary shacks of newly arrived squatters on the outskirts. This view over a part of Lagos, Nigeria, was just two blocks from the port and on the very edge of the city center. High-rise development was overtaking this area, reflecting the dual geographies of so many urban centers in such countries. This group of houses was occupied by a set of extended families; recent arrivals had been accommodated among them."

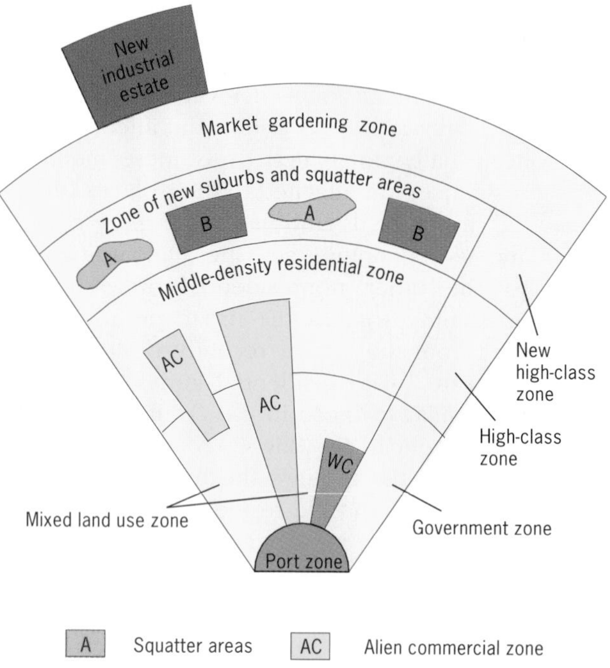

Figure 20-4 A Generalized Model of Land Use Areas in the Large Southeast Asian City. A model of land use in the large Southeast Asian city includes port zone, government zone, mixed land use zone, high-class zone, new high-class zone, middle-density residential zone, zone of new suburbs and squatter areas, market gardening zone, and new industrial zone. *Source: From T. G. McGee,* The Southeast Asian City, *London: Bell, 1967, p. 128. Reprinted by permission of the publisher.*

But the pace of urbanization throughout the realm is quickening.

As in Southeast Asia, the imprint of colonialism can be seen in many African cities. In Africa, the traditional city occurs mainly in the Muslim zone in the west. Kano, Kaduna, Zaria, and other cities in this zone retain their precolonial structures in part because of their remoteness from the routes of European colonial invasion.

But it was the Europeans who laid out such prominent urban centers as Kinshasa, Nairobi, and Harare in the interior, and Dakar, Abidjan, Luanda, Maputo, and other ports along the coast. Africa even has cities that are neither traditional nor colonial. South Africa's major urban centers (Johannesburg, Cape Town, and Durban) are essentially Western, with elements of European as well as American models, including high-rise CBDs and sprawling suburbs.

As a result of this diversity, it is difficult to formulate a model African city that would account for all or even most of what we see. Studies of African cities indicate that the central city often consists of not one but three CBDs (Fig. 20-5): a remnant of the colonial CBD, an informal and sometimes periodic market zone, and a transitional business center where commerce is conducted from curbside, stalls, or storefronts. Vertical development occurs mainly in the for-

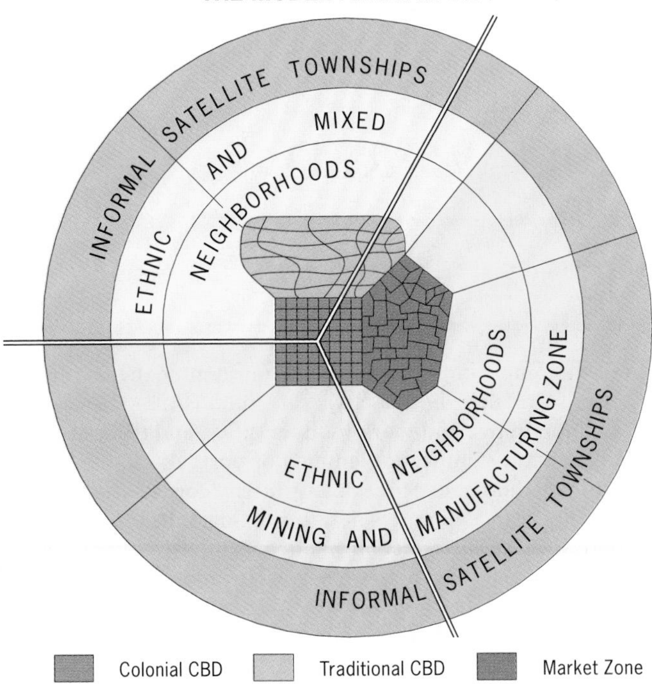

Figure 20-5 A Model African City. One model of the African city includes colonial CBD, traditional CBD, and market zone.

mer colonial CBD; the traditional business center is usually a zone of single-story buildings with some traditional architecture; and the market zone tends to be open-air, informal, yet still important. Sector development marks the encircling zone of ethnic and mixed neighborhoods (often characterized by strong ethnic identities); manufacturing or mining operations are found next to some parts of this zone. Finally, many African cities are ringed by satellite townships; these are, in effect, squatter settlements.

In Part Six, we have viewed the evolution and maturation of the city from ancient to modern times, and we have seen that the Industrial Revolution brought the most far-reaching transformation to the cities it affected. Coupled with this urban transformation was an economic one: not just cities but entire regions were drastically changed. Raw materials that previously had no value became critical resources. Formerly remote countries found that they possessed fossil-fuel and mineral reserves over which powerful empires would fight wars. We turn next to this industrial and technological transformation and the regions and landscapes it has generated.

◆ KEY TERMS ◆

central business district (CBD)
commercialization
deglomeration
disamenity sector
gentrification
globalization
inner city
microdistrict
suburbanization
world city

◆ APPLYING GEOGRAPHIC KNOWLEDGE ◆

1. The urban geography of Western European cities differs considerably from that of North American cities, despite their similar functions. European cities tend to be more compact, less sprawlingly suburbanized, and centered on generally healthier downtowns. Why have these contrasts arisen? Are European cities likely to follow the North American path toward polycentrism?

2. In the United States today, the central cities tend to be the most troubled sectors of the urban area. If you were serving on a City Council, what steps would you advocate to reverse the decline that marks the inner city? Cite examples of places where your proposals have had some positive effect.

Part Six
THE URBANIZING WORLD

Should the central city be saved, and should suburbanites, who commute downtown everyday to earn their salaries, help pay for this? Or should it be left to be transformed by the forces that are reshaping America's urban areas? The exodus to the suburbs has slowed in many American cities, and in a few places there is even some movement back into the central city. But these trends have not been of sufficient magnitude to offset the problems of the urban core. Moreover, the continuing dispersal of economic activity is working together with the telecommunications revolution to undermine the original purpose of the central city. Yet millions of Americans continue to live and work in inner cities, and these areas also contain significant elements of our cultural life and historical heritage. Since many urban cores cannot be kept alive and vibrant solely by taxing those who live there, subsidies from suburbanites using the central city are one of the few alternatives to stagnation and decline. The willingness to implement and sustain such subsidies will tell us much about the social and landscape priorities of Americans in the years ahead.

◆ SELECTED BIBLIOGRAPHY ◆

Part Six The Urbanizing World

Abbott, C. *The New Urban America: Growth and Politics in Sunbelt Cities* (Chapel Hill: University of North Carolina Press, 1981).

Adams, J., ed. *Contemporary Metropolitan America* (Cambridge, Mass.: Ballinger, 4 vols., 1976).

Agnew, J., et al., eds. *The City in Cultural Context* (Winchester, Mass.: Allen & Unwin, 1984).

Arreola, D. D., & Curtis, J. R. *The Mexican Border Cities: Landscape Anatomy and Place Personality* (Tucson: University of Arizona Press, 1993).

Bairoch, P. *Cities and Economic Development* (Chicago: University of Chicago Press, trans. C. Braider, 1989).

Berry, B.J.L. *Comparative Urbanization: Divergent Paths in the Twentieth Century* (New York: St. Martin's Press, 2nd rev. ed., 1981).

Borchert, J. "American Metropolitan Evolution," *Geographical Review* 57 (1967), 301–332.

Bourne, L., ed. *Internal Structure of the City: Readings on Urban Form, Growth, and Policy* (New York: Oxford University Press, 2nd rev. ed., 1982).

Bourne, L., et al., ed. *Urbanization and Settlement Systems: International Perspectives* (New York: Oxford University Press, 1984).

Bourne, L. S., & Ley, D., eds. *The Changing Social Geography of Canadian Cities* (Montreal, Quebec: McGill-Queen's University Press, 1993).

Brunn, S., & Williams, J., eds. *Cities of the World: World Regional Urban Development* (New York: Harper & Row, 1983).

Burgess, E. "The Growth of the City." In R. Park et al., eds., *The City* (Chicago: University of Chicago Press, 1925), pp. 47–62.

Burnett, J. A. *A Social History of Housing, 1815–1970* (North Pomfret, Vt.: David & Charles, 1978).

Carter, H. *The Study of Urban Geography.* (New York: Edward Arnold, 4th ed., 1995).

Castells, M., ed. *High Technology Space and Society* (Beverly Hills, Calif.: Sage Publications, 1985).

Castells, M., & Hall, P. *Technopoles of the World: The Making of Twenty-First-Century Industrial Complexes* (New York: Routledge, 1994).

Christaller, W. *Central Places in Southern Germany* (Englewood Cliffs, N.J.: Prentice-Hall, trans. C. Baskin, 1966 [originally published 1933]).

Christaller, W. "The Foundations of Spatial Organization in Europe," *Frankfurter Geographische Hefte* 24 (1950).

Chudacoff, H. *The Evolution of American Urban Society* (Englewood Cliffs, N.J.: Prentice-Hall, 4th rev. ed., 1994).

Clark, D. *Post-Industrial America: A Geographical Perspective* (New York and London: Methuen, 1985).

Clay, G. *Close-Up: How to Read the American City* (Chicago: University of Chicago Press, 1980 [reprint of 1973 original]).

Costa, F. J., et al. *Asian Urbanization: Problems and Processes* (Berlin: Gebruder Bomtraeger, 1988).

de Blij, H. J. *Mombasa: An African City* (Evanston, Ill.: Northwestern University Press, 1968).

Ford, L. R. "A New and Improved Model of Latin American City Structure," *Geographical Review* 86 (1996), 437–440.

Gaubatz, P. R. *Beyond the Great Wall: Urban Form and Transformation on the Chinese Frontiers* (Palo Alto, Calif.: Stanford University Press, 1996).

Gilbert, A., & Gugler, J. *Cities, Poverty and Development: Urbanization in the Third World* (New York: Oxford University Press, 2nd ed., 1992).

Gottman, J. *Megalopolis: The Urbanized Northeastern Seaboard of the United States* (New York: Twentieth Century Fund, 1961).

Griffin, E., & Ford, L. R. "A Model of Latin American City Structure," *Geographical Review* 70 (1980), 387–422.

Gugler, J., ed. *The Urbanization of the Third World* (New York: Oxford University Press, 1988).

Guldin, G. E., ed. *Urbanizing China* (Westport, Conn.: Greenwood Press, 1992).

Hall, P. *Cities of Tomorrow: An Intellectual History of Urban Planning and Design in the Twentieth Century* (Cambridge, Mass.: Blackwell Publishers, 1996).

Hall, P. *The World Cities* (New York: St. Martin's Press, 3rd rev. ed., 1984).

Hall, P., & Markusen, A., eds. *Silicon Landscapes* (Winchester, Mass.: Allen & Unwin, 1985).

Harris, C. "A Functional Classification of Cities in the United States," *Geographical Review* 33 (1943), 86–99.

Harris, C. D., & Ullman, E. L. "The Nature of Cities," *Annals of the American Academy of Political and Social Science* 242 (1945), 7–17.

Hartshorn, T. *Interpreting the City: An Urban Geography* (New York: John Wiley & Sons, 3rd rev. ed., 1992).

Harvey, D. *Social Justice and the City* (Baltimore, Md.: Johns Hopkins University Press, 1973).

Harvey, D. *The Urbanization of Capital: Studies in the History and Theory of Capitalist Urbanization* (Baltimore, Md.: Johns Hopkins University Press, 1985).

Hoyt, H. *The Structure and Growth of Residential Neighborhoods in American Cities* (Washington, D.C.: U.S. Federal Housing Administration, 1939).

Jefferson, M. "The Law of the Primate City," *Geographical Review* 29 (1939), 226–232.

Johnson, J. H., ed. *Suburban Growth: Geographical Processes at the Edge of the Western City* (London: John Wiley & Sons, 1974).

Johnson, J. H., Jones, C. K., Farrell, W. C., and Oliver, M. L. "The Los Angeles Rebellion: A Retrospective in View," *Economic Development Quarterly* 6 (4) (1992), 356–372.

Johnston, R. J. *City and Society: An Outline for Urban Geography* (London: Hutchinson, 1984).

Kim, W. B., ed. *Culture and the City in East Asia* (New York: Oxford University Press, 1997).

King, L. *Central Place Theory* (Beverly Hills, Calif.: Sage Publications, 1984).

Knox, P. L. *Urbanization: An Introduction to Urban Geography* (Englewood Cliffs, N.J.: Prentice-Hall, 1994).

Knox, P. L., ed. *The Restless Urban Landscape* (Englewood Cliffs, N.J.: Prentice-Hall, 1993).

Knox, P. L., & Taylor, P. J., eds. *World Cities in a World-system* (Cambridge, U.K.: Cambridge University Press, 1995).

Leitner, H. A. "Urban Geography: Responding to New Challenges," *Progress in Human Geography* 16 (1992), 105–118.

Ley, D. *The New Middle Class and the Remaking of the Central City* (Oxford, U.K.: Oxford University Press, 1996).

Ley, D. *A Social Geography of the City* (New York: Harper & Row, 1983).

McGee, T. G. *The Southeast Asian City: A Social Geography of the Primate Cities of Southeast Asia* (New York: Praeger, 1967).

McGee, T. G., & Robinson, I. R., eds. *The Mega-Urban Regions of Southeast Asia* (Vancouver, BC: UBC Press, 1995).

Meinig, D., ed. *The Interpretation of Ordinary Landscapes: Geographical Essays* (New York: Oxford University Press, 1979).

Mitchell, R., & Groves, P., eds. *The Shaping of North America: An Historical Geography* (Totowa, N.J.: Rowman & Allanheld, 1986).

Muller, P. O. *Contemporary Suburban America* (Englewood Cliffs, N.J.: Prentice-Hall, 1981).

Mumford, L. *The City in History: Its Origins, Its Transformations, and Its Prospects* (New York: Harcourt, Brace, 1961).

Pacione, M., ed. *Britain's Cities: Geographies of Division in Urban Britain* (New York: Routledge, 1997).

Palm, R. *The Geography of American Cities* (New York: Oxford University Press, 1981).

Rapoport, A. *House Form and Culture* (Englewood Cliffs, N.J.: Prentice-Hall, 1969).

Rotenberg, R., & McDonogh, G., eds. *The Cultural Meaning of Urban Space* (Westport, Conn.: Bergin & Garvey, 1993).

Sjoberg, G. *The Preindustrial City: Past, and Present* (Glencoe, Ill.: Free Press, 1960).

Skinner, G. W. "Marketing and Social Structure in Rural China," Part I, *Journal of Asian Studies* 24 (1964), 3–43.

Stilgoe, J. R. *Borderland: Origins of the American Suburb, 1820–1939* (New Haven, Conn.: Yale University Press, 1988).

Stren, R. E., & White, R. R., eds. *African Cities in Crisis: Managing Rapid Urban Growth* (Boulder, Colo.: Westview Press, 1989).

United Nations. Population Division. *World Urbanization Prospects, 1950–2025* (1994 revision, New York: United Nations, 1995).

Vance, J. E., Jr. *The Continuing City: Urban Morphology in Western Civilization* (Baltimore: Johns Hopkins University Press, 1990).

Ward, D. *Poverty, Ethnicity, and the American City, 1840–1925: Conceptions of the Slum and the Ghetto* (New York: Cambridge University Press, 1989).

Western, J. *Outcast Cape Town* (Minneapolis: University of Minnesota Press, 1981).

Zelinsky, W. *The Cultural Geography of the United States* (Englewood Cliffs, N.J.: Prentice-Hall, 1973).

Part Seven

THE GEOGRAPHY OF MODERN ECONOMIC CHANGE

At Issue

What price development? The Industrial Revolution propelled the world into a new age, and its environmental impacts reach from the ocean floors to the stratosphere. When the Iron Curtain lifted, the full measure of ecological damage to streams, forests, pastures, and groundwater caused by unchecked industrial activity in Eastern Europe became evident. Following the collapse of the Soviet Union, environmental damage ranging from nuclear waste pollution in the Arctic Ocean to radiation contamination in Siberia was found to be widespread. At issue is responsibility: in the formerly communist countries, state-owned enterprises created ecological disasters. But in Western countries, environmental laws failed to forestall oil and chemical spills and other devastation. ***Should a global system be established to regulate industrial pollution and cope with industrial accidents?***

On the road of good intentions . . . a billboard in Goa, India.

Part Outline

Chapter 21

Concepts of Development

From the field notes

"Why do some economies forge ahead while others do not? I spent a morning at the port of Moroni in the Federal Islamic Republic of the Comoros just after having visited the bustling economic hub of Mauritius. A boatload of wheat flour was being offloaded, bag by bag; several broke and the flour dusted the dock. Meanwhile, workers waiting to unload a cargo of wood sat motionless, unable to get started until the single crane became available. With poor infrastructure, negligible natural resources, and limited education, the Republic of the Comoros is one of the world's poorest countries. But Mauritius was very poor also, and has progressed remarkably since it began to attract foreign investment in its textile and other manufactures. Here in the Comoros, the sole opportunity may be tourism: the scenery is magnificent and flights from the Arabian Peninsula and South Africa are stopping on Grande Comore (now called Njazidja)."

KEY POINTS

- ◆ **The global economic picture is characterized by enormous gaps between rich and poor countries, but the geography of economic well-being also reveals regional disparities within countries.**
- ◆ **Economic disparities are usually believed to be due to different levels of development, but in reality development is more complex and cannot be reduced to simple categories.**
- ◆ **Underlying economic disparities is a core-periphery relationship among different regions of the world. This affects how economies develop in both the core and the periphery.**
- ◆ **As the twenty-first century approaches, some states are still subsistence-based and poor, whereas others are in the "takeoff" stage.**
- ◆ **Rapid development is taking place under widely different political systems; it is often associated with democratization, but it is also occurring under authoritarian regimes.**

In 1997, the per capita ***gross national product*** (GNP) in Japan in U.S. dollars was $39,640. In the United States it was $26,980. In Western Europe it averaged $25,010. But in India it was $290, in Nigeria it was $340, and in Indonesia, the world's fourth most populous country, it was $980. This enormous range reflects the often searing contrasts between the rich world and the poor (Table 21-1).

The economic and social geography of the contemporary world is a patchwork of almost inconceivable contrasts. On the crude fields of shifting cultivators in equatorial American and African forests, root crops are still grown using ancient methods and the most rudimentary tools. On the Great Plains of North America, in Ukraine, and in eastern Australia, modern machines plow the land, seed the grain, and harvest the wheat. Toolmakers in the villages of Papua New Guinea still fashion their implements by hand, as they did many centuries ago, while the factories of Japan disgorge automobiles by the shipload for distribution to markets thousands of miles away. Between these extremes, the range and variety of productive activities are virtually endless.

Despite the worldwide impact of the Industrial Revolution, there are areas even within the industrialized countries where change is slow in coming. Parts of the rural South in the United States still experience significant poverty and remain comparatively remote from the effects of national economic growth. In remote areas of western and northern Japan, life has changed little while modernization has occurred elsewhere in the country. In Europe, areas of isolation and stagnation persist. At the same time, there are places in poorer, less industrialized countries where clusters of industries have emerged, rapid urban growth is taking place, and local conditions differ sharply from those prevailing in surrounding areas. Recent eco-

Table 21-1 Per Capita GNP for Selected Countries, 1996 (In U.S. $)

Europe		South Asia	
United Kingdom	19,600	India	380
Sweden	25,710	Bangladesh	260
France	26,720	Pakistan	480
Germany	28,870	Sri Lanka	740
Hungary	4,340	Southeast Asias	
Italy	19,880	Indonesia	1,080
Spain	14,350	Malaysia	4,370
Greece	11,460	Singapore	30,550
North America		Thailand	5,960
Canada	19,020	Southwest Asia–North Africa	
United States	28,020	Egypt	1,080
Middle America		Kuwait	19,010
Mexico	3,670	Morocco	1,290
Costa Rica	2,640	Qatar	12,900
Nicaragua	380	Saudi Arabia	9,080
Haiti	310	UAE	19,000
South America		Subsaharan Africa	
Argentina	8,380	Nigeria	240
Brazil	4,400	Ethiopia	100
Bolivia	830	Kenya	320
Guyana	590	Moçambique	80
Peru	2,420	Gabon	3,950
East Asia		Siera Leone	200
China	750	South Africa	3,520
Japan	40,940		
South Korea	10,160		

Source: World Bank, *1998 World Development Indicators.* Washington, D.C., 1998, pp. 12–14. Figures for Kuwait, Qatar, Saudi Arabia, and UAE are estimates.

nomic growth on the Pacific Rim of East Asia has created huge regional disparities in economic conditions between some coastal provinces of China and distant interior provinces. Such regional contrasts have significant social as well as political consequences, and China is by no means the only country affected. Regional economic disparities are increasing throughout the world.

◆ CONCEPTS AND APPROACHES

Economists and geographers use a variety of approaches to describe the wide disparities in the global economy. Countries with high levels of urbanization and industrialization and high standards of living have long been referred to as ***developed countries (DCs)***, in contrast to ***underdeveloped countries (UDCs)***. This approach divides the world into two major categories, but it is also based on the idea that all countries are at some stage of development. However, the concept of ***development*** is a complicated one. How should development be measured? The GNP index provides one approach, but it has many shortcomings (see "Focus on: Gross National Product"). It does not measure any aspect of the informal economy, it says nothing about contrasts within countries, and it provides no sense of the degree to which wealth is concentrated in the hands of a few. Other approaches provide a richer basis for thinking about development (see "Focus on: Measures of Development"), but none of these approaches produces a clear dividing line between developed and underdeveloped countries. Instead, UDCs and DCs lie along a development continuum, and any division between them is arbitrary.

The problem of classifying countries into two categories of development became even more acute in the 1960s and 1970s, when some countries traditionally classified as underdeveloped, such as South Korea and Taiwan, began shooting ahead. Hence, the term ***developing countries*** came into use to describe a third category of development consisting of countries that show evidence of moving toward the developed category as measured by the indexes of development described in the boxes just mentioned. The term *underdeveloped* has such a negative connotation, however, that no country wanted to be so classified. The term came to be seen as condescending, conveying the notion that a country was poor culturally as well as economically. Such sensitivity is understandable when one realizes that ideas about development tend to come from scholars in the developed world. Moreover, terms such as *developed* and *underdeveloped* also mean rich and poor, haves and have-nots—which carry with them emotionally laden notions of advantaged and disadvantaged. Hence, the term **underde-**

Focus On

Gross National Product

The Gross National Product (GNP) of a country refers to the total value of all goods and services produced by its economy during a given year. It includes all incomes achieved by a country's citizens and businesses, whether earned within the country or abroad. It therefore is broader than Gross Domestic Product, which encompasses only goods and services produced within a country during a given year.

GNP is widely used for measuring the development status of countries. But it has its shortcomings, and not just because it conceals regional variations within countries. Most obviously, it says nothing about the distribution of wealth. Consider, for example, the GNP data for such countries as Kuwait and the United Arab Emirates (UAE). In 1995 the per capita GNP (GNP divided by the population of the country) of both countries was over $17,000. This figure is larger than those of many countries that are regarded as part of the developed world, including several European countries. Also note the high per capita GNPs for such countries as Saudi Arabia and Qatar. Are these "developed" countries in an economic and social sense? The answer is that large amounts of money derived from the sale of a single product (in this case oil) do not automatically or even quickly result in overall national development. Thus, the bare figures give us no hint of the degree of overall participation in the country's economy or the average citizen's material standard of living. National statistics (such as population data) can conceal enormous regional and demographic diversity.

Beyond these matters, GNP is a limited measure because it includes only transactions in the formal economy. Quite a few countries have a per capita GNP of less than $300 per year—a figure so low that it might seem impossible to survive in those countries. The answer to this apparent dilemma lies in the informal economy, which includes everything from a garden plot in a yard to the black market and the drug trade. Collectively, these are quite significant elements of the economic picture in many areas, but they are entirely omitted from GNP statistics.

Measures of Development

What distinguishes a developed or core economy from a less developed or peripheral one? To answer this question, we need to compare countries on the basis of certain standardized measures. Divisions between well-off and less well-off economies are arbitrary, and the dividing line is a topic of debate. There is also the problem of data. Statistics for many countries are inadequate, unreliable, and incompatible with those for other countries, or simply unavailable.

Despite those drawbacks, the following measures are normally used to gauge levels of economic development:

1. ***National Product per Person*** This figure is determined by taking the sum of all incomes accumulated in a year by all of a country's citizens and dividing it by the total population. Figures for all countries are then converted into a single currency index for purposes of comparison. In core countries, the index can exceed $25,000; in the periphery, it is as low as $100.
2. ***Occupational Structure of the Labor Force*** This is the percentage of workers employed in various sectors of the economy. A high percentage of laborers engaged in the production of food staples, for instance, signals a low overall level of development.
3. ***Productivity per Worker*** This is the sum of production over the course of a year, divided by the total number of persons in the labor force.
4. ***Consumption of Energy per Person*** The greater the use of electricity and other forms of power, the higher the level of economic development. To some extent, these data must be viewed in the context of climate.
5. ***Transportation and Communications Facilities per Person*** This measure reduces railway, road, airline connections, telephone, radio, television, and so forth to a per capita index. The higher the index, the higher the level of development.
6. ***Consumption of Manufactured Metals per Person*** A strong indicator of development levels is the quantity of iron and steel, copper, aluminum, and other metals utilized by a population during a given year.
7. ***Rates*** A number of additional measures are employed, including literacy rates, caloric intake per person, percentage of family income spent on food, and amount of savings per capita.

veloped was used less and less, and the developed–underdeveloped distinction was largely replaced by a developed–developing distinction. The latter had the advantage of sounding more optimistic, and it could encompass countries such as South Korea and Taiwan. But it was also misleading because it suggested that *all* countries were achieving higher levels of socioeconomic prosperity when that was not the case.

Beyond problems of terminology, the very effort to classify countries in terms of levels of development has come under increasing attack during the last two decades. One concern is that a scale of development suggests that all countries have moved or will move through the same process of development. Hence, like the demographic transition model (see Chapter 5), the development model does not take geographical differences very seriously. Just because Japan moved from a rural, agrarian state to an urbanized, industrial one does not mean that Sudan will—or at least that it will in the same way. Others criticize the development model because of the Western bias in the way development is conceptualized. They argue that some of the measures taken in poorer countries that are viewed as progress (attracting industry, mechanized agriculture, etc.) can lead to worse social and environmental conditions—at least in the long run. Still others criticize the development model because it does not reflect the ways in which some parts of the world influence socioeconomic changes in others. Instead, the model treats countries as autonomous units moving through a process of development at different speeds.

The Core-Periphery Model

In light of these criticisms, some scholars have argued for a new approach to describing global economic disparities—one that is more sensitive to geographical differences and the relationships among development processes occurring in different places. They propose that the geography of the world economy can be understood in terms of a ***core-periphery model***. This model, which is also used in discussions of political power, views the world as characterized by a ***core***, ***semi-periphery***, and ***periphery***. Core regions are those that have achieved high levels of socioeconomic prosperity and are dominant players in the global economic game. By contrast, periphery regions are poor regions that are dependent in significant ways on the core and do not have as much control over their own affairs. The semi-periphery, as the name implies, con-

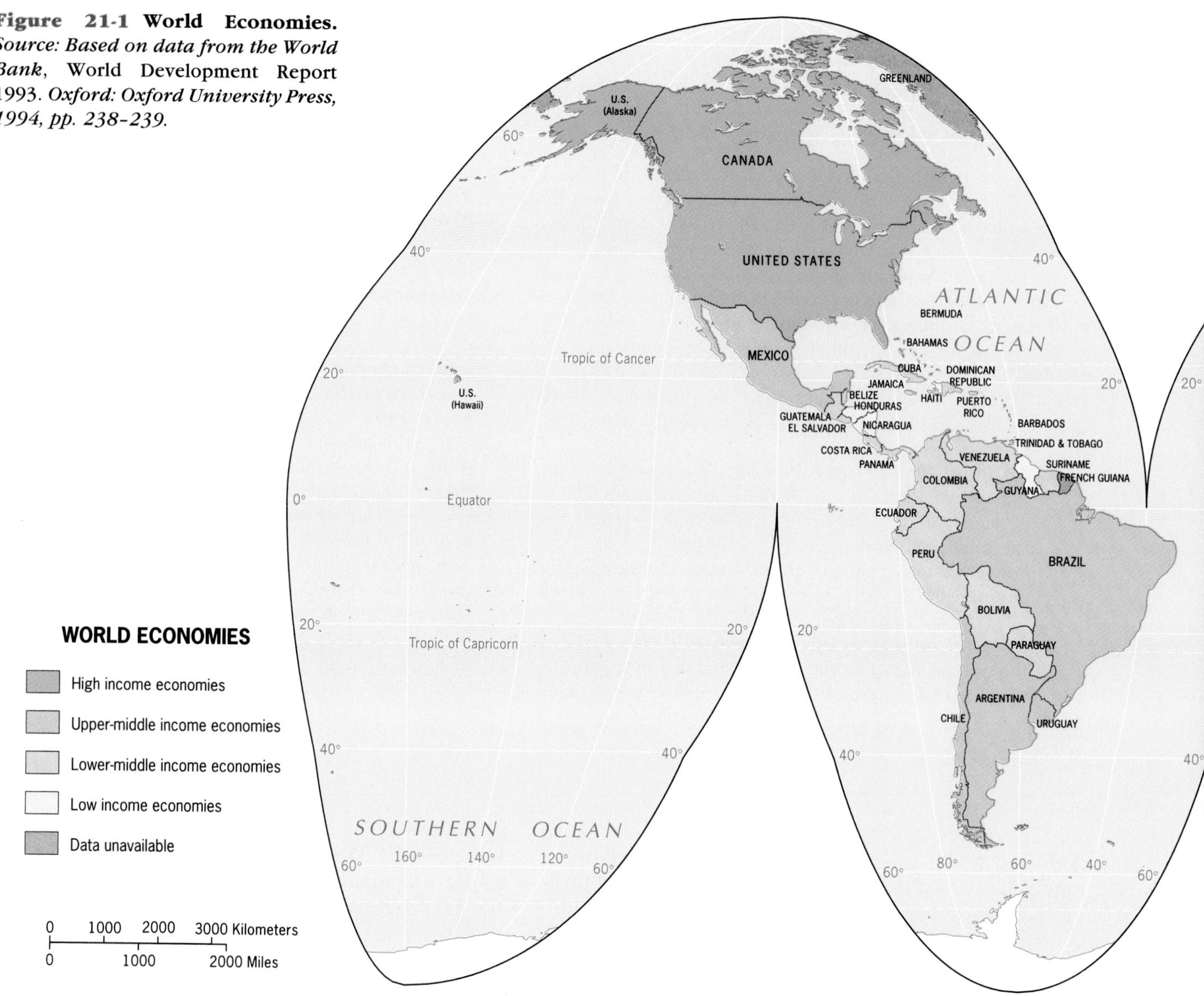

Figure 21-1 World Economies. *Source: Based on data from the World Bank,* World Development Report 1993. *Oxford: Oxford University Press, 1994, pp. 238–239.*

sists of regions that exert more power than peripheral regions but are dominated to some degree by the core regions. Since the core-periphery model focuses attention on the economic relationships among places, it is a key component of many theories that treat the global economy as a large system. The best known of these theories—World Systems Theory—was pioneered by Immanuel Wallerstein, whose work has done much to promote the core-periphery concept.

Dividing the world into cores, semi-peripheries, and peripheries, might seem to do little more than replace *developed–developing–underdeveloped* with a new set of terms. But the core-periphery model is actually quite different because it makes the power relations among places explicit and does not assume that socioeconomic change will occur in the same way in all places. It also has the advantage of being able to describe developments at any spatial scale, be they local, regional, national, or global. Thus a core-periphery relationship can exist within a region (Los Angeles can be described as the economic and social core region of Southern California); within an individual country (the Johannesburg area can be described as the economic core region of South Africa); or in a global context (Japan can be described as an economic core region of the world).

Patterns on the Map

The core-periphery model is a useful frame of reference for understanding the geography of modern economic change. But development concepts are still widely used, and despite their limitations, they provide a useful indication of the character and extent of economic disparities at the scale of the state. These

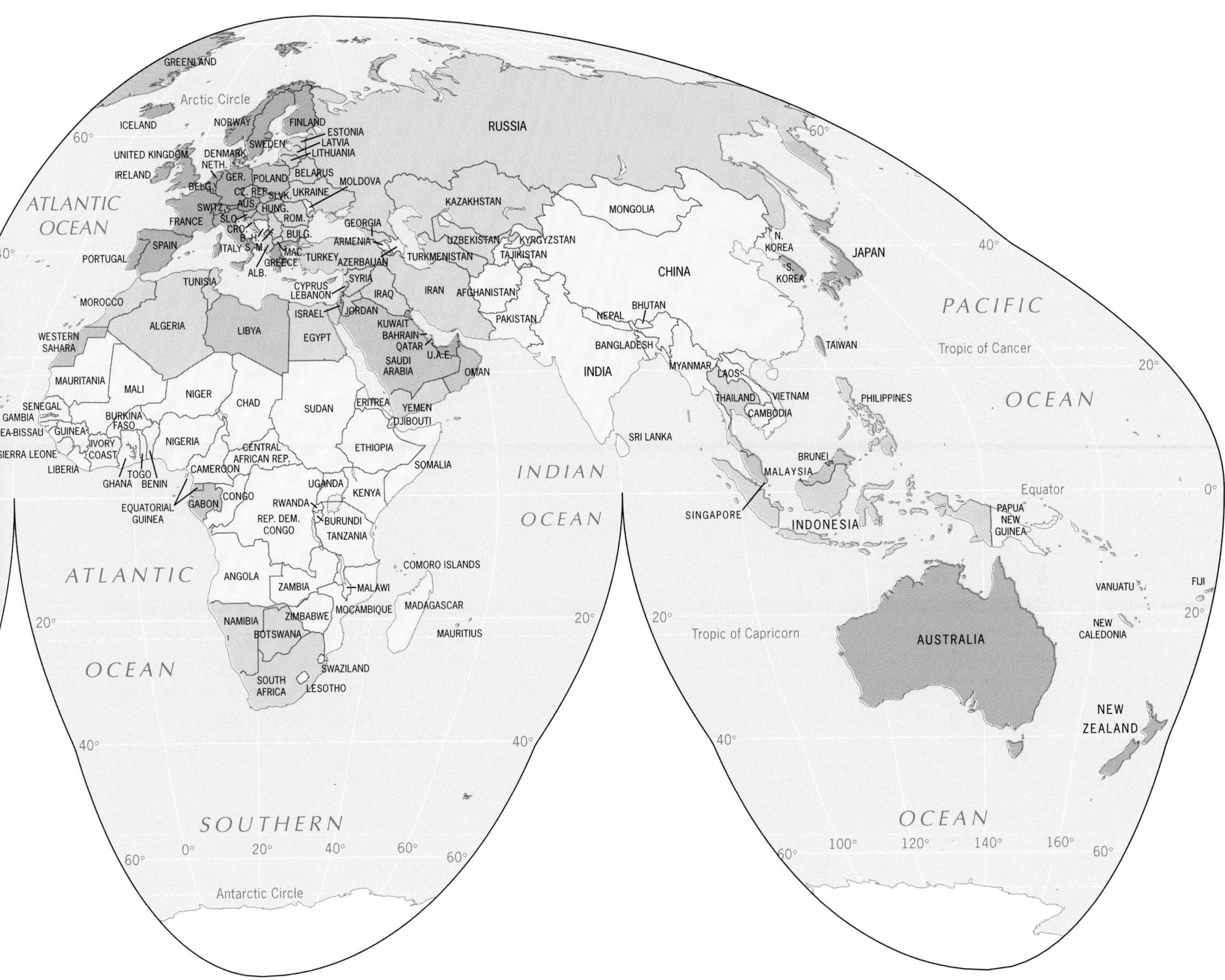

can be seen vividly in Figure 21-1. This map is based on four categories of development used by the World Bank, the Washington, D.C.-based agency that is involved in global development projects. The World Bank groups countries into four categories based on income: low-income economies, lower-middle-income economies, upper-middle-income economies, and high-income economies. The low-income countries are concentrated in Africa and South, Southeast, and East Asia. In the late 1990s the countries with the world's lowest incomes were Cambodia in Asia and Moçambique, Ethiopia, Chad, Tanzania, and Congo in Africa. In all, some 56 of the world's countries are still designated as low-income states; four of them—Guyana, Haiti, Honduras, and Nicaragua—are in the Western Hemisphere.

It is encouraging to note that middle-income countries outnumber the poorer states. According to World Bank statistics, there are 65 middle-income countries, including many in Middle and South America. Forty-seven of these are in the lower-middle-income group and 18 in the upper-middle-income group.

The high-income economies include oil-rich Southwest Asian states as well as prosperous Western European countries. When Figure 21-1 is compared to Table 21-1, some inconsistencies seem to arise. But remember that per capita GNP (Table 21-1) is only one criterion for development; Figure 21-1 is based on a wider range of indicators. Development is measured by various means, as described in the box.

◆ GLOBAL ECONOMIC DISPARITIES

Figure 21-1 is in large measure a reflection of the course of history. The sequence of events that led to the present divisions began long before the Industrial Revolution. Even by the middle of the eighteenth century, Europe had laid the foundations for its colonial expansion and global economic domination. The Industrial Revolution increased Europe's need for raw materials, while its products increased the efficiency of its control over the colonies. While Western countries gained an enormous head start, their colonies continued to supply raw materials and consume the products of Western industries. Thus a system of international exchange was born, along with a flow of capital that changed little when the age of colonialism came to an end in the mid-twentieth century. Countries in the periphery accuse the core of perpetuating its advantage through ***neo-colonialism***—the entrenchment of the old system of dominance under an economic rather than political guise.

Conditions in the Periphery

The world economic system works to the disadvantage of the periphery, but it is not the only obstacle that the poorer countries face. Political instability, corrupt leaders, misdirected priorities, misuse of aid, and cultural resistance to modernization are among the conditions that hamper development.

Countries in the periphery suffer from numerous demographic, economic, and social ills. Their populations tend to have high birth rates and moderate to high death rates, and life expectancy at birth is comparatively low (see Part Two). As much as half the population is 15 years old or younger. Infant mortality is high. Nutrition is inadequate, and diets are not well balanced; protein deficiency is a common problem. The incidence of disease is high; health-care facilities are inadequate. There is an excessively high number of persons per available doctor, and too few hospital beds are available. Sanitation is poor. Large numbers of school-age children do not go to school; illiteracy rates are high.

Rural areas are overcrowded, and surface communications are of low quality. Men and women often do not share equally in the work that must be done; women's workloads tend to be much heavier, and children are required to work. Landholdings are often fragmented, and the small plots are farmed with outdated, inefficient tools and equipment. The main crops tend to be grains and roots; little protein is produced because its demand on the available land is higher. Little is produced for the local market because distribution systems are poorly organized and demand is low. On the farms, yields per unit area are low, subsistence modes of life prevail, and many families are constantly in debt. These conditions preclude investment of money and time in such luxuries as fertilizers and soil conservation methods. As a result, soil erosion is commonplace in most peripheral countries. Where areas of larger-scale, modernized agriculture have developed, these produce exports for foreign markets and have a minimal impact on conditions in their own country.

In urban areas, overcrowding, poor housing, inadequate sanitation, and lack of services prevail. Unemployment is high. (Yet rural conditions are perceived to be so much worse that rural-urban migration continues at very high rates.) Per capita income remains low, savings per person are minimal, and credit facilities are poor. Families spend a very large portion of their income on food and basic necessities. The middle class remains small, and a large percentage of its members are foreign immigrants.

These are just some of the conditions prevailing in the periphery. Geographically, peripheral countries tend to be marked by severe regional disparities. The capital city may be a symbol of urban modernization, with thriving farms in the immediate surroundings and factories on the outskirts. Road and rail connect to a bustling port, where luxury automobiles are unloaded for use by the privileged elite. Here in the country's core area, the rush of "progress" may be evident, but if you travel a few miles into the countryside you will find a very different picture. Just as the core countries become richer and leave the poorer countries even farther behind, so the gap between progressing and stagnant regions *within* peripheral countries grows wider. This is a global problem, and it is growing worse.

Levels of Industrialization

Obviously, levels of industrialization in the core differ from those in the periphery. Certainly some industries exist in virtually all periphery countries, however modest and local; the differences lie in the *kinds* of industries and their dimensions. As noted earlier, the level of development in a country is indicated by productivity per worker in the labor force, consumption of energy per person, the quantity of metal used, and the transport facilities that have been developed. These indicators also reflect a country's industrialization, because output per worker goes up when industry becomes mechanized, commercial energy is consumed in greater quantities, metals play a leading role in manufacturing, and transport networks are more highly developed.

Small wonder, then, that some countries seeking to accelerate their economic development have undergone massive industrialization. In the Soviet Union under Stalin, planners poured huge quantities of resources into industry. Similarly, peripheral countries from Indonesia to Egypt have built their own steel mills and national airlines to serve as symbols of "progress."

Tourism: Boon or Bane?

Peripheral countries in the Caribbean region of Middle America and in other parts of the world have become leading destinations for millions of tourists from richer nations. However, the tourist industry contributes little to those countries' development—and may have serious negative effects on their cultures.

With respect to economic geography, the investment that must be made by the "host" country is substantial. Often, imports of building materials and equipment strain the country's supply system, and funds are diverted to hotel construction that should be spent on other needs such as housing for citizens. Moreover, many hotels and other tourist facilities are owned not by the host country but by large multinational corporations. These corporations earn enormous profits, which are sent back to headquarters in the home country.

Some countries do earn substantial income from tourism; they include Thailand, Kenya, Barbados, and Fiji, among others. However, that income does not truly benefit local economies. Some of the income may result from tourists' consumption of scarce commodities such as food, water, and electricity. Much of it must be reinvested in the construction of airports, cruise-ports, and other amenities. As for the creation of employment, neither the number nor the nature of jobs in the tourist industry is encouraging.

Tourism frequently strains the fabric of local communities. The invasion of poor communities by wealthier visitors sometimes creates hostility among the hosts. For some local residents, tourists have a "demonstration effect" that causes them to behave in ways that may please or interest the visitors but is disapproved of by the larger community. Free-spending, sometimes raucous tourists contribute to anger and resentment. Moreover, tourism can have the effect of debasing local culture, which is adapted to suit the visitors' taste. Many workers say that employment in the tourist industry is dehumanizing because it demands displays of friendliness and servitude that locals find insulting.

A flood of affluent tourists may be appealing to the government of a poor country (whose elite may have a financial stake in the hotels where they can share the pleasures of the wealthy), but local entrepreneurs usually take a different view. Powerful multinational corporations and the government may intervene to limit the opportunities of local, small-scale operators in favor of mass, prearranged tour promotions that isolate the tourist from local society.

The cultural landscape of tourism is a study in harsh contrasts: gleaming hotels tower over modest, often poor housing; luxury liners glide past poverty-stricken villages; opulent meals are served in hotels while, down the street, children suffer from malnutrition. If the tourist industry offered real prospects for economic progress in the periphery countries, such circumstances might be viewed as temporary, unfortunate byproducts. However, the evidence indicates otherwise.

Nevertheless, tourist travel heightens knowledge and awareness and can promote intercultural contact and understanding. "Ecotourism" aims to inform about the natural environment, whereas "geotourism" involves scholars in tourists' travel experience. Such initiatives help improve the image of what is sometimes called the "irritant industry."

Not all poorer countries, however, have made this decision. Some have realized that economic progress is achieved not just through industrial growth but through the transformation of an entire society. A steel mill or other symbolic industry will do little to speed that transformation. Some governments, therefore, have made agriculture, not industry, their main priority.

Whatever the course chosen (see "Focus on: Tourism: Boon or Bane?"), all peripheral countries in the late 1990s continue to face enormous obstacles. These arise not only from their own internal circumstances (rapid population growth, limited capital, etc.) but also from global economic conditions over which they have little control. The core countries constitute two-thirds of the market for all the products of the periphery combined, but market prices, tariffs, demand, and other conditions can change quickly and sometimes disastrously. When oil costs rose during the 1970s, the UDCs suffered severely. When inflation rose in the core, the periphery's exports were severely affected. Now the foreign debt crisis is affecting the economic well-being of low- and middle-income countries.

◆ MODELS OF DEVELOPMENT

What processes dictate the rate and extent of economic development? In the last few decades various models have been proposed to describe the economic processes that facilitate or inhibit a country's drive toward material and social prosperity. These models are of two broad types: liberal and structuralist.

Liberal models are based on the ideas about development discussed earlier. They assume that all countries are at the same stage along a development trajectory and that economic disparities between countries are the result of short-term inefficiencies in local or regional market forces. Over the long term, liberal models assume that all countries are capable of development. On the other hand, ***structuralist models*** view regional economic disparities as a *structural* feature of the global economy. Disparities exist because things have come to be organized or structured in a certain way that cannot be changed easily. For many structuralist theorists, the development of the global economy brought into being a set of large-scale orders or structures—the concentration of wealth in certain areas, unequal relations among places, and so forth—that make it very difficult for poorer regions to improve their situation. Hence, they believe that it is misleading to assume that all areas will go through the same process of development.

The Modernization Model

One of the most influential liberal models was formulated by the economist Walt Rostow in the 1960s and is referred to as the ***modernization model***. Rostow's model suggests that all countries follow a similar path through five stages of development.

In the first stage the society is *traditional* and the dominant activity is subsistence farming. The social structure is rigid and unchanging, and there is much resistance to technological change.

The second stage brings the *preconditions of takeoff.* Progressive leadership moves the country toward greater flexibility, openness, and diversification.

This, in turn, will lead to the third stage, *takeoff.* Now the country experiences something akin to an industrial revolution, and sustained growth takes hold. Urbanization increases, industrialization proceeds, and technological and mass-production breakthroughs occur.

Next, the economy enters the fourth stage, *drive to maturity.* Technologies diffuse, industrial specialization occurs throughout the nation, and international trade expands. Modernization is evident in the core areas of the country; the rate of population growth is reduced.

Some countries reach the final stage, that of high mass consumption, which is marked by high incomes and widespread production of many goods and services. A majority of workers enter the service sector of the economy.

Dependency Theory

Rostow's model provides a useful view of how certain parts of the world have changed over time, but it has been criticized because it does not take into account the different constraints that regions face and because it suggests a single development path that is not influenced by cultural differences. The principal structuralist alternative to Rostow's model, known as ***dependency theory***, addresses some of these criticisms but not all. Dependency theorists hold that the political and economic relationships between countries and regions of the world control and limit the economic development possibilities of less well-off areas. They note, for example, that colonialism created political and economic structures that caused the colonies to become dependent on the imperial powers. They further argue that such dependency helps sustain the prosperity of dominant regions and the poverty of other regions. Dependency theory thus sees very little hope for economic prosperity in regions and countries that have traditionally been dominated by external powers. This aspect of dependency theory has been criticized, since some traditionally "dependent" regions have made economic gains. Indeed, like modernization theory, dependency theory is based on generalizations about economic change that pay relatively little attention to geographical differences in culture, politics, and society. While both models provide some insights into the development process, neither is greatly concerned with the spatial and cultural situation of places—central elements of geographical analysis.

◆ A CHANGING WORLD

Today the world remains divided, but change is occurring almost everywhere. In many countries change continues to be localized, so that "national" statistics suggesting overall progress mask growing regional inequalities. Nevertheless, there are some grounds for optimism. In many countries significant indicators—rates of population growth, levels of education, percentages of workers in nonagricultural jobs—are showing improvement.

One reason for the achievement of "takeoff" levels by such countries as Mexico, Brazil, Thailand, and Malaysia lies in major political and economic changes. Until the end of the 1980s there were three major political-economic blocs: the capitalist First World, the communist Second World, and an uncommitted Third World consisting mainly of mixed economies tending toward state control. Both the First and Second Worlds sought to influence the Third World by encouraging the adoption of their economic models. The results were often disastrous, as when Tanzania and Ethiopia imposed collective farming, which was not well suited to local conditions. The collapse of the Soviet Union, however, ushered in a period of tumultuous transition whose outcome is still uncertain. But the distinctions and concerns associated with the previous divisions no longer apply, and the notion of a Third World is obsolete.

While communist economics failed in the Soviet Union and Eastern Europe, the same cannot yet be said of China. In the late 1990s, China remains a bastion of socialist planning, having overcome the challenge of democratization by military force in 1989. In China, unlike Tanzania or Ethiopia, the collectivization of agriculture brought success in the war against famine. Also, unlike the Soviet Union, China did not experience a steadily worsening economy in the 1980s. So while communism was abandoned in Russia and its neighbors, China, along with North Korea and Cuba, became its last stronghold. Even in China, however, a process of market liberalization is producing rapid changes in some parts of the country and undermining the state's grip on all aspects of the economy.

Despite the current shift toward free-market practices, we should remember that there are many routes to development. Just as there always were hard-line communist states (such as Albania and North Korea) and less rigid systems (as in Yugoslavia and Hungary), so there are variations in capitalism. For example, the economic systems of Sweden and New Zealand are essentially capitalist, but many socialist principles prevail there as well. This is less true in the Netherlands and the United Kingdom, and still less true in the United States.

Politics and economics are closely intertwined. In the Soviet Union, the end of Communist Party domination was a precondition for economic as well as political change. In South Africa, the end of *apartheid* and a changing political order were followed by an economic transformation. But the key question may well be this: Can China prove that communist political systems are able to coexist with capitalist economic practices? If the authoritarianism of China's political system survives the economic transition that is now under way, other countries may conclude that such a combination constitutes a model worth emulating. In that case the world could become polarized all over again.

◆ KEY TERMS ◆

core-periphery model
core region
dependency theory
developed country (DC)
developing country
development
gross national product (GNP)
liberal model
modernization model
neo-colonialism
peripheral region
semi-peripheral region
structuralist model
underdeveloped country (UDC)
underdevelopment

◆ APPLYING GEOGRAPHIC KNOWLEDGE ◆

1. Group the countries of Asia into the following categories: (1) developed and developing, and (2) core, semi-periphery, and periphery. What criteria did you use in categorizing the countries in each of the two classifications? What are the strengths and weaknesses of the approach to categorization that you chose?
2. You are charged with drafting a report assessing whether a bank should make a loan to Indonesia to help finance a new road across Java. What would you look at in preparing your report? How might you use the figures showing changes in the gross national product of Indonesia since 1970? Why might those figures offer only limited insight into the economic performance of the country?
3. In the box entitled "Focus on: Tourism: Boon or Bane?" we discuss some of the advantages and disadvantages of tourism as it affects countries—especially small countries. Identify a country in which tourism's advantages eclipse any disadvantages, and another country in which tourism has manifestly negative consequences. If you were to generalize from your cases, what would you say in terms of core-periphery relationships?

Chapter 22

Industrial Activity and Geographic Location

From the field notes

"Large ports provide many advantages for industry. They are transport hubs at the center of water, rail, and often air networks. They tend to have dependable energy supply because the ingredients (coal, oil) arrive here first, before national distribution. They are likely to have ample labor availability. The port area of St. Petersburg, Russia, is a growing industrial complex today. Trains and ships exchange goods ranging from raw materials to finished products."

KEY POINTS

◆ **Location theory helps explain the spatial positioning of industries and their success or failure.**

◆ **Weber's least cost theory accounted for the location of a manufacturing plant in terms of transportation, labor, and agglomeration (shared talents, services, and facilities).**

◆ **Transportation costs played a key role in the location of heavy industries; raw-material acquisition and finished-product distribution determined the options.**

◆ **Other factors influencing the location of industries also include labor costs, energy availability, and infrastructure.**

◆ **The growth or decline of secondary industries is also influenced by factors that are not accounted for by models, such as political changes and environmental fluctuations.**

In Chapter 14 we noted that economic activities can be categorized according to their purpose, their relationship to the natural resources on which they are based, and their complexity. The primary or *extractive* industries exist to feed and supply. They develop where the resources are: the soils to be farmed, the minerals to be mined, the forests to be cut. Secondary and tertiary economic activities function to convert raw materials into finished products and facilitate trade and other interactions between producers and consumers. Not only are these manufacturing and service industries more complex than primary industries, but they are also much less closely tied to the location of natural resources. During the second half of the twentieth century, Hong Kong developed one of the world's most powerful economies on the basis of secondary and tertiary industries. It could never have done so on the basis of a primary industry.

Economic geographers investigate the reasons behind the location of economic activity. What made Hong Kong an economic tiger? The Portuguese colony of Macau was nearby, but Macau never came close to matching Hong Kong's meteoric rise. Today the world is a vast panorama of primary economic activity within which are clusters of secondary industries, symbolized by the great manufacturing belts of Japan, the United States, Europe, and Russia. What geographic factors created this arrangement, and what will happen next?

Answers to such questions come from the field of ***location theory***, which attempts to explain the locational pattern of an economic activity in terms of the factors that influence this pattern. But before we look into the future, let us take note of the past. The modern map of world industries carries imprints of a time, long before the Industrial Revolution, when manufacturing centers had already become established in many parts of the world.

◆ THE "PREINDUSTRIAL" WORLD

It is accurate to describe our modern age as one of *industrial intensification.* Industrial development did not begin with the Industrial Revolution. Instead, it accelerated during that period and diffused from certain areas of innovation to other parts of the world. But long before that time industries existed in many parts of the world, and trade in their products was widespread.

For example, in the towns and villages of India, workshops produced goods made of iron, gold, silver, and brass. India's carpenters were artists as well as artisans, and their work was in demand wherever it could be bought. India's textiles, made on individual spinning wheels and hand looms, were considered the best in the world. These industries were sustained not only by local aristocrats, but also by international trade. So good were India's textiles that British textile makers rioted in 1721, demanding legislative protection against imports from India.

China, too, possessed a substantial industrial base long before the Industrial Revolution, and so did Japan. Even European industries, from the textile makers of Flanders and Britain to the iron smelters of Thüringen, had developed considerably, but in price and quality Europe's products could not match those of other parts of the world.

What Europe's products lacked in quality, its merchants more than made up for in aggressiveness. Commercial companies, such as the Dutch and British East

India Companies, laid the groundwork for Europe's colonial expansion. They gained control over local industries in India, Indonesia, and elsewhere, profited from political chaos, and played off allies against enemies. British merchants could import about as many tons of raw fiber for the textile industries as they wanted, and all they needed to do was find ways to mass-produce these raw materials into finished products. They would then bury the remaining local industries in Asia and Africa under growing volumes and declining prices. Even China, where local manufactures long prevailed over inferior and more expensive European goods, would eventually succumb.

◆ THE INDUSTRIAL REVOLUTION

During the eighteenth century European markets were growing, and there was not enough labor to keep pace with either local or overseas trade. Better machines were urgently needed, especially improved spinning and weaving machines. The first steps in the ***Industrial Revolution*** were not so revolutionary; the new machines were still driven by water running downslope. However, James Watt and others succeeded in developing a steam-driven engine, and this new invention was adapted for various uses. At about the same time, it was realized that coal could be transformed into high-carbon coke, which was far superior to charcoal in the smelting of iron.

These innovations had dramatic effects. The power loom revolutionized the weaving industry. Freed from their dependence on charcoal, iron smelters could be located near the coalfields—the same fields that supplied fuel for the new textile mills. One invention led to another, with each being applied to more and more industries. Pumps could keep water out of mines. Engines could move power looms. There was plenty of capital available for investment, because British industrialists had been drawing wealth from the overseas empire for many years.

The Industrial Revolution also affected transportation and communications. The first railroad in England was opened in 1825. In 1830 Manchester was connected by rail to the nearby port of Liverpool, and in the next several decades thousands of miles of iron and then steel track were laid. Ocean shipping also entered a new age when the first steam-powered vessel crossed the Atlantic in 1819. Now England enjoyed even greater advantages than it had at the beginning of the Industrial Revolution. Not only did Britain hold a monopoly over products that were in demand around the world, but it alone possessed the skills necessary to make the machines that manufactured them. Europe and America wanted railroads and locomotives; England had the know-how, the experience, and the capital to supply them. Soon British influence around the world was reaching its peak.

Meanwhile, the spatial pattern of modern Europe began to take shape. In Britain, densely populated and heavily urbanized industrial regions developed in the "Black Country" near the coalfields. The largest such region was (and remains) the Midlands of north-central England. In mainland Europe, a belt of major coalfields extends from west to east, roughly along the southern margins of the North European Lowland—across northern France and southern Belgium, the Netherlands, the German Rühr, western Bohemia in the Czech Republic, and Silesia in Poland. Iron ore is dispersed along a similar belt, and the industrial map of Europe reflects the resulting concentrations of economic activity (Fig. 22-1). Nowhere on the continent, however, were the coalfields, iron ore deposits, and ports located in such close proximity as they were in Britain.

As Figure 22-1 shows, the Industrial Revolution rapidly diffused eastward. Some industrial regions emerged because of their raw material combinations (such as the Rühr, Saxony, Silesia, and the Donbas); others were based on enormous urban markets (such as London and Paris). These urban centers became, and remain, important industrial complexes for other reasons besides availability of resources.

The Industrial Revolution transformed the world's economic map, but while it had dramatic impact in certain areas, it totally bypassed others. Understanding the forces and factors that shaped the world's industrial layout is a prime objective of economic geographers.

◆ THE LOCATION DECISION

Industrial activity takes place in certain locations and not in others. We have already accounted for the spatial character of primary industries: the location of resources is the determining factor. ***Secondary industries*** are less dependent on resource location. Raw materials can be transported to distant locations to be converted into manufactured products—if the resulting profits outweigh the costs.

Any attempt to establish a model for the location of secondary industry runs into complications much greater than those confronting von Thünen, who dealt only with primary industries. The location of secondary industries depends to a larger extent on human behavior and decision making, on cultural and political as well as economic factors, even on intuition or whim. Since models must be based on assumptions, economic geographers have to assume that decision makers are trying to maximize their advantages over competitors, that they want to make as much profit as

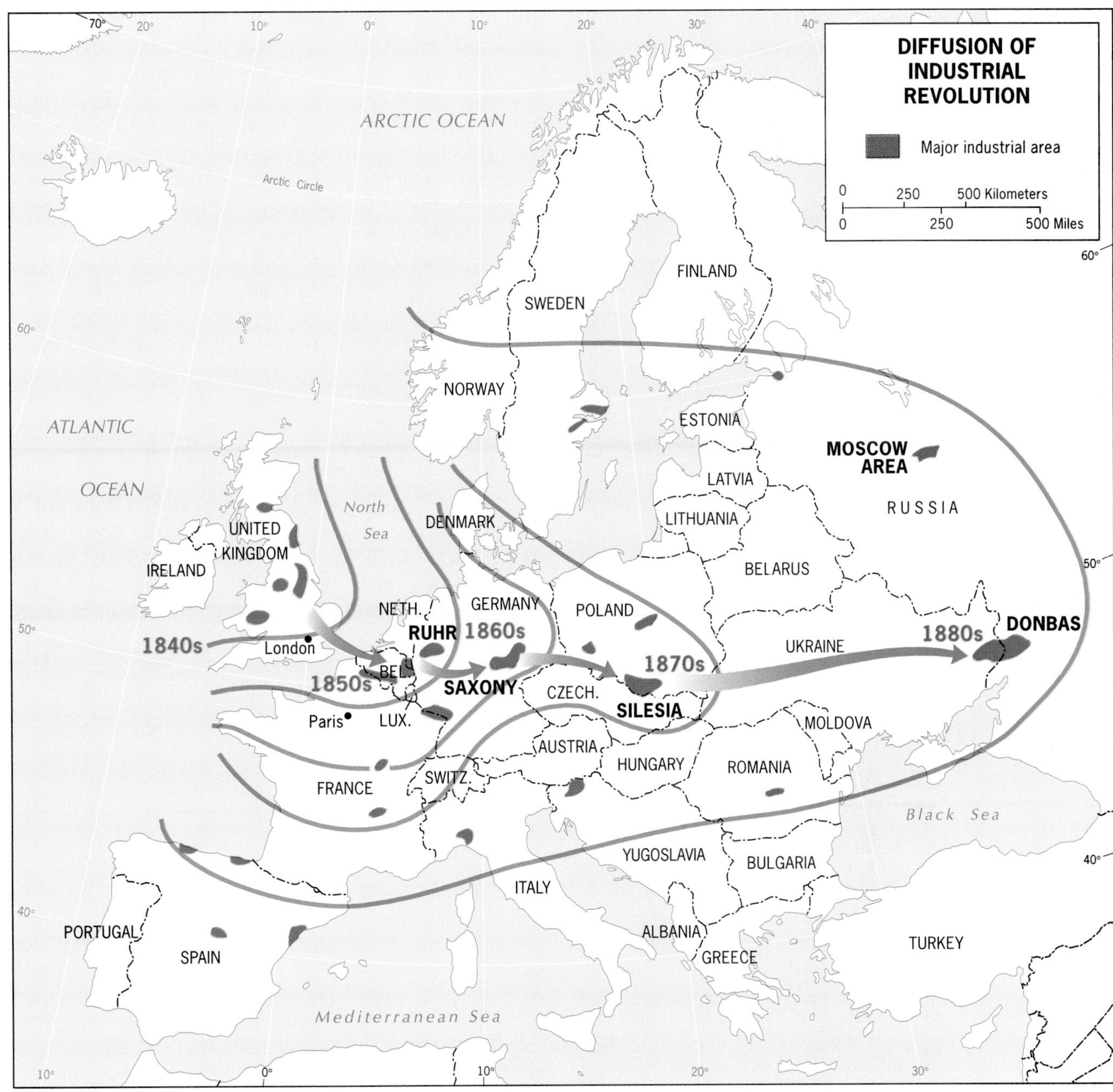

Figure 22-1 Diffusion of Industrial Revolution. The eastward diffusion of the Industrial Revolution during the second half of the nineteenth century is depicted on this map.

possible, and that they will take into account ***variable costs*** such as energy supply, transport expenses, labor costs, and other needs.

Weber's Model

The German economic geographer Alfred Weber (1868–1958) did for the secondary industries what von Thünen had done for agriculture: he developed a model for the location of manufacturing establishments. Weber's ***least cost theory*** accounted for the location of a manufacturing plant in terms of the owner's desire to minimize three categories of costs. The first and most important of these was *transportation*: the site chosen must entail the lowest possible cost of moving raw materials to the factory and finished products to the market. The second cost was that of *labor*. Higher labor costs reduce the margin of profit, so a factory might do better farther from raw materials and markets if cheap labor made up for the added transport costs. (The current economic boom on the Pacific Rim is based largely on low labor costs, which have caused industries to move from Japan and Taiwan to China and Vietnam.)

The third factor in Weber's model was what he called ***agglomeration***. When a substantial number of enterprises cluster in the same area, as happens in a large industrial city, they can provide assistance to each other through shared talents, services, and facilities. All manufacturers need office furniture and equipment; the presence of one or more producers in a large city satisfies this need for all. Thus agglomeration makes a big-city location more attractive, perhaps overcoming some increase in transport and labor costs. Excessive agglomeration, however, leads to high rents, rising wages, circulation problems (resulting in increased transport costs and loss of efficiency), and other problems. These may eventually negate the advantages of agglomeration. Such factors have led many industries to leave the crowded urban centers of the U.S. eastern megalopolis and move to other locations.

Like von Thünen's model, Weber's least cost theory gave rise to a long and spirited debate among economic geographers. Some argued that Weber's model did not adequately account for variations in costs over time. For example, when relative labor costs decline or when land rent goes down, an industry can sustain an increase in transport costs. While Weber's model might indicate that a location had become unprofitable, this ***substitution principle*** suggests otherwise. Also, the model suggests that one particular site would be optimal for a manufacturer's location, but in reality the business might be quite profitable within a larger area. Other factors that are not accounted for by the model, such as taxation policies, also complicate the picture. Despite these criticisms, Alfred Weber set in motion a debate over the spatial aspects of economic activity that continues today (see "Focus on: Industrial Location Theory").

Factors of Industrial Location

Our discussion of models of industrial location is based on circumstances prevailing in commercial economies—that is, economies guided by market mechanisms and relationships between supply and demand. However, some important industrial regions

Industrial Location Theory

Europe's rapid industrialization during the nineteenth century attracted the attention of economic geographers at an early stage. Much of this pioneering research was incorporated into Alfred Weber's *Theory of the Location of Industries* (1909). Like von Thünen before him, Weber began with a set of assumptions in order to minimize the complexities of the real world. However, unlike von Thünen, Weber dealt with activities that took place at particular points rather than across large areas. Manufacturing plants, mines, and markets are located at specific places, so Weber created a model region marked by sets of points where these activities would occur. He eliminated labor mobility and varying wage rates, and this enabled him to calculate the "pulls" exerted on each point in his theoretical region.

In the process, Weber discerned various factors that affected industrial location. For example, he recognized what he called "general" factors that would affect all industries, such as transportation costs for raw materials and finished products, and "special" factors, such as the perishability of foods. He also distinguished between "regional" factors (transport and labor costs) and "local" factors. Local factors, Weber argued, involved agglomerative and deglomerative forces. Thus the advantages of clustering drew manufacturing plants to large existing urban centers, thereby promoting growth, but disadvantages of congestion caused some plants to move outward.

Weber singled out transportation costs as the critical determinant of regional industrial location. He suggested that the site where transportation costs are lowest is the place where it would be least expensive to bring raw materials to the point of production and distribute finished products to consumers. However, economic geographers since Weber's time have concluded that the usefulness of Weber's theory was weakened by some of his assumptions, especially his notions concerning markets and consumer demand. Consumption does not take place at a single location but over a wide (in some cases a worldwide) area. Despite this criticism, practically all modern analytical studies of industrial location have a direct relationship to Weber's work.

Other economic geographers later extended Weber's theories. A major contribution was made by August Lösch, whose book, *The Spatial Structure of the Economy* (1940), was published in English translation in 1954 as *The Economics of Location*. Lösch countered Weber's studies of least cost location by seeking ways to determine maximum profit locations. He inserted the spatial influence of consumer demand, as well as production costs, into his calculations. This was a major step forward in the analysis of factors shaping the economic landscape.

evolved under state planning, which tolerated large losses for the sake of rapid industrialization. As we saw earlier, the Industrial Revolution reached Ukraine and Russia before the Soviet Union was created. But Soviet economic policy changed the direction of industrial growth, so that by the end of the Soviet era (1991) the imprints of the old commercial era were mingled with those of the era of state planning. Today the market rules again in Russia, but it is distorted by the huge Russian black market and the influence of entrenched interests. The Soviet framework persists, hampering efforts at reform.

One of the first decisions faced by the capitalists who built the great iron works of Europe had to do with the need to move either coal to the iron ores or iron ore to the coalfields. As you can see from any map of the time, the iron smelters were built near the coalfields of the British Midlands (the Black Towns were aptly named for the soot that hung permanently in the air and coated the entire landscape). The practice of moving the iron ore to the coal spread throughout Europe's industrial axis, but it is only one of three options. The other two are (1) to move the coal to the iron ore reserves or (2) to transport both materials to an intermediate location. (The planned economy of the former Soviet Union offered still another option: steel mills were built on the coalfields as well as on the iron ore reserves, and trains carried coal in one direction and iron ore in the other.)

From the field notes

"The insatiable demand for raw materials in the world's industrialized regions has had a huge environmental impact on countries near and far. In Tasmania, the Australian island known for its scenic beauty, we saw what open-pit as well as shaft mining can to do the countryside. Here, near Queenstown, a copper mine was surrounded by denuded slopes, slag heaps, and gaping scars in the landscape. It reminded me of what I had seen in Zambia (Africa) and Chile (South America). The extractive primary industries can be very destructive."

In commercial economies, iron ore is usually transported to the coalfields, often after some waste and impurities have been removed. But there are exceptions. For example, large quantitites of coal are transported to France's iron-rich Lorraine region, where coal is scarce. When an industrial complex develops near a coalfield and the coal is used up, it may be less expensive to import coal than to relocate the factories. Even when both coal and iron ore are shipped over large distances to some intermediate site, the iron ore usually travels farthest.

Raw Materials Numerous factors enter into location decisions; these factors are of great interest to economic geographers who seek to discover the processes whereby manufacturing activity organizes and adjusts economic space. Obviously, the resources involved—that is, ***raw materials***—play a major role. One example is the location of steel plants along the U.S. northeastern seaboard. Those industrial facilities were built there largely because they used iron ore shipped from Venezuela, Labrador, Liberia, and other overseas sources. Instead of transferring these materials from ocean-going ships onto trains and transporting them inland, the plants used them right where they arrived—practically at the point of unloading at such huge steel-mill complexes as Sparrows Point, near Baltimore, and Fairless, near Philadelphia. So in this case distant ore deposits affected the location of industry in the United States. Thus transport costs affect the location of industry in important ways. (Transportation is discussed in a separate section because this factor involves finished products as well as raw materials.)

In the case of raw materials, we have already noted the spatial relationships between Europe's zone of coalfields and iron ores and the spread of manufacturing throughout the region. However, not all of the world's great industrial regions lie near major sources of raw materials. Japanese industries must import raw materials from distant sources because Japan's domestic resource base is quite limited. This has not prevented Japan from developing into one of the world's great industrial nations, but it does present special problems of availability and cost. Japan's early industrial progress was based on its own manufacturing traditions and, initially, on its own resources. The rapid depletion of these raw materials was among the motives that led Japan to embark on its expansion into East Asia, where Korea and Northeast China became Japanese dependencies and sources of raw materials for Japanese industries.

Even after Japan lost its colonial empire, its industries continued to be sustained by a large, highly skilled labor force (which, before recent wage increases, was relatively cheap). Japanese products dominated markets around the world and allowed Japanese industries to purchase needed raw materials virtually anywhere. Australia, for example, became one of Japan's leading suppliers.

For many decades European countries also controlled sources of raw materials through colonization. (Britain's example had much to do with Japan's colonial expansion for similar purposes.) In the postcolonial era, materials have continued to flow from the source countries to manufacturers in the core countries, many of which are former colonial powers. This not-so-new pattern of trade spells disadvantage for countries in the periphery, since they must sell their raw materials in order to secure foreign capital even when commodity prices fall because of oversupply or recession. The core countries, on the other hand, can keep prices low by shifting from one supplier to another. When a peripheral country loses customers for its raw materials, the effect on its economy may be disastrous.

Countries in the periphery have tried to band together in cartels in order to control vital commodities that the core needs, but such efforts have not succeeded. Usually the buyers are in a stronger position than the sellers because they can find other sources (including countries that have not joined the cartels). When OPEC (the Organization of Petroleum Exporting Countries) took control of world oil supplies in the 1970s, it succeeded in driving up the price of petroleum. But countries that did not join OPEC increased their production and gave the developed countries a chance to break OPEC's hold; oil supplies recovered, prices collapsed, and the producers—not the consumers—were again the losers.

Labor *Labor* was one of the three fundamentals of Weber's least cost model, and availability of cheap semiskilled labor has had an immense impact on regional industrial development. Even in an era of automated assembly lines and computerized processing, the prospect of a large, low-wage, trainable labor force continues to attract manufacturers.

As noted earlier, Japan's postwar success was based in large measure on the skills *and* the low wages of its labor force, which allowed manufacturers to flood foreign markets with low-priced goods. Into the 1950s Japanese goods had little reputation for quality but were known for their affordability. But then Japan's factories began to excel in quality as well. This in turn led to higher prices, higher wages, and, inevitably, competition from countries where cheaper labor could be found. Taiwan and South Korea competed with Japan in goods ranging from electronics to automobiles, and in the mid-1990s Japan was in a recession while Taiwan and South Korea boomed.

The next stage of economic transformation on the Pacific Rim was already under way in the 1980s. This was the entry of China with its huge labor force. In 1994 the daily wage of a factory worker in Shanghai's Pudong district was one-fortieth that of a Japanese worker in a similar job and one-thirtieth that of a Taiwanese worker. These low wages, coupled with favorable tax regulations, are attracting thousands of enterprises to China's Special Economic Zones, transforming cities and towns in the region.

What is happening on China's Pacific Rim is nothing new; similar developments are affecting Thailand and Malaysia. And like South Korea and Japan before it, China will feel the effects of cheaper labor when Vietnam enters the picture. Similar developments are occurring elsewhere as well. Before the United States, Canada, and Mexico joined in the North American Free Trade Agreement (NAFTA) in 1994, there was intense debate over the relocation of industries from the United States across the border to Mexico, where wages were lower and profits would be higher. Thus the cost of labor still looms large in the location of industry.

Transportation As Weber noted, ***transportation*** facilities and costs are crucial in industrial location. A huge market may exist for a given product, but if that market is not served by an efficient transportation system, much of the advantage is lost. The maps in Chapter 23 underscore the fact that highly developed industrial areas are also the places that are served most effectively by transportation facilities. Industrialization and the development of modern transport systems go hand in hand. In a sense, the Industrial Revolution was a transportation revolution—a revolution that is still going on. Every year more freight is carried by air, and in the United States trucks increasingly haul goods that were formerly carried on trains.

Efficient transportation systems enable manufacturers to purchase raw materials from distant sources and distribute finished products to a widely dispersed population of consumers. Manufacturers desire maximum transport effectiveness at the lowest possible cost. They will also consider the availability of alternative systems in the event of emergencies (e.g., truck routes when rail service is interrupted). An important innovation in bulk transport was the development of container systems that facilitate the transfer of goods from one type of carrier to another (from rail-to-ship and ship-to-truck). This change lowered costs and increased flexibility, permitting many manufacturers to pay less attention to transportation in their location decisions.

For most goods, truck transport is cheapest over short distances. Railroads are cheapest over medium distances, and ships are cheapest over the longest distances. However, numerous aspects of transportation must be taken into account when location decisions are made. For example, when goods are hauled, costs are incurred at the terminal where trucks, trains, and ships are unloaded. These costs are much higher for ships than for trucks. Then, of course, there is the actual cost of transportation itself. This increases with distance, but at a decreasing rate, making long-distance transportation cheaper per mile and allowing manufacturers to reach out to distant suppliers of raw materials and also to sell to faraway customers. Still another factor has to do with the weight and volume of the freight. Certain goods may be light but occupy a lot of space inside railroad cars or ships' holds; thus they may still be expensive to transport.

Infrastructure When Weber considered the role of agglomeration in location decisions, he could not foresee the dimensions of urban areas or industrial complexes a century hence. In his time, the world population was about the size of China's today; few cities had more than 1 million inhabitants. Today's urban populations are much larger—and so are the problems and benefits of agglomeration. If you wished to build a factory in Shanghai to benefit from low-cost labor, you would have many needs, ranging from transportation facilities to markets both in China and overseas to telephones and utilities such as electricity and water supply. All these facilities, and others such as banks, postal and messenger services, hotels, and social services, are collectively referred to as ***infrastructure***. Airports, roads, docks, railways, and taxis are also included.

Infrastructure is an important factor in industrial location decisions. One reason the communist regime in China has tried to slow the rate of industrialization along the Pacific Rim lies in the inadequacy of local and regional infrastructures: the demand for such facilities as telephones and administrative assistance far exceeds what is available. Factories are having difficulty importing raw materials; market distribution systems cannot yet meet the demand. Public utilities are also inadequate. (In 1994 Shanghai brought a major new coal-burning power plant on line, but demand is expected to overtake supply in a few years.)

Given such shortcomings in infrastructures, why does the influx of enterprises continue? The answer is not found in any formal economic-geographic model. It has to do with the perception of future disadvantage. Not to gain a place on the new industrial frontier is to risk falling behind in the future. So the Chinese economic hot spots continue to grow and prosper, even with inadequate infrastructures.

Compared to China, Vietnam (which some observers regard as the next economic "tiger" on the Pacific Rim) has an even weaker infrastructure. For all its advantages (self-sufficiency in food, good relative location, a large educated labor force, and a domestic market of nearly 80 million), Vietnam has infrastructure problems that will not soon be overcome. Inadequate power and water supply and a poor surface transportation network are just two of these weaknesses.

In many Western cities, the disadvantages of excessive agglomeration are driving firms away from crowded and decaying urban areas, despite their highly developed infrastructures. Meanwhile, industries are entering non-Western cities in the expectation that their infrastructures will improve. Thus the economic landscape is constantly shifting.

Energy Another factor in the location of industry is the availability of an ***energy*** supply. This factor used to be much more important than it is today. The early British textile mills, because they depended on water rushing down hillsides to drive the looms, had few choices in deciding where to locate. However, today power comes from different sources and can be transmitted via high-voltage electrical lines over long distances. Manufacturers are therefore able to base location decisions on considerations other than power. Exceptions occur when an industry needs very large

From the field notes

"Sailing up the waterway from the Baltic Sea to Stockholm, Sweden's capital, I saw evidence of a significant difference between this country and its peninsular neighbor Norway: Sweden does not have domestic sources of oil and natural gas while Norway, by virtue of its large North Sea reserves, is well endowed in this respect. Along the entrance to Stockholm's port lie clusters of holding tanks for oil, and tankers arrive daily to fill them. It is not surprising that Sweden has sought to reduce this dependence on foreign energy supplies: this country is among the top ten hydroelectric power *and* nuclear power producers."

amounts of energy—for example, certain metallurgical (aluminum and copper processing) and chemical industries (fertilizer production). Such industries are attracted to sites where abundant energy is available, as is the case near hydroelectric plants. In the United States, the growth of aluminum production in the Pacific Northwest and the Tennessee Valley is based mainly on the ready availability of cheap electricity; this is also the case in Canada's Saint Maurice and Saguenay River Basins.

The role of energy supply as a factor in industrial location decisions has changed over time. Whereas during the Industrial Revolution manufacturing plants were often established on or near coalfields, today major industrial complexes are not found near oil fields. Instead, a huge system of pipelines and tankers delivers oil and natural gas to manufacturing regions throughout the world.

For some time during and after the global oil supply crises of the 1970s, fears of future rises in oil costs led some industries that require large amounts of electricity to move to sites where the environment is moderate and heating and air-conditioning costs are low. But when the crisis waned, national energy-conservation goals were modified, and in the late 1990s the United States' reliance on foreign energy resources was even greater than it had been in the 1970s. So just as energy supply has become a less significant factor in industrial location, so energy security is not a national priority today.

Other Factors Factors other than those we have identified may also influence industrial location decisions. If several plants have already located in a certain area, others might be influenced to do the same—not only because of the advantages of the site, but also because of a clustering or agglomeration effect. Had those already established plants not been there, the newer industries might have been located elsewhere. Still other factors are political stability and receptiveness to investment. Industries are frightened away when there are signs of uncertainty in the political future of a country, or when a government indicates that it intends to nationalize industries owned by foreigners. Taxation policies can also play a role. Some countries try to attract industries by offering huge tax exemptions over long periods.

Sometimes, influential industrialists can simply decide to locate a major plant in a particular area for personal reasons, ignoring the principles of industrial location. The directors of multinational corporations can affect the course of regional industrial development in many countries almost at will. Moreover, some industries are located where they are because of environmental conditions. The film industry is concentrated in Southern California because of the large number of clear, cloudless days there—an environmental factor that has also attracted aircraft manufacturers, which need good weather for flight-testing new planes.

Much as we may theorize, therefore, the location and success of industries may depend on unanticipated, even unaccountable factors as well. In hindsight we can explain Hong Kong's success in terms of its location, but when the colony was just a rivermouth trading port there was little to suggest its phenomenal future growth. Then China was ostracized for its role in the Korean War, and Hong Kong's links to the mainland were cut. Manufacturers had to look for new products and markets, and textiles were the answer. The political situation ensured a huge supply of labor at low wages, and the textile industry, based on imported raw materials and exported clothing, thrived. The money made in the textile industries was invested in the development of other manufactures, and the rest is—geography.

But Hong Kong would not have achieved what it did without another advantage. China, isolated as it was, needed a back door to the outside world, a route along which to funnel finances, crucial imports, and messages. That route lay through Hong Kong. As the door opened wider, Hong Kong prospered and even spawned a "twin": Shenzhen across the border.

As we have seen throughout this chapter, explaining industrial location and predicting its growth are complex matters. This will become even clearer when we discuss the regional maps in Chapter 23.

◆ KEY TERMS ◆

agglomeration
energy
Industrial Revolution
infrastructure
labor
least cost theory
location theory
raw materials
secondary industries
substitution principle
transportation
variable cost

◆ APPLYING GEOGRAPHIC KNOWLEDGE ◆

1. Invention, industrial intensification, and diffusion are among the processes that propelled the Industrial Revolution. What geographic factors help explain the locational aspects of this momentous process and its dissemination around the world? Has it run its course, or is industrialization still continuing?

2. Although the location of raw materials, labor, and markets still plays a role in the decision-making processes that determine where industrial plants will be situated, these factors have less influence today than in the past. What are the circumstances—economic as well as political—that allow more leeway in the location of industries?

Chapter 23

World Industrial Regions

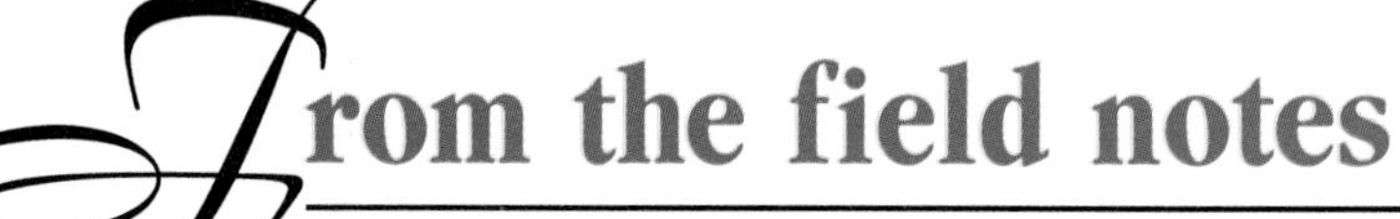

From the field notes

"Paris and the Paris Basin form the industrial as well as agricultural heart of France. The city and region are served by the Seine River, along which lies a string of ports from Le Havre at the mouth to Rouen at the head of navigation for ocean-going ships. Rouen has become a vital center on France's industrial map. As we approached on the river, you could see the famous cathedral and the city's historic cultural landscape to the left (north), but on the right bank lay a major industrial complex including coal-fired power facilities (although France leads Europe in nuclear energy), petrochemical plants, and oil installations. It is all part of the industrial region centered in Paris."

KEY POINTS

◆ **Four major industrial regions have developed, all in the Northern Hemisphere: Western and Central Europe, Eastern North America, Russia-Ukraine, and Eastern Asia. Each consists of core areas with subsidiary clusters.**

◆ **The location of Europe's primary industrial regions still reflects the spatial diffusion of the Industrial Revolution. An axis of manufacturing extends from Britain to Poland and the Czech Republic, and onward to Ukraine.**

◆ **North America's manufacturing complex, anchored by the American Manufacturing Belt, is the largest in the world today.**

◆ **Despite Ukraine's political separation from the former Soviet Union (and hence from Russia), Ukrainian and Russian industries are interdependent: Ukraine needs Russian fuels and Russia needs Ukrainian raw materials.**

◆ **Industrial regions in East Asia are the fastest growing in the world. The Asian Pacific Rim, from Japan to Indonesia, includes several of the most rapidly expanding economies, recent setbacks notwithstanding.**

When the Bolsheviks took control of the Russian Empire, they found themselves in charge of a vast realm with a mainly agricultural economy. The Industrial Revolution had penetrated the Soviet Union, but in only a few areas could its impact be seen in the landscape. The Donbas region on both sides of the Russian-Ukrainian border was such a place, and the Moscow and (then) Leningrad areas had also attracted secondary industries. But there was nothing in the Soviet Union of the 1920s to rival what was happening in Europe or North America.

Soviet communist rulers were determined to change this. They wanted to transform the Soviet economy into an industrial one. To accomplish this transformation, the dictator Josef Stalin ordered the seizure of private land and the collectivization of agriculture, so that labor would be freed for manufacturing jobs and capital could be diverted from farm to factory use. The human cost of this giant scheme was dreadful: millions of farmers were executed or starved to death when they failed to comply or were suspected of opposition (as countless Ukrainians were). But the desired transformation was accomplished. The Soviet Union became a major industrial power with vast manufacturing complexes that produced enough material to defeat the German armies during World War II, less than 20 years after Lenin's death. In the 1950s, the USSR launched the world's first artificial satellite, and a Soviet cosmonaut became the first human being in space. In the early 1960s, Soviet industries were pouring out products ranging from toys to tanks, and confidence in the superiority of communist planning was at an all-time high.

While the Soviets were forging their ***planned industrial economy***, industrial development took a very different course elsewhere. Market forces, not state planning, had propelled the Industrial Revolution in Europe and North America, and industrial economies on both sides of the Atlantic Ocean rose to global prominence. For more than four decades after World War II, the Soviets imposed their ideology on Eastern Europe's industrial development. As a result, Eastern Europe's economic geography, begun through free enterprise, was constrained by communist planning. Western Europe's industrial growth proceeded more freely, and in the postwar period Japan, Taiwan, and South Korea industrialized under free-enterprise rules as well. China, on the other hand, followed a modified Soviet model, collectivizing its farming and putting its industries under state control.

◆ MAJOR INDUSTRIAL REGIONS

Whatever the ideological basis (market-commercial, communist-state, or some combination), the world map of major regional-industrial development reveals that only a small minority of countries have become major industrial economies. Many factors are involved—resource endowment, relative location, political circumstances, economic leadership, and labor force capacity, among others. The legacy of the Industrial Revolution is evident in many older industrial complexes, such as Germany's Rühr, Poland's Silesia, and Ukraine's Donbas. But major industrial centers are emerging in such countries as India, Brazil, and China. What follows, therefore, is a picture of a fast-changing world in which new competitors are challenging the old economic order.

When industrial concentrations are mapped, four ***primary industrial regions*** stand out:

1. Western and Central Europe
2. Eastern North America
3. Russia and Ukraine
4. Eastern Asia

Each of these regions consists of one or more core areas of industrial development with subsidiary clusters some distance away. While the older manufacturing regions are quite entrenched, notable shifts are occurring. This dispersal is especially evident in East Asia, where Japan's dominance is being challenged by the "Four Tigers" of East Asia. In Europe, the Rühr is being affected by a southward shift of German industry. In North America, the old eastern core of industries is still dominant, but the balance is shifting toward subsidiary clusters to the west and south.

◆ MANUFACTURING REGIONS IN EUROPE

It is appropriate to begin with Europe, for it is here that the Industrial Revolution was launched. The manufacturing regions of Europe (Fig. 23-1) are the continent's heartland, the focus of the evolving European Union.

Britain

As noted previously, Britain's coal-fired industries produced a pattern of functional specialization that, for a time, had no equal in the world. Today that pattern has been diluted by diversification, relocation, and failure. In Britain, for example, aging plants are still operating even though they are inefficient, expensive to run, slow, and wasteful. With the relative decline of the manufacturing cities of the Midlands and northern England, industrial enterprises tend to relocate near London. This still is the greatest domestic market of the British Isles, and it is increasingly important to local manufacturers. The changes in Britain's economic geography reflect the decreasing importance of coal in the energy-supply picture, the desire to start afresh with up-to-date machinery, and the fact that London, in addition to forming a huge domestic market, is also a good port through which to import raw materials. It also reflects fundamental changes in the global economy that we will examine in the next chapter. Thus London, too, shows up in Figure 23-1 as a key industrial district within the European region.

Continental Europe

When the Industrial Revolution diffused onto the mainland, Paris was already continental Europe's greatest city—but like London it did not have coal or iron deposits in its immediate vicinity. Nevertheless, Paris was the largest local market for manufacturers for hundreds of miles around, and when a railroad system was added to the existing network of road and waterway connections, the city's centrality was further strengthened. Like London, Paris soon began to attract major industries, and the city, long a center for the manufacture of luxury items (jewelry, perfumes, and fashions), experienced substantial growth in such industries as automobile manufacturing and assembly, metallurgy, and chemical manufacturing. With a ready labor force, an ideal regional position for the distribution of finished products, the presence of governmental agencies, a nearby ocean port (Le Havre), and France's largest domestic market, Paris's development as a major industrial center was no accident.

Europe's coal deposits, however, lie in a belt across northern France, Belgium, north-central Ger-

From the field notes

"The rise of Europe to a modern world power was inextricably tied to its industrial might. The extraction of resources from far-flung colonies was important to building that might, but it was also tied to the exploitation of indigenous resources. Indeed, the manufacturing core of Europe developed around places with easy access to such key raw materials as coal and steel. This modern plant in coal-rich southern Poland shows that manufacturing regions which developed in association with accessible raw materials continue to be important sites of heavy industry."

Figure 23-1 Europe's Core and Regions. This map shows core and urban areas as well as industrial districts.

many, the northwestern Czech Republic, and southern Poland—and it was along this zone that mainland Europe's major concentrations of heavy industry developed. Three manufacturing districts lay in Germany: the *Rühr*, based on the Westphalian coalfield, the *Saxony* district, near the border of the former Czechoslovakia, and *Silesia* (now part of Poland). Germany still ranks among the world's leading producers of both coal and steel and remains Europe's leading industrial power (Table 23-1).

The Ruhr became Europe's greatest industrial complex. Named after a small tributary of the Rhine River, the Ruhr reveals the combined advantages of high-quality resources, good accessibility, and proximity to large markets. When local iron ore reserves became depleted, ores could be brought in from overseas. Since the 1870s the Ruhr has poured forth the products of heavy industry, including tanks and other weapons for Hitler's armies.

Saxony, on the other hand, was always oriented toward skill and quality. Anchored by Leipzig and Dresden, it became known for such products as opti-

Table 23-1 World Production of Raw Steel, 1996 (Thousands of Net Tons)

China	110,640
Japan	108,932
United States	105,309
Russia	54,202
Germany	43,873
South Korea	42,892
Brazil	27,827
Italy	26,775
Ukraine	25,717
India	24,030
United Kingdom	19,838
Canada	16,135
France	19,441
Turkey	14,754
Mexico	14,519

Source: American Iron and Steel Institute *Annual Statistical Report 1997.*

cal equipment and cameras, refined textiles, and ceramics. The Saxony district suffered from its inclusion in the former East Germany, and its revival is a prime objective of Germany's economic planners.

Farther east, the industrial district of Silesia was originally part of Germany, but now lies in Poland and extends into the Czech Republic (Fig. 23-1). The development of the Silesian district was based on high-quality coal resources and lesser iron ores that were later supplemented by imports from Ukraine.

Europe's industrial success was not based solely on raw materials, however. The skills of its labor force and the high degree of specialization achieved in various industrial zones led to intensive exchange of products. This exchange was facilitated by natural transport routes, augmented by artificial ones. Thus industry diffused far from the original sources to such areas as northern Italy, now one of Europe's major industrial hearths, Catalonia (anchored by Barcelona) and northern Spain, southern Sweden, and southern Finland. These and other European industrial zones are just districts within the continent's massive industrial structure; each would stand out as a major center of manufacturing activity in most other parts of the world.

◆ MANUFACTURING REGIONS IN NORTH AMERICA

In North America, industrialization occurred first in the East. Served by a wide array of natural resources and supported by networks of natural as well as artificial transportation systems, remote from the destruction caused by wars in other industrial regions, and on the doorstep of the world's richest market, North American manufacturing developed rapidly. Ample capital, mass production, specialization, and diversification marked the robust growth of this region, which benefited from ample energy supplies (see "Focus on: Industry and Energy").

Industry and Energy

North America's industrial prowess is based in part on a large and varied regional resource base and sustained by its capacity to acquire needed raw materials from overseas sources. Coal was the chief fuel for the industries that helped achieve this primacy. There was never any threat of a shortage of coal: U.S. coal reserves are among the world's largest and are widely distributed, from Appalachian Pennsylvania to the northwestern Great Plains (Fig. 23-2). The United States still vies with China as the world's largest coal producer, but the situation with respect to petroleum is quite different.

During the twentieth century the United States has become increasingly dependent on oil and natural gas. U.S. consumption of petroleum and natural gas today is about 27 percent and 37 percent, respectively, of the annual world total. In the early 1990s the United States required no fewer than 17 million barrels of petroleum *per day* to keep its power plants, machinery, vehicles, aircraft, and ships functioning. However, U.S. production of oil in recent years has averaged about 18 percent of the world total, and, even including the known Alaskan potential, U.S. oil reserves are estimated to amount to only about 4 percent of the world total. The result is heavy dependence on foreign oil supplies, with all the uncertainties involved.

Petroleum is not the only energy source for which the United States leads world demand and consumption. As Figure 23-2 shows, natural gas often occurs in association with oil deposits. The use of natural gas has increased enormously since World War II. In the 1990s, the United States consumed about 37 percent of the natural gas used in the world, and even this was barely enough to meet the demand. One result of the increased use of natural gas is the proliferation of pipelines shown in Figure 23-2. In North America in 1997 there were over 2.5 million miles (4 million kilometers) of pipelines, including parts of a new pipeline designed to carry Alaskan natural gas across Canada to the U.S. market.

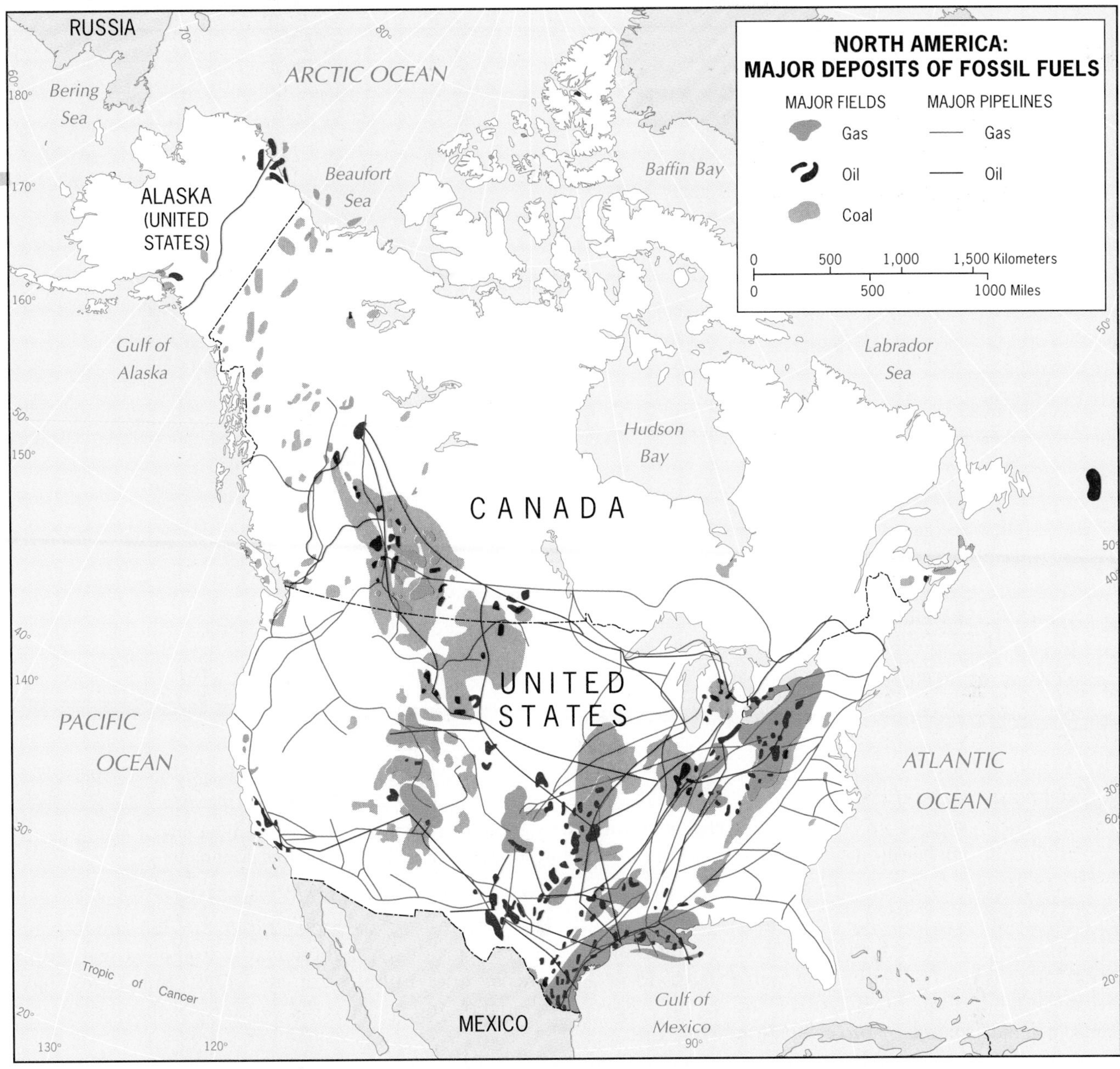

Figure 23-2 North America's Major Deposits of Fossil Fuels. The world's largest energy consumer, North America is also endowed with substantial energy resources.

Dependence on external fuel supplies affects three of the four world industrial regions discussed in this chapter. Despite discoveries of oil and gas in the North Sea, Europe still depends on foreign shipments of petroleum. The United States has two neighbors with substantial fossil fuel reserves (Mexico's oil and gas may rank among the world's largest), but its own supplies remain rather limited. Japan is almost totally dependent on oil from distant sources.

The American Manufacturing Belt

The bulk of manufacturing in the United States and Canada is concentrated in the rectangular region shown in Figure 23-3, the *American Manufacturing Belt,* which extends from the northeastern seaboard to Iowa, and from the St. Lawrence Valley to the confluence of the Ohio and Mississippi Rivers.

Manufacturing in North America began in New England as early as late colonial times, but these Northeastern states are not especially rich in mineral resources. Still, this oldest manufacturing district continues to produce high-quality light manufactures.

Industrialization also began early in New York, which today is at the heart of the Bosnywash megalopolis and home to tens of thousands of industrial establishments. An early start, large urban growth and agglomeration played roles in this development. The New York area is not especially well endowed with

Figure 23-3 North America's Manufacturing Regions. North American manufacturing has dispersed westward and southward, but the eastern core area remains dominant.

mineral resources, but, like Paris and London, it is a large market. It also has a huge skilled and semiskilled labor force, is the focus of an intensive transport network, and has long been one of the world's great ports, a major ***break-of-bulk*** location. This term refers to the transfer of transported cargo from one kind of carrier (e.g., a ship) to another (truck or train). Such transfers generate much economic activity.

Southward, the light industries of New England and New York give way to heavier manufacturing. Here lies the Southeast Pennsylvania district, centered on metropolitan Philadelphia and encompassing the Baltimore area. Iron ores shipped from distant locations like Canada and South America are smelted right on the waterfront in tidewater steel mills. Major chemical industries (notably in northern Delaware), pharmaceutical industries, and lighter manufacturing plants have been established there.

Farther west lies the well-defined Upstate New York district, extending from Albany, on the Hudson River, to Buffalo, on the shore of Lake Erie. Growth there was originally stimulated by the Erie Canal, which was dug in the early nineteenth century to connect the East Coast to the Great Lakes. Since about 1970, however, industry has declined in this district. In some ways, this is similar to what happened in Britain. Rochester was long known for its cameras and optical products, Schenectady for electrical appliances, and Buffalo for its steel. But times have changed, and so have the fortunes of this district.

Canada's Major Manufacturing Region

Canada's Southern Ontario district extends from the western end of Lake Ontario to the industrial zone at the western end of Lake Erie. As Figure 23-3 shows, this district links two parts of the U.S. manufacturing belt anchored by Buffalo and Detroit; the most direct route between these two industrial cities is through Ontario.

Canadian and U.S. manufacturing complexes meet in two great horseshoe-shaped zones around the western ends of Lakes Ontario and Erie. In the Northeast is the so-called Golden Horseshoe, which curls from Oshawa through Toronto and Hamilton to Buffalo. Westward, around the western end of Lake Erie, is the "Erie Horseshoe," which extends from Windsor in Ontario through Detroit and Toledo to Cleveland. The first of these zones is mainly Canadian and the second is largely American, but the effect of the ***North American Free Trade Agreement (NAFTA)*** is diminishing their political separation and increasing their economic interconnection.

As Figure 23-3 shows, the Montreal area along the upper St. Lawrence River also forms part of the Canadian industrial zone. This area is no match for the Ontario district, but it has one big advantage: cheap hydroelectric power. Aluminum-refining and paper-making industries therefore are located there.

Westward lies the remainder of the U.S. industrial heartland. This comprises the interior industrial district, with nodes such as the Pittsburgh–Cleveland area, the Detroit–Southeast Michigan area, Chicago–Gary–Milwaukee, and smaller areas centered on Minneapolis, St. Louis, Cincinnati, and other areas. There industrial power truly transforms the landscape as Appalachian coal and Mesabi iron ore are converted and autos, bulldozers, harvesters, armored cars, and tanks roll off the assembly lines. Refrigerators, televisions, toys, cornflakes, and pills—these and thousands of other products pour from the factories of the Midwest.

Other North American Regions

Figure 23-3 reminds us that the industrial heartland is not the only significant industrial region in the United States. The Southeastern district extends from Birmingham, Alabama, to Richmond, Virginia. The name of Birmingham has long been associated with iron and steel. Local raw materials sustained this industry for many years, but it is now declining rapidly. Atlanta, the regional focus of the South, has a growing industrial base. High-tech industries are changing the industrial structure of this region, but older industries, such as cotton, tobacco, and furniture, still prevail.

On the Gulf of Mexico, a Southwestern district is emerging, centered on the thriving urban areas of Houston and the Dallas–Forth Worth "Metroplex" and extending along the Gulf coast to New Orleans. The oil industry is dominant here, but a wide range of other activities (including meat packing and flour milling) are also located in this area. Aerospace and high-tech industries have also contributed to the development of this district.

Among industrial districts in the western half of the United States, three stand out. The Southern California district, centered on Los Angeles and San Diego, was originally based on agricultural products, but today it is a vast industrial complex with a highly diversified base. The Northern California district, anchored by San Francisco and San Jose but extending westward of San Francisco Bay, is home to Silicon Valley, the manufacturing and research leader in the computer industry. And the Northwest district, extending from Seattle northward to Vancouver, Canada, and southward to Portland, Oregon, has long been the focus of America's aerospace industry. The three West Coast districts shown in Figure 23-3 are all located on the Pacific Rim, and this advantageous location is boosting their growth and prospects.

As noted earlier, political decisions as well as economic forces can change the map. Long before NAFTA took effect on January 1, 1995, a manufacturing zone was developing in northern Mexico. This district's ***maquiladora*** plants, owned mainly by large U.S. companies, transform imported, duty-free components or raw materials into finished industrial products. At least 80 percent of these goods are then reexported to the United States, whose import tariffs are limited to the value added to the products during the Mexican fabrication stage.

Although the maquiladora process started during the 1960s, it did not really take off until the 1980s, stimulated by the wage differences between U.S. and Mexican workers and by changed political conditions. Today about 2000 assembly plants employ more than 600,000 workers, accounting for well over 20 percent of Mexico's entire industrial labor force.

The maquiladora plants produce such goods as electronic equipment, electrical appliances, automobiles, textiles, plastics, and furniture. Tertiary-sector industries, including data-processing operations, are also relocating from the United States to Mexico. Most of the new plants are located in two districts: Tijuana on the Pacific coast, linked to San Diego across the border, and Ciudad Juarez on the Rio Grande across from El Paso, Texas. These Mexican manufacturing nodes are as yet no match for those discussed earlier, but they remind us that the factors governing industrial location are changing.

◆ MANUFACTURING REGIONS OF UKRAINE AND RUSSIA

When the Soviet Union collapsed, 15 independent countries emerged from it. Political and economic geographers had to revise their views in the post-Soviet era. The economies of Russia and Ukraine confronted new challenges as capitalism replaced communism.

Ukraine

The most important country detached from the Soviet Empire (after Russia itself) was Ukraine. In the new Europe, Ukraine would be the largest territorial state and one of the most populous. As we saw previously, prior to its incorporation into the Soviet Empire Ukraine had been strongly affected by the Industrial Revolution; its Donetsk Basin (Donbas) was a major manufacturing center before the end of the nineteenth century. Afterward, Ukraine produced as much as 90 percent of all the coal mined in the then Soviet Union and, with iron ores from the Krivoy Rog reserve and later from Russia's Kursk Magnetic Anomaly, grew into one of the world's largest manufacturing complexes. The integration of eastern Ukraine and southern Russia was nearly complete: electrical transmission lines, roads, railroads, pipelines for oil and gas, and other facilities crossed the border as though it did not exist.

Today Ukraine is a divided country with a largely agrarian, nationalist west and a Russified, industrial east. Ukraine's industries need Russian raw materials and energy supplies, whereas Russia needs Ukrainian products, including foods—but what lies on the Russian side of the boundary is no match for what lies in Ukraine. When Ukraine became independent, Soviet Russia lost one of its key industrial heartlands, and with it a substantial Russian population living in Ukraine. In the late 1990s this situation still clouded the future of relations between the two giants of the former Soviet Empire.

Western Russia

Russia's economic geography (minus Ukraine) reflects both the arrival of the Industrial Revolution in precommunist times and the planned economy of the Soviet era, as well as the eastward shift of industry that occurred during World War II, when Russia was invaded from the west. Several industrial districts have developed within this huge state. The Central Industrial Region is anchored by Moscow, where industry first clustered for the same reasons that it did near London and Paris: an important local market, converging transport routes, a large labor force, and strong centrality (Fig. 23-4). Light manufacturing dominated in this district during Tsarist times, but under communist rule heavy industries were added. Nizhni Novgorod (then named Gorkiy) became the "Soviet Detroit," with huge automobile factories.

The St. Petersburg area is one of Russia's oldest manufacturing centers. It was chosen by Czar Peter the Great not only to serve as Russia's capital but also to become the country's modern industrial focus. The skills and specializations that Peter the Great nurtured with the help of Western European artisans still mark the area's key industries: high-quality machine building, optical products, and medical equipment. But St. Petersburg has become a large metropolis, and industries such as shipbuilding, chemical production, food processing, and textile making are also located there.

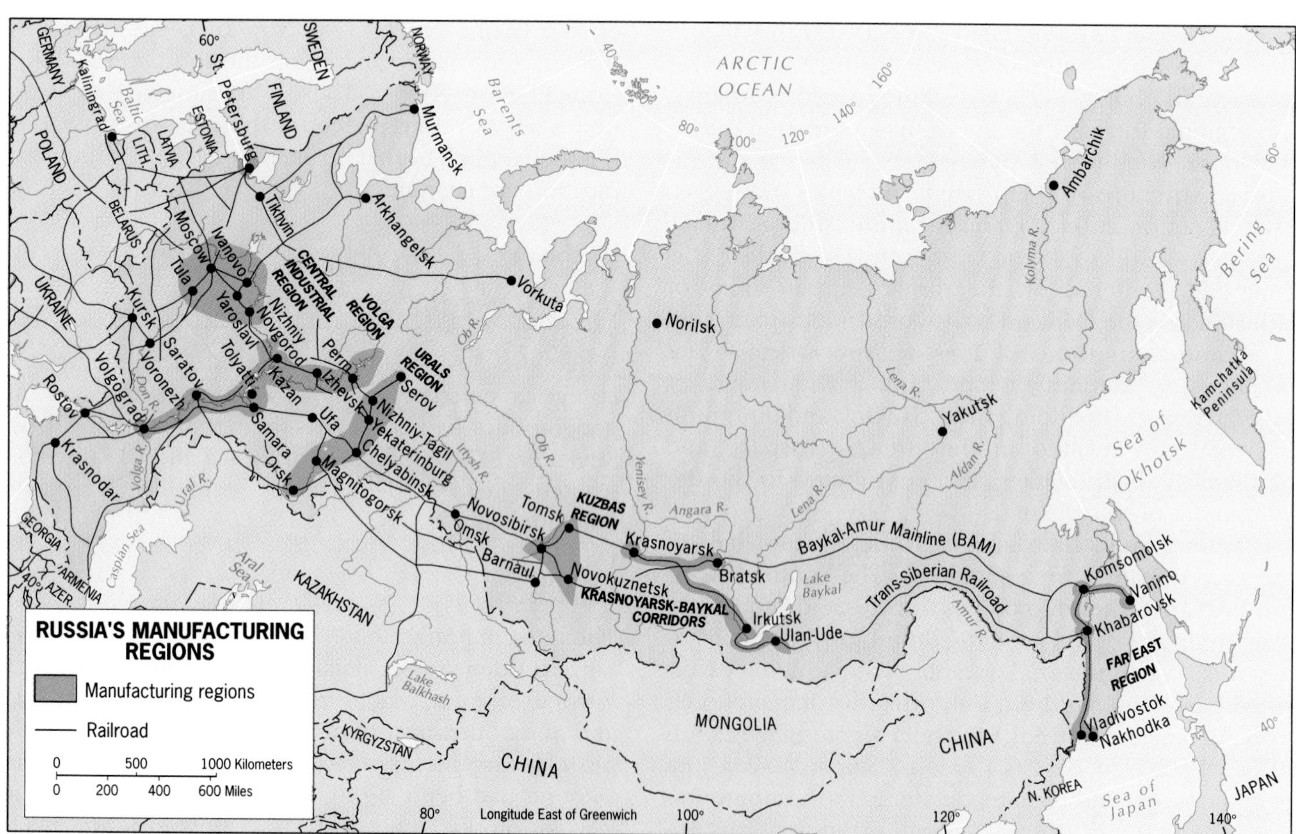

Figure 23-4 Russia's Manufacturing Regions. The major manufacturing regions of Russia reflect the dominance of the west in the country's economic geography.

Two elongated regions lie to the east of the Central Industrial Region (Fig. 23-4). The Volga has experienced major development since the mid-1930s. With the Ukraine and Moscow areas threatened by the German armies, whole industrial plants were dismantled and reassembled in Volga cities, protected from the war by distance. Samara (formerly Kuibyshev) even served as the Soviet capital for a time during World War II. After the war, progress continued. A series of dams, constructed on the Volga River, made electrical power plentiful. Known oil and natural gas reserves were larger than anywhere else in the former USSR. Canals linked the Volga to both Moscow and the Don River, making it easy to import raw materials. The cities lining the Volga, spaced at remarkably regular intervals, were assigned particular industrial functions in the state-planned economy. Samara became an oil refinery center, Saratov acquired a chemical industry, and Volgograd became known for its metallurgical industries. Today the Volga district's contribution to the Russian economy continues.

East of the Volga region lies the Urals region. This area also developed rapidly during World War II. However, there has been nothing artificial in its growth. The Ural Mountains yield an enormous variety of metallic ores, including iron, copper, nickel, chromite, bauxite, and many more. The only serious problem is coal—there is not enough of it, and the little it has is of poor quality. So coal is shipped in by rail from reserves near Novosibirsk to the east. In the cities of the Urals district, metals, metal products, and machinery are produced in great quantities. Together with the Siberian centers, the Urals district now produces more than half of all the iron and steel made in Russia.

Siberia

Three industrial regions are developing in Siberia. About 1900 kilometers (1200 miles) east-southeast of the Urals is the Kuznetsk Basin, or Kuzbas. In the 1930s this area supplied raw materials, especially coal for the Urals, but this function has diminished as local industrial growth has accelerated. The original plan was to move coal from the Kuzbas to the Urals, with returning trains carrying iron ore to the coalfields. However, good iron ores were later discovered in the Kuznetsk Basin itself.

As the resource-based Kuzbas industries grew, so did its urban centers: Novosibirsk, with nearly 2 million inhabitants, is located where the Trans-Siberian Railroad crosses the Ob River. To the northeast lies Tomsk, one of the oldest towns in the eastern region; it was founded three centuries before the Bolshevik takeover and is now caught up in the modern development of the Kuznetsk area. Southeast of Novosibirsk lies Novokuznetsk, with nearly 1 million inhabitants. In its heyday it specialized in the manufacture of heavy engineering products such as rolling stock for the railroads, as well as aluminum products using bauxite from the Urals.

Between the Kuzbas and Lake Baykal lies the Krasnoyarsk-Baykal Corridors region. Served by the Trans-Siberian Railroad and several important rivers, this 1600 kilometer-long (1000 mile-long) region contains impressive resources, including coal, timber, and water. Large hydroelectric facilities at Krasnoyarsk, Irkutsk, and Bratsk supply power to factories that produce mining equipment, chemicals, aircraft, and railway rolling stock. The weaknesses of the region include lack of oil fields, distance from Russia's major population center, and poor infrastructure.

Finally, there is the Far East region, long focused on the Pacific port of Vladivostok and more recently on the new port of Nakhodka. Today industrial growth is also occurring in the hinterlands of such cities as Komsomolsk (the first steel producer in the region) and Khabarovsk (with metal and chemical industries). The region's rich raw materials are finally being extracted, and there is enormous potential for development beyond the low-grade coal and iron ore found to date. Already the zinc and tin deposits mined here constitute Russia's largest sources of these metals. Development of this region, located on the Pacific Rim and on the doorstep of China, should be a leading objective of reformers in Moscow, 10 time zones away.

◆ MANUFACTURING REGIONS OF EASTERN ASIA

Two centuries after the onset of the Industrial Revolution, East Asia is the cauldron of industrialization. From Japan to Guangdong and from South Korea to Singapore, the islands, countries, provinces, and cities fronting the Pacific Ocean are caught up in a frenzy of industrialization that has made the geographic term *Pacific Rim* synonymous with economic opportunity. In cities such as Dalian, Shanghai, Zhuhai, Xiamen, and Shenzhen, pollution-belching smokestacks rise above a smog-choked urban landscape. Streets are jammed with traffic ranging from animal-drawn carts and overloaded bicycles to trucks and buses. Bulldozers are sweeping away vestiges of the old China; cottages with porches and tile roofs on the outskirts of the expanding city must make way for faceless gray tenements. Decaying vestiges of the old city stand amid glass-encased towers that symbolize the new economic order.

Not all of the Pacific Rim displays such symptoms. China's coastal provinces are industrializing, but the process has already run its course in Japan and Singapore. Taiwan and South Korea are in an intermediate stage, and Vietnam lags behind China. But taken as a whole, East Asia is becoming the world's most productive cluster of industrial regions. China's economy is now the world's third largest (after the United States and Japan). And as we will see in the next chapter, the economies of South Korea, Taiwan, Hong Kong, and Singapore are becoming important players as well.

Japan

In less than a century after the beginning of the Industrial Revolution, Japan became one of the world's leading industrial nations. This is all the more remarkable when one realizes that Japan has limited natural resources. Much of what Japan manufactures is made from raw materials imported from all over the world. Japan's national territory is just one twenty-fifth the size of the United States, and its population is less than half the U.S. total. Its transformation into the world's second-largest economy has rightfully been described as a miracle.

Japan's economic development began during the second half of the nineteenth century, when it embarked on a campaign of modernization and colonization. Under the banner of the Meiji Restoration, reformers modernized Japan's domestic industries, moved the capital from the interior to the coast, organized its armed forces, and obtained advice from British experts on issues ranging from education to transportation (which is why the Japanese drive on the left side of the road). The Japanese also established colonies, and soon raw materials were flowing to Japan from an expanding colonial empire in Korea, Taiwan, and mainland China.

World War II brought triumph and disaster: triumph in the form of a military campaign that included a surprise attack on Pearl Harbor in Hawaii and vast conquests in the Pacific, East Asia, and Southeast Asia, and disaster when Japanese forces were driven back with great loss of life. The war ended with the destruction of two Japanese cities by atomic bombs. When U.S. forces took control of Japan in 1945, the nation's economy was in a shambles. Yet decades later Japan had not only recovered but become a global economic power. And so for the second time in little more than a century Japan converted chaos into conquest.

In the late 1990s, Japan's economy experienced a downturn—not because of changes in the country's energy or raw-material supply, but as a result of government mismanagement and financial mistakes. Japan's problems posed a risk to the global economic system, because world economies are interconnected. But Japan's troubles are likely to be temporary, to be solved by policy changes.

Japan's industries depend on external sources of supply. This, along with its mountainous topography, caused manufacturing plants to be located in coastal areas, which are also advantageous because most goods produced by the factories are exported.

The Kanto Plain As Figure 23-5 shows, Japan's dominant region of industrialization and urbanization is the Kanto Plain, which contains about one-third of the population and includes the Tokyo–Yokohama–Kawasaki metropolitan area (27 million). This gigantic cluster of cities and suburbs (the world's largest urban agglomeration), interspersed with intensively cultivated farmlands, forms the eastern anchor of the country's core area. Besides its flatness, the Kanto Plain possesses other advantages: its fine natural harbor at Yokohama, its relatively mild and moist climate, and its central location with respect to the country as a whole. It has also benefited from Tokyo's designation as the nation's capital, when Japan embarked on its planned course of economic development. Many industries and businesses chose Tokyo as their headquarters in order to be near government decision makers.

The Tokyo–Yokohama–Kawasaki metropolitan area has become Japan's leading manufacturing complex, producing more than 20 percent of the country's annual output. The raw materials for all this industry, however, come from far away. For example, the To-

From the field notes

"Sail up Japan's Inland Sea toward Kobe, and it seems as though the country's entire waterfront has been turned into one vast system for unloading raw materials and loading finished products. Large freighters can be offloaded in just a few hours by massive cranes that lift out hold-sized containers, empty them into trucks and return them to the ship. A never-ending lineup of railroad cars and flatbed trucks circulates through the port of Kobe (seen here), picking up incoming freight and delivering goods for export. Such infrastructure and efficiency have combined to help make Japan's one of the most competitive economies in the world."

Figure 23-5 East Asia's Manufacturing Regions. For decades, the Northeast was China's most rapidly growing industrial area. Now the Chang District is taking the lead.

kyo area is among the chief producers of steel, using iron ores from the Philippines, Malaysia, Australia, India, and even Africa; most of the coal is imported from Australia and North America; and the petroleum from Southwest Asia and Indonesia. The Kanto Plain cannot produce nearly enough food for its massive resident population. Food must be imported from Canada, the United States, and Australia as well as from other areas in Japan. Thus Tokyo depends on external trade for all things ranging from food to energy.

The Kansai District Japan's second largest industrial complex extends from the eastern end of the Seto Inland Sea to the Nagoya area and includes the Kobe–Kyoto–Osaka triangle. This, the Kansai district, comes close to rivaling the Kanto area: it is a vast industrial region with steel mills, a major chemical industry, automobile manufacturing, shipbuilding, textile factories, and many other types of production. The urban agglomeration developing here is often called the *Tokaido* megalopolis.

The Kitakyushu District The Seto Inland Sea is Japan's pivotal waterway, and the Kansai district has benefited from its location at the eastern end of it. During the nineteenth century, raw materials from Korea and later from Northeast China moved in large quantities along this route. At the western entrance to the sea lies the focus of Japan's third industrial district, called Kitakyushu, a conurbation of five northern Kyushu Island cities. Japan's first coal mines were located there, as well as its first steel mills, which for many years remained the largest in the country. Today heavy industries dominate, with shipbuilding and steel-making in the lead, supplemented by a large chemical industry and numerous lighter manufacturing plants. This district will develop even faster if trade with China continues to expand. No place in Japan is better located to do business with mainland Asia.

The Toyama District Only one manufacturing district in the area depicted by our map lies outside the belt extending from Tokyo in the east to Kitakyushu in the west. It is the secondary district centered on Toyama, on the Sea of Japan. The advantage there is cheap electricity from nearby hydroelectric stations, and this is reflected by the cluster of industries located in this district: paper manufacturing, chemical industries, and textile plants. Of course, our map gives an inadequate picture of the variety and range of industries that exist throughout Japan, many of them oriented to local markets. Thousands of manufacturing plants operate in cities and towns other than those shown on the map, even on the cold northern island of Hokkaido. As we did in the case of Europe, North America, Russia, and Ukraine, we have focused here only on the truly outstanding manufacturing districts of Japan.

China

Although some industrial growth occurred in China during the period of European colonial influence, and later during the Japanese occupation, China's major industrial expansion occurred during the communist period. When the communist planners took over in 1949, one of their leading priorities was to develop China's resources and industries as rapidly as possible.

China is a vast country, and it is likely that some of its natural resources have yet to be discovered. Even so, China already has a substantial resource base. The quality of its coal is good, the quantity enormous, and many of the deposits are near the surface and easily extracted. China's iron ores are not so productive and are generally of rather low grade, but new finds are frequently made and the picture has improved steadily. This is also true in the case of oil. In recent years, with the aid of Western companies, China has intensified its search for oil reserves, and in two areas—the western interior and the continental shelf—this effort has achieved some good results. Nevertheless, the energy picture remains uncertain. In the late 1990s China's known reserves amounted to about 4 percent of the world total.

China's communist-era industrial development, aided until the early 1960s by Soviet planners, was spatially constrained by the location of raw materials, the development that had taken place before the 1949 communist takeover, the pattern of long-term urbanization in the country, the existing transport network, and the eastern clustering of the population. Like their Soviet allies, China's rulers were determined to speed the industrialization of the economy, and their decisions created several major and lesser industrial districts.

The Northeast District Under state planning rules, the Northeast district (formerly known as Manchuria and called Dongbei in China today) became China's industrial heartland, a complex of heavy industries based on the region's coal and iron deposits located in the basin of the Liao River. Shenyang, with a population of 5 million, became the "Chinese Pittsburgh," with metallurgical, machine-making, engineering, and other large factories. Anshan, to the south, emerged as China's leading iron- and steel-producing center. Harbin to the north (China's northernmost large city, with more than 2 million inhabitants) produced textiles, farm equipment, and light manufactures of many kinds (Fig. 23-5).

The Northern industrial district was established around the capital and its major port, Tianjin. Although it benefited from nearby coalfields, an ample labor force, and large agricultural production, this district did not match the Northeast in any respect. Heavy industry was located in the Tianjin area, and textile-making and food-processing plants handled local products.

Shanghai and the Chang (Yangzi) District The second largest industrial region in China developed in and around the country's biggest city, Shanghai. The communist planners never allowed Shanghai to attain its full potential, often favoring the Beijing–Tianjin complex over the great port at the mouth of the Chang called the Yangzi River in its lower course. Nevertheless, the Chang district, containing both Shanghai and Wuhan, rose to prominence and, by some measures, exceeded the Northeast as a contributor to the national economy. As Figure 23-5 shows, still another industrial complex developed farther upstream along the Chang River focused on the city of Chongqing. Whether we view the Chang district as one industrial zone or three, it is a pacesetter for Chinese industrial growth, if not in terms of iron and steel production, then in terms of its diversified production and local specializations. Railroad cars, ships, books, foods, chemicals—an endless variety of products come from the thriving Chang districts. These districts will be strongly affected by the construction of the Three Gorges Dam in the middle course of the Chang River.

The Guangdong District In the south, the Guangdong industrial district remained in fourth place under communist state planning. China's rulers tended to favor northern provinces over southern ones, and Guangzhou (formerly called Canton) never was a favorite. China's uneasy relationship with Hong Kong, located on the estuary of the Pearl River, further diminished Beijing's interest in the south. In the absence of major mineral or fuel resources, the Guangdong industrial zone could not rival the complexes of the north.

Special Economic Zones Note that the foregoing paragraphs are written in the past tense. Today economic policies in China are very different. The communist regime is still in control, but it has chosen to pursue a market-driven economic course. Moreover, certain cities and areas facing the Pacific coast have been designated as ***Special Economic Zones (SEZs)***, "open cities," and "open coastal areas" to encourage foreign investment. Shanghai is no longer shackled: a gigantic development project is transforming the right bank of the Huangpu into an industrial complex (named Pudong) that is expected to rival Hong Kong. In the meantime Shenzhen, across the border from Hong Kong, has undergone massive industrialization and become the world's fastest-growing urban area. Once-dormant Guangdong Province has become a major contributor to China's export economy.

At the same time, the Northeast has become China's rustbelt. Many of its state-run factories have been sold or closed, or are operating below capacity. Unemployment is high, and economic growth has stopped. Eventually the Northeast is likely to recover because its resources and its geography favor it. But under the new economic policies the dynamic eastern and southern provinces are producing their own industrial revolution and changing the map of this part of the Pacific Rim.

◆ INDUSTRIALIZATION ELSEWHERE

As this chapter has underscored, major industrialization has taken place in the Northern Hemisphere in a resource-rich zone that extends eastward from Britain, across the heart of Europe, through Ukraine and along the southern margins of Russia, through northern China, and across the U.S. Midwest and East. Industrialization of the kind that transformed Central Europe and its cities did not fully reach the other side of the world until China's communist rulers decided to industrialize their country, almost two centuries after the Industrial Revolution.

But we have learned another lesson. The rules of industrialization are changing. Japan did it even though it lacked raw materials of its own. Guangdong, with limited natural resources, is thriving, while China's once formidable Northeast is declining. And there are fewer rules hindering the development of secondary industries.

At present, industrial development beyond the regions discussed here remains limited. We can identify a ***secondary industrial region*** south of the world's primary industrial region (Fig. 23-6). Thailand, Malaysia, Indonesia, and Vietnam (and possibly the Philippines) are sharing in the economic growth of the Pacific Rim. Elsewhere, however, industrialization proceeds slowly. In the Western Hemisphere, only

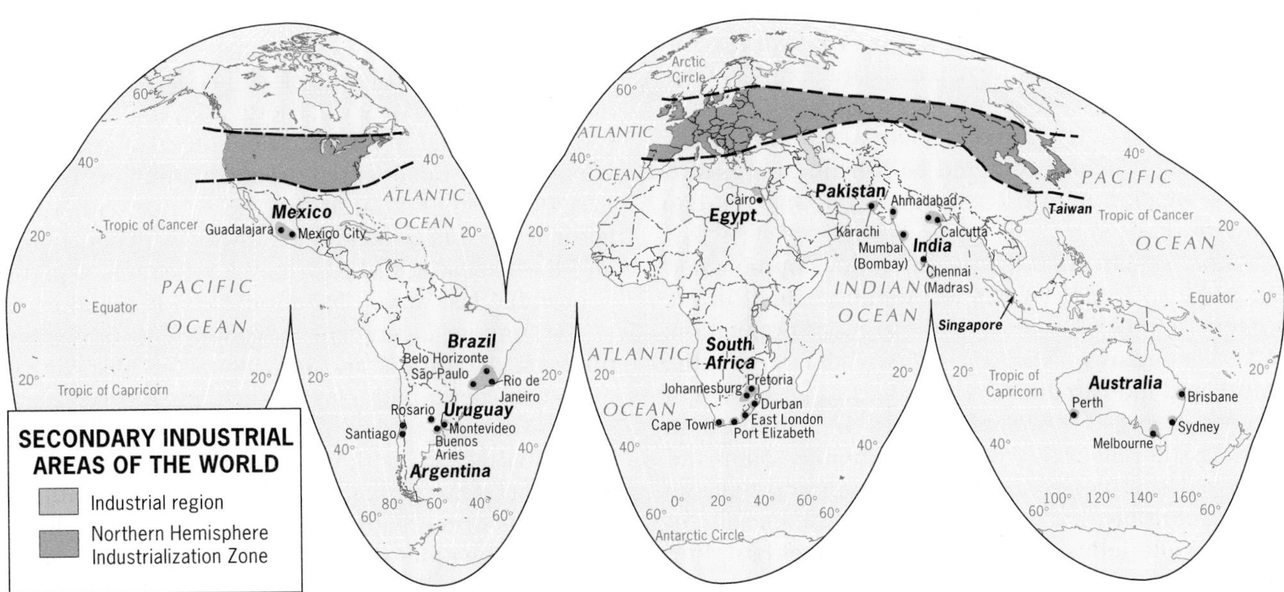

Figure 23-6 Secondary Industrial Areas of the World.

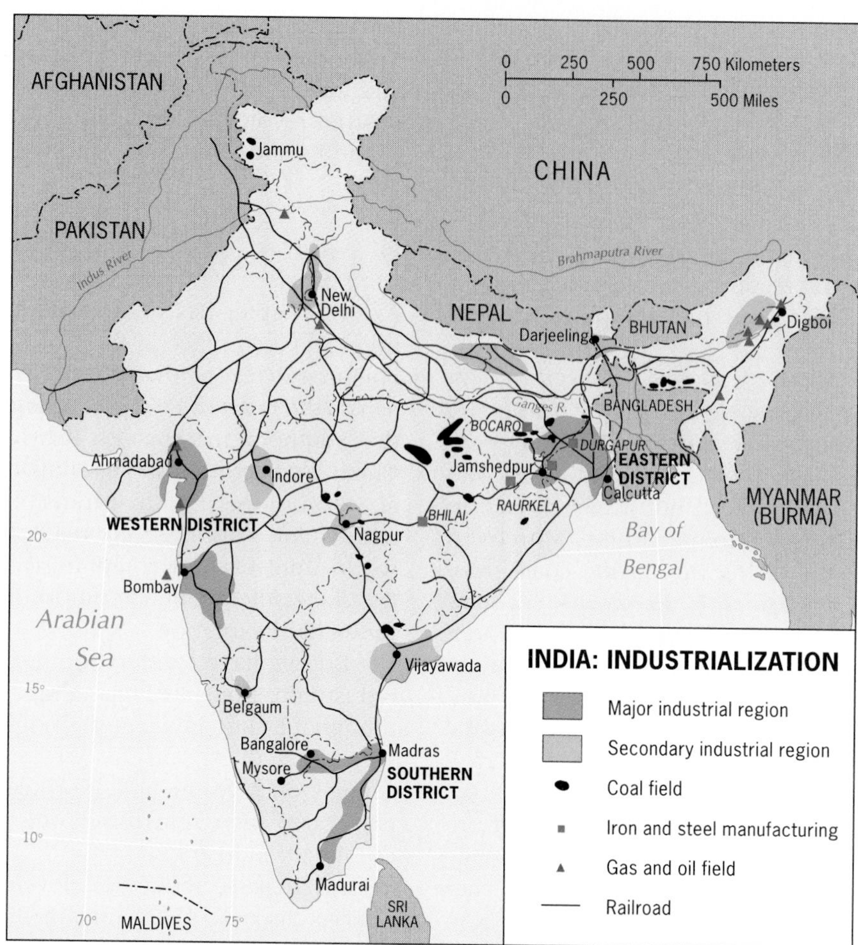

Figure 23-7 India's Industrial Areas. India's industrial areas are widely dispersed. India has large coal deposits, but its oil reserves are small.

Brazil and Mexico have substantial manufacturing industries: Brazil in the São Paulo–Rio de Janeiro–Belo Horizonte triangle (with output ranging from automobiles and weapons to chemicals and textiles) and Mexico in the Mexico City–Guadalajara complex (Fig. 23-6). In Africa, some industrialization is occurring in the hinterland of Cairo and in South Africa, principally in Gauteng Province centered on Johannesburg. Australia's smaller industries lie near the local urban markets.

More significant is the industrial development taking place in India (Fig. 23-7). Although small in the context of India's huge size and enormous population, India's economy now ranks as the eighth largest in the world, and industrialization is expanding as a result of recently changed economic policies. Industrialization in India still reflects its colonial beginnings, but major industrial complexes are developing around Calcutta (the Eastern district, with engineering, chemical, cotton, and jute industries, plus iron and steel based on the Chota Nagpur reserves), Mumbai (the Western district, where cheap electricity helps the cotton and chemical industries), and Chennai (the Southern district, with an emphasis on light engineering and textiles).

India suffers from a lack of major oil reserves, so it must spend heavily on energy. On the other hand, India has much hydroelectric potential and ample coal, and its Bihar and Karnataka iron ore reserves may be among the largest in the world. With a large labor force and a location midway between Europe and the Pacific Rim, India may yet become a participant in the last wave of the Industrial Revolution.

To understand recent industrial developments in places such as India and Brazil—or the Mexican maquiladora described earlier—we need to consider some of the sweeping changes that have occurred in the global economy during the twentieth century. As the next chapter explains, these changes have affected most parts of the planet and account for both the decline of some older manufacturing regions and the rise of some new ones.

◆ KEY TERMS ◆

break-of-bulk
maquiladora
North American Free Trade Agreement (NAFTA)
planned industrial economy
primary industrial region
secondary industrial region
Special Economic Zone (SEZ)

◆ APPLYING GEOGRAPHIC KNOWLEDGE ◆

1. After a surge of nuclear power-plant building and plans for a growing substitution of coal-fired power plants by nuclear facilities, the drive toward nuclear power in the United States slowed and then virtually stopped. In other countries, however, the expansion of nuclear power generation continued; France has the lead in Europe. What factors explain the differences between the United States and France?

2. Most of North America's manufacturing industries remain concentrated in the core area shown in Figure 23-3, but other industrial areas are developing. Unlike the massive core area, these subsidiary areas tend to be specialized around some product or combination of products. Explain the locational characteristics of the subsidiary areas shown on the map in the context of their particular products.

Chapter 24

Deindustrialization and the Rise of the Service Sector

From the field notes

"Leaving the Eastern Malaysian city of Kota Kinabalu on my way to the town of Beaufort, I see some familiar names in a most unlikely place! Education is one of the major service industries, and like others (banking, finance, tourism) it is globalizing. University and college linkages around the world are multiplying, and it is a hopeful sign: out of such interaction comes intercultural understanding. It also will have an effect on the dissemination of English; this billboard stands in a country where Malays and Chinese make up most of the population, and where Malay is the official language."

KEY POINTS

◆ **The declining cost of transportation and communication, along with changes in the production process, have led to an enormous expansion of the service sector in the twentieth century, particularly in the industrialized core.**

◆ **Deindustrialization in the core has not altered basic global patterns of economic well-being, but it has led to the growth of labor-intensive manufacturing in the periphery.**

◆ **The resulting new international division of labor has linked the world's economies more closely together, but it carries with it patterns of interaction that favor some areas over others.**

◆ **A global economic geography dominated by nation-states is giving way to one in which world cities and multinational corporations play an increasingly significant role.**

◆ **Developments such as the World Wide Web are accelerating the pace of life and changing the relationship among places.**

Ever since the Industrial Revolution, the growing demand for resources, the expansion of manufacturing and trade, and technological innovation have worked together to produce an increasingly interconnected global economy. Almost all places are in some way part of the web of production, exchange, and consumption that make up that economy—and their position in that web has significant social consequences. As we have seen, those in the developed core tend to be in the driver's seat, whereas those in the periphery have far less control. Someone living and working in the banana-producing part of Ecuador has little to say about the global price of bananas, and the banana-growing firms that dominate the economy may not even be locally owned. Yet what happens to banana prices on the global market, and the decisions that are made about that banana-growing firm, can have profound local consequences.

Tracing the historical geography of industrialization can tell us much about why some areas are in a more advantageous position than others, but that is not the entire story. Over the past 30 years many of the core industrial economies have experienced significant deindustrialization, accompanied by growth in service-related activities. This shift has its roots in dramatic decreases in the cost of transporting goods, the increasing mechanization of production, the growth of the public sector, and the rise of new information and communication technologies. The changes of the past three decades have not fundamentally altered global patterns of economic well-being, but they have produced significant new spatial orders. They have caused shifts in the locus of production, altered patterns of regional specialization, and fostered new centers of economic growth.

◆ CATEGORIES OF SERVICE INDUSTRIES

The origins of the manufacturing boom of the twentieth century can be traced to early innovations in the production process. Perhaps the most significant of these was the mass-production assembly line pioneered by Henry Ford, which allowed for the production of consumer goods at a single site on a previously unknown scale. So significant was Ford's idea that the dominant mode of large-scale manufacture that endured for much of the century is known as "***Fordist***."

By the end of World War II, the increasing saturation of consumer markets, the tremendous growth in governmental activity, rising labor activism, and declines in the cost of transportation and communication began to challenge the Fordist order. The challenge shifted into high gear in the early 1970s, when a sharp rise in oil prices during a period of international financial instability and inflation produced a dramatic downturn in the global economy. Under these circumstances, it became increasingly difficult for the core industrial regions to sustain their competitive advantage without significant readjustment. The direction that readjustment would take was signaled by the movement toward mechanization and the development of service and information industries. These trends worked together with the need for new markets and the growth of multinational concerns to create a shift toward a "postindustrial" or "post-Fordist" economic order in many of the developed, core economies.

Service industries are commonly referred to as ***tertiary industries***. These industries do not generate an actual, tangible product; instead, they include the range of services that are found in modern societies. So many different types of activities can be thought of as service activities that no one term can encompass them all. Hence, the service sector is sometimes broken down into three categories: tertiary industries, quaternary industries, and quinary industries. There is some disagreement about the scope of these terms, but tertiary industries are generally considered to be the basic business and personal services that are associated with an exchange economy (retailing, restaurants/hotels, transportation, communication, utilities, etc.). The term ***quaternary industries*** refers to the collection, processing, and manipulation of information and capital (finance, administration, insurance, legal services, computer services, etc.). People working in the quaternary sector tend to have high levels of specialized knowledge or technical skills. The term ***quinary industries*** denotes activities that facilitate complex decision making and the advancement of human capacities (scientific research, high-level management, etc.). This sector encompasses the activities of research professors, the heads of corporations, and top government officials.

Distinguishing among types of services is useful, given the extraordinary growth in the size and complexity of the service sector. In the core, service industries employ more workers than the primary and secondary industries combined, yet these service industries range from small-scale retailing to tourism services (see "Focus on: Tourism, A Service Industry Giant") to research on the causes of cancer. Placing all of these in a single category seems unwarranted. Specificity in terminology is also useful in highlighting different phases in the development of the service sector.

Focus On

Tourism, A Service Industry Giant

What is the largest industry in the world today? farming? automobile manufacturing? No, it is neither a primary nor a secondary industry. By every measure—number of jobs, total value—the leading industry is tourism and travel. Tourism accounts for 11 percent of all the jobs around the world, creating work for about 260 million people. If recent trends continue, that total will exceed 400 million a decade from now.

Tourism's growth results from several factors. Rising incomes in many countries make recreational travel possible for a fast-growing segment of the world's population. The number of East and Southeast Asian tourists has risen much faster than the global average, reflecting the economic boom in many of the Pacific Rim countries. Political barriers to international travel have fallen dramatically. Even repressive regimes such as Myanmar's and Nigeria's invite tourists to spend their currencies in these countries. Leisure time available to potential travelers is increasing through longer paid vacations, earlier retirement, and lengthier lives. Infrastructure continues to expand as hotel and resort capacity increases as much as 8 percent annually. And the global fleet of jet aircraft similarly continues to grow, along with new or expanded airports to accommodate them. Denver, Hong Kong, and Kuala Lumpur (Malaysia) are among cities opening new airports recently; Chicago, London, and Tokyo are contemplating additional airports.

One of the fastest-growing segments of the tourist industry is cruising. Until the 1960s, ocean-going liners provided transportation rather than recreation, but the advent of the jet plane ended that era. Today, ships several times as large as their predecessors, up to 135,000 tons, carry as many as 3000 passengers on vacation cruises that begin and end at the same port. Only one liner still maintains an abbreviated Transatlantic schedule. One cruise ship carrying 2000 passengers on week-long cruises can accommodate 100,000 passengers per year and generate $100 million in gross revenues while keeping 1200 officers and crew employed.

The tourist industry has transformed downtowns, ports, hinterlands, parks, and waterfronts. High-rise, ultramodern hotels dominate urban skylines from Boston to Brisbane. The Port of Miami and Fort Lauderdale's Port Everglades have been reconstructed to serve the cruise industry, and many ports from Tokyo to Tampa have added cruise terminals complete with shopping malls and restaurants. Theme parks such as Disney's establishments near Orlando, Paris, Tokyo, and Los Angeles draw millions of visitors and directly and indirectly employ thousands of workers. Once-remote wildlife parks and nature reserves in East Africa and South Asia now receive thousands of visitors, requiring expanded facilities and sometimes causing ecological damage. Isolated beaches are now lined by high-rise hotels and resorts; in the Caribbean and the Pacific, some entire islands have been taken over by tour operators.

The geographic impact of the tourist industry is far-reaching, and its economic influence on national economies grows every year. In 1997, the economic value of goods and services associated with tourism approached $4 trillion, or about 11 percent of the combined GNP of all the countries of the world. It is a dramatic example of the rise of the service sector in the world economy.

In the early decades of the twentieth century, the domestic and quasi-domestic tertiary industries were experiencing rapid growth in the global economic core. With the approach of World War II, the quaternary sector began expanding rapidly, and this expansion continued after the war. During the last three decades, both the quaternary and quinary sectors have experienced very rapid growth, giving greater meaning to the term *postindustrial.*

The expanding service sector in the core economies is only one aspect of the changing global economy. Accompanying, and in some cases driving, this expansion are several other developments that have already been mentioned: the increasing mechanization of production, particularly in manufacturing enterprises operating in the core; the growth of large multinational corporations; and the dispersal of the production process, with components for complex products such as automobiles and consumer electronics coming from factories in many different countries.

◆ GEOGRAPHICAL DIMENSIONS OF ECONOMIC ACTIVITY

The trends just outlined unfolded on a stage that was already characterized by wide socioeconomic disparities—disparities that shaped the changing economic geography of the planet. Only areas that had industry could deindustrialize, of course, and at the global scale the wealthier industrial regions were the most successful in establishing a postindustrial service economy. Thus, we should not be surprised that deindustrialization did little to change the basic disparities between core and periphery that have long characterized the global economy. Indeed, even in the manufacturing realm, mechanization and innovative production strategies allowed the core industrial regions to retain their dominance. In the late 1990s eastern Asia, western Russia and Ukraine, Western Europe, and North America still account for well over 75 percent of the world's total output of manufactured goods.

Despite its continued dominance in the manufacturing arena, the developed core has experienced some wrenching changes associated with the economic shifts of the past three decades. Anyone who has ever spent time in northern Indiana, the British Midlands, or Silesia (southern Poland and northeastern Czech Republic) knows that there are pockets of significant hardship within the core. In many cases older factories simply could not compete against newer, mechanized competitors, leading to the shutdown of the older plants. Sometimes the newer factories were not even located in the same place, and even when they were, they often required a labor force with different skills from those of the workers in the old factories. Hence, many of the older industrial districts experienced significant unemployment. The local governments of such districts also were in a poor position to respond. The closing of factories drastically reduced the tax base of many areas, making it all but impossible to invest in economic restructuring.

To understand the economic shifts that have occurred over the past few decades, however, we must look beyond individual places to the global scale—for as we have already seen, the hardships of an older industrial region are just one part of a much larger story. Part of that story involves changing business and investment practices and social arrangements, and much has been written about them by economists and sociologists. But geography is also central to the story, for some of its most fundamental elements can be seen in the changing spatial structure of economic

From the field notes

"During the communist era, much of the traditional housing stock in Eastern Europe was replaced with cinder-block structures that were minimally functional, but grim. This example from Silesia (southern Poland) is a case in point. Such structures now house a population facing high unemployment as Poland privatizes or closes outdated industries in an effort both to decentralize its economy and to shift its economic base from manufacturing to more of a service-based orientation."

Figure 24-1 Increases in Value of Manufacturing Exports to OECD Countries. This map shows the percentage of increases in value of manufacturing exports to OECD countries from major low- and middle-income trading partners, 1970–1992. *Source: The World Bank* World Development Report 1994. Infrastructure for Development, *Oxford: Oxford University Press*.

activity. Three matters are of particular importance: the rise of new economic relationships binding together different parts of the world; a shift in the locational features of certain industries and activities; and the emergence of specialized zones of economic activity. Let us look at each of these.

The New International Division of Labor

The phrase ***new international division of labor*** refers to the set of relationships that define the contemporary world economy. Whereas earlier in the century economic relations were defined by an industrialized core and a resource-exporting periphery, today the geography of the global economy is more complex. As we have seen, the traditional industrial core regions remain dominant, but important shifts have occurred in their relative importance, and new regions have emerged as major players. The countries and regions outside the core that have increased their manufacturing output most rapidly in recent decades are shown in Figure 24-1. Among the core areas, the United States and the United Kingdom are no longer as significant as they once were, whereas Japan's manufacturing base has grown dramatically. Even more striking is the emergence of a number of new large-scale contributors to the global manufacturing base. These so-called newly industrializing countries include the "***Four Tigers***" of the Pacific Rim (see "Focus on: The 'Four Tigers' "), Brazil and Mexico in the Americas, and countries at the southwestern and southeastern edges of Europe.

Lying behind the patterns shown in Figure 24-1 is a set of developments and connections that give

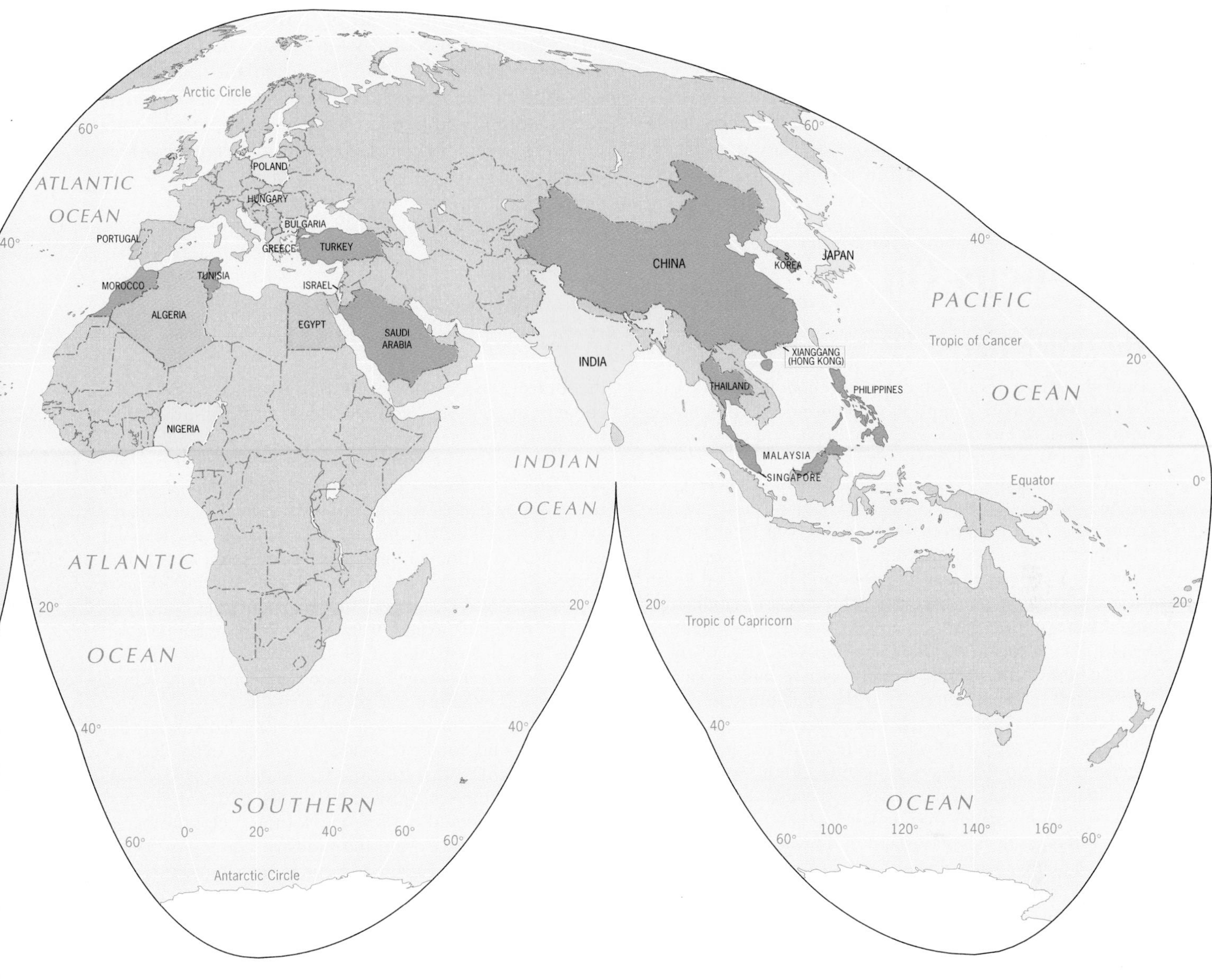

meaning to the phrase "new international division of labor." On the one hand, there is the shift away from heavy industry and toward the service sector that has occurred in parts of the traditional industrial core. On the other hand, there is the rise of labor-intensive manufacturing in new locations. And then there are the multinational corporations that have helped engineer the new international division of labor. Some of the larger multinationals, such as General Motors, Philips, Union Carbide, and Exxon, are major global economic players, with annual earnings that exceed the gross national products of many smaller states. Taking advantage of low transportation costs, favorable governmental regulations, and expanding information technology, they have constructed vast economic networks in which different facets of production are carried out in different places in order to benefit from the advantages of specific locations (see "A Sense of Scale: Nike and Economic Globalization"). Research and development activities tend to be concentrated in the core, where high levels of education and access to technology are the norm. Technologically sophisticated manufacturing also tends to be situated in the core, because both the expertise and the infrastructure are there. More labor-intensive manufacturing, particularly assembly activities, is more likely to be located in peripheral countries where labor is cheap, regulations are few, and tax rates are low.

Supporting the economic web at the heart of the new international division of labor are elaborate trading networks and financial relations. Trade itself is a tertiary economic activity of considerable importance to the global economy. Patterns of trade vary by industry, but the character of the new international division of labor ensures that the dominant flow of trade is among the core countries and between those countries and newly industrializing countries. The core countries are those with the highest levels of demand, as well as major suppliers of manufactured goods, and the newly industrializing countries are key exporters of manufactured goods used in the industries of the core. By contrast, the level of trade between peripheral countries—even between newly industrializing countries—is low because the dominant flow of exports is to the core, not to other peripheral countries. Indeed, some peripheral countries compete with one another in producing similar commodities destined for the core.

The "Four Tigers"

Until about two decades ago, Japan's economic dominance of East Asia was beyond doubt. Other nodes of manufacturing existed, but these were no threat, and certainly no match, for Japan's industrial might.

Over the past 20 years, however, Japan has been challenged. Although it remains the undisputed leader, it faces growing competition from the so-called Four Tigers of East and Southeast Asia: South Korea, Taiwan, Hong Kong, and Singapore. Among these, populous and productive South Korea is a major industrial rival. Three major manufacturing districts export products ranging from automobiles and grand pianos to calculators and computers. One of these is centered on the capital, Seoul (with 18 million inhabitants), and the two others lie at the southern end of the peninsula, anchored by Pusan and Kwangju, respectively (Fig. 23-5). If the two Koreas were reunited, the combination of the North's heavy industries and the South's major manufacturing would create a formidable industrial power just a few miles from Japan.

To the south lies the island of Taiwan. Although the island is neither large nor populous (it has 21 million inhabitants, compared to 46 million in South Korea), its industrial power is growing. In recent years Taiwan's economic planners have been moving the secondary sector away from labor-intensive manufacturing toward high-technology industries, thus meeting Japanese competition head-on. Personal computers, telecommunications equipment, precision electronic instruments, and other high-tech products flow from Taiwanese plants, which benefit from a skilled labor force. The capital, Taipei (with 7 million inhabitants), is the focus of the country's industrial complex, which is situated on the northern and northwestern zone of the island.

Just a trading colony five decades ago, Hong Kong exploded onto the world economic scene during the 1950s with textiles and light manufactures. The success of these industries, based on plentiful, cheap labor, was followed by growing production of electrical equipment, appliances, and other household products. Hong Kong is constricted by its limited land area, but situational advantages have contributed enormously to its economic fortunes. The colony became mainland China's gateway to the world, a bustling port, financial center, and break-of-bulk point. In 1997 China took over the government of Hong Kong from the British, and a showplace of capitalism came under communist control. Today the future of this third "Tiger" is in doubt.

The industrial growth of Singapore also can be attributed largely to geography. Strategically located at the tip of the Malay Peninsula, Singapore is a small island inhabited by under 3 million people, mostly ethnic Chinese but with Malay and Indian minorities. Forty years ago, Singapore was mainly an *entrepôt* (transshipment point) for such products as rubber, timber, and oil; today, the bulk of its foreign revenues come from exports of manufactured goods and, increasingly, high-technology products. Singapore is also a center for quaternary industries, selling services and expertise to a global market.

Rapid economic growth entails risks. To varying degrees, East and Southeast Asia's economies expanded under circumstances that contained potentials for trouble. Autocratic governments protected banks and state-owned industries that could not survive without help; the banks lent too much money and the industries grew lax. Those same governments engaged in sometimes grandiose construction projects requiring huge loans. Cronyism (giving special favors such as mining permits and import licenses to family and friends) and corruption continued, their costs hidden by the economic boom. Legal systems to protect foreign businesses on Asian soil were in some ways inadequate. Currencies (the money of the countries) were weakened by the resulting pressures, and some were seriously overvalued against, say, the U.S. dollar and the British pound.

In 1997, the region suffered a severe economic setback resulting from these circumstances. Thailand's currency collapsed, followed by its stock market; banks closed and bankruptcies abounded. Soon Malaysia and Indonesia were affected, and by early 1998 one of the Four Tigers, South Korea, required a massive infusion of dollars (provided by the International Monetary Fund, a Washington-based bank) to prevent economic chaos.

These economic troubles on the Pacific Rim will not, however, mark the end of the region's economic expansion. The reforms required to overcome them will serve to strengthen East and Southeast Asia's economies, and the Four Tigers and their neighbors will roar again.

A SENSE OF SCALE

Nike and Economic Globalization

Economic globalization and the new international division of labor are associated with very different local economic and social arrangements from those in prior eras. A U.S. shoe manufacturing concern 50 years ago might well have imported some materials, but its headquarters and production facilities would probably have been located in the same place, and it would have drawn a mix of skilled and unskilled labor from the community. Some secondary industries still conform to this characterization, but a great many do not.

Nike Headquarters in the Portland, Oregon, metropolitan area, where business and marketing decisions—but not shoes—are made.

Consider, for example, the modern American athletic shoe manufacturer, Nike. Nike was founded in Oregon in 1972 by a former competitive runner, and it has grown to be one of the giants of the shoe and apparel business. With headquarters in Beaverton, Oregon, a suburb of Portland, the company is far more than a Beaverton concern. Despite an Oregon work force of over 20,000 people, not a single individual in Oregon is directly involved in the process of putting a shoe together. Nike began by contracting with an Asian firm to manufacture its shoes. In 1974, Nike set up its first domestic shoe manufacturing facility in the small town of Exeter, New Hampshire. By the end of that year, Nike's work force was still modest in number, but the Oregon contingent focused on running the company and expanding sales, whereas the New Hampshire and the Asian contingents focused primarily on the production of athletic shoes.

As Nike grew to become the world's leading manufacturer of athletic shoes (with almost a 40 percent share of the world's athletic shoe market), its employment numbers skyrocketed and many new manufacturing plants were established in Asia and beyond. This transformation did not translate into manufacturing jobs in Beaverton, Oregon, however. The employment opportunities now provided by Nike at its world headquarters are for the financial administrators, marketing and sales specialists, information technology directors, computer technicians, lawyers, and support personnel needed to run an international company with over $9 billion in annual revenues. Thus, the local social and economic geography of Beaverton bears little resemblance to what one might have expected in a town housing an important shoe company a few decades ago. Instead, it is a local geography influenced, and profoundly tied into, an elaborate network of international exchange. And each node of that network is functionally specialized, dependent on other nodes, and influenced by the niche it occupies in the network.

The production of television receivers provides an example of how changing multinational networks function in a particular industry. Commercial production of television sets began after World War II. During the industry's early decades, a variety of small and medium-sized firms in Europe, Asia, and North America were involved in it, although the United States was the dominant producer. During the 1970s and 1980s a dramatic shift occurred, with a small number of large Asian producers—particularly in Japan—seizing a much larger percentage of the market and with a few European firms increasing their position as well. By 1990 ten large firms were responsible for 80 percent of the world's color television sets; eight of them were Japanese and two European. Only one U.S. firm—Zenith—remained, and its share of the global market was relatively small.

Behind this rather simple picture lies a more complicated story. The television production industry has three key elements: research and design, manufacture

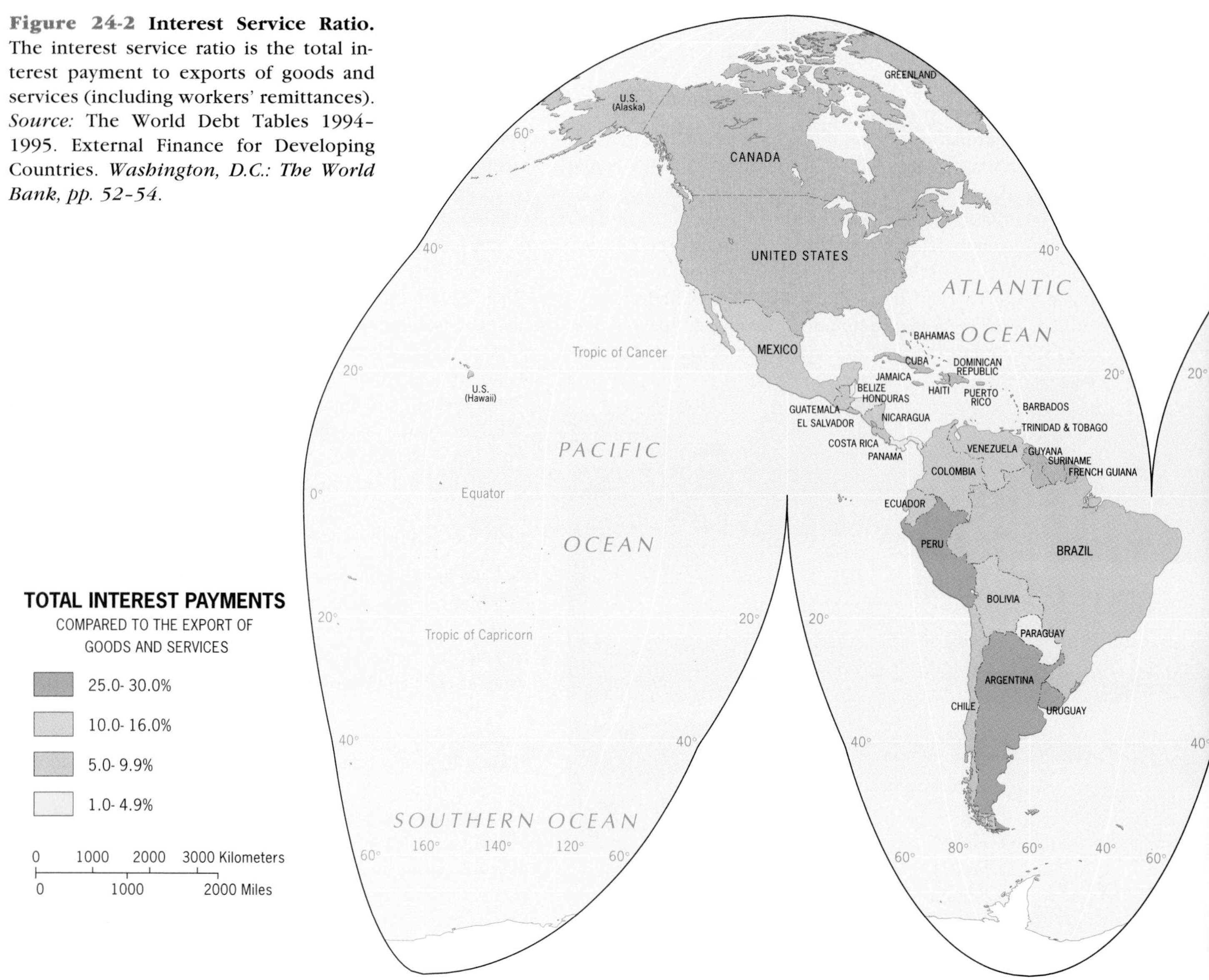

Figure 24-2 Interest Service Ratio. The interest service ratio is the total interest payment to exports of goods and services (including workers' remittances). *Source:* The World Debt Tables 1994-1995. External Finance for Developing Countries. *Washington, D.C.: The World Bank, pp. 52-54.*

of components, and assembly. Research and design has always been located in the countries where the major television manufacturers were based. During the 1970s the major firms began to move the manufacture of components and assembly "offshore." U.S. firms moved these functions to locations in Mexico (particularly the *maquiladora*, the special manufacturing districts described in the preceding chapter); Japanese firms moved them to Taiwan, Singapore, Malaysia, and South Korea. The assembly stage was the most labor intensive, so it went not just to Mexico and newly industrializing Southeast Asian countries but to places such as China, India, and Brazil as well. The Southeast Asian countries began to develop their own competing consumer electronics industries but continued to supply components to major Japanese and European manufacturers. And then a move toward greater mechanization in the production and assembly process in the 1980s led the then-dominant Japanese producers, as well as some of their Pacific Asian counterparts, to locate a growing number of their offshore production sites in Europe and the United States—places where there was a combination of suitable infrastructure, skilled labor, and accessible markets. These developments brought with them a set of trade links that both reflect and define the relationships that characterize the new international division of labor.

Patterns of financial relations mirror those of trade, but with some interesting twists. One key component of international finance is foreign direct investment. A few of the largest economies in the core are responsible for an overwhelming percentage of that investment—notably the United States, Japan, Italy, Germany, France, and the United Kingdom. Most

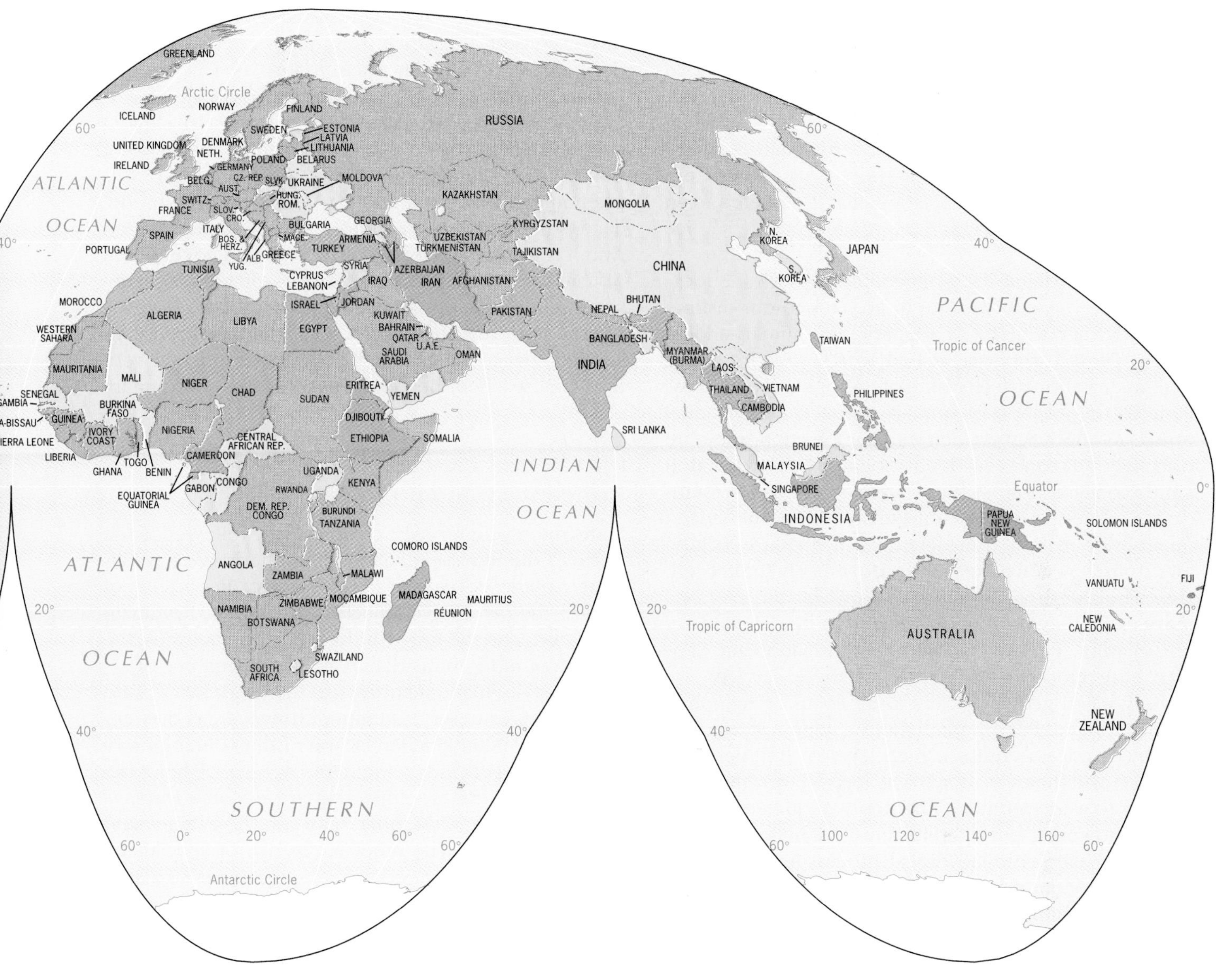

foreign direct investment goes to other core countries and the newly industrializing periphery. The major exception to this pattern is the growth of foreign direct investment by multinational corporations based in newly industrializing countries such as Taiwan, Korea, and Singapore. Companies such as Tatung, Hyundai, and Samsung are increasingly significant actors in the global economic arena.

The other part of the finance picture is the pattern of loans and payments handled by banks. Recent decades have seen an extraordinary expansion of international banking, with the banks of Japan, the United States, and key European countries leading the way. The need for capital in the periphery led to significant borrowing, especially by governments seeking to promote development. The returns on development projects have often been much lower than anticipated, however, and this has led to a debt problem of global proportions. For many countries, the cost of servicing their debts (that is, the cost of repayments plus interest) has greatly exceeded revenues (Fig. 24-2). Countries in this position have great difficulty bridging the gap between their situation and that of the developed core. They are in a weak position to attract new investment, and any excess local revenues must go to debt service.

New Influences on Location

Despite changes in the global economic environment in the late twentieth century, location decisions continue to be driven by the factors of production discussed in Chapter 22. Yet with the striking growth of the service sector and information technologies, new factors have come into play that are affecting patterns of economic activity. Most obviously, many service industries are not tied to raw materials and do not need large amounts of energy. Hence, those factors of production are markedly less important for service industries than for manufacturing concerns. Market accessibility is more relevant for the service sector, but advances in telecommunications have rendered even that factor less important for some types of service industries.

To understand these new influences on the location of services, it is useful to go back to our distinction between tertiary, quaternary, and quinary industries. Tertiary services related to transportation and communication are closely tied to population patterns and to the location of primary and secondary industries. As the basic facilitators of interaction, they are strongly linked to the basic geography of production and consumption. Other tertiary services—restaurants, hotels, retail establishments—are influenced mainly by market considerations. If they are located far from their consumers, they are unlikely to succeed.

The locational influences on quaternary services—high-level services aimed at the collection, processing, and manipulation of information and capital—are more diverse. Some of these services are strongly tied geographically to the locus of economic activity. Retail banking and various types of administrative services require a high level of interpersonal contact and therefore tend to be located near the businesses they are serving. Other types of quaternary services, however, can operate almost anywhere as long as they have access to digital processing equipment and telecommunications. When you send in your credit card bill, it is unlikely to go to the city where the headquarters of the issuing bank is located. Instead, it is likely to go to North Dakota, or Nebraska, or Colorado. Similarly, many "back-office" tasks related to insurance are performed in places such as Des Moines, Iowa, not Chicago or Hartford. These locational curiosities occur because technological advances in the telecommunications sector have made it possible for all sorts of quaternary industries to be located far away from either producers or consumers. What matters most is infrastructure, a work force that is sufficiently skilled but not too expensive, and favorable tax rates.

Those working in the quinary sector tend to be concentrated around nodes of quinary activity—governmental seats, universities, and corporate headquarters. The latter tend to be in large metropolitan areas, but seats of government and universities can be found in places that were chosen long ago as appropriate sites for administrative or educational activities based on cultural values or political compromises. The American ideal of the university town (which originated in Germany) led to the establishment of many universities at a distance from major commercial and population centers, in such towns as Champaign-Urbana, Illinois; Norman, Oklahoma; and Eugene, Oregon. Political compromises led to the establishment of major seats of government in small towns. Ottawa, Canada, and Canberra, Australia, are examples of this phenomenon. The point is that historical location decisions influence the geography of the quinary sector. And it is not just university professors and government officials who are affected. All sorts of high-level research and development activities are located on the fringes of universities, and a host of specialized consultants are concentrated around governmental centers. These then become major nodes of quinary activity.

Specialized Patterns of Economic Concentration and Interaction

Many more geographical changes have followed in the wake of the developments outlined here. We have already reviewed some of the most important of these—the growing connections between the developed core and the newly industrializing countries, the decline of older industrial areas, the emergence of assembly-style manufacturing in the periphery. Two other changes deserve attention, however, as they are altering the economic landscape of the contemporary world. One is the development of a set of links between ***world cities***—links that are in some respects more intense than the links between those cities and their hinterlands. The other is the rise of specialized economic zones devoted to particular types of activities.

World Cities The array of economic links that have developed between different parts of the globe can no longer be adequately described or understood solely in national terms. Corporate structures and flows of capital transcend national boundaries, and decisions about what happens in one corner of the world may well be made in a city thousands of miles away. In this new economic environment it is often as meaningful to look at the connections between cities in different countries as it is to focus on patterns of economic activity within a given country. This is particularly true with respect to the major urban centers of multinational business and finance—the world cities. John Friedmann, who popularized this term in the mid-1980s, calls world cities the control centers of the world economy. These cities are not necessarily the largest in terms of population, nor are they the greatest centers of manufacturing. Instead, they are the places where the world's most important financial and corporate institutions are located and where decisions are made that drive the world economy.

It is hard to come up with a definitive list of world cities, but Figure 24-3 shows the basic pattern. As the map reveals, most of the major world cities are located in the developed core. New York, London, and Tokyo are not only the dominant international actors but the focal points of the three major regional subsystems: Pacific Asia, Western Europe, and North America. The Southern Hemisphere is linked to the system primarily through Sydney, Johannesburg, and São Paulo.

Figure 24-3 is interesting not only for what it shows about the relationship among cities but also for what it implies about the world's changing human geography. Someone living and working in London may well be in closer contact and even feel greater affinity with people in New York and Tokyo than with people in Yorkshire. We must be careful not to overstate the case; these relationships and sensitivities are likely to be confined to people working in the quaternary and quinary sectors. Nevertheless, these are usually the people who exercise the most power, and their changing worldviews therefore are of considerable importance. In a different vein, people living far from the network of world cities can find it difficult to influence decisions made in that network. Note that these same points play out as one moves down the urban hierarchy. A map of connections in South America would show significant links between Buenos Aires and Santiago that are enormously influential in defining the regional economy of, say, northwestern Argentina.

From the field notes

"Looking back toward Sydney from near the shore (the ocean is behind us) confirms the dominance of this city in Australian and Southern Hemisphere affairs. This is a world-city skyline, and what you see here are the highrises of banks, financial institutions, hotels, and corporations—the embodiment of the service-sector economy."

Specialized Economic Zones Beyond the phenomenon of world cities, global economic change has produced specialized economic zones that did not exist before the late twentieth century. Specific economic activities have long been concentrated in particular places; for decades Detroit was synonymous with automobile production in the United States, and the Ruhr Valley with iron and steel production in Germany. But with the increasingly global economy, we now see two new economic concentrations: special ***manufacturing export zones*** in poorer countries and ***high technology corridors*** in wealthier countries.

In their efforts to attract manufacturing, the governments of many countries in the global economic periphery have set up special manufacturing export zones where favorable tax, regulatory, and trade arrangements are offered to foreign firms. By the mid-1990s more than 60 countries had established such zones, and many of these had become major manufacturing centers. Two of the best known of these zones were discussed in the last chapter: the Mexican maquiladora and the special economic zones of China. These are just two examples of a more widespread phenomenon. Such zones are often created in places with easy access to export markets—in Mexico, directly across the border from the United States; in China, near major ports. They typically play host to a mix of manufacturing operations that are suited to the skill levels of the labor force and the available infrastructure.

A related, but very different, type of development can be seen in the high-technology corridors that have sprung up in the global economic core. The catalyst for these corridors is technology: computers, semiconductors, telecommunications, sophisticated medical equipment, and the like. California's "Silicon Valley"

Figure 24-3 Major World Cities. In 1995 John Friedman delineated the major world cities according to global financial, multinational, national, subnational/regional articulations. *Source: J. Friedman, "Where We Stand in a Decade of World City Research," in P. C. Knox and P. J. Taylor, eds.*, World Cities in a World System. *Cambridge: Cambridge University Press, pp. 21–47.*

is a well-known example of a high-technology corridor. Several decades ago a number of innovative technology companies located their research and development activities in the area around the University of California, Berkeley, and Stanford University. They were attracted by the prospect of developing links with existing research communities and the availability of a highly educated work force. Once some of these businesses located there, others were attracted as well. The resulting collection of high-technology industries produced what Manuel Castells and Peter Hall call a ***technopole***. A similar sort of technopole developed outside Boston, where the concentration of technology-based businesses close to Harvard and the Massachusetts Institute of Technology gave rise to what is called the Route 128 high-technology corridor.

Technopoles can be found in a number of countries in Western Europe, Eastern Asia, North America, and Australia. Few are of the scale of Silicon Valley, but they are noticeable elements of the economic landscape. Many of these have sprung up on the edges of good-sized cities, particularly near airports. In Brussels, for example, the route into the city from the airport passes an array of buildings occupied by computer, communication, and electronics firms. Many of these firms are multinationals, and like their counterparts in other countries, they function in an information environment and market their products all over the world. Being near raw materials or even a particular market is unimportant for these firms; what matters to them is proximity to major networks of transportation and communication.

From the field notes

"The presence of high-tech industry often symbolizes economic success in a world in which important segments of the global economic core have moved from manufacturing industries. The landscape of this street in former East Berlin celebrates the arrival of the international high-tech in this former bastion of manufacturing-focused communism. The signs seem to proclaim that all of Berlin is now part of the global economic core."

High-technology industries have become such a symbol of the postindustrial world that local, regional, and national governments often pursue aggressive policies to attract firms in this sector. These industries are thought to be pollution free and to offer positive benefits for the communities in which they are located. Hence, bidding wars sometimes develop between communities seeking to attract such industries. High-technology industries do bring a variety of economic benefits, but they have some drawbacks as well. Communities that have attracted production facilities find that the manufacture of computer chips, semiconductors, and the like requires toxic chemicals and large quantities of water. And even more research-oriented establishments sometimes have negative environmental impacts in that land must be cleared and buildings constructed to house them. Despite these drawbacks, the high-technology sector is clearly here to stay, and areas that can tap into it are likely to find themselves in an advantageous economic position in coming years.

◆ TIME-SPACE COMPRESSION AND ITS IMPACT

A key theme of the last few decades is captured by the phrase ***time-space compression***. This phrase, coined by geographer David Harvey, refers to a set of developments that have dramatically changed the way we think about time and space in the global economic arena. It is an offshoot of the concept of ***time-space convergence***, which refers to a reduction in the importance of distance when, for example, a transportation innovation makes it possible for people or goods to move from one place to another more easily or more cheaply. A variety of developments during the twentieth century have promoted time-space conver-

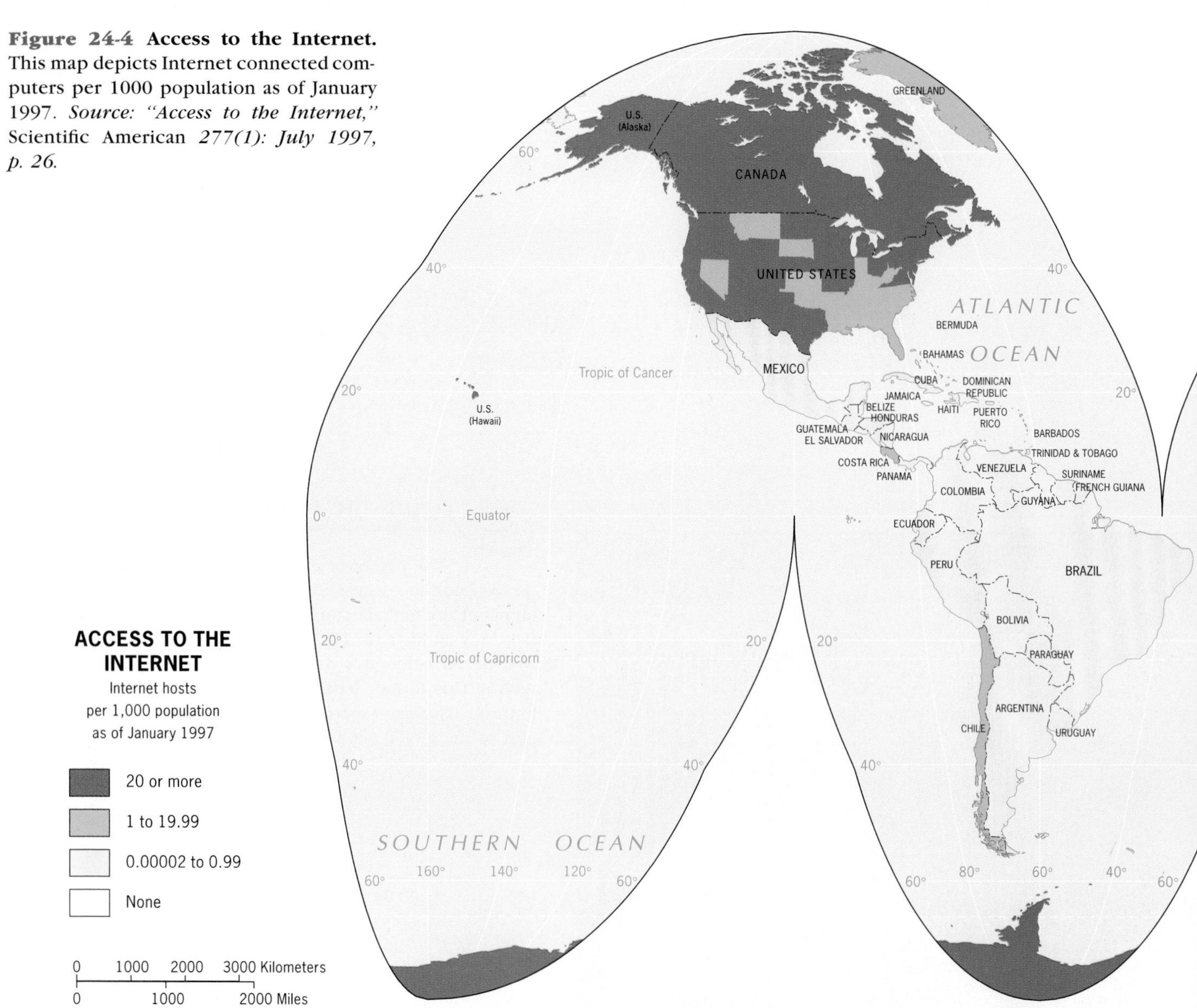

Figure 24-4 Access to the Internet. This map depicts Internet connected computers per 1000 population as of January 1997. *Source: "Access to the Internet,"* Scientific American *277(1): July 1997, p. 26.*

gence, especially technological developments that make possible faster, less expensive transportation and communication across significant distances. But Harvey argues that time-space convergence is too limited a term to encompass what has happened in recent decades. He believes that modern capitalism has so accelerated the pace of life and so changed the nature of the relationship between places that "the world seems to collapse inwards upon us (p. 240)."

There is some debate about the causes and extent of the compression about which Harvey has written, but few would deny the basic concept. The transition away from a Fordist industrial system to a more flexible set of production practices has speeded up production, opened new markets, and brought places closer together in time and space than would have been imaginable at the beginning of the twentieth century. Fluctuations in the Tokyo stock market can have impacts in New York hours, if not minutes, later. Overnight, marketing campaigns can turn a product innovation into a fad in far-flung corners of the globe. Apples picked in New Zealand yesterday can be in the lunch boxes of boys and girls in Canada tomorrow. And decisions made in London can make or break a fast-developing deal over a transport link between Kenya and Tanzania.

The rise of the World Wide Web plays into the time-space compression. It is too early to know what the full impact of the Web might be, but its role in reducing the importance of distance is self-evident. It also clearly plays a role in the decentralization of economic activity. Anyone with a computer and a network connection can establish a home page and a marketing enterprise with little up-front investment. There are no accurate estimates of the economic significance of the World Wide Web, but it is clearly of growing importance. If those trends continue, it may be harder for traditional businesses to exert as much control over certain economic sectors as they have in the past.

The importance of these trends is evident, but we

must be cautious in interpreting them. First, it is not yet clear precisely what impact the World Wide Web will have. Moreover, the geographical distribution of people with access to network connections closely mirrors the map of "haves" and "have-nots" (see Fig. 24-4). At the global scale, this means that the developed core will continue to exert a disproportionate influence on Web-based economic innovations. At the regional scale, it means that traditional centers of economic and political power—especially large cities—could strengthen their position relative to areas that are less well-off. Thus, there are clear limits to the potential of the Web to significantly alter the existing set of relationships that define the global economy.

The sensation of a shrinking world is so strong that a few commentators have proposed that we are entering an era characterized by the "end of geography." Alvin Toffler first suggested this idea in his 1970 book *Future Shock*. More recently, Richard O'Brien dealt with similar concepts in *Global Financial Integration: The End of Geography* (1992). Both Toffler and O'Brien argue that a combination of technological changes and developments in the global economy have reduced the significance of location and place to the point where they no longer matter much. There is no question that the nature and meaning of location and place have changed greatly in recent times, but the developments discussed in this chapter show that those changes have not created an undifferentiated world. Rather, they have reshaped the economic geography of the planet so profoundly and rapidly that they cry out for understanding and analysis. That is one of the reasons why geography is attracting renewed attention and why geographical understanding will be increasingly critical in the years ahead. It is therefore important not just to appreciate the forces that are remaking the world's economic geography but to be aware of the changing political context that helps shape these forces. It is to that context that we turn in the next part of this book.

◆ KEY TERMS ◆

Fordist
"Four Tigers"
high-technology corridors
manufacturing export zones
new international division of labor
quaternary industries
quinary industries
technopole
tertiary industries
time-space compression
time-space convergence
world cities

◆ APPLYING GEOGRAPHIC KNOWLEDGE ◆

1. Evaluate the strengths and weaknesses of the argument that buying a car from an American car manufacturer will support the workers of the United States and the U.S. economy.
2. Which of the world cities shown in Figure 24-3 would not have been on a map of world cities created 25 years ago? What helps to explain why they are on the map now? What cities not currently on the map would you expect to be there 25 years from now? Why?
3. In what ways has time-space compression affected your daily life? Think of at least five examples that you would cite to explain the concept of time-space compression to someone who was not familiar with it.

Part Seven
THE GEOGRAPHY OF MODERN ECONOMIC CHANGE

At Issue: Revisited

Should a global system be established to regulate industrial pollution and cope with industrial accidents? Industrial pollution represents a serious threat to the global environment, but it is not easily regulated on a state-by-state basis. Pollution does not stay within national boundaries, and accidents can occur on the high seas as well as within national territories. Moreover, the general trend toward the internationalization of economic activity complicates state efforts to regulate environmental practices, and the disadvantaged economic position of countries in the periphery often leads to a soft approach to environmental protection. Under the circumstances, efforts to cope with industrial pollution must necessarily involve multinational institutions and arrangements. There may not be the political will to establish a comprehensive global environmental security system, but the trend toward including environmental guarantees in multinational agreements is likely to intensify as the magnitude and significance of industrial pollution become increasingly evident.

◆ SELECTED BIBLIOGRAPHY ◆

Part Seven **The Geography of Modern Economic Change**

Allen, J., & Hamnett, C., eds. *A Shrinking World? Global Unevenness and Inequality* (Oxford, U.K.: Oxford University Press, 1995).

Berry, B.J.L., Conkling, E. C., & Ray, D. M. *The Global Economy in Transition* (Upper Saddle River, N.J.: Prentice-Hall, 2nd ed., 1997).

Birdsall, S. S., & Florin, J. W. *Regional Landscapes of the United States and Canada* (New York: John Wiley & Sons, 4th ed., 1992).

Blakeley, E. J., & Stimson, R. J., eds. *New Cities of the Pacific Rim*, Monograph 43 (Berkeley: University of California, Institute of Urban and Regional Development, 1992).

Blouet, B. W., & Blouet, O. M., eds. *Latin America and the Caribbean: A Systematic and Regional Survey* (New York: John Wiley & Sons, 2d ed., 1993).

Borthwick, M. *Pacific Century: The Emergence of Modern Pacific Asia* (Boulder, Colo.: Westview Press, 1992).

Boserup, E. *Economic and Demographic Relationships in Development* (Baltimore, Md.: Johns Hopkins University Press, 1990).

Burks, A. W. *Japan: A Postindustrial Power* (Boulder, Colo.: Westview Press, 3rd ed., 1991).

Chowdhury, A., & Islam, I. *The Newly Industrializing Economies of East Asia* (New York: Routledge, 1993).

Cole, J. P., & Cole, F. J. *The Geography of the European Community* (New York: Routledge, 1993).

Corbridge, S. *Debt and Development* (Cambridge, Mass.: Blackwell, 1993).

Dicken, P. *Global Shift: The Internalization of Economic Activity* (London: Paul Chapman, 2nd ed., 1992).

Drakakis-Smith, D. *Pacific Asia* (New York: Routledge, 1992).

Freeman, M. *Atlas of the World Economy* (New York: Simon & Schuster, 1991).

Friedmann, J. "The World City Hypothesis," *Development & Change* 17 (1986), 69–83.

Glasmeier, A. K., & Howland, M. *From Combines to Computers: Rural Services in the Age of Information Technology* (Albany, N.Y.: State University of New York Press, 1995).

Gleave, M. B., ed. *Tropical African Development: Geographical Perspectives* (New York: Wiley/Longman, 1992).

Hanink, D. M. *The International Economy: A Geographical Perspective* (New York: John Wiley & Sons, 1994).

Harvey, D. *The Condition of Postmodernity: An Enquiry into the Origins of Cultural Change* (Cambridge, Mass.: Blackwell, 1989).

Hussey, A. "Rapid Industrialization in Thailand, 1986–1991," *Geographical Review* 83 (1993), 14–28.

Knox, P. & Agnew, J. *The Geography of the World Economy: An Introduction to Economic Geography* (London: Edward Arnold, 2nd ed., 1994).

Knox, P., & Taylor, P. J., eds. *World Cities in a World-System* (Cambridge, U.K.: Cambridge University Press, 1995).

Kotler, P., et al. *Marketing Places: Attracting Investment, Industry, and Tourism to Cities, States, and Nations* (New York: Free Press, 1993).

Leeming, F. *The Changing Geography of China* (Cambridge, Mass.: Blackwell, 1993).

Lewis, R. A., ed. *Geographic Perspectives on Soviet Central Asia* (New York: Routledge, 1992).

Lockhart, D. G., et al., eds. *The Development Process in Small Island States* (New York: Routledge, 1993).

Lösch, A. *The Economics of Location.* Translated by W. Woglom & W. Stolper (New York: Wiley Science Editions, 1967; originally published in 1940).

Massey, D. *Spatial Divisions of Labor: Social Structures and the Geography of Production* (New York: Routledge, 2nd ed., 1995).

Murphy, A. B. "Economic Regionalization and Pacific Asia: Problems and Prospects." *Geographical Review* 85 (2), 1995, 127–140.

Murphy, R. T. *The Weight of the Yen* (New York: W.W. Norton, 1996).

O'Brien, R. *Global Financial Integration: The End of Geography* (New York: Council on Foreign Relations Press, 1992).

Pounds, N.J.G. *An Historical Geography of Europe, 1800–1914* (New York: Cambridge University Press, 1985).

Rostow, W. W. *The Stages of Economic Growth* (New York: Cambridge University Press, 2nd ed., 1971).

Smith, D. M. *Industrial Location: An Economic Geographical Analysis* (New York: John Wiley & Sons, 2nd ed., 1981).

Smith, N. *Uneven Development: Nature, Capital and the Production of Space* (New York: Blackwell, 1984).

Songqiao, Z. *Geography of China: Environment, Resources, and Development* (New York: John Wiley & Sons, 1994).

Stewart, J. M., ed. *The Soviet Environment: Problems, Policies and Politics* (New York: Cambridge University Press, 1992).

Szekely, G., ed. *Manufacturing Across Borders and Oceans: Japan, the United States and Mexico* (La Jolla, Calif.: Center for U.S.-Mexican Studies, University of California, San Diego, 1991).

Toffler, A. *Future Shock* (New York: Random House, 1970).

Vogel, E. F. *The Four Little Dragons: The Spread of Industrialization in East Asia* (Cambridge, Mass.: Harvard University Press, 1991).

Weber, A. *Theory of the Location of Industries.* Translated by C. Friedrich (Chicago: University of Chicago Press, 1929; originally published in 1909).

Wheeler, J. O., Muller, P. O., & Thrall, G. I. *Economic Geography* (New York: John Wiley & Sons, 3rd ed., 1998).

World Bank. *World Development Report 1993* (Oxford, U.K.: Oxford University Press, 1994).

Part Eight

THE POLITICAL IMPRINT

At Issue

The political world is in transition. Some scholars envisage a multipolar world in which the United States, a unified Europe, Russia, and China constitute four power cores balanced to ensure a stable global system. At the turn of the twenty-first century, however, the United States was the dominant superpower, Europe was about to embark on a contentious road toward monetary union, Russia was in substantial disarray, and China was in ascendancy but in the grip of significant internal divisions and not yet a world force. In the face of such uncertainties, a new world order may be at hand, but its outlines are unclear. At issue is which of the following questions might be answered in the affirmative and whether the transitions suggested by them can be accomplished without serious instability. ***Can Europe create a powerful economic/political union despite concerns about economic and political centralization? Can Russia overcome economic trauma and corruption to emerge as a major world power once again? Can China create the political and social institutions that can foster sustained growth and unity?***

European Union flag, Maastricht.

Part Outline

Chapter 25

Political Culture and the Evolving State

From the field notes

"I arrived in Ghana just after there had been an assassination attempt on the country's first President, Kwame Nkrumah. His statue had been draped in a hospital gown, his head bandaged. The end of colonialism in Africa seemed near, and hopes were high for the newly independent states. I knew no one who would disagree with the proclamations on Nkrumah's statue: 'To me the liberation of Ghana will be meaningless unless is it linked up with the liberation of Africa' and 'We prefer self-government with danger to servitude in tranquility.' But decolonization did not eliminate the economic and cultural problems faced by Africa's emerging states. President Nkrumah was to die in exile, his country ruled by the military, its economy severely damaged. The new African states found themselves in the periphery, their economies at the mercy of the core, their politics subject to cold war competition between the superpowers, their peoples fragmented by tribalism. Now, nearly a half century later, African statecraft has its own success stories, economies are growing again, democracy has footholds, and Nkrumah's hope may not have been in vain."

KEY POINTS

◆ **The world's living space is divided into nearly 200 states ranging in size from microstates to subcontinental giants; a minority of these states are nation-states.**

◆ **The European state model was exported through migration and colonialism, but it has not always worked well in the non-Western world.**

◆ **State territory varies in morphology as well as size; different territorial characteristics can present opportunities and challenges, depending on the historical and political-economic context.**

◆ **State territories are defined by international boundaries that mark the limits of national jurisdiction. Boundary lines on the ground mark the position of vertical planes that separate states; these planes cut through airspace as well as subsoil.**

Political activity is as basic to human culture as food production or religion. It undoubtedly began when individuals first asserted themselves as leaders of village or clan, when competition for such leadership roles, for territorial rights, or for other goals became a part of life. Ever since, political behavior by individuals, groups, communities, and nations has expressed the human desire for power and influence in the pursuit of personal and public goals. All of us are caught up in these processes, whose effects range from the composition of school boards to the conduct of war.

Political geography is the study of political activity in spatial context. Since political activity has spatial expression and focus, its outcome is revealed on the map. The present-day layout of the world political map is a product of humanity's endless politico-geographic accommodation and adjustment. A mosaic of more than 200 countries and territories separated by boundaries, the world looks like a jigsaw puzzle (Fig. 25-1). The map depicting that jigsaw puzzle is the most familiar and widely used map of the world—so widely used that we often fail to think about the patterns it contains. Yet even a brief examination of the nature and significance of the patterns on the political map provides valuable insights. It shows, for example, the inequality of countries in terms of territory (certain countries are hundreds of times as large as others) and relative location. Some countries are ***landlocked***, without coasts on the open sea, while the majority benefit from coastal frontage.

Political geographers study the spatial manifestations of political processes at various levels of scale. Much of their research focuses on the functioning of individual countries as political regions. From this research we have learned how countries are organized, how they overcome (or fail to overcome) divisive forces, how their boundaries function, and much more. In recent decades we have witnessed the collapse of colonial empires, and the problems of newly independent entities in the postcolonial era have taken political geography in new directions. In the meantime, some countries are banding together in international alliances, associations, and unions to further their common objectives.

◆ POLITICAL CULTURE

From congressional district boundaries to international borders, the maps we draw reflect ***political culture***. And political cultures vary. People adhere to political ideas just as they profess a religion and speak a native language. Today, many political systems are designed to keep religion and politics separate, but other states are ***theocracies***: their leaders are deemed to be under divine guidance, their actions representing the will of a supreme being.

If contemporary political cultures have a common element, it lies in the centrality of territory to political life. Indeed, some have argued that the effort to control pieces of the Earth's surface for political and social ends is a fundamental dynamic in human affairs and must be a key component of geographical research. In a book published in 1986, Robert Sack used the term ***human territoriality*** to describe this effort. He sees human territoriality as a key ingredient in the construction of social and political spaces. Sack's approach to territoriality differs from that taken by the social anthropologist Robert Ardrey in *The Territorial Imperative* (1966). Ardrey argued that human territoriality is analogous to the instinct in animals to control

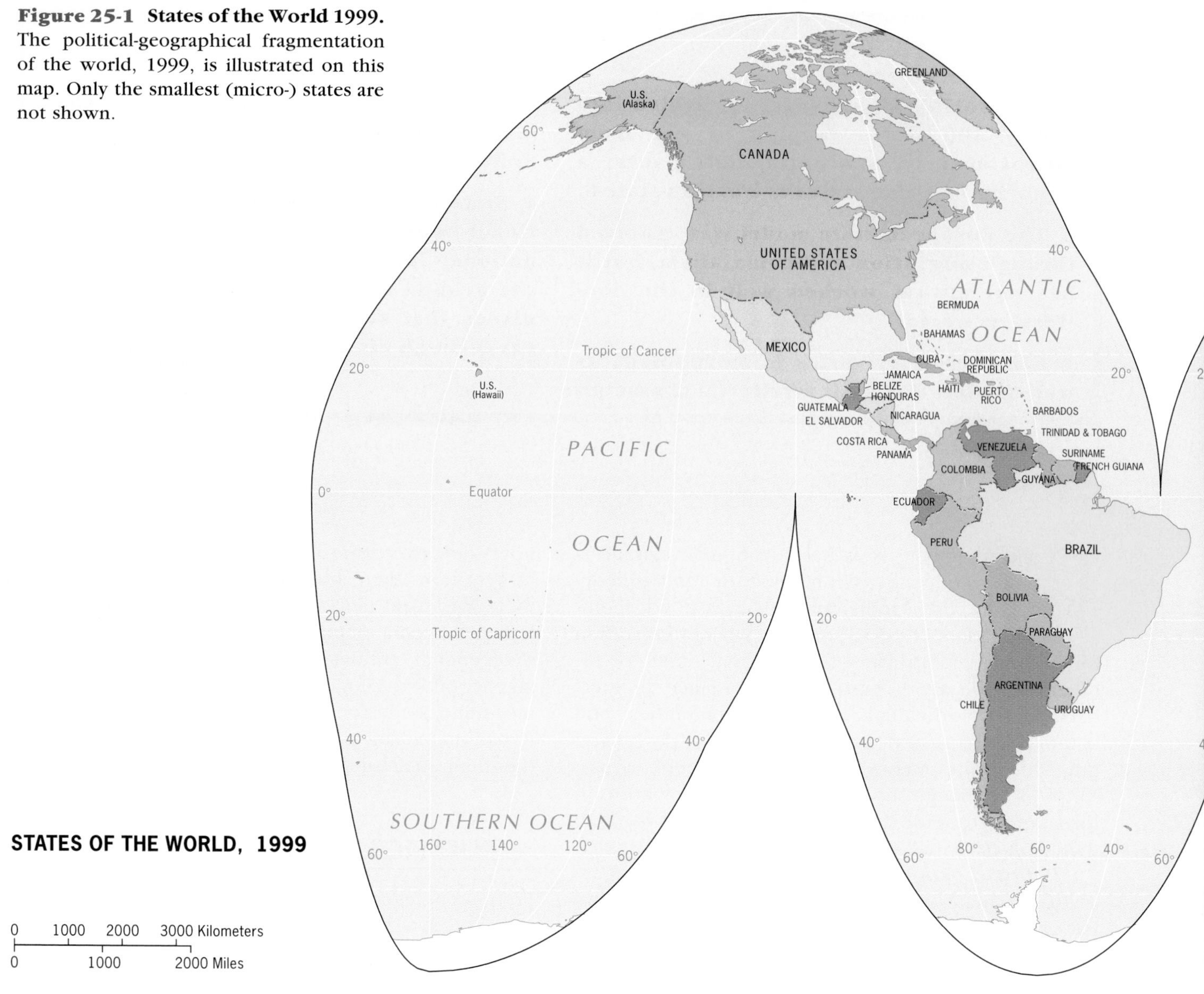

Figure 25-1 States of the World 1999. The political-geographical fragmentation of the world, 1999, is illustrated on this map. Only the smallest (micro-) states are not shown.

and defend territory. Sack, by contrast, argues that human territoriality takes many different forms, depending on the social and geographical context, and that it should not be compared to an animal instinct. Instead, he calls for a better understanding of the human organization of the planet through a consideration of how and why different territorial strategies are pursued at different times and in different places.

Territoriality attracts so much attention because it is a key element of political culture. This trait manifests itself in different ways. At the village level, for example, land is held communally in some cultures and individually in others. Such differences also mark larger groups and even entire nations. Attitudes toward land and territory differ from one society to another and from one country to another.

The rise of the modern state system carried with it a distinctive view of territory as a fixed, exclusive element of political identification and group survival. As a result, few issues can agitate a people the way a perceived violation of territory can. A neighbor's annexation of even the smallest piece of land is likely to unify even the most divided society. Conversely, the prospect of having to yield any area over which a government has jurisdiction can cause violent opposition among otherwise peaceable citizens.

The current contest over the Golan Heights provides a good example. This territory has been under Israeli control since the 1967 war, when it was captured from Syria. The prospect of its return to Syria has created deep division in Israeli society. But if Syria sought to annex any other part of Israel there would

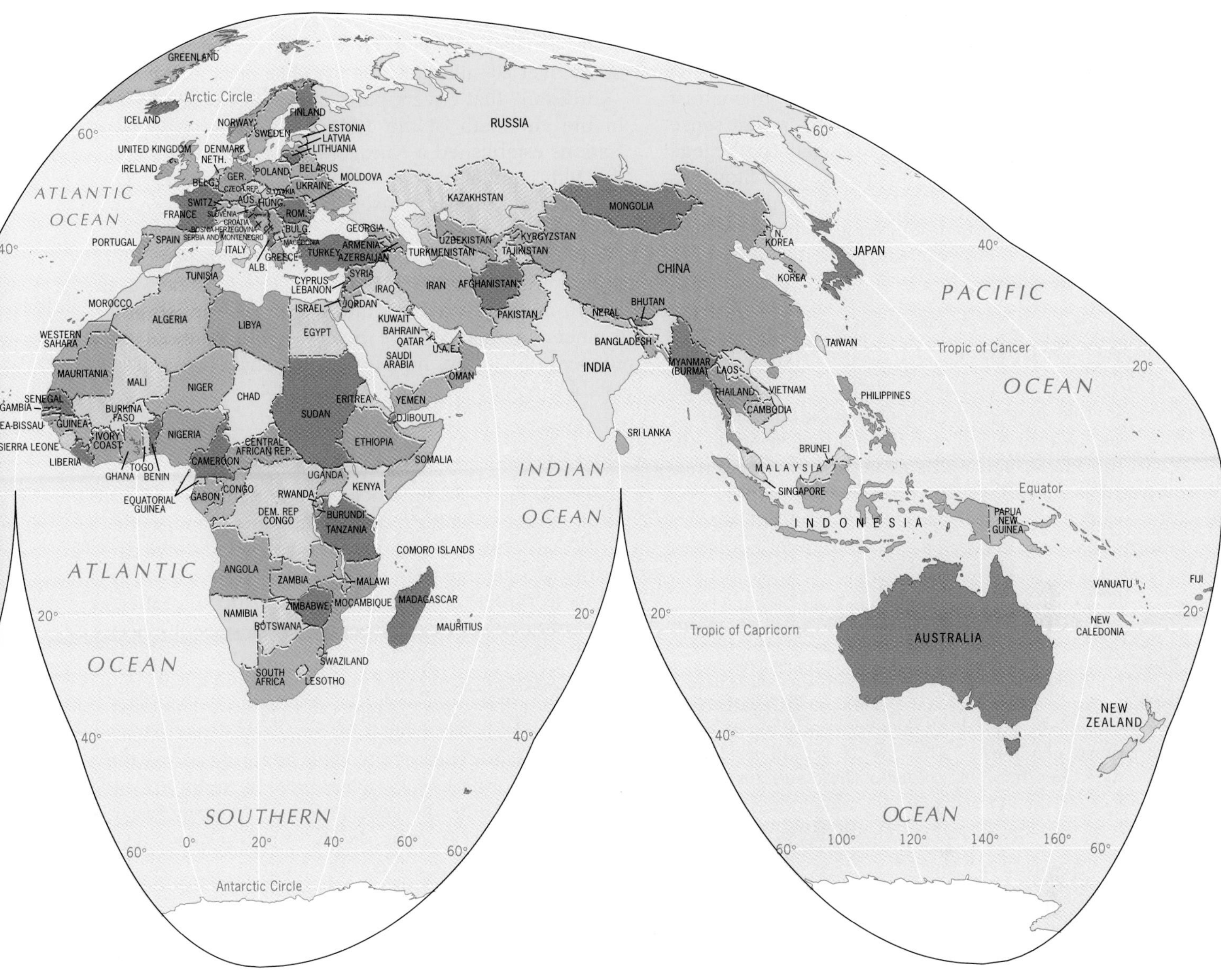

be no such division, and Israelis would be unified in opposition. Challenges to existing territorial arrangements thus remain a strong motivator for political, and even military, action in the modern world.

◆ STATE AND NATION

Up to now we have referred to national political entities as *countries*. This word is derived from the Latin *contra*, which actually means "against" or "on the opposite side." That may seem to be a rather strange derivation for a term denoting a political unit inhabited by a people of common nationality, but as we have noted before, the meaning of words often changes over time.

Political geographers prefer the term ***state***, which comes from the Latin *status*, meaning "standing." This leads to a problem: certain countries have internal divisions that are also called states, as in the United States of America. The solution is to capitalize *State* when it refers to such an internal division, as in the State of Michigan or the State of Uttar Pradesh (India).

The terms "country" and "state," therefore, are interchangeable, but the same is not true for ***nation*** and state or country. This is one of the most common geographic errors you will see in the press and popular literature, and it is understandable because legally people in a state have a shared nationality. The term "nation," however, has historic, ethnic, and often linguistic and religious connotations. It refers to a people's sense of belonging to such an entity. Sometimes a nation is even larger than the state that gave birth to it; the French form a nation, but many French-speaking and French-cultured people living outside France feel that they are part of the French nation. In contrast, Yugoslavia never achieved nationhood in that sense. Millions of people of Yugoslav nationality (in the legal sense) always identified themselves as Slovenes, Croats, Serbs, or members of other ethnic groups. Yugoslavia thus was a *state* but never a *nation*, and eventually the state collapsed. Many other countries are states but not nations.

Stateless Nations

Still another complication is that some nations are *stateless*; that is, they do not possess a national territory even within a larger multinational state. In the 1990s the Palestinian Arabs gained control over fragments of territory that may form the foundations of a future state, but most of the 6.5 million Palestinians continued to live in Israel and several other countries, including Jordan (2.1 million), Lebanon (400,000), and Syria (350,000). A much larger stateless nation is that of the over 20 million Kurds who live in an area called "Kurdistan" that covers parts of six states (Fig. 25-2). In the aftermath of the 1991 Gulf War, the United Nations established a Kurdish Security Zone north of the 36th parallel in Iraq, but subsequent events have dashed any Kurdish hopes that this might become the core of a future state. The Kurds form the largest minority in Turkey, and the city of Diyarbakir is the unofficial Kurdish capital; however, relations between the 10 million Kurds in Turkey and the Turkish government in Ankara have been volatile. Without the consent of Turkey, no Kurdish national state will be established anywhere in "Kurdistan."

From the field notes

"Walking up embassy row in the outskirts of Colombo, capital of Sri Lanka, I came across evidence of Palestinian efforts to establish the trappings of a state in the international community. There is as yet no Palestinian nation-state, but here in Colombo the non-state has an embassy."

The Rise of the Modern State

States are the building blocks of international society. Although the economic and technological changes described in Part 7 are undermining the traditional authority of states, nations still depend on their governments to represent them in the international arena—to secure needed resources such as oil, to create markets for their products, to join in alliances in order to protect their security. Of course, governments are not always wholly representative of a state's inhabitants; some states are controlled by minorities and oligarchies. In such instances the state primarily serves the interests of a ruling class, which may be an ethnic minority. Outwardly, the state functions like any other, but its internal politics are likely to reflect major divisions, as we will see later in the chapter.

The European Model In earlier chapters we traced the diffusion of the state idea to Greece and later to Rome, and the spread of the concept of statehood into Europe. There, in the post–Roman period of political fragmentation, these ideas lay dormant until feudalism began to break down. The Norman invasion of England in 1066 was perhaps the most significant event in this process. The Normans destroyed the Anglo-Saxon nobility, created a whole new political order, and achieved great national strength under William the Conqueror. On the European mainland, the continuity of dynastic rule and the strength of certain rulers led to greater national cohesiveness. In present-day Germany, France, and Spain, sizable states existed, and some of the trespass lines of the twelfth century were to become modern-day political boundaries (for example, the border between France and Spanish Aragon along the Pyrenees). At the same time, Europe experienced something of an economic revival, and internal as well as foreign trade increased. Ports and other cities came back to life, and while much of the wealth went to the nobility and the rich

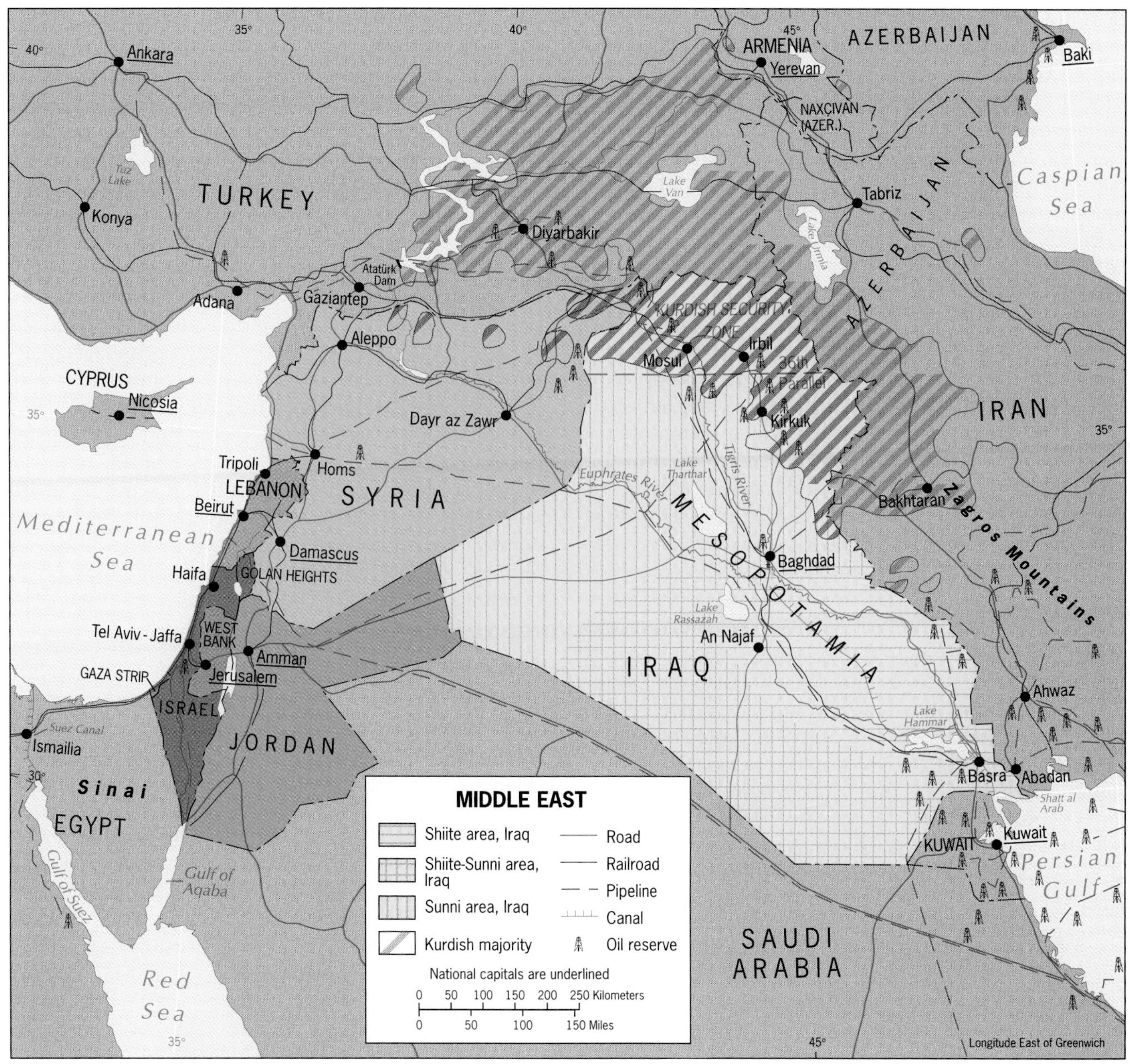

Figure 25-2 States and Territories of the Middle East. Kurdistan is a stateless nation divided under six flags. *Source: From a map in H. J. de Blij and P. O. Muller,* Geography: Regions, Realms, and Concepts, *8th ed. New York: Wiley, 1997.*

merchants, the lifestyles of many more disadvantaged people improved. Now the Muslim invaders in southern Spain could be repelled, and the Crusades to the Middle East could be financed. Crucial technological innovations occurred. The collar, for example, enormously increased the efficiency of the horse for plowing, transport, and other work. Windmills dotted the countryside. The Dark Ages were over, and a new Europe was emerging.

From a political-geographic perspective, the Peace of Westphalia can be seen as the first major step in the emergence of the European state. The treaties signed at the end of the Thirty Years' War (1648) contained language that recognized statehood and nationhood, clearly defined boundaries, and guarantees of security. Such agreements eventually were broken (and they continue to be broken today), but the language of the treaties laid the foundations for a Europe made up of national states. They provided a framework through which Spain, the Dutch United Provinces, France, and the Holy Roman Empire would gain regional stability. In Western Europe, the strong monarchies began to represent something more than mere authority. Increasingly, they became the focal points of national consciousness. They developed increasingly integrated political economies focused on the capital city, in the process breaking down regionalisms and bringing people together in the pursuit of larger-scale political and military ends. The aristocracies, which had strongly opposed monarchical rule, were brought under control. In some places parliaments reappeared, although their power was limited. There was renewed interest in Greek and Roman achievements, in politics as well as in the sciences and arts.

Power and Primacy Europe's rebirth or ***Renaissance*** would not be painless. The emerging political nationalism was accompanied by economic nationalism in the form of mercantilism, which sought to acquire wealth through plunder, colonization, and the protection of home industries and foreign markets. Rivalry and competition intensified in Europe as well as abroad. Superimposed on these conflicts was a series of religious wars (a reaction to the new secular values of the Renaissance), which ravaged Europe for many years. Catholicism and Protestantism, Reformation and Counter-Reformation fired the conflicts that devastated not only Europe's towns and cities but also the parliaments and assemblies that had become a part of the political culture. In the end the monarchies benefited most. Louis XIV of France was the personification of the absolute rule that prevailed in Europe in the late Renaissance.

Thus the politico-geographical map of Europe was slow in taking shape. In the mid-seventeenth century such states as the Republic of Venice, Brandenburg, the Papal States of central Italy, the Kingdom of Hungary, and several minor German states were all part of a complicated patchwork of political entities, many with poorly defined boundaries. Powerful royal families struggled for dominance in Eastern and Southern Europe. Instability was the rule, and strife occurred frequently. Repressive government prevailed. Europe was still far from achieving the ideal of the nation-state, the state of and for the people.

Ultimately, Europe's growing economic power proved to be the undoing of absolute rule. City-based merchants gained wealth and prestige, while the nobility declined. Money and influence were increasingly concentrated in the cities, and the traditional measure of affluence—land—became less important. The merchants and businessmen demanded political recognition. In the 1780s a series of upheavals began that would change the sociopolitical face of the Continent. Overshadowing these events was the French Revolution (1789–1795), but this momentous event was only one in a series of political upheavals. Europe's political revolution continued into the twentieth century and is not over even now.

◆ THE NATION-STATE

As Europe evolved, its influence in the rest of the world intensified. In the process, the European states were enriched as their colonial acquisitions produced wealth in various forms. England, benefiting from its political stability and its growing maritime power, gained an empire that spanned the world.

Europe's politico-geographical evolution was to have enormous significance, because variations of the European model of the state—the ***nation-state***—would eventually be adopted around the world. Literally a nation-state is a politically organized area in which nation and state occupy the same space. Since there are few examples of true nation-states, even in Europe, the importance of the nation-state concept lies primarily in the idea behind it. That idea involves more than bringing the map of nations and states into alignment. It also embodies the notion that ***sovereignty*** (final authority over a territory's political and military affairs) rests with the nation—that is, the people.

From the field notes

"The majority of European states abolished their monarchies, but some, such as the United Kingdom and the Netherlands, became parliamentary democracies while retaining their monarchs as titular heads of state. In those monarchies, the royal palaces remain icons in the cultural landscape, as are Buckingham Palace and, shown here, the Royal Palace overlooking the historic Dam Square at the heart of Amsterdam, Netherlands."

Focus On

Defining the Nation-State

As Europe went through its periods of rebirth and revolutionary change, the politico-geographical map was transformed. Smaller entities were absorbed into larger units, conflicts resolved (by force as well as by negotiation), boundaries defined, and internal divisions reorganized. The European nation-states were being formed.

What is a nation-state and what is not? The answer depends in part on the definition of the term *nation*. The definition is usually understood to involve measures of homogeneity: a nation's people should speak a single language, have a common history, share the same ethnic background, and be united by common political institutions. Generally accepted definitions of the term suggest that most states are not nation-states, because their populations are divided in one or more important ways.

Yet cultural homogeneity may not be as important as "national spirit" or emotional commitment to the state and what it stands for. One of Europe's oldest states, Switzerland, has a population that is divided along linguistic, religious, and historical lines, but Switzerland has endured because of a widespread commitment to the state ideal. Therefore, a nation-state could be defined as a political unit comprising a clearly delineated territory and inhabited by a substantial population, well enough organized to possess some power, the people considering themselves to share a political-cultural history, with certain emotional and other ties that are expressed in the state's legal institutions, political system, and ideological strength.

This definition essentially identifies the European model that emerged in the course of the region's long period of evolution and revolutionary change. France is often cited as the best example, but Germany (before World War I), Denmark, Portugal, Poland, Hungary, the Czech Republic, Slovenia, and Sweden also satisfy the terms of the definition to a great extent. European states that cannot at present be designated as nation-states include Bosnia, Latvia, Slovakia, Moldova, and Belgium.

Emerging from Europe's agricultural, industrial, and political revolutions was a modern state founded on democratic principles. To be sure, this ideal was not achieved everywhere. Although absolute rule persisted, a process of maturation occurred in many states. While some states, such as France and Italy, abolished monarchy altogether, others, including the United Kingdom and the Netherlands, became parliamentary democracies with the monarch remaining as titular head of state. And almost everywhere nationalism became the dominant political force, leading in some cases to efforts to integrate a country's population into an ever more cohesive national whole (e.g., France, Spain), in other cases to efforts to bring peoples with shared cultural characteristics within a single state (for example, Germany, Italy), and in yet other cases to successful separatist movements among nationally self-conscious populations living within states or empires (Ireland, Norway, Poland).

Europe's nation-states thus unified and nationalized large populations, and they did so within clearly defined territories. The modern map of Europe is still fragmented, but much less so than in the 1600s. Moreover, national territories were separated by boundaries, not by uncertain frontiers or vague trespass lines. The new states became organized in other areas as well, including education, health, and the military. They possessed varying degrees of power, which enabled them not only to assert themselves in Europe but also to engage in colonial campaigns.

These qualities (a population that considers itself to be a nation, a substantial and defined territory, well-developed organization, and a measure of power) are sometimes called the "four pillars" of the nation-state (see "Focus on: Defining the Nation-State"). On the map, they are expressed by the state's external and internal boundary systems, its core area and surface communications networks, and its capital city. Other manifestations of the nation-state appear on maps of resources, land use, military installations, and the like.

With Europe in control of so much of the world, Europeans defined the ground rules of the emerging international state system, and the modern European nation-state became the model that was adopted around the world. During the mid-nineteenth century, Japan reorganized itself on the European model, even moving its capital from Kyoto in the interior to Edo, renamed Tokyo, on the coast. Later, when colonial empires disintegrated, newly liberated peoples created nation-states on the European model. They hoped to forge nations from still-divided peoples, to secure their national territory, to develop economic (as well as other) systems of organization, and to assert national strength (sometimes, unfortunately, through excessive spending on military forces and equipment). On the map, former colonial provinces became new national states, with their administrative borders now transformed into international boundaries. Colonial administrative towns became national capitals. London and Paris were symbols of national progress and power in Europe, and so were the headquarters of the new states. Therefore, in countless ways, the European state became the world model.

◆ GEOGRAPHIC CHARACTERISTICS OF STATES

Even an outline map such as Figure 25-1 reveals that states are not all alike. There may be a "European model" of the nation-state, but even in Europe states differ in as many ways as they are similar. States vary in territorial size and morphology, demography, organizational structures, resources, development, power, and a host of other ways. We live in a world where one state has nearly 17 million square kilometers of territory (6.6 million sq mi) and several others exceed 7.5 million square kilometers (3 million sq mi), while some ***microstates*** do not even have 1000 square kilometers (400 sq mi). In terms of population, too, the contrasts are huge. China has over 1.2 billion people; Iceland 0.25 million.

The state is a complex system with many interacting parts. It is far more than a piece of territory and a number of people: it is a region of cities, towns, and hinterlands, railroad and road networks, administrative subdivisions, schools, and hospitals. It is a maze of circulation and movement: of people, raw materials, finished products, foodstuffs, money, and ideas. It both provides services for the people and demands their taxes, their adherence to the law, and often their service in the armed forces. To succeed, it must foster a sense of legitimacy.

As noted in the box on defining the nation-state, the inclusion of a body of people within a political boundary does not automatically make those people members of a nation. Instead, that happens through the development of a national attitude and an emotional attachment to the country and what it stands for. This attitude can be fostered in various ways; many states engage in programmed education and propaganda to encourage it. Periods of adversity or war can also strengthen national attachments. On the other hand, the spirit of nationhood is fragile and can be damaged by divisive issues. Efforts to promote a common sense of nationhood can backfire when peoples feel they are being forced to adopt an identity that is not their own. In the United States, the Vietnam War of the 1960s and early 1970s had a strong impact on commitment to the national ideal. In Canada, the national fabric has been frayed by efforts to make Quebec a separate nation. In Argentina, the costly invasion of the Falkland Islands caused observers to refer to that nation's "troubled soul."

The world politico-geographical map reveals that some states' boundaries enclose nations, or very nearly so. Iceland, Portugal, Denmark, and Poland are often cited as nation-states; outside Europe, Tunisia, Japan, and Uruguay also are identified as such. However, more often than not, state boundaries have the effect of separating and dividing peoples with shared cultural characteristics and throwing culturally diverse peoples together. The language map of Europe (Fig. 8-3) reminds us of the former effect; the colonial map of Africa is evidence of the latter. As will be noted later, boundaries often were established not by those whom they affect most directly but by outside forces. Imperial campaigns in Europe and colonial operations in Africa and Asia created boundary frameworks that often did not coincide with cultural divisions.

The European model of the nation-state has proven difficult to imitate even in Europe itself. Nevertheless, today a large majority of states possess all four of the main features of that model: a clearly defined territory, a substantial population, certain types of organizational structures, and some power. We focus next on the key geographic ingredient: territory.

◆ TERRITORY

No state can exist without territory, although the United Nations does recognize the Palestinians as a stateless nation. Within the state's territory lie the resources that make up the state. Yet a glance at a political map shows how different the world's states are in the amount of territory they control. Those differences, in turn, have translated into opportunities and challenges. The territorial character of states has long interested geographers, who have focused on matters of territorial size, shape, and relative location, together referred to as their ***territorial morphology***. Not long ago, in fact, efforts were made to draw broad generalizations about the advantages and disadvantages of a state with a large territory, a compact shape, and a strategic location. There is no question that the nature of a state's territory can have social and political significance, but we must be careful. Focusing just on territory without considering other aspects of a state's geographical context can be misleading. Being small and landlocked can mean very different things for a state in the economic core than for one in the periphery.

Different territorial characteristics can present opportunities and challenges, depending on the historical and political-economic context. Thus, the United States' large size, large population, and abundant resources helped it emerge as a major global power. For the former Soviet Union, however, the vast distances over which people and resources were distributed presented a serious obstacle and helped bring about its collapse. Similar contrasts can be seen when the issue of shape is considered. Particularly before the advent of modern transportation and communication, it was easier for a central government to knit together the territory of a ***compact*** state—one in which the distance from the geometric center to any point on the boundary did not vary greatly—than it was for states lacking this characteristic. Some states are ***fragmented***, consisting of two or more separate pieces; examples include the Philippines and East and West Pakistan before they were divided. This fragmentation makes certain kinds of interactions more difficult. Other states are ***elongated*** or attenuated (Chile, Vietnam), with historical consequences that are still evident today. Still others have a ***protruded*** area—one that extends out from a more compact core; this area sometimes has developed in different ways from the core (e.g., the southern portion of Thailand). Such states are sometimes called ***prorupt states***. Finally, a few states are ***perforated*** by another country (e.g., South Africa by Lesotho, Italy by San Marino and Vatican City).

Exclaves and Enclaves

A particularly interesting type of territorial irregularity occurs where historical circumstances have led to the existence of small outliers of territory that are separated from the state by the territory of another state. These ***exclaves*** can lie on coasts (e.g., the territory of Cabinda, which is part of Angola), but more often they are landlocked within another country, in which case they are known as ***enclaves*** within the country that surrounds them.

Figure 25-3 shows Nagorno-Karabakh, an exclave of Christian Armenia, lying totally within Muslim Azerbaijan. This situation was created by Soviet political planners, who designated specific homelands for sizable ethnic or cultural minorities in the communist empire. Christian Armenia was made a republic, and so was Muslim Azerbaijan. The problem created by having a large cluster of Christian Armenians within Azerbaijan was solved by awarding the Armenians their own territory but giving Azerbaijan the right to administer it.

All this worked while Soviet rule kept the lid on potential conflict, but when the USSR collapsed, old animosities resurfaced. The Republic of Armenia demanded that Nagorno-Karabakh be included in its territory, if necessary by a corridor linking the exclave to the main territory. (They are separated by only about 16 kilometers, or 10 miles, of mountainous terrain.) As Figure 25-3 shows, Nagorno-Karabakh is not the only exclave in this region. Azerbaijan itself has a sizable exclave, Nakhichevan, which is separated from it by Armenian territory. But note that Nakhichevan is *not* an enclave; that is, it is not completely surrounded by one country. It has borders on Armenia to the north and Iran to the south.

Exclaves and enclaves are special cases. The more general point is that territorial size and shape can influence the development of regions and states, but they do not determine their political, social, or economic well-being. Norway does very well despite its elongated shape, and Zimbabwe faces some serious internal tensions despite its relatively compact shape. The location of a state can have more important effects. Most obviously, states in the global economic core are at a competitive economic and political ad-

Figure 25-3 Spatial Relationships in Transcaucasia. This map shows spatial relations in Transcaucasia. *Source: From a map in H. J. de Blij and P. O. Muller,* Geography: Realms, Regions, and Concepts, *7th ed. New York: Wiley, 1994.*

vantage. States located in resource-rich regions can also be in an advantageous position. We must remember, however, that not all such states are in a position to tap those resources for their own benefit (for example, Congo) and that national wealth can be achieved even without a resource-rich territory—witness Switzerland and Japan. Another important consideration is a state's situation in relation to global mainstreams of activity. Singapore's rise to global economic significance is tied to its position at the crossroads of some of the world's busiest shipping routes. Conversely, isolation from flows of goods and capital puts such states as Sierra Leone, Myanmar (Burma), and Suriname at a disadvantage.

Landlocked Countries

Landlocked countries in particular face locational challenges because they have no ready access to the seas. Landlocked Bolivia, for example, suffered considerably after a war with its neighbors ended its rights to use ports on the Pacific coast. The Czech Republic is also landlocked, but its isolation is far less serious because it is connected to the outside world by waterways and surface transport routes. In Asia, Mongolia and Nepal are severely landlocked, with distance, terrain, and limited communications all contributing to their condition. In Africa, the realm with the most landlocked states of all, the resulting problems are especially severe. States in the Sahel are poorly linked to coastal entry points; in East Africa, Uganda has a rail link to the coast but Rwanda and Burundi are among the world's most isolated places. To the south, Zimbabwe has access to the sea via South Africa and Moçambique, but Zambia and Malawi suffer from poor connections as well as from political instability in their coastal neighbors.

◆ LAND BOUNDARIES

The territories of individual states are separated by international boundaries. Boundaries may appear on maps as straight lines or twist and turn to conform to the bends of rivers and the curves of hills and valleys. But a boundary is more than a line, far more than a fence or wall on the ground. A ***boundary*** between states is actually a vertical plane that cuts through the rocks below (called the ***subsoil*** in legal papers when countries argue about it) and the airspace above (Fig. 25-4). Only where this vertical plane intersects the Earth's surface (on land or at sea) does it form the line we see on a map.

When boundaries were established, the resources below the surface were much less well-known than they are today. As a result, coal seams extend from one country to another, oil reserves are split between states, and gas reserves are shared as well. Europe's coal reserves, for example, extend from Belgium underneath the Netherlands and on into Germany. Soon after mining began, these three neighbors began to accuse each other of mining coal that did not lie directly below their own national territories. (The underground surveys that were available at the time were too inaccurate to pinpoint the ownership of each coal seam.)

More recently, Germany and the Netherlands argued over a gas reserve that lies in the subsoil across

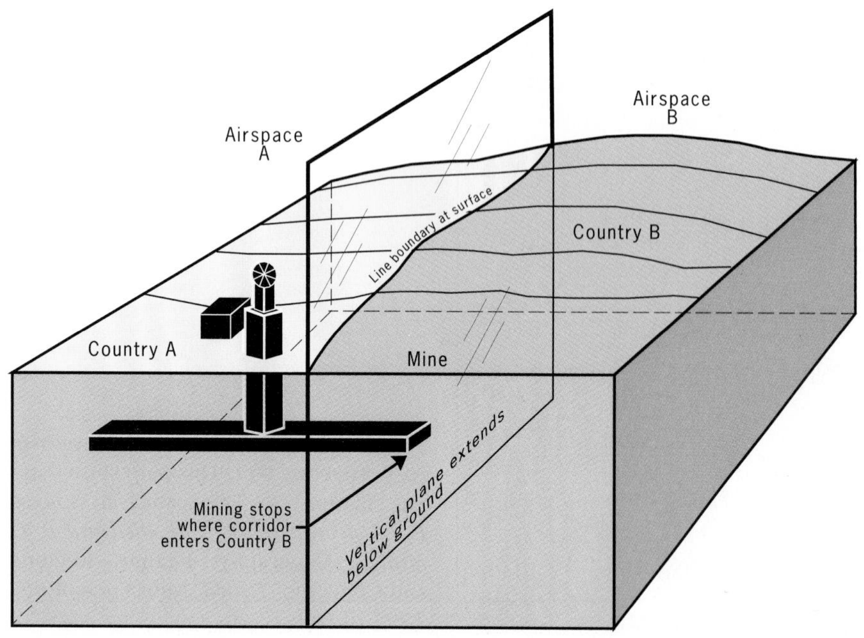

Figure 25-4 Political Boundaries on a Vertical Plane. A political boundary is a vertical plane, not merely a line on the ground.

their boundary. The Germans argued that the Dutch were withdrawing so much natural gas that the gas was flowing from beneath German land to the Dutch side of the border. The Germans wanted compensation for their "lost" gas. Similarly, a major issue between Iraq and Kuwait, which led to Iraq's invasion of Kuwait in 1990, was the oil in the Rumaylah reserve, which lies underneath the desert and crosses the boundary between the two states. The Iraqis not only asserted that the Kuwaitis were drilling too many wells and draining the reserve too quickly; they also alleged that the Kuwaitis were drilling *oblique* boreholes that penetrated the vertical plane extending downward along the border. But at the time that the Iraq–Kuwait border was established, no one knew that this giant oil reserve lay in the subsoil or that it would help create an international crisis (Fig. 25-5).

Above the ground, too, the interpretation of boundaries as vertical planes has serious implications. A state's "airspace" is defined by the atmosphere above its land area as marked by its boundaries, as well as by what lies beyond, at higher altitudes. But how high does that airspace extend? States that insist on controlling the airline traffic over their territories have not yet done the same in regard to satellite orbits, but that time may come. In addition, air circulates from one airspace to another, often carrying the pollutants of one state across the vertical plane to another state. Acid rain (see Part 10) knows no political boundaries, but it can cause serious political disputes.

The Evolution of Boundaries

Boundaries evolve through three stages. First, agreement is reached on the rough positioning of the border. Then the exact location is established through the process of ***definition***, whereby a treatylike, legal-sounding document is drawn up in which actual points in the landscape are described (or, where a straight-line boundary is involved, points of latitude and longitude). Next cartographers put the boundary on the map in a process called ***delimitation***. If either or both of the states so desire, the boundary is actually marked on the ground by steel posts, concrete pillars, fences (sometimes even a wall), or some other visible means. That final stage is the ***demarcation*** of the boundary. By no means are all boundaries on the world map demarcated. There are thousands of miles

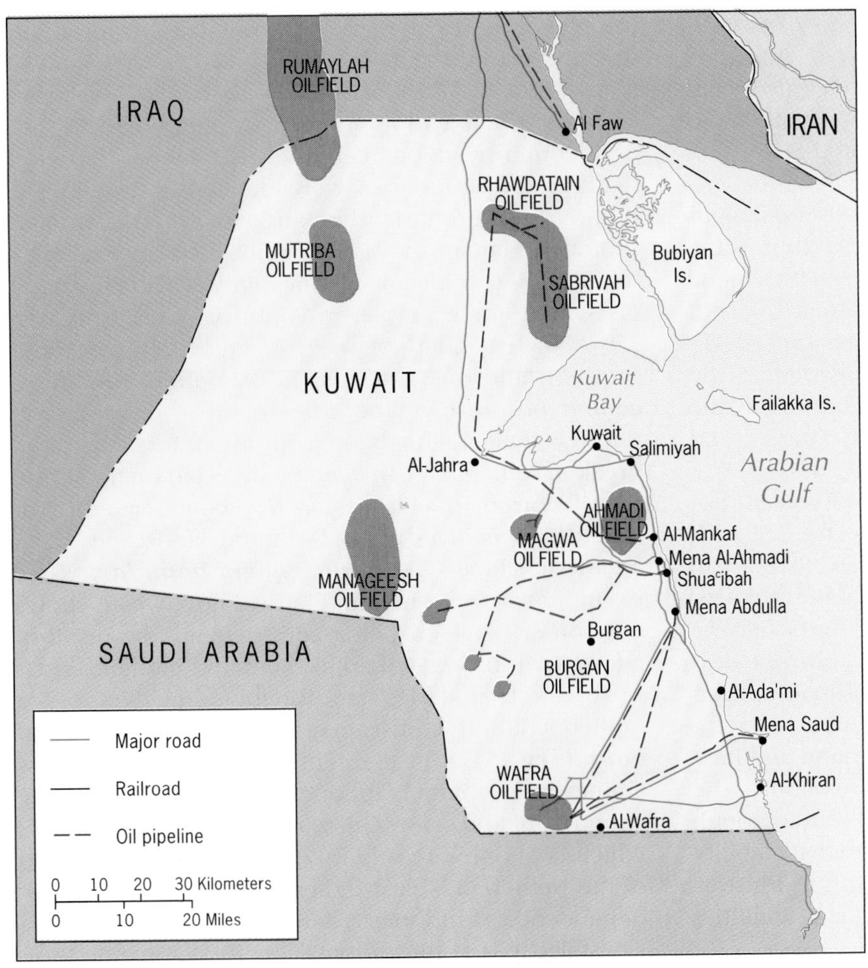

Figure 25-5 Relative Location of Kuwait. Kuwait's northern boundary was redefined and delimited by a United Nations boundary commission; it was demarcated by a series of concrete pillars 2 km (1.24 mi) apart.

where you could cross from one state into another without knowing it. Demarcating a lengthy boundary by any means at all is expensive, and it is hardly worth the effort in high mountains, vast deserts, frigid polar lands, or other places where there are few permanent settlements.

Types of Boundaries

Even the most casual glance at the world's boundary framework reveals that boundaries differ in morphological terms. Some conform to lines of latitude or longitude (Egypt occupies Africa's northeastern corner), others conform to natural features such as rivers, and still others separate societies with contrasting ethnic backgrounds or cultural characteristics. Political geographers use the term ***geometric boundary*** to identify straight-line boundaries such as that between the United States and Canada west of the Great Lakes. Such boundaries are totally unrelated to any aspects of the cultural or physical landscape. The colonial powers made extensive use of such boundaries in Africa.

Certain boundaries conform to physiographic features in the landscape, such as rivers or the crests of mountain ranges. These are referred to as ***physical-political*** or sometimes ***natural-political boundaries***, and many of them are modern versions of old trespass lines. The Rio Grande is an important physical-political boundary between the United States and Mexico; an older border follows crest lines of the Pyrenees between Spain and France. Lakes sometimes serve as boundaries as well—for example, four of the five Great Lakes of North America (between the United States and Canada) and several of the Great Lakes of East Africa (between Congo and its eastern neighbors). At first, national jurisdiction extended to the banks of rivers and the shores of lakes, but today, the waters themselves are divided between riparian and littoral states.

Physical features sometimes make convenient political boundaries, but the nature and meaning of such boundaries change over time and space. Rivers can unify as well as divide, and a mountain range that separates two states now may not have done so in the past. But a combination of perception and practical circumstances has led to the creation of many physical-political boundaries. Some of these are stable (for example, the boundary between Switzerland and Italy in the Alps), and others are not (for example, the boundary between India and China in the Karakoram Range). Thus, it is important to recognize that stability of boundaries often has more to do with local historical and geographical circumstances than with the physical character of the boundary itself.

Boundaries that mark breaks in the human landscape were formerly called anthropo-geographic boundaries, but they are now known as ***cultural-political boundaries***. When communist planners laid out their grand design for the Soviet Union, they tried to create a patchwork of nationalities, delimiting many miles of cultural-political boundaries in the process. For example, the boundary between Christian Armenia and Muslim Azerbaijan mentioned earlier was a cultural-political boundary. The map of European languages and political borders (Fig. 8-3) suggests how common such boundaries still are. Cultural breaks in the human landscape tend to shift over time, which is one reason why cultural-political boundaries often lead to conflict. Nevertheless, when peacemakers tried to draw a new map of Bosnia to help end the conflict among Serbs, Croats, and Muslims there, their attempts were based on cultural-political principles. The proposed Muslim "safe zones" were essentially cultural enclaves. However, the intermixing of the population and the highly generalized maps from which the peacemakers worked made boundary delimitation highly problematic.

Origin-Based Classification

Another way to view boundaries has to do with their evolution or genesis. This *genetic boundary classification* was pioneered by Richard Hartshorne (1899–1992), a leading American political geographer of the mid-twentieth century. Hartshorne reasoned that certain boundaries were defined and delimited before the present-day human landscape developed. Although Hartshorne used mainly Western examples to illustrate this idea, its applicability is also illustrated elsewhere, for example, in Southeast Asia. In Figure 25-6A, the boundary between Malaysia and Indonesia on the island of Borneo is an example of this ***antecedent boundary*** type. Most of this border passes through sparsely inhabited tropical rainforest, and the break in settlement can even be detected on the world population map (Fig. 4-1). A second category of boundaries evolved as the cultural landscape of an area took shape. These ***subsequent boundaries*** are exemplified by the map in Figure 25-6B, which shows the border between China and Vietnam, the result of a long-term process of adjustment and modification.

Some boundaries are forcibly drawn across a unified cultural landscape. Such a ***superimposed boundary*** exists in the center of the island of New Guinea and separates Indonesia's West Irian from the country of Papua New Guinea (Fig. 25-6C). West Irian, which is peopled mostly by ethnic Papuans, was part of the Netherlands East Indies that did not receive independence as Indonesia did in 1949. After many tension-filled years, the Indonesians finally invaded this territory in 1962 to drive out the remaining Dutch; following UN mediation and an eventual plebiscite, West Irian was formally attached to Indonesia in 1969—thereby perpetuating the boundary that the colonial administrators had originally superimposed on New Guinea in the early nineteenth century. The fourth genetic boundary type is the ***relict boundary***—a border that has ceased to function but whose imprints are still evident on the cultural landscape. The boundary between former North Vietnam and South Vietnam (Fig. 25-6D), is a classic example: once demarcated militarily, it has had relict status since 1976 following the reunification of Vietnam in the aftermath of the Indochina War (1964–1975).

Frontiers

The term ***frontier*** is misused almost as often as *nation.* "Boundary" and "frontier" are used interchangeably, as though they were synonyms, but they are not. A frontier is a *zone* of separation, an area between communities, clusters, groups, and states. It is a sort of territorial cushion that keeps rivals apart. Such "cushions" may be swamplands, impenetrable forests, wide deserts, mountain ranges, or river basins. Before the present world boundary framework jelled, many societies were separated by such natural frontiers. Eventually, even the most remote parts of the planet were settled, and boundaries were drawn through the last frontiers—even in Antarctica, the Earth's last land frontier, and, as we will see later, in the seas and oceans.

◆ FUNCTIONS OF BOUNDARIES

There was a time when states and empires built walls to fortify their borders, to keep out adversaries, and, sometimes, to keep inhabitants from wandering too far from the seat of authority. China's Great Wall and Hadrian's Wall in Britain (built by the Romans) still stand

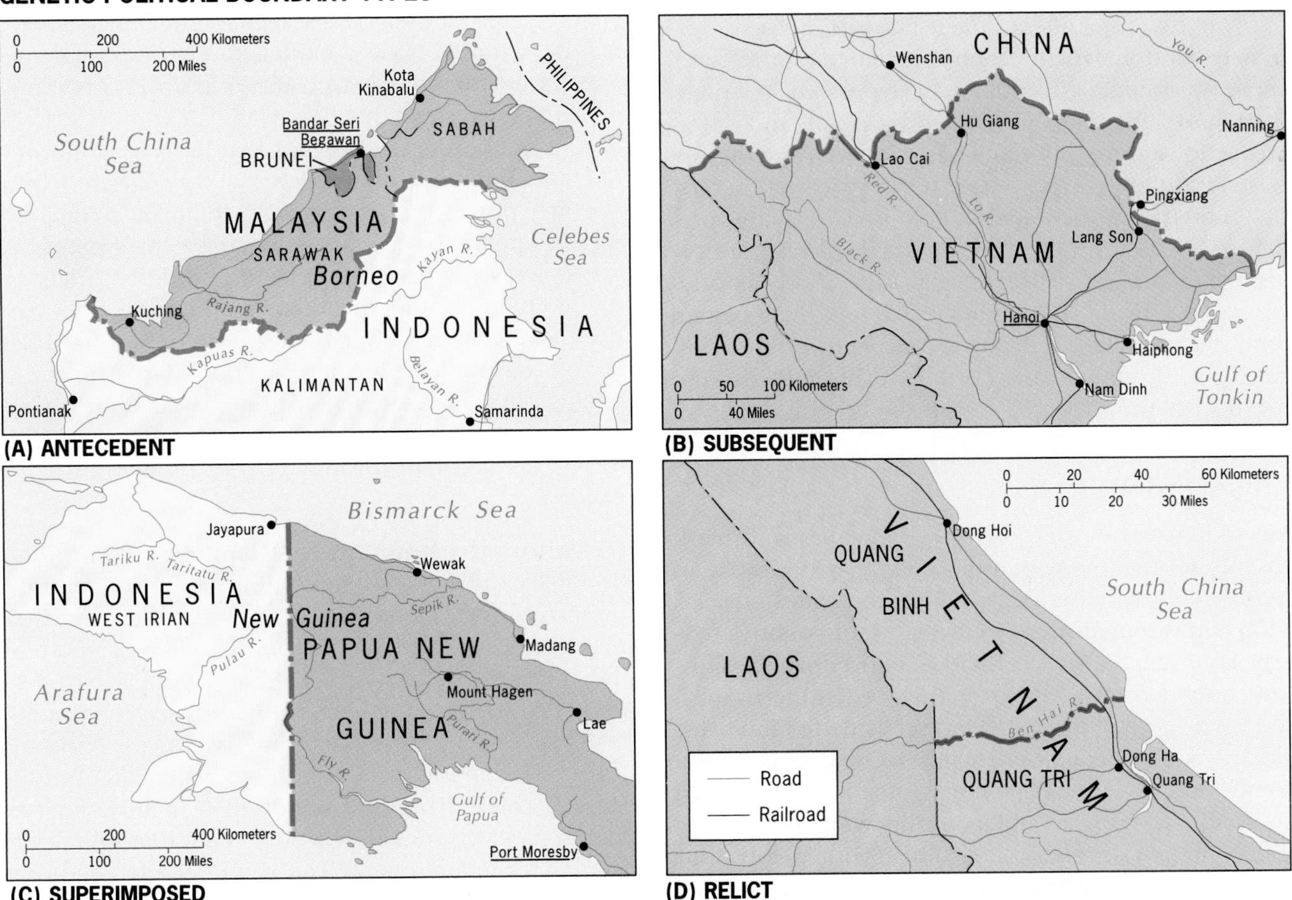

Figure 25-6 Genetic Political Boundary Types. Genetic political boundary types are (A) antecedent, (B) subsequent, (C) superimposed, and (D) relict. *Source: From a map in H. J. de Blij and P. O. Muller,* Realms, Regions, and Concepts, *7th ed. New York: Wiley, 1994.*

as evidence of such intentions. Indeed, the notion that boundaries could serve as fortifications endured into the mid-twentieth century; during World War II there were several attempts to fortify boundaries. And boundaries continue to be reinforced in order to stop people from moving across them without authorization. The Berlin Wall was built to keep East Germans from crossing into the Western enclave of West Berlin and seeking asylum from communist rule. More recently, the border between Mexico and the United States was walled and fenced in order to reduce illegal migration. Thus boundaries still serve defensive functions, though in a different context.

Today, boundaries mark the limits of state jurisdiction. They serve as symbols of state *sovereignty*. States often display maps of their national territory on the front pages of newspapers, on school books, on stamps, and even on flags. This contributes to the building of a national consciousness, a sense of inclusion that fosters ***nationalism***. Modern nationalism is a sense of national (often ethnic) consciousness and loyalty to nation and state, exalting it above all others and promoting its culture and interests over those of other nations. It is a potent force in the world today.

The governments of some states do not exert effective control over the entire territory of the state. There is no single government in Cyprus; the southern portion of Lebanon is controlled by Israel; and different factions are fighting for control over Afghanistan. In general, however, the state territory as outlined by its boundaries is the region within which its laws prevail, its taxes are collected, its armed forces are recruited or drafted, its language(s) are used, its educational curricula are implemented, and, in certain countries, the state religion is practiced. Boundaries, therefore, do much to keep the world divided—and not just politically.

Internal Boundaries

For administrative purposes, and sometimes to mark off cultural regions within the state, it is necessary to divide countries internally. The United States consists of 50 States that are in turn divided into counties (except Louisiana, which is divided into parishes). Canada is divided into 10 provinces, 2 federal territories, and 1 self-governing homeland set aside for Inuit residents. One of Canada's provinces, Quebec, is itself a homeland for French-speaking Canadians, although Quebec's borders do not coincide with the area in which French speakers live. India, with nearly four times as many inhabitants as the United States, has 25 States and 7 union territories, and some of the States have more people than most countries. If you cross from the State of Maharashtra into Karnataka, you will hear a different language. India's internal boundaries represent more cultural variation than do many international boundaries.

Political geographers have identified another kind of internal boundary, a kind that does not show up on administrative maps. As we have seen, numerous countries are culturally divided. Take the case of the former Yugoslavia: although there were internal "republics" for the country's Serbian, Croatian, Slovenian, Macedonian, and other major cultural components, this administrative structure did not accurately reflect the real situation. There were Serbs in Croatia, Croatians in Bosnia, and so on. Figure 25-7 is a simplification of the cultural mosaic of Yugoslavia before it was engulfed by civil war. Such internal boundaries can be seen in Belgium, Sri Lanka, Malaysia, Moldova, and a host of other countries, including several African states.

Boundary Disputes

Nations, like families and individuals, can become very territorial when they feel that their space has been violated. In suburban areas in the United States, quarrels over fence lines and surveys rank high among social disputes that must be solved by legal means. So it is with states. As noted earlier, the boundary we see as a line on an atlas map is the product of a complex series of legal steps that begins with a written description of the border. Sometimes that legal description is old and imprecise. Sometimes it was dictated by a stronger power that is now less dominant, giving the weaker neighbor a reason to argue for change. At other times the geography of the borderland has actually changed: the river that marked the boundary may have changed course, or a portion of it has been cut off. Resources lying across a boundary can lead to conflict. In short, states often argue about their boundaries. These boundary disputes take four principal forms: definitional, locational, operational, and allocational.

Definitional Boundary Disputes *Definitional* boundary disputes focus on the legal language of the boundary agreement. For example, a boundary definition may stipulate that the border will be marked by the median line of a river. That would seem clear enough, but the water levels of rivers vary. If the valley is asymmetrical, the median line will move back and forth between low-water and high-water stages of the stream. This may involve hundreds of meters of movement—not very much, it would seem, but enough to cause serious argument. The solution is to refine the definition to suit both parties.

Locational Boundary Disputes *Locational* boundary disputes center on the delimitation and possibly the demarcation of the border. The definition is not in dis-

Figure 25-7 The Former Yugoslavia. The ethnic mosaic of the former Yugoslavia is illustrated on this map. *Source: Based on maps drawn in the Office of the Geographer of the U.S. Department of State, Washington, D.C., 1991.*

pute, but its interpretation is. Sometimes the language of boundary treaties is vague enough to allow mapmakers to delimit the line in various ways. For example, when the colonial powers defined their empires in Africa and Asia, they specified their international boundaries rather carefully. But internal administrative boundaries often were not strictly defined. When those internal boundaries became the boundaries of independent states, there was plenty of room for argument.

In a few instances, locational disputes arise because no definition of the boundary exists at all. An important case involves Saudi Arabia and Yemen, whose potentially oil-rich border area is not covered by a treaty.

Operational Boundary Disputes *Operational* boundary disputes involve neighbors who differ over the way their boundary should function. When two adjoining countries agree that cross-border migration should be controlled, the boundary functions satisfactorily. But if one state wants to limit migration while the other does not, a dispute may arise. Similarly, efforts to prevent smuggling across borders sometimes lead to operational disputes when one state's efforts are not matched (or are possibly even sabotaged) by its neighbor's. And in areas where nomadic lifeways still prevail, the movement of people and their livestock across international borders can lead to conflict.

Allocational Boundary Disputes *Allocational* disputes of the kind described earlier, involving the Netherlands and Germany over natural gas and Iraq and Kuwait over oil, are becoming more common as the search for resources intensifies. Today many such disputes involve international boundaries at sea. Oil reserves under the seafloor in coastal waters sometimes lie in areas where exact boundary delimitation may be difficult or subject to debate. Another growing area of allocational dispute has to do with water supplies: the Tigris, Nile, Colorado, and other rivers are subject to such disputes. When a river crosses an international boundary, the rights of the upstream and downstream users of the river often come into conflict.

In this chapter we have examined various geographic aspects of the territory of states, including its development and its spatial limits. As we noted, the territorial attributes of states vary widely, and so do the advantages of their relative locations. Whatever their territorial circumstances, however, states achieve strength, durability, and power by organizing their resources effectively. Some states have overcome severe geographic disadvantages and attained prosperity and security; others, with more available resources, have not. We turn next to the role of spatial organization in the well-being of states.

◆ KEY TERMS ◆

antecedent boundary
boundary
boundary definition
boundary delimitation
boundary demarcation
compact state
cultural-political boundary
elongated state
enclave
exclave
fragmented state
frontier
geometric boundary
human territoriality
landlocked
microstate
nation
nationalism
nation-state
natural-political boundary
perforated state
physical-political boundary
prorupted state
protruded state
political culture
political geography
relict boundary
Renaissance
sovereignty
state
subsequent boundary
subsoil
superimposed boundary
territorial morphology
theocracy

◆ APPLYING GEOGRAPHIC KNOWLEDGE ◆

1. Just after the beginning of the twentieth century, the world numbered just 60 independent countries, and in 1946 there were 74. Today, the map shows 193 sovereign states. Has the proliferation of states reached a peak, or is the number of states likely to grow still further? What maps might you reference in support of your answer?
2. Political boundaries, it is often said, have become all but irrelevant in this world of global interaction and international cooperation. Still, boundary disputes continue in many parts of the world, and some countries (Cyprus, Somalia, Sri Lanka) threaten to split along newly delimited borders. Discuss the modern functions of boundaries and suggest ways in which such boundary roles may change during the twenty-first century.

Chapter 26

State Organization and National Power

From the field notes

"China's Chairman Mao used to say that political power comes from the barrel of a gun. Of course there are other ways for a state to exercise power, but here in Mumbai, India, he seems to have been taken literally. This port is bristling with weaponry: aircraft carriers, cruisers, submarines, and dozens of other navy vessels. India aspires to be a global as well as a regional power, but the country has a history of conflict with two of its neighbors: Pakistan and China. A power struggle in the form of an arms race may be in the offing." (Note: in May, 1998, India exploded five nuclear bombs at a test site in the Thar Desert, underscoring its drive to become a major military power on the global stage).

KEY POINTS

◆ **A well-developed primary core area and a mature capital city are essential components of a well-integrated state.**

◆ **The European state model had a centralized, unitary framework. Federal systems were developed in the New World and in former colonies elsewhere.**

◆ **States are held together by centripetal forces such as nationalism, education, circulation, and the institutions of government; but they are also subject to centrifugal forces in the form of ethnic disunity, cultural differences, or regional disparities.**

◆ **Geopolitics, a century-old part of political geography, studies the power relationships among states. Current developments in the states of the Pacific Rim fuel an old debate on Eurasian power relationships.**

Most political geographers believe that the number of independent states will surpass 200 in the near future. These 200 countries will occupy the surface of a small planet of which over two-thirds is covered by water or ice! With such a large number of entities, some large and others very small, it is inevitable that equality will remain a mirage. Not only are there large as well as small states: there are well-endowed and poor states, states in the global economic core and states on the disadvantaged periphery. To understand these matters we must consider the human and organizational dimensions of the state.

◆ ORGANIZATION AND POPULATION

For several years China has been undergoing dramatic economic growth. While economies in Western Europe and North America are experiencing growth of 1 to 3 percent annually, China has been reporting growth of 9 to 13 percent—such a high rate that Chinese rulers are trying to restrain it. In the late 1990s China's economy was the third largest in the world, behind those of the United States and Japan.

Yet in 1998 the Chinese people were earning just a tiny fraction of what Americans or Japanese earn per capita. In terms of development, China still ranks in the lower category by many measures. Why is this so? The answer lies in part in China's vast population. With over 1.2 billion people, and adding 13 million every year, every measure of progress must be divided by twelve hundred million. No matter how fast an economy grows, that kind of arithmetic will produce low per capita figures.

Economic success and political power are closely linked. When Western Europe's leading states established colonial empires, they were able to do so because they already were economically successful and the colonies, in turn, helped to further that success. Japan, too, used its economic reforms to mount a campaign of territorial expansion. The colonial acquisitions thus helped small European countries become imperial powers.

Today the fragments of those colonial empires are independent states. Earlier we noted the differences in the amounts of territory controlled by different states. In terms of population, the range is even greater. Over half the world's states have populations below 5 million; nearly 50 have fewer than 1 million citizens. These very small states are called ***ministates*** (unlike *microstates*, which do not have all the elements of statehood), and most have little power in a world where decisions are made by their larger neighbors (Singapore is an exception). Nevertheless, they have been given disproportionately strong representation in various international agencies, including the United Nations.

There is no "ideal" population for a state of a particular territorial size. With a territory the size of Montana, Japan has achieved what giant Brazil has not. "Overpopulated" Singapore thrives, while Liberia fractures. To understand this situation, we must consider people's *capacities* for organization in light of local circumstances and their position in the global political and economic order. Japan, Hong Kong, and Guangdong are examples of places where favorable shifts in the global economy worked together with a well-educated workforce to produce greater economic gains than those found among places with access to abundant natural resources. More generally, efforts to bring countries together and promote economic development are evident in the building of everything from school systems to road networks. Two important geographical clues to the organizational character of the state can be found in the nature of the state's core area(s) and in the size and functions of its capital city.

Core Areas

Several of the most influential European states grew over many centuries from a ***core area***, expanding into a regional entity and absorbing territory along their frontiers. Eventually their expansion was halted when neighboring entities blocked them, boundaries were defined, and their internal organization matured.

The original nucleus of these states still functions as a core area. Many countries elsewhere in the world also have well-defined core areas, even though they are often much younger than their European counterparts. You can discern core areas even on a small-scale atlas map: here lie a country's major cities (usually including the capital), its largest and densest population cluster, its most intensive transport networks, and often its most intensively cultivated farmlands. Here the national economy is best developed and circulation is most efficient. If you travel away from the core area, you see smaller towns, fewer factories, and more open land.

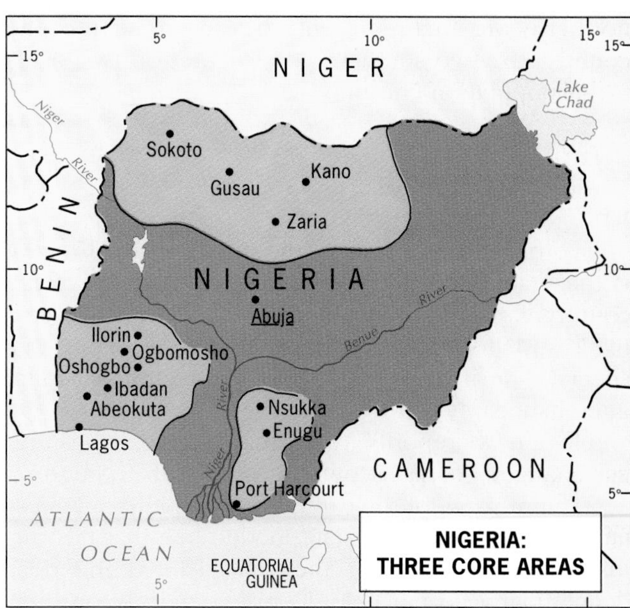

Figure 26-1 Nigeria's Three Core Areas. Nigeria is a multicore state; its northern core area lies in the Muslim realm, while the southern core areas lie in Christian-influenced Africa. Nigeria's political survival is a major African political achievement. But pressures on Nigeria are rising, and devolution remains a threat.

Japan's Kanto Plain is one of the world's leading national cores, centered on the primate city of Tokyo. Note that intensive agriculture still plays a role in this highly urbanized heartland. France's Paris Basin is a more ancient core area, centered on one of Europe's greatest primate cities. In Egypt, the Cairo-Alexandria axis and the Nile Delta form the national core, and in Chile, Santiago lies in what the Chileans call their country's *nucleo central.*

Is a well-developed core area essential for a well-functioning state? Apparently it is. Countries without recognizable cores (Congo, Chad, Mongolia, Bangladesh) may have notable capitals, but these alone do not produce a well-integrated state.

Some states possess more than one core area, and such ***multicore states*** confront particular problems. If the primary core area is dominant, as in the United States, such problems may be slight. In the United States the core area still lies in the East and Northeast, corresponding approximately with the economic region mapped in Figure 23-3, and includes the federal capital. Subsidiary core areas are not competitive or divisive. In Nigeria, on the other hand, three core areas mark ethnically and culturally diverse parts of the state, and none is truly dominant (Fig. 26-1). Nigeria's

From the field notes

"Singapore, a ministate that also is a city-state, is the product of organization as well as location. With an area of just 240 square miles (622 sq km) and a population of nearly 3 million, Singapore, the world's most urbanized state, has to be organized strictly in order to function. With the largest port in the world (in terms of number of ships served) and the third-largest oil refinery complex, Singapore is one of the Pacific Rim's economic tigers. This view, from the 68th floor of Asia's tallest hotel, shows Singapore's still-evolving skyline, a reflection of its success."

northern core area represents the Muslim heart of the country; the two southern cores center on two of its major population clusters.

Capital Cities

The core area is the heart of the state; the ***capital city*** is the brain. This is the political nerve center of the country, its national headquarters and seat of government, and the center of national life. We recognize this special status by using the name of a country's capital interchangeably with that of the state itself; for example, a news report may say that "London's position has changed" or "Moscow is at odds with Ukraine."

The primacy of the capital is yet another manifestation of the European state model, one that has diffused worldwide. After they had gained independence, many former colonies spent lavishly on their capitals, not because this was essential to political or economic success but because the European image, drawn from London or Paris or Lisbon or Brussels, compelled it.

Some newly independent states decided to relocate their capital cities, again at enormous expense. Several did so in order to move the capital from a geographically peripheral situation to a more central one. Until recently Nigeria's capital was Lagos, on the coast in the southwest of the country. A new capital has been constructed at Abuja, nearer the geographic center of the state. Malawi moved its capital from Zomba, deep in the south, to more central Lilongwe. In Pakistan, the capital was moved from the colonial headquarters of Karachi to Islamabad in the far north.

In the late 1990s Malaysia was in the process of relocating its capital from Kuala Lumpur, the former British colonial headquarters, to a completely new center called Putrajaya about 40 km (25 mi) to the south. This move was prompted by the Malaysian government's desire to build a brand-new, ultramodern capital to symbolize the country's rapid economic growth and modernization.

Capital cities are of interest to cultural as well as political geographers because they are occasionally used to focus a society's attention on a national objective. In Pakistan's case, the transfer of the capital to Islamabad was part of a plan to orient the nation toward its historic focus in the interior and toward the north, where the country narrows between Kashmir, China, and Afghanistan. In Brazil, the decision to move the capital from historic Rio de Janeiro to Brasília was made, in large part, to direct the nation's attention toward the huge, sparsely populated yet poorly integrated interior. We have already noted Japan's transfer of its capital from Kyoto to Tokyo, a move that also had specific national objectives. The capital city thus can be used to achieve national aims and promote change. Geographers sometimes refer to such cities as ***forward capitals***.

Berlin once served as such a forward capital. During the nineteenth century, when the German state was forming, its western boundaries (with the Netherlands, Belgium, and, until 1870, France) were relatively stable. To the east, however, lay the frontier. There the Germans confronted the Poles and other Slavic nations, and the growing empire expanded into much of what is today Poland.

This eastward march was underscored by the choice of Berlin as the capital. Berlin lies not far from the Oder River, whose basin was Germany's easternmost territory until the 1860s. Most of Germany lay to the west of Berlin, but the capital confirmed Germany's eastern orientation.

A century later Germany lay defeated and divided. West Germany chose a new capital, Bonn; East Germany, under Soviet control, was governed from East Berlin. The German empire had lost all of its eastern frontier, and Poland now extended to the Oder River, on Berlin's doorstep.

When Germany was reunified in 1990, Germans debated the choice of a new capital. Many favored Bonn, located near the country's western border and symbolic of its new role in Europe. Many others preferred a return to Berlin. Still others wanted to put the past behind them and argued for a totally new choice, such as Hanover, near the center of the country. In the end, Berlin was selected—raising fears among those who remembered the city's role during times of war. In the late 1990s those memories were being erased by a giant construction program that transformed Berlin and symbolized its new era. The move from Bonn, however, still was on hold pending the completion of Berlin's government complex and the final decision to make the move. Moving the capital of a large state is no small undertaking.

In general, the capital city is the pride of the state, and its layout, prominent architectural landmarks, public art, historic buildings and monuments, and often its religious structures reflect the society's values and priorities. It may be employed as a unifying force and can assert the state's values internally as well as externally. It is the focus of the state as a political region.

Unitary and Federal Systems

A well-integrated state consists of a stable, clearly bounded territory served by an adequate infrastructure, an effective administrative framework, a productive core area, and a prominent capital. All states, however, confront divisive forces—some strong enough to threaten their very survival. The question is how best to adjust the workings of the state to ensure its continuity.

When the nation-state evolved in Europe, this was not a serious problem. Democracy as we know it today had not yet matured; governments controlled the use of force and could suppress dissent by forceful means. Most European governments were highly centralized; the capital city represented authority that stretched to the limits of the state. There seemed to be no need to accommodate minorities or outlying regions where the sense of national identity was weaker. Europe's nation-states were ***unitary states***, and their administrative frameworks were designed to ensure the central government's authority over all parts of the state. France, for example, was divided into more than 90 *départements*, whose representatives came to Paris less to express regional concerns than to implement governmental decisions back home.

European notions of the state diffused to much of the rest of the world, but in the New World these notions did not always work well. When colonies freed themselves of European dominance, many found that conditions in their newly independent countries did not lend themselves to unitary systems of government. In the United States, Canada, and Australia the newness of the culture, the absence of an old primate city, the lack of a clear core area, the vastness of the national territory, and the emergence of regionalism all required something other than highly centralized government. In Europe itself, some political philosophers had already theorized about alternatives to the unitary system, and regionalism in Scotland and Wales had become a concern in London. It was situations like these that led to the emergence of the ***federal state***. Federalism accommodated regional interests by vesting primary power in provinces, States, or other regional units over all matters except those explicitly given to the national government. The Australian geographer K. W. Robinson described federation as "the most geographically expressive of all political systems, based as it is on the existence and accommodation of regional differences . . . federation does not create unity out of diversity; rather, it enables the two to coexist."

In Europe, the only genuine, long-term federation was Switzerland, but conditions there were too different from those in the New World to allow it to serve as a model. For example, the choice of a capital city was a challenge for many federations. No region would agree to locate the capital in another region. As a result, federations often created new capitals, built on federal territories carved from one or more States. Thus the U.S. capital became neither New York nor Philadelphia, but Washington, DC, built on a federal territory initially taken from Maryland and Virginia. The Australian capital became neither Sydney nor Melbourne but Canberra, established on federal territory taken from the State of New South Wales.

Federalism spread even to countries whose European settlers came from highly centralized unitary states. In Europe, few states were more strongly centralized than Spain and Portugal, yet Mexico and Brazil established federal systems. (Brazil moved its capital functions from the primate city, Rio de Janeiro, to interior Brasília in the 1950s.)

While the European colonial powers retained control over their empires in Africa and Asia, colonial rule mirrored the unitary system— only more so. Overseas domains were run with little or no consideration for local or regional cultures. But when the colonial era came to an end, the federal idea seemed to hold promise for newly independent, ethnically and culturally divided countries. The British in particular attempted to create federal frameworks as the end of the empire approached. Their greatest success was India, where the transition to independence *and* the subsequent survival of the state may be attributed in large part to the federal framework created by British and Indian negotiators during the 1940s. In Africa, in contrast, the mechanisms of federation were put in place hastily and were based on contested territorial configurations (for example, in Nigeria and Uganda), and as a result they failed to stabilize.

Today the divisive forces of regionalism are affecting not only recently formed federations but also the older unitary states of Europe (this topic is discussed in Part Ten). In response, European states are reconstructing their administrative frameworks; France, for example, has recognized 22 "regions" which consist of groupings of the 96 *départements* dating back to the time of Napoleon (Fig. 26-2). These regions are geographic evidence of France's attempt to decentralize governmental control. In similar ways, Spain, Italy, the United Kingdom, and other older unitary states are adjusting to new political-geographical circumstances—new to Europe but well known to federal governments elsewhere.

Opposing Forces

Adjusting the internal organization of the state is one way to reduce the divisive forces that put stress on it. All states suffer in some measure from disruptive forces, and all states possess unifying bonds. Strengthening these bonds to overcome actual and potential divisions is a principal task of government.

Centripetal Forces By manipulating the system, many countries have managed to enhance the ***centripetal forces*** that promote national unity. This may involve changing the administrative structure of the

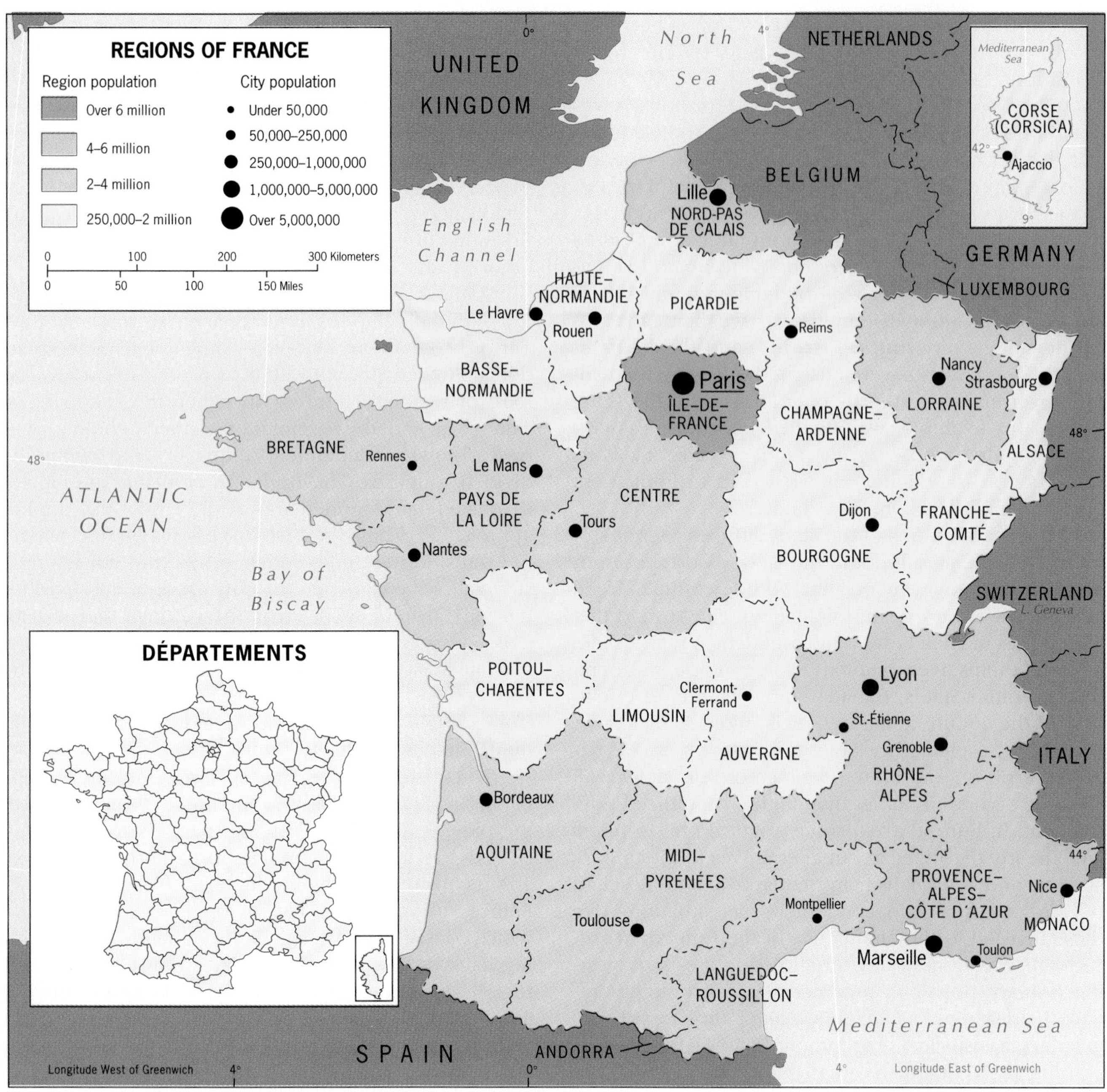

Figure 26-2 Regions of France. This map shows the new 22-region France, including Corsica. *Source: From a map in H. J. de Blij and P. O. Muller*, Geography: Realms, Regions, and Concepts, *8th ed. New York: Wiley, 1998.*

state either to strengthen central authority or to assign more power to the provinces or regions. Although India is often cited as an example of successful manipulation of the federal framework, Nigeria is also a good example. When Nigeria became independent in 1960 after centuries of British colonial rule, it had a federal framework consisting of three regions based on the core areas shown in Figure 26-1. Soon a fourth region was added, but this was not enough to stave off a disastrous war brought on by the Eastern Region's efforts to secede from the federation. After that war, it was clear to Nigerian leaders that the original regions had been too large; they were large enough to regard themselves as national entities capable of going it alone. They therefore decided to redivide Nigeria into a larger number of regions (and to call them States). The smaller States would be less able to mount separatist campaigns. Today, on paper, Nigeria is still a federation of 30 States, although successive military regimes have eroded their power and centralized the government. Given the religious division of Nigeria between a Muslim north and a non-Muslim south, the country's cultural fragmentation into some 200 peoples, and economic troubles arising from the drop in price of its leading export commodity (oil), the continued cohesion of the Nigerian federation is noteworthy.

Manipulating the system, however, may not be enough; this approach recently failed in the Soviet Union, Yugoslavia, and Czechoslovakia. Governments therefore seek to foster unity in other ways as well. Being a citizen of a country and carrying its passport are not enough to create an emotional commitment to the ideals for which the state stands. Such commitment is expressed as a sense of nationalism, an allegiance and loyalty that transcend other feelings of attachment. In a multicultural state such as South Africa, loyalties are divided: many people feel greater allegiance to their own ethnic group than to the state as a whole. In newly independent countries throughout Africa, ***tribalism*** has threatened "national" unity. Governments everywhere therefore seek to promote nationalism in order to overcome more local loyalties. One way to accomplish this is by ensuring that minorities are represented in government (see "Focus on: Electoral Geography").

Another centripetal force is the *leadership* of a charismatic individual who personifies the state and captures the public's imagination. (The origin of the word *charisma* lies in a Greek expression that means "divine gift.") At times such leaders can stimulate nationalism, as Perón did in Argentina, de Gaulle in France, and Tito in Yugoslavia. Conversely, the demise of such a leader may be followed by a weakening of nationalist sentiment.

Still another unifying force can come from a real or perceived *external threat.* When a country is confronted by an aggressive neighbor or by the loss of something vital (a critical resource or access to the sea, for example), the people are likely to rally to the national cause. Some governments have taken advantage of this tendency by creating artificial crises to divert attention from internal problems.

More durable sources of nationalism are *education* and other national institutions, including, in some countries, the church. In all countries, the state's history and geography, its symbols and songs, its traditions and values are taught in the schools. This practice builds a sense of belonging that later translates into nationalism. Where the church still dominates everyday life, as in many Muslim countries and in some Roman Catholic societies, its contribution to national cohesion can be enormous.

Directly related to this institutional force is national *ideology.* Nazism was a powerful ideological force that rallied the German nation during the 1930s; communism fired the emotions of hundreds of millions of people for nearly 80 years beginning early in this century. Communist ideology helped unify different peoples, persuaded them to make terrible sacrifices, and blinded them to dreadful excesses carried out under its banner. Indoctrination made communism the cornerstone of national culture. Communist leaders who took control of states from Poland to Cuba and from Albania to North Korea made ideology a strong centripetal force.

Communist states were walled off (literally in some instances) from the rest of the world, and when cracks opened in those walls, communist ideology alone was not enough to withstand the flow of ideas from the outside world. This underscores the importance of *circulation* as a nation-building factor. When a population is mobile, moving to and from various parts of a country and diffusing national norms in the process, regionalism and separatism often decline. Stagnant, isolated regions within a state are potentially divisive. Integration into the nation through effective circulation and communication systems reduces this threat if it is accompanied by policies of tolerance and inclusion. In a multilingual country, circulation enhances the likelihood that each language will be known and used by a substantial percentage of the population and will be regarded as part of the national culture. Low mobility, on the other hand, reinforces the separateness produced by different languages.

Centrifugal Forces All states must deal with divisive or ***centrifugal forces***. When these centrifugal forces outweigh the centripetal ones just described, the state will collapse. In recent times we have witnessed the disintegration of the world's largest colonial empires, including, in the late 1980s, the Soviet Union. We have seen the collapse of Yugoslavia, where a quasi-federal system failed to withstand the forces of division. Czechoslovakia has broken up into two countries. Cyprus is divided; Sri Lanka is wracked by war. Eritrea has separated from Ethiopia. In the late twentieth century, centrifugal forces seem to be on the rampage.

In the concluding chapter of this book we consider several of the forces that are splintering states, even older European states that up to now have been models of durability. For the moment, we should note that geography itself is a powerful factor: regionalism and real or perceived regional inequality are strong centrifugal forces. When regionalism marks religious or linguistic or other cultural contrasts, the threat to state and nation is increased.

◆ POWER RELATIONSHIPS

Just as some states are large and others small, some rich and others poor, so there are powerful states and weak ones. Measuring the relative power of states is a

Electoral Geography

"All politics is local," it is often said, and in truth a voter's most direct and important contact with government is at the local level. Voters who feel that they can have little impact on national elections but clearly have a voice in local elections still feel that they are participating in the political system. This can be a crucial factor in building a sense of commitment to the nation and what it stands for.

Electoral geography deals with various spatial aspects of voting systems, voting behavior, and voter representation. Various countries use different voting systems to elect their governments. In the 1994 South African election we could observe how the leaders of that society formulated a system that would provide majority rule while awarding some power to each of nine newly formed regions. The overall effect was to protect, to an extent, the rights of minorities in those regions. In the United States, proportional representation prevails in the House of Representatives (Congress), while the rights of States with small populations are protected in the Senate.

The geographic study of voting behavior is especially interesting because it relates the way people vote to their geographic environments. Maps of voting patterns often produce surprises that can be explained by other maps, and GIS technology has raised this kind of analysis to new levels. Church affiliation, income level, ethnic background, education level, and numerous other social factors are studied to learn why voters voted the way they did.

Probably the most practical area of electoral geography is the geography of representation. When there is a certain fixed number of seats for representatives in an elected legislature (such as the 435 congressional seats in the U.S. House of Representatives), there must be a fixed number of electoral districts from which those representatives are elected. Since the congressional seats are based on State population totals, it is up to each State to draw a map of congressional districts from which representatives will be elected.

Or is it? Can the States be trusted to draw their districting maps fairly, giving minorities an opportunity to elect their own representatives? After all, if a State has a population that is 80 percent white, 10 percent African American, and 10 percent Hispanic, an electoral district map could easily result in white majorities in all districts and no minority representatives at all. After the 1990 census the U.S. government instructed all States with substantial minority populations to construct so-called majority–minority districts (districts within which a minority would have the majority of the voters). In the hypothetical State described here, this districting would lead to the election of at least one African American and one Hispanic representative from among ten districts.

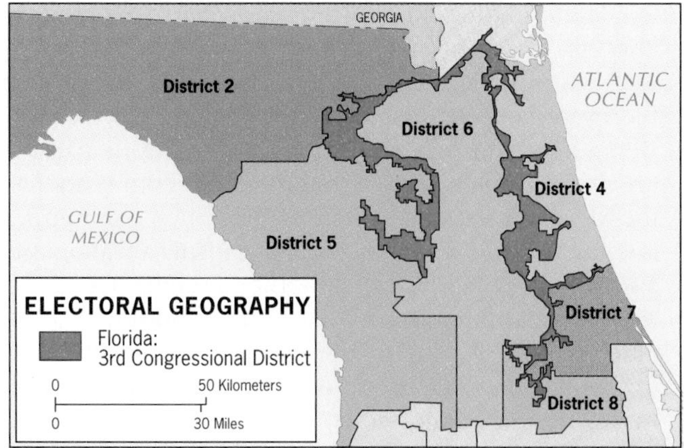

Figure 26-3 Electoral Geography. **Florida Congressional District No. 3 is an example of the spatial manipulation necessary to create majority-minority districts. In 1990, District 3 had about 310,000 African-American residents, 240,000 whites, and 16,000 Hispanics. In places, District 3 is no wider than U.S. Highway 90.** ***Source: Map and data provided by Tanya de Blij, Geographer/Analyst for the Florida House of Representatives.***

Reapportionment of the total number of representatives among the States goes on all the time because the population shifts: some States gain seats, others lose. As a result, redistricting also occurs after every census, and within States (for State legislatures) it occurs more frequently than that. Ideally, a State's congressional districts would, on the map, look relatively compact and contain roughly the same number of voters. In reality, our pluralistic society requires the construction of some oddly shaped districts in order to adhere to the majority–minority rule (Fig. 26-3).

Strange-looking districts that have been constructed to attain certain political ends are nothing new in American politics. In 1812, Governor Elbridge Gerry (pronounced with a soft *G*) of Massachusetts signed into law a district designed to give an advantage to his party—a district that looked so odd to artist Gilbert Stuart that he drew it with a head, wings, and claws. Stuart called it the "salamander district," but a colleague immortalized it by naming it a ***gerrymander***. Ever since, the term "gerrymandering" has been used to describe "redistricting for advantage." Certainly many of the districts now on the U.S. electoral map may be seen as gerrymanders, but for an important purpose: to provide representation to minorities who, without it, would not be represented as effectively in the national legislature.

complex and imprecise business. There can be no doubt, however, that a state's power is directly related to its capacity for organization.

In *The Might of Nations* (1961), J. G. Stoessinger defines power as "the capacity of a nation to use its tangible and intangible resources in such a way as to affect the behavior of other nations." Again, this does not mean solely or even primarily the use of military force; rather, it involves economic strength and political organization. A state can win concessions or reciprocal agreements with other states through its economic and political strength. It can outbid other states in the competition for access to resources in the territories of economically peripheral countries. Growth and development require organization, and organization generates power.

As noted earlier, ***colonialism*** projected European power into the non-European world. The height of the colonial era came during the eighteenth and nineteenth centuries, when the British, French, Spanish, Portuguese, Dutch, and Belgians consolidated their overseas holdings. The Germans and Italians were latecomers on the colonial scene (Fig. 26-4). Spain and Portugal lost their American possessions even before the Berlin Conference laid out the colonial map of Africa, and early in the twentieth century it was evident that small European countries would not be able to control large, distant empires forever.

Elsewhere in the world, two other colonial powers built major empires: Russia and Japan. The Russian empire was vast, and unlike others, it was contiguous: only in what is today Alaska did Russia acquire an "overseas" domain—which it sold to the United States in 1867. Japan came late to the colonial scene, but in a few decades it acquired major holdings in East Asia.

The colonial powers were able to gain control over their empires by virtue of their economic, political, and military organization; when that organization failed, they lost their advantage. Russia's internal weaknesses were exposed by its losses in the Far East (Japan decisively defeated the Russian armies in 1905). But during the heyday of colonialism the imperial powers exercised ruthless control over their domains and organized them for maximum economic exploitation. The capacity to install the infrastructures necessary for such efficient profiteering is itself evidence of the power relationships involved: entire populations were regimented in the service of the colonial ruler. Flows of raw materials were organized for the benefit of the colonial power, and the tangible evidence of that organization (mines, railroads, ports, plantations) can still be seen. Moreover, these economic systems have survived the end of colonialism. Raw material flows are much as they were before the colonial era came to an end. And while the former colonies are now independent states, the influence of

From the field notes

"Symbol of power: the Panama Canal. You cannot traverse this marvel of twentieth-century engineering without being reminded of the power of the United States to intervene in the affairs of foreign countries. There was no Panama when the United States decided to try where the French had failed: this narrow stretch of land between Atlantic and Pacific waters belonged to Colombia. But the U.S. fomented a local rebellion, helped and then recognized the victors, and created not only the Panama Canal but the Republic of Panama itself. There was no need to colonize the country; control over the vital waterway and its adjacent Canal Zone was enough. As we looked back toward the city of Colon on the Caribbean Sea side, we saw one of the world's largest ocean liners, the Queen Elizabeth II, approach the Gatun locks. Imagine: a two-way system of locks and channels engineered and built by 1914 can still accommodate most of the large ships of the 1990s. This is a monument to planning and organization in the national interest."

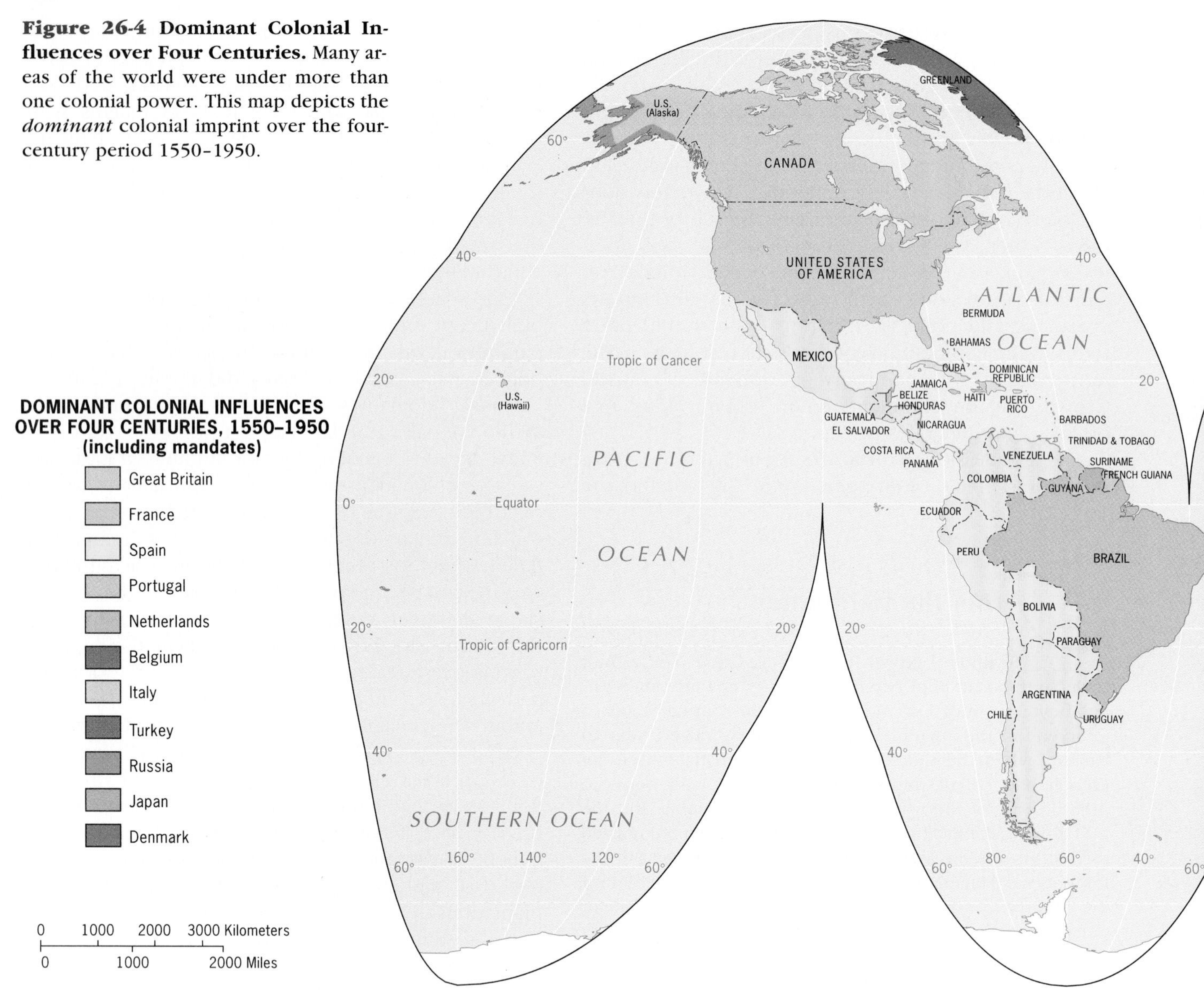

Figure 26-4 Dominant Colonial Influences over Four Centuries. Many areas of the world were under more than one colonial power. This map depicts the *dominant* colonial imprint over the four-century period 1550–1950.

their former rulers continues, notably in the former French empire.

Geopolitics

Just as economic, cultural, and urban geographers have suggested general principles governing locational behavior and processes, political geographers have sought to understand the complex political world. The first political geographer who studied the state and its power relationships in detail was Friedrich Ratzel (1844–1904). Ratzel focused on the behavioral dynamics of states. He postulated that the state resembles a biological organism whose life cycle extends from birth through maturity and, ultimately, decline and death. To prolong its existence, the state requires nourishment, just as an organism needs food. Such nourishment is provided by the acquisition of less powerful competitors' territories and their cultural contents. If a state is confined within permanent and static boundaries and deprived of overseas domains, Ratzel argued, it will atrophy. Space is the state's essential, life-giving force.

Ratzel's ***organic theory*** held that a nation, which is an aggregate of organisms (human beings), would itself function and behave as an organism. This was an extreme form of the environmental determinism that was to dominate human geography for decades to come, but it was so speculative that it would probably have soon been forgotten—except that it gave rise to a subfield of political geography called ***geopolitics***. Some of Ratzel's students translated his abstract writings into practical policies, and this led directly to the expansionist Nazi philosophies of the

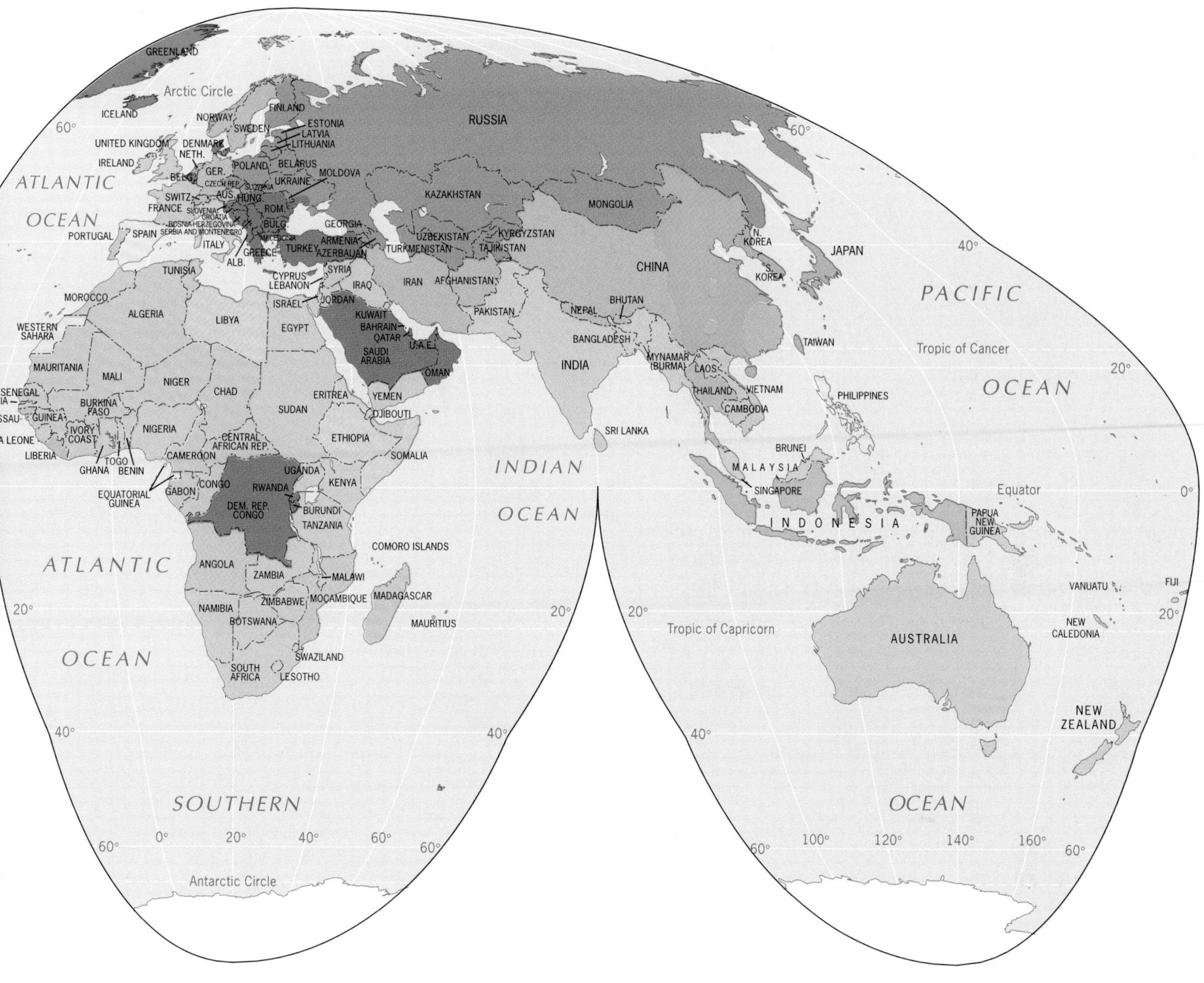

1930s. One of Hitler's associates was a political geographer, Karl Haushofer, who was a strong advocate of geopolitics.

For some decades after World War II, the term "geopolitics" had such negative connotations that few political geographers, even those studying power relationships, would identify themselves as students of geopolitics. Time, along with more balanced perspectives, has reinstated geopolitics as an appropriate name for the study of power relationships past, present, and future.

The Heartland Theory Other geographers trying to find order in the class of Europe's modern evolution were more specific than Ratzel. They linked their conclusions to the fortunes of existing states. Prominent among them was Sir Halford Mackinder (1861–1947). In 1904 he published an article titled "The Geographical Pivot of History" in the Royal Geographical Society's *Geographical Journal.* That article became one of the most intensely debated geographic publications of all time.

Mackinder, too, was concerned with power relationships, at a time when Britain had acquired a global empire through its naval supremacy. To many of his contemporaries, the oceans—avenues of colonial conquest—were the key to world domination, but not to Mackinder. He concluded that a land-based power, not a sea power, would ultimately rule the world. His famous article contained a lengthy appraisal of the largest and most populous landmass on Earth—Eurasia. At the heart of Eurasia, he argued, lay an impregnable, resource-rich "pivot area" extending from Eastern Europe to eastern Siberia (Fig. 26-5). This would

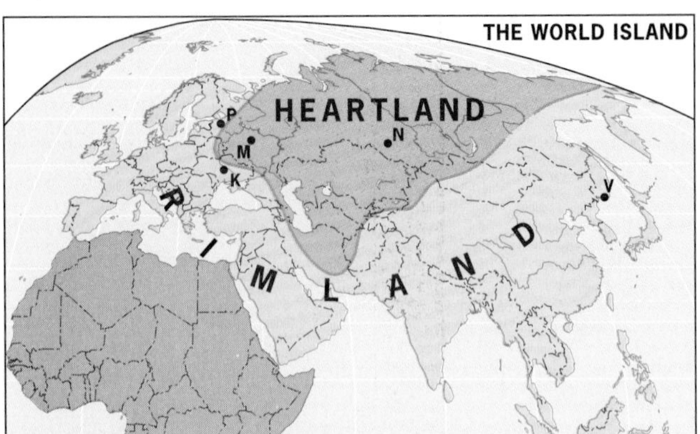

Figure 26-5 Eurasia. Eurasia is a "World Island" divided into Heartland and Rimland.

become the base for world conquest, and the key to it was Eastern Europe.

Mackinder later renamed his "pivot area" the *heartland*, and his notion became known as the ***heartland theory***. In his book *Democratic Ideals and Reality* (1919) he stated the theory as follows:

> Who rules East Europe commands the Heartland
>
> Who rules the Heartland commands the World Island
>
> Who rules the World Island commands the World

When Mackinder proposed his heartland theory, there was little to foretell the rise of a superpower in the heartland. Russia was in disarray. It had lost a war against Japan and was facing revolution. Eastern Europe was fractured. Germany, not Russia, was gaining power. But when the Soviet Union emerged and World War II gave Moscow control over much of Eastern Europe, the heartland theory attracted renewed attention.

The Rimland Theory Not all political geographers agreed with Mackinder's assessment of the heartland. One of Mackinder's critics, Nicholas Spykman, coined a geographic term that is still in use: ***rimland***. Spykman argued that the Eurasian rim, not its heart, held the key to global power. In his book *The Geography of the Peace* (1944) he parodied Mackinder:

> Who controls the Rimland rules Eurasia
>
> Who rules Eurasia controls the destinies of the world

As Figure 26-5 shows, the rimland is a fragmented zone that is unlikely to fall under the sway of one superpower, as the heartland might. Spykman, who was more of a pragmatist than a theorist, saw a divided rimland as a key to the world's balance of power. Today the rimland is still divided, but it encompasses powerful states in Western Europe as well as a potential superpower: China.

A Multipolar World—Again?

In Chapter 35 we return to the topic of global geopolitics, but it is appropriate here to reflect on the evolving power relationships that will shape the world in the twenty-first century. When Mackinder foresaw a world dominated by a single superpower, that notion, too, was revolutionary. The nineteenth century had produced (or was in the process of producing) a large number of states seeking global influence: the United Kingdom, France, Germany, Russia, the United States, and Japan among them. This was a *multipolar* world that was soon engulfed in a global war (1914–1918) and then another (1939–1945). World War I was global as a result of the colonial empires of the combatants; German and Allied forces fought battles in East Africa and elsewhere. World War II was global for additional reasons: it spilled southward and eastward beyond the confines of Europe, and it involved the United States and Japan.

Out of World War II came two newly strengthened powers, the United States and the Soviet Union. The older powers in devastated Europe were losing their colonies and were in political and economic disarray. Although the United States aided Europe through its Marshall Plan and Japan through its enlightened postwar administration, no European or Asian power regained its former status. In the aftermath of World War II there were two clear superpowers. The world was a *bipolar* one divided into capitalist and communist camps. The Soviet Union dominated almost all of the heartland as Mackinder had defined it. The United States proved that Mackinder had underestimated the capacities of lands beyond his "world island" in Eurasia.

In the mid-1990s, after the collapse of the Soviet Union, the United States found itself the only surviving superpower. However, it was constrained by the unprecedented worldwide diffusion of weapons, including nuclear weapons. Briefly after World War II the United States, which used nuclear bombs to end that conflict, was the only state possessing the weapons that could have given it global supremacy. Today it is again the dominant force in world affairs. But this dominance is likely to be short-lived, because the outlines of a new multipolar world are forming.

What are these outlines? Both Mackinder and Spykman might claim that their analyses were correct. A multipolar world is emerging in which the heartland *and* the rimland are represented by power cores. There are four potential superpowers on the "world island:" (1) Russia, in disarray after the collapse of communism but still possessing an enormous military complex and major resources; (2) Europe, if it can find a way to sustain its drive toward integration and unification; (3) China, now energized by the spectacular economic growth of its eastern provinces; and (4) the United States, facing China across a Pacific that has become a highway of trade and diffusion. So the world today resembles that of Mackinder's time, an unstable multipolar world with much potential for conflict.

◆ KEY TERMS ◆

capital city
centrifugal force
centripetal force
colonialism
core area
electoral geography
federal state
forward capital
geopolitics
gerrymander
heartland theory
ministate
multicore state
organic theory
rimland
tribalism
unitary state

◆ APPLYING GEOGRAPHIC KNOWLEDGE ◆

1. Virtually all states confront centrifugal (divisive) forces, some of them more or less permanent, others rising and ebbing over time. Consider the United States or Canada over the past half-century, and identify (a) the centrifugal forces that have affected these countries continuously throughout that period and (b) centrifugal forces that have come and gone, testing the fabric of the state. Have any of these forces threatened the territorial integrity of the two countries?
2. Consider the heartland theory, a century after its publication. Is the kind of power analysis that undergirded Mackinder's construct, which focused on Eurasia as the key to global geopolitics in the future, still relevant today?

Chapter 27

Multinationalism on the Map

From the field notes

"The expanding size and authority of multinational institutions such as the European Union raise fundamental questions for those living in Europe. Should we participate in building a more integrated Europe? Will we lose control over our own affairs if we do? Can we afford not to participate in an era when the power of the state is giving way to the power of multinational arrangements and structures? This truck, parked in the central square of Kalmar, Sweden, during the lead-up to Sweden's EU membership vote, was financed by government and business interests that sought one set of answers to these questions. They won the day in the Swedish vote, but concerns linger about how much sovereignty Sweden should concede in a world simultaneously buffeted by forces of consolidation and fragmentation."

KEY POINTS

◆ **Supranational unions range from global organizations such as the United Nations and its predecessor, the League of Nations, to regional associations such as the European Union. All signify the inadequacy of the state system as a framework for dealing with important issues and problems.**

◆ **Imposition of international sanctions and mobilization of peacekeeping operations are among the functions of the United Nations. Today the UN is active militarily in more than a dozen countries.**

◆ **The United Nations has channeled the extension of national claims over the oceans through its law of the sea.**

◆ **Among many regional multinational associations, the European Union is the most complex and far reaching. Its 15 member states are likely to be joined by others within a decade.**

◆ **Economic, military, cultural, and political forces are affecting the activities of more than 60 major international organizations. Economic prosperity and a shared military threat are the strongest factors promoting international cooperation.**

Ours is a world of contradictions. On television we see Quebecers demanding independence from Canada even as Canada joins the United States in NAFTA (North American Free Trade Agreement). At a soccer game in Scotland, fans drown out "God Save the Queen" with a thunderous rendition of "Flower of Scotland," while in London Parliament debates Britain's entry into the European Monetary Union. At every turn we are reminded of the interconnectedness of nations, states, and regions, yet separatism and calls for autonomy are rampant. In the 1990s we appear to be caught between the forces of division and those of unification.

Despite the conflicts arising from these contradictory forces, today hardly a country exists that is not involved in some multinational association. There is ample proof that such association is advantageous to the partners and that being left out can have serious negative effects on state and nation. In this chapter we look at the geographic dimensions of the progress that has been made toward unity and cooperation.

◆ SUPRANATIONALISM

The phenomenon of interstate cooperation is quite old. In ancient Greece city-states formed leagues to protect and promote mutual benefit. This practice was imitated many centuries later by the cities of Europe's Hanseatic League. But the degree to which this idea has taken root in the modern world is unprecedented. The twentieth century has witnessed the establishment of numerous international associations in political, economic, cultural, and military spheres, giving rise to the term ***supranationalism***.

Technically, supranationalism refers to efforts by three or more states to forge associations for mutual benefit and in pursuit of shared goals. Today there are over 60 major supranational organizations, many of which have subsidiaries that bring the total to more than 100. The more states participate in such multilateral associations, the less likely they are to act alone in pursuit of a self-interest that might put them at odds with neighbors.

International Sanctions

These days we hear a great deal about ***international sanctions*** designed to induce states to change their behavior. Sanctions isolate a country that behaves in a way that is deemed inappropriate by the international community, and such isolation can be very costly. For example, sanctions were implemented against South Africa to put pressure on its minority government to abolish its *apartheid* policies. Foreign firms left South Africa; foreign investment almost dried up. How much the sanctions contributed to the ending of *apartheid* is still debated, but of their impact on the economy there is no doubt. When the government of Haiti defied international demands for the reinstatement of its democratically elected president, sanctions were imposed. When North Korea defied international efforts to inspect its nuclear program, sanctions were threatened. For sanctions to succeed, international agreement is needed, and such agreement itself is evidence of supranationalism.

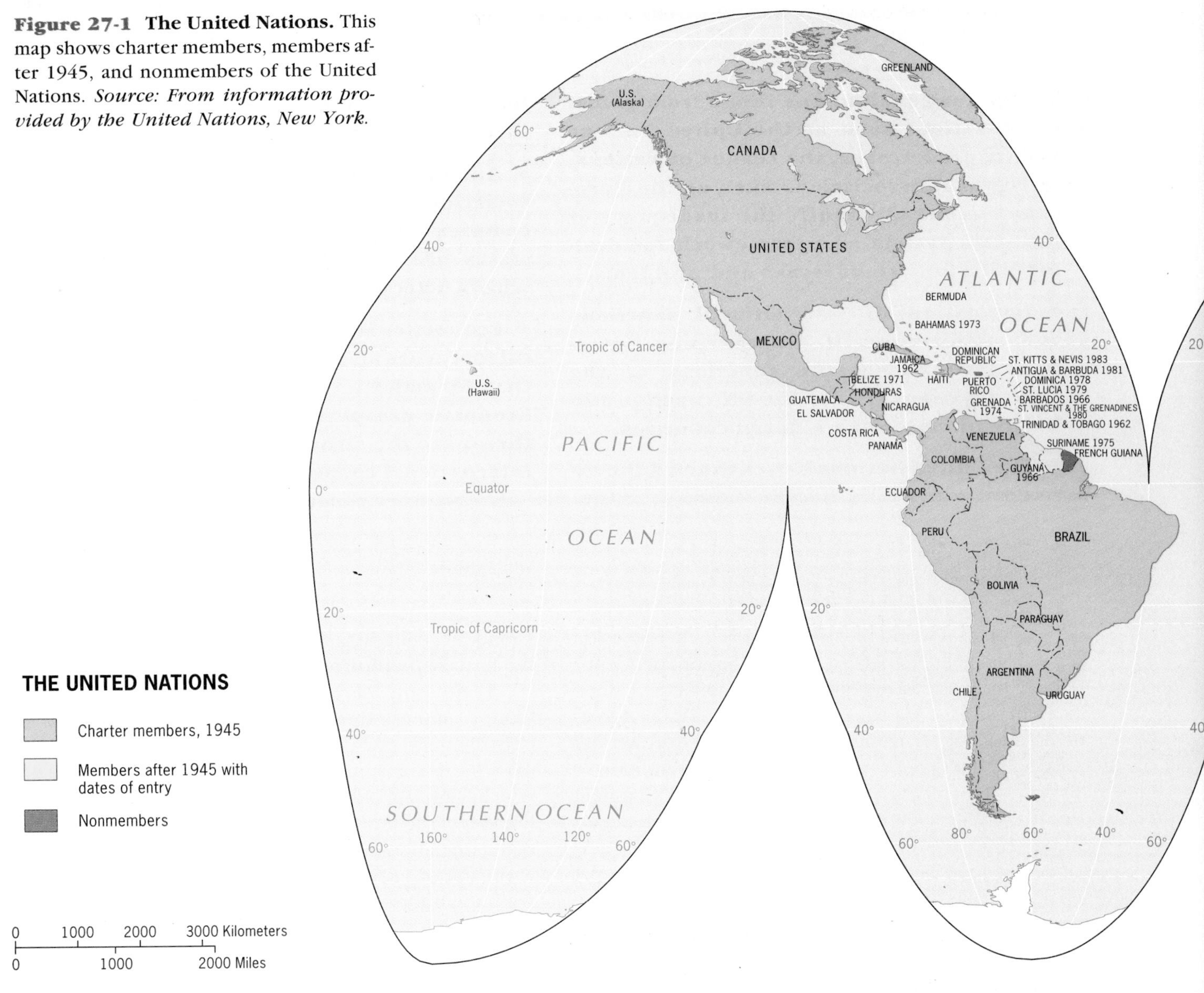

Figure 27-1 The United Nations. This map shows charter members, members after 1945, and nonmembers of the United Nations. *Source: From information provided by the United Nations, New York.*

From League of Nations to United Nations

The modern beginnings of the supranational movement came with the conferences that followed the end of World War I. The concept of an international organization that would include all the states of the world led to the creation of the League of Nations in 1919. The United States, however, was among the countries that did not join this organization. In all, 63 states participated in the League, although the total membership at any single time never reached that number. Costa Rica and Brazil left the League even before 1930; Germany departed in 1933, shortly before the Soviet Union joined in 1934. The League was born of a worldwide desire to prevent future aggression, but the failure of the United States to join dealt the organization a severe blow. In the mid-1930s the League had a major opportunity when Ethiopia's Haile Selassie made a dramatic appeal for help in the face of an invasion by Italy, a member state until 1937. However, the League failed to take action, and in the chaos of the beginning of World War II it collapsed.

Nonetheless, the interwar period witnessed significant progress toward interstate cooperation. The League of Nations spawned other international organizations. Prominent among these was the Permanent Court of International Justice, created to adjudicate legal issues between states, such as boundary disputes and fishing rights.

The League of Nations also initiated international negotiations on maritime boundaries and related as-

pects of the law of the sea. The conferences organized by the League laid the groundwork for the final resolution of this problem decades later.

◆ THE UNITED NATIONS

After the end of World War II a new organization was formed to foster international security and cooperation: the United Nations. Just as the United Nations in many ways was a renewal of the League of Nations, so its International Court of Justice succeeded the Permanent Court of the interwar period.

The representation of countries in the United Nations has been more universal than it was in the League (Fig. 27-1). A handful of states still do not belong to the United Nations, but in 1998 the United Nations had 185 member states (including the People's Republic of China, admitted in 1971). The UN's General Assembly and Security Council have overshadowed the cooperative efforts of numerous less visible but enormously productive subsidiaries, such as the FAO (Food and Agriculture Organization), UNESCO (United Nations Educational, Scientific and Cultural Organization), and WHO (World Health Organization). Membership in these organizations is less complete than in the UN as a whole, but their work has benefited all humanity.

Participation in the United Nations also serves to commit states to internationally approved standards of behavior. Many states still violate the standards, embodied in the UN Charter, but such violations can lead to collective action, for example, in the cases of South Africa, Iraq, and North Korea. It is noteworthy that states, even when censured or subjected to UN-sponsored military action, do not withdraw from the organization. Membership is too valuable to lose; thus national governments develop an understanding of the advantages of international cooperation.

Peacekeeping Operations

The United Nations is not a world government; member states participate voluntarily. Although member states do not formally yield any sovereignty to the UN, they may agree to abide by specific UN decisions, for example, those made by the International Court of Justice or those involving the law of the sea. In recent years individual states have also asked the United Nations to intervene in internal conflicts, monitor elections, and care for refugees.

Among these and numerous other functions, peacekeeping has become a costly and controversial UN responsibility. The United Nations does not have its own armed force; any UN army or police force consists of soldiers assigned to UN duty by member states. This situation can lead to disputes over leadership. A multinational UN army consists of national forces, each commanded by its own officers. These officers, however, are under the command of a UN-appointed general. Disagreements over tactics may cause individual officers to act in ways that do not conform to the UN command. For example, when a UN force consisting of United States, Pakistani, and Italian soldiers attempted to alleviate hunger in Somalia, the mission changed from humanitarian to political—and there were costly disagreements over tactics that led to many casualties among the UN peacekeepers.

Since 1994, UN peacekeeping operations have faced their most difficult challenge in the former Yugoslavia, where a civil war among Serbs, Croats, and Muslims, chiefly in Bosnia, long defied UN efforts to relieve the crisis. Disputes over leadership and tactics weakened a mission that was already overwhelmed by the dimensions of the task. The mission did have positive effects, however. The UN peacekeepers managed to keep the parties to the conflict at bay until U.S. diplomatic intervention, achieved at Dayton, Ohio, in late 1995, produced a revised map of Bosnia. After the Dayton Agreement was signed, a UN peacekeeping force of 60,000, including more than 20,000 American soldiers, implemented the accords and helped rebuild Bosnia's infrastructure. But the potential for failure still exists. Suspicion and hostility among Muslims, Serbs, and Croats persist, resettlement of refugees and political accommodation have not yet been achieved, and war criminals still function as public figures and even as civic leaders in the area.

Despite these problems, the United Nations' peacekeeping role has continued to grow, and its successes have far outweighed its failures. In late 1998, more than 70,000 peacekeepers from some 70 UN member states were serving in Angola, Bosnia, Cyprus, El Salvador, Georgia, Haiti, Kashmir, Lebanon, Liberia, Macedonia, various parts of the Middle East, Rwanda, and Western Sahara. Considering the small size of most UN peacekeeping units and the enormity of their tasks, the organization's peacekeeping function provides major benefits to the international community.

Unrepresented Peoples

In Chapter 25 we noted the plight of stateless nations. Here, too, the United Nations provides an international forum and thus relieves tensions. In 1991 the UN created the Unrepresented Nations and Peoples Organization (UNPO), which by 1998 had 49 members

From the field notes

"Walking through The Hague recently I was attracted by a demonstration in the historic center of the city. Moving closer to find out what was happening, I saw posters of the sort depicted here, protesting the treatment of Kurds in Turkey. As I watched the demonstration, I was reminded of how truly international ethnic conflicts have become. Many are not confined to single countries, or even regions, and the pressure that is exerted from afar can at times be just as significant as that which happens at home."

and 15 applicants. Four former members (Armenia, Estonia, Latvia, and Georgia), having achieved full UN membership, no longer needed UNPO's help.

The roster of UNPO membership, and the appeals that arrive at UNPO's offices from would-be members, form a barometer of the world's political condition. Albanians in Greece, Tatars of the Crimea, Ogoni in Nigeria, the Ka Lahui Hawai'i (Hawai'i's indigenous nation), North Dakota's Lakota Nation, Abkhazians in Georgia, Tibetans under China's rule, Zanzibaris hoping for independence from Tanzania, Basques in Spain, and dozens of other peoples seeking some form of redress or a stronger voice, approach UNPO for assistance.

UNPO cannot by itself solve the problems of stateless or otherwise "unheard" peoples, but it can give them a platform. In addition, UNPO ensures that appeals from its members, applicants, and others are channeled to appropriate agencies and not lost in the UN bureaucracy. In so doing, it has already cleared up misunderstandings and forestalled conflict.

◆ THE LAW OF THE SEA

Another arena in which the United Nations has accomplished much is the ***law of the sea***. As noted earlier, the League of Nations led the way, but the international negotiations were continued under UN auspices until 1982, when a United Nations Convention on the Law of the Sea was achieved.

National claims to adjacent waters (the ***territorial sea***) originated in Europe many centuries ago. A fourteenth-century Italian legal scholar is credited with the first formal proposal that states should be awarded sovereignty over a strip of water next to their coastlines; this proposal led to a lengthy legal debate over the width of that offshore zone. One suggestion was that this width should be determined by the distance a shore-based cannon could fire a cannonball; once within cannon-shot range, a ship would be in territorial waters.

Not surprisingly, various states chose different widths. Western European countries liked a 3-mile territorial sea. (Maritime distances are measured in *nautical miles*; about 1.15 statute mile equals 1 nautical mile.) Scandinavian countries preferred 4 nautical miles. Mediterranean states chose a 6-mile limit.

During the sixteenth and seventeenth centuries, some countries tried to broaden their maritime jurisdictions by closing off large bays with *baselines* (lines drawn across the open mouths of bays) and claiming fishing grounds far from shore. But until the meetings of the League of Nations, territorial seas remained relatively narrow and the open oceans remained open or, to use the technical language, remained "high seas."

The League did get a hint of what lay ahead. The Soviet Union proposed widening the territorial sea to an unheard-of 12 nautical miles, which would mean that many straits could be closed off by the littoral states and that bays up to 24 miles wide could be closed as well. The matter of delimitation—exactly how maritime boundaries should be constructed on the map—also received much attention. In addition, participating states expressed the need for protection against smuggling, pollution, and other threats from the sea (not the least of which was concern over security). But World War II intervened, and no followup conference could be held.

The Truman Proclamation

Even before the newly formed United Nations could address these issues again, a critical event occurred. In September 1945 President Truman issued two proclamations pertaining to territorial waters. The first of these stated that the United States would henceforth regulate fisheries' activities in areas of the high seas adjacent to its coastlines, but that in other respects these maritime regions would continue to function as free and open high seas. The second proclamation had a much greater impact. It announced, in part, that

> the Government of the United States regards the natural resources of the subsoil and seabed of the continental shelf beneath the high seas but contiguous to the coasts of the United States as appertaining to the United States, subject to its jurisdiction and control.

The ***Truman Proclamation***, as this pronouncement has since become known, specified that the United States' jurisdiction over the continental shelf and its contents would be limited to the region within the 600-foot *isobath* (line connecting points of equal depth). It also reconfirmed that the high seas above the continental shelf would remain open.

The Truman Proclamation focused world attention on the potential of the continental shelves. It also underscored the unequal distribution of shelf areas among the world's coastal countries. With its large eastern continental shelf, the United States gained more than 2.5 million square kilometers (900,000 square miles) of offshore territory. Neighboring Mexico, which shares the continental shelf off North America with the United States, was among the better-endowed countries, and it immediately claimed this region for itself. Next Argentina announced, in 1946, that it claimed not only its wide continental shelf but also the waters lying above it. This was a significant step because it closed an enormous area of high seas and designated them territorial waters instead.

Widening Maritime Claims

States without extensive continental shelves now began to follow Argentina's example, claiming as much as 200 miles of territorial sea. In 1947, Chile and Peru took the lead, proclaiming that their seaward boundaries henceforth lay 200 miles into the Pacific Ocean. This had the effect of closing the rich fishing grounds of the Humboldt (Peru) Current to ships of countries other than Chile and Peru. Peru soon confirmed its control over its new maritime sphere by arresting fishing vessels and fining the companies and countries where they were based.

Thus economic motives have been the driving force behind the maritime expansion of coastal states. However, the situation was complicated by the end of the colonial era. After gaining independence, the former colonies could make their own decisions. Not surprisingly, many of them concluded that if narrow territorial waters were advantageous to the colonial powers, wider territorial seas would serve their own interests better. They were encouraged in this thinking by the former Soviet Union and by China, both of which claimed 12 miles when 3 miles was still the general rule.

The UNCLOS Process

This was the chaotic situation facing the first United Nations Conference on the Law of the Sea (UNCLOS I) when it convened in 1958. Although some technical matters were resolved during this meeting, key issues, such as the width of the territorial sea and the exclusive use of fishing grounds, remained unsettled. UNCLOS II met just two years later and it, too, was unsuccessful. But then came UNCLOS III, beginning in 1973 and ending in 1982 with a convention opposed by only four countries (the United States among them) and signed by 157 states within two years of its completion. While the United Nations had not yet established an enforceable law of the sea, it had created a consensus on what that law should contain. The key provisions were the following:

1. ***The Territorial Sea.*** The convention permits states to delimit their territorial seas up to 12 nautical miles (just under 14 statute miles) from their shorelines. State sovereignty in all its forms extends over this zone. Ships of other countries, however, have the right of passage through such territorial seas, so that narrow straits remain open to transit.
2. ***The Exclusive Economic Zone (EEZ).*** The convention recognizes a state's economic rights up to 200 nautical miles (just over 230 statute miles) from shore. Here the coastal state has the right to control exploration and exploitation of natural resources in the water, seabed, and subsoil below. All resources—fish, minerals on the seafloor, oil in the continental shelf—are the property of the coastal state and may be used or sold to foreign interests. If the continental shelf extends beyond 200 nautical miles from shore, the coastal state has exclusive rights to the resources it contains up to 350 nautical miles (400 statute miles) away.

Another provision, this one having to do with the remaining high seas and what lies beneath them, caused the United States not to sign or ratify the UNCLOS III Treaty. According to this clause, mineral resources beneath the high seas constitute a "common heritage of humankind," and their exploitation is subject to UN management. The purpose of this provision was to enable states without any coasts at all to derive some benefit from the Earth's marine resources. (The world's landlocked states are part of a UN group called the "Geographically Disadvantaged States.") The United States and three other countries argued that a UN bureaucracy set up for this purpose might inhibit exploitation of such deep-sea resources by the only countries that could actually mine them, the technologically advanced states.

During the Carter (Democratic) administration the United States played a leading role in UNCLOS III, but the convention was not completed until the Reagan (Republican) administration had taken office. The new administration decided against ratifying the treaty, which cannot become law until one year after 60 states have ratified it. When the Clinton (Democratic) administration came to office, the prospect of ratification improved, and in June 1994, after some modification of the seabed provision, the treaty was accepted.

Median Lines

During the past two decades the UNCLOS III Treaty's provisions have been generally adopted in international relations. Figure 27-2 shows the effect of the 200-mile EEZ on the high seas: huge expanses of ocean have been assigned to coastal countries, some of them mere specks of islands.

What happens when countries lie closer than 400 nautical miles to each other, so that neither can have a full 200-mile EEZ? In such cases (for example, in the Caribbean, North, Baltic, and Mediterranean Seas) the ***median-line principle*** takes effect. States on opposite coasts divide the waters separating them, creating an intricate system of maritime boundaries. Often such boundaries cross resource-rich zones, for example, in the North Sea between Norway and Britain, and allocational boundary disputes may arise as a result.

The effect of EEZ and median-line calculations can

be seen on a map of Southeast Asia (Fig. 27-3), which also reminds us that the UNCLOS III Treaty may represent broad consensus but cannot prevent disputes. The South China Sea, in particular, is a problematic maritime region. The black line shows China's share of the South China Sea based on its possession of numerous small islands there, including the Paracels. The red line represents China's published claims to the region, based on "historic" association with it. A key geographic element is the Spratly Islands, which are potentially rich in oil and are claimed by China and *five* other states.

This type of problem, however, is the exception, not the rule. The UN-sponsored conferences that led to the 1982 treaty rank among the great achievements of international diplomacy and stand as an example of what can be accomplished when states choose to cooperate for the common good.

From the field notes

"As we sailed from the port of Invergordon, Scotland, we could see a row of oil-drilling platforms under construction, in repair, or being towed out into the North Sea. The shallow, oil- and gas-rich North Sea subsoil has made it necessary to divide this maritime region through median lines. The wealth of energy resources off the Scottish coast has been a factor in the rise of Scottish nationalism and notions of greater autonomy or even independence."

◆ REGIONAL MULTINATIONAL UNIONS

The League of Nations and the United Nations are global manifestations of a phenomenon that is expressed even more strongly at the regional level. This century has been a period of growing cultural-regional awareness and assertiveness and intensifying economic competition. States have begun to join together to further their shared political ideologies, economic objectives, and strategic goals. In 1998 there were more than 60 such ***multinational unions***, many of them with subsidiaries focusing on particular issues or areas. Today, interstate cooperation is so widespread around the world that a new era has clearly arrived.

The first major experiments in interstate cooperation were undertaken in Europe, with the Netherlands, Belgium, and Luxembourg leading the way. It had long been thought that all three might benefit from mutual agreements that would reduce the divisiveness of their political boundaries. Certainly, they have much in common. Residents of northern Belgium speak Flemish, which is very close to Dutch, and residents of Luxembourg speak French, as do those of southern Belgium. Even more important, these countries complement one another economically. Dutch farm products are sold on Belgian markets, and Belgian industrial goods go to the Netherlands and Luxembourg. Would it not be reasonable to create common tariffs and eliminate import licenses and quotas? Representatives of the three countries thought so. Even before the end of World War II they met in London to sign an agreement of cooperation, creating what came to be known as ***Benelux***. Other European countries watched the experiment with great interest, and soon there was talk of larger economic unions.

This movement proved to be crucial to the reconstruction of postwar Europe, and it was given an enormous boost in 1947 when U.S. Secretary of State George Marshall proposed that the United States finance a European recovery program. A committee representing 16 Western European states plus (then) West Germany presented the U.S. Congress with a joint program for economic rehabilitation, and Congress approved it. From 1948 to 1952 the United States gave Europe about $12 billion under what became known as the Marshall Plan. This investment not only revived European national economies, with American encouragement, but it also spurred a movement toward cooperation among European states.

Toward European Union

Out of that original committee of 16 was born the Organization for European Economic Cooperation

(OEEC), and this body in turn gave rise to other cooperative organizations. Soon after the OEEC was established, France proposed the creation of a European Coal and Steel Community (ECSC) with the goal of lifting the restrictions and obstacles that impeded the flow of coal, iron ore, and steel among the mainland's six primary producers: France, West Germany, Italy, and the three Benelux countries. This proposal was also implemented, but the six participants did not stop there. Gradually, through negotiations and agreement, they enlarged their sphere of cooperation to include reductions and even eliminations of certain tariffs and a freer flow of labor, capital, and nonsteel commodities. This led, in 1958, to the creation of the European Economic Community (EEC), also called the ***Common Market***.

The success of the EEC induced other countries to apply for membership. Denmark, Ireland, and the United Kingdom (which had initially declined to participate and formed EFTA, the European Free Trade Agreement) joined in 1973, Greece in 1981, and Spain and Portugal in 1986. The organization became known as the ***European Community*** (EC) because it was seen not only as an economic union but, in effect, as a future United States of Europe. By the late 1980s the EC had 12 members: the three giants (Germany, France, and the United Kingdom); the four southern countries (Italy, Spain, Portugal, and Greece); and the five small states (the Netherlands, Belgium, Luxembourg, Denmark, and Ireland). These 12 members initiated a program of cooperation and unification that led to the formal establishment of a ***European Union*** (EU) in 1992. Subsequently, Austria, Sweden, and Finland joined the EU, bringing the total number of members to 15 (Fig. 27-4).

Under the EU's unification program, member states yield more power to the Union's central authority. Not all member countries were equally supportive

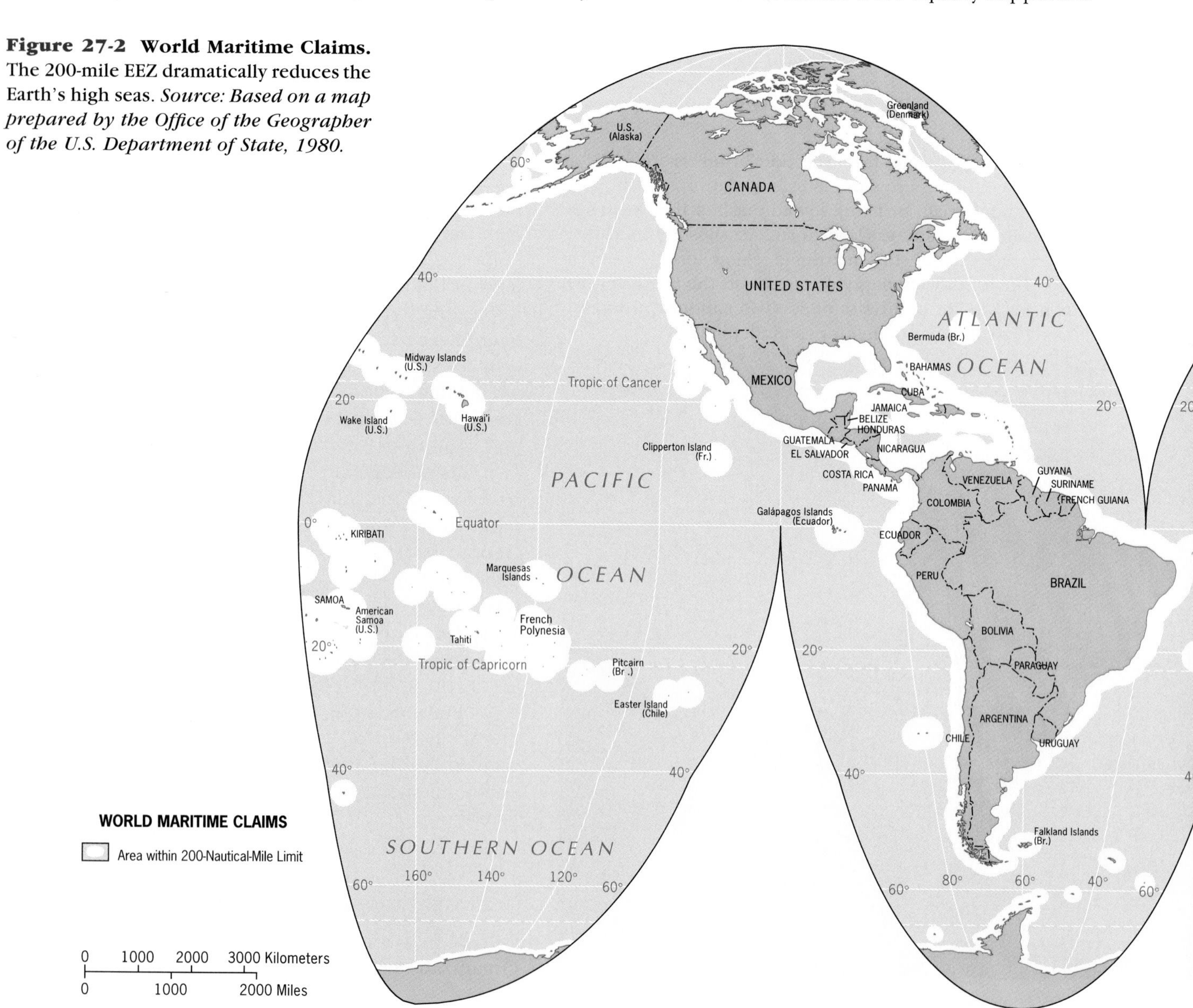

Figure 27-2 World Maritime Claims. The 200-mile EEZ dramatically reduces the Earth's high seas. *Source: Based on a map prepared by the Office of the Geographer of the U.S. Department of State, 1980.*

of this plan. A major stumbling block was money: if the European Union were to have a single currency, other currencies would eventually have to be abandoned. Imagine France without its franc, the United Kingdom without its pound, and Germany without its mark! Many voters in the member countries were reluctant to let go of such national symbols; others did not wish to see their national parliaments subservient to that of the European Union. But the program of unification continued, and in the late 1990s the EU was preparing for the establishment of a single currency—the Euro. Not all EU member states will be party to the Euro in its early years, but it is likely to be an increasingly important, if potentially controversial, element of Europe's integration process.

The Future of European Supranationalism The formation of the European Union is the most significant development of its kind in the world today. At the same time, it is a difficult process in which the anticipated advantages are increasingly being weighed against the loss of local autonomy that sometimes follows. Moreover, integration often requires painful adjustments because of the diversity of the European states. For example, agricultural practices and policies have always varied widely. Yet some general policy must govern agriculture throughout the European Union if the EU is to have real meaning. Individual states have found these adjustments problematic, and the EU parliament has had to devise policies that accommodate regional contrasts and delays in implementation.

Another concern is Germany's dominant position in the European Union. Germany is by far the most populous and economically powerful of the EU's members and will undoubtedly dominate the Union's politics as well. Memories of two world wars and fears of German dominance are potential centrifugal forces in the European Union. The Union is a patchwork of

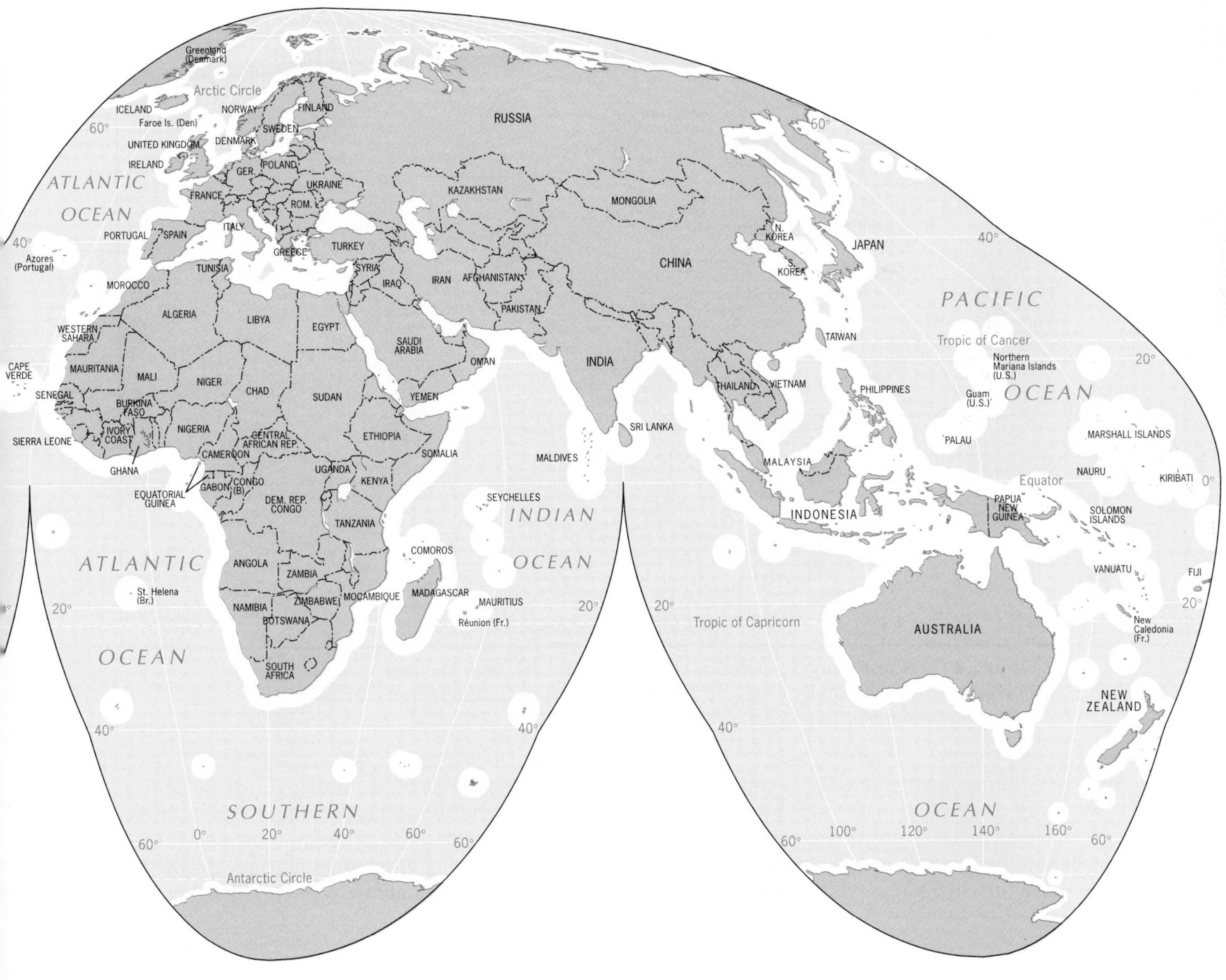

Figure 27-3 Conflicting Maritime Claims in Southeast Asia. The potential for conflict over maritime claims in the seas of Southeast Asia remains strong. *Source: From U.N., U.S., and Chinese maps as well as press reports.*

states with many different ethnic traditions and histories of conflict and competition. Economic success and growing well-being tend to submerge such differences, but should the Union face difficult economic or social times, these divisive forces will emerge again.

Such concerns have created strong division over EU membership in some member states, especially the United Kingdom. Whereas other countries have held referendums allowing all eligible citizens to vote on participation (Denmark at first voted no, then yes in a second round), the issue was not put to a vote in Britain. Some polls suggest that British voters would pull out of the EU, but the decision has been left to the Parliament. There, EU membership is supported by the majority, but the Conservative government of the early 1990s resisted most initiatives designed to promote greater integration. The Labor government of the late 1990s took a more conciliatory view toward a strengthened EU, but the integration concept continues to divide rather than unite the British people.

Expansion Still another problematic issue is the desire of many countries to join the Union at some future time. As long as these potential members are economically strong and politically stable, this does not pose a major problem. But as the EU expands eastward, perhaps someday including such states as Slovakia and Bulgaria and possibly Turkey, there will be powerful strains on the organization.

In late 1997, the EU authorized the initiation of membership negotiations with six prospective mem-

Figure 27-4 European Supranationalism. This map shows how the European states have aligned with supranationalist organizations.

A SENSE OF SCALE:

"Euroregions"

Economic globalization and suprastate nationalism are altering the political geographic context of local places as well as affecting the traditional functions and role of the state in Europe. Consider the situation in southwestern Poland, near the German and Czech borders. For decades the citizens of this region lived in an area dominated by Warsaw, although they were situated right across the border from then-communist East Germany and Czechoslovakia—countries that belonged to the same economic and political bloc as Poland. Yet, transboundary contact was not extensive, and planning decisions were made separately in the border regions of each country.

Since the collapse of communism, the political geographic situation has fundamentally changed. Anxious to encourage external investment and to take advantage of programs promoting transnational cooperation, local authorities in southwestern Poland began actively pursuing cross-boundary cooperation with their counterparts in adjacent parts of Germany and the Czech Republic. They soon succeeded in achieving "Euroregion" status for the transboundary region. ***Euroregions*** are formal entities designed to promote cooperation and reduce inequalities across international boundaries in Europe. The so-called Neisse Euroregion was created in the Polish-German-Czech border region in 1991. Plagued by some serious environmental problems—it is sometimes referred to as the Black Triangle—the Euroregion has paved the way for transboundary cooperation on environmental initiatives. In addition, a coordinated strategy has developed in the Neisse Euroregion to attract investment and encourage economic development. Poles, Germans, and Czechs in the region also engage in various forms of cross-border cultural activities (for example, music competitions) and sporting events (for example, track and field and soccer matches).

These developments have clearly transformed the political geography of the Polish-German-Czech border region. Most obviously, the inhabitants of the region no longer see themselves as living in an area fundamentally fragmented by national boundaries. Not only have new institutions emerged that link peoples and activities on different sides of the border, but also governmental authorities in Warsaw, Berlin/Bonn, and Prague have themselves encouraged the Euroregion initiative. With region-wide coordinated plans being developed to deal with matters ranging from land-use planning to historic preservation to enhancing the communications infrastructure, it is increasingly clear that the political geographic context of the Polish-German-Czech border region is no longer defined largely in terms of the map of so-called sovereign states.

Euroregions. The Neisse Euroregion is but one of many that lie along Poland's boundaries, as shown in this map of existing and developing Euroregions around Poland. *Source:* PANORAMA EUROREGIONÓW/THE PANORAMIC OF EUROREGIONS, *Statistical Office of Jelenia Góra, Poland, 1997 p. 59.*

bers: Estonia, Poland, the Czech Republic, Hungary, Slovenia, and Cyprus. Other Eastern European states are hoping to follow their lead. Under the rules of the EU, the richer countries must subsidize (provide fixed subsidies to) the poorer ones; therefore the entry of Eastern European states will add to the burden this rule imposes on the wealthier Western and Northern European members. But an even more difficult problem will involve Turkey. Some Western Europeans would like to see Turkey join the EU, thereby widening the organization's reach into the Muslim world. Turkey has indicated its interest in joining, but a referendum in Greece showed that more than 90 percent of voters there are opposed to Turkey's admission. Other EU members have expressed concern over Turkey's human rights record, specifically its treatment of the Kurdish minority, which would not meet the standards set by the Union. Behind these claims lies an unspoken sense among many that Turkey is not "European" enough to warrant membership. In early 1998, Turkey's hopes for membership were dashed by the EU's decision to consider and prioritize all applications—except Turkey's.

Even as the debate over expansion goes on, the center of the EU is experiencing other stresses. Many of the goals set during a key meeting in the Dutch town of Maastricht in 1992 are proving to be elusive; enthusiasm for the Union is fading in key countries, notably France. But progress toward supranational goals tends to be cyclical. Visions of a political United States of Europe may be sustained by the maturing of a European Parliament and the designation of a European capital (Brussels or Strasbourg), but progress toward European unification continues to depend on economics. When economic times are good, supranationalism flourishes. And until recently, Europe (especially the old EEC countries) prospered. When times became more difficult, so did the path toward unification.

Supranationalism Elsewhere

The notion of international association for mutual benefit is a worldwide phenomenon. As noted earlier, the EU originated in efforts to reduce economic barriers. Economic motives also lay behind the formation of the original North American Free Trade Agreement (NAFTA), formalized on January 1, 1994, which linked Canada, the United States, and Mexico in an economic community. The goals of NAFTA, however, are far more modest than those of the European Union—partly because the economic disparities between the United States and Mexico are much greater than those between EU member states. The lowering and eventual elimination of trade barriers is but one of the many goals of the EU; others include free movement of labor, a common currency, and even a coordinated foreign policy. NAFTA has no comparable financial or political dimensions, and it does not look forward to a NAFTA parliament or a single monetary unit.

Nevertheless, supranationalism is active in the Americas. The majority of the Caribbean island-states, with Belize in Middle America and Guyana in South America, are linked in the Caribbean Community (CARICOM), an evolving common market in the region. In the late 1990s CARICOM was growing into an organization called the Association of Caribbean States (ACS), which included not just Belize and Guyana but all interested states around the edge of the Caribbean. Also developing is the Central American Common Market, with seven members extending from Guatemala to Panama.

In South America, two major supranational groups are developing: the Andean Group and the Southern Cone Community Market (MERCOSUR). The Andean Group links together Venezuela, Colombia, Ecuador, Peru, and Bolivia, and hopes to achieve shared economic objectives through open markets. The second group, MERCOSUR, consists of giant Brazil, powerful Argentina, comparatively prosperous Uruguay, and developing Paraguay. Chile and Bolivia may join MERCOSUR, which is on track to become a full-fledged customs union (eliminating customs charges on goods moving between them) early in the twenty-first century.

Economic objectives also were the key to the formation of ECOWAS, the Economic Community of West African States. With far fewer fiscal assets than most multinational organizations and many divisive forces in the region, ECOWAS nonetheless supports economic cooperation and integration, joint development efforts, and a reduction in tariff and other barriers in West Africa. It played an important role when Liberia was engulfed in civil war in 1990. Several West African states organized a multinational peacekeeping force and sent it to Liberia, thus helping to end this costly conflict.

So numerous are the various economic unions that they clearly represent a new force on the world map. From APEC (Asia-Pacific Economic Council) to CIS (Commonwealth of Independent States, an attempt to reintegrate the former republics of the USSR), countries are joining, treaties are being drawn up, and new associations are emerging. Not all of these alliances are successful, of course; OPEC, the cartel of oil exporting states, has lost the advantages it once held. But economic supranationalism is a sign of the times, a grand experiment still in progress.

Other Forms of Supranationalism

The main motives for supranational cooperation are economic, but they are not the only ones. Often the formation of one supranational union stimulates the creation of another (either a rival or a cooperative one). The development of economic supranationalism in Europe was paralleled by the formation of a ***military alliance***, the North Atlantic Treaty Organization (NATO). This, in turn, led to the creation of the Warsaw Treaty, which combined the USSR and its Eastern European satellites into an opposing military alliance. Today the Warsaw Treaty is defunct, and NATO is expanding eastward into the former Soviet sphere. In 1997 Poland, the Czech Republic, and Hungary were admitted to the alliance, and Romania and Slovenia, whose applications were denied, appeared likely to be invited in the next round.

The growth of NATO in the former Soviet sphere

is of major concern to Russia, where this has become a leading political issue. Russia's sense of encirclement on the Eurasian landmass has always been a factor in Russian nationalism. NATO's expansion is therefore touching sensitive nerves there despite official acceptance of the process. Future Russian governments may not be so cooperative, especially if NATO invites the Baltic states to join.

Like economic unions, military alliances come and go. Among those that no longer exist are the Baghdad Pact, a Western-oriented alliance of Middle Eastern states, and SEATO (Southeast Asia Treaty Organization). Both alliances were dissolved in response to changing national policies.

Military alliances are especially significant because they normally require member states to allow other members' forces to establish bases and facilities on their territory, which involves surrendering some sovereignty. This is a more significant dimension of supranationalism than economic cooperation; military forces symbolize power and intrusion, and their presence on foreign territory can be a sensitive matter.

Other supranational organizations are based on *cultural* objectives, although the distinction between cultural and political goals is sometimes blurred. The Organization of African Unity (OAU) is often described as a cultural alliance to promote shared goals and resolve disputes, but the OAU also has clear political objectives (among which was the ending of *apartheid* in South Africa). Most African states are members of the OAU. Another ***cultural organization*** with political overtones is the Arab League, a multinational alliance of Muslim states in North Africa and Southwest Asia. Founded in 1945, it is still a major force in regional affairs, although it has been weakened by the divisions created by the Gulf War.

Some supranational organizations are primarily *political.* Europe's Parliament is the political manifestation of the EU's overall unification effort. Without economic underpinnings, though, ***political unions*** tend to be short-lived or inconsequential. The Commonwealth of Nations (successor to the British Commonwealth) is little more than a relic of Britain's imperial past, its economic benefits weakened by the United Kingdom's involvement in the European Union. The French Community has also lost much of its political relevance. The Federation of the West Indies is long forgotten. Nothing in the political arena matches the economic unions functioning today.

The many manifestations of supranationalism all point to one important reality: the sovereign state alone cannot meet all the needs of its people in modern times. We still recognize the state as the most significant unit of political-geographical organization, since states are still the principal actors in the international arena. All over the world, however, states are joining supranational unions to further economic, strategic, or other aims. This situation reflects a loss of confidence in the state as the bastion of security and prosperity. Has the state system run its course and will something else replace it? It is too early to tell, but the answer depends on the ability of existing institutions to deal with the myriad social, environmental, and political forces remaking the world—the subject of the last two parts of this book.

◆ KEY TERMS ◆

Benelux
Common Market
cultural organization
European Community
European Union
Euroregions
Exclusive Economic Zone (EEZ)
international sanctions
law of the sea
median-line principle
military alliance
multinational union
political union
supranationalism
territorial sea
Truman Proclamation

◆ APPLYING GEOGRAPHIC KNOWLEDGE ◆

1. The lengthy process that has led to the formation of the still-expanding European Union often is cited as the most significant example of supranationalism in world history. How does the EU compare to NAFTA in terms of social, economic, and political geography?
2. The United Nations has managed to control and channel many conflicts that might otherwise have had serious consequences. One of these involved the world's oceans and seas: a United Nations Law of the Sea now exists. One feature of UNCLOS regulations is the so-called Exclusive Economic Zone (EEZ). How has the EEZ functioned to expand as well as inhibit states' maritime activities? What has been the impact on marine resources?

Part Eight
THE POLITICAL IMPRINT

At Issue: Revisited

Can Europe create a powerful economic/political union despite concerns about economic and political centralization? Can Russia overcome economic trauma and corruption to emerge as a major world power once again? Can China create the political and social institutions that can foster sustained growth and unity? There are multiple obstacles to the creation of a stable, multipolar international order. These do not relate solely to international difficulties faced by Europe, Russia, and China in a quest for superpower status. Creating new superpowers also ushers in new international issues and problems. The establishment of a strong European currency could pit the United States against Europe in a destabilizing international fiscal confrontation that some believe could lead to a global depression. The rise of a strong Russia could raise serious concerns among neighbors who have only recently extracted themselves from the Soviet shadow. The ideological gap between the United States and China, which has been overlooked for a time in pursuit of economic interests, could once again come to the fore as China's regional and global influence broadens. All of this suggests that the end of the Cold War did not signal the end to large-scale threats to stability. Instead, one of the critical challenges for the twenty-first century will be to manage changing global power relations through peaceful channels.

◆ SELECTED BIBLIOGRAPHY ◆

Part Eight THE POLITICAL IMPRINT

Agnew, J. A. *Place and Politics: The Geographical Mediation of State and Society* (Boston: Allen & Unwin, 1987).

Agnew, J. A., ed. *Political Geography: A Reader* (London: Arnold, 1997).

Anderson, J., Brook, C., & Cochrane, A., eds. *A Global World?: Re-ordering Political Space* (Oxford, U.K.: Oxford University Press, 1995).

Ardrey, R. *The Territorial Imperative* (New York: Atheneum, 1966).

Barakat, H. *The Arab World: Society, Culture, and State* (Berkeley: University of California Press, 1993).

Barton, J. R. *A Political Geography of Latin America* (London: Routledge, 1997).

Boateng, E. A. *A Political Geography of Africa* (Cambridge, U.K.: Cambridge University Press, 1978).

Booth, J. A., & Walker, T. W. *Understanding Central America* (Boulder, Colo.: Westview Press, 2nd ed., 1993).

Boyd, A. *An Atlas of World Affairs* (New York: Routledge, 9th ed., 1992).

Cohen, L. J. *Broken Bonds: The Rise and Fall of Yugoslavia* (Boulder, Colo.: Westview Press, 1993).

Crossette, B. *India: Facing the Twenty-first Century* (Bloomington: Indiana University Press, 1993).

Davidson, B. *The Black Man's Burden: Africa and the Curse of the Nation-State* (New York: Times Books/Random House, 1992).

Dawson, A. H. *The Geography of European Integration: A Common European Home?* (New York: Belhaven, 1993).

Demko, G. J., & Wood, W. B., eds. *Reordering the World: Geopolitical Perspectives on the Twenty-first Century* (Boulder, Colo.: Westview Press, 1994).

Dink, N., & Karatnycky, A. *New Nations Rising: The Fall of the Soviets and the Challenge of Independence* (New York: John Wiley & Sons, 1993).

Esposito, J. L. *The Islamic Threat: Myth or Reality?* (New York: Oxford University Press, 1992).

Finkelstein, N. *The Separation of Quebec and the Constitution of Canada* (North York, Ontario: York University Centre for Public Law and Public Policy, 1992).

Freeman-Grenville, G.S.P. *The New Atlas of African History* (New York: Simon & Schuster, 1991).

Glassner, M. I. *Neptune's Domain: A Political Geography of the Sea* (Boston: Unwin Hyman, 1990).

Glassner, M. I. *Political Geography* (New York: John Wiley & Sons, 2nd ed., 1996).

Hancock, M. D., & Welsh, H., eds. *German Unification: Process and Outcomes* (Boulder, Colo.: Westview Press, 1993).

Held, C. C. *Middle East Patterns: Places, Peoples, and Politics* (Boulder, Colo.: Westview Press, 2nd ed., 1993).

Johnston, R. J. *Geography and the State: An Essay in Political Geography* (New York: St. Martin's Press, 1983).

Johnston, R. J., Knight, D. B., & Kofman, E., eds. *Nationalism, Self-Determination, and Political Geography* (New York: Croom & Helm, 1988).

Johnston, R. J., Shelley, F. M., & Taylor, P. J. *Developments in Electoral Geography* (New York: Routledge, 1990).

Lewis, R. A., ed. *Geographic Perspectives on Soviet Central Asia* (New York: Routledge, 1992).

Mackinder, H. J. *Democratic Ideals and Reality: A Study in the Politics of Reconstruction* (New York: Holt, 1919).

Mackinder, H. J. "The Geographical Pivot of History." *Geographical Journal* 23 (1904), pp. 421–444.

Mikesell, M. A., & Murphy, A. B. "A Framework for Comparative Study of Minority-Group Aspirations." *Annals of the Association of American Geographers* 81 (4) (1991), pp. 581–604.

Muir, R. *Political Geography: A New Introduction* (New York: John Wiley & Sons, 1997).

Muni, S. D. *Pangs of Proximity: India and Sri Lanka's Ethnic Crisis* (Newbury Park, Calif.: Sage Publications, 1993).

Murphy, A. B. "The Sovereign State System as Political-Territorial Ideal: Historical and Contemporary Considerations." In T. Biersteker & C. Weber, eds., *State Sovereignty as Social Construct* (Cambridge: Cambridge University Press, 1996), pp. 81–120.

Nahaylo, B., & Swoboda, V. *Soviet Disunion: A History of the Nationalities Problem in the USSR* (New York: Free Press, 1990).

Nijman, J. *The Geopolitics of Power and Conflict: Superpowers in the International System, 1945–1992* (London: Belhaven, 1993).

O'Loughlin, J. V., & Van der Wusten, H., eds. *The New Political Geography of Eastern Europe* (New York: Belhaven/Wiley, 1993).

Painter, J. *Politics, Geography, and 'Political Geography': A Critical Perspective* (London: Arnold, 1995).

Prescott, J.R.V. *Political Frontiers and Boundaries* (London: Allen & Unwin, 1987).

Ratzel, F. "Laws of the Spatial Growth of States." In R. E. Kasperson & J. Minghi, eds., *The Structure of Political Geography*, translated by R. L. Bolin (Chicago: Aldine, 1969).

Robinson, K. W. "Sixty Years of Federation in Australia," *Geographical Review* 51 (1961), pp. 1–20.

Rumley, D., & Minghi, J. V., eds. *The Geography of Border Landscapes* (New York: Routledge, 1991).

Sack, R. D. *Human Territoriality: Its Theory and History* (Cambridge: Cambridge University Press, 1986).

Spykman, N. J. *The Geography of the Peace* (New York: Harcourt, Brace, 1944).

Stoessinger, J. *The Might of Nations* (New York: Random House, 1961).

Taylor, P. *Political Geography: World-Economy, Nation-State, and Locality* (New York: John Wiley & Sons, 3rd ed., 1993).

Taylor, P. J., ed. *Political Geography of the Twentieth Century: A Global Analysis* (New York: Halsted Press, 1993).

Van Dyke, J. M., et al. *Freedom for the Seas in the 21st Century: Ocean Governance and Environmental Harmony* (Washington, D.C.: Island Press, 1993).

Vasciannie, S. C. *Landlocked and Geographically Disadvantaged States in the International Law of the Sea* (New York: Oxford University Press, 1990).

William, C. H., ed. *The Political Geography of the New World Order* (New York: Halsted Press, 1993).

Part Nine

SOCIAL GEOGRAPHIES OF THE MODERN WORLD

At Issue

Ours is a world divided by differences in people's health and well-being, as well as by race, ethnicity, and gender. We are all too familiar with large-scale economic differences, which profoundly influence patterns of food consumption and access to health care. Yet the social divisions created by societies also affect the lives and livelihoods of the world's peoples. Some groups have used differences in physical appearance to justify discrimination and even murder.

Will her life change for the better? Saigon, Vietnam.

Ethnic conflicts have caused enormous loss of life in recent decades. Gender-based inequalities are evident not just in the economic and social constraints still present for women in our own society; in some places they even result in female infanticide and the merciless exploitation of girls. At issue: ***Can the smaller world created by transport, information, and communication technologies help overcome some of these divisions?***

Part Outline

Chapter 28

A Geography of Nutrition

From the field notes

"We watched the small fleet of fishing boats return from the North Sea to the port of Oslo, and talked to the crews. Every one of them complained that catches "these days" were small, a fraction of those of a decade ago. Prices are higher now, but this would not compensate for the loss of volume, said this fisherman. I had heard the same refrain in Scotland, Portugal, Canada, Sri Lanka, and elsewhere. Time after time on the high seas, I saw huge fleets of high-tech fishing boats complete with "factory ships" where catches are processed and prepared for canning. Marine food webs are disrupted by overfishing, and a critical food resource is endangered."

KEY POINTS

◆ Daily calorie consumption varies from high levels in the richer countries such as the United States and Canada, European states, Japan, and Australia to very low levels in poorer countries in Africa. The overall situation, however, has improved markedly over the past two decades.

◆ The Green Revolution, which resulted in the development of higher-yielding, faster-growing types of rice, wheat, and some other cereals, has had far greater effect in Asia and the Americas than in Africa.

◆ Malnutrition occurs even within many of the better-nourished countries, where pockets of poverty still exist.

◆ Although global food production is sufficient to feed the world's people (if it were evenly distributed), concerns are rising that a food emergency may develop as a result of population growth, climate change, and energy costs.

◆ The mitigation of a future food crisis depends on policies and practices ranging from family planning and women's rights to improvement of distribution systems and expansion of farmlands.

Although continued rapid growth is propelling the world's population beyond the 6 billion mark, newspaper headlines no longer warn of any threats to the global food supply. Just two decades ago, predictions of regional famines in countries with large populations and high growth rates regularly made the headlines and the evening news. And these warnings seemed to have a sound basis: population growth was outpacing the Earth's capacity to provide enough food, let alone distribute it where it was most needed. Only a miracle could save the planet, it was thought.

Then the miracle happened—in the form of ***miracle rice*** and other high-yielding grains developed by technicians working in agricultural research stations. Crop yields rose dramatically, especially in Asia's paddies but also on wheat fields throughout the world. As fast as the world's population grew, food production grew faster, and the gap between demand and supply narrowed. India, long dependent on food imports, managed to feed itself. In China the threat of famine receded. Even Bangladesh came close to self-sufficiency.

But is the threat really gone? Not according to some of those who raised the alarm many years ago. In their book *Full House* (1994), Lester Brown and Hal Kane argue that 90 million people will be added to the world's population each year, bringing the total to nearly 9 billion by 2030, and that world grain output will not keep pace. They predict that grain production will increase by only about 370 million tons over the next four decades, far below the rate of increase in the 1980s. This will mean that population growth will once again outstrip food supplies, leading to crises in Subsaharan Africa, South Asia, and China. Brown and Kane suggest that the recent narrowing of the food gap, followed by the widening they predict, forms a cycle that will periodically threaten human survival.

Grain production will not expand as rapidly as in the recent past, according to Brown and Kane, because there are signs that the so-called ***Green Revolution*** (the introduction of new, more productive strains of grain and the resulting harvest increases) has run its course. In Japan, for example, production of rice rose rapidly to 4.7 tons per hectare (1.9 tons per acre) by 1984 but has not increased at all since then. In India, there is evidence that the fertilizers needed to grow the more productive types of grain are losing their effectiveness. Another concern is water: future shortages would lead to smaller harvests. And then there is the loss of farmland to urbanization. All this will lead to a substantial decline in the amount of grain available per person, reviving the threat of widespread malnutrition or worse.

Not all observers see the situation this bleakly. Experts at the United Nations and the World Bank who monitor world food production say that global grain production continues to increase at a healthy pace and shows no sign of slowing down. Japan's experience, they suggest, is due to special circumstances and does not represent the worldwide picture.

There is more to the issue than supply alone. Food availability is also a matter of geography. Whether or not supply was adequate (as measured in global terms), there have always been—and still are—people who are deprived of food. To a large extent this de-

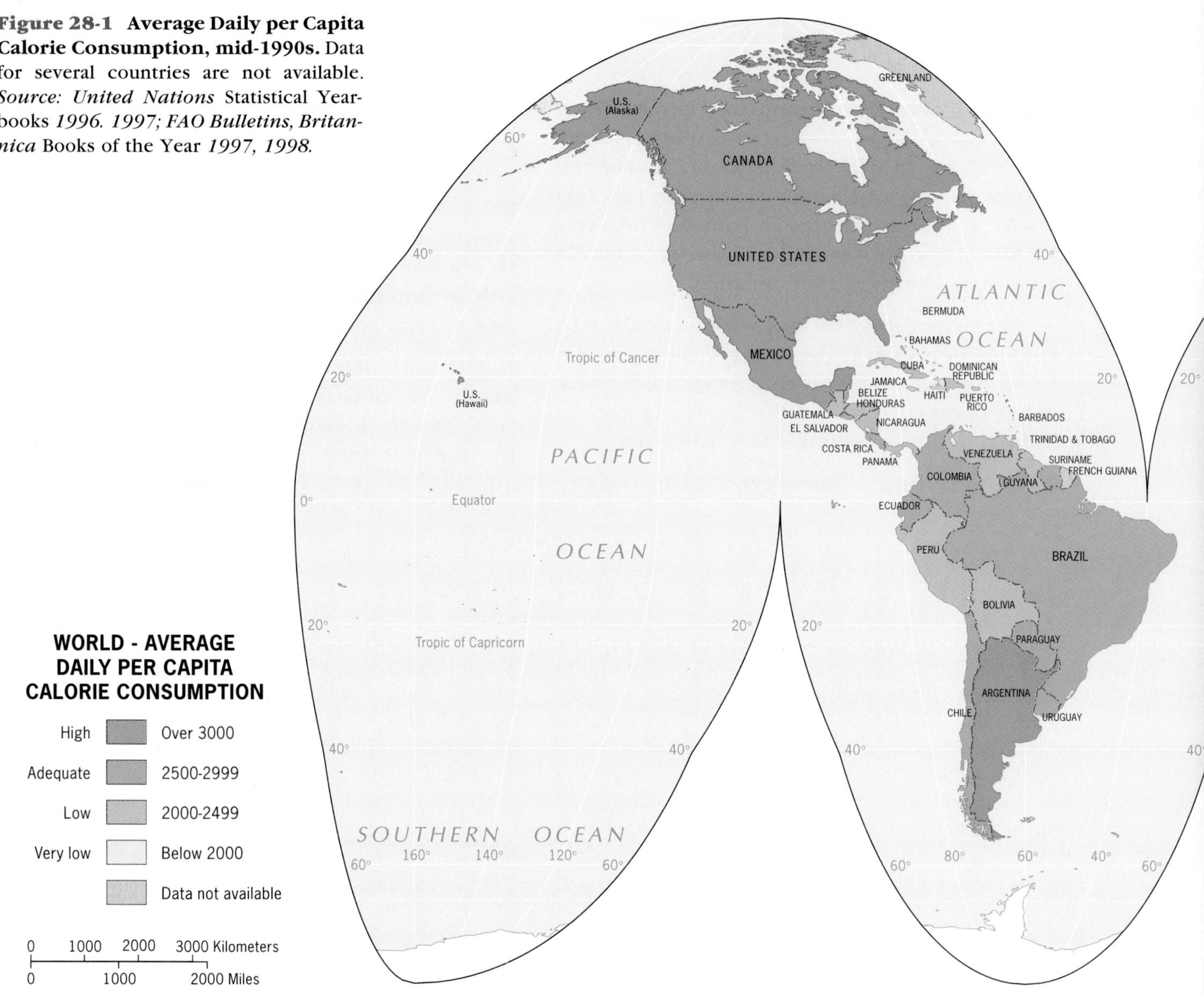

Figure 28-1 Average Daily per Capita Calorie Consumption, mid-1990s. Data for several countries are not available. *Source: United Nations* Statistical Yearbooks *1996. 1997; FAO Bulletins, Britannica* Books of the Year *1997, 1998.*

privation has to do with inadequate transport systems. Many countries lack transport networks that reach all people in need. It is also related to deliberate policy; some regimes still use food as a weapon, depriving civilian populations in war zones as a matter of strategy. Some food crises result from a combination of environmental impact and governmental ineptitude. In North Korea in the late 1990s, a series of floods followed by devastating droughts reduced grain production so severely that malnutrition was widespread and famine threatened; yet the communist regime in Pyongyang failed to facilitate the delivery of aid. In today's world, starvation results from human shortcomings, not nature's shortfalls.

◆ NUTRITION AND DIETARY BALANCE

In this chapter we examine spatial aspects of food and nutrition. There is more to nutrition than quantity; it also is a matter of quality, that is, of dietary balance. In large areas of the world, even in this time of comparative food sufficiency, that balance is still lacking.

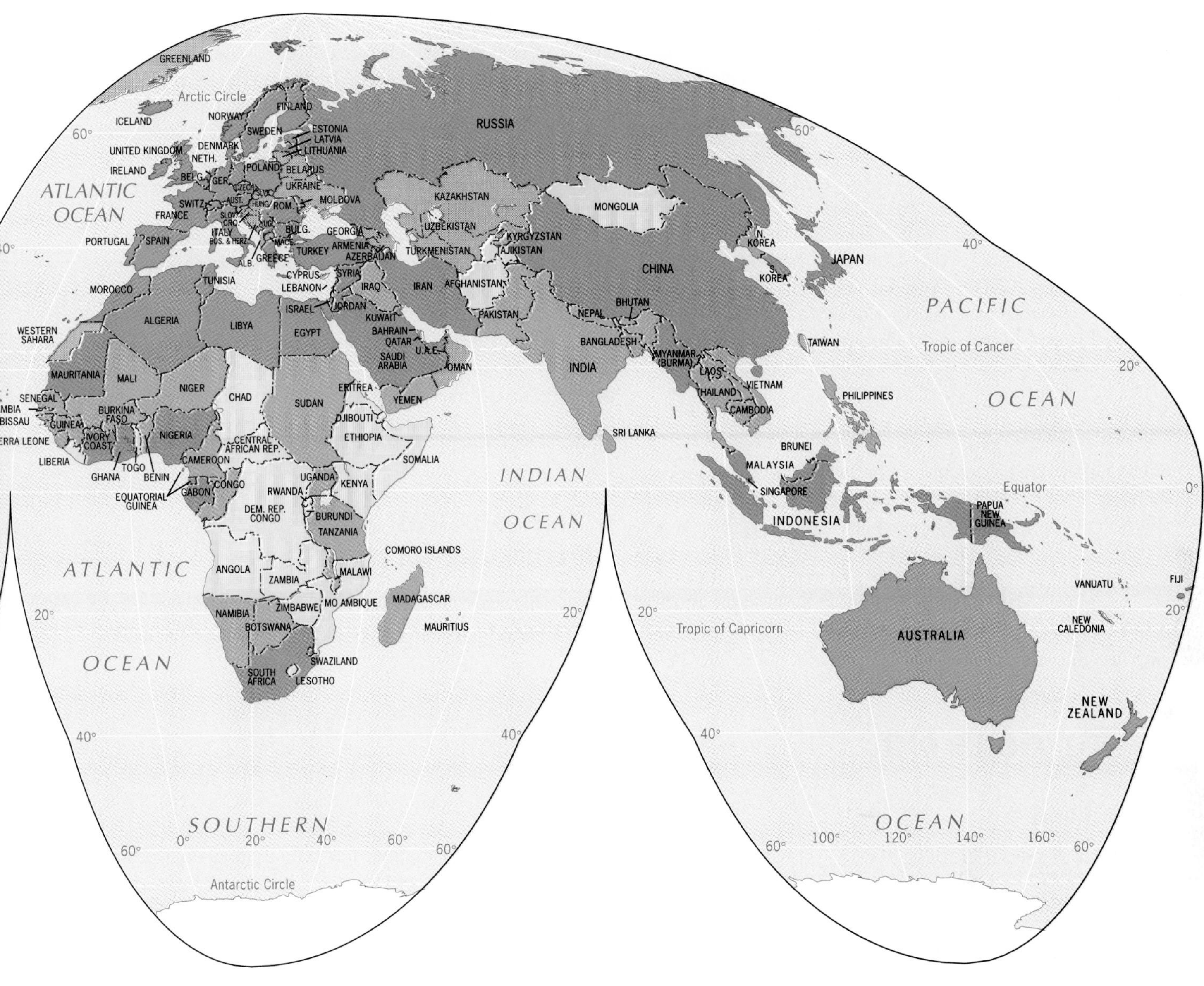

A balanced diet includes carbohydrates (derived from staples such as rice, corn, wheat, and potatoes), proteins (from meat, poultry, fish, eggs, and dairy products), vitamins (from fruits and vegetables, as well as other sources), fats, and minerals. Proteins are a critical element and may be derived from plant sources, including soybeans, peas, peanuts, and wheat as well as from meat and dairy products.

Caloric Intake

Food intake is measured in terms of *calories*, which are units of "fuel" for energy production in the body. Calorie requirements are not the same among the population. Males, for example, need more calories, on average, than females; young adults need more calories than children or old persons; larger people require more calories than smaller people.

Figure 28-1 reveals the wide range of ***caloric intake*** throughout the world. The World Bank groups countries according to caloric intake into four levels, ranging from high (over 3000 calories) to very low (below 2000). The World Bank regards 2500 calories and over as "adequate," whereas the United Nations regards 2360 calories as adequate.

Researching the current literature on global food and nutrition, you will find that the urgency of this issue has diminished. The World Bank's *Development Indicators 1998*, for example, no longer provides per-country data on calorie intake. United Nations data are available for 1995, but not for all countries, as Figure 28-1 shows.

Nevertheless, in the mid-1990s as many as 21 countries still reported a per-capita daily calorie intake of under 2000, and several of the countries for which no data were available almost certainly fell into this category (in addition, North Korea in the late 1990s suffered from widespread famine). The specter of hunger may have receded, but it has not disappeared.

Dietary Balance

What Figure 28-1 does not show is the dietary balance in these countries. With few exceptions, the countries where caloric intake is low are also those where protein is in short supply. Recent studies have indicated that the first six months of life are critical in this respect: inadequate protein intake can damage brain and body for life. Moreover, the food sources that are richest in proteins—meat, fish, and dairy products—are in short supply where they are most needed. It takes food to raise the animals that produce meat, and that food cannot be spared to feed animals when it is needed to keep people alive (see "Focus on: The Food Web"). In addition, fish is not readily available in distant, interior areas, and canned or dried fish may be expensive.

People's ***diets*** are determined by three factors: their economic circumstances, their traditions, and what the soil and climate can produce. In some places taboos limit people's access to products that might improve their diet, but nearly always the problem is a shortage of surplus food. The result is that even people whose caloric intake is marginally adequate are malnourished. "Hidden hunger" exists even in areas identified as having "adequate calories" (Fig. 28-1).

◆ THE DISTRIBUTION OF DIETARY PATTERNS

The world map of average daily calorie consumption (Fig. 28-1) is based on data that are not always reliable,

The Food Web

Plants, cultivated and wild, are the basic source of food for all the animal populations of the world, including humans. We acquire nutrients and energy by eating plant foods (vegetables, fruits, and grains) and consuming meat from animals that have eaten plant foods (cattle, hogs, chickens, etc.). Human beings therefore are part of a ***food chain***, a sequence of consumption that starts with green plants. Plants grow through the process of *photosynthesis*, the use of energy from the sun to convert carbon dioxide, water, and soil nutrients into living tissue.

Plants, the producers, are the first link in the food chain. The *primary consumers* are *herbivores*, animals that eat plants. They form the second link in the chain. The third link is *carnivores*, animals that eat herbivores. These are the *secondary consumers*. There are carnivores that eat other carnivores, and they are the next link, the *tertiary consumers*. Thus the chain goes on.

Human beings are *omnivores* (both herbivores and carnivores), eating plants as well as meat. We therefore are primary as well as secondary consumers. When we eat fish, we are tertiary consumers. The living world thus consists of an intricate network of food chains called the ***food web***.

Consumption at each level of a food chain involves a large loss of energy. It may take 12,000 pounds of grain to feed a cow until it weighs 1000 pounds. Slaughtered and eaten by human beings, that cow's 1000 pounds may produce barely 100 pounds of human weight. However, had humans eaten the grain directly, they—and not the cow—would have gained those 1000 pounds. Much more usable energy therefore is available to consumers lower on the food chain. (Primary consumers are thus in the best position.)

Cattle are especially "expensive" in the food chain. The conversion ratio (the quantity of food required to raise the weight of a consumer at the next link in the food chain by one pound) is 23:1 for cattle, 11:1 for hogs, and only 3:1 for chickens (although calculations vary). Thus one element of a solution to future food supply problems will involve more human consumers at lower levels of the food chain and the consumption of fewer meat products, especially beef. During the late 1990s more than 35 percent of the food consumed in the United States, Canada, Australia, the United Kingdom, (former West) Germany, and France came from animals. The proportion was less than 10 percent in such countries as Indonesia, India, Algeria, and Ethiopia. A narrowing of that gap would signal expanded food production and improved diets.

so it gives only a general impression of the global situation. Statistical information about caloric intake, especially for countries in the periphery, is often based on rough estimates rather than on accurate counts. Nevertheless, the map reveals rather clearly the world distribution of hunger and ***malnutrition***. In the Americas, the best-fed countries (by this measure) are the northern- and southernmost ones. These include Canada, the United States, Argentina, and Uruguay. Calorie availability in Mexico has risen markedly since 1965, from 2570 to 3136 per capita. Brazil has been in the "adequate" category for many years, while chronically underfed Haiti is still plagued by low food availability.

In Europe, calorie availability and intake are high virtually everywhere. If data from the former Soviet Union can be believed, that realm, too, was in the high-consumption category—despite frequent harvest failures and massive grain imports. In the aftermath of the collapse of the USSR, the situation may not be so favorable.

In Africa, conditions remain bleak. Many countries are in the "low" and "very low" categories, and in several countries calorie availability is lower today than in 1965. In 1996 not a single mainland Subsaharan African country had a high caloric intake, and many had an intake of 2000 or less (Table 28-1). Figure 28-1 reflects the economic, political, and environmental dislocations the African realm has suffered over the past 30 years.

In Asia, a tier of countries containing huge populations also have low or very low calorie availability. Again, political and social disarray has contributed to this situation; the long war in Afghanistan made refugees of millions of people, and Iraq also suffered from the aftermath of conflict. India continues to have low calorie availability, but Indonesia's situation has improved significantly (2732 calories compared to 1796 in 1965).

Table 28-1 reveals the wide range of available calories in different parts of the world. In New Zealand and the United States, people consume nearly twice the calories available to people in Haiti and Moçambique. Again, the table should be read with caution. All the countries in the "large supply" category have a combined population as great as that of India, where calorie supplies are low. It is worth comparing Figure 28-1 and Table 28-1 to the map of world population distribution in Figure 4-1. As will be apparent, malnutrition still afflicts and shortens the lives of hundreds of millions of people.

Table 28-1 Daily Calorie Supply per Capita in Selected Countries mid-1990s

Large Supply		Low Supply	
Denmark	3704	Pakistan	2475
United States	3603	Nicaragua	2311
France	3588	Peru	2277
Italy	3458	Laos	2117
New Zealand	3379	Malawi	2038
Syria	3296		
Mexico	3136	**Very Low Supply**	
Canada	3093		
		Kenya	1991
Adequate Supply		Mongolia	1897
		Haiti	1706
Latvia	2967	Liberia	1640
Malaysia	2807	Afghanistan	1523
Colombia	2758	Tajikistan	1400
Jamaica	2647		
Moldova	2525		

Source: United Nations, *Statistical Yearbooks* 1996, 1997, FAO Bulletins, Britannica *Books of the Year* 1997, 1998.

Effects on Children

It is especially tragic that undernutrition and malnutrition affect so many children. When food supply in a village dwindles, the social order frequently falls apart and children are the first victims.

Even when food is available in reasonable quantities, dietary imbalances can have serious effects during early childhood. A child's brain grows to about 80 percent of its adult size in the first three years of life, and an adequate supply of protein is vital in this development. Without enough protein, brain growth is inhibited and mental capacities can be permanently impaired. There can be no recovery from this loss after early childhood. Both mental capacity and physical growth are adversely affected by inadequate nutrition, so infants born into an environment of deprivation face lifelong handicaps.

Protein availability is only one requirement for good health. Other deficiencies also have a devastating impact on young bodies. For example, vitamin-A deficiency occurs in many poor countries (and in poverty-stricken regions of better-off countries as well). Vitamin A is ingested with eggs, dairy products, and animal liver; it is also contained in fruits and vegetables. None of these foods is part of the diets of millions of children. The decline in breast feeding has further reduced protein and vitamin intake, with the result that many suffer from skin diseases, low resistance to respiratory diseases, and gum and eye disorders. World Health Organization (WHO) experts report that vitamin-A deficiency is a major cause of blindness in India, Indonesia, Bangladesh, northeastern Brazil, and El Salvador. In eastern Asia alone, about 100,000 children become blind every year.

When we consider the nutritional data for Asian and African countries, therefore, we should remember that it is the children who are most severely affected by malnutrition, as well as the aged, who often can no longer fend for themselves. As noted in Chapter 5, young children make up a disproportionate percentage of the populations of the world's poorer countries, where the population explosion still takes a heavy toll.

◆ REGIONAL ASPECTS OF NUTRITION

If you were to compare Figure 28-1 in this edition of *Human Geography* with Figure 3-1 in the first edition, published more than 20 years ago, you would be encouraged by the changes. Many countries in South America, Africa, and Asia show increases in per capita calorie consumption. Far fewer countries are now in the lowest category than was the case in the mid-1970s. Countries in the low category have moved up to the adequate category, and for the first time high consumption appears in regions such as North Africa and Southwest Asia.

As noted earlier, some experts believe that in the future the food supply will once again be reduced. They may or may not be correct in this prediction, but meanwhile there is much to be concerned about as Figure 28-1 makes clear, no matter how favorable the trends. While citizens of many countries are better fed than they were two decades ago, significant numbers of people still have too little to eat and suffer from poorly balanced diets as well. Africa south of the Sahara is the worst off. In the late 1990s countries in Subsaharan Africa and in the transition zone between this realm and North Africa were among the world's hungriest and most dependent on food imports. A major cause of this situation is political and social dislocation in these ex-colonial, economically peripheral countries. The worst-fed countries, such as Ethiopia, Liberia, Congo, Moçambique, Chad, Angola, and Rwanda, have experienced civil wars, creating vast numbers of migrants and refugees. But this is not the only reason people in many African countries are poorly nourished. Even countries that are comparatively unaffected by conflict are not doing as well as the rest of the world.

Causes of Food Shortages

In part, this situation can be attributed to Africa's rapid population growth rates, which must be matched by increased food availability. But there is another major cause: Africa has benefited less from the Green Revolution than Asia. In the first place, the peoples of Asia depend mainly on two crops, rice and wheat, which are grown mainly under irrigation. In Africa the variety of crops is much greater, including corn, millet, sorghum, wheat, some rice, and others. The Green Revolution has not yet affected all of these crops, although a new strain of sorghum has been developed that yields three times as much as the standard variety and has increased harvests in the Sudan. More problematic is the soil. In Asia, most rice and wheat is planted in fertile, deep soil. Africa's soils usually are not irrigated and are thin, fragile, and easily damaged. Such soils can easily be depleted by overcropping.

Although it may seem unlikely, populous Africa also has labor problems. Africa's population is growing rapidly, but the labor force in the farming areas is not always large enough to handle the farming chores at the times when they must be done to ensure the best yields. Add to these conditions the poorly developed state of African agriculture generally—from equipment to farming methods to education to transportation—and the Green Revolution's lesser impact on Africa is understandable.

Recent Developments

In the late 1980s a development occurred that raised hopes for Africa's farmers. Scientists announced that a new "miracle maize," a strain of corn first developed during the early 1980s and subsequently modified, was ready for distribution. This new maize, also called QPM (Quality-Protein Maize), is rich in the very protein that is so severely lacking in many African diets. Some researchers are predicting that this new corn will significantly improve the nutritional balance for as many as 200 million people now primarily dependent on this grain.

Not everyone, however, is so optimistic. In *The Changing World Food Prospect* (1988), Lester Brown points out that the decline of grain production in Africa is not the only case in which yields have fallen, and that "miracle strains" may not be enough to reverse the trend. There is the possibility that climatic fluctuations will increase, causing droughts, floods, heat waves, and cold spells. Against this background, consider the drop in grain production in the United States in the middle and late 1980s: from 345 million tons in 1985 to 277 million tons in 1987, to 190 million tons in 1988. Corn harvests declined even more, from 212 million tons in 1985 to 116 million tons in 1988. In subsequent years production rose again, but such enormous swings underscore the fact that even the highly mechanized, modern U.S. grain-farming industry is not immune to wide fluctuations. In Africa, such variability spells disaster for subsistence farmers.

Another plan to increase food supplies in Africa was announced by the Food and Agriculture Organization (FAO) in 1990. Under this program large amounts of fertilizer would be provided in order to slow land degradation and soil erosion, prolong the productivity of fields, and thus encourage peasants and farmers not to abandon overused land. To put this plan in perspective, we should note that the average African farmer can afford very little fertilizer. A European farmer is likely to use more than 50 times as much fertilizer as an African farmer. Reliance on fertilizer when it is in chemical form has some negative effects, including groundwater pollution and altered soil chemistry, but it does allow for continued high yields in most places. Without such inputs, soils become exhausted and deteriorate. The FAO reasoned that supplying fertilizer directly to African farmers in quantities up to 10 times those used previously would result in enhanced yields and reduced soil loss. And direct supply of fertilizers rather than cash to purchase them, coupled with an educational program, might succeed where previous efforts did not.

Will a combination of improved maize strains and more fertilizers reverse the downward slide of African agricultural production and begin a Green Revolution there? The prospects are poor as long as populations continue to double in little more than 20 years.

Areas of Improvement

The improving situation in South and Middle America, by contrast, is directly related to the widespread decline in population growth rates noted in Chapter 5. Bolivia has long been the most poorly nourished country in South America, but even there, per capita consumption in 1995 crossed the 2000-calorie level. In Middle America, only Haiti remains poorly fed, largely because of its political troubles.

Undoubtedly, the most dramatic improvements revealed by Figure 28-1 have occurred in the tier of countries extending from North Africa through Southwest and South Asia into Southeast and East Asia. Here the Green Revolution had its fullest impact, lifting numerous countries from the very low and low categories into the adequate category—and some into the high-consumption category. In Southeast Asia, Thailand and Vietnam are major rice exporters; India has achieved self-sufficiency; and even Bangladesh, long subject to famine, is closing the gap between demand and supply.

The situation in Russia and its former empire, especially the countries in Central Asia (Turkestan), is uncertain. For some years no dependable figures have been published for many countries of the former Soviet Union, but there can be no doubt that the realm's economic troubles are translating into food and nutritional problems. In late 1994 a sample study of the Russian population indicated that male life expectancy had dropped below 60 years; in 1997 it stood at 58 years. (The national mean still stood at 65 only because women outlived men, on average, by 14 years.)

Regional Variations

Just as a world map of population growth cannot convey demographic contrasts *within* individual countries, so Figure 28-1, which is based on national statistics, conceals regional variations. People in the northwestern area of India, for example, are better fed than those in the northeast. Brazil's northeastern region has a history of malnutrition and even famine.

Nor is regional hunger a monopoly of the poorest, least developed countries. Even in the United States there is malnutrition. Hundreds of thousands of families in low-income urban areas and poverty-stricken rural areas cannot afford to spend what is necessary to achieve a balanced diet. People surviving on food stamps often run out of food. Although regional contrasts defined by hunger are not as sharp in the United States as they are in India or Brazil, such contrasts do exist.

People in North America are accustomed to shopping in supermarkets where they can find potatoes from Idaho, cereals from the Midwest, oranges from Florida, and many products from foreign countries—fruits and wines from Chile, coffee from Colombia, cheeses from Holland. Indeed, our food preferences affect land use in distant parts of the world, for example, through the conversion of forest to pastureland and the use of grains to feed meat-providing animals rather than people (see "Focus on: Feed Grains and Food Grains"). Such luxury sometimes makes it difficult to understand the factors that create regional food scarcities. If people in Southeast Brazil are better fed than people in the Northeast, why not distribute the food differently so that the Northeast is better fed? How can one part of India be reasonably well-fed while people beg for food in the streets in another part of the same country? Getting food to the people who need it immediately and most urgently is a huge problem. This was especially evident during the 1970s, when a severe drought struck the region known as the Sahel. People in the region faced starvation, but there was no system for getting food supplies to them. Airplanes were used to drop bags of grain to people far removed from highways, roads, and trucks—but it was impossible to provide enough food to meet the

Focus On

Feed Grains and Food Grains

Various ***food grains***—rice, wheat, corn, and others—produce about 53 percent of the world's food supply by direct consumption. Additional amounts of ***feed grains*** are fed to livestock and thus indirectly consumed. In the United States and Canada, we consume as much as 1 ton of grain per person per year, but only 150 pounds of this comes in the form of bread or cereal; the rest is consumed indirectly, in the form of meat and dairy products. In food-poor countries, on the other hand, only about 400 pounds of grains, less than one-fifth the U.S. supply, is available for each person. Obviously, little of this meager amount can be spared for raising livestock. As a result, dairy products and meat are in short supply and poor nourishment is made worse by protein deficiencies.

To put it another way, it takes five times as much soil, water, and fertilizer to sustain a person in the United States as it does to feed someone in India, Ghana, or Peru. The wealthier a nation becomes, the greater its demands on food supplies. In the United States, people were eating an average of 55 pounds of beef in 1940. In 1998, Americans consumed about three times as many pounds of beef. The consumption of poultry more than tripled over the same period. Consider the increased amount of feed grains required to meet this demand—feed grains that could have been food grains available for export to hungry people in other parts of the world.

immense demand. The cost was enormous, and many people were too far from where the planes brought the supplies and therefore never received any food.

But that was a crisis situation, and the Sahel food distribution effort was neither the first nor the last of its kind to fail. It always takes time to organize a massive relief program and get it under way; in the 1990s the refugee crisis in and around Rwanda proved this once again. Lives are lost while the operation gets started, and sometimes ruling regimes actually interfere with the supply lines.

In reality, regional malnutrition is only partly a function of the remoteness of the people afflicted by it. Northeastern Brazil, which periodically faces food shortages, *is* adequately connected to other parts of the country. But poverty reigns there, and unless food is brought in as part of a relief program, people cannot afford what they need. So the poorer, hungrier parts of otherwise adequately fed countries are left to survive as best they can—until a crisis occurs. Once the crisis is over, the normal situation of insufficient calories and inadequate dietary balance returns.

A larger-scale map than Figure 28-1 would reveal pockets of food poverty even in the higher categories of consumption. Such a map would underscore the need for continued improvement in access, which in some places is a matter of economics and in others is a function of gaps in the global system of food production and distribution. The continued existence of areas characterized by persistent food shortages and malnutrition has impelled some scholars to warn that greater problems may lie ahead.

◆ A FUTURE GLOBAL FOOD EMERGENCY?

When global warming became an international concern during the 1980s, concerted action was taken to reduce the contributions humanity was making to heating the "greenhouse." A comparable effort could soften the impact of a future emergency in food supplies. What might cause a food crisis?

Possible Causes

Among the factors and circumstances that may contribute to future food emergencies are population growth, climate change, rising energy costs, overfishing in the oceans, misuse of farmland, loss of soil, and changing food preferences.

Population Growth We have already indicated that *population growth* is a major factor. In Africa, for example, the food problem is made worse by high rates of population increase. It is true that the global rate of population growth is slowing and populations are not growing as fast in very large countries such as China and India as they were in the 1960s and 1970s. Even so, some 90 million people are added to the world's population per year. Even if that rate declines to 70 million during the 2020s, the world will have to produce ever more food just to keep pace.

Climate Change *Climate change* is also a risk factor. If the predictions of some physical geographers are correct, the primary environmental problem of the first quarter of the twenty-first century may not be drought but, rather, wide fluctuations in weather conditions that may bring storms, floods, freezes, heat waves, and other extremes capable of destroying crops and farmlands. These extremes may be related to the warming trend that led climatologists to believe that human activity was raising global temperatures. There are signs that nature itself is getting ready for one of its cyclic changes. If so, sustaining food production, let alone increasing it as required, may become more difficult.

Crop Yields Some scholars also identify *crop yields* as a concern. They believe that the Green Revolution has run its course. It has closed the gap between demand and supply but will not be able to continue to do so. Paddies and wheat fields cannot be expected to produce ever larger harvests, and as production levels off, the food gap will widen again. The failure of the Green Revolution in Africa is seen as a sign of what may occur throughout the world in the future.

Energy Costs Concern is also rising over the possibility that the *cost of energy* will rise again, as it did during the last major food crisis. When energy costs rise, so does the cost of fertilizers. Farmers also need to be able to buy fuel to run irrigation pumps and other equipment. The impact of the last energy crisis has faded from memory; in the United States it is remembered mainly as a shortage at the gasoline pump. But for farmers in many other countries a renewed increase in energy prices would be disastrous.

Failure of Alternative Sources Still another worry for the future lies in the apparent failure of *alternative sources* as dependable providers of calories *and* dietary balance. As the demand for food has grown and technologies have become more efficient, one of the planet's last bounties—fish, a valuable source of proteins—is declining rapidly. From mid-century to the late 1980s, the fish harvest from oceans and seas increased fivefold, and there seemed to be no limit to it. Nations quarreled over fishing rights, poor nations leased fishing grounds to richer ones, and fleets of trawlers plied the oceans. International attempts to regulate these industries failed. Meanwhile, there were signals that overfishing was destroying fish stocks. Several regional fishing industries, such as the cod fisheries on Canada's Grand Banks off Newfoundland, collapsed. In 1975 biologists estimated the Atlantic bluefin tuna population at 250,000; today there may be about 20,000 left, and the species may be placed on the endangered species list. From ocean perch and king crabs off Alaska to rock lobsters and roughies off New Zealand, fish and shellfish populations are depleted. The total annual catch is also declining and may already be beyond the point of recovery.

Food Taboos As a reminder of the power of culture, it is interesting that, in a time of food scarcity and dietary imbalance, ***food taboos*** are still in evidence—even when they stand in the way of a more balanced, nutrionally rich diet. All the world's major religions prohibit the eating of certain foods, either on particular days or at any time. Christian faiths prohibit the consumption of fish, meat, or animal products on fast days (here the Greek Orthodox religion has the most stringent rules). Judaism classifies numerous animals, including the pig, the camel, and certain species of fish, as unclean. Islam also prohibits the eating of pork. Hindu society bans the eating of meat and even eggs, although meat other than beef is consumed by members of lower castes. Buddhism discourages the taking of an animal's life for purposes of routine nutrition. People in various societies do not eat fish, eggs, or other potentially nourishing foods.

Persistence of Colonial Systems Yet another concern lies in the persistence of *colonial systems* in countries that gained independence from imperial powers. Trapped in a world economic order they cannot change, they have maintained the cash-crop estates and plantations of the colonial period. There, often on the country's best soils, crops are produced to be sold on foreign markets. Senegal's peanuts, Angola's coffee, Zimbabwe's tobacco, Kenya's tea, and Sudan's cotton still flow to those markets, even while food production is inadequate to feed those countries' own populations. In any future global food crisis, the failure to restructure production in such areas will have serious consequences.

Loss of Farmland Concern is rising over the *loss of farmland* to urban growth—not only in the wealthiest countries but also in the poorer ones, where urbanization is speeding up. Although this loss seems small in statistical terms, much of the lost acreage consists of the best, most fertile soils. Many cities were originally established amid productive farmlands that could supply the needs of their inhabitants. Now they are absorbing those farmlands as they expand. The American Farmland Trust, for example, reported in 1993 that 12 U.S. areas are severely affected, including California's Central Valley, South Florida, California's coastal zone, North Carolina's Piedmont, and the Chicago–Milwaukee–Madison triangle in Illinois-Wisconsin. These 12 areas represent only 5 percent of U.S. farmland, but they produce 17 percent of total agricultural sales, 67 percent of all fruit, 55 percent of all vegetables, and one-quarter of all dairy products. Figures for other countries in the richer parts of the world (such as Japan) as well as for poorer countries (such as Egypt) prove that this is a global problem with serious implications for the future.

Changing Food Preferences Finally, but possibly most ominous of all, are developments on the East Asian Pacific Rim. The combination of continued population growth (China alone adds 13 million people annually) and rising incomes is producing a change in East Asian *food preferences.* The demand for pork, chicken, and beef is growing as diets change, and more and more grain is being used to feed livestock rather than people. Add the loss of farmland (Japan has lost more than half of its farmland since 1950, Taiwan more than a third), and China could precipitate a world food crisis. Its demand will grow more rapidly than the food exporting nations' supplies, and its capacity to pay will limit the availability of food in other needy regions and countries ranging from tropical Africa to South Asia. Thus the benefits of the Green Revolution may last only decades, not the generations it seemed to promise just 20 years ago.

Is the world facing a food emergency comparable to that of the 1950s and 1960s? Perhaps. This time the fundamental causes may *not* be alleviated by another Green Revolution. The structure of food consumption is changing, and that problem will be harder to solve.

A More Secure Future

What can be done to prevent another food crisis from developing, or at least to reduce its severity? The ten arenas for action presented in the following list can of course be supplemented by others, but in combination they would go a long way toward achieving a crucial global goal. It is clear that only effective international action can produce results in several of these arenas, such as the regulation of ocean fishing, and such cooperation is difficult to achieve. Here are the ten key arenas:

1. ***Formulate Population Policies.*** As noted earlier, perhaps the most direct way to alleviate food crises is to reduce population growth rates. Family planning requires education and effective distribution of food supplies, a considerable challenge for poorer countries.
2. ***Sustain the Green Revolution.*** And expand it while developing policies to reduce some of its negative environmental and social consequences. "Miracle rice" allowed the Philippines to end five decades of dependence on food imports, and Mexico tripled its production of wheat in a few years. But higher-yielding grains need to be supplemented by strains that are drought-resistant and can withstand the weather extremes predicted by some environmentalists. Lesser grains such as millet and sorghum also must be improved through genetic engineering. And efforts must be made to stem the growth in chemical pollutants and rural-urban migration that have followed in the wake of Green Revolution farming.
3. ***Expand Farmlands.*** Some experts believe that the amount of land under cultivation could be expanded, perhaps more than doubled, through massive investments in irrigation and "soil reconstruction." If billions of dollars were diverted from military to agricultural investment, they argue, infertile soils could be reconstituted with organic and inorganic fertilizers and farmed with crops especially developed to grow there. This strategy, however, must take into consideration the potential negative environmental consequences of expanding farmland in some areas. The Amazon and Congo Basins are identified as regions with agricultural potential, but any significant expansions in these areas could work against efforts to preserve the rainforest and its biodiversity.
4. ***Stimulate Local Production.*** A surprisingly large percentage of food is produced in small gardens and on small plots cultivated with great care by people who use household waste and compost to improve their patch of soil and know just what to plant on it. In the former Soviet Union, people who worked on collective farms were allowed to cultivate a small plot for themselves (and to sell what they raised there). Crop yields of those small gardens far outweighed those of the collective farms.
5. ***Encourage Land Reform.*** Farmers who own their land tend to cultivate it more carefully and productively than those who work on someone else's soil. Yet much of the world's farmland remains in the hands of a comparatively small number of landowners or under the control of inefficient communal groups. Land reform introduced by the United States in Japan put small farms in the hands of former tenant farmers; the result was a tripling of output. Other countries have made progress in land reform, including Mexico and Egypt, where production also rose as a result. The process is slow and controversial, but it must be pursued throughout the world.
6. ***Improve Food Distribution Systems.*** If a food crisis develops during the first decades of the next century, geographers know where it will have the strongest impact. During the 1960s and 1970s, inefficiencies in distribution systems led to enormous waste and loss of food. Challenges arising from the continuing refugee problem signal the difficulties that lie ahead should a more massive emergency arise. Road, rail, and bridge building should be geared to anticipate regional needs.
7. ***Develop Alternative Food Sources.*** There are still opportunities to develop new food sources,

and a prominent one is ***aquaculture***. While the oceans' fish resources may not survive the current wave of overfishing, the raising of fish in ponds and controlled saltwater hatcheries is a growing industry. Compared to what the oceans have been producing (even in these years of declining production), aquaculture is but a small industry. But it has considerable potential and should be developed as rapidly as possible. Food scientists are also trying to achieve a "Food Revolution" in the laboratory, seeking to make food from grass, leaves, algae, even oil.

8. ***Strengthen Controls over Ocean Fishing.*** Although it may be too late, the international community should organize to combat violations of ocean fishing regulations. Japan and Norway are among the countries that have violated international agreements on whaling. This is a matter of great significance. If countries such as Haiti and North Korea can be threatened with sanctions over various offenses against the international community, already-rich countries that are depleting the oceans should also face sanctions.

9. ***Reduce Meat Consumption.*** This is an important arena of action. Meat consumption by people in the wealthier countries puts an enormous strain on economies and ecologies elsewhere. Apart from the fact that reducing consumption of red meat is good for health and well-being, such reduction has good effects in a wider sphere by reducing the amount of grain used to feed livestock and limiting the conversion of forest into pasture in poorer countries where beef cattle are raised cheaply to provide meat for wealthier markets.

10. ***Promote Social Change.*** In many parts of the world, notably Subsaharan Africa and South and East Asia, food emergencies afflict women more severely than men. In traditional societies, the male predominates to such a degree that he demands and takes a disproportionate share of the family's food supply. Thus women are the most severely malnourished among the adults. Among the children, too, the male tends to be favored in the allocation of food. In traditional African societies, it is not uncommon for women not only to be more severely malnourished than men, but to be responsible for hoeing the croplands, making the family's clothing, walking endless miles for water and firewood, cooking the meals, and numerous other tasks, in addition to bearing the children. Men do not perform nearly the share of work that they could, and often they abandon the family and go to the city. It is obviously unrealistic to expect rapid change in traditions that are nearly as old as those societies themselves. However, it *is* possible to direct aid primarily to women and children.

In the late 1990s the condition of world food supplies requires action on a broad range of fronts, as well as global cooperation in several areas of concern. The crisis of the early 1970s generated the first steps toward international action, but when the emergency receded, the lessons learned were soon forgotten. Yet the events of the 1970s were harbingers of the future. In time, a rising tide of world hunger may again threaten world order. Even the most selfish interests in the well-fed countries thus have a stake in the war on malnutrition.

◆ KEY TERMS ◆

aquaculture
caloric intake
diets
feed grains
food chain
food grains
food taboos
food web
Green Revolution
malnutrition
miracle rice

◆ APPLYING GEOGRAPHIC KNOWLEDGE ◆

1. Two northeast corners of continents, Africa and South America, periodically suffer from climatic extremes (mainly droughts, but also floods) and resulting food shortages. In Brazil's northeast, the government never has been able to forestall starvation; in Somalia, a relief effort under UN auspices ended in failure. Compare these two areas from environmental, cultural, and political standpoints and explain why they continue to defy attempts to reduce their problems.

2. As a geographer, you have been asked by a government to assist in promoting land reform as a partial solution to food shortages. But the task is difficult and sensitive: some of the large landholdings targeted for reform produced not only food harvests, but also cash crops for which the government receives taxes. How will your advice attempt to balance the losses and gains inherent in land reform, and project a favorable long-range outcome?

Chapter 29

Spatial Patterns of Health and Disease

From the field notes

"AIDS may have originated in Africa, but today this disease is a worldwide threat. Countries in the periphery do not have adequate resources to cope with it, but wherever you go, posters and billboards warn the people of the risk of exposure. I saw this one on the heavily traveled road from Da Nang to Hue in Vietnam—near a beach where an international corporation is building a large resort. Obviously the lesson of Thailand has been learned here."

KEY POINTS

- **Protein deficiencies still afflict populations, especially children, despite the general adequacy of available calories. In addition, dietary deficiencies continue to inhibit the development of young bodies, particularly in tropical areas.**
- **Average life expectancy maps conceal the far greater life expectancies of women virtually everywhere, but they do underscore the aging of many populations.**
- **Tropical areas are zones of intense biological activity and hence are the sources of many disease-transmitting viruses and parasites.**
- **Certain major diseases remain contained within tropical or near-tropical latitudes, but others have spread into all parts of the world; AIDS originated in tropical Africa and is now a global pandemic.**
- **Densely populated urban shantytowns with inadequate sanitation and contaminated water supplies are highly susceptible to outbreaks of disease; the South American cholera epidemic of the 1990s began in the slums of Lima, Peru.**
- **Despite the worldwide attention focused on AIDS, the leading killers in the Western world are the chronic diseases, including heart diseases, cancer, and strokes.**

Good health, like adequate food, is unevenly distributed. Sufficient calories and balanced diets help the body develop fully and well. When people are inadequately fed, however, they are susceptible to many debilitating diseases. Similarly, women who are healthy tend to bear healthy babies, but women who suffer from malnutrition and related maladies are less fortunate. It is estimated that 16 percent of babies born in the 1990s—nearly one in six—are underweight and therefore are at a disadvantage. The vast majority of these births occur in poorer countries, and millions of those babies do not survive past their first birthday.

There are stark regional differences in the distribution of food, but patterns of health show even greater contrasts. In North America, where food is generally adequate and is inspected for quality, drinking water is purified and treated, and hunger and malnutrition are rare, the general condition of the population is reflected more by obesity than by any other condition. But an air trip of just a few hours can transport us to places where people, especially children, are visibly malnourished. The resulting disadvantages will be with them for life—if they survive childhood.

The crowded, unsanitary shantytowns that have developed on the outskirts of cities in many poorer countries are reservoirs of risk where people are exposed to diseases that have been eradicated in wealthier countries. In 1990, an outbreak of cholera in Peru led to an epidemic reminiscent of another century, when such diseases killed millions in Europe. That a disease whose cause is known, whose transmission is understood, and whose cure is possible should kill more than 10,000 people and infect a million more is a sad reflection on the overall state of health in the poorer areas of the world. The fact that by mid-1991 cholera cases arising from the South American epidemic had already been recorded in the United States reminds us how interconnected our world is.

The study of health in geographic context is called ***medical geography***. Many diseases have their origin in the environment. They have source (core) areas, spread (diffuse) through populations along identifiable routes, and affect clusters of populations (regions) when at their widest distribution. Mapping disease patterns can produce insights into relationships between disease and environment. Associations between natural environments and ***contagious diseases*** (diseases that can be transmitted) are of special interest to medical geographers, since geography deals with natural (physical) as well as human problems. Medical geographers also concern themselves with the location of health-care facilities for people who need them. If a poor country receives funding to establish 25 clinics, where should those clinics be located so as to serve the greatest number of potential patients?

◆ CHILD AND INFANT MORTALITY

When examining disease, it is appropriate to return to the topic of the previous chapters, nutrition, because regions where malnutrition prevails are also areas of poverty, inadequate medical services, inadequate sanitation, and substandard housing. It is difficult to identify the specific effects of malnutrition on people's susceptibility to disease, because so many other factors are present. However, there is little doubt about the effects of malnutrition on growth and development. The impact on children is especially important.

Malnutrition and Child Mortality

In the protein-poor tropical and subtropical countries, children are ravaged by ***kwashiorkor***. The child's belly grows disproportionately large, while the skin loses its tone and becomes discolored. The hair develops a reddish tinge and begins to fall out. Later, liquids collect in swelling limbs, the digestive system fails, and the child is overcome by apathy. Death may not be far away.

In poor countries the ***child mortality rate*** (the number of children who die between the ages of 1 and 5) is directly related to the incidence of kwashiorkor. Note that a child can develop kwashiorkor even when enough calories are available. Kwashiorkor is a result of *mal*nutrition, not necessarily *under*nutrition. Often it develops when a mother stops breast feeding the child (perhaps because of the birth of a new baby) and the child is put on a starchy diet.

Where both deficiencies—lack of protein *and* insufficient calories—prevail, a child is likely to develop ***marasmus***. With this disease, the body is thin and bony, the skin shrivels, and the eyes appear huge. Staple foods with low protein content, such as the banana, the sweet potato, and the cassava (a root crop

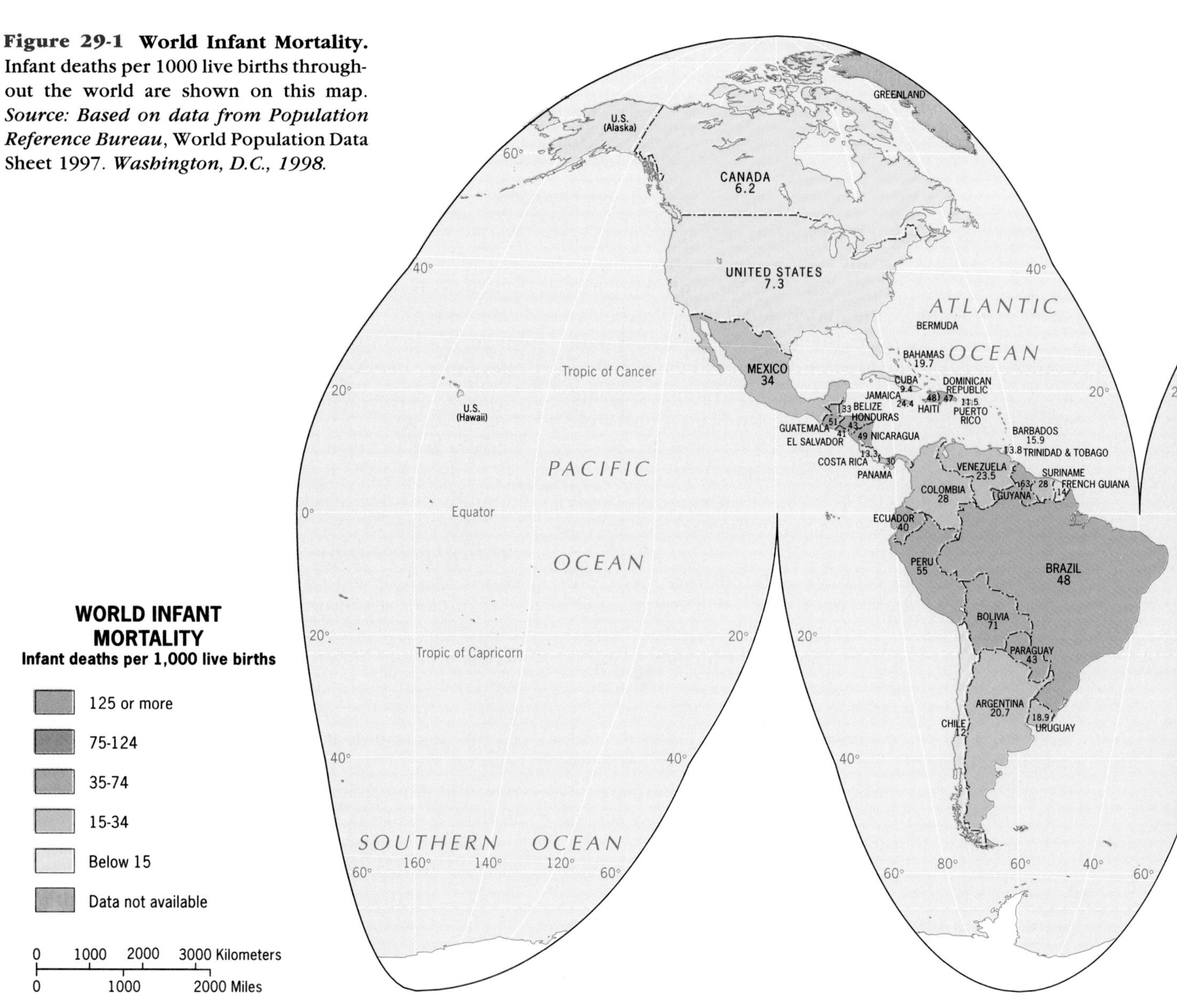

Figure 29-1 World Infant Mortality. Infant deaths per 1000 live births throughout the world are shown on this map. *Source: Based on data from Population Reference Bureau*, World Population Data Sheet 1997. *Washington, D.C., 1998.*

grown in the tropics), are eaten in sufficient quantities to stave off marasmus in some areas, but they are not nutritionally rich enough to prevent kwashiorkor. In some places where a combination of protein deficiency and insufficient calories prevails, as many as half the children never reach their fifth birthday.

Infant Mortality Rates

As noted earlier, a key measure of the human condition is the ***infant mortality rate (IMR)***. Infant mortality is recorded as a baby's death during the first year following its birth (unlike *child mortality*, which records death between ages 1 and 5). Like other population statistics, infant mortality is normally given as the number of cases per thousand, that is, per thousand live births.

Infant and child mortality reflect the overall health of a society. High infant mortality has a variety of causes. The physical health of the mother is a key factor. In societies where women bear a large number of babies, those women also tend to be inadequately nourished, exhausted from overwork, suffering from disease, and poorly educated. Many infants die because they are improperly weaned. Demographers report that more children die because their parents do not know how to cope with the routine childhood problem of diarrhea than because of epidemics. This, together with malnutrition, is the leading killer of children throughout the world. Poor sanitation is yet another threat to infants and children. It is estimated that more than one-fifth of the world's population lacks ready access to clean drinking water or hygienic human waste-disposal facilities.

The map showing the world distribution of infant mortality (Fig. 29-1) reveals the high rates in many poorer countries. The map shows infant mortality patterns at five levels ranging from 125 or more per thou-

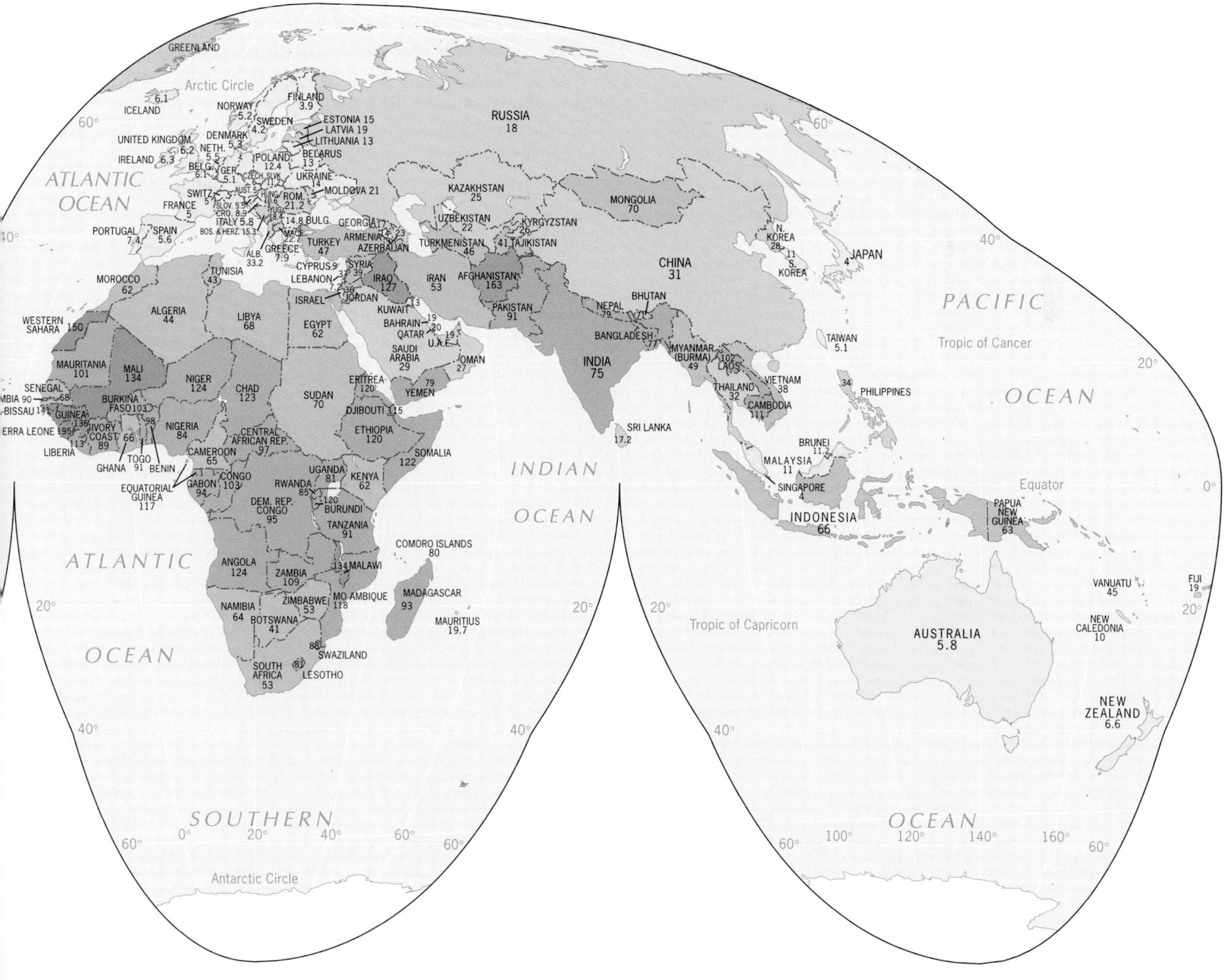

sand (one death for every eight live births) to fewer than 15. If you compare this map to that of overall crude death rate (CDR) on Figure 5-7, the role of infant mortality in societies with high death rates is evident.

Figure 29-1 shows clearly the relationship between social disorder and high IMRs. Sierra Leone, an already-poor country wracked by civil war and economic collapse during the 1990s, had the world's highest IMR. Afghanistan, whose traditionally fractious society fell victim to a Soviet invasion during the Cold War, also has a very high IMR. Conflict, dislocation, and refugee movements produce high IMRs, and the map reflects this.

The lowest infant mortality rate among larger populations has long been reported by Japan, with 4.0 deaths per 1000 live births. (Singapore matches Japan; Sweden reports 4.2.) Japan's achievement is related to its stability, strong social fabric, and prosperity. The infant mortality rate is also quite uniform throughout the country, for Japan does not have any significant ethnocultural minorities with different growth rates. As is so often the case, a map based on national statistics conceals internal regional, ethnic, or other variation, but not in the case of Japan.

In the United States, on the other hand, infant mortality rates are higher in some sectors of the population than in others; the national IMR of 7.3 represents an average. To take a more extreme case, the IMR of South Africa is an average of those of several nations within that country's borders. The IMR for South African whites is near the European average; for black Africans it is nearer the African average; and for the Coloured and Asian population sectors it lies between these two figures. The reported average of 53 per thousand therefore does not tell the "national" story as Japan's does.

In the late 1990s as many as 25 countries still reported an IMR of 100 or more, and of these, 8 had rates of 125 or higher—that is, one death or more among every eight newborns. Nevertheless, these numbers are a considerable improvement over the situation 20 or even 10 years ago. Globally, infant mortality has been declining, even in the most severely afflicted regions. Still, the situation in many African and Asian countries remains grim.

Europe Particularly jarring is the sharp contrast between tropical African and some Asian countries and the higher-latitude countries in both hemispheres. Although Japan regularly reports the lowest IMR among larger countries, Europe has very low rates as well, ranging from 5.0 in the Scandinavian countries to 7.0 in the Mediterranean states; the rate rises substantially toward the east. In Eastern Europe, Romania has long had the worst record, resulting in part from the harsh population policies imposed by the former communist regime. The contrast between Greece (7.9) and its neighbor Turkey (47.0) is noteworthy. Geographically, Turkey is in a very different geoeconomic and geopolitical situation than Greece; and unlike that of Greece, Turkey's IMR represents a heterogeneous society that includes a relatively poor Kurdish minority numbering over 10 million.

The Americas In the Americas, the map reveals some unexpected patterns. It is not surprising, given the material well-being of the United States and Canada and their superior medical facilities, that these two countries should have the hemisphere's lowest infant mortality rates (7.3 and 6.2, respectively, in the late 1990s). It should also be expected that Haiti, the poorest country of the Americas and beset by conflict and disruption, would have the highest rate. But given the demographic transition in progress in Middle and South America (see Chapter 5), some IMRs there remain remarkably high. Peru still records 55 infant deaths per 1000 live births; between 1991 and 1993 its IMR actually rose from 76 to 81 before declining somewhat. Bolivia still records an IMR of 71, Brazil 48, Ecuador 40, and Paraguay 43. These are very high IMRs when compared to the overall CDRs for the same countries.

In Middle America, too, infant mortality rates reveal how much progress still needs to be made. The contrast between the United States and Mexico (34) is similar to that between Greece and Turkey. Other countries with comparatively high IMRs include Nicaragua (49), Guatemala (51), and Honduras (43). In the Caribbean, the two countries on the island of Hispaniola—Haiti and the Dominican Republic—have the highest IMRs. Other Caribbean countries do better, for example, Cuba (9.4), and Puerto Rico (11.5), and Jamaica (24.4).

Asia The situation in Asia is a mixture of progress and stagnation. The population-control program begun by China during the 1970s continues to lower its IMR. In 1990 it still was 33, far lower even than that of most South American countries; today it is 31. In India, the IMR declined even more during the same period, but it remains high at 75. As Figure 29-1 shows, a tier of countries extending from Yemen to Cambodia and including Pakistan and Bangladesh continues to display IMRs as high as those of many African countries. Note the contrast between Indonesia (66) and Australia (5.8).

Numerous conditions play a role in creating the distribution revealed by Figure 29-1. Nutrition is one of them. Social conditions, exposure to infectious and parasitic diseases, and access to medical help also influence the pattern, and we will examine these and related issues in a later chapter. Figure 29-1 reflects the sharp contrasts and variations in the well-being of different societies. In a sense, it is an index of sanitary conditions, medical services, the health of mothers—in short, the general welfare.

◆ LIFE EXPECTANCY

In August 1994 newspapers around the world carried a brief report with important implications. The report stated that the ***life expectancy*** of Russian men had dropped below 60 and might be as low as 58. There was no evidence of a significant decline in the life expectancy of women, which held steady at 74. Just five years earlier, Russian men could expect to live to the age of 62. A rapid drop of several years over a short period revealed serious trouble in Russian society. Life expectancy for women also has dropped, from 74 to 72 today.

Russian census counts have never been very reliable, and male life expectancy may not have declined as much as the report indicates. Nevertheless, the report reminds us that life expectancy, which is rising almost everywhere in the world, can take a downturn even when a country is not at war or in the grip of an environmental crisis. It also emphasizes that women tend to be more resilient—and longer-lived—than men when the going gets rough. Virtually everywhere in the world, women's life expectancy is significantly greater than men's.

Life expectancy is another key measure of the well-being of a population. Again, the range is enormous. A girl born in the United States in the late 1990s can expect to live to the age of 79; female life expectancy is even greater in Canada (81). But a boy born in Uganda has a life expectancy of just 40 years, and a girl 42 years.

Gender Contrasts

Figure 29-2 maps *average* life expectancies as of the late 1990s. Taking each geographic realm as a whole, women outlive men by about 4 years in Europe, 4 years in East Asia, 3 years in Subsaharan Africa, 7 years in South America, and 6 years in North America. In Russia the difference may be as much as 14 years, possibly even more.

Regional Contrasts

Given this variation by sex, the map also reveals huge regional contrasts. In the late 1990s, the world average life expectancy was 68 for women and 64 for men. Most tropical African countries fell well short of these averages, but they were reached or exceeded by the majority of Middle and South American states. In Southwest, South, and Southeast Asian countries, life expectancies range from high (Jordan, Sri Lanka) to low (Nepal, Cambodia). India reported life expectancies of 59 years for both males and females.

Remarkable progress has been made in East Asia. Not only is Japan's average life expectancy among the highest in the world, but those of South Korea and Taiwan rank among the highest as well. Most important of all, in 1998 life expectancies in China were 72 for females and 68 for males.

Age Contrasts

These life expectancy figures do not mean that everyone lives to those ages. The figure is an average that takes account of the children who die young and the people who survive well beyond the average. Thus the dramatically lower figures for the world's poorer countries primarily reflect high infant mortality. A person who has survived beyond childhood is likely to survive well beyond the recorded life expectancy. The low life expectancy figures for the food-short countries remind us again how hard hit children are in poorer parts of the world.

Life expectancies have increased significantly over the past half-century. More progress has been made toward reducing death rates than toward lowering birth rates, and as a result life expectancies are slowly rising—even in the global economic core, where they are already high. It has been predicted that life expectancies may reach 85 years by the early twenty-first century, but that they will then level off because of the natural failure of vital organs in the aging body. In the meantime, we should expect a continued increase in life expectancies in poorer countries as improvements in medical facilities, hygiene, and drug availability suppress death rates.

Even now, the effects of these improvements can be observed from maps showing life expectancies (that is, remaining years of life) at advanced ages (for example, 20 and 40 years). Such maps show much less contrast between core and peripheral countries. As we will note later, although infant mortality has been dramatically reduced in better-off societies, much less progress has been made in combating the diseases of middle and advanced age. The great contrast between advantaged and disadvantaged countries lies at the base of the population pyramid, in rates of survival in the first few years of life.

It is natural that increases in life expectancy should be seen as evidence of progress. But the implications of longer life expectancies must also be considered. There will be ever-larger numbers of old people in the population, and they will require ever more support. According to World Bank data, throughout the world there are 500 million people age 60 or above, accounting for about 9 percent of the total pop-

Figure 29-2 Life Expectancy at Birth.

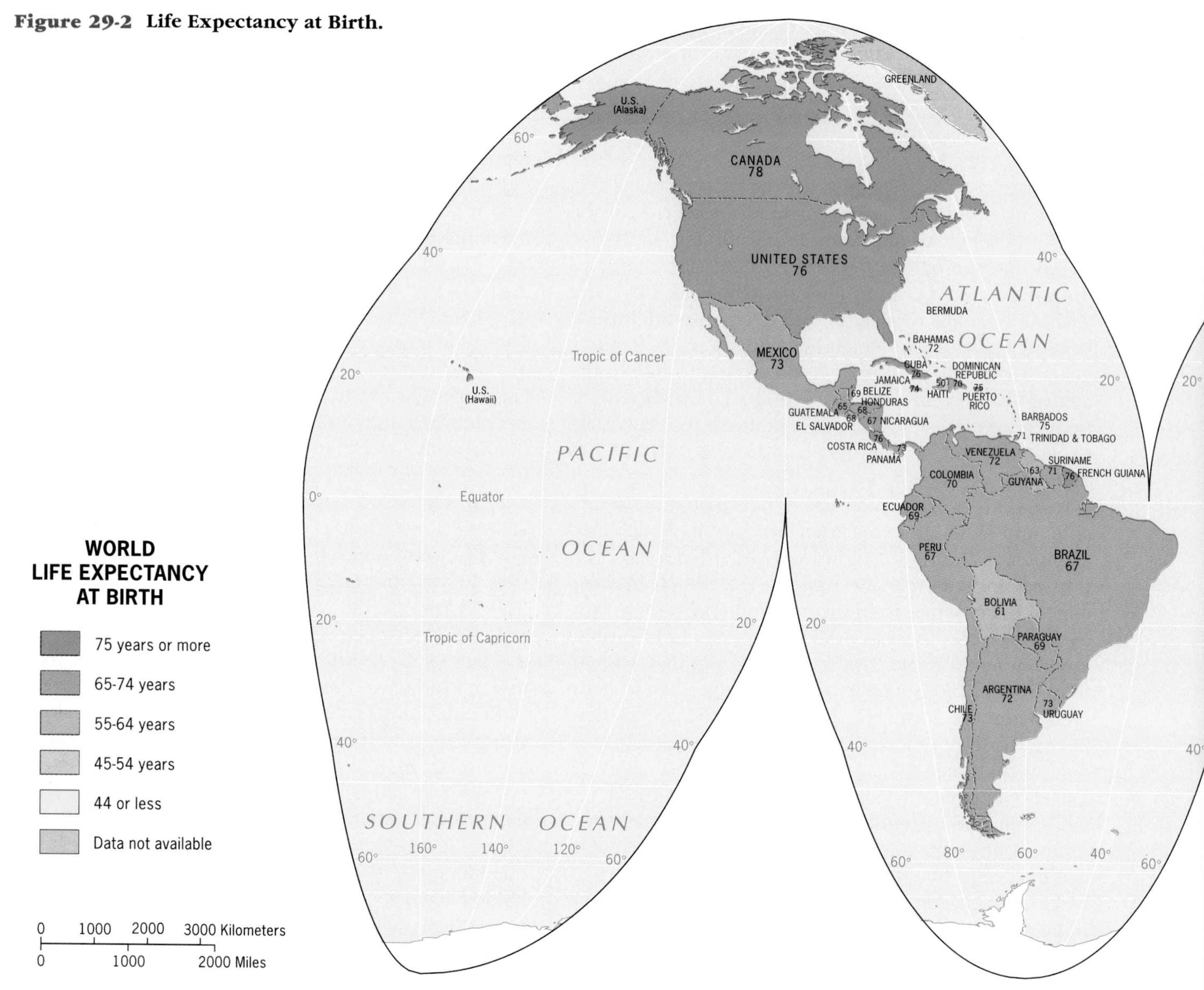

ulation. By 2030 the number of people age 60 and over will exceed 1.5 billion, and they will make up some 16 percent of the world's population. This figure—16 percent—already has been exceeded in Western Europe, where in 1998 nearly one-fifth of the population was 60 or older. By 2030, as much as *one-third* of Western Europeans are likely to be in this age bracket, and if life expectancy and growth figures can be trusted, the same will be true of *one-quarter* of the population of China.

Earlier we discussed the problems faced by societies where a large percentage of the population is young. Figure 29-2 reveals that quite a different set of challenges faces countries with aging populations, challenges that are already felt in some European countries and in Japan. In order to support growing numbers of older people, younger workers will have to be more productive and will be taxed more heavily than before. Governments will be hard-pressed to cope with the demand for services and the political impact of raising taxes for social security purposes.

◆ TYPES AND PATTERNS OF DISEASE

Life expectancy is only one manifestation of the overall health of a society, and as noted earlier, national averages tend to conceal variations by sex, age, and location. The incidence and types of diseases that affect a population also reveal the conditions in which people live. Certain kinds of environments harbor dangerous disease carriers, and diseases have ways of spreading from one population to another.

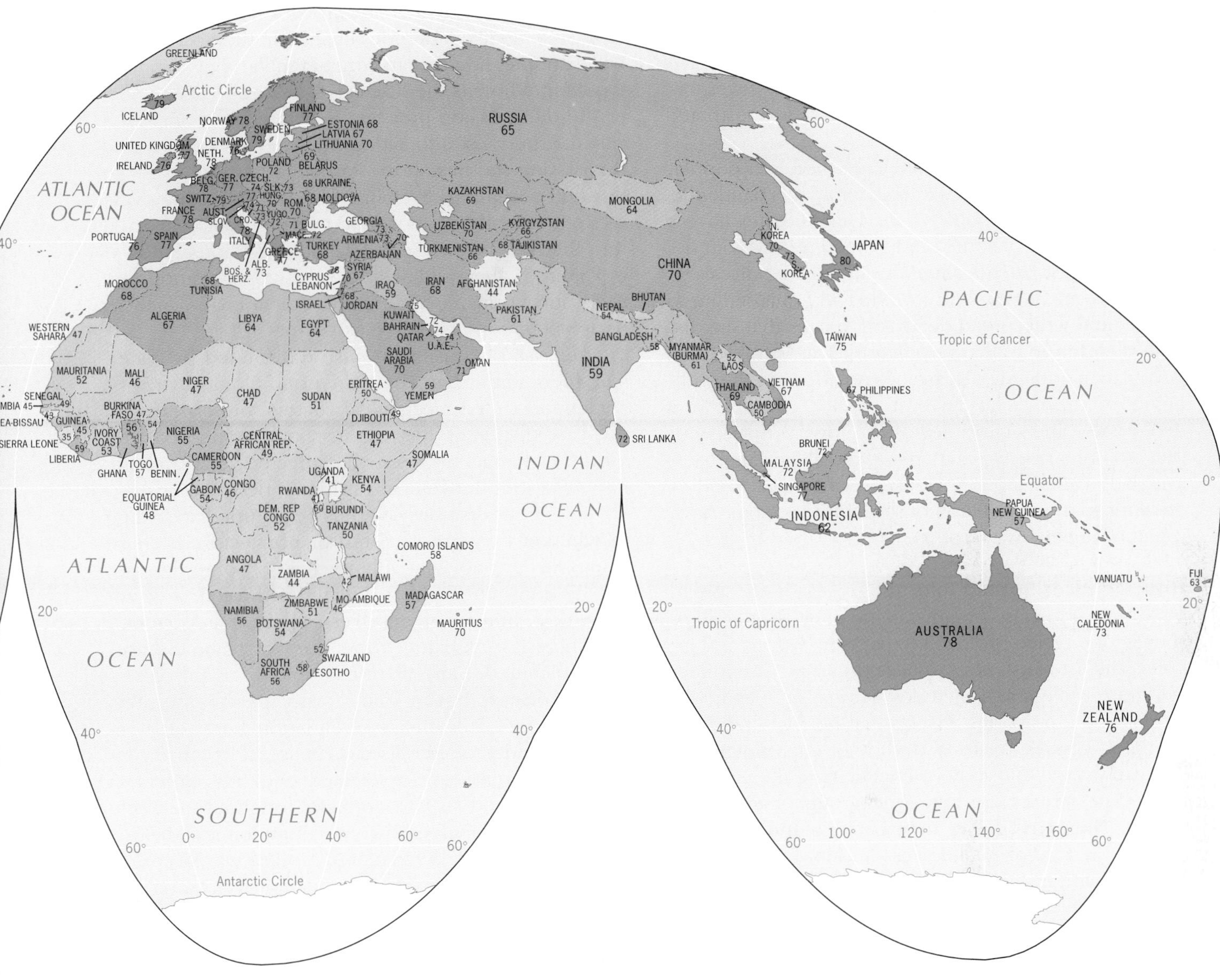

Medical geographers are interested in both the regional distribution of diseases and the processes and paths whereby diseases spread or diffuse. These are matters that can be analyzed by cartographic methods, and maps allow geographers to make important predictions. For example, a map showing the location and extent of an outbreak of diarrheal diseases can provide an early warning of the development of kwashiorkor. Maps showing the distribution of unvaccinated populations in urban areas can assist in preparation for crisis situations.

Major Types of Diseases Let us begin by classifying the types of diseases we will discuss in the remainder of the chapter:

1. ***Infectious Diseases*** About 65 percent of all human illnesses are of the infectious type. They result from an invasion of parasites and their multiplication in the body. Malaria is an example.
2. ***Chronic or Degenerative Diseases*** These are diseases of longevity or age. They do not kill instantly; instead, they cause long-term deterioration of the body. Cancer and heart disease are common chronic diseases in our society.
3. ***Genetic or Inherited Diseases*** Certain diseases can be traced directly to genetic factors. Hemophilia, sickle-cell anemia, and lactose intolerance are among these inherited maladies.

Some diseases occur in confined regions; others spread throughout the world. When a sudden outbreak leads to a high percentage of cases and a large number of deaths in a region, it is called an ***epidemic***. Peru's recent cholera outbreak had epidemic proportions. When the outbreak spreads around the world, as various forms of influenza have done since the beginning of the twentieth century, a ***pandemic*** develops. Many diseases have a limited range, however, because the organisms that transmit them are restricted by environmental conditions.

Certain diseases become established in a population without a spectacular epidemic or pandemic. Even today, many people in the United States have a venereal disease of some kind, sometimes without being aware of it. Such a situation, in which a disease is carried by many people (or ***hosts***) without leading to a rapid and widespread death toll, means that the disease is ***endemic*** to that population. This is not to suggest that an endemic disease has no effect on the well-being of those who have it. General health *does* deteriorate, and energy levels are lowered; susceptibility to other diseases may rise. On college campuses, a malady called mononucleosis is often described as endemic to the population of students (and some have it without being aware of it).

How Diseases Spread Infectious diseases are spread by disease-causing organisms ranging from microscopic, one-celled protozoa to parasitic worms and insects. The list of ***agents***, as these organisms are called, is almost endless and includes worms, such as hookworms and tapeworms; insects that burrow under the skin; and viruses, bacteria, and other microorganisms that can invade the body or contaminate the environment. The viruses are a unique group of infectious agents. They are smaller than bacteria and are composed of a core of nucleic acid and layers of protein and, in some instances, fatty substances. Viruses can infect animal cells and cause diseases such as measles, influenza, polio, and probably certain forms of cancer.

When we are afflicted by an infectious disease, we are hosts to a particular disease organism. When a population contains a large number of hosts, a ***reservoir*** has been formed from which the disease may expand or diffuse. Those to whom it spreads become additional hosts, strengthening the disease reservoir.

Diseases spread in several ways. Some agents are transmitted from one person directly to another by contact. In this case the disease is carried from one host to the next without any intermediate host. A handshake, a kiss, or some other form of touching can transmit the agents. Even standing close enough to a person so that tiny moisture particles from exhaled air reach you can have the same effect. Diseases that are transmitted in this way are termed *nonvectored* diseases; examples are the common cold, measles, venereal diseases, and mononucleosis.

When a disease is carried from one host to the next by an intermediate host, the disease is said to be *vectored.* The intermediate host or ***vector*** plays a critical role in the transmission process because the parasite (the agent) undergoes change in the host's body. For example, no one can contract malaria by touching a person who has the disease. A mosquito is essential to the transmission process. Moreover, it is not just a case of the mosquito biting the infected person and then biting the new host. Rather, a parasite must go through a significant change as part of its life cycle while it inhabits the mosquito and before it is injected into the new host. Insects (including various kinds of mosquitoes, flies, and ticks) are the most common vectors, but worms, snails, and larger animals, such as house pets, can also serve as vectors.

Disease organisms are also transmitted by water, soil, food, and feces. These are nonbiological vectors, sometimes called mechanical vectors, or ***vehicles***. In this case the agent does not necessarily undergo a biological change between the infected host and the new host, but the vehicle sustains it between hosts.

Infectious diseases can thus be grouped according to whether they are vectored or nonvectored. These categories are not mutually exclusive. Some diseases can be transmitted either directly or through a vector or vehicle; humans themselves can serve as vectors.

There is uncertainty about the way some diseases are transmitted. Cancer, for example, is classified as a chronic disease but in some forms may be an infectious disease. Still, the differentiation between nonvectored and vectored diseases is useful because geographic contrasts are associated with it. Cholera, a vehicle-vectored disease, spread throughout the world during several nineteenth-century pandemics. Malaria, on the other hand, is a vectored disease whose spread is limited by the environmental constraints on the mosquito that transmits it.

Data on population numbers, growth rates, and demographic structures do not provide a complete picture of the degree of well-being of the people they represent. Hundreds of millions of people, especially in equatorial and tropical regions, face a combination of undernourishment, malnutrition, and prevalent disease.

Let us therefore take a closer look at some of the more common diseases affecting people in various parts of the world.

Vectored Infectious Diseases

As noted earlier, tropical (and especially equatorial) environments enhance biological activity. Vectors and agents abound in such environments, and infectious diseases spread rapidly through host populations.

Malaria As Figure 29-3 shows, ***malaria*** occurs throughout the world, except in higher latitudes and drier environments. Although people in the tropical portions of Africa suffer most from this disease, malaria also prevails in India, Southeast Asia, China, and the tropical Americas.

There are several types of malaria, some more severe than others; not only human beings but also various species of monkeys, rats, birds, and even snakes can be affected by it. Malaria's virulence results from the effectiveness of its vectors, three African mosquitoes (*Anopheles gambiae*, *A. arabiensis*, and *A. funestus*). The role of these mosquitoes in the diffusion of the disease was not determined until the late eighteenth century, but the sequence is now well known: the mosquito stings an infected host and sucks up some of the disease agents. In the mosquito's stomach, the parasites reproduce and multiply, eventually reaching its saliva. When the mosquito stings the next person, some of the parasites are injected into that person's bloodstream. Now the person who has been stung develops malaria and becomes a host.

Malaria has killed or incapacitated countless millions of people. The efficiency of one of its vectors, *A. gambiae*, was revealed in 1938 when this mosquito was accidentally introduced into Brazil. Within months Brazil experienced its most serious malaria epidemic, with more than 14,000 deaths in less than a year. A quick eradication campaign wiped out *A. gambiae* before it could spread far from its Brazilian base; if the mosquito had diffused into the Amazon Basin, South America might today suffer as severely from malaria as Africa does.

Compared to the death toll in Africa and Asia, however, Brazil's epidemic was a minor incident. During the 1950s health authorities estimated that malaria caused 1 million deaths *per year* in India alone, and in Africa the toll was much higher.

Malaria is a major factor in infant and child mortality. Most of the victims are children age 5 or younger. If they survive, they develop a certain degree of immunity, although someone infected by malaria is likely to be weak and lack energy. Whole populations are afflicted, and entire regions have been abandoned because of the prevalence of the disease. The abandonment of ancient irrigation systems and apparently fertile lands, sometimes ascribed to climatic change, was in some instances probably due to the spread of malaria.

Malaria manifests itself as a recurrent fever and chills, with associated symptoms such as anemia and an enlarged spleen. The victim is not only deprived of energy, but also faces an increased risk of other diseases taking hold in the weakened body. Antimalarial drugs exist, but to defeat malaria it is necessary to eliminate the vector, the mosquito. In 1955 the World Health Organization launched a massive worldwide program against malaria following a remarkably successful campaign in Sri Lanka (then Ceylon). As Figure 29-3 shows, Sri Lanka was freed of malaria in the mid-1940s, when a massive attack on the mosquito was launched with the aid of a pesticide called *dichloro diphenyl trichloroethane* (DDT). The results were dramatic; the mosquito was practically wiped out, and

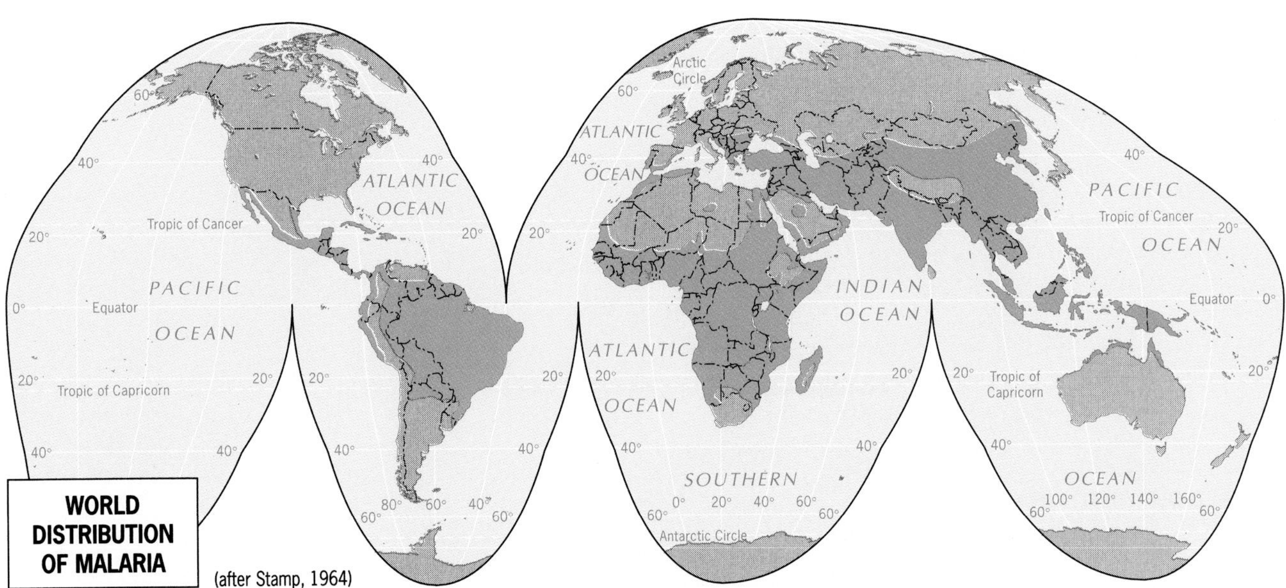

Figure 29-3 World Distribution of Malaria. Thirty-five years ago, malaria's global distribution was similar to today's; the battle against it is a stalemate. *Source: From L. D. Stamp,* The Geography of Life and Death. *Ithaca: Cornell University Press, 1964, p. 132.*

the rate of deaths attributable to malaria fell. In 1945, Sri Lanka's death rate overall had been 22 per 1000; in 1972, it reported a death rate of only 8 per 1000. The figure was further reduced to 6 per 1000 by 1985. Malaria had been defeated.

The conquest of malaria produced other problems, however. DDT proved to be highly carcinogenic and to have negative health and environmental consequences of its own. Also, the birth rate did not decline—it was 32 per 1000 in 1945, and in 1972 it was still 30 per 1000. Thus, while malaria was eradicated, the population growth rate rose substantially, creating new problems for Sri Lanka. By the time the birth rate dropped, the island had experienced a population explosion.

Success in combating major diseases often is only temporary. Following the Sri Lanka experiment, a massive assault was initiated against the malaria mosquito in India, and the number of new cases of the disease declined dramatically. But ten years later India reported that 60 million people were infected with malaria, more than half the number who had the disease before the antimalaria campaign began. This proved the mosquito population's ability to rebound quickly after even the most intensive application of insecticides. Today the war against malaria is taking a new tack: genetic interference with the mosquito so that its capacity to transmit the malaria parasite, *Plasmodium*, is destroyed. By introducing "engineered" mosquitoes into the general population, it is anticipated that those that cannot transmit malaria will eventually replace *A. gambiae*.

But all this will take many years; in the meantime malaria remains a worldwide scourge. The mosquito is surviving pesticide campaigns, and the effectiveness of antimalaria drugs is declining. The amount of misery caused by this disease remains immense.

Yellow Fever Yellow fever is now confined to tropical and near-tropical areas (Fig. 29-4), but in past centuries its distribution was much wider. The disease, which is caused by a virus transmitted by various kinds of mosquitoes, has killed vast numbers of people. In the Americas, devastating epidemics and serious outbreaks erupted in the Caribbean islands, in tropical Middle and South America, and as far north as Boston. The southern United States was repeatedly invaded by yellow fever; the last major outbreak struck coastal cities, especially New Orleans, as recently as 1905. Europe, too, experienced severe attacks of yellow fever; not even England and France were spared.

Today yellow fever has been driven back to the areas where it has long been endemic, and a vaccine is available that can provide long-term immunity. Eradicating the disease is difficult, however, since yellow fever also affects monkeys and several species of small forest animals. In the tropics, therefore, immunization of humans is the only solution.

Yellow fever contributed to the failure of Ferdinand de Lesseps, the builder of the Suez Canal, in his first attempt to cut a canal across Panama's mosquito-infested swamps in 1876. Not until a massive campaign of eradication had been waged could a second attempt at building the Panama Canal be made. This was done in 1905, but yellow fever and malaria still took a heavy toll among the workers.

The onset of yellow fever, which occurs some days after the bite of the vector mosquito, is marked

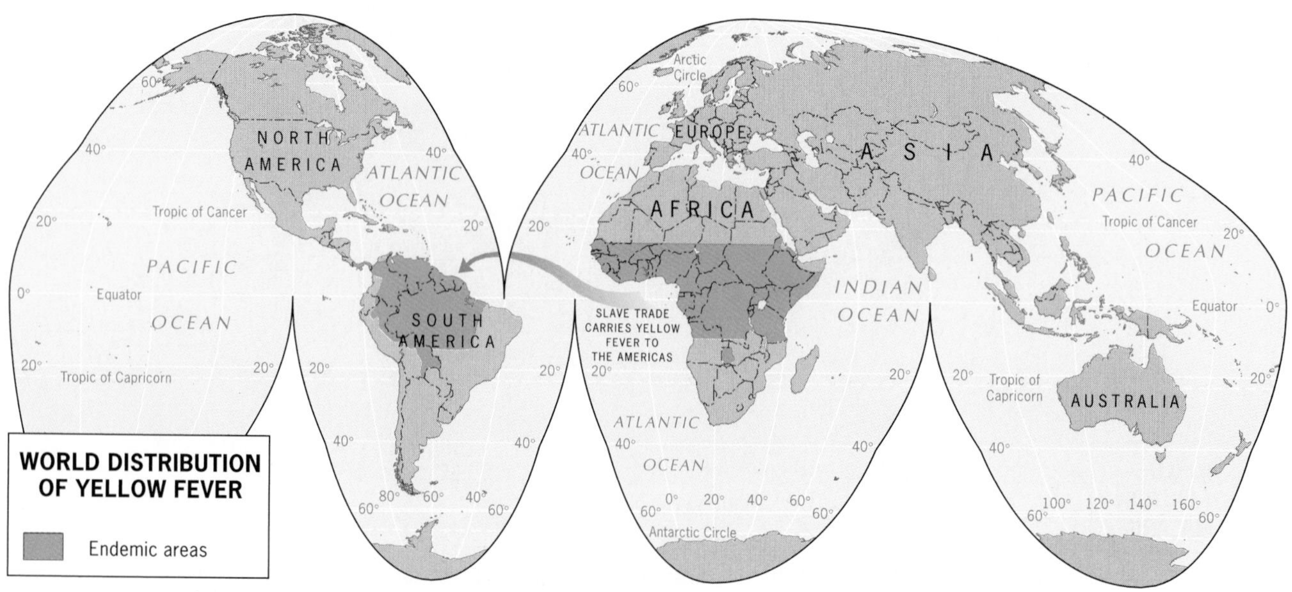

Figure 29-4 World Distribution of Yellow Fever. This maps shows the approximate areas in Africa and South America where yellow fever has long been endemic.

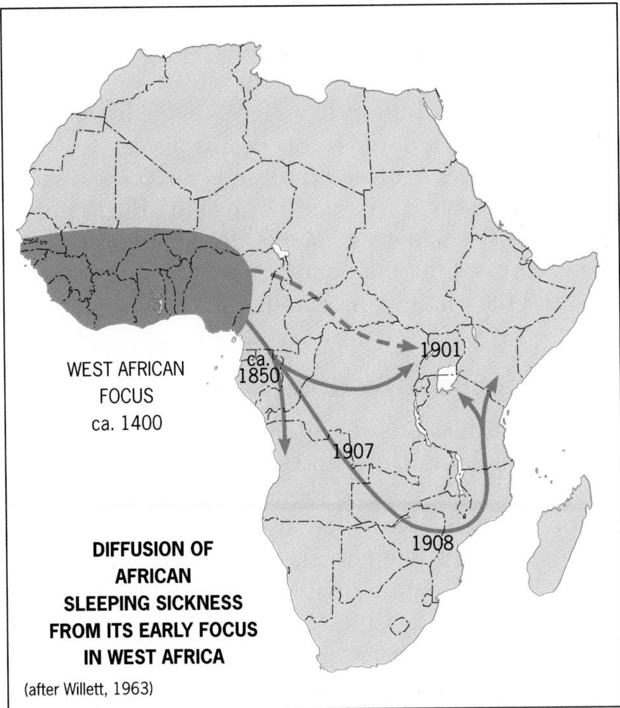

Figure 29-5 Diffusion of African Sleeping Sickness. African sleeping sickness diffusion from its early focus in West Africa is illustrated here. *Source: From K. C. Willett, "Trypanosomiasis and the Tsetse Fly Problem in Africa,"* Annual Review of Entomology, *Vol. 8, 1963, p. 197.*

by high temperatures. The fever is accompanied by headache, backache, and vomiting. Sometimes unchecked vomiting leads to death. In less acute cases jaundice occurs, and the deposition of bile pigment colors the eyes and skin quite yellow. Since there is no treatment for the disease, it has to run its course. In areas where yellow fever is endemic people have developed a degree of immunity. Still, there is always a sufficient reservoir of susceptible people to sustain a severe outbreak, and the threat of yellow fever continues for millions of people.

Sleeping Sickness The diffusion of African ***sleeping sickness*** from a source area in West Africa is thought to have begun about A.D. 1400 (Fig. 29-5). The tsetse fly, of which Africa has many species, is the vector. The fly sucks blood from an infected animal or person and in doing so ingests the single-celled agents or trypanosomes. These trypanosomes reproduce in the fly's body and eventually reach the insect's salivary glands. When the fly next bites a person or an animal, it spreads the infection to new hosts.

Africa's immense wildlife population acts as a reservoir for sleeping sickness because antelope are among the carriers of the disease (Fig. 29-6). The fly infects livestock as well as people, limiting the development of herds in places where meat and milk would improve diets that are seriously imbalanced. It also prevented the adoption of the animal-drawn plow and cart before Europeans arrived in Africa. In addition, it channeled the diffusion of cattle into Eastern and Southern Africa through corridors that were free of tsetse flies, destroying herds that moved into infested zones nearby. Most of all, it ravaged the population.

In humans, sleeping sickness begins with a fever, followed by swelling of the lymph nodes. Next the inflammation spreads to the brain and the spinal cord, producing the lethargy and listlessness that give the disease its name. Death may follow. The impact on livestock is equally severe: sick animals wither away and die within a year of infection. In some areas the disease is accompanied by a grotesque swelling of the limbs, which soon cannot be controlled. The animal stumbles about, becomes crazed, and then dies.

Although progress has been made in combating this dreaded disease, much of Africa is still affected by it (Fig. 29-7). The most promising line of attack is at the vector—killing tsetse flies in massive eradication campaigns. Sometimes whole villages have been moved from infested areas to tsetse-free zones. Killing of infected wildlife, destruction of the bush that the tsetse fly needs as its habitat, and other methods have been attempted. Africa is large, however—some 11.7 million square miles (over 30 million square kilometers)—and so the tsetse fly still rules over much of the continent.

Malaria, yellow fever, and sleeping sickness are just three of dozens of vectored infectious diseases that occur in tropical regions. A fourth is *schistosomiasis*, also known as ***bilharzia***, a debilitating disease

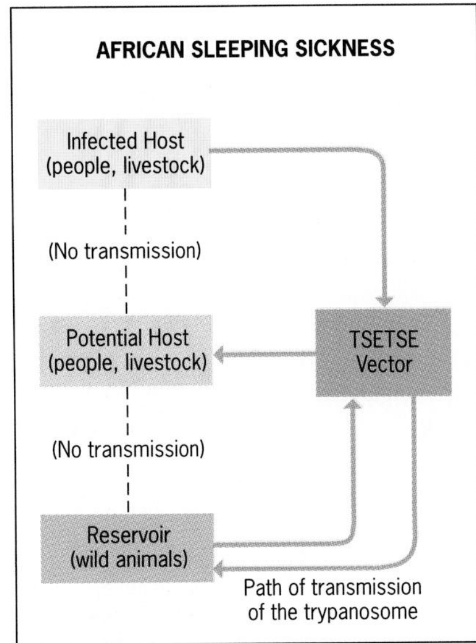

Figure 29-6 Transmission of African Sleeping Sickness. This diagram shows the path of transmission of African sleeping sickness.

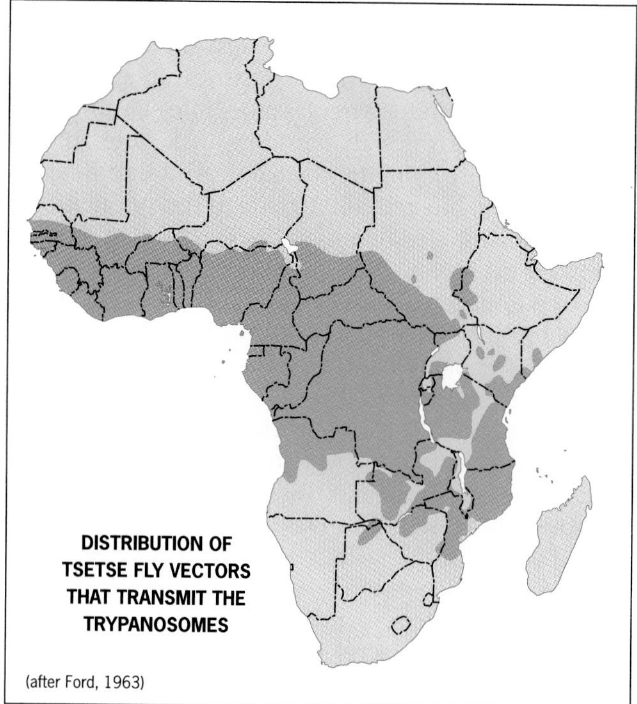

Figure 29-7 Distribution of Tsetse Fly Vectors. This map shows the distributionof tsetse fly vectors that transmit the trypanosomes. *Source: From J. Ford, "The Distribution of the Vectors of African Pathogenic Trypanosomes,"* Bulletin of the WHO, *Vol. 28, 1963, p. 655.*

transmitted by freshwater snails. The vector sends infected larva into still or slow-moving water, and when these penetrate the skin, they develop into mature, egg-laying worms. The eggs wreak havoc in the liver and other organs. When fast-moving streams in tropical areas were dammed for electricity-generating or agricultural purposes, the dams became ideal environments for the snails that transmit schistosomiasis, and local people paid the price. Figure 29-8 shows world areas at risk from three forms of this disease.

Still another vectored disease is *onchocerciasis* or ***river blindness***, so named because it afflicts people living in river valleys in West Africa and elsewhere. The vector is a fly; the parasite eventually reaches the eyes and the victim goes blind.

Nonvectored Infectious Diseases

Direct transmission of an infectious disease takes place through (1) close bodily contact, as in the case of venereal diseases and mononucleosis; (2) contamination of water and food by fecal material, which spreads diseases like cholera and infectious hepatitis; and (3) contamination of air when tiny droplets of saliva are expelled by infected persons and inhaled by others, as in the case of tuberculosis, influenza, and the common cold.

Cholera Perhaps the most frightening disease in this group is ***cholera***, also called Asiatic cholera, a term used to denote a set of diseases in which diarrhea and dehydration are the chief symptoms. Cholera is an ancient disease and was confined to India until the beginning of the nineteenth century. In 1816 it spread to China, Japan, East Africa, and Mediterranean Europe in the first of several pandemics. This initial wave abated by 1823, but by then the very name cholera was feared throughout the world, for it had killed people everywhere by the hundreds, even thousands. Death

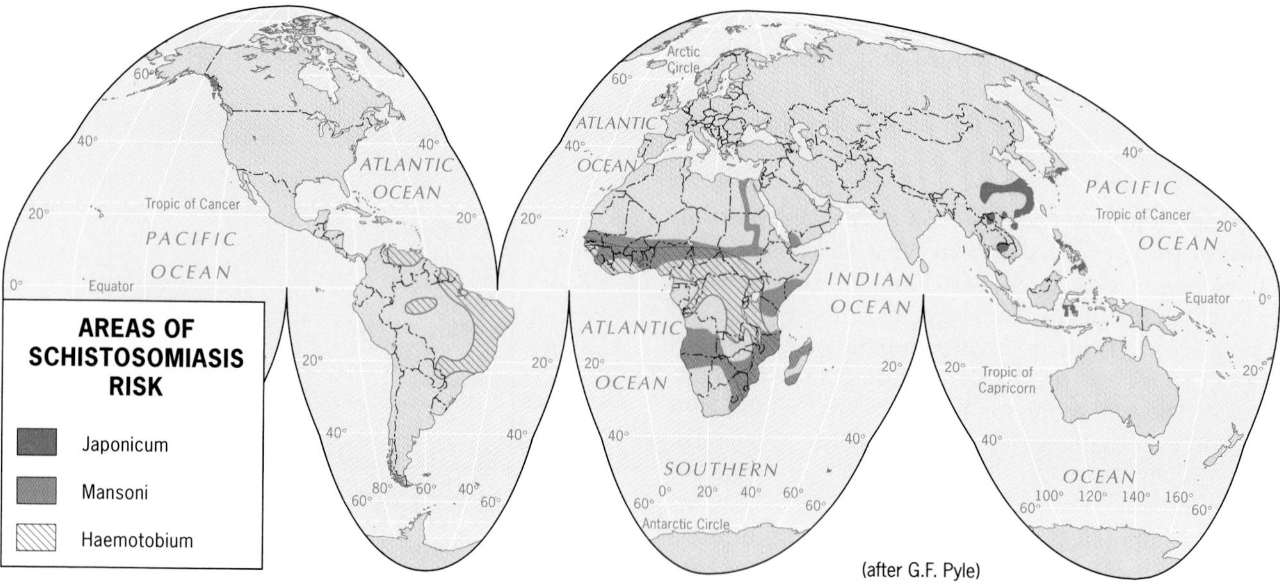

Figure 29-8 Areas of Schistosomiasis Risk. Areas where people are at risk from three types of schistosomiasis (bilharzia) are shown here. *Source: From G. Pyle,* Applied Medical Geography. *Silver Spring, Md.: Winston/Halsted, 1979, p. 47.*

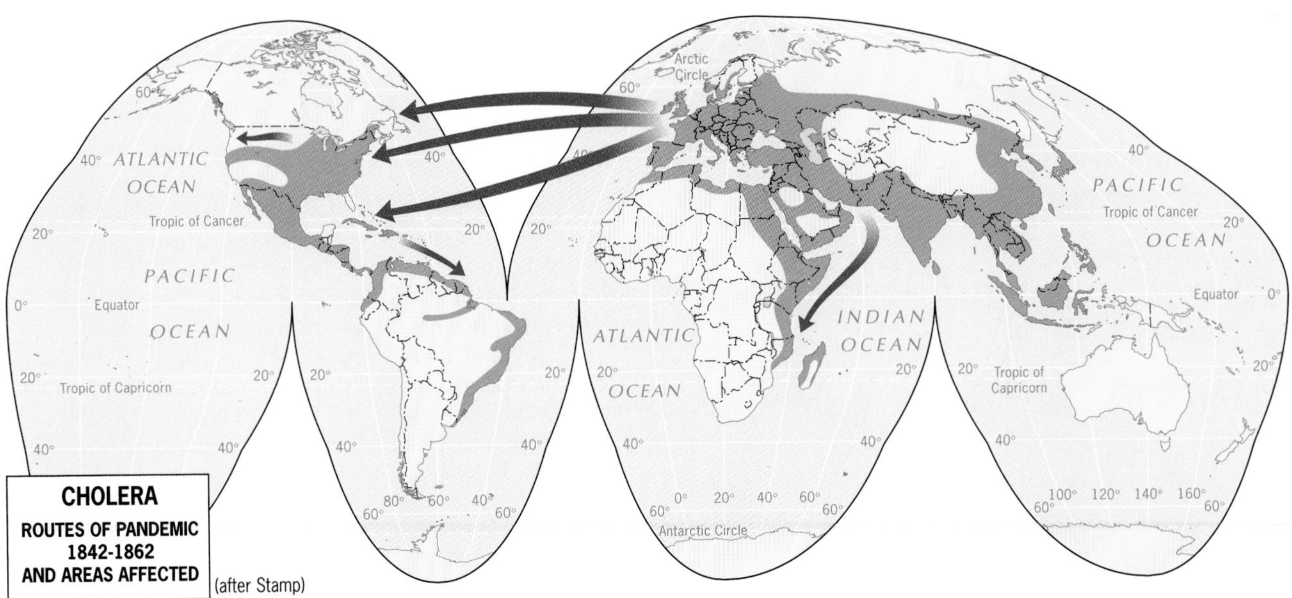

Figure 29-9 Routes of Cholera Pandemic, 1842–1862. The areas affected by the 1842–1862 cholera pandemic and the routes it took are depicted here. *Source: From L. D. Stamp,* The Geography of Life and Death *(Ithaca: Cornell University Press 1964).*

was horribly convulsive and would come in a matter of days, perhaps a week, and no one knew what caused the disease or how to avoid it when it invaded.

It was not long before a second pandemic struck. It lasted from 1826 to 1837, when cholera crossed the Atlantic and attacked North America. During the next pandemic, from 1842 to 1862, England was severely hit, and cholera again spread into North America (Fig. 29-9). During this period the vehicle for cholera was discovered (see "Focus on: Cholera and the Map"), and for the first time it was possible to take action. As Figure 29-9 shows, during the 1842–1862 pandemic, cholera spread southward along the East African coast and reached what is today northern Moçambique and Madagascar. It then spread through the Middle East to Europe and was carried across the Atlantic to North America. The disease diffused across the United States in the patterns shown in Figure 29-11. Arriving in New York and New Orleans in December 1848, it soon spread into the interior, mainly northward along the Mississippi Valley. It reached Chicago on April 29, 1850, at the same time that it was traveling westward to San Francisco, where it struck late in the same year.

There was only a brief respite before the last great world cholera pandemic began in 1865. Now, however, people knew to take precautions against contaminated water, and although the disease spread throughout the world, this was the last of the great cholera waves. In the United States cholera reached the East Coast in May 1866 and spread rapidly into the interior, reaching Detroit on May 29 and Chicago on July 21. This time it moved southward through the Mississippi Valley, meeting a northward attack that had originated in New Orleans in July as well. However, the disease failed to reach the West Coast during the 1865 to 1875 pandemic.

Although there have been later epidemics of cholera, for decades it has been confined to its South Asian endemic zone. Nevertheless, predictions that it had been defeated everywhere except in Asia proved premature. After being free from cholera for 50 years, Europe had an outbreak in 1972 in Naples, Italy. Also in the 1970s, parts of Africa that had not recently been affected reported cholera cases in a pandemic that invaded 29 countries in two years and had not totally receded by the late 1990s.

The refugee crisis that sent more than 1 million people from Rwanda to makeshift camps in Zaïre (now Congo) in mid-1994 was made worse by another cholera outbreak. River and lake waters were contaminated by thousands of corpses, and cholera spread rapidly. An international relief effort was needed to stem the tide.

The most alarming outbreak of cholera in this century, however, was the epidemic that began in Peru in December 1990. The Americas had been free from cholera for more than a hundred years, but the fast-spreading epidemic infected nearly 400,000 people during its first year and killed almost 4000. By the end of 1991 only four countries in the Americas remained untouched, and in 1992 every country in the hemisphere was affected. In early 1995 more than 1 million cases had been reported, and about 10,000 people had succumbed.

Focus On

Cholera and the Map

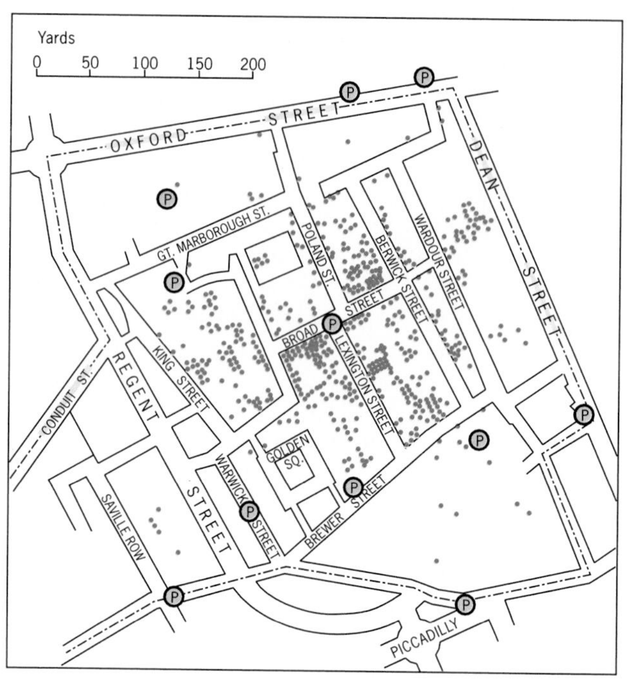

Figure 29-10 Cholera in the Soho District of London in 1854.

The map in Figure 29-10 was drawn by Dr. John Snow in 1854. It represents the streets and squares of Soho, a district of London. In those days people still drew water at municipal pumps and carried it home. Each *P* symbol on the map represents the location of such a pump.

Snow had been working on the problem of cholera for many years, and he had become convinced that contaminated water was to blame for carrying the disease to its victims. When the pandemic that began in 1842 reached England, the Soho district was severely hit. On his street map Snow located every cholera death in Soho by marking the residence of each victim with a dot. Approximately 500 deaths occurred in Soho, and as the map took shape, it became evident that an especially large number of those deaths were clustered around the pump on Broad Street. At the doctor's request, city authorities removed the handle from that pump, making it impossible to draw water there. The result was dramatic: almost immediately the number of reported new cases fell to almost zero. Snow's theory about the role of water in the spread of cholera was confirmed.

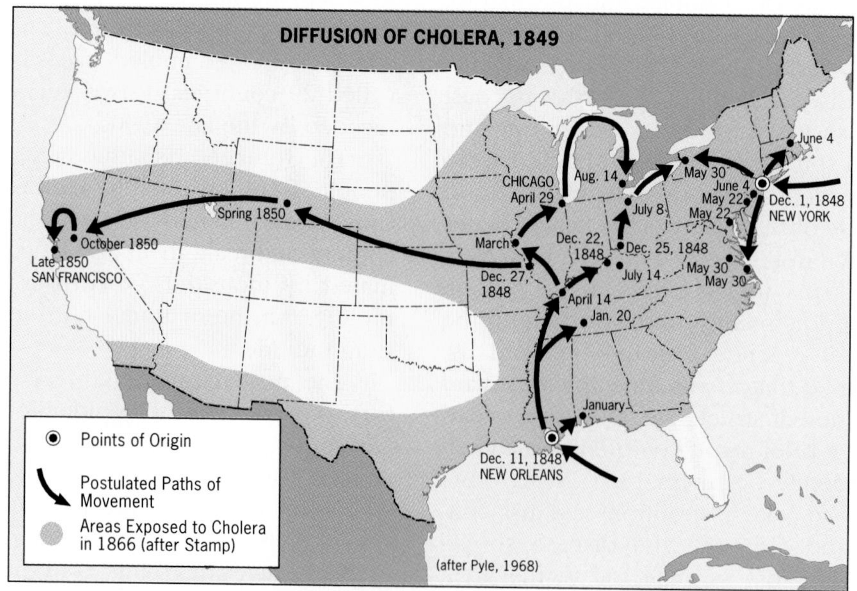

Figure 29-11 Diffusion of Cholera, 1849. This map shows the diffusion of cholera in the United States in 1849. *Source: From L. D. Stamp (see Figure 29-9), 1964, and G. F. Pyle, "The Diffusion of Cholera in the United States in the 19th Century,"* Geographical Analysis, 1, 1969, *p. 59.*

The epidemic that began in Peru was apparently caused by fecal contamination of the municipal water supply in one of Lima's shantytowns, but the diffusion of cholera through Ecuador and Chile was blamed on contaminated shellfish and raw vegetables irrigated with sewage-contaminated water. Cholera is defeated by high standards of sanitation, but urban populations form ready reservoirs when hygiene breaks down—as continues to happen in tropical Asia. A cholera vaccine exists but remains effective for only six months. If it is difficult to vaccinate an entire population even once, one can imagine the chances of doing so twice a year.

Influenza Every year tens of thousands of people succumb to the "flu," a malady that strikes millions of people throughout the world. The great majority recover, but many do not. In the United States in a typical year, ***influenza*** is the cause of death for some 20,000 people. Older people, and those who are weak, are especially susceptible.

Flu outbreaks are much worse in some years than others. In 1918 a worldwide pandemic killed between 20 and 30 million people after an especially virulent strain of the virus diffused throughout the world. Once a new strain of influenza has begun to spread, the disease is transmitted when people inhale the airborne virus, and it diffuses rapidly. A single infected person in an airplane or bus can transmit it to dozens of others.

Why do new epidemics and pandemics of influenza occur? The answer apparently lies in the life cycle of the influenza A virus, which comes from China (hence the names given to recent pandemics, such as "Chinese flu" and "Hong Kong flu"). There the virus resides in birds, especially waterfowl. The virus cannot be transmitted directly from birds to people, but it *is* transmitted from birds to pigs and from pigs to humans.

Chinese farming practices put ducks (major carriers of the influenza A virus) in close proximity to pigs and in turn to people. People with the flu can transmit the virus to pigs. Medical geographers therefore believe that the pig is host to strains of influenza A virus from both birds and humans. This means that new strains of the virus can form in the host and be transmitted to people, perhaps causing an epidemic or pandemic (Fig. 29-12).

In late 1997, a new strain of influenza, apparently originating in chickens (and possibly other fowl), broke out in Hong Kong, causing much alarm worldwide. All poultry and ducks in Hong Kong were destroyed, and imports from China were stopped. Although only a few dozen cases of the "chicken flu" appeared in humans, and human-to-human transmission was minimal, the new and unfamiliar strain raised much concern.

Influenza therefore has a vector at its source, but once it spreads away from its core area, it is diffused by contact. As noted previously, the distinction between vectored and nonvectored infectious diseases is not always hard and fast.

AIDS The last two decades of the twentieth century witnessed a medical catastrophe: the global spread of a disease called ***AIDS*** (Acquired Immune Deficiency Syndrome). Firm evidence of the existence of AIDS was recorded in 1981, and before the end of the

Figure 29-12 The Life Cycle of a New Strain of Influenza Virus.

decade a pandemic was in progress. AIDS is spread when individuals come into contact with the bodily fluids (especially blood) of other individuals—usually through sexual activity and blood transfusions. HIV (Human Immunodeficiency Virus), the virus that causes AIDS, got into the blood supply, and people in need of blood transfusions risked exposure to the virus. Despite a massive research effort on several continents in the early years, AIDS defied treatment. To be diagnosed with AIDS meant certain death. The disease struck indiscriminately, infecting the ordinary and the prominent alike—sports figures, actors, scholars, artists. Writers compared the fear of AIDS to the fear of cholera during the 1800s.

The dimensions of the AIDS pandemic are not fully known. People infected by HIV do not immediately display visible symptoms of the disease. In the early stages only a blood test will reveal infection, and then only by indicating that the body is mobilizing antibodies to fight HIV. People can carry the virus for years without being aware of it, and during that period they can unwittingly transmit it to others. Official reports of actual cases of AIDS therefore lag far behind the reservoir of infected individuals. In early 1994 the Centers for Disease Control recorded 860,000 AIDS cases in North America. Estimates of the number of people infected surpassed 1 million.

The data for the United States, however, pale before those for Africa. Official statistics for African countries still give no indication of the magnitude of the AIDS epidemic there. The medical system, already overwhelmed by the long-prevailing maladies of the region, cannot cope with this new onslaught. Many of those who are ill with AIDS live in remote villages or in the vast shantytowns of Nairobi, Kinshasa, and other large cities, and do not see a doctor. But staggering evidence of the impact of AIDS is everywhere, and surveys by the World Health Organization have begun to reveal the true magnitude of the epidemic: there were over 20.8 million HIV cases in Africa in 1997.

Most disconcerting are the trends surrounding AIDS. Since AIDS is transmitted most efficiently through blood and bodily fluid contact, sexual practices can spread the disease. Patronage of prostitutes along the Kampala (Uganda)–Nairobi (Kenya)–Mombasa highway in East Africa, for example, is known to be a diffusion route. In *The Geography of AIDS* (1991), medical geographers G. Shannon, G. Pyle, and R. Bashshur report on a series of tests of female prostitutes in Nairobi: in 1981, 4 percent tested positive for the virus; in 1984, 61 percent; and in 1986, 85 percent. In Blantyre, the largest city of Malawi, pregnant women showed an infection rate of 2 percent in 1984; in 1990 the rate was 22 percent. About one-third of babies born to infected women are themselves infected with HIV.

Infection rates in East and Equatorial African cities are high, ranging from 8 percent of adults in Congo's capital of Kinshasa to 30 percent in Kigali, capital of Rwanda. These levels have been reached relatively recently, so that the real devastation of the epidemic in Africa has only begun. Here lies Africa's "AIDS Belt," a group of tropical countries where the incidence of AIDS is the highest in the world (Fig. 29-13). The cities were the large reservoirs, but the rural areas have not escaped. Surveys conducted in rural areas of Uganda and Congo indicate that between 8 and 12 percent of adults there are infected. Medical knowledge about AIDS is improving, but no cure is in sight. Hence, before the end of the century AIDS will alter the population growth rates of much of tropical Africa.

HIV continues to defy all efforts to contain it. From its African source area it has diffused widely, although with varying intensity. In Southeast Asia, Thailand has become, in the words of geographer P. R. Gould, "[an AIDS] catastrophe in the making . . . in its eventual magnitude it may well exceed the terror of the killing fields of civil war in neighboring Cambodia." In *The Slow Plague* (1993), Gould alerts us not only to the geographic dimensions of AIDS but also to the prospect that this disease may be just one of several that are poised to assail our populous, vulnerable world.

Chronic Diseases

Dramatic as the AIDS pandemic is, the number of AIDS cases throughout the world is far smaller than those of heart disease, cancer, stroke, and lung ailments. The chronic diseases have always been the leading causes

Table 29-1 Leading Causes of Death in the United States, 1996 (thousands)

Cause	Number	Rate per 100,000
1. Heart disease	842.2	317.8
2. Cancer	539.5	203.6
3. Stroke	157.9	59.6
4. Accident	90.4	34.1
5. Influenza, pneumonia	82.2	31.0
6. Diabetes	58.8	22.2
7. HIV infection	42.4	16.0
8. Suicide	29.9	11.3
9. Cirrhosis of the liver	25.1	9.5
10. Homicide, legal action	22.5	8.5

Source: Britannica *Book of the Year, 1997,* p. 296.

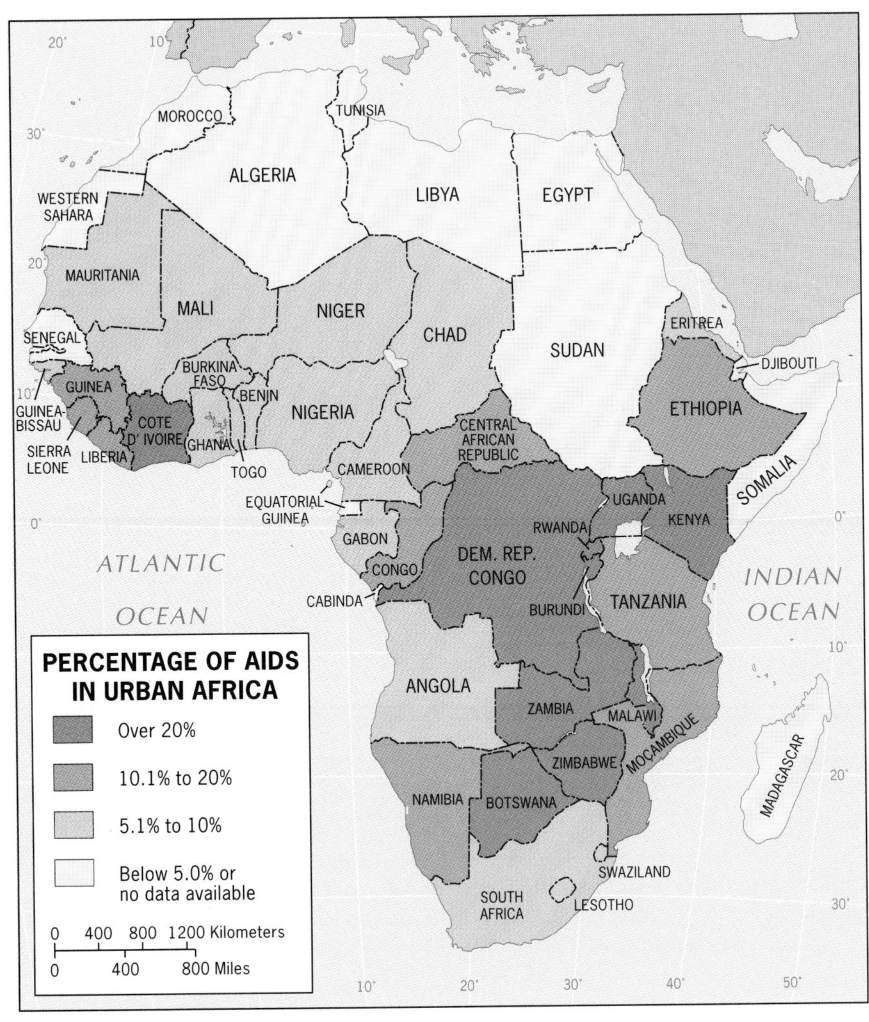

Figure 29-13 AIDS Distribution in Africa. This map shows the percentage of AIDS cases in urban Africa. *Source: Based on medical and press reports as of January 1998.*

of death; in the United States a century ago, tuberculosis, pneumonia, diarrheal diseases, and heart diseases (in that order) were the chief killers. Today, heart disease and cancer head the list, with cerebral hemorrhage (stroke) next and accidents high on the list as well (Table 29-1). At the turn of the century, tuberculosis and pneumonia caused 20 percent of all deaths; today, they cause fewer than 5 percent. The diarrheal diseases, which were so high on the old list, are now primarily children's maladies. Today, these diseases are not even on the list of the ten leading causes of death. The modern deadly diseases are the afflictions of middle and old age, reflecting higher life expectancies.

Table 29-1 reflects other realities, some of which are not so positive. Although the diseases of infancy have been largely defeated and such infectious diseases as tuberculosis and pneumonia are less serious threats than they were, the battles against cancer and heart disease are far from won. Modernization has brought with it new lifestyles, new pressures, new consumption patterns, and exposure to new chemicals, and we do not know how these affect our health. People often smoke cigarettes because they find it relaxing, but lung cancer—a major modern killer—has been linked to smoking. In order to distribute adequate food supplies to populations in huge urban areas, we add various kinds of preservatives to foods without knowing exactly how they will affect our health in the long run. We substitute artificial flavoring for sugar and other calorie-rich substances, but some of those substitutes have been proven to be dangerous. The map of cancer and heart disease shows that these problems are as heavily concentrated in the urban, industrial core as some of the major infectious diseases prevail in the periphery (Fig. 29-14).

The chronic diseases are also known as degenerative diseases and tend to be associated with old age. Arteriosclerosis involves the narrowing and sometimes the blocking of arteries carrying blood to vital organs, including the heart, brain, and kidneys. This appears to be the result of long-term accumulation of fatty ma-

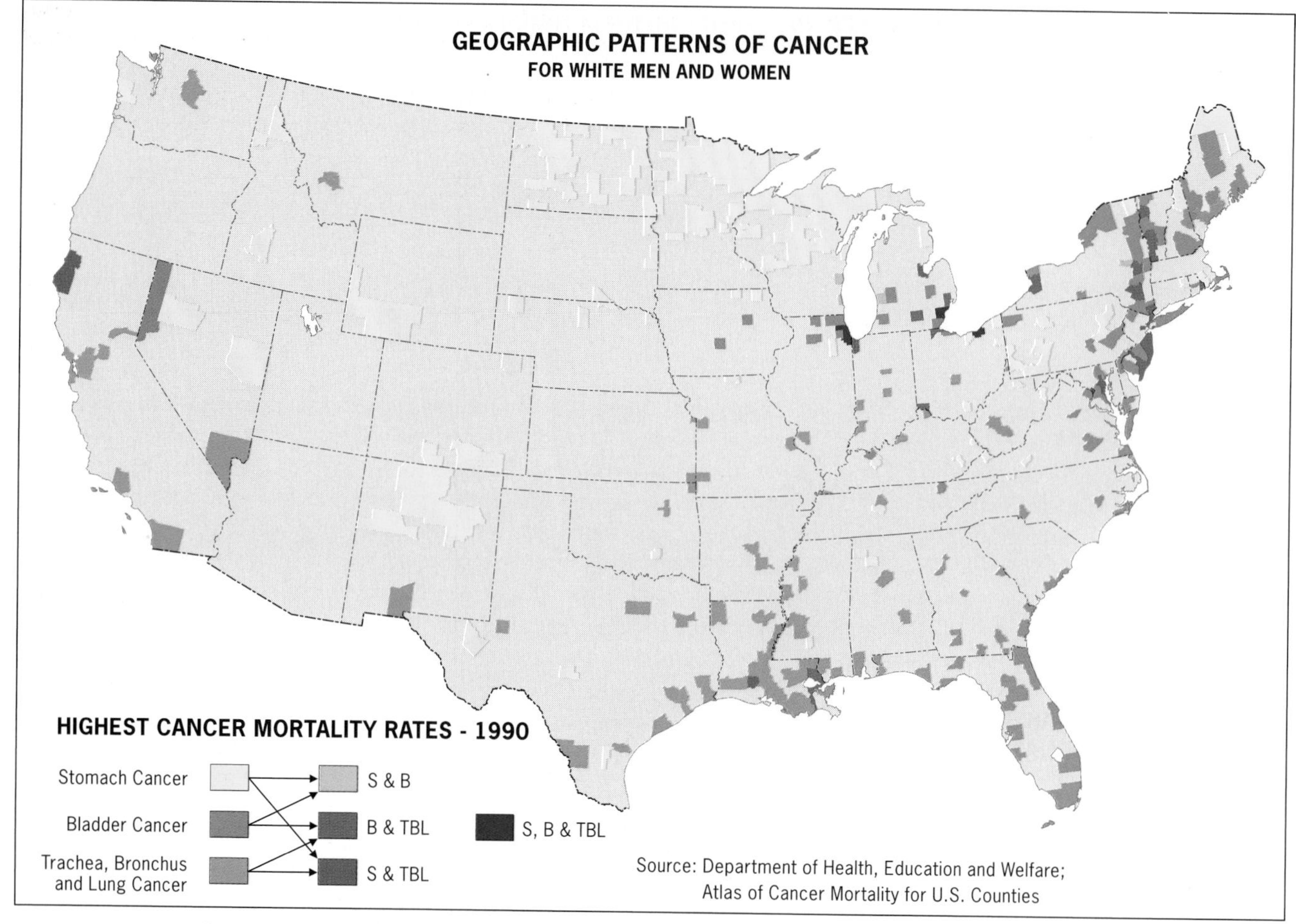

Figure 29-14 Highest Cancer Mortality Rates, 1990. The regional aspects of cancer incidence in the United States as of 1990 are illustrated in this map. *Source: Department of Health, Education and Welfare;* Atlas of Cancer Mortality for U.S. Counties.

terial and calcium on the interior walls of arteries; the risk increases with age. High-cholesterol diets over long periods contribute to the blockages, and the sedentary habits of urban life apparently are also partly responsible.

At the opposite end of the life cycle, children confront new dangers. As everyone knows, children will chew on almost anything—toys, utensils, and whatever else is in reach. In the poorer areas of the cities and towns, where many families live in substandard housing, paint peels off the walls and children pull at the slivers and chew on them. The paint contains lead, and it is now known that many children contract lead poisoning in this way, as well as from drinking water that has flowed through old lead pipes. Lead poisoning has several negative effects, including brain damage.

In addition, in many parts of the country drinking water contains substances that may be conducive to the development of cancer. Chlorine and fluoride are added to water to reduce the risk of contamination, and other chemicals are used to treat water pollution of various kinds. We are not sure of the long-term effects of consuming treated water, however, and we may be substituting one risk for another. It is one thing to start using treated water at middle age, but it is another to begin consuming it at birth. When something is consumed from birth, damaging substances have a long time to build up. Water treatment on the scale at which it occurs today is a relatively new phenomenon, and only the most recent generation has been using chemically treated water from birth. The results in terms of disease and mortality are not yet known.

Genetic Diseases

The origins of genetic or inherited diseases lie in the chromosomes and genes, and these maladies can be transferred from one generation to the next. Genetic diseases are not well understood, although some, such as sickle-cell anemia, have been studied intensively.

Genetic diseases result from gene mutations or accidents to the chromosomes. In some cases, a mutation may occur in the fetus before birth and affect the child even if both parents are completely normal; mongolism is an example. Radiation and viruses may also damage a parent's chromosomes, but the role of drugs in gene mutations is still uncertain. From a geographic standpoint, other forms of inherited disease are of greater interest. Certain genetic diseases are concentrated in specific populations, and others appear to be associated with particular natural environments. Phenylketonuria, for example, occurs mostly among Europeans. People who have this disorder cannot convert one kind of amino acid into another, and unless it is diagnosed and treated early, mental retardation results.

Metabolic problems—the inability to process all elements of the diet—are a major category of genetic diseases. Enzymes facilitate critical reactions within the body, and failure to produce an adequate quantity of a particular enzyme (or to produce any at all) leads to metabolic malfunction. Such a disorder can be inherited. A prominent example is primary adult lactose intolerance. People who suffer from this disorder lack an adequate supply of an enzyme needed to break down the milk sugar lactose. When it is severe, this "milk allergy," or galactosemia, leads to damage of the liver and spleen; young children display swelling of the abdomen, face, hands, and feet due to the accumulation of fluid. Mental retardation can result, but this effect is rare. The symptoms are more likely to be mild, including stomach and intestinal pain after milk is consumed or foods containing lactose are eaten. People who experience such discomforts will reduce or eliminate their intake of milk.

People who cannot comfortably consume milk and other foods containing lactose may suffer from deficiencies in nutrients that these foods contribute to the body, especially calcium. This has led to some unusual supplementing of diets, including the ancient custom of earth-eating, or *geophagy*. In West Africa this time-honored practice involves the eating of clay for medicinal and dietary reasons.

Lactose intolerance does not occur randomly. For example, it is much more prevalent among African Americans than among whites. In India, primary adult lactose intolerance is the rule rather than the exception. (About 80 percent of India's population probably has some intolerance, and in China the figure may be even higher.) In Africa, the peoples of the forest zone, who do not have livestock that give milk, are highly lactose intolerant, while those of the savanna, who are pastoralists, have much lower intolerance. As these regional differences illustrate, lactose intolerance and other diseases of metabolic origin can be studied from a geographic perspective, in terms of migration routes, acculturation (see Chapter 2), natural environments, ethnic distributions, and other spatial phenomena.

This chapter has focused on only a few of the topics related to the health of the world's population. The problems of medical geography should not be viewed in isolation from other issues related to population. Improved medical systems in poorer countries may prevent diseases from claiming as many lives as in the past—only to add to the numbers who will die of starvation. Even the wealthier countries have still not achieved satisfactory health-care systems, but the poor countries in particular need programs that combine planning efforts in nutrition, sanitation, health services, and family planning. The tasks ahead are numerous and enormous.

◆ KEY TERMS ◆

agent
AIDS
bilharzia
child mortality rate
cholera
chronic disease
contagious disease
endemic
epidemic
genetic diseases
hosts
infant mortality rate (IMR)
infectious disease
influenza
kwashiorkor
life expectancy
malaria
marasmus
medical geography
pandemic
reservoir
river blindness
sleeping sickness
vector
vehicle
yellow fever

◆ APPLYING GEOGRAPHIC KNOWLEDGE ◆

1. Despite improvements in sanitation and health care in Europe and North America over the past few decades, some infectious diseases are more rampant now than they were 40 years ago. What social, economic, and technological changes help explain this circumstance?

2. You are a member of a team of medical geographers working on AIDS. Your maps of the incidence of AIDS reveal different spatial patterns of transmission for different cultural realms of the world, and even for different societies within these realms. How are culture and AIDS interrelated?

Chapter 30

Geographies of Inequality: Race and Ethnicity

From the field notes

"Walking through the back streets of Taipei I noted the distinct identities of local neighborhoods: superficially they looked similar, but look more closely, and you saw variations in the kinds of stores, sorts of goods, types of activities (from repair shops to art studios), even the ways doors were marked and windows draped. And then I heard the sound of laughter and applause, and followed it to find a street theater in progress. The play went on for hours; pedestrians would stop and watch, other passersby got off their bikes and spent some time listening. By the time I left, the audience that was there when I arrived had been almost totally replaced. 'It's very local, very ethnic,' said a colleague whom I asked about this. 'These groups make some pretty biting criticisms of their neighbors!' Here, obviously, is one way ethnic identity is kept alive."

KEY POINTS

◆ All humanity constitutes one race, but human groups differ physically from each other. Many societies have used these differences to create distinctions in status and opportunity among individuals.

◆ Humanity is sometimes divided into four basic racial stocks, but some groups do not fit neatly within one of these stocks. The groupings are based on the assumption that some physical differences are more important than others.

◆ Racism is often associated with a degree of segregation that promotes stereotypes and influences where people go and what they do.

◆ Ethnicity differs from race because of its fundamentally cultural basis. Race and ethnicity can overlap, however, when a history of race relations creates a cultural divide among people.

◆ Ethnic conflict is often rooted in the frustrations of ethnic groups living in political territories that are defined and governed by the national ambitions of other ethnic groups.

Ours is a world of inequalities—of unequal opportunities, advantages, privileges. The disparities apply across the board, to entire countries, to majorities and minorities within those countries, and to individuals in those societies. Disadvantaged people in the peripheral regions look with envy at the material advantages of those located in the wealthy core. Dominant majorities in multicultural states create and sustain systems designed to protect their privileges. Members of minority groups find their upward path blocked by racial or ethnic discrimination. Women the world over suffer from mistreatment in male-dominated cultures.

In the next two chapters we focus on geographic aspects of inequality, especially those involving race, ethnicity, and gender. As we will find, these are sensitive topics; even the definitions of key terms are in dispute.

◆ THE HUMAN RACE

When you enter a foreign country for a visit, you may be asked to fill out a questionnaire to be presented to the immigration office. As often as not, one of the questions will be "What is your race?" The answer, of course, is "human." All human beings belong to the same *species.*

However, the answer "human" is not the one that is wanted. (In fact, it may get you into trouble.) What the questionnaire is asking is what *kind* of human being you are, that is, what recognizable group you belong to. The term *race* has become synonymous with something other than the human species. It focuses on differences rather than on similarities.

This is as frustrating to biologists and anthropologists as the misuse of geographic terms such as state, nation, or frontier is to human geographers. Indeed, many anthropologists believe that the whole concept of human "races" should be abandoned. Yet we cannot avoid the fact that humans do not all look alike and that the differences are given varying emphases in different societies.

◆ A GEOGRAPHY OF RACE

Let us look at the positive side first. There is no doubt about the biological unity of the human species: no matter where we live and whatever our physical attributes, we have the capacity to interbreed and produce offspring.

We may think that we look quite dissimilar, but some other species display a much wider variation. Take dogs, for example. All dogs belong to the same species, but a Saint Bernard does not appear to have much in common with a fox terrier, or a wolf with a Pekingese. But it is not appearance that is the key. Rather, it is the *genetic* makeup of the individuals. Within a species, the chromosomes of reproducing organisms are identical in number and size, and they carry very similar groups of *genes* (see "Focus on: Genetics").

Nevertheless, groups of individuals *within* a species display certain physical characteristics that tend to set them apart from others. In the human species, these groups (sometimes called *subspecies* or *populations*) exhibit regional variation. This results *not* from differences in the fundamental genetic makeup of each group but from differences in *gene frequencies* among populations. For example, some people are blue-eyed, others brown-eyed; the blue-eyed dominate in the populations of northern Europe while the brown-eyed prevail in southern Europe. Another variation related to gene frequencies has to do with blood type. The O type dominates in Native American populations while the A type prevails in Western Europe. These and other differences among human populations occur within the human race, not between races.

What has caused the regional variation in the appearance of humans in clustered populations? What is often called a race is in fact a combination of physical attributes in a population, the product of a particular genetic inheritance that dominates in that population (such as Australia's Aborigines, North Africa's Berbers, or Asia's Mongols). This inheritance varies from one population to another, and probably results from a long history of adaptation to different environments. For this reason, the use of the term *race* for such populations is in error.

Culture and Race

Unfortunately, our understanding of the biological concept of race does not erase the differences between the original populations that make up the human species. This is the negative side: after tens of thousands of years of movement and migration, mixing, and intermarriage in our increasingly mobile world, human populations with distinct physical attributes are still clustered in particular areas.

Let us keep one other reality in mind as we approach this sensitive topic. What is often called "racial" conflict is nothing of the sort. The recent disastrous breakdown of order in Rwanda is a case in point. The Western press implied that a genuine difference exists between the Tutsi and the Hutu "races" who killed each other by the hundreds of thousands. While Tutsi and Hutu did fight over land and primacy in areas around Rwanda long ago, those distinctions had largely faded when the most recent civil war broke out. No one can discern a Tutsi from a Hutu just by physical appearance. The war was over status, advantage, and opportunity. The conflict was cultural or ethnic, not "racial." A culturally rooted sense of ethnicity transcends "racial" stereotype. Many of Rwanda's Hutu, through social success and/or intermarriage, had "become" Tutsi, taking on the habits and privileges of this advantaged minority. Many paid the price at the hands of other resentful Hutu.

So it is culture, not the misused notion of race, that often produces conflict among human groups. In the former Yugoslavia, the Bosnian Muslims and the Serbs, as well as the Croats, are Slavs. In Northern Ireland, no one can tell a Catholic from a Protestant, but the thousands of people who have died in that conflict were almost all of Irish or distant Scottish ancestry. In Israel, nothing distinguishes Jew from Palestinian except culture and associated feelings of ethnic distinctiveness.

Human Biological Variation

As noted earlier, human populations vary and their differences are, in part, matters of physical appearance. Appearances, together with a variety of related biochemical factors, have led some anthropologists to

Focus On

Genetics

When Charles Darwin published his *Origin of Species* in 1859 (complete title: *The Origin of Species by Means of Natural Selection or the Preservation of Favoured Races in the Struggle for Life*), his critics seized upon a major weakness: Darwin failed to explain exactly how traits are passed from one generation to the next. But before the end of the nineteenth century, the broad principles of ***genetics*** were understood. This field was given its name by the English biologist William Bateson. The term *gene* was introduced to signify the physical basis of an inherited quality. Genes were defined as units of inheritance for certain traits (say, eye color or body size), which together form a ***genotype***. The expression of those traits (say, brown eyes or tall build) forms the ***phenotype***.

A century ago it was believed that groups of people of similar appearance (phenotype) would share, and therefore repeat, a single genotype. But today it is known that all individuals except identical twins are genetically unique; each has his or her own "genetic fingerprint." Members of groups such as Australian Aborigines, East African Maasai, or Japanese have similar genotypes, but each individual within those groups has a unique genetic makeup. This uniqueness makes it possible to identify a person through his or her DNA, which can be derived from even a small sample of blood, hair, or saliva.

argue that there are four basic human stocks:

1. The Negroid stock, from African sources
2. The Australoid stock of Southeast Asian origins
3. The Mongoloid stock, which arose in East Asia
4. The Caucasoid stock, from Southwest Asian and European sources

Even such seemingly straightforward classifications are controversial because some groups do not fit neatly within any of the categories and because they emphasize some traits over others. A consideration of a few of the most obvious attributes of appearance—skin color, physique, facial shape, and hair style—reveals both the logic and the complexity of such classifications.

Skin Color Human geographers and anthropologists have been challenged by one of the most obvious spatial correlations: the prevalence of dark skins in low latitudes, from tropical Africa through southern India to Australia, and the dominance of light skins in higher latitudes of the Northern Hemisphere. This generalization applies, of course, to peoples who have occupied such equatorial and near-equatorial regions for millennia. Only the first Aboriginal Australians are dark-skinned; later immigrants are not.

Obvious though it may be, skin color is not a reliable indicator of racial relationships. The peoples of southern India, New Guinea, and Australia are as dark-skinned as Africans, but black Africans, southern Indians, and Aboriginal Australians are not closely related genetically. Thus some other factor must have caused long-term inhabitants of low latitudes to have dark skins.

Skin color is a matter of pigmentation, which protects against strong radiation from the sun. The more *melanin* pigment is present, the darker the skin color. However, there are variations within as well as between groups: there are dark-skinned northern Europeans and light-skinned Africans. Nevertheless, often the first thing people notice about members of another culture is their skin color. This is true despite the fact that the color of human skin varies from nearly white to nearly black, through all the intermediate shades (Fig. 30-1).

Figure 30-1 reveals that tropical populations in South America have lighter skins than peoples of the African and Australasian tropics. Various theories have been advanced to account for this spatial distribution of skin pigmentation. Whatever the outcome of the current debate concerning the timing of the arrival of the first Americans (whether 13,000 years ago or more than 30,000 years ago), it is evident that the first human inhabitants of tropical America arrived quite recently compared to those of tropical Africa and Asia.

From the field notes

"Are these the four "racial" stocks of humanity? Women in 1) Grahamstown, South Africa; 2) Alice Springs, Australia; 3) Wuhan, China; and 4) Stockholm, Sweden."

1.

2.

3.

4.

The processes that result in high concentrations of melanin have not had enough time to run their course in the Americas.

This leads to the question of why Australia's Aboriginal peoples, who arrived there more than 50,000 years ago, display such intense pigmentation. Their arrival time does not seem sufficiently different from the time humans arrived in the Americas to explain the pattern shown in Figure 30-1. The answer is geographic: the diffusion route of the Aborigines was tropical, so that even before their migration into Australia they had inhabited low latitudes for a very long time. The first Americans, however, probably came from higher latitudes. Even after entering North America, many may not have reached tropical latitudes for thousands of years. So the difference (between Australia and the Americas) in terms of tropical habitation is far greater than the actual arrival times suggest.

If long-term exposure to equatorial and tropical environments generated dark skin, what was the ad-

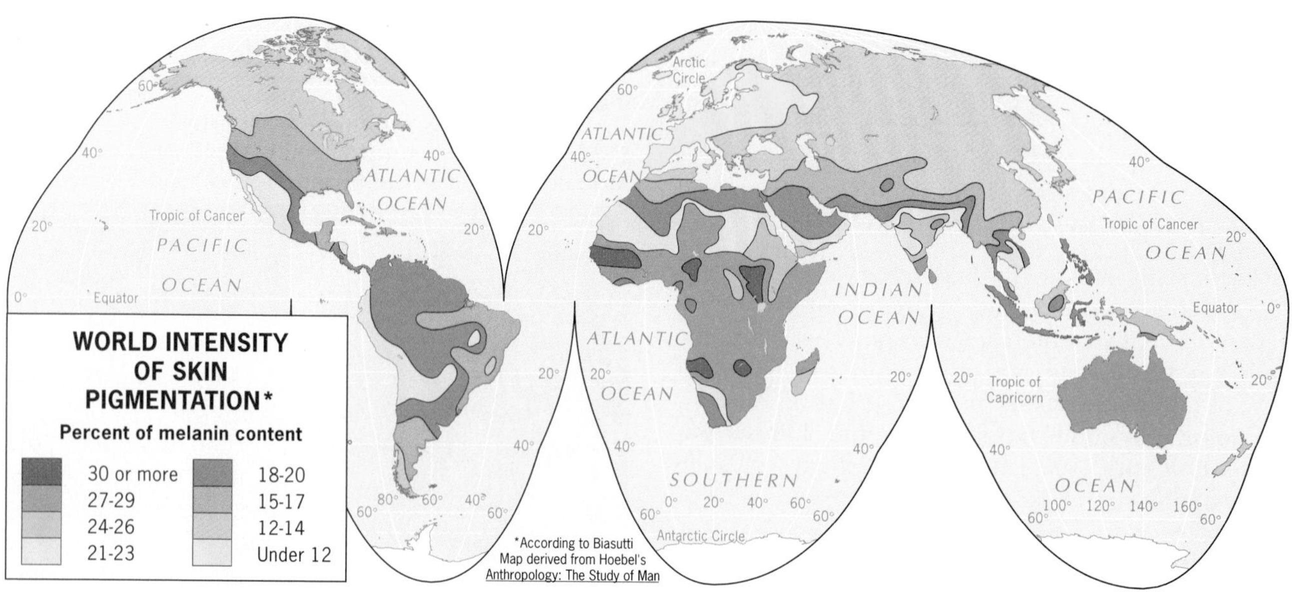

Figure 30-1 World Intensity of Skin Pigmentation. The percentage of the average melanin content of skin in countries around the globe is shown here. *Source: From a map in E. A. Hoebel,* Anthropology: The Study of Man, *4th rev. ed. New York: McGraw-Hill, 1972, p. 67.*

vantage of this trait? Melanin protects inner layers of the skin from damaging ultraviolet rays. Dark-skinned people living under the intense tropical sun are protected much more effectively than lighter-skinned people.

Another factor is vitamin D, the vitamin that fights rickets in the body. The ultraviolet radiation intercepted by darkly pigmented skin also stimulates the production of vitamin D. Excessive sunlight, however, causes softening and calcification of bones in people who cannot withstand the high intensity of ultraviolet radiation. Thus a modern theory holds that people who have lived for long periods in higher latitudes, where sunlight is weaker, have acquired light-colored skin through natural selection, in part because this allows maximum penetration by ultraviolet radiation, the production of vitamin D, and the development of a strong skeleton. But in the lower latitudes dark skins protect against excessive penetration by the sun's damaging rays and the risks of excess vitamin D in the body.

These notions do not explain all of the distributions shown in Figure 30-1, but they do suggest some of the factors behind the global pattern of skin pigmentation. Other questions remain unanswered, however. For example, there are peoples with reddish and yellowish skins whose physical appearance has not been explained.

Physique and Size When it comes to body build and size, our perceptions may again be at variance with reality. We may think of East Africa's Tutsi (Watusi) people as unusually tall, but the data show otherwise; many Tutsi appear tall because they are lean. We perceive certain peoples as short, others as short- or long-limbed, but few of these generalizations hold up against the measurements.

There is, nevertheless, a general relationship between the mean body weight in a population and the mean annual temperature of the areas in which that population is located. According to ***Bergmann's Rule***, people are naturally more slender in warmer areas and heavier in cooler zones. Put another way, Bergmann's Rule holds that the lower the mean annual temperature, the higher the population's mean body weight. But while Bergmann's Rule can be confirmed statistically, it does not explain whether this variation is due solely, or primarily, to natural selection. We noted previously that nutrition tends to be less adequate in warmer parts of the world than in cooler ones. On the other hand, Bergmann's Rule also applies to many mammals and even birds, which develop larger bulk in cooler, higher latitudes than in warmer, lower latitudes. So while proof is not available for human populations, given differences in diet and food availability, the tendency does appear to exist, and Bergmann's Rule may explain observed regional variations.

It is clear that stress, diet, and other conditions prevailing in a society can affect the mean height of its population, but again the genetic role is uncertain. Average heights can change remarkably quickly. If you visit a European museum, note the size of the suits of armor. The average European of today may be 10 inches (25 centimeters) taller than Europeans were in the Middle Ages. More recent evidence of rapid height increase comes from the United States. In a book titled *Ecology and Human Adaptation* (1975), anthropologist W. A. Stini reported that the average height of males in the United States increased by 2 inches (5 centimeters) between World War I and II. Since the end of World War II the Japanese have been growing markedly taller as well. Again, there are no totally satisfactory explanations for these variations in physical appearance.

Other Physical Traits Populations also differ in the form of their skulls, the structure of their faces, and the properties of their head hair. For a long time anthropologists believed that the *cephalic index* (the ratio of the breadth and length of the skull) might yield insight into the evolution of population groups, just as archeologists use skull analyses to chart the evolution of humanity. However, while it was possible to record a clustering of prevalent head shapes (Japanese have round heads; Western Europeans have long heads), it was not possible to derive useful conclusions from such data.

We noted previously that environment may influence body stature and weight; the same may be true for facial features. It has long been known that populations that live for long periods in the warm, moist tropics tend to have short, wide, flat noses. People living under arid conditions, including low-latitude deserts and high-latitude dry zones, are likely to have long, narrow noses. A long, thin nose may cool and warm air more effectively than a broad, short nose and may help soften the effect of dry air on the lungs.

There are also regional differences in head hair: it may be straight or woolly, fine-textured or thick. Asians tend to have straight hair, Europeans often have curly hair, and Africans have woolly hair.

One of the most characteristic facial properties is the ***epicanthic fold***, a small piece of overlapping skin that gives the eyelid a distinctive appearance. This physical trait prevails in East Asia and is associated with the Mongoloid (Asian) population group. But the epicanthic fold is not a unique Mongoloid feature. It also appears in Southern Africa's San (formerly called Bushmen) and among Native Americans.

None of these physical features (nor others not discussed, such as the form of the lips and the degree of protrusion of the lower jaw) is a satisfactory basis for racial-regional differentiation. Anthropologists could do little more than classify peoples according to individual traits and map their distribution. And therein lies one of the positive aspects of this topic: the very difficulty of explaining regional variations underscores the essential unity of humanity.

◆ RACE AS A SOCIAL CATEGORY

Despite the evidence that humans are a single species, we continue to use appearance as a basis for dividing ourselves into separate groups and creating inequalities. The importance of race is reinforced every time a visa form is filled out or a report on voting emphasizes differences among "racial" groups. Against this backdrop, it is easy to forget that the traits that societies regard as indicating racial divisions are not fixed. The darkness of skin pigmentation is a basis for "racial" divisions in parts of Africa, but in the United States anyone of African descent is regarded as being part of a single race. Moreover, as the publicity surrounding the golfer Tiger Woods reminds us, the increased intermixing of the world's populations over the past century has produced a growing number of people who do not fit neatly within any of the traditional racial categories.

Racism

The problems of using race as a social category notwithstanding, many societies around the world do treat race as significant and a large number of people believe that those of different races—however defined—are in some sense inferior. ***Racism*** is, therefore, part of the human condition, and it has both geographic expression and geographic consequences. Attacks on Turkish guestworkers in Germany are the product of a flow of people from one part of the world to another. Such attacks are concentrated in areas where social problems are more acute and nationalism has taken root among the young. In India, lighter-skinned families have for centuries enjoyed advantage and privilege as a result of a hierarchical system that came into being when Caucasoid Moghuls (Mongols) invaded the subcontinent. Some African Americans in the United States find themselves with few opportunities for educational or social advancement. In these and many other cases, racism influences the organization of people and place in ways that have significant impacts on possibilities and opportunities.

The United States has had a particularly complicated history of race relations because one racial group, African Americans, arrived in a desperately unequal situation—as slaves. This set up a system of exploitation whose worst features were ended by the Civil War but whose effects are still manifest today in everything from the paucity of African Americans in senior management positions to persistent inequalities in income. In recent decades the United States has done much to guarantee equal protection of all people under the law—most clearly in the enactment of the Civil Rights Act of 1964. Yet in many of the places where Americans live and work, race continues to be a divisive factor in American society.

Race is a particularly notable feature of the internal geography of many American urban areas. Cities such as Chicago and Washington, D.C., are remarkably segregated along racial lines. The significance of segregation goes beyond who lives where. Segregation promotes stereotypes of racial neighborhoods, and it fosters arrangements and perceptions that affect what people do and where they do it. Many Americans carry images of African-American neighborhoods as being dangerous places where crime is rampant. While some neighborhoods conform to this image, many do not. And the impacts of the visible and invisible boundaries that separate neighborhoods are often striking. Blacks can be hesitant to venture into white areas, and vice versa, for fear of discrimination or worse. City planners, investors, and business entrepreneurs make decisions that consciously or unconsciously are influenced by assumptions about the distinctiveness of racially defined neighborhoods—decisions that in turn can promote further differences among neighborhoods. These geographic processes are a critical element of the social geography of American cities. Understanding racial patterns at various scales can reveal important aspects of the way human beings create communities and relate to one another.

Race and Environment

Earlier, we encountered the notion of environmental determinism in which the natural environment, chiefly climate, was thought to control human capacities and determine their fate. But environments change and peoples migrate. While it is true that some of the most advanced technological cultures are found in the realm dominated by the European (Caucasian) population group, the pendulum has swung in other directions in the past. Civilizations in Asia and Africa developed sophisticated cultures long before most European societies managed to rise above simple tribal organization. For thousands of years the greatest achievements in administration, legislation, education, agriculture, construction, writing, and other fields were made in China, Southwest Asia, and North Africa—not in Europe. Looking at the world through the lenses of geography and history helps expose the limitations of studies that seek to equate race with capacity or intelligence.

We can condemn racial stereotypes, but we must come back to the inescapable fact that physical appearance, notably skin color, remains a critical factor in people's relationships and in their advantages and opportunities (or lack thereof). How many millions of conflicts, individual and collective, small and large, have begun because of this attribute? The "racial" stereotype remains a huge obstacle to social harmony.

◆ ETHNIC PATTERNS AND PROCESSES

Only a few decades ago, many social scientists treated ethnicity as a relic of the past that was rapidly giving way to national (state) loyalties and identities. Yet a look at any newspaper today reveals the significance of ethnicity in the contemporary world. Ethnicity is in many senses as important a category as race—sometimes even overlapping race. Yet ethnicity defies easy definition or description. Its defining characteristics differ from place to place, and a map showing all recognizable ethnic areas would look like a jigsaw puzzle of thousands of pieces, some no larger than a neighborhood, others as large as entire countries.

But size is no measure of the intensity of ethnic pride and solidarity. These feelings are deepened by shared cultural traits, a common history, a treasured cultural landscape, a real or potential threat to language or faith. "Racial" ancestry may or may not play a part in this, and ethnicity should not be equated with race-consciousness. As noted earlier, all the combatants in the former Yugoslavia are Slavs, who are in turn Europeans. In equatorial Africa, the conflict is not simply between Hutu and Tutsi, both of whom are African peoples. It is between cultures and lifestyles, and it is about power.

Certainly, ethnic conflict intensifies when hostile groups perceive themselves to be of different ancestries, for example, the Sinhalese and the Tamils in Sri Lanka. But it is culture, not race, that dominates in shaping the world's ethnic patterns and processes.

Ethnic Mosaics

We all use the term *ethnic* routinely: to describe a neighborhood, to identify a certain cuisine. In the American mosaic of cultures, ethnic enclaves are common and have names such as "Little Italy," "Chinatown," or "Little Havana." Such names signify clusters of people whose shared ancestry and cultures give them a special identity in a city's social mix. Ethnic heritage lingers in the countryside, too. Sometimes this is revealed in place names—for example, Holland (Michigan), Denmark (Wisconsin), and Stockholm (North Dakota).

Exactly what are the origins of the term *ethnic*? It comes from the ancient Greek word *ethnos*, meaning "people" or "nation." In Latin, the adjective became *ethnicus*, and hence *ethnic*, also an adjective. But note what happens when the term is used in the combined

A SENSE OF SCALE

Chinatown in Mexicali

The ethnic patterns that attract the most attention sometimes obscure important smaller-scale patterns. This was the case when Czechoslovakia was breaking up; concerns with the Czech-Slovak relationship obscured the fact that a substantial Hungarian minority lives in Slovakia. The border region between the United States and Mexico provides another case in point. This border region is generally regarded as a bicultural Anglo-Hispanic meeting point. Yet a more detailed examination of the region reveals that members of a number of different ethnic communities have shaped the region over time. Settlers from Germany, Russia, India, China, and Japan established themselves in both cities and rural areas. While many have blended into the larger community over time, distinctive ethnic patterns persist.

Take, for example, the case of the Chinese in Mexicali, Mexico, the Baja California capital city lying just south of the State of California. Not far from the historic core of this city of 600,000 residents can be found one of the largest Chinatowns in Mexico. A 1995 study of the Mexicali Chinatown by geographer James R. Curtis showed that it has been the crucible of Chinese ethnicity in the Mexicali Valley throughout much of the twentieth century. Chinese began arriving in 1902, and by 1919 more than 11,000 Chinese were either permanent or temporary residents of the valley. They established a thriving Chinatown in the heart of Mexicali that served as the uncontested center of Chinese life in the region for decades.

The Chinese of Mexicali were prominent players in the social and economic life of the city during the twentieth century. They owned and operated restaurants, retail trade establishments, commerical land developments, currency exchanges, and more. By 1989 they owned nearly 500 commercial or service properties. Moreover, in an effort to sustain their cultural traditions and to add to the cultural life

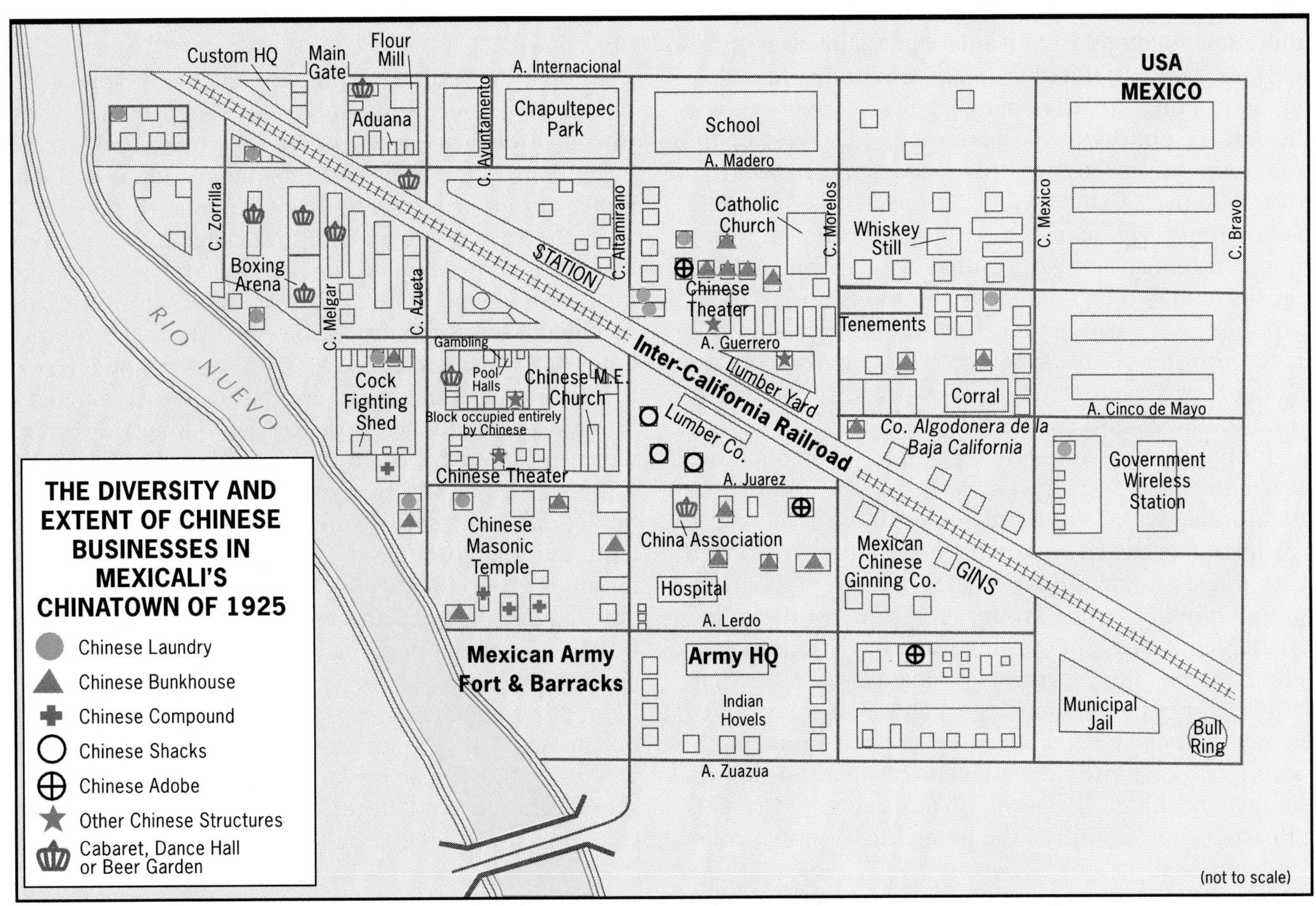

Mexicali, 1925. The diversity and extent of Chinese businesses in Mexicali's Chinatown of 1925 is shown in this map. *Source: J. R. Curtis, "Mexicali's Chinatown,"* The Geographical Review *(Lawrence, KS, 1995), p. 344.*

of the city, they established the China Association, which plays an active role in Mexicali's social and civic life.

As a result of the aging infrastructure of Mexicali's Chinatown, together with the growing affluence of some members of the Chinese community, Chinese have dispersed to the edges of the city and beyond. Relatively few Chinese continue to live in the city's Chinatown; some have even moved across the border to Calexico, while retaining business interests in Mexicali. Yet Mexicali's Chinatown continues to play an important symbolic and functional role for individuals of Chinese ancestry in the area—people who are still shaping the region's social and economic geography. The story of these people reminds us that behind many national or regional scale generalizations about ethnic patterns lie "hidden" groups. Although they may be relatively small in number, they often make substantial contributions to the character of the places they inhabit.

form, for example, *ethnology* and *ethnogeny*. In these terms race is a crucial component. The adjective *ethnic* thus refers to culture (traditions, customs, language, religion) and, in a much more general, often vague sense, to racial ancestry.

As noted earlier, this racial identity is largely a matter of self-perception. When the Yugoslavian republic of Slovenia declared its independence in 1991, local newspapers carried reports justifying that decision. Those reports frequently referred to the rights of the Slovenian "race" to control its own domain. But in the ethnic makeup of Slovenia, race is much less significant than cultural and natural environments. Slovenian is a discrete Slavic language (see the discussion in Part 3), and Slovenia lies to the northwest of the religious transition zone that crosses Yugoslavia between Roman Catholic and Eastern Orthodox areas (see Part 4). The natural environment can also play a role in forging a sense of cultural distinctiveness. Slovenians refer to their country as an Alpine, not a Balkan, republic. Slovenian nationalists may have called upon race to bolster people's feelings of nationalism, but the strength of Slovenian ethnicity is based on other cultural traditions and customs.

Ethnicity thus arises out of different combinations of cultural traditions, racial backgrounds, and natural environments. In Northern Ireland there is no racial distinction between two ethnic groups that are locked in a tragic struggle: the dominant ethnic glue is religion, Catholic for one group, Protestant for the other. In Belgium, that glue is linguistic. In Northern Belgium, the Flemings form an ethnic entity of more than 6 million people. Heirs to the rich cultural history of Flanders, they speak a language derived from Dutch. Southern Belgium is the domain of nearly 4 million French-speaking Walloons. The capital, Brussels (Bruxelles), lies north of the ethnic division that splits Belgium, a division so deep that each region has its own parliament. As in so many multiethnic countries, one ethnic group (in this case the Walloons) fears domination by a larger or more powerful ethnic group within the national boundaries.

Race can be a very strong force in the development of ethnic identity. A good example is the growing strength of the Maori (Polynesian) community in New Zealand, now numbering about 450,000 in a population of 3.5 million. Growing ethnic awareness and identity have impelled the Maoris to launch a campaign not just to improve their position in New Zealand society but also to regain about half of the national territory. Asserting that the British settlers of New Zealand have violated the 1840 Treaty of Waitangi, the Maoris have gone to court to achieve this objective.

Thus, like culture, ethnicity has many spatial dimensions. Ethnic communities in American cities and towns often are quite small, sometimes having no more than a few thousand inhabitants. On a national scale, ethnic groups may have millions of members, as in the case of Yugoslavia and Belgium. Ethnic distributions at these multiple scales are affected by many factors. In some cases, distinct ethnic areas are the product of discrimination and oppression. The "homelands" of *apartheid* South Africa were designed in part to confine African ethnic groups to particular areas. Some segregated neighborhoods in American cities were sustained by discriminatory attitudes and institutions. Yet not all segregations are pernicious; some find comfort and security in the familiarity of their own culture and cultural landscape. In smaller urban communities group identity and cohesiveness offer certain advantages: they provide a social network and a safety net. Members of a particular ethnic community may be especially successful in certain businesses and will help other members of the group succeed in such businesses. For new arrivals, an ethnic neighborhood will ease the transition with a familiar language, a shared church, and stores carrying products that are valued in the local culture.

Acculturation and Ethnicity

The persistence of urban ethnic neighborhoods seems to contradict what we noted previously about the pervasiveness of popular culture. Certainly, the diffusion of popular American culture traits affects ethnic neighborhoods and erodes their cohesiveness. This process is evident in Miami's Cuban neighborhoods, in which ethnic identity is far stronger among the old than among the young. Miami's Little Havana was created by a transplanted community that is now a generation older. The Spanish-speaking, aged domino players in the neighborhood's parks are a dwindling minority. The old values (strong family ties, regular Catholic church attendance, strict schooling) still prevail, but they are being eroded by acculturation. Young Cuban Americans, born in Florida, are adopting American cultural norms.

Does this mean that the Cuban ethnic neighborhood will disappear from Miami's urban scene? All ethnic communities go through transitions before stabilizing, and Miami's Cuban community is no exception. At present it is in transition, but eventually Miami will include stable Cuban-American ethnic neighborhoods in addition to its other ethnic clusters (Fig. 30-2).

Acculturation, even in the American "melting pot," is not resulting in rapid assimilation of ethnic cultures or neighborhoods (see "Focus on: Ethnicity and Environment"). There are two basic reasons for this: cultural revival and growing awareness of cultural linkage.

Cultural revival takes several forms. In both urban and rural settings, people from similar ethnic backgrounds initially clustered in particular areas but later diffused outward, moving some distance from the community that served as a stepping stone during the

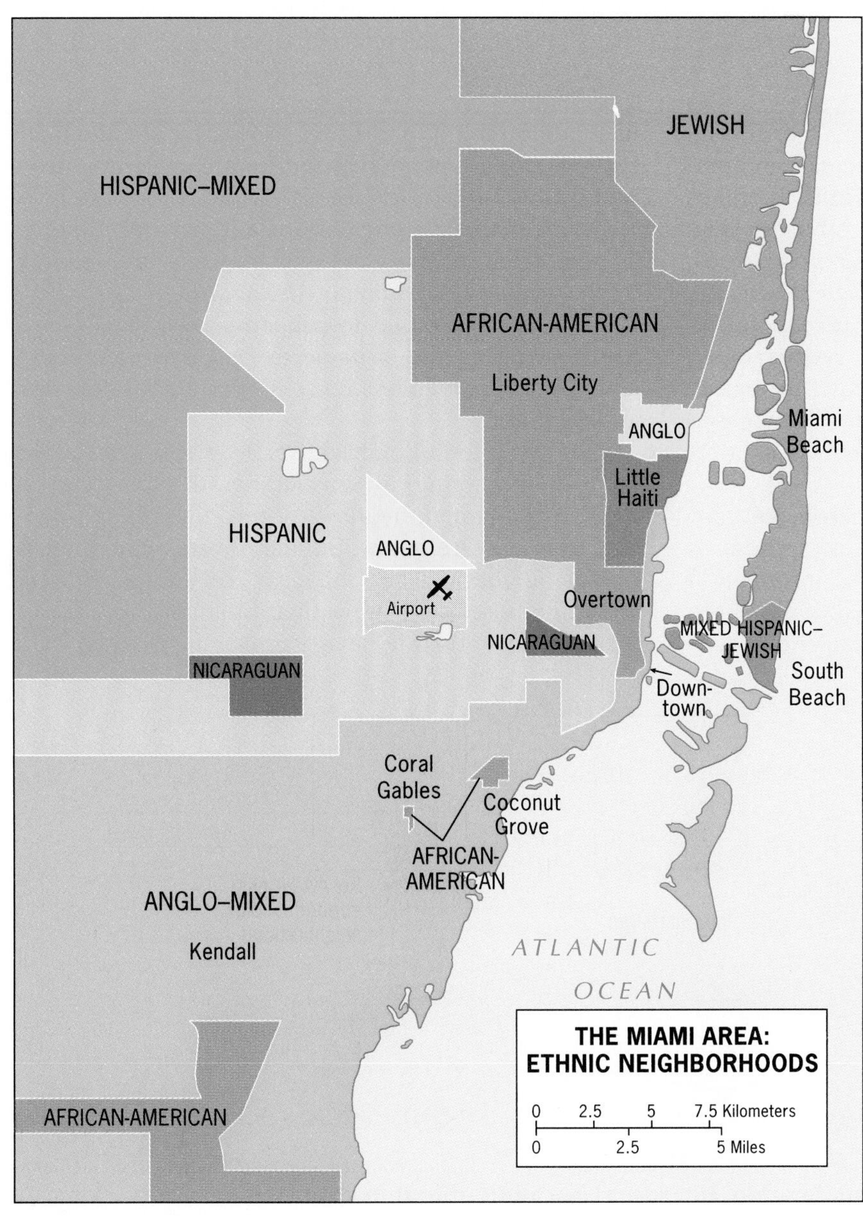

Figure 30-2 Ethnic Neighborhoods in the Miami Area. This map shows ethnic majorities in Miami-area neighborhoods in 1992. *Source: Based on information provided by T. D. Boswell and I. M. Sheskin, University of Miami.*

Focus On

Ethnicity and Environment

The ethnic neighborhoods in American cities developed as immigrants clustered in particular parts of growing metropolitan areas. Having left the crowded cities and sweatshop industries of Europe, many of these immigrants were familiar with urban life. Jobs, not climate or landscape, determined where they settled.

Other immigrants, however, came from rural areas, and so they sought a natural environment. It is no accident then that rural ethnic groups in America are often associated with natural environs similar to those of their source areas: Scandinavians in Minnesota, Finns in northern Wisconsin, Germans in central and southern Wisconsin, Hollanders in western Michigan, and Italians in California.

These rural ***ethnic islands*** in the cultural mosaic reflect the perceptions of their inhabitants, of both the natural environment they left behind and the one they selected after arriving in America. Similar landscape and vegetation did not always mean similar climate and soils, and some communities could not adjust. But many more made the right choice, and from the German and English dairy farmers of Wisconsin to the Italian winegrowers of California, they brought prosperity to the places where they settled.

difficult days of immigration (Fig. 30-3A). Over several generations these dispersed migrants increase in numbers, intermarry, and form a loose network of families that are still conscious of their shared ethnicity (Fig. 30-3B). As these families become more prosperous, funds become available for reviving their ties to the cultural source. The old neighborhood is reenergized by these renewed links (Fig. 30-3C). For example, newspapers published in various languages for particular ethnic communities have experienced increased circulation and broader regional distribution as a result of this process.

Renewed awareness of ***cultural linkage*** also tends to counter assimilation. Such awareness is strengthened by the enhanced flow of information through modern media. During the breakdown of the Soviet empire, for example, Lithuanian Americans marched on the White House in support of Lithuania's struggle for independence and Ukrainian communities in the United States rallied for Ukrainian sovereignty. Serbian and Croatian neighborhoods in North America as well as in Europe were galvanized by the struggle in the former Yugoslavia. African Americans in the United States marched in solidarity with black South Africans during the struggle to end *apartheid.* Such emotional involvement revives ethnic consciousness and culture.

Finally, the cultural landscape is a powerful element in promoting and sustaining ethnic distinctiveness. The dominant features of the cultural landscape are buildings—religious, public, private—and the layout of neighborhoods, villages, and towns. But the cultural landscape is more than buildings and layout. Signs in a particular language can be important, as can

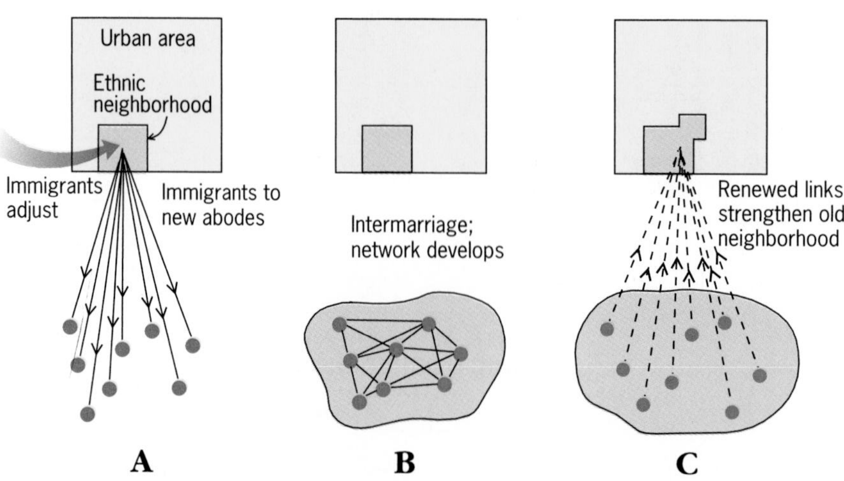

Figure 30-3 Immigration, Intermarriage, and Cultural Revival.

religious symbols. Clothing makes a statement. Headgear and footwear, adornment in the form of facial hair or tattoos, and the wearing of jewelry and other ornaments contribute to a cultural landcape that rouses a sense of belonging and helps to maintain cultural boundaries (see "Focus on: Ethnicity, Folk Culture, and Popular Culture").

◆ ETHNIC CONFLICT

Cultural revival and cultural linkage are cyclical processes. After Lithuania and Ukraine achieved independence, the common cause that aroused ethnic consciousness in American-Lithuanian and American-Ukrainian communities lost its urgency. But a conflict between Russia and Ukraine—for example, over the Crimea Peninsula—could quickly revive it.

Cultural consciousness also seems to ebb and flow without such external stimuli. Economic circumstances in a community vary over time, and prosperity plays a role in cultural perception and sensitivity. As a result, ethnic communities that have long been stable and have undergone assimilation during good economic times may erupt in disharmony and even separatism when times get tough. Other causes may lie in perceived discrimination, political leadership (a powerful political figure can inspire cultural revival), and anticipated threats to cultural identity (e.g., the growing use of English words in ethnic communities).

Territory is at the root of ethnic conflict. As we saw in Part Eight, the global political order is organized around nation-states whose governments theoretically control the territory of the state in the name of the nation. But the concept of the nation itself is often tied to a particular sense of ethnic identity, which in turn can lead members of different ethnic groups to resist the control of national governments. This is especially likely to occur when governments seek to suppress or deny the existence of ethnic minorities within their territory. Those minorities, in turn, are likely to seek some territorial autonomy within, or separation from, the states in which they are situated. This process is at work among Kurds in Turkey, Basques in Spain, Tibetans in China, Ibos in Nigeria, Albanians in Serbia, and on and on. It even plays out in places where active suppression of minority groups is more a matter of history than of policy, but intense ethnic regionalism is fueled by lingering feelings of domination. Canada and Quebec provide insight into such regionalism.

The Case of Quebec

Like the United States, Canada is a ***plural society***. Canada's population of over 27 million consists of several ethnic groups and includes people of British, French, Native American, Asian, Eastern European, and other ancestries. Territorially, Canada is even larger than the United States, although Canada's population is only slightly more than one-tenth that of the United States.

Canada is organized as a federal state. It is divided administratively into ten provinces, two territories, and the special territory of Nunavut, which has been

Focus On

Ethnicity, Folk Culture, and Popular Culture

Human geographers distinguish between material and nonmaterial culture. They also find it useful to differentiate between folk and popular culture.

Folk culture describes the dwellings, dress modes, tools, and other artifacts of material culture and the institutions and traditions of nonmaterial culture, all belonging to a usually small, often isolated, relatively changeless, community. Self-reliance, subsistence, and technological simplicity mark these fragile cultures, of which only remnants remain today. Amish communities in several rural parts of the United States exemplify this fading phenomenon.

Popular culture, in contrast, describes the changeable, nontraditional, heterogeneous cultural environment of urban industrial societies. While elements of folk culture survive in these societies, they have been overwhelmed by the mass-produced, innovative manufactures of the industrial age.

Popular culture is mass culture, regional culture, even national culture. Its landscapes have diffused far and wide, so that a small-town commercial strip and motel row in South Carolina is visually very similar to one in, say, Oregon. But the diffusion of popular culture has not erased regional distinctions. The South today may be less distinctly Southern than it was two generations ago, but its cultural heritage (much of it modified from earlier folk traits) still exists. Perceptual regions, therefore, also are called ***popular regions*** and, at larger scales, ***vernacular regions***.

A folk-culture heritage may be revived or strengthened in the interest of ethnic identity and political separatism. The resulting blend of folk and popular culture can pose a challenge to the political order.

Figure 30-4 Canada's Provinces and Territories. Canada's provinces and territories and their capitals are illustrated here. The entity entitled Nunavut was proposed in 1992 to recognize the territorial rights of indigenous peoples in this area; it formally comes into being in 1999.

set aside for the nation's indigenous peoples (Fig. 30-4). The two territories, Yukon and the Northwest Territories, together occupy an area larger than Alaska and are inhabited by fewer than 100,000 people.

Canada's provinces range in size from tiny Prince Edward Island, the size of Delaware, to vast Quebec, more than twice as large as Texas. Each province has its own legislative assembly (Quebec calls this its *national* assembly) and premier. The country is also divided into 295 federal electoral districts, from which representatives to the House of Commons (Canada's House of Representatives) are chosen.

Canada faces diverse problems in its various provinces. The economies of the Atlantic Provinces have stagnated. In the far west, British Columbia's economy is growing rapidly—but so is its immigrant population, posing a social and cultural challenge. Such regional contrasts were anticipated in 1867, when the British North America Act established the Canadian federation. At the time, not all of present-day Canada joined; much of the West had yet to be organized. But the last province to join the federation was not a western one; it was Newfoundland, a holdout until 1949.

Modern, prosperous Canada would seem to have everything: a vast territory with a wealth of resources, a small, slowly growing population, a modern economy with high incomes by world standards, and a system of government that can accommodate regional differences. Canada's provinces are accustomed to a great deal of autonomy. Yet there have been periodic crises, sparked by changes in government policy, attempts to negotiate constitutional solutions to regional concerns, and even terrorism. At the heart of these crises are issues of ethnicity and ethnic revival.

French Canada

To understand the cultural stresses that have arisen in Canada, we should examine the federation's history and relative location. Eastern Canada was first settled by aboriginal people and later (c. A.D. 1000) by the Norse in Newfoundland, and possibly by Basque fishermen between A.D. 1000 and 1500. The French, followed by the British, entered present-day Canada in the 1530s. During the seventeenth century, *New France* grew to encompass the St. Lawrence Basin, the Great Lakes region, and the Mississippi Valley. (The names of the great French missionaries and explorers who led this advance are still on the map today: Marquette, La Salle, Duluth, and others.) The late 1680s saw the beginning of a series of wars between the English and the French that ended with France's defeat and the cession of New France to Britain in 1763.

By the time Britain took control of New France, the French had made considerable progress in their American domain. French laws, the French land-tenure system, and the Roman Catholic Church prevailed, and substantial settlements (including Montreal on the St. Lawrence) had been established. The British, anxious to avoid war and preoccupied with problems in other American colonies, gave former New France (the region extending from the Great Lakes to the mouth of the St. Lawrence) the right to retain its legal and land-tenure systems, as well as freedom of religion.

After the American War of Independence, the British were left with a region that they called British North America (the name Canada was not yet in use) but whose cultural imprint still was strongly French. The war drove many thousands of British refugees northward, and soon difficulties arose between the French and the English in British North America. In 1791, heeding appeals by British settlers, the British Parliament divided Quebec into two provinces: Upper Canada, the region upstream from Montreal and centered on Lake Ontario, and Lower Canada, the valley of the St. Lawrence. Upper and Lower Canada became, respectively, the provinces of Ontario and Quebec. Under the Parliament's plan, Ontario would become English-speaking and Quebec would remain French-speaking (Fig. 30-4).

This earliest cultural division did not work well, and in 1840 the British Parliament tried again, this time reuniting the two provinces in the Act of Union. Upper and Lower Canada would have equal representation in the provincial legislature. This, too, was a failure. Efforts to find a better system led to the 1867 British North America Act, which established the Canadian federation (initially consisting of Upper and Lower Canada, New Brunswick, and Nova Scotia, later to be joined by the other provinces and territories). Under this Act, Ontario and Quebec were once again separated, but this time Quebec was given important guarantees. The French civil code was left unchanged, and the French language was protected in Parliament and in the courts.

One hundred years later a significant event in French Canada's history occurred. The president of France, Charles de Gaulle, while visiting Canada during its centennial celebration, made open appeals to French nationalism. Before a huge audience in Montreal, he ended a speech by shouting *Vive le Quebec Libre!* The thunderous response from the crowd left no doubt that he had touched a sensitive nerve in Quebec society. Quebecers did not have a strong Canadian champion, let alone an international one. Polls indicated that most felt like second-class citizens in their own country; that bilingualism meant that French-speakers had to learn English but not vice versa, and that Quebec was not getting its fair share of Canada's wealth.

Ethnic Revival

Since the 1960s the intensity of ethnic feeling in Quebec has grown, despite government efforts to satisfy Quebec's demands. In the 1970s, a Quebecer was prime minister of Canada, and it seemed that a new constitution might satisfy those demands. In 1976 a political party calling for separatism finally came to power in Quebec, but in 1980 Quebec's voters rejected separation. Yet the new constitution did not satisfy Quebec, and polls indicated that, if given another chance, the voters would support separation from Canada. To prevent a crisis, Quebec was asked to present its terms for continued membership in the Canadian federation. Its key demand was recognition of Quebec as a "distinct society" within Canada. At a meeting at Meech Lake in 1987, the prime ministers of all of Canada's provinces agreed to these terms, which were to be ratified by their parliaments. However, when the deadline for ratification came, in 1990, the parliaments of Newfoundland and Manitoba had failed to ratify, and Quebec had reason to feel rejected. Immediate demands were heard for a new referendum on separation.

In the meantime, ethnic issues in Quebec, especially those involving language, became even more intense. Over 85 percent of Quebec's more than 7 million people speak French at home, but that still leaves a substantial minority of non-French speakers. In 1977 the Quebec Parliament passed a law that compelled all businesses in the province to demonstrate that they functioned in French. As a result, many businesses and individuals moved to Ontario. Canada's Supreme

Court ruled against Quebec's language legislation, but in 1988, Quebec enacted a law that not only reinstated the legislation the Supreme Court had overturned but added a regulation that made it illegal to exhibit any outdoor commercial sign in a language other than French.

Predictably, such actions caused reactions elsewhere in Canada. With fewer than 700,000 French-speaking Canadians living outside Quebec, other provinces reconsidered the costs of bilingualism. If English could be treated as it was within Quebec, should French be accorded equality under the law in, say, Alberta or Saskatchewan? Feelings of ethnicity increased among Canada's native peoples as well. Canada has more than 500,000 native inhabitants ("First Americans") in nearly 600 distinct bands. Their leaders pointed out that if the "distinct society" clause in the Meech Lake Accord could apply to French-speaking Quebecers, it certainly should apply to them. But the Meech Lake Accord says nothing about "distinct societies" of indigenous peoples.

If Quebec were to separate from Canada, Native Canadian activism would undoubtedly increase. Canada's native peoples want the Canadian federal government to protect their rights. When they do not use their own languages, they tend to use English, a legacy of the time when they supported the British during their North American wars. Quebec's Mohawks, for example, do not wish to become part of an independent Quebec, nor do the Cree. Thus the growing ethnic consciousness among Quebec's Francophone majority is energizing ethnicity among the province's First American minorities.

Territorial Adjustments

Ethnic assertiveness among Canada's native peoples could have considerable impact on the future map of the country, and it will certainly affect the future map of Quebec. If Quebec eventually succeeds in achieving separation, other "distinct societies" are likely to claim similar rights. Among these will be the peoples of Quebec's northern frontier, the Cree, whose historic domain extends over more than half of the province of Quebec as it appears on current maps. The federal government assigned administration of the Cree to Quebec's government in 1912, an assignment that may well be nullified by Quebec's drive toward independence. In any case, the Cree probably would be empowered to seek independence themselves. This would leave the French-speaking remnant of Quebec with about 45 percent of its present area.

The territory of the Cree is not wilderness. It contains large parts of the enormous James Bay Hydroelectric Project, a vast scheme of dikes, dams, and artificial lakes that will transform a large area of northern Quebec and yield electric power for a vast market within and outside the province. Thus, the stakes of independence are high and the risks great.

None of these considerations seems to lessen the fervor of ethnic consciousness in the French community of Quebec. The province is a prime example of ethnic revival; it also exemplifies ethnic linkage. De Gaulle sought to stimulate Quebec's emotional linkages to France, and today those ties are stronger than ever. The Quebec government has established an official presence in Paris that is as strong as that of Canada itself. *Maison Quebec* (House of Quebec) is a virtual embassy in the French capital.

Yet compared to ethnic minorities in many other countries, Quebec's has had a very favorable role in Canada. On average, people in Quebec earn nearly as much as Canadians throughout the nation. For 30 of the past 47 years Canada's prime minister has been a Quebecer. Few, if any, countries have done so much to encourage bilingualism and provide government services in two official languages.

Quebec's grievances, ranging from unfair taxation to proportional representation, have been heard and have been largely resolved. Even so, these actions have not successfully warded off divisive forces. The forces of ethnicity can disrupt even the most stable governmental system, especially when ethnicity is coupled with spatial identity as in the case of Quebec.

◆ KEY TERMS ◆

Bergmann's Rule
cultural linkage
cultural revival
epicanthic fold
ethnic islands
folk culture
genetics
genotype
phenotype
plural society
popular culture
popular regions
racism
vernacular regions

◆ APPLYING GEOGRAPHIC KNOWLEDGE ◆

1. Current research results indicate that Africa is the cradle of humanity and that *Homo sapiens* emigrated from there into Eurasia and, most recently, the Americas. What geographic factors may have contributed to the subsequent differentiation of humanity into "races"? Is the question of human "stocks" settled?

2. It is sometimes said that territorial identity lies at the root of ethnic conflict. Explain how the meaning of this proposition might differ if one were looking at it on the scale of a State or province as opposed to the scale of a city.

Chapter 31

Gender and the Geography of Inequality

From the field notes

"During a taping session on the Indonesian island of Bali, I saw a brick-making facility and visited it. Young boys were bringing the wet mud from a quarry near a creek and poured it from their wheelbarrows into wooden forms. Once the bricks begin to dry and harden in the sun, they must be turned to prevent cracking. This woman told me that she worked ten hours a day, stacking and restacking the bricks, six days per week. At about 45 cents (U.S.) per hour, she was better paid than some factory workers I had visited in Sumatera. But what about her quality of life?"

KEY POINTS

◆ **Demographic statistics for individual countries (or divisions within countries) tend to conceal gender gaps, differences between females and males ranging from life expectancies to literacy rates.**

◆ **In all but three countries of the world, women outlive men for periods ranging from less than one year to ten years or more. In this context, the gender gap is widest in the richer countries and smallest in the poorer.**

◆ **Female infanticide and the abortion of female fetuses occur widely in India, China, and other countries where tradition and economics combine to threaten girls and women. Population-control policies have contributed to this human disaster of massive proportions.**

◆ **Work performed by women as unpaid labor in households and on the land would, if measured in monetary value, increase the world's total paid production by about one-third. In the poorer countries women produce more than half the food, transport water and firewood, build dwellings, and perform numerous other tasks.**

◆ A GEOGRAPHY OF GENDER

As we have seen, ours is a world of racial diversity, cultural variety, and economic disparity. We view these variations spatially, and we study ethnic homelands, culture hearths, and regional economic contrasts. There is another kind of inequality, however: inequality between the sexes, sometimes referred to by the term ***gender***—a term that connotes social situation, not just biology.

When topics such as population growth or migration or food production arise, they tend to be discussed in the aggregate. When a country's high population growth rate is cited as a threat to its future stability or its development potential, we may not consider the situation of the women who bear the children and raise them, who are confined to a village, probably for life, as their mothers and grandmothers were. Their husbands and brothers suffer no such constraints; men and women born and raised in the same village live in completely different worlds.

So it is with migration. We read the total numbers: a half-million Ethiopians dislocated by war, a million Soviet Jews leaving their homes for Israel or the United States. Behind those numbers lie vastly different, gender-related experiences. In refugee camps, women and female children are the worst off in the struggle for survival. In voluntary migrations, males tend to dominate the decision-making process and, in their new destinations, quickly form new social networks. Again, the man's and the woman's perspectives on the experience differ strongly, and male dominance remains the rule rather than the exception.

Modernization and economic development reduce inequalities between men and women. But even in Western Europe and the United States equality has not been achieved. Large wage differentials remain. Women and men are not always paid the same amount for the same work, and barriers to economic and social advancement persist. In corporate, political, and many other settings, maps of inequality can still be drawn.

In a 1987 study, geographers Susan Hanson and Geraldine Pratt found that men in Worcester, Massachusetts, had an average wage per hour of $15.45, compared to $9.34 per hour for women. Women took jobs closer to home than men, and they worked hours that made it easier for them to handle domestic chores, mainly the care of children. This put them at a disadvantage when it came to advancement in their jobs. Asked whether proximity to the man's job is more important than proximity to the woman's job, more than twice as many people—men *and* women—said that they would move nearer the man's job rather than nearer the woman's job. From such data, Hanson and Pratt derived a pattern of occupational segregation that results when women take lower-paying jobs in more restricted locations and with less hope of advancement. Patterns of this kind may not be as obvious as those created by racial segregation or ethnic concentration, but they prove the continuing existence of gender inequality.

Despite the persistence of gender inequality, women in urban, industrial societies have made enormous progress during the twentieth century, in stark contrast to what has occurred in more traditional societies. Vivid proof that wealth and economic prosperity do not automatically improve the rights and opportunities of women came from Saudi Arabia in 1990. In this oil-rich, high-income country, women are not permitted to drive automobiles. During the Gulf War foreign troops, including female soldiers driving vehicles, entered Saudi Arabia. Perhaps emboldened by their presence, several dozen Saudi women, many of whom had been educated abroad, got into their families' cars and drove through the streets in defiance of the law. But they were arrested, and the ban on driving by women in Saudi Arabia was reaffirmed.

In this chapter we assess the circumstances under which women live and work in five geographic contexts: demography and health; family and social conditions; education and opportunity; economy and productivity; and politics and public life. At times we will depend on anecdotal and subjective information because data on the conditions, roles, and contributions of women often are inadequate or incomplete. This insufficiency in itself is a reflection on gender inequality in the majority of the world's countries.

◆ DEMOGRAPHY AND HEALTH

In Chapter 5 we noted that population pyramids for certain countries show that women outrank men, especially in the higher age categories. On average, women live about four years longer than men, but this differential varies spatially. In the economic core, the ***longevity gap*** widened from five years to seven years between 1950 and 1990. In *Women: A World Survey*

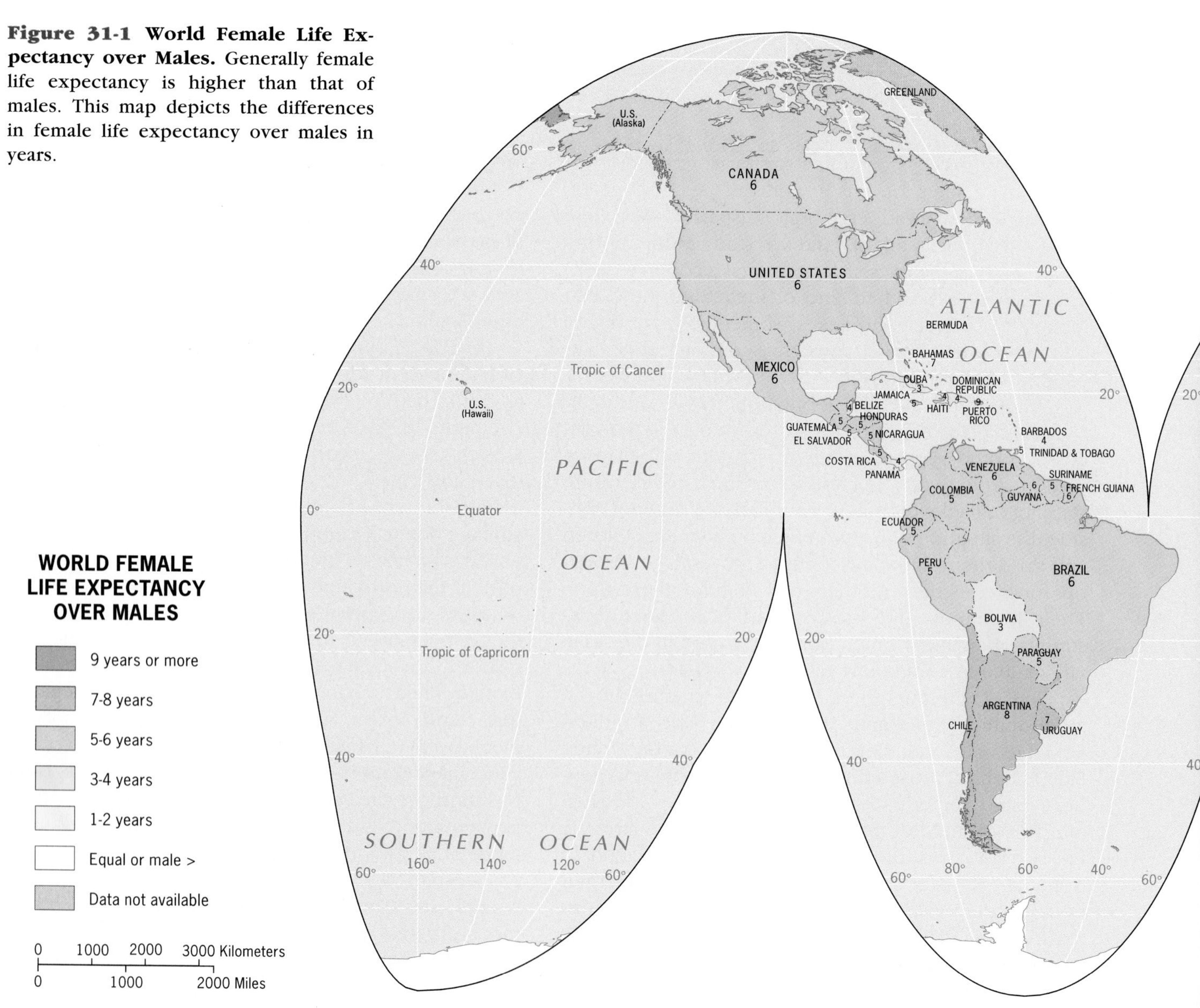

Figure 31-1 World Female Life Expectancy over Males. Generally female life expectancy is higher than that of males. This map depicts the differences in female life expectancy over males in years.

(1985), Ruth Leger Sivard noted that this widening gap resulted not only from medical and other advantages associated with socioeconomic progress but also from the fact that

> women seem to have been less inclined to adopt some of the unhealthy habits often associated with affluence: cigarette smoking in particular, but also the excessive consumption of food and alcohol, fast driving (and high accident rates), high levels of stress (p. 7).

However, Sivard points out, the increased stresses on women who are trying to deal with the competing demands of home and workplace, as well as lifestyle changes associated with modern times, may erode the gender-longevity gap.

In the late 1990s women outlived men in all but three of the world's approximately 200 countries and territories (Fig. 31-1). In Bangladesh, India, and Pakistan, men and women are officially reported to have equal life expectancies. According to data from the United Nations, the Population Reference Bureau, and the World Bank, women live three years longer than men in Africa, seven years longer in South America, seven years longer in Europe, and six years longer in the United States. Note that all three of the countries in which men live as long as women are located in South Asia. Here life is especially difficult for women, and the closing of the longevity gap reflects this hardship.

In virtually all cultures, men tend to marry women younger than they. Married women therefore can expect to outlive their husbands, sometimes by as much

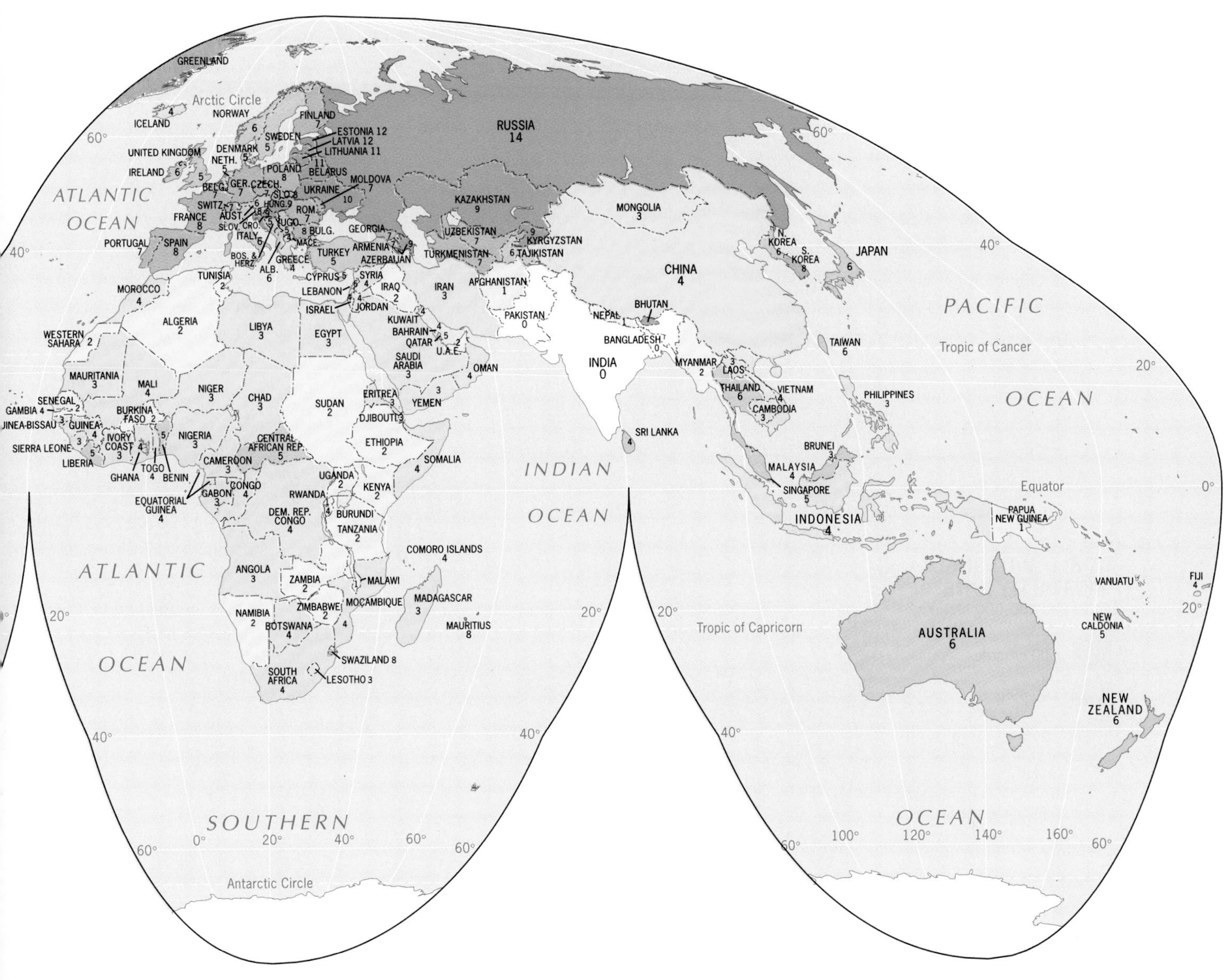

as ten years. This statistic seems to favor women until we note that widows often lack adequate support. Hundreds of millions of women who have spent their lives sustaining their families die alone, in poverty, without sufficient support from their deceased husband's pension, the state, their children, or savings.

Quality of Life

Figures on life expectancy say nothing about quality of life. During their lifetimes, women's health problems and concerns differ from those of men. According to a UN study titled *The World's Women 1970–1990*, women in poorer realms who become pregnant face health risks 80 to 600 times greater than those faced by women in the richer countries. In this respect, South Asian women suffer the highest ***maternal mortality rate***, with approximately 650 maternal deaths per 100,000 births. The risk for African women is nearly as high. In the better-off countries of the Western world, these deaths may number as few as 5 per 100,000. Inadequate medical services, an excessive number of pregnancies, and malnutrition are among the leading causes of maternal death in poorer countries (Fig. 31-2). Add to this the fact that an estimated 250,000 women die from illegal abortions each year.

In Chapter 28, we discussed world nutritional patterns, using average calorie consumption as the key measure. Again, such averages conceal gender differ-

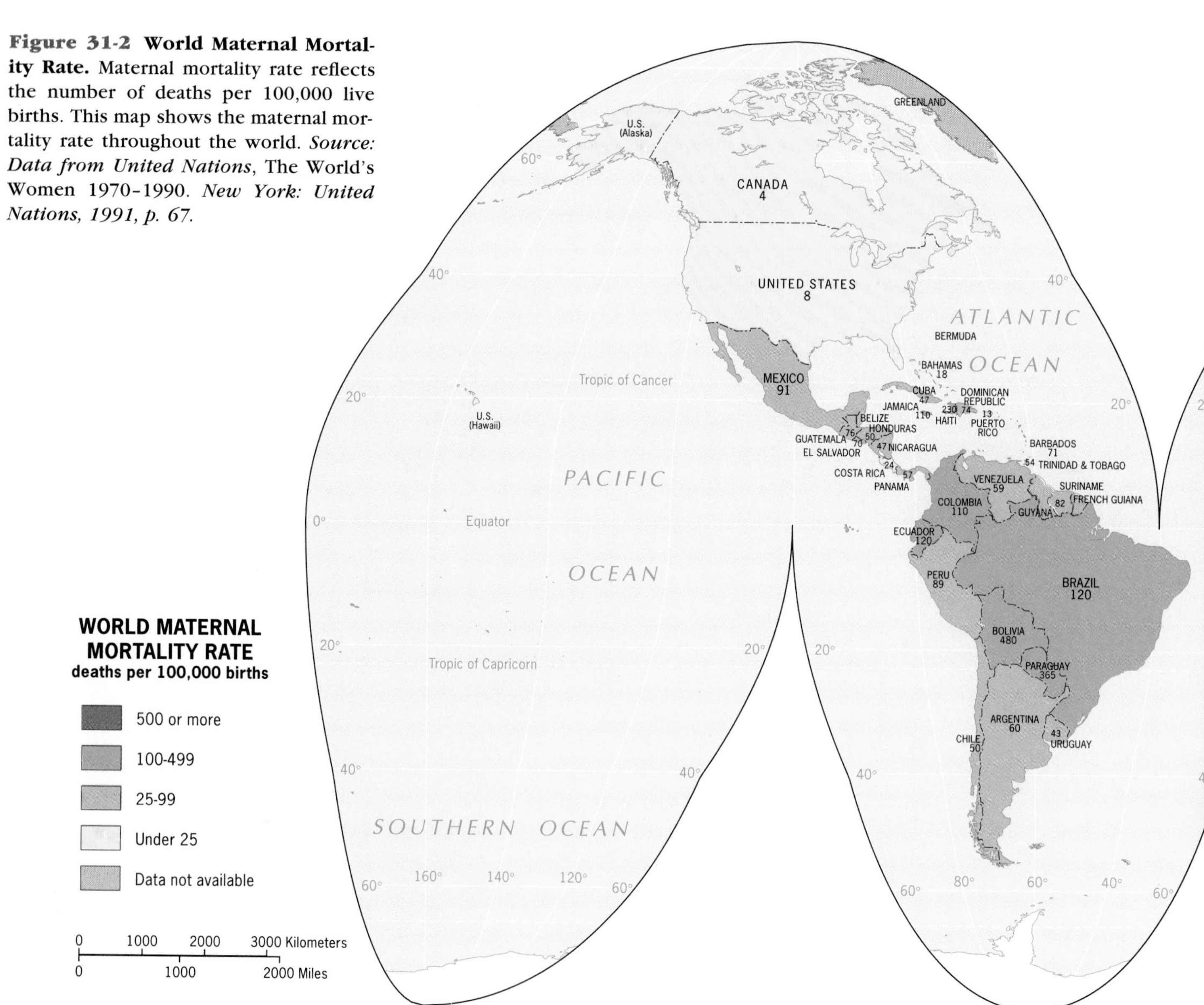

Figure 31-2 World Maternal Mortality Rate. Maternal mortality rate reflects the number of deaths per 100,000 live births. This map shows the maternal mortality rate throughout the world. *Source: Data from United Nations,* The World's Women 1970–1990. *New York: United Nations, 1991, p. 67.*

ences: in the periphery, women are less well nourished than men, and female children are even worse off. World Health Organization (WHO) reports indicate that anemia, a consequence of malnutrition, affects the majority of women in these regions, as well as two-thirds of all pregnant women in Africa and South and Southwest Asia. During their reproductive years, women need nearly three times as much iron in their daily diets as men, but they are often unable to satisfy this dietary requirement.

Under these circumstances, it is all the more remarkable that women's life expectancies—even in poorer countries—exceed those of men. According to Sivard, women are genetically programmed to have lower mortality than men—they are inherently stronger. But as we have noted, the differential is not uniform, and it is affected by variations in the cultural-economic environment within which women work and bear children.

Female Infanticide

Women may live longer than men, and in the upper age categories women may outnumber men, but in early life it is another story. In October 1990 UNICEF published a disturbing report titled *The Lesser Child: The Girl in India.* It revealed that 300,000 more girls than boys die in India each year, and many more are never born—aborted after gender-detection tests.

As a result, the ratio of men to women in India

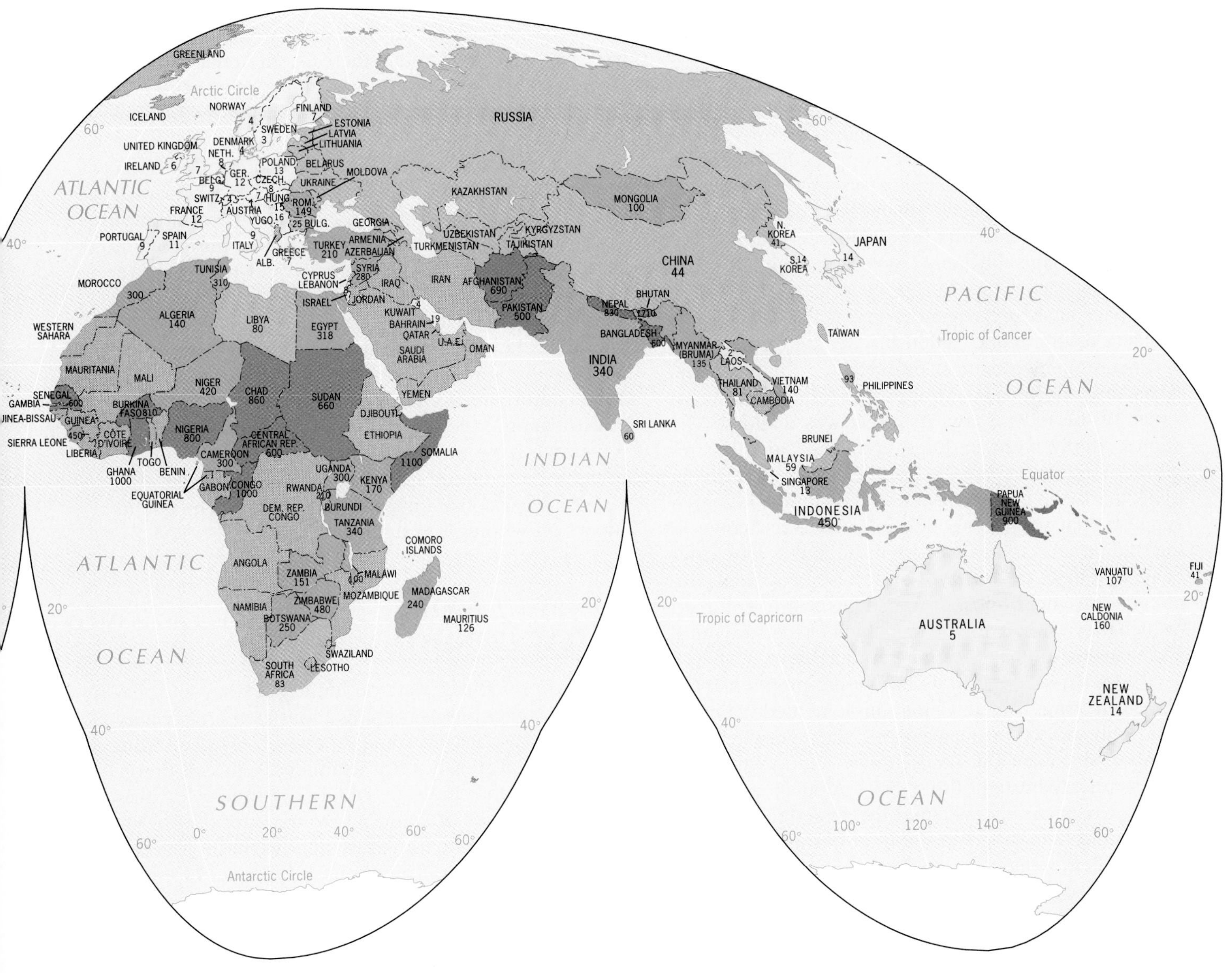

continues to widen. During the twentieth century the gap has grown from over 970 women per thousand men to under 930. In Haryana, the State in which the capital, New Delhi, is located, the 1992 figure was 873 females for every 1000 males, a disproportion so extreme that it has been known to occur only in societies that have experienced the ravages of war. In 1994 the United Nations reported that India as a whole had 133 single men for every 100 single women.

The UNICEF report indicated that many thousands of female infants are killed each year. But the modern techniques of prenatal gender detection—ultrasound and amniocentesis—contribute far more to the imbalance between male and female. Women's groups have called for a federal law that would outlaw such tests, but in India it is difficult to counter any measure that contributes to population control. In July 1994 the Indian Parliament passed a law prohibiting prenatal tests solely to determine the sex of a fetus. But a provision in the law punishes women for taking the test—even though they are often compelled to do so by male heads of families who want male heirs. Fathers want to see the family lineage preserved through males, for in Hindu society the oldest son lights the funeral pyre of the father. In addition, the supposedly outlawed, but widely practiced, tradition of dowry, by which families with sons receive payments from the brides' parents, makes male offspring valuable commodities in the marriage business, whereas daughters are liabilities.

Under such social conditions, will a law against prenatal testing work? When the debate on the issue was gaining momentum, three States (Maharashtra, Rajasthan, and Haryana) imposed a testing ban in advance of the federal law. Its effect was minimal. The clinics simply went underground, and since the required equipment can be moved easily, a thriving black market in gender detection developed. Research suggests that what is needed in India is a change in the traditional status of women in Indian society. Laws against ***female infanticide*** and dowry payments are already on the books. If those laws are enforced (which they rarely are), the result will exceed anything a law against prenatal testing could achieve.

India is not alone in its traditional preference for male offspring. When China implemented its one-child-only policy (see Part Ten), the overwhelming number of couples wanted a male child. While the policy quickly brought the overall population growth rate down, it further widened the male-female ratio. In 1995 the Chinese government published figures indicating that, while the great majority of Chinese had married by age 30, nearly 10 million people in their thirties remained single—and in this age group men outnumbered women by more than 10 to 1. The number of abortions following gender-detection tests (which are legal in China) skyrocketed after the one-child-only policy was implemented. In addition, millions of Chinese babies die through food deprivation, denial of medical care, abandonment, and murder. These conditions are having some unanticipated consequences. It is projected that the number of males unable to find wives will double, even triple, during the first decade of the twenty-first century. Chinese scholars warn that this situation may lead to social disorders ranging from increased prostitution to higher suicide rates among males, as well as other problems that could have a major impact on Chinese society in the next century.

There is an important difference between the problems in India and China. In India, female infanticide appears to be most prevalent in the poorest sectors of society, notably in remote rural areas. In China, female infanticide has long occurred in poor and remote areas, but the one-child policy has been most effective in urban and near-urban areas. This has led to a substantial increase in female infanticide in China's more developed areas, where the scarcity of female marriage partners has now become acute.

Will the lot of women in such countries as India, China, South Korea (where male births exceed female births by nearly 15 percent), and elsewhere improve as lopsided population pyramids reflect the growing need for women? Governments would have to offer incentives such as educational opportunities and tax relief to couples who have girls. They would also have to enforce laws against cultural traditions that are biased against girls and women. But governments are dominated by men, and longstanding habits are difficult to change.

As we have noted repeatedly, family planning is an important component of material progress. But without legal constraints and balanced incentives, its impact on women can be devastating.

◆ FAMILY AND SOCIAL CONDITIONS

As noted previously, data on life expectancy and maternal mortality tell us nothing about women's quality of life. We can discern some aspects of this issue from more detailed statistics, for example, from child mortality figures that indicate a higher mortality for girls between the ages of 2 and 5 than for boys (Table 31-1). Note that the rate for Pakistani boys during the late 1980s was less than 37 per thousand, whereas for girls it was over 54. In Haiti, the rate stood below 48 for boys but over 61 for girls. In Bangladesh, the ***gender gap*** was nearly 11. Such discrepancies reflect a dreadful contrast in the treatment of girls and boys, a discrimination that, even if the girls survive these early years, puts females at a lifelong physical and emotional disadvantage. As the table shows, this pattern is not confined to South Asia or the Caribbean region. It occurs in East and Southeast Asia, as well as in South America.

The infant mortality data reflect the lower status of girls and women in many societies. As the United Nations' report on women (1991) states:

> Although girls contribute much to the family—in Africa and Asia they often work seven or more hours a day—many societies consider them a burden. They are discriminated against as children and married off early. In addition, some societies expect women to start having children at a very young age . . . in Mauritania, 39 percent of girls are married by age 15 and fifteen percent have given birth. In Bangladesh, 73 percent of girls are married by age 15, and 21 percent have had at least one child. (p. 67)

Other information about women's lives in traditional societies can be obtained from sources ranging from death certificates to hospital records, from local studies to newspaper reports. However, much of what happens in rural areas is simply not known. In *Landscapes of the Home* (1982) geographers Bonnie S. Lloyd, Janice J. Monk, and Arlene C. Rengert point out that men are traditionally associated with the outdoors. The cultural landscape, they argue, is created and dominated by males; the home is an indoor, female space, which is less studied and less well known. So we have only fragmentary knowledge of the quality of life of women in rural as well as urban settings.

Table 31-1 Mortality Rates for Girls and Boys Aged 2 to 5, Selected Countries

Country	Deaths per 1000 Girls	Deaths per 1000 Boys
Pakistan	54.4	36.9
Bangladesh	68.6	57.7
Haiti	61.2	47.8
Thailand	26.8	17.3
Colombia	24.8	20.5
Costa Rica	8.1	4.8
Philippines	21.9	19.1
Turkey	19.5	18.4
South Korea	12.7	11.8
Venezuela	8.4	7.6

Source: United Nations, *The World's Women 1970–1990* (New York, 1991), p. 60.

What we do know is dismaying. Women are often victims of domestic violence because they are generally less physically strong than men. This is a global, cross-cultural phenomenon. It happens among the rich as well as the poor and in industrialized as well as traditional societies. Survey results indicate that the incidence of such violence is astonishingly high. A recent UN study investigated 1500 divorce cases in Austria; violence against the wife was cited in nearly 60 percent of these cases. In a study done in Thailand, more than 50 percent of women from a Bangkok slum area reported regular beatings by their husbands. A study from Brazil reported two dozen unpunished domestic murders in one state alone; the murdered wives had been killed by "justifiably" jealous husbands.

Women in India

Scattered information of this kind underscores the contrasting circumstances in which men and women live. In India, where Hinduism prescribes reverence for life, girls are still forced into arranged marriages. Disputes over the bride price to be paid by the bride's family to the groom's father often lead to the death of the bride, who may be punished for her father's failure to fulfill the marriage agreement. In modern times such "***dowry deaths***" should not occur at all, or at least should be declining sharply. But official figures indicate otherwise: in 1985, the number was 999, in 1987, 1786 women died at the hands of vengeful husbands or in-laws, and in 1989, the latest year for which data are available, 2436 perished. These figures report only confirmed dowry deaths; many more are believed to occur but are reported as kitchen accidents or other fatal domestic incidents.

Indian governments (federal as well as State) have set up legal aid offices to help women who seek assistance, and in 1984 the national legislature passed the Family Courts Act, creating a network of "family courts" to hear domestic cases, including dowry disputes. But the judges tend to be older males, and their chief objective, according to women's support groups, is to hold the family together, that is, to force the threatened or battered woman back into the household. Hindu culture attaches great importance to the family structure, and the family courts tend to operate on this principle.

India is a multicultural country, and powerful communities sometimes seek to institute their own laws in place of those enacted in New Delhi. With the resurgence of Muslim fundamentalism came a controversy over the rights of divorced Muslim women in India. The (national) Indian Civil Code gives some rights and protections to women who have succeeded in obtaining a legal divorce, including child support. But representatives of Muslim communities argued that the Indian Code goes against Islamic law. They therefore proposed a separate Muslim Woman's Bill that would deny divorced Muslim women even the limited rights they would have under the Indian Civil Code.

Women in Islamic Countries

The circumstances of women in the majority of traditional Muslim societies are even more restrictive than in India, where legal help and aggressive women's movements have given support and visibility to the plight of women. The story of the Saudi women who were arrested for driving the family car is a sidelight to a far more serious situation: many women in Islamic countries live an existence of isolation and servitude. Many Muslim political and social leaders deplore this situation, and some Muslim women have succeeded in breaking free from their societal handcuffs and have become doctors, lawyers, and other professionals. But Islamic laws and rules restrict certain aspects of their lives; they may wear modern, even Western dress in the privacy of their homes and compounds, but in public they must be cloaked and veiled.

The resurgence of Islamic fundamentalism, along with the severe *Sharia* laws, in some Muslim societies has had an especially strong impact on women. When the last Shah of Iran sought to modernize his country, he gave women unprecedented freedoms, including the right to wear clothing of their choice in public. This action galvanized fundamentalist opposition to his rule. After his downfall in a revolution led by the Ayatollah Khomeini, women were ordered to resume wearing the long cloaks of traditional Islamic society, as well as veils over their faces. Muslim men policed the streets to enforce this order, and many women were arrested; some, it is alleged, were even executed for flouting the fundamentalist dress code.

In 1997, the victorious Islamic Taliban movement, after taking control of the capital, Kabul, severely restricted the rights of women. A substantial number of women held professional jobs ranging from nurses to teachers; all were instructed to resign. Many women wore modern dress; all were told to don head-to-toe traditional clothing. Press reports described women being stoned to death for adultery as affairs begun during pre-Taliban days suddenly risked capital punishment. Afghanistan's return to stability came at a high price for women.

As we will note later in the chapter, the circumstances under which African women live vary widely. In parts of West Africa women control markets and commerce and have a powerful position in society. But in most of the realm men live more freely (and often more comfortably), eat better, do lighter work, and do less to support the children. As noted previously, gender inequality around the world differs only in degree, not in kind.

◆ EDUCATION AND OPPORTUNITY

Education offers a chance to escape from poverty and stagnation, improve one's circumstances, and fulfill one's potential. Where educational levels are higher, the conditions of women's lives are better. It is no accident that most of what has been said about India does not apply to the southern Indian State of Kerala, where women are better educated than elsewhere. In Kerala, the gender gap actually favors women; women's health is better and women have fewer children. Education is the key.

In North America it is normal for all girls and boys to attend school; in fact, it is the law. Imagine a situation in which the boys enter elementary school at the age of 5 or 6, but the girls stay home doing chores. In many countries of the periphery this is exactly what happened. Women's education was a lower priority, and women had less access to education than men. That produced an educational gap that still exists today. In India, for example, the overall adult literacy rate is estimated to be 55 percent. But the United Nations and UNICEF estimate that between 65 and 75 percent of all Indian women are illiterate.

The situation is improving. Long-term education data show that the gender gap is narrowing throughout the world, that girls now go to school, at least elementary school, where previously they did not (or did in far smaller numbers), and that a growing number of women obtain some higher education. Experts predict that it will take several generations for the educational gender gap to disappear, but progress is being made.

This progress varies spatially, however. In the late 1990s there were still nearly 600 million illiterate females and more than 350 million illiterate males (the great majority of them adults) in the world. Girls are now going to school in the same numbers as boys in many countries, not only in Europe, North America, and parts of East Asia but also in Middle and South America. But progress lags in South Asia and in Africa south of the Sahara. Also, sharp contrasts remain between rural and urban areas. UN studies show that these contrasts may be strongest in Middle and South America, where 1 in 4 rural women aged 15 to 24 is illiterate, compared to only 1 in 20 in urban areas. (In Subsaharan Africa, the figures are more than 7 in 10 for rural areas and more than 4 in 10 for urban areas.)

Every relevant study shows that although substantial progress has been made in the past four decades, major obstacles remain. Women still are denied access to training in such fields as forestry, fishing, and agriculture; they still have difficulty breaking into male-dominated professions. Some societies still do not allow women to teach boys (although the teaching profession is generally open to women). In the urbanized industrialized realms, women have become physicians, lawyers, and other professionals, although they still face special job-related difficulties.

Figure 31-3 summarizes the global situation in a general but revealing way. A similar map was made by Ruth Leger Sivard a decade ago in her study, *Women: A World Survey.* It was based on the question, "If male education equals 100, where does female education stand on a scale of 1 to 100?" Our map is based on the ratio of female to male enrollment at all three levels of schooling and thus is a very general average for each country. Nevertheless, the spatial pattern tells us much about the regional status of women's education. Note that the gender gap is narrowing in Middle and South America but remains very wide in tropical Africa and South Asia as well as in parts of Southwest Asia and North Africa. Rapid population growth, limited budgets, and cultural and political barriers combine to cause the disparities shown in Figure 31-3.

When reading maps like this one, it is important to remember that the validity of the data may be questionable. Recent reports from Africa and Asia suggest that progress in women's education has been halted or even reversed. Especially in Africa, economic setbacks and armed conflicts have combined to erode education systems, and women's education suffers most under such conditions. And while women's education has advanced in some Muslim countries, it has declined in others, for example in Afghanistan, where the power of fundamentalists has risen.

◆ ECONOMY AND PRODUCTIVITY

While women have made some long-term progress in the educational arena, the same cannot be said for their economic situation. When economists calculate the total annual production of goods and services in a country, they do not include the unpaid labor of women in the household, nor, usually, the work done by rural women in less developed countries.

Women's Productivity

Scholars estimate that if women's productivity in the household alone were given a dollar value (for example, by calculating what it would cost to hire people to perform these tasks), the world's total annual GNP (that is, the gross national product for all countries combined; see Part Seven) would grow by about one-third. In countries in the periphery, women produce more than half of all the food; they also build homes, dig wells, plant and harvest crops, make clothes, and do many other things that are not recorded as economically productive.

Although the circumstances of rural women in much of the periphery are generally difficult, if not desperate, the situation of African women is probably the worst. Apart from the areas in West Africa where women dominate local commerce, women in Africa south of the Sahara have heavy responsibilities and few rights. They produce an estimated 70 percent of

From the field notes

"She and her daughter came walking along the path to the village near Kanye, Botswana, carrying huge, burlap-wrapped bundles on their heads. I had seen them go earlier to fetch pails of water; in the early afternoon they were working in the field, weeding the maize (corn). Later I saw them with batches of firewood that must have weighed 60 pounds or more. In the evening, they would cook the meal. From the village I could hear men arguing, laughing."

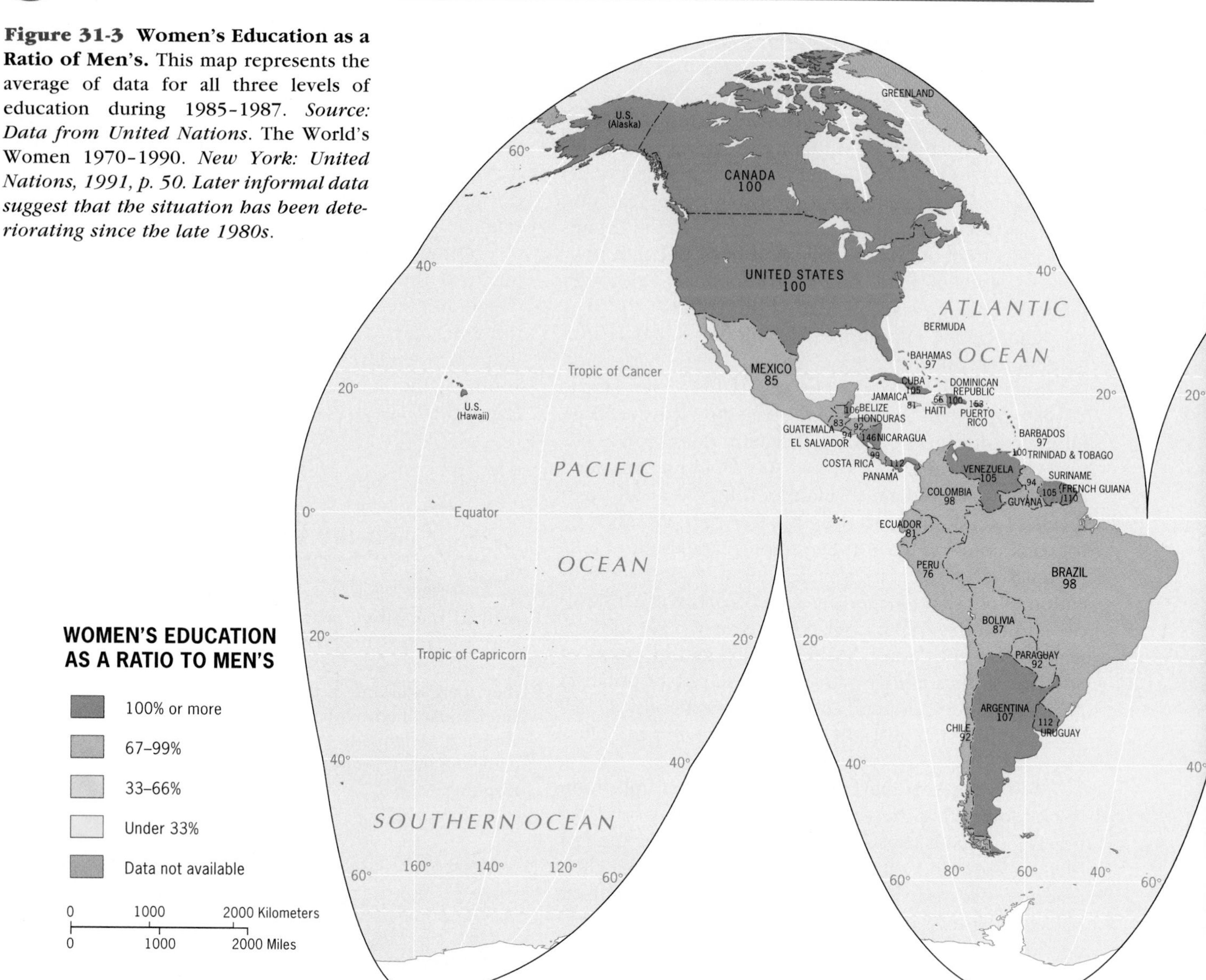

Figure 31-3 Women's Education as a Ratio of Men's. This map represents the average of data for all three levels of education during 1985–1987. *Source: Data from United Nations.* The World's Women 1970–1990. *New York: United Nations, 1991, p. 50. Later informal data suggest that the situation has been deteriorating since the late 1980s.*

the realm's food, almost all of it without any modern equipment. Their backbreaking hand-cultivation of corn and other staples is an endless task. As water supplies decrease, the exhausting walk to the nearest pump gets longer. Firewood is being cut at ever-greater distances from the village, and the task of hauling it home becomes more difficult every year. As the men leave for the towns, perhaps to marry other wives and have other children, the women left in the villages struggle for survival.

Even when she is the head of the household, however, if a woman goes to the bank for a loan she is likely to be refused: banks in Africa generally do not lend money to rural women. Not having heard from her husband for years and having reared her children, she might wish to apply for a title to the land she has occupied and farmed for decades, but land titles usually are not awarded to women. Only a small number of African women have the legal right to own property.

Young girls soon become trapped in the cycle of female poverty and overwork. Often there is little money for school fees; what is available first goes to pay for the boys. As soon as she can carry anything at all, the girl goes with her mother to weed the fields, bring back firewood, or fetch water. She will do so for an average of perhaps 12 hours a day, seven days a week, during all the years she remains capable of working. But national statistics say nothing about her contribution to the economy.

Therefore, when we study the distribution of farming and crops, as we did earlier in this book, we should remind ourselves of distributions that are not revealed by available maps. In East Africa, cash crops such as tea are called "men's crops" because the men

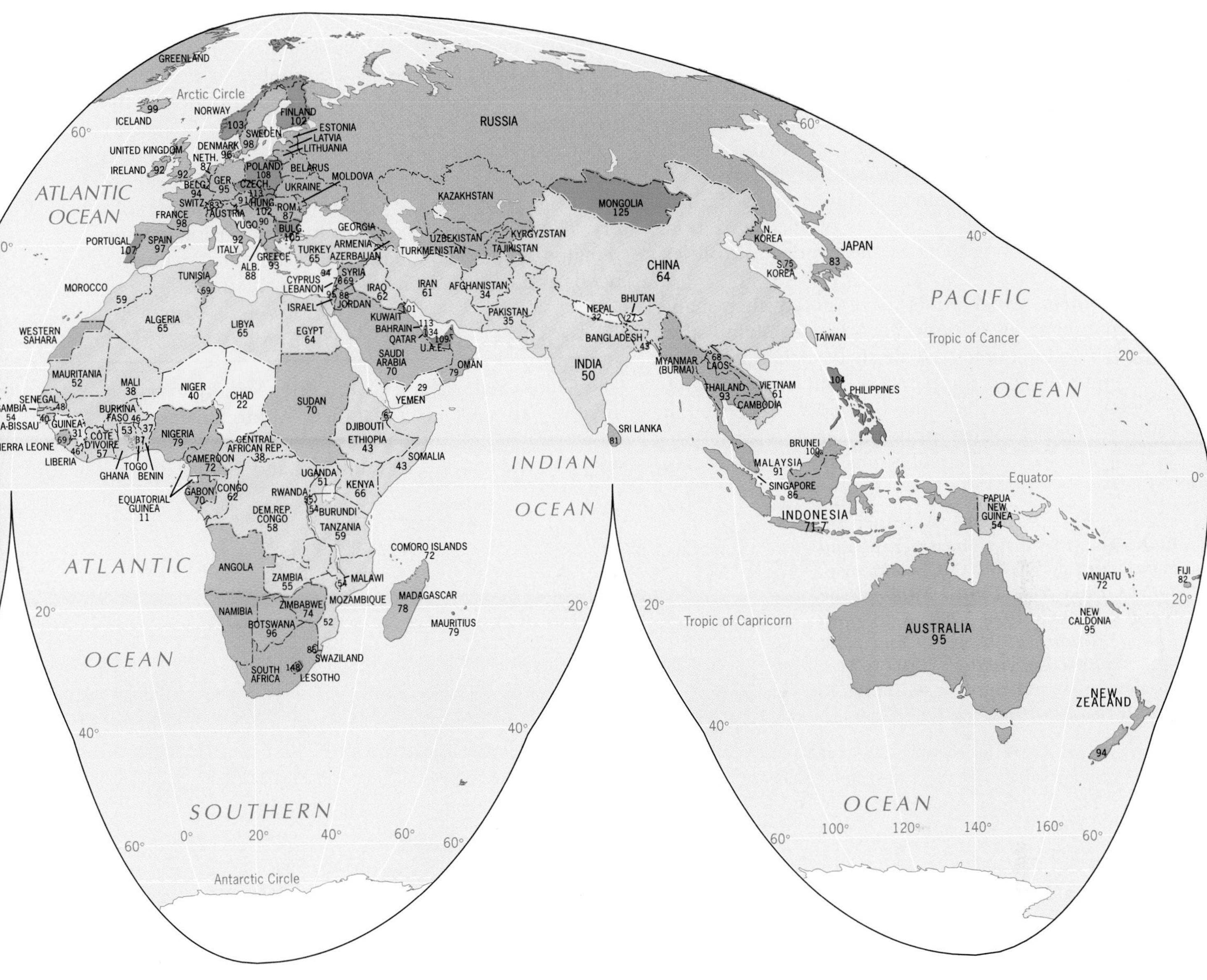

trade in what the women produce. But when the government of Kenya tried to stimulate the productivity of the tea plantations, it handed out bonuses—not to the women who did the harvesting but to the men who owned the land.

Although the quality of life for women may be lowest in rural Africa, conditions are not much better in many other regions. Village life is similar for women in South Asia or Middle and South America. But their productivity also is immense: an estimated 40 percent of all the food consumed in Middle and South America is produced by women.

Women in the Labor Force

Despite these conditions, the number of women in the "official" labor force is rising. In 1990 the United Nations estimated that there were 828 million women in the labor force. All but one geographic realm showed increases between 1970 and 1990: in the core realms, from 35 to 39 percent of the labor force; in Middle and South America, from 24 to 29 percent. In East and Southeast Asia the figure rose very slightly, to 40 and 35 percent, respectively. In Subsaharan Africa, the percentage of women in the labor force actually declined, from 39 percent in 1970 to 37 percent in 1990. As the report, *The World's Women 1970–1990*, states, women "generally continue to be the last to benefit from job expansion and the first to suffer from job contraction—particularly in the stagnant or declining economies of Africa and Latin America and the Caribbean. In Africa, due to especially severe economic conditions, the growth in the female labor force has fallen well behind population growth" (p. 17).

In most of Asia and virtually all of Africa, the great majority of wage-earning women still work in agriculture. In Subsaharan Africa, nearly 80 percent of wage-earning women work on plantations and farms; in Asia, the figure is over 50 percent. Although the number of women working in industries in these areas is comparatively small, it is rising. The increase was slowed by the global economic downturn of the late 1980s and early 1990s, as well as by mechanization, which leads to job reductions and hence to layoffs of women workers.

Economic geographers have noted that many women engage in "informal" economic activity—that is, private, often home-based activity such as tailoring, beer brewing, food preparation, and soap making. Women who seek to advance beyond subsistence but cannot enter the formal economic sector often turn to such work. In the migrant slums on the fringes of many cities, informal economic activity is the mainstay of the community. As with subsistence farming, however, it is difficult to assess the number of women involved, their productivity, or their contribution to the overall economy.

Wherever they work and at whatever job, women still face job discrimination, occupational segregation, and wage inequities, in both the core and the periphery. The world of economic gain and decision making remains a male-dominated one in which women's needs and contributions are undervalued.

◆ POLITICS AND PUBLIC LIFE

The United States is a free and open society in which anyone can seek elected office. Approximately half the voters in the United States are women. Yet in 1998 only 8 of the nation's 100 senators and 2 of its 50 gov-

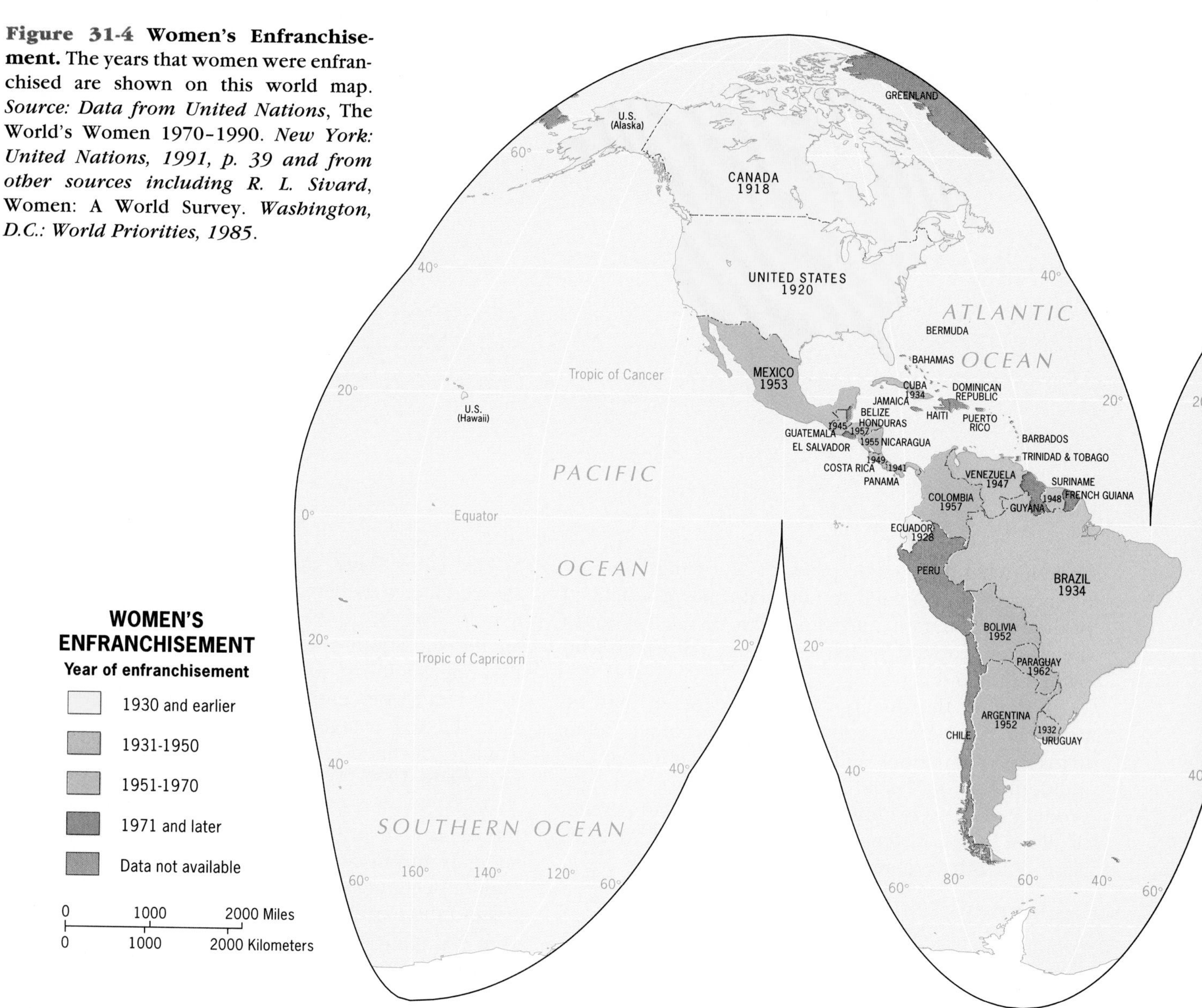

Figure 31-4 Women's Enfranchisement. The years that women were enfranchised are shown on this world map. *Source: Data from United Nations,* The World's Women 1970–1990. *New York: United Nations, 1991, p. 39 and from other sources including R. L. Sivard,* Women: A World Survey. *Washington, D.C.: World Priorities, 1985.*

ernors were women. The number of women in the House of Representatives is somewhat larger (53), but it is nowhere near the number of men. How has this male dominance developed, and why does it persist?

The answer lies in the past as well as the present. Today the idea that anyone can vote is normal and routine, but women in the United States and Canada did not achieve full ***enfranchisement***—the right to vote—until 1920. This was a half-century after the U.S. government approved the Fifteenth Amendment to the Constitution, which granted the vote to all *male* citizens "without regard to race, color, or previous condition of servitude." By the time women became able to vote (and could seek office), male dominance of political institutions and networks was deeply entrenched.

Although the United States was not the first country to respond to women's demand for the right to vote (New Zealand did so in 1893 and Australia in 1902), it was among the earliest to do so. The map in Figure 31-4 underscores the fact that, for the most part, women were unable to vote before the twentieth century. Some Western countries did not enfranchise women until as recently as 1971 (Switzerland) and 1976 (Portugal). In some Muslim countries in Southwest Asia women still cannot vote.

The legal right to vote does not immediately translate into political power or political representation. As Table 31-2 shows, women's participation in parliamentary bodies remains limited. It is strongest in the core and weakest in the periphery. Yet even where it is strongest it does not reach 40 percent; in most industrialized countries it fails to reach 15 percent. Note that the representation of women is highest in the northern European countries, averaging more than one-third of all representatives, whereas it is much

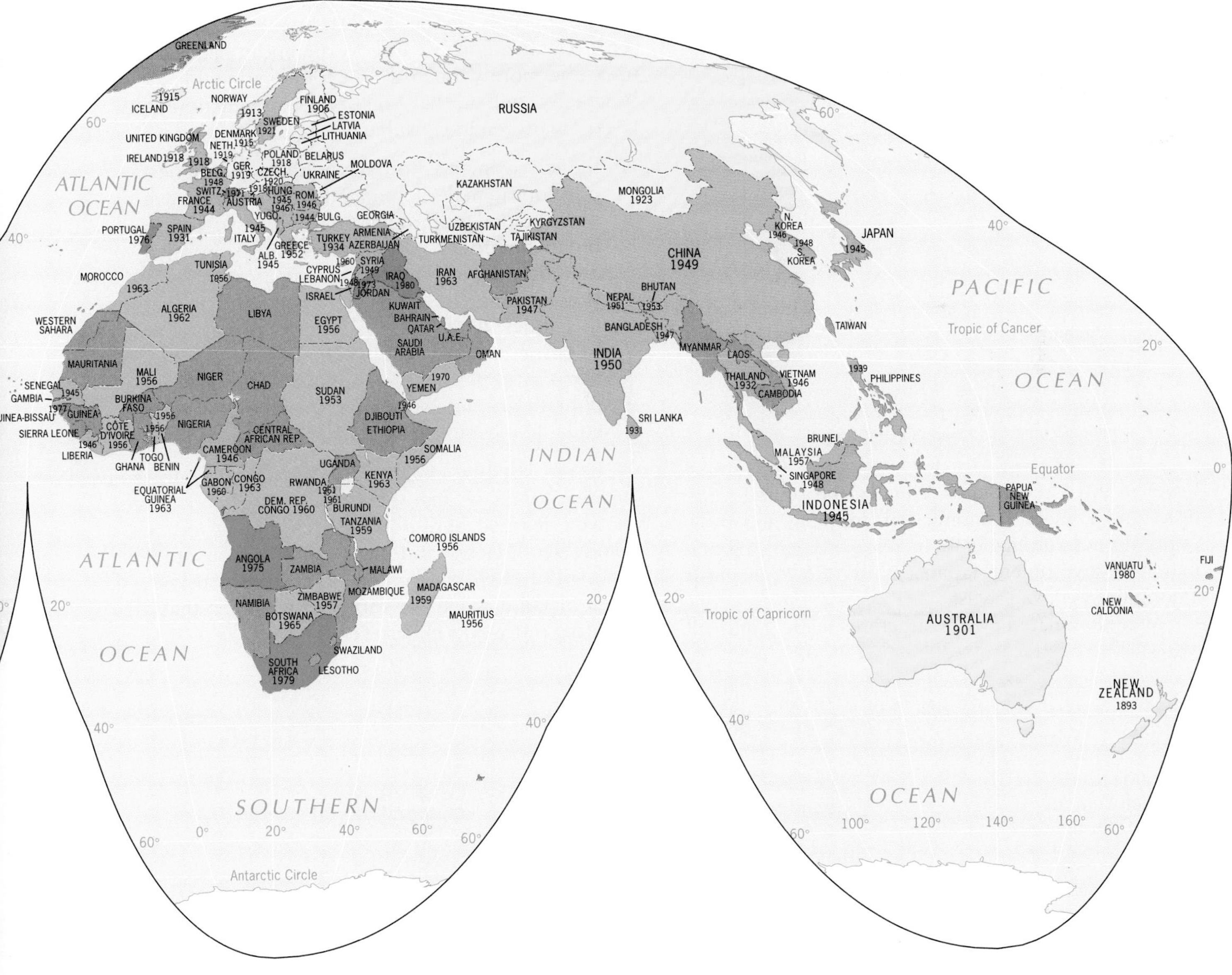

Table 31-2 Percentage of Seats in National Parliaments Occupied by Women, 1987 and 1994

	1987	1994
United States	5.3	10.9
Canada	9.6	17.3
Australia	6.1	12.6
New Zealand	14.4	21.2
Sweden	28.5	33.5
Norway	34.4	39.4
Finland	31.5	39.0
Denmark	29.1	33.0
Netherlands	20.0	29.3
France	6.4	5.7
United Kingdom	6.3	7.4
Japan	1.4	6.7
Algeria	2.4	6.7
Morocco	0.0	0.6
Egypt	3.9	2.2
Côte d'Ivoire	5.7	4.6
Kenya	1.7	3.0
Zaïre	3.5	4.2
Zimbabwe	9.0	12.0
Brazil	5.3	5.5
Argentina	4.7	14.2
Mexico	10.8	7.3
India	8.3	7.3
China	21.2	21.0
Vietnam	17.7	18.5

Source: United Nations, *The World's Women 1970–1990* (New York, 1991), pp. 32–34; and Interparliamentary Union, *Report* (Geneva, 1995), pp. 16–26.

lower in the United States, Canada, the United Kingdom, and France. Economic development and prosperity do not automatically increase women's participation in government: Japan's figure of 6.7 percent is among the world's lowest.

Male-dominated power structures make it difficult for women to enter the political arena. But the overall situation is improving, despite the figures in Table 31-2. When the 1994 data (the latest available) are compared to those for 1987, a general increase in women's representation can be discerned. For example, women's parliamentary representation more than doubled in the United States during these seven years, and it increased substantially in all the northern European countries. It also doubled in Australia and increased in New Zealand, Canada, the Netherlands, the United Kingdom, and France. And in a few countries women have become national leaders in recent decades: Corazon Aquino (Philippines), Benazir Bhutto (Pakistan), Violeta Chamorro (Nicaragua), Tansu Ciller (Turkey), Indira Gandhi (India), Chandrika Bandaranaike Kumaratunga (Sri Lanka), Mary Robinson (Ireland), Margaret Thatcher (United Kingdom), and several others have not only attained their countries' highest office but also gained international prominence and respect.

During the coming century women will achieve representative equality in government in many countries, and more women will become national leaders. What effect will this have on political interaction? Ruth Leger Sivard reminds us that

> the few women who have attained the highest positions in male-dominated governments have not avoided confrontational politics. Yet in broad opinion surveys women have revealed attitudes significantly different from men's. When women have had a chance to use power in settings where there is a deep feminist consciousness and social commitment to justice—as in the Nordic countries—government policies are noteworthy for their emphasis on equality, development, and peace. (p. 6)

In the last two chapters we have dealt with the sensitive topics of race, ethnicity, and gender. What we have learned here will help us understand contrasting worldviews and divergent reactions to the same social environment. We should keep these realities in mind when we turn to the forces that are remaking our world in Part Ten.

◆ KEY TERMS ◆

dowry deaths
enfranchisement
female infanticide
gender
gender gap
longevity gap
maternal mortality rate

◆ APPLYING GEOGRAPHIC KNOWLEDGE ◆

1. As we have seen, men outnumber women in many societies, including the world's most populous ones. Explain the factors that produce male numerical dominance in some countries, and discuss what changes would have to occur if that situation were to change.
2. Geographers Janice Monk and Arlene Rengert have argued that certain landscapes are created and dominated by men. Which landscapes in the community where you live fit this description? In what ways are those landscapes uninviting to women? Do those landscapes affect the activity patterns of women?

Part Nine

SOCIAL GEOGRAPHIES OF THE MODERN WORLD

At Issue: Revisited

Can the smaller world created by transport, information, and communication technologies help us overcome some of the divisions of race, ethnicity, and gender? Technological advances now make us more aware than ever of the social fragmentation of our world. Words and images of faraway atrocities can sometimes open possibilities for international pressure to be brought to bear on responsible parties—pressure that is organized through the use of airplanes, telephones, and computers. But those same words and images also make us aware of how deeply, even hopelessly, divided our world is. And when one considers that patterns of access to modern technology reflect the geographies of inequality surveyed in this part, technology can look as much like a part of the problem as a solution. A challenge for the decades ahead, then, is to broaden access to technology and participation in its development. Such an undertaking offers the hope that technology can help us understand the true complexity of our differences—a first critical step toward overcoming them.

◆ SELECTED BIBLIOGRAPHY ◆

Part Nine Social Geographies of the Modern World

Adepoju, A., & Oppong, C., eds. *Gender, Work & Population in Sub-Saharan Africa* (London: J. Currey, 1994).

Agarawal, B. *A Field of One's Own: Gender and Land Rights in South Asia* (Cambridge, U.K.: Cambridge University Press, 1994).

Anderson, B. *Imagined Communities: Reflections on the Origin and Spread of Nationalism* (New York: Verso, rev. ed., 1991).

Aslanbeigui, N., Pressman, S. & Summerfield, G., eds. *Women in the Age of Economic Transformation: Gender Impact of Reforms in Post-Socialist and Developing Countries* (London: Routledge, 1994).

Badran, M. *Feminists, Islam, and Nation: Gender and the Making of Modern Egypt* (Princeton, N.J.: Princeton University Press, 1995).

Bagchi, D. "Rural Energy and the Role of Women." In J. Momsen & J. Townsend, eds., *Geography of Gender in the Third World* (Albany, N.Y.: SUNY Press, 1987).

Barnett, T., & Blaikie, P. *AIDS in Africa: Its Present and Future Impact* (New York: Guilford Press, 1992).

Beneria, L., & Feldman, S., eds. *Unequal Burden: Economic Crises, Persistent Poverty and Women's Work* (Boulder, Colo.: Westview Press, 1992).

Biswas, M. R., & Gabr, M., eds. *Nutrition in the Nineties: Policy Issues* (New York: Oxford University Press, 1994).

Brooks, G. *Nine Parts of Desire: The Hidden World of Islamic Women* (New York: Anchor Books/Doubleday, 1994).

Brown, B. J., & LaPrairie, L. A. *Shades of Opportunity and Access: Ethnic and Gender Minority Issues in America with Global Reflections* (Boulder, Colo.: Department of Geography, University of Colorado, 1989).

Brown, L. R. *The Changing World Food Prospects: The Nineties and Beyond* (Washington, D.C.: Worldwatch Institute, 1988).

Brown, L. R. *Full House: Reassessing the Earth's Population Carrying Capacity* (Washington, D.C.: Worldwatch Institute, 1994).

Camilleri, J. A., Jarvis, A. P., & Paolini, A. J., eds. *The State in Transition: Reimagining Political Space* (Boulder, Colo.: Lynne Rienner, 1995).

Chatty, D., & Rabo, A., eds. *Organizing Women: Formal and Informal Women's Groups in the Middle East* (New York: Berg, 1997).

Clarke, C., Ley, D., & Peach, C., eds. *Geography and Ethnic Pluralism* (London: George Allen & Unwin, 1984).

Cliff, A., & Haggett, P. *Atlas of Disease Distribution* (Oxford, U.K.: Basil Blackwell, 1989).

Connor, W. *Ethnonationalism: The Quest for Understanding* (Princeton, N.J.: Princeton University Press, 1994).

Currey, B., & Hugo, G., eds. *Famines as a Geographical Phenomenon* (Boston: D. Reidel, 1984).

Curtis, J. A. "Mexicali's Chinatown." *Geographical Review* 85(3) (1995) 335–348.

Dando, W. *The Geography of Famine* (Silver Spring, Md.: V. H. Winston/Halsted Press, 1980).

Delaporte, F. *The History of Yellow Fever.* (Trans. A. Goldhammer. Cambridge, Mass.: MIT Press, 1991).

Gesler, W. *Health Care in Developing Countries* (Washington, D.C.: Association of American Geographers, Resource Publications in Geography, 1984).

Gibson, A., & Fast, T. *Women's Atlas of the United States* (New York: Facts on File Publications, 1986).

Gordon, A. A. *Transforming Capitalism and Patriarchy: Gender and Developments in Africa* (Boulder, Colo.: Lynne Rienner, 1996).

Gould, P. R. *The Slow Plague: A Geography of the AIDS Pandemic* (Oxford: Basil Blackwell, 1993).

Haddad, Y. Y., & Esposito, J. L., eds. *Islam, Gender & Social Change* (New York: Oxford University Press, 1998).

Hanson, S., & Pratt, G. *Gender, Work and Space* (New York: Routledge, 1995).

Hartl, D. L., & Clark, A.G. *Principles of Population Genetics* (Sunderland, Mass.: Sinauer Associates, 1989).

Hawley, J. S., ed. *Fundamentalism and Gender* (New York: Oxford University Press, 1994).

Higuchi, T. *The Visual and Spatial Structure of Landscapes* (Cambridge, Mass.: MIT Press, 1983).

House-Midambam, B., & Ekechi, F. K., eds. *African Market Women and Economic Power: The Role of Women in African Economic Development* (Westport, Conn.: Greenwood Press, 1995).

Jackson, J. B. *Discovering the Vernacular Landscape* (New Haven, Conn.: Yale University Press, 1984).

Jakle, J. A., et al. *Common Houses in America's Small Towns: The Atlantic Seaboard to the Mississippi Valley* (Athens: University of Georgia Press, 1989).

Jeffrey, R., & Jeffrey, P. *Population, Gender and Politics: Demographic Change in Rural North India* (Cambridge, U.K.: Cambridge University Press, 1997).

Jordan, T. "Perceptual Regions in Texas," *Geographical Review* 68 (1978), 293–307.

Kahne, H., & Giele, J. Z., eds. *Women's Work and Women's Lives: The Continuing Struggle Worldwide* (Boulder, Colo.: Westview Press, 1992).

Katz, M., et al. *Parasitic Diseases* (New York: Springer-Verlag, 2nd rev. ed., 1990).

Knight, D. B. "Identity and Territory: Geographical Perspectives on Nationalism and Regionalism." *Annals of the Association of American Geographers* 72 (1982), 514–531.

Lieberson, S., & Waters, M. C. *From Many Strands: Ethnic and Racial Groups in Contemporary America* (New York: Russell Sage Foundation, 1988).

Lloyd, B. S., Rengert, A. C., & Monk, J. J. "Landscapes of the Home," in A. C. Rengert, & J. J. Monk, eds., *Women and Spatial Change: Learning Resources for Social Science Courses* (Dubuque, Iowa: Kendall-Hunt, 1982).

Marty, M. E., & Appleby, R. S., eds. *Religion, Ethnicity, and Self-Identity: Nations in Turmoil* (Hanover, N.H.: University Press of New England, 1997).

Massey, D. *Space, Place and Gender* (Minneapolis: University of Minnesota Press, 1994).

McDowell, L., & Sharp, J. P., eds. *Space, Gender, Knowledge: Feminist Readings* (London: Arnold, 1997).

Meade, M., ed. *Conceptual and Methodological Issues in Medical Geography* (Chapel Hill, N.C.: Department of Geography, 1980).

Meade, M. S., et al. *Medical Geography* (New York: Guilford Press, 1988).

Mikesell, M. W. "The Myth of the Nation State." *Journal of Geography* 82 (1983), 257–260.

Mikesell, M. W., & Murphy, A. B. "A Framework for Comparative Study of Minority-Group Aspirations." *Annals of the Association of American Geographers* 81 (1991), 581–604.

Momsen, J. H., & Kinnaird, V., eds. *Different Places, Different Voices: Gender and Development in Africa, Asia, and Latin America* (London: Routledge, 1993).

Momsen, J. H., & Townsend, J., eds. *Geography of Gender in the Third World* (Albany, N.Y.: SUNY Press, 1987).

Monk, J., & Hanson, S. "On Not Excluding Half of the Human in Human Geography." *The Professional Geographer* 34 (1982), 11–23.

Montagu, A. *Man's Most Dangerous Myth: The Fallacy of Race* (Cleveland: World, 5th rev. ed., 1975).

Palca, J. "The Sobering Geography of AIDS." *Science,* 19 April 1991, pp. 372–373.

Palm, R. "Ethnic Segmentation of the Urban Housing Market by Real Estate Agents." *Annals of the Association of American Geographers* 75 (1985), 58–68.

Phillips, D. R. *Health and Health Care in the Third World* (Essex, U.K.: Longmans, 1990).

Pyle, G. *The Diffusion of Influenza: Patterns and Paradigms* (Totowa, N.J.: Rowman & Allanheld, 1986).

Relph, E. *Rational Landscapes and Humanistic Geography* (Totowa, N.J.: Barnes & Noble, 1981).

Roberts, L. "Disease and Death in the New World," *Science* 8 December 1989, pp. 1245–1247.

Rose, G. *Feminism and Geography: The Limits of Geographical Knowledge* (Minneapolis: University of Minnesota Press, 1993).

Rose, H. M., & McClain, P. D. *Race, Place and Risk: Black Homicide in Urban America* (Albany, N.Y.: State University of New York Press, 1990).

Sachs, C. *The Invisible Farmers: Women in Agricultural Production* (Totowa, N.J.: Rowman & Allanheld, 1983).

Seager, J., & Olson, A. *Women in the World: An International Atlas* (New York: Simon & Schuster, 1986).

Shannon, G. W., Pyler, G., & Bashshur, R. *The Geography of AIDS* (New York: Guilford Press, 1991).

Sheldon, K., ed. *Courtyards, Markets, City Streets: Urban Women in Africa* (Boulder, Colo.: Westview Press, 1996).

Shipman, P. *The Evolution of Racism* (New York: Simon & Schuster, 1994).

Shortridge, B. G. *Atlas on American Women* (New York: Macmillan, 1987).

Singer, M., & Berg, P. *Genes and Genomes: A Changing Perspective* (Mill Valley, Calif.: University Science Books, 1990).

Sivard, R. L. *Women: A World Survey* (Washington, D.C.: World Priorities, 1985).

Sowell, T. *Race and Culture: A World View* (New York: Basic Books, 1994).

Staudt, K., ed. *Women, International Development and Politics* (Philadelphia: Temple University Press, 1997).

Stini, W. A. *Ecology and Human Adaptation* (Dubuque, Iowa: W. C. Brown, 1975).

UNICEF. *The Lesser Child: The Girl in India* (Geneva: United Nations, 1990).

United Nations. *The World's Women, 1995: Trends and Statistics* (New York: United Nations, 1995).

Williams, C. H., & Smith, A. D. "The National Construction of Social Space." *Progress in Human Geography* 7 (1983), 502–518.

Wixman, R. *Language Aspects of Ethnic Patterns and Processes in the North Caucasus* (Chicago: University of Chicago, Department of Geography, 1980).

Yeager, P., ed. *The Geography of Identity* (Ann Arbor: University of Michigan Press, 1996).

Zelinsky, W. *The Cultural Geography of the United States* (Englewood Cliffs, N.J.: Prentice-Hall, 1973).

Part Ten

COPING WITH A RAPIDLY CHANGING WORLD

At Issue

Environmental variation (spatial as well as temporal) is one of the Earth's crucial characteristics. Temperatures rise and fall, precipitation waxes and wanes. Forests flourish and wither, deserts expand and contract. Humanity has evolved during a series of alternately warm and cold phases of an ice age that is still in progress. But today humanity itself is part of the process. The Earth has been warming, and we may be contributing to some degree to this warm-up. The world's governments are trying to find ways to combat industrial pollution and the release of "greenhouse" gases. At issue: *Should all countries be subject to the same rules? Or should the poorer countries be exempt from some of the more costly regulations? And can an effective response be organized without undermining state sovereignty?*

Should other states have a say when a government allows the forest to burn? Near Wewak, Papua New Guinea.

Part Outline

Chapter 32

Human Alteration of the Physical Environment

From the field notes

"My first field experience in one of China's Autonomous Regions, the Guangxi-Zhuang A.R., designated for non-Han minorities, had mixed results. Land degradation here was more advanced than in any other part of China visited; desertifiction seemed to be in progress in many areas. The cause: overuse of the land, and the collapse of what appeared to have been sound terracing systems. My Chinese colleague told me that China's rules for population control *and* land use were relaxed in these Autonomous regions, often leading to ecological damage."

KEY POINTS

◆ **Human alteration of the environment has been taking place for millennia, but only recently have humans acquired the ability to affect environmental change at the global scale.**

◆ **Water is a renewable resource, but water shortages threaten in many areas of the world. Future conflict over water supplies may come to rival recent conflicts over oil supplies.**

◆ **Human activity has produced an unprecedented concentration of greenhouse gases in the atmosphere, raising concerns about the prospects for significant global warming.**

◆ **Deforestation, desertification, and soil erosion pose a triple threat to the Earth's environment.**

◆ **The rapid accumulation of solid, toxic, and radioactive wastes in the technologically advanced countries is producing an increasingly serious disposal problem.**

Just a decade ago, the Soviet Union was still a formidable force in world affairs. South Africa was still in the grip of *apartheid.* Iraq and Kuwait were at peace. China was still pursuing its "Four Modernizations" campaign. NAFTA did not exist. Yugoslavia was still unified, as was Czechoslovakia.

Consider how much the world has changed in just the past ten years: the world map has been redrawn. New countries have arisen from old ones. New names by the hundreds have appeared on regional maps. New economic and political alliances have been formed. New industrial regions and new trade routes have emerged.

All this is going on against a background of global environmental change whose future is uncertain but troubling. A combination of natural cycles and human impacts may produce unprecedented climatic extremes.

In Part Ten we use geographic perspectives to help us understand, anticipate, and cope with these changes.

◆ THE HUMAN IMPACT

Biologists estimate that there may be as many as 25 million types of organisms on Earth, perhaps even more; most have not yet been identified, classified, or studied. *Homo sapiens* is only one of these, yet in ten millennia our species has developed a complex culture that is transmitted from one generation to the next through learning and is also to some degree encoded in our genes. Humans are not unique in possessing a culture: gorillas, orangutans, chimpanzees, and dolphins have cultures too. But ours is the only species with a vast and complex array of artifacts, technologies, laws, and belief systems.

No species, not even the powerful dinosaurs, ever affected their environment as strongly as humans do today. The dinosaurs (and many other species) were extinguished by what may have been an asteroid impact at the Cretaceous/Tertiary (K/T) boundary. Some biogeographers suggest that the next great extinction may be caused not by asteroids but by humans, whose numbers and demands are destroying millions of species.

Alteration of Ecosystems

This destructiveness is not just a matter of modern technology and its capacity to do unprecedented damage, whether by wartime forest defoliation, peacetime oil spills, or other means. Humans altered their environment from the beginning, when they set fires to kill herds of reindeer and bison, or hunted entire species of large mammals to extinction. The Maori, who arrived in New Zealand not much more than 1000 years ago, inflicted significant destruction on native species of animals and plants long before the advent of modern technology. Elsewhere in the Pacific realm, Polynesians reduced the forest cover to brush and, with their penchant for wearing bird-feather robes, had exterminated more than 80 percent of the regional bird species by the time the first Europeans arrived. The Europeans ravaged species ranging from Galápagos turtles to Antarctic seals. European fashions had a disastrous impact on African species ranging from snakes to leopards. Traditional as well as modern societies have had devastating impacts on their ***ecosystems*** (ecological units consisting of self-regulating associations of living and nonliving natural elements) as well as on those of areas into which they migrated.

Human alteration of the environment continues in many forms today. For the first time in history, however, the combined impact of humanity's destructive and exploitive actions is capable of producing environmental changes at the global scale. Consider for a moment the history of human life on the Earth. Early human societies had relatively small populations, and their impacts on the physical environment were limited in both duration and intensity. With the development of agrarian and preindustrial societies, human alterations of the physical environment increased, yet the effects of these early activities were still limited in scale. Even the onset of urbanization and the development of urban centers, which concentrated large numbers of people in particular places, were relatively limited. Over the last 500 years, however, both the rate and scale at which humans modify the Earth have increased dramatically. Particularly during the last half-century, the very character of human alterations of the physical world has taken on global dimensions.

Environmental Stress

The natural environment is being modified and stressed by human activity in many obvious ways and some less obvious ones. Among the more obvious actions causing ***environmental stress*** are the cutting of forests, the emission of pollutants into the atmosphere, and the spilling of oil into the oceans. Less obvious actions include the burying of toxic wastes that foul groundwater supplies, the dumping of vast amounts of garbage into the oceans, and the use of pesticides in farming. Humans have built seawalls, terraced hillslopes, dammed rivers, cut canals, and modified the environment in many constructive as well as destructive ways. All of these activities have a huge impact on the environment and have given rise to a number of key concerns. Among these are the future of water supplies, the state of the atmosphere, desertification, deforestation, soil degradation, and the disposal of industrial wastes.

◆ WATER

Economic geographers differentiate between resources that are replenished even as they are being used (*renewable* resources) and resources that are present in finite quantities and thus are *nonrenewable.* Water, the essence of life, is a renewable resource. But the available supply of fresh water is not distributed evenly across the globe. Figure 1-5 (pages 10–11) shows the world distribution of precipitation, with the

From the field notes

"Eroded river banks and damaged roads were just part of the devastation produced by the floods in East-Central Europe during the summer of 1997. The floods were a product not just of nature's fury, but of human alteration of the environment. Deforestation and the paving over of natural areas produced more rapid run-off, which in turn moved swiftly down channels modified by human hands. Downstream those channels were inadequate to handle the quantity of fast moving water flowing through them, leading to one of the worst floods in the region in decades."

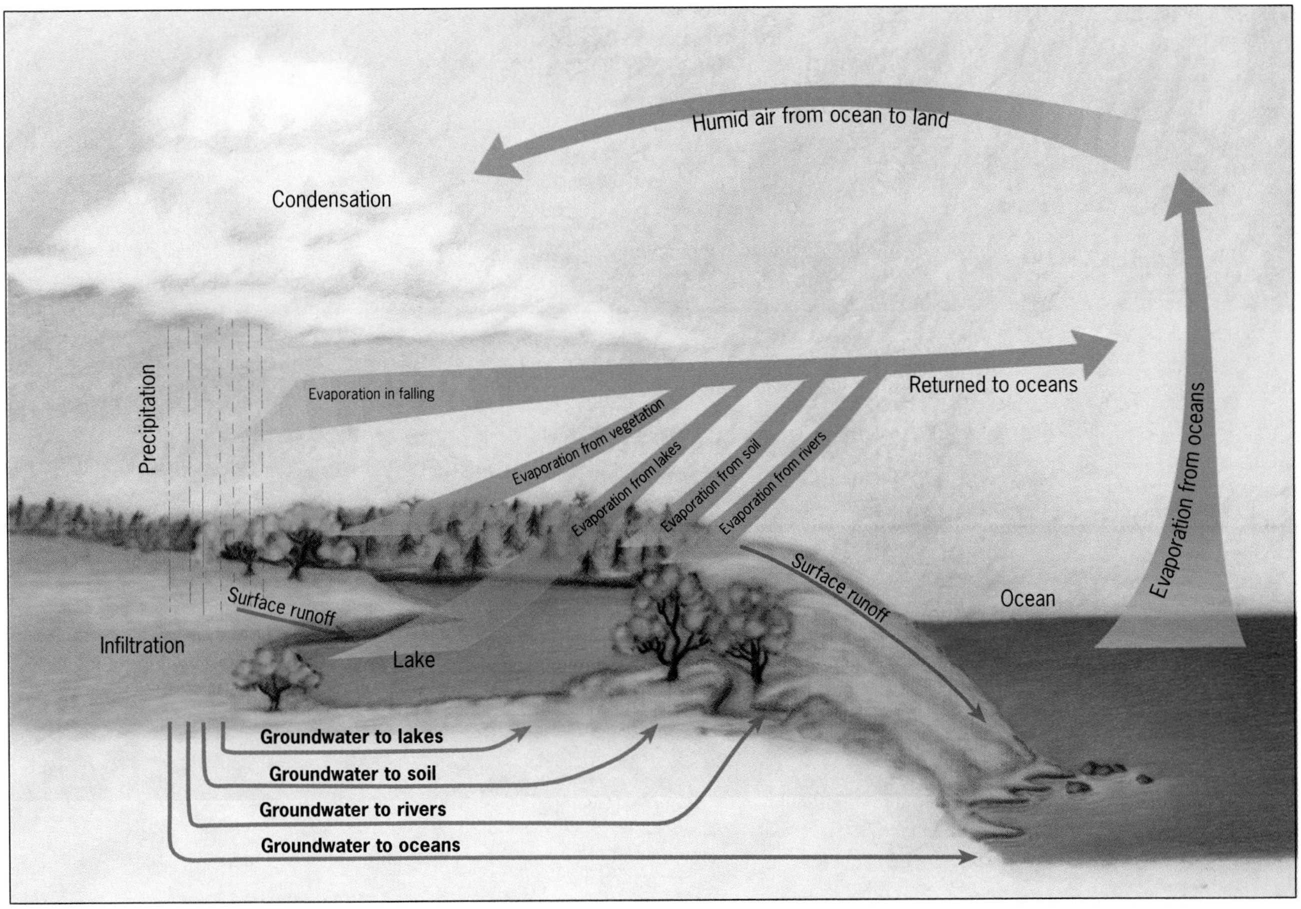

Figure 32-1 The Hydrologic Cycle. The hydrologic cycle carries moisture from the oceans and from other water bodies over the land, where precipitation, runoff, and evapotranspiration sustain the system.

From the field notes

"We drove north on Route 89 from Tucson, Arizona, across the desert. Drought rules the countryside here, and dams conserve what water there is. Snaking through the landscape are lifelines such as this, linking Coolidge Dam to distant farms and towns. In the vast, arid landscape, this narrow ribbon of water seems little more than an artificial brook—but to hundreds of thousands of people, this is what makes life possible in the Southwest."

largest totals recorded in equatorial and tropical areas of Southeast Asia, South Asia, Central and coastal West Africa, and Middle and South America. That distribution is sustained through the ***hydrologic cycle***, which brings rain and snow from the oceans to the landmasses (Fig. 32-1). The volume of precipitation in the world as a whole is enormous; spread out evenly, it would cover the land area of the planet with about 33 inches (83 cm) of water each year. Much of that water is lost through runoff and evaporation, but enough of it seeps downward into porous, water-holding rocks called ***aquifers*** to provide millions of wells with steady flows. In the United States alone it is estimated that there is 50 times as much water stored in aquifers as there is precipitation falling on the land surface every year.

Despite such favorable data, the supply of water is anything but plentiful (Fig. 32-2). Chronic water shortages afflict tens of millions of farmers in Africa and hundreds of thousands of city dwellers in Southern California; water rationing has been imposed in rainy South Florida and in Spain, which faces the Mediterranean Sea.

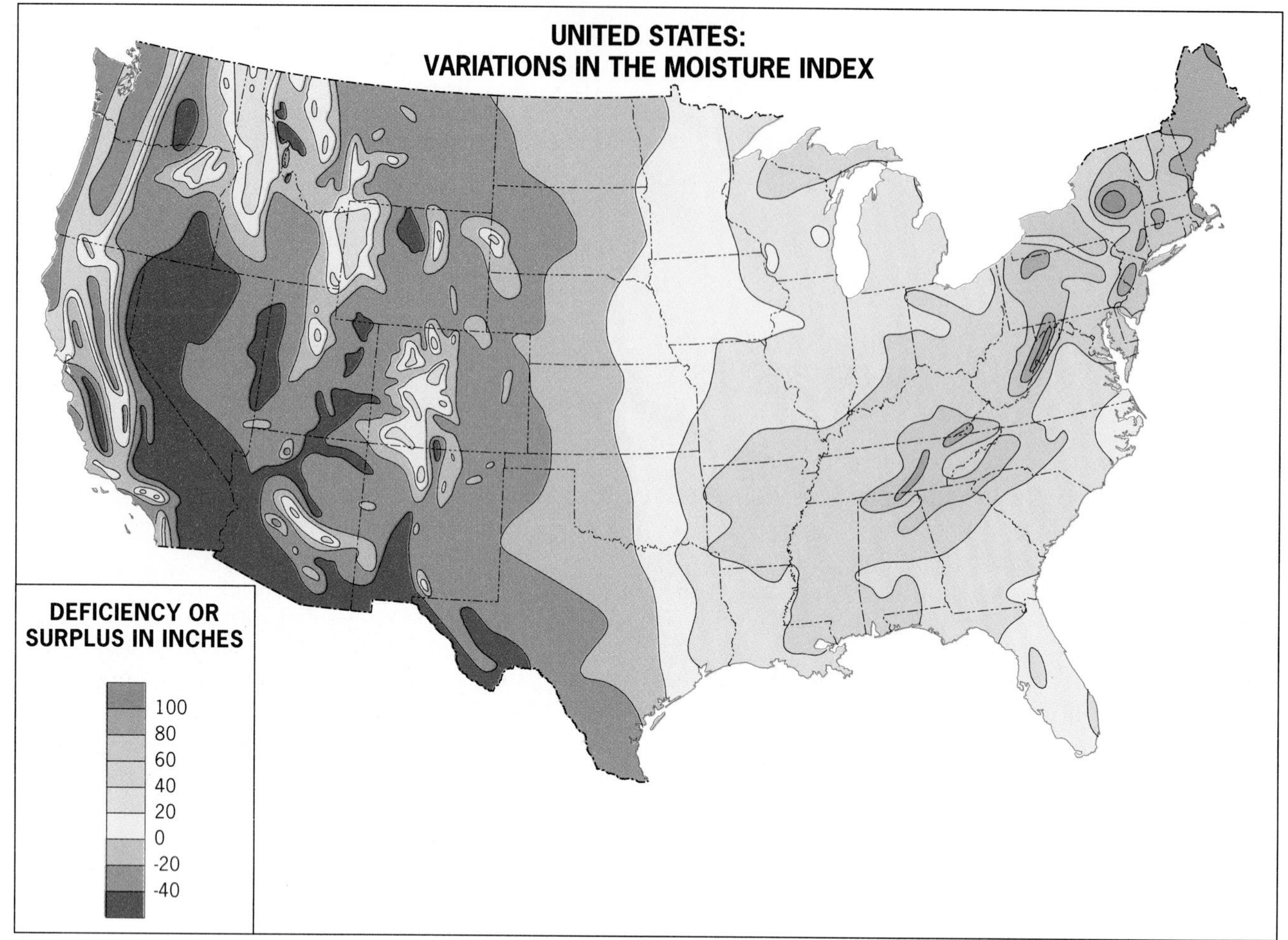

Figure 32-2 Variations in the Moisture Index in the United States. This map shows the variation in moisture surplus and deficiency in the United States. *Source: From a map in E. A. Fernald and D. J. Patton, editors,* Water Resources Atlas of Florida *(Tallahassee: Florida State University, 1984) p. 6.*

In many areas of the world people have congregated in places where water supplies are insufficient, undependable, or both. In California in the early 1990s, people were not allowed to wash their cars or refill their swimming pools; these are minor inconveniences compared to the fate faced by millions of Ethiopians trying to escape their country's civil war by fleeing to the parched borders of the Sahara. In Florida, whose urban population depends on the Biscayne Aquifer for most of its water, the long-term prospect is troubling: when seasonal rainfalls do not reach their projected averages, the Biscayne Aquifer is overused, and saltwater enters the aquifer from the nearby Atlantic Ocean. Such invasion can permanently destroy a freshwater aquifer.

It is interesting to compare Figures 1-5 and 4-1. Note how hundreds of millions of people still cluster along several of the Earth's great rivers. Indeed, nearly three-quarters of all the fresh water used annually is consumed in farming, not in cities. In California, where about 80 percent of available water is used for irrigation, this has led to an intense debate: should cities be provided with ample water at the expense of Central Valley farms, and should fruits and vegetables be bought from elsewhere, even overseas, rather than being grown locally?

Industries use another 20 percent of the world's water supply, contributing heavily to pollution when the used water is returned to streams, lakes, and aquifers. When communist rule ended in Eastern Europe, tests indicated that the region's rivers and groundwater were among the most severely polluted in the world because industries there had not been adequately regulated.

As human populations have expanded, people have increasingly settled in arid regions. One of the great ecological disasters of the twentieth century is occurring in Kazakhstan and Uzbekistan, whose common boundary runs through the ***Aral Sea***. Streams that fed this large body of water were diverted to irrigate the surrounding desert (mainly for commercial cotton production). Heavy use of chemical pesticide ruined the groundwater below, causing a health crisis that some observers describe as an "ecological Chernobyl." In the meantime the Aral Sea began to dry up, and by 1992 it had lost more than three-quarters of its total surface area (Fig. 32-3).

Throughout the world people have come to depend on water sources whose future capacity is uncertain. Rocky Mountain and Sierra Nevada snows feed the Colorado River and the aquifers that irrigate the California Central Valley. Aqueducts snake their way across the desert to urban communities. None of this slows the population's move to the Sunbelt (see Part Two), and the water situation there is becoming problematic. In coastal eastern Spain, low water pressures in city pipes often deprive the upper floors of high-rise buildings of water. In Southwest Asia and the Arabian Peninsula, growing populations strain ancient water supply systems and desalinization plants are a necessity (see "Focus on: Water and Politics in the Middle East"). As oil did in the past, water may spark regional conflicts in the future.

◆ THE ATMOSPHERE

The Earth, it is sometimes said, has six continents and seven seas—but it has only one ***atmosphere***, a thin layer of air lying directly above the lands and oceans. We depend on the atmosphere for our survival: we breathe its oxygen; it shields us from the destructive rays of the sun; it moderates temperatures; and it carries moisture from the oceans over the land, sustaining crops and forests and replenishing soils and wells.

The atmosphere has a truly amazing capacity to cleanse itself. In 1883 the Indonesian volcano Krakatau erupted catastrophically, throwing 2.5 cubic miles (10 cubic kilometers) of rock and ash into the atmosphere. Total darkness prevailed in the area for nearly three days; dust from the explosion encircled the Earth and created vividly colored sunsets for years afterward. However, eventually the atmosphere cleared and all traces of the eruption disappeared. In 1980 the eruption of Mount St. Helens in the northwestern United States caused a similar, though much smaller, globe-encircling cloud of volcanic dust in the upper atmosphere. Again, the atmosphere soon cleansed itself.

Human pollution of the atmosphere, however, may result in longer lasting, possibly even permanent damage. True, the air disperses even the densest smoke and most acrid chemical gases. But some of the waste pouring into the atmosphere may be producing irreversible change, not only in the ***troposphere*** (the lowest layer, up to about 10 miles, or 16 km, high) but also in the upper-level ***stratosphere***. The nature of the change is still being debated, but two centuries of industrial expansion have caused an enormous increase in the pollution of the troposphere. While global concern and action to limit this pollution are much in evidence, the problem may be beyond control.

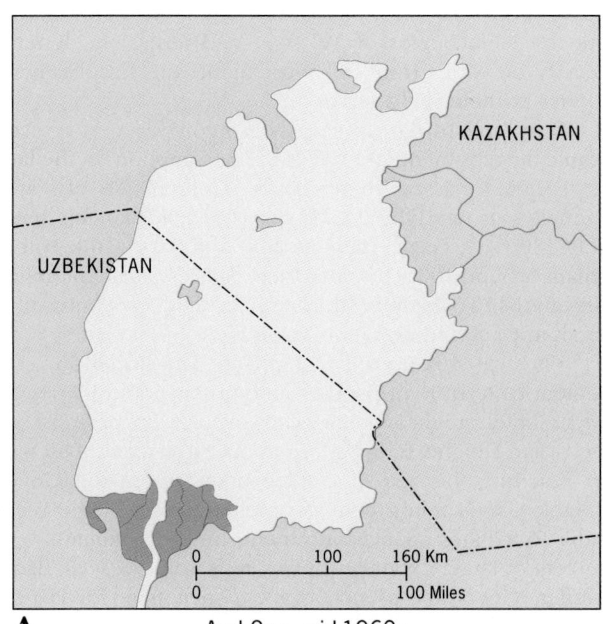

A Aral Sea, mid-1960s

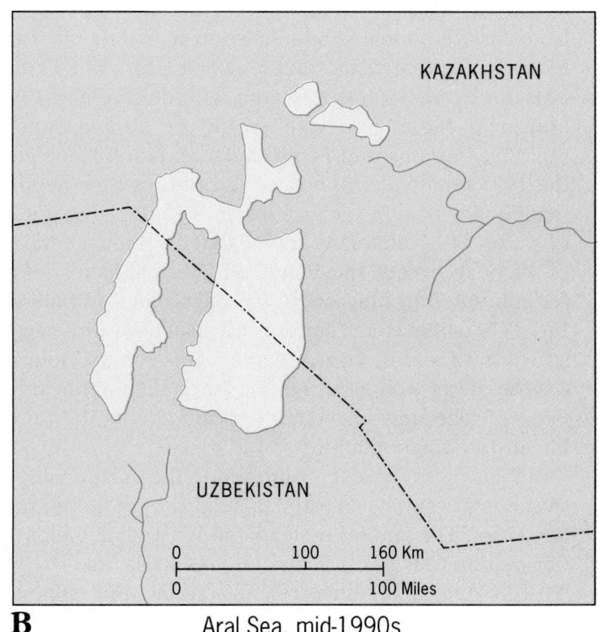

B Aral Sea, mid-1990s

Figure 32-3 The Dying Aral Sea. Affected by climatic cycles and afflicted by human interference, the Aral Sea in Turkestan (on the border of Kazakhstan and Uzbekistan) is dying. In a quarter of a century, it lost three-quarters of its surface area.

Focus On

Water and Politics in the Middle East

When relations between countries and peoples are problematic, disputes over water can make them even worse. As populations grow and as demand for water rises, fears of future shortages intensify. Control by one state over sources of water needed by another may even lead to armed conflict. In recent years, for example, relations between Turkey and its neighbors to the south have worsened, largely because of Turkey's dam-building projects at the headwaters of two rivers that are crucial to Syria and Iraq: the Euphrates and the Tigris.

Water supply is a particularly difficult problem affecting relations among Israel and its neighbors. With under 6 million people, Israel annually consumes nearly three times as much water as Jordan, the West Bank Palestinian areas, and Gaza combined (total population: about 7 million). As much as half of Israel's water comes from sources outside the Israeli state.

The key sources of water for the entire area are the Jordan River and an aquifer beneath the West Bank. When Israel captured the Golan Heights from Syria and the West Bank from Jordan during the 1967 war, it gained control over both of these sources, including the Jordan River's important tributary, the Yarmuk (Fig. 32-4). As the map shows, the Sea of Galilee forms a large freshwater reservoir in the Jordan River Valley. This is the source of most of Israel's water. (Desalting facilities do not yet contribute significantly.)

Figure 32-4 Key Water Resources in the Middle East.

The 1994 peace treaty with Jordan committed Israel to let Jordan have 200 million cubic meters (CMs) of water from surface sources under its control, chiefly the Yarmuk River. In the first year Israel would send Jordan 50 million CMs, and after 1995 the amount would double to 100 million. The 200-million level would be attained after the building of dams and facilities. Israel failed to deliver on the 1995 commitment, however, citing its own needs, the inadequacy of transfer systems, and Jordan's wasteful use of water. The Jordanians argued that this violated the terms of the peace treaty; the 50 million CMs that Israel did transfer amounted to only one-tenth of Jordan's annual needs. In 1997, when Israel announced that it would start construction of a dam on the Yarmuk that would yield water for Jordan as well as Israel, the Jordanians refused to cooperate. The unresolved water issue clouds the future of Israeli-Jordanian relations.

Water supply also complicates the relationships between Israel and its Palestinian neighbors in the West Bank and Gaza. The aquifer beneath the West Bank yields about 625 million CMs through hundreds of wells linked together by a system of pipelines. Of this, some 450 million CMs go directly to Israel; another 35 million are consumed by Israeli settlers on the West Bank, and only some 140 million are allotted to the West Bank's nearly 1.5 million Arabs.

This is unfair, say the Palestinian Arabs: if the West Bank is to become autonomous Palestinian territory, the water below the surface should belong to the Palestinians. But the Israeli cities of Tel Aviv and Jerusalem depend heavily on water from the West Bank, and Israel cannot survive without this source.

Why not? In part, the answer involves levels of economic development and habits of consumption. In the late 1990s Israel was consuming over 2 billion CMs of water annually, or nearly 400 CMs per capita. Jordanians used only 150 CMs, Gaza residents 140, and West Bank Palestinians around 100. To Arabs, these figures represent unfair allocations. To Israelis, they are justified by contrasting economic and cultural requirements.

The water issue will complicate any hoped-for settlement of territorial disputes among Israel and its neighbors. Israel might contemplate the return of most of the Golan Heights to Syria, but about 30 percent of all water reaching the Sea of Galilee comes from the Golan Heights. Israel might consider yielding most of the West Bank to a Palestinian government, but approximately 30 percent of Israel's water supply comes from the West Bank aquifer. Governments may want to negotiate for lasting peace, but at a practical level they are constrained by water needs.

Global Warming

Most scientists argue that tropospheric pollution causes the Earth to retain more heat (hence the "greenhouse" theories referred to in Part One) and that its full effect will not be felt until well into the twenty-first century. While estimates of global warming have been reduced, in the late 1990s computer models still predicted a global warming of 2°C to 3°C (about 3.5°F to 5.5°F) over the next 50 years. This might be enough to melt some glacial ice and raise sea levels as much as 6 inches (15 cm).

Moreover, changes in climate involve changes in the hydrologic cycle, affecting patterns of precipitation. These changes in turn can affect where certain types of vegetation can grow, which can alter everything from agricultural patterns to the location of animal habitats.

There is little consensus on the extent of greenhouse warming. Whatever the extent of global warming, there is no question that growing populations and increased human activity, ranging from the burning of tropical forests to pollution of the atmosphere by industry and automobiles, are having an unprecedented impact on the atmosphere. The amounts of key "greenhouse" gases, carbon dioxide (CO_2), methane, and nitrous oxides in the atmosphere have been increasing at a rate of about 2 percent per decade; steel mills, refineries, and chemical plants account for a large part of this increase. Without doubt there *will* be consequences; all that remains uncertain is *what* the consequences will be.

Acid Rain

A byproduct of the enormous volume of pollutants spewed into the atmosphere is ***acid rain***. Acid rain forms when sulfur dioxide and nitrogen oxides are released into the atmosphere by the burning of fossil fuels (coal, oil, and natural gas). These pollutants combine with water vapor in the air to form dilute solutions of sulfuric and nitric acids, which then are washed out of the atmosphere by rain or other types of precipitation, such as fog and snow.

Although acid rain usually consists of relatively mild acids, it is caustic enough to do great harm over time to certain natural ecosystems (the mutual interactions between groups of plant and animal organisms and their environment). Already we know that acid rain is causing acidification of lakes and streams (with resultant fish kills), stunted growth of forests, and loss of crops in affected areas. In cities, corrosion of buildings and monuments has accelerated.

The geography of acid rain is most closely associated with patterns of industrial concentration and middle- to long-distance wind flows. The highest densities of coal and oil burning are associated with large concentrations of heavy manufacturing, such as those in Western and Eastern Europe and the United States. As these industrial areas began to experience increasingly severe air pollution problems in the second half of the twentieth century, many countries (including the United States in 1970) enacted legislation establishing minimal clean-air standards.

Recent studies reveal that countries of the former Soviet Union, especially Russia and Ukraine, suffer severely from acid rain. Antiquated factories in the industrial heartlands continue to emit the chemicals that create acid rain. The first research studies to report on acid rain in the Asian Pacific Rim countries suggest that the situation in East and Southeast Asia is worsening, with serious effects on natural vegetation.

In the United States and Western Europe, compliance with legislated emission reductions is having positive results. In Canada as well as in Scandinavia, where acid rain from neighboring industrial regions damaged forests and acidified lakes, recovery came faster than scientists had predicted. This evidence is now encouraging other countries to impose stricter controls over factory emissions.

◆ THE LAND

Over the centuries human population growth has put increasing pressure on the land surface. More land is cleared and placed under cultivation, trees are cut down, and cities expand. The effects can be seen almost everywhere. So extensive are they that it is often difficult even to reconstruct what an area might be like in the absence of humans. The human impact on the Earth's land surface has several key aspects, of which the most significant are desertification, deforestation, soil erosion, and waste disposal.

Desertification

Climatologists have long known that the world's deserts are expanding, especially in areas with substantial human populations (Fig. 4-1). This process has the same effect as glaciation because it increases the area of uninhabitable territory at the expense of habitable land. Marginal areas that supported some vegetation have been lost to the desert, and ***desertification*** threatens similar areas throughout the world.

Desert expansion is cyclic and can result from natural causes. Some climatologists see the southward march of the Sahara as evidence of shifting climatic zones that may be related to an oncoming ice age. However, desertification is also the result of human activity. The southward expansion of the Sahara, which in the past 50 years has cost 270,000 square

Figure 32-5 Areas Threatened by Desertification. Deserts expand and contract cyclically, but nature's cycles can be distorted by human intervention. This map shows areas threatened or affected. *Source: From several sources, including J. Turk et al.*, Environmental Science *(Philadelphia: Saunders, 1984), p. 305.*

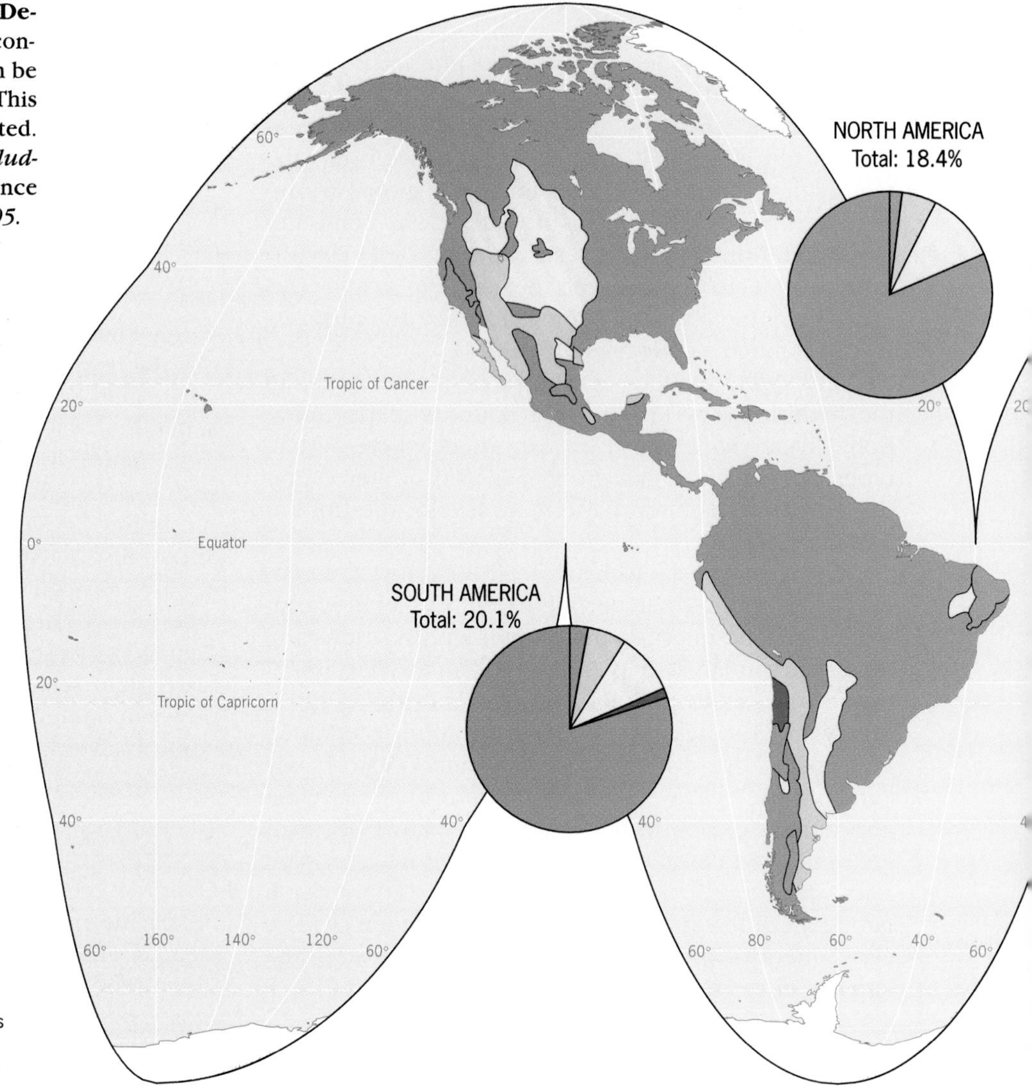

AREAS THREATENED BY DESERTIFICATION

- Extreme desert already
- Very high risk of desertification
- High risk of desertification
- Moderate risk of desertification

0 1000 2000 3000 Kilometers
0 1000 2000 Miles

miles (700,000 square kilometers) of farming and grazing land, has been accelerated by overgrazing, woodcutting, soil exhaustion, and other environmental misuse.

Desertification became a matter of serious international concern during the great Sahel drought of the 1970s (which reappeared to the east in Ethiopia and Sudan in the mid-1980s). In 1977 it was the subject of the United Nations Conference on Desertification, held in Nairobi, Kenya. It became clear that desert expansion was occurring in many areas of the world. Reports from East Africa, India, Argentina, Australia, and North America all confirmed that fragile desert-margin ecosystems were being lost (Fig. 32-5). In China and Algeria, workers were mobilized to plant vegetation that would anchor the shifting sands, but without success. As our maps indicate, rates of natural population increase are especially high in much of the desert-dominated Muslim realm. The southern margin of the Sahara lies on the edge of the fastest growing population zone on Earth. Thus desertification is likely to increase in the future.

Deforestation

As habitable space is lost to expanding deserts, the world's forests also yield to human population pressure. From the tropical Amazon Basin to high-latitude North America and Eurasia, trees are cut down and woodlands shrink.

The world's forests, especially those of lower and middle latitudes, play a critical role in what biogeographers call the ***oxygen cycle***. Atmospheric oxygen is consumed by natural processes as well as by human activities. Forests counteract this loss through photo-

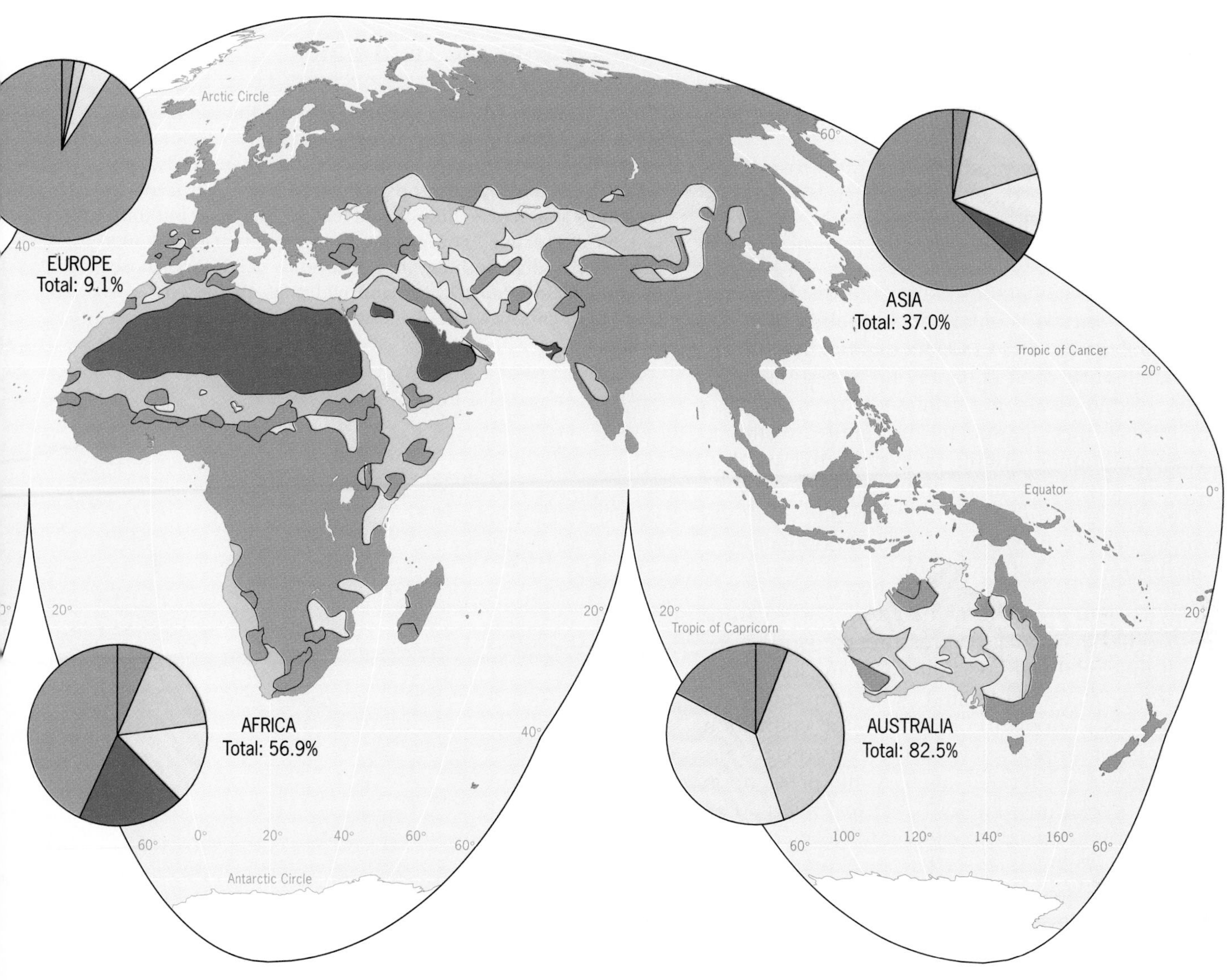

synthesis and related processes, which release oxygen into the atmosphere. The destruction of vast tracts of forest alarms ecologists and others, who warn of unforeseeable and incalculable effects—not only for the affected areas but for the planet as a whole.

In the early 1980s the Food and Agriculture Organization (FAO) of the United Nations undertook a study of the rate at which forests were being depleted. This analysis showed that 44 percent of the tropical rainforest had already been affected by cutting and that more than 1 percent was being logged every year. If this rate of cutting were to continue, the entire equatorial rainforest would be gone in less than 90 years. The situation may be even more critical. Other studies have suggested that the FAO estimate was low and that at the present rate of logging and cutting these forests will be destroyed within just 45 years.

This is what is happening in the great forested areas that still survive in South America, Africa, and Southeast Asia. The smaller surviving stands—in such places as Central America and West Africa—will be gone even earlier. Yet, the effects of ***deforestation*** are not clearly understood. The reforestation (and harvesting) of deforested areas is not the whole answer, even if it could be done on a large scale. Forests in the United States, for example, consist mainly of *second-growth* trees, which replaced the original forest after it was logged. However, the controlled second-growth forest does not (as the natural forest did) have many trees dying of old age after their trunks and limbs become soft from rot. Thus many animal species that depend on holes in trunks and hollows in tree limbs cannot find places to nest. For them the forest has ceased to be a favorable habitat. Deforestation has many causes—expanding farmland, logging, roadbuilding, mining, and human settlement—and it has been going on for centuries. However, the threat to the last great undisturbed natural forests is recent and severe.

Soil Erosion

The loss of potentially productive soil to erosion has been described as a "quiet crisis" of global proportions. Ecologists Lester Brown and Edward Wolf (1984) point out that the increasing rate of this loss

> over the past generation is not the result of a decline in the skills of farmers but rather of the pressures on farmers to produce more. In an integrated world food economy the pressures on land resources are not confined to particular countries; they permeate the entire world. Many traditional agricultural systems that were ecologically stable as recently as midcentury, when there were 2.5 billion people in the world, are breaking down as world population moves toward 5 billion. (p. 9)

Why has ***soil erosion*** increased so much? Part of the answer lies in population pressure: the world population is moving toward 6.5 billion, having long since passed the 5 billion mark cited by Brown and Wolf. Associated with population growth is the cultivation of ever-steeper slopes, with hastily constructed terraces or without any terraces at all. As the pressure on land increases, farmers are less able to leave part of their soil fallow (unused) to allow it to recover its nutrients. Shifting cultivators (see Part Five) must shorten their field rotation cycle, and as a result their soil, too, is less able to recover. As agricultural land use intensifies, water and wind erosion increases. Livestock are allowed to graze in areas where they destroy the natural vegetation; lands too dry for farming are nonetheless plowed, and wind erosion follows. It is estimated that the loss of soil to erosion amounts to more than 25 billion tons per year. According to Brown and Wolf, this is equal to 0.7 percent per year of all the soil now available, or 7 percent per decade. Soil is a renewable resource because it can recover with proper care. However, it is being "mined" as though it were a nonrenewable resource. International cooperation in food distribution, education of farmers and governments, and worldwide dissemination of soil-conservation methods are urgently needed to solve this "quiet crisis."

Waste Disposal

It is a sign of the times that the topic of waste disposal must be included in a discussion of environmental stress as it relates to population growth. If anything has grown faster than population itself, it is the waste generated by households, communities, and industries—much of it a matter of bulk, some of it a source of danger.

From the field notes

"About 10 miles (16 km) from the Kenyan town of Meru the landscape showed signs of severe erosion. We stopped to talk with the people of these homesteads, and asked them about their crops. Yes, they knew that farming on slopes as steep as these would lead to 'gullying,' but they saw no alternative. You get a crop one or two years, and that's better than nothing, they said. Some neighbors whose village had lost most of its land had gone to the city, we were told, and now the place where they lived was like a desert."

The United States, the world's largest consumer of resources, is also the largest producer of ***solid waste***, debris and garbage discarded by cities, industries, mines, and farms. According to current estimates, the United States produces about 1.7 kilograms (3.7 pounds) of solid waste per person per day, which adds up to well over 160 million metric tons (just under 180 million tons) per year. But the United States is not alone. Other high-technology economies with a high ratio of disposable materials (containers, packaging, etc.) face the same problems.

Disposal of these wastes is a major worldwide problem. The growing volume of waste must be put somewhere, but space for it is no longer easy to find. In poorer countries waste is thrown onto open dumps where vermin multiply, decomposition sends methane gas into the air, rain and waste liquids carry contaminants into the groundwater below, and fires pollute the surrounding atmosphere. In countries that can afford it, such open dumps have been replaced by ***sanitary landfills***. The waste is put in a hole that has been dug and prepared for the purpose, including a floor of materials to treat seeping liquids and soil to cover each load as it is compacted and deposited in the fill.

The number of suitable sites for sanitary landfills is decreasing, however, and it is increasingly difficult to design new sites. In the United States landfill capacity has been reached or will soon be reached in about a dozen States, most of them in the Northeast and Mid-Atlantic regions, and those States must now buy space from other States for this purpose. Trucking or sending garbage by rail to distant landfills is very expensive, but there are few alternatives (see "Focus on: The Sagas of the *Mobro* and the *Khian Sea*").

Similar problems arise on a global scale. The United States, the European Union, and Japan export solid (including hazardous) wastes to countries in Africa, Middle and South America, and East Asia. While these countries are paid for accepting the waste, they do not have the capacity to treat it properly. So the waste often is dumped in open landfills, where it creates the very hazards that the exporters want to avoid. In the late 1980s the richer countries' practice of "managing" waste by exporting it became a controversial issue, and in 1989 a treaty was drawn up to control it. The treaty did not (as many poorer countries wished) prohibit the exporting of hazardous waste, although it did require the consent of the recipient country before the waste could be transported.

It is useful to differentiate between ***toxic wastes***, in which the danger is caused by chemicals, infectious materials, and the like, and ***radioactive wastes***, which are of two types: low-level radioactive wastes that give off small amounts of radiation and are produced by industry, hospitals, research facilities, and nuclear power plants, and high-level radioactive wastes, which emit strong radiation and are produced by nuclear power plants and nuclear weapons factories. In the United States, low-level radioactive wastes have for many years been disposed of in steel drums placed in six special government-run landfills, three of which are now closed.

High-level radioactive waste is extremely dangerous and difficult to get rid of. Fuel rods from nuclear reactors will remain radioactive for thousands of years and must be stored in remote places where there is no possibility that they will contaminate water, air, or any other part of the environment. In fact, no satisfactory means or place for the disposal of high-level radioactive waste has been found. Among many suggestions are deep shafts in the bedrock, chambers dug in salt deposits (salt effectively blocks radiation), ice chambers in Antarctica, burial beneath the ocean floor, and deposition in volcanically active midocean trenches. Meanwhile, spent fuel rods (which last only about three years in the reactor) are put in specially designed drums and stored in one of about 100 sites, all of them potentially dangerous. In the mid-1990s the U.S. government was developing two major disposal sites, one at Yucca Mountain in southern Nevada, for waste from commercial nuclear power plants, and the other near Carlsbad in southern New Mexico, for military waste.

There is a related problem: transportation of waste. Even if secure and safe storage can be found

The Sagas of the *Mobro* and the *Khian Sea*

Disposing of waste can be a difficult challenge. In 1987 a barge named *Mobro*, loaded with garbage, was refused permission to unload its cargo at a landfill in Islip, New York. Towed by the tugboat *Break of Dawn*, the *Mobro* set out to sea in the hope of finding another disposal site. Arriving at the coast of North Carolina, the *Mobro* was again refused permission to unload, and the tugboat towed it out to sea again. After a journey of 6000 miles (9600 km) during which it called at six U.S. States and three countries, the *Mobro* limped back into New York waters—where State officials finally allowed the garbage to be burned in a Brooklyn incinerator.

The story of the *Khian Sea* is even less auspicious. This ship under the Bahamian flag was hired by Philadelphia to take a load of incinerated ash to Panama to be used as roadbuilding material. Incinerated ash contains toxic chemicals, and when the Panamanians realized that these materials would endanger the wetlands through which the road was being built, they refused to accept the cargo. This refusal started the *Khian Sea* on a two-year, five-continent journey in the hope of finding a country that would accept the toxic ash, but no buyer could be located. Then one day the ship appeared off the port of Singapore with its holds empty. Only the crew members know whether the ash was dumped at sea or on some remote shore.

for high-level radioactive waste, the waste has to be transported from its source to the disposal site. Such transportation presents an additional hazard; a truck or train accident could have disastrous consequences.

The dimensions of the waste-disposal problem are growing and are becoming global. The threat to the planet's environment is not just over the short term but can exist for centuries, indeed millennia.

◆ BIODIVERSITY

A significant change that is related to all of the developments discussed so far is the accelerating loss of biodiversity. An abbreviation of "biological diversity," ***biodiversity*** refers to the diversity of all aspects of life found on the Earth. Although the term is commonly used in referring to the diversity of species, it encompasses the entire range of biological diversity, from the genetic variability within individuals of a species to the diversity of ecosystems on the planet.

How many species are there? Estimates range from 10 million to 100 million, and no one is quite sure. So far only some 1.75 million species have been identified, and new species, particularly new species of insects, are being discovered regularly. Yet species are also becoming extinct at a rapid rate. It is difficult to say exactly how quickly extinctions are occurring, since we do not know how many species there are. What is clear, however, is that although extinction is a natural process, humans have dramatically increased rates of extinction, particularly over the last few hundred years. Estimates from the United Nations Environment Programme's Global Biodiversity Assessment indicate that 8 percent of plants, 5 percent of fish, 11 percent of birds, and 18 percent of the world's mammal species are currently threatened.

Human impacts on biodiversity have increased over time. The domestication of animals, followed by the agricultural domestication of plant life, caused significant changes in our relationship with other species. Large vertebrates have always been particularly hard hit by human activities. Many birds and mammals have been hunted not only for food but also for their skins, feathers, and so forth. During the eighteenth and nineteenth centuries beaver populations in North America were drastically reduced as the beavers were trapped and skinned for their pelts; many bird species were hunted for their feathers, which were sold to decorate fashionable hats. Elephants and walruses continue to be hunted for their ivory tusks. From historical records we know that over 650 species of plants and over 480 animal species have become extinct in just the last 400 years. These represent only the documented extinctions. The actual number of extinctions that occurred during this period is almost certainly much higher.

In addition to hunting species, humans have also indirectly contributed to extinctions. Human travel, for instance, introduced new species to areas around the globe—rats are among the more destructive of these; they have had devastating effects on oceanic islands. Introduced species may cause extinctions by preying upon native species or competing with them for resources. A famous example is the dodo (*Raphus cucullatus*), which was hunted to extinction by humans, dogs, and rats on the island of Mauritius. Introduced species may also carry new diseases, leading to the decimation and extinction of local populations. On oceanic islands a combination of these forces led to large numbers of extinctions after the arrival of humans. It is estimated that 2000 species of birds on tropical Pacific islands were driven to extinction following human settlement.

The extinction of the passenger pigeon (*Ectopistes migratorius*) from the Western Hemisphere is a dramatic example of the devastating effects humans can have on other species. As recently as the early 1800s, there were many millions of passenger pigeons. The birds congregated in large flocks; early accounts described the sky being darkened as the birds flew overhead. But within less than 100 years the passenger pigeon was gone. By 1900, the last known wild passenger pigeon had been shot. In 1914, the last captive passenger pigeon died in the Cincinnati Zoo. What caused the pigeon to die out so quickly? Part of its decline may have been due to natural factors, such as introduced diseases that may have spread through the large flocks, or, as some have suggested, storms that may have killed many birds at once. But regardless of these natural factors, human predation was ultimately responsible for the extinction of the passenger pigeon. Some of the human pressures on the birds were indirect, such as logging of forests, which reduced the amount of foraging habitat available to the pigeons. This was particularly damaging because beechnuts and acorns were an important food source for the birds. Other human effects were more direct. Passenger pigeons were valued for their meat, and millions were shot and then shipped by rail to urban centers like Chicago and New York. The birds' habit of congregating in large flocks made them easy targets for hunters—even when being shot at, the birds tended to remain together in large groups instead of dispersing. Thus it was a combination of human population pressures, technology, and economic forces that led to the demise of the passenger pigeon.

Identifying the nature and extent of environmental changes is only a first step toward understanding the extent of human alteration of the planet. A second, and more complicated, step is to consider the forces driving these changes. It is to this thorny issue that we turn in the next chapter.

◆ KEY TERMS ◆

acid rain
aquifer
Aral Sea
atmosphere
biodiversity
deforestation
desertification
ecosystem
environmental stress
hydrologic cycle
oxygen cycle
radioactive waste
sanitary landfill
soil erosion
solid waste
stratosphere
toxic waste
troposphere

◆ APPLYING GEOGRAPHIC KNOWLEDGE ◆

1. The Earth is warming, slightly and slowly as yet, but possibly more rapidly in the coming century. Such global warming, whether due to a natural cycle or caused primarily by human action, will result in rising sea levels and, possibly, a higher frequency of severe storms. That can be a lethal combination for densely populated, low-lying coastal areas. Using population and terrain maps, identify coastal zones that are especially vulnerable to such environmental impact.

2. The building of dams and water diversion systems has altered natural water flows in many areas of the world. Such construction sometimes creates political problems even as it mitigates water shortages—not only between sovereign states but even among subnational units. Focus your attention on the waters of the Colorado River and report on the competition for this precious resource among interested parties in the U.S. Southwest and West.

Chapter 33

Confronting Human-Induced Environmental Change

From the field notes

"It seems to me that governments of core countries all too often assume that people in peripheral countries are not really concerned about environmental issues: development there should proceed at all costs. But that is not true. Many leaders, teachers, and others in such countries as Brazil, Kenya, and India keep environmental problems in the public eye, and have attracted strong support in doing so. I ran into this demonstration in Mumbai, India in 1997: a local organization was drawing attention to the city's air pollution."

KEY POINTS

◆ Environmental change has natural as well as human causes. Current concerns over environmental change reflect humanity's role in accelerating the pace and extent of environmental change.

◆ While the populations of countries in the developed core are often smaller than those in the periphery, per capita consumption of resources in the rich countries is far greater.

◆ Modern transportation devices contribute to environmental change not just by consuming energy and producing pollution, but by facilitating global trade networks that fuel consumption in the developed core.

◆ Environmental problems frequently cross political boundaries, complicating regulation and management efforts. Nonetheless, a number of international environmental accords have been adopted on issues ranging from biodiversity to climate change.

As we have seen, there is nothing new about human alteration of the environment. Deforestation, for example, has been going on since ancient times. The ancient Greeks and Romans cut down many of the trees of the Mediterranean region, leaving a profoundly altered environment in their wake. Much later and in a different place, Spanish invaders harvested the forests of Mexico for building materials and firewood. Yet in the modern era deforestation is taking place at a pace and scale heretofore unknown. The combined impact of expanded human populations, increased consumption, and technological advances has led to environmental changes that some experts view as *irreversible*.

In view of the magnitude of humanity's impact on the environment, efforts to understand and respond to global environmental change are of critical importance. In addressing this topic we should remind ourselves that changes in the physical world are not always wrought by humans. Nature has its own cycles of change, and it is sometimes difficult to determine whether an observed change is attributable to nature or to humans. In southern Florida, for example, the struggle is on to save the Everglades—not just from human encroachment but from a drying trend. The causes of this trend are not entirely clear, but they may have natural as well as human causes. By channeling a certain amount of water into the Everglades in response to this trend, we may be counteracting natural forces.

Yet for all the power and mystery of nature, humans are now the dominant species on the planet, and the changes we observe in Earth's physical systems are being influenced, if not driven, by human activities. Geographers have long been interested in the nature and consequences of these changes, and throughout this book we have emphasized the ways in which humans shape the physical world. Geography, in fact, is one of the few academic disciplines in which the relationship between humans and the environment is a primary concern. One of the most influential nineteenth-century texts on this relationship, *Man and Nature*, was written by the geographer George Perkins Marsh. In 1955 geographers were centrally involved in an international interdisciplinary symposium on "Man's Role in Changing the Face of the Earth." This symposium, like Marsh's *Man and Nature*, focused primarily on local and regional changes. More recently, a symposium led by geographers on "The Earth as Transformed by Human Action" picked up where the 1955 discussion left off, addressing global environmental changes. The geographer's concern with how things are organized on the Earth and how they are connected in space provides a useful platform from which to consider human-induced environmental change.

As the study of environmental change has moved forward, one of the most important lessons we have learned is that global environmental systems are interconnected at numerous temporal and spatial scales. The release of ***chlorofluorocarbons*** (CFCs) in India contributes to a growing hole in the Earth's ozone layer that is centered over Antarctica. Industrial production in the Netherlands and Germany contributes to acid rain in Scandinavia. The use of water from the Rio Grande for irrigation in northern New Mexico affects the amount and quality of the river's water that reaches southern New Mexico. Human actions—

the activities we undertake individually and collectively—are increasingly important factors in all sorts of global environmental changes. To confront these changes we must consider the complex relationship between humans and the environment.

◆ UNDERSTANDING ENVIRONMENTAL CHANGE

One of the challenges of understanding global environmental changes is simply comprehending the magnitude and rates of change involved in global processes. Geographers have always been interested in phenomena that occur at various scales and the ways in which they interact. In the past, many of the environmental problems that drew our attention occurred at local or regional scales. Recent global environmental changes have forced us to recognize the larger spatial scales at which many processes operate. Only recently, with the advent of air and space travel, have we been able to identify these changes with any precision. But global changes express themselves at all scales, from local to global. For example, deforestation can have a local effect by reducing the diversity of species in a particular area. It can have regional impacts by increasing sediment runoff into streams. Finally, at a global scale, deforestation is associated with the release of carbon dioxide into the atmosphere and may affect global climate by altering processes that occur at the land surface. To fully understand deforestation we must keep all of these scales in mind.

Global changes have also forced us to think about rates of environmental change. Consider one of the issues discussed in the last chapter—the extinction of species. If we take the entire history of the planet, approximately 95 percent of all the species that have ever existed have evolved and become extinct over the past 4+ billion years. And there have been many periods of mass die-offs, such as the extinction of the dinosaurs at the end of the Cretaceous Period approximately 65 million years ago. During this time 10 percent of terrestrial families and 15 percent of marine families became extinct. Thus extinction is a natural process that occurs regardless of human action. Why, then, are we concerned about loss of biodiversity today? It is because current rates of extinction may be 1,000 to 10,000 times faster than natural extinction rates. Humans are accelerating the rate at which natural processes occur.

Several interrelated factors are responsible for the accelerated impact of humans on the environment over the past two centuries. One of these is the dramatic growth of the human population. Even considering the minimal needs for human survival, there can be little doubt that the fourfold increase in the human population in the twentieth century has had significant environmental impacts. Another factor is consumption, which has increased dramatically in parts of the modern world. Yet another is technology, which has both expanded the human capacity to alter the environment and brought with it increasing energy demands. Let us look at each of these factors in more detail.

Population

The human dimensions of global environmental changes are tied to increases in the size of the human population. Each individual requires a certain amount of resources to survive. By extension, the more people there are on the planet, the greater the demands on the Earth's environment. This relationship is so obvious that it is easy to see environmental change simply as a population issue. Although things are not that simple, population matters. A greater number of people translates into greater capacity for environmental change.

The impacts of population growth on the environment are all around us. In the United States, prime farmland is being gobbled up by expanding cities. In tropical areas, large tracts of forests are being cleared to meet the heating and cooking needs of growing populations. In China under Mao Zedong (1949–1976), when the government officially opposed population policies, deforestation was so extensive that Chairman Mao ordered every Chinese citizen to plant at least one tree. That campaign yielded an estimated 500 million trees, but today China's landscape is still marked by the scars of erosion. Whole countrysides have been laid waste, the topsoil gone soon after crops replaced natural vegetation. Now China is trying to undo the damage, but recovery is not always possible.

In light of the obvious link between population and environment, many see environmental change largely as a population issue. How helpful is this approach? It has the advantage of focusing attention on a factor whose importance is undeniable. Yet if environmental change is seen simply as a matter of numbers, some key dimensions of the issue may be overlooked. Do population numbers have the same meaning in all places? What is the role of economic and social developments in the environmental area? Where should our concern with population be directed, since the practices of peoples in one part of the world can affect environments and peoples thousands of miles away? And how do we confront population growth without treading on deeply held cultural values? Addressing these questions requires that we look beyond mere numbers to questions of consumption and technology.

From the field notes

"I watched as bulldozers attacked the tropical forest inland from the East Malaysian city of Kota Kinabalu on the northwestern coast of the island of Borneo, knocking down trees, hauling them to a clearing, and stacking them for burning. A supervisor explained that this would be the site of a new suburb of "KK," complete with shopping center, school, and medical clinic. 'Our population is growing fast,' he said, 'and soon we'll go even deeper in.' Borneo is not yet a densely peopled island, but its natural environments, habitats, and wildlife are under increasing threat. Population growth and reckless exploitation of the forest are destroying the biodiversity of this mini-continent."

Patterns of Consumption

Maps of world population tend to underscore the magnitude of populations in the poorer countries, but they fail to convey another aspect of societies and their needs: the relative demands made by different peoples on the Earth's resources. Humans, like all species, are consumers. We rely on the Earth's resources for our very survival. At the most basic level, we consume water, oxygen, and organic and mineral materials. Over time we have developed increasingly complex ways of utilizing resources, by such means as intensive agriculture and industrial production. Consequently, many societies now consume resources at a level and rate that far exceed basic subsistence needs. In a 1996 article on "Humanity's Resources" in *The Companion Encyclopedia of Geography: The Environment and Humankind*, I. G. Simmons notes that a hunter-gatherer could subsist on the resources found within an area of about 26 square kilometers, whereas today many people living in urban centers in the global economic core have access to resources from all over the planet.

The generally smaller number of people in the more affluent parts of the world make far greater demands on the Earth's resources than do the much larger numbers in the poorer countries. It has been estimated that a baby born in the United States during the 1990s will, at current rates, consume about 250 times as much energy over a lifetime as a baby born in Bangladesh over the same lifetime. In terms of food, housing, and its components, metals, paper (and thus trees), and many other materials, the consumption of individuals in affluent countries far exceeds that of people in poorer countries. Thus rapid population growth in the poorer countries tends to be a local or regional matter, keeping rural areas mired in poverty. But population growth in the richer countries is also a matter of concern, one whose impact is not just local or regional but global.

All of this underscores the importance of thinking geographically about human impacts on the natural world. People living in the global economic periphery tend to affect their immediate environment, putting pressure on soil, natural vegetation, and water supplies, and polluting the local air with the smoke from their fires. But the reach of affluent societies is much greater. The demand for low-cost meat for hamburgers in the United States led to the cutting down of trees in Central and South America to make way for pastures and cattle herds. This, in turn, has greatly increased water demand in such areas (Table 33-1). Thus the American (and European, Japanese, and Australian) consumer has an impact on distant environments.

Globally, consumption is tied to technology, for the industrialized core has access to a vast array of transportation and communication technologies that allow advertisers to stimulate demand for particular goods around the world and allow manufacturers to bring those goods from distant places. Related technological developments also allow humans to manip-

Table 33-1 Estimated Liters of Water Required to Produce 1 Kilogram of Food

Crop	Liters/Kg
Potatoes	500
Wheat	900
Corn	1400
Rice	1912
Chicken	3500
Beef	100,000

Source: D. Pimentel et al., *Bioscience,* Vol. 47, No. 2, February 1997, p. 98.

ulate atmospheric, land, oceanic, and biological systems in profound ways. Hence, we must also consider the role of technology in human-induced environmental change.

Technology

Technological advances have increased rapidly since the Industrial Revolution and today affect all aspects of our lives. We are continually developing technologies that we hope will improve our standard of living, protect us against disease, and allow us to work more efficiently. These technologies, however, have not come without a cost. Resource extraction practices

From the field notes

"This looming coal-burning power plant in southwestern Poland was built more than forty years ago. Yet as technology changed, the plant did not. Instead, it stands as a monument to the communist regime's single-minded devotion to production targets, irrespective of environmental costs or potential long-term efficiencies. Now the plant is being upgraded as part of a World Bank project, but work is proceeding slowly as project managers cope with aging infrastructure and a workforce little used to innovation."

such as mining and logging, which provide the materials to produce technologies, have created severe environmental problems. Energy is required not only to develop new technologies but to use them as well; fossil fuel consumption has contributed to many types of pollution and may be a factor in climate change. Technological innovations have produced hazardous and toxic byproducts, creating pollution and health problems that we are only now beginning to recognize. Most significant for our discussion of global environmental change, however, is the fact that technology has enabled humans to alter large portions of the planet in a short space of time.

There are many dramatic examples of the role of technology in environmental change. Great open-pit mines exist where huge machines have carved away at the Earth's surface. The enormous clear-cuts of the Pacific Northwest forests are made possible by chainsaws, trucks, and even helicopters. The heavy blanket of smog that envelops cities such as Taipei is a product of the internal combustion engine and mechanized manufacturing. Key elements of the technologies that contribute to these examples of environmental change are developments in two critical sectors of the economy: transportation and energy. Let us look at these.

Transportation Modes of transportation represent some of the most important technological advances in human history. Initially, transportation was limited to travel by foot or boat. Later, animals were domesticated and trained to carry heavy loads. Within the last few millennia, humans learned how to capture wind power with sails, which allowed ships to travel long distances and eventually enabled humans to circle the globe. The invention of the steam engine created power for ocean vessels and railroad engines, while the internal combustion engine revolutionized travel and made possible the development of the automobile and the airplane. All of these innovations have required increased resource use, not only to make the vehicles that move people and goods, but also to build and maintain the related infrastructure—roads, railroad tracks, airports, parking structures, repair facilities, and the like. And with each innovation the impacts seem to widen. As David Headrick points out in a study discussed in the *Companion Encyclopedia of Geography* (Douglas and Robinson, 1996), Chicago's O'Hare Airport covers a larger area (approximately 28 square kilometers) than Chicago's central business district (which covers approximately 8 square kilometers). Moreover, transportation innovations offer access to remote areas of the planet. There are vehicles that allow people to travel through extreme climates, to the bottoms of the ocean, and across the polar ice caps. These places, in turn, have been altered by human activity.

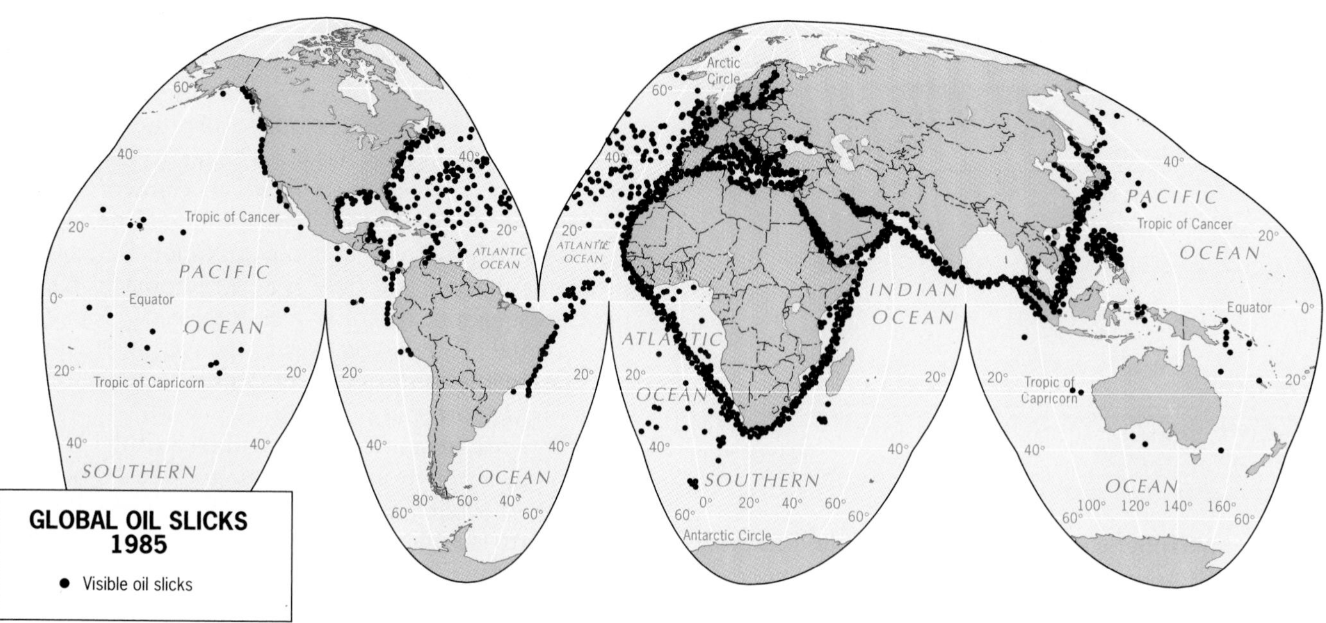

Figure 33-1 Location of Visible Oil Slicks. Oil slicks are a problem around the globe, as this map shows. *Source: Organization for Economic Co-operation and Development, 1985.* The State of the Environment 1985. *(Paris: Organization for Economic Co-operation and Development), p. 76.*

Transportation is also indirectly responsible for global environmental changes. Advances in transportation have produced significant pollution, as seen, for example, in the extent of oil spills along major shipping lanes (Fig. 33-1). Modern modes of transport have also facilitated the introduction of new species to areas where they were not found previously. Over the last few centuries, as ships became more seaworthy and global voyages more frequent, the number of species spread from one part of the globe to another increased. Some organisms attached themselves to the bottom of ships, while others stowed away on board or were transported intentionally as a food source. In modern cargo ships, the taking on of seawater as ballast facilitates the transport of ***pelagic species*** (that is, species that live in the open sea) from one side of the globe to the other. One study estimates that between 1850 and 1970 San Francisco Bay received a new species every 36 weeks, and over the last decade this rate has increased to 1 species every 12 weeks. Diseases are also spread by transportation—rapid air travel has made it common for contagious disease outbreaks in one part of the world to spread quickly to other regions.

Finally, transportation facilitates the types of global networks that are necessary to the patterns of consumption outlined earlier. Many of the products available in stores—be they electronics or clothing or food—come from distant places. Resources were required to produce and ship them, and except those that meet basic subsistence needs, they all contribute to the greater strains placed on the environment by those living in the wealthier parts of the world. This realization has led some individuals to reduce their levels of consumption or to consume more environmentally friendly, locally produced products. These changes have had some effect, but so far their impact on the geography of global consumption has been marginal.

Energy Consumption of material goods is closely linked to consumption of energy. It takes energy to produce material goods, energy to deliver them to markets, and, for many products (refrigerators, automobiles, etc.), energy to keep them running. The resulting demands for energy are a factor in environmental change. Before the 1800s human societies relied directly on solar energy in the form of plant and animal fuel sources, such as wood and animal fat. Today much of our energy supply comes from nonrenewable fossil fuels, such as coal, oil, and natural gas. Moreover, the evolution of tertiary, quaternary, and quinary economic activities has not reduced the consumption of nonrenewable resources. As populations grow, so does the demand for energy, and we can expect that over the coming decades energy production will expand to meet the increased demand. In developing countries in particular, demands for more energy are met by increasing the development of fossil-fuel sources. This helps explain why global energy production was 40 percent greater in 1993 than in 1973.

A SENSE OF SCALE

Wind Energy Parks in the European Union

The growing number of international environmental agreements signed in recent years reflects mounting international concern over the state of the global environment. The scope of these international agreements is primarily global in the sense that members of the international community agree to a global blueprint for action. How do these international agreements translate into regional or local action? What actual steps have signatory countries taken in their attempts to meet these global goals? Insights into these questions can be gained by looking at regional and local responses to a recent convention on climate change.

The UN-sponsored Framework Convention on Climate Change (FCCC) was signed by 154 countries (plus the European Union) at the June 1992 Rio de Janeiro Earth Summit. Although the stated goal of this treaty was to reduce carbon dioxide emissions globally, the agreement did not include specific emission targets or regulatory requirements.

Modern windmills that produce energy now function with increasing frequency in Europe, particularly in the Netherlands (shown here) and in Denmark.

Instead, the treaty allowed the signatory countries to develop their own national (and in the case of the European Union, regional) implementation plans. This has been happening in a number of cases, with implementation programs established that encourage both the development of "clean" renewable energy technologies and increased energy efficiency in buildings, transportation, and manufacturing.

In keeping with this approach, the European Union has mandated that a percentage of the funds it provides for regional development be used for renewable energy projects and increased energy efficiency. In 1994 alone, the EU provided ECU 175 million (US$159 million) for the development of renewable energy sources within the member states. Since 1994, the amount of EU money going toward renewable energy programs has increased even further. In one 1997 case, the EU provided ECU 43 million (US$39.1 million) for the construction of three wind energy parks in the State of Navarra in northern Spain. When completed, these wind energy parks will consist of a total of 115 wind turbines and will add 69 megawatts of "clean" electric energy to the region. And the regional government of Navarra, with the assistance of the EU, eventually hopes to add 44 additional turbines to the wind parks so that 95 megawatts of power can be generated. This amount of electricity can serve the needs of some 190,000 homes.

These wind energy parks not only help the EU meet its obligations under the FCCC; they also help Navarra achieve a goal of self-sufficiency in energy. Long-term plans call for the further expansion of Navarra's wind energy parks to provide close to 50 percent of the region's electric energy needs. As this expansion occurs, more will change than Navarra's energy situation. The wind energy parks, located in the Guerinda Mountains 30 km southeast of the city of Pamplona, will alter the local landscape and economy in ways that will shape the character of Navarra as a place in the twenty-first century.

If we look at the global distribution of fossil fuel sources of CO_2 (Fig. 33-2), we can see that production is concentrated in the highly industrialized part of the global economic core. Pollution associated with this energy production creates the acidic deposition discussed in Chapter 32. The damming of rivers for hydropower alters freshwater systems. Nuclear power is being experimented with throughout the world, but the highly volatile byproducts of this form of energy production and the potential for accidents have limited the expansion of nuclear energy.

Technology has played a key role in amplifying human-induced environmental change. At the same time, technologies are being developed to identify and solve environmental problems. In particular, remote sensing technologies help us understand the rates and

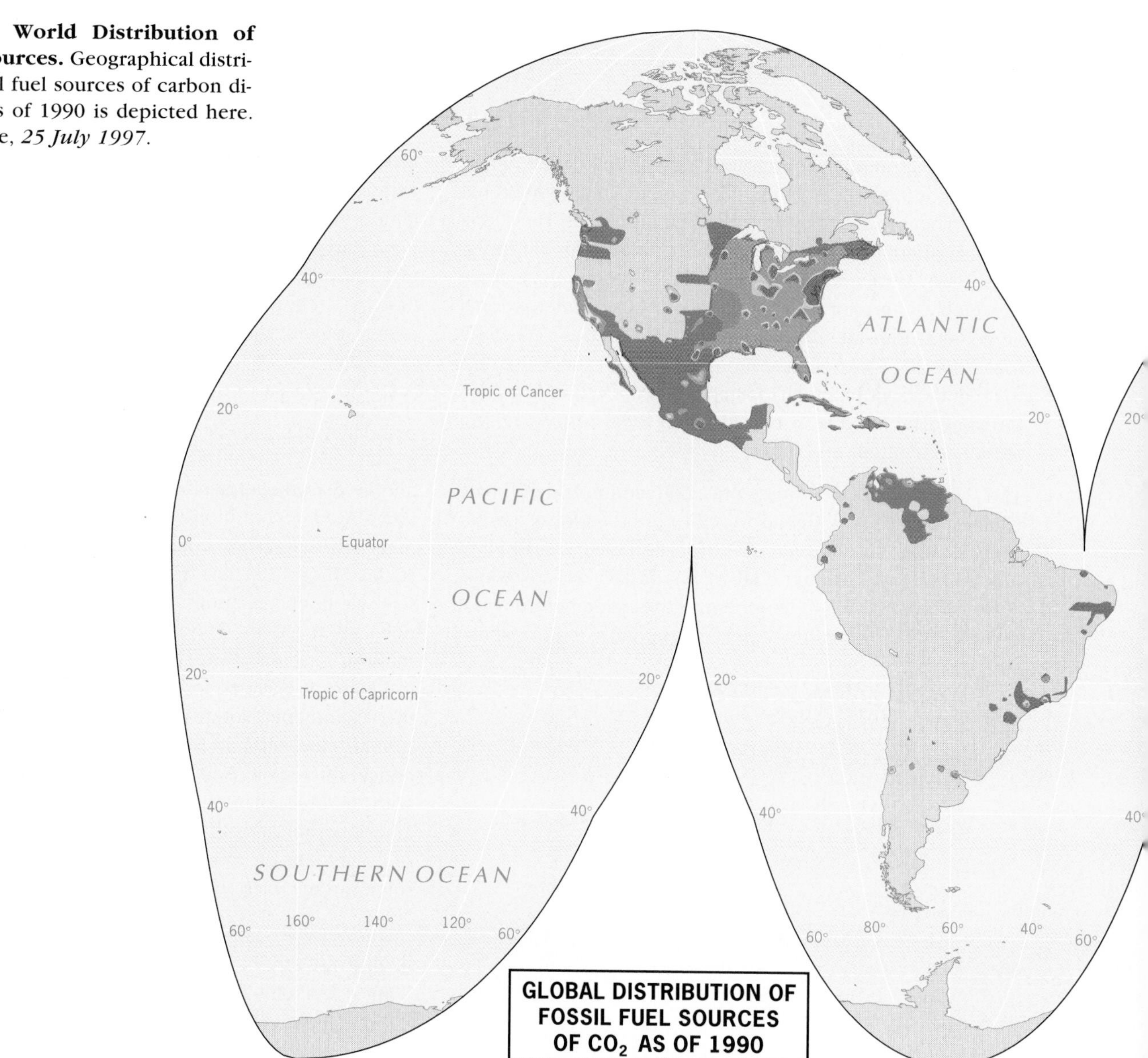

Figure 33-2 World Distribution of Fossil Fuel Sources. Geographical distribution of fossil fuel sources of carbon dioxide (CO_2) as of 1990 is depicted here. *Source:* Science, *25 July 1997.*

scales of global environmental changes. Only with the advent of satellite ***remote sensing*** systems in the 1970s, for example, were we able to gain reliable estimates of the global rate of deforestation (Fig. 33-3). Geographic information systems (GIS) are being used by geographers and others to analyze data on global change in new and useful ways. One benefit of geographic information systems is that they enable us to visualize the relationships among different environmental systems. Finally, advances in communication technologies have allowed us to transmit technological information gained in one place to people in other parts of the world, creating a global dialogue on environmental change.

◆ POLICY RESPONSES TO ENVIRONMENTAL CHANGE

Technology is only one part of the picture of the human response to environmental change. The extent and rapidity of that change have led to numerous policies aimed at protecting the environment or reversing the negative impacts of pollution. These range from local ordinances that restrict urban development in environmentally sensitive areas to global accords on topics such as biodiversity and climate change.

A major challenge in confronting environmental problems is that many of those problems do not lie within a single jurisdiction. As we saw in Part Eight,

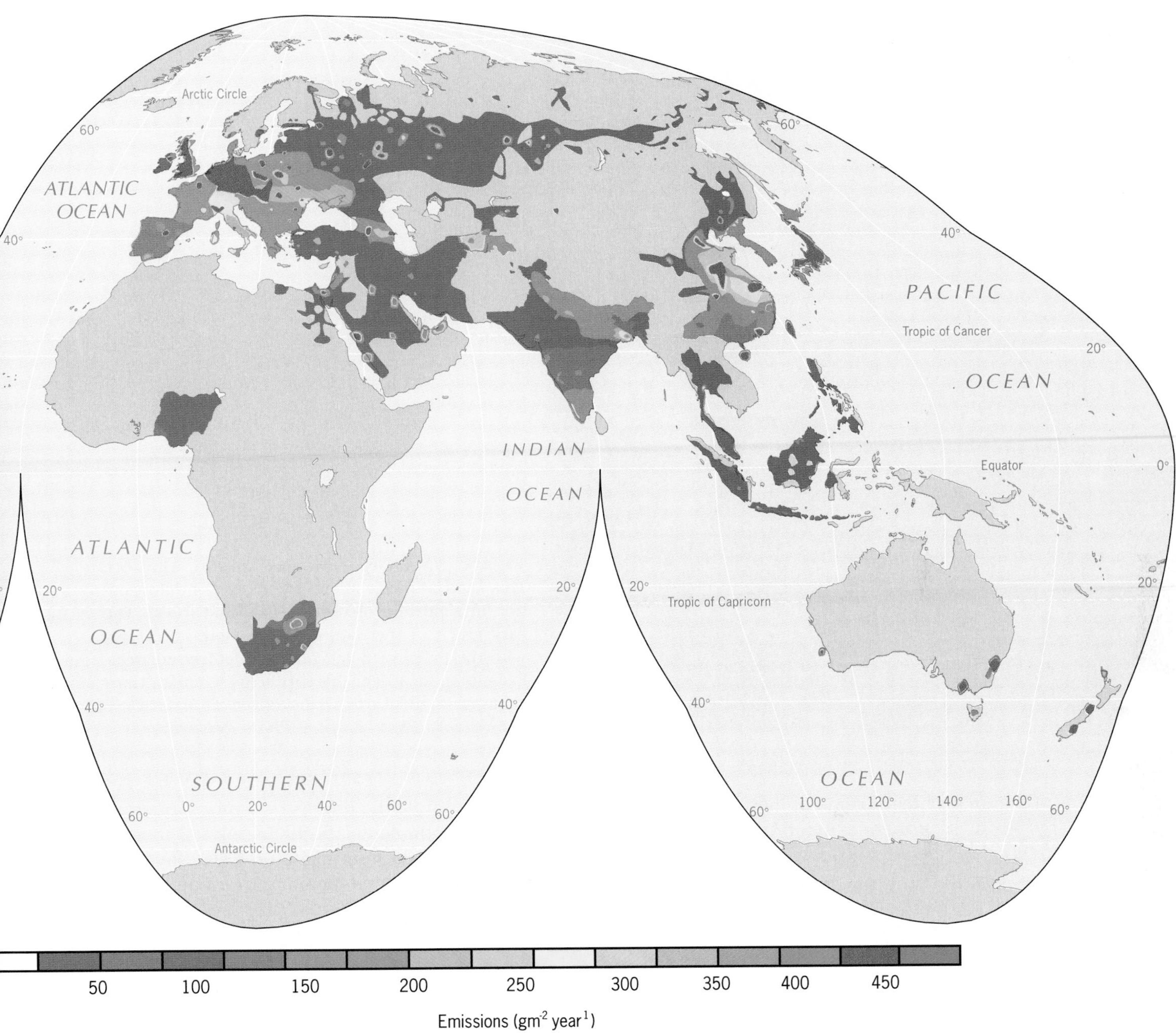

many environmental problems cross political boundaries, and people sometimes move across those boundaries in response to environmental pressures. Designing policy responses is thus complicated by the fact that the political map does not reflect the geography of environmental issues. The problem is particularly acute when environmental problems cross international boundaries, for there are few international policy-making bodies with significant authority over multinational environmental spaces. Moreover, those that do exist—the European Union, for example—often have limited authority and must heed the concerns of member states. Those concerns, in turn, may not coincide with the interests of the environment. Within democracies, politicians with an eye to the next election may hesitate to tackle long-term problems that require short-term sacrifices. Most authoritarian regimes have an even worse record, as can be seen in the policies of the Soviet-dominated governments of Eastern Europe during the communist era. Moreover, governmental leaders in peripheral countries find it very difficult to take action when, as is often the case, action requires reductions in already marginal standards of living and even greater difficulties in meeting the kinds of debt payments discussed in Chapter 24.

Despite these obstacles, the growing extent and urgency of global environmental changes have led to a number of international agreements to address some

Figure 33-3 Deforestation in the Amazon. This Landsat image shows the extent of deforestation in a portion of the Brazilian rain forest. The dark green of the natural forest contrasts sharply with the pale green and pinks of deforested areas. Examining images of this sort helps scientists track changes in the Earth's land cover. *Source: NRSC Ltd./Science Photo Library/Photo Researchers.*

of the most severe problems. Some of these are spearheaded by so-called ***nongovernmental organizations (NGOs)*** that operate outside of the formal political arena. They tend to focus on specific issues and problems, often in particular places. But beginning with the 1972 ***United Nations Conference on the Human Environment*** in Stockholm, international governmental organizations have played a growing role as well.

The framework that currently guides international governmental activity in the environmental arena evolved out of the ***United Nations Conference on Environment and Development (UNCED)*** held in Rio de Janeiro in June 1992. The delegates to UNCED gave the ***Global Environment Facility (GEF)***—a joint project of the United Nations and the World Bank—significant authority over environmental action on a global scale. The GEF funds projects related to four issues: loss of biodiversity, climate change, protection of international waters, and depletion of the ozone layer. The delegates to UNCED believed that significant progress could be made through these funded projects, along with bilateral (that is, government-to-government) aid. They also made it easier for NGOs to participate in international environmental policy making.

These actions hold the promise of a more coherent approach to environmental problem solving than is possible when decisions are made on a state-by-state basis. Yet individual states continue to influence decision making in all sorts of ways. Take the case of the GEF. Even though the GEF is charged with protecting key elements of the global environment, it still functions in a state-based world, as suggested by Figure 33-4, a map from a 1994 World Bank technical report on the forest sector in Subsaharan Africa that divides the realm into "major regions" that cut across forest zones.

A few global environmental issues are so pressing that efforts are being made to draw up guidelines for action in the form of international conventions or treaties. The most prominent examples are in the areas of biological diversity, protection of the ozone layer, and global climate change. Let us take a brief look at these.

Biological Diversity

International concern over the loss of species led to calls for a global convention (agreement) as early as 1981. By the beginning of the 1990s a group working under the auspices of the United Nations Environment Programme reached agreement on the wording of the convention, and it was submitted to UNCED for approval. It went into effect in late 1993; by 1995, 118 countries had signed it. The convention calls for the establishment of a system of protected areas and for a coordinated set of national and international regulations on activities that can have significant negative impacts on biodiversity. It also provides funding for developing countries that are trying to meet the terms of the convention.

The biodiversity convention is a step forward in that it both affirms the vital significance of preserving biological diversity and provides a framework for cooperation toward that end. However, the agreement has proved difficult to implement. In particular, there is an ongoing struggle to find a balance between the periphery's need to promote local economic development and the need to preserve biodiversity, which happens to be richest in the periphery. Also, there has been controversy over the sharing of costs for conservation programs, which has led to heated debates over ratification of the convention in some countries. Nevertheless, this convention, along with a host of voluntary efforts, has helped both to focus attention on the biodiversity issue and to promote the expansion of protected areas. Whether those areas will succeed in providing long-term species protection is an open question that will occupy geographers and biologists for years to come.

Protection of the Ozone Layer

When found in the troposphere (0 to 10 km altitude), ozone (O_3) gas is a harmful pollutant closely associated with the creation of smog. However, a naturally occurring ***ozone layer*** is found in the upper levels of the stratosphere (between 30 and 45 km altitude). The ozone layer is of vital importance, since it protects the Earth's surface from the sun's harmful ultraviolet rays. In 1985 a group of British scientists working in Antarctica discovered that the thickness of the ozone layer above the south pole had been dramatically reduced, from 300 Dobson units (DUs) in the 1960s to close to 200 DUs by 1985. Studies revealed that the main culprits in ozone depletion were a group of human-made gases collectively known as CFCs (chlorofluorocarbons). These gases, used mainly as refrigerants, in fire

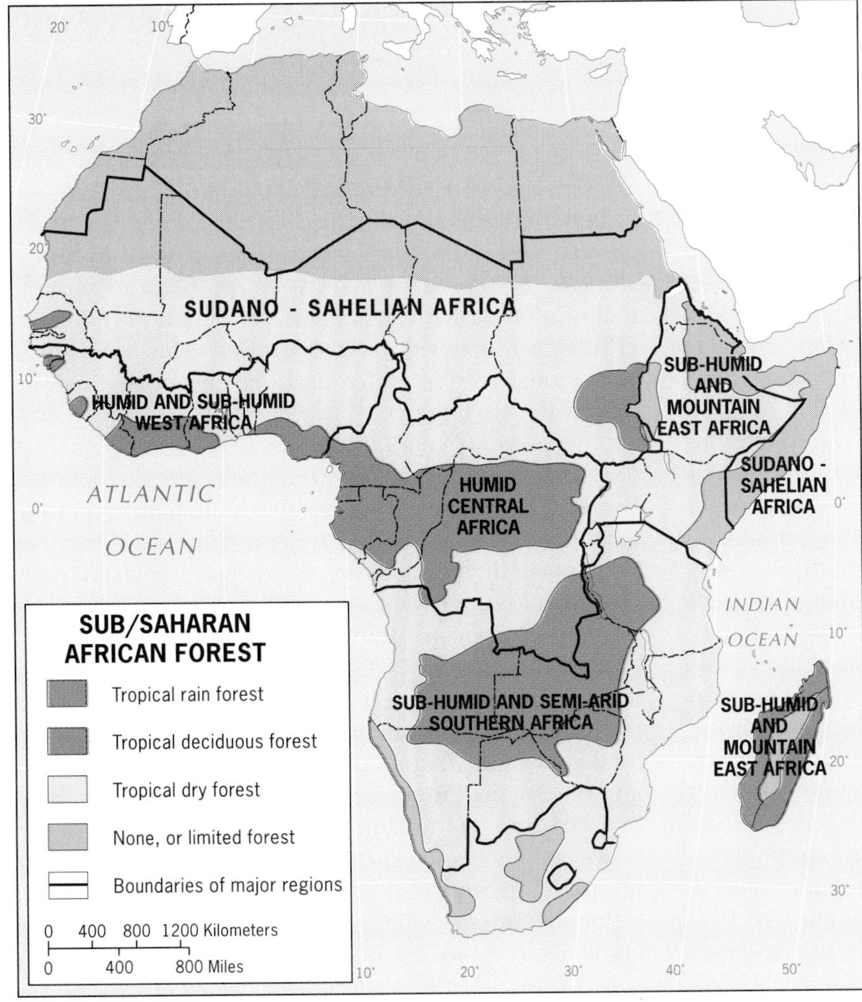

Figure 33-4 Major Regions and Forest Zones in Subsaharan Africa. This map in a World Bank technical paper on the forest sector in Subsaharan Africa shows major regions of deforestation, following state boundaries. *Source: N. P. Sharma, S. Rietbergen, C. R. Heimo, and J. Patel,* A Strategy for the Forest Sector in Sub-Saharan Africa, *World Bank Technical Paper No., 251, Africa Technical Department Series (Washington, D.C.: The World Bank, 1994).*

extinguishers, and in aerosol cans, have only been in use since the 1950s and were thought to be completely harmless to humans. The strength of the scientific evidence pointing to a rapid reduction of the ozone layer led to an unusually fast and united international response.

International cooperation began in 1985 with the negotiation of the ***Vienna Convention for the Protection of the Ozone Layer***. Specific targets and timetables for the phaseout of production and consumption of CFCs were defined and agreed upon as part of the international agreement known as the ***Montreal Protocol***, which was signed in September 1987 by 105 countries and the European Community. The original agreement called for a reduction in the production and consumption of CFCs of 50 percent by 1999. At a meeting in London in 1990, scientific data showing that ozone depletion would continue for many years after a phaseout of CFCs led the signators of the Montreal Protocol to agree to halt CFC production entirely by the year 2000. Finally, at a meeting in Copenhagen in 1992, the timetable for CFC phaseout was accelerated; participants agreed to eliminate CFC production by 1996 and to accelerate the phaseout of other ozone-depleting chemicals such as halons, hydrochlorofluorocarbons, carbon tetrachloride, methyl chloroform, and methyl bromide. This response is an encouraging example of international cooperation in the face of a significant, albeit clearly defined, problem.

From the field notes

"Some countries have to take the enhanced greenhouse-warming warning more seriously than others. As we approached the Maldives (in the Indian Ocean south of India), the islands lay like lilypads on the surface of a pond. No part of this country's natural surface lies more than 6 feet (less than 2 meters) above sea level. The upper floors of the buildings in the capital, Maale, form the Maldives's highest points. Almost any rise in sea level would threaten this outpost."

Global Climate Change

Beginning in the late 1980s, growing concern with climate changes led to a series of intergovernmental conferences on the nature and extent of the human impact on the climate system. The second of these conferences, held in Geneva in 1990, was sponsored by the World Meteorological Organization, the United Nations Environment Programme, and other international organizations. It brought together representatives from 137 states and the European Community. The delegates concluded that there was enough evidence of human impacts on climate to justify efforts to draw up a treaty on climate change. The final declaration, adopted after hard bargaining, did not specify any international targets for reducing emissions. Instead, it proclaimed climate change as a "common concern of humankind," while noting that "common but differentiated responsibilities" existed between the industrialized core and the less-industrialized periphery.

In December 1990 the United Nations General Assembly approved the start of treaty negotiations. A draft convention was prepared and submitted to UNCED for consideration. The convention was presented in general terms, but it called on the developed countries to take measures aimed at reducing their emissions to 1990 levels by the year 2000 and to provide technical and financial support for emission-reduction efforts in the developing countries. The convention was signed by 154 States and the European Community in Rio de Janeiro.

For several years after UNCED, various committees met to discuss matters relating to the convention. By 1995, mounting concerns about the nature of long-term commitments under the convention led the participants in these discussions to call for a revised treaty that would cover the post-2000 period. They appointed a group to draft an agreement to be considered at a December 1997 meeting in Kyoto, Japan. Different proposals were made in the months before this meeting, including one by the Association of Small Island States for a 20 percent cut in CO_2 by the year 2005 and one by the European Union for cuts of 7.5 percent by 2005 and 15 percent by 2010. The United States, however, was concerned about the economic effects of such cuts and the extent to which the burden of reducing emissions fell on the developed countries. It made a more modest proposal to return to 1990 CO_2

levels by 2012 and to reduce CO_2 levels below the 1990 benchmark thereafter.

After ten days of tough negotiations, an agreement was reached that involved compromises for practically every participating country. The agreement set a target period of 2008–2012 for the United States to cut its greenhouse gas emissions by 7 percent below 1990 levels, for the European Union to cut its emissions by 8 percent below 1990 levels, and for Japan to cut its emissions by 6 percent below 1990 levels. In addition, the agreement reached in Kyoto does not obligate less developed countries to adhere to specific reduction goals; instead it calls for voluntary emission reduction plans to be implemented individually by those countries with financial assistance from industrialized countries. Those plans are to be visited at periodic future summits on greenhouse gas emissions.

◆ THE FUTURE

What will the future be like? Many would agree with geographer Robert Kates (1994), who foresees a "warmer, more crowded, more connected but more diverse world" (p. 114). As we consider this prospect, we must acknowledge that global environmental changes illustrate the limits of our knowledge of the Earth. Many of today's global environmental changes were not anticipated. For example, one of the most widely used CFCs, known as Freon 12, was invented in 1931, but the thinning of the ozone hole over Antarctica was not reported until 1985, over 50 years later. Moreover, many global changes are nonlinear, and some are "chaotic" in the sense that future conditions cannot be reliably predicted. Nonlinearity means that small actions in certain situations may result in large impacts and may be more important than larger actions in causing change. Thresholds also exist in many systems which, once past, are irreversible. This occurs, for example, when the habitat for a species is diminished to the point where the species quickly dies off. Unfortunately, we may not be able to identify these thresholds until we pass them. This leaves open the possibility of "surprises," unanticipated responses by physical systems.

The complexity and urgency of the environmental challenge will tax the energies of the scientific community for some time to come. Geography will be an essential part of the effort. The major changes that are taking place have different origins and spatial expressions, and each results from a unique combination of physical and social processes. We cannot simply focus on system dynamics and generalized causal relationships. We must also consider emerging patterns of environmental change and the impacts of differences from place to place on the operation of general processes. Geography is not the backdrop to the changes taking place; it is at the very heart of the changes themselves.

◆ KEY TERMS ◆

chlorofluorocarbons (CFCs)
Global Environment Facility (GEF)
Montreal Protocol
nongovernmental organizations (NGOs)
ozone layer
pelagic species
remote sensing
United Nations Conference on Environment and Development (UNCED)
United Nations Conference on the Human Environment
Vienna Convention for the Protection of the Ozone Layer

◆ APPLYING GEOGRAPHIC KNOWLEDGE ◆

1. Suppose you were in charge of dividing up Africa into a series of regions that would become frameworks for planning and implementing policies to combat deforestation and soil erosion. What approach would you take in delimiting regions? What sources would you consult? What would your map of regions look like when it was completed?
2. Identify two areas of significant environmental degradation, one in a democratic country and one in a country with a recent or current authoritarian regime. Discuss what factors contributed to environmental degradation in each case. Specify which factors the cases have in common, and which they do not.

Chapter 34

Policy Responses to Demographic Changes

From the field notes

"China's communist regime could institute a one-child-only policy and enforce it, but India is a democracy, and India's States have considerable autonomy. Above this entrance to a suite of medical offices was some evidence of recent disputes over family planning in the State of Maharashtra: GOVERNMENT APPROVED URBAN FAMILY PLANNING CENTRE IS CLOSED FROM 11/1996, says one notice; FREE FAMILY PLANNING STERILISATION OPERATION NOT NOW CONDUCTED HERE FROM 11/1996, says another. These notices mark the outcome of decisions by the Maharashtra government to overrule federal family-planning initiatives; here is one reason why India's rate of population growth remains comparatively high."

KEY POINTS

◆ **For practical purposes population data are reported by country. But demographic variation *within* countries can be very large—as, for example, in India.**

◆ **During the twentieth century national governments have pursued three kinds of population policy: expansive, eugenic, and restrictive.**

◆ **International agreements on population policies are difficult to reach, in part because religious doctrines and governmental goals may be incompatible.**

◆ **The most dramatic population-policy reversal in recent decades was carried out by communist China.**

Population is at the center of any consideration of global change. As we have seen, despite some reduction in birth rates, population continues to grow very rapidly in some parts of the world, creating social and environmental challenges. But not all the challenges involve population growth. In some parts of the world, little or no population growth is placing strains on economic and social systems that still depend on large numbers of young people.

To understand the link between demography and policy, one must begin with the fact that population growth varies from realm to realm, from region to region, and even from province to province within individual countries. Over time, too, regional population growth has been inconsistent. Not much more than 30 years ago the world's highest rates of natural increase were in South Asia and South and Middle America, but during the late 1970s tropical Africa took the lead with an overall growth rate approaching 3 percent (representing a doubling time of 24 years). Still farther back in history Europe underwent a population explosion that was mitigated by emigration. Europeans populated the colonies and, later, the Americas and other regions.

How things change. Today Europe has the lowest growth rate in the world. Two dozen European countries have fertility rates below the replacement level. (The total fertility rate, TFR, should be above 2.1 children per childbearing-age woman to sustain a population without loss.) Europe's population will decline in the coming years, but this decline will be accompanied by difficult social problems. A population that is not replacing itself also becomes a population of older people who require pensions, social services, and other forms of support that must be paid for from a dwindling tax base. Because not enough younger people are available to take jobs (and those who are in the job market tend to take skilled positions), immigrant workers are needed, but this, too, can lead to social problems. In Germany, for example, hundreds of thousands of Turkish immigrant laborers and their families have entered the country in search of jobs. When the Berlin Wall came down and the two Germanies were reunited, thousands of former East German workers went westward in search of jobs, but the presence of immigrant workers caused tensions and violence.

Population decline is a two-edged sword. In this chapter the focus is on the practical: How do governments react to demographic problems, and what have been the results of past policies and actions? As the century draws to a close, France is the only Western European country that is encouraging its citizens, through subsidies and services, to have larger families. But France is not the only government looking for ways to cope with the consequences of negative population growth. Japan is in similar straits, but Japanese policy bars immigration of foreign workers. In Singapore, a population-control campaign (in which sterilization was encouraged, abortion was legalized, and larger families were punished) was so successful that the population stopped growing and started aging. Now Singapore's government urges families to have three or even four children. Clearly, balanced population growth is not easily achieved.

◆ GEOGRAPHY OF DEMOGRAPHY

Just as world averages, and averages for major geographic realms, conceal variations in smaller regions or individual countries, so the national data we show on such maps as Figures 5-6 and 5-7 cannot reveal internal contrasts *within* countries. These internal differences can be large, as we noted in the case of the Indian State of Kerala.

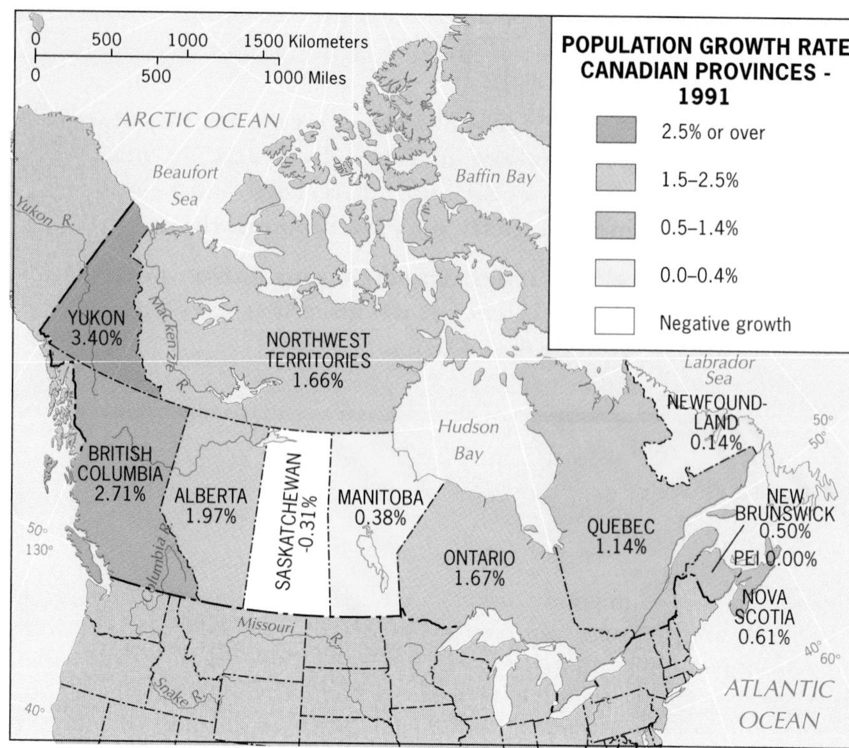

Figure 34-1 Population Growth Rate in Canadian Provinces, 1991. *Source: Data from* Statistics Canada, *1995.*

An interesting example is the situation in Quebec (Fig. 34-1). Despite being overwhelmingly Catholic, Quebec has long had the lowest birth rate among all of Canada's provinces. (Figure 34-1 reveals the effects of natural increase *and* migration, and thus reflects the outflow from the Maritime Provinces as well as immigration into the Pacific area.) In 1990 the Quebec provincial government offered women a subsidy of $6000 (Canadian) for every child born after the first two. Canada is already a low-growth country, with only 30 million people in an area even larger than the United States and a rate of natural increase of 0.6 percent. Canada's overall growth rate, taking immigration and emigration into account, is about 1.3 percent, still well below the world average. The rate of natural increase for Quebec is below Canada's, and the province's overall growth rate is near that of the country as a whole. Quebec's leaders want to encourage the rate of natural increase for political as well as economic reasons, because the great majority of people born in the province are of French-Canadian parentage.

The Canadian example reminds us of the spatial variations within countries, especially larger countries, that do not appear in national statistics. It also indicates that national population policies may not be appropriate, or even acceptable, in particular regions of a country. It was the Quebec provincial government, not Canada's federal government, that offered a subsidy for larger families. As in all federations, the objectives of one region may diverge from those of the state as a whole.

Another relevant case is that of India, where data on overall population increase should be viewed against a regional background (Fig. 34-2). From a demographic standpoint there are several Indias. Population growth is most rapid (and still explosive) in Assam and neighboring states adjacent to Bangladesh. In Nagaland and Mizoram, the rate of natural increase during the 1970s actually exceeded 4.5 percent, one of the world's highest. It has been about 2.5 percent in India's great eastern population cluster in the lower Ganges-Brahmaputra Basin. As Figure 34-2 shows, the growth rate in the southern peninsula has been below the national average. The national average for population growth does not reveal these internal spatial variations. When the food situation was less secure than it has been in recent years, hunger often afflicted the east at a time when food was adequate in the west.

The map of world population growth shows that the countries with high growth rates tend to be the "have-not" countries in the global economic periphery. These are the world's poorest countries, those least able to feed and house additional millions of people. The economic gains made by these countries under existing political and economic structures are all but wiped out by the demands of their mushrooming populations, and reduced growth rates are essential if any improvement is to occur.

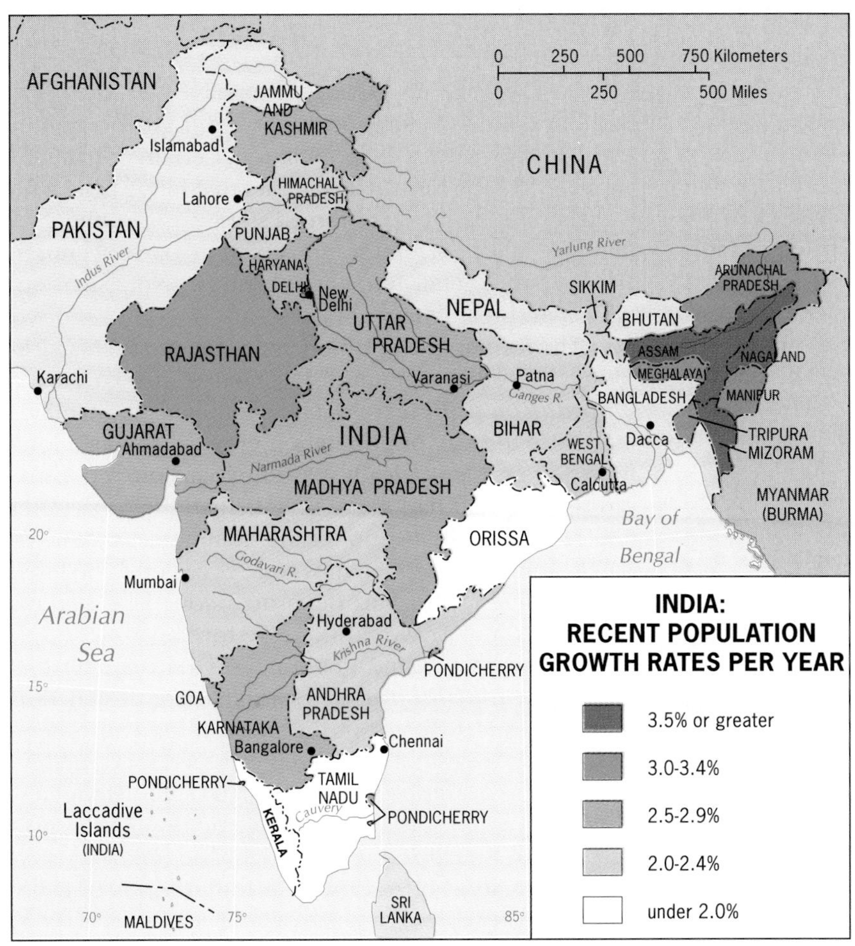

Figure 34-2 Recent Population Growth Rates in India. Data from census of India since 1970 and from demographic reports of individual state agencies were used to derive yearly population growth rates.

◆ THE UNITED NATIONS POPULATION CONFERENCES

From time to time, concern over global population trends leads to multinational discussions to seek ways to defuse the population explosion. In 1974 a gathering for this purpose took place in Bucharest, Romania. The population spiral was in full force, global hunger and dislocation were looming, and controlling population growth seemed to be a matter of overriding worldwide priority.

But the minutes of the 1974 meeting paint quite another picture, and they remind us of the cost of the Cold War and of the difficulty in reaching international agreement on any issue as sensitive as population. China, still in the aftershocks of its costly Cultural Revolution, put the Marxist view bluntly: population control was a capitalist plot designed to hamper the growth and power of communist societies, and the Chinese would not agree to any multinational plan to limit growth. On the contrary, the Chinese applauded the (then) Soviet policy of giving special recognition and awards to women who had borne ten children or more.

The Bucharest gathering was the first in a series of United Nations-sponsored conferences on population issues. While it was marred by ideological disputes, the great majority of the world's governments agreed on the urgency of the population issue. China and the Soviet Union took similar positions for different reasons: China saw family planning as a capitalist plot, while the Soviet Union promoted births because its population had not fully recovered from the enormous losses suffered during World War II. The Soviet Union encouraged large families because it saw its huge domain as underpopulated (a situation to which Stalinists had contributed by exterminating more than 30 million farmers, political opponents, and other dissidents during the 1930s). But the problems of spiraling population growth were evident to most of the participating states, communist and noncommunist alike.

UN population conferences are held every ten years. The next meeting occurred in Mexico City in

1984. The contrast between the two conferences, in terms of urgency and ideology, is striking. By 1984 the Green Revolution had narrowed the food gap, and China, in its post–Mao era, had reversed its position on population growth. China had now embarked on a severely restrictive population policy, and its growth rate had declined dramatically—so much so that the Beijing regime had been awarded a United Nations medal for achieving rapid reduction in the national birth rate. In addition, during the Reagan (Republican) era the United States did not take an active role in support of family planning. It kept a relatively low profile at the conference, and no major confrontations like those at Bucharest occurred.

The Cairo Conference

During the 1994 conference in Cairo, a new and potentially crucial division appeared, based on religious rather than political or ideological differences. The controversy centered on the issue of birth control. The Roman Catholic Church objected to the prospect that the conference would endorse abortion and artificial means of birth control. In addition, a number of Islamic countries asserted that population-control measures were inconsistent with Muslim precepts, and so Saudi Arabia and Sudan refused to participate at all. Religious fundamentalists were united on this issue.

The Impact of Fundamentalism

The Cairo Conference confirmed the growing strength of religious fundamentalism throughout the world (see Chapter 13). Not only Islamic and Christian faiths, but other religions as well are affected by this phenomenon. This was evident throughout the conference as delegations proclaimed their aversion to secularism. These arguments pushed into the background a key to reducing population growth: the education of women and the strengthening of their rights in all societies (see Chapter 31). When women have access to education and paid employment, birth rates decline and development accelerates. Data from the World Bank indicate that women without some high school education have an average of seven children; the average drops to three for women who attend high school. And because there is more time between births, the health of women and children also improves, saving medical costs for the society as a whole.

Religious fundamentalism can work against the interests of women in societies of all kinds. Many observers argue that the poverty associated with rapid population growth is best combated by improving the status of women in traditional society. On this matter the conference made little progress.

◆ POPULATION POLICIES

Many of the world's governments have instituted policies designed to influence the overall growth rate or ethnic ratios within the population. Certain policies directly affect the birth rate via laws that range from subsidization of abortion to forced sterilization. Others influence family size through taxation or subvention. These policies fall into three groups: expansive, eugenic, and restrictive.

The former Soviet Union and China under Mao Zedong led other communist societies in ***expansive population policies***, which encourage large families and raise the rate of population growth. Romania long pursued an ideologically based expansionist population policy that had some unanticipated effects. After the revolution that toppled the communist regime in 1991, Romania's orphanages were revealed to be filled with children who had been abandoned by parents who could not or would not care for them.

In the past, some governments engaged in ***eugenic population policies***, which were designed to favor one racial sector of the population over others. The ultimate example of eugenics was Nazi Germany, but other countries also pursued such strategies, though in more subtle ways. Eugenic population policies could be carried out through discriminatory taxation, allocation of resources, or other forms of racial favoritism.

Today most countries seek to reduce the rate of natural increase through ***restrictive population policies***. These policies range from toleration of officially unapproved means of birth control to outright prohibition of large families. It is important to realize how varied the situation is in Roman Catholic as well as Islamic societies. Demographic data indicate, for example, that Italians in the Catholic heartland do not adhere to the Vatican's rules, while Catholics in distant lands do obey them. And while states in the Muslim heartland do little to reduce population growth, those far from Mecca do more (see "Focus on: Indonesia and the Philippines").

Societies have experimented with a variety of techniques for achieving demographic goals, as the following discussion indicates.

Japan

The Japanese experience is a prime example of success—perhaps excessive success—in population control. During Japan's nineteenth- and early twentieth-century era of modernization, expansion, and military victories, families were encouraged to have several children. However, Japan also had growing urban centers, which tended to somewhat reduce the birth rate.

Indonesia and The Philippines

Indonesia and the Philippines are island neighbors in Southeast Asia. Indonesia, with a population of 208 million, is the world's fourth largest country and the largest Islamic nation. The Philippines is Asia's only Roman Catholic country; its population is about 75 million.

Religious fundamentalism affects both countries. In the Philippines, the powerful Roman Catholic Church opposes the use of artificial contraceptives, and church and state have been locked in a battle over birth control. Abortion is prohibited by the country's constitution. When Manila's cardinal demanded that the Philippine government boycott the Cairo Conference on Population and Development in 1994, the issue roiled the nation. But the Philippines is a democracy, and while Manila did send a delegation to Cairo, the government could not afford to ignore the pronouncements of the church. In the late 1990s the rate of population growth in the Philippines was one of Asia's highest at 2.3 percent, with a doubling time of 30 years.

Islamic Indonesia, on the other hand, has an authoritarian regime that does not tolerate the kind of opposition seen in the Philippines. In 1970 Indonesia began a nationwide family planning program, and when Muslim leaders objected, the government used a combination of coercion and inducement to counter their opposition. In Indonesia, too, the Cairo Conference was denounced by fundamentalist Muslims, but the government could afford to ignore them.

Indonesia's family planning program is generally regarded as the most successful in the Muslim world. In the 1970s, the annual population growth rate was as high as 2.5 percent; in the late 1990s, it was 1.7 percent, far below that of the Philippines. Doubling time had risen from 28 years to 41.

The contrast between these two neighbors, Christian and Muslim, reminds us that it is not possible to generalize about religion and family planning. It also underscores the authoritarian regime's advantages over a democratic government when it comes to implementing policies.

This combination of circumstances tended to stabilize the rate of population growth.

At the end of World War II, hundreds of thousands of Japanese nationals returned from the colonies. Soldiers came home and rejoined their families. During the American occupation medical services and public health were improved. The net result was an unprecedented increase in the birth rate and a simultaneous drop in death rates. Japan's rate of growth, which over the decades had averaged about 1.3 percent, suddenly rose to 2.0 percent per year. That represents a doubling time of 35 years, and with Japan's population already about 70 million at the time, it created a crisis.

In 1948 the Japanese government took action, and the results can be seen in the population pyramid in Figure 5-5. The ***Eugenic Protection Act*** legalized abortions for "social, medical, and economic reasons." Contraceptives were made available, and family planning clinics were set up throughout the country. Although contraception and female sterilization (also made widely available) helped reduce the birth rate, it was the enormous number of abortions that really brought it down. In fact, so many abortions were performed, perhaps 7 to 8 million in a decade, that the Japanese authorities began to worry about their effect on the well-being of the nation. They then began to use propaganda and educational programs to encourage contraception.

As a result of these measures, the birth rate, which had been over 34 per 1000 in 1947, had fallen to 18 per thousand just one decade later and was reduced to 13 per thousand by 1985. Meanwhile, the death rate declined from 14.2 in 1948 to 7.5 in 1958 to 6.0 in 1985. Thus in the early 1980s Japan's population, growing at less than 1 percent per year, increased by about 1 million annually. Immigration contributed little to population growth, and emigration also had little effect.

In the 1990s, Japan's demographic situation became a matter of growing concern for its leaders. The country's fertility rate had fallen to a new low of just over 1.5, far below the 2.1 needed to maintain the population without loss. (This is still higher than the prevailing TFR in West Germany just before reunification, which was below 1.3.) The effects of this decline can be seen in projections of Japan's future population, which will reach a peak of approximately 127 million and then drop to 112 to 115 million by the year 2025.

In 1991 the Japanese government increased the benefits available to parents and embarked on an expansionist population policy. But under the special conditions of Japanese life it will be difficult to reverse the trend just described. Japan is a small country, about the size of Montana. It is among the world's most highly urbanized, industrialized, and regimented societies. Living space is at a premium; living costs are high. The financial and social burdens of raising a child are great, and parents are well aware that some child benefits will not be much help. So Japan, like Germany, faces an aging population, a dwindling work force, and a shrinking tax base at a time when welfare and pension costs are rising.

What alternatives are available? Labor immigration is not an option. The Japanese refuse to allow large numbers of foreign workers into their nearly homogeneous island nation. A Singapore-style campaign to reverse the downward population spiral is not likely in Japan, nor would it be likely to work. For the time being, Japan will probably turn to an old ally—technology. It still is possible to turn over more work to robots and other advanced technologies in order to increase productivity. Some observers also suggest that many more women will enter the skilled work force in the early twenty-first century.

None of this, however, will ultimately protect Japan from the social and economic adjustments that must accompany less-than-zero or ***negative population growth***. With its borders effectively closed to immigration, its future problems will be substantially self-imposed, proving again that in this age of interaction and interconnection, cultural isolation is no guarantee of a secure future.

From the field notes

"Searing social contrasts abound in India's overcrowded cities. Even in Bombay, India's most prosperous large city, hundreds of thousands of people live like this, in the shadow of modern apartment buildings. Within seconds we were surrounded by a crowd of people asking for help of any kind, their ages ranging from the very young to the very old. Somehow this scene was more troubling here in well-off Bombay than in Calcutta or Madras, but it typified India's urban problems everywhere." ***(Note: the names of Bombay and Madras were changed after this field note was written.)***

India

Demographers predict that sometime during the first half of the twenty-first century India will overtake China as the world's most populous country—if India's political framework holds together. In the late 1990s, India's population was still growing at a rate of about 1.9 percent, adding over 18 million per year to a population approaching 1 billion.

The problems involved in carrying out a coordinated population policy in a country as culturally complex as India are enormous. India is a federation of 25 States and 7 so-called Union Territories, and the individual States differ greatly both culturally and politically. As in all true federations, the will of the federal government cannot be forcibly imposed on the States.

Population planning began on a shoestring budget in the 1950s, not long after India became independent. Limited funds were made available for family planning clinics and programs, but government leaders themselves were not aware of the real dimensions of the population explosion in progress at the time. But in the 1960s India's official census left no doubt, and the government's investment in population planning increased. A national program was instituted, and the states were encouraged to join.

Despite this national effort, rapid population growth continued, especially in the eastern States. Also, social problems arose in some of the states where the campaign was pursued most vigorously. The State of Maharashtra instituted a plan that required sterilization of anyone with three children or more. Public opposition led to rioting and the program was abandoned, but not before 3.7 million people had been sterilized. Other States also engaged in compulsory sterilization programs, but the social and political costs were heavy. Eventually, a total of 22.5 million people were sterilized, but this form of population control could not be sustained for long.

Today Indian State governments are using advertising and persuasion to encourage families to have fewer children. Almost everywhere one can see posters urging people to have small families, and a network of clinics has been established to aid women even in the remotest villages. As Figure 34-2 indicates, progress has been made in some areas, notably in the better educated areas of the south, but elsewhere as well. We should keep in mind that several of India's States have 100 million inhabitants or more, which would put them among the world's larger countries. Any reduction in population growth rates in such States is a major achievement. However, India does not have enough resources to achieve a significant decline in population growth rates in the nation as a whole.

China

For nearly 30 years after the communist government took power, China's demography was a mystery to the outside world. Estimates of China's population and its rate of natural increase varied widely. In 1978 the World Bank's *World Development Report* estimated the Chinese population at 826 million. Shortly thereafter the Chinese government announced that the 1 billion mark had been passed. Guesses about China's population had been wrong by as much as 200 million!

If there were doubts about the size of China's population, the political and social regime of Mao Zedong left no doubts about its views on family planning. At the 1974 Bucharest Conference, as noted earlier, the Chinese representative denounced population policies as imperialist tools designed to sap the strength of developing countries.

After Mao's death China's new leaders expressed very different views. If China was to modernize, they said, population growth would have to be brought under control. In 1979 they launched a policy to induce married couples to have only one child. This would have stabilized China's population at about 1.2 billion by the end of the century.

The ***one-child policy*** was applied loosely at first, but when it had less than the desired effect, it was enforced more strictly. The results were dramatic. In 1970, China's population was growing at a rate of 2.4 percent (as estimated by China's own planners); by 1985, it was down to 1.1 percent. In 1983, by which time the growth rate had been reduced to 1.2 percent, the United Nations gave China (along with India) its first Family Planning Award.

These statistics are encouraging, but they conceal the stresses the policies impose on families. After 1982 the government made it mandatory for women to use contraceptive devices after they had their one child. If a second child was born, one of the parents would have to be sterilized. Only members of China's recognized minorities (less than 3 percent of the total population) were exempt from these rules.

Such rules imposed severe hardships, especially on farming families. Many hands are needed to do farm work, and large families are common in many rural areas. Therefore, many Chinese families defied the authorities: they kept pregnant women out of sight, did not register births, and prevented inspectors from visiting villages.

In response, the government took drastic action. Those who violated the rules were fired from their jobs, had their farmlands taken away, lost many benefits, and were otherwise put at a disadvantage. In some parts of China the punishment was even worse: pregnant women known to have one or two children were arrested at work, in the fields, or at home and taken to abortion clinics to have their babies aborted—sometimes after more than six months of pregnancy. The national policies were imposed more harshly in some provinces than in others. Southeast China appears to have been targeted most severely.

China's Ministry of Public Health estimates that during the first six years of the population-control campaign, nearly 70 million abortions were performed in the country (where abortion was regarded as murder just a generation earlier). In addition, during the 1980s more than 20 million persons were sterilized *annually* (three times as many women as men), according to government reports.

The effectiveness of the Chinese population policies was ensured, not only by government incentives and punishments, but also through the actions of Communist Party officials and members. Through promises of advancements and cash payments for local compliance, party members became, in effect, the birth-control police. No village, neighborhood, factory, or collective escaped constant scrutiny.

But China is changing. In 1984, in response to a rising tide of complaints from rural areas, the government relaxed its one-child policy in the countryside. A couple whose first child was a daughter were allowed to have a second child after a four-year wait. Then the Party-imposed system of controls began to break down as enforcement weakened, people found more effective ways of circumventing the rules (sending an illegally pregnant woman to distant family members to await the birth, for example), and peasants with rising incomes could afford to pay the fine for unauthorized births. Corruption, an endemic problem in China, also enabled some people to evade punishment for violations. The results can already be seen in the statistics: fertility rates are rising, and the downward trend of the growth rate has been reversed. China's last census reported a population of 1.21 billion, and the rate of natural increase had moved upward to 1.4 percent. Although this is still a low figure for countries in the periphery, it means that China's goal for the end of the century—1.2 billion and a stable population—will be exceeded by well over 80 million. In 1997, China's government reported that the birth rate had declined again to 17 per thousand and the death rate to 7 per thousand, so that the official growth rate was 1.0 percent.

China's one-child-only policy has had a major social impact in a society where sons carry on the family name. In the cities a one-child policy was feasible. But in the tradition-bound countryside, where large families have long been the norm, the notion of one (possibly female) child was not acceptable. Observers reported that the one-child policy led to female infanticide and that hundreds of thousands of such killings went unreported at the height of the one-child-only campaign. Demographers estimated that the number of surviving male children exceeded females by 300,000 annually (see Fig. 5-5). China's own population experts have expressed concern over this imbalance. In the future males will greatly outnumber females, with unpredictable social consequences.

Thus China's relentless drive for zero population growth eroded the traditions of Chinese society and brought misery to millions of people. Chinese government and Communist Party officials admit that the policy, when strictly applied, was severe. But they argue that in a country with 100 million excess births, many millions of people will be mired in stagnation and poverty. To get ahead, they argue, the country cannot allow its material gains to be negated by an ever-growing population.

China's experience underscores the depth of the population dilemma. Even with an authoritarian government backed by party machinery, strict policies could not be enforced over the long term. Significant short-term gains were quickly wiped out. Population growth has once again become an obstacle to modernization. Given China's experience, India's regional progress is all the more remarkable and the challenge facing Africa all the more daunting.

◆ KEY TERMS ◆

eugenic population policy
Eugenic Protection Act
expansive population policy
negative population growth
one-child policy
restrictive population policy

◆ APPLYING GEOGRAPHIC KNOWLEDGE ◆

1. For many years population geographers and others have been concerned over the continuing rapid growth of the world's population. But some countries, having traversed the demographic transition, now confront the reality of stable or even declining populations. What are the impacts on countries' cultural and economic geographies of negative population growth?

2. Population policies designed to influence the growth of national populations tend to have regional ramifications; that is, their impact varies regionally. Working at the national and subnational scale, demonstrate how this statement applies to three countries that have adopted population policies.

Chapter 35

Toward A New World Order? The Changing Global Political Landscape

From the field notes

"In front of the exhibition hall on Salisbury Road in Hong Kong stood a display that was supposed to advertise an exhibit of Chinese art, but it seemed symbolic of something much more consequential than that: the red star rising over the western Pacific. This was Hong Kong before the 1997 takeover, and I went inside to ask whether this edifice was intended to do more than advertise an exhibit. "They (the communist Chinese) insisted on this design," said one of the staff members. "You may look at it as a red star rising over us. But there *is* another way of looking at it." I didn't ask, but I suppose he had in mind the reverse process. Obviously not everyone in Hong Kong was enthusiastic about what lay ahead."

KEY POINTS

◆ Devolution, the disintegration of a state along regional lines, is occurring in a growing number of countries, old and young, large and small, wealthy and poor.

◆ Visions of local or regional autonomy, notions of democracy and participation, concepts of religious fundamentalism, and economic globalization are changing the map of the modern world.

◆ The world today is burdened by a weakening state system and an antiquated boundary framework.

◆ A New World Order is said to be in the making following the end of the Cold War, but its geographic outlines cannot yet be discerned; it is likely to involve a multipolar rather than a bipolar configuration; and it is unclear how orderly it will be.

As the twentieth century draws to a close, consider how the world has changed since 1900: its human population has quadrupled; hundreds of thousands of species of animals and plants have become extinct; two world wars have been fought; weapons of mass destruction have been invented; colonial empires have collapsed; the United States has become a superpower; the Soviet Union has disintegrated; Europe has unified; Japan has achieved economic dominance; the Pacific Rim has emerged as a new force in world affairs. Add to these developments the countless breakthroughs in science and technology (notably the invention of the computer and the beginning of space travel) and medicine, and it is no exaggeration to say that in the past century the world has been transformed.

But what has happened to the world of political geography? During the early 1990s, after the collapse of the Soviet Union and the end of the bipolar world we had known for so long, there was optimistic talk of a ***New World Order***, a world in which the balance of nuclear terror between two superpowers would no longer determine the destinies of states. This New World Order would be shaped by forces that connect nations and states, by supranational unions like the European Union, and by multinational action should any state violate international rules of conduct. The risks of nuclear war would recede, and negotiation would replace confrontation. When Iraq was driven out of Kuwait by a UN coalition of states led by the United States in 1991, the framework of a New World Order seemed to be taking shape. Russia, which a few years earlier might have led the Soviet Union in support of Iraq, endorsed the UN operation. Arab as well as non-Arab forces helped repel the invaders.

Soon, however, doubts and uncertainties began to cloud hopes for a New World Order. Although states were more closely linked to each other than ever before, national self-interest still acted as a powerful centrifugal force. For all its faults, the state remained the critical building block in the new global framework. But as we have learned, today the state exists in a wide variety of forms, a diversity that stands in the way of a stable global political structure. Not only do states range enormously in size, population, economic development, culture, and traditions, but they also differ in degree of democracy, treatment of minorities, respect for human rights, and in many other ways.

In this final chapter we focus on the forces that are changing the global political landscape. These are forces with which governments, businesses, and individuals must contend. They affect travelers, consumers, government officials, business representatives, students. To be aware of these forces is to be better prepared to cope with them.

When we study the changes taking place in the world's political framework, we enter the field of ***geopolitics***. As its name implies, this field combines geography with some aspects of political science. Whereas political science tends to focus on governmental institutions, systems, and interactions, geography brings cultural, environmental, and spatial perspectives to the field. As such, geopolitics is a wide arena that helps us understand the forces that are transforming the map of the world.

◆ FORCES OF DEVOLUTION

In Part Eight we noted how states are seeking common economic, political, and cultural ground by joining in supranational unions created to benefit the participants and, by definition, to disadvantage outsiders. The European Union is designed, in part, to enhance its members' competitiveness in the world at large. In the late 1990s several major European countries were preparing to replace their historic currencies—the franc, mark, and lira, for example—with a common currency called the euro. The euro, it was hoped, would be a stronger counterweight to the dollar than the individual national currencies had been.

Such supranational unions might be expected to form an important component in any emerging new world political order. That is likely to be the case, but these unions also have a reverse effect on the state. When a state's government joins a supranational union, it does so on behalf of all its people, majorities and minorities alike. In some cases minorities are heartened by this development, for it gives them a political identity beyond the state. But minorities (or parts of a state such as a region or a province) can feel disadvantaged as well, even threatened. Paradoxically, then, supranationalism can result in stronger centrifugal forces within states.

The foregoing discussion illustrates just how fragile an apparently stable and mature state can be. Some states (China, Egypt) are products of millennia of political-geographical evolution; others, including many European states, have matured over centuries; still others are much younger, having evolved from colonial empires only a few decades ago. Revolution, civil war, and international conflict accompany the evolution of states; the United States is a case in point. Even the oldest and apparently most stable states are vulnerable to a process that is the reverse of evolution, propelled by forces that divide and destabilize. That process is called ***devolution***.

Devolutionary forces can emerge in all kinds of states, old and young, mature and still-developing. These forces arise from several sources. They can be generated by a government's decision to join a supranational union, as noted earlier. When the United Kingdom moved to join the European Union, a number of Scottish nationalists argued that Scotland would be disadvantaged by such a move. Within the United Kingdom, Scotland was a major player, one of the four components of the state. But with the United Kingdom being just one member of a European Union, Scotland would be relegated to third-level status. Thus London's decision revived devolutionary forces in Scotland. There were calls for independence for the Scots; if Denmark, with a population and territory not unlike

From the field notes

"In 1990, Scottish nationalist activism seemed to be rising; I saw makeshift booths like this in several cities and towns, urging people to sign up for 'democracy' (that is, autonomy) for Scotland. 'Scotland should be independent,' the group's representative told me. 'We have our own culture, our own history and language, and we can maintain our economy if we get control over the oil and gas in the North Sea that are really ours. We have just as much right to be an independent nation as the Danes.' Talking to political leaders in Edinburgh and Glasgow, I found only one of them to be unwilling to discuss any accommodation for the Scots: the Conservative Party leader. And the Conservative Party was in control in London! Unless the political landscape changes, Scottish aspirations will have to wait." (Note: in 1997, following the Labour Party's victory over the Conservatives, Scotland was given the opportunity to vote on a first devolutionary step: the creation of a Scottish National Assembly with limited rights. A majority voted in favor. While this option may not satisfy those demanding full independence, a significant devolutionary move has been made. Voters in Wales also approved the establishment of an assembly, but by a narrower margin).

that of Scotland, could be a full-fledged, first-rank member of the European Union, why not Scotland? During the 1990s the Scottish National Party engaged in a campaign to underscore Scotland's disadvantaged position even within the United Kingdom. If Scotland were independent, it was claimed, oil and natural gas revenues would flow from its North Sea Exclusive Economic Zone to Edinburgh, not London; Scottish taxpayers' funds would serve Scotland, not the UK as a whole. In 1997 the newly elected Labor Party gave the Scots (and the Welsh) the opportunity to vote—not for independence, but for greater autonomy, to be embodied in regional parliaments. Both Scotland and Wales voted in favor, and a major devolutionary step was taken in one of Europe's oldest and most stable states.

Cultural Forces

Although Britain has major cultural-geographic divides, English, Scottish, and Welsh histories have long been intertwined, and the resurgence of Scottish nationalism had more to do with London's supranational policies than with a sense of cultural oppression in Scotland. Cultural forces, however, are at the root of many states' devolutionary problems. Most of the world's nearly 200 states have multicultural populations, and conflict among cultural sectors can lead to devolution. This is especially true when multiculturalism is regionally expressed; that is, people of particular cultural backgrounds cluster in certain parts of the country. In Parts Eight and Nine we focused on the Canadian province of Quebec and its predominantly (though not exclusively) French-speaking population. If French speakers were distributed relatively evenly across the country, devolution would not be a threat, even if the minority objected to the government's policies. But the concentration of French-speaking Canadians in one province (with some spillover into neighboring ones) is a devolutionary force that poses a constant threat to Canada's stability.

In Europe devolutionary forces threaten a large number of older as well as younger states (Fig. 35-1). Not all of these forces have cultural bases, but several do. A prominent example is Spain, where demands for greater autonomy have come from the Basque area in the north, notably the province of Vascongadas, and from the eastern province of Catalonia. In 1979 the Spanish government signed autonomy agreements with Basque and Catalonian leaders, allowing both areas to have their own parliaments, giving their languages official status, and transferring taxation and education powers from the capital to the respective provinces. Later the government reorganized its administrative structure, creating 17 so-called Autonomous Communities and further decentralizing power. This plan reduced devolutionary pressures in strongly nationalistic Catalonia, but it was not enough for the most extreme elements in the Basque country, where a campaign of violence against Spanish targets (and

From the field notes

"The battles fought with paint on church walls along the language line in eastern Belgium send a clear message: Belgium is not a nation-state in the traditional sense of the term. Disputes over the spatial extent and autonomy of the country's language regions are played out in the press every day, and even though no one has died over this ethnolinguistic clash, the Belgian landscape reminds us that the conflict is very real—and may challenge the integrity of the Belgian state in the decades ahead."

Figure 35-1 Devolutionary Pressures in Europe. Centrifugal forces have resulted in devolutionary pressures in various places in Europe. *Source: From a map in H. J. de Blij and P. O. Muller*, Geography: Realms, Regions, and Concepts, 8th ed. *(New York: Wiley, 1997).*

even moderate Basque leaders) continued into the late 1990s.

Devolution also threatens Belgium, and here too its roots are cultural. In Chapter 10 we discussed Belgium's Flemish (Dutch) and Walloon (French) subcultures and their strong spatial expression (see Fig. 10-5). By European standards Belgium is not an old state, but it was a founding member of Benelux and the EEC, and it is a charter member of the European Union, whose headquarters are in Brussels. None of this has been enough to overcome the centrifugal forces arising from cultural differences.

The capacity of cultural forces to stimulate devolutionary processes is especially evident in Eastern Europe. Parts of the Eastern European map have changed quite drastically over the past decade, and two countries—Czechoslovakia and Yugoslavia—succumbed to devolutionary pressures. In the case of Czechoslovakia, the process was peaceful: Czechs and Slovaks divided their country along a new international boundary. As Figure 35-1 shows, however, one of the two new states, Slovakia, is not homogeneous: about 11 percent of the population is Hungarian, and that minority is concentrated along the border between Slovakia and Hungary. The Hungarian minority facing, discriminatory policies involving language and other aspects of its culture, is demanding greater autonomy to protect its heritage in the new state.

The breakup of Yugoslavia was the great tragedy of Europe in the second half of the twentieth century. Long-dormant centrifugal forces broke apart a multinational, multicultural state that had survived seven decades of turmoil and war. Yugoslavia ("Land of the South Slavs") lay between the Adriatic Sea to the west and Romania to the east, and between Austria and Hungary to the north and Bulgaria and Greece to the south. Thrown together on maps after World War I, Yugoslavia was home to 7 major and 17 smaller ethnic and cultural groups. The north, where Slovenes and Croats prevailed, was Roman Catholic; the south, Serbian Orthodox. Several million Muslims lived in enclaves surrounded by Christian populations. Two alphabets were in use.

No Yugoslav nation existed except in the legal sense. This was a zone of divergent influences that were first held together by the Royal House of Serbia and later by a communist dictatorship under the war hero Marshal Tito. But as nationalist sentiments became stronger, the various subgroups began fighting each other: Nazi-supporting Croats against anti-Hitler Serbs during World War II; Serbs, Croats, and Muslims against one another after the communist system collapsed. Ambitious leaders, often backed by the military, promoted the view that the peoples of the region were first and foremost Serbs, Croats, Slovenes, Muslims, Macedonians, or members of other, smaller cultural groups.

As a result, Yugoslavia is no more. When the communists ruled the country, they divided it into six internal "republics" on the Soviet model, all except Bosnia dominated by one major group. Now most of these republics are independent countries. Out of the collapse of Yugoslavia have come the newly recognized states of Slovenia, Croatia, Bosnia, Serbia-Montenegro (called Yugoslavia by diehard Serbs), and Macedonia.

In early 1995 the devolution of Yugoslavia was centered in Bosnia. As Figure 35-2 shows, Bosnia is shaped like a triangle with one of its points just barely touching the sea; for all intents and purposes, Bosnia is landlocked. About 44 percent of its population of 4.4 million is Muslim; 31 percent are members of the Serbian Orthodox Church; and 17 percent are Croatian Catholics. In the civil war, Muslim Bosnians and Catholic Croats fought together against the Bosnian Serbs,

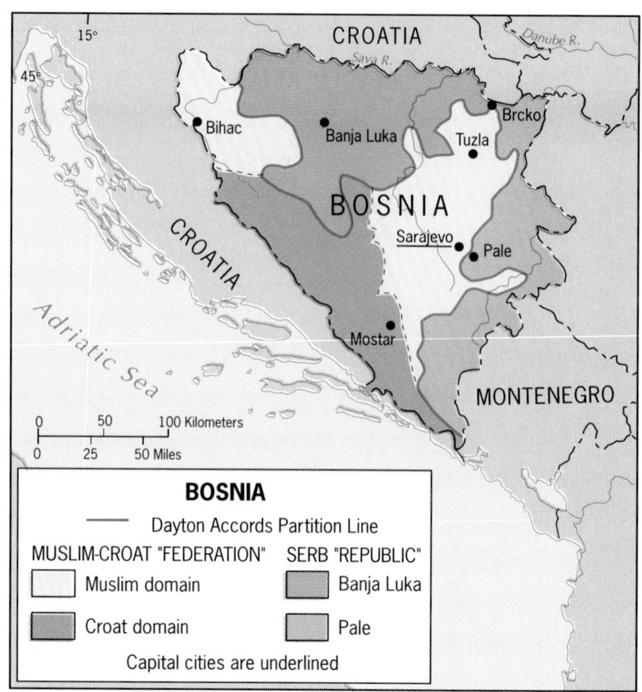

Figure 35-2 The Partition of Bosnia. The Dayton Accords Partition Line separates Serb from non-Serb entities. *Source: From a map in H. J. de Blij and P. O. Muller,* Geography: Realms, Regions, and Concepts, *8th ed. Revised (New York: Wiley, 1998).*

who were aided by the Serbs in Serbia proper (capital Belgrade). When a stalemate occurred in late 1994, the Serbs had control of about 70 percent of Bosnia and the Muslims controlled a fragmented territory west of their capital, Sarajevo.

In 1995 the United States sponsored a conference in Dayton, Ohio, to redraw the map of Bosnia. It was agreed that the country (somewhat smaller than West Virginia but with similar mountainous and hilly terrain) had to be partitioned among the Serbs, concentrated in the east and north, and the Muslims and Croats, who prevail in the center, south, and west. On a large-scale map spread out on the conference table, the conferees drew a tortuous dividing line that created a Serb "Republic" on one side and a Muslim-Croat "Federation" on the other (Fig. 35-2). This 621-mile-long, 4-mile-wide barrier runs from Bosnia's northwestern corner to its southwestern one, almost cutting the country in half near the northern town of Brcko on the Sava tributary of the Danube River.

The Dayton Accords were achieved because all the participants saw immediate or potential advantage in them. Serb-dominated territory would be reduced to 48 percent of the country. Muslims as well as Croats each got domains in their "Federation." Sarajevo was made part of the non-Serb sector of Bosnia.

But the map also contained the seeds of further

trouble. In effect it created two Serb entities, linked by the most tenuous of corridors, and the two Serbian communities had their own differences. The east (capital Pale) was far more closely aligned to Serbia proper than the north (capital Banja Luka). And Muslims and Croats were by no means unified in their "Federation." Add to this Bosnia's landlocked situation (the Dayton Accords provided no corridor to the Adriatic), and it is clear that further devolution could ocur. Once cultural differences become a source of conflict, the cycle of violence is not easily stopped.

Compared to Yugoslavia, other countries shown in Figure 35-1 have dealt with cultural-centrifugal forces more successfully. Among these are Moldova, Lithuania, and Ukraine. But elsewhere in the world devolutionary pressures have produced costly wars. Cultural forces lie at the heart of the decades-long conflict between the Muslim North and the non-Muslim South in Sudan, Africa. And similar forces have given rise to a seemingly endless civil war in Sri Lanka, South Asia, where the Sinhalese (Buddhist) majority has been unable to suppress or to accommodate the demands of the Tamil (Hindu) minority for an independent state. Thus cultural forces weaken the fabric of many states in today's global political framework.

Economic Forces

Devolutionary pressures often arise from a combination of sources. In Catalonia, for example, culture is a powerful force, but Catalonians also cite economics: with about 6 percent of Spain's territory and just 17 percent of its population, Catalonia produces some 25 percent of all Spanish exports by value and 40 percent of its industrial exports. Such economic strength lends weight to devolutionary demands based on culture as well as history.

Purely economic forces are at work in Italy and France, however. In Italy demands for autonomy for Sardinia are a result of the island's economic circumstances, with accusations of neglect by the government in Rome high on the list of grievances. But Italy faces more serious devolutionary forces on its mainland peninsula. One is the growing regional disparity between north and south. The Mezzogiorno region lies to the south, below the Ancona Line (an imaginary border extending from Rome to the Adriatic coast at Ancona). The richer, industrialized North stands in sharp contrast to this poorer, agrarian South. Despite the large subsidies granted to the Mezzogiorno, the development gap between the North, very much a part of the European core, and the South, the embodiment of the periphery, has been widening. Some politicans have exploited widespread impatience with this situation by forming organizations to promote northern interests, including devolution. The most recent of these organizations was the Northern League, which demanded independence for a proposed state called Padania, which would comprise most of Italy north of the Po River. After a surge of enthusiasm, the Padania campaign faltered. But it did push the Italian government to give more rights to the country's regions, moving it toward a more federal system. While the Northern League's efforts fell short, the fundamental reasons behind its temporary attainments have not disappeared, and Italy will confront devolutionary forces again.

Even France, often cited as the model nation-state, must cope with devolutionary forces. Its chief problem lies on the island of Corsica, where a small minority of the population of about 250,000 are engaged in a campaign for goals ranging from outright independence to greater autonomy. When this campaign began, about 25 years ago, it might have been called a cultural crusade; the activists published pamphlets that described Corsica (taken by the French from the Genoese in 1768) as a colony. Over time, however, nationalism seems to have given way to pragmatism: in return for abandoning their violent tactics, the activists want power and money. The economy has become the key issue.

Corsica has been a significant problem for France. In 1996 bombs planted by Corsicans damaged a courthouse in Aix-en-Provence and destroyed the offices of the Mayor of Bordeaux. In Corsica itself there were over 600 bomb attacks that year, and the island's tourist economy has been devastated. The fear of a more serious spillover of violence onto the mainland has compelled the French government to intensify its search for a solution.

Europe is not alone in confronting economic forces leading to devolution. During the 1990s a devolutionary movement arose in Brazil that was rooted in economics. As in northern Italy, a separatist movement arose in a well-defined region of the country (the three southernmost States of Rio Grande do Sul, Santa Catarina, and Parana). Southerners, complaining that their tax money was being misspent by the government on assistance in Amazonia, found a leader, manufactured a flag, and demanded independence for their Republic of the Pampas. The government responded by outlawing the separatists' political party, but the issue continues to affect Brazilian politics. It seems that no country is immune from devolutionary pressures.

Spatial Factors

We have seen how political decisions and cultural and economic forces can generate devolutionary processes in states. If devolutionary events have one feature in common, it is that they occur on the margins of states. Note that every one of the devolution-affected areas shown in Figure 35-1 lies on a coast or on a boundary. Distance, remoteness, and peripheral location are allies of devolution. The areas most likely to be affected are those that lie far from the national capital, are separated by water, desert, or mountains from the center of power, and adjoin neighbors that may support separatist objectives.

Note also that many islands are subject to devolutionary processes: Corsica (France), Sardinia (Italy), Taiwan (China), Singapore (Malaysia), Zanzibar (Tanzania), Jolo (Philippines), Puerto Rico (USA), Mayotte (Comoros), Cyprus, and Sri Lanka are notable examples. As this list indicates, some of these islands became independent states, while others were divided during devolution. Insularity has obvious advantages for separatist movements.

It is therefore not surprising that the United States faces its most serious devolutionary pressures on the islands of Hawai'i. While the United States has not experienced devolutionary stresses of the kind faced by Canada, it is not immune to these forces. There is a small but vocal pro-independence movement in Puerto Rico; some people in the Northwest occasionally broach the notion of a "Cascadia" that would consist of Oregon, Washington, and the Canadian province of British Columbia. But the first real brush with devolution may come in Hawai'i. In 1993, the hundred-year anniversary of the U.S. annexation of Hawai'i, a vocal minority of native Hawai'ians and their sympathizers demanded the return of rights lost during the "occupation." These demands included the right to reestablish a Hawai'ian state (before its annexation Hawai'i was a Polynesian kingdom) on several of the smaller islands. Ultimately, the island of Kauai, or at least a significant part of that island, which is considered ancestral land, would become a component of this parallel Hawai'ian state.

At present, the native Hawai'ians do not have the numbers, resources, or influence to achieve their separatist aims. The potential for some form of separation between Hawai'i and the mainland United States does exist, however. The political geographer S. B. Cohen theorized in 1991 that political entities situated in border zones between geopolitical power cores may become ***gateway states***, absorbing and assimilating diverse cultures and traditions and emerging as new entities, no longer dominated by one or the other. Hawai'i, he suggests, is a candidate for this status.

Spatial factors, then, can play a significant role in starting and sustaining devolutionary processes. Certainly they contributed to the devolution of Yugoslavia: remote frontiers and isolated valleys helped forge the complex cultural mosaic of the area in the first place, and during the country's breakup these same locales served as refuges for the adversaries who destroyed the state. Physical-geographic factors thus are a key ingredient in the devolutionary process.

From the field notes

"As I drove along a main road through a Honolulu suburb I noticed that numerous houses had the Hawai'i State flag flying upside down. I knocked on the door of this house and asked the homeowner why he was treating the State flag this way. He invited me in and we talked for more than an hour. 'This is 1993,' he said, 'and we native Hawai'ians are letting the State government and the country know that we haven't forgotten the annexation by the United States of our kingdom. I don't accept it, and we want territory to plant our flag and keep our traditions alive. Why don't you drive past the royal palace, and you'll see that we mean it.' He was right. The Iolani Palace, where the Hawai'ians' last monarch, Queen Liliuokalani, reigned until she was deposed by a group of American businessmen in 1893, was draped in black for all of Honolulu to see. Here was a touch of devolutionary stress on American soil."

◆ THE DEVOLUTION OF THE SOVIET UNION

Devolution, as we have seen, is occurring throughout the world. Governments have tried various methods to deal with the forces that drive the process, methods ranging from suppression to accommodation.

In most of the affected states, the problem remains domestic; that is, it has little or no impact on the world at large. But we must take note of one exception. When a powerful combination of political, cultural, and economic forces caused the devolution of the Soviet Union, the world was transformed.

For nearly a half-century the Soviet Union had been one of the world's two superpowers, so that, geopolitically, the world was *bipolar*. In the second half of the twentieth century the world order was determined by the relationship between Moscow and Washington. This relationship was largely competitive. In what became known as the *Cold War*, each superpower tried to hamper the other against a dangerous background of nuclear armaments. One aspect of the Cold War was a relentless arms race.

In the late 1980s an explosion of centrifugal forces in the multicultural, multinational, economically troubled Soviet Union created the conditions for sudden devolution. The first geopolitical result was the weakening of Moscow's control over the countries of Eastern Europe. The consequences were far-reaching: the Berlin Wall, symbol of communist oppression, came down, communist-ruled East Germany was freed and reunited with West Germany, and communist parties from Poland to Bulgaria lost their primacy.

The most important developments, however, occurred in the Soviet Union itself. Devolutionary forces grew rapidly throughout the empire, and its component parts asserted their independence (Fig. 35-3). In reality, the Soviet Union had been a Russian Empire, and now Russia itself, along with its 14 peripheral republics, emerged as a new, independent state. As the map shows, the Soviet Union's rapid devolution affected a huge swath of Eurasia from the Baltic Sea to Turkestan.

Even as the Soviet Union broke up, Russian leaders tried to replace the Soviet framework with a supranational entity called the Commonwealth of Independent States (CIS) with headquarters in Minsk (capital of Belarus). After some initial hesitation, all but the three Baltic states and Georgia joined the CIS (and Georgia was later forced to join after Russia helped it end a civil war). But when the Soviet flag was lowered for the last time on Christmas Day 1991, the CIS was but a skeleton organization, unable to replace what had been a cohesive empire.

The process of devolution did not stop here. While the 15 Soviet republics had become independent states, each of them also confronted centrifugal forces arising from ethnic, historic, cultural, and economic circumstances. It appeared unlikely that the Commonwealth of Independent States would withstand these divisive pressures. But the individual republics were also experiencing economic problems while trying to adjust politically. Large ethnic Russian minorities remained in each republic, as did Russian soldiers. Minorities that had been exiled by communist dictators demanded to be allowed to return home—where others had taken their homes and land. Old ethnic animosities came to the surface. Soon Muslim Azerbaijan and Christian Armenia, both in Transcaucasia (between the Black and Caspian Seas), were in a state of armed conflict.

The Near-Abroad

The presence of as many as 25 million Russians in the former Soviet Republics along Russia's rim, combined with political instability and even armed conflict, created a sphere of involvement that the Russians called their ***Near-Abroad***. The implication is that Russia's national interest extends throughout the former Soviet Empire, and Russia has given substance to that notion by intervening in several countries of its Near-Abroad. In Georgia, also in the Transcaucasian region, a political crisis soon after independence led to a civil war. Even as this conflict raged, a separatist movement in the "republic" of Abkhazia in Georgia's northwest proclaimed independence. In the costly and bitter struggle that followed, Georgia's government was compelled to ask for Russian help. This help came at a price: a permanent Russian military presence on Georgian soil.

Russia also intervened in the republics of the former Soviet Central Asia (now again called Turkestan, its pre-Soviet name). Russian interests were challenged on several fronts. The most serious crisis arose in Tajikistan, where Russian forces sustained heavy losses trying to protect a pro-Russian government against insurgents from across the border in Afghanistan.

The international community appears to recognize Russia's primacy in the Near-Abroad, in part because Moscow's problems there were caused by the Soviet communists whose system the Russians have rejected. The Soviet planners had created not only an economic system doomed to failure, but also a political framework destined to collapse. Boundaries were superimposed on a complex cultural landscape, and the friction these boundaries created was ruthlessly suppressed. Within Russia itself, 16 so-called Autonomous Soviet Socialist Republics had been designated as homelands for certain minorities—but only *some* minorities (Fig. 35-3). As times changed, and economic development occurred, population shifts took place. The Soviet national planners kept modifying the system. Boundaries were shifted in order to reward, punish, or control. Boundaries that *should* have been established (for example, between the Russian and Kazakh parts of Kazakhstan) were not. The Soviets thus left their empire with a political-geographic legacy that will remain problematic for generations to come.

The Devolution of Russia

Not only the Near-Abroad, but also Russia itself was burdened by a political-geographic system that was bound to present difficulties for the new democratic government in Moscow. Soon after the Russian tricolor

replaced the Soviet hammer and sickle above the Kremlin, leaders of the internal "republics" began to demand more autonomy, more control over their "own" resources and facilities, and, in some instances, more territory. When the Soviet Union was dissolved, there were 16 such republics within Russia, but other entities immediately demanded similar status. Within four years, the Russian Parliament had agreed to recognize five additional republics (one of which, Chechno-Ingushetia, was fragmented into two republics, Chechnya and Ingushetia).

Chechnya, in the Muslim-populated Caucasus,

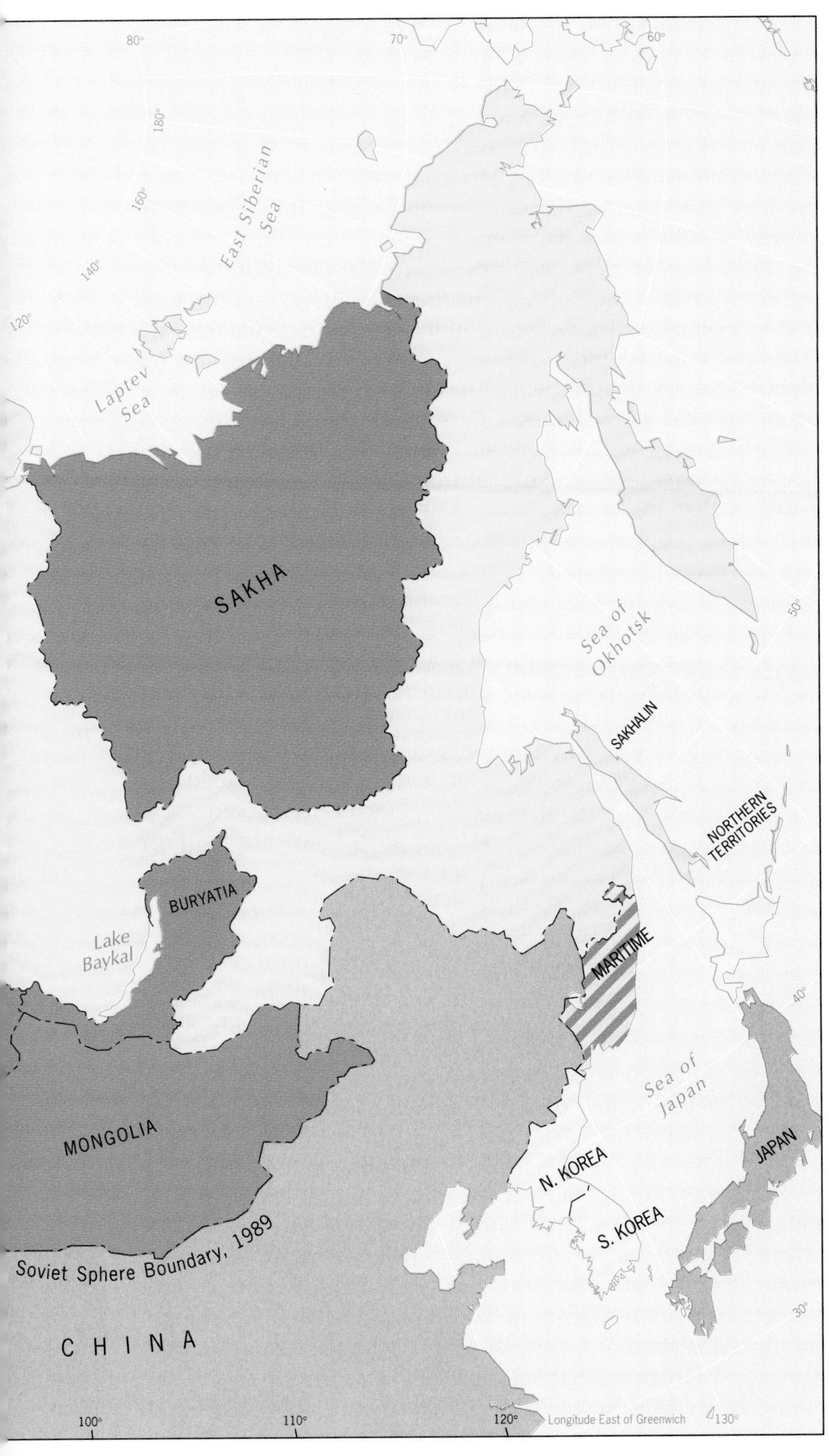

Figure 35-3 Devolution of the Soviet Union. Devolution occurred in all parts of the Soviet Union during the 1990s. *Source: From a map in H. J. de Blij and P. O. Muller*, Geography, Realms, Regions, and Concepts, *8th ed. (New York: Wiley, 1997).*

was to become Moscow's most serious devolutionary problem. Cultural forces gave rise to an anti-Russian rebellion that Russian forces proved unable to subdue. The republic's infrastructure, including its capital, Groznyy, was almost totally destroyed. In 1998 the situation was stalemated, with Chechnya having declared itself independent and Moscow refusing to acknowledge it.

The map suggests one reason for the strength of devolutionary forces in Russia: the country's vastness and the isolation of many of its population clusters. Once the process of devolution had been set in motion, the remoteness of republics and regions from Moscow seemed to perpetuate it. In Chechnya, Muslim separatists hid in the mountains of the Caucasus. In the Russian Far East, the region centered on the port of Vladivostok, ten time zones removed from the capital, demanded autonomous status, refused to pay taxes to Moscow, and argued that Russian bureaucratic constraints were ruining its chances to participate in Pacific Rim economic growth.

The new Russia is a federal state, and not just in name. Moscow's response to devolutionary pressures has been to award ever-greater power to the 21 republics and 68 regions that constitute the federal framework—thus averting a repeat of the disaster in Chechnya. In early 1998, it was clear that Russia's devolution had not yet run its course, and like other governments facing centrifugal social forces, Russia's leaders continued to seek ways to accommodate the pressure and protect the coherence of the state.

It is a measure of the importance of the Soviet Union's devolution that this giant country, territorially the largest in the world and with a population that ranked third, after China and India, broke into 15 parts of which the largest, Russia, still has more land than any other—but whose population now ranks sixth, after those of the United States, Indonesia, and Brazil. Russia today has turned inward, trying to reorganize and to control the disruptive forces of devolution. It still possesses a large arsenal of weapons, but its power to influence world affairs has dwindled, a casualty of the devolutionary events set in motion in the 1980s.

◆ THE STATE IN THE NEW WORLD ORDER

As we have learned, the state, the crucial building block in the global international framework, is vulnerable to many destructive forces. The state's weaknesses are underscored by the growing power of regions, provinces, States, and other internal entities to act independently of the national government. With or without the approval of central governments, provinces such as Catalonia, Quebec, Baden-Württemberg (Germany), Lombardy (Italy), Tatarstan (Russia), and many others have gained much more than internal autonomy: they have become economic, and to some degree political, actors on the international stage. And the cities that anchor these provinces, such as Barcelona, Stuttgart, Milan, and Lyon in Europe, Mumbai in India, and Guangzhou in China, are evolving into modern versions of the historic city-state.

Powerful provinces and their thriving urban cores engage in their own foreign commercial policies and, in some cases, pursue their own political goals as well. France's second city, Lyon, is a good example. Lyon is at the center of the Rhône-Alpes region; today it does more than twice as much business with northern Italy than with other parts of France. And Lyon's city government has opened nearly a dozen legations around the world, from Toronto and Seattle to Shanghai and Singapore. Quebec has a mission in Paris called *Maison Quebec* that draws more visitors than the official Canadian embassy in that city.

What does this portend for the future of the state? In this age of information highways, cross-border trade and travel, and global capital movements, national boundaries are losing their relevance and national governments are becoming less dominant in what were traditionally seen as national affairs. Economic activities are also being conducted on a global basis, making national boundaries far less important than in the past.

But in a different arena, national capitals and national governments are still key components of the global system. In the world of geopolitics, the state remains fundamental. States, not provinces or regions, maintain armed forces and use them in the national interest. States, not provinces or regions, enter into multinational military alliances to pursue common security goals. Perhaps most important, states continue to be the units we most frequently use to divide up the world—with all that implies for the decisions that are made and the actions that follow from those decisions.

Given these contradictions, it is not surprising that states are entering into a growing number of associations, alliances, and unions of the kind discussed in Part Eight. Multilateral relationships enhance security while supporting the economic initiatives of provinces and regions within the member states. But note that the great majority of supranational alliances bind together states that lie *within* geographic realms, not *among* them. The European Union's national boundaries may be overshadowed by economic interests, but the Christian states of Europe will have great difficulty accepting Muslim Turkey into their union, no matter how secular Turkey may be. From Mercosur (South America) to the Southern African Development Community (SADC) and from the Arab League to the Association of Southeast Asian Nations (ASEAN), supranationalism is taking on a regional form.

This may give us a glimpse of the New World Order the twenty-first century will bring. Today only one state can be described as a superpower, but American dominance will not last forever. If the state continues to be weakened, something larger may replace it, a kind of cultural umbrella that would encompass clusters of former states bound together by history, tradition, common economic interests, and mutual geopolitical advantage. Thus might arise a multipolar world composed of as many as five or six such clusters, each under the sway of one or several dominant powers.

Not all of the world's states may come under such regional domination. In particular, the states of Africa lie outside a New World Order dominated by China, India, Russia, Europe, and the United States. During the Cold War, African states became arenas of conflict fueled by the United States and the Soviet Union, so-called proxy wars that did huge amounts of damage. In the future African states may again become battlegrounds for conflicts between major powers.

Toward a New World Order

Devolution is the direct result of a vision that has diffused throughout the world: a vision of greater autonomy or independence for ethnic or cultural groups wishing to overcome real or perceived threats to their well-being or security. From native Hawai'ians to New Zealand's Maori, from Canada's Cree to Australia's Aboriginal peoples, communities are seeking previously unimagined rights and freedoms. National governments often misjudge the power of such movements or lack adequate means for dealing with them. The "window" for negotiation may be very small, and once a demand translates into violent action, it is very difficult to end the cycle of conflict.

Other major transformations are also changing our world. Prominent among these are globalization, notions of democracy, and the growing influence of religion.

Globalization The twentieth century has seen a vast spatial expansion of economic, social, and cultural interactions. These interactions affect some places more than others, but they affect such large portions of the Earth's surface that they are grouped together under the term ***globalization***. Globalization is most commonly seen as an economic phenomenon. As we saw in Chapter 24, financial and trade links now tie together peoples in distant places, and economic developments in one part of the globe can have an immediate impact on areas thousands of miles away. At the same time, the state's ability, or at least willingness, to exert control over globalized economic relations is increasingly constrained. Multinational corporations operating in a transnational legal and political environment have assumed major roles in human affairs. Financial instruments move across international boundaries with no difficulty. Investments made on one continent can and do affect the economic prospects of others.

States play an important role in these developments. They provide the territorial foundation from which producers and consumers still operate, and they continue to exert considerable regulatory powers. But economic globalization makes it increasingly difficult for the state to control economic relations. States are responding to this situation in a variety of ways, with some giving up traditional regulatory powers and others seeking to insulate themselves from the international economy. Still others are working to build supranational economic blocs that they hope will help them cope with an increasingly globalized world. The impacts of many of these developments are as yet uncertain, but it is increasingly clear that states are no longer as fundamental to international society as they once were.

The state's traditional position is being further eroded by the globalization of social and cultural relations. Networks of interaction are being constructed in ways that do not correspond to the map of states. When unrest breaks out in southern Mexico, for example, activists use the Internet to contact interested people throughout the world. Scholars and researchers in different countries work together in teams. Increased mobility has brought individuals from far-flung places into much closer contact than before. Paralleling all this change is the spread of popular culture in ways that make national boundaries virtually meaningless. The Spice Girls are all the rage in South Africa and Australia; fashions developed in northern Italy are hot items among Japanese tourists visiting Hawai'i; Thai restaurants are found in towns and cities across the United States; countless Russian women hurry home to watch the next episode of soap operas made in Mexico; and movies produced in Hollywood are seen on screens from Mumbai to Santiago.

Globalization has produced economic, social, and cultural geographies that look less and less like the map of states. At the same time, the traditional sovereign authority of the world's 200-odd states is being increasingly eroded. The state system is unlikely to disappear anytime soon, but the New World Order is likely to be one in which the spatial distribution of power is more complex than suggested by the traditional map of states. Describing that spatial distribution will be a challenge for geographers for generations to come.

Notions of Democracy While it is defined and practiced in various ways, the idea of ***democracy*** is found throughout the world. Visions of a democratic China led to the disastrous Tiananmen Square massacre in June 1989, in which communist authorities crushed a prodemocracy movement of students and workers. A desire to leave Hong Kong's population with better representation when China took over in 1997 finally led the British governor of the colony to democratize the political system there, a belated conversion that had the effect of insulting the Chinese. South Africa achieved a triumph for democracy when it held universal elections of April 1994, soon after the dismantling of *Apartheid*. From Malawi to Taiwan and from Fiji to Argentina, a global movement for democracy is under way. Not all regions of the world are equally affected: representative government has made little progress in the North African-Southwest Asian realm, for example.

When it comes to democracy, vision and practice are two different things. Some African ruling elites see no contradiction in the term *one-party democracy*, arguing that the multiple parties in many Western countries cover a narrower political spectrum than many a single African party does. Elsewhere, as in Singapore, those in control place strict limits on democratic practice. But even in countries where little progress has been made toward representative government (Indonesia, Saudi Arabia, Myanmar) the idea of democracy still stirs the hopes of millions.

Even well-functioning democracies have voters or groups of voters who feel underrepresented or even disenfranchised. Such voters do not believe that their votes can affect the course of affairs. However, there are ways to empower such voters in state and local elections (see "Focus on: Electoral Geography in Chapter 26"). By manipulating the system, a national government can ensure that state and local elections give minority voters an opportunity to influence the outcome. This crucial feature of a well-functioning democracy has the effect of involving voters who otherwise might feel alienated.

From the field notes

"The long line of cars waiting to cross from Germany into Poland provides a strong reminder of what borders once were like in western Europe—but are no longer. And the Polish car stacked high with household goods symbolizes the attempts of eastern Europeans to adjust to a rapidly changing world. Many take goods produced cheaply in Eastern Europe to sell in open markets in the West, and then return with products that are difficult to obtain or expensive in the home country."

The Growing Influence of Religion Another global phenomenon with major implications for a future world order is the revival of religion. In Chapter 12 we noted the continuing diffusion of the major faiths, especially Islam, and the renaissance of the Russian Christian churches in the post–Soviet era. This is another contrast in a world of contradictions: even in an era of science and secularism, millions of people are turning to religion to make sense of their lives and goals.

Religious fundamentalism appeals to people in societies where the prospects for democracy are dim or oppression seems inescapable. An upsurge of Shiite fundamentalism, led by an exiled *ayatollah*, ousted the Shah of Iran and transformed the political geography of a wider region. In Algeria, Islamic fundamentalists were poised to gain majority rule through democratic elections in 1992, and the country faced the prospect of an Islamic republic that would dismantle democratic institutions. The elections were canceled, and Algeria has been wracked by violence ever since. In Egypt, Islamic fundamentalists attack the government for what they regard as godless excesses and oppression, and seek to destabilize the state by destroying its tourist industry. In Sudan, the Islamic regime extended Islam's severe *sharia* criminal law to both Muslim and non-Muslim communities, causing a devolutionary conflict. In Malaysia, calls for the implementation of *sharia* law have been heard in Parliament.

None of this should lead us to conclude that the renewal of fundamentalism is exclusively or even primarily an Islamic phenomenon. Undoubtedly, the youngest of the major religions is the most energetic today, but the attraction of fundamentalism can also be observed among Christians, Hindus, Buddhists, and other believers virtually everywhere. In the United States, the evidence can be seen at the doors of abortion clinics and on the floors of political conventions, where the "religious right" has become a potent force. In India, the emergence of political parties that openly promote Hindu fundamentalism (including the powerful Bharatiya Janata Party) is a significant development. In Russia, the revival of Christian churches after seven decades of official atheism is contributing to a resurgence of political conservatism and nationalism.

Even China is affected by religious revival as controls over proselytizing have been relaxed.

Redrawing the Map

To summarize: the New World Order must come about while subnational groups strive for independence, economic and social relations are being organized at ever larger scales, notions of democracy gain strength everywhere, and religious forces influence political and social conditions. These conditions all reflect *weaknesses of the state system*, a major obstacle to achieving a future stable world order. Both supranationalism and devolution are signs of a search for alternatives, but neither process is likely to have a satisfactory outcome. Most supranational unions remain weak and do not require member states to give up much sovereignty. The products of devolution (Slovakia, Croatia, Eritrea, Moldova) in most cases do not appear to be viable alternatives to the state as we know it.

Another factor standing in the way of a New World Order is the world's *antiquated boundary framework*. We are entering the twenty-first century with a boundary system rooted in the nineteenth, which is a recipe for disorder. Changes in the social and economic geographies of entire regions have made existing boundaries irrelevant or worse. Decolonization and the demise of Soviet communism turned administrative borders into international boundaries. Many cannot function as such, yet the notion that conflicts must be resolved "within established borders" still prevails.

We have already noted the impact of cross-border migrations and the media-driven flow of ideas and images. Another influence comes from what has become known as the *domino theory*, which holds that regional destabilization results from states' proximity to one another (see "Focus on: The Domino Theory"). Also significant is the *flow of weapons* and the diffusion of nuclear arms in the modern world. During the Cold War, both superpowers supplied their allies with weaponry, and numerous smaller arms manufacturers contributed further to the diffusion of weapons. As a result, when a subnational group wishes to pursue its political goals by violent means there is no shortage of weapons to use in doing so. This obviously poses a grave threat to any future world order; any failure to agree can quickly escalate into armed conflict.

Even more critical is the ongoing *diffusion of nuclear technology*. Nuclear weapons give even small states the ability to inflict massive damage on larger and distant adversaries. Combined with missile technology, this undoubtedly is the most serious danger the world faces, which is why the United Nations in-

Focus On

The Domino Theory

During the Indochina War (1964–1975) the United States attempted to contain communist expansion by supporting the efforts of the government of South Vietnam to defeat communist insurgents. Soon the war engulfed North Vietnam as U.S. bombers attacked targets north of the border between North and South. In its later phases the conflict spilled over into Laos and Cambodia. In addition, U.S. warplanes took off from bases in Thailand. Like dominoes, one country after another fell to the ravages of war or was threatened.

Some scholars warned that this domino effect could eventually affect not only Thailand but also Malaysia, Indonesia, and Burma (today Myanmar): the whole Southeast Asian realm, they predicted, could be destabilized. But as we know, that did not happen. The war remained confined to Indochina. And the domino "theory" seemed invalid.

But is the theory totally without merit? Some political geographers continue to define this idea in terms of communist activity. However, communist insurgency is only one way in which a country may be destabilized. Right-wing rebellion (Nicaragua's Contras), ethnic conflict (Bosnia-Herzegovina), religious extremism (Algeria), and even economic and environmental causes (Somalia) can create havoc in a country. Properly defined, the ***domino theory*** holds that destabilization from any cause in one country can result in the collapse of order in a neighboring country, starting a chain of events that can affect a series of adjoining states in turn.

In fact, any visitor to Laos and especially to Cambodia will see the disastrous long-term impact of the "Vietnam" war on these countries and societies; these dominoes certainly fell. Today Indochina is relatively stable (although Cambodia suffers from sporadic strife). Now the dominoes are falling in Eastern Europe. Look at the map again: the struggle in the former Yugoslavia has moved from Slovenia to Croatia and on to Bosnia-Herzegovina and Serbia-Montenegro, and threatens to engulf Kosovo, Macedonia, Albania, and perhaps even Greece and Turkey. In 1994–1995 the United Nations attempted to contain the conflicts in the former Yugoslavia and prevent them from spreading to Kosovo and beyond. Thus there may be something to the domino theory after all.

sisted on the dismantling of Iraq's nuclear capacity after the 1991 war and why North Korea's apparent progress in the nuclear arms arena in the mid-1990s caused President Clinton to threaten military action. While it was always known that the former Soviet Union and several Western powers possessed nuclear bombs and the missiles to deliver them to enemy targets, the nuclear capabilities of other countries have been carefully guarded secrets. Thus in 1977, when reports of Iraq's nuclear program reached Israel, the Israelis attacked. But Israel itself is believed to possess a nuclear arsenal; South Africa was building one during the *apartheid* period; India and Pakistan appear to be joining the nuclear club; and there are concerns over Iran's potential as a nuclear power. As nuclear weapons became smaller and "tactical" nuclear arms were developed, the threat of nuclear weapons sales had to be taken seriously. It is now possible for a hostile state to purchase the power with which to blackmail the world.

The foregoing discussion underscores the risks that will be present if a New World Order comes about by any means other than consensus. Earlier we recorded the outlines of a four-cornered New World Order in which the United States, a united Europe, a stable Russia, and a developing China might create a mutually beneficial balance of power. Among these four powers, only the United States, is not undergoing a major transition. Whether supranationalism in Europe will eventually generate a United States of Europe is uncertain. The Russian federation, still a superpower in terms of armaments but dangerously weak at the center, also has an unclear future. Nor is the fate of China assured: failure of communist rule or instability caused by regional economic disparities may set it back. Expectations of a four-power New World Order in the twenty-first century may therefore be premature.

We live on a small, crowded, environmentally changing, economically disparate, politically unstable planet. To understand its geography is to marvel at its diversity, capacity, and continuity. Five billion years ago, the Earth was about to be born. Five million years ago, our ancestral lineage had been established. Five thousand years ago, the first cities worthy of the name, and the first complex states, had come into existence. Five hundred years ago, Europe made its fateful contact with the Americas. Fifty years ago, the world emerged from its most devastating war. Five years ago, the world was reorganizing in the aftermath of the Cold War. Where will the world be five years from now, in the early years of a new century?

Still, we expect, searching for a just and durable World Order.

◆ KEY TERMS ◆

democracy
devolution
domino theory
gateway state
geopolitics
globalization
Near-Abroad
New World Order
religious fundamentalism

◆ APPLYING GEOGRAPHIC KNOWLEDGE ◆

1. You are a member of the staff of a multinational corporation doing business in several European countries. Your management has been used to dealing with governments in the capitals of several countries including Portugal, the Netherlands, Poland, and Hungary. But now there are plans to expand operations into Spain at Barcelona, Belgium at Antwerp, the United Kingdom at Edinburgh, and France at Ajaccio. What advice will you provide, based on your knowledge of devolution?

2. Globalization and devolution are changing the role of the state in the world of today—and of the future. Using your knowledge of political and economic geography and geopolitics, try to do what Mackinder did a century ago: formulate a model for the world of the next century. Do globalization and devolution preclude the emergence of superpower-states? Can you envisage circumstances that might reverse these two processes and strengthen the state? Is Eurasia still the key, as Mackinder and Spykman argued?

Part Ten
COPING WITH A RAPIDLY CHANGING WORLD

Should all countries be subject to the same rules? Or should the poorer countries be exempt from some of the more costly regulations? And can an effective response be organized without undermining state sovereignty? The transnational character of many environmental problems poses a serious challenge to the modern state system. Organizing effective responses to global environmental problems requires international institutions with powers and authorities that have been traditionally reserved for states. As international institutions take on this critical role, they risk creating serious hardships if all places are treated alike. Instead, geographical variations in modes of livelihood, economic wealth, and social stability are unavoidable parts of the picture. In a world of increasingly globalized networks and problems, geography does not disappear. Instead, it becomes a profoundly important element of any effort to comprehend and confront changing international orders.

◆ SELECTED BIBLIOGRAPHY ◆

Part Ten Coping with a Rapidly Changing World

Alonso, W., & Starr, P., eds. *The Politics of Numbers* (New York: Russell Sage, 1987).

Bennett, R., & Estall, R., eds. *Global Change and Challenge: Geography for the 1990s* (New York: Routledge, 1991).

Berardi, G. M., ed. *World Food, Population and Development* (Totowa, N.J..: Rowman & Allanheld, 1985).

Bremmer, I., & Taras, R., ed. *New State, New Politics: Building the Post–Soviet Nations* (Cambridge: Cambridge University Press, 1997).

Brown, L., & Wolf, E. *Soil Erosion: Quiet Crisis in the World Economy* (Washington, D.C., Paper No. 60, 1984).

Brown, L. R., et al. *State of the World* (New York: W. W. Norton, Annual).

Clarke, J., ed. *Geography and Population: Approaches and Applications* (Elmsford, N.Y.: Pergamon Press, 1984).

COHMAP members. "Climatic Changes of the Last 18,000 Years: Observations and Model Simulations." *Science* 241 (1988), pp. 1043–1052.

Demko, G. J., & Wood, W. B. *Reordering the World: Geopolitical Perspectives on the 21st Century* (Boulder, Colo.: Westview Press, 2nd ed., 1998).

Douglas, I., Huggett, R., & Robinson, M., eds. *Companion Encyclopedia of Geography: The Environment and Humankind* (New York: Routledge, 1996).

Ehrlich, P., & Ehrlich, A. *The Population Explosion* (New York: Simon & Schuster, 1990).

Ehrlich, P., & Ehrlich, A. *Healing the Planet: Strategies for Resolving the Environmental Crisis* (Reading, Mass.: Addison-Wesley, 1991).

Guéhenno, J.-M. *The End of the Nation-State* (Minneapolis: University of Minnesota Press, trans. V. Elliott, 1995).

Heer, D. M., & Grigsby, J. S. *Society and Population* (Englewood Cliffs, N.J.: Prentice-Hall, 2nd ed., 1992).

Heywood, V. H., ed. *Global Biodiversity Assessment* (Cambridge: Cambridge University Press, 1995).

Huntington, S. P. *The Clash of Civilizations and the Remaking of World Order* (New York: Simon & Schuster, 1996).

Intergovernmental Panel on Climate Change. *Climate Change 1995: The Science of Climate Change.* Contributions of Working Group I, edited by J. T. Houghton, et al. (Cambridge: Cambridge University Press, 1996).

Intergovernmental Panel on Climate Change. *Climate Change 1995: Impacts, Adaptations and Mitigation of Climate Change: Scientific-Technical Analyses.* Contributions of Working Group II, edited by R. T. Watson, M. C. Zinyowera, and R. H. Moss (Cambridge: Cambridge University Press, 1996).

Intergovernmental Panel on Climate Change. *Climate Change 1995: Economic and Social Dimensions of Climate Change.* Contributions of Working Group III, edited by J. P. Bruce, H. Lee, and E. F. Haites (Cambridge: Cambridge University Press, 1996).

Johnston, R. J. *Nature, State, and Economy: A Political Economy of the Environment* (New York: John Wiley & Sons, 2nd ed., 1996).

Johnston, R. J., Taylor, P. J., and Watts, M. J., eds. *Geographies of Global Change: Remapping the World in the Late Twentieth Century* (Oxford: Blackwell, 1995).

Jordan, A. "Paying the Incremental Costs of Global Environmental Protection: The Evolving Role of GEF." *Environment* 36 (1994), 12–26.

Kates, R. W. "Sustaining Life on the Earth," *Scientific American* 271 (1994), pp. 114–122.

Lewis, M. W., & Wigen, K. E. *The Myth of Continents: A Critique of Metageography* (Berkeley, Calif.: University of California Press, 1997).

Marsh, G. P. *Man and Nature* (Cambridge, Mass.: Belknap Press of Harvard University Press, 1965).

Narendra, P. S., Rietbergen, S., Heimo, C. R., and Patel, J., eds. *A Strategy for the Forest Sector in Sub-Saharan Africa.* World Bank Technical Paper no. 251, Africa Technical Department Series (Washington, D.C.: The World Bank, 1994).

Organization for Economic Co-operation and Development. *The State of the Environment 1985* (Paris: Organization for Economic Co-operation and Development, 1985).

Park, C. C. *Tropical Rainforests* (New York: Routledge, 1992).

Population Reference Bureau. *1997 World Population Data Sheet* (Washington, D.C., 1997).

Preston, S. H., ed. *World Population: Approaching the Year 2000.* Special edition of the *Annals of the American Academy of Political and Social Science,* July 1990.

Roberts, G. *Population Policy: Contemporary Issues* (New York: Praeger, 1990).

Schrijver, N. *Sovereignty over Natural Resources: Balancing Rights and Duties* (Cambridge: Cambridge University Press, 1997).

Shafer, S., & Murphy, A. B. "The Territorial Strategies of International Governmental Organizations: Implications for Environment and Development," *Global Governance,* forthcoming.

Simmons, I. G. "Humanity's Resources." In Douglas, I., Huggett, R., & Robinson, M., eds. *The Companion Encyclopedia of Geography: The Environment and Humankind* (New York: Routledge, 1996).

Taylor, P. J. *The Way the World Works: World Hegemony to World Impasse* (New York: John Wiley & Sons, 1996).

Teitelbaum, M. S., & Winter, J. M., eds. *Population and Resources in Western Intellectual Traditions* (Cambridge: Cambridge University Press, 1989).

Tuan, Y.-F. *Topophilia: A Study of Environmental Perception, Attitudes, and Values* (Englewood Cliffs, N.J.: Prentice-Hall, 1974).

Turner, B. L., II, Clarke, W. C., Kates, R. W., Richards, J. F., Mathews, J. T., & Meyer, W. B., eds. *The Earth as Transformed by Human Action: Global and Regional Changes in the Biosphere over the Past 300 Years* (Cambridge: Cambridge University Press with Clark University, 1990).

United Nations. *World Population Prospects,* 1994 (New York: United Nations, 1995).

United Nations. *World Population: Trends and Policies* (New York: United Nations, 1988).

Vitousek, P. M., Mooney, H. A., Lubchenco, J., & Melillo, J. M. "Human Domination of the Earth's Ecosystems," *Science* 277 (25), pp. 494–499.

World Bank. *World Development Report 1997* (New York: Oxford University Press, 1997).

World Bank. *World Development Report 1990: Poverty* (New York: Oxford University Press, 1990).

Young, O. R. *International Governance: Protecting the Environment in a Stateless Society* (Ithaca, N.Y.: Cornell University Press, 1994).

Resource A

Maps

The geographer's greatest ally is the map. Maps can present enormous amounts of information very effectively, and can be used to establish theories and solve problems. Furthermore, maps often are simply fascinating, revealing things no other medium can. It has been said that if a picture is worth a thousand words, then a map is worth a million. Alfred Wegener, nearly a century ago, drew his notion of a fragmenting supercontinent on an amateurish set of four maps purporting to show how continental drift happened. He is no longer cited, but that set of maps, which at a glance summarize his entire hypothesis, continues to be reproduced in many books around the world (Fig. R-1).

Maps can be fascinating, but they often do not get the attention they deserve. You may spend 20 minutes carefully reading a page of text, but how often have you spent 20 minutes with a page-size map, studying what it reveals? No caption and no paragraph of text can begin to summarize what a map may show; it is up to the reader to make the best use of it. For example, in the chapters on population issues we study several maps that depict the human condition by country, in terms of birth and death rates, infant mortality, calorie intake, life expectancy, and so on. In the text, we can refer only to highlights (and low points) on those maps. But make a point of looking beyond the main issue to get a sense of the global distributions these maps represent. It is part of an intangible but important process: to enhance your mental map of this world.

While on the topic of maps, we should remind ourselves that a map—any map—is an incomplete representation of reality. In the first place, the map is smaller than the real world it represents. Second, it must depict the curved surface of our world on a flat plane, for example, a page of this book. And third, it must contain symbols to convey the information that must be transmitted to the reader. These are the three fundamental properties of all maps: scale, projection, and symbols.

Understanding these basics helps us interpret maps while avoiding their pitfalls. Some maps look so convincing that we may not question them as we would a paragraph of text. Yet maps, by their very nature, to some extent distort reality. Most of the time, such distortion is necessary and does not invalidate the map's message. But some maps are drawn deliberately to mislead. Propaganda maps, for example, may exaggerate or distort reality to promote political

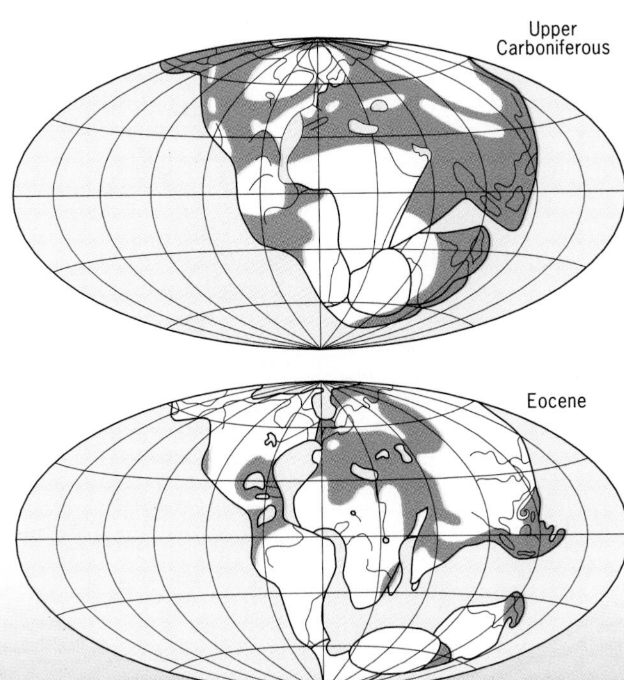

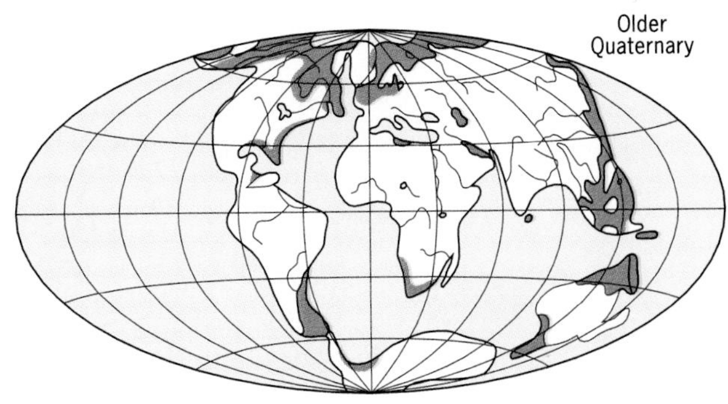

Figure R-1 A. Wegener's hypothesis of continental drift from his own sketch map in *The Origin of Continents and Oceans* (1914).

aims. We should be alert to cartographic mistakes when we read maps. The proper use of scale, projection, and symbolization ensures that a map is as accurate as it can be made.

◆ MAP SCALE

The *scale* of a map reveals how much the real world has been reduced to fit on the page or screen on which it appears. It is the ratio between an actual distance on the ground and the length given to that distance on the map, using the same units of measurement. This ratio is often represented as a fraction (e.g., 1:10,000 or 1/10,000). This means that one unit on the map represents 10,000 such units in the real world. If the unit is 1 inch, then an inch on the map represents 10,000 inches on the ground, or slightly more than 833 feet. (The metric system certainly makes things easier. One centimeter on the map would actually represent 10,000 cm or 100 meters.) Such a scale would be useful when mapping a city's downtown area, but it would be much too large for the map of an entire state. As the real-world area we want to map gets larger, we must make our map scale smaller. As small as the fraction 1/10,000 seems, it still is 10 times as large as 1/100,000, and 100 times as large as 1/1,000,000. If the world maps in this book had fractional scales, they would be even smaller. A large-scale map can contain much more detail and be far more representative of the real world than a small-scale map. Look at it this way: when we devote almost a full page of this book to a map of a major city (Fig. R-2), we are able to represent the layout of that city in considerable detail. But if the entire continental realm in which that city is located must be represented on a single page, the city becomes just a large dot on that small-scale map, and the detail is lost in favor of larger-area coverage (Fig. R-3). So the selection of scale depends on the objective of the map.

But when you examine the maps in this book, you will note that most, if not all, of them have scales that

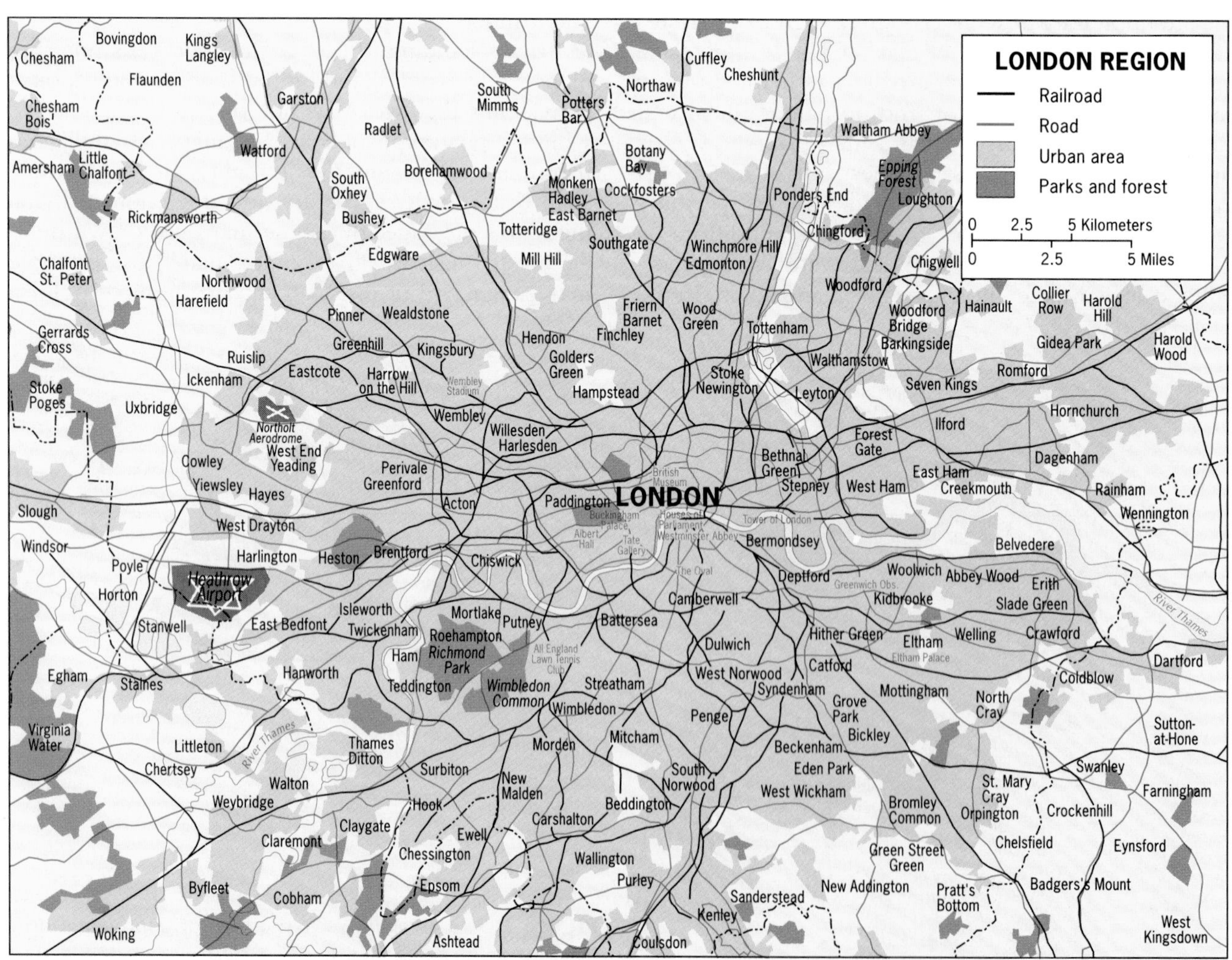

Figure R-2 The layout of a major city can be shown in considerable detail at this **large scale**.

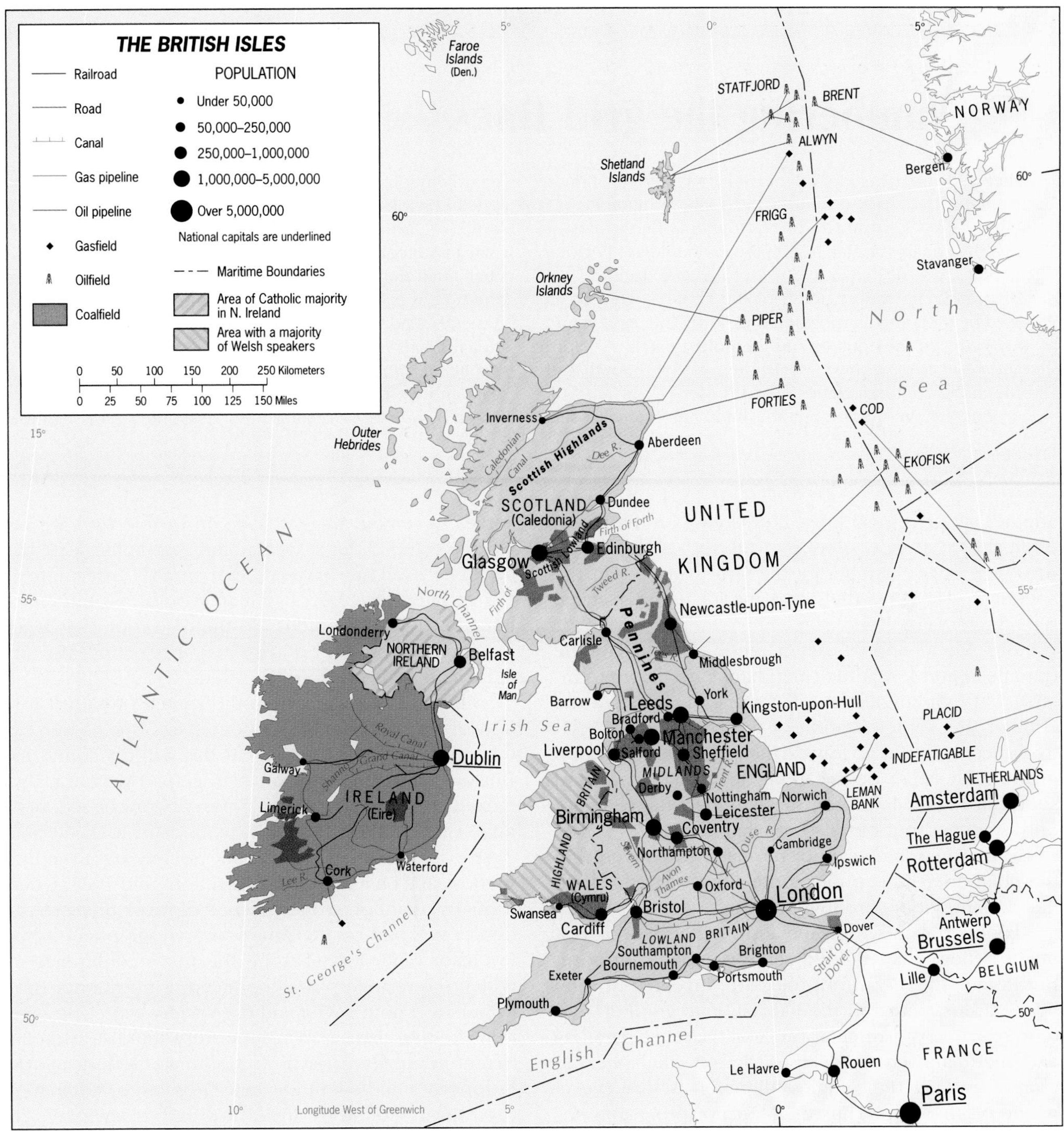

Figure R-3 Smaller scale allows display of larger area, but with less local detail.

are not given as ratios or fractions, but in graphic form. This method of representing map scale is convenient from several viewpoints. Using the edge of a piece of paper and marking the scale bar's length, the map reader can quickly—without calculation—determine approximate distances. And if a map is enlarged or reduced in reproduction, the scale bar is enlarged or reduced with it and remains accurate. That, of course, is not true of a ratio or fractional scale. Graphic scales, therefore, are preferred in this book.

◆ MAP PROJECTIONS

For centuries cartographers have faced the challenge of map projection—the representation of the spherical Earth, or part of it, on a flat surface. To get the job done, there had to be a frame of reference on the globe itself, a grid system that could be transferred to the flat page. Any modern globe shows that system: a set of horizontal lines, usually at 10-degree intervals north and south from the equator, called *parallels*, and

Numbering the grid lines

When cartographers girdled the globe with their imaginary grid lines, they had to identify each line by number, that is, by *degree.* For the (horizontal) latitude lines, that was easy: the equator, which bisects the Earth midway between the poles, was designated as 0° (zero degree) Latitude, and all parallels north and south of the equator were designated by their angular position (Fig. R-4). The parallel midway between the equator and the pole, thus, is 45° North Latitude in the Northern Hemisphere and 45° South Latitude in the Southern Hemisphere.

But the (vertical) longitude lines presented no such easy solution. Among the parallels, the equator is the only one to divide the Earth into equal halves, but *all* meridians do this. During the second half of the nineteenth century, maps with conflicting numbers multiplied, and it was clear that a solution was needed. The most powerful country at the time was Britain, and in 1884, international agreement was reached whereby the meridian drawn through the Royal Observatory in Greenwich, England, would be the *prime meridian,* 0° (zero degree) Longitude. All meridians east and west of the prime meridian could now be designated by number, from 0° to 180° East and West Longitude.

another set of vertical lines, converging on the poles, often shown at 15-degree intervals and called *meridians* (see box, "Numbering the Grid Lines"). On the spherical globe, parallels and meridians intersect at right angles (Fig. R-4).

But what happens when these lines of latitude (parallels) and longitude (meridians) are drawn to intersect at right angles on a flat piece of paper? At the equator, the representation of the real world is relatively accurate. But go toward the poles, and distortion grows with every degree until, in the northern and southern higher latitudes, the continents appear not only stretched out but also misshaped (Fig. R-5). Because the meridians cannot be made to converge in the polar areas, this projection makes Antarctica look like a giant, globe-girdling landmass.

Looking at this representation of the world, you might believe that it could serve no useful purpose. But in fact, the *Mercator* projection, invented in 1569 by Gerardus Mercator, the Flemish cartographer, had (and has) a very particular function. Because parallels and meridians cross (as they do on the spherical globe's grid) at right angles, direction is true everywhere on this map. Thus the Mercator projection enabled navigators to maintain an accurate course at sea simply by adhering to compass directions and plotting straight lines. It is used for that purpose to this day.

The spatial distortion of the Mercator projection serves to remind us that scale and projection are interconnected. What scale fraction or graphic scale bar could be used here? A scale that would be accurate at the equator on a Mercator map would be quite inaccurate at higher latitudes. So the distortion that is an inevitable byproduct of any map projection also affects map scales.

One might imagine that the spatial (areal) distortion of the Mercator projection is so obvious that no one would use it to represent the world's countries. But in fact, many popular atlas maps (Mercator also introduced the term *atlas* to describe a collection of maps) and wall maps still use a Mercator for such purposes. The National Geographic Society published its world maps on a Mercator projection until 1988, when it finally abandoned the practice in favor of a projection developed by the American cartographer Arthur Robinson (Fig. R-6). During the news conference at which the change was announced, a questioner rose to pursue a point: Why had the Society waited so long to make this change? Was it because the distortion inherent in the Mercator projection made American and European middle-latitude countries large, compared to tropical countries in Africa and elsewhere? Of course there was no such intent, but that questioner obviously understood the misleading subtleties inherent even in so apparently neutral a device as a map projection.

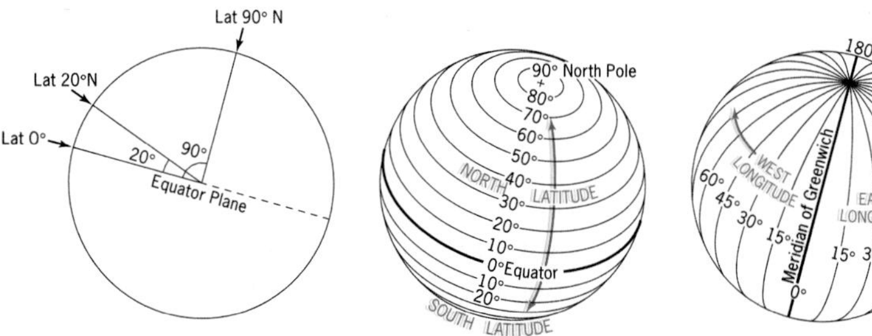

Figure R-4 Numbering of **grid lines**.

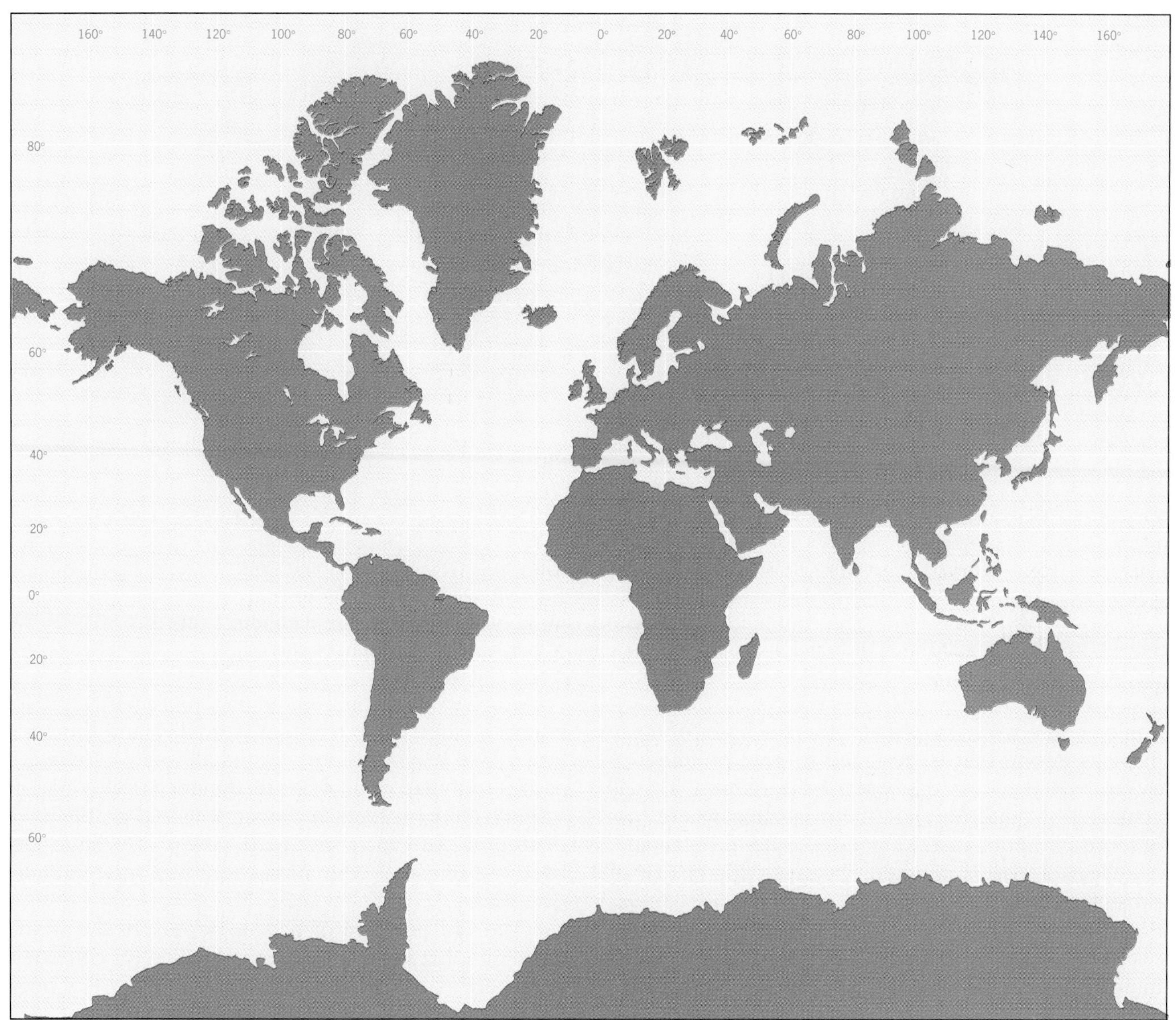

Figure R-5 Mercator's projection greatly exaggerates the dimensions of higher-latitude landmasses, but direction is true everywhere on this map.

The Mercator projection is one of a group of projections called *cylindrical* projections. Imagine the globe's lines of latitude and longitude represented by a wire grid, at the center of which we place a bright light. Wrap a piece of photographic paper around the wire grid, extending it well beyond the north and south poles, flash the bulb, and the photographic image will be that of a Mercator projection (Fig. R-7). We could do the same after placing a cone-shaped piece of paper over each hemisphere, touching the grid, say, at the 40th parallel north and south; the result would be a *conic* projection (Fig. R-8). If we wanted a map of North America or Europe, a form of conic projection would be appropriate. Now the meridians do approach each other toward the poles (unlike the Mercator projection), and there is much less shape and size distortion. And if we needed a map of Arctic and Antarctic regions, we would place the photographic paper as a flat sheet against the North and South Poles. Now the photographic image would show a set of diverging lines, as the meridians do from each pole, and the parallels would appear as circles (Fig. R-9). Such a *planar* projection is a good choice for a map of the Arctic Ocean or the Antarctic continent.

Projections are chosen for various purposes. Just as the Mercator is appropriate for navigation because direction is true, other projections are designed to preserve areal size, keep distances real, or maintain the outlines (shapes) of landmasses and countries. Projections can be manipulated for many needs. In this book, we examine global distributions of various phe-

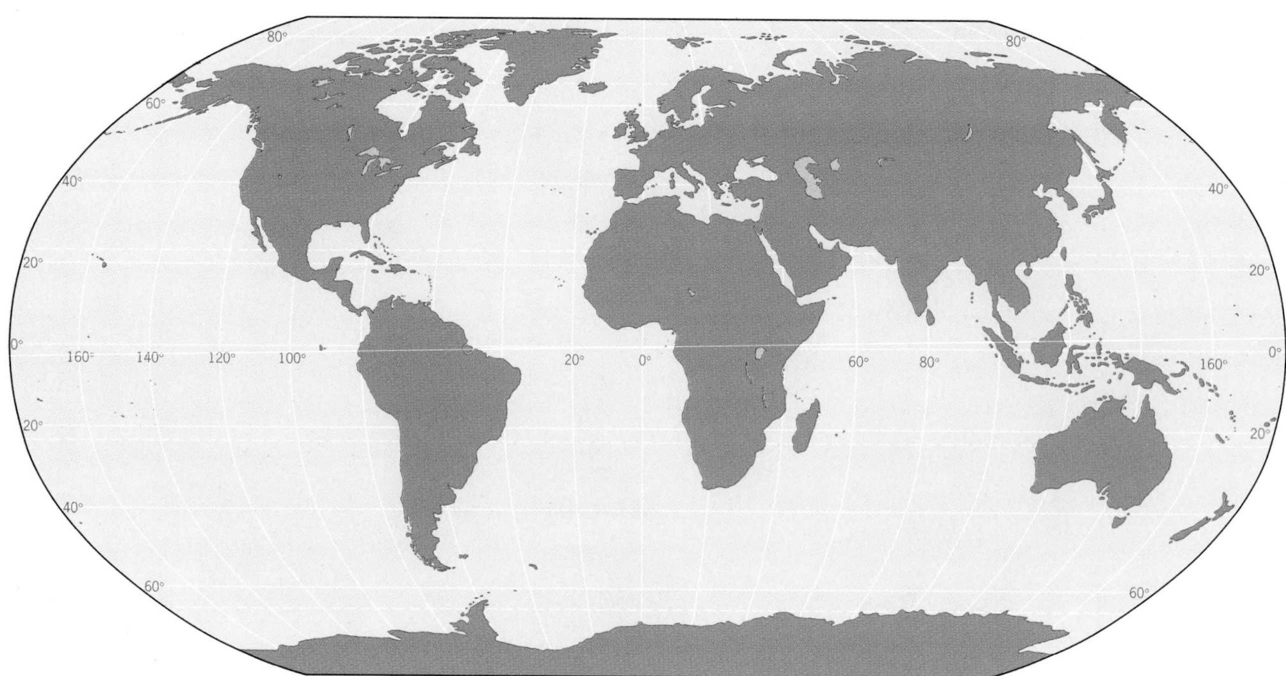

Figure R-6 The Robinson projection substantially reduces the latitudinal size magnification. It better approximates dimension, but it lacks directional utility.

nomena. The world map that forms the base for these displays is one that is designed to give prominence to land areas at the expense of the oceans. This is achieved by "interrupting" the projection where loss of territory (in this case water area) is not problematic.

When a map is planned, therefore, the choice of projection is an important part of the process. Sometimes, an inappropriate selection weakens the effectiveness of a map and may even lead to erroneous interpretations. Of course, the problem diminishes when the area to be mapped is smaller and the scale larger. We may consider various alternatives when it comes to a map of all of North America, but a map of a single State presents far fewer potential problems of distortion. And for a city map—even of a large city such as Chicago—the projection problem virtually disappears.

The old problem of how to represent the round Earth on a flat surface has been attacked for centuries, and there is no single best solution. What has been

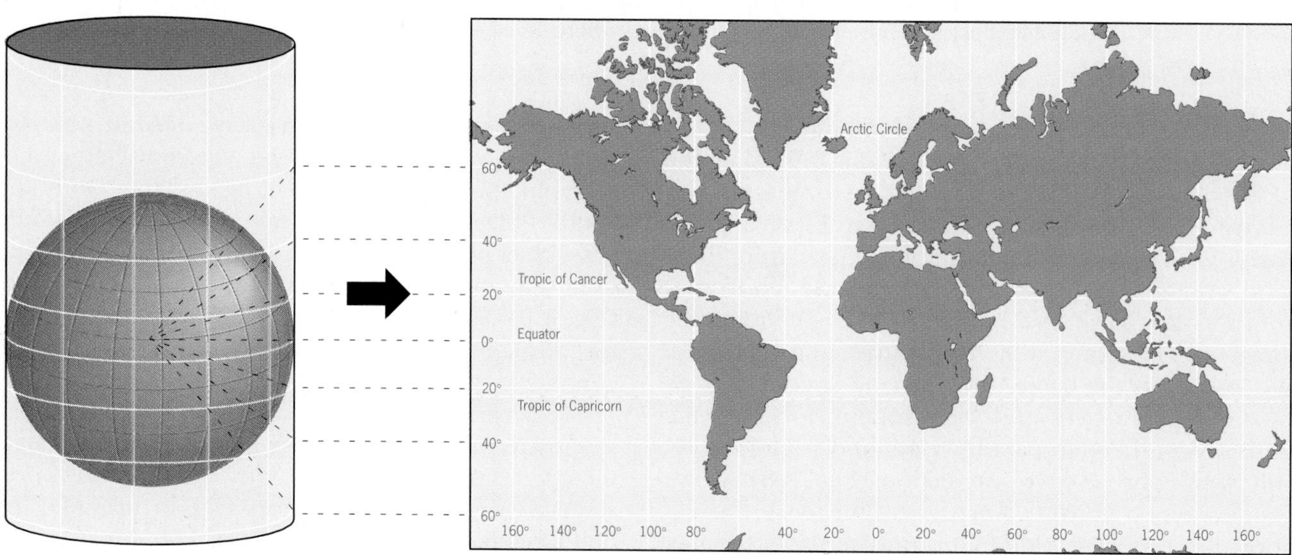

Figure R-7 Shadows of the globe's grid lines on wraparound paper: a **cylindrical projection** results.

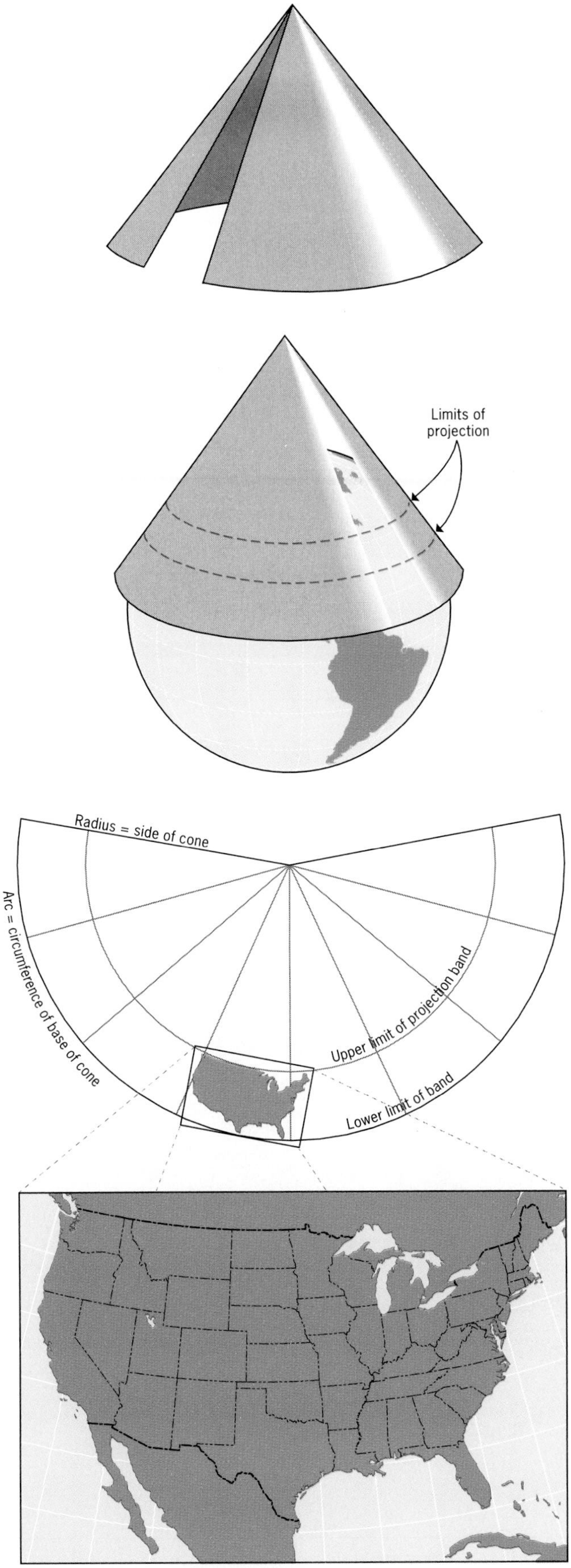

Figure R-8 Construction of a **conic projection**.

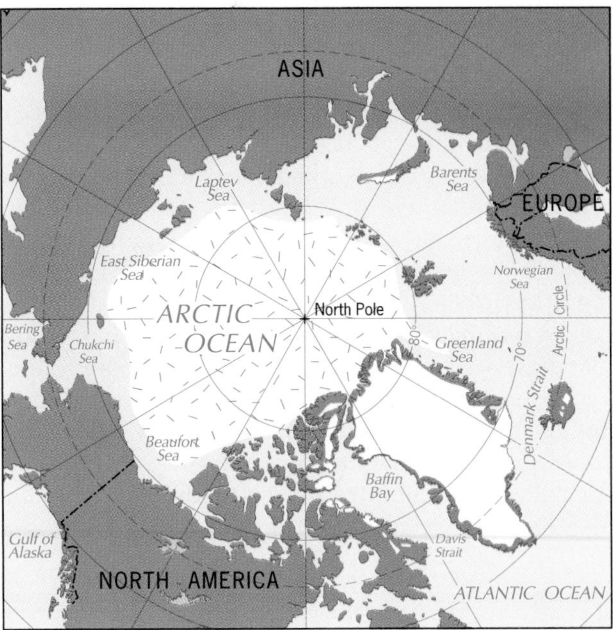

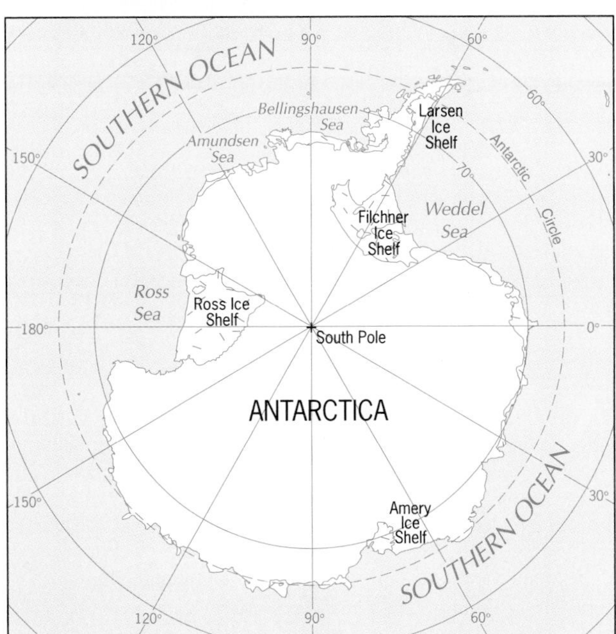

Figure R-9 Planar projection: now the light at the center of the globe projects diverging longitude lines on a flat sheet of paper placed over the North Pole (top) and the South Pole (bottom).

learned in the process, however, will be useful in fields of endeavor other than Earthly geography. As the age of planetary exploration dawns, and our space probes send back images of the surfaces of the Moon, Mars, Jupiter, and other components of our solar system, we will have to agree once again on grids, equators, and prime meridians. What has been learned in our efforts to map and represent the Earth will be useful in depicting the universe beyond.

◆ SYMBOLS ON MAPS

The third fundamental property of a map is its symbolization. Maps represent the real world, and this can be done only through the use of symbols. Anyone who has used an atlas map is familiar with some of these symbols: prominent dots (perhaps black or red) for cities; a large dot with a circle around it, or a star, for capitals; red lines for roads (double lines for four-lane highways), black lines for railroads; and patterns or colors for areas of water, forest, or farmland. Notice that these symbols respectively represent points, lines, and areas on the ground. For our purposes, we need not go further into map symbolization, which can become a very complex topic when it comes to highly specialized cartography in such fields as geology and meteorology. Nevertheless, it is useful to know why symbols such as those used on the maps in this book were chosen.

Point symbols, as we noted, are used to show individual features or places. On a large-scale map of a city block, dots can represent individual houses. But on a small-scale map, a dot has to represent an entire "city." Still, cities have various sizes, and those size differences can be put in categories and mapped accordingly (Fig. R-10). Thus New York, Chicago, and Los Angeles still appear as dots on the map, but their dots are larger than those representing Tucson, Milwaukee, or Denver. A dimensional scale is added to the map's graphic scale, and at a glance we can see the relative sizes of major cities in the United States and Canada.

Line symbols include not only roads and railroads, but also political and administrative boundaries, riv-

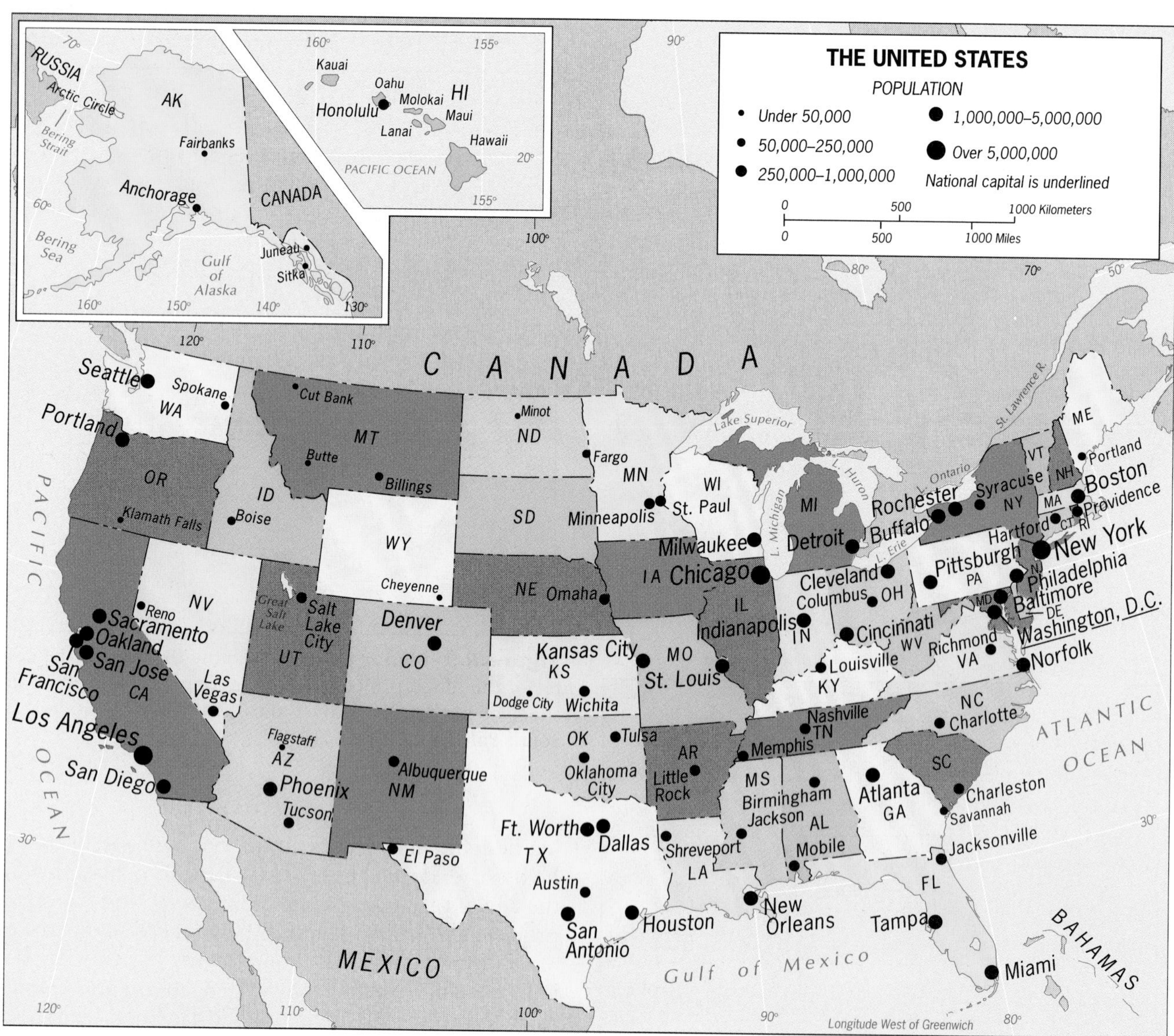

Figure R-10 This map uses **dot symbols** to indicate size categories of cities in the United States.

ers, and other linear features. Again scale plays its crucial role: on a large-scale map, it is possible to represent the fenced boundaries of a single farm, but on a small-scale map, such detail cannot be shown.

Some lines on maps do not actually exist on the ground. When physical geographers do their field work they use *contour* maps, lines that represent a certain consistent height above mean sea level (Fig. R-11). All points on such a contour line thus are at the same elevation. The spacing between contour lines immediately reveals the nature of the local topography (the natural land surface). When the contour lines at a given interval (e.g., 100 feet) are spaced closely together, the slope of the ground is steep. When they are widely separated, the land surface slopes gently. Of course contour lines cannot be found in the real world, and neither can the lines drawn on the weather maps in our daily newspaper. These lines connect points of equal pressure (isobars) and temperature (isotherms) and show the development of weather systems. Note that the letters *iso* (meaning "the same") appear in these terms. Invisible lines of this kind are collectively known as **isolines**, lines of equal or constant value. These are abstract constructions, but they can be of great value in geographic research and representation.

Area symbols take many forms, and we will see some of them on the maps in this book. Area symbols are used in various ways to represent distributions and magnitudes. Maps showing distributions (of such phenomena as regionally dominant languages or religions in human geography, and climates or soils in physical geography) show the world, or parts of it, divided into areas shaded or colored in contrasting hues. But be careful: those sharp dividing lines are likely to be transition zones in the real world, and a dominant language or religion does not imply the exclusion of all others. So distribution maps, and there are many in this book, tend to be small-scale generalizations of much more complex patterns than they can reveal. Again, maps showing magnitudes also must be read with care. Here the objective is to reveal *how much* of a phenomenon prevails in one unit (e.g., country) on the map, compared to others. The maps on population in Part 2 are examples of such maps. The important cartographic decision has to do with color (or, in black and white, graytones). Darker should mean more, and lighter implies less. That is relatively easily done when the dominant color is the same. But on a multicolored map, the use of reds, greens, and yellows can be confusing, and first impressions may have to be revised upon examination of the key.

Some students who are first drawn to the discipline of geography go on to become professional cartographers, and their work is seen in atlases, foldout magazine maps, books, and many other venues. Although cartographic technology is changing, the world's great atlases and maps still are designed and produced by researchers, compilers, draughtspeople, and other specialists.

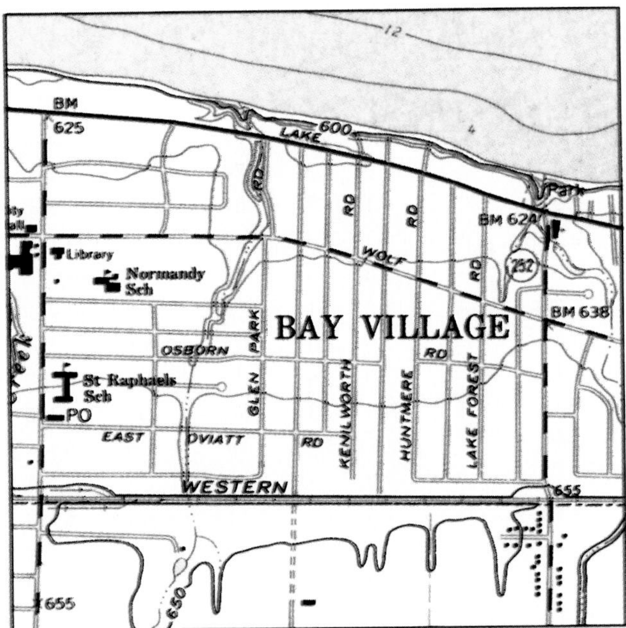

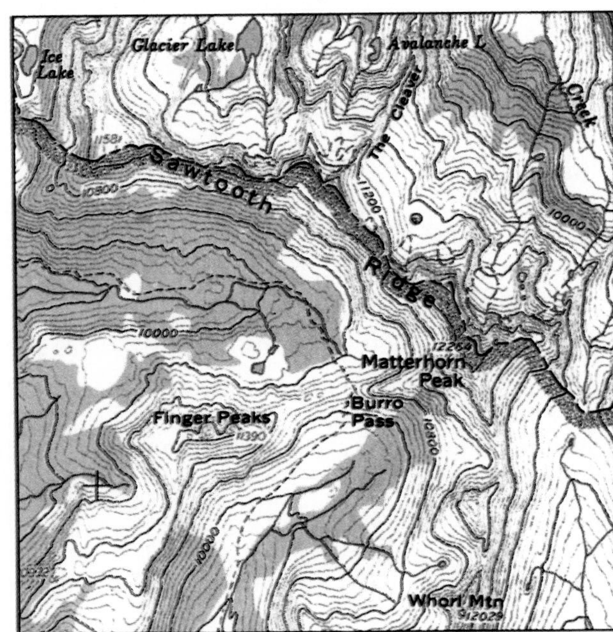

Figure R-11 **Contour lines** reflecting low relief (left) and high relief (right). The map at left is part of the U.S.G.S. North Olmstead Quadrangle, Ohio; the map at right is part of the U.S.G.S. Matterhorn Peak Quadrangle, California.

Resource **B**

1998 Area and Demographic Data for the World's States

(Smallest Microstates omitted)

	Land Area (sq mi)	Population 1998	Projected Population 2005	Population Density	Birth Rate	Death Rate	Natural Increase	Doubling Time (years)	Infant Mortality	Life Expectancy Males	Life Expectancy Females	Percent Urban	Per Capita GNP
WORLD	51,510.8	5,927.6	6,491.3	115.1	24	9	1.5%	46	59.0	64	68	44	$4,920
Europe	2,193.6	581.5	584.6	265.1	11	11	0.0%	—	8.5	71	78	72	$15,259
Albania	10.6	3.5	3.8	326.2	23	6	1.7%	41	33.2	70	76	37	$670
Austria	31.9	8.1	8.2	254.2	11	10	0.1%	693	5.0	74	80	65	$26,890
Belarus	80.1	10.3	10.2	128.1	9	13	−0.4%	—	13.0	63	74	69	$2,070
Belgium	11.8	10.2	10.3	865.3	11	10	0.1%	693	6.1	74	81	97	$24,710
Bosnia	19.7	3.6	3.8	183.8	13	7	0.6%	116	15.3	70	75	NA	NA
Bulgaria	42.7	8.3	8.2	193.4	9	14	−0.5%	—	14.8	67	75	68	$1,330
Croatia	21.6	4.8	4.6	222.2	11	11	0.0%	—	8.9	66	75	54	$3,250
Czech Rep	29.8	10.3	10.3	344.9	9	11	−0.2%	—	6.0	70	77	77	$3,870
Denmark	16.4	5.3	5.4	323.5	13	12	0.1%	693	5.3	73	78	85	$29,890
Estonia	16.3	1.5	1.4	91.6	9	14	−0.5%	—	15.0	62	74	70	$2,860
Finland	117.6	5.1	5.2	43.5	12	10	0.2%	347	3.9	73	80	65	$20,580
France	212.4	58.8	60.3	277.0	13	9	0.4%	173	5.0	74	82	74	$24,990
Germany	134.9	81.9	81.8	607.2	10	11	−0.1%	—	5.1	73	80	85	$27,510
Greece	49.8	10.5	10.6	211.1	10	9	0.1%	693	7.9	75	79	63	$8,210
Hungary	35.7	10.2	10.0	284.9	11	14	−0.3%	—	10.6	65	74	63	$4,120
Iceland	38.7	0.3	0.3	7.8	16	7	0.9%	77	6.1	77	81	92	$24,950
Ireland	26.6	3.6	3.7	136.0	14	9	0.5%	139	6.3	73	79	57	$14,710
Italy	113.5	57.4	57.5	505.7	9	9	0.0%	—	5.8	75	81	68	$19,020
Latvia	24.0	2.5	2.3	103.4	9	16	−0.7%	—	19.0	61	73	69	$2,270
Liechtenstein	0.06	0.03	0.03	502.5	12	7	0.5%	139	5.6	74	81	NA	NA
Lithuania	25.0	3.7	3.6	147.9	11	12	−0.1%	—	13.0	64	75	68	$1,900
Luxembourg	1.0	0.4	0.5	401.6	13	9	0.4%	173	5.5	73	80	86	$41,210
Macedonia	9.8	2.1	2.2	216.0	16	8	0.8%	87	22.7	70	74	58	$860
Malta	0.12	0.4	0.4	3,350.0	12	7	0.5%	139	8.9	75	79	85	NA
Moldova	12.7	4.3	4.5	338.9	13	12	0.1%	693	21.0	64	71	46	$920
Netherlands	13.1	15.6	16.3	1,194.4	12	9	0.3%	231	5.5	75	80	89	$24,000
Norway	118.5	4.4	4.6	37.3	14	10	0.4%	173	5.2	75	81	74	$31,250
Poland	117.5	38.6	39.7	328.8	11	10	0.1%	693	12.4	68	76	62	$2,790
Portugal	35.5	9.9	10.1	279.2	11	10	0.1%	693	7.4	72	79	34	$9,740
Romania	88.9	22.4	22.3	252.3	10	13	−0.3%	—	21.2	66	73	55	$1,480
Serbia	26.9	10.6	11.0	394.8	13	11	0.2%	347	14.0	70	75	51	NA

	Land Area (sq mi)	Population 1998	Projected Population 2005	Population Density	Birth Rate	eath Rate	Natural Increase	Doubling Time (years)	Infant Mortality	Life Expectancy Males	Life Expectancy Females	Percent Urban	Per Capita GNP
Slovakia	18.6	5.4	5.4	290.6	11	10	0.1%	693	11.2	69	77	57	$2,950
Slovenia	7.8	2.0	2.0	256.4	10	10	0.0%	—	5.5	70	78	50	$8,200
Spain	192.8	39.3	39.6	203.8	9	9	0.0%	—	5.6	73	81	64	$13,580
Sweden	158.9	8.9	8.8	56.0	11	11	0.0%	—	4.2	76	81	83	$23,750
Switzerland	15.3	7.1	7.4	465.4	12	9	0.3%	231	5.0	75	82	68	$40,630
Ukraine	223.7	50.4	49.7	225.5	10	15	−0.5%	—	14.0	63	73	68	$1,630
United Kingdom	93.3	59.1	58.8	633.6	13	11	0.2%	347	6.2	74	79	92	$18,700
Russia	6,550.7	146.6	143.4	22.4	9	14	−0.5%	—	18.0	58	72	73	$2,240
Armenia	10.9	3.8	3.8	350.7	13	7	0.6%	116	14.0	69	76	67	$730
Azerbaijan	33.4	7.7	8.2	230.3	19	7	1.2%	58	23.0	65	74	53	$480
Georgia	26.9	5.4	5.3	201.3	11	8	0.3%	231	17.0	69	76	56	$440
North America	7,096.5	299.5	317.9	42.2	14	9	0.6%	116	7.0	73	79	75	$26,210
Canada	3,560.2	30.3	32.2	8.5	13	7	0.6%	116	6.2	75	81	77	$19,380
United States	3,787.4	269.3	285.9	71.1	15	9	0.6%	116	7.3	73	79	75	$26,980
Middle America	1,021.9	168.6	189.3	165.0	27	6	2.2%	32	36.0	68	73	64	$2,638
Antigua and Barbuda	0.17	0.1	0.1	595.3	17	5	1.2%	58	19.0	71	75	36	NA
Bahamas	3.9	0.3	0.3	78.2	22	6	1.6%	43	19.7	68	75	86	$11,940
Barbados	0.17	0.3	0.3	1,771.8	13	9	0.4%	173	15.9	73	77	38	$6,560
Belize	8.8	0.2	0.3	23.5	38	5	3.3%	21	33.0	67	71	48	$2,630
Costa Rica	19.7	3.6	4.1	181.2	24	4	2.0%	35	13.3	73	78	44	$2,610
Cuba	42.4	11.2	11.4	263.6	14	7	0.7%	99	9.4	74	77	74	NA
Dominica	0.3	0.1	0.1	350.0	22	7	1.5%	46	18.7	74	80	NA	$2,990
Dominican Rep	18.7	8.4	9.3	447.7	27	6	2.1%	33	47.0	68	72	61	$1,460
El Salvador	8.0	6.1	6.8	756.7	32	6	2.6%	27	41.0	65	70	45	$1,610
Grenada	0.1	0.1	0.1	786.9	29	6	2.3%	30	12.0	68	73	32	$2,980
Guadeloupe	0.7	0.4	0.5	622.2	17	6	1.1%	63	12.0	71	78	99	NA
Guatemala	41.9	11.5	14.0	275.3	37	7	3.0%	23	51.0	62	67	39	$1,340
Haiti	10.6	6.7	7.5	633.8	33	15	1.8%	39	48.0	48	52	32	$250
Honduras	43.2	6.0	6.9	138.6	38	6	3.2%	22	43.0	65	70	47	$600
Jamaica	4.2	2.6	2.7	629.6	23	6	1.7%	41	24.4	71	76	50	$1,510
Martinique	0.41	0.4	0.5	985.4	16	6	1.0%	69	9.0	73	79	81	NA
Mexico	737.0	97.8	109.5	132.7	27	5	2.2%	32	34.0	70	76	71	$3,320
Netherlands Antilles	0.3	0.2	0.2	625.9	19	7	1.2%	58	6.3	72	78	90	NA
Nicaragua	46.9	4.5	5.3	96.7	37	6	3.1%	22	49.0	64	69	63	$380
Panama	28.7	2.8	3.0	95.9	24	5	1.9%	36	30.0	71	75	55	$2,750
Puerto Rico	3.4	3.8	4.0	1,128.8	18	8	1.0%	69	11.5	70	79	73	NA
Saint Lucia	0.2	0.1	0.2	424.6	25	6	1.9%	36	18.0	68	75	48	$3,370
St. Vincent and the Grenadines	0.2	0.1	0.1	676.7	22	7	1.5%	46	19.0	71	74	25	$2,280
Trinidad and Tobago	2.0	1.3	1.4	655.9	16	7	0.9%	77	13.8	68	73	65	$3,770
South America	6,763.3	329.5	362.5	48.7	24	7	1.7%	41	40.0	65	72	74	$3,620
Argentina	1,056.6	36.0	39.2	34.1	20	8	1.2%	58	20.7	68	76	87	$8,030

	Land Area (sq mi)	Population 1998	Projected Population 2005	Population Density	Birth Rate	Death Rate	Natural Increase	Doubling Time (years)	Infant Mortality	Life Expectancy Males	Life Expectancy Females	Percent Urban	Per Capita GNP
Bolivia	418.7	8.0	9.3	19.1	36	10	2.6%	27	71.0	59	62	58	$800
Brazil	3,265.1	162.7	176.6	49.8	22	7	1.5%	46	48.0	64	70	76	$3,640
Chile	289.1	14.8	16.1	51.3	21	5	1.6%	43	12.0	69	76	86	$4,160
Colombia	401.0	38.2	41.9	95.2	27	6	2.1%	33	28.0	67	72	70	$1,910
Ecuador	106.9	12.3	14.0	114.8	29	6	2.3%	30	40.0	66	71	59	$1,390
French Guiana	34.0	0.2	0.2	6.0	30	4	2.6%	27	14.0	73	79	NA	NA
Guyana	76.0	0.8	0.9	10.7	25	8	1.7%	41	63.0	60	66	31	$590
Paraguay	153.4	5.2	6.3	34.2	34	6	2.8%	25	43.0	66	71	50	$1,690
Peru	494.2	24.9	27.8	50.5	29	7	2.2%	32	55.0	64	69	70	$2,310
Suriname	60.2	0.4	0.5	6.8	25	6	1.9%	36	28.0	68	73	49	$880
Uruguay	67.5	3.2	3.4	47.8	18	10	0.8%	87	18.9	69	76	90	$5,170
Venezuela	340.6	23.1	26.2	67.7	26	5	2.1%	33	23.5	69	75	85	$3,020
North Africa/ Southwest Asia	7,659.4	495.9	577.2	64.7	32	9	2.3%	30	59.6	62	66	51	NA
Afghanistan	251.8	22.7	28.8	90.2	50	22	2.8%	25	163.0	43	44	18	NA
Algeria	919.6	30.5	35.2	33.2	31	7	2.4%	29	44.0	66	68	50	$1,600
Bahrain	0.27	0.6	0.7	2,266.7	23	3	2.0%	35	19.0	70	74	88	$7,840
Cyprus	3.6	0.7	0.8	195.8	15	8	0.7%	99	9.0	75	80	53	NA
Djibouti	9.0	0.6	0.8	68.2	39	16	2.3%	30	115.0	47	50	81	NA
Egypt	384.3	66.2	74.6	172.2	29	8	2.1%	33	62.0	62	65	44	$790
Eritrea	39.0	3.7	5.0	95.0	45	16	2.9%	24	120.0	48	51	17	NA
Iran	631.7	69.3	80.3	109.7	34	7	2.7%	26	53.0	66	69	58	NA
Iraq	168.9	21.8	26.8	129.0	38	10	2.8%	25	127.0	58	60	70	NA
Israel	8.0	5.9	6.5	735.9	21	6	1.5%	46	7.2	75	79	90	$15,920
Gaza	0.10	1.0	1.5	10,460.0	52	6	4.6%	15	33.0	70	74	NA	NA
West Bank	2.3	1.8	2.2	764.3	40	6	3.4%	20	27.0	70	74	NA	NA
Jordan	34.3	4.5	5.6	132.5	39	6	3.3%	21	36.0	66	70	78	$1,510
Kazakhstan	1,031.2	16.5	17.3	16.0	15	10	0.5%	139	25.0	64	73	56	$1,330
Kuwait	6.9	1.8	2.2	266.6	24	2	2.2%	32	13.0	73	77	96	$17,390
Kyrgyzstan	74.1	4.7	5.0	63.1	24	8	1.6%	43	26.0	61	70	35	$700
Lebanon	4.0	4.0	4.6	996.5	28	6	2.2%	32	37.0	67	73	87	$2,660
Libya	679.4	5.8	7.6	8.5	44	8	3.6%	19	68.0	62	65	85	
Morocco	172.3	28.8	31.5	166.9	26	6	2.0%	35	62.0	66	70	51	$1,110
Oman	82.0	2.4	3.0	29.0	38	4	3.4%	20	27.0	69	73	72	$4,820
Qatar	4.3	0.6	0.7	141.9	21	4	1.7%	41	20.0	71	76	91	$11,600
Saudi Arabia	830.0	20.1	25.4	24.2	35	5	3.0%	23	29.0	68	71	80	$7,040
Somalia	242.2	10.5	13.5	43.4	50	19	3.1%	22	122.0	45	49	24	NA
Sudan	917.4	28.5	33.4	31.1	35	14	2.1%	33	70.0	50	52	27	NA
Syria	71.0	15.4	18.4	217.0	33	6	2.7%	26	39.0	65	69	51	$1,120
Tajikistan	54.3	6.1	7.4	113.0	29	6	2.3%	30	41.0	65	71	28	$340
Tunisia	60.0	9.5	10.6	158.1	26	6	2.0%	35	43.0	67	69	58	$1,820
Turkey	297.2	64.7	71.7	217.8	23	7	1.6%	43	47.0	65	70	63	$2,780
Turkmenistan	181.4	4.7	5.0	25.9	28	7	2.1%	33	46.0	62	69	45	$920
United Arab Emirates	32.3	2.3	2.7	72.5	21	3	1.8%	39	19.0	73	75	82	$17,400
Uzbekistan	159.9	24.2	27.2	151.3	28	7	2.1%	33	22.0	66	73	38	$970
Western Sahara	102.7	0.2	0.3	2.0	47	18	2.9%	24	150.0	46	48	NA	NA
Yemen	203.9	15.7	20.6	77.2	46	11	3.5%	20	79.0	57	60	25	$260

	Land Area (sq mi)	Population 1998	Projected Population 2005	Population Density	Birth Rate	Death Rate	Natural Increase	Doubling Time (years)	Infant Mortality	Life Expectancy Males	Life Expectancy Females	Percent Urban	Per Capita GNP
Subsaharan Africa	7,916.3	578.1	682.5	73.0	43	15	2.8%	25	91.8	49	52	28	$509
Angola	481.4	12.0	15.0	24.9	51	19	3.2%	22	124.0	45	48	32	$410
Benin	42.7	6.1	7.6	142.9	49	15	3.4%	20	98.0	51	56	36	$370
Botswana	218.8	1.5	1.6	7.0	37	11	2.6%	27	41.0	52	56	27	$3,020
Burkina Faso	105.6	11.2	13.0	106.3	48	18	3.0%	23	103.0	46	48	15	$230
Burundi	9.9	6.3	7.4	630.9	46	20	2.6%	27	120.0	48	52	6	$160
Cameroon	179.7	14.3	17.5	79.5	41	13	2.8%	25	65.0	53	56	44	$650
Cape Verde Islands	1.6	0.4	0.5	254.8	27	8	1.9%	36	65.0	64	66	44	$960
Central African Republic	240.5	3.4	3.9	14.1	42	17	2.5%	28	97.0	46	51	39	$340
Chad	486.1	7.2	8.6	14.8	44	19	2.5%	28	123.0	45	48	22	$180
Comoros Islands	0.9	0.6	0.8	722.8	47	11	3.6%	19	80.0	56	60	29	$470
Congo (K)	875.3	49.0	60.8	55.9	48	15	3.3%	21	95.0	50	54	29	$120
Congo (B)	131.9	2.7	3.0	20.2	40	17	2.3%	30	103.0	44	48	58	$680
Equatorial Guinea	10.8	0.4	0.5	38.0	44	18	2.6%	27	117.0	46	50	37	$380
Ethiopia	386.1	60.3	72.5	156.3	46	18	2.8%	25	120.0	46	48	15	$100
Gabon	99.5	1.2	1.3	12.3	35	15	2.0%	35	94.0	52	55	73	$3,490
Gambia	3.9	1.2	1.4	315.4	45	20	2.5%	28	90.0	43	47	26	$320
Ghana	87.9	18.6	21.1	211.7	40	12	2.8%	25	66.0	54	58	36	$390
Guinea	94.9	7.7	8.7	80.9	43	19	2.4%	29	136.0	43	47	29	$550
Guinea-Bissau	10.9	1.1	1.3	102.9	42	22	2.0%	35	141.0	41	44	22	$250
Ivory Coast	122.8	15.4	18.1	125.3	39	13	2.6%	27	89.0	51	54	46	$660
Kenya	219.8	29.5	32.1	134.4	38	12	2.6%	27	62.0	53	55	27	$280
Lesotho	11.7	2.1	2.3	175.4	37	11	2.6%	27	81.0	56	59	16	$770
Liberia	37.2	2.4	3.6	63.7	43	12	3.1%	22	113.0	56	61	44	NA
Madagascar	224.5	14.6	17.8	64.9	44	11	3.3%	21	93.0	55	58	22	$230
Malawi	36.3	9.9	10.4	272.1	51	22	2.9%	24	134.0	41	42	18	$170
Mali	471.1	10.2	13.0	21.6	50	20	3.0%	23	134.0	44	48	26	$250
Mauritania	395.8	2.5	3.0	6.2	40	14	2.6%	27	101.0	50	53	39	$460
Mauritius	0.8	1.1	1.2	1,425.8	18	7	1.1%	63	19.7	66	74	43	$3,380
Moçambique	302.7	18.9	22.5	62.4	45	19	2.6%	27	118.0	44	48	28	$80
Namibia	317.9	1.7	2.2	5.5	38	12	2.6%	27	64.0	55	57	32	$2,000
Niger	489.1	10.1	12.9	20.7	53	19	3.4%	20	124.0	45	48	15	$220
Nigeria	351.7	110.3	137.8	313.7	43	13	3.0%	23	84.0	53	56	16	$260
Réunion	1.0	0.7	0.8	733.2	21	5	1.6%	43	7.0	69	79	73	NA
Rwanda	9.5	7.8	9.2	825.9	39	20	1.9%	36	85.0	40	41	5	$180
São Tome and Principe	0.29	0.1	0.2	356.6	43	9	3.4%	20	50.8	62	65	46	$350
Senegal	74.3	9.0	10.9	121.6	43	16	2.7%	26	68.0	48	50	43	$600
Seychelles	0.20	0.1	0.1	507.0	21	7	1.4%	50	18.3	68	73	50	$6,620
Sierra Leone	27.7	4.5	5.4	161.9	49	30	1.9%	36	195.0	33	36	35	$180
South Africa	471.4	43.1	44.6	91.5	27	12	1.5%	46	53.0	54	58	57	$3,160
Swaziland	6.6	1.0	1.4	156.4	43	11	3.2%	22	88.0	53	61	30	$1,170
Tanzania	341.1	30.4	33.7	89.1	45	15	3.0%	23	91.0	49	51	21	$120
Togo	21.0	4.9	6.3	231.6	46	11	3.5%	20	91.0	55	59	30	$310
Uganda	77.1	21.2	24.2	274.9	51	22	2.9%	24	81.0	40	42	11	$240

	Land Area (sq mi)	Population 1998	Projected Population 2005	Population Density	Birth Rate	Death Rate	Natural Increase	Doubling Time (years)	Infant Mortality	Life Expectancy Males	Life Expectancy Females	Percent Urban	Per Capita GNP
Zambia	287.0	9.6	10.7	33.4	45	24	2.1%	33	109.0	43	45	42	$400
Zimbabwe	149.4	11.7	11.8	78.3	40	14	2.6%	27	53.0	50	52	31	$540
South Asia	1,592.0	1,297.7	1,453.5	815.1	30	10	2.0%	34	76.1	59	59	25	$346
Bangladesh	50.3	124.6	140.7	2,478.0	31	11	2.0%	35	77.0	58	58	16	$240
Bhutan	18.2	0.8	1.0	45.3	40	9	3.1%	22	71.0			15	$420
India	1,148.0	988.1	1,101.6	860.7	29	10	1.9%	36	75.0	59	59	26	$340
Maldives	0.12	0.3	0.4	2,590.0	43	7	3.6%	19	50.0	63	66	26	$990
Nepal	52.8	23.1	27.6	437.9	35	12	2.3%	30	79.0	53	54	10	$200
Pakistan	297.6	141.7	161.9	476.0	39	11	2.8%	25	91.0	61	61	28	$460
Sri Lanka	25.0	19.0	20.3	759.2	20	5	1.5%	46	17.2	70	74	22	$700
East Asia	4,450.2	1,470.1	1,566.3	330.3	16	7	0.9%	77	29.0	69	73	36	$4,400
China	3,601.3	1,249.1	1,338.1	346.8	17	7	1.0%	69	31.0	68	72	29	$620
Japan	145.4	126.5	127.1	869.9	10	7	0.3%	231	4.0	77	83	78	$39,640
Korea, North	46.5	24.7	26.9	532.0	24	6	1.8%	39	28.0	67	73	61	NA
Korea, South	38.1	46.3	48.3	1,215.6	15	6	0.9%	77	11.0	69	77	74	$9,700
Macau	0.10	0.5	0.5	5,055.0	14	3	1.1%	63	6.0	67	71	97	NA
Mongolia	604.8	2.5	2.8	4.1	29	8	2.1%	33	70.0	62	65	55	$310
Taiwan	14.0	21.7	23.0	1,549.5	15	6	0.9%	77	5.1	72	78	75	NA
Southeast Asia	1,683.6	510.0	563.7	302.9	26	8	1.8%	39	52.0	62	66	30	$1,410
Brunei	2.0	0.3	0.4	153.5	27	4	2.3%	30	11.2	70	73	67	NA
Cambodia	68.2	11.5	14.0	169.0	45	16	2.9%	24	111.0	48	51	13	$270
Indonesia	705.2	207.8	226.8	294.6	25	8	1.7%	41	66.0	60	64	31	$980
Laos	89.1	5.2	6.4	58.8	43	15	2.8%	25	102.0	50	53	19	$350
Malaysia	126.9	21.5	24.4	169.1	27	5	2.2%	32	11.0	70	74	51	$3,890
Myanmar (Burma)	253.9	47.7	53.8	187.8	31	12	1.9%	36	49.0	60	62	25	NA
Philippines	115.1	75.1	86.1	652.4	30	7	2.3%	30	34.0	65	68	47	$1,050
Singapore	0.24	3.5	3.8	14,743.8	16	5	1.1%	63	4.0	74	79	100	$26,730
Thailand	197.3	60.8	64.3	308.0	18	7	1.1%	63	32.0	66	72	19	$2,740
Vietnam	125.7	76.3	83.5	607.0	23	7	1.6%	43	38.0	65	69	20	$240
Australia	3,055.0	22.3	23.7	7.3	14	7	0.7%	97	5.9	75	81	85	$18,007
Australia	2,951.5	18.6	19.9	6.3	14	7	0.7%	99	5.8	75	81	85	$18,720
New Zealand	103.5	3.6	3.8	35.1	16	8	0.8%	87	6.6	73	79	85	$14,340
Pacific	192.2	6.3	7.3	33.0	32	9	2.3%	30	50.5	56	58	23	NA
Federated States of Micronesia	0.27	0.1	0.1	378.5	31	9	2.2%	32	46.0	64	67	26	NA
Fiji	7.1	0.8	0.9	114.8	25	6	1.9%	36	19.0	61	65	39	$2,440
French Polynesia	1.4	0.2	0.3	145.7	25	5	2.0%	35	9.0	68	72	57	NA
Guam	0.21	0.2	0.2	975.2	28	4	2.4%	29	9.1	72	76	38	NA
Marshall Islands	0.07	0.1	0.1	1,485.7	49	9	4.0%	17	63.0	60	63	65	NA
New Caledonia	7.1	0.2	0.2	28.7	23	5	1.8%	39	10.0	70	75	70	NA
Papua New Guinea	174.9	4.5	5.3	25.8	34	10	2.4%	29	63.0	56	57	15	$1,160
Samoa	1.1	0.2	0.2	186.0	31	8	2.3%	30	21.0			21	$1,120
Solomon Islands	10.8	0.4	0.5	38.3	39	5	3.4%	20	28.0	68	73	13	$910
Vanuatu	4.7	0.2	0.2	43.8	38	9	2.9%	24	45.0			18	$1,200

Resource **C**

Glossary

Absolute direction A compass direction such as north or south.

Absolute distance The physical distance between two points usually measured in miles or kilometers.

Absolute location The position or place of a certain item on the surface of the Earth as expressed in degrees, minutes, and seconds of **latitude**, 0° to 90° north or south of the equator, and **longitude**, 0° to 180° east or west of the **prime meridian** passing through Greenwich, England (a suburb of London).

Accessibility The degree of ease with which it is possible to reach a certain location from other locations. Accessibility varies from place to place and can be measured.

Acculturation Cultural modification resulting from intercultural borrowing. In cultural geography, the term is used to designate the change that occurs in the culture of indigenous peoples when contact is made with a society that is technologically more advanced.

Acid rain A growing environmental peril whereby acidified rainwater severely damages plant and animal life. Caused by the oxides of sulfur and nitrogen that are released into the atmosphere when coal, oil, and natural gas are burned, especially in major manufacturing zones.

Acropolis Literally "high point of the city". The upper fortified part of an ancient Greek city, usually devoted to religious purposes.

Activity (or **action**) **space** The space within which daily activity occurs.

Age-sex pyramid Graphic representation (profile) of a population showing the percentages of the total population by age and sex, normally in five-year groups.

Agglomerated (nucleated) settlement A compact, closely packed settlement (usually a hamlet or larger village) sharply demarcated from adjoining farmlands.

Agglomeration A process involving the clustering or concentrating of people or activities. The term often refers to manufacturing plants and businesses that benefit from close proximity because they share skilled-labor pools and technological and financial amenities.

Agrarian Relating to the use of land in rural communities or to agricultural societies in general.

Agribusiness A general term for large-scale, mechanized industrial agriculture that is controlled by corporate interests.

Agricultural density The number of inhabitants per unit of agricultural land. As used in population geography, agricultural density excludes urban residents so that it reflects the pressure of population in rural areas. **Physiologic density** measures the total population, urban and rural, against the agricultural land.

Agricultural Revolution The revolutionary transformation of agricultural practices, systems, and production. The *First Agricultural Revolution*, dating back 10,000 years, achieved plant and animal domestication. The *Second Agricultural Revolution* dovetailed with and benefited from the *Industrial Revolution* and witnessed improved methods of cultivation, harvesting, and storage of farm produce. The *Third Agricultural Revolution*, currently in progress, is based on new high-yielding strains of grains and other crops developed by genetic engineering.

Agriculture The purposeful tending of crops and livestock in order to produce food and fiber.

Animism The belief that inanimate objects, such as hills, rocks, rivers, and other elements of the natural landscape (including trees), possess souls and can help as well as hinder human efforts on Earth.

Antecedent boundary A political boundary that existed before the **cultural landscape** emerged and stayed in place while people moved in to occupy the surrounding area. An example is the 49th parallel boundary, dividing the United States and Canada between the Pacific Ocean and Lake of the Woods in northernmost Minnesota.

Anthropogeographic boundaries Political boundaries that coincide substantially with cultural discontinuities in the human landscape, such as religious or linguistic transitions.

Apartheid Literally, "apartness". The Afrikaans term given to the policies of racial separation once practiced in South Africa and to the highly segregated sociogeographical patterns they produced—a system now being dismantled.

Aquaculture The use of a river segment or an artificial body of water such as a pond for the raising and harvesting of food products, including fish, shellfish, and even seaweed. Japan is among the world's leaders in aquaculture.

Arable Literally, cultivable. Land fit for cultivation by one farming method or another.

Area A term that refers to a part of the Earth's surface with less specificity than **region**. For example, urban area alludes very generally to a place where urban development has taken place, whereas urban region requires certain specific criteria on which a delimitation is based (e.g., the spatial extent of commuting or the built townscape).

Area symbols Portray two-dimensional spaces on a map, with colors or black-and-white areal patterns representing specific quantitative ranges (which are identified in the map legend).

Areal interdependence A term related to **functional specialization**. When one area produces certain goods or has certain raw materials or resources and another area has a different set of resources and produces different goods, their needs may be complementary; by exchanging raw materials and products, they can satisfy each other's requirements. The concepts of areal interdependence and **complementarity** are related: both have to do with exchange opportunities between regions.

Arithmetic population density The population of a country or region expressed as an average per unit area. The figure is derived by dividing the population of the areal unit by the number of square kilometers or miles that make up the unit.

Aryan From the Sanskrit Arya ("noble"), a name applied to an ancient people who spoke an Indo-European language and who moved into northern India from the northwest. Although properly a language-related term, Aryan has assumed additional meanings, especially racial ones.

Ashkenazim One of the two main ethnic groups within Jewish culture. This branch eventually settled in Central Europe after having been driven out of Jerusalem early in the first millennium AD.

Autocratic An autocratic government holds absolute power; rule is often by one person or a small group of persons who control the country by despotic means.

Balkanization The fragmentation of a region into smaller, often hostile political units.

Basic activities Economic activities whose products are exported beyond a region's limits. Nonbasic, or service, activities involve production and consumption within the region.

Bergmann's Rule A principle holding that the lower the mean annual temperature, the higher a population's mean body weight.

Biodiversity The total variety of plant and animal species in a particular place; biological diversity.

Birth rate The crude birth rate is expressed as the annual number of live births per 1000 individuals within a given population.

Brahman A Hindu of the highest caste, most often a priest, a person believed to possess sacred knowledge and to be of the greatest purity. Brahmans (or Brahmins) alone are believed capable of carrying out particular religious rituals and tasks. In India, Brahmans have for many centuries been religious, intellectual, and even political leaders.

Break-of-bulk point A location along a transport route where goods must be transferred from one carrier to another. In a port, the cargoes of oceangoing ships are unloaded and put on trains, trucks, or perhaps smaller riverboats for inland distribution.

Brick A traditional building material made of hard, oven-baked or sun-baked blocks of mud shaped into standard sizes.

Buffer zone A set of countries separating ideological or political adversaries. In southern Asia, Afghanistan, Nepal, and Bhutan were parts of a buffer zone between British and Russian-Chinese imperial spheres. Thailand was a buffer state between British and French colonial domains in mainland Southeast Asia.

Cartel An international syndicate formed to promote common interests in some economic sphere through the formulation of joint pricing policies and the limitation of market options for consumers. The Organization of Petroleum Exporting Countries (OPEC) is a classic example.

Cartography The art and science of making maps, including data compilation, layout, and design. Also concerned with the interpretation of mapped patterns.

Caste system The strict social segregation of people—specifically in India's Hindu society—on the basis of ancestry and occupation.

Cenozoic The era of recent life on the geologic time scale extending from 65 million years ago to the present; subdivided into the Tertiary and Quaternary periods.

Census A periodic and official count of a country's population.

Central business district (CBD) The downtown heart of a central city, the CBD is marked by high land values, a concentration of business and commerce, and the clustering of the tallest buildings.

Central place Any point or place in the urban hierarchy, such as a town or city, having a certain economic reach or **hinterland**.

Central place theory Theory proposed by Walter Christaller that explains how and where central places in the urban hierarchy would be functionally and spatially distributed with respect to one another.

Centrality The strength of an urban center in its capacity to attract producers and consumers to its facilities; a city's "reach" into the surrounding region.

Centrifugal forces A term employed to designate forces that tend to divide a country—such as internal religious, linguistic, ethnic, or ideological differences.

Centripetal forces Forces that unite and bind a country together—such as a strong national culture, shared ideological objectives, and a common faith.

Child mortality rate A figure that describes the number of children that die between the first and fifth years of their lives in a given population.

Chlorofluorocarbons (CFCs) Synthetic organic compounds first created in the 1950s and used primarily as refrigerants and as propellants. The role of CFCs in the destruction of the Ozone layer led to the signing of an international agreement (the **Montreal Protocol**).

Circulation In political geography, the system of integration and movement through language, education, transportation, and communications.

City-state An independent political entity consisting of a single city with (and sometimes without) an immediate **hinterland**. The ancient city-states of Greece have their modern equivalent in Singapore.

Civilization An advanced state of a society possessing historical and cultural unity whose attributes include plant and animal domestication, metallurgy, occupational specialization, writing, and cities.

Climatic optimum Period of maximal warmth during the Holocene interglaciation epoch, experienced between 7000 and 5000 years ago.

Colonialism see **imperialism**.

Compact state A politico-geographical term to describe a state that possesses a roughly circular, oval, or rectangular territory in which the distance from the geometric center to any point on the boundary exhibits little variance. Cambodia, Uruguay, and Poland are examples of this shape category.

Complementarity Regional complementarity exists when two regions, through an exchange of raw materials and/or finished products, can specifically satisfy each other's demands.

Concentric zone model A structural model of the American central city that suggests the existence of five concentric land-use rings arranged around a common center.

Condominium In political geography, this denotes the shared administration of a territory by two governments.

Confucianism A philosophy of ethics, education, and public service based on the writings of Confucius and traditionally thought of as one of the core elements of Chinese culture.

Connectivity The degree of direct linkage between one particular location and other locations in a transport network.

Conservation The careful management and use of natural resources, the achievement of significant social benefits from them, and the preservation of the natural environment.

Contagious diffusion The distance-controlled spreading of an idea, innovation, or some other item through a local population by contact from person to person—analogous to the communication of a contagious illness.

Contagious disease A disease that can be transmitted amongst people, either through direct contact or through a vector.

Continental drift The notion hypothesized by Alfred Wegener concerning the fragmentation of Pangaea and the slow movement of the modern continents away from this core supercontinent.

Continental shelf The gently sloping, relatively shallow, submerged plain just off the coast of a continent, extending to a depth of around 180 meters (600 feet/1000 fathoms).

Conurbation General term used to identify large, multimetropolitan complexes formed by the coalescence of two or more major urban areas. The Boston– Washington **megalopolis** along the U.S. northeastern seaboard is an outstanding example.

Core area In geography, a term with several connotations. Core refers to the center, heart, or focus. The core area of a **nation-state** is constituted by the national heartland—the largest population cluster, the most productive region, the area with greatest **centrality** and **accessibility**, probably containing the capital city as well.

Core-periphery model A model that describes how economic, political, and/or cultural power is spatially distributed between dominant **core regions**, and more marginal or dependent **semi-peripheral** and **peripheral regions**. The core-periphery model can be applied at a variety of spatial scales.

Core-periphery relationships The contrasting spatial characteristics of, and linkages between, the have (core) and have-not (periphery) components of a national or regional system.

Core region In terms of the **core-periphery model**, core regions are the centers of economic, political, and/or cultural power within a given territorial entity.

Corridor In general, refers to a spatial entity in which human activity is organized in a linear manner, as along a major transport route or in a valley confined by highlands. Specific meaning in politico-geographical context is a land extension that connects an otherwise **landlocked** state to the sea. History has seen several such corridors come and go. Poland once had a corridor (it now has a lengthy coastline); Bolivia lost a corridor to the Pacific Ocean between Peru and Chile.

Creole Ethnic term first applied in the Caribbean region to the native-born descendants of the Spanish conquerors and their local consorts.

Creole language A language that began as a *pidgin* but was later adopted as the mother tongue by a people in place of the mother tongue.

Cultural diffusion The process of spreading and adoption of a cultural element, from its place of origin across a wider area.

Cultural ecology The multiple interactions and relationships between a culture and its natural environment.

Cultural landscape The forms and artifacts sequentially placed on the physical landscape by the activities of various human occupants. By this progressive imprinting of the human presence, the physical landscape is modified into the cultural landscape, forming an interacting unity between the two.

Cultural linkage A culturally shared trait that gives an ethnic or cultural group a strengthened sense of awareness and self-identity.

Cultural pluralism A society in which two or more population groups, each practicing its own **culture**, live adjacent to one another without mixing inside a single **state**.

Cultural-political boundaries Political boundaries that coincide with cultural breaks in the landscape, such as language, religion, and ethnicity.

Cultural revival The process of continuous reinvigoration of cultural traits and behavior in communities geographically separated from their original source area.

Culture The sum total of the knowledge, attitudes, and habitual behavior patterns shared and transmitted by the members of a society. This is anthropologist Ralph Linton's definition; hundreds of others exist.

Culture area A distinct, culturally discrete spatial unit; a region within which certain cultural norms prevail.

Culture complex A related set of culture traits, such as prevailing dress codes and cooking and eating utensils.

Culture-environment tradition One of the four major areas of geographic research and teaching; the relationships between human societies and their natural environments.

Culture hearth Heartland, source area, innovation center; place of origin of a major culture.

Culture realm A cluster of regions in which related culture systems prevail. In North America, the United States and Canada form a culture realm, but Mexico belongs to a different culture realm.

Culture region A region within which common cultural characteristics prevail.

Culture trait A single element of normal practice in a culture, such as the wearing of a turban.

Cyclical movement Movement—for example, nomadic migration—that has a closed route repeated annually or seasonally.

Death rate The crude death rate is expressed as the annual number of deaths per 1000 individuals within a given population.

Definition In political geography, the written legal description (in a treatylike document) of a boundary between two countries or territories. See also **delimitation**.

Deforestation See **tropical deforestation**.

Deglomeration The process of industrial deconcentration in response to technological advances and/or increasing costs due to congestion and competition.

Delimitation In political geography, the translation of the written terms of a boundary treaty (the **definition**) into an official cartographic representation.

Demarcation In political geography, the actual placing of a political boundary on the landscape by means of barriers, fences, walls, or other markers.

Demographic transition model Multistage model, based on Western Europe's experience, of changes in population growth exhibited by countries undergoing industrialization. High birth rates and death rates are followed by plunging death rates, producing a huge net population gain; this is followed by the convergence of birth rates and death rates at a low overall level.

Demographic variables Births (fertility), deaths (mortality), and migration are the three basic demographic variables.

Demography The study of patterns and rates of population change, including birth and death rates, migration trends, and evolving population distribution patterns.

Density A description of the quantity per unit area of a given object or living organism.

Density of population The number of people per unit area. Also see **arithmetic density** and **physiologic density** measures.

Dependency theory A structuralist critique of the **modernization model** of development, dependency theory argues that certain types of political and economic relations (e.g., **colonialism**) between countries and regions of the world have created arrangements that both control and limit the extent to which regions can develop.

Desertification The encroachment of desert conditions on moister zones along the desert margins, where plant cover and soils are threatened by desiccation—through overuse, in part by humans and their domestic animals, and, possibly, in part because of inexorable shifts in the Earth's environmental zones.

Determinism See **environmental determinism**.

Development The economic, social, and institutional growth of national states.

Devolution The process whereby regions within a **state** demand and gain political strength and growing autonomy at the expense of the central government.

Diffusion The spatial spreading or dissemination of a culture element (such as a technological innovation) or some other phenomenon (e.g., a disease outbreak). See also **contagious**, **expansion**, **hierarchical**, and **relocation diffusion**.

Diffusion routes The spatial trajectory through which cultural traits or other phenomena spread.

Dispersed settlement In contrast to **agglomerated** or **nucleated** settlement, dispersed settlement is characterized by a much lower **density of population** and the wide spacing of individual homesteads (especially in rural North America).

Distance decay The various degenerative effects of distance on human spatial structures and interactions.

Divided capital In political geography, a country whose administrative functions are carried out in more than one city is said to have divided capitals.

Domestication The transformation of a wild animal or wild plant into a domesticated animal or a cultivated crop to gain control over food production. A necessary evolutionary step in the development of humankind—the invention of **agriculture**.

Domino theory The belief that political destabilization in one country can result in the collapse of order in a neighboring state, starting a chain reaction of collapse.

Double cropping The planting, cultivation, and harvesting of two crops successively within a single year on the same plot of farmland.

Doubling time The time required for a population to double in size.

Dualism The division of geography into broad categories: "human" and "physical"; and "regional" and "systematic."

Earth-science tradition One of the four major areas of geographic research and teaching; also known as **physical (natural) geography**.

Ecology Strictly speaking, the study of the many interrelationships between all forms of life and the natural environments in which they have evolved and continue to develop. The study of ecosystems focuses on the interactions between specific organisms and their environments. See also **cultural ecology**.

Economic reach The maximum distance people can be from a central place and still be attracted to it for business purposes. See also **hinterland**.

Economic tiger One of the burgeoning beehive countries of the Pacific Rim of Australasia. Using postwar Japan as a model, these countries have experienced significant modernization, industrialization, and Western-style economic growth since 1980. The four leading economic tigers are South Korea, Taiwan, Hong Kong, and Singapore.

Economies of scale The savings that accrue from large-scale production whereby the unit cost of manufacturing decreases as the level of operation enlarges. Supermarkets operate on this principle and are able to charge lower prices than small grocery stores.

Ecosystem A linkage of plants or animals to their environment in an open system as far as energy is concerned.

Ecumene The portion of the world's land surface that is permanently settled by human beings.

El Niño A periodic, large-scale, abnormal warming of the sea surface in the low latitudes of the eastern Pacific Ocean that produces a (temporary) reversal of surface ocean currents and airflows throughout the equatorial Pacific; these regional events have global implications, disturbing normal weather patterns in many parts of the world.

Electoral geography Subfield of geography that deals with various spatial aspects of voting systems, voting behavior, and voter representation.

Elongated state A **state** whose territory is decidedly long and narrow in that its length is at least six times greater than its average width. Chile and Vietnam are two classic examples on the world political map.

Emigrant A person migrating away from a country or area; an out-migrant.

Empirical Relating to the real world, as opposed to theoretical abstraction.

Enclave A piece of territory that is surrounded by another political unit of which it is not a part.

Endemic A disease that is particular to a locality or region.

ENSO Acronym for El Niño Southern Oscillation; the reversal of the flow of ocean currents and prevailing winds in the equatorial Pacific Ocean that disturbs global weather patterns.

Entrepôt A place, usually a port city, where goods are imported, stored, and transshipped; a **break-of-bulk point**.

Environmental determinism The view that the natural environment has a controlling influence over various aspects of human life, including cultural development. Also referred to as environmentalism.

Environmental geography A subdivision of geography concerned with the relationships and interactions between humans and the environment.

Environmental perception The total impression individuals have of their surroundings which create a mental map.

Environmental stress The threat to environmental security by human action such as atmospheric and groundwater pollution, deforestation, oil spills, and ocean dumping.

Esperanto An artificial Latin-based language, which its European proponents in the early twentieth century hoped would become a global language.

Ethnic The combination of a people's culture (traditions, customs, language, and religion) and racial ancestry.

Ethnic cleansing The slaughter and/or forced removal of one ethnic group from its homes and lands by another ethnic group.

Ethnic islands Small, usually rural and ethnically homogenous enclaves situated within a larger and more diverse cultural context.

Eugenic population policy Government policy designed to favor one racial sector over others.

Eugenic Protection Act Policy enacted by the Japanese government in 1948 that legalized abortion for social, medical, and economic reasons.

European state model A **state** consisting of a legally defined territory inhabited by a population governed from a capital city by a representative government.

Euroregions Transboundary cooperation zones in Europe that conform to the rules of the Euregion Council. The first self-designed Euroregion was established along the Dutch-German border in the early 1960s, and the number of Euroregions has expanded significantly over the past two decades.

Exclave A bounded (nonisland) piece of territory that is part of a particular state but lies separated from it by the territory of another state.

Exclusive economic zone (EEZ) An oceanic zone extending up to 200 nautical miles form a shoreline, within which the coastal state can control fishing, mineral exploration, and additional activities by all other countries.

Expansion diffusion The spread of an innovation or an idea through a population in an area in such a way that the number of those influenced grows continuously larger, resulting in an expanding area of dissemination.

Expansive population policy Government policy that encourages large families and raises the rate of population growth.

Exponential growth Cumulative or compound growth (of a population) over a given time period.

External migration Migration across an international border.

Extractive sector See **primary economic activity**.

Extraterritoriality Politico-geographical concept suggesting that the property of one **state** lying within the boundaries of another actually forms an extension of the first state.

Favela Shantytown on the outskirts or even well within an urban area in Brazil.

Federal state A political framework wherein a central government represents the various entities within a **nation-state** where they have common interests—defense, foreign affairs, and the like—yet allows these various entities to retain their own identities and to have their own laws, policies, and customs in certain spheres.

Federation See **federal state**.

Feng Shui Literally "wind-water." The Chinese art and science of placement and orientation of tombs, dwellings, buildings, and cities. Structures and objects are positioned in an effort to channel flows of *sheng-chi* ("life-breath") in favorable ways.

Fertile Crescent Crescent-shaped zone of productive lands extending from near the southeastern Mediterranean coast through Lebanon and Syria to the alluvial lowlands of Mesopotamia (in Iraq). Once more fertile than today, this is one of the world's great source areas of agricultural and other innovations.

Feudalism Prevailing politico-geographical system in Europe during the Middle Ages when land was owned by the nobility and was worked by peasants and serfs. Feudalism also existed in other parts of the world, and the system persisted into this century in Ethiopia and Iran, among other places.

Folk culture Cultural traits such as dress modes, dwellings, traditions, and institutions of usually small, tradition-bound communities.

Food web (food chain) All plants and animals are in some way connected to this organic sequence in which each life-form consumes the form below and, at the same time, is consumed by the form above. Plant life constitutes the foundation of the food web; the meat-eating animals (carnivores) stand at the top.

Fordist A highly organized and specialized system for organizing industrial production and labor. Named after automobile producer Henry Ford, Fordist production features assembly-line production of standardized components for mass consumption.

Forced migration Human **migration** flows in which the movers have no choice but to relocate.

Formal region A type of region marked by a certain degree of homogeneity in one or more phenomena; also called uniform region or homogeneous region.

Forward capital Capital city positioned in actually or potentially contested territory, usually near an international border; it confirms the **state**'s determination to maintain its presence in the region in contention.

Fragmented state A state whose territory consists of several separated parts, not a contiguous whole. The individual parts may be isolated from each other by the land area of other states or by international waters.

Francophone Describes a country or region where other languages are also spoken, but where French is the **lingua franca**, or the language of the elite. Quebec is Francophone Canada.

Frontier Zone of advance penetration, usually of contention; an area not yet fully integrated into a national **state**.

Functional differentiation A mode of distinguishing things or arrangements based on the purposes or activities to which they are devoted.

Functional region A region defined by the particular set of activities or interactions that occur within it.

Functional specialization The production of particular goods or services as a dominant activity in a particular location.

Gateway state A state, by virtue of its border location between geopolitical power cores, that absorbs and assimilates cultures and traditions of its neighbors without being dominated by them.

Gender gap The differences in levels of health, education, income, opportunity and participation in politics and public life that exist between males and females.

Gentrification The rehabilitation of deteriorated, often abandoned, housing of low-income inner-city residents.

Geographic Information System (GIS) A collection of computer hardware and software that permits spatial data to be collected, recorded, stored, retrieved, manipulated, analyzed, and displayed to the user.

Geographic realm The basic **spatial** unit in our world regionalization scheme. Each realm is defined in terms of a synthesis of its total human geography—a composite of its leading cultural, economic, historical, political, and appropriate environmental features.

Geography Literally means "Earth Description." As a modern academic discipline, it is concerned with the explanation of the physical and human characteristics of the Earth's surface. "Why are things located where they are?" is the central question that geographical scholarship seeks to answer.

Geologic time scale The standard timetable or chronicle of Earth history used by scientists; the sequential organization of geologic time units, whose dates continue to be refined by ongoing research.

Geometric boundaries Political boundaries **defined** and **delimited** (and occasionally **demarcated**) as straight lines or arcs.

Geopolitics The study of the interplay between international political relations and the territorial/environmental context in which they occur.

Gerrymandering Redistricting for advantage, or the practice of dividing areas into electoral districts to give one political party an electoral majority in a large number of districts while concentrating the voting strength of the opposition in as few districts as possible.

Ghetto An urban region marked by particular ethnic, racial, religious, and economic properties, usually (but not always) a low-income area.

Glaciation A period of global cooling during which continental ice sheets and mountain glaciers expand.

Global Environment Facility (GEF) An organization created under the auspices of the United Nations and the World Bank in 1991, the GEF is an international funding clearinghouse for global environmental initiatives.

Globalization The expansion of economic, political, and cultural activities to the point that they become global in scale and impact. This process has been aided by technological advances in transportation, information management, and telecommunications.

Gondwana The southern portion of the primeval supercontinent, Pangaea.

Gravity model A mathematical prediction of the interaction of places, the interaction being a function of population size of the respective places and the distance between them.

Green Revolution The successful recent development of higher-yield, fast-growing varieties of rice and other cereals in certain developing countries, which led to increased production per unit area and a temporary narrowing of the gap between population growth and food needs.

Greenhouse effect The widely used analogy describing the blanket-like effect of the atmosphere in the heating of the Earth's surface; shortwave insolation passes through the "glass" of the atmospheric "greenhouse," heats the surface, is converted to long-wave radiation that cannot penetrate the "glass," and thereby results in trapping heat, which raises the temperature inside the "greenhouse."

Gross national product (GNP) The total value of all goods and services produced in a country during a given year.

Growing season The number of days between the last frost in the spring and the first frost of the fall.

Growth pole An urban center with certain attributes that, if augmented by a measure of investment support, will stimulate regional economic development in its **hinterland**.

Heartland theory The hypothesis, proposed by British geographer Halford Mackinder during the first two decades of this century, that any political power based in the heart of Eurasia could gain sufficient strength to eventually dominate the world. Furthermore, since Eastern Europe controlled access to the Eurasian interior, its ruler would command the vast "heartland" to the east.

Hegemony The political dominance of a country (or even a region) by another country. The former Soviet Union's postwar grip on Eastern Europe, which lasted from 1945 to 1990, was a classic example.

Hierarchical diffusion A form of **diffusion** in which an idea or innovation spreads by trickling down from larger to smaller adoption units. An **urban hierarchy** is usually involved, encouraging the leapfrogging of innovations over wide areas, with geographic distance a less important influence.

Hierarchy An order or gradation of phenomena, with each level or rank subordinate to the one above it and superior to the one below. The levels in a national urban hierarchy are constituted by hamlets, villages, towns, cities, and (frequently) the **primate city**.

High seas Areas of the oceans away from land, beyond national jurisdiction, open and free for all to use.

High-technology corridors Areas along or near major transportation arteries that are devoted to the research, development, and sale of high technology products. These areas develop because of the networking and synergistic advantages of concentrating high-technology enterprises in close proximity to one another. "Silicon Valley" is a prime example of a high-technology corridor in the United States.

Hinterland Literally, "country behind," a term that applies to a surrounding area served by an urban center. That center is the focus of goods and services produced for its hinterland and is its dominant urban influence as well. In the case of a port city, the hinterland also includes the inland area whose trade flows through that port.

Holocene The current interglaciation epoch, extending from 10,000 years ago to the present on the geologic time scale.

Human geography One of the two major divisions of systematic geography; the spatial analysis of human population, their cultures, and activities.

Human territoriality A term associated with the work of Robert Sack that describes the efforts of human societies to influence events and achieve social goals by exerting, and attempting to enforce, control over specific geographical areas.

Hydrologic cycle The system of exchange involving water in its various forms as it continually circulates among the **atmosphere**, the oceans, and above and below the land surface.

Ice age A stretch of geologic time during which the Earth's average atmospheric temperature is lowered; causes the expansion of glacial ice in the high latitudes and the growth of mountain glaciers in lower latitudes.

Ice cap A regional mass of ice smaller than a continent-size ice sheet; while the Laurentide ice sheet covered much of North America east of the Rocky Mountains, an ice cap covered the Rockies themselves.

Ice sheet A large and thick layer of ice that flows outward in all directions from a central area where continuous accumulation of snow and thickening of ice occur. Also called continental ice sheet or continental glacier.

Iconography The identity of a region as expressed through its cherished symbols; its particular **cultural landscape** and personality.

Ideology A set of beliefs, values, assertions, and preferences about how society should be organized and focused.

Imam The political head of the Muslim community or the person who leads prayer services. In **Shiite** Islam the imam is immune from sin or error.

Immigrant A person migrating into a particular country or area; an in-migrant.

Imperialism The drive toward the creation and expansion of a colonial empire and, once established, its perpetuation.

Industrial Revolution The term applied to the social and economic changes in agriculture, commerce and manufacturing that resulted from technological innovations and specialization in late eighteenth-century Europe.

Infant mortality rate (IMR) A figure that describes the number of babies that die within the first year of their lives in a given population.

Infrastructure The foundations of a society: urban centers, transport networks, communications, energy distribution systems, farms, factories, mines, and such facilities as schools, hospitals, postal services, and police and armed forces.

Insurgent state Territorial embodiment of a successful guerrilla movement. The establishment by anti-government insurgents of a territorial base in which they exercise full control; thus, a state within a **state**.

Interactive mapping In geographic information systems (GIS) methodology, the constant dialogue via computer demands and feedback to queries between the map user and the map.

Interglaciation A period of warmer global temperatures between the most recent deglaciation and the onset of the next glaciation.

Internal migration Migration flow within a **nation-state**, such as ongoing westward and southward movements in the United States.

International migration **Migration** flow involving movement across international boundaries.

International refugees **Refugees** who have crossed one or more international boundaries during their dislocation and who now find themselves encamped in a different country.

Intervening opportunity The presence of a nearer opportunity that greatly diminishes the attractiveness of sites farther away.

Intranational refugees **Refugees** who have abandoned their town or village but not their country.

Irredentism A policy of cultural extension and potential political expansion aimed at a national group living in a neighboring country.

Irrigation The artificial watering of croplands. In Egypt's Nile valley, *basin irrigation* is an ancient method that involved the use of floodwaters that were trapped in basins on the floodplain and released in stages to augment rainfall. Today's *perennial irrigation* requires the construction of dams and irrigation canals for year-round water supply.

Isogloss A geographic boundary within which a particular linguistic feature occurs.

Karma In Hinduism and Buddhism, the force generated by a person's actions that affects transmigrations into a future existence, determining conditions and position in the next earthly stage of life.

K/T boundary Boundary between the Mesozoic and Cenozoic eras marking the extinction of many plants and animals, including the great dinosaurs.

Land bridge A narrow isthmian link between two large landmasses. They are temporary features—at least in terms of geologic time—subject to appearance and disappearance as the land or sea-level rises and falls.

Landlocked An interior country or **state** that is surrounded by land. Without coasts, a landlocked state is at a disadvantage in a number of ways—in terms of **accessibility** to international trade routes and in the scramble for possession of areas of the **continental shelf** and control of the **exclusive economic zone** beyond.

Late Cenozoic Ice Age The last great ice age that ended 10,000 years ago; spanned the entire Pleistocene epoch (2 million to 10,000 years ago) plus the latter portion of the preceding Pliocene epoch, possibly beginning as far back as 3.5 million years ago.

Latitude The angular distance, measured in degrees north or south, of a point along a parallel from the equator.

Law of the Sea The United Nations Convention on the Law of the Sea (UNCLOS), signed by 157 states (but not including the United States) in 1982; established states' rights and responsibilities concerning the ownership and use of the Earth's seas and oceans and their resources.

League of Nations A global (supranational) organization established by the victors of World War I to preserve peace and security and to promote economic and social cooperation among its members.

Least cost theory Model developed by Alfred Weber according to which the location of manufacturing establishments is determined by the minimization of three critical expenses: labor, transportation, and agglomeration.

Liberal models A general term for economic development models which assume that (1) all countries are capable of developing economically in the same way and (2) economic disparities between countries and regions are the result of short-term inefficiencies in local or regional market forces. The **modernization model** of development is an example of a liberal model.

Life expectancy A figure indicating how long, on average, a person may be expected to live. Normally expressed in the context of a particular state.

Lingua franca The term derives from "Frankish language," and applied to a tongue spoken in ancient Mediterranean ports that consisted of a mixture of Italian, French, Greek, Spanish, and even some Arabic. Today it refers to a "common language," a second language that can be spoken and understood by many peoples, although they speak other languages at home.

Location theory A logical attempt to explain the locational pattern of an economic activity and the manner in which its producing areas are interrelated. The agricultural location theory contained in the **von Thünen model** is a leading example.

Longevity gap The difference in the average length of life between males and females.

Longitude The angular distance, measured in degrees east or west, of a point along a meridian from the prime meridian.

Main Street Canada's dominant **conurbation** that is home to more than 60 percent of the country's inhabitants; stretches southwestward from Quebec City in the middle St. Lawrence valley to Windsor on the Detroit River.

Malnutrition Condition of ill health resulting from the deficiency or improper balance of essential foodstuffs in the diet, usually proteins, vitamins, and minerals. Two common forms of malnutrition among children in the world's poorer countries are *kwashiorkor*, a protein-deficient disorder, and *marasmus*, which results from insufficient protein and calories.

Malthusian Designates the early nineteenth-century viewpoint of Thomas Malthus, who argued that population growth was outrunning the Earth's capacity to produce sufficient food. Neo-Malthusian refers to those who subscribe to such positions in modern contexts.

Manufacturing export zones A feature of economic development in peripheral countries whereby the host country establishes areas with favorable tax, regulatory, and trade arrangements in order to attract foreign manufacturing operations. The goods manufactured in these export zones are primarily destined for the global market.

Map projection An orderly arrangement of meridians and parallels, produced by any systematic method, that can be used for drawing a map of the spherical Earth on a flat surface.

Maquiladora The term given to modern industrial plants in Mexico's northern (U.S.) border zone. These foreign-owned factories assemble imported components and/or raw materials and then export finished manufactures, mainly to the United States. Most import duties are minimized, bringing jobs to Mexico and the advantages of low wage rates to the foreign entrepreneurs.

Marasmus A disease that develops as a result of both a lack of protein and an insufficient caloric intake.

Median-line principle The system of drawing a political boundary midway between two states' coastlines when the territorial seas or EEZ are narrower than twice the standard or adopted limit.

Medical geography The study of health and disease within a geographic context and from a geographical perspective. Among other things, medical geography looks at sources, diffusion routes, and distributions of diseases.

Megalopolis Term used to designate large coalescing supercities that are forming in diverse parts of the world; formerly used specifically with an uppercase M to refer to the Boston–Washington multimetropolitan corridor on the northeastern seaboard of the United States, but now used generically with a lower-case m as a synonym for **conurbation**.

Mental map Image or picture of the way space (e.g., state or city) is organized as determined by an individual's perception, impression, and knowledge of that space.

Mercantilism Protectionist policy of European **states** during the sixteenth to the eighteenth centuries that promoted a state's economic position in the contest with other countries. The acquisition of gold and silver and the maintenance of a favorable trade balance (more exports than imports) were central to the policy.

Metropolitan area See **urban (metropolitan) area**.

Mesolithic period The Middle Stone Age, starting in Europe at the end of the last glacial period over 10,000 years ago.

Mesozoic The era of medieval life on the geologic time scale extending from 225 million years ago to 65 million years ago.

Migrant diffusion A form of relocation diffusion in which innovation adopted in distant places has lessened where it originated.

Migration A change in residence intended to be permanent. See also **forced**, **internal**, **international**, and **voluntary migration**.

Migratory movement Human relocation movement from a source to a destination without a return journey, as opposed to **cyclical movement**.

Milpa agriculture Middle and South American subsistence agriculture in which forest patches are cleared for temporary cultivation of corn and other crops.

Miracle rice A high-yielding variety of rice developed in the Philippines in the 1960s and now widely planted in Asia.

Model An idealized representation of reality built to demonstrate certain of its properties. A spatial model focuses on a geographic dimension of the real world.

Modernization model A liberal model of economic development most closely associated with the work of economist Walter Rostow. The modernization model (sometimes referred to as modernization theory) maintains that all countries go through five interrelated stages of development, which culminate in an economic state of self-sustained economic growth and high levels of mass consumption.

Montreal Protocol An international agreement signed in 1987 by 105 countries and the European Community (now European Union). The protocol called for a reduction in the production and consumption of **chlorofluorocarbons (CFCs)** of 50% by 2000. Subsequent meetings in London (1990) and Copenhagen (1992) accelerated the timing of CFC phase-out, and a world-wide complete ban has been in effect since 1996.

Multicore state A state that possesses more than one core or dominant region, be it economic, political or cultural.

Multinationals Internationally active corporations that can strongly influence the economic and political affairs of many countries they operate in.

Multiple nuclei model The Harris–Ullman model that showed the mid-twentieth-century American central city consisting of several land-use zones arranged around nuclear growth points.

Multiplier effect Expansion of economic activity caused by the growth or introduction of another economic activity. For example, a new basic industry will create jobs, directly or indirectly, in the non-basic sector.

Multiregional Evolution Theory Theory that human phenotypes evolved in four separate regions (Africa, Australia, East Asia, and Europe) producing, respectively, the Negroid, Australoid, Mongoloid, and Caucasoid stocks.

NAFTA The North American Free Trade Agreement which took effect January 1, 1994 creating a free-trade area between the United States,

Canada and Mexico; provides for the tariff-free movement of goods and products, financial services, telecommunications, investment, and patent protection within and between the signatories.

Nation Legally a term encompassing all the citizens of a **state**. Most definitions now tend to refer to a tightly knit group of people possessing bonds of language, ethnicity, religion, and other shared cultural attributes. Such homogeneity actually prevails within very few states.

Nationalism A sense of national consciousness and loyalty exalting one nation above all others and placing primary emphasis on the promotion of its culture and interests as opposed to those of other nations.

Nation-state A country whose population possesses a substantial degree of cultural homogeneity and unity. The ideal form to which most **nations** and **states** aspire—a political unit wherein the territorial state coincides with the area settled by a certain national group or people.

Natural increase rate Population growth measured as the excess of live births over deaths per 1000 individuals per year. Natural increase of a population does not reflect either **emigrant** or **immigrant** movements.

Natural-political boundaries See **physical-political boundaries**.

Natural resource Any valued element of (or means to an end using) the environment; includes minerals, water, vegetation, and soil.

Nautical mile By international agreement, the nautical mile—the standard measure at sea—is 6076.12 feet in length, equivalent to approximately 1.15 statute miles (1.85 kilometers).

Neocolonialism The entrenchment of the colonial order, such as trade and investment, under a new guise.

Neolithic period The New Stone Age marked by animal domestication, the beginnings of agriculture, the presence of crafts, and the diversification of tool-making industries.

Network (transport) The entire regional system of transportation connections and nodes through which movement can occur.

New industrial division of labor A late-twentieth century set of global economic relationships characterized by a growing dominance of service industries in the global economic core and an associated shift of manufacturing to parts of the developing world.

New World Order The international system resulting from the collapse of the Soviet Union in which the balance of nuclear terror theoretically no longer determines the destinies of states.

Nomadism **Cyclical movement** among a definite set of places. Nomadic peoples mostly are **pastoralists**.

Nongovernmental organizations (NGOs) International organizations that operate outside of the formal political arena but that are nevertheless influential in spearheading international initiatives on social, economic, and environmental issues.

Nonrenewable resource A resource that when used at a certain rate will ultimately be exhausted (metallic ores and petroleum are good examples).

Nuclear fusion The formation of an atomic nucleus by the union of two other nuclei having a lighter mass, a process that yields a huge amount of energy, which, if harnessed, may solve the world's power problems during the twenty-first century. A virtually inexhaustible source of fuel (hydrogen) exists, and the process does not produce dangerous radioactivity as nuclear fission does.

Nucleated settlement See **agglomerated settlement**.

Official language In multilingual countries the language selected, often by the educated and politically powerful elite, to promote internal cohesion; usually the language of the courts and government.

One-child policy Official policy launched by China in 1979 to induce married couples to have only one child in an effort to control population growth.

Organic theory A determinist view that states resemble biological organisms with life cycles that include stage of youth, maturity, and old age, now largely discredited.

Ozone layer The layer in the upper atmosphere located between 30kms and 45kms above the Earth's surface where stratospheric ozone is most densely concentrated. The ozone layer acts as a filter for the sun's harmful ultra-violet rays.

Pacific Rim A far-flung group of countries and parts of countries (extending clockwise on the map from New Zealand to Chile) sharing the following criteria: they face the Pacific Ocean; they evince relatively high levels of economic development, industrialization, and urbanization; and their imports and exports mainly move across Pacific waters.

Paleolithic period The Old Stone Age, the earliest period of human development that is approximately coextensive with the Pleistocene epoch beginning over 2 million years ago and ending between 40,000 and 10,000 years ago, when communities subsisted on hunting and gathering and used tools of stone, bone, and ivory.

Pandemic An outbreak of a disease that spreads worldwide.

Pangaea The primeval supercontinent, hypothesized by Alfred Wegener, that broke apart and formed the continents and oceans as we know them today; consisted of two parts—a northern Laurasia and a southern **Gondwana**.

Parallel An east–west line of **latitude** that is intersected at right angles by meridians of **longitude**.

Pastoralism A form of agricultural activity that involves the raising of livestock. Many peoples described as herders actually pursue mixed **agriculture**, in that they may also fish, hunt, or even grow a few crops. But pastoral peoples' lives revolve around their animals.

Pelagic species Organisms that exist in open lake waters or open ocean waters.

Per capita Capita means *individual*. Income, production, or some other measure is often given per individual.

Perceptual region A region that only exists as a conceptualization or an idea and not as a physically demarcated entity. For example, in the United States, "the South" or "the Mid-Atlantic region" are perceptual regions.

Perforated state A **state** whose territory completely surrounds that of another state. South Africa, which encloses Lesotho and is perforated by it, is an example.

Periodic movement A form of migration that involves intermittent but recurrent movement, such as temporary relocation for college attendance or service in the armed forces.

Peripheral region In terms of the **core-periphery model**, peripheral regions are the least powerful regions and therefore are often marginalized or under the control of both **semi-peripheral regions** and **core regions**.

Permanent refugee **Refugees** who have been substantially integrated into the host country or host region and who are thus seen as long-term visitors.

Physical (natural) geography One of the two major divisions of systematic geography; the spatial analysis of the structure, processes, and location of the Earth's natural phenomena such as climate, soil, plants, animals, and topography.

Physical-political (natural-political) boundaries Political boundaries that coincide with prominent physical features in the natural landscape—such as rivers or the crest ridges of mountain ranges.

Physiologic density The number of people per unit area of **arable** land.

Pidgin A **Lingua Franca** that has been simplified and modified through contact with other languages.

Plantation A large estate owned by an individual, family, or corporation and organized to produce a cash crop. Almost all plantations were established within the tropics; in recent decades, many have been divided into smaller holdings or reorganized as cooperatives.

Pleistocene The epoch that extended from about 2 million to 10,000 years ago on the geologic time scale; includes the latter half of the last great (Late Cenozoic) ice age, which began about 3.5 million years ago, as well as the emergence of humankind.

Plural society A society composed of numerous ethnic groups.

Political geography The study of the interaction of geographical area and political process; the spatial analysis of political phenomena and processes.

Pollution The release of a substance, through human activity, that chemically, physically, or biologically alters the air or water it is discharged into. Such a discharge negatively impacts the environment, with possible harmful effects on living organisms, including humans.

Popular culture Cultural traits such as dress, diet, and music that identify and are part of today's changeable, urban-based, media-influenced society.

Popular region Same as **perceptual region**.

Population density A measurement of the number of people per given unit of land.

Population explosion The rapid growth of the world's human population during the past century, attended by ever-shorter **doubling times** and accelerating rates of increase.

Population geography A subdivision of human geography that focuses on the spatial aspects of **demography** and the influences of demographic change on particular places.

Population policy Official (government) policy aimed at changing the size, composition (structure), or growth of population.

Population (age-sex) structure Graphic representation (profile) of a population according to age and sex.

Possibilism Geographic viewpoint—a response to determinism—that holds that human decision making is the crucial factor in cultural development, not environmental limitation or restricted options. Cultural heritage and learning are the key attributes in society's use of the natural environment.

Postindustrial (postmodern) economy Emerging economy, in the United States and a handful of other highly advanced countries, as traditional industry is overshadowed by a higher-technology productive complex dominated by services and information-related and managerial activities.

Precambrian The era that precedes the Paleozoic era of ancient life on the geologic time scale, named after the oldest period of the Paleozoic, the Cambrian; extends backward from 570 million years ago to the origin of the Earth, now estimated to be about 4.6 billion years ago.

Primary economic activity Activity engaged in the direct extraction of **natural resources** from the environment—such as mining, fishing, lumbering, and especially **agriculture**.

Primate city A country's largest city—ranking atop the **urban hierarchy**—most expressive of the national culture and usually (but not always) the capital city as well.

Prime meridian The north–south line on the Earth grid, passing through the Royal Observatory at Greenwich in London, defined as having a longitude of 0°.

Process Causal force that shapes a **spatial** pattern as it unfolds over time.

Protectorate In Britain's system of colonial administration, the protectorate was a designation that involved the guarantee of certain rights (such as the restriction of European settlement and land alienation) to peoples who had been placed under the control of the Crown.

Protruded state A type of **state** territorial shape that exhibits a narrow, elongated land extension leading away from the main body of territory. Thailand is an example.

Proxemics The individual and collective preferences for nearness or distance as displayed by different cultures.

Pull factor Positive conditions and perceptions that effectively attract people to new locales from other areas.

Push factor Negative conditions and perceptions that induce people to leave their abode and migrate to a new locale.

Push-pull concept The idea that **migration** flows are simultaneously stimulated by conditions in the source area, which tend to drive people away, and by the perceived attractiveness of the destination.

Quaternary The second of the two periods of the Cenozoic era of recent life on the geologic time scale extending from approximately 2 million years ago to the present.

Quaternary industries Service sector industries concerned with the collection, processing, and manipulation of information and capital. Examples include finance, administration, insurance, and legal services.

Quinary industries Service sector industries that require high level of specialized knowledge or technical skill. Examples include scientific research and high level management.

Racism The negative characterization of peoples' abilities, potential, or worth based on their race or skin color.

Radioactive waste Hazardous waste emitting radiation from nuclear power plants, nuclear weapons factories, and nuclear equipment in hospitals and industry.

Rank-size rule In a model urban hierarchy, the population of a city or town will be inversely proportional to its rank in the hierarchy.

Realm See **geographic realm**.

Recycling Conservation practice of reprocessing materials for reuse.

Refugees People who have been dislocated involuntarily from their original place of settlement.

Region A commonly used term and a geographic concept of central importance. An **area** on the Earth's surface marked by certain properties.

Regional science Discipline that emphasizes the application of modern spatial analytical techniques to regional problems and issues.

Regionalism The consciousness and loyalty to a region considered distinct and different from the state as a whole by those who occupy it.

Relative direction A culturally determined locational reference such as the "Middle East" or "Far West."

Relative distance Distance measured, not in linear terms such as miles or kilometers, but in terms such as cost and time.

Relative location The regional position or **situation** of a place relative to the position of other places. Distance, **accessibility**, and connectivity affect relative location.

Relict boundary A political boundary that has ceased to function, but the imprint of which can still be detected on the **cultural landscape**.

Religious fundamentalism Religious movement whose objectives are to return to the foundations of the faith and to influence state policy.

Relocation diffusion Sequential **diffusion** process in which the items being diffused are transmitted by their carrier agents as they evacuate the old areas and relocate to new ones. The most common form of relocation diffusion involves the spreading of innovations by a **migrating** population.

Remote sensing A method of collecting data or information through the use of instruments (e.g., satellites) that are physically distant from the area or object of study.

Renewable resource A resource that can regenerate as it is exploited.

Restrictive population policy Government policy designed to reduce the rate of natural increase.

Rimland Term coined by Nicholas Spykman referring to the coastal rim of Eurasia, which Spykman maintained held the key to global power. A counterthesis to Mackinder's heartland thesis.

Rural density A measure that indicates the number of persons per unit area living in the rural areas of a country, outside the urban concentrations.

Sahel Semiarid zone extending across most of Africa between the southern margins of the arid Sahara and the moister tropical savanna and forest zone to the south. Chronic drought, **desertification**, and overgrazing have contributed to severe famines in this area for decades.

Scale Representation of a real-world phenomenon at a certain level of reduction or generalization. In **cartography**, the ratio of map distance to ground distance; indicated on a map as a bar graph, representative fraction, and/or verbal statement.

Secondary economic activity Activity that processes raw materials and transforms them into finished industrial products; the manufacturing sector.

Sector model A structural model of the American central city that suggests that land-use areas conform to a wedge-shaped pattern focused on the downtown core.

Secularism Secularism holds that ethical and moral standards should be formulated and adhered to for life on Earth and not to accommodate the prescriptions of a deity and promises of a comfortable afterlife. A secular state is the opposite of a **theocracy**.

Sedentary Permanently attached to a particular area; a population fixed in its location. The opposite of **nomadic**.

Semi-peripheral region In terms of the **core-periphery model**, semi-peripheral regions are intermediary regions in terms of the hierarchy of power between **core regions** and **peripheral regions**.

Sephardim One of the two main ethnic groups within Jewish culture. This branch settled in Northern Africa and later in the Iberian Peninsula after having been driven away from Jerusalem early in the first millennium AD.

Sequent occupance The notion that successive societies leave their cultural imprints on a place, each contributing to the cumulative **cultural landscape**.

Service industry See **tertiary economic activity**.

Settlement density The amount of area in a country for each city with 100,000 people or more.

Shaman In traditional societies, a shaman is deemed to possess religious and mystical powers, acquired directly from supernatural sources. At times an especially strong shaman might attract a regional following; many shamans, however, remain local figures.

Shantytown Unplanned slum development on the margins of cities in the developing realms, dominated by crude dwellings and shelters mostly made of scrap wood, iron, and even pieces of cardboard.

Shatter belt Region caught between stronger, colliding external cultural-political forces, under persistent stress and often fragmented by aggressive rivals. Eastern Europe and Southeast Asia are classic examples.

Shifting agriculture Cultivation of crops in recently cut and burned tropical forest clearings, soon to be abandoned in favor of newly cleared nearby forestland. Also known as slash-and-burn agriculture.

Shiites Adherents of one of the two main divisions of Islam. Also known as Shiahs, the Shiites represent the Persian (Iranian) variation of Islam and believe in the infallibility and divine right to authority of the **Imams**, descendants of Ali.

Site The internal locational attributes of an urban center, including its local spatial organization and physical setting.

Situation The external locational attributes of an urban center; its **relative location** or regional position with reference to other nonlocal places.

Slash-and-burn agriculture See **shifting agriculture**.

Social stratification The differentiation of society into classes based on wealth, power, production, and prestige.

Southern Cone The southern, mid-latitude portion of South America constituted by the countries of Chile, Argentina, and Uruguay; often included as well is the southernmost part of Brazil, south of the Tropic of Capricorn (23½° S).

Sovereignty A principle of international relations that holds that final authority over social, economic, and political matters should rest with the legitimate rulers of independent states.

Spatial Pertaining to space on the Earth's surface; synonym for geographic.

Spatial interaction See **complementarity** and **intervening opportunity**.

Standard language The language quality of a country's dominant language that is preferred by the elite and/or the state.

State A politically organized territory that is administered by a sovereign government and is recognized by a significant portion of the international community. A state must also contain a permanent resident population, an organized economy, and a functioning internal circulation system.

State capitalism Government-controlled corporations competing under free market conditions, usually in a tightly regimented society.

Stationary population level The level at which a national population ceases to grow.

Step migration Migration to a distant destination that occurs in stages, for example, from farm to nearby village, and later to town and city.

Stratification (social) In a layered or stratified society, the population is divided into a **hierarchy** of social classes. In an industrialized society, the proletariat is at the lower end: elites that possess capital and control the means of production are at the upper level. In the traditional **caste system** of Hindu India, the "untouchables" form the lowest class or caste, whereas the still-wealthy remnants of the princely class are at the top.

Structuralist models A general term for models of economic development that treat economic disparities among countries or regions as the result of historically derived power relations within the global economic system.

Subsequent boundary A political boundary that developed contemporaneously with the evolution of the major elements of the cultural landscape through which it passes.

Subsistence The state of existing on the minimum necessities to sustain life; spending most of one's time in pursuit of survival.

Subsistence agriculture Self-sufficient agriculture that is small scale and low technology and emphasizes food production for local consumption, not for trade.

Suburb A subsidiary urban area surrounding and connected to the central city. Many are exclusively residential; others have their own commercial centers or shopping malls.

Suburban downtown Significant concentration of diversified economic activities around a highly **accessible** suburban location, including retailing, light industry, and a variety of major corporate and commercial operations. Late-twentieth-century coequal to the American central city's **central business district (CBD)**.

Sunnis Adherents to the largest branch of Muslims, called the orthodox or traditionalist. They believe in the effectiveness of family and community in the solution of life's problems, and they differ from the **Shiites** in accepting as authoritative the traditions *(sunna)* of Muhammad.

Superimposed boundary A political boundary placed by powerful outsiders on a developed human landscape. Usually ignores preexisting cultural-spatial patterns, such as the border that now divides North and South Korea.

Supranational A venture involving three or more national states—political, economic, and/or cultural cooperation to promote shared objectives. Europe's Economic Community or Common Market is one such organization.

Swidden agriculture See **shifting agriculture**.

System Any group of objects or institutions and their mutual interactions. Geography treats systems that are expressed **spatially** such as **regions**.

Systematic geography Topical geography: cultural, political, economic geography, and the like.

Takeoff Economic concept to identify a stage in a country's **development** when conditions are set for a domestic Industrial Revolution, which occurred in Britain in the late eighteenth century and in Japan in the late nineteenth century following the Meiji Restoration.

Technopole Centers or nodes of high-technology research and activity around which a **high-technology corridor** is sometimes established.

Temporary refugees **Refugees** who are encamped in a host country or host region while waiting for resettlement.

Territorial morphology A **state**'s geographical shape, which can have a decisive impact on its spatial cohesion and political viability. A **compact** shape is most desirable; among the less efficient shapes are those exhibited by **elongated**, **fragmented**, **perforated**, and **prorupt** states.

Territorial sea Zone of seawater adjacent to a country's coast, held to be part of the national territory and treated as a segment of the sovereign state.

Territoriality A country's or more local community's sense of property and attachment toward its territory, as expressed by its determination to keep it inviolable and strongly defended.

Tertiary economic activity Activity that engages in services—such as transportation, banking, retailing, education, and routine office-based jobs.

Theocracy A **state** whose government is under the control of a ruler who is deemed to be divinely guided or under the control of a group of religious leaders, as in post-Khomeini Iran. The opposite of the theocratic state is the **secular** state.

Time-Distance decay The declining degree of acceptance of an idea or innovation with increasing time and distance from its point of origin or source.

Time-space compression A term associated with the work of David Harvey that refers to the social and psychological effects of living in a world in which **time-space convergence** has rapidly reached a high level of intensity.

Time-space convergence A term coined by Donald Janelle that refers to the greatly accelerated movement of goods, information, and ideas during the twentieth century made possible by technological innovations in transportation and communications.

Toponomy (or **Toponymy**) The etymological study of place names or associated language.

Total Fertility Rate (TFR) The average number of children born to a woman during her lifetime, as expressed for a total population.

Totalitarian A government whose leaders rule by absolute control, tolerating no differences of political opinion.

Township-and-Range System A rectangular land division scheme designed by Thomas Jefferson to disperse settlers evenly across farmlands of the U.S. interior.

Toxic waste Hazardous waste causing danger from chemicals and infectious materials.

Traditional Term used in various contexts (e.g., traditional religion) to indicate originality within a culture or long-term part of an indigenous society. It is the opposite of modernized, superimposed, changed; it denotes continuity and historic association.

Transculturation Cultural borrowing that occurs when different cultures of approximately equal complexity and technological level come into close contact. In **acculturation**, by contrast, an indigenous society's culture is modified by contact with a technologically superior society.

Transhumance A seasonal periodic movement of pastoralists and their livestock between highland and lowland pastures.

Transition zone An area of **spatial** change where the peripheries of two adjacent realms or regions join; marked by a gradual shift (rather than sharp break) in the characteristics that distinguish these neighboring geographic entities from one another.

Tropical deforestation The clearing and destruction of tropical rainforests to make way for expanding settlement frontiers and the exploitation of new economic opportunities.

Truman Proclamation In September 1945, President Harry Truman proclaimed the United States would regulate fisheries' activities in areas of the high seas adjacent to its coastline, and that U.S. jurisdiction over the continental shelf and its contents would be limited to the region within the 600-foot isobath.

Underdeveloped countries (UCDs) Countries that, by various measures, suffer seriously from negative economic and social conditions, including low per capita incomes, poor nutrition, inadequate health, and related disadvantaged circumstances.

United Nations Conference on Environment and Development (UNCED) Also known as the Earth Summit, an international environmental conference held in Rio de Janeiro, Brazil, in 1992 that led to the signing of important international agreements on climate change and biodiversity.

United Nations Conference on the Human Environment The first internationally significant United Nations conference dealing with human impacts of the environment, held in 1972.

Unitary state A **nation-state** that has a centralized government and administration that exercises power equally over all parts of the state.

United Nations A global (supranational) organization established at the end of World War II to foster international security and cooperation.

Urban (metropolitan) area The entire built-up, nonrural area and its population, including the most recently constructed suburban appendages. Provides a better picture of the dimensions and population of such an area than the delimited municipality (central city) that forms its heart.

Urban geography A subfield of geography that focuses especially on urban places, their characteristics, processes of genesis and growth, their systems, relative location, and interrelationships.

Urban hierarchy A ranking of settlements (hamlet, village, town, city, metropolis) according to their size and economic functions.

Urbanization The process by which towns and cities grow and become more densely populated and spatially expansive.

Urban morphology The study of the form and structure of urban places.

Urban realms model A **spatial** generalization of the large, late-twentieth-century city in the United States. It is shown to be a widely dispersed, multicentered metropolis consisting of increasingly independent zones or realms, each focused on its own **suburban downtown**; the only exception is the shrunken central realm, which is focused on the **central business district**.

Urban system The functional and **spatial** organization of towns and cities.

Urbanization A term with several connotations. The proportion of a country's population living in urban places is its level of urbanization. The process of urbanization involves the movement of people to, and the clustering of people in towns and cities—a major force in every geographic realm today. Another kind of urbanization occurs when an expanding city absorbs rural countryside and transforms it into suburbs; in the case of cities in the developing world, this also generates peripheral **shantytowns**.

Vectored disease A disease carried from one host to another by an intermedite host.

Vernacular region(s) Same as **perceptual region** but at a larger spatial scale.

Vienna Convention for the Protection of the Ozone Layer The first international convention aimed at addressing the issue of ozone depletion. Held in 1985, the Vienna Convention was the predecessor to the **Montreal Protocol**.

Voluntary migration Population movement in which people relocate in response to perceived opportunity, not because they are forced to move.

Von Thünen model Explains the location of agricultural activities in a commercial, profit-making economy. A process of spatial competition allocates various farming activities into concentric rings around a central market city, with profit-earning capability the determining force in how far a crop locates from the market. The original (1826) Isolated State model now applies to the continental scale.

Wattle Traditional dwelling built using poles and sticks that are woven tightly together and then plastered with mud.

World cities Dominant cities in terms of their role in the global political economy. These are not the world's biggest cities in terms of population or industrial output. Instead these are centers of strategic control of the world economy.

Ziggurat A lofty ancient Babylonian temple tower that symbolized power and authority.

Zionism The movement to unite the Jewish people of the Diaspora and to establish a national homeland for them in Palestine.

Index

E

Q

R